Spain

Santiago de Compostela & Galicia
p499

Cantabria & Asturias
p454

Bilbao, the Basque Country & La Rioja
p396

Castilla y León
p139

Aragón
p359

Catalonia
p301

Barcelona
p230

Madrid
p66

Toledo & Castilla-La Mancha
p201

Extremadura
p543

Valencia & Murcia
p725

Mallorca, Menorca & Ibiza
p776

Seville & Andalucía's Hill Towns
p571

Granada & South Coast Andalucía
p650

THIS EDITION WRITTEN AND RESEARCHED BY

Anthony Ham,

A DEMOTES /GETTY IMAGES ©

LOS MALLOS P388

CARMEN MARTÍNEZ BANÚS /GETTY IMAGES ©

Contents

TAPAS P41

/GETTY IMAGES ©

MERCADO DE SAN MIGUEL,
MADRID P107

Contents

Welcome to Spain

Passionate, sophisticated and devoted to living the good life, Spain is at once a stereotype come to life and a country more diverse than you ever imagined.

An Epic Land

Spain's diverse landscapes stir the soul. The Pyrenees and the Picos de Europa are as beautiful as any mountain range on the continent, while the snowcapped Sierra Nevada rises up improbably from the sun-baked plains of Andalucía; these are hiking destinations of the highest order. The wildly beautiful cliffs of Spain's Atlantic northwest are offset by the charming coves of the Mediterranean. And everywhere you go, villages of timeless beauty perch on hilltops, huddle in valleys and cling to coastal outcrops as tiny but resilient outposts of Old Spain.

A Culinary Feast

Food and wine are national obsessions in Spain, and with good reason. The touchstones of Spanish cooking are deceptively simple: incalculable variety, traditional recipes handed down through the generations, and an innate willingness to experiment and see what comes out of the kitchen laboratory. You may experience the best meal ever over tapas in an earthy bar where everyone's shouting, or over a meal prepared by a celebrity chef in the refined surrounds of a Michelin-starred restaurant. Either way, the breadth of gastronomic experience that awaits you is breathtaking.

Art Imitates Life

Poignantly windswept Roman ruins, cathedrals of rare power and incomparable jewels of Islamic architecture speak of a country where the great civilisations of history have always risen, fallen and left behind their indelible mark. More recently, what other country could produce such rebellious and relentlessly creative spirits as Salvador Dalí, Pablo Picasso and Antoni Gaudí and place them front and centre in public life? Here, grand monuments to the past coexist alongside architectural creations of such daring that it becomes clear that Spain's future will be every bit as original as its past.

Fiestas & Flamenco

For all such talk, this is a country that lives very much in the present and there's a reason why 'fiesta' is one of the best-known words in the Spanish language. It's because life is itself a fiesta here and everyone seems to be invited. Perhaps you'll sense it along a crowded post-midnight street when all the world has come out to play. Or maybe that moment will come when a flamenco performer touches something deep in your soul. Whenever it happens, you'll find yourself nodding in recognition: *this* is Spain.

Why I Love Spain

By Anthony Ham, Author

More than a decade after I fell in love with Spain and decided to call it home, the life that courses relentlessly through the streets here still produces in me a feeling that this is a place where anything can happen. Here, the passions of Europe's most passionate country are the fabric of daily life; this is a country with music in its soul and an unshakeable spring in its step. And over time Spain's passions – for fine food, for wild landscapes, for a life lived to the full – have become very much my own.

For more about our authors, see page 912

Above: La Seo, Zaragoza (p362)

Spain

Picos de Europa
Admire Spain's most jagged mountain high (p489)

Bilbao
Explore the best of Basque culture (p399)

Salamanca
The high point of Renaissance architecture (p147)

Madrid
Linger in three of the world's finest art galleries (p66)

Toledo
Search for signs of its multifaith past (p204)

Córdoba
Amazing Islamic architecture (p640)

Seville
Embrace Andalucía's heart and very Catholic soul (p574)

Granada
Marvel at the exquisite Alhambra's perfection (p654)

Las Alpujarras
Discover ancient Moorish villages (p677)

Sierra Nevada
Ski in winter, hike in summer (p675)

ATLANTIC OCEAN

Costa da Morte

Ferrol
A Coruña
Santiago de Compostela
Pontevedra
Vigo
Rías Baixas
Lugo
Ourense
Río

Avilés Gijón
Oviedo
Torrelavega
Parque Natural Fragas do Eume
Parque Natural de Somiedo
Cordillera Cantábrica
León
Benavente
Zamora
Palencia
Valladolid
Segovia
Ávila
Salamanca
Cordillera Central
Parque Nacional de los Picos de Europa
Santander
Bilbao (Bilbo)
Miranda de Ebro
Burgos
Aranda de Duero
Río Du
Guadalaj
MADRI

PORTUGAL
LISBON
Plasencia
Sierra de Gredos
Badajoz Mérida
Zafra
Sierra Morena
Parque Natural Sierra Norte
Aranjuez
Toledo
Ciudad Real
Río Guadiana
Córdoba
Parque Natural Sierra de Andújar
Cordillera Bética
Granada
Parque Natura Sierra Nevad
Sierra Nevada Alpujar

Huelva
Parque Nacional de Doñana
Cádiz
Costa de la Luz
Parque Natural Los Alcornocales
Málaga
Costa del Sol
Algeciras Gibraltar
Strait of Gibraltar
Ceuta (Spain)
Tangier MOROCCO

FRANCE

The Pyrenees
Hike the dramatic Pyrenean
high country (p326)

Bay of Biscay

Biarritz

Golfe du Lion

**San
Sebastián**

Perpignan

**Pamplona
(Iruña)**

Pyrenees **ANDORRA
LA VELLA** **ANDORRA**

Logroño

Figueres

Girona

Riu Ter

Río Segre

Costa Brava

Zaragoza

Lleida

Barcelona

Río Ebro

La Rioja
Meander through Spain's
premier wine region (p446)

Costa Daurada

Golfo de Valencia

Menorca

Barcelona
Immerse yourself in
Spain's style city (p230)

Teruel

*Costa del
Azahar*

**Palma de
Mallorca**

Cuenca

Río Turia

Río Júcar

Valencia

Mallorca

Balearic Islands (Islas Baleares)

Río Cabriel

Ibiza

Albacete

Parque Natural
Sierras de Cazorla,
Segura y las Villas

Río Segura

**Alicante
(Alacant)**

Formentera

Costa Blanca

**Elche
(Elx)**

*MEDITERRANEAN
SEA*

Murcia

Cartagena

Costa Cálida

1°E   2°E   3°E   4°E

Parque Natural
de Cabo de
Gata-Níjar

Almería

0° (Greenwich)

ALGERIA

1°W

ELEVATION	
	2000m
	1500m
	1250m
	1000m
	800m
	600m
	400m
	200m
	100m
	0

Spain's
Top 18

Barcelona

1 Home to cutting-edge architecture, world-class dining and vertiginous nightlife, Barcelona (p230) has long been one of Europe's most alluring destinations. Days are spent wandering the cobblestone lanes of the Gothic quarter, basking on Mediterranean beaches or marvelling at Gaudí masterpieces across the city. By night, Barcelona is a whirl of vintage cocktail bars, gilded music halls, innovative eateries and dance-loving clubs, with the party extending well into the night. There are also colourful markets, hallowed arenas (like Camp Nou, p263, where FC Barcelona plays), and a calendar packed with traditional Catalan festivals. Below left: Park Güell (p258)

Sampling Tapas

2 One of the world's most enjoyable ways to eat, tapas is as much a way of life as it is Spain's most accessible culinary superstar. These bite-sized bar snacks are the accompaniment to countless Spanish nights of revelry and come in seemingly endless variations. In Andalucía, expect the best *jamón* (cured ham) or fine Spanish olives. In San Sebastián (p424) and elsewhere in the Basque Country (p407) – where they're called *pintxos* – tapas are an elaborate form of culinary art. Other great places for tapas include Madrid (p112) and Zaragoza (p366).

SAM BURT PHOTOGRAPHY / GETTY IMAGES ©

DALLAS STRIBLEY / GETTY IMAGES ©

The Alhambra

3 The palace complex of Granada's Alhambra (p655) is close to architectural perfection. It is perhaps the most refined example of Islamic art in the world, not to mention the most enduring symbol of 800 years of Moorish rule in what was known as Al-Andalus. From afar, the Alhambra's red fortress towers dominate the Granada skyline, set against a backdrop of the Sierra Nevada's snowcapped peaks. Up close, the Alhambra's perfectly proportioned Generalife gardens complement the exquisite detail of the Palacio Nazaríes. This is Spain's most beautiful monument. Above left: Generalife (p662)

La Sagrada Família

4 The Modernista brainchild of Antoni Gaudí, La Sagrada Família (p249) remains a work in progress more than 80 years after its creator's death. Fanciful and profound, inspired by nature and barely restrained by a Gothic style, Barcelona's quirky temple soars skyward with an almost playful majesty. The improbable angles and departures from architectural convention will have you shaking your head in disbelief, but the detail of the decorative flourishes on the Passion Facade, Nativity Facade and elsewhere are worth studying for hours.

Seville

5 Nowhere is as quintessentially Spanish as Seville (p574), a city of capricious moods and soulful secrets, which has played a pivotal role in the evolution of flamenco, bullfighting, baroque art and Mudéjar architecture. Blessed with year-round sunshine and a never-ending schedule of energetic festivals, everything seems more amorous here, a feeling not lost on legions of 19th-century aesthetes, who used the city as a setting in their romantic works of fiction. Head south to the home of *Carmen* and *Don Juan* and take up the story. Above: Flamenco performance, Tablao El Arenal (p595)

Madrid Nightlife

6 Madrid is not the only European city with nightlife (p113), but few can match its intensity and street clamour. As Ernest Hemingway said, 'Nobody goes to bed in Madrid until they have killed the night'. There are wall-to-wall bars, small clubs, live venues, cocktail bars and mega-clubs beloved by A-list celebrities all across the city, with unimaginable variety to suit all tastes. But it's in the *barrios* of Huertas, Malasaña, Chueca and La Latina that you'll really understand what we're talking about. Top: Why Not? bar (p124)

Sierra Nevada & Las Alpujarras

7 Dominated by the Mulhacén (3479m), mainland Spain's highest peak, the Sierra Nevada (p675) makes a stunning backdrop to the warm city of Granada. Skiing in winter and hiking in summer can be mixed with exploration of the fascinating villages of Las Alpujarras (p677), arguably Andalucía's most engaging collection of *pueblos blancos* (white towns). Suitably for one of the last outposts of Moorish settlement on Spanish soil, the hamlets of Las Alpujarras resemble North Africa, oasis-like and set amid woodlands and deep ravines.

A La Playa

8 It's easy to see why Spain's beaches are Europe's favourite summer playground, but the beach is also an obsession among Spaniards in summer when the entire country heads for the coast. There's so much more to Spain's coastline than the overcrowded beaches of Benidorm: the rugged coves of the Costa Brava (p304), Mallorca (p778), Menorca (p796) and Cabo de Gata (p721) come close to the Mediterranean ideal, while the Atlantic beaches from Tarifa (p700) to the Portuguese frontier and the dramatic coastline of Spain's northwest are spectacular. Top: Calella de Palafrugell (p306)

Semana Santa

9 Return to Spain's medieval Christian roots in the country's dramatic Easter celebrations. Religious fraternities parade elaborate *pasos* (figures) of Christ and the Virgin Mary through the streets to the emotive acclaim of the populace; the most prestigious procession is the *madrugada* (early hours) of Good Friday. Seen for the first time, it's an exotic and utterly compelling fusion of pageantry, solemnity and deep religious faith. The most extraordinary processions are in Castilla y León, Castilla La Mancha, and Andalucía, but if you choose one make it Seville (p589).

R. DURAN / GETTY IMAGES ©

Renaissance Salamanca

10 Luminous when floodlit, the elegant central square of Salamanca, the Plaza Mayor (p147), is possibly the most attractive in all of Spain. It is just one of many highlights in a city whose architectural splendour has few peers in the country. Salamanca is home to one of Europe's oldest and most prestigious universities, so student revelry also lights up the nights. It's this combination of grandeur and energy that makes so many people call Salamanca their favourite city in Spain. Above left: Plaza Mayor (p147)

Hiking in the Pyrenees

11 Spain is a walker's destination of exceptional variety, but we reckon the Pyrenees in Navarra (p438), Aragón (p370) and Catalonia (p326) offer the most special hiking country. Aragón's Parque Nacional de Ordesa y Monte Perdido is one of the high points (pun intended) of the Pyrenees, while its glories are mirrored across the provincial frontier of Parque Nacional d'Aigüestortes i Estany de Sant Maurici in Catalonia. It's a tough but rewarding world of rock walls and glacial cirques, accompanied by elusive Pyrenean wildlife. Above right: Parque Nacional de Ordesa y Monte Perdido (p379)

Bilbao: Spain's Northern Gem

12 It only took one building, a shimmering titanium fish called the Museo Guggenheim (p399), to turn Bilbao from a byword for industrial decay into a major European art centre. But while it's this most iconic of modern buildings that draws the visitors, it's the hard-working soul of this city that ends up captivating, and let's face it there's plenty to be entranced by: riverside promenades, clanky funicular railways, superb *pintxos* bars, an iconic football team, a clutch of quality museums and, yeah OK, a shimmering titanium fish. Top right: Museo Guggenheim (p399)

ALEX LINGHORN / GETTY IMAGES ©

Córdoba's Mezquita

13 A church that became a mosque before reverting to a church, Córdoba's Mezquita (p641) charts the evolution of Western and Islamic architecture over a 1000-year trajectory. Its innovative features include horseshoe arches, an intricate mihrab, and a 'forest' of 856 columns, many of them recycled from Roman ruins. The sheer scale of the Mezquita reflects Córdoba's erstwhile power as the most cultured city in 10th-century Europe. It was also inspiration for even greater buildings to come, most notably in Seville and Granada.

Madrid's Golden Art Triangle

14 Madrid is one of the fine-arts capitals of the world, with an extraordinary collection of art galleries concentrated in the city-centre. Housing works by Goya, Velázquez, El Greco and masters from across Europe, the showpiece is the Museo del Prado (p83), but also within a short stroll are the Centro de Arte Reina Sofía (p89), showcasing Picasso's *Guernica,* plus works by Dalí and Miró, and the Museo Thyssen-Bornemisza (p85), which carries all the big names spanning centuries. Below: Centro de Arte Reina Sofía (p89)

Picos de Europa

15 Jutting out in compact form just back from the rugged and ever-changing coastline of Cantabria and Asturias, the Picos (p489) comprise three dramatic limestone massifs, unique in Spain but geologically similar to the Alps and jammed with inspiring trails. These peaks and valleys form Spain's second-largest national park, with some of the most spectacular mountain scenery in the country – no small claim considering the presence of the Pyrenees and the Sierra Nevada. The Picos de Europa deservedly belong in such elite company.

TATYANA KILDISHEVA / GETTY IMAGES ©

ANDREA PISTOLESI / GETTY IMAGES ©

La Rioja Wine Country

16 La Rioja (p446) is the sort of place where you could spend weeks meandering along quiet roads in search of the finest drop. Bodegas offering wine-tastings and picturesque villages that shelter excellent wine museums are the mainstay in this region. The Frank Gehry–designed Hotel Marqués de Riscal (p452), close to Elciego, has been likened to Bilbao's Guggenheim in architectural scale and ambition, and has become the elite centre for wine tourism in the region.

Three Cultures in Toledo

17 Symbolic home to Spain's Catholic Church, once host to thriving Muslim and Jewish communities, the medieval core of Toledo (p204) is an extraordinary piece of world heritage. Known as 'the city of the three cultures', it remains a fascinating labyrinth with former mosques, synagogues and churches; the latter are still very much in use and the cathedral is one of Spain's most imposing. Given Toledo's proximity to Madrid, the city can get overrun with day-trippers. Stay overnight – that's when Toledo really comes into its own. Top right: Alcázar (p205)

Flamenco

18 The soundtrack to Europe's most passionate country, flamenco (p856) has the power to lift you out of the doldrums and stir your soul. It's as if by sharing in the pain of innumerable generations of dispossessed misfits you open a door to a secret world of musical ghosts and ancient spirits. On the other side of the coin, flamenco culture can also be surprisingly jolly, jokey and tongue-in-cheek. There's only one real proviso: you have to hear it live, preferably in its Seville-Jerez-Cádiz heartland, although anywhere in Andalucía should do.

Need to Know

For more information, see Survival Guide (p861)

Currency
Euro (€)

Language
Spanish (Castilian). Also Catalan, Basque and Galician.

Visas
Generally not required for stays of up to 90 days (not at all for members of EU or Schengen countries). Some nationalities need a Schengen visa.

Money
ATMs widely available. Credit cards accepted in most hotels, restaurants and shops.

Mobile Phones
Local SIM cards widely available and can be used in European and Australian mobile phones. Not compatible with many North American or Japanese systems.

Time
Central European time zone; GMT/UTC plus one hour.

When to Go

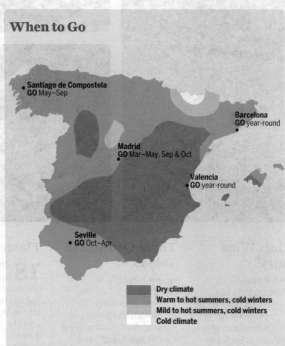

Santiago de Compostela
GO May–Sep

Barcelona
GO year-round

Madrid
GO Mar–May, Sep & Oct

Valencia
GO year-round

Seville
GO Oct–Apr

Dry climate
Warm to hot summers, cold winters
Mild to hot summers, cold winters
Cold climate

High Season
(Jun–Aug, public holidays)

➡ Accommodation books out and prices increase by up to 50%.

➡ Low season in parts of inland Spain.

➡ Expect warm, dry and sunny weather; more humid in coastal areas.

Shoulder (Mar–May, Sep & Oct)

➡ A good time to travel with mild, clear weather and fewer crowds.

➡ Local festivals can send prices soaring.

Low Season
(Nov–Feb)

➡ Cold in central Spain; rain in the north and northwest.

➡ Mild temperatures in Andalucía and the Mediterranean coast.

➡ This is high season in ski resorts.

➡ Many hotels are closed in beach areas but elsewhere prices plummet.

Useful Websites

Fiestas.net (www.fiestas.net) Festivals around the country.

Lonely Planet (www.lonely planet.com/spain) Destination information, hotel bookings, traveller forums and more.

Renfe (Red Nacional de los Ferrocarriles Españoles; www.renfe.com) Spain's rail network.

Tour Spain (www.tourspain.org) Culture, food and links to hotels and transport.

Turespaña (www.spain.info) Spanish tourist office's site.

Important Numbers

There are no area codes in Spain.

International access code	☏00
Country code	☏34
International directory inquiries	☏11825
Domestic operator	☏1009
National directory inquiries	☏11818
Emergencies	☏112

Exchange Rates

Australia	A$1	€0.66
Canada	C$1	€0.67
Japan	¥100	€0.70
New Zealand	NZ$1	€0.61
UK	UK£1	€1.21
US	US$1	€0.73

For current exchange rates see www.xe.com.

Daily Costs

Budget: less than €75

➡ Dorm bed: €18–25

➡ Double room in *hostal*: €55–65 (more in Madrid and Barcelona)

➡ Self-catering and lunch *menú del día*: €9–14

➡ Use museum and gallery 'free admission' afternoons

Midrange: €75–175

➡ Double room in midrange hotel: €65–140

➡ Lunch and/or dinner in local restaurant: €20–40

➡ Car rental: per day from €25

Top End: more than €175

➡ Double room in top-end hotel: €140 and up (€200 in Madrid, Barcelona and the Balearics)

➡ Fine dining for lunch and dinner: €150–250

➡ Regularly stay in *paradores* (luxury state-owned hotels)

Opening Hours

Standard opening hours are for high season only and tend to shorten outside that time.

Banks 8.30am–2pm weekdays; some also open 4pm–7pm Thursday, 9am–1pm Saturday

Central post offices 8.30am–9.30pm weekdays, 8.30am–2pm Saturday (most other branches 8.30am–8.30pm weekdays, 9.30am–1pm Saturday)

Nightclubs midnight or 1am to 5am or 6am

Restaurants lunch 1pm–4pm, dinner 8.30pm–11pm or midnight

Shops 10am–2pm and 4.30pm–7.30pm or 5pm–8pm; big supermarkets and department stores generally open 10am–10pm Monday to Saturday

Arriving in Spain

Barajas Airport (Madrid, p131) Metro and buses cost €4.50 to €5 and run every five to 10 minutes from 6.05am to 1.30am; it's 30 to 40 minutes to the centre. Taxis cost €30 and reach the centre in 20 minutes.

El Prat Airport (Barcelona, p297) Buses cost €5.90 and run every five to 10 minutes from 6.10am to 1.05am; it's 30 to 40 minutes to the centre. Trains cost €4.10 and run every 30 minutes from 5.42am to 11.38pm; it takes 25 to 30 minutes to reach the centre. Taxis cost €25 to €30 and reach the centre in 30 minutes.

Getting Around

Spain's system of public transport is one of the best in Europe, with a fast and super-modern train system, extensive domestic air network, an impressive and well-maintained road network, and buses that connect villages in the country's remotest corners.

Train Extremely efficient rail network from slow inter-city regional trains to some of the fastest trains on the planet with more routes being added to the network every year.

Car Vast network of motorways radiating out from Madrid to all corners of the country shadowed by smaller but often more picturesque minor roads.

Bus The workhorses of the Spanish roads, from slick express services to stop-everywhere village-to-village buses.

For much more on **getting around**, see p875

First Time Spain

For more information, see Survival Guide (p861)

Checklist

➡ With huge airfare differences, check *all* airlines before booking your flight.

➡ Check if you can use your phone in Spain and ask about roaming charges.

➡ At the very least, book your first night's accommodation to ensure an easy start to your trip.

➡ Check the calendar to work out which festivals to visit or avoid.

➡ Organise travel insurance.

What to Pack

➡ Passport and/or national ID card (EU citizens) and carry it on you.

➡ Spanish phrasebook – not everyone speaks English.

➡ Money belt, and padlock for your suitcase/backpack.

➡ Headphones for bus or train journeys and Skype calls.

➡ Two-pin continental Europe travel plug.

➡ Earplugs for noisy Spanish nights.

➡ Renfe (train) app and a hiking one downloaded to your phone.

Top Tips for Your Trip

➡ To blend in with the locals (and avoid going hungry), adjust your body clock on arrival. In no time at all you'll be eating lunch at 2.30pm and dinner at 9pm.

➡ A few words of Spanish can go a long way. English is widely (but not universally) spoken.

➡ Spain is food-obsessed and you'll miss half the fun if you don't join in – linger over meals and always ask for the local speciality.

➡ Unless you're in a hurry, avoid the motorways and take the scenic back roads.

➡ Get used to having less personal space and being surrounded by high-volume conversations.

What to Wear

Northern Spain and much of the interior can be bitterly cold in winter – come prepared with plenty of warm clothing. You should also carry some form of wet-weather gear if you're in the northwest. Spaniards are generally quite fashion-conscious and well-dressed – in the cities in particular, they rarely dip below smart casual.

Sleeping

Accommodation in Spain can be outrageously good value by European standards. Reserving a room is always recommended in the high season.

➡ **Paradors** These state-run hotels often inhabit stunning historic buildings and can be surprisingly well-priced, especially off-season.

➡ **Hotels** Everything from boutique to family-run with an equally wide range of rates.

➡ **Hostales** Small, simpler yet comfortable hotel-style places, often with private bathrooms.

➡ **Casas Rurales** Rural homes with usually rustic, simple rooms that can be reserved individually or as a block.

➡ **Camping & Youth Hostels** For the budget-minded traveller. Quality varies but they're great places to meet other travellers.

Money

Paying with a credit card is widespread in Spain (except in many bars), although there may be a minimum (€5 to €10). Visa and MasterCard are almost always accepted, American Express less so. When paying with a credit card, photo ID (eg passport or driving licence) is required, even where you're required to enter your PIN.

ATMs are everywhere and most allow you to use international credit or debit cards to withdraw money in euros (always check the display showing which cards you can use). There is usually a charge (1.5% to 2%) on ATM cash withdrawals abroad; check with your bank before leaving home.

For more information, see p869.

Bargaining

Haggling over prices is accepted in some markets, and shops *may* offer a small discount if you're spending a lot of money. Otherwise expect to pay the stated price.

Tipping

➡ **When to Tip** Tipping is almost always optional.

➡ **Restaurants** Many Spaniards leave small change, others up to 5%, which is considered generous.

➡ **Taxis** Optional, but most locals round up to the nearest euro.

➡ **Bars** It's rare to leave a tip in bars (even if the bartender gives you your change on a small dish).

Language

English is quite widely spoken, especially in larger cities and popular tourist areas, less so in rural villages and among older Spaniards. Learning a little Spanish before you come will, however, greatly increase your appreciation of the country, not least through your ability to converse with locals. Many restaurants (but by no means all) now have English-language menus, but some museums have labels only in Spanish.

Phrases to Learn Before You Go

1 **What time does it open/close?**
¿A qué hora abren/cierran? a ke o·ra ab·ren/thye·ran

The Spanish tend to observe the siesta (midday break), so opening times may surprise you.

2 **Are these complimentary?**
¿Son gratis? son gra·tees

Tapas (bar snacks) are available pretty much around the clock at Spanish bars. You'll find they're free in some places.

3 **When is admission free?**
¿Cuándo es la entrada gratuita?
kwan·do es la en·tra·da gra·twee·ta

Many museums and galleries in Spain have admission-free times, so check before buying tickets.

4 **Where can we go (salsa) dancing?**
¿Dónde podemos ir a bailar (salsa)?
don·de po·de·mos eer a bai·lar (sal·sa)

Flamenco may be the authentic viewing experience in Spain, but to actively enjoy the music you'll want to do some dancing.

5 **How do you say this in (Catalan/Galician/Basque)?**
¿Cómo se dice ésto en (catalán/gallego/euskera)?
ko·mo se dee·the es·to en (ka·ta·lan/ga·lye·go/e·oos·ke·ra)

Spain has four official languages, and people in these regions will appreciate it if you try to use their local language.

Etiquette

➡ **Greetings** Spaniards greet friends and strangers alike with a kiss on each cheek, although two males only do this if they're close friends. It is customary to say 'Hola, buenos días' or 'Hola, buenas tardes' (in the afternoon or evening) when meeting someone or when entering a shop or bar, and 'hasta luego' when leaving.

➡ **Eating & Drinking** Spanish waiters won't expect you to thank them every time they bring you something, but may expect you to keep your cutlery between courses in casual bars and restaurants.

➡ **Visiting Churches** It is considered disrespectful to visit churches for the purposes of tourism during Mass and other worship services.

➡ **Escalators** Always stand on the right to let people pass.

What's New

Jewish Andalucía

Andalucía's Jewish history finally emerges from the shadows at Seville's new Centro de Interpretación Judería de Sevilla (p583), and Granada's Palacio de los Olvidados (p663) and Museo Sefardí (p662).

Dalí in Mallorca

The Museo Can Morey de Santmartí (p782) in Palma de Mallorca is an astonishing collection of over 220 original works by Salvador Dalí.

Rise & Rise of Flamenco

New highlights of Andalucía's flamenco boom include Seville's relocated Casa de la Memoria (p584) and Casa de la Guitarra (p595), Córdoba's Centro Flamenco Fosforito (p645) and Granada's Casa del Arte Flamenco (p673).

Jamón's New Home

Finally a museum, the Museo del Jamón (p570), worthy of Spain's stunning culinary success story. It's in Extremadura's far south, in the heart of *jamón* country.

Archaeology's Return

Santander's Museo de Prehistoria y Arqueología de Cantabria (p459), Madrid's Museo Arqueológico Nacional (p92) and Logroño's Museo de la Rioja (p446) have all finally reopened. And the results, from prehistoric cave art to Spain's Roman history, are spectacular.

Rooftop Tours

The cathedrals in Lugo (p541) and Tui (p535) in Galicia now offer rooftop tours, giving fascinating perspectives on the buildings' interiors and panoramic vistas out over the rooftops.

Modernista Masterpieces

Barcelona's magnificent Modernista heritage just got better with the reopening of Gaudí's Bellesguard (☎93 250 40 93; www.bellesguardgaudi.com; Carrer de Bellesguard 16; admission €7; ⊙10am-7pm Mon-Sat Apr-Oct, 10am-3pm Mon-Sat Nov-Mar; ◾FGC Avinguda Tibidabo), Casa Amatller (by Puig i Cadafalch, p256) and Casa Lleó Morera (by Domènech i Montaner p256).

Street-Art Hotel

With its reputation for clubbing ecstasy, Ibiza has added more street cred to its portfolio with Urban Spaces (p811), an alternative bolthole where the suites are decorated by world-famous street artists.

Artisan Beers

Spain's love affair with beers has finally translated into a small but growing industry of microbrewers. Our pick of the newbies is Córdoba's Cervezas Califa (p647).

Barcelona's Design Hub

The new, ultra-modernist Disseny Hub (www.dhub-bcn.cat; Plaça de les Glòries Catalanes 37; ◾Glòries) is the vanguard of an entire neighbourhood's renewal, with a decorative arts and textiles museum among the attractions planned.

Madrid Rooftops

The newly accessible roof terraces of Madrid – the Círculo de Bellas Artes (p79) and Mirador de Madrid (p91) – offer fabulous views out over central Madrid and beyond.

For more recommendations and reviews, see **lonelyplanet.com/spain**

If You Like...

Islamic Architecture

Almost seven centuries of Muslim empires bequeathed to Spain Europe's finest accumulation of Islamic architecture, especially in the former Moorish heartland of Al-Andalus (Andalucía), which encompassed Granada, Córdoba and Seville.

Alhambra An extraordinary monument to the extravagance of Al-Andalus, breathtaking in scope and exquisite in its detail. (p655)

Mezquita Perfection wrought in stone in Córdoba's onetime great mosque, one of Al-Andalus' finest architectural moments. (p641)

Alcázar Exquisite detail amid a perfectly proportioned whole. (p579)

Giralda The former minaret represents a high point in Seville's Islamic skyline. (p575)

Aljafería A rare Moorish jewel in the north. (p365)

Alcazaba An 11th-century palace-fortress. (p684)

Teruel A splendid, little-known collection of Mudéjar design, proof that Islam's influence outlasted Islamic rule. (p390)

Incredible Art

Spain's artistic tradition is one of Europe's richest and most original, from local masters to Europe's finest, who flourished under Spanish royal patronage. The result? Art galleries of astonishing depth.

Museo del Prado Quite simply one of the world's best galleries. (p83)

Centro de Arte Reina Sofia Picasso's *Guernica,* Dalí and Miró. (p89)

Museo Thyssen-Bornemisza Works by seemingly every European master. (p85)

Museo Picasso Málaga More than 200 works by Picasso, Málaga's favourite son. (p683)

Museu Picasso Unrivalled collection from Picasso's early years. (p246)

Museu Nacional d'Art de Catalunya Epic collection that includes some extraordinary Romanesque frescoes. (p264)

Teatre-Museu Dalí As weird and wonderful as Salvador Dalí himself. (p322)

Museo Guggenheim Showpiece architecture and world-class contemporary art. (p399)

Roman Ruins

Hispania was an important part of the ancient Roman Empire for almost five centuries; it left a legacy of extraordinary sites scattered around the country.

Mérida The most extensive Roman remains in Spain. (p562)

Segovia Astonishing Roman aqueduct bisects the city. (p159)

Lugo Spain's finest preserved Roman walls encircle this Galician city. (p540)

Itálica Iberia's oldest Roman town with a fine amphitheatre, close to Seville. (p598)

Baelo Claudia Intact Roman town with views of Africa on Andalucía's far southern coast. (p633)

Zaragoza A fine theatre, beautifully restored forum, baths and a former river port. (p362)

Villa Romana La Olmeda Spain's best-preserved Roman villa laid with exquisite mosaic floors. (p177)

IF YOU LIKE...FLAMENCO

Seville (p589), in Andalucía, is the best place to catch flamenco live.

Torre de Hércules In A Coruña, this 1st-century-AD lighthouse sits on what was then the furthest tip of the civilised world. (p515)

Cathedrals

Catholicism is at the heart of Spanish identity, and cathedrals, with their rich accumulation of architectural styles, form the monumental and spiritual centrepiece of many Spanish towns.

La Sagrada Família Gaudí's unfinished masterpiece rises above Barcelona like an apparition of some fevered imagination. (p249)

Catedral de Santiago de Compostela One of Spain's most sacred (and beautiful) sites, with a magnificent Romanesque portico. (p503)

Catedral de Burgos A Gothic high point with legends of El Cid lording it over the old town. (p185)

Catedral de Toledo Extravagant monument to the power of Catholic Spain in its most devout heartland. (p204)

Catedral de Seville Vast and very beautiful Gothic cathedral with the stunning Giralda bell-tower. (p575)

Catedral de Mallorca Palma's cathedral includes breath-taking work by Gaudí and Miquel Barceló. (p780)

Beaches

Despite Spain's summer popularity, the country's surfeit of coastal riches means that an unspoiled beach experience remains a possibility. You just need to know where to look.

Above: Roman Aqueduct (p159), Segovia.

Below: Teatro Joy Eslava dance club (p114), Madrid

Cabo de Gata A wildly beautiful reminder of the Andalucian coast as it once was. (p721)

Costa de la Luz Unbroken stretches of sand along a beautiful coast from Tarifa to Cádiz. (p632)

Playa de la Concha One of the most beautiful city beaches anywhere in the world. (p417)

Menorca The Balearics before mass tourism arrived and an insight into why it did. (p799)

Costa Brava Rugged coast with windswept cliffs, pristine hidden coves and wide beaches. (p304)

Rías Baixas Dramatic long ocean inlets and islands strung with many a fine sandy strand. (p523)

Staying Out Late

From sophisticated cocktail bars to beachside *chiringuitos* (bars), from dance-until-dawn nightclubs to outdoor *terrazas* (bars with outdoor tables), Spanish nightlife is diverse, relentless and utterly intoxicating.

Ibiza Europe's club and chill-out capital and the enduring icon of Mediterranean cool. (p812)

Madrid Bars, nightclubs, live-music venues and nights that roll effortlessly into one another. (p113)

Valencia Barrio del Carmen and Russafa nights are famous throughout Spain, with a roaring soundtrack in the city's oldest quarter. (p743)

Barcelona Glamorous and gritty nightspots for an international crowd. (p287)

Zaragoza The heartbeat of Aragón with fabulous tapas bars and drinking bars that don't crank up until well after midnight. (p367)

Spanish Food

Spain obsesses about food with an eating public as eager to try something new as they are wary lest their chefs stray too far from one of Europe's richest culinary traditions.

Pintxos in San Sebastián Spain's culinary capital, with more Michelin stars than Paris and the country's best *pintxos* (Basque tapas). (p424)

Paella in Valencia The birthplace of paella and still the place for the most authentic version – think chicken, beans and rabbit. (p739)

Catalan cooking in Barcelona Home city for Catalonia's legendary cooking fuelled by Spain's top food markets. (p285)

Tapas in La Latina, Madrid Rising above Madrid's modest home-grown cuisine, this inner-city *barrio* (district) showcases the best tapas from around Spain. (p112)

Seafood in Galicia The dark arts of boiling an octopus and the Atlantic's sea creatures (goose barnacles, anyone?) are pure culinary pleasure. (p512)

Roasted meats in the interior *Cochinillo asado* (roast suckling pig) and *cordero asado lechal* (roast spring lamb) are fabulous winter staples. (p161 and p184)

Wine Tasting

In many parts of the country you won't find anything *but* wines from Spain. La Rioja is the king of Spanish wine regions, but there's so much more to be discovered.

La Rioja wine region Bodegas, wine museums and vineyards to the horizon – this is Spanish wine's heartland. (p446)

Ribera del Duero Spain's favourite wine region in waiting, with bodegas lining the riverbank. (p196)

Penedès wine country The sparkling cava wines that are Spain's favourite Christmas drink. (p350)

El Puerto de Santa María The sherry capital of the world, with numerous bodegas open for visits and tastings. (p614)

Somontano One of Spain's most underrated wine regions, with dozens of vineyards open to the public. (p386)

Galicia Up-and-coming region with fruity white *albariño* a revival of native grape varieties. (p526)

Hiking

Spanish landscapes are continental in variety and include some of Europe's premier hiking destinations, from the Pyrenees in the north to the valleys of Andalucía in the south.

Parque Nacional de Ordesa y Monte Perdido Pyrenean high country at its most spectacular. (p379)

Camino de Santiago One of the world's most famous walks, which can last a couple of days or weeks. (p49)

Picos de Europa Jagged peaks and steep trails inland from the Bay of Biscay. (p489)

Serra de Tramuntana The finest hiking in the Balearics, along Mallorca's west coast. (p786)

Sierra Nevada Wildlife and stunning views in the shadow of mainland Spain's highest mountain. (p675)

Month by Month

TOP EVENTS

Semana Santa (Holy Week), usually March or April

Las Fallas, March

Bienal de Flamenco, September

Carnaval, February or March

Feria de Abril, April

January

Ski resorts in the Pyrenees in the northeast and the Sierra Nevada, close to Granada in the south, are in full swing. School holidays run until around 8 January; book ahead.

✶✶ Three Kings

El Día de los Reyes Magos (Three Kings' Day), on 6 January, is the highlight of a Spanish kid's calendar. The night before, three local politicians dress up as the three wise men and lead a sweet-distributing frenzy (Cabalgata de Reyes) through most towns.

February

This is often the coldest month in Spain, with temperatures close to freezing, especially in the north and inland regions. If you're heading to Carnaval, accommodation is at a premium in Cádiz, Sitges and Ciudad Rodrigo.

✶✶ Carnaval

Riotously fun, Carnaval ends on the Tuesday 47 days before Easter Sunday, and involves fancy-dress parades and festivities. It's wildest in Cádiz (p611), Sitges (p347) and Ciudad Rodrigo (p154).

✶✶ Fiesta Medieval

In one of Spain's coldest corners, Teruel's inhabitants don their medieval finery and step back to the Middle Ages with markets, food stalls and a re-enactment of a local lovers' legend during the Fiesta Medieval. (p392)

✶✶ Contemporary Art Fair

One of Europe's biggest celebrations of contemporary art, Madrid's Feria Internacional de Arte Contemporánea (Arco) draws gallery reps and exhibitors from all over the world. (p101)

✶✶ Barcelona's Winter Bash

Around 12 February, the Festes de Santa Eulàlia celebrates Barcelona's first patron saint with a week of cultural events, from parades of giants to *castells* (human castles). (p272)

March

With the arrival of spring, the weather starts to warm up ever so slightly and Spaniards start dreaming of a summer by the beach.

☆ Festival de Jerez

One of Spain's most important flamenco festivals takes place in the genre's heartland in late February or early March. (p622)

✶✶ Las Fallas de San José

The extraordinary festival of Las Fallas consists of several days of all-night dancing and drinking, first-class fireworks and processions from 15 to 19 March. Its principal stage is Valencia City and the festivities culminate in the ritual burning of effigies in the streets. (p745)

April

Spain has a real spring in its step with wildflowers in full bloom, Easter celebrations and school holidays. It requires some advance planning (book ahead), but it's a great time to be here.

☆☆ Semana Santa (Holy Week)

Easter (the dates change each year) entails parades of *pasos* (holy figures), hooded penitents and huge crowds. It's extravagantly celebrated in Seville (p589), as well as Málaga (p686), Ávila (p144), Cuenca (p223), Lorca (p774) and Zamora (p171).

☆☆ Dance of Death

The Dansa de la Mort on Holy Thursday in the Catalan village of Verges is a chilling experience. This nocturnal dance of skeleton figures is the centrepiece of Holy Week celebrations. (p316)

☆☆ Los Empalaos

On Holy Thursday, Villanueva de la Vera, in northeast Extremadura, plays out an extraordinary act of Easter self-abnegation; the devotion and self-inflicted suffering of the barefoot penitents leaves most onlookers breathless. (p558)

☆☆ Moros y Cristianos (Moors & Christians)

Late-April colourful parades and mock battles between Christian and Muslim 'armies' in Alcoy, near Alicante, make this one of the most spectacular of many such festivities staged in Valencia and Alicante provinces. (p762)

☆☆ Feria de Abril

This week-long party, held in Seville in the second half of April, is the biggest of Andalucía's fairs. *Sevillanos* dress up in traditional finery, ride around on horseback and in elaborate horse-drawn carriages and dance late into the night. (p589)

☆☆ Romería de la Virgen

On the last Sunday in April, hundreds of thousands of people make a mass pilgrimage to the Santuario de la Virgen de la Cabeza near Andújar, in Jaén province. A small statue of the Virgin is paraded about, exciting great passion.

May

A glorious time to be in Spain, May sees the countryside carpeted with spring wildflowers.

☆☆ Muslim Pirates

Sóller, in northern Mallorca, is invaded by Muslim pirates in early May. The resulting 'battle' between townsfolk and invaders, known as Es Firó, recreates an infamous (and unsuccessful) 16th-century assault on the town. (p790)

☆☆ Feria del Caballo (Horse Fair)

A colourful equestrian fair in Andalucía's horse capital, Jerez de la Frontera, the Feria del Caballo is one of Andalucía's most festive and extravagant fiestas. It features parades, horse shows, bullfights and plenty of music and dance. (p622)

◉ Córdoba's Courtyards Open Up

Scores of beautiful private courtyards in Córdoba are opened to the public for the Festival de Los Patios Cordobeses. It's a rare chance to see an otherwise hidden side of Córdoba strewn with flowers and freshly painted. (p645)

☆ Titirimundi International Puppet Festival

For a week in the middle of May, puppet shows take over Segovia with all manner of street events throughout the city to celebrate this fine festival. (p161)

☆☆ Fiesta de San Isidro

Madrid's major fiesta celebrates the city's patron saint with bullfights, parades, concerts and more. Locals dress up in traditional costumes, and some of the events, such as the bullfighting season, last for a month. (p101)

June

By June, the north is shaking off its winter chill and the Camino de Santiago's trails are becoming crowded. In the south, it's warming up as the coastal resorts ready themselves for the summer onslaught.

☆☆ Romería del Rocío

Focused on Pentecost weekend (the seventh after Easter), this festive pilgrimage is undertaken by up to one million people to the shrine of the Virgin in El Rocío. This is Andalucía's Catholic tradition at its most curious and compelling. (p604)

✷✷ Feast of Corpus Christi

On the Thursday in the ninth week after Easter (sometimes May, sometimes June), religious processions and celebrations take place in Toledo (p208) and other cities. The strangest celebration is the baby-jumping tradition of Castrillo de Murcia. (p208)

✷✷ Bonfires & Fireworks

Midsummer bonfires, fireworks and roaming giants feature on the eve of the Fiesta de San Juan (24 June; Dia de Sant Joan), notably along the Mediterranean coast, particularly in Barcelona and in Ciutadella, Menorca, where you can see splendid horsemanship in parades. (p272)

☆ Electronica Festival

Performers and spectators come from all over the world for Sónar, Barcelona's two-day celebration of electronic music, which is said to be Europe's biggest festival of its kind. Dates vary each year. (p272)

🍷 Wine Battle

On 29 June Haro, one of the premier wine towns of La Rioja, enjoys the Batalla del Vino, squirting wine all over the place in one of Spain's messiest playfights, pausing only to drink the good stuff. (p450)

July

Temperatures in Andalucía and much of the interior can be fiercely hot, but it's a great time to be at the beach and is one of the

Above: Catedral de Santiago de Compostela (p503)

Below: La Tomatina festival (p748), Buñol

best months for hiking in the Pyrenees.

☆ Festival Internacional de la Guitarra

Held in Córdoba, this fine international guitar festival ranges from flamenco and classical to rock, blues and beyond. Headline performances take place in the Alcázar gardens at night. (p645)

🎊 Running of the Bulls

The Fiesta de San Fermín (Sanfermines) is the week-long nonstop festival and party in Pamplona with the daily *encierro* (running of the bulls) as its centrepiece. The anti-bullfighting event, the Running of the Nudes, takes place two days earlier. (p437)

☆ Celtic Pride

Groups from as far off as Nova Scotia come to celebrate their Celtic roots with the *gallegos* (Galicians) at Festival Ortigueira (www.festivaldeortigueira.com), a bagpipe- and fiddler-filled music fest held in the Rías Atlas, Galicia.

🎊 Día de la Virgen del Carmen

Around 16 July in most coastal towns, particularly in some parts of Andalucía, the image of the patron of fisherfolk is carried into the sea or paraded on a flotilla of small boats.

🎊 Fiestas del Apóstol Santiago

The Día de Santiago (25 July) marks the day of Spain's national saint and is spectacularly celebrated in Santiago de Compostela.

With so many pilgrims around, it's the city's most festive two weeks of the year. (p507)

☆ Festival Internacional de Benicàssim

Spain is awash with outdoor concert festivals attracting big-name acts from around the country and abroad, especially in summer. This one, in the Valencian town of Benicàssim, remains one of the original and best. (p748)

🎊 Santander Summer

Semana Grande in Santander (around 25 July) is this northern Spanish town's big summer blow-out, with music, shows and plenty of partying all day and all night. (p460)

August

Spaniards join Europeans in converging on the coastal resorts of the Mediterranean. Although the weather can be unpredictable, Spain's northwestern Atlantic coast offers a more nuanced summer experience.

🎊 Crazy for Canoeing

The Descenso Internacional del Sella takes place in Asturias on the first weekend in August when tens of thousands of people go mad for a canoeing competition between Arriondas and Ribadesella. (p480)

☆ Festival del Teatro Clásico

The peerless Roman theatre and amphitheatre in Mér-

ida, Extremadura, become the stage for the classics of ancient Greece and Rome, and the occasional newbie such as Will Shakespeare. Performances are held most nights during July and August. (p564)

🍷 Galician Wines

The fabulous wines of Galicia are the reason for the Fiesta del Albariño in Cambados on the first weekend of August. Expect five days of music, fireworks and intensive consumption of Galicia's favourite fruity white wine.

🍷 Natural Cider Festival

Gijón's Fiesta de la Sidra Natural gives expression to the Asturian obsession with cider and even includes an annual world-record attempt for the number of people simultaneously pouring cider in one place. It also involves musical concerts. (p477)

✕ Galician Octopus

Galicia's passion for octopus boils over at the Festa do Pulpo de O Carballiño on the second Sunday in August. Tens of thousands of people converge on the small town of Carballiño to eat as much of the stuff as they can.

🎊 Barcelona Street Festival

Locals compete for the most elaborately decorated street in the popular week-long Festa Major de Gràcia, held around 15 August. People pour in to listen to bands in the streets and squares, fuel up on snacks, and drink at countless street stands. (p272)

La Tomatina

Buñol's massive tomato-throwing festival, held in late August, must be one of the messiest get-togethers in the country. Thousands of people launch about 100 tonnes of tomatoes at one another in just an hour or so! (p748)

September

This is the month when Spain returns to work after a seemingly endless summer. Numerous festivals take advantage of the fact that weather generally remains warm until late September.

Bienal de Flamenco

There are flamenco festivals all over Spain throughout the year, but this is the most prestigious of them all. Held in Seville in even-numbered years (and Málaga every other year), it draws the biggest names in the genre. (p589)

Fiesta de la Virgen de Guadalupe

The pretty town of Guadalupe in Extremadura celebrates its very own Virgin Mary. A statue is paraded about on the evening of the 6th and again on the 8th, which also happens to be Extremadura's regional feast day.

Feria de Pedro Romero

The honouring of Pedro Romero, one of the legends of bullfighting, is a good excuse for the people of Ronda to host weeks of partying. Highlights include a flamenco festival, an unusual program of bullfighting and much all-night partying. (p635)

La Rioja's Grape Harvest

Logroño celebrates the feast day of St Matthew (Fiesta de San Mateo) and the year's grape harvest. There are grape-crushing ceremonies and endless opportunities to sample the fruit of the vine in liquid form. (p446)

Barcelona's Big Party

Barcelona's co-patron saint is celebrated with fervour in the massive four-day Festes de la Mercè in September. The city stages special exhibitions, free concerts and street performers galore. (p274)

San Sebastián Film Festival

It may not be Cannes, but San Sebastián's annual two-week celebration of film is one of the most prestigious dates on Europe's film-festival circuit. It's held in the second half of the month and has been gathering plaudits since 1957. (p421)

Romans & Carthaginians

In the second half of the month, locals dress up to re-enact ancient battles during the festival of Carthagineses y Romanos in Cartagena. It's among the more original mock battles staged around Spain to honour the distant past. (p771)

October

Autumn brings generally mild temperatures to Spain, although the winter chill can start to bite in central and northern parts of the country.

Fiestas del Pilar

In Zaragoza on 12 October, the faithful mix with hedonists to celebrate this festival dedicated to Our Lady of the Pillar; the pillar in question is in the cathedral, but much of the fun happens in the bars nearby. (p365)

Fiesta de Santa Teresa

The patron saint of Ávila is honoured with 10 days of processions, concerts and fireworks around her feast day. Huddled behind medieval walls, the festival brings to life the powerful cult of personality surrounding Ávila's most famous daughter. (p144)

November

A quiet time on the festival calendar, November is cool throughout the country. The ski season usually begins in this month in the Pyrenees and Sierra Nevada.

La Matanza

One of Andalucía's more macabre spectacles is November's pig massacre, known as *la matanza*, which traditionally starts on 11 November – St Martin's Day. It's an upbeat affair replicated in many mountain villages in the Spanish interior with plenty of eating and drinking.

Itineraries

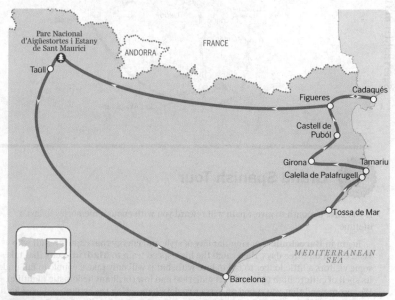

Barcelona & Around

Spend a lifetime in **Barcelona** and it may not be enough, but to get a taste of why that's the case you'll need a minimum of two days to soak up the Gaudí sights, taste the city's culinary excellence and wander its old town. When you can tear yourself away, rent a car and head north along the Mediterranean shoreline, passing through **Tossa de Mar** and its castle-backed bay, then **Calella de Palafrugell** and **Tamariu**, two beautifully sited coastal villages, before heading inland to pass the night in wonderful **Girona**. The next day is all about Salvador Dalí, from his fantasy castle **Castell de Puból**, his extraordinary theatre-museum in **Figueres**, and then his one-time home, the lovely seaside village of **Cadaqués**. The next morning, leave the Mediterranean behind and drive west in the shadow of the Pyrenees – a long day in the saddle, but a day with one jaw-dropping vista after another. Your reward is a couple of nights based in **Taüll**, gateway to the utterly magnificent **Parc Nacional d'Aigüestortes i Estany de Sant Maurici**. A loop south via Lleida then east will have you back in Barcelona by mid-afternoon on your final day.

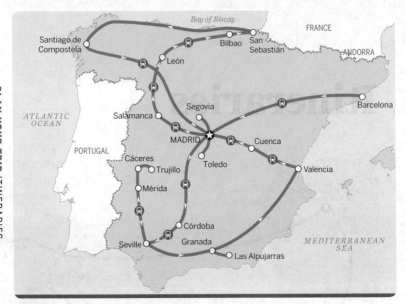

Grand Spanish Tour

4 WEEKS

If you have a month to give, Spain will reward you with enough memories to last a lifetime.

Begin in **Barcelona**, that singular city of style and energy that captivates all who visit. Count on three days, then catch the high-speed train to **Madrid**, a city that takes some visitors a little longer to fall in love with, but it will only take a couple to fall under its spell of culture high (fantastic art galleries) and low (brilliant hedonistic nightlife). We recommend that you spend an extra two days here, using the capital as a base for day trips to **Segovia** and **Toledo**. Catch another train, this time heading for **Salamanca**, that plateresque jewel of Castilla y León. After a night in Salamanca, travel north by train to **León** to stay overnight and see the extraordinary stained-glass windows of its cathedral, and then continue on to **Bilbao**, home of the Guggenheim and so much that is good about Basque culture. Spend a night here, followed by another couple in splendid **San Sebastián**. A couple of days' drive along the Cantabrian, Asturian and Galician coasts will take you along Spain's most dramatic shoreline en route to **Santiago de Compostela**, where a couple of nights is a minimum to soak up this sacred city. Wherever you travel in the north, from San Sebastián to Santiago, make food a centrepiece of your visit.

Catch the train back to Madrid, then take a high-speed train to **Córdoba** (two nights) and **Seville** (two nights). While you're in the area, detour north by bus or train to the Roman ruins of **Mérida** (one night), the fabulous old city of **Cáceres** (one night) and medieval **Trujillo** (one night). Return to Seville and make immediately for **Granada** (two nights). Add an extra couple of nights and a rental car and you can visit the lovely villages of **Las Alpujarras**. Keep the car (or catch the train) and travel from Granada to **Valencia** to spend a couple of days enjoying its architecture, paella and irresistible energy. You've just enough time to catch the high-speed train to cliff-top **Cuenca** (one night) on your way back to Madrid at journey's end.

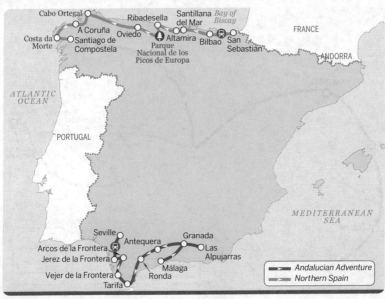

 Andalucian Adventure
10 DAYS

 Northern Spain
10 DAYS

Begin in **Málaga**, whose airport receives flights from almost every conceivable corner of Europe. Málaga has enough attractions to keep you occupied for one very full day; don't miss the Picasso Museum. No Andalucian itinerary is complete without at least a couple of nights in peerless **Granada** with its astonishing Alhambra, gilded Capilla Real and medieval Muslim quarter of Albayzín. Rent a car and make for the otherworldly valleys of **Las Alpujarras** with their fine mountain scenery and North African–style villages, where you should stay overnight. If you've kept the car, head west for three days along quiet back roads to some of Andalucía's most spectacular villages and towns – Mudéjar **Antequera**, spectacular **Ronda**, whitewashed **Tarifa** with its bohemian air, beguiling **Vejer de la Frontera** and **Arcos de la Frontera**, one of Andalucía's most glorious *pueblos blancos* (white villages). With three days left, leave the car and spend a night in **Jerez de la Frontera**, allowing time to visit its sherry bodegas, then catch a train north to flamenco-rich **Seville**, which is for many the essence of Andalucía.

There is no finer introduction to the north of the country than **San Sebastián**, with its dramatic setting and fabulous food. Two nights is a minimum. Less than three hours west of San Sebastián by train, **Bilbao** is best known as the home of the showpiece Guggenheim Museum and warrants at least a night, preferably two. To make the most of the rest of the coast, you'll need a car. Cantabria's cobblestone medieval marvel, **Santillana del Mar**, the rock art at **Altamira**, and the village of **Ribadesella** will fill one day, with another taken up by the steep valleys of the **Picos de Europa**. After a third night in irresistible **Oviedo**, tackle Galicia's coastline, one of Spain's great natural wonders, punctuated with secluded fishing villages and stunning cliffs. As you make your way around the coast for a further two nights, don't miss **Cabo Ortegal**, dynamic **A Coruña** and the **Costa da Morte**. For the last two nights, linger in **Santiago de Compostela**, a thoroughly Galician city with fine regional cuisine, a cathedral of rare power and many pilgrim footfalls.

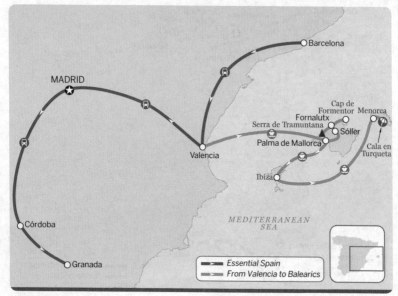

Barcelona

MADRID

Valencia

Córdoba

Granada

Cap de
Formentor Menorca
Fornalutx
Serra de Tramuntana   Sóller
Palma de Mallorca
Cala en
Turqueta

Ibiza

*MEDITERRANEAN
SEA*

Essential Spain
From Valencia to Balearics

🔟 DAYS Essential Spain

So many Spanish trails begin in **Barcelona**, Spain's second-biggest city and one of the coolest places on earth. Explore the architecture and sample the food, before catching the train down the coast to **Valencia** for another dose of nightlife and the 21st-century wonders of the Ciudad de las Artes y las Ciencias. This is the home of paella, and if you only try Spain's signature dish once, make it here. A fast train whisks you inland to the capital, mighty **Madrid**, for the irresistible street energy, the pretty plazas and one of the richest concentrations of art museums on the planet, along the iconic Paseo del Prado. Yet another fast train takes you deep into Andalucía, with **Córdoba** your entry point into this wonderful corner of Spain. The most obvious highlight is Córdoba's 7th-century Mezquita, which captures the essence of the country's formerly Islamic south. But we've saved the best until last: **Granada**, the one-time capital of Muslim Al-Andalus boasts the extraordinary Alhambra, its soulful alter ego, the Albayzín, and an eating and drinking scene that embraces Spanish culinary culture in all its variety.

1️⃣ WEEK Valencia & the Balearics

Valencia, Spain's third-largest city, has many calling cards, among them the chance to eat Spain's finest paella, the Ciudad de las Artes y las Ciencias, which may just be Spain's most extraordinary example of contemporary architecture, and the Barrio del Carmen, one of the country's liveliest quarters. After at least two days, catch a ferry to pretty **Palma de Mallorca** and spend at least a full day in the town, lingering in particular over its astonishing cathedral. Take the vintage train to **Sóller** and hire a car to drive along the **Serra de Tramuntana** coast and explore the villages of Mallorca's northwest, such as **Fornalutx**, and the fine coastal scenery at **Cap de Formentor**, where the drama of these rocky isles takes on full power. After a couple of days in the northwest, return to Palma for the ferry to **Ibiza** and dive into its world-famous nightlife, before island-hopping again, this time to **Menorca** and its wonderful south-coast beaches. If we had to choose just one of these, we'd make it **Cala en Turqueta**.

 ## Castile & Aragón

2 WEEKS

From **Madrid**, head northwest then west to some of the loveliest towns of the Spanish heartland: **Segovia** with its Disneyesque castle and Roman aqueduct, walled **Ávila** and vibrant **Salamanca** should together occupy around four days of your time with short train rides connecting the three. Trains also connect you to the cathedral towns of **León** and **Burgos**, home to two of Spain's most extraordinary churches. Spend at least a day in each. An extra night in Burgos will, if you rent a car for a day, allow you to take a day trip to the medieval village of **Covarrubias**. Cross the border into Aragón and make for **Zaragoza**, one of Spain's most vibrant cities, with a wealth of monuments and great tapas – two days is a must. Rent a car and head for the hills where **Sos del Rey Católico** looks for all the world like a Tuscan hill town – stay overnight to appreciate its quiet charm. Drive south for an overnight stop in dramatic **Daroca**, which is encircled by mountains and ruined city walls, then continue to **Teruel** with its Mudéjar gems. Finish your trip with two nights in **Albarracín**, one of Spain's most spectacular villages, with medieval architecture as extraordinary as the setting.

 ## Extreme West

10 DAYS

Extremadura is one of Spain's least-known corners, which is all the more reason to visit. Begin with a night in Extremadura's north, in **Plasencia**, which is jammed with notable buildings, churches and convents. From Plasencia, catch the bus or train to **Cáceres**, whose Ciudad Monumental is one of the finest surviving medieval cores in any Spanish city. Allow two nights here. Regular buses take an hour to nearby **Trujillo**, a smaller but equally enchanting relic of the Middle Ages. Spend two nights here, one to explore the warren of cobbled lanes, and another to rent a car for a day trip to the charming hill town and pilgrims' destination of **Guadalupe**. From Trujillo it's just over an hour by bus south to **Mérida**, but the journey spans the centuries: Mérida boasts some of Spain's most impressive Roman ruins, and you'll need at least two nights here to take it all in. Further south again by bus across the dry plains lies whitewashed **Zafra**, a precursor to Andalucía in spirit, architecture and geography. After a night in Zafra, all roads lead to magical **Seville**, one of Andalucía's (and Spain's) most captivating cities.

Off the Beaten Track: Spain

ILLAS CÍES

Galicia has many candidates for little-known secrets but the Illas Cíes, off the coast of Vigo, is our pick for its fine beaches and lack of crowds. (p533)

ZAMORA & AROUND

Zamora is a little-visited Romanesque treasure. Not far away, the medieval village of Puebla de Sanabria is stunning. (p170)

SIERRA DE FRANCIA

The timeworn Sierra de Francia contains some of Spain's least-visited back-country villages. The pick is probably La Alberca but San Martín del Castañar is utterly beguiling. (p155)

WESTERN EXTREMADURA

Western Extremadura is the land time forgot, from the quiet valleys of the Sierra de Gata and Las Hurdes (p560) to remote Alcántara (p551) with its fine Roman bridge.

CÁDIZ

Cádiz is all about narrow white-washed streets where the seafood and wine flow freely in summer. The nearby beaches are some of Spain's best. (p606)

BAEZA & ÚBEDA

These twin towns (p709 and p711) in the north of Andalucía are two of Spain's finest Renaissance gems. Better still, they're lightly touristed.

Map labels: Bay of Biscay, ATLANTIC OCEAN, Costa da Morte, Ferrol, A Coruña, Avilés, Gijón, Santander, Oviedo, Parque Natural de Somiedo, Parque Nacional de los Picos de Europa, Torrelavega, Cordillera Cantábrica, Santiago de Compostela, Lugo, León, Burgos, Pontevedra, Vigo, Ourense, ILLAS CÍES, Río Sil, Benavente, Palencia, Aranda de Duero, Valladolid, ZAMORA, Río Duero, Salamanca, Segovia, SIERRA DE FRANCIA, Ávila, Guadalajara, Cordillera Central, MADRID, PORTUGAL, Plasencia, WESTERN EXTREMADURA, Río Tajo, Aranjuez, Toledo, LISBON, Badajoz, Mérida, Ciudad Real, Río Guadiana, Zafra, Parque Natural Sierra de Andújar, ÚBEDA, Parque Natural Sierra Norte, Córdoba, BAEZA, Huelva, Seville, Cordillera Bética, Granada, Parque Natural Sierra Nevada, Parque Nacional de Doñana, CÁDIZ, Parque Los Alcornocales, Málaga, Costa de la Luz, Costa del Sol, Algeciras, Gibraltar

NORTHERN ARAGÓN

Draw near to the Pyrenees from the postcard-perfect villages of Aínsa, Alquézar and Torla on the cusp of the Parque Nacional de Ordesa y Monte Perdido. (p382)

EL MAESTRAZGO

Straddling southwestern Aragón and western Valencia, isolated El Maestrazgo specialises in meandering back roads and pretty hamlets. (p393)

FORMENTERA

Travellers in the know make for Formentera, a little-visited Balearic island south of Ibiza with some of the best beaches in the Mediterranean. (p820)

CABO DE GATA & ALMERÍA

The Cabo de Gata (p721) is dramatic, wild and an antidote to overdeveloped shorelines. Its gateway, Almería (p717), is one of Spain's most agreeable provincial towns.

Baked scallops are a Galician specialit

Plan Your Trip

Eat & Drink Like a Local

For Spaniards, eating is one of life's more pleasurable obsessions.
In this chapter, we'll help you make the most of this fabulous
culinary culture, whether it's demystifying the dark art of ordering
tapas or taking you on a journey through the regional specialities
of Spanish food.

The Year in Food

Southern Spain's relatively balmy climate ensures that, unusually for Europe, fruit and vegetables can be grown year-round.

Winter (Dec–Feb)

Across inland Spain, winter is the time for fortifying stews (such as *cocido* or *fabada*) and roasted meats, especially *cochinillo* (suckling pig) and *cordero* (spring lamb).

Winter to Spring (Nov–Apr)

Catalans salivate over *calçots*, those large spring onions that are eaten with your hands and a bib, and *romesco* (a rich red-peppers-and-ground-almond sauce). This is *pulpo* (boiled octopus) season in Galicia.

Summer (Jun–Aug)

The cold soups gazpacho and *salmorejo* (specialities of Andalucía) only appear in summer. Rice dishes by the Mediterranean are another key ingredient of the Spanish summer.

Autumn (Sep–Nov)

La Rioja's grape harvest gets underway in September. The Fiesta de San Mateo in Logroño (21 September) gets it all happening.

Food Experiences

Food & Wine Festivals

➡ **Feria del Queso** (p553) An orgy of cheese tasting and serious competition in Trujillo in late April or early May.

➡ **Feria del Vino Ribeiro** (p538) Ribadavia in Galicia's south hosts one of the region's biggest wine festivals in early July.

➡ **Fiesta del Albariño** (p31) Five days of music, fireworks and intensive consumption of Galicia's favourite fruity white wine in the first week of August.

➡ **Festa do Pulpo de O Carballiño** (p31) Carballiño in Galicia sees 70,000 people cram in for a mass octopus-eating binge on the second Sunday of August.

➡ **Batalla del Vino** (p450) Every 29 June in Haro in La Rioja, they have a really messy wine fight.

➡ **Fiesta de la Sidra Natural** (p477) This Gijón fiesta in August includes an annual world-record attempt on the number of people simultaneously pouring cider.

➡ **Fiesta de San Mateo** (p446) In Logroño, La Rioja's September grape harvest is celebrated with grape-crushing ceremonies and tastings.

Meals of a Lifetime

➡ **Arzak** (p423) This San Sebastián restaurant is the home kitchen of Spain's most revered father-daughter team.

➡ **Martín Berasategui Restaurant** (p423) One of Spain's most respected celebrity chefs. Also in San Sebastián.

➡ **El Celler de Can Roca** (p316) This Girona eatery represents everything that's good about innovative Catalan cuisine.

➡ **Sergi Arola Gastro** (p112) Catalan master-chef who has taken Madrid by storm.

➡ **Tickets** (p285) Barcelona restaurant from the stable of Spain's most decorated chef.

➡ **La Terraza del Casino** (p108) Located in Madrid, this is one of the country's temples to laboratory-led innovations.

➡ **Quique Dacosta** (p754) Molecular gastronomy brought to the Mediterranean. In Denia.

➡ **DiverXo** (p112) Madrid's only three-Michelin-starred eatery.

Cheap Treats

➡ **Tapas or Pintxos** Possibly the world's most ingenious form of snacking. Madrid's La Latina barrio, Zaragoza's El Tubo, and most Andalucian cities offer rich pickings, but a *pintxo* (Basque tapas) crawl in San Sebastián's Parte Vieja is one of life's most memorable gastronomic experiences.

➡ **Chocolate con Churros** These deep-fried doughnut strips dipped in thick hot chocolate are a Spanish favourite for breakfast, afternoon tea or at dawn on your way home from a night out. Madrid's Chocolatería de San Ginés (p114) is the most famous purveyor.

OLIVER STREWE / GETTY IMAGES ©

➡ **Bocadillos** Rolls filled with *jamón* or other cured meats, cheese, tortilla or (in Madrid) deep-fried calamari.

➡ **Pa amb Tomàquet** Bread rubbed with tomato, olive oil and garlic – a staple in Catalonia, Mallorca and elsewhere.

Cooking Courses

➡ **Alambique** (p99) Cooking classes in Madrid covering Spanish and international themes.

➡ **Cooking Club** (p99) Respected program of classes across a range of cooking styles. In Madrid.

➡ **Apunto** (Map p96; ☑91 702 10 41; www. apuntolibreria.com; Calle de Hortaleza 64; per person €30-60; Ⓜ Chueca) Excellent range of cooking styles in Madrid.

➡ **Catacurian** (☑97 782 53 41; www. catacurian.com) English-language wine and cooking classes in the Priorat region with Catalan chef Alicia Juanpere and her American partner.

➡ **Cook and Taste** (p271) One of Barcelona's best cooking schools.

➡ **Espai Boisa** (☑93 192 60 21; http:// espaiboisa.com; Ptge Lluís Pellicer 8; 3hr class €70) ✦ Excellent three-hour courses with a focus on local ingredients and recipes, and plenty of time to taste what you cook. In Barcelona.

➡ **L'Atelier** (☑958 85 75 01; www.ivu.org/ atelier/index-eng; Calle Alberca 21; cooking classes per person per day €50) Award-winning vegetarian chef Jean-Claude Juston runs vegetarian cooking courses in Andalucía's Las Alpujarras.

➡ **Cooking Holidays Mallorca** (☑971 64 82 03; www.cookingholidaysmallorca.com; Avinguda Llonga) In Cala d'Or, offering everything from tapas to gourmet offerings.

➡ **Mallorca Cuisine** (☑971 61 67 19; www. mallorcacuisine.com; Sa Mola Gran 8, Galilea) Tapas and paella classes close to Palma de Mallorca.

➡ **La Janda** (p632) In Vejer de la Frontera, combining cooking with Spanish classes.

Dare to Try

➡ **Oreja** Pig's ear, cooked on the grill. It's a little like eating gristly bacon.

➡ **Callos** Tripe cooked in a sauce of tomato, paprika, garlic and herbs. It's a speciality of Madrid.

➡ **Rabo de toro** Bull's tail, or oxtail stew. It's a particular delicacy during bullfighting season in Madrid and Andalucía, when the tail comes straight from the bullring...

➡ **Percebes** Goose barnacles from Galicia to the Balearics. The first person to try them sure was one adventurous individual, but we're glad they did.

➡ **Garrotxa** Formidable Catalan cheese that almost lives up to its name.

➡ **Caracoles** Snails. Much loved in Catalonia, Mallorca and Aragón.

➡ **Morcilla** Blood sausage. It's blended with rice in Burgos, with onion in Asturias.

➡ **Criadillas** Bull's testicles. Eaten in Andalucía.

➡ **Botillo** Spanish version of haggis from Castilla y León's Bierzo region.

Local Specialities

Food

Spaniards love to travel in their own country, and given the riches on offer, they especially love to do so in pursuit of the perfect meal. Tell a Spaniard that you're on your way to a particular place and they're sure to start salivating at the mere thought of the local speciality, and they'll surely have a favourite restaurant at which to enjoy it.

Basque Country & Catalonia

The confluence of sea and mountains has bequeathed to the Basque Country an extraordinary culinary richness – seafood and steaks are the pillars upon which Basque cuisine was traditionally built. San Sebastián, in particular, showcases the region's diversity of culinary experiences and it was from the kitchens of San Sebastián that *nueva cocina vasca* (Basque nouvelle cuisine) emerged, announcing Spain's arrival as a culinary superpower.

Catalonia blends traditional Catalan flavours with expansive geographical diversity with an openness to influences from the rest of Europe. All manner of seafood, paella, rice and pasta dishes, as well as Pyrenean game dishes, are regulars on Catalan menus. Sauces are more prevalent here than elsewhere in Spain.

ORDERING TAPAS

Unless you speak Spanish, the art of ordering can seem one of the dark arts of Spanish etiquette. Fear not – it's not as difficult as it first appears.

In the Basque Country, Zaragoza and many bars in Madrid, Barcelona and elsewhere, it couldn't be easier. With tapas varieties lined up along the bar, you either take a small plate and help yourself or point to the morsel you want. If you do this, it's customary to keep track of what you eat (by holding on to the toothpicks, for example) and then tell the bar staff how many you've had when it's time to pay. Otherwise, many places have a list of tapas, either on a menu or posted up behind the bar. If you can't choose, ask for *'la especialidad de la casa'* (the house speciality) and it's hard to go wrong.

Another way of eating tapas is to order *raciones* (literally 'rations'; large tapas servings) or *media raciones* (half-rations; smaller tapas servings). Remember, however, that after a couple of *raciones* you'll be full. In some bars you'll also get a small (free) tapa when you buy a drink.

Inland Spain

The best *jamón ibérico* comes from Extremadura, Salamanca and Teruel, while *cordero asado lechal* (roast spring lamb) and *cochinillo asado* (roast suckling pig) are winter mainstays. Of the hearty stews, the king is *cocido*, a hotpot or stew with a noodle broth, carrots, cabbage, chickpeas, chicken, *morcilla* (blood sausage), beef and lard. *Migas* (breadcrumbs, often cooked with chorizo and served with grapes) are also regulars.

Cheeses, too, are specialities here, from Extremadura's Torta del Casar (a creamy cheese) to Castilla-La Mancha's *queso manchego* (a hard sheep's-milk cheese).

Galicia & the Northwest

Galicia is known for its bewildering array of seafood, and the star is *pulpo á feira* (spicy boiled octopus, called *pulpo gallego* or spelled *pulpo á galega* in the local Galician language), a dish whose constituent elements (octopus, oil, paprika and garlic) are so simple yet whose execution is devilishly difficult. Neighbouring Asturias and Cantabria produce Spain's best *anchoas* (anchovies).

In the high mountains of Asturias and Cantabria, the cuisine is as driven by mountain pasture as it is by the daily comings and goings of fishing fleets. Cheeses are particularly sought after, with special fame reserved for the untreated cow's-milk cheese, *queso de Cabrales. Asturianos* (Asturians) are also passionate about their *fabada asturiana* (a stew made with pork, blood sausage and white beans) and *sidra* (cider) straight from the barrel.

Valencia, Murcia & the Balearic Islands

There's so much more to the cuisine of this region than oranges and paella, but these signature products capture the essence of the Mediterranean table. You can get a paella just about anywhere in Spain, but to get one cooked as it should be cooked, look no further than the restaurants in Valencia's waterfront Las Arenas district or La Albufera. In the Balearics, paella, rice dishes and lashings of seafood are similarly recurring themes.

Murcia's culinary fame brings us back to the oranges. The littoral is known simply as 'La Huerta' ('the garden'). Since Moorish times, this has been one of Spain's most prolific areas for growing fruit and vegetables.

Andalucía

Seafood is a consistent presence the length of the Andalucian coast. Andalucians are famous above all for their *pescaito frito* (fried fish). A particular speciality of Cádiz, fried fish Andalucian-style means that just about anything that emerges from the sea is rolled in chickpea and wheat flour, shaken to remove the surplus, then deep-fried ever so briefly in olive oil, just long enough to form a light, golden crust that seals the essential goodness of the fish or seafood within.

In a region where summers can be fierce, there's no better way to keep cool than with a *gazpacho andaluz* (Andalucian gazpacho), a cold soup with many manifestations. The base is almost always tomato, cucumber, vinegar and olive oil.

Wines

All of Spain's autonomous communities, with the exceptions of Asturias and Cantabria, are home to recognised wine-growing areas.

La Rioja, in the north, is Spain's best-known wine-producing region. The principal grape of Rioja is the *tempranillo*, widely believed to be a mutant form of the pinot noir. Its wine is smooth and fruity, seldom as dry as its supposed French counterpart. Look for the 'DOC Rioja' classification on the label and you'll find a good wine.

Not far behind are the wine-producing regions of Ribera del Duero in Castilla y León, Navarra, the Somontano wines of Aragón, and the Valdepeñas region of southern Castilla-La Mancha (it's famous for its quantities rather than quality, but is generally well priced and remains popular).

For white wines, the Ribeiro wines of Galicia are well regarded. Also from the area is one of Spain's most charming whites – *albariño*. This crisp, dry and refreshing drop is unusual, designated as it is by grape rather than region.

ALL ABOUT SPANISH WINE

Spanish wine is subject to a complicated system of classification. If an area meets certain strict standards for a given period, covering all aspects of planting, cultivating and ageing, it receives Denominación de Origen (DO; Denomination of Origin) status. There are more than 60 DO-recognised wine-producing areas in Spain.

An outstanding wine region gets the much-coveted Denominación de Origen Calificada (DOC), a controversial classification that some in the industry argue should apply only to specific wines, rather than every wine from within a particular region. At present, the only DOC wines come from La Rioja in northern Spain and the small Priorat area in Catalonia.

The best wines are often marked with the designation 'crianza' (aged for one year in oak barrels), 'reserva' (aged for two years, at least one of which is in oak barrels) and 'gran reserva' (two years in oak and three in the bottle).

The Penedès region in Catalonia produces whites and sparkling wine such as *cava,* the traditional champagne-like toasting drink of choice for Spaniards at Christmas.

Sherry

Sherry, the unique wine of Andalucía, is Spain's national dram and is found in almost every bar, *tasca* (tapas bar) and restaurant in the land. Dry sherry, called *fino,* begins as a fairly ordinary white wine of the palomino grape, but it's 'fortified' with grape brandy. This stops fermentation and gives the wine taste and smell constituents that enable it to age into something sublime. It's taken as an *aperitivo* (aperitif) or as a table wine with seafood.

Amontillado and Oloroso are sweeter sherries, good for after dinner. Manzanilla is grown only in Sanlúcar de Barrameda near the coast in southwestern Andalucía and develops a slightly salty taste that's very appetising. It's possible to visit bodegas (wineries) in Sanlúcar, as well as in Jerez de la Frontera and El Puerto de Santa María.

How to Eat & Drink

Having joined Spaniards around the table for years, we've come to understand what eating Spanish-style is all about. If we could distil the essence of how to make food a highlight of your trip into a few simple rules, they would be these: always ask for the local speciality; never be shy about looking around to see what others have ordered before choosing; always ask the waiter for their recommendations; and, wherever possible, make your meal a centrepiece of your day.

When to Eat

Breakfast

Desayuno (breakfast) Spanish-style is generally a no-nonsense affair taken at a bar midmorning or on the way to work. A *café con leche* (half coffee and half milk) with a *bollo* (pastry) or croissant is the typical breakfast. Another common breakfast order is a *tostada,* which is simply buttered toast.

In hotels, breakfast can begin as early as 6.30am and may continue until 10am (usually later on weekends).

THE TRAVELLERS' FRIEND – MENÚ DEL DÍA

One great way to cap prices at lunchtime Monday to Friday is to order the *menú del día*, a full three-course set menu including water, bread and wine. These meals are priced from around €10, although €12 and up is increasingly the norm. You'll be given a menu with a choice of five or six starters, the same number of mains and a handful of desserts. Choose one from each category; it's possible to order two starters, but not two mains.

Lunch

Lunch (*comida* or *almuerzo*) is the main meal of the day. During the working week few Spaniards have time to go home for lunch, so most people end up eating in restaurants, and all-inclusive three-course meals (*menús del día*) are as close as they can come to eating home-style food without breaking the bank. On weekends or in summer, Spaniards are not averse to lingering for hours over a meal with friends and family. Lunch rarely begins before 2pm (restaurants usually open from 1pm until 4pm).

Dinner

Dinner (*cena*) is usually a lighter meal, although that may differ on weekends. Going out for a drink and some tapas is a popular way of eating dinner in many cities. It does vary from region to region, but most restaurants open from 8.30pm to midnight, later on weekends.

Drinking Etiquette

Wherever you are in Spain there'll be a bar close by. More than just places to drink, bars are centres of community life. Spaniards drink often and seem up for a drink almost any time of the day or night, but they rarely do so to excess; drinking is rarely an end in itself, but rather an accompaniment to good conversation, food or music.

PRICE INDICATORS

Throughout this book, restaurants are grouped according to price range (€ to €€€). The order within each of those ranges follows the author's preference. The following price brackets refer to a standard main dish:

€ less than €10

€€ from €10 to €20

€€€ more than €20

Where to Eat & Drink

asador Restaurant specialising in roast meats.

bar de copas Gets going around midnight and serves hard drinks.

casa de comidas Basic restaurant serving well-priced home cooking.

cervecería The focus is on *cerveza* (beer) on tap.

horno de asador Restaurant with a wood-burning roasting oven.

marisquería Bar or restaurant specialising in seafood.

restaurante Restaurant.

taberna Rustic place serving tapas and *raciones* (large tapas).

tasca Tapas bar.

terraza Open-air bar, for warm-weather tippling and tapas.

vinoteca Wine bars where you order by the glass.

Menu Decoder

a la parilla grilled

asado roasted or baked

bebidas drinks

carne meat

carta menu

casera homemade

ensalada salad

entrada entree or starter

entremeses hors d'oeuvres

frito fried

menú usually refers to a set menu

menú de degustación tasting menu

pescado fish

plato combinado main-and-three-veg dish

postre dessert

raciones large-plate size serving of tapas

sopa soup

Spain's Foodie Highlights

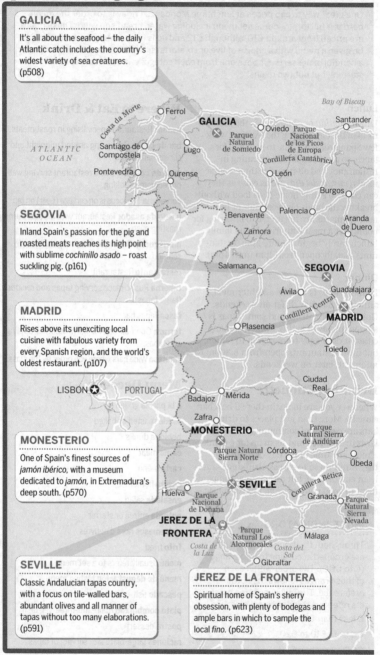

GALICIA

It's all about the seafood – the daily Atlantic catch includes the country's widest variety of sea creatures. (p508)

SEGOVIA

Inland Spain's passion for the pig and roasted meats reaches its high point with sublime *cochinillo asado* – roast suckling pig. (p161)

MADRID

Rises above its unexciting local cuisine with fabulous variety from every Spanish region, and the world's oldest restaurant. (p107)

MONESTERIO

One of Spain's finest sources of *jamón ibérico*, with a museum dedicated to *jamón*, in Extremadura's deep south. (p570)

SEVILLE

Classic Andalucian tapas country, with a focus on tile-walled bars, abundant olives and all manner of tapas without too many elaborations. (p591)

JEREZ DE LA FRONTERA

Spiritual home of Spain's sherry obsession, with plenty of bodegas and ample bars in which to sample the local *fino*. (p623)

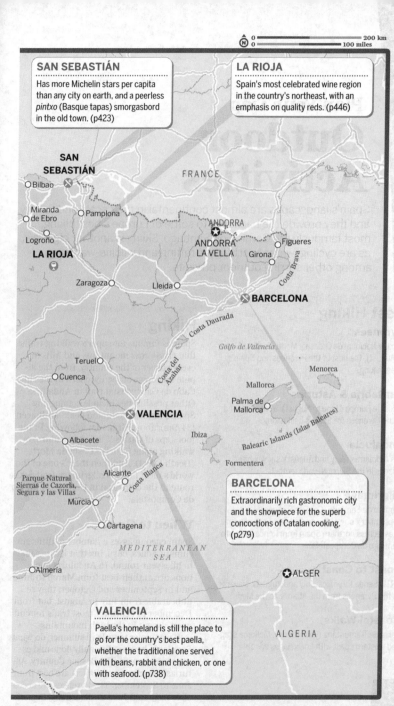

N 0 — 200 km
0 — 100 miles

SAN SEBASTIÁN

Has more Michelin stars per capita than any city on earth, and a peerless *pintxo* (Basque tapas) smorgasbord in the old town. (p423)

LA RIOJA

Spain's most celebrated wine region in the country's northeast, with an emphasis on quality reds. (p446)

FRANCE

SAN
SEBASTIÁN
○ Bilbao ✈

Miranda ○ Pamplona
de Ebro ○
Logroño ○
LA RIOJA

ANDORRA
★
ANDORRA
LA VELLA ○ Figueres
Girona ○
Costa Brava

Zaragoza ○ Lleida ○

✈ BARCELONA

Costa Daurada

Teruel ○

Golfo de Valencia

Menorca

○ Cuenca

Costa del Azahar

Mallorca

Palma de
Mallorca ○

✈ VALENCIA

Ibiza

Balearic Islands (Islas Baleares)

○ Albacete

Formentera

Alicante
○
Parque Natural *Costa Blanca*
Sierras de Cazorla,
Segura y las Villas
Murcia ○

BARCELONA

Extraordinarily rich gastronomic city and the showpiece for the superb concoctions of Catalan cooking. (p279)

○ Cartagena

*MEDITERRANEAN
SEA*

○ Almería

★ ALGER

VALENCIA

Paella's homeland is still the place to go for the country's best paella, whether the traditional one served with beans, rabbit and chicken, or one with seafood. (p738)

ALGERIA

Plan Your Trip

Outdoor Activities

Spain's landscapes are almost continental in their scale and variety, and they provide the backdrop to some of Europe's best hiking, most famously the Camino de Santiago. Skiing is another big draw, as are cycling, water sports, river-rafting and wildlife-watching, among other stirring outdoor pursuits.

Best Hiking

Pyrenees
Parque Nacional de Ordesa y Monte Perdido (June to August): the best of the Pyrenees and Spain's finest hiking.

Cantabria & Asturias
Picos de Europa (June to August): a close second to the Pyrenees for Spain's best hiking.

Andalucía
Las Alpujarras (July and August): snow-white villages in the Sierra Nevada foothills.

Pilgrimage
Camino de Santiago (Camino Francés; May to September): one of the world's favourite pilgrimages, across northern Spain from Roncesvalles to Santiago de Compostela.

Coast to Coast
GR11 (Senda Pirenáica; July and August): traverses the Pyrenees from the Atlantic to the Med.

Coastal Walks
Serra de Tramuntana (year-round): Mallorca's jagged western coast with fine villages en route.

Hiking

Spain is famous for superb walking trails that criss-cross mountains and hills in every corner of the country, from the alpine meadows of the Pyrenees to the sultry Cabo de Gata coastal trail in Andalucía. Other possibilities include conquering Spain's highest mainland peak, Mulhacén (3479m), above Granada; following in the footsteps of Carlos V in Extremadura; or walking along Galicia's Costa da Morte (Death Coast). And then there's one of the world's most famous pilgrimage trails – the route to the cathedral in Galicia's Santiago de Compostela.

When to Go

Spain encompasses a number of different climatic zones, ensuring that it's possible to hike year-round. In Andalucía conditions are at their best from March to June and in September and October: they're unbearable from July to August, but from December to February most trails remain open, except in the high mountains.

If you prefer to walk in summer, do what Spaniards have traditionally done and escape to the north. The Basque Country, Asturias, Cantabria and Galicia are best from June to September. The Pyrenees are accessible from mid-June until (usually) September; July and August are the ideal months for the high Sierra Nevada. August is the busiest month on the trails, so if you plan to head to popular national parks and stay in *refugios* (pilgrim hostels), book ahead.

Destinations

Pyrenees

For good reason, the Pyrenees, separating Spain from France, are Spain's premier walking destination. The range is utterly beautiful: prim and chocolate-box pretty on the lower slopes, wild and bleak at higher elevations, and relatively unspoilt compared to some European mountain ranges. The Pyrenees contain two outstanding national parks: Aigüestortes i Estany de Sant Maurici and Ordesa y Monte Perdido.

The spectacular GR11 (Senda Pirenáica) traverses the range, connecting the Atlantic (at Hondarribia in the Basque Country) with the Mediterranean (at Cap de Creus in Catalonia). Walking the whole 35- to 50-day route is an unforgettable challenge, but there are also magnificent day hikes in the national parks and elsewhere.

Picos de Europa

Breathtaking and accessible limestone ranges with distinctive craggy peaks (usually hot rock-climbing destinations, too) are the hallmark of Spain's first national park, the Picos de Europa, which straddles the Cantabria, Asturias and León provinces and is fast gaining a reputation as the place to walk in Spain.

Elsewhere in Spain

To walk in mountain villages, the classic spot is Las Alpujarras, near the Parque Nacional Sierra Nevada in Andalucía. The Sierra de Cazorla and Sierra de Grazalema, both also in Andalucía, are also outstanding. The long-distance GR7 trail traverses these three regions – you can walk all or just part of the route, depending on your time and inclination.

Great coastal walking abounds, even in heavily visited areas such as the south coast (try Andalucía's Cabo de Gata). The following are trails that are less known but equally rewarding:

➜ Els Ports, Valencia

➜ Ruta de Pedra en Sec, Mallorca

➜ Camí de Cavalls, Menorca

Information

For the full low-down on these walks, including the Camino de Santiago, check out Lonely Planet's *Hiking in Spain*. Region-specific walking (and climbing) guides are published by Cicerone Press (www. cicerone.co.uk).

Madrid's La Tienda Verde (p869) and Librería Desnivel (p869) both sell maps (the best Spanish ones are *Prames* and *Adrados*) and guides.

Numerous websites offer local route descriptions but the following three cover a number of Spanish regions, although you'll need to speak Spanish to take full advantage of their content:

➜ www.andarines.com

➜ http://en.wikiloc.com

➜ http://wikirutas.es

Camino de Santiago

'The door is open to all, to sick and healthy, not only to Catholics but also to pagans, Jews, heretics and vagabonds.'

So go the words of a 13th-century poem describing the Camino. Eight hundred years later these words still ring true. The Camino de Santiago (Way of St James) originated as a medieval pilgrimage and, for more than 1000 years, people have taken up the Camino's age-old symbols – the scallop shell and staff – and set off on the adventure of a lifetime to the tomb of St James the Apostle, in Santiago de Compostela, in the Iberian Peninsula's far northwest.

Today the most popular of the several *caminos* (paths) to Santiago de Compostela is the Camino Francés, which spans 783km of Spain's north from Roncesvalles, on the border with France, to Santiago de Compostela in Galicia, and attracts walkers of all backgrounds and ages, from countries across the world. And no wonder: its list of assets (culture, history, nature) is impressive, as are its accolades. Not only is it Council of Europe's first Cultural Itinerary and a Unesco World Heritage site but, for pilgrims, it's a pilgrimage equal to visiting Jerusalem, and by finishing it you're guaranteed a healthy chunk of time off purgatory.

To feel, absorb, smell and taste northern Spain's diversity, for a great physical challenge and for a unique perspective on rural and urban communities, this is an incomparable walk.

History

In the 9th century a remarkable event occurred in the poor Iberian hinterlands: following a shining star, Pelayo, a religious hermit, unearthed the tomb of the apostle James the Greater (or, in Spanish, Santiago). The news was confirmed by the local bishop, the Asturian king and later the pope. Its impact is hard to truly imagine today, but it was instant and indelible: first a trickle, then a flood of Christian Europeans began to journey towards the setting sun in search of salvation.

Compostela became the most important destination for Christians after Rome and Jerusalem. Its popularity increased with an 11th-century papal decree granting it Holy Year status: pilgrims could receive a plenary indulgence – a full remission of your lifetime's sins – during a Holy Year. These occur when Santiago's feast day (25 July) falls on a Sunday: the next one isn't until 2021.

The 11th and 12th centuries marked the heyday of the pilgrimage. The Reformation was devastating for Catholic pilgrimages, and by the 19th century, the Camino had nearly died out. In its startling late-20th-century reanimation, which continues today, it's most popular as a personal and spiritual journey of discovery, rather than one primarily motivated by religion.

Routes

Although in Spain there are many *caminos* (paths) to Santiago, by far the most popular is, and was, the Camino Francés, which originated in France, crossed the Pyrenees at Roncesvalles and then headed west for 783km across the regions of Navarra, La Rioja, Castilla y León and Galicia. Waymarked with cheerful yellow arrows and scallop shells, the 'trail' is a mishmash of rural lanes, paved secondary roads and footpaths all strung together. Starting at Roncesvalles, the Camino takes roughly two weeks cycling or five weeks walking.

But this is by no means the only route, and the summer crowds along the Camino Francés have prompted some to look at alternative routes – in 2005, nearly 85% of walkers took the Camino Francés; by 2013 this had fallen to 70%. Increasingly popular routes include the following:

Camino Portugués North to Santiago through Portugal.

Camino del Norte Via the Basque Country, Cantabria and Asturias.

Via de la Plata From Andalucía north through Extremadura, Castilla y León and on to Galicia.

A very popular alternative is to walk only the last 100km (the minimum distance allowed) from Sarria in Galicia in order to earn a *Compostela* certificate of completion given out by the Catedral de Santiago de Compostela.

Another possibility is to continue on beyond Santiago to the dramatic 'Lands End' outpost of Fisterra (Finisterre), an extra 88km.

Information

For more information about the *Credencial* (like a passport for the Camino, in which pilgrims accumulate stamps at various points along the route) and the *Compostela* certificate, visit the website of the cathedral's **Oficina del Peregrino** (Pilgrim's Office; www.peregrinossantiago.es; Rúa do Vilar 3, Santiago de Compostela).

There are a number of excellent Camino websites:

Caminolinks (www.caminolinks.co.uk) Complete, annotated guide to many Camino websites.

Mundicamino (www.mundicamino.com) Excellent, thorough descriptions and maps.

Camino de Santiago (www.caminodesantiago.me) Contains a huge selection of news groups, where you can get all of your questions answered.

PILGRIM HOSTELS

There are around 300 *refugios* (pilgrim hostels) along the Camino, owned by parishes, 'friends of the Camino' associations, private individuals, town halls and regional governments. While in the early days these places were run on donations and provided little more than hot water and a bed, today's pilgrims are charged €5 to €10 and expect showers, kitchens and washing machines. Some things haven't changed though – the *refugios* still operate on a first-come, first-served basis and are intended for those doing the Camino solely under their own steam.

Camino Francés

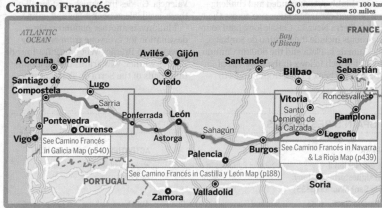

When to Walk

People walk and cycle the Camino year-round. In May and June the wildflowers are glorious and the endless fields of cereals turn from green to toasty gold, making the landscapes a huge draw. July and August bring crowds of summer holidaymakers and scorching heat, especially through Castilla y León. September is less crowded and the weather is generally pleasant. From November to May there are fewer people on the road as the season can bring snow, rain and bitter winds. Santiago's feast day, 25 July, is a popular time to converge on the city.

National & Natural Parks

Much of Spain's most spectacular and ecologically important terrain – about 40,000 sq km or 8% of the entire country, if you include national hunting reserves – is under some kind of official protection. Nearly all of these areas are at least partly open to walkers, naturalists and other outdoor enthusiasts, but degrees of conservation and access vary.

The *parques nacionales* (national parks) are areas of exceptional importance and are the country's most strictly controlled protected areas. Spain has 14 national parks – nine on the mainland, four on the Canary Islands and one in the Balearic Islands. The hundreds of other protected areas fall into at least 16 classifications and range in size from 100-sq-metre rocks off the Balearics to Andalucía's 2140-sq-km Parque Natural de Cazorla.

Canyoning

For exhilarating descents into steep-walled canyons by any means possible (but in the care of professional guides), look no further than Alquézar in Aragón, one of Europe's prime locations for this popular sport. Alquézar's numerous activities operators can also arrange rock climbing and rafting in the surrounding Sierra de Guara.

Canyoning is also possible in the following places:

➡ Cangas de Onís in Picos de Europa

➡ Torrent de Pareis and Gorg Blau in Mallorca

Cycling

Spain has a splendid variety of cycling possibilities, from gentle family rides to challenging two-week expeditions. If you avoid the cities (where cycling can be somewhat nerve-racking), Spain is also a cycle-friendly country, with drivers accustomed to sharing the roads with cyclists. The excellent network of secondary roads, usually with comfortable shoulders to ride on, is ideal for road touring.

Destinations

Every Spanish region has both off-road (called BTT in Spanish, from *bici todo terreno*, meaning 'mountain bike') and touring trails and routes. Mountain bikers can head to just about any sierra (mountain range) and use the extensive *pistas forestales* (forestry tracks).

One highly recommended and challenging off-road excursion takes you across the snowy Sierra Nevada. Classic long-haul touring routes include the Camino de Santiago, the Ruta de la Plata and the 600km Camino del Cid, which follows in the footsteps of Spain's epic hero, El Cid, from Burgos to Valencia. Guides in Spanish exist for all of these, available at bookshops and online.

Mallorca is another popular cycling destination for everyone from ordinary travellers to Bradley Wiggins, 2012 Tour de France winner, who trains on the mountain roads of the Serra de Tramuntana.

SPAIN'S BEST PARKS

PARK	FEATURES	ACTIVITIES	BEST TIME TO VISIT
Parc Nacional d'Aigüestortes i Estany de Sant Maurici (p335)	beautiful Pyrenees lake region	walking, wildlife-watching	Jun–Sep
Parque Nacional de Doñana (p602)	bird and mammal haven in Guadalquivir delta	4WD tours, walking, wildlife-watching, horse riding	year-round
Parque Nacional de Ordesa y Monte Perdido (p379)	spectacular section of the Pyrenees, with chamois, raptors and varied vegetation	walking, rock climbing	mid-Jun–Jul & mid-Aug–Sep
Parque Nacional de los Picos de Europa (p489)	beautiful mountain refuge for chamois, and a few wolves and bears	walking, rock climbing	May-Jul & Sep
Parques Nacional and Natural Sierra Nevada (p675)	mainland Spain's highest mountain range, with ibexes, 60 endemic plants and the beautiful Alpujarras valleys on its southern slopes	walking, rock climbing, mountain biking, skiing, horse riding	year-round, depending on activity
Parque Natural de las Sierras de Cazorla, Segura y Las Villas (p715)	abundant wildlife, 2300 plant species and beautiful mountain scenery	walking, mountain biking, wildlife-watching, 4WD tours	Apr-Oct
Áreas Naturales Serra de Tramuntana (p786)	spectacular mountain range on Mallorca	walking, birdwatching	late Feb-early Oct
Parque Nacional de Monfragüe (p561)	spectacular birds of prey	birdwatching	Mar-Oct
Parque Natural Sierra de Grazalema (p628)	lovely, green, mountainous area with rich bird life	walking, caving, canyoning, birdwatching, paragliding, rock climbing	Sep-Jun
Parc Natural del Cadí-Moixeró (p334)	steep pre-Pyrenees range	rock climbing, walking	Jun-Sep
Parc Natural de la Zona Volcànica de la Garrotxa (p327)	beautiful wooded region with 30 volcanic cones	walking	Apr-Oct
Parque Natural Sierra de Gredos (p146)	beautiful mountain region, home to Spain's biggest ibex population	walking, rock climbing, mountain biking	Mar-May & Sep-Nov
Parque Natural de Somiedo (p488)	dramatic section of Cordillera Cantábrica with brown bears	walking	Jul-Sep
Parque Natural de Cabo de Gata-Níjar (p721)	sandy beaches, volcanic cliffs, flamingo colony and semi-desert vegetation	swimming, birdwatching, walking, horse riding, diving	year-round

Information

Spanish-language cycling website www. amigosdelciclismo.com gives useful information on restrictions, updates on laws, circulation norms, contact information for cycling clubs and lists of guidebooks, as well as a lifetime's worth of route descriptions organised region by region.

Bike Spain (p100) in Madrid is one of the better cycling tour operators.

Many of the cycling guidebooks in publication are in Spanish:

➡ *España en bici*, by Paco Tortosa and María del Mar Fornés. A good overview guide, but quite hard to find.

➡ *Cycle Touring in Spain: Eight Detailed Routes*, by Harry Dowdell. A helpful planning tool; also practical once you're in Spain.

➡ *The Trailrider Guide – Spain: Single Track Mountain Biking in Spain*, by Nathan James and Linsey Stroud. Another good resource.

Skiing & Snowboarding

For winter powder, Spain's skiers (including the royal family) head to the Pyrenees of Aragón and Catalonia. Outside the peak periods (the beginning of December, 20 December to 6 January, Carnaval and Semana Santa), Spain's top resorts are relatively quiet, cheap and warm in comparison with their counterparts in the Alps.

The season runs from December to April, though January and February are generally the best, most reliable times for snow.

Destinations

In Aragón, two popular resorts are Formigal and Candanchú. Just above the town of Jaca, Candanchú has some 42km of runs with 51 pistes (as well as 35km of cross-country track). In Catalonia, Spain's first resort, La Molina, is still going strong and is ideal for families and beginners. Considered by many to have the Pyrenees' best snow, the 72-piste resort of Baqueira-Beret boasts 30 modern lifts and 104km of downhill runs for all levels.

Spain's other major resort is Europe's southernmost: the Sierra Nevada, outside Granada. The 80km of runs here are at their prime in March, and the slopes are particularly suited for families and novice-to-intermediate skiers.

Information

Spanish ski resorts have equipment hire, as well as ski schools. Lift tickets cost between €35 and €50 per day for adults, and €25 and €35 for children; equipment hire costs from around €20 per day. If you're planning ahead, Spanish travel agencies frequently advertise affordable single- or multi-day packages with lodging included.

An excellent source of information on snowboarding and skiing in Spain is www. skisnowboardeurope.com.

Scuba Diving & Snorkelling

There's more to Spain than what you see on the surface – literally! Delve under the ocean waves anywhere along the country's almost 5000km of shoreline and a whole new Spain opens up, crowded with marine life and including features such as wrecks, sheer walls and long cavern swim-throughs.

The numerous Mediterranean dive centres cater to an English-speaking market and offer single- and multi-day trips, equipment rental and certification courses. Their Atlantic counterparts (in San Sebastián, Santander and A Coruña) deal mostly in Spanish, but if that's not an obstacle for you, the colder waters of the Atlantic offer a different, and very rewarding, experience.

A good starting point is the reefs along the Costa Brava, especially around the Illes Medes marine reserve, off L'Estartit (near Girona). On the Costa del Sol, operators launch to such places as La Herradura Wall, the *Motril* wreck and the Cavern of Cerro Gordo. Spain's Balearic Islands are also popular dive destinations with excellent services – Port d'Andratx (Mallorca), for example, has a number of dive schools.

VIAS VERDES

Spain has a growing network of Vias Verdes (literally 'green ways', but equivalent to the 'rail trail' system in other countries), an outstanding system of decommissioned railway tracks that have been converted into bicycle (or hiking) trails. Trails range from 1.2km to 84.4km in length. For details, see www.viasverdes.com.

Paco Nadal's book *Buceo en España* provides information province by province, with descriptions of ocean floors, dive centres and equipment rental.

Surfing

The opportunity to get into the waves is a major attraction for beginners and experts alike along many of Spain's coastal regions. The north coast of Spain has, debatably, the best surf in mainland Europe.

The main surfing region is the north coast, where numerous high-class spots can be found, but Atlantic Andalucía gets decent winter swells. Despite the flow of vans loaded down with surfboards along the north coast in the summer, it's actually autumn through to spring that's the prime time for a decent swell, with October probably the best month overall. The variety of waves along the north coast is impressive: there are numerous open, swell-exposed beach breaks for the summer months, and some seriously heavy reefs and points that only really come to life during the colder, stormier months.

Destinations

The most famous wave in Spain is the legendary river-mouth left at Mundaka. On a good day, there's no doubt that it's one of the best waves in the world. However, it's not very consistent, and when it's on, it's always very busy and ugly.

Heading east, good waves can be found throughout the Basque Country. Going west, into neighbouring regions of Cantabria and Asturias, you'll also find a superb range of well-charted surf beaches, such as Rodiles in Asturias and Liencres in Can-

tabria. If you're looking for solitude, some isolated beaches along Galicia's beautiful Costa da Morte remain empty even in summer. In southwest Andalucía there are a number of powerful, winter beach breaks, and weekdays off Conil de la Frontera (located just northwest of Cabo de Trafalgar) can be sublimely lonely.

Information

In summer a shortie wetsuit (or, in the Basque Country, just board shorts) is sufficient along all coasts except Galicia, which picks up the icy Canaries current – you'll need a light full suit here.

Surf shops abound in the popular surfing areas and usually offer board and wetsuit hire. If you're a beginner joining a surf school, ask the instructor to explain the rules and to keep you away from the more experienced surfers.

There are a number of excellent surf guidebooks to Spain:

➡ Lonely Planet author Stuart Butler's English-language *Big Blue Surf Guide: Spain*.

➡ José Pellón's Spanish-language *Guía del Surf en España*.

➡ Low Pressure's superb *Stormrider Guide: Europe – the Continent*.

Windsurfing & Kitesurfing

The best sailing conditions are to be found around Tarifa, which has such strong and consistent winds that it's said that the town's once-high suicide rate was due to the wind turning people mad. Whether or not this is true, one thing is without doubt: Tarifa's 10km of white, sandy beaches and perfect year-round conditions have made this small town the windsurfing capital of Europe. However, the same wind that attracts so many devotees also makes it a less than ideal place to learn the art.

If you can't make it as far south as Tarifa, then the less-known Empuriabrava in Catalonia also has great conditions, especially from March to July, while the family resort of Oliva near Valencia, Murcia's Mar Menor, or Fornells on Menorca are also worth considering. If you're looking for waves, try Spain's northwest coast, where Galicia can have fantastic conditions.

HANG-GLIDING & PARAGLIDING

If you want to take to the skies either *ala delta* (hang-gliding) or *parapente* (paragliding), there are a number of specialised clubs and adventure-tour companies here. The **Real Federación Aeronáutica España** (www.rfae.org) gives information on recognised schools and lists clubs and events.

Information

An excellent guidebook to windsurfing and kitesurfing spots across Spain and the rest of Europe is Stoked Publications' *The Kite and Windsurfing Guide: Europe*.

Spanish-language website www.windsurfesp.com gives thorough descriptions of spots, conditions and schools all over Spain.

Kayaking & Rafting

Opportunities abound in Spain for taking off downstream in search of white-water fun along its 1800 rivers and streams. As most rivers are dammed for electric power at some point along their flow, there are many reservoirs with excellent low-level kayaking and canoeing, where you can also hire equipment.

In general, May and June are best for kayaking, rafting, canoeing and hydrospeeding (water tobogganing). Top white-water rivers include Catalonia's turbulent Noguera Pallaresa, Aragón's Gállego and Ésera, Cantabria's Carasa and Galicia's Miño.

For fun and competition, the crazy 22km, en-masse Descenso Internacional del Sella (p480) canoe race is a blast.

Patrick Santal's *White Water Pyrenees* thoroughly covers 85 rivers in France and Spain for kayakers, canoeists and rafters.

Wildlife Tourism

Spain is home to some of Europe's most interesting wildlife, from abundant resident and migratory bird species to charismatic carnivores that have made a comeback.

The following resources will help guide you when watching wildlife in Spain.

➡ Fundación Oso Pardo (p487) Spain's main resource for brown bears.

➡ Life Lince (www.lifelince.org) Up-to-the-minute news on the Iberian lynx.

➡ Iberia Nature (www.iberianature.com) An excellent English-language source of information on Spanish fauna and flora, although some sections need an update.

➡ *Wild Spain*, by Teresa Farino (2009). Practical guide to Spain's wilderness and wildlife areas.

➡ *Collins Bird Guide: The Most Complete Guide to the Birds of Britain & Europe*, by Lars Svensson et al (2009).

ROCK CLIMBING

For an overview of Spanish rock climbing, check out the Spain information on the websites of **Rockfax** (www.rockfax.com) and **Climb Europe** (www.climb-europe.com). Both include details on the best climbs in the country. Rockfax also publishes various climbing guidebooks covering Spain.

Tour Operators

Iberian Wildlife (www.iberianwildlife.com) A full portfolio of wildlife tours.

Nature Trek (www.naturetrek.co.uk) Birds, wolves and bears, and lynx-watching trips into the Parque Natural Sierra de Andújar and Doñana.

Julian Sykes Wildlife Holidays (www.juliansykeswildlife.com) Birdwatching, Iberian lynx in Parque Natural Sierra de Andújar and other small-group trips.

Wildwatching Spain (www.wildwatching spain.com) Wolves and Iberian lynx are the standouts among many tours.

Animals

There are around 85 terrestrial mammal species in Spain, 70 reptiles and amphibians and some 227 different species of butterflies.

In addition to the three predator species covered below, other wildlife highlights include:

Cabra montés (ibex) Chiefly found in Castilla y León's Sierra de Gredos and in the mountains of Andalucía.

Barbary macaques Gibraltar's 'apes' are Europe's only wild monkeys.

Marine mammals Dolphin- and whale-spotting boat trips are a popular attraction in Gibraltar and Tarifa.

Brown Bears

One of the most impressive of Spain's flagship species is the *oso pardo* (brown bear), of which an estimated 240 remain in the wild. The majority of Spain's bears inhabit the Cordillera Cantábrica. There is also a tiny population in the Pyrenees, although the last known native Pyrenean bear died in October 2010. The current population is entirely made up of introduced bears from Slovenia and their offspring.

Hunting or killing Spain's bears has been banned since 1973, and expensive conservation programs have started to pay off in the last few years, at least in the western Cordillera Cantábrica, where the population is considered viable for future survival – their numbers have almost doubled in the past decade.

The best place to see brown bears in the wild is the Parque Natural de Somiedo in southwestern Asturias. There is also a small chance of seeing bears in the Picos de Europa. A bear enclosure and breeding facility at Senda del Oso, also in Asturias, is a good chance to get a little closer.

Iberian Wolf

The *lobo ibérico* (Iberian wolf) is, like the brown bear, on the increase. Though heavily protected, wolves are still considered an enemy by many country people, although from a population low of around 500 in 1970, Spain now has between 2000 and 2500. The species is found in small populations across the north, including the Picos de Europa, but their heartland is the mountains of Galicia and northwestern Castilla y León. The most accessible population is in the Sierra de Culebra, close to Zamora, and where Zamora Natural (p173) runs wolf-watching expeditions. Riaño, close to León, is another possibility.

Iberian Lynx

The beautiful Iberian lynx, Europe's only big-cat species, is the most endangered feline species in the world. It once inhabited large areas of the peninsula, but numbers fell to as few as 120 at the beginning of the 21st century. A highly successful captive breeding program and the reintroduction of captive-bred lynx into the wild, along with restocking of rabbit populations (rabbits make up more than 80% of the lynx's diet), have seen the wild population reach an estimated 320 individuals, with a further 150 in captivity.

The two remaining lynx populations are in Andalucía: the Parque Nacional de Doñana (with 85 lynxes); and the Sierra Morena (235 lynxes) spread across the Guadalmellato (northeast of Córdoba), Guarrizas (northeast of Linares) and Andújar-Cardeña (north of Andújar) regions. There are also plans for new wild populations to be established in Portugal, north of Seville and in the Montes de Toledo in Castilla-La Mancha.

Private operators offer 4WD or horseback excursions into the Parque Nacional de Doñana and/or the adjacent natural park from the village of El Rocio or from Sanlúcar de Barrameda. Companies include Doñana Nature (p602), Doñana Ecuestre (p603), Cooperativa Marismas del Rocio (p602), Donana Reservas (p602) and Visitas Donana (p617). These represent the best opportunities to see the lynx in the wild.

Otherwise, the Parque Natural Sierra de Andújar or the Parque Natural Sierra de Cardeña y Montoro are your best bet to see these elusive creatures. While you can explore either of these parks under your own steam, **Lynxaia** (☑625 512442; www.lynxaia.com) covers the Parque Natural Sierra de Cardeña y Montoro.

Birds

With around 500 species Spain has easily the biggest and most varied bird population in Europe. Around 25 species of birds of prey, including the *águila real* (golden eagle), *buitre leonado* (griffon vulture) and *alimoche* (Egyptian vulture), breed here. Although the white stork is everywhere, much rarer is the *cigüeña negra* (black stork), which is down to about 200 pairs in Spain.

Spain's extensive wetlands make it a haven for waterbirds. The most important of the wetlands is the Parque Nacional de Doñana and surrounding areas in the Guadalquivir delta in Andalucía. Hundreds of thousands of birds winter here, and many more call in during the spring and autumn migrations. Doñana is also home to a population of the highly endangered *águila imperial* (imperial eagle).

Other outstanding birdwatching sites around the country include the following:

Parque Nacional de Monfragüe, Extremadura A spectacular place to observe birds of prey.

Laguna de Gallocanta, Aragón Thousands of *patos* (ducks) and *grullas* (cranes) winter here at Spain's biggest natural lake.

La Albufera, Valencia Important coastal wetland for migratory species.

Ebro Delta, Catalonia Important wetland area.

Laguna de Fuente de Piedra, Andalucía One of Europe's two main breeding sites for the flamenco (greater flamingo), with as many as 20,000 pairs rearing chicks in spring and summer.

Pyrenees Good for birds of prey.

Plan Your Trip

Travel with Children

Spain is a family-friendly destination with excellent transport and accommodation infrastructure, food to satisfy even the fussiest of eaters, and an extraordinary range of attractions that appeal to adults and children alike. Visiting as a family does require careful planning, but no more than for visiting any other European country.

Spain for Kids

Spain's tourism industry workers are accustomed to Spaniards travelling in family groups, and most will go out of their way to make sure children are looked after.

Eating Out

Food and children are two of the great loves for Spaniards. Spanish fare is rarely spicy and kids tend to like it.

Children are usually welcome, whether in a sit-down restaurant or in a chaotically busy bar. Indeed, it's rare that you'll be made to feel uncomfortable as your children run amok, although the more formal the place, the more uncomfortable you're likely to feel. In summer, the abundance of outdoor terraces with tables is ideal for families, although it can be easy to lose sight of wandering young ones amid the scrum of people.

You cannot rely on restaurants having *tronas* (high chairs), although many do these days. Those that do, however, rarely have more than one (a handful at most), so make the request when making your reservation or as soon as you arrive.

Very few restaurants (or other public places) have nappy-changing facilities.

A small but growing number of restaurants offer a *menú infantil* (children's

Best Regions for Kids

Mediterranean Spain

Spain's coastline may be a summer-holiday cliché, but it's a fabulous place for a family holiday. From Catalonia in the north to Andalucía in the south, most beaches have gentle waters and numerous child-friendly attractions and activities (from water parks to water sports for older kids).

Barcelona

Theme parks, a wax museum, a chocolate museum, all manner of other museums with interactive exhibits, beaches, gardens... Barcelona is one of Spain's most child-friendly cities – even its architecture seems to have sprung from a child's imagination.

Inland Spain

Spain's interior may not be the first place you think of for a family holiday, but its concentrations of castles, tiny villages and fascinating, easily negotiated cities make it worth considering.

menu), which usually includes a main course (hamburger, chicken nuggets, pasta and the like), a drink and an ice cream or milkshake for dessert.

One challenge can be adapting to Spanish eating hours – when kids get hungry between meals it's sometimes possible to zip into the nearest *tasca* (tapas bar) and get them a snack, and there are also sweet shops scattered around most towns. That said, we recommend carrying emergency supplies from a supermarket for those times when there's simply nothing open.

Transport

Spain's transport infrastructure is world-class, and high-speed AVE trains render irrelevant the distances between many major cities. Apart from anything else, most kids love the idea that they're travelling at nearly 300km/h.

Discounts are available for children (usually under 12) on public transport. Those under four generally go free.

You can hire car seats (usually for an additional cost) for infants and children from most car-hire firms, but you should always book them in advance. This is especially true during busy travel periods, such as Spanish school holidays, Navidad (Christmas) and Semana Santa (Holy Week).

It's extremely rare that taxis have child seats – unless you're carrying a portable version from home, you're expected to sit the child on your lap, with the seatbelt around you both.

Children's Highlights

Spain has a surfeit of castles, horse shows, fiestas and ferias, interactive museums, flamenco shows and even the Semana Santa processions, to name just a few highlights for kids.

For a number of cities throughout this guidebook, we've included boxed texts that highlight child-friendly attractions.

Beaches

Spain's beaches, especially those along the Mediterranean coast, are custom-made for children – many (particularly along the Costa Brava and in the Balearic Islands) are sheltered from the open ocean by protective coves, while most others are characterised by waveless waters that qui-

etly lap the shore. Yes, some can get a little overcrowded at the height of summer, but there are still plenty of tranquil stretches of sand if you choose carefully.

Playa de la Concha (p417) In San Sebastián, this is Spain's most easily accessible city beach.

Aiguablava and Fornells Sheltered, beautiful Costa Brava coves.

Cala Sant Vicenç (p794) Four of Mallorca's loveliest cove beaches.

Menorca (p799) Quiet north-coast beaches, even in summer.

Zahara de los Atunes Cádiz province beach with pristine sand.

Architecture of the Imagination

Many museums have started to incorporate an interactive element into what were once staid and static exhibits. Numerous major sights (such as the Alhambra and most art galleries) also have guidebooks aimed specifically at children. And then there's live flamenco, something that every child should see once in their lives.

Alcázar (p159) In Segovia: the inspiration for Sleeping Beauty's castle.

Park Güell (p258) and Casa Batlló (p253) Gaudí's weird-and-wonderful Barcelona creations.

Castillo de Loarre (p388) The stereotypically turreted castle in Aragón.

Casas Colgadas (p221) Houses in Cuenca that hang out over the cliff.

Estadio Santiago Bernabéu (p127) and **Camp Nou** (p263) Football, football, football...

Museo Guggenheim (p399) In Bilbao: watch them gaze in wonder.

Gardens, Theme Parks & Horse Shows

Spain has seen an explosion of Disneyfied theme parks in recent years. Parks range from places that re-create the era of the dinosaurs or the Wild West to more traditional parks with rides and animals.

Dinópolis (p392) In Teruel, this is a cross between Jurassic Park and a funfair.

PortAventura (p356) Fine amusement park close to Tarragona.

TIPS FOR TRAVELLING WITH CHILDREN

Some of our authors have travelled throughout Spain with their children. Here are a few of their tips:

➡ Expect your children to be kissed, offered sweets, have their cheeks pinched and their hair ruffled at least once a day.

➡ Always ask for extra tapas in bars, such as olives or cut, raw carrots.

➡ Adjust your children to Spanish time (ie late nights) as quickly as you can; otherwise they'll miss half of what's worth seeing.

➡ Crayons and paper are rarely given out in restaurants – bring your own.

➡ If you're willing to let your child share your bed, you won't incur a supplement. Extra beds usually incur a €20 to €30 charge.

➡ Always ask the local tourist office for the nearest children's playgrounds.

Terra Mítica (p756) In Benidorm, where the spirit of Disneyland meets the Med.

Oasys/Mini Hollywood (p720) Wild West movie sets in the deserts of Almería.

Zoo Aquarium de Madrid (p98) Probably Spain's best zoo.

Parc d'Atraccions (p262) Great rides and a puppet museum. In Barcelona.

Real Escuela Andaluza del Arte Ecuestre (p619) Andalucian horse shows in all their finery.

Planning

For general advice on travelling with young ones, see Lonely Planet's *Travel with Children* or visit the websites www.travel-withyourkids.com and www.familytravel-network.com.

What to Bring

Although you might want to bring a small supply of items that you're used to having back home (this is particularly true for baby products) in case of emergency (or a Sunday when most pharmacies and super-markets are closed), Spain is likely to have everything you need.

You can buy baby formula in powder or liquid form, as well as sterilising solutions such as Milton, at *farmacias* (pharmacies). Disposable *panales* (nappies, or diapers) are widely available at supermarkets and *farmacias*. Fresh cow's milk is sold in cartons and plastic bottles in supermarkets in big cities, but can be hard to find in small towns, where UHT is often the only option.

When to Go

If you're heading for the beach, summer (especially July and August) is the obvious choice – but it's also when Spaniards undertake a mass pilgrimage to the coast, so book well ahead. It's also a good time to travel to the mountains (the Pyrenees, Sierra Nevada). During summer, the interior can be unbearably hot – Seville and Córdoba regularly experience daytime temperatures of almost 50°C at this time.

Our favourite time for visiting Spain is in spring and autumn, particularly May, June, September and October. In all but the latter month, you might be lucky and get weather warm enough for the beach, but temperatures in these months are generally mild and the weather often fine.

Winter can be bitterly cold in much of Spain – fine if you come prepared and even better if you're heading for the snow.

Accommodation

Most hotels (but rarely budget establishments) have cots for small children, although most only have a handful, so reserve one when booking your room. If you're asking for a cot, it can be a good idea to ask for a larger room as many Spanish hotel or *hostal* rooms can be on the small side, making for very cramped conditions. Cots sometimes cost extra, while other hotels offer them for free.

In top-end hotels you can sometimes arrange for childcare, and in some places child-minding agencies cater to visitors. Some top-end hotels – particularly resorts, but also some *paradores* (luxurious state-owned hotels) – have play areas, and many also have swimming pools.

Regions at a Glance

Madrid

Galleries
Nightlife
Food

Art's Golden Mile

Madrid is one of the world's premier cities for public art with the Museo del Prado, the Centro de Arte Reina Sofía and the Museo Thyssen-Bornemisza all within easy walking distance of each other.

Killing the Night

Nightclubs that don't really get busy until 3am. Sophisticated cocktail bars where you mingle with A-list celebrities while sipping your mojito. A live-music scene that begins with flamenco before moving on to jazz and every other genre imaginable.

Tapas & Traditional Food

Traditional Madrid food is nothing to get excited about, but roasted meats in the world's oldest restaurant are memorable eating experiences. Elsewhere, the neighbourhood of La Latina is home to one of the country's finest concentrations of tapas bars.

p66

Castilla y León

Medieval Towns
Villages
Food

City as Art

Rich in history, cathedrals and other grand public monuments, the splendid towns of old Castile can be difficult to choose between. But if we have to choose, it would be plateresque Salamanca, fairy-tale Segovia and gorgeous León.

Quiet Pueblos

The villages of Castilla y León feel like Spain before mass tourism and the modern world arrived on Iberian shores, from the Sierra de Francia in the far southwest to quiet, medieval hamlets like Covarrubias, Puebla de Sanabria and Calatañazor.

Hearty Inland Fare

Roasted and grilled meats are specialities in the Spanish interior, so much so that Spaniards travel here from all over the country for a winter meal. *Jamón* and other cured meats are also a regional passion.

p139

Toledo & Castilla-La Mancha

History
Literature
Villages & Castles

City of Three Faiths

In the Middle Ages, Toledo was one of the most cosmopolitan cities in Spain, as shown by some fine landmarks from that era – a poignant mosque, fine Jewish sites and a cathedral of real power adorned with works by El Greco, Zurbarán and Velázquez.

Tilting at Windmills

The Don Quixote trail through Castilla-La Mancha offers the rare opportunity to follow the terrain trod by one of literature's most eccentric figures. Windmills and sweeping plains evoke Cervantes' novel to such an extent that you can almost hear Sancho Panza's patter.

Beautiful Villages

Amid the often-empty horizons of La Mancha, pretty villages can seem like oases. Almagro and Sigüenza are our favourites, while the castles close to Toledo – this was a longtime frontier between Moorish and Christian Spain – are simply magnificent.

p201

Barcelona

Architecture
Food
Art & History

Modernista Masterpieces

From Gaudí's wondrous Sagrada Família to Domènech i Montaner's celestial Palau de la Música Catalana, Catalan visionaries have made Barcelona one of Europe's great Modernista centres, a showcase for the surreal and captivating.

Culinary Gems

Barcelona's artistry doesn't end at the drawing board. Feasting on seafood overlooking the Mediterranean, munching on tapas at the magnificent Boqueria market, indulging in celebrated Michelin-starred restaurants: it's all part of the Barcelona experience.

Artistry of the Past

A once vibrant settlement of ancient Rome, Barcelona has over 2000 years of history hidden in its old lanes. The old Gothic centre has 14th-century churches and medieval mansions that hold more recent treasures – from a Picasso collection to pre-Columbian masterpieces.

p230

Catalonia

Food
Beaches
Hiking

The Catalan Kitchen

Vying with the Basque Country for Spain's highest per-capita ratio of celebrity chefs, Catalonia is something of a pilgrimage for gastronomes. Here, even in the smallest family establishments, they fuse ingredients from land and sea, always keeping faith with rich culinary traditions even as they head off in innovative new directions.

The Catalan Coast

The picturesque coastlines known as the Costa Brava and Costa Daurada are studded with pretty-as-a-postcard villages and beaches that are generally less crowded than those further south. And not far away, signposts to Salvador Dalí and the Romans make for fine day trips.

Spain's High Country

Northern Catalonia means the Pyrenees, where shapely peaks and quiet valleys offer some of the best hiking anywhere in the country.

p301

Aragón

Mountains
Villages
History

Head for the Hills

Perhaps the prettiest corner of the Pyrenees, northern Aragón combines the drama of steep summits with the quiet pleasures of deep valleys and endless hiking trails. The Parque Nacional de Ordesa y Monte Perdido is arguably Spain's most picturesque national park.

Stone Villages

Aragón has numerous finalists in the competition for Spain's most beautiful village, among them Aínsa, Sos del Rey Católico and Albarracín. Many sit in the Pyrenean foothills against a backdrop of snowcapped mountains.

Romans, Moors & Christians

Centred on one of Spain's most important historical kingdoms, Aragón is strewn with landmarks from the great civilisations of ancient and medieval times. Zaragoza in particular spans the millennia with grace and fervour, and Teruel is an often-missed Mudéjar jewel.

p359

Bilbao, the Basque Country & La Rioja

Food
Wine
Villages

Spain's Culinary Capital

To understand the buzz surrounding Spanish food, head for San Sebastián, which is at once *pintxos* (Basque tapas) heaven and home to outrageously talented chefs. Increasingly a match for San Sebastián are Logroño, Vitoria and Pamplona.

The Finest Drop

La Rioja is to wine what the Basque Country is to food. Wine museums, wine tastings and vineyards stretching to the horizon make this Spain's most accessible wine region. And, of course, it accompanies every meal here.

Villages

There are stunning villages to be found throughout the Basque Country and La Rioja, but those in the Pyrenean foothills and high valleys of Navarra are a match for anything the rest of Spain has to offer.

p396

Cantabria & Asturias

Coastal Scenery
Mountains
Food

The Scenic Coast

Wild rocky walls encircle a beautiful sandy cove at Playa del Silencio, just one of over 200 beaches tucked away along the rugged, emerald-green Asturian coastline, behind which rise gorgeous villages and marvellous mountainscapes.

Picos de Europa

The jagged Picos de Europa have some of the most stunning hiking country in Spain. Vertiginous precipices stretch down into the dramatic Garganta del Cares gorge, while the El Naranjo de Bulnes peak beckons from beyond high mountain passes.

Cheese & Cider

Knocking back cider is Asturias' favourite pastime, particularly along Oviedo's *el bulevar de la sidra,* while the tangy Cabrales cheese from the foothills of the Picos de Europa is one of Spain's best.

p454

Santiago de Compostela & Galicia

Coastal Scenery
History
Food

The Wildest Coast

Galicia's windswept coast is one of Europe's most dramatic and stunningly beautiful. On the Rías Altas, cliffs plunge from enormous heights into roiling Atlantic waters, interspersed with picturesque fishing villages and isolated sandy beaches.

A Sacred Past

In few places are long-gone centuries as alive as they are in Santiago de Compostela. Its magnificent cathedral, churches, streets and plazas represent 1300 uninterrupted years as the goal of that great pilgrimage route, the Camino de Santiago.

Fruits of the Sea

Galicia has some of the world's best seafood, and fine meat from its rich pastures too. Head to Santiago de Compostela's bustling market, the Mercado de Abastos, for the best of both – and the chance to enjoy them at restaurants on the spot.

p499

Extremadura

Medieval Towns
Roman Ruins
Food

Medieval Film Sets

Spain may be replete with wonderfully preserved old towns that date back to the Middle Ages, but Cáceres and Trujillo are up there with the best. Meandering along their cobblestoned lanes is a journey back into an epic past.

Roman Mérida

Spain's most beautiful Roman theatre, its longest Roman-era bridge, a breathtaking museum and a slew of other ruined glories – welcome to Emerita Augusta, now known as Mérida and Spain's finest Roman site. The fabulous bridge at Alcántara also merits a visit.

Ham & Cheese

Some of Spain's finest *jamón* comes from Extremadura, most notably from around Monesterio, which has Spain's best *jamón* museum, and Montánchez. The Torta del Casar cheese from just north of Cáceres is another culinary star.

p543

Seville & Andalucía's Hill Towns

Music
History
Gastronomy

Cradle of Flamenco

The towns and cities of Western Andalucía pretty much invented modern flamenco. Look no further than the *bulerías* of Jerez, the *alegrías* of Cádiz and the *soleares* of Seville – all of them performed with passion in local *tablaos* and *peñas*.

White Towns

They're all here, the famous white towns, with their ruined hilltop castles, geranium-filled flower boxes and small somnolent churches. Arcos, Jimena, Grazalema, Vejer...the ancient sentinels on a once volatile frontier that divided two great civilisations.

Fish & Sherry

Where the Atlantic meets the Mediterranean, you're bound to find good fish, which the Andalucians traditionally deep-fry in olive oil to create *pescaíto frito*. Then there's the sherry made from grapes that grow near the coast – a perfect pairing.

p571

Granada & South Coast Andalucía

Architecture
Beaches
Walks

Hybrid Granada

A celebrated Nasrid palace-fortress, a hilltop Moorish quarter, opulent walled 'carmens' with elaborate gardens, and a baroque-Renaissance cathedral – the city of Granada is a magnificent 'mess' of just about every architectural style known to European building.

Southern Beaches

The south coast's beaches are an industry, bagging more tourist euros than the rest of the region put together. Choose according to your budget and hipster-rating between Estepona, Marbella, Torremolinos, Málaga, Nerja and Almuñécar.

Wild Areas

Walk the dry, craggy coastline of Cabo de Gata; hitch onto the GR7 long-distance footpath in Las Alpujarras; or get lost looking for wildlife on the trails in the highlands east of Cazorla. Andalucía has its untamed side, if you know where to look.

p650

Valencia & Murcia

Fiestas
Cuisine
Beaches

Bulls, Fire & Knights in Armour

The biggest and noisiest party is Valencia's Las Fallas in March. But almost every *pueblo* has its fiesta, usually with fireworks and often with bulls. Lorca's Semana Santa (Holy Week) festivities rival those of Andalucía.

Simmering Rice

Paella first simmered over an open fire in Valencia. Rice dishes are everywhere, supplemented by fish and seafood from the Mediterranean and the freshest of vegetables grown along the fertile coastal strip down into Murcia.

Strands & Rocky Coves

From small bays to vast beaches stretching over kilometres, from tiny rocky coves to the sandy sweeps of Denia, Benidorm and Murcia's Costa Cálida (Hot Coast), there's always room to stretch out your towel.

p725

Mallorca, Menorca & Ibiza

Beaches
Walking & Cycling
Nightlife

Beaches

White sand, black sand, pebbles or rocky inlets, each of the islands offers variety with, in general, fine sand on their southern shores, rougher stuff to the north.

Outdoor Adventure

Watery fun – sailing, windsurfing, diving or simply splashing about in all the major coastal resorts – is the most popular activity, but the Balearics are also fine trekking destinations, particularly along the Serra de Tramuntana, Mallorca's wild, craggy north.

Through the Night

It's not only the megavenues of Ibiza that pound until dawn. In season, Ciutadella, on Menorca, draws in clubbers from all over the island; Palma de Mallorca is the big draw for locals there; and the smaller music bars of diminutive Formentera hold their own.

p776

On the Road

Madrid

Includes ➡

Best Places to Eat

➡ Mercado de San Miguel (p107)

➡ Restaurante Sobrino de Botín (p108)

➡ DiverXo (p112)

➡ Casa Alberto (p109)

➡ Estado Puro (p110)

Best Places to Stay

➡ Hotel Meninas (p104)

➡ Praktik Metropol (p104)

➡ Hotel Alicia (p105)

➡ Only You Hotel (p106)

➡ Hotel Silken Puerta América (p107)

Why Go?

Madrid is a miracle of human energy and peculiarly Spanish passions, a beguiling place with a simple message: this city knows how to live.

It's true Madrid doesn't have the immediate cachet of Paris, the monumental history of Rome or the reputation for cool of that other city up the road. But it's a city whose contradictory impulses are legion, the perfect expression of Europe's most passionate country writ large.

This city has transformed itself into one of Spain's premier style centres and its calling cards are many: astonishing art galleries, relentless nightlife, an exceptional live-music scene, a feast of fine restaurants and tapas bars, and a population that's mastered the art of the good life. It's not that other cities don't have these things: it's just that Madrid has all of them in bucketloads.

When to Go
Madrid

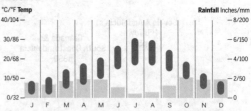

Jan–Feb Foodies and famous Spanish chefs flock to the Madrid Fusion & Gastro Festival.

Mar–Apr Warmer spring weather brings *madrileños* out into the city's *terrazas*.

Sep Madrid shakes off its summer torpor with (usually) lovely autumn weather.

Visiting Madrid's Baroque Palaces

The Spanish capital's contribution to world architectural textbooks is known as *barroco madrileño* (Madrid baroque). Its creation is largely attributed to Juan de Herrera (1530–97), perhaps the greatest figure of the Spanish Renaissance, who fused the sternness of the Renaissance style with a muted approach to its successor, the more voluptuous, ornamental baroque. Prime examples in Madrid include the Plaza Mayor, the former *ayuntamiento* (town hall) on Plaza de la Villa and the Convento de la Encarnación.

Madrid's Barrios in a Nutshell

Plaza Mayor & Royal Madrid form Madrid's oldest quarter, home to some of Madrid's grandest monuments, as well as bars, restaurants and hotels. Next door, the La Latina and Lavapiés neighbourhoods are the preserve of narrow medieval streets, great bars for tapas and drinking, and restaurants. Away to the east of the Puerta del Sol, the Huertas area is one of Madrid's nightlife capitals.

Down the hill and a world away, the Paseo del Prado and El Retiro area is downtown Madrid's greenest corner, with world-class art galleries along the Paseo's shores and the Parque del Buen Retiro up the hill to the east. Salamanca is upmarket and Madrid's home of old money, not to mention Madrid's home of designer shopping; while Malasaña and Chueca are two inner-city *barrios* with eclectic nightlife, shopping and outstanding eating options: the latter is the heartbeat of Madrid's gay community.

Northern Madrid has high-class restaurants and is the home of Real Madrid football club. Where it wraps around the city to the west, Chamberí is a wonderful residential *barrio* that offers a glimpse of Madrid away from the tourist crowds – come here to experience Madrid as the locals do.

Madrid's Best Art Galleries

➡ Museo del Prado (p83) One of the great art galleries of the world, with Goya and Velázquez the highlights.

➡ Centro de Arte Reina Sofía (p89) Stunning contemporary art gallery that's home to Picasso's *Guernica,* as well as works by Dalí, Miró and others.

➡ Museo Thyssen-Bornemisza (p85) Private art gallery with European masters from every era.

➡ Real Academia de Bellas Artes de San Fernando (p79) Goya, Picasso, Velázquez, Rubens...

➡ Ermita de San Antonio de la Florida (p95) Exquisite Goya frescoes in their original setting.

➡ Museo Sorolla (p96) Stunning Andalucian-style home in leafy northern Madrid with Sorolla's finest works.

Tapas Central

La Latina, southwest of Plaza Mayor, is one of Spain's best tapas neighbourhoods. Weekends are crazy-busy and there's Basque *pintxos* (tapas), Madrid's best tortilla and wine bars aplenty. Start along Calle de la Cava Baja, and finish with a mojito on Plaza de la Paja.

Madrid's Best Views

➡ Mirador de Madrid (p91)

➡ Círculo de Bellas Artes (p79)

➡ Gourmet Experience (p109)

➡ The Roof (p118)

➡ Room 820, Hostal Luis XV (p103)

Pretty Plazas

➡ Plaza Mayor (p72)

➡ Plaza de Oriente (p74)

➡ Plaza de Santa Ana (p79)

➡ Plaza de la Villa (p75)

➡ Plaza de la Paja (p76)

➡ Plaza de la Cibeles (p91)

Top Madrid Stages

➡ Café Central (p123; jazz)

➡ Corral de la Morería (p123; flamenco)

➡ Torres Bermejas (p125; flamenco)

➡ Candela (p125; flamenco)

➡ Sala El Sol (p124; rock)

➡ Sala Clamores (p125; jazz and other genres)

➡ Teatro de la Zarzuela (p122; *zarzuela*)

Madrid Highlights

1 Watch the masterpieces of Velázquez and Goya leap off the canvas at the world-famous **Museo del Prado** (p83).

2 Search for treasure in the Sunday **El Rastro** (p78) flea market, then join the crowds in the **Parque del Buen Retiro** (p89).

3 Soak up the buzz with a *caña* (small beer) or glass of Spanish wine on **Plaza de Santa Ana** (p79).

4 Go on a **tapas crawl** in the medieval *barrio* (district) of La Latina (p112).

5 Order *chocolate con churros* (deep-fried doughnut strips dipped in hot chocolate) close to dawn at the **Chocolatería de San Ginés** (p114).

6 Make a sporting pilgrimage to see the stars of Real Madrid play at **Estadio Santiago Bernabéu** (p127).

7 Dance the night away in one of the city's world-famous nightclubs such as **Teatro Joy Eslava** (p114).

8 Feast on roast lamb at **Café de la Iberia** (p137) in Chinchón.

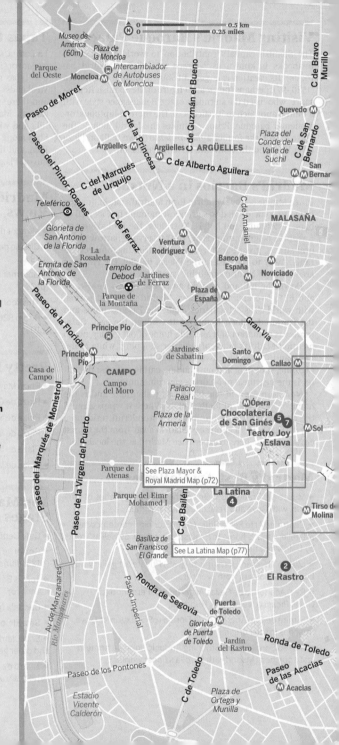

History

When Iberia's Christians began the Reconquista (c 722) – the centuries-long campaign by Christian forces to reclaim the peninsula – the Muslims of Al-Andalus constructed a chain of fortified positions through the heart of Iberia. One of these was built by Muhammad I, emir of Córdoba, in 854, on the site of what would become Madrid. The name they gave to the new settlement was Mayrit (or Magerit), which comes from the Arabic word *majira,* meaning water channel.

A Worthy Capital?

Madrid's strategic location in the centre of the peninsula saw the city change hands repeatedly, but it was not until 1309 that the travelling Cortes (royal court and parliament) sat in Madrid for the first time. Despite the growing royal attention, medieval Madrid remained dirt poor and small-scale: 'In Madrid there is nothing except what you bring with you,' observed one 15th-century writer. It simply bore no comparison with other major Spanish, let alone European, cities.

By the time Felipe II ascended the Spanish throne in 1556, Madrid was surrounded by walls that boasted 130 towers and six stone gates, but these fortifications were largely built of mud and designed more to impress than provide any meaningful defence of the city. Madrid was nonetheless chosen by Felipe II as the capital of Spain in 1561.

Madrid took centuries to grow into its new role and despite a handful of elegant churches, the imposing Alcázar and a smattering of noble residences, the city consisted of, for the most part, precarious whitewashed houses. The monumental Paseo del Prado, which now provides Madrid with so much of its grandeur, was a small creek.

During the 17th century, Spain's golden age, Madrid began to take on the aspect of a capital and was home to 175,000 people, making it the fifth-largest city in Europe (after London, Paris, Constantinople and Naples).

Carlos III (r 1759–88) gave Madrid and Spain a period of comparatively commonsense government. After he cleaned up the city, completed the Palacio Real, inaugurated the Real Jardín Botánico and carried out numerous other public works, he became known as the best 'mayor' Madrid had ever had.

Madrileños (residents of Madrid) didn't take kindly to Napoleon's invasion and subsequent occupation of Spain in 1805 and, on 2 May 1808, they attacked French troops around the Palacio Real and what is now Plaza del Dos de Mayo. The ill-fated rebellion was quickly put down by Murat, Napoleon's brother-in-law and the most powerful of his military leaders.

Wars, Franco & Terrorism

Turmoil continued to stalk the Spanish capital. The upheaval of the 19th-century Carlist Wars was followed by a two-and-a-half-year siege of Madrid by Franco's Nationalist forces from 1936 to 1939, during which the city was shelled regularly from Casa de Campo and Gran Vía became known as 'Howitzer Alley'.

After Franco's death in 1975 and the country's subsequent transition to democracy, Madrid became an icon for the new Spain as the city's young people unleashed a flood of pent-up energy. This took its most colourful form in the years of *la movida,* the endless party that swept up the city in a frenzy of creativity and open-minded freedom that has in some ways yet to abate.

On 11 March 2004, just three days before the country was due to vote in national elections, Madrid was rocked by 10 bombs on four rush-hour commuter trains heading into the capital's Atocha station. The bombs had been planted by terrorists with links to al-Qaeda, reportedly because of Spain's then support for the American-led war in Iraq. When the dust cleared, 191 people had died and 1755 were wounded, many seriously. Madrid was in shock and, for 24 hours at least, this most clamorous of cities fell silent. Then, 36 hours after the attacks, more than three million *madrileños* streamed onto the streets to protest against the bombings, making it the largest demonstration in the city's history. Although deeply traumatised, Madrid's mass act of defiance and pride began the process of healing. Visit Madrid today and you'll find a city that has resolutely returned to normal.

In the years since, Madrid has come agonisingly close in the race to host the Summer Olympics, coming third behind London and Paris in the race for 2012, second behind Rio for 2016 before falling into the also-rans for the 2020 games. And, of course, Madrid was the scene of one of the biggest celebrations in modern Spanish history when the Spanish World Cup–winning football team returned home in July 2010. These celebrations were almost matched two years later when Spain won the 2012 European Football Championships, again bringing much-needed cheer to a city affected deeply by Spain's severe economic downturn.

◉ Sights

Madrid has three of the finest art galleries in the world: if ever there existed a golden mile of fine art, it would have to be the combined charms of the Museo del Prado, the Centro de Arte Reina Sofía and the Museo Thyssen-Bornemisza. Beyond the museums' walls, the combination of stately architecture and feel-good living is nowhere easier to access than in the beautiful plazas, where *terrazas* (cafes with outdoor tables) provide a front-row seat for Madrid's fine cityscape and endlessly energetic street life. Throw in some outstanding city parks (the Parque del Buen Retiro, in particular) and areas like Chueca,

Malasaña and Salamanca, which each have their own identity, and you'll wonder why you decided to spend so little time here.

◉ Plaza Mayor & Royal Madrid

Downtown Madrid is where the story of Madrid began. As the seat of royal power, this is where the splendour of imperial Spain was at its most ostentatious and where Spain's overarching Catholicism was at its most devout – think expansive palaces, elaborate private mansions, ancient churches and imposing convents amid the clamour of modern Madrid.

MADRID SIGHTS

MADRID IN...

One Day

Begin in the **Plaza Mayor** with its architectural beauty, fine *terrazas* and endlessly fascinating passing Madrid parade. Wander down Calle Mayor, passing the delightful **Plaza de la Villa** en route, and head for the **Palacio Real**. By then you'll be ready for a coffee (or something stronger) and there's no finer place to rest than in the **Plaza de Oriente**. Double back up towards the **Plaza de la Puerta del Sol** then lose yourself in the Huertas area around **Plaza de Santa Ana**, the ideal place for a long, liquid lunch. Stroll down the hill to the incomparable **Museo del Prado**, one of Europe's best art galleries. In anticipation of a long night ahead, catch your breath in the **Parque del Buen Retiro**. As the sun nears the horizon, climb to Madrid's best views at the **Mirador de Madrid** or **Círculo de Bellas Artes**, before heading up along **Gran Vía** and into Chueca for Madrid's famously noisy and eclectic nightlife.

Three Days

Three days is a minimum for getting a real taste of Madrid. Spend a morning each on days two and three at **Centro de Arte Reina Sofía** and **Museo Thyssen-Bornemisza**. Otherwise, pause in **Plaza de la Cibeles** to admire some of the best architecture in Madrid as you work your way north to the **Gran Café de Gijón**, one of Madrid's grand old cafes. A quick metro ride across town takes you to the astonishing Goya frescoes in the **Ermita de San Antonio de la Florida**. While you're in the area, consider a chicken-and-cider meal at **Casa Mingo**. On another day, head for La Latina and the great restaurants and tapas bars along Calle de la Cava Baja, or some cod tapas at **Casa Revuelta**. If it's a Sunday, precede these outings with a wander through **El Rastro**, one of the best flea markets in Europe. In Malasaña, Calle de Manuela Malasaña offers rich pickings for a meal and the august and old-world **Café Comercial** is a fine old pit stop at any time of the day.

One Week

If you're in town for a week, begin day four with some shopping. Calle de Serrano has just about everything for the designer-conscious, while Calle de Fuencarral (casual streetwear) or Calle de Augusto Figueroa (shoes) could also occupy an hour or two. Check out the bullring at **Plaza de Toros**, and **Estadio Santiago Bernabéu**, home to Real Madrid. Other possibilities that will deepen your Madrid experience include wandering through medieval and multicultural **Lavapiés** or seeing a live **flamenco performance**. Day trips could include **Toledo** and **Segovia**. Of the numerous royal residences in the Madrid vicinity, the most impressive is **San Lorenzo de El Escorial**, but **Chinchón** is an enchanted alternative with ramshackle village charm written all over its colonnaded Plaza Mayor.

Plaza Mayor & Royal Madrid

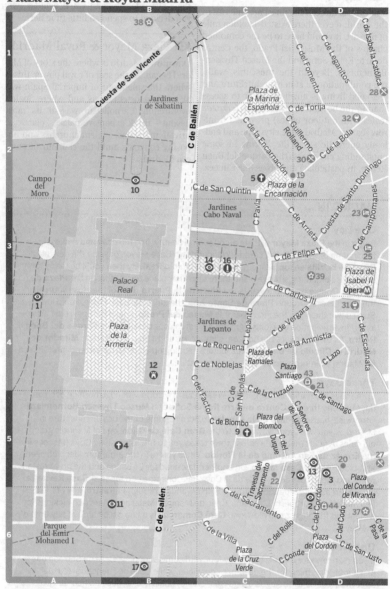

Plaza Mayor

SQUARE

(Map p72; Plaza Mayor; M Sol) Madrid's grand central square, a rare but expansive opening in the tightly packed streets of central Madrid, is one of the prettiest open spaces in Spain, a winning combination of imposing architecture, picaresque historical tales and vibrant street life coursing across its cobblestones. At once beautiful in its own right and a reference point for so many Madrid days, it also hosts the city's main tourist office (p131), a Christmas market in December

its first public ceremony was suitably auspicious – the beatification of San Isidro Labrador (St Isidro the Farm Labourer), Madrid's patron saint. Thereafter it was as if all that was controversial about Spain took place in this square. Bullfights, often in celebration of royal weddings or births, with royalty watching on from the balconies and up to 50,000 people crammed into the plaza, were a recurring theme until 1878. Far more notorious were the *autos-da-fé* (the ritual condemnations of heretics during the Spanish Inquisition) followed by executions – burnings at the stake and deaths by garrotte on the north side of the square, hangings to the south. These continued until 1790 when a fire largely destroyed the square, which was subsequently reproduced under the supervision of Juan de Villanueva, who lent his name to the building that now houses the Museo del Prado (p83). These days, the plaza is an epicentre of Madrid life.

The grandeur of the plaza is due in part to the warm colours of the uniformly ochre apartments, with 237 wrought-iron balconies offset by the exquisite frescoes of the 17th-century Real Casa de la Panadería (Royal Bakery). The present frescoes date to 1992 and are the work of artist Carlos Franco, who chose images from the signs of the zodiac and gods (eg Cybele) to provide a stunning backdrop for the plaza. The frescoes were inaugurated to coincide with Madrid's 1992 spell as European Capital of Culture.

Palacio Real   PALACE
(Map p72; ☏91 454 88 00; www.patrimonio nacional.es; Calle de Bailén; adult/concession €10/5, guide/audioguide/pamphlet €7/4/1, EU citizens last 3 hours Mon-Thu free; ☉10am-8pm Apr-Sep, to 6pm Oct-Mar; ⓜÓpera) Spain's lavish Palacio Real is a jewel box of a palace, although it's used only occasionally for royal ceremonies; the royal family moved to the modest Palacio de la Zarzuela years ago.

When the Alcázar burned down on Christmas Day 1734, Felipe V, the first of the Bourbon kings, decided to build a palace that would dwarf all its European counterparts. Felipe died before the palace was finished, which is perhaps why the Italianate baroque colossus has a mere 2800 rooms, just one quarter of the original plan.

The official tour (self-guided tours are also possible and follow the same route) leads through 50 of the palace rooms, which hold a good selection of Goyas, 215 absurdly ornate clocks, and five Stradivarius violins still used

and arches leading to so many laneways that lead out into the labyrinth.

Ah, the history the plaza has seen! Designed in 1619 by Juan Gómez de Mora and built in typical Herrerian style, of which the slate spires are the most obvious expression,

Plaza Mayor & Royal Madrid

for concerts and balls. The main **stairway** is a grand statement of imperial power, leading first to the Halberdiers' rooms and eventually to the sumptuous **Salón del Trono** (Throne Room), with its crimson-velvet wall coverings and Tiepolo ceiling. Shortly after, you reach the **Salón de Gasparini**, with its exquisite stucco ceiling and walls resplendent with embroidered silks.

Outside the main palace, visit the **Farmacia Real** (Royal Pharmacy) at the southern end of the patio known as the **Plaza de la Armería** (or Plaza de Armas). Westwards across the plaza is the **Armería Real** (Royal Armoury), a shiny collection of weapons and armour, mostly dating from the 16th and 17th centuries.

Plaza de Oriente   SQUARE
(Map p72; Ⓜ Ópera) A royal palace that once had aspirations to be the Spanish Versailles. Sophisticated cafes watched over by apartments that cost the equivalent of a royal salary. The Teatro Real (p126), Madrid's opera house and one of Spain's temples to high culture. Some of the finest sunset views in

Madrid... Welcome to Plaza de Oriente, a living, breathing monument to imperial Madrid.

At the centre of the plaza, which the palace overlooks, is an equestrian **statue of Felipe IV** (Map p72; Ⓜ Ópera). Designed by Velázquez, it's the perfect place to take it all in, with marvellous views wherever you look. If you're wondering how a heavy bronze statue of a rider and his horse rearing up can maintain that stance, the answer is simple: the hind legs are solid, while the front ones are hollow. That idea was Galileo Galilei's. Nearby are some 20 marble statues, mostly of ancient monarchs. Local legend has it that these ageing royals get down off their pedestals at night to stretch their legs.

The adjacent **Jardines Cabo Naval** adds to the sense of a sophisticated oasis of green in the heart of Madrid.

Campo del Moro & Jardines de Sabatini   GARDENS
In proper palace style, lush gardens surround the Palacio Real. To the north are the formal French-style **Jardines de Sabatini**

(Map p72; ⊙9am-10pm May-Sep, 9am-9pm Oct-Apr; Ⓜ Ópera). Directly behind the palace are the fountains of the **Campo del Moro** (Map p72; ☑91 454 88 00; www.patrimonionacional.es; Paseo de la Virgen del Puerto; ⊙10am-8pm Mon-Sat, 9am-8pm Sun & holidays Apr-Sep, 10am-6pm Mon-Sat, 9am-6pm Sun & holidays Oct-Mar; Ⓜ Príncipe Pío), so named because this is where the Muslim army camped before a 12th-century attack on the Alcázar. Now, shady paths, a thatch-roofed pagoda and palace views are the main attractions.

Catedral de Nuestra Señora de la Almudena
CATHEDRAL

(Map p72; ☑91 542 22 00; www.museocatedral.archimadrid.es; Calle de Bailén; cathedral & crypt by donation, museum adult/child €6/4; ⊙9am-8.30pm Mon-Sat, for Mass Sun, museum 10am-2.30pm Mon-Sat; Ⓜ Ópera) Paris has Notre Dame and Rome has St Peter's Basilica. In fact, almost every European city of stature has its signature cathedral, a standout monument to a glorious Christian past. Not Madrid. Although the exterior of the Catedral de Nuestra Señora de la Almudena sits in harmony with the adjacent Palacio Real, Madrid's cathedral is cavernous and largely charmless within; its colourful, modern ceilings do little to make up for the lack of old-world gravitas that so distinguishes great cathedrals.

Carlos I first proposed building a cathedral here back in 1518, but building didn't actually begin until 1879. It was finally finished in 1992 and its pristine, bright-white, neo-Gothic interior holds no pride of place in the affections of *madrileños*.

You can climb to the cathedral's summit. En route you climb through the cathedral's museum; follow the signs to the **Museo de la Catedral y Cúpula** on the northern facade, opposite the Palacio Real.

Muralla Árabe
WALLS

(Map p72; Cuesta de la Vega; Ⓜ Ópera) Behind the cathedral apse, down Cuesta de la Vega, is a short stretch of the so-called Muralla Árabe, the fortifications built by Madrid's early medieval Islamic rulers. Some of it dates as far back as the 9th century, when the initial Islamic fort was raised. Other sections date from the 12th and 13th centuries, by which time the city was in Christian hands.

Plaza de la Villa
SQUARE

(Map p72; Plaza de la Villa; Ⓜ Ópera) The intimate Plaza de la Villa is one of Madrid's prettiest. Enclosed on three sides by wonderfully preserved examples of 17th-century *barroco madrileño* (Madrid-style baroque architecture – a pleasing amalgam of brick, exposed stone and wrought iron), it was the permanent seat of Madrid's city government from the Middle Ages until recent years, when Madrid's city council relocated to the grand Palacio de Cibeles on Plaza de la Cibeles (p91).

On the western side of the square is the 17th-century **former ayuntamiento** (town hall; map p72; Ⓜ Ópera), in Habsburg-style baroque with Herrerian slate-tile spires. On the opposite side of the square is the Gothic **Casa de los Lujanes** (Map p72; Ⓜ Ópera), whose brickwork tower is said to have been 'home' to the imprisoned French monarch François I after his capture in the Battle of Pavia (1525). The plateresque (15th- and 16th-century Spanish baroque) **Casa de Cisneros** (Map p72; Ⓜ Ópera), built in 1537 with later Renaissance alterations, also catches the eye.

Convento de las Descalzas Reales
CONVENT

(Convent of the Barefoot Royals; Map p72; www.patrimonionacional.es; Plaza de las Descalzas 3; adult/child €7/4, incl Convento de la Encarnación €10/5, EU citizens Wed & Thu afternoon free; ⊙10am-2pm & 4-6.30pm Tue-Sat, 10am-3pm Sun; Ⓜ Ópera, Sol) The grim plateresque walls of the Convento de las Descalzas Reales offer no hint that behind the facade lies a sumptuous stronghold of the faith. On the obligatory guided tour you'll see a gaudily frescoed Renaissance stairway, a number of extraordinary tapestries based on works by Rubens, and a wonderful painting entitled *The Voyage of the 11,000 Virgins*. Some 33 nuns still live here and there are 33 chapels dotted around the convent.

The convent was founded in 1559 by Juana of Austria, the widowed daughter of the Spanish king Carlos I, and it remains one of Spain's richest religious houses.

Convento de la Encarnación
CONVENT

(Map p72; ☑91 454 88 00; www.patrimonionacional.es; Plaza de la Encarnación 1; adult/concession €7/4, incl Convento de las Descalzas Reales €10/5, EU citizens Wed & Thu afternoon free; ⊙10am-2pm & 4-6.30pm Tue-Sat, 10am-3pm Sun; Ⓜ Ópera) Founded by Empress Margarita de Austria, this 17th-century mansion built in the Madrid baroque style (brick, exposed stone and wrought iron) is still inhabited by nuns of the Augustine order. The large art collection dates mostly from the 17th century, and among the many gold and silver reliquaries is one that contains the blood of San Pantaleón, which purportedly liquefies each year on 27 July.

Iglesia de San Nicolás de los Servitas
CHURCH

(Map p72; ☑ 91 548 83 14; Plaza de San Nicolás 6; ⊙ 8am-1.30pm & 5.30-8.30pm Mon, 8-9.30am & 6.30-8.30pm Tue-Sat, 9.30am-2pm & 6.30-9pm Sun & holidays; Ⓜ Ópera) Considered Madrid's oldest surviving church, Iglesia de San Nicolás de los Servitas may have been built on the site of Muslim Magerit's second mosque. It offers a rare glimpse of medieval Madrid, although apart from the restored 12th-century Mudéjar bell tower, most of the present church dates back to the 15th century.

Iglesia de San Ginés
CHURCH

(Map p72; Calle del Arenal 13; ⊙ 8.45am-1pm & 6-9pm Mon-Sat, 9.45am-2pm & 6-9pm Sun; Ⓜ Sol, Ópera) Due north of Plaza Mayor, San Ginés is one of Madrid's oldest churches: it has been here in one form or another since at least the 14th century. What you see today was built in 1645 but largely reconstructed after a fire in 1824. The church houses some fine paintings, including El Greco's *Expulsion of the Moneychangers from the Temple* (1614).

It is speculated that, prior to the arrival of the Christians in 1085, a Mozarabic community (Christians in Muslim territory) lived around the stream that later became Calle del Arenal and that its parish church stood on this site.

⊙ La Latina & Lavapiés

La Latina combines some of the best things about Madrid: the Spanish capital's best selection of tapas bars and a medieval streetscape studded with elegant churches. The *barrio's* heartland is centred on the area between (and very much including) Calle de la Cava Baja and the beautiful Plaza de la Paja.

Lavapiés, on the other hand, is a world away from the sophistication of modern Madrid. This is at once one of the city's oldest and most traditional *barrios* and home to more immigrants than any other central-Madrid *barrio*. It's quirky, alternative and a melting pot all in one. It's not without its problems, and the *barrio* has a reputation both for anti-glamour cool and as a no-go zone, depending on your perspective.

Basílica de San Francisco El Grande
CHURCH

(Map p77; Plaza de San Francisco 1; adult/concession €3/2; ⊙ mass 8am-10.30am Mon-Sat, museum 10.30am-12.30pm & 4-6pm Tue-Sun; Ⓜ La Latina, Puerta de Toledo) This is one of the largest churches in the city and has an extravagantly frescoed dome which is, by some estimates, the largest in Spain and the fourth-largest in the world, with a height of 56m and diameter of 33m. The baroque basilica has some outstanding features, including frescoed cupolas and chapel ceilings by Francisco Bayeu. Goya's *The Prediction of San Bernardino of Siena for the King of Aragón* is here, too, in the Capilla de San Bernardino.

According to legend, the basilica sits atop the site where St Francis of Assisi built a chapel in 1217.

Although entry is free during morning Mass times, there is no access to the museum and the lights in the Capilla de San Bernardino won't be on (to illuminate the Goya).

Iglesia de San Andrés
CHURCH

(Map p77; Plaza de San Andrés 1; ⊙ 8am-1pm & 6-8pm Mon-Sat, 8am-1pm Sun; Ⓜ La Latina) The stately Iglesia de San Andrés crowns the plaza of the same name, providing a lovely backdrop for the impromptu parties that fill this square on Sunday afternoons as the El Rastro crowd drifts in. Gutted during Spain's civil war, it was restored to its former glory and is at its best when illuminated at night.

Around the back, overlooking the delightful Plaza de la Paja (Map p77), is the Capilla del Obispo, where San Isidro Labrador, patron saint of Madrid, was first buried.

When the saint's body was discovered here in the late 13th century, two centuries after his death, decomposition had not yet set in. San Isidro made his last move to the Basílica de Nuestra Señora del Buen Consejo (Calle de Toledo 37; ⊙ 8am-1pm & 6-9pm; Ⓜ Tirso de Molina, La Latina) in the 18th century. From Tuesday to Friday at 12.30pm, stop by for the sung service 'Oficio del Mediodía'.

Down the bottom of Plaza de la Paja, and visible from the Capilla del Obispo, is the Jardín del Príncipe Anglona (Map p77; Plaza de la Paja; ⊙ 10am-10pm Apr-Oct, 10am-6.30pm Nov-Mar), one of the quietest corners of the city.

Museo de San Isidro
MUSEUM

(Map p77; ☑ 91 366 74 15; www.madrid.es; Plaza de San Andrés 2; ⊙ 9.30am-8pm Tue-Fri, 10am-2pm Sat & Sun Sep-Jul, 9.30am-2.30pm Tue-Sat Aug;

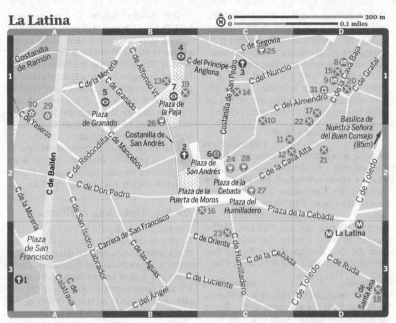

La Latina

Ⓜ La Latina) **FREE** Next door to the Iglesia de San Andrés, this engaging museum sits on the spot where San Isidro Labrador is said to have ended his days around 1172. For an overview of Madrid's history, this place is hard to beat, with archaeological finds from the Roman period, including a 4th-century mosaic found on the site of a Roman villa in the *barrio* (district) of Carabanchel, maps, scale models, paintings and photos of Madrid down through the ages.

A particular highlight is the large model based on Pedro Teixera's famous 1656 map of Madrid. Of great historical interest (though not much to look at) is the 'miraculous well', where the saint called forth water to slake his master's thirst. In another miracle, the son of the saint's master fell into a well, whereupon Isidro prayed and prayed until the water rose and lifted his son to safety. The museum is housed in a largely new building with a 16th-century Renaissance courtyard and a 17th-century chapel.

Viaducto & Jardines de las Vistillas
VIEWPOINT, GARDENS

(Map p72; M La Latina) For a great view out to the west, take a stroll down Calle de Segovia, where a *viaducto* (viaduct) provides a good vantage point. The outdoor tables in the adjacent Jardines de las Vistillas are another good spot, with views out towards Sierra de Guadarrama. During the civil war, Las Vistillas was heavily bombarded by Nationalist troops from the Casa de Campo, and they in turn were shelled from a Republican bunker here.

La Morería
NEIGHBOURHOOD

(Map p77; M La Latina) The area stretching southeast from the *viaducto* to the Iglesia de San Andrés was the heart of the *morería*. This is where the Muslim population of Magerit was concentrated in the wake of the 11th-century Christian takeover of the town. Strain the imagination a little and the maze of winding and hilly lanes even now retains a whiff of the North African medina.

Iglesia de San Pedro El Viejo
CHURCH

(Map p77; ☑ 91 365 12 84; Costanilla de San Pedro; M La Latina) With its clearly Mudéjar bell tower, Iglesia de San Pedro El Viejo is one of the few remaining windows onto the world of medieval Madrid. The church was built atop the site of the old Mezquita de la Morería (Mosque of the Muslim Quarter).

El Rastro
MARKET

(Ribera de Curtidores; ☺ 8am-3pm Sun; M La Latina) A Sunday morning at El Rastro is a Madrid institution. You could easily spend an entire morning inching your way down the Calle de la Ribera de Curtidores and through the maze of streets that hosts El Rastro flea market every Sunday morning. Cheap clothes, luggage, old flamenco records, even older photos of Madrid, faux designer purses, grungy T-shirts, household goods and electronics are the main fare. For every 10 pieces of junk, there's a real gem (a lost masterpiece, an Underwood typewriter) waiting to be found.

The crowded Sunday flea market was, back in the 17th and 18th centuries, largely a meat market (rastro means 'stain', in reference to the trail of blood left behind by animals dragged down the hill). The road leading through the market, Ribera de Curtidores, translates as 'Tanners' Alley' and further evokes this sense of a slaughterhouse past. On Sunday mornings this is the place to be, with all of Madrid (in all its diversity) here in search of a bargain.

A word of warning: pickpockets love El Rastro as much as everyone else, so keep a tight hold on your belongings and don't keep valuables in easy-to-reach pockets.

◎ Sol, Santa Ana & Huertas

The Plaza de la Puerta del Sol is Madrid's beating heart and the sum total of all Madrid's personalities, with fabulous shopping, eating and entertainment options. If nearby Huertas is known for anything, it's for nightlife that never seems to abate once the sun goes down. Such fame is well deserved, but there's so much more to Huertas than immediately meets the eye. Enjoy the height of sophisticated European cafe culture in the superb Plaza de Santa Ana, then go down the hill through Barrio de las Letras to the Centro de Arte Reina Sofía, one of the finest contemporary art galleries in Europe.

Plaza de la Puerta del Sol
SQUARE

(Map p80; Plaza de la Puerta del Sol; M Sol) The official centre point of Spain is a gracious hemisphere of elegant facades that's often very crowded. It is, above all, a crossroads. People here are forever heading somewhere else, on foot, by metro (three lines cross here) or by bus (many lines terminate and start nearby). In Madrid's earliest days, the Puerta del Sol (Gate of the Sun) was the eastern gate of the city.

The main building on the square houses the regional government of the Comunidad de Madrid. The Casa de Correos (Map p80), as it is called, was built as the city's main post office in 1768. The clock was added in 1856 and on New Year's Eve people throng the square to wait impatiently for the clock to strike midnight, and at each gong swallow a grape – not as easy as it sounds! On the footpath outside the Casa de Correos is a plaque marking Spain's Kilometre Zero, the point from which Spain's network of roads is measured.

The semicircular junction owes its present appearance in part to the Bourbon king Carlos III (r 1759–88), whose **equestrian statue** (Map p80), complete with his unmistakable nose, stands in the middle. Look out for the **statue of a bear** (Map p80) nuzzling a *madroño* (strawberry tree) at the plaza's eastern end; this is the official symbol of the city.

Real Academia de Bellas Artes de San Fernando
MUSEUM

(Map p80; ☎ 91 524 08 64; http://rabasf.insde.es; Calle de Alcalá 13; adult/child €6/free, Wed free; ⏲ 10am-3pm Tue-Sun Sep-Jun, hours vary Jul & Aug; Ⓜ Sol, Sevilla) An academic centre for up-and-coming artists since Fernando VI founded it in the 18th century (both Picasso and Dalí studied here), the Royal Fine Arts Academy houses works by some of the best-loved old masters. Highlights include works by Zurbarán, El Greco, Rubens, Tintoretto, Goya, Sorolla and Juan Gris, not to mention a couple of minor portraits by Velázquez and a few drawings by Picasso.

Gran Vía
STREET

(Map p80; Gran Vía; Ⓜ Gran Vía, Callao) Gran Vía, one of Madrid's grandest thoroughfares, climbs through the city centre from Plaza de España all the way down to Calle de Alcalá. On a rise about one-third of the way along stands the 1920s-era **Telefónica building** (Edificio Telefónica; Map p80) which was for years the tallest building in the city. At the southern end of Gran Vía, the stunning French-designed 1905 **Edificio Metrópolis** (Map p80) has a winged statue of victory sitting atop its dome.

Gran Vía has only existed since 1910, when it was bulldozed through what was then a lively labyrinth of old streets. Among the buildings torn down was the house that Goya had once lived in.

★ Círculo de Bellas Artes
CULTURAL CENTRE, LOOKOUT

(Map p80; www.circulobellasartes.com; Calle Marqués de Casa Riera 2; admission €3; ⏲ roof terrace 9am-2am Mon-Thu, 9am-2.30am Fri, 11am-2.30am Sat & Sun; Ⓜ Sevilla, Plaza de España) For some of Madrid's best views, take the lift to the 7th floor of the 'Fine Arts Circle'. You can almost reach out and touch the glorious dome of the Edificio Metrópolis and otherwise take in Madrid in all its finery, including the distant mountains. Two bars, lounge music and places to recline add to the experience.

ⓘ MADRID CARD

If you intend to do some intensive sightseeing and travelling on public transport, it might be worth looking at the **Madrid Card** (☎ 91 360 47 72; www.madridcard.com; 1/2/3 days adult €45/55/65, child age 6-12yr €32/38/42). It includes free entry to more than 50 museums in and around Madrid (some of these are already free, but it does include the Museo del Prado, Museo Thyssen-Bornemisza, Centro de Arte Reina Sofía, Estadio Santiago Bernabéu and Palacio Real); free walking tours; and discounts in a number of restaurants, shops, bars and car rental agencies. The Madrid Card can be bought online, or in person at the tourist offices on Plaza Mayor or Terminal 4 in Barajas airport, the Metro de Madrid ticket office in Terminal 2 of the airport, the Museo Thyssen-Bornemisza, and in some hotels. A list of sales outlets appears on the website.

Downstairs, the centre has exhibitions, concerts, short films and book readings. There's also a fine *belle-époque* cafe (Map p80; ☎ 91 521 69 42; Calle de Alcalá 42; ⏲ 9am-1am Sun-Thu, to 3am Fri & Sat; Ⓜ Sevilla) on the ground floor.

★ Plaza de Santa Ana
SQUARE

(Map p80; Plaza de Santa Ana; Ⓜ Sevilla, Sol, Antón Martín) Plaza de Santa Ana is a delightful confluence of elegant architecture and irresistible energy. It presides over the upper reaches of the Barrio de las Letras and this literary personality makes its presence felt with the statues of the 17th-century writer Calderón de la Barca and Federíco García Lorca, and in the Teatro Español (p122; formerly the Teatro del Príncipe) at the plaza's eastern end. Apart from anything else, the plaza is the starting point for many a long Huertas night.

Situated in the heart of Huertas, the plaza was laid out in 1810 during the controversial reign of Joseph Bonaparte, giving breathing space to what had hitherto been one of Madrid's most claustrophobic *barrios*. The plaza quickly became a focal point for intellectual life, and the cafes surrounding the plaza thronged with writers, poets and artists engaging in endless *tertulias* (literary and philosophical discussions).

Sol, Santa Ana & Huertas

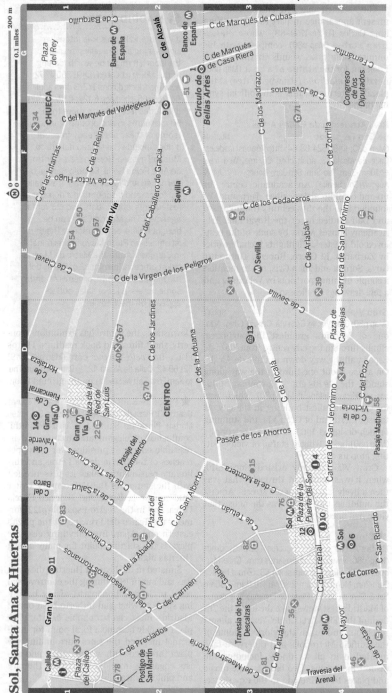

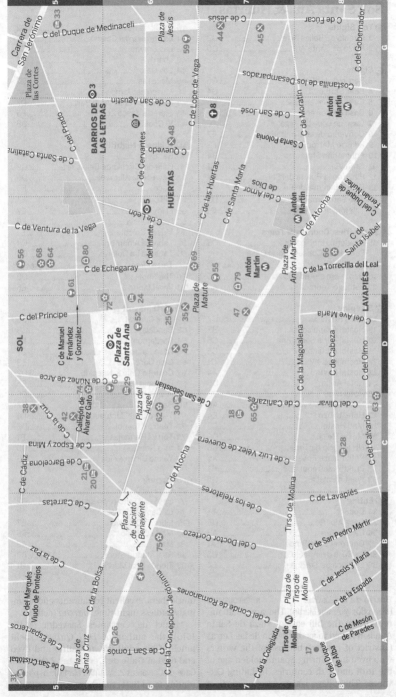

MADRID SIGHTS

Sol, Santa Ana & Huertas

Barrio de las Letras NEIGHBOURHOOD
(Map p80; M Antón Martín) The area that unfurls down the hill east of Plaza de Santa
Ana is referred to as the Barrio de las Letras
(District of Letters), because of the writers
who lived here during Spain's golden age of
the 16th and 17th centuries, including Cervantes. These days, it's an eclectic *barrio* of
quirky bars, excellent restaurants and seemingly endless night-time *marcha* (action).

Miguel de Cervantes Saavedra (1547–
1616), the author of *Don Quijote*, spent
much of his adult life in Madrid and lived
and died at Calle de Cervantes 2 (Map p80;
Calle de Cervantes 2; M Antón Martín); a plaque
(dating from 1834) sits above the door. Sadly,

the original building was torn down in the early 19th century. When Cervantes died his body was interred around the corner at the Convento de las Trinitarias (Map p80; Calle de Lope de Vega 16; M Antón Martín), which is marked by another plaque. Still home to cloistered nuns, the convent is closed to the public, which saves the authorities embarrassment: no one really knows where in the convent the bones of Cervantes lie, although there are plans afoot to try and solve the mystery once and for all. A commemorative Mass is held for him here every year on the anniversary of his death, 23 April. Another literary landmark is the Casa de Lope de Vega (Map p80; ☏ 91 429 92 16; Calle de Cervantes 11; ⊙ guided tours every 30min 10am-2pm Tue-Sat; M Antón Martín) FREE, the former home of Lope de Vega (1562–1635), Spain's premier playwright. It's now a museum containing memorabilia from Lope de Vega's life and work.

◉ El Retiro & the Art Museums

If you've just come down the hill from Huertas, you'll feel like you've left behind a madhouse for an oasis of greenery, fresh air and high culture. The Museo del Prado and the Museo Thyssen-Bornemisza are among the richest galleries of fine art in the world, and other museums lurk in the quietly elegant streets just behind the Prado. Rising up the hill to the east are the stately gardens of the glorious Parque del Buen Retiro.

Museo del Prado   MUSEUM

(Map p84; www.museodelprado.es; Paseo del Prado; adult/child €14/free, 6-8pm Mon-Sat & 5-7pm Sun free, audioguides €3.50, admission plus official guidebook €23; ⊙ 10am-8pm Mon-Sat, 10am-7pm Sun; 🖨; M Banco de España) Welcome to one of the world's premier art galleries. The more than 7000 paintings held in the Museo del Prado's collection (although only around 1500 are currently on display) are like a window onto the historical vagaries of the Spanish soul, at once grand and imperious in the royal paintings of Velázquez, darkly tumultuous in Las pinturas negras (Black Paintings) of Goya, and outward-looking with sophisticated works of art from all across Europe.

Spend as long as you can at the Prado or, better still, plan to make a couple of visits because it can be a little overwhelming if you try to absorb it all at once.

Entrance to the Prado is via the eastern Puerta de los Jerónimos (Map p84), with tickets on sale beneath the northern Puerta de Goya (Map p84). Once inside, pick up the free plan from the ticket office or information desk just inside the entrance – it lists the location of 50 of the Prado's most famous works and gives room numbers for all major artists.

➡ History

The western wing of the Prado (Edificio Villanueva) was completed in 1785, as the neoclassical Palacio de Villanueva. Originally conceived as a house of science, it later served, somewhat ignominiously, as a cavalry barracks for Napoleon's troops during their occupation of Madrid between 1808 and 1813. In 1814 King Fernando VII decided to use the palace as a museum, although his purpose was more about finding a way of storing the hundreds of royal paintings gathering dust than any high-minded civic ideals – his was an era where art was a royal preserve. Five years later the Museo del Prado opened with 311 Spanish paintings on display.

➡ Goya

Francisco José de Goya y Lucientes is found on all three floors of the Prado, but we recommend starting at the southern end of the ground or lower level. In room 65, Goya's El dos de mayo and El tres de mayo rank among Madrid's most emblematic paintings; they bring to life the 1808 anti-French revolt and subsequent execution of insurgents in Madrid. Alongside, in rooms 67 and 68, are some of his darkest and most disturbing works, Las pinturas negras; they are so called in part because of the dark browns and black that dominate, but more for the distorted animalesque appearance of their characters.

There are more Goyas on the 1st floor in rooms 34 to 37. Among them are two more of Goya's best-known and most intriguing oils: La maja vestida and La maja desnuda. These portraits, in room 73, of an unknown woman, commonly believed to be the Duquesa de Alba (who may have been Goya's lover), are identical save for the lack of clothing in the latter. There are further Goyas on the top floor.

➡ Velázquez

Diego Rodriguez de Silva y Velázquez is another of the grand masters of Spanish art who brings so much distinction to the Prado. Of all his works, Las meninas (room 12)

El Retiro & the Art Museums

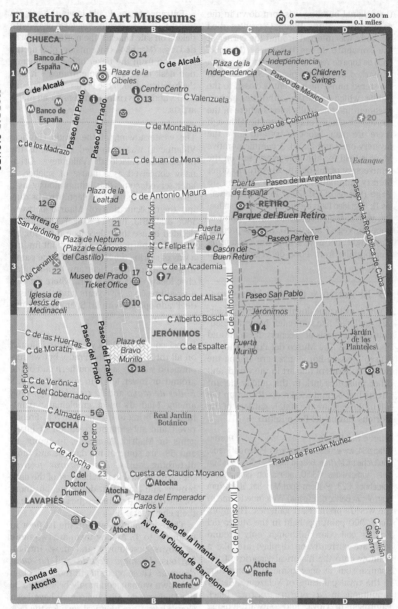

is what most people come to see. Completed in 1656, it is more properly known as *La família de Felipe IV* (The Family of Felipe IV). The rooms surrounding *Las meninas* contain more fine works by Velázquez: watch in particular for his paintings of various members of royalty who seem to spring off the canvas – Felipe II, Felipe IV, Margarita de Austria (a younger version of whom features in *Las meninas*), El Príncipe Baltasar Carlos and Isabel de Francia – on horseback.

El Retiro & the Art Museums

MADRID SIGHTS

➡ Spanish & Other European Masters

Having experienced the essence of the Prado, you're now free to select from the astonishingly diverse works that remain. If Spanish painters have piqued your curiosity, Bartolomé Esteban Murillo, José de Ribera and the stark figures of Francisco de Zurbarán should be on your itinerary. The vivid, almost surreal works by the 16th-century master and adopted Spaniard El Greco, whose figures are characteristically slender and tortured, are also perfectly executed.

Another alternative is the Prado's outstanding collection of Flemish art. The fulsome figures and bulbous cherubs of Peter Paul Rubens (1577–1640) provide a playful antidote to the darkness of many of the other Flemish artists. His signature works are *Las tres gracias* (Three Graces) and *Adoración de los reyes magos*. Other fine works in the vicinity include *The Triumph of Death* by Pieter Bruegel, Rembrandt's *Artemisa,* and those by Anton Van Dyck. And don't miss the weird-and-wonderful *The Garden of Earthly Delights* (room 56A) by Hieronymus Bosch (c 1450–1516). No one has yet been able to provide a definitive explanation for this hallucinatory work, although many have tried.

And then there are the paintings by Dürer, Rafael, Tiziano (Titian), Tintoretto, Sorolla, Gainsborough, Fra Angelico, Tiepolo...

➡ Edificio Jerónimos

In contrast to the original Edificio Villanueva, the eastern wing (Edificio Jerónimos) is part of the Prado's stunning modern extension, which opened in 2007. Dedicated to temporary exhibitions (usually to display Prado masterpieces held in storage for decades for lack of wall space), and home to the excellent bookshop and cafe, its main attraction is the 2nd-floor cloisters. Built in 1672 with local granite, the cloisters were until recently attached to the adjacent Iglesia de San Jerónimo El Real, but were in a parlous state. As part of their controversial incorporation into the Prado, they were painstakingly dismantled, restored and reassembled.

Museo Thyssen-Bornemisza MUSEUM
(Map p84; ☎ 902 760511; www.museothyssen.org; Paseo del Prado 8; adult/concession/child €10/7/ free, Mon free; ◎10am-7pm Tue-Sun, noon-4pm Mon; Ⓜ Banco de España) The Thyssen is one of the most extraordinary private collections of predominantly European art in the world. Where the Prado or Reina Sofía enable you to study the body of work of a particular artist in depth, the Thyssen is the place to immerse yourself in a breathtaking breadth of artistic styles. Most of the big names are here, sometimes with just a single painting, but the Thyssen's gift to Madrid and the art-loving public is to have them all under one roof.

Begin on the top floor and work your way down.

➡ Second Floor

The 2nd floor, which is home to medieval art, includes some real gems hidden among the mostly 13th- and 14th-century and predominantly Italian, German and Flemish religious paintings and triptychs. Unless

Museo del Prado

PLAN OF ATTACK

Begin on the 1st floor with **Las meninas** ① by Velázquez. Although it alone is worth the entry price, it's a fine introduction to the 17th-century golden age of Spanish art; nearby are more of Velázquez' royal paintings and works by Zurbarán and Murillo. While on the 1st floor, seek out Goya's **La maja vestida and La maja desnuda** ② with more of Goya's early works in neighbouring rooms. Downstairs at the southern end of the Prado, Goya's anger is evident in the searing **El dos de mayo and El tres de mayo** ③, and the torment of Goya's later years finds expression in the adjacent rooms with his **Las pinturas negras** ④, or Black Paintings. Also on the lower floor, Hieronymus Bosch's weird and wonderful **The Garden of Earthly Delights** ⑤ is one of the Prado's signature masterpieces. Returning to the 1st floor, El Greco's **Adoration of the Shepherds** ⑥ is an extraordinary work, as is Peter Paul Rubens' **Las tres gracias** ⑦ which forms the centrepiece of the Prado's gathering of Flemish masters. (Note: this painting may be moved to the 2nd floor.) A detour to the 2nd floor takes in some lesser-known Goyas, but finish in the **Edificio Jerónimos** ⑧ with a visit to the cloisters and the outstanding bookshop.

ALSO VISIT:

Nearby are Museo Thyssen-Bornemisza and Centro de Arte Reina Sofía. They form an extraordinary trio of galleries.

TOP TIPS

» **Book online** Purchase your ticket online (www.museodelprado.es) and avoid the queues.

» **Best time to visit** As soon after opening time as possible.

» **Free tours** The website (www.museo delprado.es/coleccion/que-ver/) has self-guided tours for one- to three-hour visits.

Las meninas (Velázquez)
This masterpiece depicts Velázquez and the Infanta Margarita, with the king and queen whose images appear, according to some experts, in mirrors behind Velázquez.

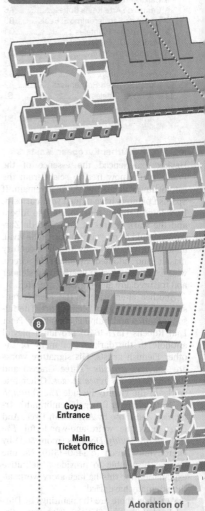

Goya Entrance

Main Ticket Office

Edificio Jerónimos
Opened in 2007, this state-of-the-art extension has rotating exhibitions of Prado masterpieces held in storage for decades for lack of wall space, and stunning 2nd-floor granite cloisters that date back to 1672.

Adoration of the Shepherds (El Greco)
There's an ecstatic quality to this intense painting. El Greco's distorted rendering of bodily forms came to characterise much of his later work.

Las tres gracias (Rubens)

A late Rubens masterpiece, *The Three Graces* is a classical and masterly expression of Rubens' preoccupation with sensuality, here portraying Aglaia, Euphrosyne and Thalia, the daughters of Zeus.

La maja vestida & La maja desnuda (Goya)

These enigmatic works scandalised early 19th-century Madrid society, fuelling the rumour mill as to the woman's identity and drawing the ire of the Spanish Inquisition.

DEA PICTURE LIBRARY/GETTY IMAGES ©

DEA/G. DAGLI ORTI/GETTY IMAGES ©

Edificio Villanueva

El dos de mayo & El tres de mayo (Goya)

Few paintings evoke a city's sense of self quite like Goya's portrayal of Madrid's valiant but ultimately unsuccessful uprising against French rule in 1808.

Las pinturas negras (Goya)

Las pinturas negras are Goya's darkest works. *Saturno devorando a su hijo* evokes a writhing mass of tortured humanity, while *La romería de San Isidro* and *El aquelarre* are profoundly unsettling.

Information Counter & Audioguides

rónimos Entrance (Main Entrance)

Gift Shop

Cafeteria

Murillo Entrance

Velázquez Entrance

The Garden of Earthly Delights (Bosch)

A fantastical painting in triptych form, this overwhelming work depicts the Garden of Eden and what the Prado describes as 'the lugubrious precincts of Hell' in exquisitely bizarre detail.

KRZYSZTOF DYDYNSKI/GETTY IMAGES ©

you've got a specialist's eye, pause in room 5 where you'll find one work by Italy's Piero della Francesca (1410–92) and the instantly recognisable *Portrait of King Henry VIII* by Holbein the Younger (1497–1543), before continuing on to room 10 for the evocative 1586 *Massacre of the Innocents* by Lucas Van Valckenberch. Room 11 is dedicated to El Greco (with three pieces) and his Venetian contemporaries Tintoretto and Titian, while Caravaggio and the Spaniard José de Ribera dominate room 12. A single painting each by Murillo and Zurbarán add further Spanish flavour in the two rooms that follow, while the exceptionally rendered views of Venice by Canaletto (1697–1768) should on no account be missed.

Best of all on this floor is the extension (rooms A to H) built to house the collection of Carmen Thyssen-Bornemisza. Room C houses paintings by Canaletto, Constable and Van Gogh, while the stunning room H includes works by Monet, Sisley, Renoir, Pissarro and Degas.

Before heading downstairs, a detour to rooms 19 through 21 will satisfy those devoted to 17th-century Dutch and Flemish masters, such as Anton van Dyck, Jan Brueghel the Elder, Rubens and Rembrandt (one painting).

ℹ MUSEUM DISCOUNTS & CLOSING TIMES

Many museums (including the Museo del Prado and Centro de Arte Reina Sofía) offer free entry at selected times – check the opening hours throughout this chapter. Remember, however, that the museums can be extremely crowded during these periods.

If you plan to visit the Museo del Prado, Museo Thyssen-Bornemisza and Centro de Arte Reina Sofía while in Madrid, the Paseo del Arte ticket covers them all in a combined ticket for €26 and is valid for one visit to each gallery during a 12-month period; buying separate tickets would cost a total of €32. A one-year ticket for unlimited visits to the Prado, Reina Sofía and eight other museums around Spain costs €36.

Free admission to the three museums (and other attractions) is included in the price of the Madrid Card (p79).

→ **First Floor**

If all that sounds impressive, the 1st floor is where the Thyssen really shines. There's a Gainsborough in room 28 and a Goya in room 31 but, if you've been skimming the surface of this overwhelming collection, room 32 is the place to linger over each and every painting. The astonishing texture of Van Gogh's *Les Vessenots* is a masterpiece, but the same could be said for *Woman in Riding Habit* by Manet, *The Thaw at Véthueil* by Monet, Renoir's *Woman with a Parasol in a Garden* and Pissarro's quintessentially Parisian *Rue Saint-Honoré in the Afternoon*. Room 33 is also something special, with Cézanne, Gauguin, Toulouse-Lautrec and Degas, while the big names continue in room 34 (Picasso, Matisse and Modigliani) and 35 (Edvard Munch and Egon Schiele).

In the 1st floor's extension (rooms I to P), the names speak for themselves. Room K has works by Monet, Pissaro, Sorolla and Sisley, while room L is the domain of Gauguin (including his iconic *Mata Mua*), Degas and Toulouse-Lautrec. Rooms M (Munch), N (Kandinsky), O (Matisse and Georges Braque) and P (Picasso, Matisse, Edward Hopper and Juan Gris) round out an outrageously rich journey through the masters. On your way to the stairs there's Edward Hopper's *Hotel Room*.

→ **Ground Floor**

On the ground floor, the foray into the 20th century that you began in the 1st-floor extension takes over with a fine spread of paintings from cubism through to pop art.

In room 41 you'll see a nice mix of the big three of cubism, Picasso, Georges Braque and Madrid's own Juan Gris, along with several other contemporaries. Kandinsky is the main drawcard in room 43, while there's an early Salvador Dalí alongside Max Ernst and Paul Klee in room 44. Picasso appears again in room 45, another one of the gallery's standout rooms; its treasures include works by Marc Chagall and Dalí's hallucinatory *Dream Caused by the Flight of a Bee Around a Pomegranate, One Second Before Waking Up*.

Room 46 is similarly rich, with Joan Miró's *Catalan Peasant with a Guitar*, the splattered craziness of Jackson Pollock's *Brown and Silver I*, and the deceptively simple but strangely pleasing *Green on Maroon* by Mark Rothko taking centre stage. In rooms 47 and 48 the Thyssen builds to a stirring climax, with Francis Bacon, Roy Lichtenstein, Henry Moore and Lucian Freud, Sigmund's Berlin-born grandson, all represented.

Centro de Arte Reina Sofía MUSEUM
(Map p84; ☑ 91 774 10 00; www.museoreinasofia.es; Calle de Santa Isabel 52; adult/concession €8/free, Sun, 7-9pm Mon & Wed-Sat free; ☉ 10am-9pm Mon, Wed, Thu & Sat, 10am-7pm Sun, closed Tue; Ⓜ Atocha) Home to Picasso's *Guernica,* arguably Spain's most famous artwork, the Centro de Arte Reina Sofía is Madrid's premier collection of contemporary art. In addition to plenty of paintings by Picasso, other major drawcards are works by Salvador Dalí (1904–1989) and Joan Miró (1893–1983). The collection principally spans the 20th century up to the 1980s. The occasional non-Spaniard artist makes an appearance (including Francis Bacon's *Lying Figure;* 1966), but most of the collection is strictly peninsular.

The permanent collection is displayed on the 2nd and 4th floors of the main wing of the museum, the Edificio Sabatini. *Guernica*'s location never changes – you'll find it in room 206 on the 2nd floor. Beyond that, the location of specific paintings can be a little confusing. The museum follows a theme-based approach, which ensures that you'll find works by Picasso or Miró, for example, spread across the two floors. The only solution if you're looking for something specific is to pick up the latest copy of the *Planos de Museo* (Museum Floorplans) from the information desk just outside the main entrance; it lists the rooms in which each artist appears (although not individual paintings).

In addition to Picasso's *Guernica,* which is worth the admission fee on its own, don't neglect the artist's preparatory sketches in the rooms surrounding room 206; they offer an intriguing insight into the development of this seminal work. If Picasso's cubist style has captured your imagination, the work of the Madrid-born Juan Gris (1887–1927) or Georges Braque (1882–1963) may appeal.

The work of Joan Miró is defined by often delightfully bright primary colours, but watch out also for a handful of his equally odd sculptures. Since his paintings became a symbol of the Barcelona Olympics in 1992, his work has begun to receive the international acclaim it so richly deserves – the museum is a fine place to get a representative sample of his innovative work.

The Reina Sofía is also home to 20 or so canvases by Salvador Dalí, of which the most

GOYA IN MADRID

Madrid has the best collection of Goyas on earth. Here's where to find them:

➡ Museo del Prado (p83)

➡ Real Academia de Bellas Artes de San Fernando (p79)

➡ Ermita de San Antonio de la Florida (p95)

➡ Museo Lázaro Galdiano (p92)

➡ Basílica de San Francisco El Grande (p76)

➡ Museo Thyssen-Bornemisza (p85)

famous is perhaps the surrealist extravaganza that is *El gran masturbador* (1929). Among his other works is a strange bust of a certain *Joelle,* which Dalí created with his friend Man Ray (1890–1976). Another well-known surrealist painter, Max Ernst (1891–1976), is also worth tracking down.

If you can tear yourself away from the big names, the Reina Sofía offers a terrific opportunity to learn more about sometimes lesser-known 20th-century Spanish artists. Among these are Miquel Barceló (b 1957); *madrileño* artist José Gutiérrez Solana (1886–1945); the renowned Basque painter Ignazio Zuloaga (1870–1945); Benjamin Palencia (1894–1980), whose paintings capture the turbulence of Spain in the 1930s; Barcelona painter Antoni Tàpies (1923–2012); pop artist Eduardo Arroyo (b 1937); and abstract painters such as Eusebio Sempere (1923–85) and members of the Equipo 57 group (founded in 1957 by a group of Spanish artists in exile in Paris), such as Pablo Palazuelo (1916–2007). Better known as a poet and playwright, Federico García Lorca (1898–1936) is represented by a number of his sketches.

Of the sculptors, watch in particular for Pablo Gargallo (1881–1934), whose work in bronze includes a bust of Picasso, and the renowned Basque sculptors Jorge Oteiza (1908–2003) and Eduardo Chillida (1924–2002).

★ Parque del Buen Retiro GARDENS
(Map p84; ☉ 6am-midnight May-Sep, to 11pm Oct-Apr; Ⓜ Retiro, Príncipe de Vergara, Ibiza, Atocha) The glorious gardens of El Retiro are as beautiful as any you'll find in a European city. Littered with marble monuments,

landscaped lawns, the occasional elegant building (the Palacio de Cristal is especially worth seeking out) and abundant greenery, it's quiet and contemplative during the week but comes to life on weekends. Put simply, this is one of our favourite places in Madrid.

Laid out in the 17th century by Felipe IV as the preserve of kings, queens and their intimates, the park was opened to the public in 1868 and ever since, whenever the weather's fine and on weekends in particular, *madrileños* from all across the city gather here to stroll, read, take a boat ride or nurse a cool drink at the numerous outdoor *terrazas*.

The focal point for so much of El Retiro's life is the artificial *estanque* (lake), which is watched over by the massive ornamental structure of the Monument to Alfonso XII on the east side, complete with marble lions; as sunset approaches on a Sunday afternoon in summer, the crowd grows, bongos sound out across the park and people start to dance. Row boats (per boat per 45min weekdays/weekends €5.80/7.50; ☺10am-8.30pm Apr-Sep, to 5.45pm Oct-Mar) can be rented from the lake's northern shore – an iconic Madrid experience. On the southern end of the lake, the odd structure decorated with sphinxes is the Fuente Egipcia (Egyptian Fountain): legend has it that an enormous fortune buried in the park by Felipe IV in the mid-18th century rests here. Hidden among the trees south of the lake is the Palacio de Cristal (☎91 574 66 14; ☺10am-10pm May-Sep, 10am-6pm Oct-Apr), a magnificent metal-and-glass structure that is arguably El Retiro's most beautiful architectural monument. It was built in 1887 as a winter garden for exotic flowers and is now used for temporary exhibitions organised by the Centro de Arte Reina Sofía. Just north of here, the 1883 Palacio de Velázquez (☺10am-10pm May-Sep, 10am-6pm Oct-Apr) is also used for temporary exhibitions.

At the southern end of the park, near La Rosaleda (Rose Garden) with its more than 4000 roses, is a statue of El Ángel Caído. Strangely, it sits 666m above sea level... In the same vein, the Puerta de Dante, in the extreme southeastern corner of the park, is watched over by a carved mural of Dante's Inferno. Occupying much of the southwestern corner of the park is the Jardín de los Planteles, one of the least-visited sections of El Retiro, where quiet pathways lead beneath an overarching canopy of trees. West of here is the moving Bosque del Recuerdo (Memorial Forest), an understated memorial to the 191 victims of the 11 March 2004 train bombings. For each victim stands an olive or cypress tree. To the north, just inside the Puerta de Felipe IV, stands what is thought to be Madrid's oldest tree, a Mexican conifer (ahuehuete) planted in 1633.

In the northeastern corner of the park is the Ermita de San Isidro (Map p94), a small country chapel noteworthy as one of the few, albeit modest, examples of Romanesque architecture in Madrid. When it was built, Madrid was a small village more than 2km away.

Real Jardín Botánico GARDENS
(Royal Botanical Garden; Map p84; ☎91 420 04 38; www.rjb.csic.es; Plaza de Bravo Murillo 2; adult/child €3/free; ☺10am-9pm May-Aug, reduced hours Sep-Apr; Ⓜ Atocha) With its manicured flower beds and neat paths, the Real Jardín Botánico is more intimate than the much-larger Parque del Buen Retiro which lies to the east. First created in 1755 on the banks of Río Manzanares, the garden was moved here in 1781 by Carlos III. These days you can see thousands of plant species.

Antigua Estación de Atocha NOTABLE BUILDING
(Map p84; Plaza del Emperador Carlos V; Ⓜ Atocha Renfe) In 1992 the northwestern wing of the Antigua Estación de Atocha (Old Atocha train station) was given a stunning overhaul. The project was the work of architect Rafael Moneo, the man behind the Museo del Prado extension and the Museo Thyssen-Bornemisza, and his landmark achievement was to create a thoroughly modern space within the grand iron-and-glass relic from the 19th century that resonates with the stately European train stations of another age.

The interior was artfully converted into a light-filled tropical garden with more than

---

REINA SOFÍA FRINGE

If you've explored the best that the Centro de Arte Reina Sofía has to offer and you're eager for more, the streets west of the museum, particularly Calle Valencia and Calle de Doctor Fourquet, have more private art galleries (13 at last count) per square metre than anywhere else in town (and in this art-obsessed city that's no small feat). Check out www.artemadrid.com for a full list of these galleries and others across Madrid.

500 plant species (and a resident turtle population), in addition to shops, cafes and the Renfe train information offices.

Caixa Forum
MUSEUM, ARCHITECTURE

(Map p84; www.fundacio.lacaixa.es; Paseo del Prado 36; ☉10am-8pm; Ⓜ Atocha) FREE This extraordinary structure is one of Madrid's most eye-catching landmarks. Seeming to hover above the ground, this brick edifice is topped by an intriguing summit of rusted iron. On an adjacent wall is the *jardín colgante* (hanging garden), a lush vertical wall of greenery almost four storeys high. Inside there are four floors of exhibition and performance space awash in stainless steel and with soaring ceilings. The exhibitions here are always worth checking out and include photography, contemporary painting and multimedia shows.

Plaza de la Cibeles
SQUARE

(Map p84; Ⓜ Banco de España) Of all the grand roundabouts along the Paseo del Prado, Plaza de la Cibeles most evokes the splendour of imperial Madrid. Built between 1904 and 1917 by Antonio Palacios, Madrid's most prolific architect of the belle époque, the Palacio de Cibeles (Palacio de Comunicaciones; Map p84) combines elements of the North American monumental style of the period with Gothic and Renaissance touches. It's a dynamic cultural centre with chillout areas and exhibition spaces, plus the exceptional views of the Mirador de Madrid (Map p84; www.centrocentro.org; 9th fl, Palacio de Comunicaciones, Plaza de la Cibeles; adult/child €2/0.50; ☉10.30am-1.30pm & 4-7pm Tue-Sun).

These views from the summit are arguably Madrid's best, sweeping west down over the Plaza de la Cibeles, up the hill towards the sublime Edificio Metrópolis and out to the mountains. But the views are splendid whichever way you look. Take the lift up to the 6th floor, from where the gates are opened every half hour. From there you can either take another lift or climb the stairs up to the 9th floor.

Other landmark buildings around the plaza's perimeter include the Palacio de Linares (Map p84; ☎91 595 48 00; www.casamerica.es; Plaza de la Cibeles 2; adult/child/student & senior €8/free/5; ☉guided tours 11am, noon & 1pm Sat & Sun Sep-Jul, ticket office 9am-8pm Mon-Fri, 11am-1pm Sat & Sun; Ⓜ Banco de España) and Casa de América, the 1769 Palacio Buenavista (Map p96; Plaza de la Cibeles) and the 1891 national Banco de España (Map p84).

The spectacular fountain of the goddess Cybele at the centre of the plaza is one of Madrid's most beautiful. Ever since it was erected in 1780 by Ventura Rodríguez, it has been a Madrid favourite. Carlos III liked it so much that he tried to have it moved to the royal gardens of the Granja de San Ildefonso, on the road to Segovia, but *madrileños* kicked up such a fuss that he let it be. The Cibeles fountain is the venue for joyous and often-destructive celebrations by players and supporters of Real Madrid whenever the side wins anything of note.

Museo Naval
MUSEUM

(Map p84; ☎91 523 87 89; www.armada.mde.es/museonaval; Paseo del Prado 5; ☉10am-7pm Tue-Sun; Ⓜ Banco de España) FREE A block south of Plaza de la Cibeles, this museum has some quite extraordinary models of ships (including from the Spanish Armada) from the earliest days of Spain's maritime history to the 20th century. Antique maps are further highlights, especially Juan de la Cosa's parchment map of the known world, put together in 1500. The accuracy of Europe and Africa is astounding, and it's supposedly the first map to show the Americas (albeit with considerably greater fantasy than fact).

Iglesia de San Jerónimo El Real
CHURCH

(Map p84; ☎91 420 35 78; Calle de Ruiz de Alarcón; ☉10am-1pm & 5-8.30pm Mon-Sat Oct-Jun, hours vary Jul-Sep; Ⓜ Atocha, Banco de España) Tucked away behind the Museo del Prado, this chapel was traditionally favoured by the Spanish royal family, and King Juan Carlos I was crowned here in 1975 upon the death of Franco. The sometimes-sober, sometimes-splendid mock-Isabelline interior is actually a 19th-century reconstruction that took its cues from the Iglesia de San Juan de los Reyes in Toledo; the original was largely destroyed during the Peninsular War. What remained of the former cloisters has been incorporated into the Museo del Prado (p83).

Puerta de Alcalá
MONUMENT

(Map p84; Plaza de la Independencia; Ⓜ Retiro) The first gate to bear this name was built in 1599, but Carlos III was singularly unimpressed and had it demolished in 1764 to be replaced by another, the one you see today. Twice a year, in autumn and spring, cars abandon the roundabout and are replaced by flocks of sheep being transferred in an age-old ritual from their summer to winter pastures (and vice versa).

WORTH A TRIP

MADRID RÍO

For decades, nay centuries, Madrid's Río Manzanares (Manzanares River) was a laughing stock. In the 17th century, renowned Madrid playwright Lope de Vega described the beautiful Puente de Segovia over the river to be a little too grand for the 'apprentice river'. He suggested the city buy a bigger river or sell the bridge. Thus it remained until the 21st century when Madrid's town hall decided to bring the river up to scratch.

Planned before the economic crisis swung a wrecking ball through the city's long list of planned infrastructure projects, the Madrid Río development saw the M-30 motorway driven underground and vast areas – up to 500,000 sq metres by some estimates – of abandoned riverside land turned into parkland that one former mayor described as 'a giant green carpet'. A summer beach à la Paris, bike paths, outdoor cafes and children's playgrounds are all part of the mix in this attractive 10km-long stretch of parkland.

To rent a bike for exploring the riverbank, try Mi Bike Río (☑ 91 139 46 52; mibikerio. com; Calle de Aniceto Marinas 26; bike per hr/day €5/30; ☺ 10.30am-2pm & 5-8.15pm Mon-Fri, 9.30am-8.15pm Sat & Sun; Ⓜ Príncipe Pío), a short hop from Príncipe Pío metro station.

Also nearby is Matadero Madrid (☑ 91 252 52 53; www.mataderomadrid.com; Paseo de la Chopera 14; Ⓜ Legazpi) FREE. This contemporary arts centre, opened in 2007, is a stunning multipurpose space south of centre. Occupying the converted buildings of the old Arganzuela livestock market and slaughterhouse, it hosts cutting-edge drama, musical and dance performances and exhibitions on architecture, fashion, literature and cinema.

Unless you're renting a bike, the three easiest ways to access Madrid Río are:

➜ Walk down the hill from La Latina to the western end of Calle de Segovia.

➜ Catch the metro to the Estadio Vicente Calderón (☑ 91 366 47 07; www. clubatleticodemadrid.com; Paseo de la Virgin del Puerto; Ⓜ Pirámides), the home football stadium of Atlético de Madrid.

➜ Follow the signs from Matadero Madrid.

In 1986, the gate was the unlikely (and, to us, inexplicable) focal point for a Spanish mega-hit. Mention *La Puerta de Alcalá* by Ana Belén and Victor Manuel to *madrileños* of a certain age and watch their eyes glaze over with nostalgia. We still don't get it...

◉ Salamanca

The *barrio* of Salamanca is Madrid's most exclusive quarter, defined by grand and restrained elegance. This is a place to put on your finest clothes and be seen (especially along Calle de Serrano or Calle de José Ortega y Gasset); to stroll into shops with an affected air and resist asking the prices; or to promenade between the fine museums and parks that make you wonder whether you've arrived at the height of civilisation.

Museo Arqueológico Nacional   MUSEUM
(Map p94; man.mcu.es; Calle de Serrano 13; admission €3, 5-8pm Sat & 9.30am-noon Sun free; ☺ 9.30am-8pm Tue-Sat, 9.30am-3pm Sun; Ⓜ Serrano) Reopened after a massive overhaul of the building, the showpiece National Archaeology Museum contains a sweeping accumulation of artefacts behind its towering facade.

The large collection includes stunning mosaics taken from Roman villas across Spain, intricate Muslim-era and Mudéjar handiwork, sculpted figures such as the *Dama de Ibiza* and *Dama de Elche*, examples of Romanesque and Gothic architectural styles and a partial copy of the prehistoric cave paintings of Altamira (Cantabria).

Museo Lázaro Galdiano   MUSEUM
(☑ 91 561 60 84; www.flg.es; Calle de Serrano 122; adult/concession €6/3, last hour free; ☺ 10am-4.30pm Mon & Wed-Sat, to 3pm Sun; Ⓜ Gregorio Marañón) In an imposing early-20th-century Italianate stone mansion, the Museo Lázaro Galdiano has some 13,000 works of art and objets d'art. Apart from works by Bosch, Zurbarán, Goya, Claudio Coello, El Greco and Constable, this is a rather oddball assembly of all sorts of collectables. In room 14 copies of some of Goya's more famous works are hung together to make a collage, including *La maja* and the frescoes of the Ermita de San Antonio de la Florida (p95).

Plaza de Toros & Museo Taurino   STADIUM
(☑ 91 725 18 57; Calle de Alcalá 237; admission free, tour adult/child €10/7; ☺ 10am-6pm; Ⓜ Las

Ventas) The Plaza de Toros Monumental de Las Ventas (often known simply as Las Ventas) is the most important bullring in the bullfighting world and the circle of sand enclosed by four storeys, which can seat up to 25,000 spectators, evokes more a sense of a theatre than a sports stadium. Guided visits (conducted in English and Spanish) take you out onto the sand and into the royal box; tours last 40 minutes and start on the hour. For reservations, contact Las Ventas Tour (☑687 739 032; www.lasventastour.com; adult/child €10/7; ☉10am-6pm, days of bullfight 10am-1pm).

A classic example of the neo-Mudéjar style, Las Ventas opened in 1931 and hosted its first *corrida* (bullfight) three years later. Even today, to be carried high on the shoulders of aficionados out through the grand and decidedly Moorish Puerta de Madrid is the ultimate dream of any *torero* (bullfighter) – if you've made it at Las Ventas, you've reached the pinnacle of the bullfighting world. The gate is known more colloquially as the 'Gate of Glory'.

If your curiosity is piqued, wander into the Museo Taurino (☑91 725 18 57; www.lasventas.com; Calle de Alcalá 237; ☉9.30am-2.30pm Mon-Fri) FREE and check out the collection of paraphernalia, costumes, photos and other bullfighting memorabilia up on the top floor above one of the two courtyards by the ring.

The area where the Plaza de Toros is located is known as Las Ventas because, in times gone by, several wayside *ventas* (taverns), along with houses of ill repute, were to be found here.

Museo al Aire Libre   SCULPTURE
(Map p94; www.munimadrid.es/museoairelibre; cnr Paseo de la Castellana & Paseo de Eduardo Dato; ☉24hr; Ⓜ Rubén Darío) FREE This fascinating open-air collection of 17 abstract sculptures includes works by the renowned Basque artist Eduardo Chillida, Catalan master Joan Miró, Eusebio Sempere and Alberto Sánchez, one of Spain's foremost sculptors of the 20th century. The sculptures are beneath the overpass where Paseo de Eduardo Dato crosses Paseo de la Castellana, but somehow the hint of traffic grime and pigeon shit only adds to the appeal. All but one are on the eastern side of Paseo de la Castellana.

Fundación Juan March   CULTURAL CENTRE
(Map p94; www.march.es; Calle de Castelló 77; ☉11am-8pm Mon-Sat, 10am-2pm Sun & holidays;

Ⓜ Núñez de Balboa) FREE This foundation organises some of the better temporary exhibitions in Madrid each year and it's always worth checking its website to see what's on. The foundation also stages concerts across a range of musical genres and other events throughout the year.

◉ Malasaña & Chueca

The inner-city *barrios* of Malasaña and Chueca are where Madrid gets up close and personal. Yes, there are rewarding museums and examples of landmark architecture sprinkled throughout. But these *barrios* are more about doing than seeing; more about experiencing life as it's lived by *madrileños* than ticking off a list of wonderful, if more static, attractions. Malasaña and Chueca are neighbourhoods with attitude and personality, where Madrid's famed nightlife, shopping and eating thrive. Malasaña is streetwise and down to earth, while Chueca, as Madrid's centre of gay culture, is more stylish and flamboyant.

Museo de Historia   MUSEUM
(Map p96; Calle de Fuencarral 78; ☉10am-8pm Tue-Fri, 10am-2pm Sat & Sun; Ⓜ Tribunal) FREE The fine Museo de Historia (formerly the Museo Municipal) has an elaborate baroque entrance, raised in 1721 by Pedro de Ribera. The museum's interior is undergoing major renovations which are unlikely to be finished before 2015. When it reopens, the collection includes paintings and other memorabilia charting the historical evolution of Madrid, of which the highlight is Goya's *Allegory of the City of Madrid*. In the meantime, the basement houses some splendid scale models of Madrid down through the ages.

Sociedad General de Autores y Editores   ARCHITECTURE
(General Society of Authors & Editors; Map p96; Calle de Fernando VI 4; Ⓜ Alonso Martínez) This swirling, melting, wedding cake of a building is as close as Madrid comes to the work of Antoni Gaudí, which so illuminates Barcelona. It's a joyously self-indulgent ode to *modernismo* and is virtually one of a kind in Madrid. Casual visitors are actively discouraged, although what you see from the street is impressive enough. The only exception at the time of writing is on the first Monday of October, International Architecture Day, when the doors are thrown open.

Salamanca

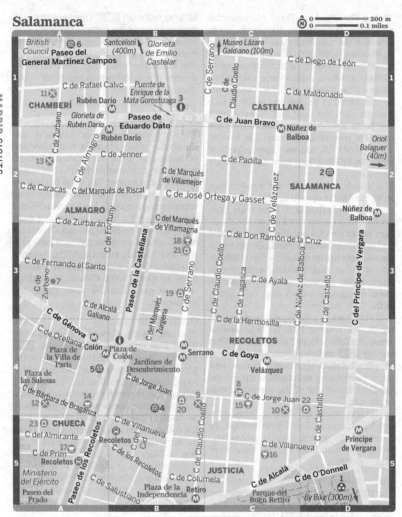

Antiguo Cuartel del
Conde Duque   NOTABLE BUILDING
(Map p96; Calle del Conde Duque 9; Ⓜ Plaza de
España, Ventura Rodríguez, San Bernardo) This
grand former barracks dominates Conde
Duque on the western fringe of Malasaña,
with its imposing, recently restored facade
stretching 228m down the hill. Its highlight
is the extravagant 18th-century doorway, a
masterpiece of the baroque churrigueresque
style. These days it's home by day to a cultural centre, which hosts government archives,
libraries, the Hemeroteca Municipal (the
biggest collection of newspapers and maga-

zines in Spain), temporary exhibitions and,
when it reopens after renovations, the Museo Municipal de Arte Contemporáneo
(Map p96; ☑ 91 588 59 28; www.madrid.es; Calle
del Conde Duque 9-11; Ⓜ Plaza de España, Ventura
Rodríguez, San Bernardo) FREE.

◉ Parque del Oeste & Northern Madrid

This area wraps around central Madrid to
the north and west and contains some fabulous sights, and outstanding (if fairly widely
spread) places to eat, drink and watch live

Salamanca

music. But it's here perhaps more than anywhere else in Madrid that you get a sense of the city as the *madrileños* experience it, away from the tourist crowds.

One *barrio* in particular captures this sense of a city as locals live it. Immediately north of Chueca and Malasaña, Chamberí has quiet, tree-lined streets and one of the city's most underrated squares, the Plaza de Olavide. It's not that Chamberí has many sights to see - it's more about soaking up the essence of Madrid with scarcely a tourist in sight.

Ermita de San Antonio de la Florida
ART GALLERY
(Glorieta de San Antonio de la Florida 5; ⊙9.30am-8pm Tue-Sun, hours vary Jul & Aug; Ⓜ Príncipe Pío) FREE The frescoed ceilings of the Ermita de San Antonio de la Florida are one of Madrid's most surprising secrets. Recently restored and also known as the **Panteón de Goya**, the southern of the two small chapels is one of the few places to see Goya's work in its original setting, as painted by the master in 1798 on the request of Carlos IV. Simply breathtaking.

The frescoes on the dome depict the miracle of St Anthony, who is calling on a young man to rise from the grave and absolve his father, unjustly accused of his murder. Around them swarms a typical Madrid crowd.

The painter is buried in front of the altar. His remains (minus the mysteriously missing head) were transferred in 1919 from Bordeaux (France), where he died in self-imposed exile in 1828.

Parque del Oeste
GARDENS
(Park of the West; Avenida del Arco de la Victoria; Ⓜ Moncloa) Sloping down the hill behind the Moncloa metro station, Parque del Oeste is quite beautiful, with plenty of shady corners where you can recline under a tree in the heat of the day, and fine views out to the west towards Casa de Campo. It has been a *madrileño* favourite ever since its creation in 1906.

Templo de Debod
RUIN
(www.munimadrid.es/templodebod; Paseo del Pintor Rosales; ⊙10am-2pm & 6-8pm Tue-Fri, 9.30am-8pm Sat & Sun Apr-Sep, 9.45am-1.45pm & 4.15-6.15pm Tue-Fri, 9.30am-8pm Sat & Sun Oct-Mar; Ⓜ Ventura Rodríguez) FREE Remarkably, this authentic 4th-century-BC Egyptian temple sits in the heart of Madrid, in the Parque de la Montaña. The Templo de Debod was saved from the rising waters of Lake Nasser, formed by the Aswan High Dam in Egypt, and sent block by block to Spain in 1968. The views from the surrounding gardens towards the Palacio Real are rather lovely.

Museo de América
MUSEUM
(www.mecd.gob.es/museodeamerica; Avenida de los Reyes Católicos 6; adult/concession €3/1.50, Sun free; ⊙9.30am-8.30pm Tue-Sat, 10am-3pm Sun May-Oct, 9.30am-6.30pm Tue-Sat, 10am-3pm Sun Nov-Apr; Ⓜ Moncloa) Travel to, and trade with, the newly discovered Americas was a central part of Spain's culture and economy from 1492 until the early 20th century. The Museo de América has a representative (if fairly uncritical) display of ceramics, statuary, jewellery and instruments of hunting,

Malasaña & Chueca

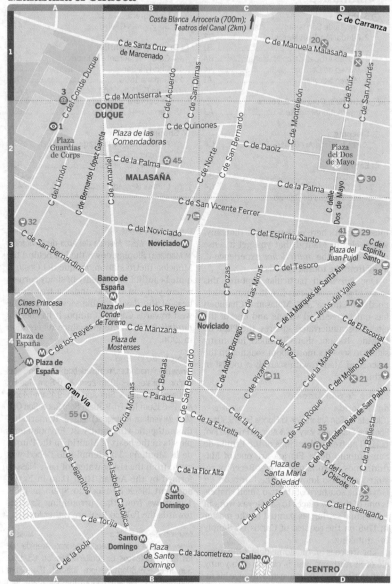

fishing and war, along with some of the paraphernalia brought back by the colonisers. The Colombian gold collection, dating back to the 2nd century AD, is particularly eye-catching.

Museo Sorolla GALLERY
(Map p94; museosorolla.mcu.es; Paseo del General Martínez Campos 37; adult/child €3/free, Sun & 2-8pm Sat free; ☺ 9.30am-8pm Tue-Sat, 10am-3pm Sun; ⓜ Iglesia, Gregorio Marañón) The Valencian artist Joaquín Sorolla immortalised the clear

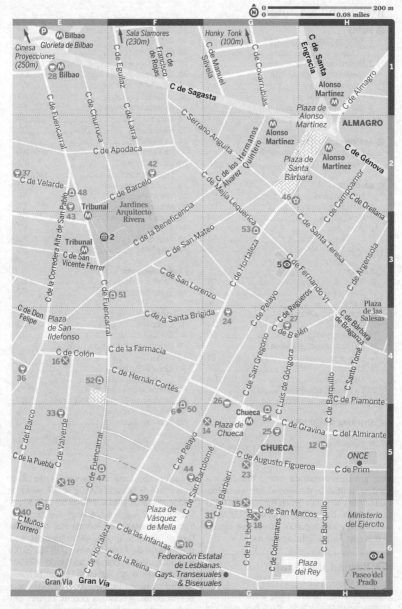

Mediterranean light of the Valencian coast. His Madrid house, a quiet mansion surrounded by lush gardens that he designed himself, was inspired by what he had seen in Andalucía and now contains the most complete collection of the artist's works.

On the ground floor there's a cool *patio cordobés,* an Andalucian courtyard off which is a room containing collections of Sorolla's drawings. The 1st floor, with the main salon and dining areas, was mostly decorated by the artist himself. On the same

Malasaña & Chueca

floor are three separate rooms that Sorolla used as studios. In the second one is a collection of his Valencian beach scenes. The third was where he usually worked. Upstairs, works spanning Sorolla's career are organised across four adjoining rooms.

◉ Beyond the Centre

Casa de Campo   PARK

(Ⓜ Batán) This 1700-hectare, somewhat unkempt semi-wilderness stretches west of Río Manzanares. There are prettier and more central parks in Madrid, but such is the scope here that nearly half a million *madrileños* visit every weekend, when cyclists, walkers and picnickers overwhelm the byways and trails that criss-cross the park.

Inside the Casa de Campo is the Zoo Aquarium de Madrid (☏ 902 345 014; www.zoo-madrid.com; adult/child €22.90/18.55; ⊙ 10.30am-8.30pm Jul & Aug, reduced hours Sep-Jun; ☐ 37 from Intercambiador de Príncipe Pío, Ⓜ Casa de Campo), home to around 3000 animals, and the Parque de Atracciones (☏ 91 463 29 00; www.parquedeatracciones.es; adult/child €29.90/free; ⊙ noon-midnight Sun-Fri, to 1am Sat Jul & Aug, reduced hours Sep-Jun; ☐ 37 from Intercambiador de Príncipe Pío, Ⓜ Batán), a decent amusement park sure to keep kids entertained.

A fun way to get to the Casa de Campo is the Teleférico (☏ 91 541 11 18; www.teleferico.com; one way/return €4/5.75; ⊙ noon-9pm Mon-Fri, to 9.30pm Sat & Sun Jun-Aug, reduced hours Sep-May; Ⓜ Argüelles) cable car. It starts at Paseo del Pintor Rosales, on the corner of Calle del Marqués de Urquijo, and ends at a high point in the middle of the park.

 Activities

Madrid is not Europe's most bicycle-friendly city, but a ride in the Casa de Campo or El Retiro is a great way to spend an afternoon.

There are public gyms scattered throughout Madrid. They generally charge a modest €4 to €8 for one-day admission. Privately owned health centres are more expensive (€10 to €15), but usually have less-crowded workout rooms.

Madrid Xanadú SKIING

(☑902 361309; www.madridsnowzone.com; Calle Puerto de Navacerrada; per hr adult/child €22/19, day pass €36/33, equipment rental €18; ☺10am-midnight; ☑528, 534) The largest covered ski centre in Europe. Open year-round, it's kept at a decidedly cool -2°C. Within the same complex are a mammoth mall, cinemas, a kart track and an amusement park. Madrid Xanadú is about 23km west of Madrid, just off the A5. To get here, take bus 528 or 534 from the Intercambiador de Príncipe Pío.

Hammam al-Andalus DAY SPA

(Map p80; ☑91 429 90 20; madrid.hammamal andalus.com; Calle de Atocha 14; treatments €30-73; ☺10am-midnight; ☑Sol) A beautiful imitation traditional Arab bathhouse; bookings required.

By Bike BICYCLE RENTAL

(☑91 154 61 08; www.bybike.info; Avenida de Menéndez Pelayo 35; per hr/day from €4/30; ☺10am-9pm Mon-Fri, 9.30am-9.30pm Sat & Sun Jun-Sep, 10am-3pm & 5-9pm Mon-Fri, 9am-9pm Sat & Sun Oct-May; ☒; ☑Ibiza) Ideally placed for the Parque del Buen Retiro and with child seats/trailers, roller blades and electric bikes for hire. Prices vary depending on the length of hire and number of people.

Centro Deportivo La Chopera GYM

(Map p84; ☑91 420 11 54; Parque del Buen Retiro; 1/10 sessions €5/42.95, court hire per adult €6.90; ☺8.30am-9.30pm, closed Aug; ☑Atocha) With a fine workout centre, and several football fields, this *centro deportivo* (sports centre and gym) in the southwestern corner of the Parque del Buen Retiro is one of Madrid's most attractive and central. It also has tennis courts, but you'll need your own racquet.

Canal de Isabel II SWIMMING

(☑91 554 69 25; Avenida de Filipinas 54; admission from €5.50; ☺11am-8pm late May-early Sep;

☑Ríos Rosas, Canal) Open only in summer, this large outdoor pool is easily accessible by metro from the city centre. The same complex also has a football field, a basketball court and a weights room, and across the road there's a running track and a golf driving range. It's around 3km north of the centre, close to where Calle de Bravo Murillo intersects with Avenida de Filipinas.

Courses

Language

Spanish-language schools of all possible categories abound in Madrid. Non-EU citizens who are wanting to study at a university or language school in Spain should, in theory, have a study visa.

Academia Inhispania LANGUAGE COURSE

(Map p80; ☑91 521 22 31; www.inhispania.com; Calle de la Montera 10-12; ☑Sol) Intensive four-week courses start at €525.

Academia Madrid Plus LANGUAGE COURSE

(Map p72; ☑91 548 11 16; www.madridplus.es; 6th fl, Calle del Arenal 21; ☑Ópera) Four-week courses start from €340; intensive courses cost up to €800.

International House LANGUAGE COURSE

(Map p94; ☑902 141517; www.ihmadrid.es; Calle de Zurbano 8; ☑Alonso Martínez) Three-week intensive courses cost from €594 (20 hours per week) to €804 (30 hours per week). Staff can organise accommodation with local families.

Universidad Complutense LANGUAGE COURSE

(☑91 394 53 25; http://pendientedemigracion. ucm.es/info/cextran/index; Secretaria de los Cursos para Extranjeros, Facultadole Filologia (Edificio A) Universidad Complutense; ☑Cuidad Universitaria) Offers a range of language and cultural courses. An intensive semester course of 120 contact hours costs €1213, while month-long courses (48 hours) start at €486.

Cooking

Alambique COOKING COURSE

(Map p72; ☑91 547 42 20; www.alambique.com; Plaza de la Encarnación 2; per person from €45; ☑Ópera, Santo Domingo) Most classes here last from 2½ to 3½ hours and cover a range of cuisines. Most are conducted in Spanish, but some are in English.

Cooking Club COOKING COURSE

(☑91 323 29 58; www.club-cooking.com; Calle de Veza 33; ☑Valdeacederas) This respected

LOCAL KNOWLEDGE

TRIBALL – THE NEW MALASAÑA

Although Malasaña is unlikely to shed its carefully cultivated retro image any time soon, one part of the *barrio* has transformed itself into one of the coolest corners of the city. Begun as a project run by local businesses to change the way people think about Malasaña, **Triángulo Ballesta** (www.triballmadrid.com) is named after the area between the once (and sometimes still) famously seedy Calle de Ballesta, close to Gran Vía, and Tribunal Metro station on Calle Fuencarral. Most of the buzz is along Calle de la Corredera Baja de San Pablo with new businesses and the avant-garde arts community transforming it into their *barrio* of choice. They have promised not to stop until they have transformed Triball into the new Soho.

program of classes encompasses a range of cooking styles.

Flamenco

Fundación Conservatorio
Casa Patas   FLAMENCO
(Map p80; www.conservatorioflamenco.org; Calle de Cañizares 10; 1-hour class from €16, per month €40-75, plus €33 joining fee; Ⓜ Antón Martín, Tirso de Molina) Every conceivable type of flamenco instruction, including dance, guitar, singing and much more. It's upstairs from the Casa Patas *tablao* (flamenco venue). Single classes are also possible.

Tours

If you're pushed for time and want to fit a lot of sightseeing into a short visit, guided tours can be the ideal way to see the city.

Visitas Guiadas Oficiales   GUIDED TOUR
(Official Guided Tours; Map p72; 🖉 902 221424; www. esmadrid.com/guidedtours; Plaza Mayor 27; adult/ child €5.90/free, cycling & roller-blade tours adult €6.90; Ⓜ Sol) Over 40 highly recommended walking, cycling and roller-blade tours conducted in Spanish and English. Organised by the Centro de Turismo de Madrid (p131). Stop by the office and pick up its *M – Visitas Guiadas/Guided Tours* catalogue.

Wellington Society   WALKING TOUR
(🖉 609 143 203; www.wellsoc.org; tours €65-90) A handful of quirky historical tours laced with anecdotes and led by the inimitable Stephen Drake-Jones. Membership costs €65 and includes a day or evening walking tour.

Letango Tours   WALKING TOUR
(Map p80; 🖉 655 818 740; www.letangospaintours. com; Plaza Tirso de Molina 12, 1ºD; per person €135; Ⓜ Tirso de Molina) Eight walking tours through Madrid with additional excursions to San Lorenzo El Escorial, Segovia and Toledo. Per person prices drop the more of you there are.

Insider's Madrid   WALKING TOUR
(🖉 91 447 38 66; www.insidersmadrid.com; tours from €60) An impressive range of tailor-made tours, including walking, tapas, flamenco and bullfighting tours.

Madrid Bike Tours   CYCLING
(🖉 680 581 782; www.madridbiketours.com; 4hr tours €55) Londoner Mike Chandler offers a guided two-wheel tour of Madrid as well as tours further afield.

Bike Spain   CYCLING
(Map p72; 🖉 91 559 06 53; www.bikespain.info; Calle del Codo; bike rental half-/full day €12/17, tours from €31; ⏱ 10am-2pm & 4-7pm Mon-Fri, 10am-2pm Sat & Sun; Ⓜ Ópera) English-language guided city tours by bicycle, by day or (Friday) night, plus longer expeditions to San Lorenzo de El Escorial (€115).

Madrid Segway Tours   GUIDED TOUR
(🖉 659 824 499; www.madsegs.com; 3hr tour per person €65, plus €15 refundable deposit) Most of these Segway tours start in Plaza de España.

Urban Movil   GUIDED TOUR
(Map p72; 🖉 91 542 77 71, 687 535 443; www. urbanmovil.com; Plaza de Santiago 2; 1hr/2hr Segway tours €40/65; ⏱ 10am-8pm) Segway tours around Madrid. Prices include 10 minutes of training before you set out and it also organises bike tours.

Madrid City Tour   BUS
(🖉 902 024758; www.esmadrid.com/en/tourist-bus; 1-day ticket adult €21, child free-€9; ⏱ 9am-10pm Mar-Oct, 10am-6pm Nov-Feb) Hop-on, hop-off open-topped buses that run every 10 minutes or so along two routes. Information, including maps, is available at tourist offices, most travel agencies and some hotels, or you can get tickets on the bus. One major stop is outside the Museo del Prado on Calle Felipe IV. It also runs night tours in summer. Two-day tickets also available.

Adventurous Appetites   FOOD TOUR
(☑639 331073; www.adventurousappetites.com; 4hr tours €50; ☺8pm-midnight Mon-Sat) Runs English-language tapas tours through central Madrid. Prices include the first drink but exclude food.

✰✰ Festivals & Events

Madrid loves to party, and seemingly any excuse is good for a fiesta. For details about national festivals and events in the city, check online at www.esmadrid.com.

January & February

Madrid Fusion & Gastro Festival   FOOD
(www.esmadrid.com/gastrofestival) All the Spanish chefs who have made it big on the national and international stage come to Madrid for this gastronomy summit. It's a cooking extravaganza where the masters of the Spanish kitchen show off their latest creations. Over 400 bars and restaurants bring the festival back down to earth with special menus. Runs from late January to mid-February.

Arco   ART
(Feria Internacional de Arte Contemporánea; www.ifema.es) One of Europe's biggest celebrations of contemporary art, Arco draws galleries and exhibitors from all over the world to the Parque Ferial Juan Carlos I exhibition centre near Barajas airport in mid-February.

March

La Noche de los Teatros   THEATRE
(www.lanochedelosteatros.com) On 'The Night of the Theatres', Madrid's streets become the stage for all manner of performances, with a focus on comedy and children's plays. It usually takes place on the last Saturday of March.

May & June

Fiesta de la Comunidad de Madrid   FESTIVAL
On 2 May 1808 Napoleon's troops quelled an uprising in Madrid, and commemoration of the day has become an opportunity for much festivity. The day is celebrated with particular energy in the bars of Malasaña.

Fiesta de San Isidro   CULTURAL
(www.esmadrid.com) Around 15 May Madrid's patron saint is honoured with a week of nonstop processions, parties and bullfights. Free concerts are held throughout the city, and this week marks the start of the city's bullfighting season.

Festimad   MUSIC
(www.festimad.es) Bands from all over the country and beyond converge on Móstoles or Leganés (on the MetroSur train network) for two days of indie music indulgence. Although usually held in May, Festimad sometimes spills over into April or June.

Fiesta de Otoño a Primavera   MUSIC, THEATRE
(www.esmadrid.com) The 'Autumn to Spring Festival' involves a busy calendar of musical and theatrical activity.

Suma Flamenca   FLAMENCO
(www.madrid.org/sumaflamenca) A soul-filled flamenco festival that draws some of the biggest names in the genre to the Teatros del Canal in June.

MADRID FESTIVALS & EVENTS

MADRID FOR CHILDREN

Madrid has plenty to keep the little ones entertained. A good place to start is Casa de Campo (p98), where there are swimming pools, the Zoo Aquarium de Madrid and the Parque de Atracciones amusement park, which has a 'Zona Infantil' with sedate rides for the really young. To get to Casa de Campo, take the Teleférico (p98), one of the world's most horizontal cable cars, which putters for 2.5km out from the slopes of La Rosaleda.

The Museo del Ferrocarril (☑902 228822; www.museodelferrocarril.org; Paseo de las Delicias 61; adult/child €6/4; ☺9.30am-3pm Tue-Fri, 10am-8pm Sat, 10am-3pm Sun, closed Aug; ⓂDelicias) is home to old railway cars, train engines and more. The free Museo Naval (p91) will appeal to those fascinated by ships.

The Museo de Cera (Map p94; ☑91 319 26 49; www.museoceramadrid.com; Paseo de los Recoletos 41; adult/child €17/12; ☺10am-2.30pm & 4.30-8.30pm Mon-Fri, 10am-8.30pm Sat & Sun; ⓂColón) is Madrid's answer to Madame Tussaud's, with more than 450 wax characters.

Other possibilities include seeing Real Madrid play at the Estadio Santiago Bernabéu (p127), wandering through the greenery of the Parque del Buen Retiro (p89), where in summer there are puppet shows and boat rides, or skiing at Madrid Xanadú (p99).

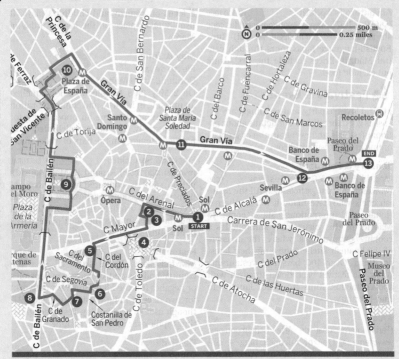

Walking Tour
Historic Madrid

START PLAZA DE LA PUERTA DEL SOL
END PLAZA DE LA CIBELES
LENGTH 5KM; THREE TO FOUR HOURS

Start in the pulsating ❶ **Plaza de la Puerta del Sol** (p78), then head northwest along Calle del Arenal to the ❷ **Iglesia de San Ginés** (p76), the site of one of Madrid's oldest places of Christian worship. Behind it is the wonderful ❸ **Chocolatería de San Ginés** (p114), a place of worship for lovers of *chocolate con churros* (deep-fried doughnut strips dipped in hot chocolate).

Continue up to and across Calle Mayor until you reach ❹ **Plaza Mayor** (p72), then turn west and head down the hill to the historic ❺ **Plaza de la Villa** (p75), home to some of the city's oldest surviving buildings.

Take the street down the left side of the Casa de Cisneros, cross Calle del Sacramento at the end, go down the stairs and follow the cobbled Calle del Cordón out onto Calle de Segovia. Almost directly in front of you is the Mudéjar tower of the 15th-century

❻ **Iglesia de San Pedro El Viejo** (p78); proceed up Costanilla de San Pedro, lingering en route in the ❼ **Plaza de la Paja** (p76).

From here, twist down through lanes of La Morería to Calle de Bailén and the wonderful *terrazas* (cafes with outdoor tables) on the edge of the ❽ **Jardines de las Vistillas** (p78). After a *cerveza* (beer), follow Calle de Bailén past the cathedral and royal palace to the elegant ❾ **Plaza de Oriente** (p74).

Head to the western side of the square and follow the walkway extension of Calle de Bailén, which leads into ❿ **Plaza de España**, surrounded by monumental towers. The eastern flank of Plaza de España marks the start of ⓫ **Gran Vía** (p79), a Haussmannesque boulevard that was slammed through tumbledown slums in the 1910s and 1920s. Head up and then down the hill past the elegant facades to the superb dome of the ⓬ **Edificio Metrópolis** (p79), where Gran Vía meets Calle de Alcalá. Down the hill you go to ⓭ **Plaza de la Cibeles** (p91), Madrid's favourite roundabout.

Día del Orgullo de Gays,
Lesbianas y Transexuales   GAY PRIDE
(www.orgullogay.org) The colourful Gay Pride
Parade, on the last Saturday in June, sets
out from the Puerta de Alcalá in the early
evening, and winds its way around the city
in an explosion of music and energy, ending
up at the Puerta del Sol.

July & August

Veranos de la Villa   SUMMER FESTIVAL
(veranosdelavilla.esmadrid.com) Madrid's town
hall stages a series of cultural events, shows
and exhibitions throughout July and August, known as 'Summers in the City'.

Summer Festivals   SUMMER FESTIVAL
Small-time but fun, the neighbourhood
summer festivals (held during the period
from mid-August to September), such as San
Cayetano in Lavapiés, and San Lorenzo and
La Paloma in La Latina, are great for cheap
entertainment.

September & October

DCode   MUSIC
(www.dcodefest.com) Held in September at
Madrid's Complutense University, this terrific music festival gets better with each
passing year. Franz Ferdinand, Amaral and
Kings of Convenience are recent headline
acts on a program that includes local and
international groups.

Arte Madrid – Apertura   ARTS
(www.artemadrid.com/apertura-que-es-apertura)
In mid- to late-September, more than 50
private art galleries inaugurate their exhibitions at the same time, with day and night
events to accompany this explosion of artistic creativity.

Semana de la Arquitectura   ARCHITECTURE
(www.esmadrid.com/semanaarquitectura/) Ma-
drid's Architecture Week includes guided
architectural visits to some of the city's
most emblematic buildings. It may begin in
September but more often happens in early
October.

November

Madrid en Danza   DANCE
(www.madrid.org/madridendanza/2013/index.
html) The best-known names of Spanish
dance, including flamenco performers, are
joined by international acts in Madrid in
November for almost three weeks of concerts at stages around the city.

🛏 Sleeping

Madrid has high-quality accommodation
across all price ranges and caters to every
taste. Where you decide to stay will play an
important role in your experience of Madrid. Plaza Mayor and Royal Madrid put
you in the heart of the busy downtown area,
while La Latina (the best *barrio* for tapas),
Lavapiés and Huertas (good for nightlife)
are ideal for those who love Madrid nights
and don't want to stagger too far to get back
to their hotel in the wee small hours. Staying
along the Paseo del Prado is ideal for those
here to spend most of their time in galleries, while Salamanca is quiet, upmarket and
perfect for serial shoppers. You don't have to
be gay to stay in Chueca, but you'll love it
if you are, while Malasaña is another inner-
city *barrio* with great restaurants and bars.

🛏 Plaza Mayor & Royal Madrid

Hostal Madrid   HOSTAL, APARTMENT €
(Map p80; ☑91 522 00 60; www.hostal-madrid.
info; Calle de Esparteros 6; s €35-62, d €45-78,
d apt per night €55-150, per month €1200-2500;
❋⚛; Ⓜ Sol) The 19 excellent apartments
here range in size from 33 sq metres to 200
sq metres and each has a fully equipped
kitchen, its own sitting area, bathroom and,
in the case of the larger ones (room 51 on
the 5th floor is one of the best), an expansive
terrace with good views over central Madrid.
The *hostal* rooms are comfortable and well-
sized and the service is friendly.

Hostal Luis XV   HOSTAL €
(Map p80; ☑91 522 10 21; www.hrluisxv.net; Calle de
la Montera 47, 8th fl; s/d from €35/50; ❋⚛; Ⓜ Gran
Vía) Everything here – especially the spacious
rooms and the attention to detail – makes
this family-run place feel pricier than it is.
You'll find it hard to tear yourself away from
the balconies outside every exterior room,
from where the views are superb (especially
from the triple in room 820), and you're so
high up that noise is rarely a problem.

Hostal Acapulco   HOSTAL €
(Map p80; ☑91 531 19 45; www.hostalacapulco.
com; Calle de la Salud 13, 4th fl; s/d €55/65; ❋⚛;
Ⓜ Gran Vía, Callao) A cut above many other
hostales in Madrid, this immaculate little
place has marble floors, renovated bathrooms (with bathtubs), double-glazed windows and comfortable beds. Street-facing
rooms have balconies overlooking a sunny
plaza and are flooded with natural light.

Los Amigos Sol Backpackers' Hostel   HOSTEL €

(Map p72; ☑ 91 559 24 72; www.losamigoshostel. com; Calle de Arenal 26, 4th fl; dm incl breakfast €17-21; @ ☎; Ⓜ Ópera, Sol) If you arrive in Madrid keen for company, this could be the place for you – lots of students stay here, the staff are savvy (and speak English) and there are bright dorm-style rooms (with free lockers) that sleep two to four people. There's also a kitchen for guests.

Hotel Meninas   BOUTIQUE HOTEL €€

(Map p72; ☑ 91 541 28 05; www.hotelmeninas. com; Calle de Campomanes 7; s/d from €89/109; ❀ ☎; Ⓜ Ópera) This is a classy, cool choice. The colour scheme is blacks, whites and greys, with dark-wood floors and splashes of fuchsia and lime green. Flat-screen TVs in every room, modern bathroom fittings, internet access points, and even a laptop in some rooms, round out the clean lines and latest innovations. Past guests include Viggo Mortensen and Natalie Portman.

Praktik Metropol   BOUTIQUE HOTEL €€

(Map p80; ☑ 91 521 29 35; www.hotelpraktik metropol.com; Calle de la Montera 47; s/d from €65/79; ❀ ☎; Ⓜ Gran Vía) You'd be hard-pressed to find better value anywhere in Europe than here in this recently overhauled hotel. The rooms have a fresh, contemporary look with white-wood furnishings, and some (especially the corner rooms) have brilliant views down to Gran Vía and out over the city. It's spread over six floors and there's a roof terrace if you don't have a room with a view.

Hotel Plaza Mayor   HOTEL €€

(Map p80; ☑ 91 360 06 06; www.h-plazamayor. com; Calle de Atocha 2; s/d from €55/70; ❀ ☎; Ⓜ Sol, Tirso de Molina) We love this place. Sitting just across from the Plaza Mayor, here you'll find stylish decor, helpful staff and charming original elements of this 150-year-old building. The rooms are attractive, some

WANT MORE?

For in-depth information, reviews and recommendations at your fingertips, head to http://shop.lonelyplanet.com to purchase a downloadable PDF of Lonely Planet's *Madrid City Guide*.

Alternatively, head to Lonely Planet (www.lonelyplanet.com/madrid) for planning advice, author recommendations, traveller reviews and insider tips.

with a light colour scheme and wrought-iron furniture. The pricier attic rooms boast dark wood and designer lamps, and have lovely little terraces with wonderful rooftop views of central Madrid.

Mario Room Mate   BOUTIQUE HOTEL €€

(Map p72; ☑ 91 548 85 48; www.room-matehotels. com; Calle de Campomanes 4; s €80-125, d €100-150; ❀ ☎; Ⓜ Ópera) Entering this swanky boutique hotel is like crossing the threshold of Madrid's latest nightclub: staff dressed all in black, black walls and swirls of red lighting in the lobby. Rooms can be small, but have high ceilings, simple furniture and light tones contrasting smoothly with muted colours and dark surfaces. Some rooms are pristine white; others have zany murals.

Petit Palace Posada del Peine   BOUTIQUE HOTEL €€

(Map p80; ☑ 91 523 81 51; www.hthoteles.com; Calle de Postas 17; r from €120; ❀ ☎; Ⓜ Sol) This hotel combines a splendid historic building (dating from 1610), a brilliant location (just 50m from the Plaza Mayor) and modern hi-tech rooms. The bathrooms sparkle with stunning fittings and hydromassage showers, and the rooms are beautifully appointed. Many historical architectural features remain in situ in the public areas. It's just a pity some of the rooms aren't larger.

🛏 La Latina & Lavapiés

Mad Hostel   HOSTEL €

(Map p80; ☑ 91 506 48 40; www.madhostel. com; Calle de la Cabeza 24; dm €16-23; ❀ @ ☎; Ⓜ Antón Martín) Mad Hostel is filled with life. The 1st-floor courtyard – with retractable roof – re-creates an old Madrid *corrala* (a traditional Madrid tenement block with long communal balconies built around a central courtyard), and is a wonderful place to chill. The four- to eight-bed rooms are smallish but clean. There's a small rooftop gym with state-of-the-art equipment.

★ Posada del León de Oro   BOUTIQUE HOTEL €€

(Map p77; ☑ 91 119 14 94; www.posadadelleon deoro.com; Calle de la Cava Baja 12; r from €121; ❀ ☎; Ⓜ La Latina) This rehabilitated inn has muted colour schemes and well-sized rooms. It also has a patio at its core and thoroughly modern rooms along one of Madrid's best-loved streets. The downstairs bar (p108) is terrific.

Posada del Dragón
BOUTIQUE HOTEL €€

(Map p77; ☑91 119 14 24; www.posadadeldragon. com; Calle de la Cava Baja 14; r from €91; ✳🛜; Ⓜ La Latina) At last, a boutique hotel in the heart of La Latina. This restored 19th-century inn sits on one of our favourite Madrid streets, and rooms either look out over the street or over the pretty internal patio. The rooms? Some are on the small side, but they've extremely comfortable beds, and bold, brassy colour schemes and designer everything. There's a terrific bar-restaurant downstairs.

Artrip
BOUTIQUE HOTEL €€

(☑91 539 32 82; www.artriphotel.com; Calle de Valencia 11; d/ste from €100/120; Ⓜ Lavapiés) For an alternative but supremely comfortable take on Madrid life, Artrip is close to the big-three art museums and surrounded by plenty of private art galleries in the heart of multicultural Lavapiés. Rooms are dazzling white offset by strong splashes of colour.

🛏 Sol, Santa Ana & Huertas

Hostal Adriano
HOSTAL €

(Map p80; ☑91 521 13 39; www.hostaladriano. com; Calle de la Cruz 26, 4th fl; s/d €45/60; ✳🛜; Ⓜ Sol) They don't come any better than this bright and friendly *hostal* wedged in the streets that mark the boundary between Sol and Huertas. Most rooms are well sized and each has its own well-considered colour scheme. On the same floor, the owners run the Hostal Adria Santa Ana (Map p80; www. hostaladriasantaana.com; Calle de la Cruz 26, 4th fl; s/d €59/68; ✳🛜), which is a step up in price, style and comfort.

Cat's Hostel
HOSTEL €

(Map p80; ☑91 369 28 07; www.catshostel.com; Calle de Cañizares 6; dm €16-22; ✳@🛜; Ⓜ Antón Martín) Forming part of a 17th-century palace, the internal courtyard here is one of Madrid's finest – lavish Andalucian tilework, a fountain, a spectacular glass ceiling and stunning Islamic decoration, surrounded on four sides by an open balcony. There's also a super-cool basement bar with free internet and fiestas, often with live music.

★ Hotel Alicia
BOUTIQUE HOTEL €€

(Map p80; ☑91 389 60 95; www.room-matehoteles. com; Calle del Prado 2; d €100-175, ste from €200; ✳🛜; Ⓜ Sol, Sevilla, Antón Martín) One of the landmark properties of the designer Room Mate chain of hotels, Hotel Alicia overlooks Plaza de Santa Ana with beautiful, spacious rooms. The style (the work of designer Pascua Ortega) is a touch more muted than in other Room Mate hotels, but the supermodern look remains intact, the downstairs bar is oh-so-cool, and the service is young and switched on.

Hotel Miau
BOUTIQUE HOTEL €€

(Map p80; ☑91 369 71 20; www.hotelmiau.com; Calle del Príncipe 26; s incl breakfast €50-85, d incl breakfast €60-105; ✳🛜; Ⓜ Sol, Antón Martín) If you want to be close to the nightlife of Huertas or can't tear yourself away from the beautiful Plaza de Santa Ana, then Hotel Miau is your place. Light tones, splashes of colour and modern art adorn the walls of the rooms, which are large and well equipped. It can be noisy, but you did choose Huertas...

NH Palacio de Tepa
HOTEL €€

(Map p80; ☑91 389 64 90; www.nh-hoteles.com; Calle de San Sebastián 2; d from €135; Ⓜ Antón Martín) With a prime Huertas location, this fine offering from the NH stable inhabits a thoroughly overhauled 17th-century palace. The interiors combine the usual clean-lined NH look of beiges, whites and splashes of citrus green with some period features such as exposed wooden beams in some rooms.

Hotel Urban
LUXURY HOTEL €€€

(Map p80; ☑91 787 77 70; www.derbyhotels.com; Carrera de San Jerónimo 34; r from €225; ✳🛜🛁; Ⓜ Sevilla) This towering glass edifice is the epitome of art-inspired designer cool. It boasts original artworks from Africa and Asia, dark-wood floors and dark walls are offset by plenty of light, while the dazzling bathrooms have wonderful designer fittings – the washbasins are sublime. The rooftop swimming pool is one of Madrid's best and the gorgeous terrace is heaven on a candlelit summer's evening.

Me by Meliá
LUXURY HOTEL €€€

(Map p80; ☑91 701 60 00; www.memadrid.com; Plaza de Santa Ana 14; r from €185; ✳🛜; Ⓜ Sol, Antón Martín) Once the landmark Gran Victoria Hotel, the Madrid home of many a famous bullfighter, this audacious new hotel is fast becoming a landmark of a different kind. Overlooking the western end of Plaza de Santa Ana, this luxury hotel is decked out in minimalist white with curves and comfort in all the right places; this is one place where it's definitely worth paying extra for the view.

🛏 El Retiro & the Art Museums

★ Hotel Ritz
LUXURY HOTEL €€€

(Map p84; ☑ 91 701 67 67; www.ritzmadrid.com; Plaza de la Lealtad 5; d from €324, ste €850-5000; ✳ 🛜; Ⓜ Banco de España) The grand old lady of Madrid, the Hotel Ritz is the height of exclusivity. One of the most lavish buildings in the city, it has classic style and impeccable service that is second to none. Unsurprisingly it's the favoured hotel of presidents, kings and celebrities. The public areas are palatial and awash with antiques, while the rooms are extravagantly large, opulent and supremely comfortable.

Westin Palace
LUXURY HOTEL €€€

(Map p80; ☑ 91 360 80 00; www.westinpalacemadrid.com; Plaza de las Cortes 7; d/ste from €289/600; ✳ 🛜; Ⓜ Banco de España, Antón Martín) An old Madrid classic, this former palace of the Duque de Lerma opened as a hotel in 1911, and was Spain's second luxury hotel. Ever since, it has looked out across Plaza de Neptuno at its rival, the Ritz, like a lover unjustly scorned. Its name may not have the world-famous cachet of the Ritz, but it's not called the Palace for nothing and is extravagant in all the right places.

🛏 Salamanca

Petit Palace Art Gallery
HOTEL €€

(Map p94; ☑ 91 435 54 11; www.hthoteles.com; Calle de Jorge Juan 17; d from €135; ✳ 🛜; Ⓜ Serrano) Occupying a stately 19th-century Salamanca building, this landmark property of the Petit Palace chain is a lovely designer hotel that combines hi-tech facilities with an artistic aesthetic, with loads of original works dotted around the public spaces and even in some of the rooms. Hydro-massage showers, laptop computers and exercise bikes in many rooms are just some of the extras.

🛏 Malasaña & Chueca

Life Hotel
HOTEL €

(Map p96; ☑ 91 531 42 96; www.antiguaposadadelpez.com; Calle de Pizarro 16; s/d from €39/55; ✳ 🛜; Ⓜ Noviciado) This place inhabits the shell of a historic Malasaña building, but the rooms are slick and contemporary with designer bathrooms. You're also just a few steps up the hill from Calle del Pez, one of Malasaña's most happening streets. It's an exceptionally good deal, even when prices head upwards.

Flat 5 Madrid
HOSTAL €

(Map p96; ☑ 91 127 24 00; www.flat5madrid.com; Calle de San Bernardo 55, 5th fl; r €60-100, without bathroom €35-50; ✳ 🛜; Ⓜ Noviciado) Unlike so many other *hostales* in Madrid, where the charm depends on a time-worn air, Flat 5 Madrid has a fresh, clean-lined look with bright colours, flat-screen TVs and flower boxes on the window sills. Even the rooms that face onto a patio have partial views over the rooftops. If the rooms and bathrooms were a little bigger, we'd consider moving in.

Hostal La Zona
HOSTAL €

(Map p96; ☑ 91 521 99 04; www.hostallazona.com; Calle de Valverde 7, 1st fl; s incl breakfast €35-55, d incl breakfast €50-70; ✳ 🛜; Ⓜ Gran Vía) Catering primarily to a gay clientele, the stylish Hostal La Zona has exposed brickwork, subtle colour shades and wooden pillars. We like a place where a sleep-in is encouraged – breakfast is served from 9am to noon, which is exactly the understanding Madrid's nightlife merits. Arnaldo and Vincent are friendly hosts.

★ Only You Hotel
BOUTIQUE HOTEL €€

(Map p96; ☑ 91 005 22 22; www.onlyyouhotels.com; Calle de Barquillo 21; d from €157; ✳ @ 🛜; Ⓜ Chueca) This stunning new boutique hotel makes perfect use of a 19th-century Chueca mansion. The look is classy and contemporary and is the latest project by respected interior designer Lázaro Rosa Violán. Nice touches include all-day á la carte breakfasts and a portable router that you can carry out into the city to stay connected.

Hotel Óscar
BOUTIQUE HOTEL €€

(Map p96; ☑ 91 701 11 73; www.room-matehoteles.com; Plaza de Vázquez de Mella 12; d €90-200, ste €150-280; ✳ 🛜; Ⓜ Gran Vía) Outstanding. Hotel Óscar belongs to the highly original Room Mate chain of hotels, and the designer rooms ooze style and sophistication. Some have floor-to-ceiling murals, the lighting is always funky, and the colour scheme is asplash with pinks, lime greens, oranges or more-minimalist black and white.

Hotel Abalú
BOUTIQUE HOTEL €€

(Map p96; ☑ 91 531 47 44; www.hotelabalu.com; Calle del Pez 19; d/apt from €80/110; ✳ 🛜; Ⓜ Noviciado) Malasaña's very own boutique hotel is an oasis of style amid the *barrio's* time-worn feel. Suitably located on cool Calle del Pez, each room here has its own design drawn from the imagination of Luis Delgado, from retro chintz to Zen, baroque and pure white (and most aesthetics in between). You're close to Gran Vía, but away from the tourist scrum.

🛏 Beyond the Centre

★Hotel Silken Puerta América
LUXURY HOTEL €€
(☎91 744 54 00; www.hoteles-silken.com; Avenida de América 41; d/ste from €125/250; ❄ 🕿; 🇲 Cartagena) When the owners of this hotel saw their location (halfway between the city and the airport), they knew they had to do something special to build a self-contained world so innovative and luxurious that you'd never want to leave. Their idea? Give 22 of world architecture's most creative names (eg Zaha Hadid, Sir Norman Foster, Ron Arad, David Chipperfield, Jean Nouvel) a floor each to design.

The result is an extravagant pastiche of styles, from zany montages of 1980s chic to bright-red bathrooms that feel like a movie star's dressing room. To get here, take Avenida de América in the direction of the airport; it's about 4km northwest of the city centre.

🍴 Eating

After holding fast to its rather unexciting local cuisine for centuries (aided by loyal locals who never saw the need for anything else), Madrid has finally become a worthy culinary capital.

There's everything to be found here, not least the rich variety of regional Spanish specialities from across the country. And there's not a *barrio* where you can't find a great meal. Restaurants in Malasaña, Chueca and Huertas range from glorious old *tabernas* (taverns) to boutique eateries across all price ranges. For more classically classy surrounds, Salamanca and Northern Madrid are generally pricey but of the highest standard, and ideal for a special occasion. In the central *barrios* of Los Austrias, Sol and Centro there's a little bit of everything. Splendid tapas bars abound everywhere, but La Latina is the undoubted queen.

🍴 Plaza Mayor & Royal Madrid

Casa Revuelta
TAPAS €
(Map p72; ☎91 366 33 32; Calle de Latoneros 3; tapas from €2.60; ⊙10.30am-4pm & 7-11pm Tue-Sat, 10.30am-4pm Sun, closed Aug; 🇲 Sol, La Latina) Casa Revuelta puts out some of Madrid's finest tapas of *bacalao* (dried and salted cod; €3), bar none. While aficionados of Casa La-

bra (p112) may disagree, the fact that the octogenarian owner, Señor Revuelta, painstakingly extracts every fish bone in the morning and serves as a waiter in the afternoon wins the argument for us.

La Gloria de Montera
SPANISH €
(Map p80; www.grupandilana.com; Calle del Caballero de Gracia 10; mains €7-12; ⊙1.15-4pm & 8.30-11.30pm; 🇲 Gran Vía) From the same stable as La Finca de Susana (p110), La Gloria de Montera combines classy decor with eminently reasonable prices. It's not that the food is especially creative, but rather the tastes are fresh and the surroundings sophisticated. You'll get a good initiation into Spanish cooking without paying too much for the experience.

★Mercado de San Miguel
TAPAS €€
(Map p72; www.mercadodesanmiguel.es; Plaza de San Miguel; tapas from €1; ⊙10am-midnight Sun-Wed, 10am-2am Thu-Sat; 🇲 Sol) One of Madrid's oldest and most beautiful markets, the Mercado de San Miguel has undergone a stunning major renovation. Within the early-20th-century glass walls, the market has become an inviting space strewn with tables. You can order tapas and sometimes more substantial plates at most of the counter-bars, and everything here (from caviar to chocolate) is as tempting as the market is alive.

Taberna La Bola
MADRILEÑO €€
(Map p72; ☎91 547 69 30; www.labola.es; Calle de la Bola 5; mains €16-24; ⊙1.30-4.30pm & 8.30-11pm Mon-Sat, 1.30-4.30pm Sun, closed Aug; 🇲 Santo

---

WHAT'S COOKING IN MADRID?

➡ *cocido a la madrileña* (Madrid meat-and-chickpea hotpot) Taberna La Bola (above), Lhardy (p110) or Malacatín (p109)

➡ *cordero o cochinillo asado* (roast lamb or suckling pig) Restaurante Sobrino de Botín (p108)

➡ *sopa de ajo* (garlic soup) Posada de la Villa (p108)

➡ *callos a la madrileña* (Madrid-style tripe) Taberna La Bola

➡ *huevos rotos* (potatoes cooked with eggs and *jamón*) Casa Lucio (p109) or Almendro 13 (p112)

LOCAL KNOWLEDGE

BOCADILLO DE CALAMARES

One of the lesser-known culinary specialties of Madrid is a *bocadillo de calamares* (a baguette-style roll filled to bursting with deep-fried calamari). You'll find them in many bars in the streets surrounding Plaza Mayor and neighbouring bars along Calle de los Botaderos, off Plaza Mayor's southeastern corner. At around €2.50, it's the perfect street snack.

Domingo) Taberna La Bola (going strong since 1870 and run by the sixth generation of the Verdasco family) is a much-loved bastion of traditional Madrid cuisine. If you're going to try *cocido a la madrileña* (meat-and-chickpea stew; €20) while in Madrid, this is a good place to do so. It's busy and noisy and very Madrid.

★Restaurante Sobrino de Botín CASTILIAN €€€

(Map p72; ☑91 366 42 17; www.botin.es; Calle de los Cuchilleros 17; mains €19-27; Ⓜ La Latina, Sol) It's not every day you can eat in the oldest restaurant in the world (the *Guinness Book of Records* has recognised it as the oldest – it was established in 1725). And it has also appeared in many novels about Madrid, from Ernest Hemingway's to Frederick Forsyth's. Roasted meats are the speciality.

The secret of its staying power is fine *cochinillo* (roast suckling pig; €25) and *cordero asado* (roast lamb; €25) cooked in wood-fired ovens. Eating in the vaulted cellar is a treat. If we have a complaint, it's that the waiters like to keep things ticking over a little too quickly. To get behind the scenes, take the Botín Experience guided tour run by Insider's Madrid (p100).

Restaurante Sandó CONTEMPORARY SPANISH €€€

(Map p72; ☑91 547 99 11; www.restaurantesando.es; Calle de Isabel la Católica 2; mains €21-28, menú degustación €49; ⊙1-4pm & 8-11pm Tue-Sat; Ⓜ Santo Domingo) Juan Mari Arzak, one of Spain's most famous chefs, has finally set up shop in Madrid, just off the Plaza de Santo Domingo. Bringing Basque innovation to bear upon local tradition, the cooking here is assured with dishes like tuna chunk with ginger and hibiscus. If you can't decide, try the *menú degustación* (tasting menu), or head around the corner to the tapas bar.

La Terraza del Casino CONTEMPORARY SPANISH €€€

(Map p80; ☑91 521 87 00; www.casinodemadrid.es; Calle de Alcalá 15; mains €32-65, set menus from €69-135; ⊙1.30-3.30pm & 9-11pm Mon-Sat; Ⓜ Sevilla) Perched atop the lavish Casino de Madrid building, this temple of haute cuisine is presided over by celebrity chef Paco Roncero and is the proud bearer of two Michelin stars. It's all about culinary experimentation, with a menu that changes as each new idea emerges from the laboratory and moves into the kitchen. The *menu degustación* (€135) is a fabulous avalanche of tastes.

✖ La Latina & Lavapiés

Enotaberna del León de Oro SPANISH €€

(Map p77; ☑91 119 14 94; www.posadadelleondeoro.com; Calle de la Cava Baja 12; mains €13-18; ⊙1-4pm & 8pm-midnight; Ⓜ La Latina) The stunning restoration work that brought to life the Posada del León de Oro (p104) also bequeathed to La Latina a fine new bar-restaurant. The emphasis is on matching carefully chosen wines with creative dishes (such as baby squid with potato emulsion and ruccola pesto) in a casual atmosphere. It's a winning combination.

Naïa Bistro FUSION €€

(Map p77; ☑91 366 27 83; www.naiabistro.com; Plaza de la Paja 3; mains €12-20, set menus €30-45; ⊙1.30-4.30pm & 8.30-11.30pm Tue-Sun; Ⓜ La Latina) On the lovely Plaza de la Paja, Naïa has a real buzz about it, with modern Spanish cuisine, a chill-out lounge downstairs and outdoor tables on lovely Plaza de la Paja. The emphasis throughout is on natural ingredients, healthy food and exciting tastes.

Ene Restaurante CONTEMPORARY SPANISH €€

(Map p77; ☑91 366 25 91; www.enerestaurante.com; Calle del Nuncio 19; mains €11-22, brunch €22; ⊙1-4pm & 8.30pm-midnight daily, brunch 12.30-4.30pm Sat & Sun; Ⓜ La Latina) Just across from Iglesia de San Pedro El Viejo, one of Madrid's oldest churches, Ene is anything but old world. The design is cutting edge and awash with reds and purples, while the young and friendly waiters circulate to the tune of lounge music. The food is Spanish-Asian fusion and there are also plenty of *pintxos* (Basque tapas) to choose from.

El Estragón VEGETARIAN €€

(Map p77; ☑91 365 89 82; www.elestragonvegetariano.com; Plaza de la Paja 10; mains €8-14; ⊙1-4.30pm & 8pm-midnight; ✐; Ⓜ La Latina) A delightful spot for crêpes, vegie burgers and other vegetarian specialities, El Estragón is undoubtedly one of Madrid's best vegetarian restaurants, although attentive vegans won't appreciate the use of butter. Apart from that, we're yet to hear a bad word about it.

Casa Lucio
SPANISH €€

(Map p77; ☎91 365 32 52; www.casalucio.es; Calle de la Cava Baja 35; mains €10-30; ☺1-4pm & 8.30pm-midnight Sun-Fri, 8.30pm-midnight Sat, closed Aug; Ⓜ La Latina) Lucio has been wowing *madrileños* with his light touch, quality ingredients and home-style local cooking for ages – think roasted meats and, a Lucio speciality, eggs in abundance. There's also *rabo de toro* (bull's tail) during the Fiestas de San Isidro Labrador, and plenty of *rioja* (red wine) to wash away the mere thought of it. Casa Lucio draws an august, well-dressed crowd.

Malacatín
MADRILEÑO €€

(Map p77; ☎91 365 52 41; www.malacatin.com; Calle de Ruda 5; mains €11-15; ☺11am-5.30pm Mon-Wed & Sat, 11am-5.30pm Thu & Fri; Ⓜ La Latina) If you want to see *madrileños* enjoying their favourite local food, this is one of the best places to do so. Conversations bounce off the tiled walls of the cramped dining area adorned with bullfighting memorabilia. The speciality is as much *cocido* (meat-and-chickpea stew) as you can eat (€19.50). The *pringa de cocido* (taste of *cocido;* €9) at the bar is a great way to try Madrid's favourite dish.

Posada de la Villa
MADRILEÑO €€€

(Map p77; ☎91 366 18 80; www.posadadelavilla.com; Calle de la Cava Baja 9; mains €19-28; ☺1-4pm & 8pm-midnight Mon-Sat, 1-4pm Sun, closed Aug; Ⓜ La Latina) This wonderfully restored 17th-century *posada* (inn) is something of a local landmark. The atmosphere is formal, the decoration sombre and traditional (heavy timber and brickwork), and the cuisine decidedly local – roast meats, *cocido* (meat-and-chickpea stew), *callos* (tripe) and *sopa de ajo* (garlic soup).

✕ Sol, Santa Ana & Huertas

★ Ramiro's Tapas Wine Bar
TAPAS €

(Map p80; ☎91 843 73 47; Calle de Atocha 51; tapas from €4.50, raciones from €10; ☺1-4.30pm & 8-11.30pm Mon-Sat, 1-4.30pm Sun; Ⓜ Antón Martín) One of the best tapas bars to open in Madrid in recent years, this fine gastrobar occupies an open, convivial space with low

wooden tables and offers up traditional tapas with subtle but original touches. Most of the cooking comes from Castilla y León and they do exceptional things with cured meats, foie gras and prawns.

Gourmet Experience
FOOD COURT €

(Map p80; 9th fl, Plaza de Callao 2; ☺10am-10pm; Ⓜ Callao) Ride the elevator up to the ninth floor of the El Corte Inglés department store for one of downtown Madrid's best eating experiences. The views here are fabulous, but the food is also excellent, with everything from top-notch tapas to gourmet hamburgers. One is StreetXo, a tapas bar watched over by David Muñoz of three-Michelin-starred DiverXo (p112) fame.

There's also an onsite gourmet food store with Spanish products.

★ Casa Alberto
SPANISH, TAPAS €€

(Map p80; ☎91 429 93 56; www.casaalberto.es; Calle de las Huertas 18; tapas from €3.25, raciones €8.50-16, mains €14-21; ☺1.30-4pm & 8pm-midnight Tue-Sat, 1.30-4pm Sun; Ⓜ Antón Martín) One of the most atmospheric old *tabernas* of Madrid, Casa Alberto has been around since 1827. The secret to its staying power is vermouth on tap, excellent tapas at the bar and fine sit-down meals; Casa Alberto's *rabo de toro* (bull's tail) is famous among aficionados.

★ Vi Cool
CONTEMPORARY SPANISH €€

(Map p80; ☎91 429 49 13; www.vi-cool.com; Calle de las Huertas 12; mains €8-19; ☺1.30-4.15pm & 8.30pm-midnight Tue-Sun; Ⓜ Antón Martín) Catalan master chef Sergi Arola is one of the most restless and relentlessly creative culinary talents in the country. Aside from his showpiece Sergi Arola Gastro (p112), he has dabbled in numerous new restaurants around the capital and in Barcelona, but this is one of his most interesting yet – a modern bar-style space with prices that enable the average mortal to sample his formidable gastronomic skills.

Dishes are either tapas or larger *raciones*, ranging from his trademark Las Bravas de Arola (a different take on the Spanish dish of roast potatoes in a spicy tomato sauce), to fried prawns with curry and mint.

Maceiras
GALICIAN €€

(Map p80; ☎91 429 15 84; Calle de las Huertas 66; mains €7-14; Ⓜ Antón Martín) Galician tapas (think octopus, green peppers etc) never tasted so good as in this agreeably rustic bar down the bottom of the Huertas hill, especially when washed down with a crisp white

Ribeiro. The simple wooden tables, loyal customers and handy location make this a fine place to rest after (or en route to) the museums along the Paseo del Prado.

La Finca de Susana
SPANISH €€

(Map p80; ☑ 91 369 35 57; www.lafinca-restaurant. com; Calle de Arlabán 4; mains €7-12; ☉ 1-3.45pm & 8.30-11.30pm Sun-Wed, 1-3.45pm & 8.15pm-midnight Thu-Sat; Ⓜ Sevilla) It's difficult to find a better combination of price, quality cooking and classy atmosphere anywhere in Huertas. The softly lit dining area is bathed in greenery and the sometimes innovative, sometimes traditional food draws a hip young crowd. The duck confit with plums, turnips and couscous is a fine choice. No reservations.

Sidrería Vasca Zeraín
BASQUE €€€

(Map p80; ☑ 91 429 79 09; www.restaurante-vasco-zerain-sidreria.es; Calle Quevedo 3; mains €14-32; ☉ 1.30-4pm & 7.30pm-midnight Mon-Sat, 1.30-4pm Sun, closed Aug; Ⓜ Antón Martín) In the heart of the Barrio de las Letras, this sophisticated Basque restaurant is one of the best places in town to sample Basque cuisine. The essential staples include cider, *bacalao* and wonderful steaks, while there are also a few splashes of creativity thrown in (the secret's in the sauce). We highly recommend the *menú sidrería* (cider-house menu; €35).

Lhardy
MADRILEÑO €€€

(Map p80; ☑ 91 521 33 85; www.lhardy.com; Carrera de San Jerónimo 8; mains €28-38; ☉ 1-3.30pm & 8.30-11pm Mon-Sat, 1-3.30pm Sun, closed Aug; Ⓜ Sol, Sevilla) Downstairs at this Madrid landmark (since 1839) is an elegant treasure trove of takeaway gourmet tapas, while the six upstairs dining areas are the upmarket preserve of traditional Madrid dishes with an occasional hint of French influence. House specialities include *cocido a la madrileña* (€35.50), pheasant and wild duck in an orange perfume. The quality and service are unimpeachable.

✖ Paseo del Prado & El Retiro

★ Estado Puro
TAPAS €

(Map p84; ☑ 91 330 24 00; www.tapasenestadopuro.com; Plaza Neptuno (Plaza de Cánovas del Castillo) 4; tapas €2-12.50; ☉ noon-midnight Mon-Sat, to 4pm Sun; Ⓜ Banco de España, Atocha) Estado Puro serves up fantastic tapas, many of which have their origins in Catalonia's world-famous elBulli restaurant, such as the *tortilla española siglo XXI* (21st-century

Spanish omelette, served in a glass). The kitchen here is overseen by Paco Roncero, the head chef at La Terraza del Casino (p108), who learned his trade with master chef Ferran Adrià.

✖ Salamanca

La Colonial de Goya
TAPAS €

(Map p94; ☑ 91 435 76 08; www.restauranterin condegoya.es; Calle de Jorge Juan 34; tapas €3-4.50, mains €11-18; ☉ 1-4pm & 8pm-midnight; Ⓜ Velázquez) Canapés are the speciality here and should be sufficient for most, but a range of carpaccios, croquettes and main dishes is also served at this engaging little tapas bar. The pheasant paté or the brie stuffed with salmon are typical of what's on offer. The atmosphere is casual, while the all-white decor of wood and exposed brick walls is as classy as the neighbourhood.

✖ Malasaña & Chueca

La T Gastrobar
TAPAS, MODERN SPANISH €

(Map p96; ☑ 91 531 14 06; www.latgastrobar.es; Calle Molino de Viento 4; mains €14-19; ☉ 1-4pm & 9pm-midnight Tue-Sat; Ⓜ Callao) This slick split-level place does variations on Spanish classics, such as thin layers of bull's tail with pastrami and baked apple or the lamb ribs with chestnuts, pine nuts and potatoes. The atmosphere is classy yet casual in the finest Madrid tradition.

Bazaar
CONTEMPORARY SPANISH €

(Map p96; www.restaurantbazaar.com; Calle de la Libertad 21; mains €6.50-10; ☉ 1.15-4pm & 8.30-11.30pm Sun-Wed, 1.15-4pm & 8.15pm-midnight Thu-Sat; Ⓜ Chueca) Bazaar's popularity among the well heeled and famous shows no sign of abating. Its pristine white interior design, with theatre-style lighting and wall-length windows, may draw a crowd that looks like it stepped out of the pages of *Hola!* magazine, but the food is well priced and the atmosphere casual. No reservations accepted, so get there early or be prepared to wait, regardless of whether you're famous or not.

★ La Carmencita
SPANISH €€

(Map p96; ☑ 91 531 09 11; www.tabernalacarmencita. es; Calle de la Libertad 16; mains €14-20; ☉ 9am-2am; Ⓜ Chueca) Around since 1854 and the bar where legendary poet Pablo Neruda was once a regular, the folk of La Carmencita has taken 75 of their favourite traditional Spanish recipes and brought them to the table, sometimes with a little updating but more often safe in the knowledge that nothing needs changing. Backed up by what they call 'wines with soul', it's hard to resist this place.

La Musa SPANISH, FUSION €€

(Map p96; ☑ 91 448 75 58; www.grupolamusa.com; Calle de Manuela Malasaña 18; tapas from €3.75, mains €7-15; ⊙ 9am-midnight Mon-Wed, 9am-1am Fri, 1pm-2am Sat, 1pm-midnight Sun; Ⓜ San Bernardo) Snug yet loud, a favourite of Madrid's hip young crowd yet utterly unpretentious, La Musa is all about designer decor, lounge music on the sound system and memorably fun food (breakfast, lunch and dinner). The menu is divided into three types of tapas – hot, cold and BBQ.

Among the hot varieties is the fantastic *jabalí con ali-oli de miel y sobrasada* (wild boar with honey mayonnaise and *sobrasada* – a soft and spreadable mildly spicy sausage from Mallorca). If you don't fancy waiting, try the sister restaurant/lounge bar nearby, Ojalá Awareness Club (p121).

La Gastrocroquetería de Chema TAPAS €€

(Map p96; ☑ 91 364 22 63; www.gastrocroqueteria. com; Calle del Barco 7; tapas €3-12.40, set menus €16-28; ⊙ 9pm-midnight Mon-Fri, 2-4.30pm & 9pm-midnight Sat & Sun; Ⓜ Tribunal) Croquetas in all their glory are what this place is all about. Try the classic version (made with *jamón* or cod) or any number of riffs on the croquette theme (with *sobrasada* – spreadable cured meat – and chocolate, for example). It also does other tapas, with a couple of set menus to guide your way.

Albur TAPAS, SPANISH €€

(Map p96; ☑ 91 594 27 33; www.restaurantealbur. com; Calle de Manuela Malasaña 15; mains €13-18; ⊙ 12:30-5pm & 7:30pm-1am Mon-Thu, 12:30-5pm & 7:30pm-2am Fri, 12:30pm-2am Sat, 12.30pm-1am Sun; Ⓜ Bilbao) This place has a wildly popular tapas bar and a classy-but-casual restaurant out the back. Albur is known for terrific rice dishes and tapas, and has a well-chosen wine list. The restaurant's waiters never seem to lose their cool, and its extremely well-priced rice dishes are the stars of the show, although in truth you could order anything here and leave well satisfied.

Mercado de San Antón TAPAS €€

(Map p96; www.mercadosananton.com; Calle de Augusto Figueroa 24; meals €10-30; ⊙ 10am-midnight Mon-Thu, to 1.30am Fri-Sun; Ⓜ Chueca) Upstairs in this recently revamped fresh food market in the heart of Chueca you'll find what they describe as a 'gastro market' or 'tapas vil-

lage' – a small but enticing selection of shopfronts selling creative cooking with a good mix of local and international cuisines on offer. Wander up to the roof for good rooftop views.

La Tasquita de Enfrente CONTEMPORARY SPANISH €€€

(Map p96; ☑ 91 532 54 49; www.latasquitadeenfrente.com; Calle de la Ballesta 6; mains €17-32, set menus €45-69; ⊙ 1.30-4.30pm & 8.30pm-midnight Mon-Sat; Ⓜ Gran Vía) For all the innovation sweeping Spanish cuisine, Spanish chefs succeed at home only if they maintain a certain fidelity to traditional bases before heading off in new directions. Chef Juanjo López's seasonal menu never ceases to surprise but also combines simple Spanish staples to stunning effect. His *menú degustación* (€49) and *menú de Juanjo* (€65) would be our choice if this is your first time. Reservations essential.

✖ Parque del Oeste & Northern Madrid

Casa Mingo ASTURIAN €

(☑ 91 547 79 18; www.casamingo.es; Paseo de la Florida 34; raciones €3.95-10.30; ⊙ 11am-midnight; Ⓜ Príncipe Pío) Built in 1916 to feed workers building the Príncipe Pío train station, Casa Mingo is a well-known and vaguely cavernous Asturian cider house. It's kept simple here, focusing primarily on the signature dish of *pollo asado* (roast chicken; €10.50) accompanied by a bottle of cider. Combine with a visit to the neighbouring Ermita de San Antonio de la Florida (p95).

Las Tortillas de Gabino SPANISH €€

(Map p94; ☑ 91 319 75 05; www.lastortillasdegabino.com; Calle de Rafael Calvo 20; tortillas €9-15.50, mains €12-20; ⊙ 1.30-4pm & 9-11.30pm Mon-Sat; Ⓜ Iglesia) It's a brave chef who messes with the iconic *tortilla de patatas* (potato-and-onion omelette), but the results here are delicious – such as tortilla with octopus, and with all manner of surprising combinations. This place also gets rave reviews for its *croquetas*. The service is excellent and the bright yet classy dining area adds to the sense of a most agreeable eating experience. Reservations are highly recommended.

Costa Blanca Arrocería SPANISH €€

(☑ 91 448 58 32; Calle de Bravo Murillo 3; mains €12-22; ⊙ 1.30-4.30pm Mon, 1.30-4.30pm & 8.30-11.30pm Tue-Fri, 2-4pm & 8.30-11.30pm Sat & Sun; Ⓜ Quevedo) Even if you don't have plans to

A TAPAS TOUR OF MADRID

La Latina

Madrid's home of tapas is La Latina, especially along Calle de la Cava Baja and the surrounding streets. Almendro 13 (Map p77; ☑ 91 365 42 52; Calle del Almendro 13; mains €7-15; ⊙ 12.30-4pm & 7.30pm-midnight Sun-Thu, 12.30-5pm & 8pm-1am Fri & Sat; Ⓜ La Latina) is famous for quality rather than frilly elaborations, with cured meats, cheeses, tortillas and *huevos rotos* (literally, 'broken eggs') the house specialities. Down on Calle de la Cava Baja, Txacolina (Map p77; ☑ 91 366 48 77; Calle de la Cava Baja 26; tapas from €3.50; ⊙ 8pm-midnight Mon & Tue, 1-4pm & 8pm-midnight Wed-Sat, 1-4pm Sun; Ⓜ La Latina) does Basque 'high cuisine in miniature'; wash it all down with a *txacoli*, a sharp Basque white. Casa Lucas (Map p77; ☑ 91 365 08 04; www.casalucas.es; Calle de la Cava Baja 30; tapas/raciones from €5/12; ⊙ 1-3.30pm & 8pm-midnight Thu-Tue, 1-3.30pm Wed; Ⓜ La Latina) and La Chata (Map p77; ☑ 91 366 14 58; Calle de la Cava Baja 24; mains €11.50-21, tapas selection for 2 people €20; ⊙ 1-4pm & 8.30pm-midnight Thu-Mon, 8.30pm-midnight Tue & Wed; Ⓜ La Latina) are also hugely popular. Not far away, Juana La Loca (Map p77; ☑ 91 364 05 25; Plaza de la Puerta de Moros 4; tapas from €4.50, mains €8-19; ⊙ noon-1am Tue-Sun, 8pm-1am Mon; Ⓜ La Latina) does a magnificent *tortilla de patatas* (potato and onion omelette), as does Txirimiri (Map p77; ☑ 91 364 11 96; www.txirimiri.es; Calle del Humilladero 6; tapas from €4; ⊙ noon-4.30pm & 8.30pm-midnight, closed Aug; Ⓜ La Latina). Taberna Matritum (Map p77; ☑ 91 365 82 37; Calle de la Cava Alta 17; mains €13-18; ⊙ 1.30-4pm & 8.30pm-midnight Wed-Sun, 8.30pm-midnight Mon & Tue; Ⓜ La Latina) serves great tapas and desserts by the master chocolatier Oriol Balaguer.

Plaza Mayor & Royal Madrid

For *bacalao* (cod), Casa Labra (Map p80; ☑ 91 532 14 05; www.casalabra.es; Calle de Tetuán 11; tapas from €0.90; ⊙ 9.30am-3.30pm & 5.30-11pm; Ⓜ Sol) has been around since 1860 and was a favourite of the poet Federico García Lorca. However, many *madrileños* wouldn't eat *bacalao* anywhere except Casa Revuelta (p107), clinched by the fact that the owner painstakingly extracts every fish bone in the morning.

Sol, Santa Ana & Huertas

In Huertas, La Casa del Abuelo (Map p80; ☑ 91 000 01 33; www.lacasadelabuelo.es; Calle de la Victoria 12; raciones from €9.60; ⊙ noon-midnight Sun-Thu, noon-1am Fri & Sat; Ⓜ Sol) is

be in Chamberí, it's worth a trip across town to this casual bar-restaurant that offers outstanding rice dishes, including paella. The quality is high and prices are among the cheapest in town. Start with *almejas a la marinera* (baby clams) and follow it up with *paella de marisco* (seafood paella) for the full experience. As always in such places, you'll need two people to make up an order.

★ DiverXo   MODERN SPANISH €€€
(☑ 915 70 07 66; diverxo.com; Calle Pensamiento 28; mains €70-90, set menus €95-140; ⊙ 2-3.30pm & 9-10.30pm Tue-Sat, closed 3 weeks in Aug; Ⓜ Cuzco) Madrid's only three-Michelín-starred restaurant, DiverXo in northern Madrid is one of Spain's true culinary indulgences. Chef David Muñoz effortlessly and creatively combines world flavours with those closer to home and the result is an exquisite array of tastes. As always in such places, we recommend that you order one of the *menús de degustación* (tast-

ing menus) and that you reserve your table months in advance.

★ Sergi Arola
Gastro   CONTEMPORARY SPANISH €€€
(Map p94; ☑ 91 310 21 69; www.sergiarola.es; Calle de Zurbano 31; mains €50-58, set menus €105-135; ⊙ 2-3.30pm & 9-11.30pm Tue-Sat; Ⓜ Alonso Martínez) Sergi Arola, a stellar Catalan acolyte of the world-renowned chef Ferran Adrià, runs this highly personalised temple to all that's innovative in Spanish gastronomy. The menus change with the seasons and you pay for the privilege of eating here. But this is culinary indulgence at its finest, the sort of place where creativity, presentation and taste are everything. And oh, what tastes... With just 26 seats, booking well in advance is necessary.

★ Santceloni   CATALAN €€€
(☑ 91 210 88 40; www.restaurantesantceloni.com; Paseo de la Castellana 57; mains €44-71, set menus

famous for *gambas a la plancha* (grilled prawns) or *gambas al ajillo* (prawns sizzling in garlic on little ceramic plates) and a *chato* (small glass) of the heavy, sweet El Abuelo red wine. For *patatas bravas* (fried potatoes lathered in a spicy tomato sauce), Las Bravas (Map p80; ☑ 91 522 85 81; www.lasbravas.com; Callejón de Álvarez Gato 3; raciones €3.55-10; ◷ 12.30-4.30pm & 7.30pm-12.30am; Ⓜ Sol, Sevilla) is the place. Another good choice down the bottom of the Huertas hill is Los Gatos (Map p80; ☑ 91 429 30 67; Calle de Jesús 2; tapas from €3.50; ◷ 11am-1am Sun-Thu, 11am-2am Fri & Sat; Ⓜ Antón Martín) with eclectic decor and terrific canapés. Ramiro's Tapas Wine Bar (p109) is another fine choice.

El Retiro, the Art Museums & Salamanca

Along the Paseo del Prado, there's only one choice for tapas and it's one of Madrid's best: Estado Puro (p110). In Salamanca, Biotza (Map p94; www.biotzarestaurante.com; Calle de Claudio Coello 27; cold/hot pintxos €2.80/3.40, raciones from €6, set menus from €17.50; ◷ 9am-2am Mon-Sat; Ⓜ Serrano) offers creative Basque *pintxos* in stylish surrounds, while La Colonial de Goya (p110) serves up some of Madrid's best canapés.

Chueca

Chueca is another stellar tapas *barrio*. Don't miss Bocaito (Map p80; ☑ 91 532 12 19; www.bocaito.com; Calle de la Libertad 4-6; tapas from €3.50, mains €10-29; ◷ 1-4pm & 8.30pm-midnight Mon-Fri, 8.30pm-midnight Sat; Ⓜ Chueca, Sevilla), another purveyor of Andalucian *jamón* (ham) and seafood and a favourite haunt of film-maker Pedro Almodóvar. Bodega de La Ardosa (Map p96; ☑ 91 521 49 79; Calle de Colón 13; tapas & raciones €3.50-11; ◷ 8.30am-2am Mon-Fri, 12.45pm-2.30am Sat & Sun; Ⓜ Tribunal) is extremely popular for its *salmorejo* (cold, tomato-based soup), *croquetas*, *patatas bravas* and *tortilla de patatas*, while Casa Julio (Map p96; ☑ 91 522 72 74; Calle de la Madera 37; 6/12 croquetas €5/10; ◷ 9.30am-3.30pm & 6.30pm-midnight Mon-Sat, closed Aug; Ⓜ Tribunal) is widely touted as the home of Madrid's best *croquetas*. Other brilliant choices include Le Cabrera (Map p94; ☑ 91 319 94 57; www.lecabrera.com; Calle de Bárbara de Braganza 2; tapas €3-22, caviar €85; ◷ 1.30-4pm & 8.30pm-midnight Mon-Sat, 1.30-4pm Sun; Ⓜ Colón, Alonso Martínez) and Baco y Beto (Map p96; ☑ 91 522 84 41; Calle de Pelayo 24; tapas from €4; ◷ 8.30-11.30pm Mon-Fri, 1-4pm & 8.30pm-midnight Sat; Ⓜ Chueca).

€150-180; ◷ 2-4pm & 9-11pm Mon-Fri, 9-11pm Sat, closed Aug; Ⓜ Gregorio Marañón) The Michelin-starred Santceloni is one of Madrid's best restaurants, with luxury decor that's the work of star interior designer Pascual Ortega, and nouvelle cuisine from the kitchen of master chef Óscar Velasco. Each dish is an exquisite work of art and the menu changes with the seasons, but we'd recommend one of the *menús gastronómicos* to really sample the breadth of surprising tastes on offer.

Zalacaín   BASQUE, NAVARRAN €€€
(☑ 91 561 48 40; www.restaurantezalacain.com; Calle de Álvarez de Baena 4; mains €27-50, set menu €106; ◷ 1.15-4pm & 9pm-midnight Mon-Fri, 9pm-midnight Sat, closed Aug; Ⓜ Gregorio Marañón) Where most other fine-dining experiences centre on innovation, Zalacaín is a bastion of tradition, with a refined air and a loyal following among Spain's great and good. Everyone who's anyone in Madrid, from the

king down, has eaten here since the doors opened in 1973; it was the first restaurant in Spain to receive three Michelin stars and still has one.

The pig's trotters filled with mushrooms and lamb is a house speciality, as is the lobster salad. The wine list is purported to be one of the best in the city (it stocks an estimated 35,000 bottles with 800 different varieties). You should certainly dress to impress (men will need a tie and a jacket).

🍷 Drinking & Nightlife

To get an idea of how much *madrileños* like to go out and have a good time, consider one simple statistic: Madrid has more bars than any city in the world – six, in fact, for every 100 inhabitants.

No *barrio* in Madrid is without a decent club or disco, but the most popular dance spots are in the centre. Don't expect the dance clubs or *discotecas* to really get going until after 1am; some won't even bat an eyelid until 3am, when bars elsewhere have closed.

Club prices vary widely, depending on the time of night you enter, the way you're dressed and the number of people inside. The standard admission fee is €12, which usually includes the first drink, although megaclubs and swankier places charge a few euros more. Even those that let you in free will play catch-up with hefty prices for drinks, so don't plan your night around looking for the cheapest ticket.

Plaza Mayor & Royal Madrid

Old taverns and the odd hidden gem rub shoulders in Madrid's centre. As a general rule, the further you stray from Plaza Mayor, the more prices drop and the fewer tourists you'll see.

Chocolatería de San Ginés
CAFE

(Map p72; Pasadizo de San Ginés 5; ⊘24hr; ⓂSol) One of the grand icons of the Madrid night, this *chocolate con churros* (Spanish donuts with chocolate) cafe sees a sprinkling of tourists throughout the day, but locals pack it out in their search for sustenance on their way home from a nightclub sometime close to dawn. Only in Madrid...

Café del Real
BAR, CAFE

(Map p72; Plaza de Isabel II 2; ⊘8am-1am Mon-Thu, 8am-2:30am Fri, 9am-2:30am Sat, 10am-11:30pm Sun; ⓂÓpera) A cafe and cocktail bar in equal parts, this intimate little place serves up creative coffees and a few cocktails to the soundtrack of chill-out music. The best seats are upstairs, where the low ceilings, wooden beams and leather chairs are a great place to pass an afternoon with friends.

Chocolatería Valor
CAFE

(Map p72; www.chocolateriasvalor.es; Postigo de San Martín; ⊘9am-10.30pm Sun, 8am-10.30pm Mon-Thu, 8am-1am Fri, 9am-1am Sat; ⓂCallao) It may be Madrid tradition to indulge in *chocolate con churros* around sunrise on your way home from a nightclub, but for everyone else who prefers a more reasonable hour, this is possibly the best *chocolatería* in town. Our favourite chocolate variety has to be *cuatro sentidos de chocolate* (four senses of chocolate; €7.95), but we'd happily try everything on the menu to make sure.

Teatro Joy Eslava
CLUB

(Joy Madrid; Map p72; ☑91 366 37 33; www.joy-eslava.com; Calle del Arenal 11; admission €12-15;

⊘11.30pm-6am; ⓂSol) The only things guaranteed at this grand old Madrid dance club (housed in a 19th-century theatre) are a crowd and the fact that it'll be open (it claims to have operated every single day for the past 31 years). Throw in occasional live acts and cabaret-style performances on stage and it's a point of reference for Madrid's professional party crowd.

Charada
CLUB

(Map p72; www.charada.es; Calle de la Bola 13; admission €12; ⊘midnight-6am Fri & Sat; ⓂSanto Domingo) Charada took the Madrid nightlife scene by storm in 2009 and has since settled back into a reliable regular on the Madrid clubbing scene. Its two rooms (one red, one black) are New York chic (with no hint of the building's former existence as a brothel). The name for Friday night sessions (El Fabuloso Club) says it all really.

La Latina & Lavapiés

Most nights (and Sunday afternoons), crowds of happy *madrileños* hop from bar to bar across La Latina. This is a *barrio* beloved by discerning 20- and 30-something urban sophisticates who ensure there's little room to move in the good places and the bad ones don't survive long. The crowd is a little more diverse on Sundays as hordes fan out from El Rastro. Most of the action takes place along Calle de la Cava Baja (where the dividing line between drinking and tapas bars is decidedly blurred), the western end of Calle del Almendro and Plaza de la Paja. Working-class, multicultural Lavapiés is completely different – think quirky bars brimming with personality that draw an alternative, often bohemian crowd. Not everyone loves Lavapiés, but we do.

Gau&Café
CAFE

(www.gaucafe.com; Calle de Tribulete 14, 4th fl; ⊘11am-midnight Mon-Fri, 1.30pm-midnight Sat; ⓂLavapiés) Decoration that's light and airy, with pop-art posters of Audrey Hepburn and James Bond. A large terrace with views over the Lavapiés rooftops. A stunning backdrop of a ruined church atop which the cafe sits. With so much else going for it, it almost seems incidental that it also serves great teas, coffees and snacks (and meals). The cafe is around 300m southwest of Plaza de Lavapiés along Calle de Tribulete; look for the glass doors.

Delic
BAR, CAFE

(Map p77; www.delic.es; Costanilla de San Andrés 14; ⏰11:30am-midnight Mon-Fri, 1:30pm-midnight Sat; Ⓜ La Latina) We could go on for hours about this long-standing cafe-bar, but we'll reduce it to its most basic elements: nursing an exceptionally good mojito (€8) or three on a warm summer's evening at Delic's outdoor tables on one of Madrid's prettiest plazas is one of life's great pleasures. Bliss.

Due to local licensing restrictions, the outdoor tables close two hours before closing time, whereafter the intimate interior is almost as good. Its new shop, a few doors up, is a treasure trove of interesting homewares and lifestyle knick-knacks.

La Escalera de Jacob
COCKTAIL BAR

(www.laescaleradejacob.es; Calle de Lavapiés 9; concerts from €6; ⏰7pm-2am Mon-Fri, 10am-2am Sat & Sun; Ⓜ Antón Martín, Tirso de Molina) As much a cocktail bar as a live-music venue or theatre, 'Jacob's Ladder' is one of Madrid's most original stages. Magicians, storytellers, children's theatre, live jazz and other genres are all part of the mix. This alternative slant on life makes for some terrific live performances.

Regardless of what's on, it's worth stopping by here for creative cocktails that you won't find anywhere else – the *fray aguacate* (Frangelico, vodka, honey, avocado and vanilla) should give you an idea of how far they go.

Bonanno
WINE BAR

(Map p77; ✆91 366 68 86; Plaza del Humilladero 4; ⏰noon-2am; Ⓜ La Latina) If much of Madrid's nightlife starts too late for your liking, Bonanno could be for you. It made its name as a cocktail bar, but many people come here for the great wines and it's usually full of young professionals from early evening onwards. Be prepared to snuggle up close to those around you if you want a spot at the bar.

Café del Nuncio
BAR, CAFE

(Map p77; Calle de Segovia 9; ⏰noon-2am Sun-Thu, to 3am Fri & Sat; Ⓜ La Latina) Café del Nuncio straggles down a laneway to Calle de Segovia. You can drink on one of several cosy levels inside or, better still, in summer enjoy the outdoor seating that one local reviewer likened to a slice of Rome. By day it's an old-world cafe, but by night it's one of the best bars in the *barrio*.

Taberna Tempranillo
WINE BAR

(Map p77; Calle de la Cava Baja 38; ⏰1-3.30pm & 8pm-midnight Tue-Sun, 8pm-midnight Mon; Ⓜ La Latina) You could come here for the tapas, but we recommend Taberna Tempranillo primarily for its wines, of which it has a selection that puts many Spanish bars to shame, and many are sold by the glass. It's not a late-night place, but it's always packed in the early evening and on Sundays after El Rastro.

El Viajero
BAR

(Map p77; ✆91 366 90 64; www.elviajeromadrid.com; Plaza de la Cebada 11; ⏰5pm-2am Tue-Fri, noon-2.30am Sat, noon-midnight Sun; Ⓜ La Latina) The undoubted highlight of this landmark of La Latina nights is the rooftop *terraza* (open-air bar), which boasts fine views down onto the thronging streets. When the weather's warm, it's nigh on impossible to get a table. Our secret? It often closes the *terraza* around 8pm to spruce it up a little; you should be ready to pounce when it reopens and thereafter guard your table with your life.

🍷 Sol, Santa Ana & Huertas

Huertas comes into its own after dark and stays that way until close to sunrise. Bars are everywhere, from Sol down to the Paseo del Prado hinterland, but it's in Plaza de Santa Ana and along Calle de las Huertas that most of the action is concentrated.

★ La Venencia
BAR

(Map p80; ✆91 429 73 13; Calle de Echegaray 7; ⏰1-3.30pm & 7.30pm-1.30am; Ⓜ Sol, Sevilla) La Venencia is a *barrio* classic, with fine sherry from Sanlúcar and manzanilla from Jeréz poured straight from the dusty wooden barrels, accompanied by a small selection of tapas with an Andalucian bent. Otherwise, there's no music, no flashy decorations; it's all about you, your *fino* (sherry) and your friends. As one reviewer put it, it's 'a classic among classics'.

Tartân Roof
LOUNGE BAR

(La Azotea; Map p80; www.azoteadelcirculo.com; Calle Marqués de Casa Riera 2; admission €3; ⏰9am-2am Mon-Thu, 9am-2.30am Fri, 11am-2.30am Sat & Sun) Order a cocktail, then lie down on the cushions and admire the view from this fabulous rooftop terrace. It's a brilliant place to chill out with the views at their best close to sunset.

El Imperfecto
COCKTAIL BAR

(Map p80; Plaza de Matute 2; ⏰3pm-2am Mon-Thu, to 2.30am Fri & Sat; Ⓜ Antón Martín) Its name

Locals' Madrid

More than most other Spanish cities, Madrid can take time to get under your skin, but once it does it rewards your patience a thousand times over. A little local knowledge is the key.

A Very Madrid Sunday

Madrileños like nothing better than Sunday morning at El Rastro flea market (p78), followed by tapas and vermouth around 1pm along Calle de la Cava Baja (p112) in La Latina. Then it's across town to the Parque del Buen Retiro (p89) where, east of the lake, crowds gather, drums start to beat and people begin to dance as the sun nears the horizon

Food Icons

In this food-obsessed city you'll find countless treasures that capture the city's culinary essence. The Mercado de San Miguel (p107) epitomises the irresistible buzz that goes with eating here. Nearby Casa Revuelta (p107) is not much to look at but it's similarly adored by locals.

1. El Rastro flea market (p78) 2. Parque del Buen Retiro (p89) 3. Mercado de San Miguel (p107), a tapas bar

Informal Flamenco

Madrid has many outstanding flamenco stages but most are pretty formal affairs. While upstairs at Candela (p125) fits this description, the downstairs bar is for true aficionados and it's a more spontaneous proposition. Sometimes it works, sometimes it doesn't, but therein lies the magic of flamenco.

Barrio Life

North of the centre, the locals reclaim their city. Plaza de Olavide (p94) is the heart and soul of Chamberí and offers an authentic slice of local life. It's not that there's much to see here: instead, the agreeable hum of local life, watched from the outdoor tables that encircle the plaza, is a fascinating window on how locals experience Madrid.

notwithstanding, the 'Imperfect One' is our ideal Huertas bar, with live jazz most Tuesdays at 9pm and a drinks menu as long as a saxophone, ranging from cocktails (€7, or two mojitos for €10) and spirits to milkshakes, teas and creative coffees. Its pina colada is one of the best we've tasted and the atmosphere is agreeably buzzy yet chilled.

The Roof
COCKTAIL BAR

(Map p80; ☎91 701 60 20; www.memadrid.com; Plaza de Santa Ana 14; admission €25; ⊙9pm-1.30am Mon-Thu, 8pm-3am Fri & Sat; Ⓜ Antón Martín, Sol) High above the Plaza de Santa Ana, this sybaritic, open-air (7th floor) cocktail bar has terrific views over Madrid's rooftops. The high admission price announces straight away that riff-raff are not welcome here – this is a place for sophisticates, with chill-out areas strewn with cushions, funky DJs and a dress policy designed to sort out the classy from the wannabes.

Taberna Alhambra
BAR

(Map p80; Calle de la Victoria 9; ⊙11am-1.30am Sun-Wed, to 2am Thu, to 2.30am Fri & Sat; Ⓜ Sol) There can be a certain sameness about the bars between Sol and Huertas, which is why this fine old *taberna* (tavern) stands out. The striking facade and exquisite tile work of the interior are quite beautiful; however, this place is anything but stuffy and the feel is cool, casual and busy. It serves tapas and, later at night, there are some fine flamenco tunes.

Cervecería Alemana
BAR

(Map p80; Plaza de Santa Ana 6; ⊙11am-12.30am Sun-Thu, to 2am Fri & Sat, closed Aug; Ⓜ Antón Martín, Sol) If you've only got time to stop at one bar on Plaza Santa Ana, let it be this classic *cervecería* (beer bar), renowned for its cold, frothy beers and a wider selection of Spanish beers than is the norm. It's fine inside, but snaffle a table outside in the plaza on a summer's evening and you won't be giving it up without a fight.

This was one of Hemingway's haunts, and neither the wood-lined bar nor the bow-tied waiters have changed much since his day.

Taberna La Dolores
BAR

(Map p80; ☎91 429 22 43; Plaza de Jesús 4; ⊙11am-1am Sun-Thu, to 2am Fri & Sat; Ⓜ Antón Martín) Old bottles and beer mugs line the shelves behind the bar at this Madrid institution, known for its blue-and-white tiled exterior and for a 30-something crowd that often includes the odd *famoso* (celebrity) or

two. You get good house wine, great anchovies and what Spaniards like to call 'well-poured beer'.

Viva Madrid
BAR

(Map p80; www.grupotartufo.es/vivamadrid; Calle de Manuel Fernández y González 7; ⊙noon-midnight Mon-Thu, noon-2am Fri & Sat; Ⓜ Antón Martín, Sol) The tiled facade of Viva Madrid is one of Madrid's most recognisable and it's an essential landmark on the Huertas nightlife scene. It's packed to the rafters on weekends, and you come here in part for fine mojitos and also for the casual, friendly atmosphere. The recently improved tapas offerings are another reason to stop by.

Kapital
CLUB

(Map p84; ☎91 420 29 06; www.grupo-kapital.com; Calle de Atocha 125; admission from €18; ⊙5.30-10.30pm & midnight-6am Fri & Sat, midnight-6am Thu & Sun; Ⓜ Atocha) One of the most famous megaclubs in Madrid, this massive, seven-storey nightclub has something for everyone: from cocktail bars and dance music to karaoke, salsa, hip hop and more chilled spaces for R&B and soul, as well as an area devoted to 'Made in Spain' music.

It's such a big place that a cross section of Madrid society (VIPs and the Real Madrid set love this place) hangs out here without ever getting in each other's way.

Coco
NIGHTCLUB

(Map p80; www.cocomadrid.com; Calle Alcalá 20; ⊙midnight-6am Fri-Sun; Ⓜ Sevilla) The designer decor is stunning and there's three nights of dancing with a sophisticated crowd. The music is nothing too challenging – the kind of music we all secretly love to dance to.

🍸 Salamanca

Salamanca is the land of the beautiful people and it's all about gloss and glamour: heels for her and hair gel for him. As you glide through the *pijos* (beautiful people or yuppies), keep your eyes peeled for Real Madrid players and celebrities.

Charly's Bar
COCKTAIL BAR

(Map p94; ☎91 435 69 30; Calle de Jorge Juan 22, 1st fl; ⊙2pm-2.30am Mon-Sat; Ⓜ Velázquez) More than 40 creative cocktails from one of Madrid's finest, celebrity bartender Carlos Moreno, mean anything from an-anything-but-humble daiquiri to daring combinations that change as each new idea occurs to Carlos. It's above Restaurante La Moraga.

Gabana 1800
CLUB

(Map p94; ☑ 91 575 18 46; www.gabana.es; Calle Velázquez 6; admission €15; ☺ midnight-5.30am Wed-Sat; Ⓜ Retiro) With its upmarket crowd that invariably includes a few *famosos,* Gabana 1800 is very Salamanca. That this place has lasted the distance where others haven't owes much to a fabulous array of drinks, a rotating cast of first-class DJs and a fairly discerning door policy – dress to impress.

Serrano 41
CLUB

(Map p94; ☑ 91 578 18 65; www.serrano41.com; Calle de Serrano 41; admission €15; ☺ 11pm-5.30am Wed-Sun; Ⓜ Serrano) If bullfighters, Real Madrid stars and other A-listers can't drag themselves away from Salamanca, chances are that you'll find them here. Danceable pop and house dominate and, as you'd imagine, the door policy is stricter than most. The outdoor terrace opens in late May and is *very* cool until it closes in mid-September.

🍸 Malasaña & Chueca

Drinking in Malasaña and Chueca is like a journey through Madrid's multifaceted past. Around the Glorieta de Bilbao and along the Paseo de los Recoletos you encounter stately old literary cafes that revel in their grandeur and late-19th-century ambience. Throughout Malasaña, rockers nostalgic for the hedonistic Madrid of the 1970s and '80s will find ample bars to indulge their memories. At the same time, across both *barrios,* but especially in gay-focussed Chueca and away to the west in Conde Duque, modern Madrid is very much on show, with chill-out spaces and swanky, sophisticated cocktail bars.

Museo Chicote
COCKTAIL BAR

(Map p80; www.museo-chicote.com; Gran Vía 12; ☺ 5pm-3am Mon-Thu, to 3.30am Fri & Sat; Ⓜ Gran Vía) The founder of this Madrid landmark (complete with 1930s-era interior) is said to have invented more than 100 cocktails, which the likes of Hemingway, Ava Gardner, Grace Kelly, Sophia Loren and Frank Sinatra have all enjoyed at one time or another. It's at its best after midnight, when a lounge atmosphere takes over, couples cuddle on the curved benches and some of the city's best DJs do their stuff.

Café Comercial
CAFE

(Map p96; Glorieta de Bilbao 7; ☺ 7.30am-midnight Mon-Thu, 7.30am-2am Fri, 8.30am-2am Sat, 9am-midnight Sun; @ 🛜; Ⓜ Bilbao) This glorious old Madrid cafe proudly fights a rearguard action against progress with heavy leather seats, abundant marble and old-style waiters. It dates back to 1887 and has changed little since those days, although the clientele has broadened to include just about anyone, from writers and their laptops to old men playing chess.

La Terraza de Óscar
LOUNGE BAR

(Map p96; Plaza de Vázquez de Mella 12; ☺ 5pm-2am Mon-Thu, 4pm-3am Fri-Sun; Ⓜ Gran Vía) Occupying one of the stunning rooftop terraces (this one with a small swimming pool) atop Hotel Óscar (p106), this chilled space with gorgeous skyline views has become a cause *célèbre* among A-list celebrities.

★ La Realidad
BAR

(Map p96; ☑ 91 532 80 55; Calle de la Corredera Baja de San Pablo 51; ☺ 9.30am-1.30am Sun-Thu, to 2.30am Fri & Sat; Ⓜ Tribunal) Great place. Part hip cafe, part funky bar to start your Malasaña night, at once bohemian and yet appealing enough to draw the mainstream punter, La Realidad (The Reality) serves up fine tapas to accompany its equally fine cocktails. It also does brunch, displays contemporary art, has weird-and-wonderful furnishings and generally proves that it *is* possible to be all things to all people.

El Jardín Secreto
BAR, CAFE

(Map p96; www.eljardinsecretomadrid; Calle del Conde Duque 2; ☺ 5.30pm-12.30am Sun-Thu, 6.30pm-2.30am Fri & Sat; Ⓜ Plaza de España) Lit

---

LA HORA DEL VERMUT

Sunday. One o'clock in the afternoon. A dark bar off Calle de la Cava Baja. In any civilised city the bar would be shut tight, but in Madrid the place is packed because it's *la hora del vermut* (vermouth hour), a long-standing tradition whereby friends and families head out for a quick apéritif before Sunday lunch. Sometimes referred to as *ir de Rastro* (going to the Rastro) because so many of the traditional vermouth bars are in and around El Rastro market, this Sunday tradition is deeply ingrained in *madrileño* culture. Some of the best bars for vermouth are along La Latina's Calle de la Cava Baja, while Casa Alberto (p109) is another legendary part of this fine tradition.

MADRID DRINKING & NIGHTLIFE

CLANDESTINE BARS

A small but growing trend of the Madrid night is that of *bares clandestinos* (clandestine bars). While it may sound vaguely illicit, it's all above board and involves places that are shops by days morphing effortlessly into cool bars after dark. Our favourite is **Kikekeller** (Map p96; www.kikekeller.com; Calle de la Corredera Baja de San Pedro 17; ⊘ shop 5-9pm Mon, noon-3pm & 5-9pm Tue-Fri, 12.30-9.30pm Sat; bar 7pm-2.30am Thu-Sat; Ⓜ Callao), an avant-garde furniture and interior decoration shop a short distance north of Gran Vía and where they can't even wait for the shop to close on Saturday before opening the bar. It's one of the more original places to enjoy the Madrid night.

by Spanish designer candles, draped in organza from India and serving up chocolates from the Caribbean, 'The Secret Garden' ranks among our favourite drinking corners in Conde Duque, at the western end of Malasaña. It serves milkshakes, teas, cocktails and everything in between. It's at its best on a summer's evening, but the atmosphere never misses a beat, with a loyal, young professional crowd.

Café Belén
BAR

(Map p96; Calle de Belén 5; ⊘ 3.30pm-2am Sun-Thu, 3.30pm-3.30am Fri & Sat; Ⓜ Chueca) Café Belén is cool in all the right places – lounge and chill-out music, dim lighting, a great range of drinks (the mojitos are especially good) and a low-key crowd that's the height of casual sophistication. In short, it's one of our favourite Chueca watering holes.

Gorila
BAR

(Map p96; ☑ 91 007 08 88; Calle de la Corredera Baja de San Pablo 47; ⊘ 10am-1am; Ⓜ Tribunal) One of those multi-purpose Malasaña bars that's as good for breakfast as for a night-time beer or cocktail, split-level Gorila is watched over by a giant painted gorilla and populated by a casual Malasaña crowd.

Lolina Vintage Café
CAFE

(Map p96; www.lolinacafe.com; Calle del Espíritu Santo 9; ⊘ 10am-12.30am Sun-Thu, 10am-2am Fri & Sat; Ⓜ Tribunal) Lolina seems to have captured the essence of the *barrio* in one small space. With a studied retro look (comfy old-style chairs and sofas, gilded mirrors and 1970s-era wallpaper), it confirms that the new Malasaña is not unlike the old. It's low-key and full from breakfast to closing time, catering to every taste from salads to cocktails.

La Vía Láctea
BAR, CLUB

(Map p96; Calle de Velarde 18; ⊘ 8pm-3am Sun-Thu, 8pm-3.30am Fri & Sat; Ⓜ Tribunal) A living, breathing and delightfully grungy relic of *la*

movida, La Vía Láctea remains a Malasaña favourite for a mixed, informal crowd that seems to live for the 1980s. The music ranges across rock, pop, garage, rockabilly and indie. There are plenty of drinks to choose from, and by late Saturday night anything goes. Expect long queues to get in on weekends.

Café-Restaurante El Espejo
CAFE

(Map p94; Paseo de los Recoletos 31; ⊘ 8am-midnight; Ⓜ Colón) Once a haunt of writers and intellectuals, this architectural gem blends Modernista and art-deco styles, and its interior could overwhelm you with all the mirrors, chandeliers and bow-tied service of another era. The atmosphere is suitably quiet and refined, although our favourite corner is the elegant glass pavilion out on the Paseo de los Recoletos, where the outdoor tables are hugely popular in summer.

Fábrica Maravillas
BAR, BREWERY

(Map p96; ☑ 915 21 87 53; fabricamaravillas.com; Calle de Valverde 29; ⊘ 6pm-midnight Mon-Fri, 12.30pm-midnight Sat & Sun; Ⓜ Tribunal, Gran Vía) Spain has taken its time in getting behind the worldwide trend of boutique or artisane beers, but it's finally starting to happen. The finest example in Madrid is Fábrica Maravillas, a microbrewery known for its 'Malasaña Ale'.

Café Pepe Botella
CAFE, BAR

(Map p96; Calle de San Andrés 12; ⊘ 10am-2am Mon-Thu, 10am-2.30am Fri & Sat, 11am-2am Sun; ☏; Ⓜ Bilbao, Tribunal) Pepe Botella has hit on a fine if simple formula for success. As good around midnight as it is in the afternoon, when its wi-fi access draws the laptop-toting crowd, it's a classy bar with green velvet benches, marble-topped tables and old photos and mirrors covering the walls.

Areia
LOUNGE

(Map p96; www.areiachillout.com; Calle de Hortaleza 92; ⊘ 2pm-3am Mon-Fri, 1pm-3am Sat &

Sun; M Chueca, Alonso Martínez) The ultimate lounge bar by day (cushions, chill-out music and dark secluded corners, where you can hear yourself talk or even canoodle quietly), this place is equally enjoyable by night. That's when groovy DJs take over (from 11pm Sunday to Wednesday, and from 9pm the rest of the week) with deep and chill house, nu jazz, bossa and electronica. It's cool, funky and low-key all at once.

Gran Café de Gijón
CAFE

(Map p94; www.cafegijon.com; Paseo de los Recoletos 21; ⊙ 7am-1.30am; M Chueca, Banco de España) This graceful old cafe has been serving coffee and meals since 1888 and has long been a favourite with Madrid's literati for a drink or a meal – *all* of Spain's great 20th-century literary figures came here for coffee and *tertulias* (literary discussions). You'll find yourself among intellectuals, conservative Franco diehards and young *madrileños* looking for a quiet drink.

Ojalá Awareness Club
LOUNGE

(Map p96; Calle de San Andrés 1; ⊙ 9am-1am Mon-Wed, 9am-1.30am Thu, 9am-2am Fri, 11am-2am Sat, 11am-1am Sun; M Tribunal) Yes, you eat well here, but we love it first and foremost for a drink (especially a daiquiri) at any time of day. Its lime-green colour scheme, zany lighting and hip, cafe-style ambience make it an extremely cool place to hang out, but the sandy floor and cushions downstairs (open from 6pm) take chilled to a whole new level.

Martínez Bar
COCKTAIL BAR

(Map p96; ☑ 91 080 26 83; Calle del Barco 4; ⊙ 5pm-2.30am Mon-Fri, 1pm-2.30am Sat, 1pm-1am Sun; M Gran Vía) This fine old cocktail bar re-creates a 1920s-era ambience with plenty of wood-panelling. The gin and tonics are excellent and the mojito-with-a-free-tapa for €5 from Monday to Thursday is outrageous value.

Café Manuela
CAFE

(Map p96; Calle de San Vicente Ferrer 29; ⊙ 4pm-2am Sun-Thu, 4pm-2.30am Fri & Sat; M Tribunal) This graciously restored throwback to the 1950s is a refuge from Malasaña's gritty streets. There's a luminous quality to it when you come in out of the night and, like so many Madrid cafes, it's a surprisingly multifaceted space, serving cocktails, delicious milkshakes and offering board games atop the marble tables in the unlikely event that you get bored.

T-Club
CLUB

(Map p96; www.tclub.es; Calle de Barceló 11; ⊙ midnight-6am Wed-Sat; M Tribunal) Once known as Pachá and a longstanding icon of the Madrid night, the odd celebrity turns up at this Ibiza-style megaclub and gets all sweaty dancing to house and related genres across the three dance floors.

Tupperware
BAR, CLUB

(Map p96; ☑ 91 446 42 04; Calle de la Corredera Alta de San Pablo 26; ⊙ 9pm-3am Mon-Wed, 8pm-3.30am Thu-Sat, 8pm-3am Sun; M Tribunal) A classic of the Malasaña night and prime candidate for the bar that best catches the *barrio*'s enduring *rockero* spirit. Tupperware draws a 30-something crowd, spins indie rock with a bit of soul and classics from the '60s and '70s, and generally revels in kitsch (eyeballs stuck to the ceiling, and plastic TVs with action-figure dioramas lined up behind the bar). By the way, locals pronounce it 'Tupper-warry'.

☆ Entertainment

All of the following publications and websites provide comprehensive, updated listings of showings at Madrid's theatres, cinemas and concert halls:

EsMadrid Magazine (www.esmadrid.com) Monthly tourist-office listings for concerts and other performances; available at tourist offices, some hotels and online.

CHUECA COCKTAIL BARS

Chueca has Madrid's richest concentration of sophisticated cocktail bars beloved by the city's A-list celebrities. In addition to Museo Chicote (p119), there's **Del Diego** (Map p80; ☑ 91 523 31 06; Calle de la Reina 12; ⊙ 7pm-3am Mon-Thu, to 3.30am Fri & Sat; M Gran Vía), where the decor blends old-world-cafe with New York style and there are 75 cocktails to choose from. Other places we highly recommend include old-world **Bar Cock** (Map p80; ☑ 91 532 28 26; www.barcock.com; Calle de la Reina 16; ⊙ 4pm-3am Mon-Fri, 7pm-3am Sat & Sun; M Gran Vía), where drinks prices double after 10pm, and achingly chic **Le Cabrera** (Map p94; ☑ 91 319 94 57; www.lecabrera.com; Calle de Bárbara de Braganza 2; ⊙ 4pm-2am Mon-Thu, 4pm-2.30am Fri, 1pm-2.30am Sat, 1.30pm-2am Sun; M Colón, Alonso Martínez).

Guía del Ocio (www.guiadelocio.com) Spanish-only weekly magazine that comes every Friday with *El País* newspaper.

In Madrid (www.in-madrid.com) Monthly English-language expat publication given out free (check the website for locations), with lots of information about what to see and do in town.

La Netro (www.lanetro.com/madrid) Comprehensive online guide to Madrid events.

Metropoli (www.elmundo.es/metropoli) *El Mundo's* Friday supplement magazine has information on the week's offerings.

Cinemas

Movie tickets at most cinemas are considerably cheaper (usually €3.90) on Wednesdays.

Cine Doré   CINEMA
(Map p80; ☑ 91 369 11 25; www.mcu.es/cine/MC/FE/CineDore/Programacion; Calle de Santa Isabel 3; tickets €2.50; ⊘ Tue-Sun; Ⓜ Antón Martín) The National Film Library offers fantastic classic and vanguard films.

Cinesa Proyecciones   CINEMA
(☑ 902 333231; www.cinesa.es; Calle de Fuencarral 136; tickets €3.90-10.50; Ⓜ Bilbao, Quevedo) Wonderful art-deco exterior; modern cinema within.

Cines Princesa   CINEMA
(☑ 902 229122, 91 541 41 00; www.cinesrenoir.com; Calle de la Princesa 3; tickets from €3.90-10; Ⓜ Plaza de España) Screens all kinds of original-version films, from Hollywood blockbusters to arty flicks.

LA ZARZUELA

What began in the late 17th century as a way to amuse King Felipe IV and his court has become Spain's own unique theatre style. With a light-hearted combination of music and dance, and a focus on everyday people's problems, *zarzuelas* quickly became popular in Madrid, which remains the genre's capital. Although you're likely to have trouble following the storyline (*zarzuelas* are notoriously full of local references and jokes), seeing a *zarzuela* gives an entertaining look into local culture. The best place to catch a show is the Teatro de la Zarzuela.

Yelmo Cineplex Ideal   CINEMA
(Map p80; ☑ 902 220922; www.yelmocines.es; Calle del Doctor Cortezo 6; tickets €9.20; Ⓜ Sol, Tirso de Molina) Close to Plaza Mayor; offers a wide selection of films.

Theatre & Dance

Madrid's theatre scene is a year-round affair. Most shows are in Spanish, but those who don't speak the language may still enjoy musicals or *zarzuela,* Spain's own singing and dancing version of musical theatre. Tickets for all shows start at around €10 and run up to around €50.

Compañía Nacional de Danza   DANCE
(www.cndanza.mcu.es) Under director José Carlos Martínez, this dynamic company performs worldwide and has won accolades for its innovation, marvellous technicality and style. The company, made up mostly of international dancers, performs original, contemporary pieces and is considered a leading player on the international dance scene.

Ballet Nacional de España   DANCE
(☑ 91 517 99 99; balletnacional.mcu.es) A classical company that's known for its unique mix of ballet and traditional Spanish styles, such as flamenco and *zarzuela*. When in Madrid, it's usually on stage at the Teatro Real or the Teatro de la Zarzuela.

Teatro de la Zarzuela   THEATRE
(Map p80; ☑ 91 524 54 00; teatrodelazarzuela.mcu.es; Calle de Jovellanos 4; tickets €5-50; ⊘ box office noon-6pm Mon-Fri, 3-6pm Sat & Sun; Ⓜ Banco de España, Sevilla) This theatre, built in 1856, is the premier place to see *zarzuela*. It also hosts a smattering of classical music and opera performances, as well as the cutting-edge Compañía Nacional de Danza.

Teatro Español   THEATRE
(Map p80; ☑ 91 360 14 84; www.teatroespanol.es; Calle del Príncipe 25; Ⓜ Sevilla, Sol, Antón Martín) This theatre, which fronts onto the Plaza de Santa Ana, has been here in one form or another since the 16th century and is still one of the best places to catch mainstream Spanish drama, from the works of Lope de Vega to more recent playwrights.

Teatros del Canal   THEATRE
(☑ 91 308 99 99; www.teatroscanal.org; Calle de Cea Bermúdez 1; Ⓜ Canal) A state-of-the-art theatre complex opened in 2009, Teatros del Canal hosts major theatre performances, as well as musical and dance concerts. It also

---

LOCAL KNOWLEDGE

MICROTHEATRE

It is one of the more innovating trends to sweep Madrid's live theatre scene. The *microteatro* (microtheatre) phenomenon takes performances out of more formal theatre settings and involves the performances of short theatrical works (some as short as 15 minutes) for tiny audiences in private homes, bars and other offbeat stages. Among the better examples are:

Microteatro por Dinero (www.teatropordinero.com)

La Casa de la Portera (lacasadelaportera.com)

La Pensión de las Pulgas (lacasadelaportera.com/la-pension-de-las-pulgas/)

---

runs numerous concerts during the Suma Flamenca (p101) festival in June.

Live Music

Madrid made its name as a live music city back in the 1980s, when drugs and rock music fuelled the decade-long fiesta known as *la movida madrileña*. While rock remains a Madrid mainstay and the doors of a handful of classic venues remain open, the live music scene is in rude health, covering every genre – flamenco and jazz are the star attractions – just about every night of the week. Many concert venues double as clubs where DJs follow the live acts, making it possible to start off the night with a great concert and stay on to party until late.

Madrid may not be the spiritual home of flamenco, and its big names may feel more at home in the atmospheric flamenco taverns of Andalucía, but Madrid remains one of Spain's premier flamenco stages.

Seeing flamenco in Madrid is, with some worthy exceptions, expensive – at the *tablaos* (restaurants where flamenco is performed) expect to pay €25 to €35 just to see the show. The admission price usually includes your first drink, but you pay extra for meals that, put simply, are rarely worth the money (up to €50 per person). For that reason, we suggest you eat elsewhere and simply pay for the show (after having bought tickets in advance), albeit on the understanding that you won't have a front-row seat. The other important thing to remember is that most of these shows are geared towards tourists. That's not to say that the quality isn't often top-notch. On the contrary, often it's magnificent, spine-tingling stuff. It's just that they sometimes lack the genuine, raw emotion of real flamenco.

In addition to checking the websites of individual clubs, a good website to find out what's happening is La Noche En Vivo (www.lanocheenvivo.com); click on 'Las Salas' for a list of venues.

For first-class flamenco, jazz and other musical genres in a more formal concert setting (usually the Auditorio Nacional de Música, p126), check out the website of the Centro Nacional de Difusión Musical (www.cndm.mcu.es).

Corral de la Morería   FLAMENCO
(Map p77; ☎91 365 84 46; www.corraldelamor eria.com; Calle de la Morería 17; admission incl drink €50, mains from €21, set menus €37.50-55; ☉7pm-12.15am, shows 9pm & 10.55pm; ⓂÓpera) This is one of the most prestigious flamenco stages in Madrid, with 50 years' experience as a leading flamenco venue and top performers most nights. The stage area has a rustic feel, and tables are pushed up close. The performances have a far better price: quality ratio than the meals.

★**Café Central**   JAZZ
(Map p80; ☎91 369 41 43; www.cafecentral madrid.com; Plaza del Ángel 10; admission €12-18; ☉12.30pm-2.30am Sun-Thu, 12.30pm-3.30am Fri & Sat; ⓂAntón Martín, Sol) In 2011, the respected jazz magazine *Down Beat* included this art-deco bar on the list of the world's best jazz clubs, the only place in Spain to earn the prestigious accolade (said by some to be the jazz equivalent of earning a Michelin star) and with well over 9000 gigs under its belt, it rarely misses a beat.

Big international names such as Chano Domínguez, Tal Farlow and Wynton Marsalis have all played here and you'll hear everything from Latin jazz and fusion to tango and classical jazz. Performers usually play here for a week and then move on, so getting tickets shouldn't be a problem (except on weekends). Shows start at 9pm and tickets go on sale from 6pm before the set starts.

★ **Sala El Sol**   LIVE MUSIC
(Map p80; ☎ 91 532 64 90; www.elsolmad.com;
Calle de los Jardines 3; admission incl drink €10,
concert tickets €8-25; ☺ midnight-5.30am Tue-Sat
Jul-Sep; Ⓜ Gran Vía) Madrid institutions don't
come any more beloved than Sala El Sol. It
opened in 1979, just in time for *la movida*,
and quickly established itself as a leading
stage for all the icons of the era. *La movida*
may have faded into history, but it lives on
at El Sol, where the music rocks and rolls,
while soul and funk also get a run.

It's a terrific venue and although most
concerts start at 11pm (despite the official
opening hours), some acts take to the stage
as early as 10pm. After the show, DJs spin
rock, fusion and electronica. Check the website for upcoming acts.

GAY & LESBIAN MADRID

Madrid is one of Europe's most gay-friendly cities. The heartbeat of gay Madrid is the
inner-city *barrio* of Chueca, where Madrid didn't just come out of the closet, but ripped
the doors off in the process. But even here the crowd is almost always mixed gay/
straight. The best time of all to be in town if you're gay or lesbian is around the last Saturday in June, for Madrid's gay and lesbian pride march, Día del Orgullo de Gays, Lesbianas y Transexuales (p103). An excellent place to stay is Hostal La Zona (p106).

Librería Berkana (Map p96; ☎ 91 522 55 99; www.libreriaberkana.com; Calle de Hortaleza
62; ☺ 10.30am-9pm Mon-Fri, 11.30am-9pm Sat, noon-2pm & 5-9pm Sun; Ⓜ Chueca) One of the
most important gay and lesbian bookshops in Madrid, Librería Berkana operates like
an unofficial information centre for gay Madrid; here you'll find the biweekly *Shanguide*,
jammed with listings and contact ads, as well as books, magazines and videos.

Mamá Inés (Map p96; www.mamaines.com; Calle de Hortaleza 22; ☺ 10am-2am Sun-Thu, to
3am Fri & Sat; Ⓜ Chueca) A gay meeting place with its low lights and low music, this cafe-
bar is where you'll hear the word on where the night's hotspot will be. There's a steady
stream of people coming and going throughout the day and they turn the lights down
low and crank up the music as evening turns into night.

Café Acuarela (Map p96; www.cafeacuarela.es; Calle de Gravina 10; ☺ 11am-2am Sun-Thu,
to 3am Fri & Sat; Ⓜ Chueca) A few steps up the hill from Plaza de Chueca and long a centrepiece of gay Madrid – a huge statue of a nude male angel guards the doorway – this
is an agreeable, dimly lit salon decorated with, among other things, religious icons. It's
ideal for quiet conversation and catching the weekend buzz as people plan their forays
into the more clamorous clubs in the vicinity.

Club 54 Studio (Map p96; www.studio54madrid.com; Calle de Barbieri 7; ☺ 11.30am-
3.30am Wed-Sun; Ⓜ Chueca) Modelled on the famous New York club Studio 54, this nightclub draws a predominantly gay crowd, but its target market is more upmarket than
many in the *barrio*. Unlike other Madrid nightclubs where paid dancers up on stage try
to get things moving, here they let the punters set the pace.

Liquid Madrid (Map p96; www.liquid.es; Calle de Barbieri 7; ☺ 8pm-3am Mon-Thu, to 3.30am
Fri & Sat; Ⓜ Chueca) An essential stop on any gay itinerary through Chueca, Liquid is a
little overwhelming with its multiple video screens and endless movement of people.

Why Not? (Map p96; www.whynotmadrid.com; Calle de San Bartolomé 7; admission €10;
☺ 10.30pm-6am; Ⓜ Chueca) Underground, narrow and packed with bodies, gay-friendly
Why Not? is the sort of place where nothing's left to the imagination (the gay and
straight crowd who come here are pretty amorous) and it's full nearly every night of the
week. Pop and top-40 music are the standard here. We're not huge fans of the bouncers
here but, once you get past them, it's all good fun.

Black & White (Map p96; www.discoblack-white.net; Calle de la Libertad 34; ☺ 10pm-5.30am
Sun-Thu, to 6am Fri & Sat; Ⓜ Chueca) People still talk about the opening party of Black &
White way back in 1982, and ever since it's been a pioneer of Chueca's gay nights. This
place is extravagantly gay with drag acts, male strippers and a refreshingly no-holds-
barred approach to life.

Las Tablas   FLAMENCO

(Map p72; ☎91 542 05 20; www.lastablasmadrid.
com; Plaza de España 9; admission incl drink €27;
◎8pm & 10pm; Ⓜ Plaza de España) Las Tablas has
a reputation for quality flamenco and reasonable prices; it could just be the best choice in
town. Most nights you'll see a classic flamenco
show, with plenty of throaty singing and soul-
baring dancing. Antonia Moya and Marisol
Navarro, leading lights in the flamenco world,
are regular performers here.

Casa Patas   FLAMENCO

(Map p80; ☎91 369 04 96; www.casapatas.com;
Calle de Cañizares 10; admission incl drink €34;
◎shows 10.30pm Mon-Thu, 9pm & midnight Fri &
Sat; Ⓜ Antón Martín, Tirso de Molina) One of the
top flamenco stages in Madrid, this *tablao*
offers flawless quality and serves as a good
introduction to the art. It's not the friendliest place in town, especially if you're only
here for the show, and you're likely to be
crammed in a little, but no one complains
about the standard of the performances.

Villa Rosa   FLAMENCO

(Map p80; ☎91 521 36 89; www.tablaoflamenco
villarosa.com; Plaza de Santa Ana 15; admission €32;
◎11pm-6am Mon-Sat, shows 8.30pm & 10.45pm
Sun-Thu, 8.30pm, 10.45pm & 12.15am Fri & Sat;
Ⓜ Sol) The extraordinary tiled facade (the
1928 work of Alfonso Romero, who was responsible for the tile work in Madrid's Plaza
de Toros) of this longstanding nightclub is a
tourist attraction in itself; the club even appeared in the Pedro Almodóvar film *Tacones
lejanos* (High Heels; 1991). It's been going
strong since 1914 and has recently returned
to its roots with top-notch performances.

Costello Café & Niteclub   LIVE MUSIC

(Map p80; www.costelloclub.com; Calle del Caballero de Gracia 10; admission €5-10; ◎8pm-3am Sun-
Wed, 6pm-3.30am Thu-Sat; Ⓜ Gran Vía) Very cool.
Costello Café & Niteclub weds smooth-as-
silk ambience to an innovative mix of pop,
rock and fusion in Warholesque surrounds.
There's live music at 9.30pm every night except Sundays, with resident and visiting DJs
keeping you on your feet until closing time
from Thursday to Saturday.

Las Carboneras   FLAMENCO

(Map p72; ☎91 542 86 77; www.tablaolascarbon
eras.com; Plaza del Conde de Miranda 1; admission
incl drink €33.40; ◎shows 8.30pm & 10.30pm
Mon-Thu, 8.30pm & 11pm Fri & Sat; Ⓜ Ópera, Sol,
La Latina) Like most of the *tablaos* around
town, this place sees far more tourists than

locals, but the quality is nonetheless unimpeachable. It's not the place for gritty, soul-
moving spontaneity, but it's still an excellent
introduction and one of the few places that
flamenco aficionados seem to have no com-
plaints about.

Torres Bermejas   FLAMENCO

(Map p80; ☎91 532 33 22; torresbermejas.com;
Calle de Mesonero Romanos 11; admission €35;
◎shows 9pm-midnight, doors open 8pm) For
decades this was the Madrid stage for flamenco legend Camarón de la Isla, and it's
once again a good place to see flamenco. The
atmosphere is aided by the extravagantly
tiled interior.

Cardamomo   FLAMENCO

(Map p80; ☎91 369 07 57; www.cardamomo.es;
Calle de Echegaray 15; admission incl drink €39;
◎10pm-3.30am, live shows 9pm Oct-May, 10pm
Jun-Sep; Ⓜ Sevilla) One of the better flamenco
stages in town, Cardamomo draws more
tourists than aficionados, but the flamenco
is top-notch.

Candela   BAR

(Map p80; ☎91 467 33 82; www.candelaflamenco.
com; Calle del Olmo 3; admission €10; ◎10.30pm-
late; Ⓜ Antón Martín) Candela draws a foreign
crowd upstairs for formal, wel-priced flamenco, while many of Madrid's young performers hang out with locals downstairs in
an informal bar where spontaneous music
often breaks out late in the evening. To see
Candela at its best, come after 1am and respect the atmosphere.

Popular   JAZZ

(Map p80; ☎91 429 84 07; www.populart.es; Calle
de las Huertas 22; ◎6pm-2.30am Sun-Thu, to
3.30am Fri & Sat; Ⓜ Antón Martín, Sol) 𝗙𝗥𝗘𝗘 One
of Madrid's classic jazz clubs, this place offers a low-key atmosphere and top-quality
music, which is mostly jazz with occasional
blues, swing and even flamenco thrown into
the mix. Compay Segundo, Sonny Fortune
and the Canal Street Jazz Band have all
played here. Shows start at 10.45pm but, if
you want a seat, get here early.

Sala Clamores   LIVE MUSIC

(☎91 445 79 38; www.clamores.es; Calle de Alburquerque 14; admission €5-25; ◎6.30pm-2am
Sun-Thu, 6.30pm-5.30am Fri & Sat; Ⓜ Bilbao) This
one-time classic jazz cafe has morphed into
one of the most diverse music stages in Madrid – it's been going for three decades and
hasn't changed the decor once. Jazz is still

a staple, but world music, flamenco, soul fusion, singer-songwriter, pop and rock all make regular appearances. Live shows can begin as early as 7pm on weekends, but sometimes really only get going after 1am.

It's in the neighbourhood of Chamberí, just off Calle de Trafalgar.

Café Berlin   JAZZ
(Map p72; ☑ 91 521 57 52; berlincafe.es; Calle de Jacometrezo 4; admission €5-12; ⊗ 10pm-5.30am Tue-Sun Sep-Jul; Ⓜ Callao, Santo Domingo) El Berlín has been something of a Madrid jazz stalwart since the 1950s, although a recent makeover has brought flamenco, R&B, soul, funk and fusion. The art-deco interior adds to the charm. Headline acts play at 11.30pm on Fridays and Saturdays, with other performances sprinkled throughout the week.

El Junco Jazz Club   JAZZ
(Map p96; ☑ 91 319 20 81; www.eljunco.com; Plaza de Santa Bárbara 10; concerts €5-9, Sun free; ⊗ 11pm-5.30am Tue-Thu & Sun, 11pm-6am Fri & Sat, concerts 11pm Tue-Sun; Ⓜ Alonso Martínez) El Junco has established itself on the Madrid nightlife scene by appealing as much to jazz aficionados as to clubbers. Its secret is high-quality live jazz gigs from Spain and around the world, followed by DJs spinning funk, soul, nu jazz, blues and innovative groove beats. The emphasis is on music from the American South and the crowd is classy and casual.

ContraClub   LIVE MUSIC
(Map p77; ☑ 91 365 55 45; www.contraclub.es; Calle de Bailén 16; admission €6-12; ⊗ 10pm-6am Wed-Sat; Ⓜ La Latina) ContraClub is a crossover live-music venue and nightclub, with live flamenco on Wednesday and an eclectic mix of other live music (jazz, blues, world music and rock) from Thursday to Saturday. After the live acts (which start at 10.30pm), the resident DJs serve up equally eclectic beats (indie, pop, funk and soul) to make sure you don't move elsewhere.

Café La Palma   ROCK
(Map p96; ☑ 91 522 50 31; www.cafelapalma.com; Calle de la Palma 62; admission free-€12; ⊗ 5pm-3am Sun-Thu, 5pm-3.30am Fri & Sat; Ⓜ Noviciado) It's amazing how much variety Café La Palma has packed into its labyrinth of rooms. Live shows featuring hot local bands are held at the back, while DJs mix it up at the front. Shows either start at 9pm or 10pm from Thursday to Saturday, but you might find live music other nights as well.

Honky Tonk   ROCK
(☑ 91 445 61 91; www.clubhonky.com; Calle de Covarrubias 24; ⊗ 9.30pm-5am Sun-Thu, 9.30pm-6am; Ⓜ Alonso Martínez) FREE Despite the name, this is a great place to see blues or local rock 'n' roll, though many acts have a little country, jazz or R&B thrown into the mix. It's a fun vibe in a smallish club that's been around since the heady 1980s and opens 365 days a year. It's a reliable late-night option, and the range of malt whiskies is impressive.

La Boca del Lobo   LIVE MUSIC
(Map p80; ☑ 91 429 70 13; www.labocadellobo.com; Calle de Echegaray 11; admission free-€10; ⊗ 9pm-3.30am Tue-Sat; Ⓜ Sol, Sevilla) Known for offering mostly rock and alternative concerts, La Boca del Lobo (The Wolf's Mouth) is as dark as its name suggests and has broadened its horizons to include just about anything – roots, reggae, jazz, soul, ska, flamenco, funk and fusion. Concerts start between 9.30pm and 11pm (check the website) Wednesday to Saturday, then DJs take over until closing time.

Classical Music & Opera

Auditorio Nacional de Música   CLASSICAL MUSIC
(☑ 91 337 01 40; www.auditorionacional.mcu.es; Calle del Príncipe de Vergara 146; Ⓜ Cruz del Rayo) When it's not playing the Teatro Real, Madrid's venerable Orquesta Sinfonía plays at this modern venue, which also attracts famous conductors from across the world to its two concert halls. It's usually fairly easy to get your hands on tickets at the box office. It's north of the Salamanca neighbourhood, 1km beyond Calle del Príncipe de Vergara's intersection with Avenida de América.

Teatro Real   OPERA
(Map p72; ☑ 902 244848; www.teatro-real.com; Plaza de Oriente; Ⓜ Ópera) After spending €100 million-plus on a long rebuilding project, the Teatro Real is as technologically advanced as any venue in Europe, and is the city's grandest stage for elaborate operas, ballets and classical music. Come for a performance or take the guided tour (or both!).

You'll pay as little as €7 for a spot so far away you'll need a telescope, although the sound quality is consistent throughout. For the best seats, don't expect change from €130. If it's the building that captures your interest, there are daily one-hour tours (per person €8 to €16) – they leave every half hour from 10.30am to 1pm.

LA MOVIDA MADRILEÑA

Anyone who went wild when they first moved out of their parents' house can identify with *la movida madrileña* (literally, 'the Madrid scene'). After the long, dark years of dictatorship and conservative Catholicism, Spaniards, especially *madrileños,* emerged onto the streets in the late 1970s with all the zeal of ex-convent schoolgirls. Nothing was taboo as *madrileños* discovered the '60s, '70s and early '80s all at once. Drinking, drugs and sex suddenly were OK. All-night partying was the norm, cannabis was virtually legalised and the city howled.

La movida was presided over by Enrique Tierno Galván, an ageing former university professor who had been a leading opposition figure under Franco and was affectionately known throughout Spain as 'the old teacher'. A socialist, he became mayor of Madrid in 1979 and, for many, launched *la movida* by telling a public gathering '*a colocarse y ponerse al loro',* which loosely translates as 'get stoned and do what's cool'. Not surprisingly, he was Madrid's most popular mayor ever. When he died in 1986, a million *madrileños* turned out for his funeral.

But *la movida* was not just about rediscovering the Spanish art of *salir de copas* (going out to drink). It was also accompanied by an explosion of creativity among the country's musicians, designers and film-makers. The most famous of these was film director Pedro Almodóvar. Still one of Europe's most creative directors, his riotously colourful films captured the spirit of *la movida,* featuring larger-than-life characters who pushed the limits of sex and drugs. Among the other names from *la movida* that still resonate, the designer Agatha Ruiz de la Prada stands out. And play anything by Alaska, Los Rebeldes, Radio Futura or Nacha Pop and watch *madrileños* get nostalgic.

Sport

Estadio Santiago Bernabéu   FOOTBALL
(📞902 291709, 91 398 43 00; www.realmadrid.com; Avenida de Concha Espina 1; tour adult/child €19/13; ◷10am-7pm Mon-Sat, 10.30am-6.30pm Sun, except match days; Ⓜ Santiago Bernabéu) The home of Real Madrid, Estadio Santiago Bernabéu is a temple to football and is one of the world's great sporting arenas. For a self-guided tour of the stadium, buy your ticket at ticket window 10 (next to gate 7). Tickets for matches start at €40 and can be bought online at www.realmadrid.com, while the all-important telephone number for booking tickets (which you later pick up at gate 42) is 📞902 324324, which only works if you're calling from within Spain.

Watching a game here is akin to a pilgrimage for sports fans. When the players strut their stuff with 80,000 passionate *madrileños* in attendance, you'll get chills down your spine. If you haven't purchased online or over the phone, turn up at the ticket office at gate 42 on Avenida de Concha Espina early in the week before a scheduled game. If you're in town when Real Madrid wins a major trophy, head to Plaza de la Cibeles and wait for the all-night party to begin.

Otherwise, the tour takes you through the Exposición de Trofeos (Trophy Exhibit), the presidential box, the press room, dressing rooms and the players' tunnel, and onto the pitch itself. On match days, tours cease five hours before the game is scheduled to start, although the Exposición de Trofeos is open until two hours before game time.

The stadium is north of the city, along the Paseo de la Castellana, around 3.5km north of the Plaza de la Cibeles.

🏠 Shopping

Madrid is a fantastic city in which to shop and *madrileños* are some of the finest exponents of the art.

The peak shopping season is during *las rebajas,* the annual winter and summer sales period when prices are slashed on just about everything. The winter sales begin around 7 January, just after Three Kings' Day, and last well into February. Summer sales begin in early July and last into August.

All shops may (and many usually do) open on the first Sunday of every month and throughout December.

🏠 Plaza Mayor & Royal Madrid

Antigua Casa Talavera   CERAMICS
(Map p72; Calle de Isabel la Católica 2; ◷10am-1.30pm & 5-8pm Mon-Fri, 10am-1.30pm Sat; Ⓜ Santo Domingo) The extraordinary tiled facade of this wonderful old shop conceals an Aladdin's cave of ceramics from all over Spain. This is not the mass-produced stuff aimed at

a tourist market, but comes from the small family potters of Andalucía and Toledo, ranging from the decorative (tiles) to the useful (plates, jugs and other kitchen items).

El Arco Artesanía   HANDICRAFTS

(Map p72; www.artesaniaelarco.com; Plaza Mayor 9; ⊙11am-9pm; MSol, La Latina) This original shop in the southwestern corner of Plaza Mayor sells an outstanding array of home-made designer souvenirs, from stone and glass work to jewellery and home fittings. The papier mâché figures are gorgeous.

El Flamenco Vive   FLAMENCO

(Map p72; www.elflamencovive.es; Calle Conde de Lemos 7; ⊙10.30am-2pm & 5-9pm Mon-Sat; MÓpera) This temple to flamenco has it all, from guitars and songbooks to well-priced CDs, polka-dotted dancing costumes, shoes, colourful plastic jewellery and literature about flamenco. It's the sort of place that will appeal as much to curious first timers as to serious students of the art. It also organises classes in flamenco guitar.

El Jardín del Convento   FOOD

(Map p72; ☑91 541 22 99; www.eljardindelconvento. net; Calle del Cordón 1; ⊙11am-3pm & 5.30-9pm Tue-Sun) In a quiet lane just south of Plaza de la Villa, this appealing little shop sells home-made sweets baked by nuns in abbeys, convents and monasteries all across Spain.

Salvador Bachiller   ACCESSORIES

(Map p96; www.salvadorbachiller.com; Gran Vía 65; ⊙10am-9.30pm Mon-Sat, 11am-9pm Sun; MPlaza de España, Santo Domingo) The stylish and high-quality leather bags, wallets, suitcases and other accessories of Salvador Bachiller are a staple of Spanish shopping aficionados. This is leather with a typically Spanish twist – the colours are dazzling in bright pinks, yellows and greens. Sound garish? You'll change your mind once you step inside. It also has an **outlet** (Map p96; ☑91 523 30 37; Calle de Gravina 11; ⊙10.30am-9.30pm Mon-Thu, 10.30am-11pm Fri & Sat, noon-9pm Sun; MChueca) in Chueca for superseded stock.

Casa Hernanz   SHOES

(Map p72; Calle de Toledo 18; ⊙9am-1.30pm & 4.30-8pm Mon-Fri, 10am-2pm Sat; MLa Latina, Sol) Comfy, rope-soled *alpargatas* (espadrilles), Spain's traditional summer footwear, are worn by everyone from the King of Spain down, and you can buy your own pair at this humble workshop, which has been hand-making the shoes for five generations; you

can even get them made to order. Prices range from €5 to €40.

Maty   FLAMENCO

(Map p80; ☑91 531 32 91; www.maty.es; Calle del Maestro Victoria 2; ⊙10am-1.45pm & 4.30-8pm Mon-Fri, 10am-2pm & 4.30-8pm Sat & 1st Sun of month; MSol) Wandering around central Madrid, it's easy to imagine that flamenco outfits have been reduced to imitation dresses sold as souvenirs to tourists. That's why places like Maty matter. Here you'll find dresses, shoes and all the accessories that go with the genre, with sizes for children and adults. These are the real deal, with prices to match, but they make brilliant gifts.

🏠 La Latina & Lavapiés

On a Sunday morning, don't forget El Rastro (p78), Madrid's epic flea market.

Helena Rohner   JEWELLERY

(Map p77; www.helenarohner.com.es; Calle del Almendro 4; ⊙9am-8.30pm Mon-Fri, noon-2.30pm & 3.30-8pm Sat, noon-3pm Sun; MLa Latina, Tirso de Molina) One of Europe's most creative jewellery designers, Helena Rohner has a spacious boutique in La Latina. Working with silver, stone, porcelain, wood and Murano glass, she makes inventive pieces and her work is a regular feature of Paris fashion shows. In her own words, she seeks to recreate 'the magic of Florence, the vitality of London and the luminosity of Madrid'.

🏠 Sol, Santa Ana & Huertas

Casa de Diego   ACCESSORIES

(Map p80; personales.ya.com/jlleran; Plaza de la Puerta del Sol 12; ⊙9.30am-8pm Mon-Sat; MSol) This classic shop has been around since 1858, making, selling and repairing Spanish fans, shawls, umbrellas and canes. The fans are works of antique art. There's another **branch** (Map p80; ☑91 531 02 23; personales.ya.com/jlleran; Calle del los Mesoneros Romanos 4; ⊙9.30am-1.30pm & 4.45-8pm Mon-Sat; MCallao, Sol) nearby.

María Cabello   WINE

(Map p80; Calle de Echegaray 19; ⊙9.30am-2.30pm & 5.30-9pm Mon-Fri, 10am-2.30pm & 6.30-9.30pm Sat; MSevilla, Antón Martín) All wine shops should be like this. This family-run corner shop really knows its wines and the interior has scarcely changed since 1913. There are fine wines in abundance (mostly Spanish, and a few foreign bottles), with some 500 labels on show or tucked away out the back.

Tienda Real Madrid   SPORTS
(Map p80; www.realmadrid.com; Gran Vía 31; ⏱10am-9pm Mon-Sat, 11am-9pm Sun; Ⓜ Metro Gran Vía, Callao) The Real Madrid club shop sells replica shirts, posters, caps and just about everything under the sun to which it could attach a club logo. From the shop window, you can see down onto the stadium itself. There's another branch (Map p80; ☑915 21 79 50; Calle del Carmen 3; ⏱10am-8.45pm Mon-Sat, 10am-6.45pm Sun; Ⓜ Sol) in the centre of town, and another (Gate 57, Estadio Santiago Bernabéu, Avenida de Concha Espina 1; ⏱10am-8.30pm; Ⓜ Santiago Bernabéu) at the stadium in the city's north.

La Central de Callao   BOOKSHOP, SOUVENIRS
(Map p80; ☑917 90 99 30; www.lacentral.com; Postigo de San Martín 8; ⏱9.30am-10pm Mon-Fri, 10am-10pm Sat, 10am-9.30pm Sun; Ⓜ Callao) Inhabiting an old palace is this fabulous multi-storey bookstore, cafe and purveyor of better-than-average Madrid souvenirs.

🏠 Salamanca

Agatha Ruiz de la Prada   FASHION
(Map p94; www.agatharuizdelaprada.com; Calle de Serrano 27; ⏱10am-8.30pm Mon-Sat; Ⓜ Serrano) This exuberant boutique has serious and highly original fashion. Agatha Ruiz de la Prada is one of the enduring icons of *la movida,* Madrid's 1980s outpouring of creativity.

Gallery   CLOTHING, ACCESSORIES
(Map p94; ☑91 576 79 31; www.gallerymadrid.com; Calle de Jorge Juan 38; ⏱10.30am-8.30pm Mon-Sat; Ⓜ Príncipe de Vergara, Velázquez) This stunning showpiece of men's fashion and accessories is Madrid in a nutshell – stylish, brand-conscious and all about having the right look. There are creams and fragrances to indulge the metrosexual in you, as well as quirkier items such as designer crash helmets. With an interior designed by Tomas Alia, and a growing line in women's fashion, it's one of the city's coolest shops.

Oriol Balaguer   FOOD
(www.oriolbalaguer.com; Calle de José Ortega y Gasset 44; ⏱9am-8pm Mon-Fri, 10am-8pm Sat, 10am-2.30pm Sun; Ⓜ Nuñez de Balboa) Catalan pastry chef Oriol Balaguer has a formidable CV – he worked in the kitchens of Ferran Adrià in Catalonia and won the prize for the World's Best Dessert (his 'Seven Textures of Chocolate') in 2001. His chocolate boutique is presented like a small art gallery, except that it's dedicated to exquisite, finely crafted chocolate collections and cakes. You'll never be able to buy ordinary chocolate again.

Camper   SHOES
(Map p94; www.camper.es; Calle de Serrano 24; ⏱10am-9pm Mon-Sat, noon-8pm Sun; Ⓜ Serrano) This world-famous cool and quirky shoe brand from Mallorca offers bowling-shoe chic with colourful, fun designs that are all about quality coupled with comfort. There are other outlets throughout the city, including a branch (Map p96; ☑91 531 23 47; www.camper.com; Calle de Fuencarral 42; ⏱10am-8pm Mon-Sat; Ⓜ Gran Vía, Tribunal) in Malasaña – check out its website for locations.

🏠 Malasaña & Chueca

Mercado de Fuencarral   CLOTHING
(Map p96; www.mdf.es; Calle de Fuencarral 45; ⏱11am-9pm Mon-Sat; Ⓜ Tribunal) Madrid's home of alternative club cool revels in its reverse snobbery. With shops like Fuck, Ugly Shop and Black Kiss, it's funky, grungy and filled to the rafters with torn T-shirts, black leather and silver studs. This is a Madrid icon and when it was threatened with closure in 2008, there was nearly an uprising.

Lurdes Bergada   FASHION
(Map p94; ☑91 531 99 58; www.lurdesbergada.es; Calle del Conde de Xiquena 8; ⏱10am-2.30pm & 4.30-8.30pm Mon-Sat; Ⓜ Chueca, Colón) Lurdes Bergada and Syngman Cucala, a mother-son designer team from Barcelona, offer classy and original men's and women's fashions using neutral colours and all-natural fibres. They have another branch (Map p96; Calle de Fuencarral 70; ⏱10.30am-8.30pm Mon-Sat; Ⓜ Tribunal) in Malasaña.

Patrimonio Comunal Olivarero   FOOD
(Map p96; www.pco.es; Calle de Mejía Lequerica 1; ⏱10am-2pm & 5-8pm Mon-Fri, 10am-2pm Sat; Ⓜ Alonso Martínez) To pick some of the country's olive-oil varieties (Spain is the world's largest producer), Patrimonio Comunal Olivarero is perfect. The staff know their oil and are happy to help out if you speak a little Spanish.

Curiosite   GIFTS
(Map p96; www.curiosite.es; Calle de la Corredera Alta de San Pablo 28; ⏱11am-9pm Mon-Sat; Ⓜ Tribunal) Some of Madrid's more original gifts are on offer in this quirky shop that combines old favourites (eg Star Wars Lego, Voodoo dolls) and a sideways glance at mundane household items. We couldn't resist the *jamón*-shaped cushions.

Delicatessen Hermanos López Pascual FOOD

(Map p96; www.lopezpascual.com; Calle de la Corredera Baja de San Pablo 13; ⊙10.30am-2pm & 5.30-8.30pm Mon-Fri, 9.30am-2pm Sat) This fine delicatessen sells what many consider to be the best *jamón ibérico* in Madrid.

ℹ️ Information

DANGERS & ANNOYANCES

Madrid is a generally safe city although you should, as in most European cities, be wary of pickpockets in the city centre, on the metro and around major tourist sights. You need to be especially careful in the most heavily touristed parts of town, notably the Plaza Mayor and surrounding streets, the Puerta del Sol, El Rastro and around the Museo del Prado. Tricks abound and they usually involve a team of two or more (sometimes one of them is an attractive woman to distract male victims). While one diverts your attention, the other empties your pockets. But don't be paranoid: remember that the overwhelming majority of travellers to Madrid rarely encounter any problems.

More unsettling than dangerous, the central Calle de la Montera has long been the haunt of prostitutes, pimps and a fair share of shady characters, although the street has recently been pedestrianised, and furnished with CCTV cameras and a police station.

The *barrio* of Lavapiés is a gritty, multicultural melting pot. We love it, but it's not without its problems, with drug-related crime an occasional but persistent problem. It's probably best avoided if you're on your own at night.

EMERGENCY

Emergency (☎112)

Policía Nacional (☎091)

Servicio de Atención al Turista Extranjero (Foreign Tourist Assistance Service; ☎91 548 80 08, 91 548 85 37, 902 102112; www.es madrid.com/satemadrid; Calle de Leganitos 19; ⊙9am-midnight; Ⓜ Plaza de España, Santo Domingo) To report thefts or other crime-related matters, cancel your credit cards, contact your embassy and other related matters, this is your best bet.

Teléfono de la Víctima (☎902 180995) Hotline for victims of racial or sexual violence.

INTERNET ACCESS

Most midrange and top-end hotels have either wi-fi or cable ADSL in-room connections; even some of the better hotels can run out of cables for the latter so ask for one as soon as you arrive.

For a reasonable (but by no means exhaustive) list of wi-fi hotspots, check out www.madrid memata.es/madrid-wifi.

For another option with a range of plans (from free to €10 for one month), try www.gowex.com.

You'll find plenty of small *locutorios* (small shops selling phonecards and cheap phone calls) all over the city and many have a few computers out the back. In the downtown area, your best options include the Centro de Turismo de Madrid, which has a couple of computers with time-limited access. In Malasaña, try upstairs in Café Comercial (p119).

MEDICAL SERVICES

Farmacia Mayor (☎91 366 46 16; Calle Mayor 13; ⊙24hr; Ⓜ Sol) Open around the clock.

Farmacia Velázquez 70 (☎91 575 60 28; Calle de Velázquez 70; ⊙24hr; Ⓜ Velázquez)

Hospital General Gregorio Marañón (☎91 586 80 00; www.hggm.es; Calle del Doctor Esquerdo 46; Ⓜ Sáinz de Baranda, O'Donnell, Ibiza) One of the city's main (and more central) hospitals.

Unidad Medica (Anglo American; ☎91 435 18 23; www.unidadmedica.com; Calle del Conde de Aranda 1; ⊙9am-8pm Mon-Fri, 10am-1pm Sat; Ⓜ Retiro) A private clinic with a wide range of specialisations and where all doctors speak Spanish and English, with some also speaking French and German. Each consultation costs around €125.

POST

Main Post Office (Map p84; www.correos.es; Paseo del Prado 1; ⊙8.30am-9.30pm Mon-Fri, to 2pm Sat; Ⓜ Banco de España) The main post office is in the gigantic Palacio de Cibeles on Plaza de la Cibeles.

TOURIST INFORMATION

Centro de Turismo de Madrid (Map p72; ☎91 588 16 36; www.esmadrid.com; Plaza Mayor 27; ⊙9.30am-8.30pm; @; Ⓜ Sol) Excellent city tourist office with a smaller office underneath Plaza de Colón (Map p94; Plaza de Colón; ⊙9.30am-8.30pm; Ⓜ Colón) and the Palacio de Cibeles (Map p84; Plaza de Cibeles 1; ⊙10am-8pm Tue-Sun; Ⓜ Plaza de España), as well as information points at Plaza de la Cibeles (Map p84; Plaza de la Cibeles; ⊙9.30am-8.30pm; Ⓜ Banco de España), Plaza del Callao (Map p80; Plaza del Callao; Ⓜ Callao, closed for renovations at the time of writing), outside the Centro de Arte Reina Sofía (Map p84; cnr Calle de Santa Isabel & Plaza del Emperador Carlos V; ⊙9.30am-8.30pm; Ⓜ Atocha) and at the T2 and T4 terminals at Barajas airport.

WEBSITES

EsMadrid.com (www.esmadrid.com) The *ayuntamiento's* (town hall) supersexy website with info on upcoming events.

Le Cool (madrid.lecool.com) Weekly updates on upcoming events in Madrid with an emphasis on the alternative, offbeat and avant-garde.

Lonely Planet (www.lonelyplanet.com/madrid) An overview of Madrid with hundreds of useful links.

Turismo Madrid (www.turismomadrid.es) Portal of the regional Comunidad de Madrid tourist office that's especially good for areas outside the city but still within the Comunidad de Madrid.

Madrid Diferente (madriddiferente.com) Good for restaurants, shops, upcoming events with a refreshingly offbeat style.

ℹ Getting There & Away

AIR

Madrid's **Barajas airport** (☎ 902 404704; www. aena.es; Ⓜ Aeropuerto T1, T2 & T3, Aeropuerto T4) lies 15km northeast of the city. It's Europe's sixth-busiest hub (between 45 and 50 million passengers pass through here annually).

Although all airlines conduct check-in *(facturación)* in the airport's departure areas, some also allow check-in at the Nuevos Ministerios metro stop and transport interchange in Madrid itself – ask your airline.

A full list of airlines flying to Madrid (and which of Madrid's four terminals they use) is available on the Madrid-Barajas section of www.aena.es; click on 'Airlines'.

BUS

Estación Sur de Autobuses (☎ 91 468 42 00; www.estaciondeautobuses.com; Calle de Méndez Álvaro 83; Ⓜ Méndez Álvaro), just south of the M30 ring road, is the city's principal bus station. To get here, take Calle de Méndez Alvaro around 2km southeast of Atocha train station. It serves most destinations to the south and many in other parts of the country. Most bus companies have a ticket office here, even if their buses depart from elsewhere.

Northwest of the centre and connected to lines 1 and 3 of the Metro, the subterranean **Intercambiador de Autobuses de Moncloa** sends buses out to the surrounding villages and satellite suburbs that lie north and west of the city.

Major bus companies include:

ALSA (☎ 902 422242; www.alsa.es) One of the largest Spanish companies with many services throughout Spain. Most depart from Estación Sur but some buses headed north (including to Bilbao and Zaragoza, and some services to Barcelona) leave from the Intercambiador de Avenida de América, with occasional services from T4 of Madrid's Barajas airport.

Avanzabus (☎ 902 020052; www.avanzabus. com) Services to Extremadura (eg Cáceres),

Castilla y León (eg Salamanca and Zamora) and Valencia via Cuenca, as well as Lisbon in Portugal. All leave from the Estación Sur.

CAR & MOTORCYCLE

Madrid is surrounded by two main ring roads, the outermost M40 and the inner M30; there are also two partial ring roads, the M45 and the more-distant M50. The R5 and R3 are part of a series of toll roads built to ease traffic jams.

The big-name car-rental agencies have offices all over Madrid and offices at the airport, and some have branches at Atocha and Chamartín train stations.

Avis (☎ 902 180 854; www.avis.es; Gran Vía 60; Ⓜ Santo Domingo, Plaza de España)

Enterprise/Atesa (☎ 902 100101; www.atesa. es; Plaza de España , underground parking area; Ⓜ Plaza de España)

Europcar (☎ 902 105030; www.europcar.es; Calle de San Leonardo de Dios 8; Ⓜ Plaza de España)

Hertz (☎ 902 402405; www.hertz.es; Edificio de España, Calle de la Princesa 14; Ⓜ Plaza de España)

Pepecar (☎ 807 414243; www.pepecar.com; Plaza de España, underground parking area; Ⓜ Plaza de España) Specialises in low-cost rentals. Bookings are best made over the internet.

TRAIN

Madrid is served by two main train stations. The bigger of the two is **Puerta de Atocha** (Ⓜ Atocha Renfe), at the southern end of the city centre, while **Chamartín** (Ⓜ Chamartín) lies in the north of the city. The bulk of trains for Spanish destinations depart from Atocha, especially those going south. International services arrive at and leave from Chamartín. For bookings, contact **Renfe** (☎ 902 240202; www.renfe.es) at either train station.

High-speed **Tren de Alta Velocidad Española** (AVE) services connect Madrid with Seville (via Córdoba), Valladolid (via Segovia), Toledo, Valencia (via Cuenca), Burgos, Málaga and Barcelona (via Zaragoza, Huesca, Lerida and/or Tarragona). Most high-speed services operate from Madrid's Puerta de Atocha station. The Madrid–Segovia/Valladolid service leaves from the Chamartín station.

ℹ Getting Around

Madrid is well served by an ever-expanding metro system and an extensive bus service. In addition, you can get from the north to the south of the city quickly by using *cercanías (*local trains) between Chamartín and Atocha train stations. Taxis are also a reasonably priced option.

RED DE METRO Y METRO LIGERO *Metro a*

SIMBOLOGÍA - Key

	Línea / Line
1	Pinar de Chamartín / Valdecarros
O 2	Las Rosas / Cuatro Caminos
3	Villaverde Alto / Moncloa
4	Argüelles / Pinar de Chamartín
5	Alameda de Osuna / Casa de Campo
6	Circular
7	Hospital del Henares / Pitis
8	Nuevos Ministerios / Aeropuerto
9	Mirasierra / Arganda del Rey
10	Hospital Infanta Sofía / Puerta del Sur
11	Plaza Elíptica / La Fortuna
12	MetroSur
R	Ópera / Príncipe Pío

mℓ
1	Pinar de Chamartín / Las Tablas
2	Colonia Jardín / Estación de Aravaca
3	Colonia Jardín / Puerta de Boadilla

Key

- Transbordo corto / Metro interchange
- Transbordo largo / Metro interchange with long walking distance
- Cambio de tren / Change of trains
- Horario restringido / Restricted opening times
- Metro Ligero / Light Rail
- Cercanías Renfe / Suburban railway
- Grandes intercambiadores / Transfer Terminal
- Autobuses interurbanos / Suburban buses
- Autobuses largo recorrido / Interegional bus station
- Autobuses nocturnos / Night bus line
- Estación de tren / Railway station
- Aeropuerto Madrid-Barajas / Madrid-Barajas Airport
- Zonas tarifarias / Fare zones

- Estación accesible / ascensor: Ver al dorso / Step-free access / lift: See behind
- Suplemento Aeropuerto / Airport extra charge
- Oficina de gestión tarjeta transporte público / Public Transport Card Office
- Centro de Información / Travel Information Centre
- Aparcamiento disuasorio gratuito / Free Park and Ride
- Aparcamiento disuasorio de pago / Paid Park and Ride
- Productos Oficiales de Metro / Official Metro Merchandising

(Station names on map, partial list:)

Las Tablas · Mirasierra · Tres Olivos · Pitis · Montecarmelo · María Tudor · Blasco Ibáñez · Fuencarral · Begoña · Chamartín · Pinar de Chamartín · Herrera Oria · Barrio del Pilar · Ventilla · Bambú · Duque de Pastrana · Pío XII · Colombia · Plaza de Castilla · Valdeacederas · Tetuán · Cuzco · Santiago Bernabéu · Concha Espina · Estrecho · Alvarado · Cuatro Caminos · Nuevos Ministerios · República Argentina · Cruz del Rayo · Avda. de América · Guzmán el Bueno · Ríos Rosas · Gregorio Marañón · Diego de León · Metropolitano · Canal · Alonso Cano · Iglesia · Bilbao · Rubén Darío · Núñez de Balboa · Lista · Ciudad Universitaria · Islas Filipinas · Quevedo · Moncloa · Argüelles · San Bernardo · Ventura Rodríguez · Tribunal · Colón · Serrano · Velázquez · Goya · Príncipe de Vergara · Plaza de España · Noviciado · Alonso Martínez · Chueca · Príncipe Pío · Santo Domingo · Gran Vía · Callao · Sevilla · Banco de España · Retiro · Ibiza · Ópera · Sol · Tirso de Molina · Antón Martín · La Latina · Puerta del Ángel · Puerta de Toledo · Alto de Extremadura · Lucero · Lavapiés · Atocha · Acacias · Embajadores · Atocha Renfe · Pirámides · Menéndez Pelayo · Palos de la Frontera · Pacífico · Marqués de Vadillo · Delicias · Méndez Álvaro · Urgel · Oporto · Carpetena · Puente · Vista Alegre · Plaza Elíptica · Usera · Legazpi · Arganzuela-Planetario · Abrantes · Opañel · Carabanchel · Almendrales · Pan Bendito · San Francisco · Hospital 12 de Octubre · La Peseta · Carabanchel Alto · San Fermín-Orcasur · Ciudad de los Ángeles · Villaverde Bajo-Cruce · San Cristóbal · Villaverde Alto · El Carrascal

Metro Ligero (Left side)

Estación de Aravaca · Berna · Avenida de Europa · Campus Somosaguas · Dos Castillas · Bélgica · Pozuelo Oeste · Somosaguas Centro · Somosaguas Sur · Prado del Rey · Colonia de los Ángeles · Prado de la Vega · Ventorro del Espino · Montepríncipe · Retamares · Cocheras · Ciudad del Cine / la Imagen · Colonia Jardín · Aviación Española · Campamento · Empalme · Aluche · Eugenia de Montijo · Carabanchel · Joaquín Vilumbrales · La Fortuna · Alcorcón Central · Parque Lisboa · Parque Oeste · Universidad Rey Juan Carlos · Móstoles Central · Pradillo · Hospital de Móstoles · Manuela Malasaña · Loranca · Parque Europa · Hospital de Fuenlabrada · Fuenlabrada Central · Parque de los Estados · Puerta del Sur · San Nicasio · Leganés Central · Casa del Reloj · Hospital Severo Ochoa · El Bercial · Julián Besteiro · Los Espartales · El Casar · Juan de la Cierva · Getafe Central · Alonso de Mendoza · Conservatorio · Arroyo Culebro

Puerta de Boadilla · Siglo XXI · Boadilla Centro · Ferial de Boadilla · Infante Don Luis · Nuevo Mundo · Cantabria · José Isbert

Reyes Católicos · Baunat · Manuel de Falla · Marqués · La Moraleja · La Granja · Ronda de la Comunicación · Palas de Rey · Lacoma · Avda. de la Ilustración · Peñagrande · Antonio Machado · Valdezarza · Francos Rodríguez

ZONA B1 / Zone B1 · **ZONA A** / Zone A · **ZONA B2** / Zone B2

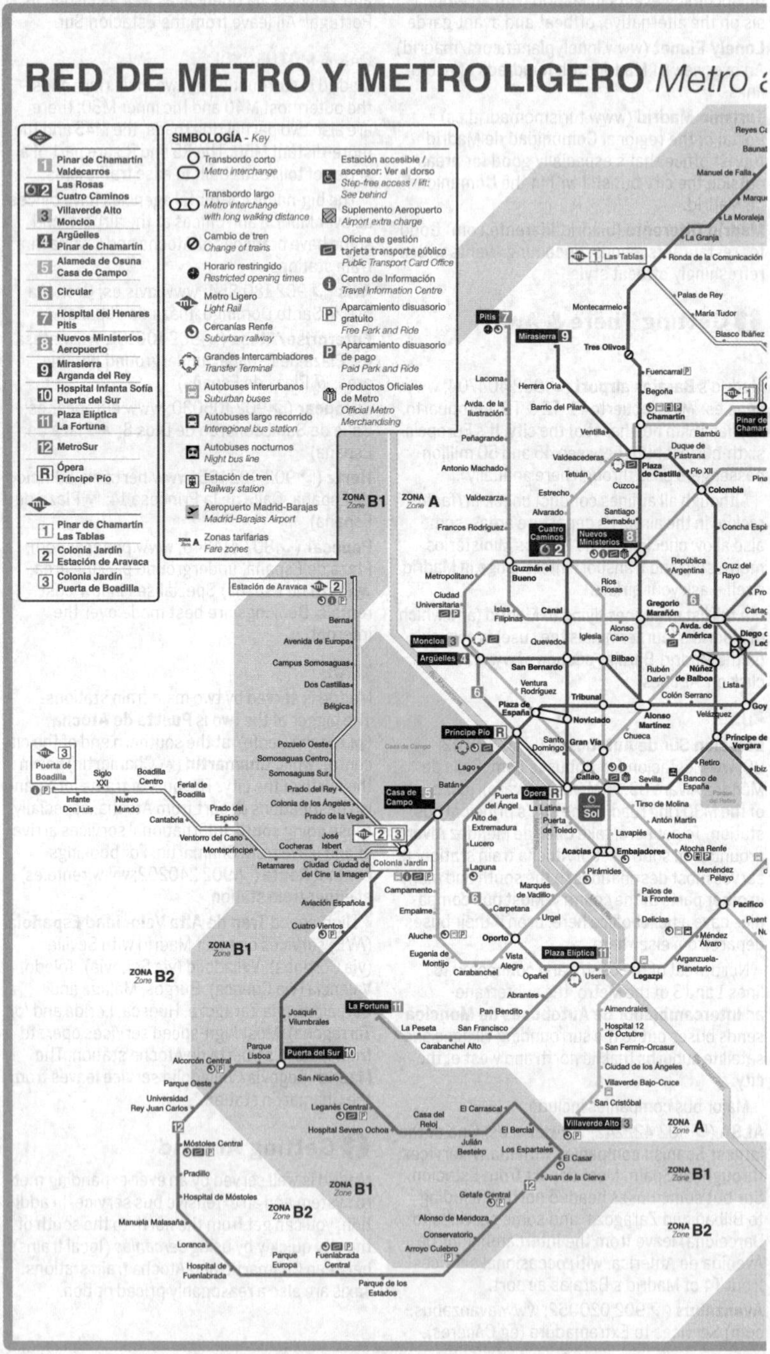

and Light Rail Network

Hospital Infanta Sofia 10

ólicos

s de la Valdavia

ZONA **B1**

ZONA **A**
Zone

lvarez de Villaamil
Antonio Saura
Virgen del Cortijo
Fuente de la Mora

Manoteras

Hortaleza

Parque de Santa María

San Lorenzo

Mar de Cristal

Campo de las Naciones

del Rey

Canillas

Esperanza

Arturo Soria

Avda. de la Paz

Alfonso XIII

peridad

Parque de las Avenidas

Barrio de la Concepción

Barrio de la Mora

Ventas El Carmen

Quintana

Manuel Becerra

Ascao

García Noblejas

San Blas

La Elipa

La Almudena

Avda. de Guadalajara

O'Donnell

Alsacia

Aeropuerto T4 8

Barajas

Aeropuerto T1-T2-T3

Alameda de Osuna 5

Canillejas

Tomé Arias

Suanzes

Ciudad Lineal

Estadio Olímpico

Coslada Central

Barrio del Puerto

La Rambla

San Fernando

Jarama

Henares

Las Rosas 2

Hospital del Henares 7

Sáinz de Baranda

Estrella

Vinateros

ZONA **A**
Zone

Conde Casal

Artilleros

Pavones

Valdebernardo

de Vallecas

va Numancia

Portazgo

Buenos Aires

Alto del Arenal

Miguel Hernández

Sierra de Guadalupe

Villa de Vallecas

Congosto

La Gavia

Las Suertes

Valdecarros

Vicálvaro

San Cipriano

Rivas-Urbanizaciones

Rivas Futura

Rivas Vaciamadrid

La Poveda

Arganda del Rey 9

ZONA **B1**
Zone

ZONA **B2**
Zone

Puerta de Arganda

ZONA **B3**
Zone

◀ Metro ▶

CONSORCIO TRANSPORTES MADRID
www.crtm.es

EM
Comunidad de Madrid
www.madrid.org

TO/FROM THE AIRPORT

A taxi to/from the city centre will cost you a flat rate €30.

Exprés Aeropuerto (Airport Express; www.emtmadrid.es; per person €5; ☉24hr; ☎) The Exprés Aeropuerto runs between Puerta de Atocha train station and the airport. Buses run every 13 to 23 minutes from 6am to 11.30pm, and every 35 minutes throughout the rest of the night. The trip takes 40 minutes. From 11.55pm until 5.35am, departures are from the Plaza de la Cibeles, not the train station.

Metro (www.metromadrid.es) Line 8 of the metro runs from the airport to the Nuevos Ministerios transport interchange on Paseo de la Castella, where it connects with lines 10 and 6. It operates from 6.05am to 2am. A one-way ticket to/from the airport costs €4.50 (10-trip Metrobús ticket €12.20). Even if you have a 10-trip ticket, you'll need to buy the airport supplement from machines at any metro station. The journey to Nuevos Ministerios takes around 15 minutes, around 25 minutes from T4.

AeroCITY (☎91 747 75 70; www.aerocity.com; per person from €20, express service per minibus from €35) Private minibus service.

BUS

Buses operated by **Empresa Municipal de Transportes de Madrid** (EMT; ☎902 507850; www.emtmadrid.es) travel along most city routes regularly between about 6.30am and 11.30pm. There are 26 night-bus *búhos* (owls) routes operating from midnight to 6am, with all routes originating in Plaza de la Cibeles.

CERCANÍAS

The short-range *cercanías* regional trains operated by **Renfe** (www.renfe.es/cercanias) go as far afield as El Escorial, Alcalá de Henares, Aranjuez and other points in the Comunidad de Madrid. Tickets range between €1.65 and €5.40, depending on how far you're travelling. In Madrid itself they're handy for making a quick, north–south hop between Chamartín and Atocha train stations (with stops at Nuevos Ministerios and Sol).

METRO

Madrid's modern metro (www.metromadrid.es), Europe's second-largest, is a fast, efficient and safe way to navigate Madrid, and generally easier than getting to grips with bus routes. There are 11 colour-coded lines in central Madrid, in addition to the modern southern suburban MetroSur system, as well as lines heading east to the major population centres of Pozuelo and Boadilla del Monte. Colour maps showing the metro system are available from any metro station. The metro operates from 6.05am to 2am, although there is talk of ceasing the service at midnight. A single ticket costs €1.50; a 10-ride Metrobús ticket is €12.20.

TAXI

You can pick up a taxi at ranks throughout town or simply flag one down. Flag fall is €2.40 from 6am to 9pm daily, €2.90 the rest of the time. You pay between €1 and €1.20 per kilometre depending on the hour. Several supplementary charges, usually posted inside the taxi, may apply. There's no charge for luggage.

Radio-Teléfono Taxi (☎91 547 82 00; www.radiotelefono-taxi.com)

Tele-Taxi (☎91 371 21 31; www.tele-taxi.es)

AROUND MADRID

The Comunidad de Madrid may be small but there are plenty of rewarding excursions that allow you to escape the clamour of city life without straying too far. Imposing San Lorenzo de El Escorial and graceful Aranjuez guard the western and southern gateways to Madrid. Also to the south, the beguiling village of Chinchón is a must-see, while Alcalá de Henares is a stunning university town east of the capital. To the north, picturesque villages (and skiing opportunities) abound in Sierra de Guadarrama and Sierra del Pobre.

San Lorenzo de El Escorial

POP 18,495 / ELEV 1032M

The Unesco World Heritage-listed palace and monastery complex of San Lorenzo de El Escorial is an impressive place, rising up from the foothills of the mountains that shelter Madrid from the north and west. The one-time royal getaway is now a prim little town overflowing with quaint shops, restaurants and hotels catering primarily to throngs of weekending *madrileños*. The fresh, cool air here has been drawing city dwellers since the complex was first ordered to be built by Felipe II in the 16th century. Most visitors come on a day trip from Madrid.

History

After Felipe II's decisive victory in the Battle of St Quentin against the French on St Lawrence's Day, 10 August 1557, he ordered the construction of the complex in the saint's name above the hamlet of El Escorial. Several villages were razed to make way for the huge monastery, royal palace and mausoleum for Felipe's parents, Carlos I and Isabel. It all flourished under the watchful eye of the architect Juan de Herrera, a towering figure of the Spanish Renaissance.

The palace-monastery became an important intellectual centre, with a burgeoning library and art collection, and even a laboratory where scientists could dabble in alchemy. Felipe II died here on 13 September 1598.

In 1854 the monks belonging to the Hieronymite order, who had occupied the monastery from the beginning, were obliged to leave during one of the 19th-century waves of confiscation of religious property by the Spanish state, only to be replaced 30 years later by Augustinians.

◉ Sights

The main entrance to the **Real Monasterio de San Lorenzo** (☎91 890 78 18; www.patrimonionacional.es; adult/concession €10/5, guide/audioguide €7/4, EU citizens free 3 three hours Wed & Thu; ☉10am-8pm Apr-Sep, 10am-6pm Oct-Mar, closed Mon) is on its western facade. Above the gateway a statue of St Lawrence stands guard, holding a symbolic gridiron, the instrument of his martyrdom (he was roasted alive on one). From here you'll first enter the **Patio de los Reyes**, which houses the statues of the six kings of Judah.

Directly ahead lies the sombre **basilica**. As you enter, look up at the unusual flat vaulting by the choir stalls. Once inside the church proper, turn left to view Benvenuto Cellini's white Carrara marble statue of Christ crucified (1576).

The remainder of the ground floor contains various treasures, including some tapestries and an El Greco painting – impressive as it is, it's a far cry from El Greco's dream of decorating the whole complex. Continue downstairs to the northeastern corner of the complex. You pass through the **Museo de Arquitectura** and the **Museo de Pintura**. The former tells (in Spanish) the story of how the complex was built; the latter contains a range of 16th- and 17th-century Italian, Spanish and Flemish art.

Head upstairs into a gallery around the eastern part of the complex known as the **Palacio de Felipe II** or **Palacio de los Austrias**. You'll then descend to the 17th-century **Panteón de los Reyes** (Crypt of the Kings), where almost all Spain's monarchs since Carlos I are interred. Backtracking a little, you'll find yourself in the Panteón de los Infantes (Crypt of the Princesses).

Stairs lead up from the Patio de los Evangelistas (Patio of the Gospels) to the Salas Capitulares (chapter houses) in the southeastern corner of the monastery. These bright, airy rooms, with their richly frescoed ceilings, contain works by El Greco, Titian, Tintoretto, José de Ribera and Hieronymus Bosch (known as 'El Bosco' to Spaniards).

Just south of the monastery is the Huerta de los Frailes (Friars Garden; ⊙ 10am-7pm Apr-Sep, 10am-6pm Oct-Mar, closed Mon), which merits a stroll, while the Jardín del Príncipe (⊙ 10am-7pm Apr-Sep, 10am-6pm Oct-Mar, closed Mon), which leads down to the town of El Escorial (and the train station), contains the Casita del Príncipe (⊙ 10am-8pm Apr-Sep, 10am-6pm Oct-Mar, closed Mon), a little neoclassical gem built in 1772 by Juan de Villanueva under Carlos III for his heir, Carlos IV.

Eating

Restaurante Charolés MADRILEÑO €€€
(☎ 91 890 59 75; Calle floridablanca 24, San Lorenzo de El Escorial; mains €17-23, cocido per person €29; ⊙ 1-4pm & 9pm-midnight) One of the most popular destinations for *madrileños* heading for the hills, Charolés does grilled or roasted meats to perfection, and it's much loved for its *cocido madrileño* (chickpea-and-meat hotpot), which is perfect on a cold winter's day.

ⓘ Information

Tourist Office (☎ 91 890 53 13; www.san lorenzoturismo.org; Calle de Grimaldi 4, El Escorial; ⊙ 10am-2pm & 3-6pm Tue-Sat, 10am-2pm Sun).

ⓘ Getting There & Away

Every 15 minutes (every 30 minutes on weekends) buses 661 and 664 run to El Escorial (€4.20, one hour) from platform 30 at the Intercambiador de Autobuses de Moncloa in Madrid.

San Lorenzo de El Escorial is 59km northwest of Madrid and it takes 40 minutes to drive there. Take the A6 highway to the M600, then follow the signs to El Escorial.

A few dozen **Renfe** (☎ 902 240202; www. renfe.es) C8 *cercanías* make the trip daily from Madrid's Atocha or Chamartín train station to El Escorial (€5.40, one hour).

South of Madrid

Aranjuez
POP 57,728

Unesco World Heritage–listed Aranjuez was founded as a royal pleasure retreat, away from the riff-raff of Madrid, and it remains an easy day trip to escape the rigours of city life. The palace is opulent, but the fresh air and ample gardens are what really stand out.

⊙ Sights

Palacio Real PALACE
(☎ 91 891 07 40; www.patrimonionacional.es; palace adult/concession €9/4, guide/audioguide €6/4, EU citizens free last 3 hours Wed & Thu, gardens free; ⊙ palace 10am-8pm Apr-Sep, 10am-6pm Oct-Mar, gardens 8am-9.30pm mid-Jun–mid-Aug, reduced hours mid-Aug–mid-Jun) The Royal Palace started as one of Felipe II's modest summer palaces but took on a life of its own as a succession of royals, inspired by the palace at Versailles in France, lavished money upon it. By the 18th century its 300-plus rooms had turned the palace into a sprawling, gracefully symmetrical complex filled with a cornucopia of ornamentation that you see today.

The obligatory guided tour (in Spanish) provides insight into the palace's art and history. And a stroll in the lush gardens takes you through a mix of local and exotic species, the product of seeds brought back by Spanish botanists and explorers from Spain's colonies all over the world. Within their shady perimeter, which stretches a few kilometres from the palace, you'll find the Casa de Marinos, which contains the Museo de Falúas, a museum of royal pleasure boats from days gone by. The 18th-century neoclassical Casa de Labrador is also worth a visit. Further away, towards Chinchón, is the Jardín del Príncipe, an extension of the massive gardens.

Eating

Casa Pablete TAPAS €
(Calle de Stuart 108; tapas from €4, raciones €8-13; ⊙ noon-4pm & 8pm-midnight Wed-Mon, closed Aug) Going strong since 1946, this casual tapas bar has a loyal following far beyond Aranjuez. Its *croquetas* are a major drawcard, as is the stuffed squid, and it's all about traditional cooking at its best without too many elaborations.

THE STRAWBERRY TRAIN

You could take a normal train from Madrid to Aranjuez, but for romance it's hard to beat the Tren de la Fresa (Strawberry Train; ☑902 240202; www.museodelferrocarril.org; return adult/child €29/21; ⊙10am Sat & Sun early May-late Oct). Begun in 1985 to commemorate the Madrid–Aranjuez route (Madrid's first and Spain's third rail line, which was inaugurated in the 1850s) the Strawberry Train is a throwback to the time when Spanish royalty would escape the summer heat and head for the royal palace at Aranjuez.

The journey begins when an antique Mikado 141F-2413 steam engine pulls out from Madrid's Museo del Ferrocarril, pulling behind it four passenger carriages that date from the early 20th century and have old-style front and back balconies. During the 50-minute journey, rail staff in period dress provide samples of local strawberries: one of the original train's purposes was to allow royalty to sample the summer strawberry crop from the Aranjuez orchards. Upon arrival in Aranjuez, your ticket fare includes a guided tour of the Palacio Real, Museo de Falúas and other Aranjuez sights, not to mention more strawberry samplings. The train leaves Aranjuez for Madrid at 6pm for the return journey.

Casa José SPANISH €€€
(☑91 891 14 88; www.casajose.es; Calle de Abastos 32; mains €21-32, set menus €64-75; ⊙1.45-3.30pm & 9-11.30pm Tue-Sat, 1.45-3.30pm Sun, closed Aug) The quietly elegant Casa José is the proud owner of a Michelin star and is packed on weekends with *madrileños*, drawn by the beautifully prepared meats and local dishes with some surprising innovations. It's pricey but worth every euro.

ℹ Information

Tourist Office (☑91 891 04 27; turismo enaranjuez.com; Plaza de San Antonio; ⊙10am-8.30pm May-Oct) The tourist office is in the heart of town, a few hundred metres southwest of the Palacio Real.

ℹ Getting There & Away

Coming by car from Madrid, take the N-IV south to the M305, which leads to the city centre.

AISA Bus Company (☑902 198788; www. aisa-grupo.com) bus 423 runs to Aranjuez from Madrid's Estación Sur every 15 minutes or so (€4.20, 45 minutes).

From Madrid's Atocha station, C3 *cercanías* trains leave every 15 or 20 minutes for Aranjuez (€3.35, 45 minutes).

Chinchón

POP 5428
Chinchón is just 45km from Madrid but worlds apart. Although it has grown beyond its village confines, visiting its antique heart is like stepping back into a charming, ramshackle past. It's worth an overnight stay to really soak it up, and lunch in one of the

méson (tavern)-style restaurants around the plaza is another must.

◉ Sights

The heart of town is its unique, almost circular Plaza Mayor, which is lined with sagging, tiered balconies – it wins our vote as one of the most evocative *plazas mayores* in Spain. In summer the plaza is converted into a bullring, and it's also the stage for a popular Passion play shown at Easter.

Chinchón's historical monuments won't detain you long, but you should take a quick look at the 16th-century Iglesia de la Asunción, which rises above Plaza Mayor, and the late-16th-century Renaissance Castillo de los Condes, out of town to the south. The castle was abandoned in the 1700s and was last used as a liquor factory. Ask at the tourist office to see if they're open.

✦ Festivals & Events

Fiesta Mayor VILLAGE FESTIVAL
Chinchón's main annual festival, with religious processions, bullfights and other merriment centred on the Plaza Mayor. It starts in the second week of August and usually lasts for a week.

🛏 Sleeping

Hostal Chinchón HOSTAL €
(☑91 893 53 98; www.hostalchinchon.com; Calle Grande 16; s/d/tr €40/50/65; ❖🄿🄿🄿) The public areas here are nicer than the smallish rooms, which are clean but worn around the edges. The highlight is the surprise rooftop pool overlooking Plaza Mayor.

Parador de Chinchón LUXURY HOTEL €€

(✆91 894 08 36; www.parador.es; Avenida Generalísimo 1; r €85-176; ❇☎) The former Convento de Agustinos (Augustine Convent), Parador de Chinchón is one of the town's most important historical buildings and can't be beaten for luxury. It's worth stopping by for a meal or coffee (and a peek around) even if you don't stay here.

✖ Eating

Chinchón is loaded with traditional-style restaurants dishing up *cordero asado* (roast lamb). But if you're after something a little lighter, there is nothing better than savouring a few tapas and drinks on sunny Plaza Mayor.

Mesón Cuevas del Vino SPANISH €€

(✆91 894 02 06; www.cuevasdelvino.com; Calle Benito Hortelano 13; mains €14-27; ⊙noon-11pm Mon-Fri, 11am-midnight Sat, 11am-8pm Sun) From the huge goatskins filled with wine and the barrels covered in famous signatures, to the atmospheric caves underground, this is sure to be a memorable eating experience with delicious home-style cooking.

Café de la Iberia SPANISH €€

(✆91 894 08 47; www.cafedelaiberia.com; Plaza Mayor 17; mains €13-22) This is definitely our favourite of the *mesones* (home-style restaurants) on the Plaza Mayor perimeter. It offers wonderful food, including succulent *cordero asado* (roast lamb), served by attentive staff in an atmospheric dining area set around a light-filled internal courtyard (where Goya is said to have visited). Or, if you can get a table, you can eat out on the balcony.

ℹ Information

Tourist Office (✆91 893 53 23; www.ciudad-chinchon.com; Plaza Mayor 6; ⊙10am-7pm) A small office with helpful staff.

ℹ Getting There & Away

La Veloz (✆91 409 76 02; Avenida del Mediterráneo 49; Ⓜ Conde de Casal) runs bus 337 half-hourly from Madrid to Chinchón (€4.20, 55 minutes). Buses leave from Madrid's Avenida del Mediterráneo, 100m east of Plaza del Conde de Casal.

Sitting 45km southeast of Madrid, Chinchón is easy to reach by car. Take the N-IV motorway and exit onto the M404, which makes its way to Chinchón.

Alcalá de Henares
POP 204,823

East of Madrid, Alcalá de Henares is full of surprises with historical sandstone buildings seemingly at every turn. Throw in some sunny squares and a legendary university, and it's a terrific place to escape the capital for a few hours.

◉ Sights

Universidad de Alcalá UNIVERSITY

(✆91 883 43 84; guided tours €4; ⊙9am-9pm) FREE Founded in 1486 by Cardinal Cisneros, this is one of the country's principal seats of learning. A guided tour gives a peek into the Mudéjar chapel and the magnificent Paraninfo auditorium, where the King and Queen of Spain give out the prestigious Premio Cervantes literary award every year.

Museo Casa Natal de Miguel de Cervantes MUSEUM

(✆91 889 96 54; www.museo-casa-natal-cervantes.org; Calle Mayor 48; ⊙10am-6pm Tue-Sun) FREE The town is dear to Spaniards because it's the birthplace of literary figurehead Miguel de Cervantes Saavedra. The site, believed by many to be Cervantes' birthplace, is recreated in this illuminating museum, which lies along the beautiful, colonnaded Calle Mayor.

✖ Eating

Baratería TAPAS €€

(✆91 888 59 25; Calle de los Cerrajeros 18; tapas from €3.50, mains €9-15; ⊙12.30-4pm & 8pm-midnight Mon-Sat, 12.30-4pm Sun) A wine bar, tapas bar and restaurant all rolled into one, Baratería is a fine place to eat whatever your mood. Grilled meats are the star of the show: the ribs with honey, in particular, are a local favourite.

Hostería del Estudiante CASTILIAN €€

(✆91 888 03 30; www.parador.es; Calle de los Colegios 3; mains €13-22; ⊙1-4pm & 8.30-11pm) Based in the *parador*, this charming restaurant has wonderful Castilian cooking and a classy ambience in a dining room decorated with artefacts from the city's illustrious history.

ℹ Information

Tourist Office (✆91 881 06 34; www.turismoalcala.es; Plaza de los Santos Niños; ⊙10am-8pm) Free guided tours of 'Alcalá Monumental' (Alcalá's monuments/architecture) at noon and 4.30pm Saturday and Sunday.

Getting There & Away

Alcalá de Henares is just 35km east of Madrid, heading towards Zaragoza along the A2.

Buses depart every five to 15 minutes from Madrid's Intercambiador de Avenida de América (€3.60, one hour).

The C2 and C7 *cercanías* trains make the trip to Alcalá de Henares daily (€2.40, 50 minutes).

Sierra de Guadarrama

North of Madrid lies the Sierra de Guadarrama, a popular skiing destination and home to several charming towns. In **Manzanares El Real** you can explore the small 15th-century **Castillo de los Mendoza** (☎91 853 00 08; admission incl guided tour €3; ⏲10am-5pm Tue-Fri, 10am-7.30pm Sat & Sun), a storybook castle with round towers at its corners and a Gothic interior patio.

Cercedilla is a popular base for hikers and mountain bikers. There are several marked trails, the main one known as the **Cuerda Larga** or **Cuerda Castellana**. This is a forest track that takes in 55 peaks between the **Puerto de Somosierra** in the north and **Puerto de la Cruz Verde** in the southwest. Small ski resorts, such as **Valdesqui** (☎902 886446; www.valdesqui.es; Puerto de Cotos; lift tickets day/afternoon €37/22; ⏲9am-4pm) and **Navacerrada** (☎902 882328; www.puertonavacerrada.com; lift tickets €27-32; ⏲9.30am-5pm) welcome weekend skiers from the city.

Information

Centro de Información Valle de la Fuenfría (☎91 852 22 13; Carretera de las Dehesas; ⏲10am-6pm) Information centre located 2km outside Cercedilla on the M614.

Navacerrada Tourist Office (☎91 856 03 08; www.navacerrada.es; ⏲9am-5pm).

Getting There & Away

By car from Madrid, take the A-6 motorway to Cercedilla.

Bus 724 runs to Manzanares El Real from Plaza de Castilla in Madrid (€4.20, 45 minutes). From Madrid's Intercambiador de Autobuses de Moncloa, bus 691 heads to Navacerrada (€5.10, one hour) and bus 684 runs to Cercedilla (€5.10, one hour).

From Chamartín train station you can get to Puerto de Navacerrada on the C8B *cercanías* line (€5.40, 1¾ hours with train change in Cercedilla, four daily), and Cercedilla on the C2 *cercanías* line (€4, 1½ hours, 15 daily).

Buitrago & Sierra Pobre

The 'Poor Sierra' is a toned-down version of its more refined western neighbour, the Sierra de Guadarrama. Popular with hikers and others looking for nature without quite so many creature comforts or crowds, the sleepy Sierra Pobre has yet to develop the tourism industry of its neighbours. And that's just why we like it.

Head first to **Buitrago**, the largest town in the area, where you can stroll along part of the old **city walls**. You can also take a peek into the 15th-century Mudéjar and Romanesque **Iglesia de Santa María del Castillo** and into the small and unlikely **Picasso Museum** (☎91 868 00 56; www.madrid.org/museo_picasso; Plaza Picasso 1; ⏲11am-1.45pm & 4-6pm Tue, Thu & Fri, 11am-1.45pm Wed, 10am-2pm & 4-7pm Sat, 10am-2pm Sun) FREE, which contains a few works that the artist gave to his barber, Eugenio Arias, and is one of those rural treasures one stumbles across in the strangest places in Spain.

Hamlets are scattered throughout the rest of the sierra; some, like **Puebla de la Sierra** and **El Atazar**, make for pretty walks and are the starting point for winding hill trails.

Eating

El Arco NORTHERN SPANISH €€€
(☎918 68 09 11; Calle Arco 6; meals €35-45; ⏲1-4pm Fri-Sun mid-Sep–mid-Jun, 1-4pm & 8.30-11pm Tue-Sat, 1-4pm Sun mid-Jun–mid-Sep) The best restaurant in the region, El Arco is located in Villavieja del Lozoya, close to Buitrago, and is known for its fresh, creative cuisine based on local ingredients and traditional northern Spanish dishes. The desserts and wine list also stand out.

Information

Buitrago Tourist Office (☎91 868 16 15; Calle Tahona 19; ⏲9am-3pm Jul-Sep) For more information on Picasso Museum, visit the tourist office.

Getting There & Away

By car from Madrid, take the N-I highway to Buitrago.

Bus 191 leaves hourly from Madrid's Plaza de la Castilla to Buitrago (€5.10, 1½ hours).

Castilla y León

Best Places to Eat

➜ Restaurante El Fogón Sefardí (p162)

➜ Zazu Bistro (p152)

➜ Martín Quiroga (p165)

➜ Delirios (p181)

➜ El Huerto de Roque (p188)

Best Places to Stay

➜ Posada Real La Cartería (p172)

➜ La Posada Regia (p180)

➜ Don Gregorio (p151)

➜ Rimbombin (p187)

➜ Hotel Mozart (p164)

➜ Hospedería La Gran Casa Mudéjar (p161)

Why Go?

If you're looking for a window on the Spanish soul, head to Castilla y León. This is Spain without the stereotypes, with vast plains, spectacular mountain peaks and evocative medieval towns. Experience fabled cities like Salamanca, with its lively student population, and Segovia, famed for a fairy-tale fortress that inspired Disneyland's Sleeping Beauty castle. The multiturreted walls of Ávila have similar magical appeal, while the lofty cathedrals of León and Burgos are among Europe's most impressive. And, like most of Spain, food here is an agreeable obsession, promising the country's best *jamón* (cured ham), roast lamb and suckling pig.

The region's story is equally told through its quiet back roads, half-timbered hamlets and isolated castles. From the scenic Sierra de Francia in the southwest to Covarrubias, Calatañazor and Medinaceli in the east, this is the hidden Spain most travellers never imagined still existed.

When to Go
León

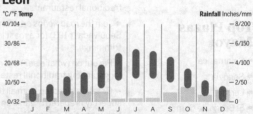

Mar & Apr Enjoy wild flowers in the countryside and soul-stirring Semana Santa processions.

Jun Get into holiday mode during annual fiesta time in Burgos, Soria and Segovia.

Sep Capture the youthful buzz of Salamanca as universities return to class.

DON'T MISS

The tapas bars in León's Barrio Húmedo are among the best in the province with delectable tapas ranging from traditional morsels to mini artworks on a plate.

Iberia's Finest Roman Villa

Okay, it's not Pompeii, but it is Spain (and Portugal's) most exciting and best-preserved Roman Villa. Located seemingly in the middle of nowhere, the Villa Romana La Olmeda (p177) is surrounded by fertile plains and hidden behind an incongruous futuristic-looking building. Step inside, however, to be transported back, like some zany time traveller, to the 4th century AD and the villa of a wealthy aristocrat and land owner whose property spans some 1000 sq metres and contains some of the finest mosaics to be discovered in a private Roman villa anywhere in Europe.

Prettiest Villages

➡ Covarrubias (p190)

➡ Pedraza de la Sierra (p163)

➡ San Martín del Castañar (p156)

➡ Puebla de Sanabria (p172)

➡ La Alberca (p156)

➡ Calatañazor (p199)

SMALL IS BEAUTIFUL

Most people associate this province with its magnificent cities, like Salamanca and León. But downsize drastically and you discover villages that look, well, like nowhere else in Spain. Stone-and-timber buildings, sandy main squares, earthy local bars, porticoed walkways held up by ancient wooden columns – and locals who stare. Consider learning enough Spanish to order a *cerveza* (beer) and take a sidestep from the city heavyweights to discover some of Spain's most extraordinary medieval villages (covered in this chapter). Staying overnight can add to this tangible sense of the past. The lack of traffic, the cobbled streets, the ancient buildings and the slow pace of life are a marvellous antidote to stressful living – along with no wi-fi (if you're lucky!).

Top Tipple

Over the last two decades, Ribera del Duero has seriously challenged Rioja for Spain's top wine region tiara. There are over 200 wineries here and some 9229 hectares of vines. And the jewel in the crown has to be world famous Vega Sicilia, Spain's most celebrated wine.

Top Plazas Mayor

➡ Salamanca

➡ Segovia

➡ Lerma

➡ El Burgo de Osma

➡ Medinaceli

Top Five Food Experiences

➡ Stop by León's La Casa de los Quesos (p181) for a wheel of locally produced goat or sheep's cheese (the perfect accompaniment to that bottle of Ribera del Duero wine you bought earlier).

➡ Indulge in the local speciality, *morcilla de Burgos* (blood sausage from Burgos; p188) at one of this city's fine traditional restaurants.

➡ Join the *madrileños* on a Sunday and head to picturesque Sepúlveda (p193) for a roast lamb lunch and all the trimmings.

➡ Pig out on (what else?) but roast suckling pig at one of the longstanding traditional restaurants in Segovia (p161).

➡ Or take a sidestep from all that meaty fare and enjoy superbly prepared organic and vegetarian cuisine at Salamanca's La Boca Abierta (p152) or El Laurel (p152); restaurants that reflect the diverse culinary tastes of a city with a substantial foreign student population.

Castilla y León Highlights

1 Revel in the architectural elegance and irresistible energy of **Salamanca** (p147).

2 Savour the sepulchral light in **León's** cathedral, a kaleidoscopic vision of glass and stone (p177).

3 Leave well-travelled paths behind and explore the **Montaña Palentina** (p175).

4 Dine on *cordero asado* (roast lamb) in the pretty hilltop towns of **Lerma** (p192) and **Sepúlveda** (p193).

5 Escape city life in the historic villages of **Covarrubias** (p190) or **Medinaceli** (p199).

6 Imagine you're somewhere between ancient Rome and Disneyland in **Segovia** (p157).

7 Go in search of wolves in the **Sierra de la Culebra** (p173), close to medieval **Puebla de Sanabria** (p172).

8 Shop for local gourmet goodies in **La Alberca** (p156).

9 Learn more about the oldest-known European discovered at the **Atapuerca** (p191) archaeological site.

THE SOUTHWEST

Ávila

POP 59,010 / ELEV 1130M

Ávila's old city, surrounded by imposing city walls comprising eight monumental gates, 88 watchtowers and more than 2500 turrets, is one of the best-preserved medieval bastions in Spain. In winter, when an icy wind whistles in off the plains, the old city huddles behind the high stone walls as if seeking protection from the harsh Castilian climate. At night, when the walls are illuminated to magical effect, you'll wonder if you've stumbled into a fairy tale. It's a deeply religious city that, for centuries, has drawn pilgrims to the cult of Santa Teresa de Ávila, with many churches, convents and high-walled palaces. As such, Ávila is the essence of Castilla, the epitome of old Spain.

◉ Sights

★ **Murallas**   WALLS
(adult/child under 12yr €5/free; ⊘ 10am-8pm Tue-Sun; ⊞) Ávila's splendid 12th-century walls stretch for 2.5km atop the remains of earlier Roman and Muslim battlements and rank among the world's best-preserved medieval defensive perimeters. Two sections of the walls can be climbed – a 300m stretch that can be accessed from just inside the Puerta del Alcázar, and a 1300m stretch that runs the length of the old city's northern perimeter. The admission price includes a multilingual audioguide.

Raised to a height of 12m between the 11th and 12th centuries, the walls have been much restored and modified, with various Gothic and Renaissance touches, and even some Roman stones reused in the construction. At dusk they attract swirls of swooping and diving swallows.

★ **Catedral del Salvador**   CATHEDRAL
(Plaza de la Catedral; admission €4; ⊘ 10am-7.30pm Mon-Fri, 10am-8pm Sat, noon-6.30pm Sun) Ávila's 12th-century cathedral is both a house of worship and an ingenious fortress: its stout granite apse forms the central bulwark in the historic city walls. The sombre Gothic-style facade conceals a magnificent interior with an exquisite early 16th-century altar frieze showing the life of Jesus, plus Renaissance-era carved choir stalls and a museum with an El Greco painting and a splendid silver monstrance by Juan de Arfe.

The first Gothic church in Spain, the cathedral's famous altar frieze of 24 paintings was completed by Juan de Borgoña in 1515; the year of Santa Teresa's birth. Above, the stunning ochre-stained limestone columns and cantilevered ceilings in the side aisles produce an effect unlike any other cathedral in the country.

Monasterio de Santo Tomás   MONASTERY
(www.monasteriosantotomas.com; Plaza de Granada 1; admission €4; ⊘ 10am-1pm & 4-8pm) Commissioned by the Reyes Católicos (Catholic Monarchs), Fernando and Isabel, and completed in 1492, this monastery is an exquisite example of Isabelline architecture, rich in historical resonance. Three interconnected cloisters lead to the church that contains the alabaster tomb of Don Juan, the monarchs' only son. There's also the impressive Museo Oriental (Oriental Museum) with 11 rooms of Far Eastern art, plus a more modest Museo de Historia Natural (Natural History Museum); both are included in the admission price.

To get here, head southeast from Jardín de San Vicente along Calle de Ferrol Hernandez and Avenida del Alférez Provisional.

Convento de Santa Teresa   MUSEUM
(Plaza de la Santa; ⊘ 8.45am-1.30pm & 3.30-9pm Tue-Sun) FREE Built in 1636 around the room where the saint was born in 1515, this is the epicentre of the cult surrounding Teresa. There are three attractions in one here: the church, a relics room and a museum. Highlights include the gold-adorned chapel (built over the room she was born), the baroque altar and the relic of the saint's ring finger (complete with ring). Apparently Franco kept it beside his bedside throughout his rule.

The elaborate chapel is lorded over by a baroque altar by Gregorio Fernández which features a statue of the saint. There's also a modest basement museum dedicated to Santa Teresa, accessible from Calle Aizpuru.

Monasterio de la Encarnación   MONASTERY
(Calle de la Encarnación; admission €2; ⊘ 9.30am-1.30pm & 3.30-6pm Mon-Fri, 10am-1pm & 4-6pm Sat & Sun) North of the city walls, this unadorned Renaissance monastery is where Santa Teresa fully took on the monastic life and lived for 27 years. One of the three main rooms open to the public is where the saint is said to have had a vision of the baby Jesus. Also on display are relics like the piece of wood used by Teresa as a pillow (ouch!) and

Ávila

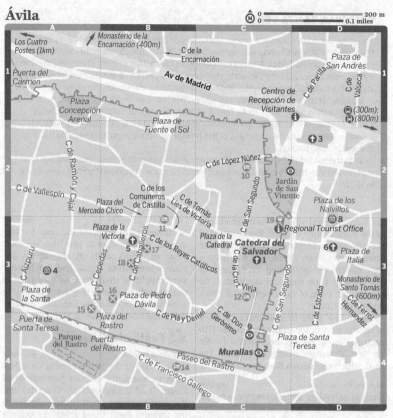

Ávila

the chair upon which St John of the Cross made his confessions.

To reach here, head north from Plaza de Fuente el Sol, via Calle de la Encarnación, for approximately 500m.

Basílica de San Vicente CHURCH
(Plaza de San Vicente; admission €2; ⊙ 10am-6.30pm Mon-Sat, 4-6pm Sun) This graceful church is a masterpiece of Romanesque simplicity: a series of largely Gothic modifications in sober

WHO WAS SANTA TERESA?

Teresa de Cepeda y Ahumada, probably the most important woman in the history of the Spanish Catholic Church, was born in Ávila on 28 March 1515, one of 10 children of a merchant family. Raised by Augustinian nuns after her mother's death, she joined the Carmelite order at age 20. After her early, undistinguished years as a nun, she was shaken by a vision of hell in 1560, which crystallised her true vocation: she would reform the Carmelites.

In stark contrast to the opulence of the church in 16th-century Spain, her reforms called for the church to return to its roots, taking on the suffering and simple lifestyle of Jesus Christ. The Carmelites demanded the strictest of piety and even employed flagellation to atone for their sins. Not surprisingly, all this proved extremely unpopular with the mainstream Catholic Church.

With the help of many supporters, Teresa founded convents all over Spain and her writings proved enormously popular. She died in 1582 and was canonised by Pope Gregory XV in 1622.

granite contrasted with the warm sandstone of the Romanesque original. Work started in the 11th century, supposedly on the site where three martyrs – San Vicente and his sisters – were slaughtered by the Romans in the early 4th century. Their canopied cenotaph is an outstanding piece of Romanesque style with nods to the Gothic.

Take a look at the headstones on the floor of the main nave; some date back to the 17th century. Also of note is the peaceful Jardín de San Vicente (◷8am-10pm) across the road, which was once a Roman cemetery.

Museo Provincial   MUSEUM
(Plaza de los Nalvillos; admission incl Iglesia de Santo Tomé El Viejo €1.20, Sat & Sun free; ◷10am-2pm & 5-8pm Tue-Sat, 10am-2pm Sun) This regional museum includes local ethnographic exhibits (the 1932 photos by Albert Klemm are particularly interesting), as well as Roman artefacts and some fine medieval paintings.

Iglesia de Santo Tomé El Viejo   CHURCH
(Plaza de Italia; admission incl Museo Provincial €1.20, Sat & Sun free; ◷10am-2pm & 5-8pm Tue-Sat, 10am-2pm Sun) This church dates from the 13th century, and it was from this pulpit that Santa Teresa was castigated most vehemently for her reforms. It has been restored to house mostly Roman foundation stones and a splendid floor mosaic.

Iglesia de San Juan Bautista   CHURCH
(Plaza de la Victoria; ◷Mass 10am & 7.30pm Mon-Sat, noon Sun) FREE This quiet parish church dates from the 16th century and contains the font in which Santa Teresa was baptised on 4 April 1515. The church can be visited before and after Mass.

Los Cuatro Postes   VIEWPOINT
Northwest of the city, on the road to Salamanca, this viewpoint provides the best views of Ávila's walls. It also marks the place where Santa Teresa and her brother were caught by their uncle as they tried to run away from home (they were hoping to achieve martyrdom at the hands of the Muslims). The best views are at night.

⚜ Festivals & Events

Semana Santa   HOLY WEEK
Ávila is one of the best places in Castilla y León to watch the solemn processions of Easter. It all begins on Holy Thursday and the most evocative event is the early morning (around 5am) Good Friday procession which circles the city wall.

Fiesta de Santa Teresa   CULTURAL FESTIVAL
Annual festival during the second week of October honouring the city's patron saint with processions, concerts and fireworks.

🛏 Sleeping

★ **Hotel El Rastro**   HISTORIC HOTEL €
(☑920 35 22 25; www.elrastroavila.com; Calle Cepedas; s/d €35/55; ❉🐾) This atmospheric hotel occupies a former 16th-century palace with original stone, exposed brickwork and an earth-toned colour scheme exuding a calm understated elegance. Each room has a different form, but most have high ceilings and plenty of space. The owners also run a marginally cheaper, same name hostal around the corner.

Hostal San Juan   HOSTAL €
(☑920 25 14 75; www.hostalsanjuan.es; Calle de los Comuneros de Castilla 3; s/d Sun-Thu €24/30, Fri &

Sat €32/40; 🛜) With warm tones throughout, well-kept rooms and a location close to everything in Ávila, Hostal San Juan is pleasant, friendly and very good value. The addition of a fitness room (with exercise machines) is a real one-off in this budget category.

Hostería Las Cancelas HISTORIC HOTEL €€
(📞920 21 22 49; www.lascancelas.com; Calle de la Cruz Vieja 6; r €70; ⊙Feb-Dec; 🕸🛜) Set above an excellent restaurant, the rooms here have a no-frills, traditional charm with terracotta tiles and Castilian dark-wood furniture. Bathrooms are freshly tiled and modern, but the vast reception is anything but, exuding all the evocative atmosphere of the building's former 15th-century *posada* (inn) roots.

Hostal Arco San Vicente HOSTAL €€
(📞920 22 24 98; www.arcosanvicente.com; Calle de López Núñez 6; s/d €40/66; 🕸🛜) This gleaming *hostal* has small, blue-carpeted rooms with pale paintwork and wrought-iron bedheads. Rooms on the 2nd floor have attic windows and air-con, some on the 1st floor look out at the Puerta de San Vicente; corner room 109 is particularly spacious and attractive.

Hotel Las Leyendas HISTORIC HOTEL €€
(📞920 35 20 42; www.lasleyendas.es; Calle de Francisco Gallego 3; s/d incl breakfast €56/79; 🕸🛜) Occupying the house of 16th-century Ávila nobility, this intimate hotel overflows with period touches wedded to modern amenities. Some rooms have views out across the plains, others look onto an internal garden. The decor varies between original wooden beams, exposed brick and stonework and more modern rooms with walls washed in muted earth tones. Breakfast is a little sparse.

Eating

Ávila is famous for its *chuleton de Ávila* (T-bone steak) and *judías del barco de Ávila* (white beans, often with chorizo, in a thick sauce).

Trattoria Roberto TRATTORIA €
(www.trattoriaroberto.es; Calle de Caballeros 12; mains €8.50-10; ⊙10.30am-4.30pm & 7.30pm-midnight Tue-Sun; 🖉🖬) If you feel like sidestepping from Avila's more traditional cuisine, this Italian menu includes some two dozen pasta sauces, ranging from pesto to *puttanesca* (with anchovies, tomatoes and garlic). The ebullient owner has a passion for soul music, hence the entertaining Motown-style decor of posters, pictures and vinyl, along with the foot-tapping soundtrack.

★Soul Kitchen CONTEMPORARY CASTILIAN €€
(www.soulkitchen.es; Calle de Caballeros 13; mains €9-€18.50; ⊙10am-midnight Mon-Fri, 11am-2am Sat, 11am-midnight Sun; 🖉🖬) Opened in 2013, this restaurant has the kind of contemporary energy that can seem lacking in Avila's staider restaurants. The eclectic menu changes regularly and ranges from salads, with dressings like chestnut and fig, to hamburgers with cream of *setas* (oyster mushrooms). Lighter eats include *bruschetta* with tasty toppings. Live music, poetry readings (and similar) take place in summer.

Mesón del Rastro CASTILIAN €€
(www.elrastroavila.com; Plaza del Rastro 1, Ávila; mains €12-21; ⊙1-4pm & 9-11pm) The dark-wood-beamed interior announces immediately that this is a bastion of robust Castilian cooking and has been since 1881. Expect delicious mainstays such as *judías del barco de Ávila* and *cordero asado,* mercifully light salads and, regrettably, the occasional coach tour. The *menú degustacó*n, priced for two people (€30), comes warmly recommended, but only if you're *really* hungry.

Hostería Las Cancelas CASTILIAN €€
(📞920 21 22 49; www.lascancelas.com; Calle de la Cruz Vieja 6; mains €16-25; ⊙1-4pm & 7.30-11pm) This courtyard restaurant occupies a delightful interior patio dating back to the 15th century. Renowned for being a mainstay of

---

CASTILLA Y LEÓN'S BEST FESTIVALS

Semana Santa Almost all of of Castilla y León's cities and villages host evocative processions (March/April)

Fiesta de Santa Teresa (p144) Honours Ávila's revered patron saint (October)

Carnaval (p154) Ciudad Rodrigo hosts the region's celebrations (February)

Concierto de las Velas (p163) Eerie candlelit concerts in Pedraza de la Sierra (July)

Titirimundi International Puppet Festival (www.titirimundi.es; ⊙mid-May; 🖬) Celebrates puppetry and puppet theatre in Segovia (mid-May)

Baby-jumping (p193) Strange Corpus Cristi festival in Castrillo de Murcia (May/June)

Ávila cuisine, traditional meals are prepared with a salutary attention to detail; the *solo-millo con salsa al ron y nueces* (sirloin in a rum and walnut sauce) is a rare deviation from tradition. Reservations recommended.

Posada de la Fruta CASTILIAN, INTERNATIONAL **€€**
(www.posadadelafruta.com; Plaza de Pedro Dávila 8; bar mains €8-10, restaurant mains €12-20; ⊙1-4pm & 7.30pm-midnight) Simple, tasty bar-style meals can be had in a light-filled, covered courtyard, while the traditional *comedor* (dining room) is all about hearty meat dishes offset by simple fresh salads. The unusual international meat dishes, which include gazelle and kangaroo, are the standout.

Drinking & Nightlife

Ávila is long on saints but short on discos, so nights can be church mouse quiet.

⭐ **La Bodeguita de San Segundo** WINE BAR
(www.vinoavila.com; Calle de San Segundo 19; ⊙11am-midnight Thu-Tue) Situated in the 16th-century Casa de la Misericordia, this superb wine bar is standing-room only most nights and more tranquil in the quieter afternoon hours. Its wine list is renowned throughout Spain with over 1000 wines to choose from, with tapas-sized servings of cheeses and cured meats the perfect accompaniment.

❶ Information

Centro de Recepción de Visitantes (☑920 35 40 00, ext 790; www.avilaturismo.com; Avenida de Madrid 39; ⊙9am-8pm) Municipal tourist office.

Regional Tourist Office (☑920 21 13 87; www.turismocastillayleon.com; Casa de las Carnicerías, Calle de San Segundo 17; ⊙9am-2pm & 5-8pm Mon-Sat, 9.30am-5pm Sun)

❶ Getting There & Away

Bus Frequent services to Segovia (€5.85, one hour), Salamanca (€7.60, 1½ hours) and Madrid (€9.45, 1½ hours); a couple of daily buses head for the main towns in the Sierra de Gredos.

Car & Motorcycle From Madrid the driving time is around one hour; the toll costs €9.70.

Train There are services to Madrid (from €8.75, 1¼ to two hours), Salamanca (from €12,1¼ hours, eight daily) and León (from €22, three hours, three daily).

❶ Getting Around

Local bus 1 runs past the train station to Plaza de la Catedral.

Sierra de Gredos

South of Ávila, the plains of Castilla yield to the precipitous Sierra de Gredos, a secret world of lakes and granite mountains rising up to the Pico de Almanzor (2592m). While the occasional castle or sanctuary may catch the eye, the overriding appeal is the scenery. The sierra is also popular with walkers, mountain bikers and rock climbers, the best seasons being spring and autumn.

A convenient gateway to the southern Sierra de Gredos is Arenas de San Pedro while, nearby, Guisando, El Hornillo and El Arenal, a trio of villages at a distance of 5km, 6km and 9km from Arenas, respectively, have access to walking trails.

Sleeping & Eating

Camping Los Galayos CAMPGROUND **€**
(☑920 37 40 21; www.campinglosgalayos.com; Carretera Linarejos; adult/sites/car €3.90/3.80/3.60, 4-person bungalow €93; P ♨) One of the best camping grounds in the region with the option of well-equipped bungalows, Los Galayos has a stunning position on the Rio Pelayo with mountain views. Ideal for families, there is easy access to a small waterfall and pools of shallow turquoise water for paddling tots.

El Fogon de Gredos RURAL HOTEL **€**
(☑920 37 40 18; www.fogondegredos.com; Carretera Linarejos, Guisando; s/d incl breakfast €28/55, mains €8-14; P ❄ ♨) This is the most attractive option in Guisando, offering spacious rooms with sweeping pine-clad mountain views. El Fogon is even better known as a restaurant serving satisfying, meat-dominated local cuisine. It's located around 1.5km beyond the town centre, by the Rio Pelayo.

⭐ **El Milano Real** BOUTIQUE HOTEL **€€**
(☑920 34 91 08; www.elmilanoreal.com; Calle de Toledo, Hoyos del Espino; r incl breakfast from €95, mains €12-18; P ❄ ♨ ♨) This is a gorgeous place to stay, with wonderful views, a peaceful setting and a fine restaurant. Each room's decor reflects its name, ranging from a Zen-feel Japanese room to the Nordic choice with its very own sauna. All have agreeable extras like hydro-massage baths and breakfast is a gourmet affair. There is also a spa.

La Casa de Arriba RURAL HOTEL **€€**
(☑920 34 80 24; www.casadearriba.com; Calle de la Cruz 19, Navarredonda de Gredos; s/d €68/80, mains €8-15; ❄ ♨) At the top of the village, this lovely hotel dates from the 17th cen-

A PICTURESQUE HIKE

Running west off the N502, near Puerta de Pico, the scenic C500 passes Navarredonda de Gredos and on to Hoyos del Espino, from where the small AV931 leads into the sierra, ending after 12km at La Plataforma. This is the jumping-off point for one of the region's most picturesque walks, leading to the Laguna Grande, a glassy mountain lake in the shadow of the Pico de Almanzor. The easy-to-moderate walk along a well-marked 8km trail takes about 2½ hours each way. Next to the lake is a *refugio* (mountain shelter), which is often full, and good camping. From here it's possible to climb to the top of the Pico de Almanzor (difficult) in about two hours or continue for two hours west to the Circo de Cinco Lagunas (easy to moderate). From there you could either backtrack or descend via the Garganta del Pinar towards the town of Navalperral de Tormes, a rigorous undertaking that can take five hours.

For organised activities, including horse riding, trekking and abseiling, check out the eco-friendly Alternativas en el Medio Natural (☑ 920 34 83 85; www.amngredos.com; Hoyos del Espino) ✐. You can book the *refugio* in advance by calling ☑ 920 207 576 or 91 847 6253.

tury and brims with rustic charm: wooden beams and floors, antique furnishings and thick stone walls. The restaurant is highly regarded.

ℹ Information

Tourist Office (☑ 920 37 23 68; Plaza de San Pedro; ◷ 10am-1.30pm & 4-8pm Mon-Sat) Has information on local hikes.

ℹ Getting There & Away

Public transport is intermittent at best – renting a car is essential. Daily buses connect Arenas de San Pedro with Madrid (€12.75, 2½ hours, nine daily) and Ávila (€8, 1¼ hours, two daily).

Salamanca

POP 155,619

Whether floodlit by night or bathed in the sunset, there's something magical about Salamanca. This is a city of rare beauty, awash with golden sandstone overlaid with ochre-tinted Latin inscriptions; an extraordinary virtuosity of plateresque and Renaissance styles. The monumental highlights are many, with the exceptional Plaza Mayor (illuminated to stunning effect at night) an unforgettable highlight. But this is also Castilla's liveliest city, home to a massive Spanish and international student population that throngs the streets at night and provides the city with so much youth and vitality.

History

In 220 BC Celtiberian Salamanca was besieged by Hannibal. Later, under Roman rule, it was an important staging post on the Ruta de la Plata (Silver Route) from the mines in Asturias to Andalucía. After the Muslim invasion of Spain, the city repeatedly changed hands. The greatest turning point was the founding of the university in 1218, which grew to become the equal of Oxford and Bologna. The city followed the rest of Castilla into decline in the 17th century, although by the time Spanish literary hero Miguel de Unamuno became rector at the university in 1900 Salamanca had essentially recovered. Throughout the 20th century, especially during the Civil War, Salamanca's university became both the centre for liberal resistance to fascism and the object of Franco's efforts to impose a compliant academic philosophy at Spain's most prestigious university. To a small degree, that liberal–conservative tension still defines the character of the town.

◉ Sights & Activities

★ Plaza Mayor   SQUARE

Built between 1729 and 1755, Salamanca's exceptional grand square is widely considered to be Spain's most beautiful central plaza. The square is particularly memorable at night when illuminated (until midnight) to magical effect. Designed by Alberto Churriguera, it's a remarkably harmonious and controlled baroque display. The medallions placed around the square bear the busts of famous figures.

Look for the controversial inclusion of Franco in the northeast corner – it looks different from the others, being unceremoniously covered with what looks like a humble

Salamanca

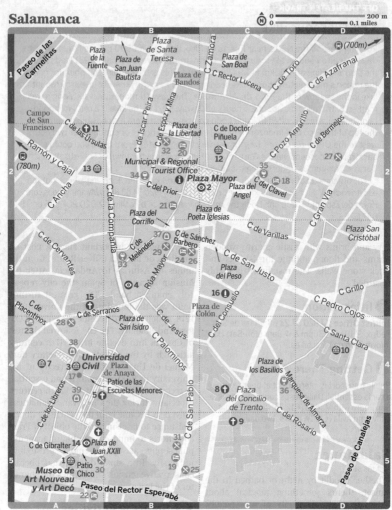

plastic bag (to counter its regular subjection to vandalism). Bullfights were held here well into the 19th century; the last ceremonial *corrida* (bullfight) took place in 1992.

★**Universidad Civil**　　HISTORIC BUILDING
(Calle de los Libreros; adult/concession €4/2, Mon morning free; ⊙9.30am-1.30pm & 4-6.30pm Mon-Sat, 10am-1.30pm Sun) The visual feast of the entrance facade is a tapestry in sandstone, bursting with images of mythical heroes, religious scenes and coats of arms. It's dominated by busts of Fernando and Isabel. Founded initially as the Estudio Generál

in 1218, the university reached the peak of its renown in the 15th and 16th centuries. Behind the facade, the highlight of an otherwise modest collection of rooms lies upstairs: the extraordinary university library, the oldest university library in Europe.

★**Museo de Art Nouveau y Art Decó**　　MUSEUM
(Casa Lis, Calle de Gibraltar; adult/child under 12yr €4/free, Thu morning free; ⊙11am-2pm & 5-9pm Tue-Fri, 11am-9pm Sat & Sun; ⊕) Utterly unlike any other Salamanca museum, this stunning collection of sculpture, paintings and

Salamanca

art deco and art nouveau pieces inhabits a beautiful, light-filled Modernista (Catalan art nouveau) house. There's abundant stained glass and exhibits that include Lalique glass, toys by Steiff (inventor of the teddy bear), Limoges porcelain, Fabergé watches, fabulous bronze and marble figurines and a vast collection of 19th-century children's dolls (some strangely macabre...) which kids will love. There's also a cafe and an excellent gift shop.

Catedral Nueva   CATHEDRAL
(Plaza de Anaya; ◎ 9am-8pm) **FREE** The tower of this late-Gothic cathedral lords over the city centre, its compelling *churrigueresco* (ornate style of baroque) dome visible from almost every angle. The interior is similarly impressive, with elaborate choir stalls, main chapel and retrochoir all courtesy of the prolific José Churriguera. The ceilings are also exceptional, along with the Renaissance doorways, particularly the Puerta del Nacimiento on the western face, that stands out as one of several miracles worked in the city's native sandstone.

The Puerta de Ramos, facing Plaza de Anaya, contains an encore to the 'frog spotting' challenge on the university facade. Look for the little astronaut and ice-cream cone chiselled into the portal by stonemasons during restoration work in 1992.

Catedral Vieja   CATHEDRAL
(Plaza de Anaya; admission €4.75; ◎ 10am-7.30pm) The Catedral Nueva's largely Romanesque predecessor, the Catedral Vieja is adorned with an exquisite 15th-century altarpiece, one of the finest outside Italy, with 53 panels depicting scenes from the lives of Christ and Mary, topped by a representation of the Final Judgment. The cloister was largely ruined in an earthquake in 1755, but the Capilla de Anaya houses an extravagant alabaster sepulchre and one of Europe's oldest organs, a Mudéjar work of art dating from the 16th century.

The cathedral was begun in 1120 and remains something of a hybrid: there are Gothic elements, while the unusual ribbed cupola, the Torre del Gallo, reflects a Byzantine influence.

Convento de San Esteban   CONVENT
(Plaza del Concilio de Trento; admission €3; ◎ 10am-1.30pm & 4-7.30pm) Just down the hill from the cathedral, the lordly Convento de San Esteban's church has an extraordinary altarlike facade, with the stoning of San Esteban (St Stephen) as its central motif. Inside is

DON'T MISS

FROG-SPOTTING

Arguably a lot more interesting than trainspotting, a compulsory task facing all visitors to Salamanca is to search out the frog sculpted into the facade of the Universidad Civil (p148). Once pointed out, it's easily enough seen, but the uninitiated can spend considerable time searching. Why bother? Well, they say that those who detect it without help can be assured of good luck and even marriage within a year. Some hopeful students see a guaranteed examination's victory in it. If you believe all this, stop reading now. If you need help, look at the busts of Fernando and Isabel. From there, turn your gaze to the largest column on the extreme right of the front. Slightly above the level of the busts is a series of skulls, atop the leftmost of which sits our little amphibious friend (or what's left of his eroded self).

a well-presented museum dedicated to the Dominicans, a splendid Gothic-Renaissance cloister and an elaborate church built in the form of a Latin cross and adorned by an overwhelming 17th-century altar by José Churriguera.

Convento y Museo de las Úrsulas CONVENT
(Calle de las Úrsulas 2; admission €2; ⊙11am-1pm & 4.30-6pm Tue-Sun) A late-Gothic nunnery founded by Archbishop Alonso de Fonseca in 1512, the religious museum is fairly modest with some interesting paintings by Juan de Borgoña, who completed the stunning altar in Avila's Catedral del Salvador (p142), but do take a look at the magnificent marble tomb within the church, sculpted by Diego de Siloé.

Casa de las Conchas HISTORICAL BUILDING
(House of Shells; Calle de la Compañia 2; ⊙9am-9pm Mon-Fri, 10am-2pm & 4-7pm Sat & Sun) FREE
One of the city's most endearing buildings, named after the 300 scallop shells clinging to its facade. The house's original owner, Dr Rodrigo Maldonado de Talavera, was a doctor at the court of Isabel and a member of the Order of Santiago, whose symbol is the shell. It now houses the public library, entered via a charming colonnaded courtyard with a central fountain and intricate stone tracery.

Convento de Santa Clara MUSEUM
(Calle Santa Clara 2; adult/concession €3/2; ⊙9.30am-12.45pm & 4.20-6.10pm Mon-Fri, 9.30am-2.10pm Sat & Sun) This much-modified convent started life as a Romanesque structure and now houses a small museum. You can admire the beautiful frescoes and climb up some stairs to inspect at close quarters the 14th- and 15th-century wooden Mudéjar ceiling. You can only visit as part of a (Spanish-language) guided tour which run roughly every hour.

Puerta de la Torre VIEWPOINT
(Jeronimus; Plaza de Juan XXIII; admission €3.75; ⊙10am-7.15pm) For fine views over Salamanca, head to the tower at the southwestern corner of the Catedral Nueva's facade. From here, stairs lead up through the tower, past labyrinthine but well-presented exhibitions of cathedral memorabilia, then along the interior balconies of the sanctuaries of the Catedral Nueva and Catedral Vieja and out onto the exterior balconies. There's another entrance inside the Catedral Vieja.

Real Clericía de San Marcos CHURCH, TOWER
(San Marcos; Calle de la Compañia; San Marcos €3, Scala Coeli €3.75; ⊙San Marcos 10.30am-12.30pm & 5-6.30pm Tue-Fri, 10am-1pm & 5-7.15pm Sat, 10am-1pm Sun, Scala Coeli 10am-7pm) Visits to this colossal baroque church and the attached Catholic university are via obligatory guided tours (in Spanish), which run every 45 minutes. You can also climb the Scala Coeli (tower), some 166 steps, including the bell tower, with superb panoramic views.

Convento de las Dueñas CONVENT
(Calle Gran Vía; admission €2; ⊙11am-12.45pm & 4.30-6.45pm Mon-Sat) This Dominican convent is home to the city's most beautiful cloister, with some decidedly ghoulish carvings on the capitals.

Torre del Clavero TOWER
(Calle del Consuelo) This 15th-century octagonal fortress has an unusual square base and smaller cylindrical towers.

Palacio de Monterrey HISTORIC BUILDING
(Calle del Prior) Off the southwestern corner of Plaza Mayor, take Calle del Prior, which leads to the 16th-century holiday home of the Duques de Alba and a seminal piece of Spanish Renaissance architecture; it's not open to the public but the facade is superb.

Cielo de Salamanca HISTORIC BUILDING
(Patio de las Escuelas Menores; ☉ 9.30am-1.30pm Tue-Fri, 10am-2pm Sat & Sun) FREE The main (and only) attraction here is the beautiful pale-blue ceiling fresco of the zodiac; give yourself a few moments to adjust to the light before gazing aloft.

Museo Taurino MUSEUM
(Calle de Doctor Piñuela 5-7; admission €3; ☉ 11.30am-1.30pm & 6-8pm Tue-Sat, 11.30am-1.30pm Sun) Salamanca lies in one of Spain's bullfighting heartlands and this small museum is packed with bullfighting memorabilia.

🎓 Courses

In addition to the following, the municipal tourist office has a list of accredited private colleges.

University of Salamanca LANGUAGE COURSE
(Cursos Internacionales, Universidad Civil; ☎ 923 29 44 18; www.cursosinternacionales.usal.es; Patio de las Escuelas Menores) Salamanca is one of the most popular places in Spain to study Spanish and the University of Salamanca is the most respected language school. Courses range from a three-hour daily course spread over two weeks (€425) to a 10-week course of five hours daily (€1975). Accommodation can be arranged.

👉 Tours

The Municipal tourist office (p153) organises two-hour guided tours of the city. These depart at 2pm on weekdays from in front of the tourist office in Plaza Mayor and cost €20 per person. They are held in Spanish, French or English and include admission to the cathedral. Reservations essential.

🛏️ Sleeping

★ Hostal Concejo HOSTAL €
(☎ 923 21 47 37; www.hconcejo.com; Plaza de la Libertad 1; s/d €45/60; P ❀ 🐾 🛜) A cut above the average *hostal*, the stylish Concejo has polished-wood floors, tasteful furnishings, light-filled rooms and a superb central location. Try and snag one of the corner rooms (like number 104) with traditional glassed-in balcony, complete with a table, chairs and people-watching views.

Hostal Plaza Mayor HOSTAL €
(☎ 923 26 20 20; www.hostalplazamayor.es; Plaza del Corrillo 20; s/d €33/55; ❀ @ 🛜) Near Plaza Mayor, this friendly, family owned *hostal* has simple but well-tended rooms washed in

pale peach with dark wood furniture, some with wooden beams. Three of the outside rooms have small balconies which are pleasant for people watching but noisy for sleeping; interior rooms are far quieter.

Microtel Placentinos BOUTIQUE HOTEL €€
(☎ 923 28 15 31; www.microtelplacentinos.com; Calle de Placentinos 9; s/d incl breakfast Sun-Thu €57/73, Fri & Sat €88/100; ❀ 🛜) One of Salamanca's most charming boutique hotels, Microtel Placentinos is tucked away on a quiet street and has rooms with exposed stone walls and wooden beams. The service is faultless, and the overall atmosphere is one of intimacy and discretion. All rooms have a hydromassage shower or tub and there's a summer-only outside whirpool spa.

Aparthotel El Toboso APARTMENT €€
(☎ 923 27 14 62; www.hoteltoboso.com; Calle del Clavel 7; 3-/4-/5-person apt €75/85/105; ❀ 🛜 🖶) These apartments don't have heaps of character but are super value, especially the larger ones which come with kitchens (including washing machines) and renovated bathrooms; ideal for families. Don't miss the fabulous 100-year-old tiled mural of Don Quijote in the bar.

Rúa Hotel HOTEL €€
(☎ 923 27 22 72; www.hotelrua.com; Calle de Sánchez Barbero 11; r incl breakfast from €80; ❀ @ 🛜) The former apartments here have been converted to seriously spacious rooms with sofas and fridges. Light-wood floors, rag rolled walls and arty prints set the tone. You couldn't be more central than this.

★ Don Gregorio BOUTIQUE HOTEL €€€
(☎ 923 21 70 15; www.hoteldongregorio.com; Calle de San Pablo 80; r/ste incl breakfast from €180/300; P ❀ 🛜) A palatial hotel with part of the city's Roman Wall flanking the garden. Rooms are decorated in soothing shades of cappuccino with crisp white linens and extravagant extras, including private saunas, espresso machines and two TVs (in the suites), complimentary mini-bar, kingsize beds and vast hydromassage tubs (in the standard rooms). Sumptuous antiques and medieval tapestries adorn the public areas.

Hotel Rector HOTEL €€€
(☎ 923 21 84 82; www.hotelrector.com; Paseo del Rector Esperabé 10; r €150; ❀ 🛜) This luxurious hotel is an oasis of calm and luxury, and the antithesis of the cookie-cut homogeneity of the five-star chains. Expect vases of orchids,

stained-glass windows, finely carved antiques and excellent service, as well as sumptuous, carpeted rooms.

Eating

★ La Boca Abierta · INTERNATIONAL €
(www.labocaabierta.com; Calle Sánchez Barbero 9; tapas €3-3.80, mains €10; ☉1-4pm & 8-11pm; 🖉) Enjoy delicious, freshly prepared dishes including healthy salads, risottos, mini pizzas, burgers (ranging from black pudding to vegetarian), and similar. The tapas are generously sized (try the vegetable tempura) and the desserts original and varied. The muted lights and subtle decor set the scene nicely, along with the smooth jazz on the sound system.

El Laurel · VEGETARIAN €
(Calle de San Pablo 49; menú del día €10.40, mains €8-9; ☉1.30-5pm & 8.30pm-12.30am Tue-Sat, 1.30-5pm Sun; 🖉🖢) A great value three course *menú* (with wine, beer or soft drink) including a vegetarian choice based on Spanish favourite dishes, like garbonzos with chestnuts (instead of *chorizo*), vegetable paella, *croquetas* of pumpkin, pinenuts and carrot, and soy burgers. The decor and ambience is suitably soothing and intimate with just a handful of tables.

Mandala Café · MEDITERRANEAN €
(Calle de Serranos 9-11; set menu €10; ☉8am-11pm; 🖢) Come here with an appetite as cool and casual Mandala offers a three-course set menu (unusually available for lunch *and* dinner) with dishes like black rice with seafood, and vegetable lasagne. There are also 18 flavours of hot chocolate, 45 types of milkshakes, 56 juice combinations and more teas than we could count.

★ Zazu Bistro · BISTRO €€
(www.restaurantezazu.com; Plaza de la Libertad 8; mains €11-19; ☉2-4pm & 9-11.30pm) Enjoy a romantic, intimate ambience and Italian-inspired dishes like prawn and wild mush-

room risotto and duck confit tagliatelle. There are some culinary surprises as well, like that delectable British standard, sticky toffee pudding, for dessert. Every dish is executed to perfection. Snag a table by the window overlooking this tranquil square.

La Cocina de Toño · TAPAS €€
(www.lacocinadetoño.es; Calle Gran Via 20; tapas €1.30-3.80, mains €7-20; ☉2-4pm & 8-10pm Tue-Sat, 2-5pm Sun) This place owes its loyal following to its creative *pinchos* (snacks) and half-servings of dishes such as escalope of foie gras with roast apple and passionfruit gelatin. The restaurant serves more traditional fare as befits the decor, but the bar is one of Salamanca's gastronomic stars. Slightly removed from the old city, it draws a predominantly Spanish crowd.

Mesón Las Conchas · CASTILIAN €€
(Rúa Mayor 16; mains €10-21; ☉bar 8am-midnight, restaurant 1-4pm & 8pm-midnight; 🖢) Enjoy a choice of outdoor tables, an atmospheric bar or the upstairs, wood-beamed dining area. The bar caters mainly to locals who know their *embutidos* (cured meats). For sit-down meals, there's a good mix of roasts, *platos combinados* and *raciones* (full-plate-size tapas). It serves a couple of cured meat platters (€35 for two people), and a highly rated oven-baked turbot.

Restaurante Lis · CONTEMPORARY CASTILIAN €€
(☑923 21 62 60; www.restaurantelis.es; Patio Chico 18; mains €14-18, set menus €28-32; ☉2-4pm & 8.30pm-late Tue-Sat, 4-8.30pm Sun) This classy restaurant specialises in set menus with a choice of five starters for sharing, followed by an elected meat or fish main, and dessert. The atmosphere is intimate and the cooking assured with riffs on well-known dishes such as duck hamburger or mango ravioli. Reservations recommended.

Victor Gutierrez · CONTEMPORARY SPANISH €€€
(☑923 26 29 73; www.restaurantevictorgutierrez.com; Calle de San Pablo 66-80; set menus €36-80; ☉2-4pm & 8-11pm Tue-Sat, 2-4pm Sun; 🕾) Justifiably exclusive vibe with an emphasis on innovative dishes with plenty of colourful drizzle. The choice of what to order is largely made for you with some excellent set menus. Reservations essential.

Drinking & Nightlife

Salamanca's large student population equals a lively nightlife. Many cafe-bars morph into dance clubs after midnight.

★ **Tío Vivo** MUSIC BAR
(www.tiovivosalamanca.com; Calle del Clavel 3-5; ☺3.30pm-late) Sip drinks by flickering candlelight to a background of '80s music, enjoying the whimsical decor of carousel horses and oddball antiquities. There is live music Tuesday to Thursday from midnight, sometimes with a €5 admission.

Vinodiario WINE BAR
(Plaza de los Basilios 1; ☺9.30am-1am Sun-Thu, to 1.30am Fri & Sat) Away from the crowds of the old-city centre, this quiet but classy neighbourhood wine bar is staffed by knowledgeable bar staff and loved by locals who, in summer, fill the outdoor tables for early evening drinks. The tapas are good.

Café El Corrillo MUSIC BAR
(www.cafecorrillo.com;CalledeMeléndez;☺8.30am-3am) Great for a beer and tapas at any time, with live music on Wednesday and Thursday nights from 10pm. The *terraza* out back is perfect on a warm summer's evening.

Garamond CLUB
(Calle del Prior 24; ☺9pm-late) A stalwart of Salamanca nightlife with medieval-style decor, Garamond has music that's good to dance to without straying too far from the mainstream.

🛍 **Shopping**

Salamanca overflows with souvenir shops, running the whole gamut from the tasteful to the tacky; the following fall into the former category. All over the centre of town, you'll come across places serving the finest Salamanca *jamón serrano* (ham made from white pigs), usually vacuum sealed and ready to carry home.

La Galatea BOOKS
(Calle de los Libreros 28; ☺4.30-8.30pm Mon, 10.30am-2.30pm & 4.30-8.30pm Tue-Sat, 10.30am-2.30pm Sun) The first bookshop in decades to open along Salamanca's 'Street of the Booksellers' (there were once more than 50), this fine space combines a bargain table (with some books in English), some gorgeous Spanish-language rare antique books and a carefully chosen collection of LPs.

Mercatus SOUVENIRS
(Calle de Cardenal Pla y Deniel; ☺10am-8.15pm Mon-Sat, 10.15am-2pm Sun) The official shop of the University of Salamanca has a stunning range of stationery items, leather-bound

books and other carefully selected reminders of your Salamanca visit.

El Fotografo SOUVENIRS
(Calle de Meléndez 5; ☺10.30am-1.30pm & 5-8pm Mon-Fri, 11am-2pm & 6-8.30pm Sat) This small photography shop sells beautiful B&W photos of Salamanca, coffee-table books and photographic equipment.

ℹ **Information**

Municipal & Regional Tourist Office (☎923 21 83 42; www.turismodesalamanca.com; Plaza Mayor 14; ☺9am-2pm & 4.30-8pm Mon-Fri, 10am-8pm Sat, 10am-2pm Sun) The Regional Tourist Office shares an office with the municipal office on Plaza Mayor. An audio city barcode guide (www.audioguiasalamanca.es) is available with the appropriate app.

ℹ **Getting There & Away**

The bus and train stations are a 10- and 15-minute walk, respectively, from Plaza Mayor.
Bus Buses include the following destinations: Madrid (regular/express €16.45/24.05, 2½ to three hours, hourly), Ávila (€7.60, 1½ hours, five daily), Segovia (€14, 2½ hours, four daily) and Valladolid (€9.95, 1½ hours, eight daily). There is a limited service to smaller towns with just one daily bus, except on Sunday, to La Alberca (€6.15, around 1½ hours), with stops in the villages of the Sierra de Francia such as Mogarraz and San Martín del Castañar.
Train Regular departures to Madrid's Chamartín station (€23.20, 2½ hours), Ávila (€11.75, 1¾ hour) and Valladolid (from €11.75, 1½ hours).

ℹ **Getting Around**

Bus 4 runs past the bus station and around the old-city perimeter to Calle Gran Vía. From the train station, the best bet is bus 1, which heads into the centre along Calle de Azafranal.

Around Salamanca

The town of Alba de Tormes makes for an interesting half-day excursion from Salamanca. People come here from far and wide to pay homage to Santa Teresa, who is buried in the Convento de las Carmelitas she founded in 1570. There's also the stout Torreón, the only surviving section of the former castle of the Dukes of Alba. There are regular buses (every two hours on weekends) from Salamanca's bus station to Alba de Tormes (€1.80, 40 minutes).

Ciudad Rodrigo

POP 13,710

Close to the Portuguese border and away from well-travelled tourist routes, somnambulant Ciudad Rodrigo is one of the prettier towns in western Castilla y León. It's an easy day trip from Salamanca, 80km away, but sleeping within the sanctuary of its walls enables you to better appreciate the town's medieval charm – and you'll have the Plaza Mayor to yourself after the day trippers head home.

◉ Sights

Ciudad Rodrigo's walled old town is home to some of the best-preserved plateresque architecture outside Salamanca.

★ Plaza Mayor
SQUARE

The long, sloping Plaza Mayor is a fine centrepiece for this beautiful town. At the top of the hill, the double-storey arches of the Casa Consistorial (Town Hall; ⊙ 1st floor gallery 9am-2pm Mon-Fri) are stunning, but the plaza's prettiest building is the Casa del Marqués de Cerralbo, an early 16th-century town house with a wonderful facade.

Catedral de Santa María
CATHEDRAL

(Plaza de San Salvador 1; adult/concession €3/2.50, Sun afternoon free, tower €2; ⊙ 11am-2pm Mon, 11am-2pm & 4-6pm Tue-Sat, noon-2pm & 4-6pm Sun) The elegant, weathered sandstone cathedral, begun in 1165, towers over the historic centre. Of particular interest are the Puerta de las Cadenas, with splendid Gothic reliefs of Old Testament figures; the elegant Pórtico del Perdón; and, inside, the exquisite carved-oak choir stalls. You can also climb the tower at 1.15pm on Saturday and Sunday; the views are Ciudad Rodrigo's best.

Murallas
WALLS

FREE There are numerous stairs leading up onto the crumbling ramparts of the city walls that encircle the old town. You can follow their length for about 2.2km around the town and enjoy fabulous views over the surrounding plains.

Casa de los Vázquez
HISTORIC BUILDING

(Correos; Calle de San Juan 12; ⊙ 8.30am-2.30pm Mon-Fri, 9.30am-1pm Sat) FREE Even if you've nothing to post, the correos (post office) is worth passing by to admire the magnificent artesonado (wooden Mudéjar ceiling), stained glass and medieval-style pictorial tiled friezes.

Iglesia de San Pedro & San Isidro
CHURCH

(Plaza Cristobal de Castillo; ⊙ before & after Mass) FREE The fusion of various 12th-century Romanesque-Mudéjar elements with later Gothic modifications makes this church worth seeking out. Don't miss the porticoes in the cloister. Discovered in 1994, the 12th-century reliefs of a Roman queen, Arab king and Catholic bishop reflect the various cultures of the region over the years.

Palacio de los Ávila y Tiedra
HISTORIC BUILDING

(Plaza del Conde 3; ⊙ 9am-7pm Mon-Sat) The 16th-century Palacio de los Ávila y Tiedra boasts one of the town's most engaging plateresque facades, and it's the pick of a handful of fine examples that surround the Plaza del Conde.

★ Festivals & Events

Carnaval
CARNIVAL

(🎭) Celebrated with great enthusiasm in February. In addition to the outlandish fancy dress, you can witness (or join in) a colourful encierro (running of the bulls) and capeas (amateur bullfights).

⌂ Sleeping

Hostal Arcos 11
HOSTAL €

(☑ 923 46 06 64; Campo de Toledo 17; s/d €25/45; ❋) Barbie would love the pink walls and floral bedspreads here (Ken may go elsewhere). The chip marble flooring and small bathrooms are acceptable at this price and the views of the Plaza Mayor a bonus.

★ Hospedería Audiencia Real
HISTORIC HOTEL €€

(☑ 923 49 84 98; www.audienciareal.com; Plaza Mayor 17; d €50-80; ❋ 🛜) Right on Plaza Mayor, this fine 16th-century inn has been beautifully reformed and retains a tangible historic feel with lovely exposed stone walls. Rooms have wrought-iron furniture and several sport narrow balconies overlooking the square; the very best has a private glassed-in alcove containing a romantic table for two.

Hotel Conde Rodrigo 1
HISTORIC HOTEL €€

(☑ 923 46 14 08; www.hotelesciudadrodrigo.com; Plaza de San Salvador 9; s/d €78/85; ❋ 🛜) Housed in a 16th-century former palace, the refurbished rooms are washed in pale yellow with dark-wood furnishings, shiny parquet floors and smart burgundy-and-white fabrics. The large flat-screen TV, minibar and well-equipped bathrooms are similarly agreeable, given the price.

GOING POTTY

Chamber pots, commodes, bed pans... Ciudad Rodrigo's Museo del Orinal (Chamber Pot Museum; adult/child under 12yr €2/free; ⊙ 11am-2pm Tue, Wed, Fri & Sun, 11am-2pm & 4-7pm Sat & Mon; 🖶) is opposite the cathedral, but its theme is definitely more down-to-earth than otherworldly. This city is home to Spain's (possibly the world's) only museum dedicated to the not-so-humble chamber pot (or potty, as it is known in the UK). The private collection of former local resident José Maria del Arco comprises a staggering 1300 exhibits. Hailing from 27 countries, there are some truly historic pieces here.

Highlights include a 12th-century Islamic version from Cordoba and some wonderful one-offs, like a 19th-century French chamber pot shaped like a bra and a Chinese example with a narrow opening, apparently used on rice boats. If you need a tinkle yourself, you will have to go elsewhere; there are no public toilets at the Museo del Orinal.

Parador Enrique II   HISTORIC HOTEL €€
(☎ 923 46 01 50; www.parador.es; Plaza del Castillo 1; r €125-145; 🅿 ❄ @ 🖧) Ciudad Rodrigo's premier address is a plushly renovated 14th-century castle built into the town's western wall. Converted in 1931, it's the third-oldest *parador* (luxurious state-owned hotel) in Spain. The views are good, the rooms are comfortable and the terraced gardens overlook Río Agueda. Shame about the Muzak.

🍴 Eating & Drinking

Zascandil   MODERN TAPAS €
(Correo Viejo 5; pinchos €2.50, tostas €5.50-7; ⊙ 1-4pm & 7-11pm) 🍴 A fashionable spot with an art deco look to accompany the pretty-as-a-picture gastro tapas, like sashimi and gourmet mini burgers. Organic veg come from the owner's *huerta* (market garden) and eco-wines are served. Live music in summer.

El Sanatorio   TAPAS, RACIONES €
(Plaza Mayor 12; raciones €5.50-10, mains €4.50-11; ⊙ 11am-late) Dating from 1937, the interior here doubles as a fascinating social history of the town. The walls are papered floor to ceiling with B&W photos (the oldest dated 1928), mainly of the annual Carnaval when the square used to be used as a bullring. Order a beer and peruse the pics. The tapas and *raciones* are good, as well.

La Pulpería   SEAFOOD €€
(Correo Viejo 7; mains €9.50-12; ⊙ 11.30am-4.30pm & 8-10pm Thu-Tue) Brightly lit and decorated with nets and fishing paraphernalia, the seafood here is arguably the best in town. The long menu includes paella, *bacalau* (cod) prepared a variety of ways and fried seafood with shellfish. Half *raciones* are also available if you fancy an inexpensive taster of such tentacle temptations as *pulpo a la gallego* (Galician-style octopus).

ℹ Information

Tourist Office (☎ 923 49 84 00; www.ayto ciudadrodrigo.es; Plaza Mayor 27; ⊙ 10am-1.30pm & 4-7pm Tue-Sun)

Regional Tourist Office (www.turismocastilla yleon.com; Plaza de Amayuelas 5; ⊙ 9am-2pm & 5-7pm Mon-Fri, 10am-2pm & 5-8pm Sat & Sun) Staff can arrange guided tours of the old town (€5).

ℹ Getting There & Away

Bus From the **bus station** (Campo de Toledo) there are up to 13 daily services (fewer on weekends) to Salamanca (€6.90, one hour). For the Sierra de Francia, you'll need to go via Salamanca.

Sierra de Francia

Hidden away in a remote corner of southwestern Castilla y León and, until recently, secluded for centuries, this mountainous region with wooded hillsides and pretty stone and timber villages is among Castilla y León's best-kept secrets. Quiet mountain roads connect villages that you could easily spend days exploring and where the pace of life remains relatively untouched by the modern world. This was once one of Spain's most godforsaken regions; malaria-ridden until the early 20th century.

Having your own car enables you to immerse yourself in quiet villages such as Mogarraz, east of La Alberca. It has some of the most evocative old houses in the region and is famous for its *embutidos* (cured meats), as well as the more recent novelty of over 400 portraits of past and present residents, painted by local artist Florencio Maillo and on display outside the family homes. The history of this extraordinary project dates from the 1960s when poverty was rife and many

ROAD TRIP: NORTH OF CIUDAD RODRIGO

One of the most dramatic landforms in Castilla y León, the Parque Natural Arribes del Duero is a little known gem, and this road trip takes you through some of the most picturesque country and villages.

The quiet SA324 north from Ciudad Rodrigo gives no hint of what lies ahead. At Castillo de Martín Viejo, 17km northwest of Ciudad Rodrigo, take the turn-off for Siega Verde (guided visit adult/concession €5/4; ⊘ 11am-2pm & 4-7pm Thu-Sun), the Unesco World Heritage–listed archaeological site with 645 prehistoric rock carvings of animals and ancient symbols – it's one of the richest such collections in Europe. San Felices de los Gallegos, 40km north of Ciudad Rodrigo, has a pretty Plaza Mayor and a well-preserved castle. After Lumbrales, a further 10km to the north, the road (now the SA330) narrows and passes among stone walls and begins to buck and weave with the increasingly steep contours of the land. The Mirador del Cachón de Caneces (lookout) offers the first precipitous views. The road then drops down to the Puerto de la Molinero, before climbing again to Saucelle (24km from Lumbrales) and then on to Vilvestre (31km), with pleasing views out towards the Río Duero and Portugal.

But it's at Aldeadávila, around 35km to the north, that you find the views that make this trip worthwhile. Before entering the village, turn left at the large purple sign. After 5.1km, a 2.5km walking track leads to the Mirador El Picón de Felipe, with fabulous views down into the canyon. Returning to the road, it's a further 1km down to the Mirador del Fraile – the views of the impossibly deep canyon with plunging cliffs on both sides are utterly extraordinary. This is prime birdwatching territory with numerous raptors nesting on the cliffs and griffon vultures wheeling high overhead on the thermals.

For an entirely different perspective, return to Aldeadávila, and at the eastern exit to the town follow the signs down to the lovely Playa del Rostro, from where 1½-hour boat journeys (⚓ 627 63 73 49; www.corazondelasarribes.com; adult/child 3-9yr €16/8; ⊘ noon & 6pm Aug, 6pm Mon-Fri, noon & 6pm Sat & Sun Jun & Jul, shorter hours rest of the year; ⛴) follow the canyon to the base of the cliffs.

---

locals were seeking work, mainly in South America. They needed identity cards and it is these that inspired the portraits.

Miranda del Castañar, further east, is similarly intriguing, strung out along a narrow ridge, but San Martín del Castañar is the most enchanting, with half-timbered stone houses, flowers cascading from balconies, a bubbling stream and a small bullring at the top of the town, next to the renovated castle with its *Centro de Interpretación* (Interpretation Centre) and historic cemetery.

Hotels are rare in these parts, but *casas rurales* (village or farmstead accommodation) abound, with a handful in each village. Alternatively, Abadía de San Martín (☎ 923 43 73 50/666 88 21 88; www.abadiadesanmartin. com; Calle Paipérez 24, San Martín del Castañar; d/ste €75/85) and Hotel Spa Villa de Mogarraz (hotelspamogarraz.com; Calle Miguel Ángel Maillo 54, Mogarraz; s/d €70/100; ⚛) are wonderful choices.

For further information and maps, visit the tourist offices in Salamanca or Ciudad Rodrigo.

La Alberca

POP 1210 / ELEV 1048M

La Alberca is one of the largest and most beautifully preserved of Sierra de Francia's villages; a historic and harmonious huddle of narrow alleys flanked by gloriously ramshackle houses built of stone, wood beams and plaster. Look for the date they were built (typically late 18th century) carved into the door lintels. Numerous stores sell local products such as *jamón*, as well as baskets and the inevitable tackier souvenirs. The centre is pretty-as-a-postcard Plaza Mayor; there's a market here on Saturday mornings.

🍴 Sleeping & Eating

Weekends are the busiest time, when Spanish tourists threaten to overwhelm the town. Come during the week to see La Alberca at its best.

Hostal La Alberca   HOSTAL €

(☎ 923 41 51 16; www.hostallaalberca.com; Plaza Padre Arsenio; s/d/tr €29/35/49) Housed in one of La Alberca's most evocative half-timbered buildings, above a restaurant, this charming place has comfortable, renovated rooms. Balconies overlook a small square at the entrance to the village.

Hostal La Balsa HOSTAL €
(☑ 923 41 53 37; La Balsada 4; s/d/tr €22/33/45; ☜) Tidy small rooms with large bathrooms and tubs for enjoying a post-hike soak. Located a few steps from Plaza Mayor, above a popular bar-cafeteria.

Hotel Doña Teresa HOTEL €€
(☑ 923 41 53 08; www.hoteldeteresa.com; Carretera Mogarraz; s/d €60/90; P ❄ ☜) Doña Teresa is a perfect modern fit for the village's old-world charm but can be booked up by Spanish tour groups. The large rooms combine character (wooden beams and exposed stone) with all the necessary mod cons; some open onto a garden. The owners also run a spa 1.5km away with various treatments available at reduced rates for guests.

La Taberna CASTILIAN €€
(www.latabernadelaalberca.com; Plaza Mayor 5; mains €10-15; ☉ 1-4pm, plus 8pm-12.30am Sat; ⛊) Right on Plaza Mayor with daily three-course menus including such surf to turf choices as *rabo de toro* (oxtail) and grilled trout, plus gut-busting *parrilladas* (grills) of various meats.

❶ Getting There & Away

Buses travel between La Alberca and Salamanca (€6.15, around 30 minutes) twice daily on weekdays and once a day on weekends.

Valle de las Batuecas

The drive south into Extremadura through this dreamy valley is spectacular. Just beyond La Alberca, a sweeping panorama of cascading lower mountain ranges opens up before you. The road corkscrews down into the valley before passing through beautiful terrain that has been praised by poets and the writer/academic Miguel de Unamuno. Time your visit for spring when purple heather and yellow rapeseed blanket the hillsides.

Peña de Francia

Head north from La Alberca along the C512 and you'll soon strike the turn-off to the highest peak in the area, Peña de Francia (1732m), topped by a monastery and reached by a road that turns perilous after rain. Views extend

east to the Sierra de Gredos, south into Extremadura and west towards Portugal.

Sierra de Béjar

Between the Sierra de Francia and the Sierra de Gredos, the Sierra de Béjar is home to more delightful villages and rolling mountain scenery, normally snowcapped until well after Easter. It is an excellent region for outdoor activities. The centre of the region is Béjar, with a partly walled, but somewhat neglected, old quarter straddling the western end of a high ridge.

Just east of the mountains, the C500 leads to El Barco de Ávila on the Río Tormes and lorded over by a proud, if ruined, castle.

The most scenic village in the region is tiny Candelario (population 1033), a 5km detour from Béjar. Nudging against a steep rock face, this charming village is dominated by mountain architecture of stone-and-wood houses clustered closely together to protect against the harsh winter climate. It is a popular summer resort and a great base for hiking. Contact Tormes (☑ 923 40 80 89; www.aventur.es; Calle Tormes 7) for organised hikes and other activities.

Béjar and Candelario are served by sporadic bus services from Salamanca and various other destinations, including Madrid and Plasencia.

THE CENTRAL PLATEAU

There's something soul-stirring about the high *meseta* (plateau) with its seemingly endless horizon. But from the plains spring the delightful towns of the Castilian heartland – magical Segovia, energetic Valladolid, the Romanesque glories of Zamora and the exceptional cathedral of Palencia.

Segovia

POP 56,660 / ELEV 1002M

Unesco World Heritage–listed Segovia has always had a whiff of legend about it, not least in the myths that the city was founded by Hercules or by the son of Noah. It may also have something to do with the fact that nowhere else in Spain has such a stunning monument to Roman grandeur (the soaring aqueduct) survived in the heart of a vibrant modern city. Or maybe it's because art really has imitated life Segovia-style – Walt

Segovia

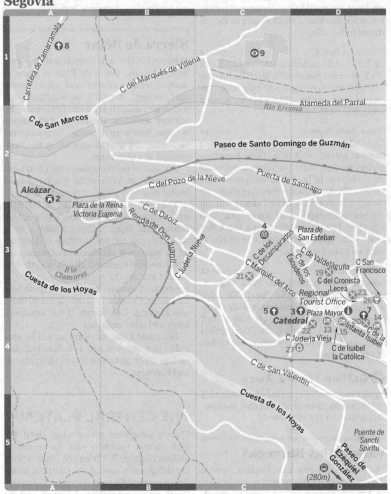

Disney is said to have modelled Sleeping Beauty's castle in California's Disneyland on Segovia's Alcázar. Whatever it is, the effect is stunning: a city of warm terracotta and sandstone hues set amid the rolling hills of Castilla and against the backdrop of the Sierra de Guadarrama.

History

Founded by Celtiberian tribes, Segovia was occupied by the Romans in 80 BC and rose to become an important town of Roman Hispania. As Christian Spain recovered from the initial shock of the Muslim attack, Sego-

via became something of a frontline city until the invaders were evicted in 1085. Later a favourite residence of Castilla's roaming royalty, the city backed Isabel and saw her proclaimed queen in the Iglesia de San Miguel in 1474. Segovia subsequently slid into obscurity until the 1960s, when tourism helped regenerate the town. This rebirth gained added momentum in 1985 when the historic centre and aqueduct were added to Unesco's World Heritage list, bringing Segovia to the attention of the world and sparking a tourist boom that has not yet abated.

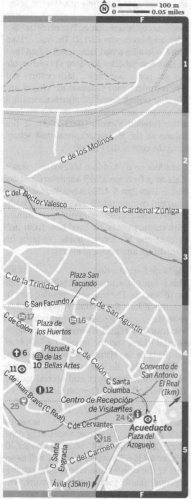

Segovia

⦿ Top Sights

⦿ Sights

🛏 Sleeping

🍴 Eating

🍷 Drinking & Nightlife

🛍 Shopping

⦿ Sights

★ Acueducto
ROMAN AQUEDUCT

Segovia's most recognisable symbol is El Acueducto (Roman Aqueduct), an 894m-long engineering wonder that looks like an enormous comb plunged into Segovia. First raised here by the Romans in the 1st century AD, the aqueduct was built with not a drop of mortar to hold the more than 20,000 uneven granite blocks together. It's made up of 163 arches and, at its highest point in Plaza del Azoguejo, rises 28m high.

The aquaduct was originally part of a complex system of aqueducts and underground canals that brought water from the mountains more than 15km away. Its pristine condition is attributable to a major restoration project in the 1990s. For a different perspective, climb the stairs next to the aqueduct that begin behind the tourist office.

★ Alcázar
CASTLE

(www.alcazardesegovia.com; Plaza de la Reina Victoria Eugenia; adult/concession/child under 6yr €5/3/free, tower €2, EU citizens 3rd Tue of the month free; ⏱10am-7pm; 🚻) Rapunzel towers, turrets topped with slate witches' hats and a *deep* moat at its base make the Alcázar a prototype fairytale castle, so much so that its design inspired Walt Disney's vision of

Sleeping Beauty's castle. Fortified since Roman days, the site takes its name from the Arabic *al-qasr* (fortress). It was rebuilt in the 13th and 14th centuries, but the whole lot burned down in 1862. What you see today is an evocative, over-the-top reconstruction of the original.

Highlights include the Sala de las Piñas, with its ceiling of 392 pineapple-shaped 'stalactites', and the Sala de Reyes, featuring a three-dimensional frieze of 52 sculptures of kings who fought during the Reconquista. The views from the summit of the Torre de Juan II are truly exceptional.

★ **Catedral** CATHEDRAL
(Plaza Mayor; adult/concession €3/2, Sun morning free; ⊙9.30am-6.30pm) Started in 1525 on the site of a former chapel, Segovia's cathedral is a powerful expression of Gothic architecture that took almost 200 years to complete. The austere three-nave interior is anchored by an imposing choir stall and enlivened by 20-odd chapels, including the Capilla del Cristo del Consuelo, which houses a magnificent Romanesque doorway, and the Capilla de la Piedad containing an important altarpiece by Juan de Juni.

The Capilla del Cristo Yacente (with its fine ceiling) and Capilla del Santísimo Sacramento are also especially beautiful, along with the Gothic cloister. The attached Museo Catedralicio will appeal to devotees of religious art.

Iglesia de Vera Cruz CHURCH
(Carretera de Zamarramala; admission €1.75; ⊙10.30am-1.30pm & 4-7pm Tue-Sun Dec-Oct) This 12-sided church is one of the best-preserved of its kind in Europe. Built in the early 13th century by the Knights Templar and based on Jerusalem's Church of the Holy Sepulchre, it once housed a piece of the Vera Cruz (True Cross), now in the nearby village church of Zamarramala (on view only at Easter).

The curious two-storey chamber in the circular nave (the inner temple) is where the knights' secret rites took place.

> **ⓘ BEST VIEW OF TOWN**
>
> For *the* shot of Segovia for your screensaver, head out of town due north (towards Cuéllar) for around 2km. The view of the city unfolds in all its movie-style magic, with the aqueduct taking a deserved star role.

Museo de Arte Contemporáneo Esteban Vicente GALLERY
(www.museoestebanvicente.es; Plazuela de las Bellas Artes; adult/concession €3/1.50, Thu free; ⊙11am-2pm & 4-7pm Tue & Wed, 11am-2pm & 4-8pm Thu & Fri, 11am-8pm Sat, 11am-3pm Sun) This adventurous art space occupies a 15th-century palace, complete with Renaissance chapel and Mudéjar ceiling. Some 153 abstract paintings, lithographs and sculptures by Segovia-born artist Esteban Vicente (1903–2000), a fine painter of the abstract expressionist school, form the core of the exhibit.

Casa-Museo de Antonio Machado MUSEUM
(Calle de los Desamparados 5; admission €2.50, Wed free; ⊙11am-2pm & 4.30-7.30pm Wed-Sun) This museum commemorates Antonio Machado, a *segoviano* and one of Spain's pre-eminent 20th-century poets. He lived here from 1919 to 1932 and his former home contains his furnishings and personal effects.

Plaza de San Martín SQUARE
This is one of the most captivating small plazas in Segovia. The square is presided over by a statue of Juan Bravo, the 14th-century Torreón de Lozoya (⊙5-9pm Tue-Fri, noon-2pm & 5-9pm Sat & Sun) FREE, a tower that now houses exhibitions, and the Iglesia de San Martín (Plaza de San Martín; ⊙before & after Mass) FREE, a pièce de Romanesque résistance with its Mudéjar tower and arched gallery. The interior boasts a Flemish Gothic chapel.

Monasterio de Santa María del Parral MONASTERY
(Calle Del Marqués de Villena; admission by donation; ⊙10am-12.30pm & 4.15-6.30pm Mon-Sat, 10-11.30am & 4.15-6.30pm Sun) Ring the bell to see part of the cloister and church; the latter is a proud, flamboyant Gothic structure. The monks chant a Gregorian Mass at noon on Sundays, and at 1pm daily in summer.

Convento de San Antonio El Real CONVENT
(Calle de San Antonio El Real 6; adult/child under 12yr €2/free; ⊙10am-2pm Wed-Sun) About 1.3km southeast of the aqueduct, this was once the summer residence of Enrique IV. The Gothic-Mudéjar church has a splendid ceiling.

Iglesia de San Miguel CHURCH
(Plaza Mayor; ⊙11.30am-2pm Thu & Sun, 11am-2pm & 5-7pm Fri & Sat) FREE On Plaza Mayor, this church – where Isabel was proclaimed Queen of Castile – recedes humbly into the background before the splendour of the cathedral across the square.

✰✰ Festivals & Events

Titirimundi International Puppet Festival
PUPPETRY

(www.titirimundi.es; ⊙ mid-May; 🖭) A week-long festival in mid-May that celebrates puppetry and puppet theatre with shows and street events throughout the city.

Fiestas de San Juan y San Pedro
PILGRIMAGE

(⊙ 24-29 Jun; 🖭) On San Juan's day (29 June), a pilgrimage takes place to a hermitage outside town. Throughout the six days of festivities, there are parades, concerts and bullfights.

Fiesta San Frutos
PATRON SAINT FESTIVAL

(⊙ 25 Oct) Segovia celebrates the town's patron saint, who is said to be the healer of hernias and bodily fractures. The event is marked in the cathedral with choral singing.

⏏ Sleeping

Hostal Fornos
HOSTAL €

(📞 921 46 01 98; www.hostalfornos.com; Calle de la Infanta Isabel 13; s/d €41/55; 🌐) This tidy little *hostal* is a cut above most other places in this price category. It has a bright cheerful atmosphere and rooms with a fresh white-linen-and-wicker look. Some rooms are larger than others, but the value is excellent. On the downside, some readers have complained of street noise.

Natura – La Hostería
HOTEL €

(📞 921 46 67 10; www.naturadesegovia.com; Calle de Colón 5-7; r €60; 🌐🛜) An eclectic choice a few streets back from Plaza Mayor. The owner obviously has a penchant for Dalí prints and the rooms have plenty of character, with chunky wooden furnishings and bright paintwork.

★ Hospedería La Gran Casa Mudéjar
HISTORIC HOTEL €€

(📞 921 46 62 50; www.lacasamudejar.com; Calle de Isabel la Católica 8; r €80; 🌐@🛜) Spread over two buildings, this place has been magnificently renovated, blending genuine 15th-century Mudéjar carved wooden ceilings in some rooms with modern amenities. In the newer wing, the rooms on the top floors have fine mountain views out over the rooftops of Segovia's old Jewish quarter. Adding to the appeal, the restaurant comes highly recommended and there's a small spa.

Hotel Infanta Isabel
HOTEL €€

(📞 921 46 13 00; www.hotelinfantaisabel.com; Plaza Mayor 12; r €55-95; 🅿🌐🛜) The colonnaded

ⓘ TOP 'TO DO' WEBSITE

For guided tours, bicycle hire, restaurant discounts, hot-air balloon and helicopter rides, horseriding and, well, just about anything else, check out the reliable www.reservasdesegovia.com website run by the *Turismo de Segovia*.

building fits well with the hotel's interior of period furnishings in most of the spacious rooms. The style may be classic in orientation, but there's a lovely sense of light and space here and the bathrooms are being gradually updated. Some rooms overlook Plaza Mayor.

Hotel Palacio San Facundo
HISTORIC HOTEL €€

(📞 921 46 30 61; www.hotelpalaciosanfacundo.com; Plaza San Facundo 4; s/d incl breakfast €90/120; 🌐@🛜) Segovia's hotels are proving adept at fusing stylishly appointed modern rooms onto centuries-old architecture. This place is one of the best, with an attractive columned courtyard, a warm colour scheme, chic room decor and a central location. The breakfast buffet is more generous than most.

✕ Eating

Segovianos love their pigs to the point of obsession. Just about every restaurant boasts its *horno de asar* (roasts). The main speciality is *cochinillo asado* (roast suckling pig), but *judiones de la granja* (butter beans with pork chunks) also looms large.

★ La Almuzara
ITALIAN, VEGETARIAN €

(Calle Marqués del Arco 3; mains €7.50-10; ⊙ noon-4pm & 8pm-midnight Wed-Sun, 8pm-midnight Tue; 🖉🖭) If you're a vegetarian, you don't need to feel like an outcast in this resolutely carnivorous city. La Almuzara offers a dedicated vegetarian menu, as well as pizzas, pastas and close to 18 innovative salads. They are not too pious to scrimp on desserts either with some decadent daily-changing choices. The ambience is warm and artsy.

Tuma
LEBANESE, SYRIAN €

(Calle Santa Columba 5; mains €8-10; menú del día €12; ⊙ 12.30pm-4.30pm & 7-11.30pm) Just around the corner from the main tourist office, this welcome addition to Segovia's restaurant scene serves such Middle Eastern favourites as hummus, falafel, shawarma, stuffed vine leaves and moussaka. The interior is all warm fabrics and overstuffed cushions; all that's missing is the hookah (water pipe, that is).

★ **Restaurante**
El Fogón Sefardí SEPHARDIC €€
(📞 921 46 62 50; www.lacasamudejar.com; Calle de Isabel la Católica 8; mains €20-25, tapas from €2.50; ⏰ 1.30-4.30pm & 5.30-11.30pm) Located within the Hospedería La Gran Casa Mudéjar, this is one of the most original places in town. Sephardic and Jewish cuisine is served either on the intimate patio or in the splendid dining hall with original, 15th-century Mudéjar flourishes. The theme in the bar is equally diverse. Stop here for a taste of the award-winning tapas. Reservations recommended.

Casa Duque GRILL €€
(📞 921 46 24 87; www.restauranteduque.es; Calle de Cervantes 12; mains €9-20; ⏰ 12.30-4.30pm & 8.30-11.30pm) *Cochinillo asado* has been served at this atmospheric *mesón* (tavern) since the 1890s. For the uninitiated, try the *menú segoviano* (€32), which includes *cochinillo*, or the *menú gastronómico* (€39). Downstairs is the informal *cueva* (cave), where you can get tapas and full-bodied *cazuelas* (stews). Reservations recommended.

El Sitio CASTILIAN €€
(Calle de la Infanta Isabel 9; mains €14-20, menú del día €11, tapas from €1.50; ⏰ 9am-3pm & 7pm-11.30pm) The tapas bar is always crowded with locals here for the exceptionally fresh, inexpensive and appertising palate ticklers like a creamy *patatas ali-oli*, stuffed mussels, homemade croquettes and quality *chorizo*. The menu is traditional and well priced, served in a dining room with exposed stone, stained-glass windows and muted lighting (for a change...).

DON'T MISS

SWEET TREATS

If you are one of those people who scoffs all the marzipan off the Christmas cake, you will love Segovia's speciality: *ponche segoviano* (literally 'Segovian punch', but far removed from that insipid low-alcohol drink you used to consume as a spotty teenager). This is a rich lemon-infused sponge cake coated with marzipan and topped with icing sugar in a distinctive criss-cross pattern. A good place to indulge in your *ponche* passion is the patisserie **Limón y Menta** (Calle de Isabel La Católica 2; ⏰ 8am-11pm), just off Plaza Mayor.

Di Vino MODERN SPANISH €€
(📞 921 46 16 50; www.restaurantedivino.com; Calle de Valdeláguila 7; mains €15-25; ⏰ 1-4pm & 7.30-11.30pm) Dine in snazzy modern surroundings on dishes that combine the traditional, like *pierna de cabrito al horno* (roasted leg of lamb), with the innovative, like the starter of *bacalau bloody mary* (cod-infused bloody mary) or kangaroo steak with Jamaican pepper. Di Vino prides itself on its extensive wine list. Reservations recommended.

Mesón José María CASTILIAN €€
(www.rtejosemaria.com; Calle del Cronista Lecea 11; mains €16-26; ⏰ 1-4pm & 8-11.30pm; 🛗) Offers fine bar tapas and five dining rooms serving exquisite *cochinillo asado* and other local specialities, most of which, including the suckling pig, are displayed in the window.

Drinking & Nightlife

In fine weather Plaza Mayor is the obvious place for hanging out and people-watching. Calle de la Infanta Isabel is one of those Spanish streets that you'll hear before you see; locals call it 'Calle de los Bares' (Street of the Bars). Another good street for bars and nightclubs is nearby Calle de los Escuderos.

Bodega del Barbero WINE BAR
(Calle Alhóndiga 2; ⏰ 10am-1am Mon-Fri, noon-1am Sat & Sun) Tucked down a narrow street, this intimate bar has a wide range of *vino* by the glass, regular art exhibitions and live music on the outside terrace on summer weekends.

Canavan's Theatre CLUB
(Plaza de la Rubia; ⏰ midnight-6.30am Thu-Sat) Opened in 2013, this is no cheesy disco, the decor is sumptuous with exquisite friezes, flocked wallpaper, chandeliers and an overall extravagant theatrical feel.

Shopping

Artesanía La Gárgola ARTS & CRAFTS
(www.gargolart.com; Calle Judería Vieja 4; ⏰ 10am-8pm Mon-Sat) Check out these unusual, high-quality handmade crafts and souvenirs in ceramic, wood and textile.

ℹ Information

Centro de Recepción de Visitantes (Tourist Office; 📞 921 46 67 20; www.turismodesegovia.com; Plaza del Azoguejo 1; ⏰ 10am-7pm Sun-Fri, 10am-8pm Sat) Segovia's main tourist office runs two-hour guided tours, departing daily at 11.15am for a minimum of four people (€13.50 per person). Reserve ahead.

Regional Tourist Office (www.segoviaturismo. es; Plaza Mayor 10; ⊘9am-8pm Sun-Thu, 9am-9pm Fri & Sat)

ℹ Getting There & Away

Bus The bus station is just off Paseo de Ezequiel González. Buses run half-hourly to Segovia from Madrid's Paseo de la Florida bus stop (€8, 1½ hours). Buses depart to Ávila (€6, one hour, eight daily) and Salamanca (€14, 2½ hours, four daily), among other destinations.

Car & Motorcycle Of the two main roads down to the AP6, which links Madrid and Galicia, the N603 is the prettier. The nearest underground car park to the historic centre is in Plaza de la Artillería near the aqueduct.

Train Just two normal trains run daily from Madrid to Segovia (€8, two hours), leaving you at the main train station 2.5km from the aqueduct. The faster option is the high-speed Avant (€12.50, 28 minutes), which deposits you at the newer Segovia-Guiomar station, 5km from the aqueduct.

ℹ Getting Around

Bus 9 does a circuit through the historic centre, bus 8 goes to Segovia train station and bus 11 goes to Segovia-Guiomar station. All services cost €1.10 and leave from just outside the aqueduct.

Around Segovia

Pedraza de la Sierra

POP 200

The captivating walled village of Pedraza de la Sierra, about 37km northeast of Segovia, is eerily quiet during the week; its restaurants, bars and eclectic shops spring to life with the swarms of weekend visitors. Bus services to Pedraza are sporadic at best.

◉ Sights

At the far end of town stands the lonely **Castillo de Pedraza** (Pedraza de la Sierra; admission €5; ⊘11am-2pm & 5-8pm Wed-Sun), unusual for its intact outer wall. The 14th-century **Plaza Mayor** is similarly evocative with its ancient columned arcades.

✾ Festivals & Events

Concierto de las Velas   MUSIC FESTIVAL
(⊘1st & 2nd Sun in Jul) On the first and second Sunday in July, Pedraza hosts the atmospheric Concierto de las Velas, when the electricity is shut down and live music is performed in a village lit only by candles.

A SPANISH VERSAILLES
••

La Granja de San Ildefonso (Sierra de Guadarrama; gardens free, Palacio Real adult/child under 12yr €9/free; ⊘10am-8pm; 🅿🚻) These magnificent gardens date from 1720 when French architects and gardeners, together with some Italian help, began laying out these elaborate baroque gardens, famous for their 28 extravagant fountains that depict ancient myths. There is also a maze. The 300-room **Palacio Real**, once a favoured summer residence for Spanish royalty and restored after a fire in 1918, is similarly impressive and includes the colourful **Museo de Tapices** (Tapestry Museum).

The palace was built for the Bourbon King Felipe V who chose this site in the western foothills of the Sierra de Guadarrama, to recreate in miniature his version of Versailles, the palace of his French grandfather, Louis XIV. If you time your visit for Wednesday, Saturday or Sunday at 5.30pm you can see the fountains in action (adult/child €4/2).

Up to a dozen daily buses to La Granja depart regularly from Segovia's bus station (€2, 20 minutes).

🛏 Sleeping

Hospedería de Santo Domingo   HOTEL €€
(📱921 50 99 71; www.hospederiadesantodomingo. com; Calle Matadero 3; d from €89) This excellent *hospedería* has terrific rooms decked out in warm ochre and earth colours. Most have large terraces overlooking the low hills nearby, criss-crossed with dry stone walls.

🛍 Shopping

Sánchez Muñoz   ART
(www.artepedraza.com; Calle Mayor; ⊘11am-2pm & 4-8pm daily Apr-Oct, 11am-2pm & 4-8pm Sat & Sun Oct-Apr) Sánchez Muñoz is an established *madrileño* artist who has a small studio here. His watercolours of the local villages are vibrant and colourful and based on subtle abstract forms. Prints available from €7.

ℹ Getting There & Away

Linecar (www.linecar.es) runs from Segovia to Pedraza just twice weekly at 1pm on Tuesday and Friday (€3.90, one hour).

Valladolid

POP 317,864

Valladolid is a city on the upswing and a convenient gateway to northern Spain. An attractive place with a very Spanish character, the city's appeal is in its sprinkling of monuments, the fine Plaza Mayor and some excellent museums. By night, Valladolid comes alive as its large student population overflows from the city's boisterous bars.

⊙ Sights

The historical centre of Valladolid is compact and easy to cover on foot, with most sights in the narrow streets north and east of the vast and magnificent Plaza Mayor.

★**Museo Nacional de Escultura**   MUSEUM
(www.museoescultura.mcu.es; Calle de San Gregorio 2; adult/concession €3/1.50, Sat afternoon & Sun free; ⊙10am-2pm & 4-7.30pm Tue-Sat, 10am-2pm Sun) Spain's premier showcase of polychrome wood sculpture is housed in the former Colegio de San Gregorio (1496), a flamboyant Isabelline Gothic–style building where exhibition rooms line a splendid two-storey galleried courtyard. Works by Alonso de Berruguete, Juan de Juní and Gregorio Fernández are the star attractions. Downstairs is a small wing dedicated to Fernández. Don't miss his painfully lifelike sculpture of a dead Christ.

★**Plaza de San Pablo**   SQUARE
This open square is dominated by the exquisite Iglesia de San Pablo. The church's main facade is an extravagant masterpiece of Isabelline Gothic, with every square centimetre finely worked, carved and twisted to produce a unique fabric in stone. Also fronting the square is the Palacio de Pimentel (⊙10am-2pm & 5-7pm Tue-Sat), where, on 12 July 1527, Felipe II was born. A tiled mural in the palace's entrance hall depicts scenes from the life of the king. The palace hosts occasional exhibitions.

★**Casa-Museo de Colón**   MUSEUM
(Calle de Colón; adult/child €2/free, Wed €1; ⊙10am-2pm & 5-8.30pm Tue-Sun; ⊕) The Casa-Museo de Colón is a superb museum spread over four floors. It has interactive exhibits, and wonderful old maps take you on a journey through Christopher Columbus' (Cristóbal Colón in Spanish) journeys to the Americas. The top floor describes Valladolid

in the days of the great explorer (who died here in 1506).

Museo Patio Herreriano   GALLERY
(www.museopatioherreriano.org; Calle de Jorge Guillén 6; adult/concession €3/2, Wed & Sun €1; ⊙11am-2pm & 5-8pm Tue-Fri, 11am-8pm Sat, 10am-3pm Sun) Dedicated to post-WWI Spanish art, this museum contains works by Salvador Dalí, Joan Miró, Basque sculptor Eduardo Chillida, Jorge Oteiza, Antoni Tàpies and Esteban Vicente, arrayed around the cloisters of a former monastery.

Catedral   CATHEDRAL
(Calle Arribas 1; museum adult/concession €3/1.50; ⊙10am-1.30pm & 4.30-7pm Tue-Sat, 10am-2pm Sun) Valladolid's 16th-century cathedral is not Castilla's finest, but it does have an extravagant altarpiece by Juní and a processional monstrance by Juan de Arfe in the attached Museo Diocesano y Catedralicio. Outside, check out the 13th-century ruins of the Collegiate Church (atop which the cathedral was built) on the cathedral's northeastern perimeter.

Casa de Cervantes   MUSEUM
(museocasacervantes.mcu.es; Calle del Rastro; adult/child under 12yr €3/free, Sun free; ⊙9.30am-3pm Tue-Sat, 10am-3pm Sun) Cervantes was briefly imprisoned in Valladolid; his house is preserved behind a quiet little garden.

Colegio de Santa Cruz   HISTORIC BUILDING
(Calle Cardenal Mendoza; ⊙hours vary) FREE
Check out the colonnaded patio and chapel with super-realistic *Cristo de la Luz* sculpture. The Colegio also hosts temporary exhibitions.

Iglesia de Santa María la Antigua   CHURCH
(Calle Antigua 1; ⊙before & after Mass) FREE
Stunning 14th-century Gothic church with elegant Romanesque tower.

Iglesia de San Benito El Real   CHURCH
(Calle de San Benito; ⊙before & after Mass) FREE
One of the loveliest church facades in Valladolid with unusual 16th-century octagonal columns.

⊨ Sleeping

Valladolid's hotels see more business folk than tourists during the week, so prices can drop considerably from Friday to Sunday.

★**Hotel Mozart**   HOTEL €
(www.hotelmozart.net; Calle Menéndez Pelayo 7; s/d €50/60; ❈🌐⊕) Extremely well-priced

hotel given the recently refurbished quality of the rooms. Kingsize beds, plush earth-colour furnishings and fabrics, polished parquet floors, dazzling marble bathrooms and space enough for a comfortable armchair. The entrance has a whiff of grandeur about it as well, which contributes to the surprise of this budget bracket price.

Hostal París
HOSTAL €

(☑ 983 37 06 25; www.hostalparis.com; Calle de la Especería 2; s/d €40/50; ❈ ☎) One of the closest places to Plaza Mayor, Hostal París has had the interior designers in. Washed in pale pastel colours with striking abstract art panels, good-size desks and flat-screen TVs, the rooms successfully combine comfort with a classy feel.

Hotel Meliá Recoletos
HOTEL €€

(☑ 983 21 62 00; www.solmelia.com; Acera de Recoletos 13; s/d €75/100; ⓟ ❈ @ ☎) This excellent four-star hotel has a touch of class that elevates it above other hotels in this category. Part of a chain but with a boutique-hotel intimacy, it offers large luxurious rooms with a classic look and impeccable service. With a predominantly business clientele, the hotel lowers its rates at weekends.

Hotel El Nogal
HOTEL €€

(☑ 983 34 03 33; www.hotelelnogal.com; Calle del Conde Ansúrez 10-12; s/d €50/60; ⓟ ❈ ☎) Hotel El Nogal's rooms sport polished floorboards, colourful crimson drapes and bedspreads, and modern bathrooms, most with hydromassage showers. All rooms face either a square or a quiet street.

Hotel Imperial
HOTEL €€

(☑ 983 33 03 00; www.himperial.com; Calle Peso 4; s/d €60/66; ❈ ☎) This solid, comfortable hotel around the corner from Plaza Mayor has a warm old-fashioned feel in its public spaces, while the carpeted rooms are more modern, with sunny cream-and-yellow paintwork. The bathrooms are large and glossy.

✗ Eating

El Corcho
TAPAS €

(Calle de Correos 2; tostas from €1.40; ⊙ 11am-4pm & 7-11pm) This spit-and-sawdust place located on the city's top street for tapas bars wins the prize of public opinion with its excellent selection of *tostas* (toasts), with tasty toppings.

EGGS FOR BREAKFAST?

For those who have grown weary of *tostadas,* stop by **Cafeteria Oxford** (Calle Claudio Moyano 6; breakfast €2.30-4; ⊙ 7am-10pm Mon-Sat; ☎ ❒), in the centre of town, which has 12 choices of inexpensive breakfast menus ranging from eggs and bacon to cappuccino and homemade plum cake.

★ Martín Quiroga
CONTEMPORARY CASTILIAN €€

(☑ 605 787117; Calle San Ignacio 17; mains €16-18; ⊙ 1.30-3.30pm & 8.30-11.30pm) With just four tables and a typical waiting list of a month, you would imagine that this extraordinarily high quality gastrobar would have prices to match. It doesn't. There is no menu, dishes depend on what's fresh in season and available from the market that day, but there's plenty of choice. Special diets are catered to with advance notice. Reservations essential.

Los Zagales de Abadía
CONTEMPORARY CASTILIAN €€

(☑ 983 38 08 92; www.loszagales.com; Calle de la Pasión 13; mains €18-21, set menus €19-26; ⊙ 1-4pm & 7-11pm Mon-Sat, 1-4pm Sun) The bar here is awash with hanging local produce, all represented in the prize-winning tapas displayed along the bar – this place has done well, not just at local competitions but nationwide. Even so, Los Zagales is best known for its restaurant, where the servings are generous and the food excellent. Reservations recommended.

El Caballo de Troya
SPANISH €€

(☑ 983 33 93 55; www.restaurantesanti.es; Calle de Correos 1; mains €9.20-25; ⊙ 1.30-3.30pm & 9-11.30pm Mon-Sat, 2-4pm Sun) The 'Trojan Horse' is a Valladolid treat, set around a stunning Renaissance-style courtyard with a *taberna* downstairs for brilliant *raciones* – choose the *bandeja surtidas* (tasting platters) for a rich and varied combination of tastes. The restaurant is as sophisticated in flavours as the dining room is classy in design. Reservations recommended.

Vinotinto
CASTILIAN €€

(Calle de Campanas 4; mains €12-20, tapas from €2; ⊙ 10.30am-4pm & 8-11.30pm) This is where wine bar meets steakhouse, sizzling nightly with local gossip, spare ribs and other grilled meats in a fashionable tavern-style atmosphere. Shame about the bright lights.

Valladolid

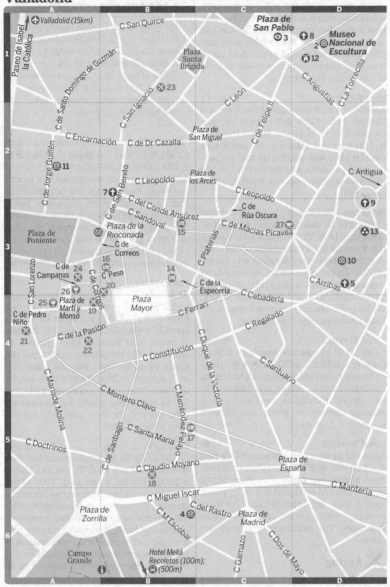

The local *jamón ibérico* (Iberian ham) is particularly good, sliced so finely as to melt in the mouth. The modern Vinotinto Joven, opposite, has a more intimate, younger feel and does some fabulous tapas.

La Parrilla de San Lorenzo   CASTILIAN **€€**
(983 33 50 88; www.hotel-convento.com; Calle de Pedro Niño; mains €14-22; 2-4pm & 9pm-midnight Mon-Sat, 1.30-4.30pm Sun) Both a stand-up bar and a much-lauded restaurant in the evocative setting of a former 16th-century

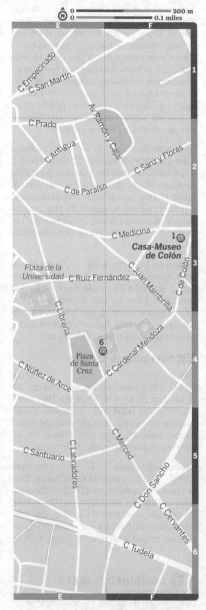

Valladolid

🍷 Drinking & Nightlife

Café de la Comedia COCKTAIL BAR
(Plaza de Martí y Monsó; ☺3.30pm-late) Decor is suitably comedic with Laurel and Hardy on the screen and Chaplin pics (and similar) decorating the walls. Very popular and serves good cocktails and wines by the glass.

El Minuto CAFE, BAR
(Calle de Macias Picavea 15; ☺8am-1am Mon-Sat, 10am-10pm Sun) This smooth cafe-bar is famed for its superb coffee and popular with students. The nearby Calle de Librería is an epicentre of early evening student drinking.

Be Bop CLUB
(Plaza de Martí y Monsó; ☺3pm-late) One of an energetic strip of bars and clubs overlooking this pretty square.

monastery, La Parilla de San Lorenzo specialises in upmarket Castilian cuisine (hearty stews, legumes and steaks). Check out the historic grill and giant domed oven, used specifically for roast lamb and suckling pig. Reservations recommended.

ⓘ Information

Tourist Office (📞 983 21 93 10; www.asomateavalladolid.org; Acera de Recoletos; ⊘9am-8pm)

ⓘ Getting There & Away

Air Ryanair (www.ryanair.com) has flights to Valladolid from Barcelona and Málaga. **Iberia** (www.iberia.es) operates up to five daily flights to Barcelona, with connections to other cities in Spain.

Train More than a dozen daily high-speed AVE train services connect Valladolid with Madrid (€32.90, one hour), and there are slower services (2¾ hours) for as little as €23. Other regular trains run to León (from €17.40, about two hours), Burgos (from €10.95, about 1½ hours) and Salamanca (from €11.75, 1½ hours).

ⓘ Getting Around

Air Valladolid's airport is 15km northwest of the city centre. **Linecar** (www.linecar.es) has up to five daily bus services from Valladolid to the airport (€4). A taxi between the airport and the city centre costs around €20.

Bus Local buses 2 and 10 pass the train and bus stations on their way to Plaza de España.

Around Valladolid

Medina de Rioseco

POP 5000

Medina de Rioseco, a once-wealthy trading centre, still has a tangible medieval feel although, given the number of boarded up frontages around Plaza Mayor, is sadly a lot poorer these days. Head for Calle Mayor with its colonnaded arcades held up by ancient wooden columns; market stalls set up here on Wednesday mornings.

⊙ Sights

Iglesia de Santa María de Mediavilla CHURCH
(Calle Santa María; guided visits in Spanish €2; ⊘11am-noon & 5-7pm Tue-Sun) This grandiose Isabelline Gothic work has three star-vaulted naves and the rightfully famous **Capilla de los Benavente** chapel. Anchored by an extravagant altarpiece by Juan de Juní and carved over eight years from 1543, it's sometimes referred to as the 'Sistine Chapel of Castilla'; it's certainly one of Spain's finest examples of Renaissance-era religious art.

Museo de Semana Santa MUSEUM
(Calle de Lázaro Alonso; admission €3.50; ⊘11am-2pm & 4-7pm Tue-Sun Apr-Sep, weekends only Oct-Mar) Medina de Rioseco is famous for its Easter processions, but if you can't be here during Holy Week, this museum provides an insight into the ceremonial passion of Easter here. Like its sister museum in Zamora (p170), it's dedicated to *pasos* (floats carried in Semana Santa processions) and an extensive range of other Easter artefacts.

Iglesia de Santiago CHURCH
(Calle Santa María; admission €2; ⊘11am-noon & 4-7pm Tue-Sun) Down the hill from the Iglesia de Santa María, the portals of this church blend Gothic, neoclassical and plateresque architectural styles. Access to the interior outside of summer is only possible as part of the guided tour of the Iglesia de Santa María de Mediavilla.

Museo de San Francisco CHURCH, MUSEUM
(www.museosanfrancisco.es; Paseo de San Francisco 1; admission €3; ⊘guided visits in Spanish 11am-1pm & 4-6pm Tue-Sun) This 16th-century former convent has an extravagant *retablo* (altarpiece) by Fray Jacinto de Sierra and a wide-ranging collection of sacred art.

🛏 Sleeping & Eating

Vittoria Colonna HOTEL €
(📞 983 72 50 87; www.hotelvittoriacolonna.es; Calle de San Juan 2b; s/d €30/50; ❄🛜) This modern three-star hotel with its raspberry-pink frontage offers well-sized and well-appointed rooms. Some are nicer than others, but all have smart grey-and-white bathrooms.

Restaurante Pasos CASTILIAN €€
(📞 983 72 00 21; www.restaurantepasos.es; Calle de Lázaro Alonso 44; mains €13-22; ⊘11am-5pm & 8pm-midnight Tue-Sat, 2-10pm Sun) Come here for well-prepared typical Castilian fare that courts various flavours but stays firmly in classical mould with reliable dishes such as

---

ⓘ COMBINED TICKETS

If you plan on visiting all four of Medina de Rioseco's sights, consider buying the combined 'Un Viaje a la Emoción' ticket for €7. It can be purchased at each of the four participating sights, and will save you €3.50. Note that between April and September, this *bono* can only be purchased at weekends.

chuletillas de lechazo (lamb chops). Reservations recommended.

Casa Manolo CASTILIAN €€
(Calle Las Armas 4; mains €9-12; ⏲8am-midnight Fri-Wed) The best of a clutch of restaurants on this sidestreet in the historic centre. The courtyard provides a pleasant setting for enjoying reliably good Castilian dishes.

Information

Tourist Office (☎983 72 03 19; www.medinaderioseco.com; Paseo de San Francisco 1; ⏲10am-2pm & 4-6pm Tue-Sat, 10am-2pm Sun) Alongside the Museo de San Francisco.

Getting There & Away

Up to eight daily buses run to León (€7.10, 1¼ hours) and up to 10 go to Valladolid (€3.15, 30 minutes).

Tordesillas

POP 9186

Commanding a rise on the northern flank of Río Duero, this pretty little town has a historical significance that belies its size. Originally a Roman settlement, it later played a major role in world history when, in 1494, Isabel and Fernando, the Catholic Monarchs, sat down with Portugal here to hammer out a treaty determining who got what in Latin America. Portugal got Brazil and much of the rest went to Spain.

Sights

Real Convento de Santa Clara CONVENT
(www.patrimonionacional.es; adult/concession €7/4, EU citizens & residents Wed & Thu afternoon free; ⏲10am-2pm & 4-6.30pm Tue-Sat, 10.30am-3pm Sun) Still home to a few Franciscan nuns living in near-total isolation, this Mudéjar-style convent dates from 1340 when it was begun as a palace for Alfonso XI. In 1494, the Treaty of Tordesillas was signed here. A 50-minute guided tour (in Spanish) takes in a wonderful Mudéjar patio left over from the palace and the church with its stunning *techumbre* (roof).

Other highlights include the Mudéjar door, Gothic arches, superb Arabic inscriptions and the Arab baths.

Museo del Tratado del Tordesillas MUSEUM
(Calle de Casas del Tratado; ⏲10am-1.30pm & 5-7.30pm Tue-Sat, 10am-2pm Sun) FREE Dedicated to the 1494 Treaty of Tordesillas, the informative displays in this museum look at the world as it was before and after the treaty, with some fabulous old maps taking centre stage. There's also a multilingual video presentation.

Exposición Permanente de Maquetas MUSEUM
(Calle de Casas del Tratado; ⏲10am-1.30pm & 5-7.30pm Tue-Sat, 10am-2pm Sun) FREE This small display of scale models includes Leon's Gaudí-designed Casa de Botines.

Plaza Mayor SQUARE
The heart of town is formed by the delightful porticoed and cobbled Plaza Mayor, its mustard-yellow paintwork offset by dark-brown woodwork and black grilles.

Sleeping & Eating

Hostal San Antolín HOSTAL €
(☎983 79 67 71; www.hostalsanantolin.com; Calle San Antolín 8; s/d/tr €25/40/50; ❄📶) Located near Plaza Mayor, the overall aesthetic is modern with rooms painted in bright pastel tones. Its main focus is the attached restaurant, with *raciones* downstairs in the bar, a pretty flower-decked inner patio and an elegant restaurant (mains €12 to €19).

Parador de Tordesillas LUXURY HOTEL €€
(☎983 77 00 51; www.parador.es; Carretera de Salamanca 5; r €125; P❄📶🏊👪) Tordesillas' most sophisticated hotel is this low-rise, ochre-toned *parador,* surrounded by pine trees just outside town. Some rooms have four-poster beds, all are large and many look out onto the tranquil gardens.

Viky TAPAS €
(Plaza Mayor 14; tapas from €0.60, mains €5-16; ⏲8am-11pm Tue-Sun) The pick of the eateries that encircle the Plaza Mayor, tiny Viky has tapas lined up along the bar, and a varied menu of canapés, *raciones* and other tapas. Service can be gruff.

Information

Tourist Office (☎983 77 10 67; www.tordesillas.net; Calle de Casas del Tratado; ⏲10am-1.30pm & 5-7.30pm Tue-Sat, 10am-2pm Sun May-Sep, shorter hours rest of the year) In Casas del Tratado, near the Iglesia de San Antolín.

Getting There & Away

The **bus station** (☎983 77 00 72; Avenida de Valladolid) is near Calle de Santa María. Regular buses depart for Valladolid (€2.50, 30 minutes) and Zamora (€5.45, one hour).

Toro

POP 1078

With a name that couldn't be more Spanish and a stirring history that overshadows its present, Toro is your archetypal Castilian town. It was here that Fernando and Isabel cemented their primacy in Christian Spain at the Battle of Toro in 1476. The town sits on a rise high above the north bank of Río Duero and has a charming historic centre with half-timbered houses and Romanesque churches.

⊙ Sights

Colegiata Santa María La Mayor   CHURCH
(Plaza de la Colegiata; admission €2; ⊙10.30am-2pm & 5.30-7.30pm Tue-Sun) This 12th-century church rises above the town and boasts the magnificent Romanesque-Gothic **Pórtico de la Majestad**. Treasures inside include the famous 15th-century painting called *Virgen de la mosca* (Virgin of the Fly); see if you can spot the fly on the virgin's robe. Entrance to the main sanctuary is free; the admission fee applies to the sacristy.

Monasterio Sancti Spiritus   MONASTERY
(Calle del Canto 27; admission €4; ⊙guided tours in Spanish 10.30am-12.30pm & 4.30-5.30pm Tue-Sun) Southwest of town, this monastery features a fine Renaissance cloister and the striking alabaster tomb of Beatriz de Portugal, wife of Juan I.

Alcázar   CASTLE
(Paseo del Espolón) Not far from the Colegiata Santa María La Mayor, this former fortress dates to the 10th century and still boasts seven towers.

🛏️ Sleeping & Eating

Plaza Mayor and nearby streets bustle with plenty of places to eat and sample local wines.

Zaravencia   HOTEL €
(☑980 69 49 98; www.hotelzaravencia.com; Plaza Mayor 17; s/d incl breakfast €38/55; ❄️ 🤵) Overlooking the lovely Plaza Mayor, this friendly place has a bar-restaurant downstairs and good-sized rooms, albeit with an anaemic decor of light pine furniture and cream walls. Pay €10 more for a plaza view and balcony (it's worth it).

Hotel Juan II   HOTEL €€
(☑980 69 03 00; www.hotelesentoro.es; Paseo del Espolón 1; s/d €54/72; 🅿️❄️🤵🏊) Despite its modern red-brick exterior, the rooms here are charming with warm terracotta-tiled floors, dark-wood furniture and large terraces. Request room 201 if you can for its fabulous double-whammy vista of the Río Duero to one side and the Colegiata Santa María La Mayor to the other. The restaurant is one of Toro's best (mains €15 to €21), specialising in hearty meat dishes.

ℹ️ Information

Tourist Office (☑980 69 47 47; www.turismocastillayleon.com; Plaza Mayor 6; ⊙10am-2pm & 4-8pm)

ℹ️ Getting There & Away

Regular buses operate to Valladolid (€5.20, one hour) and Zamora (€2.75, 30 minutes), and there are two direct services to Salamanca (€6, 1½ hours) on weekdays.

Zamora

POP 66,293

First appearances can be deceiving: as in so many Spanish towns, your introduction to provincial Zamora is likely to be nondescript apartment blocks. But persevere as the *casco historico* (old town) is hauntingly beautiful with sumptuous medieval monuments that have earned Zamora the popular sobriquet 'Romanesque Museum'. It's a subdued encore to the monumental splendour of Salamanca and one of the best places to be during Semana Santa.

⊙ Sights

Catedral   CATHEDRAL
(Plaza de la Catedral; adult/concession €4/2; ⊙10am-2pm & 5-8pm) Zamora's largely Romanesque cathedral features a square tower, an unusual Byzantine-style dome surrounded by turrets, and the ornate Puerta del Obispo. The **Museo Catedralicio** is the star attraction with a collection of Flemish tapestries dating from the 15th century. Inside the 12th-century cathedral itself, the magnificent early-Renaissance choir stalls depict clerics, animals and a naughty encounter between a monk and a nun. Another major highlight is the **Capilla de San Ildefonso**, with its lovely Gothic frescoes.

Museo de Semana Santa   MUSEUM
(Plaza de Santa María La Nueva; adult/concession €4/2; ⊙10am-2pm & 5-8pm Tue-Sat, 10am-2pm Sun) This museum will initiate you into the weird-and-wonderful rites of Easter, Span-

ish-style. It showcases the carved and painted *pasos* (figures) that are paraded around town during the colourful processions. The hooded models are eerily lifelike.

Churches
CHURCHES

(⊙10am-1pm & 5-8pm Tue-Sun) Among those churches retaining some of their Romanesque charm are the Iglesia de San Pedro y San Ildefonso (Rúa de Francos 39), which has Gothic touches; Iglesia de la Magdalena (Rúa de los Francos), the southern doorway of which is considered the city's finest, with its preponderance of floral motifs; and Iglesia de San Juan de Puerta Nueva (Plaza Mayor). Iglesia de Santa María La Nueva (Calle de San Martín Carniceros) is actually a medieval replica of a 7th-century church destroyed by fire in 1158. Sporadic opening hours apply to all.

Castillo
CASTLE

(⊙10am-2pm & 7-10pm Tue-Sun; 🔊) FREE This fine aesthetically restored castle of 11th-century origin is filled with local sculptures and you can climb the tower and walk the ramparts. The surrounding park is a lovely place for a picnic.

🎆 Festivals & Events

Semana Santa
HOLY WEEK

If you're in Spain during Holy Week, make your way to Zamora, a town made famous for its elaborate celebrations. It's one of the most evocative places in the country to view the hooded processions. Watching the penitents weave their way through the historic streets, sometimes in near-total silence, is an experience you'll never forget.

🛏 Sleeping

Prices can almost double here during Semana Santa.

Hostal La Reina
HOSTAL €

(☑980 53 39 39; Plaza Mayor 1 & 3; s/d €22/30, with shared bathroom €15/20; 🕸) Watched over by delightful older owners, Hostal La Reina offers large (albeit mildly shabby) rooms, the best of which have balconies overlooking Plaza Mayor.

NH Palacio del Duero
HOTEL €€

(☑980 50 82 62; www.nh-hotels.com; Plaza de la Horta 1; r €75; P🕸@🛜) In a superb position, next to a lovely Romanesque church, the seemingly modern building has cleverly encompassed part of the former convent, as well as (somewhat bizarrely) a 1940s power

CASTILLA Y LEÓN'S BEST CASTLES

While Segovia's Disneyesque Alcázar may get all the attention, lonely hilltop castles are something of a regional speciality. Top choices include the following:

Pedraza de la Sierra (p163) An unusually intact outer wall northeast of Segovia.

Turégano (admission €2; ⊙11am-2pm & 4-7.30pm Sat, 11am-2pm Sun) A unique 15th-century castle-church complex 30km north of Segovia.

Coca (www.castillodecoca.com; guided tours €2.70; ⊙tours 10.30am-1pm & 4.30-6pm Mon-Fri, 11am-1pm & 4-7pm Sat & Sun) An all-brick, virtuouso piece of Gothic-Mudéjar architecture 50km northwest of Segovia.

Ponferrada (adult/concession €4/2, Wed free; ⊙10am-2pm & 4.30-8.30pm Tue-Sun) A fortress-monastery west of León built by the Knights Templar in the 13th century.

Peñafiel (p194) One of the longest in Spain and now a wine museum.

Gormaz A 10th-century, Muslim-era fortress with 21 towers; 14km south of El Burgo de Osma.

station; the lofty brick chimney still remains. Rooms are large and plushly furnished.

Parador Condes de Alba y Aliste
HISTORIC HOTEL €€€

(☑980 51 44 97; www.parador.es; Plaza Viriato 5; r €100-168; 🕸@🛜🏊) Set in a sumptuous 15th-century palace, this is modern luxury with myriad period touches (mostly in the public areas). There's a swimming pool and, unlike many *paradores,* it's right in the heart of town. On the downside, there is very limited parking available (just eight places). The restaurant is predictable *parador* quality (*menú del día* €33).

🍴 Eating & Drinking

The richest pickings for restaurants and tapas bars are around Plaza Mayor and Plaza del Maestro. One local dish worth seeking out is *arroz a la zamorana* (rice with pork and ham).

Agape
TAPAS €

(Plazuela de San Miguel 3; tapas from €1.70; ⊙noon-11.30pm; 🖶) Of the many bars and restaurants fanning out from Plaza Mayor, this is probably the best. Ignore the pizza and pasta menu and order one of its artful, well-sized tapas, such as *tosta de solomillo de tres mostazas* (sirloin toast with three mustards). Larger appetites can opt for the *menú del día* (€8) with its seven choices of entrée and main.

El Rincón de Antonio
CONTEMPORARY CASTILIAN €€

(🖉980 53 53 70; www.elrincondeantonio.com; Rúa de los Francos 6; mains €19.50-26, set menus €11-65; ⊙1.30-4pm & 8.30-11.30pm Mon-Sat, 1.30-4.30pm Sun) A fine place offering tapas in the bar as well as sit-down meals in a classy, softly lit dining area. Amid the range of tasting menus, there's one consisting of four tapas for €11, including a glass of wine. In the restaurant, dishes are classic with a contemporary twist, like Galician scallops served in onion leaves. Reservations recommended.

ℹ️ Information

Municipal Tourist Office (🖉980 54 82 00; www.zamora.es; Plaza de Arias Gonzalo; ⊙10am-2pm & 5-8pm)

Regional Tourist Office (🖉980 53 18 45; www.turismocastillayleon.com; Avenida Príncipe de Asturias 1; ⊙9am-8pm) Organises guided tours (free to €7), including nocturnal explorations of the city. Note that at the time of research the Municipal Tourist Office was in the early planning stages of a possible move here, as well.

ℹ️ Getting There & Away

Bus Almost hourly bus services operate to/from Salamanca (from €5.50, one hour, five to 13 daily), with less-frequent departures on weekends. Other regular services include to León (€9.25, 1½ hours), Valladolid (€8.15, 1½ hours) and Burgos (€17.75, 4½ hours).

Train Trains head to Valladolid (€11.95, 1½ hours, one daily) and Madrid (€30.60, two to four hours, four daily).

Around Zamora

The lonely 7th-century San Pedro de la Nave (⊙10am-1pm & 5-8pm Tue-Sun) FREE, about 24km northwest of Zamora, is a rare and outstanding example of Visigoth church architecture, with blended Celtic, Germanic and Byzantine elements. Of special note are the intricately sculpted capitals. To get there from Zamora, take the N122, then follow the signs to Campillo.

Puebla de Sanabria
POP 1700

Close to the Portuguese border, this captivating village is a tangle of medieval alleyways that unfold around a 15th-century castle and trickle down the hill. This is one of Spain's loveliest hamlets and it's well worth stopping overnight: the quiet cobblestone lanes make it feel like you've stepped back centuries.

👁️ Sights

Castillo
CASTLE

(adult/child under 12yr €3/free; ⊙11am-2pm & 4-8pm Mon-Sat, 4-7pm Sun; 🅿🖶) Crowning the village's high point and dominating its skyline for kilometres around, the castle has some interesting displays on local history, flora and fauna, a slide show about the culture and history of the village and a camera obscura. Kids will love the chance to try on the pieces of armour. The views from the ramparts are also superb.

Plaza Mayor
SQUARE

At the top of the village, this striking town square is surrounded by some fine historical buildings. The 17th-century *ayuntamiento* (town hall) has a lovely arched facade and faces across the square to Iglesia de Nuestra Señora del Azogue (admission free; ⊙11am-2pm & 4-8pm Sat & Sun), a pretty village church which was first built in the 12th century.

🛌 Sleeping

Hostal Carlos V
HOSTAL €

(🖉980 62 06 18; www.hostalcarlos.es; Avenida Braganza 6; r €50; ❄🛜🖶) One of the best deals in town with pleasant rooms, dazzling white bedding, extra-fluffy towels, firm mattresses, rainforest shower heads and quality toiletries. There's a good cafe-restaurant here, too.

⭐ Posada Real La Cartería
HISTORIC HOTEL €€

(🖉980 62 03 12; www.lacarteria.com; Calle de Rúa 16; r €136; ❄@🛜) This stunning old inn is one of the best hotels in this part of the country. It blends modern comforts with all the old-world atmosphere of the village itself, featuring delightful, large rooms with exposed stone walls and wooden beams. The bathrooms have Jacuzzi tubs and there is even a small gym (as if walking around this hilly village wasn't exercise enough!).

LOOKING FOR WOLVES

Spain is home to Western Europe's largest contingent of wolves – an estimated 2000 to 2500 survive, which represents 30% of Europe's wolves outside of Eastern Europe. Spain's wolves are largely restricted to the country's northwest, with the largest population present in the Sierra de la Culebra, southeast of Puebla de Sanabria. If you're keen to catch a glimpse of this charismatic predator, contact **Zamora Natural** (☑655 821899; www.zamoranatural.com; per person €35; ☉10am-2pm Tue-Fri), which runs year-round excursions in search of wolves, including a handful every month devoted to tracking wolves; sightings are certainly not guaranteed with the chances ranging between 20% and 40%. An interpretation centre devoted to the region and its wolves is also under construction in the small village of Robledo, around 8km southwest of Puebla de Sanabria.

CASTILLA Y LEÓN PALENCIA

La Hoja de Roble　　　HISTORIC HOTEL **€€**
(☑980 62 01 90; www.lahojaderoble.com; Calle Constanilla 13; s €45, d €55-85; ❉ ☎) At the bottom of the hill where you begin the climb up into the old town, this hotel is an outstanding choice. The building dates to the 17th century and the rooms have a real sense of history (exposed stone walls, original wooden beams) without being oppressive. There is also a wine bar and a good restaurant.

 Eating

★ **Posada Real La Cartería**　　CASTILIAN **€€**
(Calle de Rúa 16; mains €9-18; ☉1-4pm & 9pm-midnight) The local obsession with wild mushrooms (*setas, boletus*) and *trucha* (trout) caught in the river down below the village is alive and well here.

La Posada de Puebla de Sanabria　　　CASTILIAN **€€**
(www.laposadadelavilla.com; Plaza Mayor 3; mains €8-18; ☉1.30-4pm & 8.30-11pm Thu-Tue) This excellent restaurant right on Plaza Mayor has a white-tableclothed elegance and serves up local steaks and the wild mushrooms for which this region is famed.

ℹ Information

Tourist Office (☑980 62 07 34; www.turismo sanabria.es; ☉11am-2pm & 5-8pm) Inside the castle.

ℹ Getting There & Away

There are sporadic bus services to Puebla de Sanabria from Zamora (from €7.50, 1¼ hours).

Parque Natural Lago de Sanabria

Around 15km north of Puebla de Sanabria, this protected area centres on Spain's largest glacier lake – Lago de Sanabria covers 368 hectares and is an astonishing 55m deep.

At least 10 hiking trails fan out across the park and surrounding areas. One comparatively easy circular three-hour (6km) walk, starts at **Sotillo** (signposted *camino tradicional,* just beyond the church) and takes in a stunning waterfall, while the main **Lago de Sanabria** and the lovely high-altitude **Lago de los Peces** can only be reached by car. For maps and further information, stop at the **Casa del Parque** (☉10am-2pm & 5-8pm Jul & Aug, shorter hours rest of the year), 5km before reaching the park entrance close to the village of Rabanillo. In addition to an information office, there's also an informative **Centro de Interpretación** (San Martín de Castañeda; admission €1; ☉10am-1pm & 5-7pm Jul-Sep) with information on the park's wildlife and geology.

Palencia

POP 81,198

Subdued Palencia boasts an immense Gothic cathedral, the sober exterior of which belies the extraordinary riches that await within; it's widely known as 'La Bella Desconocida' (Unknown Beauty). Otherwise, you'll find some pretty squares and a colonnaded main pedestrian street (Calle Mayor), flanked by shops and several other churches.

◉ Sights

★ **Catedral**　　　　CATHEDRAL
(Calle Mayor Antigua 29; cathedral & crypt €2, incl museum €3; ☉10am-1.30pm & 4.30-7.30pm Mon-Fri, 10am-2pm & 4-5.30pm Sat, 4.30-8pm Sun) The **Puerta del Obispo** (Bishop's Door) is the highlight of the facade of the imposing cathedral, among the largest in Castilla.

One of the most stunning chapels is the **Capilla El Sagrario**: its ceiling-high altarpiece tells the story of Christ in dozens of exquisitely carved and painted panels. The stone screen behind the choir stalls is a masterpiece of bas-relief attributed to Gil de Siloé.

From the retrochoir, a plateresque stairwell leads to the crypt, a remnant of the original Visigoth church. Near the stairwell is the oak pulpit, with delicate carvings of the Evangelists by Juan de Ortiz. In the attached **Museo Catedralicio** a whimsical highlight is a trick painting by 16th-century German artist Lucas Cranach the Elder. Looking straight on, it seems to be a surreal dreamscape that predates Dalí by some 400 years. Only when viewed from the side is the true image revealed – a portrait of Emperor Carlos V.

Iglesia de San Miguel CHURCH
(Calle de Mayor Antigua; ☉ 9.30am-1.30pm & 6.30-7.30pm Mon-Sat, 9.30am-1.30pm & 6.30-8pm Sun) This church stands out for its tall Gothic tower with a castle-like turret. San Miguel's interior is unadorned and austerely beautiful. According to legend, El Cid was betrothed to his Doña Jimena here.

Museo Diocesano MUSEUM
(Calle de Mayor Antigua; guided tours in Spanish €4; ☉ tours 10.30am, 11.30am & 12.30pm Mon-Sat) Located within the 18th-century Palacio Episcopal, this museum showcases art from the Middle Ages through to the Renaissance. Pride of place goes to works by Pedro de Berruguete and an altarpiece starring the Virgin (attributed to Diego de Siloé).

Modernista Architecture ARCHITECTURE
Palencia is embellished with some real architectural gems, including the 19th-century Modernista **Mercado de Abastos** (Fresh Food Market) on Calle Colón, the eye-catching **Collegio Vallandrando** on Calle Mayor and the extraordinarily ornate neo-plateresque **Palacio Provincial** on Calle Burgos. Step into the lobby of the latter to admire the ceiling

CASTILLA Y LÉON'S (DOC) WINE REGIONS

The wineries here are, overall, known for their robust reds, the perfect accompaniment to the traditional hearty meat dishes. Increasingly, however, the region is producing quality white and *rosado* (rosé) wines.

Arlanza Known for its red crianzas made from tempranillo grapes and produced by several bodegas, including the Señorío de Valdesneros.

Arribes One of the oldest wine regions, dating from Roman times, rufete is the main grape variety here. Look for La Casita organic wines, including aromatic whites made from malvasía grapes.

Bierzo Best known for young red wines made with 70% mencía grape. Home of Spain's second-most expensive red wine: La Faraona produced by Bodega Descendientes de J Palacios.

Cigales Look for aromatic *rosados* made from tempranillo and garnacha grape varietals which also form the basis of some robust red vintages.

Ribera del Duero The largest wine-producing region covering some 9229 hectares. Tempranillo, cabernet sauvignon, malbec and merlot are the most popular grape varieties. Spain's celebrated Vega Sicilia comes from here, as well as the country's most expensive wine: Dominio de Pingus.

Rueda Known for its dry aromatic white wines made primarily from verdejo grapes.

Tierra de León The youngest DO region. Main grape varietals are prieto picudo, mencía for reds and verdejo, albarín blanco and godello for young aged reds, as well as rosés.

Tierra del Vino de Zamora Look for Bodegas Viñas del Cenit wines, including their namesake Cenit produced from 100% tempranillo grapes – highly rated by La Guía Peñín, Spain's most-famous wine guide.

Toro Produces heavy tempranillo-based reds and famed for Bodega Namanthia's fruity and aromatic Termanthia, one of Spain's finest red wines.

Valles de Benavente Main grape varieties are tempranillo, prieto picudo, mencía for reds and verdejo and malvasia for white wines. Look for the light sparkling Rosado de Aguja (rosé).

frieze of the city under attack by the Roman legions, dating from 1904 and painted by local artist Eugenio Oliva.

Iglesia de San Pablo CHURCH
(Plaza de San Pablo; ⊙7.30am-12.30pm & 6.30-8.15pm) Has a Renaissance facade and an enormous plateresque altarpiece in the main chapel.

🛏 Sleeping

Hotel Colón 27 HOTEL €
(☑979 74 07 00; www.hotelcolon27.com; Calle de Colón 27; s/d/tr €30/40/50; ❋🕲) This place is excellent value, with comfortable carpeted rooms sporting pine furniture, good firm mattresses, shiny green-tiled bathrooms and small flat-screen TVs. Located opposite a school, it can be noisy at recess time.

Eurostars Diana Palace HOTEL €€
(☑979 01 80 50; www.eurostarsdianapalace.com; Avenida Santander 12; s/d incl breakfast €60/80; P❋🕲) A comfortable, albeit modern, block of a hotel within walking distance of the town centre.

🍴 Eating & Drinking

★Gloria Bendita CONTEMPORARY CASTILIAN €€
(☑979 10 65 04; Calle la Puebla 8; mains €15-25; ⊙1-11.30pm Mon-Sat, 1-5pm Sun; 🕲) Ignore the drab surroundings of modern apartment blocks and seek out this, one of Palencia's new breed of elegant restaurants serving sophisticated Castilian cuisine with a modern twist. Meat and fish dishes are the emphasis here with classics like braised beef served with oyster mushrooms. There are just a handful of tables in an intimate space so reservations are essential.

Restaurante Casa Lucio CASTILIAN €€
(☑979 74 81 90; www.restaurantecasalucio.com; Calle de Don Sancho 2; mains €14.50-33; ⊙10am-midnight Mon-Sat, 10am-4pm Sun) That great Spanish tradition of an overcrowded bar laden with tapas yielding to a quieter, more elegant restaurant is alive and well. Sidle up to the bar for creative tapas or consider the Castilian speciality of *cordero asado* (€36 for two). Reservations recommended.

ℹ Information

Patronato de Turismo (☑979 70 65 23; www.palencia-turismo.com; Calle Mayor 31; ⊙9am-2pm & 5-8pm Mon-Fri, 10.30am-2.30pm Sat) Information about Palencia province and city,

encompassing both the municipal and regional tourst offices.

ℹ Getting There & Away

Bus From the **bus station** (Carerra del Cementerio) there are regular services to Valladolid (€4.25, 45 minutes), Madrid (€18.58, 3½ hours) and Aguilar de Campóo (€7, 1½ hours).

Train Regular trains run to Madrid (from €29, 3¼ hours), Burgos (from €7.45, 45 minutes), León (from €12.40, 1¼ hours) and Valladolid (from €5.85, 45 minutes).

Around Palencia

Baños de Cerrato

Located around 13km southeast of Palencia is Spain's oldest church, the 7th-century **Basílica de San Juan** (admission €2, Wed free; ⊙10am-1.30pm & 4.50-8pm Tue-Sun). Built by the Visigoths in AD 661 and modified many times since, its stone-and-terracotta facade exudes a pleasing, austere simplicity. Check out the 7th-century fountain east of the entrance.

Frómista

POP 830

The main (and some would say only) reason for stopping here is the village's exceptional Romanesque church, the **Iglesia de San Martín** (admission €1; ⊙9.30am-2pm & 4.30-8pm). Dating from 1066 and restored in the early 20th century, this harmoniously proportioned church is one of the premier Romanesque churches in rural Spain, adorned with a veritable menagerie of human and zoomorphic figures just below the eaves. The capitals within are also richly decorated.

ℹ Getting There & Away

There are two buses daily from Palencia (€3.80, 30 minutes).

Montaña Palentina

These hills in the far north of Castilla y León offer a beautiful preview of the Cordillera Cantábrica, which divides Castilla from Spain's northern Atlantic regions. And the scenery around here is some of the prettiest in the region.

Aguilar de Campóo

POP 7203

Aguilar de Campóo is a bustling town with some interesting monuments. It's well placed for exploring the stunning scenery and Romanesque churches of the Montaña Palentina.

⊙ Sights

Overlooking the town and providing its picturesque backdrop is a 12th-century castillo and the graceful Romanesque Ermita de Santa Cecilia (admission €1; ⊙ 11am-2pm & 5-8pm Tue-Sun).

Down in the town itself, the elongated Plaza de España is capped at its eastern end by the Colegiata de San Miguel, a 14th-century Gothic church with a fine Romanesque entrance.

Just outside town, on the highway to Cervera de Pisuerga, is the restored Romanesque Monasterio de Santa María la Real (☑ 979 12 30 53; www.santamarialareal.org; Carretera de Cervera; admission with/without guided visit €5/3; ⊙ 4-8pm Tue-Fri, 10.30am-2pm & 4.30-7.30pm Sat & Sun Oct-Jun, 10.30am-2pm & 4.30-7.30pm Jul-Sep). Its 13th-century Gothic cloister with delicate capitals is glorious.

⌂ Sleeping & Eating

There's plenty of accommodation around town and the square is flanked by bars and restaurants.

Posada Santa María
La Real   HISTORIC HOTEL €€
(☑ 979 12 20 00; www.santamarialareal.org; Carretera de Cervera; s/d €60/80; P ❋ 🖳) Inhabiting part of the Romanesque monastery of the same name, this charming *posada* is the most atmospheric place to stay in the region. Some rooms have stone walls, others are split-level and all are decked out in wood. The restaurant offers medieval-themed dinners and several set menus (from €15).

Hotel Restaurante Valentín   HOTEL €€
(☑ 979 12 21 25; www.hotelvalentin.com; Avenida Ronda 23; s/d €52/71; 🖳) This sprawling, central hotel has little character but does boast large comfortable rooms, and there's a bustling on-site restaurant (mains €8 to €15).

ℹ Information

Tourist Office (www.turismocastillayleon.com; Plaza de España 30; ⊙ 10am-1.45pm & 4-5.45pm Tue-Sat, 10am-1.45pm Sun)

ℹ Getting There & Away

Regular trains link Aguilar de Campóo with Palencia (from €7, 1½ hours), but the station is 4km from town. Buses bound for Burgos, Palencia and Santander depart at least once daily.

Romanesque Circuit

There are no fewer than 55 Romanesque churches in the cool, hilly countryside surrounding Aguila de Campóo, and you could easily spend a day tracking them as you meander along quiet country trails.

At Olleros de Pisuerga there's a little church carved into rock; it's signposted as 'Ermita Rupestre'. Ask at Bar Feli on the main road through town for someone to open it up for you.

Further south, on a quiet back road, the Benedictine Monasterio de Santa María de Mave FREE has an interesting 13th-century Romanesque church, the only part of the complex open to visitors; ask at the cafe next door for the key. It's off the main highway around 8km south of Aguilar de Campóo. Nearby, the Monasterio de San Andrés de Arroyo (www.sanandresdearroyo.es; guided tours €3; ⊙ 10am-12.30pm & 4-6pm) is an outstanding Romanesque gem, especially its cloister, which dates from the 13th century. Guided tours in Spanish run hourly.

Cervera de Pisuerga & Around

Around 25km northwest of Aguilar de Campóo along the CL626, Cervera de Pisuerga is an important regional crossroads. If you decide to stay, the parador (www.parador.es; r with/without views €175/135; P 🖳), 3km west of town along the P210, is suitably classy with fabulous mountain views.

From Cervera you've a choice of routes. The N621 north from Cervera is a lovely road into Cantabria and to the southern face of the Picos de Europa.

If you've time, the sinuous P210 that follows the mountainous foothills for 61km from Cervera to Guardo is one of the loveliest drives in Castilla y León. The road climbs to the mountain pass Alto de La Varga (1413m), while the prettiest views are further on, along the shores of the Embalse de Camporredondo, particularly around Alba de Cardaños. From comparatively ugly Guardo, it's possible to loop back to Aguilar de Campóo along the CL626, or head south to the Roman villa of La Olmeda near Saldaña.

VISIT A ROMAN VILLA

Villa Romana La Olmeda (www.villaromanalaolmeda.com; off CL615; adult/concession/child under 12yr €5/3/free, 3-6.30pm Tue free ; ☉10.30am-6.30pm Tue-Sun; P ♿) contains some of the most beautiful remnants of a Roman villa anywhere on the Iberian Peninsula. The villa was built around the 1st or 2nd centuriy AD, but was completely overhauled in the middle of the 4th century. It was then that the simply extraordinary mosaics were added; the hunting scenes in **El Oecus** (principal salon) are especially impressive. Elevated boardwalks guide you around the 4400-sq-metre villa with multimedia presentations in Spanish, English and French.

Located on the fertile plains south of the Montaña Palentina, the turn-off to the site is 3km south of Saldaña, along the CL615. If you want to delve further, ask at the ticket office here about details on the monographic museum in Saldaña where many of the excavated artifacts are on display.

THE NORTHWEST

León

POP 134,305527M / ELEV 527M

León is a wonderful city, combining stunning historical architecture with an irresistible energy. Its standout attraction is the cathedral, one of the most beautiful in Spain. By day you'll encounter a city with its roots firmly planted in the soil of northern Castilla, with its grand monuments, loyal Catholic heritage and role as an important staging post along the Camino de Santiago. By night León is taken over by its large student population, who provide it with a deep-into-the-night soundtrack of revelry that floods the narrow streets and plazas of the picturesque old quarter, the Barrio Húmedo. It's a fabulous mix.

History

A Roman legion set up camp here in AD 70 as a base for controlling the gold mines of Las Médulas. In the 10th century the Asturian king Ordoño II moved his capital here from Oviedo and, although it was later sacked by the Muslim armies of Al-Mansour, León was maintained by Alfonso V as the capital of his growing kingdom. As the centre of power shifted south, León went into decline. Mining brought the city back to life in the 1800s. Throughout the 20th century, León's fame revolved around its role as a major staging post along the Camino de Santiago. The city came within the newly autonomous region of Castilla y León in 1983.

On 18 June, 2013, León was declared by UNESCO to hold the oldest documentary testimony of the European parliamentary system. This dates back to 1188 when King

Alfonso IX recognised the pre-democratic rights of citizens to vote and intervene in the decisions of public affairs.

☉ Sights

★**Catedral** CATHEDRAL
(www.catedraldeleon.org; adult/concession/child under 12yr €5/4/free; ☉8.30am-1.30pm & 4-8pm Mon-Sat, 8.30am-2.30pm & 5-8pm Sun) León's 13th-century cathedral, with its soaring towers, flying buttresses and breathtaking interior, is the city's spiritual heart. Whether spotlit by night or bathed in glorious sunshine, the cathedral, arguably Spain's premier Gothic masterpiece, exudes a glorious, almost luminous quality. The show-stopping facade has a radiant rose window, three richly sculpted doorways and two muscular towers. After going through the main entrance, lorded over by the scene of the Last Supper, an extraordinary gallery of *vidrieras* (stained-glass windows) awaits.

French in inspiration and mostly executed from the 13th to the 16th centuries, the windows' kaleidoscope of coloured light is offset by the otherwise gloomy interior. There seems to be more glass than brick – 128 windows with a surface of 1800 sq metres in all – but mere numbers cannot convey the ethereal quality of light permeating this cathedral.

Other treasures include a silver urn on the altar, by Enrique de Arfe, containing the remains of San Froilán, León's patron saint. Also note the magnificent choir stalls and the peaceful, light-filled claustro, its 15th-century frescoes providing a perfect complement to the main sanctuary. The **Museo Catedralicio-Diocesano**, off the cloisters, has an impressive collection encompassing works by Juní and Gaspar Becerra alongside

León

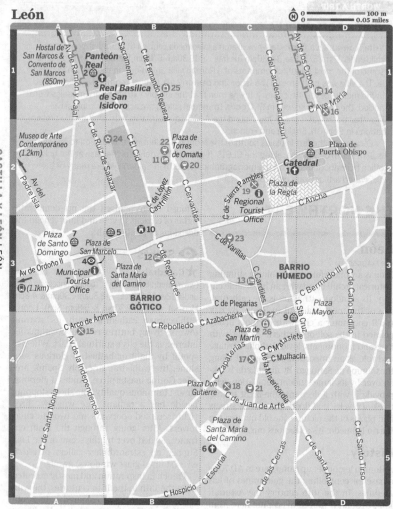

Hostal de
San Marcos &
Convento de
San Marcos
(850m)

Panteón
Real
2 🏛
3 🏛
Real Basílica 🏛 25
de San
Isidoro

Museo de Arte
Contemporáneo
(1.2km)

C Sacramento

C de Fernando Regueral

⭐ 24
C El Cid

22
11 🏛
Plaza de
Torres
de Omaña
🏛 20

C de López
Castrillón

C Cervantes

C de Sierra Pambley

C del Cardenal Landázuri

Av de los Cubos

🏛 14
C Aye María
🏛 16

8
Catedral
1 🏛
Plaza de
Puerta Obispo

Plaza de
la Regla

19 🏛
Regional
Tourist
Office

C Ancha

Plaza
de Santo
Domingo

7 🏛
🏛 5
🏛 10

Plaza de
San Marcelo

4 🏛
Municipal 🏛
Tourist
Office

🏛 (1.1km)

C de Regidores

🏛 23
C de Varillas

C Cardiles

13 🏛

BARRIO
HÚMEDO

C Bermudo III

C de Caño Badillo

C de Ordoño II

Plaza de
Santa María
del Camino

BARRIO
GÓTICO

C Arco de Ánimas

🏛 15

C Rebolledo

C Azabachería

C de Plegarias

Plaza de
San Martín

🏛 27
26

9 🏛

C Sta Cruz

Plaza
Mayor

Av de la Independencia

C de Santa Nonia

C de Zapaterías

17 🏛

C Matasiete

C Mulhacín

Plaza Don
Gutierre

🏛 18 🏛 21

C de Juan de Arfe

C de la Misericordia

Plaza de
Santa María
del Camino

6 🏛

C Escurial

C Hospicio

C de las Cercas

C de Santa Ana

C de Santo Tirso

a precious assemblage of early-Romanesque
carved statues of the Virgin Mary.

Part of the cathedral is under restoration, but this has been turned cleverly to its
advantage, by allowing you to climb up to
one of the platforms high in the main sanctuary from where there are stunning views.
Guided visits leave on the hour (€3) and are
accessed from outside the cathedral next to
its northern wall. In addition to the official
opening hours, ask about its summer-only
night visits, which begin at 11.30pm (€6,
weekends only) and coincide with the turning off of the external floodlights and turn-

ing on the church's interior lighting. The
change is extraordinary.

⭐ **Real Basílica de San Isidoro** CHURCH
(⊙ 7.30am-11pm) **FREE** Even older than León's
cathedral, the Real Basílica de San Isidoro
provides a stunning Romanesque counterpoint to the former's Gothic strains, with extraordinary frescoes in the attached Panteón
the main highlight.

Fernando I and Doña Sancha founded the
church in 1063 to house the remains of the
saint, as well as the remains of themselves
and 21 other early Leónese and Castilian

León

monarchs. Sadly, Napoleon's troops sacked San Isidoro in the early 19th century, although there's still plenty to catch the eye.

The main basilica is a hotchpotch of styles, but the two main portals on the southern facade are pure Romanesque. Of particular note is the Puerta del Perdón, attributed to Maestro Mateo, the genius of the cathedral at Santiago de Compostela.

★ **Panteón Real**   HISTORIC BUILDING
(admission €5; ⊙10am-1.30pm & 4-6.30pm Mon-Sat, 10am-1.30pm Sun) Attached to the Real Basílica de San Isidoro, Panteón Real houses the remaining sarcophagi, which rest with quiet dignity beneath a canopy of some of the finest Romanesque frescoes in Spain. Motif after colourful motif of biblical scenes drench the vaults and arches of this extraordinary hall, held aloft by marble columns with intricately carved capitals.

The pantheon also houses a small museum where you can admire the shrine of San Isidoro, a mummified finger of the saint (!) and other treasures.

Abutting the southwestern corner of the basilica is a fragment of the former *muralla* (old city wall).

Museo Sierra-Pambley   MUSEUM
(www.sierrapambley.org/museo; Plaza de la Regla 4; adult/concession €3/2; ⊙11am-2pm & 5-8pm Tue-Sun; 🎦) This stately house dates from the 19th century and was built by Segundo Sierra-Pambley, who founded one of the first schools in the region in 1887. The rooms cover two floors with original furniture (much of it French) and unexpected treasures, like 19th-century schoolbooks, children's toys and a very early movie projector.

Barrio Gótico   HISTORIC QUARTER
Stately Plaza de San Marcelo is home to the ayuntamiento (town hall), which occupies a charmingly compact Renaissance-era palace. The Renaissance theme continues in the form of the splendid Palacio de los Guzmanes (1560), where the facade and patio stand out; the latter is accessible only on a free guided tour that leaves regularly from 11.30am to 4.30pm. Next door is Antoni Gaudí's contribution to León's skyline, the castle-like, neo-Gothic Casa de Botines (1893), now a bank.

Down the hill, the delightful Plaza de Santa María del Camino feels like a cobblestone Castilian village square and is overlooked by the careworn Romanesque Iglesia de Santa María del Mercado.

At the northeastern end of the old town is the beautiful and time-worn 17th-century Plaza Mayor. Sealed off on three sides by porticoes, this sleepy plaza is home to a bustling produce market on Wednesday and Saturday. On the west side of the square is the late-17th-century baroque old town hall.

Museo de Arte Contemporáneo   ART
(Musac; www.musac.org.es; Avenida de los Reyes Leóneses 24; admission €5, 5-9pm Sun free; ⊙10am-3pm & 5-8pm Tue-Fri, 11am-3pm & 5-9pm Sat & Sun) León's showpiece Museo de Arte

Contemporáneo has been acclaimed for the 37 shades of coloured glass that adorn the facade; they were gleaned from the pixelisation of a fragment of one of the stained-glass windows in León's cathedral. The airy galleries mostly display temporary displays of cutting-edge Spanish and international photography, video installations and other similar forms and also has a growing permanent collection. Concerts are regularly held here.

Museo de León
MUSEUM

(www.museodeleon.com; Plaza de Santo Domingo 8; admission €1.20, Sat & Sun free; ☉10am-2pm & 5-8pm Tue-Sat, 10am-2pm Sun) Spread over four floors, the exhibits in this well-presented city museum begin with stone artefacts in the basement, and thereafter journey through the Middle Ages up to the 19th century. There are rooftop views towards the cathedral from the 3rd floor. The informative descriptions are in Spanish and English.

Convento de San Marcos
CONVENT, PARADOR

(Plaza de San Marcos) **FREE** You will have to check into the Hostal de San Marcos parador to appreciate most of this palatial former monastery, although the historic chapter house and magnificent cloister can be viewed. The platetersque exterior is also superb, sectioned off by slender columns and decorated with delicate medallions and friezes that date from 1513.

✦✥ Festivals & Events

Semana Santa
RELIGIOUS

(Holy Week) León is an excellent place to see solemn Holy Week processions of hooded penitents.

Fiestas de San Juan y San Pedro
LOCAL FIESTA

(☉21-30 Jun; ♣) The city lets its hair down on the cusp of summer with concerts, street stalls and general merriment.

🛏 Sleeping

Le Petit León
BOUTIQUE HOTEL €

(☑987 07 55 08; www.lepetitleonhotel.com; Calle Cardiles; s/d €55/65; ✳🛜) One of the city's latest hotels right in the centre of the Barrio Húmedo (the double glazing helps a little...), the rooms here are small and chic with underfloor heating. Decorated with a contemporary combo of stylish wallpaper and pastel-washed walls, several have small terraces overlooking the pedestrian street.

The same management runs the chilled-out wine bar, plus restaurant next door.

Hostal San Martín
HOSTAL €

(☑987 87 51 87; www.sanmartinhostales.com; Plaza de Torres de Omaña 1, 2nd fl; s/d/tr €31/43/55, s without bathroom €22; 🛜) In a splendid central position occupying an 18th-century building, the rooms are light, airy and painted in candy colours. All have small terraces. The spotless bathrooms have excellent water pressure and tubs, as well as showers. There's a comfortable sitting area and the friendly owner can provide advice and a map.

★La Posada Regia
HISTORIC HOTEL €€

(☑987 21 31 73; www.regialeon.com; Calle de Regidores 9-11; s/d incl breakfast €55/90; ✳🛜) This place has the feel of a *casa rural* despite being in the city centre. The secret is a 14th-century building, magnificently restored (wooden beams, exposed brick and understated antique furniture), with individually styled rooms and supremely comfortable beds and bathrooms. As with anywhere in the Barri Gòtic, weekend nights can be noisy.

Q!H
BOUTIQUE HOTEL €€

(☑987 87 55 80; www.qhhoteles.com; Avenida de los Cubos 6; s/d €45/65; ✳🛜🖳) Located within confessional distance of the cathedral, this boutique spa hotel occupies an historic 19th-century building that provides a suitable aesthetic canvas for the sharp modern design of the interior. Rooms have cathedral views, a bold accented colour scheme and steely grey bathrooms. Prices increase with use of the spa and treatments.

★Hostal de San Marcos
HISTORIC HOTEL €€€

(☑987 23 73 00; www.parador.es; Plaza de San Marcos 7; d incl breakfast from €198; ✳@🛜) Despite the confusing '*hostal*' in the name, León's sumptuous *parador* is one of the finest hotels in Spain. With palatial rooms fit for royalty and filled with old-world luxury and decor, this is one of the Parador chain's flagship properties, and as you'd expect, the service and attention to detail are faultless. It also houses the Convento de San Marcos.

✗ Eating

La Trébede
TAPAS €

(Plaza de Torres de Omaña; tapas from €2.50; ☉noon-4pm & 8pm-midnight Mon-Sat) As good for tapas (try the croquettes) as for first drinks (wines by the glass start at €1.50), La Trébede is always full. The decor is eclectic –

deer's antlers, historic wirelesses and the scales of justice – and the sign outside promising 350km to Santiago may prompt you to abandon the Camino and stay a little longer.

★ Delirios
CONTEMPORARY CASTILIAN €€

(☏987 23 76 99; www.restaurantedelirios.com; Calle Ave Maria 2; mains €15-18; ⏱1.30-3.30pm & 9pm-11.30 Tue-Sat, 1.30-3.30pm Sun) One of the city's more adventurous dining options where innovative combinations like tuna tataki with orange and ginger, and brie and foie gras with coconut hit the mark virtually every time. Staider tastebuds can opt for dishes like steak with parsnip chips, while the chocolate mousse with passionfruit is designed to put a satisfied waddle in every diner's step. Reservations recommended.

El Llar
CASTILIAN €€

(Plaza de San Martín 9; mains €8-15; ⏱1.30-3.45pm & 8.30-11.45pm; ✐) This old León *taberna* is a great place to *tapear* (eat tapas) with its innovative selection of *raciones* that includes baked potatoes filled with wild mushrooms and prawns au gratin. The upstairs restaurant has a fine classic look and the menu includes vegetarian options and other fine dishes such as León trout in a crab sauce.

La Mary
MEDITERRANEAN €€

(www.lamaryrestaurant.com; Plaza Don Gutierre 5; mains €8-12, menú del día €9.95; ⏱noon-4pm & 8pm-midnight) The daily lunch menu is excellent value. Dishes include Italian options like caprese salad and risottos, plus seafood with imaginative sides, like broccoli purée. The atmosphere is bright and contemporary and there are outside tables.

Alfonso Valderas
SEAFOOD €€

(☏987 20 05 05; Calle Arco de Ánimas 1; mains €13.65-18.90; ⏱1.30-4pm & 9-11.30pm Mon-Sat, 1.30-4pm Sun) The city's most famous restaurant for *bacalao* (salt cod), prepared around 25 different ways. If this is your first encounter with this versatile fish, order it *al pil-pil* (with a mild chilli sauce). Otherwise, you might want to try the pig's trotters filled with cod. The dining room is grandly elegant, with a magnificent grandfather clock and a baffling display cabinet of antique shoes. Reservations recommended.

Restaurante Zuloaga
CONTEMPORARY SPANISH €€

(☏987 23 78 14; www.restaurantezuloaga.com; Calle de Sierra Pambley 3; menú del día €16, mains €16-20; ⏱1-4pm & 8pm-midnight) Located in the vaults of an early-20th-century palace,

PAPA QUIJANO
....

Visit **La Lola** (www.papaquijano.com; Calle de Ruiz de Salazar 22; ⏱9pm-5am Wed-Sat, live music from midnight) to hear legendary Papa Quijano, a *latino*-rock crooner who, since the 1970s, has run this dimly lit atmospheric bar with a back alcove encompassing part of the Roman wall. Papa has recorded several CDs and accrued quite a fan base – along with his three sons, better known as *Café Quijano*, although they are now pursuing separate careers.

this sophisticated place has a well-stocked cellar and an adventurous menu – the Icelandic cod confit on a bed of deboned pig's trotters is typical of what you may find here.

 Drinking & Nightlife

★ Camarote Madrid
WINE BAR

(www.camarotemadrid.com; Calle Cervantes 8; ⏱10am-4pm & 8pm-12.30am) With legs of ham displayed like a some meaty Broadway chorus line, this popular bar is famed for its tapas (the little ceramic cup of *salmorejo* is rightly famous). But the extensive wine list wins the day amid the buzz of a happy crowd swirling around the central bar.

Soho Vintage
COCKTAIL BAR

(Calle de Varillas 1; ⏱4pm-3.30am) Sultry lighting and a Victoriana-themed decor with cabinets of dolls and model ships, and art deco prints (plus some edgy contemporary artwork and photographs) equal a chic space for enjoying a pre-dining cocktail.

Delicatessen
MUSIC BAR

(www.delicatessenclub.com; Calle de Juan de Arfe 10; ⏱10.30pm-4am) Just down the hill from Plaza de San Martín, this place is two bars in one. Head for La Galocha downstairs for indie rock or for the smarter slick feel upstairs, where every night is different. Monday begins with jazz, and the DJ-spun beats get faster as the week gathers momentum.

🛍 Shopping

★ La Casa de los Quesos
FOOD

(Calle de Plegarias 14; ⏱10am-2pm & 5-7.30pm Mon-Fri, 11am-2.30pm Sat) Cheese lovers will want to stop here; you'll find every imaginable variety with plenty of regional choices.

El Escribano HANDICRAFTS
(Calle de Fernando Regueral 6; ⊙11.30am-1.30pm & 6-8.30pm Mon-Fri) Some lovely etchings and reproductions of medieval art are among the many attractions of this classy shop.

Iguazú BOOKS
(Calle de Plegarias 7; ⊙10am-2pm & 5-8.30pm Mon-Fri, 10.30am-2.30pm Sat) A fine little travel bookshop, with regional hiking maps.

ℹ Information

Municipal Tourist Office (✆987 87 83 27; Plaza de San Marcelo; ⊙9.30am-2pm & 5-7.30pm)
Regional Tourist Office (✆987 23 70 82; www.turismocastillayleon.com; Calle el Cid 2; ⊙9am-8pm)

ℹ Getting There & Away

The train and bus stations lie on the western bank of Río Bernesga, off the western end of Avenida de Ordoño II.

Bus Departing from the **bus station** (Paseo del Ingeniero Sáez de Miera) to Madrid (€24.95, 3½ hours, eight daily), Astorga (€3.80, one hour, 17 daily), Burgos (€15.30, two hours, three daily), and Valladolid (€10.20, two hours, nine daily).

Car & Motorcycle Parking bays (€12 to €16 for 12 hours) are found in the streets surrounding Plaza de Santo Domingo.

Train Regular daily trains travel to Valladolid (from €13.90, two hours), Burgos (from €21.10, two hours), and Madrid (from €27.25, 4¼ hours).

East of León

Sahagún

POP 2846 / ELEV 807M

A modest, albeit picturesque town today, Sahagún was once home to one of Spain's more powerful abbeys and remains an important waystation for pilgrims en route to Santiago.

◉ Sights

Santuario de La Peregrina CONVENT
(off Avenida Fernando de Castro; admission €2; ⊙noon-2pm & 6-8pm Tue-Sun) This 13th-century former convent has been stunningly restored with glimpses of elaborate 13th-century frescoes and 17th-century Mudéjar plasterwork; the latter is in the chapel to the right of the main nave. A modern addition to the convent houses some excellent scale models of Sahagún's major monuments. An interpretation centre dedicated to the Camino de Santiago should be open by the time you read this.

Iglesia de San Tirso CHURCH
(Plaza de San Tirso; ⊙10.15am-2pm & 4.30-8pm Wed-Sat, 10.15am-2pm Sun) FREE The early-12th-century Iglesia de San Tirso, at the western entrance to town, is an important stop on the Camino de Santiago; it's known for its pure Romanesque design and Mudéjar bell tower laced with rounded arches. The Iglesia San Lorenzo, just north of Plaza Mayor, has a similar bell tower.

Museo Benedictinas MUSEUM
(Avenida de Doctores Bermejo y Calderón; admission by donation; ⊙guided visits in Spanish hourly 10am-noon & 4-5pm Tue-Sat, 10am-noon Sun) The more important remnants of Sahagún's abbey are kept in this small museum.

🛏 Sleeping & Eating

La Bastide du Chemìn HOSTAL €
(✆987 78 11 83; www.labastideduchemin.es; Calle Arco 66; s/d €28/40; 🅰) Opened in 2013, this cosy small *hostal*, opposite the Albergue de Peregrinos (Hostel for Pilgrims), has pleasant rustic rooms with beamed ceilings.

San Facundo CASTILIAN €€
(Avenida de la Constitución 97-99; mains €16-25; ⊙noon-4pm & 8pm-midnight; 🅰🅰) Part of the Hostal La Codorniz, this traditional restaurant has an impressive carved Mudéjar ceiling and specialises in succulent roasted meats.

ℹ Information

Tourist Office (✆987 78 21 17; www.sahagun.org; Calle del Arco 87; ⊙noon-2pm & 6-9pm Mon-Thu, 11am-2pm & 4-9pm Fri-Sun) Located within the Albergue de Peregrinos.

ℹ Getting There & Away

Trains run regularly throughout the day from León (from €5.25, 40 minutes) and Palencia (from €5.25, 35 minutes).

West of León

Astorga

POP 11,826 / ELEV 870M

Perched on a hilltop on the frontier between the bleak plains of northern Castilla and the mountains that rise up to the west towards Galicia, Astorga is a fascinating small town with a wealth of attractions out of proportion to its size. In addition to its fine cathedral, the city boasts a Gaudí-designed palace, a smattering of Roman ruins and

---

WORTH A TRIP

AN ECCLESIASTICAL TREASURE

Rising from Castilla's northern plains, Monasterio de San Miguel de Escalada (admission by donation; ⊙ 10.15am-2pm & 4.30-8pm Tue-Sun) is a typically remote Castilian church rich in history. It was built in the 9th century by refugee monks from Córdoba on the remains of a Visigoth church, and various orders of monks and nuns lived here from the 9th to 19th century. It's best known for its beautifully simple horseshoe arches of the kind rarely seen this far north in Spain.

The graceful exterior porch with its portico is balanced by the impressive marble columns within; all of the interior columns (and three of those outside) are of Roman origin. Inside, two stone slabs and an arch are all that remains of the original Visigoth church, while other features are clearly Mozarabic (post Islamic).

To get here, take the N601 southeast of León. After about 14km, take the small LE213 to the east; the church is 16km after the turn-off.

---

a personality dominated by the Camino de Santiago.

History

The Romans built the first settlement, Astúrica Augusta, at the head of the Ruta del Oro. During the Middle Ages Astorga was well established as a way station along one of Europe's most important pilgrimage routes. By the 15th century its growing significance inspired the construction of the cathedral and the rebuilding of its 3rd-century walls.

⊙ Sights

Catedral   CATHEDRAL

(Plaza de la Catedral; cathedral free, museum €3, incl Palacio Episcopal €5; ⊙ church 9-10.30am Mon-Sat, 11am-1pm Sun, museum 10am-2pm & 4-8pm Tue-Sun) The cathedral's striking plateresque southern facade is created from caramel-coloured sandstone with elaborate sculptural detail. Work began in 1471 and continued over three centuries, resulting in a mix of styles. The mainly Gothic interior has soaring ceilings and a superb 16th-century altarpiece by Gaspar Becerra. The attached Museo Catedralicio features the usual religious art, documents and artefacts.

Palacio Episcopal   MUSEUM, ARCHITECTURE

(Museo de los Caminos; Calle de Los Sitios; admission €3, incl Museo Catedralicio €5; ⊙ 10am-2pm & 4-8pm Tue-Sat, 10am-2pm Sun) Catalan architect Antoni Gaudí left his mark on Astorga in the fairytale turrets and frilly facade of the Palacio Episcopal. Built in the 19th century, it now houses the Museo de los Caminos, an eclectic collection with Roman artefacts and coins in the basement; contemporary paintings on the top floor; and medieval sculpture, Gothic

tombs and silver crosses dominating the ground and 1st floors. The highlight is the chapel, with its stunning murals and stained glass.

Museo del Chocolate   MUSEUM

(Calle de José María Goy 5; adult/child under 12yr €2.50/free, incl Museo Romano €3; ⊙ 10.30am-2pm & 4-6pm Tue-Sat, 11am-2pm Sun; 🖈) Proof that Astorga does not exist solely for the virtuous souls of the Camino comes in the form of this small and quirky private museum. Chocolate ruled Astorga's local economy in the 18th and 19th centuries, as evidenced by this eclectic collection of old machinery, colourful advertising and lithographs. Best of all, you get a free chocolate sample at the end.

Museo Romano   MUSEUM

(Plaza de San Bartolomé 2; adult/child under 12yr €2.50/free, incl Museo del Chocolate €3; ⊙ 10am-2pm & 4-6pm Tue-Sun; 🖈) Housed in the Roman *ergástula* (slave prison), the Museo Romano has a modest selection of artefacts and an enjoyable big-screen slide show on Roman Astorga.

✷ Festivals & Events

Festividad de Santa Marta   RELIGIOUS

(⊙ last week of Aug; 🖈) Astorga awakes from its customary slumber to celebrate this saint with fireworks and bullfights.

🛏 Sleeping

Hotel Vía de la Plata   HOTEL €€

(📞 987 61 90 00; www.hotelviadelaplata.es; Calle Padres Redentoristas 5; d/ste incl breakfast €80/105; ❄@🛜) Opened in 2012, this spa hotel occupies a handsome former monastery, just off Plaza España. Guests receive a considerable discount for the spa treatments which include the deliciously decadent sounding *chocoterapia*. The rooms are slick and modern with fashionable mushroom browns and creams, tubular lights and full-size tubs, as well as showers.

Hotel Astur Plaza　　　　HOTEL €€
(☑987 61 89 00; www.hotelasturplaza.com; Plaza de España 2; s/d/ste from €55/75/110; ❈@🖘) Opt for one of the supremely comfortable rooms that face pretty Plaza de España. On weekends, you'll want to forsake the view for a quieter room out the back. The suites have hydromassage tubs, and there are three VIP double rooms with 'super kingsize' beds (€85).

✖ Eating

The local speciality is *cocido maragato,* a stew of chickpeas, various meats, potatoes and cabbage – the *cocido*. Portions are huge, so one order usually feeds two. Several pastry shops sell the traditional local *mantecadas,* a cake-like sweet peculiar to Astorga.

Restaurante Serrano CONTEMPORARY SPANISH €€
(☑987 61 78 66; www.restauranteserrano.es; Calle de la Portería 2; mains €12-20; ⊘noon-4pm & 8-11.30pm Tue-Sun) The menu at upmarket Restaurante Serrano has a subtle gourmet flourish, with fresh summery starters like *ensalada de mango y centollo* (mango and crab salad) with raspberry vinaigrette, innovative meat and fish mains, and plenty of tempting desserts with chocolate. It also serves *cocido* and other local dishes. Reservations recommended.

Aizkorri CONTEMPORARY CASTILIAN €€
(www.aizkorri.es; Plaza España 5; pinchos €3, mains €11-13; ⊘10am-4pm & 7pm-midnight) The mod-

ern steely grey-and-black bar here is generally packed with locals here for the palate pleasing *pinchos,* like tuna with tartar sauce. More substantial dishes range from tasty salads with artichoke hearts and roasted peppers to innovative takes on traditional cuisine such as baked rabbit on puff pastry with roasted vegetables.

Restaurante Las Termas CASTILIAN €€
(☑987 60 22 12; Calle de Santiago Postas 1; mains €9-15; ⊘1-4pm Tue-Sun; 🖈) This lunchtime restaurant is run by Santiago (a popular name in these parts) who, apart from being a charming host, oversees a menu renowned for the quality of its *cocido* and *ensalada maragata* (salad of chickpeas and cod).

❶ Information

Tourist Office (☑987 61 82 22; www.turismo castillayleon.com; ⊘10am-2pm & 4-8pm) In the northwestern corner of the *casco* (historic centre).

❶ Getting There & Away

Regular bus services connect Astorga with León (€3.80, one hour, 12 daily) and Madrid (from €28.70, 4½ hours, three daily). The train station is inconveniently located a couple of kilometres north of town.

Las Médulas

The ancient Roman gold mines at Las Médulas, about 20km southwest of Ponferrada, once served as the main source of gold for the entire Roman Empire – the final tally came to a remarkable three million kilograms. An army of slaves honeycombed the area with canals and tunnels (some over

---

WHAT'S COOKING IN CASTILLA Y LEÓN

Castilla y León's cuisine owes everything to climate. There's no better way to fortify yourself against the bitterly cold winters of the high plateau than with *cordero asado* (roast lamb), a speciality all over the province, including at Segovia's excellent Casa Duque (p162). Other regional delights include *chuleton de Ávila* (T-bone steak, from Ávila) available at this city's traditional restaurants, like Méson del Rastro (p145). Still on the meaty route, it's a fact that an estimated 60% of Spain's famous *jamón ibérico* (cured ham) comes from the Salamanca region. Sample some of the very best at Valledolid's Vinotinto (p165) where it takes pride of place on the menu. Heading north, León is one of Spain's top cities to *tapear* at great bars like La Trébede (p180), which serves regional tasty bites like a *pincho de morcilla* (blood sausage) free with your drink. Seeking more sophistication? No problem. This region is also home to an increasing number of exciting contemporary restaurants where traditional dishes are combined with innovative ingredients and expertise. Soria's Baluarte (p198) and Delirios (p181) in Léon are foodie favourites in this genre.

40km long!) through which they pumped water to break up the rock and free it from the precious metal. The result is a singularly unnatural natural phenomenon and one of the more bizarre landscapes you'll see in Spain. It's breathtaking at sunset.

To get to the heart of the former quarries, drive beyond Las Médulas village (4km south of Carucedo and the N536 Hwy). Several trails weave among chestnut trees and bizarre formations left behind by the miners. There are also fine views to be had in the vicinity of neighbouring Orellan.

THE EAST

Burgos

POP 179,906 / ELEV 861M

The extraordinary Gothic cathedral of Burgos is one of Spain's glittering jewels of religious architecture and looms large over the city and skyline. On the surface, conservative Burgos seems to embody all the stereotypes of a north-central Spanish town, with sombre grey-stone architecture, the fortifying cuisine of the high *meseta* (plateau) and a climate of extremes. But this is a city that rewards deeper exploration: below the surface lie good restaurants and, when the sun's shining, pretty streetscapes that extend far beyond the landmark cathedral. There's even a whiff of legend about the place: beneath the majestic spires of the cathedral lies Burgos' favourite and most roguish son, El Cid.

History

Burgos began life in 884 as a strategic fortress on the frontline between the Muslims and the rival kingdom of Navarra. It was surrounded by several *burgos* (villages), which eventually melded together to form the basis of a new city. Centuries later, Burgos thrived as a staging post for pilgrims on the Camino de Santiago and as a trading centre between the interior and the northern ports. During the Spanish Civil War, General Franco used Burgos as the base for his government-in-waiting.

◉ Sights

★**Cathedral**   CHURCH
(Plaza del Rey Fernando; adult/child under 14yr incl multilingual audioguide €6/1.50; ◷10am-6pm)

This Unesco World Heritage–listed cathedral is a masterpiece. A former modest Romanesque church, work began on a grander scale in 1221. Remarkably, within 40 years most of the French Gothic structure had been completed. You can enter the cathedral from Plaza de Santa María for free, and have access to the Capilla del Santísimo Cristo, with its much-revered 13th-century crucifix, and the Capilla de Santa Tecla, with its extraordinary ceiling. However, we recommend that you visit the cathedral in its entirety.

The cathedral's twin towers went up in the 15th century. Each represent 84m of richly decorated Gothic fantasy surrounded by a sea of similarly intricate spires. Probably the most impressive of the portals is the Puerta del Sarmental, the main entrance for visitors, although the honour could also go to the Puerta de la Coronería, on the northwestern side, which shows Christ surrounded by the Evangelists.

Inside the main sanctuary, a host of other chapels showcase the diversity of the interior, from the light and airy Capilla de la Presentación to the Capilla de la Concepción with its gilded, 15th-century altar. The Capilla del Condestable, behind the main altar, bridges Gothic and plateresque styles. Highlights here include three altars watched over by unusual star-shaped vaulting in the dome. The sculptures facing the entrance to the chapel are 15th- and 16th-century masterpieces of stone carving, portraying the Passion, death, resurrection and ascension of Christ.

The main altar is a typically overwhelming piece of gold-encrusted extravagance, while directly beneath the star-vaulted central dome lies the tomb of El Cid. Another highlight is Diego de Siloé's Escalera Dorada (Gilded Stairway) on the cathedral's northwestern flank.

Also worth a look is the peaceful cloister, with its sculpted medieval tombs. Off the cloister is the Capilla de Corpus Cristi, where, high on the northwestern wall, hangs the coffin of El Cid. The adjoining Museo Catedralicio has a wealth of oil paintings, tapestries and ornate chalices, while the lower cloister covers the history of the cathedral's development, with a scale model to help you take it all in.

Historic Centre   NEIGHBOURHOOD
Burgos' historic centre is austerely elegant, guarded by monumental gates and with the

Burgos

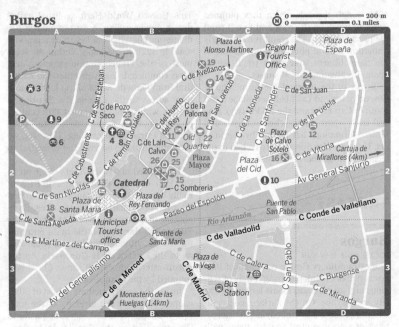

0 — 200 m
0 — 0.1 miles

Burgos

◉ Top Sights
1 Catedral	B2

◉ Sights
2 Arco de Santa María	B2
3 Castillo de Burgos	A1
4 Iglesia de San Esteban	B2
5 Iglesia de San Nicolás	A2
6 Mirador	A2
7 Museo de Burgos	C3
8 Museo del Retablo	B2
9 Parque de Castillo	A1
10 Statue of El Cid	C2

⊜ Sleeping
11 Hotel Entrearcos	B2
12 Hotel La Puebla	D2
13 Hotel Meson del Cid	A2
14 Hotel Norte y Londres	C1

15 Rimbombin	B2

⊗ Eating
16 Casa Ojeda	C2
17 Cervecería Morito	B2
18 El Huerto de Roque	A2
19 La Favorita	C1
20 La Mejillonera	B2

◉ Drinking & Nightlife
21 Café de Las Artes	C1
22 Café España	C2
23 Chocolatería Candilejas	B1
24 El Bosque Encantado	D1

⊞ Shopping
25 Casa Quintanilla	B2
26 Jorge Revilla	B2

cathedral as its centrepiece. This quarter can be accessed via two main bridges: the **Puente de San Pablo**, beyond which looms a romanticised **statue of El Cid** and, about 300m to the west, the **Puente de Santa María** leading to the splendid **Arco de Santa María** (☑ 947 28 88 68; ⏱ 11am-2pm & 5-9pm Tue-Sat, 11am-2pm Sun) FREE, once the main

gate to the old city and part of the 14th-century walls.

The Arco de Santa María also hosts temporary free exhibitions. Running along the riverbank between the two bridges is the Paseo del Espolón, an attractive tree-lined pedestrian area. Just back from the *paseo* (promenade) is the Plaza Mayor, with some striking facades.

Monasterio de las Huelgas
MONASTERY

(guided tours €7, Wed free; ⊙ 10am-1pm & 4-5.30pm Tue-Sat, 10.30am-2pm Sun) A 30-minute walk west of the city centre on the southern river bank, this monastery was once among the most prominent monasteries in Spain. Founded in 1187 by Eleanor of Aquitaine, daughter of Henry II of England and wife of Alfonso VIII of Castilla, it's still home to 35 Cistercian nuns. If you've come this far, join a guided tour (otherwise only a small section of the church is accessible), which takes you through the three main naves of the church.

This veritable royal pantheon contains the tombs of numerous kings and queens, as well as a spectacular gilded Renaissance altar. The highlight, though, is the **Museo de Ricas Telas**, reached via a lovely Romanesque cloister and containing bejewelled robes and royal garments.

To get here follow the river via Calle de la Merced and Avenida de Palencia, turning left on Calle Reina Leonor. The monastery is signposted.

Iglesia de San Esteban
CHURCH, MUSEUM

(Calle de Pozo Seco; admission incl museum €2; ⊙ 10am-2pm & 5-8pm Mon-Sat, shorter hours rest of the year) Just west of the cathedral, this is a solid 14th-century Gothic structure with an unusual porch and a **Museo del Retablo** (Altar Museum) with a display of some 18 altars dating from the 15th to 18th centuries.

Cartuja de Miraflores
MONASTERY

(⊙ 10.15am-3pm & 4-6pm Mon, Tue & Thu-Sat, 11am-3pm & 4-6pm Sun) FREE Set in peaceful woodlands 4km east of the city centre, this monastery contains a trio of 15th-century masterworks by Gil de Siloé. The walk to the monastery along Río Arlanzón takes about one hour. To get here, head north along Paseo de la Quinta (flanking the river) from where the monastery is clearly signposted.

Castillo de Burgos
CASTLE

(adult/child under 14yr €3.70/2.60; ⊙ 11am-2pm & 4-7pm Sat & Sun; 🖰) Crowning the leafy hilltop **Parque de Castillo** are the massive fortifications of the rebuilt Castillo de Burgos. Dating from the 9th century, the castle has witnessed a turbulent history, suffering a fire in 1736 before finally being blown up by Napoleon's troops in 1813. There's a small museum covering the town's history and some of the original castle foundations are on view. Just south of the car park is a **mirador** (lookout) with great views.

Museo de Burgos
MUSEUM

(Calle de Calera 25; admission €1.20, Sat & Sun free; ⊙ 10am-2pm & 5-8pm Tue-Sat, 10am-2pm Sun) This museum, housed in the 16th-century Casa de Miranda, contains some fine Gothic tombs and other archaeological artefacts covering a wide period.

Iglesia de San Nicolás
CHURCH

(Calle de San Nicolás; admission €1.50, Mon free; ⊙ 10am-2pm & 5-7pm Mon-Sat) Close to the cathedral, this place boasts an enormous stone-carved altar by Francisco de Colonia, with scenes from the life of St Nicolás.

🎊 Festivals & Events

Festividad de San Lesmes
PATRON SAINT FESTIVAL

(⊙ 30 Jan) Celebrates the city's patron saint.

Festividad de San Pedro y San Pablo
RELIGIOUS

(⊙ early Jul; 🖰) The Feast of Sts Peter and Paul is celebrated with bullfights, processions and much merry-making, particularly on the first Sunday of July, the **Día de las Peñas**.

🛏 Sleeping

⭐ **Rimbombín**
HOSTAL €

(🕿 947 97 76 82; www.rimbombin.com; Calle Sombrería 6; s/d/apt €40/60/90; 🅿 ✳ 🛜) Opened in 2013, this *hostal* has an upbeat contemporary feel with its slick white furnishings and decor, matched with light pine beams and modular furniture. Three of the rooms have balconies overlooking the pedestrian street. The apartment is excellent value for longer stays with the same chic modern look and two bedrooms. Continental breakfast is a paltry €2 extra.

Hotel Entrearcos
BOUTIQUE HOTEL €

(🕿 947 25 29 11; www.hotelentrearcos.com; Calle de la Paloma 4; s/d €50/60; ✳ 🛜) This stylish little hotel is as central as you'll find. Its rooms are beautifully presented and the bathrooms have hydromassage showers. Some rooms look onto the main pedestrian street, while Rooms 502 and 503 have castle and partial cathedral views. On the downside, the service can be lacklustre.

Hotel Norte y Londres
HISTORIC HOTEL €€

(🕿 947 26 41 25; www.hotelnorteylondres.com; Plaza de Alonso Martínez 10; s/d €66/100; 🅿 @ 🛜) Set in a former 16th-century palace and with understated period charm, this fine hotel

Camino Francés in Castilla y León

promises spacious rooms with antique furnishings, polished wooden floors and pretty balconies; those on the 4th floor are more modern. The bathrooms are exceptionally large, the service exceptionally efficient.

Hotel La Puebla
BOUTIQUE HOTEL €€

(947 20 00 11; www.hotellapuebla.com; Calle de la Puebla 20; s/d €45/66; ❄@🖥) This boutique hotel adds a touch of style to the Burgos hotel scene. The rooms aren't huge and most don't have views, but they're softly lit, beautifully designed and supremely comfortable. Extra perks include bikes and a pillow menu while, on the downside, some readers have complained about the level of street noise.

Hotel Meson del Cid
HISTORIC HOTEL €€

(947 20 87 15; www.mesondelcid.es; Plaza de Santa María 8; s/d €70/100; 🅿❄🖥) Facing the cathedral, this hotel occupies a centuries-old building. Rooms have burgundy-and-cream Regency-style fabrics, aptly combined with dark-wood furnishings and terracotta tiles. Several have stunning front-row seats of the cathedral (for a supplement of €10).

✕ Eating

Burgos is famous for its *queso* (cheese), *morcilla* (blood sausage) and *cordero asado* (roast lamb).

Cervecería Morito
TAPAS €

(Calle Sombrerería 27; tapas €3, raciones €5-7; 12.30-3.30pm & 7-11.30pm) This is the undisputed king of Burgos tapas bars and it's always crowded, deservedly so. A typical order is *alpargata* (lashings of cured ham with bread, tomato and olive oil) or the *pincho de*

morcilla (small tapa of local blood sausage). The presentation is surprising nouvelle, especially the visual feast of salads.

La Mejillonera
SEAFOOD €

(Calle de la Paloma 33; tapas from €2.50; 11.30-3pm & 6.30-11pm) A popular stand-up place, La Mejillonera serves great mussels, while the *patatas bravas* (potatoes with spicy tomato sauce) and *calamares* (calamari) are other popular orders.

★ El Huerto de Roque
CONTEMPORARY CASTILIAN €€

(www.elhuertoderoque.com; Calle de Santa Águeda 10; mains €10-12, menú del día €15; restaurant 1-4pm Tue-Sat, gastrobar 8pm-2am Thu-Sat;) Come here for an inexpensive lunch with plenty of choices. The emphasis is on fresh and ecological produce with typical plates including vegetable spring rolls with a sweet and sour sauce, and crab in a Thai green curry sauce. It's a boho-rustic place with original tiles, wooden furniture and edgy artwork. The adjacent gastropub reflects a similar cuisine, tapas style.

La Favorita
TAPAS €€

(www.lafavorita-taberna.com; Calle de Avellanos 8; tapas from €2; 10am-midnight Mon-Fri, noon-1.30am Sat & Sun) Away from the main Burgos tapas hub and close to the cathedral, La Favorita has a barn-like interior of exposed brick and wooden beams, and attracts slicked-back-hair businessmen at midday. The emphasis is on local cured meats and cheeses (try the cheese platter for €12.90), and wine by the glass starts at €1.90. The tapas include beef sirloin with foie gras.

Casa Ojeda
CASTILIAN €€

(☑947 20 90 52; www.grupojeda.com; Calle de Vitoria 5; mains €15-25; ⊙1-3pm & 8-11pm Mon-Sat, 1-4pm Sun) Dating from 1912, this Burgos institution, sheathed in dark wood with stunning mullioned windows, is one of the best places in town to try *cordero asado* or *morcilla de Burgos*. The upstairs dining room has outstanding food and faultless service. A more limited range of *platos combinados* (meat-and-three-veg dishes) is available in the downstairs bar. Reservations recommended.

Drinking & Nightlife

There are two main hubs of nightlife. The first is along Calle de San Juan and Calle de la Puebla. For later nights on weekends, Calle del Huerto del Rey, northeast of the cathedral, has dozens of bars.

Chocolatería Candilejas
CAFE

(Calle de Fernán González 36; desserts from €3; ⊙6.30-11pm Mon-Thu, to 1am Fri & Sat) For delicious milkshakes, including unusual flavours like raspberry and walnut, *chocolate con churros* (deep-fried spiral doughnuts dipped in hot chocolate) and homemade cakes, check out this cross between a Spanish bar and tea room.

Café España
CAFE

(Calle de Lain Calvo 12; ⊙9am-midnight Mon-Fri, 9am-2am Sat & Sun) With its old-world elegance, Café España has been a bastion of the Burgos cafe scene for more than 80 years. These days some 20 different coffees are available. A pianist plays jazz here most weekends from 11pm.

Café de Las Artes
BAR, CAFE

(Calle de Lain Calvo 31; ⊙10am-midnight; 🛜) This cafe is famed for its tasty *lazos* (puff pastry delicacies), as well as excellent coffee served straight up or flavoured with vanilla, cinnamon or hazlenut. The place has an artsy vibe accentuated by sultry background music.

El Bosque Encantado
BAR

(Calle de San Juan 31; ⊙4.30pm-1am) 'The Enchanted Garden' revels in its kitsch decor and is good for early evening drinks.

Shopping

Jorge Revilla
JEWELLERY

(www.jorgerevilla.com; Calle de la Paloma 29; ⊙10am-2pm & 5-8pm Mon-Fri, 10am-2pm Sat) Local Burgos jewellery designer Jorge Revilla is becoming a global name with his exquisite and sophisticated silver pieces.

Casa Quintanilla
FOOD

(Calle de la Paloma 22; ⊙10am-8.30pm Mon-Sat, 10am-2pm Sun) This is the pick of many stores around the town centre offering local produce that's ideal for a picnic or a gift for back home.

Information

Municipal Tourist office (☑947 28 88 74; www.aytoburgos.es; Plaza de Santa María;

CAMINO DE SANTIAGO

Burgos to León

Many pilgrims avoid this stretch of the Camino and take the bus, which is a pity as they are missing out on the subtle and ever-changing play of colours on the *meseta* (plateau). Contrary to popular opinion, it is not flat. Villages here are set low in long valleys, with occasional rivers, which rise up to the high barren plains. There are large limestone rocks everywhere and evocative sights, such as flocks of sheep led by solitary shepherds and isolated adobe villages. The path passes via **Castrojeriz**, with its castle dominating the town while, in better-known **Frómista**, the Iglesia de San Martín (p175) is one of the jewels of early Spanish Romanesque architecture. Between **Carrión de los Condes** and **Calzadilla de la Cueza**, the Camino coincides with a stretch of Roman road. Further on, despite appearances, **Sahagún** was an immensely powerful and wealthy Benedictine centre by the 12th century. The Mudéjar-influenced brick Romanesque churches merit a visit. Before reaching León, the Camino becomes monotonous, running through a long series of villages along paved, busy roads.

Day Walk

The comparatively short stretch between **Rabé de las Calzadas** and **Hontanas** (18.8km, five hours) is best in springtime – this rolling *meseta* walk brings solitude amid the wheat, allowing you to appreciate the region's uniquely lonely landscapes and villages.

⊙10am-8pm) Pick up its 24-hour, 48-hour and 72-hour guides to Burgos; they can also be downloaded as PDFs online.

Regional Tourist Office (www.turismocastil-layleon.com; Plaza de Alonso Martínez 7; ⊙9am-8pm Sun-Thu, 9am-9pm Fri & Sat)

❶ Getting There & Away

The **bus station** (Calle de Miranda 4) is south of the river, in the newer part of town. The train station is a considerable hike northeast of the town centre – bus 2 (€1.10) connects the train station with Plaza de España. **Renfe** (✎ 947 20 91 31; Calle de la Moneda 21; ⊙9.30am-1.30pm & 4.30-7.30pm Mon-Fri), the national rail network, has a convenient sales office in the centre of town.

Bus Regular buses run to Madrid (€18.50, three hours, up to 20 daily), Bilbao (€13.20, two hours, eight daily) and León (€15.30, two hours, three daily).

Train Destinations include Madrid (from €35.80, 2½ to 4½ hours, seven daily), Bilbao (from €22.90, three hours, four daily), León (from €21.10, two hours) and Salamanca (from €16.20, 2½ hours, three daily).

Around Burgos

Ermita de Santa María de Lara

If you take the N234 southeast of Burgos, a worthwhile stop some 35km out is the 7th-century Ermita de Santa María de Lara, close to Quintanilla de las Viñas. This modest Visigothic hermitage has some fine bas-reliefs around its external walls, which are among the best surviving regional examples of religious art from the 7th century.

Covarrubias

POP 630 / ELEV 975M

A breath away from the Middle Ages, the picturesque hamlet of Covarrubias is one of Castilla y León's hidden gems. Spread out along the shady banks of Río Arlanza, its distinctive arcaded half-timbered houses overlook intimate cobblestone squares.

A good time to be here is the second weekend of July, when the village hosts its **Medieval Market** and **Cherry Festival**.

◉ Sights

Although the main attraction is simply wandering the atmospheric cobbled streets, there are a few sights, too.

★**Colegiata de San Cosme y Damián**   CHURCH
(admission €2.50; ⊙10.30am-2pm & 4-7pm Mon & Wed-Sat, 4.30-6pm Sun) This 15th-century Gothic church has the evocative atmosphere of a mini cathedral. It is home to Spain's oldest still-functioning church organ and has a gloriously ostentatious altar, fronted by several Roman stone tombs, plus that of Fernán González, the 10th-century founder of Castilla. Don't miss the graceful cloisters and the *sacristia* with its vibrant 15th-century paintings by Van Eyck and tryptic *Adoracion de los Magis*.

EL CID: THE HEROIC MERCENARY

Few names resonate through Spanish history quite like El Cid, the 11th-century soldier of fortune and adventurer whose story tells in microcosm the tumultuous years when Spain was divided into Muslim and Christian zones. That El Cid became a romantic, idealised figure of history, known for his unswerving loyalty and superhuman strength, owes much to the 1961 film starring Charlton Heston and Sophia Loren. Reality, though, presents a different picture.

El Cid (from the Arabic *sidi* for 'chief' or 'lord') was born Rodrígo Diaz in Vivar, a hamlet about 10km north of Burgos, in 1043. After the death of Ferdinand I, he dabbled in the murky world of royal succession, which led to his banishment from Castilla in 1076. With few scruples, El Cid offered his services to a host of rulers, both Christian and Muslim. With each battle, he became ever more powerful and wealthy.

It's not known whether he suddenly developed a loyalty to the Christian kings or smelled the wind and saw that Spain's future would be Christian. Either way, when he heard that the Muslim armies had taken Valencia and expelled all the Christians, El Cid marched on the city, recaptured it and became its ruler in 1094 after a devastating siege. At the height of his powers and reputation, the man also known as El Campeador (Champion) retired to spend the remainder of his days in Valencia, where he died in 1099. His remains were returned to Burgos, where he lies buried in the town's cathedral (p185).

WORTH A TRIP

THE OLDEST EUROPEAN

Atapuerca (902 02 42 46; www.atapuerca.org; guided tours in Spanish €6; tours hourly from 10am-1pm, plus 4pm & 5pm Jul-Sep, shorter hours rest of the year; P) The archaeological site of Atapuerca, around 15km west of Burgos, has long excited students of early human history. But archaeologists made their greatest discovery here in July 2007 when they uncovered a jawbone and teeth of what is believed to be the oldest-known European: 1.2 million years old, some 500,000 years older than any other remains discovered in Western Europe. A Unesco World Heritage–listed site and still under excavation, the site is open to visitors with advance reservations.

Ceramics, cave paintings, carvings and burial sites have been discovered here, as well as remains of occupation in the area by homo sapiens from around 40,000 years ago, human settlements from the Neolithic age and evidence of cannibalism. There's a diverse programme of courses and study groups for adults, students and children (in Spanish).

Torreón de Doña Urraca
TOWER

This squat 10th-century tower dominates the remains of the town's medieval walls.

Sleeping & Eating

Casa Galín
HOSTAL €

(947 40 65 52; www.casagalin.com; Plaza de Doña Urraca 4; s/d €25/42;) A cut above your average provincial *hostal,* Casa Galín has comfortable, rustic-style rooms in a traditional timbered building overlooking the main square. It's home to a popular restaurant for tapas, fish and roasted meats, with a well-priced menu (€10).

Hotel Rey Chindasvinto
HOTEL €

(947 40 65 60; hotelchindas@wanadoo.es; Plaza del Rey Chindasvinto 5; s/d incl breakfast €35/55;) The best hotel in town, the Rey Chindasvinto has lovely spacious rooms with wooden beams, exposed brickwork and a good restaurant. The owners are friendly but the service sometimes goes missing.

Restaurante de Galo
CASTILIAN €€

(www.degalo.com; Calle Monseñor Vargas 10; mains €8.50-31; 1.30-4pm Thu-Tue) This fine restaurant in the heart of the village is recommended for its robust traditional dishes cooked in a wood-fired oven. This is a good place to sample the regional speciality of *cordero asado* (roast lamb).

Shopping

La Alacena
FOOD

(Calle de Monseñor Vargas 8; 10am-2pm & 5-7.30pm Tue-Sun) For homemade chocolates, local honey and other gourmet goodies, step inside this friendly shop.

Information

Tourist Office (947 40 64 61; www.eco-varrubias.com; Calle de Monseñor Vargas; 10.30am-2pm & 5-8pm Tue-Sat, 11am-2pm Sun) Located under the arches of the imposing northern gate, pick up the *Talleres Artesanos de Covarrubias* booklet which lists (and maps) seven art and craft workshops in the village.

Getting There & Away

Two buses travel between Burgos and Covarrubias on weekdays, and one runs on Saturday (€4, one hour).

Santo Domingo de Silos
POP 320

Nestled in the rolling hills south of Burgos, this tranquil, pretty village has an unusual claim to fame: monks from its monastery made the British pop charts in the mid-1990s with recordings of Gregorian chants. The monastery is one of the most famous in central Spain, known for its stunning cloister.

Sights

For sweeping views over the town, pass under the **Arco de San Juan** and climb the grassy hill to the south to the **Ermita del Camino y Via Crucis**.

Cloister
MONASTERY

(admission €3.50; 10am-1pm & 4.30-6pm Tue-Sat, 4.30-6pm Sun) This is a two-storey treasure chest of some of Spain's most imaginative Romanesque art. Although the overall effect is spectacular, the sculpted capitals are especially exquisite, with lions intermingled with floral and geometrical motifs betraying the never-distant influence of Islamic art in Spain. The guided tour covers the 17th-century **botica** (pharmacy) and a small

HIDDEN VILLAGES

The N623 Hwy carves a pretty trail from Burgos, particularly between the mountain passes of **Portillo de Fresno** and **Puerto de Carrales**. About 15km north of the former, a side road takes you through a series of intriguing villages in the **Valle de Sedano**. The town of the same name has a fine 17th-century church, but more interesting is the little Romanesque one above **Moradillo de Sedano**: the sculpted main doorway is outstanding.

Villages flank the highway on the way north, but **Orbaneja del Castillo** is the area's best-kept secret. Take the turn-off for Escalada and follow the signs. A dramatic backdrop of strange rock walls lends this spot an enchanting air. The N623 then continues north into the Valderredible region of Cantabria with its rock-hewn churches.

museum containing religious artworks, Flemish tapestries and the odd medieval sarcophagus. Guided tours are in Spanish only, and other visitors are usually allowed to wander more freely.

Church CHURCH
(⊙6am-2pm & 4.30-10pm, chant 6am, 7.30am, 9am, 1.45pm, 4pm, 7pm & 9.30pm) FREE Notable for its pleasingly unadorned Romanesque sanctuary dominated by a multidomed ceiling, this is where you can hear monks chant; times of the chants are subject to change.

Museo Los Sonidos de la Tierra MUSEUM
(Calle Las Condesas 10; ⊙10.30am-2pm & 5-7pm May-Oct, shorter hours rest of the year; ⊕) FREE Showcases musical instruments from the region and around the world.

🛏 Sleeping & Eating

Hotel Santo Domingo de Silos HOTEL, HOSTAL €
(☑947 39 00 53; www.hotelsantodomingodesilos. com; Calle Santo Domingo 14; s €36-48, d €40-65, apt €70-105; P✳🛜🏊) This place combines a simple *hostal* with a three-star hotel with large, comfortable rooms, some with whirlpool bathtubs, right opposite the monastery. It also has several nearby apartments, a swimming pool and underground parking. There is a reasonable restaurant (mains €7 to €17).

Hotel Tres Coronas HISTORIC HOTEL €€
(☑947 39 00 47; www.hoteltrescoronasdesilos. com; Plaza Mayor 6; s incl breakfast €57-73, d incl breakfast €71-93; P✳🛜) Set in a former 17th-century palace, this hotel is brimming with character with rooms of thick stone walls and old-world charm. The rooms at the front have lovely views over the square. The atmospheric restaurant (*menú del día* €12), which specialises in meats roasted in a wood-fire oven, is the village's best.

ℹ Information

Tourist Office (☑947 39 00 70; www.turismo-castillayleon.com; Calle de Cuatro Cantones 10; ⊙10am-1.30pm & 4-6pm Tue-Sun)

ℹ Getting There & Away

There is one daily bus (Monday to Saturday) from Burgos to Santo Domingo de Silos (€6.95, 1½ hours).

Desfiladero de Yecla

A mere 1.3km down the back road (BU911) to Caleruega from Santo Domingo, the spectacular Desfiladero de Yecla, a splendid gorge of limestone cliffs, opens up. It's easily visited thanks to a walkway – the stairs lead down from just past the tunnel exit.

South to Río Duero

Lerma

POP 2830 / ELEV 827M

If you're travelling between Burgos and Madrid and finding the passing scenery none too eye-catching, Lerma rises up from the roadside like a welcome apparition. An ancient settlement, Lerma hit the big time in the early 17th century when Grand Duke Don Francisco de Rojas y Sandoval, a minister under Felipe II, launched an ambitious project to create another El Escorial. He failed, but the cobbled streets and delightful plazas of the historic quarter are his most enduring legacy.

◉ Sights

Pass through the **Arco de la Cárcel** (Prison Gate), off the main road to Burgos, climbing up the long Calle del General Mola to the massive **Plaza Mayor**, which is fronted by the oversized **Palacio Ducal**, now a *parador* notable for its courtyards and 210 balconies. To the right of the square is the Dominican nuns' Convento de San Blas, which can be visited as part of the tourist office tour.

A short distance northwest of Plaza Mayor, a pretty passageway and viewpoint, Mirador de los Arcos, opens up over Río Arlanza. Its arches connect with the 17th-century Convento de Santa Teresa.

The Pasadizo de Duque de Lerma (admission €2) is a restored 17th-century subterranean passage that connects the palace with the Iglesia Colegial de San Pedro Apóstol – buy tickets at the tourist office.

🛏 Sleeping & Eating

Posada La Hacienda de Mi Señor HISTORIC HOTEL €€
(☎947 17 70 52; www.lahaciendademisenor.com; Calle El Barco 6; s/d incl breakfast €45/65; ❄@🛜) This is your best midrange bet, with enormous rooms in a renovated, historic building a couple of blocks down the hill from the square. The candy-floss colour scheme will start to grate if you stay too long; request room 205 for a more muted paint palette.

⭐ Parador de Lerma HISTORIC HOTEL €€€
(☎947 17 71 10; www.parador.es; Plaza Mayor 1; r €90-185; P❄@🛜) Undoubtedly the most elegant place to stay, this *parador* occupies the renovated splendour of the old Palacio Ducal and is thankfully devoid of the ostentacious decor (suits of armour and similar) you find in some *paradors*. Even if you are not staying here, take a look at the graceful cloistered inner patio. The rooms oooze luxury and character, and the service is impeccable.

Asador Casa Brigante CASTILIAN €€
(☎947 17 05 94; www.casabrigante.com; Plaza Mayor 5; mains €15-22; ⊙1.30-4pm) You're in the heart of Castilian wood-fired-oven territory and Plaza Mayor is encircled by high-quality restaurants with *cordero asado* on the menu (€35 for two is a good price to pay). A favourite is the cosy and friendly Asador Casa Brigante – you won't taste better roast lamb anywhere. Ask about its accommodation options nearby.

❶ Information

Tourist Office (☎947 17 70 02; www.citlerma.com; Casa Consistorial; ⊙10am-2pm & 4-7pm Tue-Sun) Offers 1¼-hour guided tours (€4) of the town and most of its monuments up to three times daily from April to September.

❶ Getting There & Away

There are eight daily buses from Burgos (€4.10, 30 minutes), with only four on Saturday or Sunday. Some buses coming from Aranda de Duero or Madrid also pass through.

Sepúlveda

POP 1230 / ELEV 1313M
With its houses staggered along a ridge carved out by the gorge of Río Duratón and famous for its *cordero asado* and *cochinillo*, Sepúlveda is a favourite weekend escape for *madrileños* (Madrid residents). Indeed, the Tuscan-style warm tones of Sepúlveda's buildings, fronting the central Plaza de España, are an enviable setting for a hot Sunday roast. Wednesday is market day.

The *ayuntamiento* (town hall) backs onto what remains of the old castle, while high above it all rises the 11th-century Iglesia del Salvador. It's considered the prototype of Castilian Romanesque, marked by the single arched portico.

🛏 Sleeping & Eating

Hospedería de los Templarios BOUTIQUE HOTEL €€
(☎665 593 551; www.hospederiadelostemplarios; Plaza de España 19-20; r from €70) This

---

ONLY IN SPAIN...

Spain's weird and wonderful fiestas have always left the rest of the world shaking their heads, from the Running of the Bulls in Pamplona to the tomato-throwing extravaganza of La Tomatina in Buñol. But surely there's no festival quite as strange as the baby-jumping festival of Castrillo de Murcia, a village just south of the A231, 25km west of Burgos.

Every year since 1620, this tiny village of around 250 inhabitants has marked the feast of Corpus Cristi by lining up the babies of the village on a mattress, while grown men dressed as 'El Colacho', a figure representing the devil, leap over up to six prostrate and, it must be said, somewhat bewildered babies at a time. Like all Spanish rites, it does have a purpose: the ritual is thought to ward off the devil. But why jumping over babies? We have no idea and the villagers aren't telling. They do, however, assure us that no baby has been injured in the recorded history of the fiesta.

aesthetically restored hotel has delightful rooms furnished with antiques but exuding an ambience that is far from old fashioned with stylish bathrooms, warm washes of colour on the walls and some edgy artwork. Small terraces afford superb views.

Restaurante Figón
Zute el Mayor CASTILIAN €€
(☑921 54 01 65; www.figondetinin.com; Calle de Lope Tablada 6; mains €11-24; ⊙1.30-4.30pm) A warmly recommended place, Figón Zute el Mayor is impossibly crowded on winter weekends, so be sure to reserve in advance.

Filka
CASTILIAN €€
(☑921 54 02 91; Plaza de España 4; main €16-22; ⊙2-4pm & 8-11pm Wed-Mon) One of the few places in the centre that is open for dinner. However, if you are yearning after the local speciality *cordero asado*, you need to let them know (aside from weekends). Otherwise, the lamb chops are a sound meaty choice.

❶ Getting There & Away

At least two buses link Sepúlveda daily with Madrid.

Parque Natural del Hoz del Duratón

A sizeable chunk of land northwest of Sepúlveda has been constituted as a natural park, the centrepiece of which is the Hoz del Duratón (Duratón Gorge). A dirt track leads 5km west from the hamlet of Villaseca to the Ermita de San Frutos. In ruins now, the hermitage was founded in the 7th century by San Frutos and his siblings, San Valentín and Santa Engracia. They lie buried in a tiny chapel nearby. This is a magical place, overlooking one of the many serpentine bends in the gorge, with squadrons of buzzards and eagles soaring above. The Parque Natural del Hoz del Duratón is a popular weekend excursion and some people take kayaks up to Burgomillodo to launch themselves down the waters of the canyon.

There is an excellent Centro de Interpretación (☑921 54 05 86; www.miespacionatural.es; Calle del Conde de Sepúlveda 34; ⊙10am-7pm; ⓘ) in Sepúlveda that also has an informative permanent exhibition about all aspects of the natural park, including the flora and fauna. It is housed in part of the Iglesia de Santiago.

West along Río Duero

Peñafiel
POP 5620
Peñafiel is the gateway to the Ribera del Duero wine region and it makes a wonderful base for getting to know the region's celebrated wines.

◉ Sights

★ **Plaza del Coso** SQUARE
Get your camera lens poised for one of Spain's most stunningly picturesque plazas. This rectangular 15th-century 'square' was one of the first to be laid out for this purpose and is considered one of the most important forerunners to the *plazas mayores* across Spain. It's still used for bullfights on ceremonial occasions, and it's watched over by distinctive half-wooden facades – as well as the grande dame of the castle up on the hill.

Castillo de Peñafiel CASTLE, MUSEUM
(Museo Provincial del Vino; Peñafiel; castle €3, incl museum €7, audioguides €2; ⊙11am-2.30pm & 4.30-8.30pm Tue-Sun) Dramatically watching over Peñafiel, this castle houses the state-of-the-art Museo Provincial del Vino. Telling a comprehensive story of the region's wines, this wonderful museum is informative and entertaining with interactive displays, dioramas, backlit panels and computer terminals. The pleasures of the end product are not neglected: wine tasting costs €7 if you do it solo, €10 with an expert to explain it all. The castle itself, is one of the longest and narrowest in Spain, and also worth exploring.

The castle's crenulated walls and towers stretch over 200m, but are little more than 20m across, and were raised and modified over 400 years from the 10th century onwards. The sight of it in the distance alone is worth the effort of getting here.

🛏 Sleeping & Eating

Hotel Convento Las Claras HISTORIC HOTEL €€
(☑983 87 81 68; www.hotelconventolasclaras.com; Plaza de los Comuneros 1; s/d €115/130; ❈ 🐾 ⓦ) This cool, classy hotel is an unexpected find in little Peñafiel. A former convent, the rooms are luxurious and there's a full spa available with thermal baths and treatments, and an excellent restaurant with, as you'd expect, a carefully chosen wine list. There are also lighter meals available in the cafeteria.

Hotel Castillo de Curiel HISTORIC HOTEL €€€
(📞 983 88 04 01; www.castillodecuriel.com; r from €140) Just north of Peñafiel, in the village of Curiel de Duero, this should be the hotel of choice for castle romantics. Occupying the oldest castle, dating from the 9th century, in the region (albeit extensively reformed), the hotel has lovely antique-filled rooms, all with sweeping views. It also has a well-regarded restaurant.

ℹ Information

Tourist Office (www.turismopenafiel.com; Plaza del Coso 31-32; ⏰ 10.30am-2.30pm & 5-8pm Tue-Sun)

ℹ Getting There & Away

Four or five buses a day run to Valladolid (€5.20, 45 minutes), 60km west of Peñafiel.

East along Río Duero

El Burgo de Osma

POP 5270 / ELEV 943M
Some 12km east of San Esteban de Gormaz, El Burgo de Osma is a real surprise. Once important enough to host its own university, it still has a feel of gracious, albeit mildly faded, elegance and is dominated by a remarkable cathedral.

◉ Sights

Your initiation into the old town is likely to be along the broad Calle Mayor, its portico borne by an uneven phalanx of stone and wooden pillars. Not far along, it leads into Plaza Mayor, fronted by the 18th-century ayuntamiento and the more sumptuous Hospital de San Agustín, which is where you'll find the tourist office.

If you exit El Burgo from near the cathedral on Plaza de San Pedro de Osma, take a left for the village of Osma, high above which stand the ruins of the 10th-century Castillo de Osma.

Catedral CATHEDRAL
(Plaza de San Pedro de Osma; ⏰ 10.30am-1pm & 4-7pm Tue-Sun) FREE Dating back to the Romanesque 12th century, the cathedral's architecture evolved as a combination of Gothic and, subsequently, Baroque – as in the weighty tower. The sanctuary is filled with art treasures, including the 16th-century main altarpiece and the so-called Beato de Osma, a precious 11th-century codex (manu-

BEST FOR KIDS

Castillo, Puebla de Sanabria (p172) Kids can try on armour and clamber up towers.

Casa-Museo de Colón, Valladolid (p164) Fun interactive exhibits about Columbus.

Museo del Orinal, Ciudad Rodrigo (p155) The Potty Museum will put a smirk on every kid's face.

Museo de Art Nouveau y Art Decó, Salamanca (p148) There are loads of fabulous toys here, including three rooms of historic dolls.

Alcázar, Segovia (p159) The inspiration for Walt Disney's Sleeping Beauty castle. Enough said.

Titirimundi International Puppet Festival, Segovia (p161) Time your visit for this wonderful family-geared festival (mid-May).

Museo del Chocolate, Astorga (p183) Chocolate pleases kids (of all ages).

script) that can be seen in the Capilla Mayor. Also of note is the light-flooded, circular Capilla de Palafox, a rare example of the neoclassical style in this region.

🛏 Sleeping & Eating

Hostal Mayor 71 HOSTAL €
(📞 975 36 80 24; www.mayor71.es; Calle Mayor 71; s/d €42/48; 🏠) This is a good central option, with modern, simple rooms. The best ones overlook Calle Mayor, and there are also some apartments nearby.

Posada del Canónigo HISTORIC HOTEL €€
(📞 975 36 03 62; www.posadadelcanonigo.es; Plaza San Pedro de Osma 19; s/d incl breakfast €50/65; ⏰ Apr-Oct; ❄🏠) This is certainly the most imaginative choice, with some rooms overlooking the cathedral from a handsome 16th-century building. There are two comfortable sitting rooms, one with a fireplace and library, and the rooms, all of them different, are overflowing with period charm, although it's rarely overdone.

Hotel II Virrey HOTEL €€
(📞 975 34 13 11; www.virreypalafox.com; Calle Mayor 2; s/d/ste €60/85/120; ❄🏠) This place has recently overhauled its decor, and it's now

WINE TASTING IN THE RIBERA DEL DUERO

The Ribero del Duero vintage wines are possibly the oldest in Spain and discerning Spanish wine lovers frequently claim that the wines of this region are the equal of the more famous Rioja wines.This is the largest wine-growing region in Castilla y León and Spain's most celebrated wine, Vega Sicilia, comes from here.

Not all the 200-plus wineries here are open for tours and/or tasting (including, unfortunately, Vega Sicilia), but around 50 are. For a full list, including details about tours and tastings, pick up the excellent *Wine Tourism Guide* (Ribera del Duero Wine Route) from the tourist office (p195) in Peñafiel. Another good resource is the website www.rutadelvinoriberadelduero.es.

Most of the wineries are located in the countryside surrounding Peñafiel; those that run tours and tastings include:

Matarromera (☑ 983 10 71 00; www.matarromera.es; Valbuena de Duero; tasting & tour €10; ⊙10am-2pm & 3-7pm Mon-Fri, 10am-2pm & 4-8pm Sat)

Legaris (☑ 983 87 80 88; www.legaris.es; Curiel de Duero; tasting & tour €10; ⊙ noon-7pm)

Protos (☑ 983 87 80 11; www.bodegasprotos.com; Calle Bodegas Protos 24-28; tours €10; ⊙10am-1pm & 4.30-6pm Tue-Fri, 10am-1pm & 4.30-6.30pm Sat & Sun) It's right in Peñafiel.

Aside from cellar-door sales at the wineries themselves, Peñafiel has numerous wine sellers dotted around the village. They really know their wines and most have every conceivable Ribera del Duero wine.

a curious mix of old Spanish charm and contemporary – public areas remain dominated by heavily gilded furniture, porcelain cherubs, dripping chandeliers and a sweeping staircase. Room rates soar on weekends in February and March, when people flock here for the *matanza* (ritual slaughter) of pigs, after which diners indulge in all-you-can-eat feasts.

The *matanza* costs €48 per head – not bad for one of the more unusual dining experiences. There's even a pig museum. The hotel also has a good restaurant, as well as a cafeteria for lighter meals.

Casa Engracia   GRILL €
(Calle Ruiz Zorrilla 3; mains €8-14; ⊙ 1-4.30pm Mon, 1-4pm & 7-11pm Tue-Sun) One of a rare breed of restaurants in this town that opens during the week. Expect sound rather than sensational meals, with an emphasis on grilled meats and fish.

ⓘ Information

Tourist Office (www.burgosma.es; Plaza Mayor 9; ⊙10am-2pm & 4-7pm Wed-Sun)

ⓘ Getting There & Away

Buses link El Burgo with Soria (€4.20, 50 minutes, two daily, one on Sunday) and Valladolid (€11.10, two hours, three daily).

Parque Natural del Cañón del Río Lobos

Some 15km north of El Burgo de Osma, this park promises forbidding rockscapes and a magnificent, deep river canyon, not forgetting abundant vultures and other birds of prey. About 4km in from the road stands the Romanesque **Ermita de San Bartolomé**. You can walk deeper into the park, but free camping is forbidden. If you're driving through the park between El Burgo de Osma and San Leonardo de Yagüe, don't miss the wonderful views from the **Mirador de La Galiana**, which is signposted off the SO920.

Camping Cañón del Río Lobos (☑ 975 36 35 65; camping.riolobos@hotmail.com; sites per person/tent/car €5/5/6.25; ⊙ Easter–mid-Sep;) **FREE** is near Ucero. If you're heading north along the switchback road that climbs up the canyon, you'll have some fine views back towards Ucero.

Soria

POP 40,000 / ELEV 1055M

Small-town Soria is one of Spain's smaller provincial capitals. Set on Río Duero in the heart of backwoods Castilian countryside, it's a great place to escape tourist Spain, with an appealing and compact old centre, and a sprinkling of stunning monuments.

Sights

Monasterio de San Juan de Duero RUIN
(Camino Monte de las Ánimas; admission €0.60, Sat & Sun free; ⏲10am-2pm & 5-8pm Tue-Sat, 10am-2pm Sun) The most striking of Soria's sights, this wonderfully evocative and partially ruined cloister boasts exposed and gracefully interlaced arches; the arches artfully blend Mudéjar and Romanesque influences and no two capitals are the same. Inside the church, the carvings are worth a closer look for their intense iconography. It's on the riverbank down the hill from the historic centre.

Ermita de San Saturio HISTORIC BUILDING
(Paseo de San Saturio; ⏲10.30am-2pm & 4.30-7.30pm Tue-Sun) FREE A lovely riverside walk south for 2.3km from the Monasterio de San Juan de Duero will take you past the 13th-century church of the former Knights Templar, the Monasterio de San Polo (not open to the public), and on to the fascinating, baroque Ermita de San Saturio.

The hermitage is one of Castilla y León's most beautifully sited structures, an octagonal structure that perches high on the riverbank and over the cave where Soria's patron saint spent much of his life. Climb through a series of fascinating rooms hewn from the rock, but linger most of all in the Capilla, an extravagantly frescoed chapel near the building's summit.

Concatedral de San Pedro CATHEDRAL
(Calle de San Agustín; cloister €1; ⏲cloister 11am-1pm Mon, 10.30am-1.30pm & 4.30-7.30pm Tue-Sun) Climbing back up the hill towards the historic centre, the Concatedral de San Pedro has a plateresque facade. The 12th-century **cloister** is the most charming feature here. Its delicate arches are divided by slender double pillars topped with capitals adorned with floral, human and animal motifs.

Casco Viejo OLD TOWN
The narrow streets of Soria's old town centre on Plaza Mayor. The plaza's appeal lies in its lack of uniformity, and in the attractive Renaissance-era **ayuntamiento** and the **Iglesia de Santa María la Mayor**, with its unadorned Romanesque facade and gilt-edged interior. A block north is the majestic, sandstone, 16th-century **Palacio de los Condes Gomara** (Calle de Aguirre), while Soria's **Casa de las Poetas** (3rd fl, Calle Mayor 23; admission free; ⏲10am-2pm & 4-8pm Tue-Sun) pays homage to Antonio Machado and other Spanish poets with a connection to the town.

Further north is the beautiful Romanesque **Iglesia de Santo Domingo** (Calle de Santo Tomé Hospicio; ⏲7am-9pm). Its small but exquisitely sculpted portal is something special, particularly at sunset when its reddish stone seems to be aglow. At the **Iglesia de San Juan de Rabanera** (Calle de San Juan de Rabanera; ⏲before & after Mass), which was first built in the 12th century, hints of Gothic and even Byzantine art gleam through the mainly Romanesque hue.

Museo Numantino MUSEUM
(Paseo del Espolón 8; admission €1.20; ⏲10am-2pm & 5-8pm Tue-Sat, 10am-2pm Sun) Archaeology buffs with a passable knowledge of Spanish should enjoy this well-organised museum, dedicated to finds from ancient sites across the province of Soria (especially Numancia). It has everything from mammoth bones to ceramics and jewellery, accompanied by detailed explanations of the historical developments in various major Celtiberian and Roman settlements.

Festivals & Events

Fiestas de San Juan y de la Madre de Dios LOCAL FIESTA
Since the 13th century, the 12 *barrios* (districts) of Soria have celebrated this annual festival with considerable fervour. Held during the second half of June, the main festivities take place on Jueves (Thursday) La Saca, when each of the districts presents a bull to be fought the next day.

Sleeping

Hostería Solar de Tejada BOUTIQUE HOTEL €
(☎975 23 00 54; www.hosteriasolardetejada.es; Calle de Claustrilla 1; s/d €52/56; ❄📶) This handsome boutique hotel right along the historic quarter's pedestrianised zone has individually designed, albeit small, rooms with homey decor. Several sport balconies overlooking the bustling pedestrian street.

Apolonia BOUTIQUE HOTEL €€
(☎975 23 90 56; www.hotelapoloniasoria.com; Puertas de Pro 5; s/d/ste incl breakfast €60/66/90; ❄@📶) This smart hotel has a contemporary urban feel with its charcoal, brown and cream colour scheme, abundance of glass, abstract artwork and, in four of the rooms, an interesting, if revealing, optional colour light effect between the main room and the large walk-in shower – possibly best for romancing couples. The youthful management can arrange excursions.

Hotel Soria Plaza Mayor   HOTEL €€
(☑ 975 24 08 64; www.hotelsoriaplazamayor.com; Plaza Mayor 10; s/d/ste €65/72/91; ✳ @) This hotel has terrific rooms, each with its own style of decor, overlooking either Plaza Mayor or a quiet side street. There are so many balconies that even some bathrooms have their own. The suites are *very* comfortable.

Hotel Leonor Centro   HOTEL €€
(☑ 975 23 93 03; www.hotel-leonor.com; Plaza Ramón y Cajal 5; s/d €70/90; ✳ 🛜) Just off the main pedestrian street through the historic centre, this fine four-star hotel has contemporary carpeted rooms with tasteful furnishings and a neutral colour scheme with splashes of burgundy and light wood panels. The bathrooms have hydromassage tubs, plus there is a small spa.

🍴 Eating & Drinking

Soria's restaurants are mainly centred around the main squares, namely Plaza El Salvador, Plaza Ramón Benito Aceñal and Plaza Mayor. Soria's surprisingly raucous drinking scene has its epicentre on Plaza Ramón Benito Aceñal, with Plaza San Clemente, just off Calle Mayor, offering strong competition.

Olé!   TAPAS €
(Marqués de Vadillo 5; cazuelas & tapas €3; ☺ 7.30am-11pm; 🍴) This airy contemporary place specialises in *cazuelas,* small terracotta dishes containing a wide range of surprisingly substantial dishes, like *pisto* (ratoutuille) topped with a fried egg, pasta *carbonara, morcilla* (blood sausage) and the all time favourite *patatas ali oli* (fried potatoes with garlic mayonnaise). A couple of these is easily equal to a main dish elsewhere, equalling an extraordinarily inexpensive (and tasty) meal.

Capote   SANDWICHES €
(Plaza Ramón Benito Aceñal; montaditos €1.30; ☺ 8am-midnight; 🍴) You'll have to fight through the crowd to reach the counter at this popular bar where you can fill up happily on the tasty and varied *montaditos* (open sandwiches).

Fogon del Salvador   CASTILIAN €€
(Plaza El Salvador 1; mains €14.50-22; ☺ 1.30-4pm & 9pm-midnight; 🍴) A Soria culinary stalwart and fronted by a popular bar, Fogon del Salvador has a wine list as long as your arm (literally) and a fabulous wood-fired oven churning out succulent meat-based dishes.

There is also (surprisingly) a healthy list of vegetarian dishes and the *raciones* include some rarely found dishes, such as *anguila ahumada* (smoked baby eels).

⭐ Baluarte   CONTEMPORARY CASTILIAN €€€
(☑ 975 21 36 58; www; Caballeros 14; mains €20-33, menú degustación €50; ☺ 1.45-3.45pm & 9-11pm Tue-Sat, 1.30-3.30pm Sun) Oscar Garcia is one of Spain's most exciting new chefs and this comparitively new venture in Soria appropriately showcases his culinary talents. Dishes are based on classic Castilian ingredients but treated with just enough foam and drizzle to ensure that they are both exciting and satisfying, without being too pretentious. Reservations essential.

ℹ Information

Municipal Tourist Office (☑ 975 22 27 64; www.soria.es; Plaza Ramón y Cajal; ☺ 10am-2pm & 4-8pm Tue-Sun) Offers guided tours at weekends at noon (€5) departing from the tourist office. Reserve in advance.

Regional Tourist Office (☑ 975 21 20 52; www.turismocastillayleon.com; Calle de Medinaceli 2; ☺ 9.30am-2pm & 5-8pm)

ℹ Getting There & Away

Bus From the **bus station** (☑ 975 22 51 60; Avenida de Valladolid), a 15-minute walk west of the city centre, there are regular services to Burgos (€12.15, 2½ hours), Madrid (€16.10, 2½ hours) and Valladolid (€16, three hours), as well as main provincial towns.

Train The **train station** (Carretera de Madrid) is 2.5km southwest of the city centre. Trains connect Soria with Madrid (€21.70, 2¾ hours, three daily), but there are few other direct services.

Around Soria

Numancia's Roman Ruins   RUINS
(www.numanciasoria.es; Numancia; adult/concession/child under 13yr €4/3/free, Sat & Sun free; ☺ 10am-2pm & 4-8pm Tue-Sat, 10am-2pm Sun) The mainly Roman ruins of Numancia, 8km north of Soria, have a lonely, windswept aspect with little to suggest the long history of a settlement inhabited as early as the Bronze Age. Numancia proved one of the most resistant cities to Roman rule. Finally Scipio, who had crushed Carthage, starved the city into submission in 134 BC. Under Roman rule, Numancia was an important stop on the road from Caesaraugustus (Zaragoza) to Astúrica Augusta (Astorga). Now the city

exists in outline only and will appeal more to budding archaeologists than to casual visitors.

Sierra de Urbión & Laguna Negra

The Sierra de Urbión, northwest of Soria, is home to the beautiful Laguna Negra (Black Lake), a small glacial lake that resembles a black mirror at the base of brooding rock walls amid partially wooded hills. Located 18km north of the village of Vinuesa, the lake is reached by a winding and scenic road (there's no public transport) that's bumpy in patches. The road ends at a car park, where there's a small information office (⊙ Jun-Oct). It's a further 2km uphill to the lake, either on foot or via the bus (return €1, departing half-hourly from 10am to 2pm and 4pm to 6.30pm June to October), which leaves you 300m short of the lake. From the lake, a steep trail leads up to the Laguna de Urbión in La Rioja or to the summit of the Pico de Urbión, above the village of Duruelo de la Sierra, and on to a series of other tiny glacial lakes.

Calatañazor

POP 40 / ELEV 1071M

One of Castilla y León's most romantic tiny hilltop villages, Calatañazor is a charming detour. It's not visible from the highway just 1km away, and has a crumbling medieval air. Pass through the town gate and climb the crooked, cobbled lanes, wandering through narrow streets lined by ochre stone and adobe houses topped with red-tiled roofs and conical chimneys. Scenes from the movie *Doctor Zhivago* were shot here.

Towering above the village is the one-time Muslim fortress that gave Calatañazor its name (which comes from the Arabic Qala'at an-Nassur, literally 'The Vulture's Citadel'). Now in ruins, it has exceptional views from the walls and watchtowers, both down over the rooftops and north over a vast field called Valle de la Sangre (Valley of Blood). This was the setting of an epic 1002 battle that saw the Muslim ruler Almanzor defeated.

There's also a church and a handful of artisan shops selling local products. There are three well-signposted *casas rurales* if you fancy staying the night.

There's no regular public transport to Calatañazor. If you're driving, the village lies around 1km north of the N122 – the well-signposted turn-off is about 29km west of Soria and about 27km northeast of El Burgo de Osma.

South of Soria

Medinaceli

POP 820 / ELEV 1270M

Modern Medinaceli, along a slip road just north of the A2 motorway, is the contemporary equivalent of a one-horse town, but don't be fooled: old Medinaceli is one of Castilla y León's most beautiful *pueblos* (villages), draped along a high, windswept ridge 3km to the north.

⊙ Sights

In addition to the sights listed following, there's the moderately interesting Gothic Colegiata de Santa María (Plaza de la Iglesia; admission by donation; ⊙11am-2pm & 4-7pm Tue-Sun), and the evocative remains of a synagogue: San Román.

But Medinaceli's charm consists of rambling through tranquil cobblestone lanes and being surrounded by delightful stone houses redolent of the noble families that lived here after the town fell to the Reconquista in 1124. The area between Plaza de Santiueste and the lovely, partly colonnaded Plaza Mayor is Medinaceli at its best. The oldest remaining building is the 16th-century Alhónidga, formerly used for storing and selling grain.

Palacio Ducal　　　　ARCHITECTURE, GALLERY
(Plaza Mayor; admission €2; ⊙10am-8pm) This largely 17th-century palace overlooks the Plaza Mayor, and hosts regular and high-quality exhibitions of contemporary art in rooms arrayed around the stunning two-storey Renaissance courtyard. In one of the rooms is a 2nd-century Roman mosaic.

Roman Sites　　　　　　　　RUIN
Once a strategic Roman outpost, Medinaceli boasts a 1st-century-AD Arco Romano (Roman triumphal arch) at the entrance to town, a mosaic (from a Roman villa) in situ under glass on Plaza San Pedro and another mosaic in the Palacio Ducal.

✦ Festivals & Events

Festival Internacional de Música　　MUSIC
(⊙weekends Jul) On Saturdays and/or Sundays in July, the Colegiata de Santa María

hosts mostly classical concerts by international performers.

🛏 Sleeping & Eating

Medina Salim BOUTIQUE HOTEL €€
(📞975 32 69 74; www.hotelmedinasalim.com; Calle Barranco 15; s/d incl breakfast €60/80; 🅿🏧🛜) A welcoming boutique hotel which sports large airy rooms with fridges and terraces that overlook either the sweeping valley or medieval cobbles out front. Decor is contemporary and light with pale woodwork and colour scheme. Perks include a small spa and a delightful breakfast room-cum-cafeteria which overlooks part of the original Roman wall.

La Ceramica RURAL HOTEL €€
(📞975 32 63 81; www.laceramicacasarural.es; Calle de Santa Isabel 2; s/d €40/60, d incl breakfast & dinner €91; ⊙Feb–mid-Dec; 🛜) Located in the centre of the historic quarter, the rooms here are intimate and comfortable, with a strong dose of rustic charm; the attic room 22 is lovely, but the CR2 apartment which sleeps four feels just like home. There's sometimes a two-night minimum stay. The restaurant is excellent (mains €8 to €17).

Asador de la Villa El Granero CASTILIAN €€
(📞975 32 61 89; Calle de Yedra 10; mains €13-20; ⊙1.30-4pm & 9-11pm May-Oct, shorter hours rest of the year) This well-signposted place, with a shop selling local food products at the front, is thought by many to be Medinaceli's best restaurant. The *setas de campo* (wild mushrooms) are something of a local speciality. Book ahead on weekends.

Iglesia Convento Santa Isabel SWEETS €
(Calle de Campo San Nicolás; cookies from €6; ⊙10am-2pm & 4-7pm) The nuns at this pretty convent bake up tasty cookies and other sweets; ring the bell and then make your selection through the revolving window.

ℹ Information

Tourist Office (📞975 32 63 47; Calle Campo de San Nicolás; ⊙10am-2pm & 4-7pm Wed-Sun) At the entrance to town, just around the corner from the arch.

ℹ Getting There & Away

Two daily buses to Soria (€6.75, 45 minutes) leave from outside the *ayuntamiento* in the new town. There's no transport between the old and new towns; it's a steep hike.

Santa María de la Huerta

POP 370

This largely insignificant village, just short of the Aragonese frontier, contains a wonderful Cistercian monastery (admission €3; ⊙10am-1pm & 4-6pm Mon-Sat, 10-11.15am & 4-6.30pm Sun), founded in 1162, where monks lived until the monastery was expropriated in 1835. The order was allowed to return in 1930 and 25 Cistercians are now in residence. Before entering the monastery, note the church's impressive 12th-century facade with its magnificent rose window.

Inside the monastery you pass through two cloisters, the second of which is the more beautiful. Known as the Claustro de los Caballeros, it's Spanish-Gothic in style, although the medallions on the 2nd floor, bearing coats of arms and assorted illustrious busts, such as that of Christopher Columbus, are a successful plateresque touch. Off this cloister is the *refectorio* (dining hall). Built in the 13th century, it's notable for the absence of columns to support the vault.

A couple of buses per day connect the village with Soria.

Toledo & Castilla-La Mancha

Best Places to Eat

➡ Calle Mayor (p229)
➡ El Corregidor (p217)
➡ La Bodeguilla de Basilio (p224)
➡ Kumera (p211)
➡ Figón del Huécar (p224)

Best Places to Stay

➡ Palacio de la Serna (p215)
➡ La Casa del Rector (p216)
➡ Hotel Albamanjón (p220)
➡ Antiguo Palacio de Atienza (p229)
➡ Parador de Cuenca (p224)

Why Go?

Castilla-La Mancha's landscape is richly patterned and dramatic: undulating plains of rich henna-coloured earth, neatly striped and spotted with olive groves, and golden wheat fields and grapevines – all stretching to a horizon you never seem to reach. This is Don Quijote country, and you'll find references to the fictional knight throughout the region, including a fistful of picturesque windmills. And in many ways, this really is storybook Spain, a land of hearty meals, cheese and wine, lonely hilltop castles and towns stocked with churches.

The area's best-known city is glorious Toledo, an open-air museum of medieval buildings and cultural sights. Cuenca is another wondrous place, seemingly about to topple off its eagle-eyrie perch high above a gorge. There are quiet mountainous stretches here as well, including the Sierra de Alcaraz and the Serranía de Cuenca.

When to Go
Toledo

°C/°F Temp — Rainfall Inches/mm

Mar & Apr Enjoy the countryside's colourful dazzle of wildflowers against a lush green landscape.

May Stroll the evocative streets of medieval Toledo and Cuenca before the sizzle of high summer.

Sep & Oct Hike across Castilla-La Mancha's natural parks and picturesque villages.

FESTIVALS

Corpus Christi in Toledo (p208) is one of the most important religious events, while Cuenca is renowned for its eerily silent Semana Santa (p223) processions. If you can, also catch Toledo's Virgen del Sagrario (p209), or Almagro's Festival Internacional de Teatro Clásico (p216).

Best Paradors

➡ Parador Conde de Orgaz, Toledo (p211)

➡ Parador de Oropesa (p213)

➡ Parador de Almagro (p216)

➡ Parador de Cuenca (p224)

➡ Parador de Alarcón (p226)

➡ Parador de Sigüenza (p229)

Architectural Oddities

➡ Transparente in Toledo's Catedral – an otherworldly light behind the main altar.

➡ Valeria – Spain's best-preserved Roman-era Forum.

➡ Sinagoga del Tránsito, Toledo – one of the last synagogues built in Spain.

➡ Casas Colgadas, Cuenca – houses hanging out over a gorge.

➡ Corral de Comedias, Almagro – ancient Shakespeare-esque theatre.

➡ Windmills, Consuegra – Cervantes' classic novel comes alive.

Off the Beaten Track

If you divert even a little from the main tourist-trail axis of Toledo and El Quijote, you're likely to come across some of Spain's least-visited regions. Evocative Roman ruins don't come any quieter than Segóbriga (p226) and Valeria (p226), while nearby Pastrana (p226) and Atienza (p229) are two of Spain's most beautiful medieval villages – come during the week and you'll find no one here. South of Toledo, deserted hilltop castles such as the Castillo de Montalbán (p213) whisper, in near silence, of an epic past. In the region's far southeast, Alcalá del Júcar (p220) is typical of the villages time forgot in the Río Júcar valley, while the Sierra de Alcaraz (p225) is like Castilla-La Mancha's lost world.

ICONIC MUSEUMS

Castilla-La Mancha is best known for its role as the backdrop for one of the world's greatest-ever novels, and two museums – Museo del Quijote y Biblioteca Cervantina (p215) in Ciudad Real and the Casa-Museo de Dulcinea (p219) in El Toboso – provide fascinating insights into this quixotic literary heritage. But other museums, too, offer a chance to get under the skin of the region. In Talavera de la Reina, for example, the Museo Ruiz de Luna (p213) takes you into the wonderful world of ceramics, a centuries-old artisan tradition that's so different from the mass-produced stuff you see elsewhere in Spain. Holy Week celebrations in Cuenca are some of the most stirring in Spain, the city's Museo de la Semana Santa (p222) is the next best thing if you can't be there at Easter.

Top Five Food Experiences

➡ Visit Villadiego (p216), southwest of Ciudad Real, to learn all about queso manchego (a hard sheep's milk cheese).

➡ Get to know the wines of the prolific wine-producing region of Valdepeñas at Bodega de las Estrellas (p220).

➡ Dine on venison at Cuenca's best table at Mesón Casas Colgadas (p224).

➡ Try the famous local eggplants from Almagro at Restaurante Abrasador (p217).

➡ Sample the best in local cooking with the Menú de Montes de Toledo at La Abadía (p211).

Castilla-La Mancha Highlights

1 Stroll the tangle of medieval streets and explore the monuments of **Toledo** (p204).

2 Wind down in the picture-perfect medieval town of **Atienza** (p229).

3 Take *the* Don Quijote shot of the windmills overlooking **Consuegra** (p214).

4 Kick back with a beer at a riverside bar in **Alcalá del Júcar** (p220) beneath the cascade of houses and its castle.

5 Visit the exceptional **Museo de Arte Abstracto Español** (p221) in one of the extraordinary hanging houses of Cuenca.

6 Marvel at the handsome plaza and historic theatre in enticing **Almagro** (p215).

7 Be king or queen of the castle by visiting the **castillos** (p213) south of Toledo.

8 Check out the chunky cathedral, hilltop castle and great restaurants in pleasing **Sigüenza** (p227).

TOLEDO

POP 85,593 / ELEV 655M

Though one of the smaller of Spain's provincial capitals, Toledo looms large in the nation's history and consciousness as a religious centre, bulwark of the Spanish church, and once-flourishing symbol of a multicultural medieval society. The old town today is a treasure chest of churches, museums, synagogues and mosques set in a labyrinth of narrow streets, plazas and inner patios in a lofty setting high above the Río Tajo. Crowded by day, Toledo changes dramatically after dark when the streets take on a moody, other-worldly air.

History

Already an important pre-Roman settlement, Toledo was eventually chosen as capital of the post-Roman Visigothic kingdom. After being taken by the Moors in AD 711, the city rapidly grew to become the capital of an independent Arab *taifa* (small kingdom) and *the* centre of learning and arts in Spain.

Alfonso VI marched into Toledo in 1085 and, shortly thereafter, the Vatican recognised Toledo as a seat of the Spanish Church. Initially, Toledo's Christians, Jews and Muslims coexisted tolerably well. However, the eventual convert-or-get-out dictates issued to the Jews and Muslims stripped this multifaith city of the backbone of its social and economic life. Once Felipe II chose Madrid as his capital in the mid-16th century, Toledo went into decline, although its religious power within the Catholic Church remains undimmed.

⊙ Sights

★ **Catedral** CATHEDRAL

(Plaza del Ayuntamiento; adult/child €8/free; ⊙10.30am-6.30pm Mon-Sat, 2-6.30pm Sun) Toledo's cathedral reflects the city's historical significance as the heart of Catholic Spain and it's one of the most extravagant cathedrals in the country. The heavy interior, with sturdy columns dividing the space into five naves, is on a monumental scale. Every one of the numerous side chapels has artistic treasures, with the other main highlights being the *coro* (choir), Capilla Mayor, Transparente, sacristia and belltower (for €3 extra).

From the earliest days of the Visigothic occupation, the current site of the cathedral has been a centre of worship. During Muslim rule, it contained Toledo's central mosque, destroyed in 1085. Dating from the 13th century and essentially a Gothic structure, the cathedral is nevertheless a melting pot of styles, including Mudéjar and Renaissance. The Visigothic influence continues today in the unique celebration of the Mozarabic Rite, a 6th-century liturgy that was allowed to endure after Cardinal Cisneros put its legitimacy to the test by burning missals in a fire of faith; they survived more or less intact. The rite is celebrated in the Capilla Mozarabe at 9am Monday to Saturday, and at 9.45am on Sundays.

The high altar sits in the extravagant **Capilla Mayor**, whose masterpiece is the *retablo* (altarpiece), with painted wooden sculptures depicting scenes from the lives of Christ and the Virgin Mary; it's flanked by royal tombs. The oldest of the cathedral's magnificent stained-glass pieces is the **rose window** above the Puerta del Reloj. Behind the main altar lies a mesmerising piece of 18th-century churrigueresque (lavish Baroque ornamentation), the **Transparente**, which is illuminated by a light well carved into the dome above.

In the centre of things, the **coro** is a feast of sculpture and carved wooden stalls. The 15th-century lower tier depicts the various stages of the conquest of Granada.

The **tesoro**, however, deals in treasure of the glittery kind. It's dominated by the extraordinary **Custodia de Arfe**: with 18kg of pure gold and 183kg of silver, this 16th-century processional monstrance bristles with some 260 statuettes. Its big day out is the Feast of Corpus Christi (p208), when it is paraded around Toledo's streets.

Other noteworthy features include the sober **cloister**, off which is the 14th-century **Capilla de San Blas**, with Gothic tombs and stunning frescoes, the gilded **Capilla de Reyes Nuevos**, and the **sala capitular** (chapterhouse), with its remarkable 500-year-old *artesonado* (wooden Mudéjar

---

ⓘ **TAKE THE ESCALATOR**

A **remonte peatonal** (⊙7am-11pm Mon-Fri, 8am-2am Sat, 8am-10pm Sun), which starts near the Puerta de Alfonso VI and ends near the Monasterio de Santo Domingo El Antiguo, is a good way to avoid the steep uphill climb to reach the historic quarter of town.

ceiling) and portraits of all the archbishops of Toledo.

The highlight of all, however, is the **sacristía** (sacristy), which contains a gallery with paintings by such masters as El Greco, Zurbarán, Caravaggio, Titian, Raphael and Velázquez. It can be difficult to appreciate the packed-together, poorly lit artworks, but it's a stunning assemblage in a small space. In an adjacent chamber, don't miss the spectacular Moorish standard captured in the Battle of Salado in 1340.

An extra €3 gets you entrance to the upper level of the cloister, and the **belltower**, which offers predictably wonderful views over the centre of historic Toledo.

Termas Romanas & Tolmo Museum   RUIN, ART GALLERY
(Plaza Amador de los Rios; ⏱10am-2pm & 5-9pm Tue-Sat Jun-Sep, 10am-2pm & 4-8pm Tue-Sat Oct-May, 10am-2pm Sun year-round) **FREE** The modest remains of Toledo's Roman baths (down the stairs) are combined with a small but extraordinary collection of artworks, including a single sketch each from (among others) Picasso, Miró, Barceló, Tapies, Chillida and Antonio López. A series of sketches documenting Toledo's history is also worth lingering over.

Alcázar   FORTRESS, MUSEUM
(Museo del Ejército; Calle Alféreces Provisionales; adult/child €5/free; ⏱11am-5pm) At the highest point in the city looms the foreboding Alcázar. Rebuilt under Franco, it has been reopened as a vast military museum. The usual displays of uniforms and medals are here, but the best part is the exhaustive historical section, with an in-depth overview of the nation's history in Spanish and English.

Abd ar-Rahman III raised an *al-qasr* (fortress) here in the 10th century, which was thereafter altered by the Christians. Alonso Covarrubias rebuilt it as a royal residence for Carlos I, but the court moved to Madrid and the fortress eventually became a military academy. The Alcázar was heavily damaged during the siege of the garrison by loyalist militias at the start of the Civil War in 1936. The soldiers' dogged resistance, and the famous refusal of their commander, Moscardó, to give it up in exchange for his son's life, made the Alcázar a powerful Nationalist symbol.

The exhibition is epic in scale and by the time you get to the end of the 19th century your feet will be begging for mercy, but relief is at hand: sensibly the Civil War is essentially skipped over in one sensitively conceived paragraph to avoid controversy. You can, however, see a re-creation of Moscardó's office; other highlights include the monumental central patio decorated with Habsburg coats of arms, and archaeological remains from Moorish times.

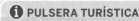

❶ PULSERA TURÍSTICA
The Pulsera Turística is a bracelet (€8) that gets you into six key Toledo sights (no time limit), all of which cost €2.50 on their own. Buy the bracelet at any of the sights covered, which are Monasterio San Juan de los Reyes, Sinagoga de Santa María La Blanca, Iglesia de Santo Tomé, Iglesia del Salvador, Iglesia San Ildefonso and Mezquita del Cristo de la Luz.

Museo de Santa Cruz   MUSEUM
(Calle de Cervantes 3; ⏱10am-7pm Mon-Sat, to 2pm Sun) **FREE** The 16th-century Museo de Santa Cruz is a beguiling combination of Gothic and plateresque styles. The cloisters and carved wooden ceilings are superb, as is the collection of Spanish ceramics. Also upstairs is an atmospheric cruciform gallery that contains an archaeological display, some fine Flemish religious art, a number of El Grecos, a crucifixion attributed to Goya, a flag from the Battle of Lepanto, and the wonderful 15th-century *Tapestry of the Astrolabes*.

Mezquita del Cristo de la Luz   MOSQUE
(Calle Cristo de la Luz; admission €2.50; ⏱10am-2pm & 3.30-6.45pm Mon-Fri, 10am-6.45pm Sat & Sun) On the northern slopes of town you'll find a modest, yet beautiful, mosque (the only one remaining of Toledo's 10) where architectural traces of Toledo's medieval Muslim conquerors are still in evidence. Built around AD 1000, it suffered the usual fate of being converted into a church (hence the religious frescoes), but the original vaulting and arches survived.

According to local legend (which explains the mosque's unusal name), when Alfonso VI conquered Toledo for the Christians in 1085, his horse stopped outside the mosque and refused to continue. Closer investigations revealed a statue of Christ with its oil lamp still burning more than three centuries after it was left there…

Toledo

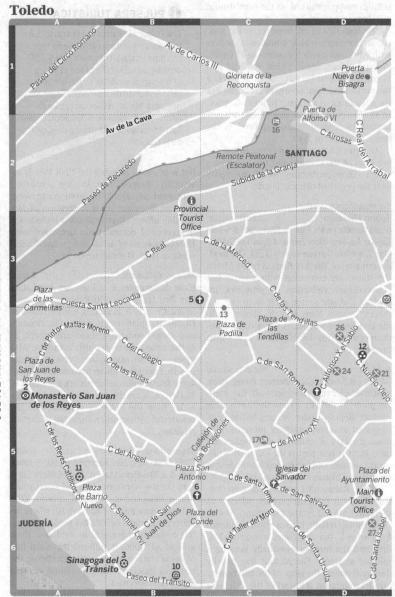

★**Monasterio San Juan
de los Reyes**　　　　　　MONASTERY
(Calle San Juan de los Reyes 2; admission €2.50;
⊙10am-6.30pm Jun-Sep, to 5.30pm Oct-May)
This imposing 15th-century Franciscan
monastery and church was provocatively

founded in the heart of the Jewish quarter
by the Catholic monarchs Isabel and Fernando to demonstrate the supremacy of their
faith. The rulers had planned to be buried
here but eventually ended up in their prize
conquest, Granada. The highlight is the

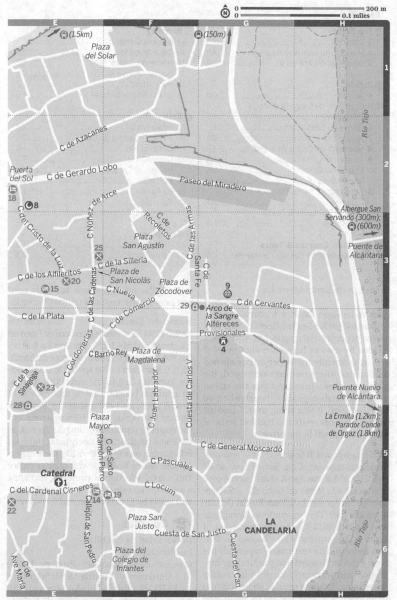

amazing two-level cloister, a harmonious fusion of late (flamboyant) Gothic downstairs and Mudéjar architecture upstairs, with superb statuary, arches, vaulting, elaborate pinnacles and gargoyles surrounding a lush garden with orange trees and roses.

The adjacent church has a series of enormous coats of arms of the Catholic monarchs. Outside, note the chains dangling from the northeastern facade – they once belonged to Christian prisoners liberated from Muslim Granada.

Toledo

Sinagoga de Santa María La Blanca
SYNAGOGUE

(Calle de los Reyes Católicos 4; admission €2.50; ⊙10am-6.45pm Jun-Sep, to 5.45pm Oct-May) This pretty Mudéjar synagogue has five naves divided by rows of horseshoe and multifoil arches. Originally the upper arches opened onto rooms where women worshipped; the men were down below. Admire the stucco work and ornate capitals, although when we were last here, it was being freshly painted (rather than restored) and had lost some of its ancient appeal in the process.

★ Sinagoga del Tránsito
SYNAGOGUE

(museosefardi.mcu.es; Calle Samuel Leví; adult/child €3/1.50, Sat after 2pm & all day Sun free, combined ticket with Museo del Greco €5; ⊙9.30am-8pm Tue-Sat Apr-Sep, to 6.30pm Tue-Sat Oct-Mar, 10am-3pm Sun) This magnificent synagogue was built in 1355 by special permission of Pedro I. The synagogue now houses the **Museo Sefardí**. The vast main prayer hall has been expertly restored and the Mudéjar decoration and intricately carved pine ceiling are striking. Exhibits provide an insight into the history of Jewish culture in Spain, and include archaeological finds, a memorial garden, costumes and ceremonial artefacts.

Toledo's former *judería* (Jewish quarter) was once home to 10 synagogues and comprised some 10% of the walled city's area. After the expulsion of the Jews from Spain in 1492, the synagogue was variously used as a priory, hermitage and military barracks.

Museo del Greco
MUSEUM, GALLERY

(☑925 22 44 05; museodelgreco.mcu.es; Paseo del Tránsito; adult/child €3/1.50, after 2pm Sat & all day Sun free, combined ticket with Sinagoga del Tránsito €5; ⊙9.30am-8pm Tue-Sat Apr-Sep, to 6.30pm Oct-Mar, 10am-3pm Sun) In the early 20th century, an aristocrat bought what he thought was El Greco's house and did a stunning job of returning it to period style. He was wrong, but the museum remains worthwhile. As well as the house itself, with its lovely patio and good information on the painter's life, there are excavated cellars from a Jewish-quarter palace and a good selection of paintings, including a set of the apostles by El Greco, a Zurbarán, and works by El Greco's son and followers.

Courses

Universidad de Castilla-La Mancha
SPANISH

(www.uclm.es/fundacion/esto; Plaza de Padilla) The University of Castilla-La Mancha runs an ESTO (Spanish in Toledo) program with various language courses. Visit its website for more details.

🎉 Festivals & Events

Corpus Christi
RELIGIOUS

This is one of the finest Corpus Christi celebrations in Spain, taking place on the Thursday 60 days after Easter Sunday. Several days of festivities reach a crescendo with a procession featuring the massive Custodia de Arfe.

Virgen del Sagrario
LOCAL FIESTA

Taking place on 15 August (Assumption Day), this is when you can drink of the cathedral's well water, believed to have miraculous qualities – the queues for a swig from an earthenware *botijo* (jug) can be equally astonishing. It's also the city's main fiesta, with plenty of partying guaranteed.

☞ Tours

Various companies offer guided (and usually themed) walking tours around the town. Themes include Three Cultures (Muslim, Christian and Jewish) and El Greco, while there are also night tours based around local legends.

Toledo Cultura y Vino
WALKING TOUR

(www.toledoculturayvino.com; per person €12-20) Tours focused on El Greco and the city's Sefardi Jewish culture.

Toledo Tres Culturas
GUIDED TOURS

(☑603 420 820; www.toledo3culturas.com; per person €10-12) A range of day and night tours.

Rutas de Toledo
WALKING TOUR

(☑630 793 338; www.rutasdetoledo.es; per person €5-12) A good mix of standard tours (El Greco, Sefardi) with more creative night tours (including some with actors in traditional dress).

Toledo City Tour
BUS TOUR

(www.toledocitytour.es; adult single/day €5.50/9, child €2.75/4.50) Open-top bus tour that circles the city, with some fabulous panoramic views of the town. Unusually, there's a hop-on-hop-off *or* single-trip option.

🛏 Sleeping

Toledo's plentiful accommodation is offset by the visiting tourists, especially from July to September. Many visitors prefer to visit on a day-trip from Madrid.

Albergue San Servando
HOSTEL €

(☑925 22 45 58; www.reaj.com; Subida del Castillo; dm under/over 30 €14.05/16.90; ❈@☎) This well-appointed official hostel has modern installations inside a 14th-century fort. Dorms have either two single beds or two double bunks, and there's a cafeteria serving meals. If you're not an HI member, you'll need to buy a card here. To get here, cross the bridge northeast of the centre, keep going and the hostel is up a street on the right.

Hostal Alfonso XII
HOSTAL €

(☑925 25 25 09; www.hostal-alfonso12.com; Calle de Alfonso XII; s €27-40, d €35-50; ❈☎) In a great location in the *judería*, this quality *hostal* (budget hotel) occupies an 18th-century Toledo house, meaning twisty passages and stairs, and compact rooms in curious places. It's got plenty of charm.

Casa de Cisneros
BOUTIQUE HOTEL €€

(☑925 22 88 28; www.hostal-casa-de-cisneros.com; Calle del Cardenal Cisneros; s/d €40/66; ❈☎) Right by the cathedral, this lovely 16th-century house was once the home of the cardinal and Grand Inquisitor Cisneros (often known as Ximénes). It's a top choice, with cosy, seductive rooms with original wooden beams and walls and voguish bathrooms. Archaeological works have revealed the remains of Roman baths and part of an 11th-century Moorish palace in the basement.

Hotel Abad
HOTEL €€

(☑925 28 35 00; www.hotelabad.com; Calle Real del Arrabal 1; r/apt from €58/120; ℙ❈☎) Compact, pretty and pleasing, this hotel sits on the lower slopes of the old town and offers good value. Rooms blend modern comfort with exposed old brick very successfully;

TOP TOLEDO VIEWS

For superb city views, head over the Puente de Alcántara to the other side of Río Tajo and head along the road that rises to your right, where the vista becomes more marvellous with every step. If you're staying overnight, along this road, the Parador Conde de Orgaz (p211) has superlative views, as does the restaurant known as La Ermita (www.laermitarestaurante.com; Carretera de Circunvalación; mains €18-22, degustation menu €48; ⊙1.30-4pm & 8.45-11pm), which has a short, quality menu of elaborate Spanish cuisine.

You can also climb the towers at the Iglesia San Ildefonso (Iglesia de los Jesuitas; Plaza Juan de Mariana 1; admission €2.50; ⊙10am-6.45pm Apr-Sep, to 5.45pm Oct-Mar), surely one of the few churches to boast a Coke machine, for more camera-clicking views of the cathedral and Alcázar.

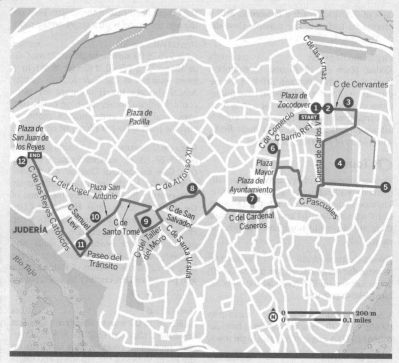

🏃 City Walk
A Stroll Through History

START PLAZA DE ZOCODOVER
END MONASTERIO SAN JUAN DE LOS REYES
LENGTH 2KM; 1½–2½ HOURS

Start off in central ❶ **Plaza de Zocodover**, for centuries the city's marketplace and scene for bullfights and Inquisition-led burnings at the stake, then pass through the ❷ **Arco de la Sangre** on the eastern side of the square to admire the facade of the ❸ **Museo de Santa Cruz** (p205). Up the hill to the south is Toledo's signature ❹ **Alcázar** (p205), beyond which (follow Cuesta de Carlos V along the west wall of the Alcázar and then turn left to walk down Calle de General Moscardó) there are some fine ❺ **views over the Río Tajo**; as the Alcázar's commanding position and sweeping views attest, Toledo was perfectly sited for medieval defences.

Follow the spires down the hill to the west, passing the remnants of a mosque, ❻ **Mezquita de las Tornerías**, before reaching the ❼ **Catedral** (p204), the spiritual home of Catholic Spain. Twist your way northwest to the ❽ **Centro Cultural San Marcos**, housed in the 17th-century San Marcos church where the original domed roof, complete with ceiling frescoes, creates an evocative gallery space for temporary art exhibitions. Southwest of here, the 14th-century ❾ **Taller del Moro** is interesting for its classic Mudéjar architecture.

Down the hill you enter the heart of Toledo's old Jewish quarter. Admire the swords in the shops along ❿ **Calle de San Juan de Dios** and head past the ⓫ **Sinagoga del Tránsito** (p208) for clifftop views over the river. The synagogue takes on a special poignancy if you continue along Calle de los Reyes Católicos to the splendid ⓬ **Monasterio San Juan de los Reyes** (p206). Spain's Catholic rulers hoped this church would represent the ultimate triumph of their religion over others. This is a fine spot to end your walk, but you could drop down from here to the riverside pathway that will take you on a half-circuit of the old town back to near your starting point (an additional 2km).

some have small balconies, but those at the back are notably quieter. There are also apartments available next door.

Casa de los Mozárabes
APARTMENT €€

(☏925 21 17 01; www.casadelosmozarabes.com; Callejón de Menores 10; apt €90-155; ❄🐾) Occupying an historic Toledo house on a quiet central lane, these excellent apartments have modern furnishings that combine well with the exposed brick and historic features of the building. There's a common lounge area with a pool table and a few weights.

Hacienda del Cardenal
HISTORIC HOTEL €€

(☏925 22 49 00; www.hostaldelcardenal.com; Paseo de Recaredo 24; r incl breakfast €55-120; ❄🐾) This wonderful 18th-century mansion has soft ochre-coloured walls, arches and columns. Some rooms are grand, others are spartan, and all come with dark furniture, plush fabrics and parquet floors. Several overlook the glorious terraced gardens.

La Posada de Manolo
BOUTIQUE HOTEL €€

(☏925 28 22 50; www.laposadademanolo.com; Calle de Sixto Ramón Parro 8; s/d €33/61; ❄🐾) This memorable hotel has themed each floor with furnishings and decor reflecting one of the three cultures of Toledo: Christian, Islamic and Jewish. There are stunning views of the old town and cathedral from the terrace.

★Parador Conde de Orgaz
HOTEL €€€

(☏925 22 18 50; www.parador.es; Cerro del Emperador; r €105-207; P❄🐾🏊) High above the southern bank of Río Tajo, Toledo's low-rise *parador* (luxurious state-owned hotel) boasts a classy interior and breathtaking city views. The *parador* is well signposted: turn right just after crossing the bridge northeast of the old centre. You'll need a car or be prepared to pay taxis.

✕ Eating

★Kumera
MODERN SPANISH €

(☏925 25 75 53; www.restaurantekumera.com; Calle Alfonso X El Sabio 2; meals €9-10, set menus €20-35; ⏱8am-2.30am Mon-Fri, 11am-2.30am Sat & Sun) With arguably the best price-quality ratio in town, this place serves up innovative takes on local traditional dishes such as *cochinito* (suckling pig), *rabo de toro* (bull's tail) or *croquetas* (croquettes, filled with *jamón*, squid, cod or wild mushrooms), alongside gigantic toasts and other creatively conceived dishes. The dishes with foie gras as the centrepiece are especially memorable.

Palacios
SPANISH €

(www.hostalpalaciostoledo.com; Calle Alfonso X el Sabio 3; set menus €8.50-25, mains €6-14; ⏱noon-11pm) An unpretentious place, where stained glass, beams and efficient old-fashioned service combine with traditional no-nonsense cuisine. Hungry? Try a gut-busting bowl of traditional *judías con perdiz* (white beans with partridge) for starters. It's very popular so be prepared to wait a while for a table.

Alfileritos 24
MODERN SPANISH €€

(www.alfileritos24.com; Calle de los Alfileritos 24; mains €15-20, bar food €4.50-12; ⏱9.30am-midnight, to 1am Fri & Sat) The 14th-century surroundings of columns, beams and barrel-vault ceilings are snazzily coupled with modern artwork and bright dining rooms in an atrium space spread over four floors. The menu demonstrates an innovative flourish in the kitchen, with dishes like green rice with quail or loins of venison with baked-in-the-bag Reineta apple.

La Abadía
CASTILIAN, TAPAS €€

(www.abadiatoledo.com; Plaza de San Nicolás 3; raciones €4-15) In a former 16th-century palace, this atmospheric bar and restaurant has arches, niches and subtle lighting spread over a warren of brick-and-stone-clad rooms. The menu includes lightweight dishes and tapas, but the 'Menú de Montes de Toledo' (€19) is a fabulous collection of tastes from the nearby mountains.

Asador Palencia de Lara
GRILL €€

(☏925 25 67 46; www.asadorpalenciadelara.es; Calle Nuncio Viejo 6; mains €17-20; ⏱1-4pm & 8.30-11pm Mon-Sat, 1-4pm Sun, closed Jul & Aug) This smart place with a modern dining room set in an historic patio specialises in grilled meats and it does them pretty well. Eschew the overpriced starters and start your meal in the bar area, which turns out a delicious series of €2 tapas, then head through for the meaty mains. The wine list looks amazingly cheap, but be aware that €8 is added to each bottle – don't ask us why.

Taberna El Botero
SPANISH €€

(☏925 22 90 88; www.tabernaelbotero.com; Calle de la Ciudad 5; raciones €9-17; ⏱noon-4pm & 8pm-midnight Wed-Sun, noon-4pm Mon & Tue) Handy for the cathedral, this atmospheric bar and restaurant offers up elaborately presented dishes based on traditional Spanish ingredients like octopus, hake and game. It also does a nice line in expertly prepared cocktails and mixed drinks.

EL GRECO IN TOLEDO

Born in Crete in 1541, Domenikos Theotokopoulos, more succinctly known as 'El Greco' (The Greek), made Toledo his own. After being schooled as a Renaissance artist in Venice and Rome, where he learned from the likes of Titian and Tintoretto, El Greco came to Spain in 1577 and settled in Toledo, where there were several patrons to support him. The painter did not suffer from a lack of modesty: 'As surely as the rate of payment is inferior to the value of my sublime work, so will my name go down to posterity as one of the greatest geniuses of Spanish painting', he pronounced.

Controversial, arrogant, wildly individual and extravagant, El Greco liked the high life; as Toledo's fortunes declined, however, so did the artist's personal finances. Although his final paintings are among his best, he often found himself unable to pay the rent. At the time of his death in 1614, he wasn't rated highly, and it was only in the late 19th century that people began to appreciate his work again. His striking use of colour and the almost abstract nature of some of his figures make his Spanish paintings instantly recognisable.

Iglesia de Santo Tomé (www.santotome.org; Plaza del Conde; admission €2.50; ⊙10am-6pm, to 7pm mid-Mar–mid-Oct) contains El Greco's masterpiece *El entierro del Conde de Orgaz* (The Burial of the Count of Orgaz). When the count was buried in 1322, St Augustine and St Stephen supposedly descended from heaven to attend the funeral. El Greco's work depicts the event, complete with miracle guests including himself, his son and Cervantes. The nearby Museo del Greco (p208) also has a solid collection of El Greco's works.

One of the oldest convents in Toledo, the 11th-century **Convento de Santo Domingo El Antiguo** (☑925 22 29 30; Plaza de Santo Domingo el Antiguo; admission €2; ⊙11am-1.30pm & 4-7pm Mon-Sat, 4-7pm Sun) includes some of El Greco's early commissions, other copies and signed contracts of the artist. Visible through a hole in the floor is the crypt and wooden coffin of the painter himself.

Other spots in Toledo where you can contemplate El Greco's works include the Museo de Santa Cruz (p205) and *sacristía* (sacristy) at the Catedral (p204).

Hostal del Cardenal SPANISH €€€

(☑925 22 49 00; www.hostaldelcardenal.com; Paseo de Recaredo 24; mains €18-25) This hotel-restaurant enjoys one of Toledo's most magical locations for eating alfresco; it's tucked into a private garden entered via its own gate in the city walls. The food is classic Spanish, with roast meats – suckling pig and lamb are the best dishes on show here – to the fore. It's a bit touristy, but the location is unforgettable on a warm summer's night.

Casa Aurelio SPANISH €€€

(☑925 22 41 05; www.casa-aurelio.com; Calle de la Sinagoga 6; mains €18-22; ⊙1-4.30pm & 8-11.30pm Tue-Sat, 1-4.30pm Mon) This place ranks among the best of Toledo's traditional eateries. Game, fresh produce and time-honoured dishes are prepared with panache. There's another **branch** (Plaza del Ayuntamiento) near the cathedral.

 Shopping

For centuries Toledo was renowned for the excellence of its swords and you'll see them for sale everywhere (although be wary of taking them in your hand luggage through customs!). Another big seller is anything decorated with *damasquinado* (damascene), a fine inlay of gold or silver in the Arab artistic tradition.

Santo Tomé FOOD

(☑925 22 11 68; www.mazapan.com; Plaza de Zocodover 7; ⊙9am-10pm) Not a marzipan fan? Think again. You probably won't have tasted it so good anywhere else. Toledo is famed for this wonderful almond-based confectionery (even the local nuns get in on the marzipan act; most of the convents sell the sweets) and the Santo Tomé marzipan brand is highly regarded.

Casa Cuatero FOOD & DRINK

(☑925 22 26 14; www.casacuartero.com; Calle Hombre de Palo 5; ⊙10am-2pm & 5-8pm Mon-Fri, 10am-3pm & 4-8pm Sat) Just north of the cathedral, this fabulous food shop (here since 1920) sells marzipan, cured meats, wines, cheeses and all manner of local delicacies from around Castilla-La Mancha. It's ideal for gifts to take back home or a picnic.

ℹ Information

Main Tourist Office (☎ 925 25 40 30; www.toledo-turismo.com; Plaza del Ayuntamiento; ⊙10am-6pm) Within sight of the cathedral. There's another branch (Estación de Renfe; ⊙10am-3pm) at the train station.

Provincial Tourist Office (www.diputoledo.es; Subida de la Granja; ⊙8am-6pm Mon-Fri, 10am-5pm Sat, 10am-3pm Sun) At the top of the escalator.

ℹ Getting There & Away

For most major destinations, you'll need to backtrack to Madrid.

From Toledo's **bus station** (Avenida de Castilla La Mancha), buses depart for Madrid's Plaza Eliptica roughly every half hour (from €5.35, one hour to 1¾ hrs), some direct, some via villages. There are also services to Cuenca (€14, 2¼ hours).

From the pretty **train station** (☎ 902 240 202; Paseo de la Rosa) high-speed AVE (Alta Velocidad Española) trains run every hour or so to Madrid (one way/return €12/20, 30 minutes).

ℹ Getting Around

Buses (€1.50) run between Plaza de Zocodover and the bus station (bus 5) and train station (buses 61 and 62). Bus 12 does a circuit within the old town.

Driving in the old town is a nightmare. There are several underground car parks throughout the area. Zones blocked off by bollards can be accessed if you have a hotel reservation. At the base of the old town are several large free car parks.

AROUND TOLEDO

The area around Toledo is rich with castles in varying states of upkeep. Most are only accessible by car.

Situated some 20km southeast of Toledo along the CM42 is the dramatic ruined Arab castle of Almonacid de Toledo. A few kilometres further down the road is a smaller castle in the village of Mascaraque. Continue on to Mora, where the 12th-century Castillo Peñas Negras, 3km from town, is on the site of a prehistoric necropolis; follow the sandy track to reach the castle for stunning big-sky views of the surrounding plains. Next, head for the small, pretty town of Orgaz, which has a handsome, well-preserved 15th-century castle (☎ 925 31 76 85; www.ayto-orgaz.es/castillo; adult/concession €3/2; ⊙guided

visits 1pm Mon-Fri, 11am, noon, 1pm, 4pm & 5pm Sat, 11pm, noon & 1pm Sun).

Around 30km southwest of Toledo, the hulking 12th-century Templar ruin of Castillo de Montalbán stands majestically over the Río Torcón valley. It's open only sporadically, but there's little to stop you wandering around at any time.

THE WEST

Talavera de la Reina

POP 88,548

Talavera de la Reina, long famous for its ceramics, has a laid-back appeal. The finest example of its many tiled buildings is the gold-and-blue facade of the Teatro Victoria, just off Plaza del Padre Juan de Mariana.

Within the old city walls is Museo Ruiz de Luna (Pl de San Agustín; adult/child €0.60/free; ⊙9am-3.15pm Tue-Fri, 9.45am-2pm & 3.45-7pm Sat, 10am-2.30pm Sun), housing local ceramics dating from the 16th to 20th centuries in a handsome brick monastery. To buy contemporary ceramics, check out the factories and shops along the road leading west to the A5 motorway.

The tourist office (☎ 925 82 63 22; www.talavera.org/turismo; Ronda del Cañillo 22; ⊙9.30am-2pm & 5-7pm Mon-Fri, 10am-2pm Sat & Sun) doubles as a gallery displaying (you guessed it) ceramics.

The bus station is in the town centre. Regular buses between Madrid and Badajoz stop in Talavera de la Reina, and there are services to Toledo (from €5.30, 1½ hours) roughly hourly.

Oropesa

The delightful village of Oropesa, 34km west of Talavera de la Reina and enticingly visible south from the N5 motorway, is one of western Castilla-La Mancha's most appealing settlements. Atop the town is the 14th-century castle (adult/child €3/1.50; ⊙10am-2pm & 4-6pm Tue-Sun; 🏃) looking north across the plains towards the Sierra de Gredos.

Across from here, sharing a courtyard, is a 14th-century palace that houses Spain's second-oldest parador (☎ 925 43 00 00; www.parador.es; Plaza Palacio 1; r €75-145; P ❀ 🌐), which has managed to retain a heady historical feel without 'over-heritaging'. The rooms are large and luxurious, with heavy brocade curtains and antiques. Read Somerset

Maugham's rave review of the place in the lobby and ask to see San Pedro de Alcántara's 16th-century sleeping quarters, hidden in the bowels of this former palace.

There's also **La Hostería** (☏ 925 43 08 75; www.lahosteriadeoropesa.com; Plaza del Palacio 5; s/d incl breakfast €50/65; [P][✳]), just below the castle, which has pretty, individually decorated rooms with beamed ceilings and a popular restaurant (mains €8 to €14) with tables spilling out into a flower-festooned courtyard.

From Talavera de la Reina, buses (€3.60) travel here three or four times daily.

THE SOUTH

Consuegra

POP 10,668

If you choose one place to go windmill-spotting in Castilla-La Mancha, make it Consuegra where you can get that classic shot of nine *molinos de viento* (windmills) flanking Consuegra's 12th-century **castle** (adult/child €4/free; ☉ 10am-1.30pm & 4.30-6.30pm Mon-Fri, 10.30am-1.30pm & 4.30-6.30pm Sat & Sun Jun-Sep, 10am-1.30pm & 3.30-5.30pm Mon-Fri, 10.30am-1.30pm & 3.30-5.30pm Sat & Sun Oct-May; [✈]). Consuegra once belonged to the Knights of Malta; a few rooms in the castle have been re-created to give a good indication of how the knights would have lived. Information boards include English and French. There's a **tourist office** (☏ 925 47 57 31; www.consuegra. es; ☉ 9am-2pm & 4.30-7pm Mon-Fri, from 10.30am Sat & Sun Jun-Sep) in the Bolero mill, which

---

WHAT'S COOKING IN CASTILLA-LA MANCHA?

➡ *queso manchego* (La Mancha cheese) – most Castilla-La Mancha restaurants offer this as an entrée; Villadiego (p216) takes you to the source

➡ *berenjenas de Almagro* (eggplants from Almagro) – Restaurante Abrasador (p217)

➡ *perdiz a la toledana* (partridge stewed Toledo-style) – Casa Aurelio (p212)

➡ *cochinillo asado* (roast suckling pig) – Asador Palencia de Lara (p211)

➡ *mazapan* (marzipan) – Santo Tomé (p212)

---

is the first you come to as the road winds up from the town – it opens and closes one hour earlier in low season. You can climb the steps here and see the original machinery.

Down in the town, it's worth tracking down the **Plaza Mayor**, with its pretty 1st-floor balconies.

Sleeping & Eating

There are plenty of bars dotted around, particularly close to the Plaza Mayor.

La Vida de Antes HOTEL €€
(☏ 925 48 06 09; www.lavidadeantes.com; Calle Colón 2; s/d incl breakfast €50/70; [P][✳][⊛][≋][♿]) Charming La Vida de Antes has old tiled floors, antique furnishings and a pretty patio that really evoke a bygone era. The duplex rooms are particularly cosy and there's interesting art exhibited throughout the building.

Getting There & Away

There are regular weekday buses (three on weekends) running between Consuegra and Toledo (€7.25, one hour) and up to seven buses daily to Madrid (€10, two hours).

Campo de Criptana

POP 14,594

One of the most popular stops on the El Quijote route, Campo de Criptana is crowned by 10 windmills visible from miles around. Revered contemporary film-maker, Pedro Almodóvar, was born here, but left for Madrid in his teens, later remarking that in this conservative provincial town, 'I felt as if I'd fallen from another planet'.

Sights

It's all about the top of the town here: 10 spectacular **windmills** straddle the summit and their proximity to the surrounding houses makes an interesting contrast with Consuegra. One of the windmills has a **ticket office** (per mill €0.60; ☉ 10am-2pm & 5-7pm Tue-Sat, 11am-2pm Sun) selling admission to three other mills that hold a variety of displays, including one on Sara Montiel, femme fatale of the Spanish silver screen in the 1950s and '60s, who was born in this town.

Sleeping & Eating

Hospedería Casa de la Torrecilla HOTEL €€
(☏ 926 58 91 30; Calle Cardenal Monescillo 17; s/d €45/80; [✳][@][☎]) This lovely hotel has a vivid-

ly patterned and tiled interior patio. Housed in an early-20th-century nobleman's house, the rooms have parquet floors and are spacious and atmospheric.

Cueva La Martina SPANISH €€
(☑926 56 14 76; www.cuevalamartina.com; Rocinante 13; mains €16-20; ☺1-4pm & 8.30-11pm Tue-Sun) The best place to eat is atmospheric Cueva La Martina, opposite the windmills. The cave-like dining area is dug into the rock, and there's a breezy upstairs terrace with views over town.

ℹ Information

Tourist Office (☑926 56 22 31; www.campodecriptana.info; Molino Poyatos, Calle Barbero 1; ☺10am-2pm & 4-6pm Mon-Fri, 11am-2pm & 4-6pm Sat & Sun) In addition to local information, there's a small handicrafts display here.

ℹ Getting There & Away

Campo de Criptana and Ciudad Real are linked by two buses Monday to Friday and one on Saturday (€8.95, 1¼ hours).

Ciudad Real

POP 74,872

Despite being the one-time royal counterpart of Toledo, these days Ciudad Real is an unspectacular Spanish working town. Unless you're on the trail of every last Don Quijote landmark or possess an interest in provincial Spanish towns where tourists rarely venture, there's probably not enough here to warrant a detour off the main highway.

◉ Sights

The town centre has a certain charm with its pedestrianised shopping streets and distinctive Plaza Mayor, complete with carillon clock (topped by Cupid), flamboyant neo-Gothic town-hall facade and modern tiered fountain.

Museo del Quijote y Biblioteca Cervantina MUSEUM
(☑926 20 04 57; www.ciudad-real.es/turismo/quijote; Ronda de Alarcos 1; ☺10am-2pm & 6-9pm Tue-Sat) FREE For Don Quijote fans, the Museo del Quijote has audiovisual displays, plus a Cervantes library stocked with 3500 Don Quijote books, including some in Esperanto and Braille, with most of them now digitised, and others dating back to 1724. It helps if you speak Spanish. Entry is by guided tour every half-hour.

🛏 Sleeping & Eating

★Palacio de la Serna HOTEL €€
(☑926 84 22 08; www.hotelpalaciodelaserna.com; Calle Cervantes 18; r €89-140, ste €180-220; P✳✦⍨) Just 20 minutes' drive south of Ciudad Real (and an equivalent distance from Almagro) in the sleepy village of Ballesteros de Calatrava, this superb hotel feels a world away. Set around a courtyard, it combines rural comfort with appealing design; the owner's evocative modern sculptures feature heavily. Rooms are a little avant-garde, with open showers and numerous thoughtful touches. There's a good on-site restaurant.

La Vinoteca SPANISH €€
(Calle Hernán Pérez de Pulgar 3; lunch menus €15, mains €12-18) Willing service and high-quality dishes with a daily changing menu make this one of Ciudad Real's best lunching options. On weekends the set menu rises to €18, but you might get *arroz con bogavante* (rice with lobster) or roast lamb.

ℹ Getting There & Away

From the **bus station** (Carretera Calzada), southwest of the town centre, up to three daily buses head to Toledo (€11, two hours) and Madrid (€15, 2½ hours).

Most trains linking Madrid with Andalucía stop at Ciudad Real's **train station** (Av Europa), east of the town centre. Regular departures include high-speed services to Madrid (from €21, one hour).

Almagro

POP 9100

The jewel in Almagro's crown is the extraordinary 16th-century Plaza Mayor, with its wavy tiled roofs, stumpy columns and faded bottle-green porticoes. The town is a delight to wander around, although it can be deathly quiet in the depths of winter.

◉ Sights

Corral de Comedias NOTABLE BUILDING
(www.corraldecomedias.com; Plaza Mayor 18; adult/child incl English audioguide €3/free; ☺10am-2pm & 5-8pm Mon-Fri, to 6pm Sat, 11am-2pm Sun Apr-Oct, 10am-2pm & 4-7pm Mon-Fri, to 5pm Sat, to 1pm Sun Nov-Mar) Opening onto the plaza is the oldest theatre in Spain. The 17th-century Corral de Comedias is an evocative tribute to the golden age of Spanish theatre, with rows of wooden balconies facing the original stage, complete with dressing

rooms. At various intervals visits become 'theatrised' with costumed actors replacing the audioguide: this costs €1 more. It's used for performances on Saturday evenings during daylight saving (from the end of March to the end of October); buy tickets online.

Museo Nacional de Teatro MUSEUM
(museoteatro.mcu.es; Calle de Gran Maestre 2; adult/child €3/free, Sat afternoon & Sun free; ⊙10am-2pm & 4-7pm Tue-Fri, 11am-2pm & 4-6pm Sat, 11am-2pm Sun) Just off the main square, this museum has exhibits on Spanish theatre from the golden age of the 17th century displayed in rooms surrounding a magnificent 13th-century courtyard.

Tours

Two companies offer almost identical Spanish-language walking tours of central Almagro. Advance reservations are essential and the price in both cases includes entry into the Corral de Comedias.

Alarcos Turismo WALKING TOUR
(☑926 26 13 82; Calle Mayor de Carnicerías 5; per person €12; ⊙11am & 6.30pm Jul & Aug, 11am & 6pm Jun & Sep, 11am & 5pm Oct-May) Two-hour guided tours of all the major local landmarks.

Visitas Guiadas a Almagro WALKING TOUR
(☑609 793 654; per person €12) A small-scale but professional operator.

Festivals & Events

Festival Internacional de Teatro Clásico THEATRE
(www.festivaldealmagro.com) In July the Corral de Comedias holds a month-long international theatre festival, attracting world-class theatre companies performing primarily classical plays.

Sleeping

La Posada de Almagro GUESTHOUSE €
(☑926 88 22 44; www.laposadadealmagro.com; Calle Gran Maestre 5; s €24-44, d €35-60; ✳️🔊) A short hop from the Plaza Mayor, this fine inn has simple, tidy rooms with wrought-iron bedheads, thoughtfully decorated walls and tiled bathrooms. Bring earplugs if you're here on a weekend as the noise from the restaurant can be loud and long.

★La Casa del Rector HOTEL €€
(☑926 26 12 59; www.lacasadelrector.com; Calle Pedro Oviedo 8; s/d €80/90; ✳️@🔊✖️) This extraordinary hotel has a wide variety of rooms ranging from sumptuous antique-filled classics to those reflecting cutting-edge modern design, complete with vast private hot tubs and dramatic artwork. Service is faultless and facilities include a classy spa.

Retiro del Maestre HOTEL €€
(☑926 26 11 85; www.retirodelmaestre.com; Calle San Bartolomé 5; s incl breakfast €60-90, d €78-112; P✳️🔊) Enjoy cosseted treatment and style without the hurly-burly of a big hotel. The rooms here are spacious and washed in warm yellow and blue; go for those on the upper floor with private balconies. The location, a five-minute walk from the Plaza Mayor, couldn't be better.

Parador de Almagro HISTORIC HOTEL €€€
(☑926 86 01 00; www.parador.es; Ronda de San Francisco 31; r €80-164; P✳️@🔊✖️) A sumptuous ivy-clad former convent in a quiet corner of Almagro, this *parador* has a luxurious, old-

---

THE QUESO MANCHEGO EXPERIENCE

More than two dozen Castilla-La Mancha foods and wines have been given DO (Denominación de Origen) status, offering both protection and recognition of high-quality traditional products. *Queso manchego* (Manchego cheese) is the best known of these. Peer into any cheese counter in the country and you'll find great wheels of this cheese in varying sizes and displaying a baffling range of labels and prices. For many visitors, their Manchego initiation will be the neat little tapas triangles often served free with a drink. These are usually *semicurado* (semi-cured) rather than the crumbly stronger (and more expensive) *curado* (cured); the former is aged for approximately three to four months, the latter six to eight months. To receive the Manchego denomination, the milk must come from a local Manchegan breed of sheep that has evolved over hundreds of years.

If you want more than a tapa, visiting **Villadiego** (www.quesosvilladiego.com; Carretera Poblete-Alarcos Km2.2, Poblete), 7km southwest of Ciudad Real along the CM420, is the cheese equivalent of visiting a winery. During a one-hour tour of the farm (where they've been making the cheese since 1840), you learn what it takes to make *queso manchego*; tasting is an essential part of the visit. There's a shop where you can buy what you've tried.

world charm, despite the mildly incongruous, brightly coloured beams in the rooms.

Eating

Bar El Gordo
TAPAS €

(Plaza Mayor 12; raciones €6-12; ☺noon-4pm & 8-11pm) The best and liveliest tapas option on the square, this has a good mix of visitors and locals and buzzes with good cheer on weekend evenings.

Restaurante Abrasador
CASTILIAN €€

(☑926 88 26 56; www.abrasador.com; Calle San Agustín 18; tostas €1.50, mains €11.50-25, set menus from €25; ☺noon-4pm & 8-11pm Mon, Tue & Thu-Sat, noon-4pm Sun) Thoughtfully prepared cooking dominates the restaurant out the back (snaffle the table next to the open fire in winter if you can), with perfectly grilled meats. Out the front, you'll find some of the most creative tapas in Almagro – the famed local eggplant features prominently and it's our pick of the orders whatever guise it's in.

★ El Corregidor
SPANISH €€€

(☑658 81 93 67; www.elcorregidor.com; Calle de Jerónimo Ceballos 2; mains €18-24; ☺noon-5pm & 8.30-11.30pm Thu-Sun, noon-5pm Tue & Wed) The town's best restaurant has several lively bars flanking a leafy courtyard and a hotchpotch decor that somehow works. The upstairs restaurant features high-quality Manchegan cooking; check out the wall of culinary awards. Reservations recommended.

ℹ Information

Tourist Office (☑926 86 07 17; www.ciudad-almagro.com; Plaza Mayor 1; ☺10am-2pm & 5-8pm Tue-Fri, 10am-2pm & 5-7pm Sat, 10am-2pm Sun) Afternoon opening and closing is one hour earlier from November to March.

ℹ Getting There & Away

At least one train goes daily to Madrid (€26, 2½ hours); for destinations to the south, change in Ciudad Real (€3.60, 15 minutes). Buses run to Ciudad Real (€3.15, 30 minutes, up to five daily Monday to Saturday).

Castillo de Calatrava

This magnificent castle-monastery (Calatrava La Nueva; adult/child €3/1.50; ☺11am-2pm & 5.30-8.30pm Tue-Fri, 10am-2pm & 5.30-8.30pm Sat, 10am-2pm & 5-9pm Sun) looms high in the sky some 6km south of the town of Calzada de Calatrava and 30km south of Almagro.

WORTH A TRIP

BELMONTE

About 17km northeast of Mota del Cuervo, quiet little Belmonte is notable for its fine castle, the Castillo de Belmonte. This is how castles *should* look, with turrets, largely intact walls and a commanding position over the village. If you'd like to stay overnight, Palacio Buenavista Hospedería (☑967 18 75 80; www.palaciobuenavista.es; Calle José Antonio González 2; s/d/ste incl breakfast €46/73/91; ℙ❄☎) is a classy boutique hotel and fine restaurant set in a 17th-century palace next to the Colegiata.

A steep stony road leads to the top, where breathtaking views, as well as the imposingly preserved fortress, are your reward. The complex was once a base of the medieval order of knights who controlled this frontier area during the Reconquista. Seasonal opening hours vary.

Parque Nacional Tablas de Daimiel

Forty kilometres northeast of Ciudad Real, this small wetland national park is great for birdwatching. From the visitor centre (☑926 69 31 18; www.mma.es/parques; ☺8.30am-6pm Oct-Mar, to 9pm Apr-Sep), which has an exhibition on the fragile local ecosystem, three trails lead out along the lakeshore and over boardwalks. From these, and the various observation hides (bring binoculars) you can see an astonishing variety of wildlife, including ducks, geese, kingfishers, flamingos, herons and other waders, tortoises and otters. Early morning and late afternoon are the best times. The park is 10km from the town of Daimiel, which is linked by regular buses to Ciudad Real.

Parque Natural de las Lagunas de Ruidera

This ribbon of 14 small lakes is surrounded by lush parkland, camping grounds, picnic areas, and discreetly situated restaurants and hotels. Turn off along the lakeshore in the town of Ruidera; along this road there are several places hiring pedalos, canoes and bikes, or offering horse-riding to explore the area.

On the Trail of Don Quixote

Few literary landscapes have come to define an actual terrain quite like the La Mancha portrayed in Miguel de Cervantes's *El ingenioso hidalgo don Quijote de la Mancha*, better known as *El Quijote* (in Spanish) or *Don Quixote* (in English).

The Man from La Mancha

'In a village in La Mancha whose name I cannot recall, there lived long ago a country gentleman...'. Thus begins the novel and thus it was that the village where our picaresque hero began his journey had always remained a mystery. That was, at least, until 10 eminent Spanish academics marked the 400th anniversary of the book's publication in 1605 by carefully following the clues left by Cervantes. Their conclusion? That Villanueva de los Infantes (population 5581) in Castilla-La Mancha's far south was Don Quixote's starting point. These days, the town is otherwise most memorable for its ochre-hued Plaza Mayor, surrounded by wood-and-stone balconies and watched over by the 15th-century Iglesia de San Andrés. If you're staying overnight, look no further than **La Morada de Juan de Vargas** (☏926 36 17 69; www.lamoradadevargas.com; Calle Cervantes 3; d €50-75; ❋🛜).

Staying for the Knight

There is little consensus as to where Don Quixote went next, and there are as many *rutas de Don Quijote* (Don Quixote routes) as there are La Mancha towns eager to claim an impeccable Cervantes

1. Windmills of
Consuegra (p214)
2. Iglesia de San
Andrés, Villanueva de
los Infantes **3.** Don
Quixote statue, Plaza de
Espana, Madrid

pedigree. In fact, few towns are actually
mentioned by name in the book.

One that does appear is the now-
unremarkable town of Puerto Lápice,
southeast of Toledo. It was here that Don
Quixote stayed in an inn that he mistook
for a castle and, after keeping watch all
night, convinced the innkeeper to knight
him. El Toboso, northeast of Alcázar de
San Juan, also appears in the book as
the home of Dulcinea, the platonic love
of Quixote. Nowadays you'll find in El
Toboso the 16th-century **Casa-Museo
de Dulcinea** (Calle Don Quijote 1; admission
€0.60; ☺10am-2pm & 4.30-7.30pm Tue-Fri,
until 6.30pm Sat, 10am-2pm Sun), as well as
the obligatory Don Quixote statue and a
library with more than 300 editions of
the book in various languages.

Windmills

Don Quixote may have spent much of
his quest tilting at windmills *(molinos
de viento)*, but nowhere is the exact
location of these 'monstrous giants',
against whom honourable battles must be
fought, revealed. The finest windmills are
arguably the nine of Consuegra (p214),
strung out along a ridge line that rises
from the pancake-flat plains, and clearly
visible from far away. Mota del Cuervo,
northeast of Alcázar de San Juan, also
has some seven candidates, but Campo
de Criptana (p214) is Consuegra's main
rival. Only 10 of Campo de Criptana's
original 32 windmills remain, but they
sit dramatically above the town. Local
legend also maintains that Cervantes was
baptised in the town's Iglesia de Santa
Maria.

A great place to stay is Hotel Albaman-jón (📞926 69 90 48; www.albamanjon.net; Laguna de San Pedro 16; d incl breakfast €112-186; ❄️🛜). Running up the hill behind the main building, these super suites are all separate from each other and have a private terrace with lake views, wood fires for winter, and most have a Jacuzzi. The windmill suite has a vista of the turquoise lake that's worth pushing the boat out for. The restaurant has great views and is decorated exuberantly with tiles and curios. Leafy camping ground Camping Los Batanes (📞926 69 90 20; www.losbatanes.com; sites incl 2 people, tent & car €17-32, bungalows €53-120; 🅿️🐕🛝) is on Laguna Redondilla. During summer there's an entertainment program for children.

Alcalá del Júcar

Northeast of Albacete, the deep, tree-filled gorge of Río Júcar makes for a stunning detour. About halfway along the CM3201, the breathtaking town of Alcalá del Júcar comes into view as you descend via hairpin turns. Its landmark castle (adult/child €2/1.50; ⏰11am-2pm & 5-8pm May-Sep, 11am-2pm & 3-6pm Oct-Apr), dating mostly from the 15th century, towers over the houses that spill down the steep bank of the river gorge. At the foot of the town there's a medieval bridge with Roman origins and a leafy meeting-and-greeting plaza. It's a good destination for young kids, with a large traffic-free area, and safe paddling in a bend of the river.

Activities here include river trips and local walking trails. Several companies offer a full range of land and water excursions. Avenjúcar (📞967 47 41 34; www.avenjucar.com; Calle San Roque, Tolosa) is an operator that comes reader recommended, and they have accommodation as well.

🛏️ Sleeping & Eating

Hostal Rambla   HOSTAL €
(📞967 47 40 64; www.hostalrambla.es; Paseo Los Robles 2; s/d incl breakfast €45/55; ❄️🛜) There are several well-priced hotels, including Hostal Rambla by the 'Roman' bridge. Rooms are compact, but it's friendly and well located, and there's a pleasant restaurant with a large terrace, specialising in chargrilled meats served with green peppers and potatoes.

Bodega-Cueva La Asomada   BODEGA €
(📞652 18 24 40; Calle de la Asomada 107; mains €7-13; ⏰ 8.30-10.30pm Fri, 1.30-3.30pm & 8.30-10.30pm Sat & Sun) 🍴 La Asomada, at the top of the village, should be sought out by eco folks. Located in a cave and former bodega, owner Pilar Escusa uses organic produce and prepares delicious seasonal dishes. Reservations essential.

THE WINES OF VALDEPEÑAS

From last count, Castilla-La Mancha has nine recognised wine regions: Almansa, Jumila, La Mancha, Manchuela, Mentrida, Mondejar, Ribera del Júcar, Ucles and Valdepeñas. But it's the latter that has the most interesting story.

Situated midway between Madrid and Córdoba, the large and otherwise uninviting town of Valdepeñas offers weary travellers one (and only one) good reason to break the journey. Surrounding the town is what some experts believe to be the largest expanse of vineyards in the world (although many of these belong to the larger, if lesser-known, La Mancha wine region). True aficionados of the humble grape argue that quantity does not easily translate into quality and there's an element of truth to this view – Valdepeñas has historically been to the mass market what La Rioja is to the quality end of the wine trade.

That said, things are changing. You're still more likely to come across Valdepeñas wines in the cheap, cask variety than served in Spain's finest restaurants, but some of the Valdepeñas bodegas have begun making inroads into the quality end of the market. Most of the bodegas offer tours, tastings and short wine courses only by appointment, and charge to boot. Check the websites for details to avoid going thirsty.

Bodegas Arúspide (📞926 34 70 75; www.aruspide.com; Calle Franci Morales 102; tour €5) Bodegas Arúspide offers tours and a tasting of two or more wines.

Bodega de las Estrellas (📞650 552976; www.labodegadelasestrellas.com; Calle Unión 82; tour €6-10) Bodega de las Estrellas makes organic wine and also has a tour and tasting option that includes a meal in the bodega.

ℹ Information

Tourist Office (☎967 47 30 90; www.turis-mocastillalamancha.com; ☉10am-2pm daily, also 4-7pm Sat & Sun) The small tourist office has a wealth of information about *casas rurales* (farmstead accommodation), cave accommodation and activities, including maps showing local walking trails.

ℹ Getting There & Away

There are one to two buses daily except Sunday between Albacete and Alcalá (€6.90, 1½ hours).

THE NORTHEAST

Cuenca

POP 56,107

Cuenca, with its extraordinary setting, is one of Spain's most memorable cities. Its old centre is a World Heritage stage-set of evocative medieval buildings, the most emblematic of which are the *casas colgadas* (hanging houses), which cling like swallows' nests above the deep gorges that surround the town.

◉ Sights

Most of the sights are in the spectacular old town, on a hill between the gorges of Ríos Júcar and Huécar. Just wandering the narrow streets, tunnels and staircases, stopping every now and again to admire the majestic views (and catch your breath) is the chief pleasure of Cuenca. The new town spreads out at the base of the hill; this is where you'll find normal Cuenca life – the old town is a little museum-like and few locals live there.

★ Museo de Arte Abstracto Español
MUSEUM

(Museum of Abstract Art; www.march.es/arte/cuenca; Calle Canónigos; adult/concession/child €3/1.50/free; ☉11am-2pm & 4-6pm Tue-Fri, 11am-2pm & 4-8pm Sat, 11am-2.30pm Sun) This impressive contemporary art museum is one of several spaces in Cuenca devoted to modern art and sculpture, its galleries memorably occupying one of the *casas colgadas*. Begun as an attempt by Fernando Zóbel to unite the works of his fellow artists from the so-called Abstract Generation of the 1950s and '60s, the museum's constantly evolving displays include works by Eduardo Chillida, Antoni Tàpies and Manuel Millares.

★ Casas Colgadas
HISTORIC BUILDINGS

The most striking element of medieval Cuenca, the *casas colgadas* jut out precariously over the steep defile of Río Huécar. Dating from the 14th century, the houses, with their layers of wooden balconies, seem to emerge from the rock as if an extension of the cliffs. For the best views of the *casas colgadas*, cross the Puente de San Pablo footbridge or walk to the mirador (lookout) at the northernmost tip of the old town.

Museo de Cuenca
MUSEUM

(www.patrimoniohistoricoclm.es/museo-de-cuenca; Calle Obispo Valero 12; adult/child €1.20/free, Sat & Sun free; ☉10am-2pm & 4-7pm Tue-Sat, 10am-2pm Sun) Exceptionally well laid out and well documented (in Spanish), exhibits here range from the Bronze Age to the 18th century. Sala 7 is particularly awe-inspiring, with its original Roman statues, including Emperor Augustus, plus columns and pediments discovered at nearby Segóbriga and Valeria.

Museo de las Ciencias
MUSEUM

(pagina.jccm.es/museociencias; Plaza de la Merced; adult/child €3/free, Sat & Sun free; ☉10am-2pm & 4-7pm Tue-Sat, 10am-2pm Sun; 🚼) This family-friendly science museum has displays that range from a time machine to plenty of interactive gadgets to keep the kiddies happy. There is also a planetarium with hourly sessions beginning at 10.30am.

Museo Diocesano
MUSEUM

(Calle Obispo Valero 1; admission €2.50, incl cathedral €5; ☉11am-2pm & 4-6pm Tue-Sat, 11am-2pm Sun Nov-Mar, 11am-2pm & 4-7pm Tue-Sat, 11am-2pm Sun Apr-Oct) Better than the average museum of religious art in Spain, this has an excellent collection of Flemish tapestries, some fine Romanesque and Gothic sculpture, and a notable collection of paintings that includes two canvases by El Greco, one a particularly moving Christ carrying the cross.

Catedral
CATHEDRAL

(Plaza Mayor; adult/child €3.80/2, incl Museo Diocesano & audioguide €5; ☉10am-1pm & 4-6pm) Dominating the Plaza Mayor, Cuenca's cathedral was built on the site of the main mosque after the city's reconquest by Alfonso VIII in 1177. Highlights within include the Gothic tombs of the Montemayor family, an impressive sacristy, the chapterhouse *artesonado* ceiling and several stunning stained-glass windows.

Cuenca

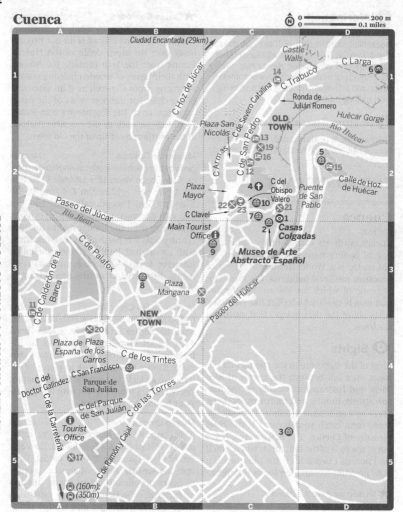

Espacio Torner   GALLERY

(www.espaciotorner.com; Calle de Hoz de Huécar, Iglesia San Pablo; adult/child €3/free; ⊙ 11am-2pm & 4-6pm Tue-Sat, 11am-2pm Sun) One of several Cuenca spaces placing contemporary art in historic buildings, this is set in a Gothic church with great views of the old town. It displays abstract paintings and sculptures by Gustavo Torner, one of several artists who made Cuenca their home in the 1960s. The soaring vaulted ceilings and combination of space and height are exceptionally powerful.

Museo de la Semana Santa   MUSEUM

(www.msscuenca.org; Calle Andrés de Cabrera 13; adult/child €3/free; ⊙ 11am-2pm & 4.30-7.30pm Thu-Sat, 11am-2pm Sun; 👪) This museum is the next best thing to experiencing Semana Santa firsthand. Spread over two floors are audiovisual displays showing the processions by local brotherhoods against a background of sombre music. Displays include costumes and a 20-minute film (in Spanish), in which the locals explain their passion for this annual religious ritual.

Cuenca

Ars Natura MUSEUM
(www.centroarsnatura.es; Calle Diego Ramírez de Villaescusa; adult/child €3/free; 🅿) 🖉 This impressive environmental museum has several vast galleries with interactive exhibits on local flora and fauna, climate change, local geology and environmental impact studies as well as basket-weaving video demonstrations. All information is in Spanish, but there's enough here to keep nonspeakers interested, including a river-fish aquarium and an outdoor section with examples of different wetland environments and sustainable technologies. Bus 7 stops outside. It was closed for renovation when we visited but should be open by the time you read this.

✹ Festivals & Events

Semana Santa HOLY WEEK
(www.juntacofradiascuenca.es) Cuenca's Easter celebrations are renowned throughout Spain for the eerie, silent processions through the streets of the old town.

🛏 Sleeping

Many of the hotel rooms in the atmospheric old town have stunning views, so always ask for a room *con vista*. That said, there are some good options in the livelier new town below, too. Phone ahead for budget accommodations in the old town, as the owners tend to live elsewhere.

★**Hostal Tabanqueta** HOSTAL €
(☎969 21 40 76; www.hostaltabanqueta.com; Calle Trabuco 13; d €45, apt €50-100; 🅿🌢🛜) Up the hill from Plaza Mayor, this friendly spot has free parking nearby and top-of-the-town

views. The accommodation is excellent, with heating, stylish tiled bathrooms, attractive artwork, and hotel-standard amenities like toiletries, an espresso machine and hospitality tray with pastries. They've also a number of apartments nearby.

Hostal San Pedro HOSTAL €
(☎969 23 45 43, 628 407 601; www.hostalsanpedro.es; Calle de San Pedro 34; s/d €35/60; 🛜) In this excellently priced and positioned *hostal*, rooms have butter-coloured paintwork, wrought-iron bedheads and rustic wood furniture, and the bathrooms are shiny and modern. The owners live elsewhere, so call first.

Posada de San José HISTORIC HOTEL €€
(☎969 21 13 00; www.posadasanjose.com; Ronda de Julián Romero 4; s with/without bathroom €58/31, d €95/44) This 17th-century former choir school retains an extraordinary monastic charm with its labyrinth of rooms, eclectic artwork, uneven floors and original tiles. All rooms are different; cheaper ones are in former priests' cells, while more costly doubles combine homey comfort with old-world charm. Several have balconies with dramatic views of the gorge. There's a tapas restaurant and the owners also rent out tastefully furnished self-contained apartments.

Convento del Giraldo HOTEL €€
(☎969 23 27 00; www.hotelconventodelgiraldo.com; Calle de San Pedro 12; s/d €82/88; 🌢@🛜) Just above the cathedral, this conversion of a 17th-century convent wins points for location and style, though there aren't too many

original features left. Nevertheless, the attractive rooms feature dark wooden furniture, big bathrooms and great views from many of them. You can find good discounts online.

CH Victoria Alojamientos HOSTAL €€
(☑620 782937; www.chvictorialojamientos.com; Calle Mateo Miguel Ayllón 2; s €25-40, d €45-95; 🅿🛜) Blurring the lines between *hostal* and hotel, the rooms at this excellent new town place offer every comfort, with stylish decoration, modern bathrooms, firm mattresses and plenty of thoughtful extras.

★Parador de Cuenca HISTORIC HOTEL €€€
(☑969 23 23 20; www.parador.es; Calle de Hoz de Huécar; d €90-202; 🅿🌀🛜🏊) This majestic former convent commands stunning views of the *casas colgadas*. The revamped rooms have a luxury corporate feel, while the public areas are headily historic with giant tapestries and antiques.

🍴 Eating

The Plaza Mayor (in the Old Town) and Plaza de España (New Town) are the centres of their respective eating zones. There is a good choice in and surrounding both squares.

★La Bodeguilla de Basilio TAPAS €
(☑969 23 52 74; Calle Fray Luis de León 3; raciones €10-13; ☺1-4pm & 8-11pm Mon-Sat, 1-4pm Sun) Arrive here with an appetite, as you're presented with a complimentary plate of tapas when you order a drink – typical freebies are a combo of quail eggs, ham, fried potatoes, lettuce hearts and zucchinis (courgettes).

Understandably, it gets packed out, so head to the restaurant at the back for specials like *patatas a lo pobre* (potatoes with onions, garlic and peppers) or lamb chops.

El Bodegón SPANISH €
(Cerrillo de San Roque A1; mains €6-14; ☺1-4pm & 8.30-11.30pm Tue-Sun) Up a narrow lane in the new town, this sociable bar has a peaceful terrace and several indoor tables where you can watch your meat being expertly grilled on the wood stove in the corner. No frills; great value.

San Juan Plaza Mayor SPANISH €
(Plaza Mayor 5; mains €7-14; ☺12.30-4pm & 8pm-midnight Tue-Sat, 12.30-4pm Sun) This bright and buzzy tapas bar on Plaza Mayor has fine cathedral views from its terrace and a good selection of tasty bar snacks. The dining room offers a broad range of cheap eats,

including a wide selection of rice dishes for two, as well as salads and grilled meats. Simpler dishes are the way to go here. Service is scatty.

Mesón Casas Colgadas TRADITIONAL SPANISH €€
(☑969 22 35 52; Calle de los Canónigos 3; mains €14-25, menus €28) Housed in one of the *casas colgadas*, Cuenca's gourmet pride and joy fuses an amazing location with delicious traditional food on the menu, such as venison stew and the quaintly translated 'boned little pork hands stew' (pig-trotter stew). Reservations are recommended.

El Secreto SPANISH €€
(www.elsecretocuenca.com; Calle de Alfonso VIII 81; mains €10-17; ☺11am-4.30pm Mon & Tue, 11am-4.30pm & 8pm-midnight Thu-Sun; 🖊) Exuberant decor featuring painted tiles and a friendly, laid-back attitude characterise this place, which has a pretty dining room with vistas behind a small front bar. There's a good selection of pastas and salads, and meat dishes include a tasty venison burger.

★Figón del Huécar SPANISH €€€
(☑969 24 00 62; www.figondelhuecar.es; Ronda de Julián Romero 6; mains €17-25; ☺1.30-4pm & 9-11pm Tue-Sat, 1.30-4pm Sun) With a romantic terrace offering spectacular views, this is a highlight of old town eating. Roast suckling pig, lamb stuffed with raisins, pine nuts and foie gras and a host of Castilian specialities are presented and served with panache. The house used to be the home of Spanish singer José Luis Perales.

Ars Natura MODERN SPANISH €€€
(☑969 21 95 12; www.restaurantearsnatura.com; Calle Río Gritos 5, Cerro Molina; mains €21-26, set menus €25-70; ☺1-4pm & 8.30pm-midnight Tue-Sat, 1-4pm Sun) Celebrated chef Manuel de la Osa's second restaurant at Ars Natura showcases unique dishes using traditional local ingredients, like red partridge salad with butter beans and oyster mushrooms. The decor is suitably elegant. Reservations essential.

🍷 Drinking & Nightlife

Cuenca is a student town with lively nightlife. Calle San Francisco in the new town has an energetic row of terrace bars with a pre-clubbing party feel from around 9pm on weekends. There are several more sophisticated venues around Plaza Mayor. For later action, head for the disco-pubs on Calle del Doctor Galíndez, near Plaza de España.

SIERRA DE ALCARAZ

Stretching across the southern strip of Albacete province, the cool, green peaks of the Sierra de Alcaraz offer a great escape from the dusty plains around Albacete. The gateway to the region, sleepy hilltop **Alcaraz**, has a lovely Renaissance Plaza Mayor and a lattice of narrow cobbled streets. The most scenic countryside is to be found along the **CM412**, particularly between **Puerto de las Crucetas** (elev 1300m) and **Elche de la Sierra**.

And then there's the spectacular **Nacimiento del Río Mundo** (Source of the River Mundo; ☉10am-dusk), around 8km from Riópar and signposted off the Siles road. From the car park, it's a short walk through the forest of mainly coniferous trees to the bottom of the falls – above towers an awesomely high concave cliff face. It's a steep climb to the second viewpoint above, but worth the effort. Water emerges from the rocks just above the platform in a dramatic drop of some 24m (spraying you liberally en route). The falls are surrounded by dense forest stretching to a rocky horizon.

The two best places to stay are the **Mirador Sierra de Alcaraz** (☎967 38 00 17; www.alcarazmirador.com; Calle Granada 1; d €48-70; ✸) in Alcaraz, and **Las Salegas del Maguillo** (☎660 24 96 92; www.lassalegasdelmaguillo.com; Carretera Riópar-Siles Km11; d €90, 4-/6-person apt €150/210; Ⓟ✸🐾), which is high up in the hills above the road 11km west of Riópar, beyond the Nacimiento del Río Mundo turn-off.

Lolita Lounge Bar BAR
(www.lolitaloungebar.es; Calle Clavel 7; ☉7.30pm-late Fri, noon-late Sat & Sun) A slick minimalist bar with lots of steely metal and slate. Cocktails, a huge range of gin, imported beers and a good mix of music attract the high-heeled and slicked-back-hair set.

❶ Information

Main Tourist Office (☎969 24 10 51; turismo.cuenca.es; Calle Alfonso VIII 2; ☉9am-9pm Mon-Sat, to 2.30pm Sun) Ask about visiting the medieval tunnels that honeycomb the old town and are under ongoing investigation.

Tourist Office (☎969 23 58 15; Plaza Hispanidad; ☉10am-2pm & 5-8pm Mon-Thu, 10am-8pm Fri-Sun) Cuenca's second slightly smaller tourist office in the new town, open somewhat reduced hours on weekends in winter.

❶ Getting There & Away

The train and bus stations are located almost across from each other, southwest of Calle de Fermín Caballero. Fast AVE trains use the Fernando Zóbel station, southwest of town. Bus 12 links it with the town centre.

There are up to nine buses daily to Madrid (€15, 2¼ hours) and regular services to other cities in Castilla-La Mancha as well as Valencia.

Numerous daily trains run to Madrid, ranging from slow *regionales* (trains operating within one region, usually stopping all stations; €15, three hours) to swift AVEs (€35, 55 minutes). The other way, to Valencia, is a similar deal (€16 to €38).

❶ Getting Around

Local buses 1 and 2 do the circuit from the new town to Plaza Mayor (€0.75, every 30 minutes), stopping outside the train station. There's a large free car park on Calle Larga above the arch at the top of the old town.

Around Cuenca

Serranía de Cuenca

Spreading north and east of Cuenca, the Serranía de Cuenca is a heavily wooded and fertile zone of craggy mountains, sandstone gorges and green fields. Ríos Júcar and Huécar flow through the high hinterland, through landscapes well worth exploring with your own transport.

Head out from Cuenca 30km via the CM2105 to extraordinary **Ciudad Encantada** (adult/child €3/free; ☉10am-dusk). Surrounded by pine woods, limestone rocks have been eroded into fantastical shapes by nature. It's a shaded 40-minute circuit around the open-air rock museum but it gets crowded on weekends. The CM2105 continues north via the picturesque village of Uña, the crystal-clear waters of **Embalse del Tobar** and past the **Reserva Natural de El Hosquillo**, a protected park where reintroduced brown bears roam wild.

Beteta has a charming porticoed Plaza Mayor with half-timbered buildings, and a crumbly hilltop castle. Lodging options in town include a couple of *casas rurales*. You

WORTH A TRIP

VALERIA'S ROMAN RUINS

The fascinating archaeological site of Valeria (www.valeriaromana.es; ⊙10.30am-2pm & 5.30-8.30pm Apr-Oct, 10.30am-2pm & 3-5pm Mon-Sat, 10am-3pm Sun Nov-Mar) FREE is located 34km south of Cuenca. It's fairly untouristed, giving the pleasure of wandering around a sizeable Roman town without the distraction of bus tours and school groups. The location is sublime, amid wild meadows and dramatic gorges. A ruined medieval castle crowns the hillside; below are remains of a forum, as well as a basilica, four reservoirs, urban streets and the well-preserved remains of a vast extravagant fountain. There is also the original *casa colgada* (hanging house) here, its upper floor still clearly constructed to cling to the rock side, with the lower floors visible below.

can return to Cuenca via the CM210, a quiet rural route that passes several traditional villages, the source of Spain's trademark blue-bottled water, Solán de Cabras (with summer spa hotel), as well as Priego, a lovely valley town that dates from Roman times and has sights including medieval churches, Roman arches and Moorish towers.

If you're heading on to Sigüenza, track northeast from Beteta to Molina de Aragón, a pretty town utterly dominated by one of Spain's most spectacular castles, built by the Moors before being embellished after falling into Christian hands.

Alarcón

One hundred kilometres or so south of Cuenca is the seductive medieval village of Alarcón. The approach is via a narrow road winding through three medieval defensive arches. The most famous sight here is the triangular-based Islamic castle, now a sumptuous parador (Marqués de Villena; ☑969 33 03 15; www.parador.es; d from €186; P ❋ ☎), offering old-world charm and supremely comfortable rooms with exposed brick-and-stone walls, and plush fabrics and furnishings. Alternatively, Meson Don Julián (☑969 33 03 00; Plaza Autónomo 1; s/d €40/50; ❋ ☎), near the castle entrance, has pretty, rustic rooms with balconies and fridges, and a friendly bar-restaurant. The best restaurant in town is the enchanting La Cabaña de Alarcón (Álvaro de Lara 21; mains €11-19; ⊙1-4pm & 8.30-11pm Mon-Sat, 1-4pm Sun), with dark-pink paintwork, contemporary artwork and well-priced, well-executed local dishes.

Segóbriga

These Roman ruins (adult/concession/child €5/2.50/free; ⊙10am-9pm Apr-Sep, to 6pm Oct-Mar, closed Mon) may date as far back as the

5th century BC. The best-preserved structures are a Roman theatre and amphitheatre on the fringes of the ancient city, looking out over a valley. Other remains include the outlines of a Visigothic basilica and a section of the aqueduct, which helped keep the city green in what was otherwise a desert. A small museum (included in the price) has some striking exhibits.

The site is near Saelices, 2km south of the A3 motorway between Madrid and Albacete. From Cuenca, drive west 55km on the N400, then turn south on the CM202.

Pastrana

POP 1054

Pastrana, 42km south of the regional capital of Guadalajara along the CM200, should not be missed. It's an unspoilt place with twisting cobbled streets flanked by honey-coloured stone buildings.

◉ Sights

The heart and soul of the place is the Plaza de la Hora, a large square dotted with acacias and fronted by the sturdy Palacio Ducal. It's in Pastrana that the one-eyed princess of Éboli, Ana Mendoza de la Cerda, was confined in 1581 for a love affair with the Spanish king Felipe II's secretary. You can see the caged window of her 'cell', where she died 10 years later, and arrange a tour (Spanish only; €2) via the tourist office (☑949 37 06 72; www.pastrana.org; Plaza de la Hora 5; ⊙10am-2pm & 4-7pm Mon-Fri, 10am-2pm & 4-8pm Sat, 10am-2pm Sun).

Iglesia de Nuestra Señora de la Asunción Museum　MUSEUM
(Colegiata; adult/child €2.50/free; ⊙11.30am-2pm & 4.30-7pm Tue-Fri, 1-2pm & 4.30-7pm Sun) Walk from the square along Calle Mayor and you'll soon reach the massive Iglesia de Nuestra

Señora de la Asunción. Inside, the interesting little museum contains the jewels of the princess of Éboli, some exquisite 15th-century tapestries and even an El Greco.

🛏 Sleeping & Eating

Hotel Palaterna   HOTEL €

(☏ 949 37 01 27; www.hotelpalaterna.com; Plaza de los Cuatro Caños; s/d/ste €50/65/95; ❀ ⓦ) Hotel Palaterna is a pleasant modern hotel overlooking a small square complete with bubbling fountain. Rooms are painted in cool colours, contrasting with dark wood furniture.

Casa Seco   TAPAS €

(Calle Mayor 36; tapas from €2.50) Don't miss the locals' local, Casa Seco, with all four walls, plus ceiling, papered with faded bullfighting posters. It's run by a wonderfully matriarchal lady who keeps the flat-cap clientele under control.

ⓘ Getting There & Away

If travelling by public transport from either Madrid or Cuenca, you'll need to take a bus or train to Guadalajara, from where there's a daily bus to/from Pastrana (1¼ hours).

Recópolis

Thirteen kilometres south of Pastrana, signposted off the Tarancón road (turn right just after passing the nuclear power plant), Recópolis (www.patrimoniohistoricoclm.es; Zorita de los Canes; adult/concession/child €5/2.50/1; ⓣ 10am-6pm mid-Sep–Apr, 10am-2pm & 5-9pm May–mid-Sep) is an intriguing ruin in a lovely situation above Río Tajo. The word Visigoth usually calls up images of horned-helmeted lager louts urinating on the dying embers of Roman civilisation, but it's not a fair portrayal of these skilled metalworkers and early Christian monarchs. After uniting most of the peninsula under his rule, King Leovigildo, whose capital was at Toledo, founded Recópolis in AD 578 as a planned walled city named after his son Recaredo. You can see the royal palace complex, workshops and the main street, though later modifications by the Moors and others muddy the waters slightly. There's an interpretation centre and good information in English throughout. Admission includes a nature trail and entrance to the nearby ruined castle at Zorita de los Canes.

Sigüenza

POP 4335

Sleepy, historic and filled with the ghosts of a turbulent past, Sigüenza is well worth a detour. The town is built on a low hill cradled by Río Henares and boasts a castle, a cathedral and several excellent restaurants set among twisting lanes of medieval buildings. Start your ambling at the beautiful 16th-century Plaza Mayor.

◉ Sights

★Catedral   CATHEDRAL

(ⓣ 9.30am-2pm & 4-8pm Tue-Sat, noon-5.30pm Sun) Rising up from the heart of the old town is the city's centrepiece, the cathedral. Begun as a Romanesque structure in 1130, work continued for four centuries as the church was expanded and adorned. The largely Gothic result is laced with elements of other styles, from plateresque through to Renaissance to Mudéjar. The church was heavily damaged during the civil war, but was subsequently rebuilt. The dark interior has a broodingly ancient feel and some fine stained glass, plus an impressive 15th-century altarpiece.

To enter the chapels, sacristy and Gothic cloister, you'll need to join a Spanish-language-only guided tour (per person €5; noon, 1pm, 4.30pm and 5.30pm Tuesday to Sunday). A highlight of the tour is the Capilla Mayor, home of the reclining marble statue of Don Martín Vázquez de Arce (the statue is named *El Doncel*), who died fighting the Muslims in the final stages of the Reconquista. Particularly beautiful is the Sacristía de las Cabezas, with a ceiling adorned with hundreds of heads sculpted by Covarrubias. The Capilla del Espíritu Santo boasts a doorway combining plateresque, Mudéjar and Gothic styles; inside is a remarkable dome and an *Anunciación* by El Greco.

Museo Diocesano de Arte   RELIGIOUS, ART

(admission €3; ⓣ 11am-2pm & 4-7pm Tue-Sat, 11am-2pm Sun) Across the square from the cathedral, this well-presented museum houses a mediocre collection of religious art from Sigüenza and the surrounding area. Its saving grace is an Immaculate Virgin hovering over Seville by Zurbarán. Afternoon opening is 5pm to 8pm in summer.

Castillo   CASTLE

Calle Mayor heads south up the hill from the cathedral to a magnificent-looking

Sigüenza

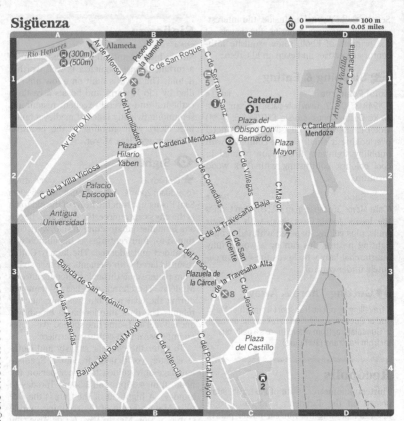

Sigüenza

castle, which was originally built by the Romans and was, in turn, a Moorish *alcázar* (fortress), royal palace, asylum and army barracks. Virtually destroyed during the Spanish Civil War, it was subsequently rebuilt under Franco as a *parador*.

🛏 Sleeping

El Doncel HOTEL €€
(📞949 39 00 01; www.eldoncel.com; Paseo de la Alameda 3; d €48-85; ❇🌐) With earthy colours, lots of exposed stone, spot lighting, minibars, and marshmallow-soft duvets and pillows, this place is aimed squarely at couples on a romantic weekend away from Madrid. It's comfortable and attractive, and there's a good restaurant. Prices drop substantially midweek.

Hostal Puerta Medina HOSTAL €€
(📞949 39 15 65; www.puertamedina.es; Calle Serrano Sanz 17; s/d €52/70; 🌐) Tucked away in a noble 18th-century building a block downhill from the cathedral, this *hostal* offers a genuine welcome and bright, spacious, quiet rooms with plenty of original character. The

affable owner puts on a good breakfast (included) with home-baked bread. Easy parking on this street. Much cheaper outside the high summer season.

Parador de Sigüenza HISTORIC HOTEL €€€
(949 39 01 00; www.parador.es; Plaza del Castillo; d €90-175; P🅿❄🛜) Sigüenza's luxurious *parador* is set in the castle, which dates back to the 12th century, and overlooks the town. The magnificent courtyard is a wonderful place to pass the time. The rooms have period furnishings and castle-style windows so can be on the dark side: ask for one with a balcony to make the most of natural light and views.

✕ Eating

Cafe-Bar Alameda TAPAS €
(Paseo de la Alameda 2; raciones €6-10) Join the local card players at this down-home bar. Its counter groans with tempting tapas and *pinchos* (canapes), including *caracoles* (snails) and *orejas* (pig's ears) for the intrepid, as well as more-digestible choices like tortilla stuffed with bacon and cheese.

★Calle Mayor SPANISH €€
(949 39 17 48; www.restaurantecallemayor.com; Calle Mayor 21; mains €12-18; 1-3.30pm & 8.30-11pm) A standout meal stop on the hill between the cathedral and castle. Traditional dishes like delicious roast goat or fried lamb's brains take their place alongside more elaborate creations in a stylish but comfortable dining area.

Gurugú de la Plazuela TAPAS €€
(www.gurugudelaplazuela.com; Plaza de la Cárcel; mushroom dishes €12-18; 12.30-4pm & 8-11pm Thu-Sat, 12.30-4pm Sun;) The speciality of this historic tavern is mushrooms, lots of them, with some 16 varieties on the menu, prepared all sorts of ways. Other choices include a nice line in game dishes. There are regular art and photography exhibitions.

ℹ Information

Tourist Office (949 34 70 07; www.turismocastillalamancha.es; Calle Serrano Sanz 9; 10am-2pm & 4-6pm Mon-Thu & Sat, 10am-2pm & 4-8pm Fri, 10am-2pm Sun) Just down the hill from the cathedral. Opens and closes an hour later in the afternoon in summer.

ℹ Getting There & Away

Buses are infrequent and mainly serve towns around Sigüenza. They stop on Avenida de Alfonso VI. Five daily regional trains go to Madrid's Chamartín station (€12 to €14, 1½ to 1¾ hours) via Guadalajara; some go on to Soria in the other direction.

Atienza
POP 482

Some 30km northwest of Sigüenza lies Atienza, a charming walled medieval village crowned by yet another castle ruin. Wandering the streets here is utterly enchanting; this is one of Spain's most beautiful villages.

◉ Sights

The main half-timbered square and former 16th-century market place, Plaza del Trigo, is overlooked by the Renaissance Iglesia San Juan Bautista, which has an impressive organ and lavish gilt *retablo*. There are several more mostly Romanesque churches, three of which hold small museums. One of these is devoted to the Caballada, a spectacular procession of horses on Corpus Christi.

🛏 Sleeping

Hostal El Mirador HOSTAL €
(949 39 90 38; www.elmiradordeatienza.com; Calle Barruelo; s/d/tw €24/40/45; ❄🛜) El Mirado, with spotless rooms that are a steal at this price, is a budget option in a modern whitewashed building offering great panoramic views over the fields below. The excellent restaurant shares the vistas and has creative dishes, as well as the standard *cordero* (lamb) and *cabrito* (kid).

★Antiguo Palacio de Atienza RURAL HOTEL €€
(949 39 91 80; www.palaciodeatienza.com; Plaza de Agustín González 1; d €49-89; ❄🛜♨) The best place to stay, this former palace has handsome rooms featuring well-chosen artworks, comfortable beds and exposed beams. The variation in price relates to the size of the room and option of a hot tub in the stylish little bathrooms. Balconies overlook the lawns and pool. and there's a good restaurant. It's a perfect place to base yourself for a few days to explore the area.

ℹ Getting There & Away

A couple of buses leave early in the morning, bound for Madrid (€10, 2¾ hours) and Sigüenza (€3.65, 45 minutes).

Barcelona

Best Places to Eat

➡ Tickets (p285)
➡ Cinc Sentits (p284)
➡ Tapas 24 (p284)
➡ La Vinateria del Call (p280)
➡ Quimet i Quimet (p287)

Best Places to Stay

➡ DO (p275)
➡ Hotel Banys Orientals (p276)
➡ Five Rooms (p278)
➡ Cami Bed & Gallery (p278)
➡ Casa Gràcia (p279)

Why Go?

Barcelona is a mix of sunny Mediterranean charm and European urban style, where dedicated hedonists and culture vultures feel equally at home. From Gothic to Gaudí, the city bursts with art and architecture; Catalan cooking is among the country's best; summer sun seekers fill the beaches in and beyond the city; and the bars and clubs heave year-round.

From its origins as a middle-ranking Roman town, of which vestiges can be seen today, Barcelona became a medieval trade juggernaut. Its old centre holds one of the greatest concentrations of Gothic architecture in Europe. Beyond this are some of the world's more bizarre buildings: surreal spectacles capped by Antoni Gaudí's Sagrada Família.

Barcelona has been breaking ground in art, architecture and style since the late 19th century. From Picasso and Miró to today's modern wonders, Barcelona's racing pulse has barely skipped a beat. Equally busy are the city's avant-garde chefs, who compete with old-time classics for gourmets' attention.

When to Go
Barcelona

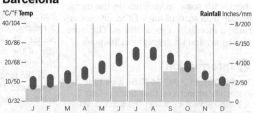

May Plaça del Fòrum rocks during Primavera Sound, a long weekend of outdoor concerts.	**Jun** Sónar, Europe's biggest celebration of electronic music, is held across the city.	**Sep** Festes de la Mercè is Barcelona's end-of-summer finale and biggest party.

Culinary Riches

Great Catalan restaurants can be found in nearly every neighbourhood around town. The settings can be a huge part of the appeal – with candlelit medieval chambers in the Ciutat Vella (old city) and Modernista design in the Eixample setting the stage for a memorable feast. Although there are plenty of high-end places in this city, *barcelonins* aren't averse to eating at humbler, less elegant places – which sometimes offer the most memorable dining experiences. Along those lines, you can't always judge the quality of the food from the restaurant interior. The size of the crowds gathering inside (or even outside) is usually a better indicator.

CATALAN CULTURE

Barcelona is famous for being the capital of Catalonia, which is home to unique traditions seen nowhere else in Spain. Catalan pride manifests itself in many aspects, including raucous festivals where you can see awe-inspiring *castells* (human towers) and frightening *correfocs* (fire runs). The biggest events are Festes de Santa Eulàlia (p272) in February and Festes de la Mercè (p274) in September. But no matter what time of year you visit, you can catch Catalan folk dancing: see the *sardana* performed in front of La Catedral from 6pm on Saturdays or around noon on Sundays. The Catalan language is widely spoken, and you'll earn much goodwill by learning a few phrases. *Bon dia* (good day/good morning), *bona tarda* (good afternoon) or *bona nit* (good evening) are good places to start.

Top Modernista Gems

➔ La Sagrada Família (p249), Antoni Gaudí's unfinished symphony, is a soaring cathedral that people love or loathe. Work continues apace on this controversial project.

➔ Palau de la Música Catalana (p244), a gaudily sumptuous home for music to suit the most eclectic of tastes, is a giddy example of Modernista fantasy.

➔ La Pedrera (p257), Gaudí's wavy corner apartment block with an exquisite period apartment and a sci-fi roof, is one of the best examples of the star architect's work.

➔ Casa Batlló (p253), possibly kookier than La Pedrera, looks at first glance like some strange sea creature frozen into a building facade. Inside, it's all curls and swirls.

➔ Recinte Modernista de Sant Pau (p257), long one of the city's main hospitals, features 16 uniquely decorated pavilions.

SEASIDE ALLURE

No matter the season, taking a stroll or a bike ride along Barcelona's revitalised waterfront makes a splendid complement to exploring medieval lanes and Modernista architecture. In summer, open-air beach bars provide refreshing pit stops.

Top Tips

➔ Beat the crowds by buying tickets online for the Museu Picasso and La Sagrada Família.

➔ Have a seafood feast in Barceloneta.

➔ Take a biking tour, walking tour (many are free) or a gourmand's stroll.

➔ Explore the latest new bars in up-and-coming Sant Antoni and Poble Sec.

Best Drinking Spots

➔ Ocaña (p287)

➔ Sor Rita (p287)

➔ La Caseta del Migdia (p291)

➔ Dry Martini (p290)

➔ Bar Marsella (p289)

Resources

➔ Barcelona Turisme (www.barcelonaturisme.com) Official tourism website.

➔ Miniguide (www.miniguide.es) Art, film, shops, eateries, bars and clubs.

➔ Barcelona Rocks.com (www.barcelonarocks.com) Bars, clubs and gigs.

BARCELONA

Barcelona Highlights

❶ Marvel at **La Sagrada Família** (p249), Antoni Gaudí's still-unfolding Modernista masterpiece.

❷ Stroll the narrow medieval lanes of the enchanting **Barri Gòtic** (p235).

❸ See a concert in the extravagant concert hall of **Palau de la Música Catalana** (p244).

❹ Join the riotous carnival at an FC Barça match in hallowed **Camp Nou** (p263).

❺ Drink in the views from Gaudí's **Park Güell** (p258).

❻ Dine (p283) and drink (p289) amid the architecturally rich streetscape of **L'Eixample**.

❼ Discover Pablo's early masterpieces inside the atmospheric **Museu Picasso** (p246).

❽ Feast on fresh seafood, followed by a stroll along the boardwalk in **La Barceloneta** (p247).

❾ Take in the nightlife of bohemian-loving **El Raval** (p288).

❿ Explore **Montjuïc** (p264), home to Romanesque art, a brooding fort, Miró and beautiful gardens.

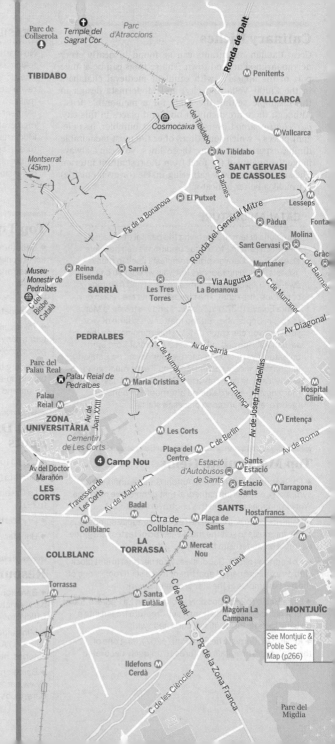

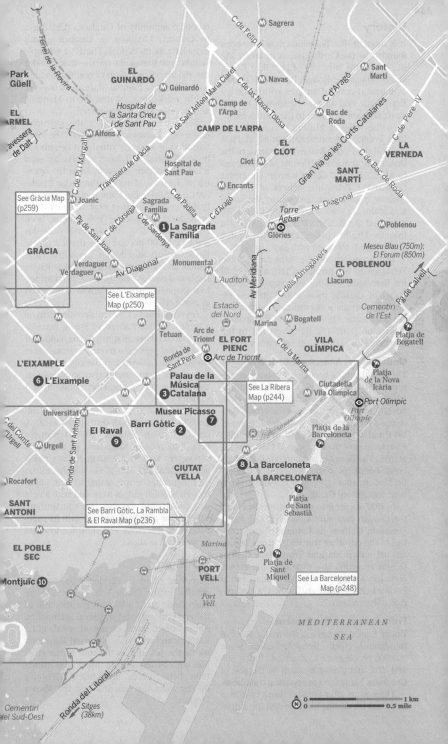

History

It is thought that Barcelona may have been founded by the Carthaginians in about 230 BC, taking the surname of Hamilcar Barca, Hannibal's father. Roman Barcelona (known as Barcino) covered an area within today's Barri Gòtic and was overshadowed by Tarraco (Tarragona), 90km to the southwest.

In the wake of Muslim occupation and then Frankish domination, Guifré el Pilós (Wilfrid the Hairy) founded the house of the Comtes de Barcelona (Counts of Barcelona) in AD 878. In 1137 Count Ramon Berenguer IV married Petronilla, heiress of Aragón, creating a joint state and setting the scene for Catalonia's golden age. Jaume I (1213–76) wrenched the Balearic Islands and Valencia from the Muslims in the 1230s to '40s. Jaume I's son Pere II followed with Sicily in 1282.

The accession of the Aragonese noble Fernando to the throne in 1479 augured ill for Barcelona, and his marriage to Queen Isabel of Castilla more still. Catalonia effectively became a subordinate part of the Castilian state. After the War of the Spanish Succession (1702–13), Barcelona fell to the Bourbon king, Felipe V, in September 1714.

Modernisme, Anarchy & Civil War

The 19th century brought economic resurgence. Wine, cotton, cork and iron industries developed, as did urban working-class poverty and unrest. To ease the crush, Barcelona's medieval walls were demolished in 1854, and in 1869 work began on L'Eixample, an extension of the city beyond Plaça de Catalunya. The flourishing bourgeoisie paid for lavish buildings, many of them in the eclectic Modernisme style, whose leading exponent was Antoni Gaudí.

In 1937, a year into the Spanish Civil War, the Catalan communist party (PSUC; Partit Socialista Unificat de Catalunya) took control of the city after fratricidal street battles against anarchists and Trotskyists. George Orwell recorded the events in his classic *Homage to Catalonia*. Barcelona fell to Franco in 1939 and there followed a long period of repression.

From Franco to the Present

Under Franco, Barcelona received a flood of immigrants, chiefly from Andalucía. Some 750,000 people came to Barcelona in the '50s and '60s, and almost as many to the rest of Catalonia. Many lived in appalling conditions.

Three years after Franco's death in 1975, a new Spanish constitution created the autonomous community of Catalonia (Catalunya in Catalan; Cataluña in Castilian), with Barcelona as its capital. The 1992 Olympic Games put Barcelona on the map. Under the visionary leadership of popular Catalan Socialist mayor Pasqual Maragall, a burst of public works brought new life to Montjuïc and the once shabby waterfront.

Flush with success after the Olympics makeover, Barcelona continued the revitalisation of formerly run-down neighbourhoods. El Raval, still dodgy in parts, has seen a host of building projects, from the opening of Richard Meier's cutting-edge Macba (p243) in 1995 to the Filmoteca de Catalunya (p292) in 2012. Further west, the once derelict industrial district of Poble Nou has been reinvented as 22@ (pronounced 'vint-i-dos arroba'), a 200-hectare zone that's a centre for technology and design. Innovative companies and futuristic architecture (such as the brand-new Museu del Disseny) continue to reshape the urban landscape of this ever-evolving city.

On other fronts, Catalonia continues to be a trendsetter for the rest of Spain. Barcelona's shared biking program Bicing, launched in 2007, has become a model for sustainable transport initiatives, and the city continues to invest in green energy (particularly in its use of solar power and electric and hybrid vehicles).

Once a great kingdom unto its own, Catalonia has a long independent streak. In 2013, on the Catalan National Day (11 September), hundreds of thousands of separatist supporters formed a 400km human chain across Catalonia. In 2014, a referendum on independence was slated to take place, though Spanish judges have said such a vote was illegal and violates the constitution. Whether or not Catalonia will gain its independence, Barcelona will continue to chart its own course ahead.

◉ Sights

Barcelona could be divided into thematic chunks. In the Ciutat Vella (especially the Barri Gòtic and La Ribera) are the bulk of the city's ancient and medieval splendours. Along with El Raval, on the other side of La Rambla, and Port Vell, where old Barcelona meets the sea, this is the core of the city's life, both by day and by night. Top attractions here include the Museu d'Història de Barcelona, La Catedral and the Museu Picasso.

L'Eixample is where the Modernistas went to town. Attractions here are more spread out. Passeig de Gràcia is a concentrated showcase for some of their most outlandish work, but La Sagrada Família, Gaudí's masterpiece, is a long walk (or short metro ride) from there.

Other areas of interest include the beaches and seafood restaurants of the working-class district of La Barceloneta. Montjuïc, with its gardens, museums, art galleries and Olympic Games sites, forms a microcosm on its own. Not to be missed are the Museu Nacional d'Art de Catalunya and the Fundació Joan Miró.

Gaudí's Park Güell is just beyond the area of Gràcia, whose narrow lanes and interlocking squares set the scene for much lively nightlife.

Futher out, you'll find the amusement park and church of high-up Tibidabo, the wooded hills of Parc de Collserola, FC Barcelona's Camp Nou football stadium and the peaceful haven of the Museu-Monestir de Pedralbes.

◉ La Rambla

Head to Spain's most famous street for that first taste of Barcelona's vibrant atmosphere.

Flanked by narrow traffic lanes and plane trees, the middle of La Rambla is a broad pedestrian boulevard, crowded every day until the wee hours with a cross section of *barcelonins* and out-of-towners. Dotted with cafes, restaurants, kiosks and news stands, and enlivened by buskers, pavement artists, mimes and living statues, La Rambla rarely allows a dull moment.

La Rambla gets its name from a seasonal stream (*raml* in Arabic) that once ran here. It was outside the city walls until the 14th century and was built up with monastic buildings and palaces in the 16th to 18th centuries. Unofficially La Rambla is divided into five sections, each with its own name.

Gran Teatre del Liceu   ARCHITECTURE
(Map p236; ☑ 93 485 99 14; www.liceubarce lona.com; La Rambla dels Caputxins 51-59; tour 20/80min €5.50/11.50; ◔ guided tour 10am, short tour 11.30am, noon, 12.30pm & 1pm; Ⓜ Liceu) If you can't catch a night at the opera, you can still have a look around one of Europe's greatest opera houses, known to locals as the Liceu. Smaller than Milan's La Scala but bigger than Venice's La Fenice, it can seat up to 2300 people in its grand horseshoe-shaped auditorium.

Mirador de Colom   VIEWPOINT
(Map p236; ☑ 93 302 52 24; Plaça del Portal de la Pau; lift adult/child €4.50/3; ◔ 8.30am-8pm; Ⓜ Drassanes) High above the swirl of traffic on the roundabout below, Columbus keeps permanent watch, pointing vaguely out to the Mediterranean. Built for the Universal Exhibition in 1888, the monument allows you to zip up 60m in the lift for bird's-eye views back up La Rambla and across the ports of Barcelona.

◉ Barri Gòtic

Barcelona's 'Gothic Quarter', east of La Rambla, is a medieval warren of narrow, winding streets, quaint *plaças* (plazas), and grand mansions and monuments from the city's golden age. Many of its buildings date from the 15th century or earlier. The district is liberally seasoned with restaurants, cafes and bars, so relief from sightseeing is always close by.

★La Catedral   CHURCH
(Map p236; ☑ 93 342 82 62; www.catedralbcn.org; Plaça de la Seu; admission free, special visit €6, choir admission €2.80; ◔ 8am-12.45pm & 5.15-7.30pm Mon-Sat, special visit 1-5pm Mon-Sat, 2-5pm Sun & holidays; Ⓜ Jaume I) Barcelona's central place of worship presents a magnificent image. The richly decorated main facade, laced with gargoyles and the stone intricacies you would expect of northern European Gothic, sets it quite apart from other churches in Barcelona. The facade was actually added in 1870, although the rest of the building was built between 1298 and 1460. The other facades are sparse in decoration, and the octagonal, flat-roofed towers are a clear reminder that, even here, Catalan Gothic architectural principles prevailed.

Museu Diocesà   MUSEUM
(Casa de la Pia Almoina; Map p236; ☑ 93 315 22 13; www.arqbcn.org; Avinguda de la Catedral 4; adult/child €6/3; ◔ 10am-2pm & 5-8pm Tue-Sat, 11am-2pm Sun; Ⓜ Jaume I) Next to the cathedral, the Diocesan Museum has a handful of exhibits on Gaudí (including a fascinating documentary on his life and philosophy) on the upper floors. There's also a sparse collection of medieval and romanesque religious art usually supplemented by a temporary exhibition or two.

Plaça de Sant Jaume   SQUARE
(Map p236; Ⓜ Liceu or Jaume I) In the 2000 or so years since the Romans settled here, the

Barri Gòtic, La Rambla & El Raval

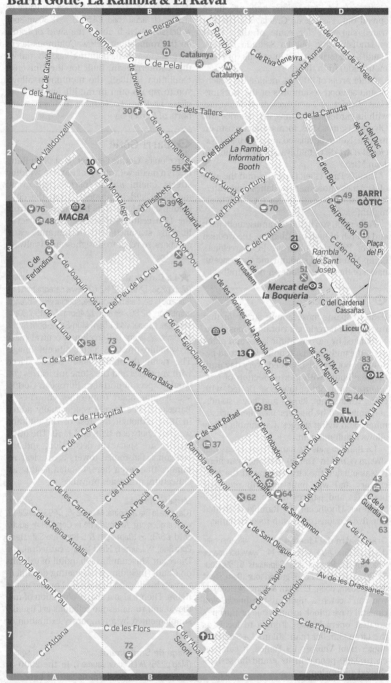

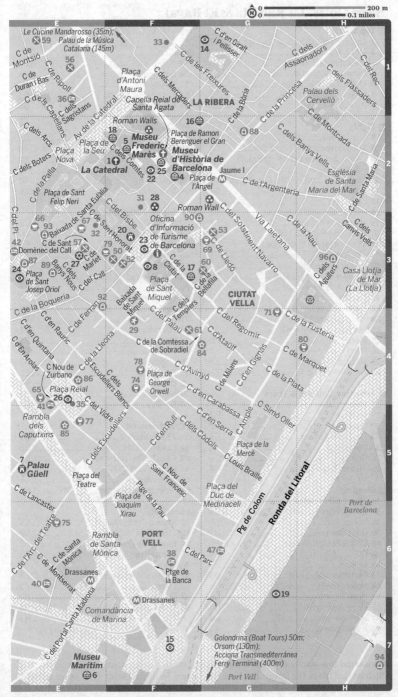

Le Cucine Mandarosso (35m);
Palau de la Música
Catalana (145m)

C de Montsió
59
56
33
14
C d'en Giralt
i Pellisser
C dels
Assaonadors

C de
Duran i Bas
C de les Freixures
C de la Bòria
C dels Flassaders
C del Rec

C de ls Ripoll
36
C dels
Sagristans
C dels Mercaders
LA RIBERA
C de la Princesa
Palau dels
Cervelló

C dels Arcs
Plaça
d'Antoni
Maura
Capella Reial de
Santa Àgata
16
C de Montcada
C dels Banys Vells

Av de la Catedral
Roman Walls
18
5
Museu
Frederic
Marès
Plaça de Ramon
Berenguer el Gran
88

Plaça de
la Seu
1
Museu
d'Història de
Barcelona
Església
de Santa
Maria del Mar

La Catedral
C dels Comtes
22
25
4
Plaça de
l'Àngel
Jaume I

Plaça de Sant
Felip Neri
31
28
Roman Wall
C de l'Argenteria

C de la Palla
C del Pi
66
93
Baixada de Santa Eulàlia
C del Bisbe
67
20
90
Oficina
d'Informació
de Turisme
de Barcelona
53
C de la Nau
Canvis Vells

42
Domènec del Call
57
C de Sant Honorat
32
23
69
C de Lledó
60

87
89
27
C dels
Banys Nous
C de la
Market
50
79
52
8
17
C de la
Ciutat
C de la
Bellafila
96
Casa Llotja
de Mar
(La Llotja)

24
Plaça de
Sant
Josep Oriol
Plaça
de Sant
Miquel
CIUTAT
VELLA

C de la Boqueria
92
Baixada
de Sant
Miquel
C dels
Templers
C del Regomir
71
C de la Fusteria

C d'en Rauric
C de Ferran
29
C del Palau
61
C d'Atàulf
84

C d'en Quintana
78
C de la Comtessa
de Sobradiel
80
C de Marquet

C d'En Arolas
86
74
C d'Avinyó
C de Milans
C de la Plata

C Nou de
Zurbano
Plaça de
George
Orwell
C d'en Gignàs

65
26
35
C dels Escudellers Blancs
C d'en Carabassa
C Simó Oller

41
C del Vidre
C d'en Serra
C Ample

Rambla
dels
Caputxins
85
77
C dels Còdols
Plaça de la
Mercè
C Louis Braille

7
Palau
Güell
C dels Escudellers
Nou de
Sant Francesc
Plaça del
Duc de
Medinaceli

C de Lancaster
Plaça del
Teatre
Pg de Colom
Ronda del Litoral
Port de
Barcelona

75
Plaça de
Joaquim
Xirau
Plaça
de la Pau

C de l'Arc del Teatre
C de Santa
Mònica
Rambla
de Santa
Mònica
PORT
VELL
38
47
C del Parc

40
Drassanes
Ptge de
la Banca
19

Drassanes
Comandància
de Marina

C del Portal Santa Madrona
15
Golondrina (Boat Tours) 50m;
Orsom (130m);
Acciona Transmediterránea
Ferry Terminal (400m)
94

Museu
Marítim
6
Port Vell

BARCELONA SIGHTS

Barri Gòtic, La Rambla & El Raval

area around this square (often remodelled), which started life as the forum, has been the focus of Barcelona's civic life. This is still the central staging area for Barcelona's traditional festivals. Facing each other across the square are the Palau de la Generalitat (seat

EL CALL

One of our favourite places to wander around in the Ciutat Vella is El Call (pronounced 'kye'), which is the name of the medieval Jewish quarter that flourished here until a tragic pogrom in the 14th century. Today, its narrow lanes hide some surprising sites (including an ancient synagogue unearthed in the 1990s and the fragments of a women's bathhouse inside the basement of the cafe, Caelum, p286). Some of the old town's most unusual shops are here – selling exquisite antiques, handmade leather products, even kosher wine. Its well-concealed dining rooms and candlelit bars and cafes make a fine destination in the evening.

El Call (the name probably derives from the Hebrew word '*kahal*', meaning 'community') is a tiny area, and a little tricky to find. The boundaries are roughly Carrer del Call, Carrer dels Banys Nous, Baixada de Santa Eulalia and Carrer de Sant Honorat.

of Catalonia's regional government) on the north side and the *ajuntament* (town hall) to the south.

Palau de la Generalitat
PALACE

(Map p236; www.president.cat; Plaça de Sant Jaume; ⊙ 2nd & 4th weekend of month; Ⓜ Liceu, Jaume I) Founded in the early 15th century, the Palau de la Generalitat is open on limited occasions only (the second and fourth weekends of the month, plus open-door days). The most impressive of the ceremonial halls is the Saló de Sant Jordi, named after St George, the region's patron saint. To see inside, book on the website (unfortunately in Catalan only).

Ajuntament
ARCHITECTURE

(Map p236; ☑ 93 402 70 00; www.bcn.cat; Plaça de Sant Jaume; ⊙ 10.30am-1.30pm Sun; Ⓜ Liceu, Jaume I) FREE The *ajuntament,* otherwise known as the Casa de la Ciutat, has been the seat of power for centuries. The Consell de Cent (the city's ruling council) first sat here in the 14th century, but the building has lamentably undergone many changes since the days of Barcelona's Gothic-era splendour.

Museu d'Idees i Invents de Barcelona
MUSEUM

(Museum of Ideas and Inventions; Map p236; ☑ 93 332 79 30; www.mibamuseum.com; Carrer de la Ciutat 7; adult/child €8/6; ⊙ 10am-2pm & 4-7pm Tue-Fri, 10am-8pm Sat, to 2pm Sun; Ⓜ Jaume I) Although the price is a bit steep for such a small museum, the collection makes for an amusing browse over an hour or so. On display, you'll find both brilliant and bizarre inventions: square egg makers, absorbent pillows for flatulent folks, a chair for inserting suppositories, as well as more useful devices like the Lifestraw (filters contaminants

from any drinking source) and gas glasses (adaptive eyecare for any prescription).

Plaça Reial
SQUARE

(Map p236; Ⓜ Liceu) One of the most photogenic squares in Barcelona, the Plaça Reial is a delightful retreat from the traffic and pedestrian mobs on the nearby Rambla. Numerous eateries, bars and nightspots lie beneath the arcades of 19th-century neoclassical buildings, with a buzz of activity at all hours.

Temple Romà d'August
RUIN

(Map p236; Carrer del Paradis 10; ⊙ 10am-2pm Mon, to 7pm Tue-Sun; Ⓜ Jaume I) FREE Opposite the southeast end of La Catedral, narrow Carrer del Paradis leads towards Plaça de Sant Jaume. Inside No 10, itself an intriguing building with Gothic and baroque touches, are four columns and the architrave of Barcelona's main Roman temple, dedicated to Caesar Augustus and built to worship his imperial highness in the 1st century AD.

Plaça del Rei
MUSEUM, SQUARE

(Map p236) Plaça del Rei (King's Sq) is a picturesque plaza where Fernando and Isabel received Columbus following his first New World voyage. It is the courtyard of the former Palau Reial Major. The palace today houses a superb history museum, with significant Roman ruins underground.

★ Museu d'Història de Barcelona
MUSEUM

(Map p236; ☑ 93 256 21 00; www.museuhistoria. bcn.cat; Plaça del Rei; adult/child €7/free, free 1st Sun of month & 3-8pm Sun; ⊙ 10am-7pm Tue-Sat, 10am-8pm Sun; Ⓜ Jaume I) One of Barcelona's most fascinating museums takes you back through the centuries to the very foundations of Roman Barcino. You'll stroll over ruins of the old streets, sewers, laundries and wine- and fish-making factories that

La Rambla

A TIMELINE

Look beyond the human statues and tourist-swarmed restaurants, and you'll find a fascinating piece of Barcelona history dating back many centuries.

13th century A serpentine seasonal stream (called ramla in Arabic) runs outside the city walls. As Barcelona grows, the stream will eventually become an open sewer until it's later paved over.

1500–1800 During this early period, La Rambla was dotted with convents and monasteries, including the baroque **Església de Betlem ❶**, completed in the early 1700s.

1835 The city erupts in anticlericism, with riots and the burning of convents. Along La Rambla, many religious assets are destroyed or seized by the state. This paves the way for new developments, including the **Mercat de la Boqueria ❷** in 1840, **Gran Teatre del Liceu ❸** in 1847 and **Plaça Reial ❹** in 1848.

Teatre Poliorama
Built in 1894 as the seat of the Royal Academy of Sciences and Arts, it later served as a cinema, and a strategic lookout for one communist faction during the Spanish Civil War.

Església de Betlem
Dedicated to the Holy Family, this is the last standing of the many churches once lining La Rambla. Its once sumptuous interior was gutted during the Spanish Civil War.

Via Sepulcral Romana

Ⓜ **Font de Canaletes**

La Rambla

❼

Palau Moja

Centre de la Imatge ❶

Palau de la Virreina

Plaça del Pi

Plaça St Jos Orió

❺

❷

Mercat de la Boqueria
The official name of Barcelona's most photogenic market is El Mercat de Sant Josep, which references the convent of St Josep that once stood here.

Gran Teatre del Liceu
Although badly damaged by fire in 1994, this gorgeous opera house was restored and reborn in 1999, and remains one of Europe's finest theatres.

1883 Architect Josep Vilaseca refurbishes the **Casa Bruno Cuadros** ❺. As Modernisme is sweeping across the city, Vilaseca creates an eclectic work using stained glass, wrought iron, Egyptian imagery and Japanese prints.

1888 Barcelona hosts the Universal Exhibition. The city sees massive urban renewal projects, with the first electric lights coming to La Rambla, and the building of the **Mirador de Colom** ❻.

1936–39 La Rambla becomes the site of bloody street fighting during the Spanish Civil War. British journalist and author George Orwell, who spends three days holed up in the **Teatre Poliorama** ❼ during street battles, later describes the tumultuous days in his excellent book, *Homage to Catalonia*.

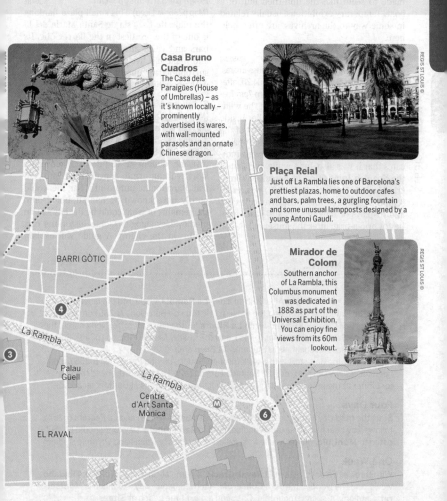

Casa Bruno Cuadros
The Casa dels Paraigües (House of Umbrellas) – as it's known locally – prominently advertised its wares, with wall-mounted parasols and an ornate Chinese dragon.

REGIS ST LOUIS ©

Plaça Reial
Just off La Rambla lies one of Barcelona's prettiest plazas, home to outdoor cafes and bars, palm trees, a gurgling fountain and some unusual lampposts designed by a young Antoni Gaudí.

Mirador de Colom
Southern anchor of La Rambla, this Columbus monument was dedicated in 1888 as part of the Universal Exhibition. You can enjoy fine views from its 60m lookout.

REGIS ST LOUIS ©

BARRI GÒTIC

❹

La Rambla

❸

Palau Güell

La Rambla

Centre d'Art Santa Mònica

Ⓜ

❻

EL RAVAL

flourished here following the town's founding by Emperor Augustus around 10 BC. Equally impressive is the building itself, which was once part of the Palau Reial Major (Grand Royal Palace) on Plaça del Rei, among the key locations of medieval princely power in Barcelona.

Palau del Lloctinent
HISTORIC SITE

(Map p236; Carrer dels Comtes; ⊙10am-7pm; Ⓜ Jaume I) FREE This converted 16th-century palace has a peaceful courtyard worth wandering through. Have a look upwards from the main staircase to admire the extraordinary timber *artesonado,* a sculpted ceiling made to seem like the upturned hull of a boat. Temporary exhibitions, usually related in some way to the archives, are often held here.

★ Museu Frederic Marès
MUSEUM

(Map p236; ☑93 256 35 00; www.museumares. bcn.es; Plaça de Sant Iu 5; admission €4.20, after 3pm Sun & 1st Sun of month free; ⊙10am-7pm Tue-Sat, 11am-8pm Sun; Ⓜ Jaume I) One of the wildest collections of historical curios lies inside this vast medieval complex, once part of the royal palace of the counts of Barcelona. A rather worn coat of arms on the wall indicates that it was also, for a while, the seat of the Spanish Inquisition in Barcelona. Frederic Marès i Deulovol (1893–1991) was a rich sculptor, traveller and obsessive collector, and displays of religious art and vast varieties of bric-a-brac litter the museum.

Roman Walls
RUIN

(Map p236) From Plaça del Rei it's worth a detour to see the two best surviving stretches of Barcelona's Roman walls, which once boasted 78 towers (as much a matter of prestige as of defence). One section is on the southeast side of Plaça de Ramon Berenguer el Gran, with the Capella Reial de Santa Àgata atop. The other is a little further south, by the northern end of Carrer del Sots-tinent Navarro. They date from the 3rd and 4th centuries, when the Romans rebuilt their walls after the first attacks by Germanic tribes from the north.

Plaça de Sant Josep Oriol
SQUARE

(Map p236; Ⓜ Liceu) This small plaza flanking the majestic Església de Santa Maria del Pi is one of the prettiest in the Barri Gòtic. Its bars and cafes attract buskers and artists and make it a lively place to hang out. It is surrounded by quaint streets, many dotted with appealing cafes, restaurants and shops.

Sinagoga Major
SYNAGOGUE

(Map p236; ☑93 317 07 90; www.calldebarcelona. org; Carrer de Marlet 5; admission by suggested donation €2.50; ⊙10.30am-6.30pm Mon-Fri, to 2.30pm Sat & Sun; Ⓜ Liceu) When an Argentine investor bought a run-down electrician's store with an eye to converting it into central Barcelona's umpteenth bar, he could hardly have known he had stumbled onto the remains of what could be the city's main medieval synagogue (some historians cast doubt on the claim). A guide will explain

---

BARCELONA IN...

Two Days

Start with the **Barri Gòtic**. After a stroll along **La Rambla**, wade into the labyrinth to admire La Catedral (p235) and the Museu d'Història de Barcelona (p239) on historic Plaça del Rei. Cross Via Laietana into **La Ribera** for the city's most beloved church, the Basilica de Santa Maria del Mar (p245), and the nearby Museu Picasso (p246). Round off with a meal and cocktails in the funky **El Born** area.

The following day, start with a walk through Gaudí's unique Park Güell (p258), then head for his work in progress, La Sagrada Família (p249). Afterwards, head to El Raval for dinner at the innovative Suculent (p281) followed by drinks at Bar Marsella (p289).

Four Days

Start the third day with more Gaudí, visiting Casa Batlló (p253) and La Pedrera (p257), followed by beachside relaxation and seafood in **Barceloneta**. Day four should be dedicated to **Montjuïc**, with its museums, galleries, fortress, gardens and Olympic stadium.

One Week

With three extra days, take in **El Raval**, **Gràcia**, a game at Camp Nou (p263), **Tibidabo** views, and the wooded paths of **Collserola**. A tempting one-day excursion is **Montserrat**, Catalonia's 'sacred mountain'. Or spend a day at the beach at **Sitges**.

what is thought to be the significance of the site in various languages.

⊙ El Raval

West of La Rambla, Ciutat Vella spreads to Ronda de Sant Antoni, Ronda de Sant Pau and Avinguda del Paral·lel, which together trace the line of Barcelona's 14th-century walls. Known as El Raval, the area contains what remains of one of the city's slums, the dwindling but still seedy red-light zone and drug abusers' haunt of the Barri Xinès, at its south end. It's not nearly as tricky as it once was, but watch your pockets nonetheless.

★ MACBA   MUSEUM
(Museu d'Art Contemporani de Barcelona; Map p236; ☑ 93 412 08 10; www.macba.cat; Plaça dels Àngels 1; adult/concession €10/8; ⊙ 11am-7.30pm Mon & Wed-Fri, 10am-9pm Sat, 10am-3pm Sun & holidays; Ⓜ Universitat) Designed by Richard Meier and opened in 1995, MACBA has become the city's foremost contemporary art centre, with captivating exhibitions for the serious art lover. The permanent collection is on the ground floor and dedicates itself to Spanish and Catalan art from the second half of the 20th century, with works by Antoni Tàpies, Joan Brossa and Miquel Barceló, among others, though international artists, such as Paul Klee, Bruce Nauman and John Cage, are also represented.

Centre de Cultura Contemporània
de Barcelona   CULTURAL BUILDING
(CCCB; Map p236; ☑ 93 306 41 00; www.cccb. org; Carrer de Montalegre 5; 2 exhibitions adult/ child under 16yr/senior & student €8/free/6, 1 exhibition €6/free/4, 3-8pm Sun free; ⊙ 11am-8pm Tue-Sun; Ⓜ Universitat) A complex of auditoriums, exhibition spaces and conference halls opened here in 1994 in what had been an 18th-century hospice, the Casa de la Caritat. The courtyard, with a vast glass wall on one side, is spectacular. With 4500 sq metres of exhibition space in four separate areas, the centre hosts a constantly changing program of exhibitions, film cycles and other events.

Antic Hospital de la
Santa Creu   HISTORIC BUILDING
(Former Hospital of the Holy Cross; Map p236; ☑ 93 270 16 21; www.bnc.cat; Carrer de l'Hospital 56; ⊙ 9am-8pm Mon-Fri, to 2pm Sat; Ⓜ Liceu) FREE Behind La Boqueria stands the Antic Hospital de la Santa Creu, which was once the city's main hospital. Begun in 1401, it functioned until the 1930s, and was considered

one of the best in Europe in its medieval heyday – it is famously the place where Antoni Gaudí died in 1926. Today it houses the **Biblioteca de Catalunya**, and the **Institut d'Estudis Catalans** (Institute for Catalan Studies). The hospital's Gothic chapel, **La Capella** (Map p236; ☑ 93 442 71 71; www.bcn.cat/lacapella; ⊙ noon-2pm & 4-8pm Tue-Sat, 11am-2pm Sun & holidays; Ⓜ Liceu) FREE, shows temporary exhibitions.

★ Palau Güell   PALACE
(Map p236; ☑ 93 472 57 75; www.palauguell.cat; Carrer Nou de la Rambla 3-5; adult/concession €12/8; ⊙ 10am-8pm Tue-Sun; Ⓜ Drassanes) Finally reopened in its entirety in May 2012 after several years of refurbishment, this is a magnificent example of the early days of Gaudí's fevered architectural imagination – the extraordinary neo-Gothic mansion, one of the few major buildings of that era raised in Ciutat Vella, gives an insight into its maker's prodigious genius.

Església de Sant Pau del Camp   CHURCH
(Map p236; Carrer de Sant Pau 101; adult/concession €3/2; ⊙ 10am-1.30pm & 4-7.30pm Mon-Sat; Ⓜ Paral·lel) The best example of Romanesque architecture in the city is the dainty little cloister of this church. Set in a somewhat dusty garden, the 12th-century church also boasts some Visigothic sculptural detail on the main entrance.

BARCELONA SIGHTS

★ **Museu Marítim** MUSEUM
(Map p236; 📞93 342 99 20; www.mmb.cat; Avinguda de les Drassanes; adult/child €5/2, 3-8pm Sun free; 🕙10am-8pm; 🛜; Ⓜ Drassanes) These mighty Gothic shipyards shelter the Museu Marítim, a remarkable relic from Barcelona's days as the seat of a seafaring empire. Highlights include a full-sized replica (made in the 1970s) of Don Juan of Austria's 16th-century flagship, fishing vessels, antique navigation charts and dioramas of the Barcelona waterfront.

◉ **La Ribera**

La Ribera is cut off from the Barri Gòtic by noisy Via Laietana, which was driven through the city in 1908. La Ribera, whose name refers to the waterfront that once lay much further inland, was the pumping commercial heart of medieval Barcelona. Its intriguing, narrow streets house major sights, and good bars and restaurants, mainly in El Born around Passeig del Born.

Palau de la Música Catalana ARCHITECTURE
(📞93 295 72 00; www.palaumusica.org; Carrer de Sant Francesc de Paula 2; adult/child €17/free;

BARCELONA SIGHTS

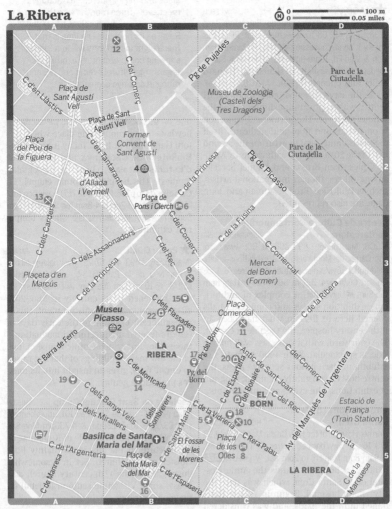

La Ribera

⊘ guided tours 10am-3.30pm daily; Ⓜ Urquinaona) This concert hall is a high point of Barcelona's Modernista architecture, a symphony in tile, brick, sculpted stone and stained glass. Built by Domènech i Montaner between 1905 and 1908 for the Orfeo Català musical society, it was conceived as a temple for the Catalan Renaixença (Renaissance).

Carrer de Montcada
STREET
(Map p244; Ⓜ Jaume I) An early example of town planning, this medieval high street was driven towards the sea from the road that in the 12th century led northeast from the city walls. It was the city's most coveted address for the merchant classes. The bulk of the great mansions that remain today mostly date to the 14th and 15th centuries.

★ Basílica de Santa Maria del Mar
CHURCH
(Map p244; ✆ 93 310 23 90; Plaça de Santa Maria del Mar; ⊘ 9am-1.30pm & 4.30-8.30pm Mon-Sat, from 10.30am Sun; Ⓜ Jaume I) FREE At the southwest end of Passeig del Born stands the apse of Barcelona's finest Catalan Gothic church, Santa Maria del Mar (Our Lady of the Sea). Built in the 14th century with record-breaking alacrity for the time (it took just 54 years), the church is remarkable for its architectural harmony and simplicity.

Mercat de Santa Caterina
MARKET
(Map p236; ✆ 93 319 17 40; www.mercatsantacaterina.com; Avinguda de Francesc Cambó 16; ⊘ 7.30am-2pm Mon, to 3.30pm Tue, Wed & Sat, to 8.30pm Thu & Fri, closed afternoons Jul & Aug; 🛜; Ⓜ Jaume I) Come shopping for your tomatoes at this extraordinary-looking produce market, designed by Enric Miralles and Benedetta Tagliabue to replace its 19th-century predecessor. Finished in 2005, it is distinguished by its kaleidoscopic and undulating roof, held up above the bustling produce stands, restaurants, cafes and bars by twisting slender branches of what look like grey steel trees.

Museu de la Xocolata
MUSEUM
(Map p244; ✆ 93 268 78 78; www.museuxocolata.cat; Carrer del Comerç 36; adult/child under 7yr/senior & student €5/free/4.25; ⊘ 10am-7pm Mon-Sat, to 3pm Sun & holidays; 🛜 ♿; Ⓜ Jaume I) Chocoholics have a hard time containing themselves in this museum dedicated to the fundamental foodstuff – particularly when faced with tempting displays of cocoa-based treats in the cafe at the exit. The displays trace the origins of chocolate, its arrival in Europe, and the many myths and images associated with it. Among the informative stuff and machinery used in the production of chocolate are large chocolate models of emblematic buildings such as the Sagrada Família, along with various characters, local and international.

Arxiu Fotogràfic de Barcelona
GALLERY
(Map p244; ✆ 93 256 34 20; www.bcn.cat/arxiu/fotografic; Plaça de Pons i Clerch 2, 2A; ⊘ 10am-7pm Mon-Sat; Ⓜ Jaume I) FREE On the 2nd floor of the former Convent de Sant Agustí is the modest exhibition space of this city photo archive. Photos on show are generally related to the city, as the photo collection is principally devoted to that theme, from the late 19th century until the late 20th century.

BARCELONA SIGHTS

La Ribera

Museu del Rei de la Magia　MUSEUM
(Map p236; ☑ 93 318 71 92; www.elreydelamagia.
com; Carrer de les Jonqueres 15; admission €3;
⏱ 11am-2pm & 4-8pm Thu-Sun, closed Sun morning Jul & Aug; ⓓ; Ⓜ Jaume I) This museum is
a timeless curio. It is the scene of magic
shows, home to collections of material that
hark back to the 19th-century origins of the
associated **magic shop** (Map p236; ☑ 93 319
39 20; www.elreydelamagia.com; ⏱ 11am-2pm &
5-8pm Mon-Fri, 11am-2pm Sat; Ⓜ Jaume I) at Carrer de la Princesa 11 (which holds everything
from old posters and books for learning
tricks to magic wands and trick cards) and
the place for budding magicians of all ages
to enrol in courses. Seeing is believing.

Parc de la Ciutadella　PARK
(Map p248; Passeig de Picasso; Ⓜ Arc de Triomf)
FREE Come for a stroll, a picnic, a visit to
the zoo or to inspect Catalonia's regional
parliament, but don't miss a visit to this, the
most central green lung in the city. Parc de la
Ciutadella is perfect for winding down.

Parlament de Catalunya　NOTABLE BUILDING
(Map p248; www.parlament.cat; ⏱ guided tours
10am-1pm Sat, Sun & holidays) Southeast, in the
fort's former arsenal, is the regional Parlament de Catalunya. You can join free guided
tours, in Catalan and Spanish (Castilian)
only, on Saturdays and Sundays. The building is open for independent visiting on 11
September from 10am to 7pm. The most
interesting is the sweeping **Escala d'Honor**
(Stairway of Honour) and the several solemn
halls that lead to the **Saló de Sessions**, the
semicircular auditorium where parliament
sits. At the centre of the garden in front of
the *parlament* is a statue of a seemingly
heartbroken woman, *Desconsol* (Distress;
1907), by Josep Llimona.

Zoo de Barcelona　ZOO
(Map p248; ☑ 902 457545; www.zoobarcelona.cat;
Parc de la Ciutadella; adult/child €19.90/€11.95;
⏱ 10am-5.30pm Nov-Mar, 10am-7pm Apr, May, Sep,
& Oct, 10am-8pm Jun-Aug; ⓓ; Ⓜ Barceloneta) The
zoo is a great day out for kids, with 7500 critters that range from geckos to gorillas, lions
and elephants. There are more than 400 species, plus picnic areas dotted all around and
a wonderful adventure playground. There
are pony rides, a petting zoo and a minitrain meandering through the grounds. A
new marine zoo being built on the coast of
El Fòrum northeast of the city centre will
ease the currently slightly crowded space,
although the recession has meant plans are
stalled for the time being.

◉ Port Vell

Barcelona's old port at the bottom of La
Rambla, to the west of La Barceloneta, was
transformed in the 1990s to become a popular leisure zone.

MUSEU PICASSO

The setting alone, in five contiguous medieval stone mansions, makes the **Museu Picasso** (Map p244; ☑ 93 256 30 00; www.museupicasso.bcn.cat; Carrer de Montcada 15-23;
adult/child €14/free, temporary exhibitions adult/child €6.50/free, 3-8pm Sun & 1st Sun of
month free; ⏱ 9am-7pm daily, until 9.30pm Thu; 🛜; Ⓜ Jaume I) unique (and worth the prob-
able queues). The pretty courtyards, galleries and staircases preserved in the first three
of these buildings are nearly as delightful as the collection inside.

The collection, which includes more than 3500 artworks, is strongest on Picasso's
earliest years, up until 1904, which is apt considering that the artist spent his formative
creative years in Barcelona.

A visit starts with sketches and oils from Picasso's earliest years in Málaga and La
Coruña – around 1893–95. Some of his self-portraits and the portraits of his father,
which date from 1896, are evidence enough of his precocious talent. The enormous
Ciència i Caritat (Science and Charity) showcases his masterful academic techniques
of portraiture.

His nocturnal blue-tinted views of *Terrats de Barcelona* (Roofs of Barcelona) and *El
foll* (The Madman) are cold and cheerless, yet somehow spectrally alive.

Among the later works, done in Cannes in 1957, *Las meninas* is a complex technical
series of studies on Diego Velázquez' masterpiece of the same name (which hangs in the
Prado in Madrid).

Moll de la Fusta PROMENADE
Northeast from the quay stretches the promenade Moll de la Fusta. Usually the **Pailebot de Santa Eulàlia** (Map p236; Moll de la Fusta; adult/child €1/free; ⊙ 10am-8.30pm Tue-Fri & Sun, 2-8.30pm Sat; Ⓜ Drassanes), a fully functioning 1918 schooner restored by the Museu Marítim, is moored here for visits, although sometimes it's off on the high seas; admission is free with a Museu Marítim ticket.

Moll d'Espanya PROMENADE
The heart of the redeveloped harbour is Moll d'Espanya, a former wharf linked to Moll de la Fusta by a wave-shaped footbridge, **Rambla de Mar**, which rotates to let boats enter the marina behind it. At the end of Moll d'Espanya is the glossy **Maremàgnum** shopping and eating complex, but the major attraction is **L'Aquàrium** (Map p248; ☑ 93 221 74 74; www.aquariumbcn.com; Moll d'Espanya; adult/child €20/15, dive €300; ⊙ 9.30am-11pm Jul & Aug, to 9pm Sep-Jun; Ⓜ Drassanes), with its 80m-long shark tunnel. Short of diving among them (which can be arranged here too), this is as close as you can get to a set of shark teeth without being bitten. Beyond L'Aquàrium is the big-screen **Imax cinema**.

⊙ Barceloneta & the Waterfront
Barceloneta, laid out in the 18th century and subsequently heavily overdeveloped, was once a factory workers' and fishing quarter. Today the smokestacks are gone (as are most of the fishing families), though an authentic, ungentrified air still permeates these narrow gridlike streets. You'll find some excellent seafood restaurants here and a few bohemian neighbourhood bars. Barceloneta meets the sea at the city's sparkling new waterfront, with a beachside promenade extending some 4.5km past artificial beaches, parks and new high-rises to El Fòrum.

Museu d'Història de Catalunya MUSEUM
(Museum of Catalonian History; Map p248; ☑ 93 225 47 00; www.mhcat.net; Plaça de Pau Vila 3; adult/child €4.50/3.50, 1st Sun of month free; ⊙ 10am-7pm Tue & Thu-Sat, to 8pm Wed, to 2.30pm Sun; Ⓜ Barceloneta) Inside the **Palau de Mar** (Map p248), this worthwhile museum takes you from the Stone Age through to the early 1980s. It is a busy hotchpotch of dioramas, artefacts, videos, models, documents and interactive bits: all up, an entertaining exploration of 2000 years of Catalan history.

---

❶ FREE BARCELONA
Entry to some sights is free on occasion, most commonly on the first Sunday of the month. Other attractions are free on Sunday afternoons. Here are some sights that offer free admission days:

➡ Museu Picasso (p246) Sundays 3pm to 8pm and all day on first Sunday of the month.

➡ La Catedral (p235) From 8am to 12.45pm and 5.15pm to 8pm Monday to Saturday.

➡ Museu d'Història de Barcelona (p239) From 3pm to 8pm Sunday and first Sunday of the month.

➡ Museu d'Història de Catalunya (p247) First Sunday of the month.

➡ Museu Marítim (p244) From 3pm to 8pm Sunday.

➡ Museu Nacional d'Art de Catalunya (p264) First Sunday of the month.

➡ Palau Güell (p243) First Sunday of the month November to March, and 5pm to 8pm Sundays from April to October.

➡ Museu de la Música (p256) From 3pm to 8pm Sunday.

Passeig Marítim de la Barceloneta PROMENADE
(Ⓜ Barceloneta or Ciutadella Vila Olímpica) On La Barceloneta's seaward side are the first of Barcelona's **beaches**, which are popular on summer weekends. The pleasant Passeig Marítim de la Barceloneta, a 1.25km promenade from La Barceloneta to Port Olímpic, is a haunt for strollers and rollers, so bring your rollerblades.

Port Olímpic MARINA
(Ⓜ Ciutadella Vila Olímpica) A busy marina built for the Olympic sailing events, Port Olímpic is surrounded by bars and restaurants. An eye-catcher on the approach from La Barceloneta is Frank Gehry's giant copper *Peix* (Fish) sculpture. The area behind Port Olímpic, dominated by twin-tower blocks (the luxury Hotel Arts Barcelona and the Torre Mapfre office block), is the former Vila Olímpica living quarters for the Olympic competitors, which was later sold off as apartments.

La Barceloneta

N 0 ————————— 200 m
0 ————————— 0.1 miles

Teatre Nacional de
Catalunya (1.1km);
Els Encants
Vells (1.6km)

C de Wellington

C de Villena

C de la Marina

C de Joan Miró

25

C de Salvador Espriu

Razzmatazz
(1km)

Av del Litoral

4 5

C de Ramon Trias Fargas

Ciutadella
Vila
Olímpica

Torre
Mapfre

Xiringuito
D'Escribà (680m);
Base Nautica
Municipal
(1.1km)

Pg de Picasso

7

8
Peix
Sculpture

23

Pg de Circumval·lació

Ronda del Litoral

Av del Marquès de l'Argentera

C de Trelawny

1

C d'Ocata

C del Doctor Aiguader

C del Gasòmetre

Platja de la
Barceloneta

Barceloneta
M

22 12

C del Doctor Aiguader

20 18

Plaça
de Pau
Vila

C Carbonell

C Pizarro

C de Balboa

C de Ginebra

LA BARCELONETA

Parc de la
Barceloneta

Pg Marítim de la Barceloneta

3

13

17

26

14

Plaça de la
Barceloneta

C de la Maquinista

C del Baluard

Plaça de la Font

24

19

Plaça
del Poeta
Bosca

C de Sant
Carles

15

21

Platja
de Sant
Sebastià

C de l'Almirall Cervera

Pg del Mar

Pg de Joan de Borbó

Marina

16

C del Almirall
Aixada

C del Judici

Moll de la Barceloneta

2

11

9

Plaça
del Mar

Moll de Balears

Port
Vell

6

10

Platja
de Sant
Miquel

MEDITERRANEAN
SEA

Pg Escullera

La Barceloneta

El Fòrum NEIGHBOURHOOD

(☎93 356 10 50; Ⓜ El Maresme Fòrum) Once an urban wasteland, this area has seen dramatic changes in recent years, with sparkling new buildings, open plazas and waterfront recreation areas. The most striking element is the eerily blue, triangular *2001: A Space Odyssey*–style **Edifici Fòrum** building by Swiss architects Herzog & de Meuron.

◎ L'Eixample

Stretching north, east and west of Plaça de Catalunya, L'Eixample (the Extension) was Barcelona's 19th-century answer to overcrowding in the medieval city.

Work on it began in 1869, following a design by Ildefons Cerdà, who specified a grid of wide streets with plazas that were formed by their cut-off corners. Cerdà also planned numerous public green spaces, but few survived the ensuing scramble for real estate.

The development of L'Eixample coincided with the city's Modernisme period and so it's home to many Modernista creations. Apart from La Sagrada Família, the principal ones are clustered on or near L'Eixample's main avenue, Passeig de Gràcia.

Along the area's grid of straight streets are the majority of the city's most expensive shops and hotels, plus a range of eateries, bars and clubs.

★ **La Sagrada Família** CHURCH

(☎93 207 30 31; www.sagradafamilia.cat; Carrer de Mallorca 401; adult/child under 11yr/senior & student €14.80/free/12.80; ⊙9am-8pm Apr-Sep, to 6pm Oct-Mar; Ⓜ Sagrada Família) If you have time for only one sightseeing outing, this should be it. La Sagrada Família inspires awe by its sheer verticality, and in the manner of the medieval cathedrals it emulates, it's still under construction after more than 100 years. When completed, the highest tower will be more than half as high again as those that stand today.

Unfinished it may be, but it attracts around 2.8 million visitors a year and is the most visited monument in Spain. The most important recent tourist was Pope Benedict XVI, who consecrated the church in a huge ceremony in November 2010.

The Temple Expiatori de la Sagrada Família (Expiatory Temple of the Holy Family) was Antoni Gaudí's all-consuming obsession. Given the commission by a conservative society that wished to build a temple as atonement for the city's sins of modernity, Gaudí saw its completion as his holy mission. As funds dried up, he contributed his own, and in the last years of his life he was never shy of pleading with anyone he thought a likely donor.

Gaudí devised a temple 95m long and 60m wide, able to seat 13,000 people, with a central tower 170m high above the transept (representing Christ) and another 17 of 100m or more. The 12 along the three facades represent the Apostles, while the remaining five represent the Virgin Mary and the four Evangelists. With his characteristic dislike for straight lines (there were

L'Eixample

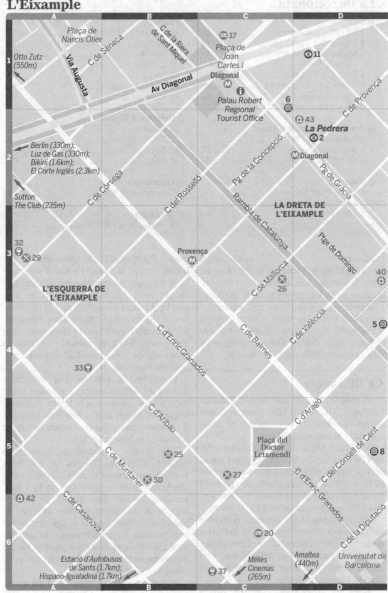

Otto Zutz (550m)

Plaça de Narcís Oller

C de Sèneca

Via Augusta

C de la Riera de Sant Miquel

Av Diagonal

17

Plaça de Joan Carles I

Diagonal

Palau Robert Regional Tourist Office

11

6

43

La Pedrera

2

Diagonal

Berlin (330m); Luz de Gas (330m); Bikini (1.6km); El Corte Inglés (2.3km)

Sutton The Club (235m)

C de Còrsega

C del Rosselló

Pg de la Concepció

Rambla de Catalunya

C de Provença

Pg de Gràcia

LA DRETA DE L'EIXAMPLE

Ptge de Domingo

32

29

Provença

L'ESQUERRA DE L'EIXAMPLE

C de Mallorca

26

40

C de Balmes

C de València

5

C d'Enric Granados

33

C d'Aribau

C d'Aragó

Plaça del Doctor Letamendi

25

C de Muntaner

30

27

C del Consell de Cent

8

42

C de Casanova

C d'Enric Granados

20

C de la Diputació

Estació d'Autobusos de Sants (1.7km); Hispano-Igualadina (1.7km)

37

Méliès Cinemas (265m)

Amaltea (440m)

Universitat de Barcelona

BARCELONA SIGHTS

none in nature, he said), Gaudí gave his towers swelling outlines inspired by the weird peaks of the holy mountain Montserrat outside Barcelona, and encrusted them with a tangle of sculpture that seems an outgrowth of the stone.

At Gaudí's death, only the crypt, the apse walls, one portal and one tower had been finished. Three more towers were added by 1930, completing the northeast (Nativity) facade. In 1936 anarchists burned and smashed the interior, including workshops,

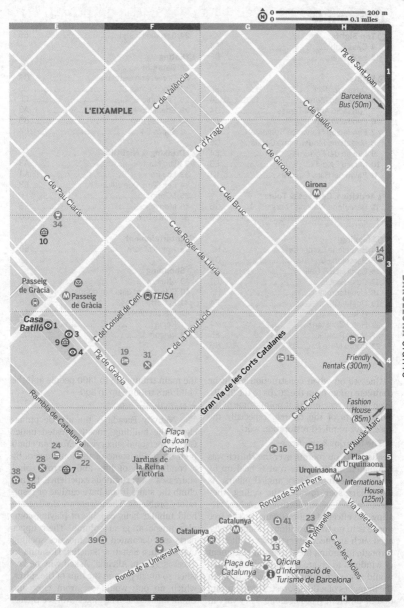

plans and models. Work began again in 1952, but controversy has always clouded progress. Opponents of the continuation of the project claim that the computer models based on what little of Gaudí's plans survived the anarchists' ire have led to the creation of a monster that has little to do with Gaudí's plans and style. It is a debate that appears to have little hope of resolution. Like or hate what is being done, the fascination it awakens is undeniable.

L'Eixample

Guesses on when construction might be complete range from the 2020s to the 2040s. Even before reaching that point, some of the oldest parts of the church, especially the apse, have required restoration work.

➡ The Interior & the Apse

Inside, work on roofing over the church was completed in 2010. The roof is held up by a forest of extraordinary angled pillars. As the pillars soar towards the ceiling, they sprout a web of supporting branches, creating the effect of a forest canopy. The tree image is in no way fortuitous – Gaudí envisaged such an effect. Everything was thought through, including the shape and placement of windows to create the mottled effect one would see with sunlight pouring through the branches of a thick forest. The pillars are of four different types of stone. They vary in colour and load-bearing strength, from the soft Montjuïc stone pillars along the lateral aisles through to granite, dark grey basalt and finally burgundy-tinged Iranian porphyry for the key columns at the intersection of the nave and transept. Tribunes built high above the aisles can host two choirs;

the main tribune up to 1300 people and the children's tribune up to 300.

➡ Nativity Facade

The Nativity Facade is the artistic pinnacle of the building, mostly created under Gaudí's personal supervision. You can climb high up inside some of the four towers by a combination of lifts and narrow spiral staircases – a vertiginous experience. Do not climb the stairs if you have cardiac or respiratory problems. The towers are destined to hold tubular bells capable of playing complex music at great volume. Their upper parts are decorated with mosaics spelling out 'Sanctus, Sanctus, Sanctus, Hosanna in Excelsis, Amen, Alleluia'. Asked why he lavished so much care on the tops of the spires, which no one would see from close up, Gaudí answered: 'The angels will see them.'

Three sections of the portal represent, from left to right, Hope, Charity and Faith. Among the forest of sculpture on the Charity portal you can see, low down, the manger surrounded by an ox, an ass, the shepherds and kings, and angel musicians. Some 30 different species of plant from around Catalonia are reproduced here, and the faces of the many figures are taken from plaster casts done of local people and the occasional one made from corpses in the local morgue!

Directly above the blue stained-glass window is the Archangel Gabriel's Annunciation to Mary. At the top is a green cypress tree, a refuge in a storm for the white doves of peace dotted over it. The mosaic work at the pinnacle of the towers is made from Murano glass, from Venice.

To the right of the facade is the curious **Claustre del Roser**, a Gothic style mini-cloister tacked on to the outside of the church (rather than the classic square enclosure of the great Gothic church monasteries). Once inside, look back to the intricately decorated entrance. On the lower right-hand side, you'll notice the sculpture of a reptilian devil handing a terrorist a bomb. Barcelona was regularly rocked by political violence and bombings were frequent in the decades prior to the civil war. The sculpture is one of several on the 'temptations of men and women'.

➡ **Passion Facade**

The southwest Passion Facade, on the theme of Christ's last days and death, was built between 1954 and 1978 based on surviving drawings by Gaudí, with four towers and a large, sculpture-bedecked portal. The sculptor, Josep Subirachs, worked on its decoration from 1986 to 2006. He did not attempt to imitate Gaudí, rather producing angular, controversial images of his own. The main series of sculptures, on three levels, are in an S-shaped sequence, starting with the Last Supper at the bottom left and ending with Christ's burial at the top right. Decorative work on the Passion Facade continues even today, as construction of the Glory Facade moves ahead.

To the right, in front of the Passion Facade, the **Escoles de Gaudí** is one of his simpler gems. Gaudí built this as a children's school, creating an original, undulating roof of brick that continues to charm architects to this day. Inside is a re-creation of Gaudí's modest office as it was when he died, and explanations of the geometric patterns and plans at the heart of his building techniques.

➡ **Glory Facade**

The Glory Facade is under construction and will, like the others, be crowned by four towers – the total of 12 representing the Twelve Apostles. Gaudí wanted it to be the most magnificent facade of the church. Inside

will be the narthex, a kind of foyer made up of 16 'lanterns', a series of hyperboloid forms topped by cones. Further decoration will make the whole building a microcosmic symbol of the Christian church, with Christ represented by a massive 170m central tower above the transept, and the five remaining planned towers symbolising the Virgin Mary and the four evangelists.

➡ **Museu Gaudí**

Open the same times as the church, the Museu Gaudí, below ground level, includes interesting material on Gaudí's life and other works, as well as models and photos of La Sagrada Família. You can see a good example of his plumb-line models that showed him the stresses and strains he could get away with in construction. A side hall towards the eastern end of the museum leads to a viewing point above the simple crypt in which the genius is buried. The crypt, where Masses are now held, can also be visited from the Carrer de Mallorca side of the church.

➡ **Exploring La Sagrada**

Although essentially a building site, the completed sections and museum may be explored at leisure. Fifty-minute guided tours (€4) are offered. Alternatively, pick up an audio tour (€4), for which you need ID. Enter from Carrer de Sardenya and Carrer de la Marina. Once inside, €2.50 will get you into lifts that rise up inside towers in the Nativity and Passion facades. These two facades, each with four sky-scraping towers, are the sides of the church. The main Glory Facade, on which work is underway, closes off the southeast end on Carrer de Mallorca.

⭐ **Casa Batlló**   ARCHITECTURE
(Map p250; ☑ 93 216 03 06; www.casabatllo.es; Passeig de Gràcia 43; adult/concessions/child under 7yr €21.50/€18.50/free; ☺ 9am-9pm daily; Ⓜ Passeig de Gràcia) One of the strangest residential

---

WANT MORE?

For in-depth information, reviews and recommendations at your fingertips, head to http://shop.lonelyplanet.com to purchase a downloadable PDF of Lonely Planet's *Barcelona City Guide*.

Alternatively, go to **Lonely Planet** (www.lonelyplanet.com/Spain/Barcelona) for planning advice, author recommendations, traveller reviews and insider tips.

La Sagrada Família

A TIMELINE

1882 Francesc del Villar is commissioned to construct a neo-Gothic church.

1883 Antoni Gaudí takes over as chief architect, and plans a far more ambitious church to hold 13,000 faithful.

1926 Death of Gaudí; work continues under Domènec Sugrañes. Much of the **apse** ❶ and **Nativity Facade** ❷ is complete.

1930 **Bell towers** ❸ of the Nativity Facade completed.

1936 Construction is interrupted by Spanish Civil War; anarchists destroy Gaudí's plans.

1939-40 Architect Francesc de Paula Quintana i Vidal restores the crypt and meticulously reassembles many of Gaudí's lost models, some of which can be seen in the **museum** ❹.

1976 Completion of **Passion Facade** ❺.

1986-2006 Sculptor Josep Subirachs adds sculptural details to the Passion Facade including the panels telling the story of Christ's last days, amid much criticism for employing a style far removed from what was thought typical of Gaudí.

2000 **Central nave vault** ❻ completed.

2010 Church completely roofed over; Pope Benedict XVI consecrates the church; work begins on a high-speed rail tunnel that will pass beneath the church's **Glory Facade** ❼.

2020-40 Projected completion date.

TOP TIPS

» **Light** The best light through the stained-glass windows of the Passion Facade bursts through into the heart of the church in the late afternoon.

» **Time** Visit at opening time on week-days to avoid the worst of the crowds.

» **Views** Head up the Nativity Facade bell towers for the views, as long queues generally await at the Passion Facade towers.

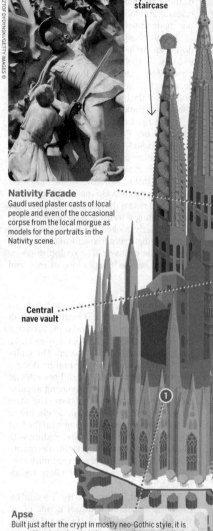

Spiral staircase

Nativity Facade
Gaudí used plaster casts of local people and even of the occasional corpse from the local morgue as models for the portraits in the Nativity scene.

Central nave vault

Apse
Built just after the crypt in mostly neo-Gothic style, it is capped by pinnacles that show a hint of the genius that Gaudí would later deploy in the rest of the church.

Bell towers
The towers (eight completed) of the three facades represent the 12 Apostles. Lifts whisk visitors up one tower of the Nativity and Passion Facades (the latter gets longer queues) for fine views.

NIKADA/GETTY IMAGES ©

Completed church
Along with the Glory Facade and its four towers, six other towers remain to be completed. They will represent the four Evangelists, the Virgin Mary and, soaring above them all over the transept, a 170m colossus symbolising Christ.

Glory Facade
This will be the most fanciful facade of all, with a narthex boasting 16 hyperboloid lanterns topped by cones that will look something like an organ made of melting ice cream.

Museu Gaudí
Jammed with old photos, drawings and restored plaster models that bring Gaudí's ambitions to life, the museum also houses an extraordinarily complex plumb-line device he used to calculate his constructions.

Escoles de Gaudí

Crypt
The first completed part of the church, the crypt is in largely neo-Gothic style and lies under the transept. Gaudí's burial place here can be seen from the Museu Gaudí.

JEKATERINA NIKITINA/GETTY IMAGES ©

Passion Facade
See the story of Christ's last days from Last Supper to burial in an S-shaped sequence from bottom to top of the facade. Check out the cryptogram in which the numbers always add up to 33, Christ's age at his death.

STEPHEN SAKS/GETTY IMAGES ©

buildings in Europe, this is Gaudí at his hallucinogenic best. The facade, sprinkled with bits of blue, mauve and green tiles and studded with wave-shaped window frames and balconies, rises to an uneven blue-tiled roof with a solitary tower.

It is one of the three houses on the block between Carrer del Consell de Cent and Carrer d'Aragó that gave it the playful name Manzana de la Discordia, meaning 'Apple (Block) of Discord'. The others are Puig i Cadafalch's Casa Amatller and Domènech i Montaner's Casa Lleó Morera. They were all renovated between 1898 and 1906 and show how eclectic a 'style' Modernisme was.

Locals know Casa Batlló variously as the *casa dels ossos* (house of bones) or *casa del drac* (house of the dragon). It's easy enough to see why. The balconies look like the bony jaws of some strange beast and the roof represents Sant Jordi (St George) and the dragon. Even the roof was built to look like the shape of an animal's back, with shiny scales – the 'spine' changes colour as you walk around. If you stare long enough at the building, it seems almost to be a living being. Before going inside, take a look at the pavement. Each paving piece carries stylised images of an octopus and a starfish, Gaudí designs originally cooked up for Casa Batlló.

When Gaudí was commissioned to refashion this building, he went to town inside and out. The internal light wells shimmer with tiles of deep sea blue. Gaudí eschewed the straight line, and so the staircase wafts you up to the 1st (main) floor, where the salon looks on to Passeig de Gràcia. Everything

swirls: the ceiling is twisted into a vortex around its sunlike lamp; the doors, window and skylights are dreamy waves of wood and coloured glass. The same themes continue in the other rooms and covered terrace. The attic is characterised by Gaudí trademark hyperboloid arches. Twisting, tiled chimney pots add a surreal touch to the roof.

Museu de la Música   MUSEUM

(☑ 93 256 36 50; www.museumusica.bcn.cat; Carrer de Lepant 150; adult/student €5/4, 3-8pm Sun free; ⊙ 10am-6pm Tue-Sat, to 8pm Sun; M Monumental) Some 500 instruments (less than a third of those held) are on show in this museum, housed on the 2nd floor of the administration building in L'Auditori, the city's main classical-music concert hall.

Instruments range from a 17th-century baroque guitar through to lutes (look out for the many-stringed 1641 archilute from Venice), violins, Japanese kotos, sitars from India, eight organs (some dating from the 18th century), pianos, a varied collection of drums and other percussion instruments from across Spain and beyond, along with all sorts of phonographs and gramophones. There are some odd pieces indeed, like the *buccèn*, a snake-head-adorned brass instrument. Much of the documentary and sound material can be enjoyed through audiovisual displays as you proceed.

From Tuesday to Sunday at 3.30pm, the museum holds a **concert** (€15, including museum admission), in which musicians perform on rare instruments held in the collection.

Casa Amatller   ARCHITECTURE

(Map p250; ☑ 93 487 72 17; www.amatller.org; Passeig de Gràcia 41; tour €10; ⊙ tour Sat; M Passeig de Gràcia) **FREE** One of Puig i Cadafalch's most striking bits of Modernista fantasy, Casa Amatller combines Gothic window frames with a stepped gable borrowed from Dutch urban architecture. But the busts and reliefs of dragons, knights and other characters dripping off the main facade are pure caprice.

Casa Lleó Morera   ARCHITECTURE

(Map p250; ☑ 93 676 27 33; www.casalleomorera.com; Passeig de Gràcia 35; adult/concession/child under 12yr €15/€13.50/free; ⊙ guided tour in English 10am Mon-Sat; M Passeig de Gràcia) Domènech i Montaner's 1905 contribution to the Manzana de la Discordia, with Modernista carving outside and a bright, tiled lobby in which floral motifs predominate, is perhaps the least odd-looking of the three

APPLE OF DISCORD

Casa Batlló is the centrepiece of the so-called Manzana de la Discordia (Apple of Discord – in a play on words, *manzana* means both city block and apple), along with Casa Lleó Morera and Casa Amatller, on the western side of Passeig de Gràcia between Carrer del Consell de Cent and Carrer d'Aragó. All three buildings were completed between 1898 and 1906. According to Greek myth, the original Apple of Discord was tossed onto Mt Olympus by Eris (Discord) with orders that it be given to the most beautiful goddess, sparking jealousies that helped start the Trojan War.

main buildings on the block. In 2014 part of the building was opened to the public (by guided tour only), so you can appreciate the 1st floor, giddy with swirling sculptures, rich mosaics and whimsical decor.

Museu del Perfum   MUSEUM
(Map p250; ☑ 93 216 01 21; www.museudelperfum.com; Passeig de Gràcia 39; adult/child €5/3; ⊙10.30am-2pm & 4.30-8pm Mon-Fri, 11am-2pm Sat; M Passeig de Gràcia) Housed in the back of the Regia (Map p250; ☑ 93 216 01 21; www.regia.es; Passeig de Gràcia 39; ⊙ 9.30am-8.30pm Mon-Fri, 10.30am-8.30pm Sat; M Passeig de Gràcia) perfume store, this museum contains everything from ancient Egyptian and Roman (the latter mostly from the 1st to 3rd centuries AD) scent receptacles to classic eau de cologne bottles – all in all, some 5000 bottles of infinite shapes, sizes and histories.

★ La Pedrera   ARCHITECTURE
(Casa Milà; Map p250; ☑ 93 484 59 00; www.lapedrera.com; Carrer de Provença 261-265; adult/student/child €16.50/14.85/8.25; ⊙ 9am-8pm Mar-Oct, to 6.30pm Nov-Feb; M Diagonal) This undulating beast is another madcap Gaudí masterpiece, built in 1905–10 as a combined apartment and office block. Formally called Casa Milà, after the businessman who commissioned it, it is better known as La Pedrera (the Quarry) because of its uneven grey stone facade, which ripples around the corner of Carrer de Provença.

Fundació Antoni Tàpies   GALLERY
(Map p250; ☑ 93 487 03 15; www.fundaciotapies.org; Carrer d'Aragó 255; adult/concession €7/5.60; ⊙10am-7pm Tue-Sun; M Passeig de Gràcia) The Fundació Antoni Tàpies is both a pioneering Modernista building (completed in 1885) and the major collection of leading 20th-century Catalan artist Antoni Tàpies. A man known for his esoteric work, Tàpies died in February 2012, aged 88; he leaves behind a powerful range of paintings and a foundation intended to promote contemporary artists.

Museu del Modernisme Català   MUSEUM
(Map p250; ☑ 93 272 28 96; www.mmcat.cat; Carrer de Balmes 48; adult/concession €10/€8.50; ⊙10am-8pm Mon-Sat, to 2pm Sun; M Passeig de Gràcia) Housed in a Modernista building, the ground floor seems like a big Modernista furniture showroom. Several items by Antoni Gaudí, including chairs from Casa Batlló and a mirror from Casa Calvet, are supplemented by a host of items by his lesser-known contemporaries, including

DON'T MISS

TOP FIVE FOR ART LOVERS
....
➡ Museu Nacional d'Art de Catalunya (p264)

➡ Museu Picasso (p246)

➡ Fundació Joan Miró (p264)

➡ Macba (Museu d'Art Contemporani de Barcelona; p243)

➡ Fundació Antoni Tàpies

some typically whimsical, mock medieval pieces by Puig i Cadafalch.

Palau del Baró Quadras   ARCHITECTURE
(Map p250; ☑ 93 467 80 00; Avinguda Diagonal 373; ⊙8am-8pm Mon-Fri; M Diagonal) FREE Puig i Cadafalch designed Palau del Baró Quadras (built 1902–06) in an exuberant Gothic-inspired style. The main facade is its most intriguing, with a soaring, glassed-in gallery. Take a closer look at the gargoyles and reliefs – the pair of toothy fish and the sword-wielding knight clearly have the same artistic signature as the architect behind Casa Amatller. Decor inside is eclectic, but dominated by Middle Eastern and East Asian themes.

Recinte Modernista de Sant Pau   ARCHITECTURE
(☑ 93 553 78 01; www.santpaubarcelona.org; Carrer de Cartagena 167; adult/concession/child €8/5.60/free; ⊙10am-6.30pm Mon-Sat, to 2.30pm Sun; M Hospital de Sant Pau) Domènech i Montaner outdid himself as architect and philanthropist with the Modernista Hospital de la Santa Creu i de Sant Pau, redubbed in 2014 the 'Recinte Modernista'. It was long considered one of the city's most important hospitals, and only recently repurposed, its various spaces becoming cultural centres, offices and something of a monument. The complex, including 16 pavilions – together with the Palau de la Música Catalana, a joint World Heritage site – is lavishly decorated and each pavilion is unique.

Torre Agbar   ARCHITECTURE
(www.torreagbar.com; Avinguda Diagonal 225; M Glòries) Barcelona's very own cucumber-shaped tower, Jean Nouvel's luminous Torre Agbar, is among the most daring additions to the skyline since the first towers of La Sagrada Família went up. Completed in 2005, it shimmers at night in shades of midnight blue and lipstick red. At the time

of publication, the Hyatt group was in negotiations to purchase the building and transform it into a luxury hotel.

Fundación Francisco Godia
GALLERY

(Map p250; ☑93 272 31 80; www.fundacionfgodia.org; Carrer de la Diputació 250; adult/child under 6yr/student €6/free/3; ☉10am-8pm Mon & Wed-Sat, 10am-3pm Sun; Ⓜ Passeig de Gràcia) Francisco Godia (1921–90), head of one of Barcelona's great establishment families, liked fast cars (he came sixth in the 1956 Grand Prix season driving Maseratis) and fine art. An intriguing mix of medieval art, ceramics and modern paintings make up this varied private collection.

Museu Egipci
MUSEUM

(Map p250; ☑93 488 01 88; www.museuegipci.com; Carrer de València 284; adult/senior & student €11/8; ☉10am-8pm Mon-Sat, to 2pm Sun; Ⓜ Passeig de Gràcia) Hotel magnate Jordi Clos has spent much of his life collecting ancient Egyptian artefacts, brought together in this private museum. It's divided into different thematic areas (the Pharaoh, religion, funerary practices, mummification, crafts etc) and boasts an interesting variety of exhibits.

Fundació Suñol
GALLERY

(Map p250; ☑93 496 10 32; www.fundaciosunol.org; Passeig de Gràcia 98; adult/concession/child €4/2/free; ☉11am-2pm & 4-8pm Mon-Fri, 4-8pm Sat; Ⓜ Diagonal) Rotating exhibitions of portions of this private collection of mostly 20th-century art (some 1200 works in total) offer anything from Man Ray's photography to sculptures by Alberto Giacometti. Over two floors, you are most likely to run into Spanish artists, anyone from Picasso to Jaume Plensa, along with a sprinkling of others from abroad.

DEADLY SERIOUS

Museu de Carrosses Fúnebres
(☑93 484 19 99; www.cbsa.cat; Carrer de la Mare de Déu de Port 56-58; ☉10am-2pm Wed-Sun; ☐9, 21) FREE is probably the weirdest museum in town. This basement hearse museum is the place to come if you want to see how the great and good have been transported to their final resting places in Barcelona since the 18th century. Solemn, wigged mannequins and life-size model horses accompany a series of dark hearses.

◉ Gràcia

Gràcia lies north of L'Eixample. Once a separate village and, in the 19th century, an industrial district famous for its Republican and liberal ideas, it became fashionable among radical and bohemian types in the 1960s and '70s. Now more sedate and gentrified, it retains a very Catalan feel, a mixed-class population (with a high rate of students, both local and from abroad) and a slightly rebellious air (witness all the Catalan nationalist youth graffiti and the occasional surviving squat). Gràcia's interest lies in the atmosphere of its narrow streets, small plazas and its multitude of bars and restaurants.

The liveliest plazas are Plaça del Sol, Plaça de la Vila de Gràcia with its clock tower (a favourite meeting place) and Plaça de la Virreina with the 17th-century Església de Sant Joan (Map p259). Approximately five blocks west of Plaça de la Vila de Gràcia, there's a big covered market, the Mercat de la Llibertat (☑93 217 09 95; www.mercatllibertat.com; Plaça de la Llibertat 27; ☉8am-8pm Mon-Fri, 8am-3pm Sat; ☐FGC Gràcia) FREE. West of Gràcia's main street, Carrer Gran de Gràcia (from Fontana metro station, walk one block north to Carrer de les Carolines and turn left), seek out an early Gaudí house, the turreted, vaguely Mudéjar Casa Vicens (Carrer de les Carolines 22; ☐FGC Plaça Molina); it's not open to the public.

Park Güell
PARK

(☑93 409 18 31; www.parkguell.cat; Carrer d'Olot 7; adult/child €7/€4.50 admission to central area; ☉8am-9.30pm daily; ☐24 or 32, Ⓜ Lesseps or Vallcarca) North of Gràcia and about 4km from Plaça de Catalunya, Park Güell is where Gaudí turned his hand to landscape gardening. It's a strange, enchanting place where his passion for natural forms really took flight – to the point where the artificial almost seems more natural than the natural.

Park Güell originated in 1900, when Count Eusebi Güell bought a tree-covered hillside (then outside Barcelona) and hired Gaudí to create a miniature city of houses for the wealthy in landscaped grounds. The project was a commercial flop and was abandoned in 1914 – but not before Gaudí had created 3km of roads and walks, steps, a plaza and two gatehouses in his inimitable manner. In 1922 the city bought the estate for use as a public park.

Just inside the main entrance on Carrer d'Olot, recognisable by the two Hansel-and-Gretel gatehouses, is the park's Centre d'Interpretaciò, in the Pavelló de Consergeria, which is a typically curvaceous former porter's home that hosts a display on Gaudí's building methods and the history of the park. There are nice views from the top floor.

The steps up from the entrance, guarded by a mosaic dragon/lizard (a copy of which you can buy in many downtown souvenir shops), lead to the **Sala Hipóstila** (aka the Doric Temple). This is a forest of 88 stone columns, some of which lean like mighty trees bent by the weight of time, originally intended as a market. To the left curves a gallery whose twisted stonework columns and roof give the effect of a cloister beneath tree roots – a motif repeated in several places in the park. On top of the Sala Hipóstila is a broad open space whose centrepiece is the **Banc de Trencadís**, a tiled bench curving sinuously around its perimeter and designed by one of Gaudí's closest colleagues, architect Josep Maria Jujol (1879–1949). With Gaudí, however, there is always more than meets the eye. This giant platform was designed as a kind of catchment area for rainwater washing down the hillside. The water is filtered through a layer of stone and sand, and it drains down through the columns to an underground cistern.

The spired house over to the right is the **Casa-Museu Gaudí**, where Gaudí lived for most of his last 20 years (1906–26). It contains furniture by him (including items that were once at home in La Pedrera, Casa Batlló and Casa Calvet) and other memorabilia. The house was built in 1904 by Francesc Berenguer i Mestres as a prototype for the 60 or so houses that were originally planned here.

Much of the park is still wooded, but it's laced with pathways. The best views are from the cross-topped **Turó del Calvari** in the southwest corner.

The walk from metro stop Lesseps is signposted. From the Vallcarca stop, it is marginally shorter and the uphill trek eased by escalators. Bus 24 drops you at an entrance near the top of the park.

The park is extremely popular (it gets an estimated 4 million visitors a year, about 86% of them tourists) and in 2013 an entrance fee was imposed on the central area containing most of its attractions. Access is limited to a certain number of people every half-hour, and it's wise to book ahead online.

Gràcia

◎ Sights
1 Església de Sant Joan A1

⚏ Sleeping
2 Aparteasy B4

✖ Eating
3 El Tossal B3
4 La Nena A2
5 Les Tres a la Cuina B1
6 Sol i Lluna A1

◎ Drinking & Nightlife
7 La Cigale B2
8 Le Journal A3
9 Raïm B3
10 Viblioteca A2

✪ Entertainment
11 Verdi A1

⬡ Shopping
12 Mercat de l'Abaceria Central B2

The Genius of Gaudí

The name Gaudí has become a byword for Barcelona and, through his unique architectural wonders, one of the principal magnets for visitors to the city.

A Catholic & a Catalan

Born in Reus and initially trained in metalwork, Antoni Gaudí i Cornet (1852–1926) personifies, and largely transcends, the Modernisme movement that brought a thunderclap of innovative greatness to turn-of-the-century Barcelona. Gaudí was a devout Catholic and Catalan nationalist, and his creations were a conscious expression of Catalan identity and, in some cases, great piety.

The Masterworks

He devoted much of the latter part of his life to what remains Barcelona's call sign: the unfinished Sagrada Família. His inspiration in the first instance was Gothic, but he also sought to emulate the harmony he observed in nature, eschewing the straight line and favouring curvaceous forms.

Gaudí used complex string models weighted with plumb lines to make his calculations. You can see examples in the upstairs mini-museum in La Pedrera.

The architect's work evokes sinuous movement often with a dreamlike or surreal quality. The private apartment house Casa Batlló is a fine example in which all appears as a riot of the unnaturally natural – or the naturally unnatural. Not only are straight lines eliminated, but the lines between real and unreal, sober and dream-drunk, good sense and play are all blurred. Depending

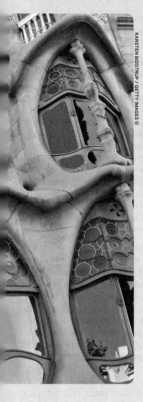

1. Casa Batlló
2. Palau Güell
3. La Pedrera

KARSTEN BIDSTRUP / GETTY IMAGES ©

CHRISTOPHER GROENHOUT / GETTY IMAGES ©

MAREMAGNUM / GETTY IMAGES ©

on how you look at the facade, you might see St George defeating a dragon, or a series of fleshless sea monsters straining out of the wall.

He seems to have particularly enjoyed himself with rooftops. At La Pedrera and Palau Güell, in particular, he created all sorts of fantastical, multicoloured tile figures as chimney pots looking like anything from *Alice in Wonderland* mushrooms to *Star Wars* imperial troopers.

Saint Gaudí?

Much like his work in progress, La Sagrada Família, Gaudí's story is far from over. In March 2000 the Vatican decided to proceed with the examination of the case for canonising him, and pilgrims already stop by the crypt to pay homage

to him. One of the key sculptors at work on the church, the Japanese Etsuro Sotoo, converted to Catholicism because of his passion for Gaudí.

GREATEST HITS

➡ La Sagrada Família (p249), a symphony of religious devotion.

➡ La Pedrera (p257), dubbed 'the Quarry' because of its flowing facade.

➡ Casa Batlló (p253), a fairy-tale dragon.

➡ Park Güell (p258), a park full of Modernista twists.

➡ Palau Güell (p243), one of Gaudí's earliest commissions.

⊙ Tibidabo

Tibidabo (512m) is the highest hill in the wooded range that forms the backdrop to Barcelona and is a good place for some fresh air and fine views. It gets its name from the devil, who, trying to tempt Christ, took him to a high place and said, in the Latin version: *'Haec omnia tibi dabo si cadens adoraberis me'* ('All this I will give you, if you will fall down and worship me').

CosmoCaixa MUSEUM
(Museu de la Ciència; ☎ 93 212 60 50; www.fundacio.lacaixa.es; Carrer de Isaac Newton 26; adult/child €4/free; ⊙ 10am-8pm Tue-Sun; 🚌 60, 🚇 FGC Avinguda Tibidabo) Kids (and kids at heart) are fascinated by displays here and this science museum has become one of the city's most popular attractions. The single greatest highlight is the recreation over 1 sq km of a chunk of flooded Amazon rainforest (Bosc Inundat). More than 100 species of Amazon flora and fauna (including anacondas, colourful poisonous frogs and caymans) prosper in this unique, living diorama in which you can even experience a tropical downpour.

Parc d'Atraccions AMUSEMENT PARK
(☎ 93 211 79 42; www.tibidabo.cat; Plaça de Tibidabo 3-4; adult/child €29/10.30; ⊙ closed Jan-Feb) The reason most *barcelonins* come up to Tibidabo is for some thrills in this funfair, close to the top funicular station. Here you'll find whirling high-speed rides and high-tech 4D cinema, as well as old-fashioned amusement, including an old steam train and the

Museu d'Autòmats, with its collection of automated puppets going as far back as 1880. Check the website for opening times.

Temple del Sagrat Cor CHURCH
(Church of the Sacred Heart; ☎ 93 417 56 86; Plaça de Tibidabo; lift €2; ⊙ 7am-8pm, lift 10am-8pm) FREE The Church of the Sacred Heart, looming above the top funicular station, is meant to be Barcelona's answer to Paris' Sacré-Cœur. The church, built from 1902 to 1961 in a mix of styles with some Modernista influence, is certainly as visible as its Parisian namesake, and even more vilified by aesthetes. It's actually two churches, one on top of the other. The top one is surmounted by a giant statue of Christ and has a lift to take you to the roof for the panoramic (and often wind-chilled) views.

Jardins del Laberint d'Horta GARDENS
(☎ 93 413 24 00; Passeig del Castanyers 1; adult/student €2.23/1.42, Wed & Sun free; ⊙ 10am-sunset; 🚹; 🚇 Mundet) Laid out in the twilight years of the 18th century by Antoni Desvalls, Marquès d'Alfarras i de Llupià, this carefully manicured park remained a private family idyll until the 1970s, when it was opened to the public. Many a fine party and theatrical performance was held here over the years, but it now serves as a kind of museum-park. The gardens take their name from a maze in their centre, but other paths take you past a pleasant artificial lake *(estany)*, waterfalls, a neoclassical pavilion and a false cemetery. The last is inspired by 19th-century romanticism, characterised by an obsession with a swooning, anaemic (some might say silly)

ℹ GETTING TO TIBIDABO

Take one of the frequent Ferrocarrils de la Generalitat de Catalunya (FGC) trains to Avinguda de Tibidabo from Catalunya station on Plaça de Catalunya (€2, 10 minutes). Outside Avinguda de Tibidabo station, hop on the *tramvia blau* (one way €4.20, 15 minutes, every 15 or 30 minutes 10am to 6pm Saturdays, Sundays and holidays), Barcelona's last surviving old-style tram. It runs between fancy Modernista mansions – of particular note is Casa Roviralta, now home to a well-known grill restaurant, El Asador de Aranda (☎ 93 417 01 15; www.asadordearanda.com; Av del Tibidabo 31; mains €20-22; ⊙ 1-4pm daily & 8-11pm Mon-Sat; 🚇 Av Tibidabo) – and Plaça del Doctor Andreu and has been doing so since 1901. When the tram isn't in operation, a bus serves the route.

From Plaça del Doctor Andreu (also called Plaça del Funicular), the Tibidabo funicular railway climbs through the woods to Plaça de Tibidabo at the top of the hill (return €7.70, five minutes). Departures start at 10.15am and continue until shortly after the park's closing time.

An alternative is bus T2, the 'Tibibús', from Plaça de Catalunya to Plaça de Tibidabo (€3, 30 minutes). It runs every 30 to 50 minutes on Saturday, Sunday and holidays; purchase tickets on the bus. The last bus down leaves Tibidabo 30 minutes after the Parc d'Atraccions closes.

vision of death. The labyrinth, in the middle of these cool gardens (somehow odd in this environment, with modern apartments and ring roads nearby), can be surprisingly frustrating! Aim to reach the centre from the bottom end, and then exit towards the ponds and neoclassical pavilion. This is a good one for kids. Scenes of the film adaptation of Patrick Süskind's novel *Perfume* were shot in the gardens. To reach the gardens, take the right exit upstairs at Mundet Metro station; on emerging, turn right and then left along the main road (with football fields on your left) and then the first left uphill to the gardens (about five minutes).

◉ Collserola

Parc de Collserola PARK
(☏93 280 35 52; www.parcnaturalcollserola.cat; Carretera de l'Església 92; ⊙ Centre d'Informació 9.30am-3pm, Can Coll 9.30am-3pm Sun & holidays, closed Jul & Aug; ⓡFGC Peu del Funicular, funicular Baixador de Vallvidrera) *Barcelonins* needing an escape from the city without heading too far into the countryside seek out this extensive, 8000-hectare park in the hills. It is a great place to hike and bike and bristles with eateries and snack bars. Pick up a map from the **Centre d'Informació**. The principal point of interest is the sprawling **Museu-Casa Verdaguer**. Catalonia's revered writer Jacint Verdaguer lived in this late-18th-century country house before his death on 10 July 1902. Beyond, the park has various other minor highlights, including a smattering of country chapels (some Romanesque), the ragged ruins of the 14th-century Castellciuro castle in the west, various lookout points and, to the north, the 15th-century **Can Coll**, a grand farmhouse. It's used as an environmental education centre where you can see how richer farmers lived around the 17th to 19th centuries.

Torre de Collserola LOOKOUT
(☏93 406 93 54; www.torredecollserola.com; Carretera de Vallvidrera al Tibidabo; adult/child €6/4; ⊙noon-2pm & 3.30-8pm Wed-Sun Jul & Aug, noon-2pm & 3.15-6pm Sat, Sun & holidays Sep-Jun, closed Jan & Feb; ⓘ111, Funicular de Vallvidrera) Sir Norman Foster designed the 288m-high Torre de Collserola telecommunications tower, which was completed in 1992. There is an external glass lift to the visitors' observation area, 115m up, where there are some magnificent views – up to 70km on a clear day. All of Barcelona's TV and radio sets are

DON'T MISS

TOP HISTORIC SITES
• •
➜ Museu d'Història de Barcelona (p239)

➜ Museu d'Història de Catalunya (p247)

➜ Museu-Monestir de Pedralbes (p263)

➜ Museu Marítim (p244)

➜ MUHBA Refugi 307 (p264)

transmitted from here, and repeater stations across Catalonia are also controlled from this tower.

◉ Pedralbes

A wealthy residential area north of the Zona Universitària, Pedralbes is named after the eponymous convent that is a key attraction in the area.

Jardins del Palau de Pedralbes PARK
(Avinguda Diagonal 686; ⊙10am-8pm Apr-Oct, to 6pm Nov-Mar; ⓂPalau Reial) **FREE** A few steps from busy Avinguda Diagonal lies this small enchanting green space. Sculptures, fountains, citrus trees, bamboo groves, fragrant eucalyptus, towering cypresses and bougainvillea-covered nooks lie scattered along the paths criss-crossing these peaceful gardens. Among the little-known treasures here are a vine-covered parabolic pergola and a gurgling fountain of Hercules, both designed by Antoni Gaudí.

Museu-Monestir de Pedralbes MONASTERY
(☏93 256 34 34; www.bcn.cat/monestirpedralbes; Baixada del Monestir 9; adult/child €7/5, free 3-8pm Sun; ⊙10am-5pm Tue-Fri, to 7pm Sat, to 8pm Sun; ⓘ22, 63, 64 or 75, ⓡFGC Reina Elisenda) This peaceful old convent was first opened to the public in 1983 and is now a museum of monastic life (the few remaining nuns have moved into more modern neighbouring buildings). It stands at the top of Avinguda de Pedralbes in a residential area that was countryside until the 20th century, but which remains a divinely quiet corner of Barcelona.

Camp Nou STADIUM
(☏902 189900; www.fcbarcelona.com; Carrer d'Aristides Maillol; adult/child €23/17; ⊙10am-7.30pm Mon-Sat, to 2.30pm Sun; ⓂPalau Reial) Among Barcelona's most-visited sites is

the massive stadium of Camp Nou (which means New Field in Catalan), home to the legendary Futbol Club Barcelona. Attending a game amid the roar of the crowds is an unforgettable experience. Football fans who aren't able to see a game can get a taste of all the excitement at the museum, with its multimedia exhibits, and a self-guided tour of the stadium.

◉ El Poble Sec

Draped on the eastern slopes of Montjuïc down to Avinguda del Paral·lel, working-class El Poble Sec (the Dry Village) is short on sights but hides several interesting bars and eateries. Until the 1960s the neighbourhood was the centre of Barcelona nightlife, crammed with theatres and cabarets. A handful of them survives and one, the Sala Apolo (p293), converted itself successfully into a club.

MUHBA Refugi 307　　　　HISTORIC SITE
(Map p266; ☑ 93 256 21 22; www.museuhistoria. bcn.cat; Carrer Nou de la Rambla 169; admission incl tour adult/child under 7yr €3.40/free; ☺ tours 10.30am, 11.30am & 2.30pm Sun; Ⓜ Paral·lel) Part of the Museu d'Història de Barcelona (MUHBA), this is a shelter that dates back to the days of the Spanish Civil War. Barcelona was the city most heavily bombed from the air during this war and had more than 1300 air-raid shelters. Local citizens started digging this one under a fold of Montjuïc in March 1937.

◉ Montjuïc

Montjuïc, the hill overlooking the city centre from the southwest, is dotted with museums, soothing gardens and the main group of 1992 Olympic sites, along with a handful of theatres and clubs.

The name Montjuïc (Jewish Mountain) indicates there was once a Jewish cemetery, and possibly settlement, here. Montjuïc also has a darker history: its castle was used as a political prison and execution site by various governments, including the Republicans during the civil war and Franco thereafter.

The first main burst of building on Montjuïc came in the 1920s, when it was chosen as the stage for Barcelona's 1929 World Exhibition. The Estadi Olímpic, the Poble Espanyol and some museums all date from this time. Montjuïc got a facelift and more new buildings for the 1992 Olympics.

Abundant roads and paths, with occasional escalators, plus buses and a chairlift, allow you to visit Montjuïc's sights in any order you choose. The main attractions – the Museu Nacional d'Art de Catalunya, CaixaForum, the Poble Espanyol, the Pavelló Mies van der Rohe, the Fundació Joan Miró, the Estadi Olímpic and the views from the castle – make for a full couple of days' sightseeing.

Plaça d'Espanya　　　　SQUARE
(Map p266) The approach to Montjuïc from Plaça d'Espanya gives you the full benefit of the landscaping on the hill's northern side and allows Montjuïc to unfold for you from the bottom up. On Plaça d'Espanya's northern side is the former Plaça de Braus Les Arenes bullring, built in 1900 and slowly being converted into a shopping and leisure centre by Sir Richard Rogers.

Behind the bullring is Parc Joan Miró, created in the 1980s, and worth a quick detour for Miró's giant, highly phallic sculpture *Dona i Ocell* (Woman and Bird) in the northwest corner.

★ **Museu Nacional d'Art de Catalunya (MNAC)**　　MUSEUM
(Map p266; ☑ 93 622 03 76; www.museunacional. cat; Mirador del Palau Nacional; adult/senior & child under 16yr/student €12/free/€8.40, 1st Sun of month free; ☺ 10am-8pm Tue-Sat, to 3pm Sun, library 10am-6pm Mon-Fri; Ⓜ Espanya) From across the city, the bombastic neobaroque silhouette of the Palau Nacional can be seen on the slopes of Montjuïc. Built for the 1929 World Exhibition and restored in 2005, it houses a vast collection of mostly Catalan art spanning the early Middle Ages to the early 20th century. The high point is the collection of extraordinary Romanesque frescoes.

★ **Fundació Joan Miró**　　MUSEUM
(Map p266; ☑ 93 443 94 70; www.fundaciomiro-bcn.org; Parc de Montjuïc; adult/child €11/free; ☺ 10am-8pm Tue-Sat, to 9.30pm Thu, to 2.30pm Sun & holidays; ☐ 55, 150, funicular Paral·lel) Joan Miró, the city's best-known 20th-century artistic progeny, bequeathed this art foundation to his hometown in 1971. Its light-filled buildings, designed by close friend and architect Josep Lluís Sert (who also built Miró's Mallorca studios), are crammed with seminal works, from Miró's earliest timid sketches to paintings from his last years.

Castell de Montjuïc　　FORTRESS, GARDENS
(Map p266; ☑ 93 256 44 45; www.bcn.cat/castell-demontjuic; Carretera de Montjuïc 66; adult/conces-

ROMANESQUE TREASURES IN THE MUSEU NACIONAL D'ART DE CATALUNYA

The Romanesque art section in the Museu Nacional d'Art de Catalunya constitutes one of Europe's greatest such collections and is an absolute must for lovers of medieval art – and an excellent place to learn about it for those who have had few previous opportunities. The collection consists mainly of 11th- and 12th-century murals, woodcarvings and altar frontals – painted, bas-relief wooden panels that were forerunners of the elaborate *retablos* (altarpieces) that adorned later churches. Gathered from decaying rural churches in northern Catalonia early last century, they are a surprising treasure of vivid colour, discrediting the idea that medieval churches were bereft of decoration. The two outstanding items are an image of Christ in Majesty, done around 1123 and taken from the apse of the Església de Sant Climent de Taüll in northwest Catalonia, and an apse image of the Virgin Mary and Christ Child from the nearby Església de Santa Maria de Taüll.

sions/child €5/€3/free, Sun pm & 1st Sun of month free; ☉10am-8pm; ☐150, cable car Telefèric de Montjuïc to Castell de Montjuïc) This forbidding *castell* (castle or fort) dominates the southeastern heights of Montjuïc and enjoys commanding views over the Mediterranean. It dates, in its present form, from the late 17th and 18th centuries. For most of its dark history, it has been used to watch over the city and as a political prison and killing ground.

Jardins GARDENS
Towards the foot of the fortress, above the main road to Tarragona, the Jardins de Mossèn Costa i Llobera (Map p266; www.bcn. cat/parcsijardins; Carretera de Miramar 1; ☉10am-sunset; cable car Transbordador Aeri to Miramar) FREE have a good collection of tropical and desert plants – including a veritable forest of cacti. Near the Estació Parc Montjuïc (funicular station) are the ornamental Jardins de Mossèn Cinto Verdaguer, full of beautiful bulbs and aquatic plants. East across the road are the landscaped Jardins Joan Brossa (Map p266; ☉10am-sunset; cable car Telefèric de Montjuïc to Mirador) FREE. These gardens contain many Mediterranean species, from cypresses to pines and a few palms. From the Jardins del Mirador, opposite the Estació Mirador, you have fine views over the port of Barcelona.

Poble Espanyol CULTURAL CENTRE
(Map p266; www.poble-espanyol.com; Avinguda de Francesc Ferrer i Guàrdia 13; adult/child €11/6.25; ☉9am-8pm Mon, to midnight Tue-Thu & Sun, to 3am Fri, to 4am Sat; ☐13, 23, 150, Ⓜ Espanya) Welcome to Spain! All of it! This 'Spanish Village' is both a cheesy souvenir hunters' haunt and an intriguing scrapbook of Spanish architecture built for the Spanish crafts section of the 1929 World Exhibition. You

can meander from Andalucía to the Balearic Islands in the space of a couple of hours, visiting surprisingly good copies of Spain's characteristic buildings.

Fundació Fran Daurel MUSEUM
(Map p266; www.fundaciofrandaurel.com; Avinguda Francesc Ferrer i Guàrdia 13; ☉10am-7pm) FREE The Fundació Fran Daurel (in Poble Espanyol) is an eclectic collection of 300 works of art including sculptures, prints, ceramics and tapestries by modern artists ranging from Picasso and Miró to more contemporary figures, including Miquel Barceló. The foundation also has a sculpture garden, boasting 27 pieces, nearby the Fundació and within the grounds of Poble Espanyol (look for the Montblanc gate). Frequent temporary exhibitions broaden the offerings further.

Font Màgica FOUNTAIN
(Map p266; ☎93 316 10 00; Avinguda de la Reina Maria Cristina; ☉every 30min 7-9pm Fri & Sat Oct-Apr, 9.30-11pm Thu-Sun May-Sep; Ⓜ Espanya) A huge fountain that crowns the long sweep of the Avinguda de la Reina Maria Cristina to the grand facade of the Palau Nacional, Font Màgica is a unique performance in which the water can look like seething fireworks or a mystical cauldron of colour.

Pavelló Mies van der Rohe ARCHITECTURE
(Map p266; ☎93 423 40 16; www.miesbcn.com; Avinguda de Francesc Ferrer i Guàrdia 7; adult/child €5/free; ☉10am-8pm; Ⓜ Espanya) The Pavelló Mies van der Rohe is not only a work of breathtaking beauty and simplicity, it is a highly influential building emblematic of the modern movement. The structure has been the subject of many studies and interpretations, and it has inspired several generations of architects.

Montjuïc & Poble Sec

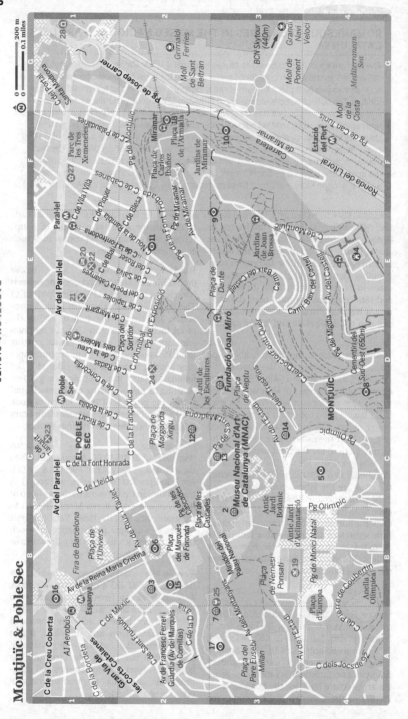

Montjuïc & Poble Sec

CaixaForum GALLERY
(Map p266; ☏93 476 86 00; www.fundacio.lacaixa.es; Avinguda de Francesc Ferrer i Guàrdia 6-8; adult/student & child €4/free, 1st Sun of month free; ☺10am-8pm Mon-Fri, to 9pm Sat & Sun; ℗; ⓂEspanya) The Caixa building society prides itself on its involvement in (and ownership of) art, in particular all that is contemporary. Its premier art expo space in Barcelona hosts part of the bank's extensive collection from around the globe. The setting is a completely renovated former factory, the Fàbrica Casaramona, an outstanding Modernista brick structure designed by Puig i Cadafalch. From 1940 to 1993 it housed the First Squadron of the police cavalry unit – 120 horses in all.

Museu Etnològic MUSEUM
(Map p266; www.museuetnologic.bcn.cat; Passeig de Santa Madrona 16-22; ◻55) Barcelona's ethnology museum presents a curious permanent collection that explores how various societies have worked down the centuries, as seen through collections of all sorts of objects. The entire museum was closed at the time of writing for major refurbishments. Check the website for the reopening date.

**Museu d'Arqueologia
de Catalunya** MUSEUM
(MAC; Map p266; ☏93 423 21 49; www.mac.cat; Passeig de Santa Madrona 39-41; adult/student €4.50/3.50; ☺9.30am-7pm Tue-Sat, 10am-2.30pm Sun; ⓂPoble Sec) This archaeology museum, housed in what was the Graphic Arts palace during the 1929 World Exhibition, covers Catalonia and cultures from elsewhere in Spain. Items range from copies of pre-Neanderthal skulls to Carthaginian necklaces and jewel-studded Visigothic crosses.

Anella Olímpica OLYMPIC SITE
(☺8am-9pm Apr-Sep, 8am-7pm Oct-Mar) The 'Olympic Ring' is the group of sports installations where the main events of the 1992 Olympics were held. Westernmost is the **Institut Nacional d'Educació Física de Catalunya (INEFC)** , a kind of sports university, designed by one of Catalonia's best-known contemporary architects, Ricardo Bofill. Past a circular arena, Plaça d'Europa, with the Torre Calatrava telecommunications tower behind it, is the **Piscines Bernat Picornell**, where the swimming and diving events were held.

Estadi Olímpic Lluís Companys STADIUM
(Map p266; ☏93 426 20 89; Avinguda de l'Estadi; ☺10am-8pm; ◻150) FREE The Estadi Olímpic was the main stadium of Barcelona's Olympic Games. If you saw the Olympics on TV, the 65,000-capacity stadium may seem surprisingly small. So might the Olympic flame holder into which an archer spectacularly fired a flaming arrow during the opening ceremony. The stadium was opened in 1929 and restored for 1992.

Montjuïc

A ONE-DAY ITINERARY

Montjuïc, perhaps once the site of pre-Roman settlements, is today a hilltop green lung looking over city and sea. Interspersed across varied gardens are major art collections, a fortress, an Olympic stadium and more. A solid one-day itinerary can take in the key spots.

Alight at Espanya metro stop and make for **CaixaForum ❶**, always host to three or four free top-class exhibitions. The nearby **Pavelló Mies van der Rohe ❷** is an intriguing study in 1920s futurist housing by one of the 20th century's greatest architects. Uphill, the Romanesque art collection in the **Museu Nacional d'Art de Catalunya ❸** is a must, and its restaurant is a pleasant lunch stop. Escalators lead further up the hill towards the **Estadi Olímpic ❹**, scene of the 1992 Olympic Games. The road leads east to the **Fundació Joan Miró ❺**, a shrine to the master surrealist's creativity. Contemplate ancient relics in the **Museu d'Arqueologia de Catalunya ❻**, then have a break in the peaceful **Jardins de Mossèn Cinto Verdaguer ❼**, the prettiest on the hill, before taking the cable car to the **Castell de Montjuïc ❽**. If you pick the right day, you can round off with the gorgeously kitsch **La Font Màgica ❾** sound and light show, followed by drinks and dancing in an open-air nightspot in **Poble Espanyol ❿**.

TOP TIPS

» **Moving views** Ride the Transbordador Aeri from Barceloneta for a bird's eye approach to Montjuïc. Or take the Teleféric de Montjuïc cable car to the Castell for more aerial views.

» **Summer fun** The Castell de Montjuïc features outdoor summer cinema and concerts (see http://sala montjuic.org).

» **Beautiful bloomers** Bursting with colour and serenity, the Jardins de Mossèn Cinto Verdaguer are exquisitely laid out with bulbs, especially tulips, and aquatic flowers.

JEAN-PIERRE LESCOURRET/GETTY IMAGES ©

CaixaForum
This former factory and barracks designed by Josep Puig i Cadafalch is an outstanding work of Modernista architecture; like a Lego fantasy in brick.

Olympic Needle

Piscines Bernat Picornell

Poble Espanyol
Amid the rich variety of traditional Spanish architecture created in replica for the 1929 Barcelona World Exhibition, browse the art on show in the Fundació Fran Daurel.

TRAVEL INK/GETTY IMAGES ©

Pavelló Mies van der Rohe
Admire the inventiveness of the great German architect Ludwig Mies van der Rohe in this recreation of his avant garde German pavillion for the 1929 World Exhibition.

La Font Màgica
Take a summer evening to behold the Magic Fountain come to life in a unique 15-minute sound and light performance, when the water glows like a cauldron of colour.

PAUL BIRIS/GETTY IMAGES ©

Museu Nacional d'Art de Catalunya
Make a beeline for the Romanesque art selection and the 12th-century polychrome image of Christ in majesty, which was recovered from the apse of a country chapel in northwest Catalonia.

Fundació Joan Miró
Take in some of Joan Miró's giant canvases, and discover little-known works from his early years in the Sala Joan Prats and Sala Pilar Juncosa.

9

3

6

Museu Etnològic

Teatre Grec

5

7

Museu Olímpic i de l'Esport

4

Estadi Olímpic

Jardí Botànic

8

Jardins de Mossèn Cinto Verdaguer

Castell de Montjuïc
Enjoy the sweeping views of the sea and city from atop this 17th-century fortress, once a political prison and long a symbol of oppression.

ELAN FLEISHER/GETTY IMAGES ©

Museu d'Arqueologia de Catalunya
Seek out the Roman mosaic depicting the Three Graces, one of the most beautiful items in this museum, which was dedicated to the ancient past of Catalonia and neighbouring parts of Spain.

CULTURA TRAVEL/QUIM ROSER/GETTY IMAGES ©

ℹ️ GETTING TO MONTJUÏC

You *could* walk from Ciutat Vella (the foot of La Rambla is 700m from the eastern end of Montjuïc). Escalators run up to the Palau Nacional from Avinguda de Rius i Taulet and Passeig de les Cascades. They continue as far as Avinguda de l'Estadi.

Bus

Several buses make their way up here, including buses 50, 55 and 61. Local bus 193 does a circle trip from Plaça d'Espanya to the castle.

Metro & Funicular

Take the metro (lines 2 and 3) to Paral·lel station and get on the **funicular railway** (☉ 9am-10pm Apr-Oct, 9am-8pm Nov-Mar) from there to Estació Parc Montjuïc.

Telefèric de Montjuïc

From Estació Parc Montjuïc, this **cable car** (adult/child one way €6.80/5.20; ☉ 10am-9pm) carries you to the Castell de Montjuïc via the *mirador* (lookout point).

Transbordador Aeri

To get to the mountain from the beach, take the **Transbordador Aeri** (Map p248; www.telefericodebarcelona.com; Passeig Escullera; one way/return €11/16.50; ☉ 11am-7pm; ☐ 17, 39 or 64, Ⓜ Barceloneta). This cable car runs between Torre de Sant Sebastià in La Barceloneta and the Miramar stop on Montjuïc.

Museu Olímpic i de l'Esport MUSEUM
(Map p266; ☎ 93 292 53 79; www.museuolimpicbcn.com; Avinguda de l'Estadi 60; adult/student €5.10/3.20; ☉ 10am-8pm Tue-Sat, 10am-2.30pm Sun; ☐ 55, 150) The Museu Olímpic i de l'Esport is an information-packed interactive museum dedicated to the history of sport and the Olympic Games. After picking up tickets, you wander down a ramp that snakes below ground level and is lined with displays on the history of sport, starting with the ancients.

Jardí Botànic GARDENS
(Map p266; www.jardibotanic.bcn.cat; Carrer del Doctor Font i Quer 2; adult/child €3.50/free; ☉ 10am-7pm; ☐ 55, 150) This garden is dedicated to Mediterranean flora and has a collection of some 40,000 plants and 1500 species that thrive in areas with a climate similar to that of the Mediterranean, such as the Eastern Mediterranean, Spain, North Africa, Australia, California, Chile and South Africa.

Cementiri del Sud-Oest CEMETERY
(☎ 93 484 19 70; www.cbsa.cat; Carrer de la Mare de Déu de Port 56-58; ☉ 8am-6pm; ☐ 9, 21) **FREE** On the hill to the south of the Anella Olímpica stretches this huge cemetery, the Cementiri del Sud-Oest (or 'Cementiri Nou'), which extends down the southern side of the hill. Opened in 1883, it's an odd combination of elaborate architect-designed tombs for rich families and small niches for the rest. It includes the graves of numerous Catalan art-

ists and politicians, and, at the entrance, the Col·lecció de Carrosses Fúnebres (p258).

Transbordador Aeri CABLE CAR
(Map p266; www.telefericodebarcelona.com; Av de Miramar, Jardins de Miramar; one way/return €11/16.50; ☉ 11am-7pm; ☐ 50 & 153)

🏃 Activities

Popular places for a run or a bike ride are in Montjuïc and in the Parc de Collserola (among the best trails there is the 9km-long Carretera de les Aigües): both are hilly but much less stressful than the rest of the city in terms of traffic. Another good place for a spin or a jog is along the esplanade from Barceloneta beach up to El Fòrum.

Club Natació Atlètic-Barcelona SWIMMING
(Map p248; www.cnab.cat; Plaça del Mar; daypass adult/child €12.20/7.10; ☉ 7am-11pm Mon-Sat, 8am-8pm Sun; ☐ 17, 39, 57 or 64, Ⓜ Barceloneta) This athletic club has one indoor and two outdoor pools. Of the latter, one is heated for lap swimming in winter. Admission includes use of the gym and private beach access.

Golondrina BOAT TOUR
(Map p236; ☎ 93 442 31 06; www.lasgolondrinas.com; Moll de les Drassanes; adult/child €14.50/5.25; ☉ Mar-Nov; Ⓜ Drassanes) For a view of the harbour from the water, you can take a *golondrina* from in front of the Mirador a Colom. The 90-minute round trip takes you to Port Olímpic, El Fòrum and back again.

The number of departures depends largely on season and demand. As a rule, trips are only done between March and November. If you just want to discover the area around the port, you can opt for a 35-minute excursion to the breakwater and back (€7/3 per adult/child).

Orsom   CRUISE
(☎93 441 05 37; www.barcelona-orsom.com; Moll de les Drassanes; adult/child €16.50/11; ☺Apr-Oct; ⓜDrassanes) Aboard a large sailing catamaran, Orsom makes the 90-minute journey to Port Olímpic and back. There are three departures per day (four on weekends in July and August), and the last is a jazz cruise, scheduled around sunset. The same company also runs five daily, 50-minute speedboat tours (adult/child €12.50/11).

Piscines Bernat Picornell   SWIMMING
(Map p266; ☎93 423 40 41; www.picornell.cat; Avinguda de l'Estadi 30-38; adult/child €6.50/4.50; ☺6.45am-midnight Mon-Fri, 7am-9pm Sat, 7.30am-4pm Sun; ☐50, 61 or 193) Barcelona's official Olympic pool on Montjuïc. On Saturday nights, between 9pm and 11pm, the pool (with access to sauna and steam bath) is open only to nudists. On Sundays between October and May the indoor pool also opens for nudists only from 4.15pm to 6pm.

🎓 Courses

Barcelona is bristling with schools offering Spanish- and Catalan-language courses. You can learn lots more in Barcelona, too, such as salsa and sauces.

Cook and Taste   COOKING COURSE
(Map p236; ☎93 302 13 20; www.cookandtaste.net; Carrer del Paradís 3; half-day workshop €65; ⓜLiceu) Learn to whip up a paella or stir a gazpacho in this Spanish cookery school.

International House   LANGUAGE COURSE
(☎93 268 45 11; www.ihes.com/bcn; Carrer de Trafalgar 14; ⓜArc de Triomf) Intensive courses from around €410 for two weeks. Staff can also organise accommodation.

👉 Tours

There are a number of tour options if you want a hand getting around the sights.

Barcelona Walking Tours   WALKING TOUR
(Map p250; ☎93 285 38 34; www.barcelonaturisme.com; Plaça de Catalunya 17-S; ⓜCatalunya) The Oficina d'Informació de Turisme de Barcelona organises guided walking tours.

One explores the Barri Gòtic (adult/child €15.50/free; ☺in English 9.30am daily); another follows in the footsteps of Picasso (adult/child €21.50/7; ☺in English 3pm Tue, Thu & Sat) and winds up at the Museu Picasso, entry to which is included in the price, and a third takes in the main jewels of Modernisme (adult/child €15.50/free; ☺in English 4pm Fri). Also offered is a gourmet tour (adult/child €21.50/7; ☺in English 10am Fri & Sat) of traditional purveyors of fine foodstuffs across the old city; it includes a couple of chances to taste some of the products.

Bus Turístic   BUS TOUR
(☎93 285 38 32; www.barcelonabusturistic.cat/en; day ticket adult/child €27/16; ☺9am-8pm) This hop-on, hop-off service covers three circuits (44 stops) linking virtually all the major tourist sights. Tourist offices, TMB transport authority offices and many hotels have leaflets explaining the system. Each of the two main circuits takes approximately two hours. The third circuit, from Port Olímpic to El Fòrum, runs from April to September and is less interesting. A Bus Turístic ticket entitles you to discounts to some museums.

Catalunya Bus Turístic   BUS TOUR
(Map p250; ☎93 285 38 32; www.catalunyabusturistic.com/; Plaça de Catalunya) Routes include a day in Vic (€35), north of Barcelona, visiting the old town and huge weekly market; Girona and Figueres (€71); a Penedès wine and cava (sparkling wine) jaunt with three winery tours and lunch (€59); Montserrat and Sitges (€69). All tours leave at 8.30am from late March to October from Plaça de Catalunya.

FREE WALKING TOURS

Numerous companies offer pay-what-you-wish walking tours. These typically take in the Barri Gòtic or the Modernista sites of L'Eixample.

Runner Bean Tours (Map p236; ☎636 108776; www.runnerbeantours.com; ☺11am year-round & 4.30pm Apr-Sep),

Feel Free Tours (www.feelfreetours.com)

Orange Donut Tours (www.orangedonuttours.com; ☺tours 11am & 3pm)

Discover Walks (www.discoverwalks.com; ☺10.30am, 3pm & 5pm Fri-Mon Apr-Oct)

Travel Bound (www.travelbar.com).

Barcelona Scooter
DRIVING TOUR

(Map p248; ☏ 93 221 40 70; tour €50; ☺ 10.30am Sat, 3.30pm Thu) Run by Cooltra, Barcelona Scooter offers a three-hour tour by scooter around the city (€50) in conjunction with the city tourism office. Departure is from the Cooltra rental outlet.

Gocar
DRIVING TOUR

(Map p236; ☏ 93 269 17 92; www.gocartours.es; Carrer de Freixures 23; tours 2½/8hrs €70/160; ☺ 9am-9pm) These GPS-guided 'cars' (really two-seat, three-wheel mopeds) allow you to tour around town, park where motorbikes are allowed and listen to commentaries on major sites as you go. The GPS system makes it virtually impossible to get lost.

My Favourite Things
TOUR

(☏ 637 265405; www.myft.net; tours from €26; max 10 people) Offers tours based on numerous themes: street art, shopping, culinary tours, musical journeys and forgotten neighbourhoods are among the offerings. Other activities include flamenco and salsa classes and bicycle rides in and out of Barcelona. Some of the more unusual activities cost more and times vary

---

BICYCLE TOURS

Barcelona is awash with companies offering bicycle tours. Tours typically cost around €22, take two to four hours and generally stick to the old city, La Sagrada Família and the beaches.

Barcelona By Bike (Map p248; ☏ 671 307325; www.barcelonabybike.com; Carrer de la Marina 13; €22; Ⓜ Cuitadella/Vila Olimpica)

CicloTour (Map p236; ☏ 93 317 19 70; www.barcelonaciclotour.com/eng; Carrer dels Tallers 45; €22; ☺ 11am daily, 4.30pm mid-Apr-Oct, 7.30pm Thu-Sun Jun-Sep)

Barcelona by Bicycle (Map p244; ☏ 93 268 21 05; www.bicicletabarcelona.com; Carrer de l'Esparteria 3; €22)

Barcelona Biking (Map p236; ☏ 656 356300; www.barcelonabiking.com; Baixada de Sant Miquel 6; bike hire per hr/24hr €5/15, €21; ☺ 10am-8pm, tour 11am daily; Ⓜ Jaume I or Liceu)

Fat Tire Bike Tours (Map p236; ☏ 93 342 92 75; http://fattirebiketours.com; Carrer Sant Honorat 7; bike hire per hr/half-day €3/8, tour €24; ☺ 10am-8pm; Ⓜ Jaume I or Liceu)

🎊 Festivals & Events

Reis/Reyes
EPIPHANY

Epifanía (the Epiphany) on 6 January is also known as the Dia dels Reis Mags/Día de los Reyes Magos (Three Kings' Day). The night before, children delight in the Cavalcada dels Reis Mags (Parade of the Three Kings), a colourful parade of floats and music during which tons of sweets are thrown into the crowd of eager kids (and not a few adults!).

Festes de Santa Eulàlia
CITY FESTIVAL

(www.bcn.cat/santaeulalia) Celebrates Barcelona's first patron saint with a week of cultural events, including *castells* (human castles).

Dia de Sant Jordi
PATRON SAINT FESTIVAL

This is the day of Catalonia's patron saint (George) and also the Day of the Book: men give women a rose, women give men a book, publishers launch new titles. La Rambla and Plaça de Sant Jaume and other central city streets and squares are filled with book and flower stalls. Celebrated on 23 April.

Pride Barcelona
GAY PRIDE

(www.pridebarcelona.org) The Barcelona gay-pride festival is a week of celebrations held towards the end of June with a program of culture and concerts, and the gay-pride march on the last Sunday of the month.

Sónar
MUSIC

(www.sonar.es) A celebration of electronic music is said to be Europe's biggest such event. Locations and dates change each year.

Primavera Sound
MUSIC

(www.primaverasound.com) For three days in late May or early June, the Auditori Fòrum and other locations around town become the combined stage for a host of international DJs and musicians.

Dia de Sant Joan
MIDSUMMER

This is a colourful midsummer celebration on 24 June with bonfires, even in the squares of L'Eixample, and fireworks marking the evening that precedes this holiday.

Festival del Grec
MUSIC, DANCE

(www.barcelonafestival.com) Held from late June to August, this festival involves music, dance and theatre at many locations across the city.

Festa Major de Gràcia
CITY FESTIVAL

(www.festamajordegracia.org) This is a madcap local festival held in Gràcia around 15 August, with decorated streets, dancing and concerts.

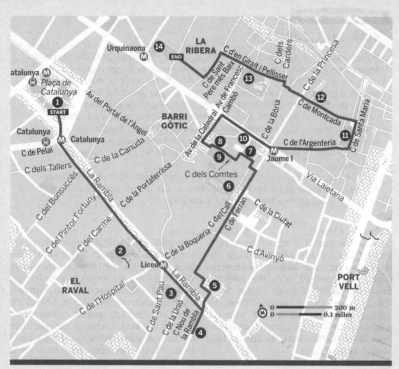

🏃 City Walk
Old Town

START PLAÇA DE CATALUNYA
END PALAU DE LA MÚSICA CATALANA
LENGTH 3.5KM; 1½ HOURS

Much of what makes Barcelona fascinating is crowded into a relatively compact space, making a strolling tour a great way to make the city's acquaintance. First, follow the crowds – wander down La Rambla from ❶ **Plaça de Catalunya**. Along the way, sniff around the ❷ **Mercat de la Boqueria** (p280), one of Europe's most colourful and well-stocked produce markets. Pop into the ❸ **Gran Teatre del Liceu**, the city's main opera house, and then visit one of Gaudí's earlier efforts, the ❹ **Palau Güell** (p243). From here, cross La Rambla and linger in scenic ❺ **Plaça Reial** (p239). Make your way to ❻ **Plaça de Sant Jaume** (p235), at the core of the Barri Gòtic and the political heart of the city for 2000 years. You can examine the city's Roman origins in the nearby ❼ **Museu d'Història de Barcelona** (p239), which also leads you to a fine Catalan Gothic hall and medieval chapel. From the complex

of buildings huddled around the museum and Plaça del Rei, you pass the ❽ **Museu Frederic Marès** (p242) en route to the main facade of the ❾ **Catedral** (p235) – make time to spend inside and to head up to the roof for bird's-eye views of the medieval city. From there, make the loop down Vía Laietana to admire what remains of the ❿ **Roman walls** (p242), and then branch off along Carrer de l'Argenteria (once home to Barcelona's silversmiths) to reach the splendid Gothic ⓫ **Església de Santa Maria del Mar** (p245), a striking symbol of Catalan identity. Circle around it and up noble Carrer de Montcada, home to fine centuries-old mansions, several of which house museums – including the ⓬ **Museu Picasso** (p246). Proceed north past the ⓭ **Mercat de Santa Caterina** (p245), a daring 21st-century reincarnation of a grand 19th-century produce market on the site of a medieval monastery, and then dogleg on to the stunning Modernista ⓮ **Palau de la Música Catalana** (p244), best visited for a performance of anything from flamenco to Portuguese *fado*.

LOCAL KNOWLEDGE

SUMMER CELEBRATION

In the summer, there are loads of great events on. From June to August, the city hosts **Música als Parcs** (Music in the Parks), a series of open-air concerts held in different parks and green spaces around the city. Over 40 different concerts feature classical, blues and jazz groups. Popular venues include Parc de la Ciutadella, Parc de Joan Miró (Carrer de Tarragona, Sant Antoni) and Parc Turó (Avinguda de Pau Casals 19, Sant Gervasi). Stop in at the tourist office or go online (www.bcn.cat) for a schedule.

Another ongoing summertime event is the **Festival Piknic Electronik** (piknic-electronik.es/en). Every Sunday from June through September, you can enjoy a day of electronic music at an outdoor space on Montjuïc. It attracts a mix of young families and party people.

And for big-name concerts, don't miss the **Festival Pedralbes** (www.festivalpe-dralbes.com), featuring top talent (George Benson, Carla Bruni, Kool & the Gang) performing in lovely gardens from mid-June to early July.

Festes de la Mercè
CITY FESTIVAL

(www.bcn.cat/merce) The city's biggest party involves four days of concerts, dancing, *castellers* (human-castle builders), a fireworks display synchronised with the Montjuïc fountains, dances of giants on the Saturday, and *correfocs* – a parade of fireworks-spitting monsters and demons who run with the crowd – spitting dragons and devils from all over Catalonia, on the Sunday. Held around 24 September.

🛏 Sleeping

Those looking for cheaper accommodation close to the action should check out the Barri Gòtic and El Raval. Some good lower-end *pensiones* (small private hotels) are also scattered about L'Eixample. A range of boutique-style hotels with real charm in all categories has enriched the offerings in the past few years. Many midrange and top-end places are spread across L'Eixample, most of them within easy striking distance of the old town. There's a handful of options near the beaches at La Barceloneta.

🛏 Barri Gòtic

Alberg Hostel Itaca
HOSTEL €

(Map p236; ☑93 301 97 51; www.itacahostel. com; Carrer de Ripoll 21; dm €21-24, tw/d €60/70, apt €90-150; @ 🛜; Ⓜ Jaume I) A bright, quiet hostel near the cathedral, Itaca has spacious dorms (sleeping six to 10 people) with parquet floors and spring colours, and two doubles. There's a lively vibe, and the hostel organises activities (pub crawls, flamenco concerts, free daily walking tour), making it a good option for solo travellers.

Bonic
B&B €€

(Map p236; ☑626 053434; www.bonic-barcelona. com; Carrer de Josep Anselm Clavé 9; s €55, d €90-95; ❄ @ 🛜; Ⓜ Drassanes) Bonic is a small, cosy B&B that has eight rooms in varied styles, with wood or decorative tile floors, high ceilings and attractive furnishings. Several are bright and cheerfully painted, and some lack exterior windows. Owing to the restrictive layout – all guest rooms share three bathrooms – maximum occupancy is six or seven guests a night, although groups of friends can book the whole place to themselves.

El Jardí
HOTEL €€

(Map p236; ☑93 301 59 00; www.eljardi-barcelona. com; Plaça de Sant Josep Oriol 1; d €90-120; ❄ 🛜; Ⓜ Liceu) 'The Garden' has no garden but a handful of boxy doubles with balcony overlooking one of the prettiest squares in Barcelona. If you can snag one of them, it is well worth climbing up the stairs. If you can't get a room with a view, you are better off looking elsewhere.

Vrabac
GUESTHOUSE €€

(Map p236; ☑663 494029; vrabacguesthouse. wordpress.com; Carrer de Portaferrissa 14; d €95-145, s/d without bathroom from €55/65; ❄ 🛜; Ⓜ Liceu or Catalunya) In a central location just off La Rambla, Vrabac is set in a beautifully restored heritage building complete with original decorative ceilings, exposed sandstone walls and large oil paintings. Rooms vary in size and equipment – the best have elegant ceramic tile floors and sizeable balconies with private bathrooms. The cheapest are small and basic and lack a bathroom, and aren't recommended. Cash only.

DO BOUTIQUE HOTEL €€€
(Map p236; ☑93 481 36 66; www.hoteldoreial.com; Plaça Reial 1; s/d from €230/280; ❄🛜♨; Ⓜ Liceu) Overlooking the magnificent plaza for which it is named, this 18-room property has handsomely designed rooms, set with beamed ceilings, wide plank floors and all-important soundproofing. The service is excellent, and the facilities extensive, with roof terrace (with bar in summer), dipping pool, solarium and spa. Its excellent market-to-table restaurants draw in visiting foodies.

🛏 El Raval

Hotel Peninsular HOTEL €
(Map p236; ☑93 302 31 38; www.hotelpeninsular.net; Carrer de Sant Pau 34; s/d €57/80; ❄@🛜; Ⓜ Liceu) An oasis on the edge of the slightly dicey Barri Xinès, this former convent (which was connected by tunnel to the Església de Sant Agustí) has a plant-draped atrium extending its height and most of its length. The 60 rooms are simple, with tiled floors and whitewash, but mostly spacious and well kept. There are some great bargains to be had on quiet dates.

Chic & Basic Tallers HOSTAL €
(☑93 302 51 83; www.chicandbasic.com; Carrer dels Tallers 82; s/d from €71/84; ❄@; Ⓜ Universitat) The colour scheme here is predominantly white, with exceptions like the screaming orange fridge in the communal kitchen and chill-out area. Rooms are also themed lily white, from the floors to the sheets. Finishing touches include the plasma-screen TVs and the option of plugging your iPod into your room's sound system. The street can get noisy.

★ Barceló Raval DESIGN HOTEL €€
(Map p236; ☑93 320 14 90; www.barceloraval.com; Rambla del Raval 17-21; r from €128; ❄@; Ⓜ Liceu) Part of the city's plans to pull the El Raval district up by the bootstraps, this oval-shaped designer hotel tower makes a 21st-century splash. The rooftop terrace offers fabulous views and the B-Lounge bar-restaurant is the toast of the town for meals and cocktails. Rooms have slick aesthetics (white with lime green or ruby-red splashes of colour), Nespresso machines and iPod docks.

Chic & Basic Ramblas DESIGN HOTEL €€
(Map p236; ☑93 302 71 11; www.chicandbasicramblashotel.com; Passatge Gutenberg 7; s & d €106-116; ❄🛜; Ⓜ Drassanes) The latest in the Chic & Basic chain is the most riotous to date, with quirky and colourful interiors that hit you from the second you walk in and see a vintage Seat 600 car in the foyer. The rooms themselves are solid blocks of colour, and each loosely pays homage to an aspect of Barcelona life in the 1960s. All have balconies and small kitchens. Note that the name is misleading – the hotel is a couple of blocks into the Raval.

BARCELONA SLEEPING

BARCELONA FOR CHILDREN

There's plenty to interest kids, from street theatre on La Rambla to the beaches. Transport is good, many attractions are huddled fairly close together and children are generally welcome in restaurants and cafes.

An initial stroll along La Rambla is full of potential distractions and wonders, particularly the living statues and buskers.

At the bottom end of La Rambla, more options present themselves: a ride up to the top of the Mirador de Colom (p235) or seeing sharks at L'Aquàrium (p247).

The Transbordador Aeri (p270), strung across the harbour between La Barceloneta and Montjuïc, is an irresistible ride. Or scare the wits out of them with hair-raising rides at Tibidabo's Parc d'Atraccions (p262) amusement park.

Of the city's museums, those most likely to capture children's imaginations as much as those of their adult companions are the Museu Marítim (p244), the Museu de la Xocolata (p245) and the popular interactive Cosmocaixa (p262) science museum.

In the summer months, you will doubtless be rewarded by squeals of delight if you take the bairns to one of the city's **swimming pools** or the **beach**. In cooler weather, parks can be a good choice. A walk in the gardens of Montjuïc, including some exploration of Castell de Montjuïc (p264), will appeal to everyone. Adults find the maze of the Jardins del Laberint d'Horta (p262) hard to work out, too. Another old favourite with most children is a visit to see the animals at the Zoo de Barcelona (p246).

Hotel Sant Agustí
HOTEL €€

(Map p236; ☑ 93 318 16 58; www.hotelsa.com; Plaça de Sant Agustí 3; r from €125; ❄ @ �; Ⓜ Liceu) This former 18th-century monastery opened as a hotel in 1840, making it the city's oldest. The location is perfect – a quick stroll off La Rambla on a curious square. Rooms sparkle, and are mostly spacious and light filled. Consider an attic double with sloping ceiling and bird's-eye views.

Hotel España
HOTEL €€

(Map p236; ☑ 93 550 00 00; www.hotelespanya. com; Carrer de Sant Pau 9-11; r €164; ❄ @ ຈ ▨; Ⓜ Liceu) Best known for its wonderful Modernista interiors in the dining rooms and bar, in which architect Domènech i Montaner, sculptor Eusebi Arnau and painter Ramon Casas had a hand, this hotel offers clean, straightforward rooms in a building that still manages to ooze a little history. In the 1920s it was a favourite with bullfighters.

Raval Rooms
HOSTAL €€

(Map p236; ☑ 93 481 66 70; www.ravalrooms.com; Carrer de Joaquín Costa 44; s/d €90/95; ❄ @ ຈ; Ⓜ Universitat) There's pea-green and lemon-lime decor in this hip 2nd-floor *hostal* located on a bar-lined lane dominated by resident migrants and wandering bands of uni students. The rooms are pleasant and secure, if snug, and enlivened with colourful artworks.

Casa Camper
DESIGN HOTEL €€€

(Map p236; ☑ 93 342 62 80; www.casacamper.com; Carrer d'Elisabets 11; s/d from €238/260; ❄ @ ຈ; Ⓜ Catalunya) The massive foyer looks like a contemporary-art museum, but the rooms are the real surprise. Decorated in red, black and white, each room has a sleeping and bathroom area, where you can put on your Camper slippers, enjoy the Vinçon furniture and contemplate the hanging gardens. Across the corridor is a separate, private sitting room with balcony, TV and hammock. Get to the rooftop for sweeping cityscapes.

🛏 La Ribera

Pensión Francia
HOSTEL €

(Map p244; ☑ 93 319 03 76; www.pensionfrancia-barcelona.com; Carrer de Rera Palau 4; s/d without bathroom €30/55; ຈ; Ⓜ Barceloneta) The homey smell of laundry pervades this quaint little hostel in a great location close to the shore, the Parc de la Ciutadella and the nightlife of El Born. The 11 simple rooms are kept spick and span, with nothing much in the way of frills. Rooms with balconies

benefit from plenty of natural light but little noise, as the lane is set away from the busy nearby thoroughfares.

Pensió 2000
PENSIÓN €

(☑ 93 310 74 66; www.pensio2000.com; Carrer de Sant Pere més Alt 6; d €70-80; ❄ @ ຈ; Ⓜ Urquinaona) This 1st-floor, family-run place is opposite the anything-but-simple Palau de la Música Catalana. Seven reasonably spacious doubles have mosaic-tiled floors, and after a recent renovation all have private bathrooms. You can eat your breakfast in the little courtyard.

Chic & Basic
DESIGN HOTEL €€

(Map p244; ☑ 93 295 46 52; www.chicandbasic. com; Carrer de la Princesa 50; s €81-87, d €103-150; ❄ @ ຈ; Ⓜ Jaume I) This is a very cool hotel indeed, with its 31 spotlessly white rooms and fairy-light curtains that change colour, adding an entirely new atmosphere to the space. The rooms are small, but the ceilings are high and the beds enormous. Many beautiful old features of the original building have been retained, such as the marble staircase. Chic & Basic also runs a *hostal* and other hotels and apartments around town.

Hotel Banys Orientals
BOUTIQUE HOTEL €€

(Map p244; ☑ 93 268 84 60; www.hotelbanysorientals.com; Carrer de l'Argenteria 37; s €96, d €115.50-143; ❄ ຈ; Ⓜ Jaume I) Book well ahead to get into this magnetically popular designer haunt. Cool blues and aquamarines combine with dark-hued floors to lend this clean-lined, boutique hotel a quiet charm. All rooms, on the small side, look onto the street or back lanes. There are more spacious suites in two other nearby buildings.

🛏 Port Vell & Barceloneta

Hotel Marina Folch
HOTEL €

(Map p248; ☑ 93 310 37 09; Carrer del Mar 16; s/d/tr from €45/65/85; ❄ ❄; Ⓜ Barceloneta) Simple digs above a busy seafood restaurant. This hotel has just one teeny single and nine doubles of varying sizes and quality. The best have small balconies facing out towards the marina. The rooms are basic but well maintained, and the location is unbeatable, just a couple of minutes from the beach.

Equity Point Sea Hostel
HOSTEL €

(Map p248; ☑ 93 231 20 45; www.equity-point.com; Plaça del Mar 1-4; dm €19-34; ❄ @ ຈ; ▭ 17, 39, 57 or 64, Ⓜ Barceloneta) Perched near the sea in a rather ugly high-rise is this busy backpackers hostel. Rooms are basic, cramped and noisy (bring earplugs) but you will not find a room closer to the beach.

Marina View
B&B €€

(Map p236; ☑678 854456; www.marinaview-bcn.com; Passeig de Colom; d without/with view €116/139, tr €136/165; 🕸🛜; Ⓜ Drassanes) In an excellent location near both the old city and the waterfront, this Irish-run B&B has six airy, comfortably furnished rooms, some with small balconies sporting sunlit views over the marina. The welcome is genuinely warm, and Paddy, the owner, has loads of tips on how to make the most of your visit.

Hotel del Mar
HOTEL €€

(Map p248; ☑93 319 30 47; www.gargallo-hotels.com; Pla del Palau 19; d €96-150; 🕸@🛜; Ⓜ Barceloneta) The nicely modernised Hotel del Mar is strategically placed between Port Vell and El Born. Rooms are bright, clean and comfortable, though not luxurious. The best chambers have balconies with waterfront views. It's a fairly peaceful spot only 10 minutes' walk from the beaches and seafood of La Barceloneta, and the nightlife of El Born.

🛏 Poblenou & Port Olímpic

Amistat Beach Hostel
HOSTEL €

(☑93 221 32 81; www.amistatbeachhostel.com; Carrer Amistat 21; dm €21-33; 🛜; Ⓜ Poblenou) A stylish new addition to Poblenou, Amistat has attractively designed common areas, with a beanbag-filled lounge with DJ set-up, a low-lit TV room and a guest kitchen. The rooms, which sleep from four to 12, are clean, but basic – aside from a splash of colour on the ceilings. Friendly staff organise pub crawls, club nights and other events.

Poblenou Bed & Breakfast
HOTEL €€

(☑93 221 26 01; www.hostalpoblenou.com; Carrer del Taulat 30; s/d from €50/80; 🕸@🛜; Ⓜ Llacuna) Experience this colourful working-class neighbourhood, just back from the beach, a few steps from the restaurant-lined Rambla del Poblenou, and increasingly home to a diverse population of loft-inhabiting gentrifiers. The 1930s house, with its high ceilings and beautiful tile floors, has six appealing rooms, all with a fresh feel, light colours, comfortable beds andsome with a balcony.

🛏 L'Eixample

Hostal Oliva
HOSTAL €

(Map p250; ☑93 488 01 62; www.hostaloliva.com; Passeig de Gràcia 32; d €51-91, s/d without bathroom €41-71; 🕸🛜; Ⓜ Passeig de Gràcia) A picturesque antique lift wheezes its way up to this 4th-floor *hostal*, a terrific, reliable cheapie in one of the city's most expensive neighbourhoods. Some of the single rooms can barely fit a bed but the doubles are big enough, light and airy (some with tiled floors, others with parquet and dark old wardrobes).

Hostal Muntaner
HOSTAL €

(☑93 410 94 74; www.hostalmuntaner.com; Carrer de Muntaner 175; s/d €60, without bathroom €50;

GAY STAYS

Barcelona has a few excellent gay-friendly options, some in the heart of the 'Gaixample'.

Hotel Axel (Map p250; ☑93 323 93 93; www.axelhotels.com; Carrer d'Aribau 33; r from €129; 🕸@🛜🖥; Ⓜ Universitat) Favoured by a mixed fashion and gay set, Axel occupies a sleek corner block and offers modern touches in its 105 designer rooms. A subtle, light colour scheme, plasma TVs and (in the double rooms) king-sized beds are just some of the pluses. Take a break in the rooftop pool, the Finnish sauna or the spa bath. The rooftop Skybar is open for cocktails from May to September.

Room Mate Pau (Map p250; ☑93 343 63 00; pau.room-matehotels.com; Carrer de Fontanella 7; d €125-170; 🕸🛜; Ⓜ Urquinaona, Catalunya) Just a short stroll from Plaça de Catalunya, Room Mate Pau sits somewhere between upscale hostel and boutique hotel. The rooms are small and minimalist, but cleverly designed (with USB-connected flat screen TVs and good mattresses). The enticing interior terrace with bar draws a young and hip crowd.

Casa de Billy Barcelona (☑93 426 30 48; www.casabillybarcelona.com; Gran Via de les Corts Catalanes 420; s & d from €40, without bathroom from €35; @; Ⓜ Rocafort) Set in a rambling apartment, a stone's throw from the Gaixample bars, this is an intriguing, gay-friendly stop. The rooms are largely decorated in flamboyant Art Deco style and guests may use the kitchen. There is a two-night-minimum policy.

LONGER-STAY ACCOMMODATION

An alternative accommodation option can be apartment rental. Typical short-term prices are around €80 to €100 for two people per night. An excellent option, with hundreds of listings is **Air BnB** (www.airbnb.com). In addition to full apartments, the site also lists rooms available, which can be a good way to meet locals and/or other travellers if you don't mind sharing common areas. Prices for a room range from €30 to €60 on average.

There are scores of rental services: **Oh-Barcelona** (www.oh-barcelona.com)

Aparteasy (Map p259; ☑ 93 451 67 66; www.aparteasy.com; Carrer de Santa Tecla 3; Ⓜ Diagonal)

Feelathomebarcelona.com (Map p236; ☑ 651 894141; www.feelathomebarcelona.com; Carrer Nou de la Rambla 15)

Barcelona On Line (Map p250; ☑ 902 887017, 93 343 79 93; www.barcelona-on-line.es; Gran Vía de les Corts Catalanes, 662, 1º 1A)

Friendly Rentals (☑ 93 268 80 51; www.friendlyrentals.com; Passatge de Sert 4)

Rent a Flat in Barcelona (☑ 93 342 73 00; www.rentaflatinbarcelona.com; Ronda del Guinardó 2).

※; Ⓜ Hospital Clínic) Within a five-block walk of Passeig de Gràcia and Diagonal, this is a busy residential location surrounded by restaurants and bars (especially along nearby Carrer d'Aribau, a block away). Crisp, simple rooms are comfy and light. Be aware of traffic noise at the front of the house – a room deeper inside will guarantee tranquillity.

Fashion House
B&B €

(☑ 637 904044; www.bcnfashionhouse.com; Carrer del Bruc 13; s/d €51/91, without bathroom €41/71; ※ ⑦; Ⓜ Urquinaona) The name is a little silly but this typical, broad 1st-floor L'Eixample flat contains eight rooms of varying size done in tasteful style, with 4.5m-high ceilings, parquet floors and, in some cases, a little balcony onto the street. Bathrooms are located along the broad corridor, one for every two rooms.

Somnio Hostel
HOSTEL €

(Map p250; ☑ 93 272 53 08; www.somniohostels.com; Carrer de la Diputació 251; dm €25, d €87, s/d without bathroom €44/78; ※ @ ⑦; Ⓜ Passeig de Gràcia) A crisp, tranquil hostel with 10 rooms (two of them six-bed dorms and all with a simple white and light-blue paint job), Somnio is nicely located in the thick of things in L'Eixample and a short walk from the old city. Rain showers and thick flex mattresses are nice features in these 2nd-floor digs.

★ Five Rooms
BOUTIQUE HOTEL €€

(Map p250; ☑ 93 342 78 80; www.thefiverooms.com; Carrer de Pau Claris 72; s/d from €155/165; ※ @ ⑦; Ⓜ Urquinaona) Like they say, there are five rooms (standard rooms and suites) in this 1st-floor flat virtually on the border between L'Eixample and the old centre of town. Each is different and features include broad, firm beds, stretches of exposed brick wall, restored mosaic tiles and minimalist decor. There are also two apartments.

Cami Bed & Gallery
B&B €€

(Map p250; ☑ 93 270 17 48; www.camibedandgallery.com; Carrer de Casp 22, prl 1º; s/d from €135, s/d without bathroom from €110; ※ ⑦; Ⓜ Catalunya) A new, luxury B&B in a handsome Modernista building that could not be more central, just metres from the Plaça Catalunya. Seven airy rooms, with high ceilings, are meticulously designed and each slightly different in character, though only one has a private bathroom. It was conceived by art lovers, and also functions as a gallery, staging exhibtions and cultural events.

Hotel Constanza
BOUTIQUE HOTEL €€

(Map p250; ☑ 93 270 19 10; www.hotelconstanza.com; Carrer del Bruc 33; s/d €80/100; ※ @ ⑦; Ⓜ Girona, Urquinaona) This boutique beauty has stolen the hearts of many a visitor to Barcelona. Design touches abound, and little details like flowers in the bathroom add charm. Suites and studios are further options. The terrace is a nice spot to relax looking over the rooftops of L'Eixample.

Barcelona Center Inn
HOTEL €€

(Map p250; ☑ 93 265 25 60; www.hostalcenter-inn.com; Gran Via de les Corts Catalanes 688; s/d €75/89; ※ @ ⑦; Ⓜ Tetuan) A charming simplicity pervades the rooms here. Wrought-iron bedsteads are overshadowed by flowing drapes. Room decor varies, with a vaguely Andalucian flavour in the bathrooms. Some rooms have little terraces. Get a back room if you can, as Gran Via is noisy.

Hotel Praktik
BOUTIQUE HOTEL €€

(Map p250; ☑93 343 66 90; www.hotelpraktik rambla.com; Rambla de Catalunya 27; r €119-129; ✴️🛜; MPasseig de Gràcia) This Modernista gem hides a gorgeous little boutique number. While the high ceilings and the bulk of the original tile floors have been maintained, the 43 rooms have daring ceramic touches, spot lighting and contemporary art. There is a chilled reading area and deck-style lounge terrace. The handy location on a tree-lined boulevard is a bonus.

🛏 Gràcia

★Casa Gràcia
HOSTEL €

(Map p250; ☑93 187 44 97; www.casagraciabcn. com; Passeig de Gràcia 116; dm from €27, d from €50; ✴️@🛜; MDiagonal) A hostel with a difference (several differences), the tasteful Casa Gràcia has raised the bar for budget accommodation. There are dorm rooms and a couple of private rooms, and all are decorated in crisp white with bursts of colour. There's a huge terrace where communal dinners are held, along with film screenings and various other events, and art exhibitions adorn its walls. There's also a kitchen and TV room for those colder months.

🛏 Montjuïc, Poble Sec & Sant Antoni

★Hotel Market
BOUTIQUE HOTEL €

(☑93 325 12 05; www.forkandpillow.com; Passatge de Sant Antoni Abad 10; s/d from €72/76; ✴️@🛜; MSant Antoni) Attractively located in a renovated building along a narrow lane just north of the grand old Sant Antoni market (now shut for renovation), this place has an air of simple chic. Room decor is a pleasing combination of white, dark nut browns, light wood and reds.

Sant Jordi Mambo Tango
HOSTEL €

(Map p266; ☑93 442 51 64; www.hostelmambotango.com; Carrer del Poeta Cabanyes 23; dm from €27; @🛜; MParal·lel) A fun, international hostel to hang out in, the Mambo Tango has basic dorms (sleeping from six to nine people) and a welcoming, somewhat chaotic atmosphere. This playful vibe is reflected in the kooky colour scheme in the bathrooms. Advice on what to do and where to go out is always on hand.

Urban Suites
HOTEL, APARTMENT €€

(☑93 201 51 64; www.theurbansuites.com; Carrer de Sant Nicolau 3; ste from €130; P✴️@🛜; MSants Estació) Directed largely at the trade-fair crowd, this contemporary spot with 16 suites and four apartments makes for a convenient and comfortable home away from home. You get a bedroom, living room and kitchen, DVD player and free wi-fi, and the configuration is good for families. Prices fluctuate enormously according to demand. There is a two-night minimum stay.

🛏 La Zona Alta

Inout Hostel
HOSTEL €

(☑93 280 09 85; www.inouthostel.com; Major del Rectoret 2; dm €18; ✴️@🛜♿; FGC Baixador de Vallvidrera) One of Spain's most extraordinary hostels, Inout is a beautifully located property with a strong social ethos. Over 90% of staff here have disabilities. It's a friendly and welcoming place with extensive facilities, including an enticing pool, sports courts, and a low-key restaurant with panoramic views. It's a 12-minute uphill walk from the Baixador de Vallvidrera FGC station.

🍴 Eating

Barcelona is something of a foodies' paradise, combining rich Catalan cooking traditions with a new wave of culinary wizardry by chefs at the vanguard of *nueva cocina española*.

Traditional restaurants, often quite affordable, are scattered across the Barri Gòtic and El Raval, where you'll also find plenty of hip little places. The El Born area of La Ribera teems with eateries, ranging from high-end experimental to many atmospheric spots in historic buildings.

Barceloneta and the waterfront is famed for its seafood eateries, while Gràcia offers a diverse range of tapas bars, inexpensive Middle Eastern and Greek joints and classic Spanish eateries.

Across the broad expanse of L'Eixample, the Zona Alta and further outlying districts, you'll find all sorts of places, from designer sushi bars and top-end dining rooms to festive old-world eateries. You need to know where you are going, however, as wandering about aimlessly and picking whatever takes your fancy is not as feasible as in the old city.

Cartas (menus) may be in Catalan, Spanish or both; quite a few establishments also have foreign-language menus.

✕ Barri Gòtic

Butifarring
SANDWICHES €

(Map p236; Carrer del Call 26; sandwiches €4-5; ⊙9am-9pm Mon-Thu, to 11pm Fri & Sat, to 6pm Sat; 🛜; Ⓜ Liceu, Jaume I) Gourmet sausage sandwiches are grilled to perfection at this friendly and appealing new eatery just off Plaça Sant Jaume. You'll find around six different sausages on the menu including seasonal varieties (like calçots in winter), plus homemade sauces, roasted potatoes, Montseny craft beer and chocolate coulant (soufflé) for dessert.

Rasoterra
VEGETARIAN €

(Map p236; 📄93 318 69 26; Carrer del Palau 5; tapas €5-8, lunch specials €7-10; ⊙noon-5pm Tue, to midnight Wed-Sun; 📄; Ⓜ Jaume I) A delightful addition to the Gothic quarter, Rasoterra cooks

---

MARKET FEASTING

Barcelona has some fantastic food markets. Foodies will enjoy the sounds, smells and most importantly tastes of the Mercat de la Boqueria (Map p236; 📄93 318 25 84; www.boqueria.info; La Rambla 91; ⊙8am-8.30pm Mon-Sat, closed Sun; Ⓜ Liceu). This is probably Spain's biggest and best market, and it's conveniently located right off La Rambla. Here you'll find countless temptations, including an array of tapas bars where you can sample amazingly fresh dishes cooked to perfection.

Other recommended markets for produce or tapas-style dining:

Mercat de Sant Antoni (📄93 209 31 58; www.mercatdesantantoni.com; Carrer de Comte d'Urgell 1; ⊙7am-2.30pm & 5-8.30pm Mon-Thu, 7am-8.30pm Fri & Sat; Ⓜ Sant Antoni)

Mercat de Santa Caterina (p245)

Mercat del Ninot (Map p250; Carrer de Mallorca 157; Ⓜ Hospital Clínic)

Mercat de la Llibertat (p258)

Mercat de la Barceloneta (Map p248; 📄93 221 64 71; www.mercatde-labarceloneta.com; Plaça de la Font 1; ⊙7am-3pm Mon-Thu & Sat, 7am-8pm Fri; Ⓜ Barceloneta)

Mercat de l'Abaceria Central (Map p259; Travessera de Gràcia 186; ⊙7am-2.30pm & 5.30-8pm Mon-Sat; Ⓜ Fontana)

---

up first-rate vegetarian dishes in a Zen-like setting with tall ceilings, low-playing jazz and fresh flowers on the tables. The creative, globally influenced menu changes regularly and might feature Vietnamese-style coconut pancakes with tofu and vegetables, beluga lentils with basmati rice, and pear and goat cheese quesadillas. Good vegan and gluten-free options.

Allium
CATALAN, FUSION €€

(Map p236; 📄93 302 30 03; Carrer del Call 17; mains €8-16; ⊙noon-4pm Mon-Tue, to 10.30pm Wed-Sat; Ⓜ Liceu) This inviting newcomer to Barri Gòtic serves beautifully prepared tapas dishes and changing specials (including seafood paella for one). The menu, which changes every two or three weeks, focuses on seasonal, organic cuisine. Its bright, modern interior sets it apart from other neighbourhood options; it's also open continuously, making it a good bet for those who don't want to wait until 9pm for a meal.

La Vinateria del Call
SPANISH €€

(Map p236; 📄93 302 60 92; www.lavinateriadelcall. com; Carrer de Sant Domènec del Call 9; small plates €7-12; ⊙7.30pm-1am; Ⓜ Jaume I) In a magical setting in the former Jewish quarter, this tiny jewel box of a restaurant serves up tasty Iberian dishes including Galician octopus, cider-cooked chorizo and the Catalan escalivada (roasted peppers, aubergine and onions) with anchovies. Portions are small and made for sharing, and there's a good and affordable selection of wines.

Cafè de l'Acadèmia
CATALAN €€

(Map p236; 📄93 319 82 53; Carrer dels Lledó 1; mains €13-19; ⊙1.30-4pm & 8.45-11.30pm Mon-Fri; Ⓜ Jaume I) Expect a mix of traditional dishes with the occasional creative twist. At lunchtime, local ajuntament (town hall) office workers pounce on the menú del día. In the evening it is rather more romantic, as low lighting emphasises the intimacy of the timber ceiling and wooden decor. On warm days, you can also dine on the pretty square at the front.

Onofre
SPANISH €€

(Map p236; 📄93 317 69 37; www.onofre.net; Carrer de les Magdalenes 19; mains €9-14; ⊙10am-4pm & 7.30pm-midnight Mon-Sat; Ⓜ Jaume I) Famed for its wine selections, Onofre is a small, modern eatery (and wine shop and delicatessen) that has a strong local following for its delicious tapas plates, good affordable wines and great-value lunch specials (three-course prix-fixe for €10.75). Among the delectable tapas selections: Italian greens with foie shavings, duck confit, codfish carpaccio, oven-baked prawns, and warm goat cheese salad with ham and anchovies.

★ Koy Shunka   JAPANESE €€€

(Map p236; ☑ 93 412 79 39; www.koyshunka.com; Carrer de Copons 7; multicourse menus €77-110; ⊙ 1.30-3pm Tue-Sun & 8.30-11pm Tue-Sat; Ⓜ Urquinaona) Down a narrow lane north of the cathedral, Koy Shunka opens a portal to exquisite dishes from the East – mouthwatering sushi, sashimi, seared Wagyu beef and flavour-rich seaweed salads are served alongside inventive cooked fushion dishes like steamed clams with sake or tempura of scallops and king prawns with Japanese mushrooms. Don't miss the house speciality of tender *toro* (tuna belly).

Pla   FUSION €€€

(Map p236; ☑ 93 412 65 52; www.elpla.cat; Carrer de la Bellafila 5; mains €18-25; ⊙ 7.30pm-midnight; ☑; Ⓜ Jaume I) One of Gòtic's long-standing favourites, Pla is a stylish, romantically lit medieval dining room where the cooks churn out such temptations as oxtail braised in red wine, seared tuna with oven-roasted peppers, and polenta with seasonal mushrooms. It has a tasting menu for €38 Sunday to Thursday.

✗ El Raval

Elisabets   CATALAN €

(Map p236; ☑ 93 317 58 26; Carrer d'Elisabets 2-4; mains €8-10; ⊙ 7.30am-11pm Mon-Thu & Sat, until 2am Fri, closed Aug; Ⓜ Catalunya) This unassuming restaurant is popular for no-nonsense local fare. The walls are dotted with old radio sets and the *menú del día* (€10.85) varies daily. If you prefer *a la carta*, try the *ragú de jabalí* (wild boar stew) and finish with *mel i mató* (a Catalan dessert made from cheese and honey). Those with a post-midnight hunger on Friday nights can probably get a meal here as late as 1am.

Sésamo   VEGETARIAN €

(☑ 93 441 64 11; Carrer de Sant Antoni Abat 52; tapas €6; ⊙ 8pm-midnight Tue-Sun; ☑; Ⓜ Sant Antoni) Widely held to be the best veggie restaurant in the city (admittedly not as great an accolade as it might be elsewhere), Sésamo is a cosy, fun place. The menu is mostly tapas, and most people go for the seven-course tapas menu (wine included; €25), but there are a few more substantial dishes. Nice touches include the home-baked bread and cakes.

★ Caravelle   INTERNATIONAL €€

(Map p236; ☑ 93 317 98 92; Carrer del Pintor Fortuny 31; mains €10-13; ⊙ 8.30am-6.30pm Mon-Wed, 8.30am-1am Thu, 10.30am-1am Sat, 10.30am-6.30pm Sun; Ⓜ Liceu) A bright little joint, beloved by the hipster element of the Raval and anyone with a discerning palate. Tacos as you've never tasted them (cod, lime *alioli* and radish; pulled pork with roast corn and avocado), a superior steak sandwich on homemade brioche with pickled celeriac, and all manner of soul food. Drinks are every bit as inventive – try the homemade ginger beer or grapefruit soda.

★ Mam i Teca   CATALAN €€

(Map p236; ☑ 93 441 33 35; Carrer de la Lluna 4; mains €9-12; ⊙ 1-4pm & 8pm-midnight Mon & Wed-Sun, closed Sat lunch; Ⓜ Sant Antoni) A tiny place with half a dozen tables, Mam i Teca is as much a lifestyle choice as a restaurant. Locals drop in and hang about at the bar, and diners are treated to Catalan dishes made with locally sourced products and adhering to Slow Food principles. Try, for example, cod fried in olive oil with garlic and red pepper, or pork ribs with chickpeas.

Bar Pinotxo   TAPAS €€

(Map p236; www.pinotxobar.com; Mercat de la Boqueria; mains €8-15; ⊙ 6am-4pm Mon-Sat; Ⓜ Liceu) Bar Pinotxo is arguably La Boqueria's, and even Barcelona's, best tapas bar. It sits among the half-dozen or so informal eateries within the market, and the popular owner, Juanito, might serve up chickpeas with a sweet sauce of pine nuts and raisins, a fantastically soft mix of potato and spinach sprinkled with coarse salt, soft baby squid with cannellini beans, or a quivering cube of caramel-sweet pork belly.

Suculent   CATALAN €€

(Map p236; ☑ 93 443 65 79; www.suculent.com; Rambla del Raval 39; mains €11-20; ⊙ 1-4pm & 8.30-11.30pm Wed-Sun, closed Sun dinner; Ⓜ Liceu) Michelin-starred chef Carles Abellán (of Comerç 24 fame) adds to his stable with this old-style bistro, which showcases the best of Catalan cuisine. From the cod brandade to the oxtail stew with truffled sweet potato, only the best ingredients are used, so be warned that the prices can mount up a bit, but this is a great place to sample the regional highlights.

La Ribera

★ Bormuth
TAPAS €

(Map p244; ☑ 93 310 21 86; Carrer del Rec 31; tapas from €3.50; ⊙ 5pm-midnight Mon & Tue, noon-1am Wed, Thu & Sun, noon-2.30am Fri & Sat; Ⓜ Jaume I) Opened on the pedestrian Carrer del Rec in 2013, Bormuth has tapped into the vogue for old-school tapas with modern-times service and decor, and serves all the old favourites – *patatas bravas, ensaladilla* (Russian salad), tortilla – along with some less predictable and superbly prepared numbers (try the chargrilled red pepper with black pudding). The split-level dining room is never less than animated, but there's a more peaceful space with a single long table if you can assemble a group.

★ En Aparté
FRENCH €

(☑ 93 269 13 35; www.enaparte.es; Carrer Lluis el Piados 2; mains €7-10; ⊙ 10am-1am Tue-Thu, 10am-2am Fri & Sat, noon-1am Sun; 🖘; Ⓜ Arc de Triomf or Urquinaona) A great low-key place to eat good-quality French food, just off the quiet Plaça de Sant Pere. The restaurant is small but spacious, with sewing-machine tables and vintage details, and floor-to-ceiling windows that bring in some wonderful early-afternoon sunlight.

The lunch menu (€11) is excellent, offering a salad (such as beetroot and apple and walnut), and a quiche or other dish, such as stuffed peppers with a potato gratin. Brunch (French toast, eggs Benedict and muesli with yoghurt) is served on weekends.

★ El Atril
INTERNATIONAL €€

(Map p244; ☑ 93 310 12 20; www.atrilbarcelona. com; Carrer dels Carders 23; mains €11-15; ⊙ 6pm-midnight Mon, noon-midnight Tue-Thu, noon-1am Fri & Sat, 11.30am-11.30pm Sun; Ⓜ Jaume I) Aussie owner Brenden is influenced by culinary influences from all over the globe, so while you'll see plenty of tapas (the *patatas bravas* are recommended for their homemade sauce), you'll also find kangaroo fillet, salmon and date rolls with mascarpone, chargrilled turkey with fried yucca, and plenty more. If the weather is good or there's no room in the cosy dining room, there are tables outside in a lively square.

Casa Delfín
SPANISH €€

(Map p244; ☑ 93 319 50 88; www.tallerdetapas. com; Passeig del Born 36; mains €10-15; ⊙ 8am-midnight daily, until 1am Fri & Sat; Ⓜ Barceloneta) One of Barcelona's culinary delights, Casa

Delfín is everything you dream of when you think of Catalan (and Mediterranean) cooking. Start with the tangy and sweet *calçots* (a cross between a leek and an onion; February and March only) or salt-strewn *padron* peppers, moving on to grilled sardines speckled with parsley, then tackle the meaty monkfish roasted in white wine and garlic.

Cal Pep
TAPAS €€

(Map p244; ☑ 93 310 79 61; www.calpep.com; Plaça de les Olles 8; mains €12-20; ⊙ 7.30-11.30pm Mon, 1-3.45pm & 7.30-11.30pm Tue-Fri, 1-3.45pm Sat, closed last 3 weeks Aug; Ⓜ Barceloneta) Getting a foot in the door here is the problem – there can be queues out into the square with people trying to get in. And if you want one of the five tables out the back, you'll need to call ahead. Most people are happy elbowing their way to the bar for some of the tastiest gourmet seafood tapas in town.

★ Comerç 24
INTERNATIONAL €€€

(Map p244; ☑ 93 319 21 02; www.carlesabellan. com; Carrer del Comerç 24; mains €24-32; ⊙ 1.30-3.30pm & 8.30-11pm Tue-Sat; Ⓜ Barceloneta) Michelin-starred chef Carles Abellán playfully reinterprets the traditional (suckling pig 'Hanoi style'), as well as more international classics, such as the bite-sized mini-pizza sashimi with tuna; *melón con jamón*, a millefeuille of layered caramelised Iberian ham and thinly sliced melon, or oxtail with cauliflower purée. If your budget will stretch to it, try a little of almost everything with the 'Menú del Gran Festival' (€116).

Port Vell & Barceloneta

Baluard Barceloneta
BAKERY €

(Map p248; Carrer del Baluard 36; pastries €1-2.70; ⊙ 8am-9pm; Ⓜ Barceloneta) One of the best bakeries in the city, Baluard serves up warm flaky croissants, perfect baguettes, moist muffins, and a range of tempting pastries and tarts (try one with figs or wild berries).

Can Maño
SPANISH €

(Map p248; Carrer del Baluard 12; mains €7-12; ⊙ 9am-4pm Tue-Sat & 8-11pm Mon-Fri; Ⓜ Barceloneta) It may look like a dive, but you'll need to be prepared to wait before being squeezed in at a packed table for a raucous night of *raciones* (full-plate-size tapas serving; posted on a board at the back) over a bottle of *turbio* – a cloudy white plonk. The seafood is abundant with first-rate squid, shrimp and fish served at rock-bottom prices.

Vaso de Oro TAPAS €
(Map p248; Carrer de Balboa 6; tapas €4-12;
☺10am-midnight; MBarceloneta) Always
packed, this narrow bar gathers a festive,
beer-swilling crowd who come for fantastic
tapas. Fast-talking, white-jacketed waiters
will serve up a few quick quips with your
plates of grilled *gambes* (prawns), *foie a la
plancha* (grilled liver pâté) or *solomillo* (sirloin) chunks. Want something a bit different
to drink? Ask for a *flauta cincuenta* – half
lager and half dark beer.

La Cova Fumada TAPAS €
(Map p248; ☑93 221 40 61; Carrer del Baluard 56;
tapas €3.50-7.50; ☺9am-3.20pm Mon-Wed, 9am-
3.20pm & 6-8.20pm Thu & Fri, 9am-1.20pm Sat;
MBarceloneta) There's no sign and the setting
is decidedly downmarket, but this tiny, buzzing family-run tapas spot always packs in a
crowd. The secret? Mouthwatering *pulpo*
(octopus), *calamar, sardinias* and 15 or so
other small plates cooked up to perfection
in the small open kitchen near the door.
The *bombas* (potato croquettes served with
alioli) and grilled *carxofes* (artichokes) are
good, but everything is amazingly fresh.

Jai-Ca SEAFOOD €
(Map p248; ☑93 268 32 65; Carrer de Ginebra 13;
tapas €4-7; ☺9am-11.30pm Mon-Sat; MBarceloneta) Jai-Ca is a much-loved eatery that
serves up juicy grilled prawns, flavour-rich
anchovies, tender octopus, decadent razor
clams and other seafood favourites to ever-
growing crowds as the evening progresses.
The *turbio* (Galician white wine), sangria
and cold draughts are ideal refreshment after a day on the beach.

Barraca SEAFOOD €€€
(Map p248; ☑93 224 12 53; www.barraca-
barcelona.com; Passeig Maritim de la Barceloneta
1; mains €19-29; ☺1pm-midnight; MBarceloneta)
Recently opened, this buzzing space has a
great location fronting the Mediterranean –
a key reference point in the excellent seafood dishes served up here. Start off with a
cauldron of chili-infused clams, cockles and
mussels before moving on to the lavish paellas and other rice dishes, which steal the
show.

Can Majó SEAFOOD €€€
(Map p248; ☑93 221 54 55; www.canmajo.es; Car-
rer del Almirall Aixada 23; mains €16-26; ☺1-4pm
Tue-Sun & 8-11.30pm Tue-Sat; ☐45, 57, 59, 64 or 157,
MBarceloneta) Virtually on the beach (with
tables outside in summer), Can Majó has a

EAT WITH LOCALS
A handful of new websites allow travellers to eat in the homes of locals for
about the same price as you'd pay to
eat in a restaurant. The biggest and best
of the bunch is **EatWith.com** (www.
eatwith.com)– the airbnb of the dining
world – which lists hundreds of aspiring
hosts throwing dinner parties and food-
related events (wine tastings, cooking
tutorials, gourmet walking tours) in
Barcelona and beyond. Read profiles
of hosts, plus reviews by recent guests,
then take the plunge. It's a great way to
experience an authentic side of the city.

long and steady reputation for fine seafood,
particularly its rice dishes and bountiful *su-
quets* (fish stews). The bouillabaisse of fish
and seafood is succulent. Sit outside (there
are heat lamps in winter) and admire the
beach goers.

🍴 Poblenou & Port Olímpic

★ Can Recasens CATALAN €€
(☑93 300 81 23; Rambla del Poblenou 102; mains
€6-14; ☺9pm-1am Mon-Sat & 1-4pm Sat; MPoble-
nou) One of Poblenou's most romantic settings, Can Recasens hides a warren of warmly lit rooms full of oil paintings, flickering
candles, fairy lights and baskets of fruit. The
food is outstanding, with a mix of salads,
fondues, smoked meats, cheeses, and open-
faced sandwiches piled high with delicacies
like wild mushrooms and brie, *escalivada*
(grilled vegetables) and gruyere, and spicy
chorizo.

🍴 L'Eixample

★ Cerveseria Catalana TAPAS €
(Map p250; ☑93 216 03 68; Carrer de Mallorca
236; tapas €4-11; ☺9.30am-1.30am; MPasseig
de Gràcia) The 'Catalan Brewery' is good for
breakfast, lunch and dinner. Come for your
morning coffee and croissant, or wait until
lunch to enjoy choosing from the abundance
of tapas and *montaditos* (canapés). You can
sit at the bar, on the pavement terrace or in
the restaurant at the back. The variety of hot
tapas, salads and other snacks draws a well-
dressed crowd of locals and outsiders.

Copasetic
CAFE €

(☑93 532 76 66; www.copaseticbarcelona.com; Carrer de la Diputació 55; mains €8-12; ☺7pm-midnight Mon, noon-midnight Tue & Wed, noon-1am Thu, noon-3am Fri, 10.30am-3am Sat, 10.30am-6pm Sun; ⓂRocafort) A fun and friendly new cafe, decked out with retro furniture. There's plenty for everyone, whether your thing is eggs Benedict, wild-berry tartlets or a juicy fat burger, lots of vegetarian, gluten-free and organic options, and superb (and reasonably priced) brunches on weekends. Wednesday night is ladies' night, with cheap cocktails.

Fastvínic
CAFE €

(Map p250; ☑93 487 32 41; www.fastvinic.com; Carrer de la Diputació 251; sandwiches €4.25-12; ☺noon-midnight Mon-Sat; ⓂPasseig de Gracia) 🖉 A project in sustainability all round, this is Slow Food done fast, with ingredients, wine and building materials all sourced from Catalonia. Designed by Alfons Tost, there are air-purifying plants, energy-efficient LED lighting, and a water and food recycling system.

Amaltea
VEGETARIAN €

(www.amalteaygovinda.com; Carrer de la Diputació 164; mains €5-9; ☺1-4pm & 8-11.30pm Mon-Sat; 🖉; ⓂUrgell) The ceiling fresco of blue sky sets the scene in this popular vegetarian eatery. The *menú del día* (€10.70) offers a series of dishes that change frequently with the seasons and homemade desserts are tempting. At night, the set two-course dinner (€15) offers good value. The place is something of an alternative lifestyle centre, with yoga, t'ai chi and belly-dancing classes.

★Tapas 24
TAPAS €€

(Map p250; ☑93 488 09 77; www.carlesabellan. com; Carrer de la Diputació 269; tapas €4-9; ☺9am-midnight Mon-Sat; ⓂPasseig de Gràcia) Carles Abellán, master of Comerç 24 in La Ribera, runs this basement tapas haven known for its gourmet versions of old faves. Specials include the *bikini* (toasted ham and cheese sandwich – here the ham is cured and the truffle makes all the difference) and a thick *arròs negre de sípia* (squid-ink black rice).

Cata 1.81
TAPAS €€

(Map p250; ☑93 323 68 18; www.cata181.com; Carrer de València 181; tapas €6-8; ☺7pm-midnight Mon-Sat; ⓂPasseig de Gràcia) A beautifully designed venue (with lots of small lights, some trapped in birdcages), this is the place to come for fine wines and dainty gourmet dishes like *raviolis amb bacallà* (salt-cod

dumplings) or *truita de patates i tòfona negre* (thick potato tortilla with a delicate trace of black truffle). The best option is to choose from one of several tasting-menu options ranging from €29 to €45.

Can Kenji
JAPANESE €€

(☑93 476 18 23; www.cankenji.com; Carrer del Rosselló 325; mains €8-14; ☺1-3.30pm & 8.30-11pm Mon-Sat; ⓂVerdaguer) If you want to go Japanese in Barcelona, this is the place. The chef of this understated little *izakaya* (the Japanese version of a tavern) gets his ingredients fresh from the city's markets, with traditional Japanese recipes receiving a Mediterranean touch, so you'll get things like sardine tempura with an aubergine, miso and anchovy purée, or *tataki* (lightly grilled meat) of *bonito* (tuna) with *salmorejo* (a Córdoban cold tomato and bread soup).

Taktika Berri
BASQUE, TAPAS €€

(Map p250; ☑93 453 47 59; Carrer de València 169; tapas from €3; ☺1-4pm & 8.30-11pm Mon-Fri, 1-4pm Sat; ⓂHospital Clínic) Get in early because the bar teems with punters anxious to try some of the best Basque tapas in town. The hot morsels are all snapped up as soon as they arrive from the kitchen, so keep your eyes peeled. The seated dining area out the back is also good. In the evening, it's all over by about 10.30pm.

★Cinc Sentits
INTERNATIONAL €€€

(Map p250; ☑93 323 94 90; www.cincsentits. com; Carrer d'Aribau 58; tasting menus €65-109; ☺1.30-3pm & 8.30-10pm Tue-Sat; ⓂPasseig de Gràcia) Enter the realm of the 'Five Senses' to indulge in a jaw-dropping tasting menu (there is no à la carte, although dishes can be tweaked to suit diners' requests), consisting of a series of small, experimental dishes. A key is the use of fresh local produce, such as fish landed on the Costa Brava and top-quality suckling pig from Extremadura, along with the kind of creative genius that has earned chef Jordi Artal a Michelin star.

✕ Gràcia

★Les Tres a la Cuina
INTERNATIONAL €

(Map p259; ☑93 105 49 47; Carrer de Sant Lluis 35; menú del día €9, brunch menú €10; ☺10am-6pm Mon-Fri, 11.30am-4.30pm Sat & Sun; ⓂJoanic) Colourful, Instagrammable food that tastes superb and uses ingredients you won't find in most other restaurants around town. The menu changes daily but you can choose from the likes of chicken with apricots, prunes and tamarind sauce, or quinoa salad with baked fennel and avocado, and finish up with pistachio and lemon drizzle cake. All this prepared with love and Slow Food principles for an unbeatable price. There are few tables, so arrive early.

★ **El Tossal**   SPANISH €€

(Map p259; ☑ 93 457 63 82; www.eltossalbcn.com; Carrer de Tordera 12; mains €10-16; ⊙ 1.30-4pm & 8.30-11pm Tue-Sat; M Joanic) A proper old-fashioned, no-frills Catalan restaurant, of the sort in which Gràcia excels, with tables arrayed around a central bar area and into a low-ceilinged dining annexe. The speciality is game and similarly hearty fare – the oxtail stew is excellent, as is the duck magret with caramelised onions and a port reduction – and there is a short but well-chosen list of suitably robust wines.

Sol i Lluna   FRENCH €€

(Map p259; ☑ 93 237 10 52; Carrer de Verdi 50; mains €10.50-16.50; ⊙ 7.30-11pm Mon-Fri, 1-4pm & 7.30pm-midnight Sat & Sun; M Fontana) Bright and sunny by day, softly lit at night, Sol i Lluna is a peaceful, elegant place that has as its distinguishing feature a giant wooden hippo in the window. The food is mostly French, but draws in influences from around the globe, such as the 'lasagne' of ratatouille with goat's cheese or the vegetarian Puy lentil 'meatballs'.

Botafumeiro   SEAFOOD €€€

(☑ 93 218 42 30; www.botafumeiro.es; Carrer Gran de Gràcia 81; mains €16-28; ⊙ noon-1am; M Fontana) It is hard not to mention this classic temple of Galician shellfish and other briny delights, long a magnet for VIPs visiting Barcelona. You can bring the price down by sharing a few *medias raciones* (large tapas plates) to taste a range of marine offerings or a *safata especial del Mar Cantàbric* (seafood platter) between two. Try the *percebes,* the strangely twisted goose barnacles harvested along Galicia's north Atlantic coast, which many Spaniards consider the ultimate seafood delicacy.

✖ La Zona Alta

Mitja Vida   TAPAS €

(Carrer de Brusi 39; tapas €2-6; ⊙ 6-11pm Mon-Thu, noon-4pm & 6-11pm Fri & Sat, noon-4pm Sun; ℝ FGC Sant Gervasi) A fun, youthful mostly local crowd gathers around the stainless-steel tapas bar of tiny Mitja Vida. It's a jovial eating and drinking spot, with servings of anchovies, *calamares,* smoked herring, cheeses and *mojama* (salt-cured tuna). The drink of choice is housemade vermouth.

Ajoblanco   TAPAS €€

(☑ 93 667 87 66; Carrer de Tuset 20; sharing plates €8-20; ⊙ noon-3am; ℝ FGC Gràcia) New in 2014, this beautifully designed space serves a mix

BARCELONA EATING

CELEBRATED CATALAN CHEFS

Barcelona has a growing number of Michelin-starred chefs. Albert Adrià, brother of Ferran of El Bulli fame, has brought even more culinary fame to Barcelona with his growing empire of restaurants. His tapas restaurant **Tickets** (Map p266; www.ticketsbar.es; Avinguda del Paral·lel 164; tapas €6-15; ⊙ 7-11.30pm Tue-Fri, 1.30-3.30pm & 7-11.30pm Sat, closed Aug; M Paral·lel) is a delectable showcase of whimsy and imagination, with deconstructed dishes like liquid olives, 'air baguettes' (made with Iberian ham) and cotton-candy-covered trees with edible dark chocolate 'soil'.

Other great chefs continue to redefine contemporary cuisine. Carles Abellán, creator of Comerç 24 (p282), Tapas 24 (p284) and other restaurants, playfully reinterprets traditional tapas with dishes like the bite-sized mini-pizza sashimi with tuna; melón con *jamón,* a millefeuille of layered carmelised Iberian ham and thinly sliced melon; oxtail with cauliflower purée; and an ever-changing parade of other mouth-watering bites.

Another star of the Catalan cooking scene is Jordi Vilà, who continues to wow diners at **Alkimia** (☑ 93 207 61 15; www.alkimia.cat; Carrer de l'Indústria 79; mains €18-29; ⊙ 1.30-3.30pm & 8-11pm Mon-Fri; M Sagrada Família) and **Vivanda** (☑ 93 203 19 18; www.vivanda. cat; Carrer Major de Sarrià 134; sharing plates €9-15; ⊙ 1.30-3.30pm Tue-Sun, 9-11pm Tue-Sat; ℝ FGC Reina Elisenda) with reinvented Catalan classics. Other major players on the Catalan dining scene are Jordi Artal at Cinc Sentits (p284), Xavier Pellicer at **ABaC** (☑ 93 319 66 00; www.abacbarcelona.com; Av del Tibidabo 1; mains €42-72, tasting menu €135-155; ⊙ 1.30-4pm & 8.30-11pm Tue-Sat) and Barraca (p283), and Carles Gaig, whose family has roots in Catalan culinary traditions dating back to the 1860s.

of classic and creative tapas plates that go nicely with the imaginative cocktail menu. Sip the house vermouth while feasting on oxtail tacos, jumbo prawns with avocado and cherry tomato, or arugula salad with goat cheese, strawberries and toasted almonds.

✖ Montjuïc, Poble Sec & Sant Antoni

Barramón
CANARIAN €

(Map p266; ☑ 93 442 30 80; www.barramon.es; Carrer de Blai 28; mains €9-11; ☉ 7-11.30pm Mon-Thu, 1pm-midnight Fri-Sun; Ⓜ Paral·lel) On the lively Carrer de Blai, Barramón is a great little bar that serves Canarian food and is a bit rock and roll at the same time. Try the *ropa vieja* (an infinitely more flavoursome version of its Cuban cousin), a wonderful stew of chickpeas and shredded pork; *papas arrugadas* (baked new potatoes with a spicy sauce); and *almogrote* (cured cheese topped with olive oil, garlic and red pepper).

★ Quimet i Quimet
TAPAS €€

(Map p266; ☑ 93 442 31 42; Carrer del Poeta Cabanyes 25; tapas €4-11; ☉ noon-4pm & 7-10.30pm Mon-Fri, noon-4pm Sat & Sun; Ⓜ Paral·lel) Quimet i Quimet is a family-run business that has been passed down from generation to generation. There's barely space to swing a *calamar* in this bottle-lined, standing-room-only place, but it is a treat for the palate, with *montaditos* (tapas on a slice of bread) made to order. Let the folk behind the bar advise you, and order a drop of fine wine to accompany the food.

Federal
CAFE €€

(☑ 93 187 36 07; www.federalcafe.es; Carrer del Parlament 39; snacks from €8; ☉ 8am-11pm Mon-Thu, 8am-1am Fri, 9am-1am Sat, 9am-5.30pm Sun;

BEST CAFES

Some of Barcelona's most atmospheric cafes lie hidden in the cobbled lanes of the Ciutat Vella. A round-up of our favourite spots for a pick-me-up:

Salterio (Map p236; Carrer de Sant Domènec del Call 4; ☉ 2pm-midnight; Ⓜ Jaume I) A wonderfully photogenic spot tucked down a tiny lane in the Call, Salterio serves refreshing teas, Turkish coffee, authentic mint teas and snacks amid stone walls, incense and ambient Middle Eastern music. If hunger strikes, try the *sardo* (grilled flat-bread covered with pesto, cheese or other toppings).

Čaj Chai (Map p236; ☑ 93 301 95 92; www.cajchai.com; Carrer de Sant Domènec del Call 12; ☉ 3-10pm Mon, 10.30am-10pm Tue-Sun; Ⓜ Jaume I) Inspired by Prague's bohemian tearooms, this bright and buzzing cafe in the heart of the old Jewish quarter is a tea connoisseur's paradise. Čaj Chai stocks over 100 teas from China, India, Korea, Japan, Nepal, Morocco and beyond. It's a much-loved local haunt.

Caelum (Map p236; ☑ 93 302 69 93; www.caelumbarcelona.com; Carrer de la Palla 8; ☉ 10.30am-8.30pm Mon-Thu, 10.30am-11.30pm Fri & Sat, 11.30am-9pm Sun; Ⓜ Liceu) Centuries of heavenly gastronomic tradition from across Spain are concentrated in this exquisite medieval space in the heart of the city. The upstairs cafe is a dainty setting for decadent cakes and pastries, while descending into the underground chamber with its stone walls and flickering candles is like stepping into the Middle Ages.

Granja M Viader (Map p236; ☑ 93 318 34 86; www.granjaviader.cat; Carrer d'en Xuclà 6; ☉ 9am-1.30pm & 5-9pm Mon-Sat; Ⓜ Liceu) For more than a century, people have flocked down this alley to get to the cups of homemade hot chocolate and whipped cream (ask for a *suís*) ladled out in this classic Catalan-style milk bar-cum-deli. The Viader clan invented Cacaolat, a forerunner of kids' powdered-chocolate beverages. The interior is delightfully vintage and the atmosphere always upbeat.

La Nena (Map p259; ☑ 93 285 14 76; Carrer de Ramon i Cajal 36; snacks from €3; ☉ 9am-10.30pm; ♿; Ⓜ Fontana) A French team has created this delightfully chaotic space for indulging in cups of *suïssos* (rich hot chocolate) served with a plate of heavy homemade whipped cream and *melindros* (spongy sweet biscuits), fine desserts and even a few savoury dishes (including crêpes). The place is strewn with books and the area out the back is designed to keep kids busy, with toys, books and a blackboard with chalk, making it an ideal family rest stop.

Ⓜ Sant Antoni) On a stretch that now teems with cafes, Australian-run Federal was the trailblazer, with its breezy chic and superb brunches. Later in the day there is healthy, tasty cooking from veggie burgers to a ploughman's, and cupcakes and good coffee are available all day. Head to the roof for a small, leafy terrace on which to browse the day's papers.

Xemei
ITALIAN €€

(Map p266; ☑93 553 51 40; Passeig de l'Exposició 85; mains €15-24; ⊙1.30-3.30pm & 9-11.30pm Mon-Fri, 2-4pm & 9pm-midnight Sat & Sun; Ⓜ Poble Sec) Xemei ('twins' in Venetian, because it is run by twins from Italy's lagoon city) is a wonderful slice of Venice in Barcelona. To the accompaniment of gentle jazz, you might try a starter of mixed *cicheti* (Venetian seafood tapas), followed by *bigoi in salsa veneziana* (thick spaghetti in an anchovy and onion sauce).

Drinking & Nightlife

Barcelona's bars run the gamut from wood-panelled wine cellars to bright waterfront places and trendy cocktail lounges. Most are at their liveliest around midnight. Barcelona's clubs are spread a little more thinly than bars across the city. They tend to open from around midnight until 6am.

The old town is jammed with venues. One of the hippest areas is El Born, at the lower end of La Ribera, but there is an impressive scattering of bars across the lower half of the Barri Gòtic and in El Raval too. The last especially is home to some fine old drinking institutions as well as a new wave of funky, inner-city places.

Elsewhere, a series of squares and some streets in Gràcia are loaded up with bars. In the broad expanse of L'Eixample you need to know where to go. The upper end of Carrer d'Aribau is the busiest area (late in the week), along with the area around its continuation northwest of Avinguda Diagonal.

Some useful sources of information on bars, clubs and gigs include www.barcelonarocks.com, www.clubbingspain.com and www.lanetro.com/barcelona.

Barri Gòtic

Ocaña
BAR

(Map p236; ☑93 676 48 14; www.ocana.cat; Plaça Reial 13; ⊙5pm-2.30am Mon-Fri, from 11am Sat & Sun; Ⓜ Liceu) Named after a flamboyant artist who once lived on Plaça Reial, Ocaña is a beautifully designed space with fluted columns, stone walls, candlelit chandeliers and plush furnishings. Have a seat on the terrace and watch the passing people parade, or head downstairs to the Moorish-inspired Apotheke bar or the chic lounge a few steps away, where DJs spin for a mix of beauties and bohemians on weekend nights.

Sor Rita
BAR

(Map p236; Carrer de la Mercè 27; ⊙7pm-2.30am; Ⓜ Jaume I) A lover of all things kitsch, Sor Rita is pure eye candy, from its leopard-print wallpaper to its high-heel festooned ceiling, and deliciously irreverent decorations inspired by the films of Almodóvar. It's a fun and festive scene, with special-event nights throughout the week, including tarot readings on Mondays, €5 all-you-can-eat snack buffets on Tuesdays, karaoke Wednesdays and gin specials on Thursdays.

Ginger
COCKTAIL BAR

(Map p236; www.ginger.cat; Carrer de Palma de Sant Just 1; ⊙7.30pm-2.30am Tue-Sat; Ⓜ Jaume I) Tucked away just off peaceful Plaça de Sant Just, Ginger is an art deco–style multilevel drinking den with low lighting, finely crafted cocktails and good ambient sounds (provided by vinyl-spinning DJs some nights). It's a mellow spot that's great for sipping wine and sampling from the small tapas menu.

Oviso
BAR

(Map p236; Carrer d'Arai 5; ⊙10am-2.30am; 🛜; Ⓜ Liceu) Oviso is a popular budget-friendly restaurant with outdoor tables on the plaza, but shows its true bohemian colours by night, with a mixed crowd, a rock-and-roll vibe and a rustic decorated two-room interior plastered with curious murals – geese taking flight, leaping dolphins and blue peacocks framing the brightly painted concrete walls.

La Cerveteca
BAR

(Map p236; Carrer de Gignàs 25; ⊙6-11pm Sun-Thu, to midnight Fri & Sat; Ⓜ Jaume I) An unmissable stop for beer lovers, La Cerveteca serves an impressive variety of global craft brews. In addition to scores of bottled brews, there's a frequent rotation of what's on draught. Cheeses, *jamon ibérico* and other charcuterie selections are on hand, including *cecina* (cured horse meat). The standing cask tables (with a few seats at the back) are a fine setting for an early evening pick-me-up.

Marula Cafè BAR

(Map p236; www.marulacafe.com; Carrer dels Escudellers 49; ⊙11pm-5am Wed-Sun; MLiceu) A fantastic funk find in the heart of the Barri Gòtic, Marula will transport you to the 1970s and the best in funk and soul. James Brown fans will think they've died and gone to heaven. It's not, however, a monothematic place and DJs slip in other tunes, from breakbeat to house. Samba and other Brazilian dance sounds also penetrate here.

Barcelona Pipa Club BAR

(Map p236; ☑93 302 47 32; www.bpipaclub.com; Plaça Reial 3; ⊙10pm-4am; MLiceu) This pipe-smokers' club is like an apartment, with all sorts of interconnecting rooms and knick-knacks – notably the pipes after which the place is named. Buzz at the door and head two floors up. Note there's no longer any smoking here, though there is occasional live music.

🍸 El Raval

★Casa Almirall BAR

(Map p236; www.casaalmirall.com; Carrer de Joaquín Costa 33; ⊙6pm-2.30am Mon-Thu, 6.30-3am Fri, noon-3am Sat, noon-1.30am Sun; MUniversitat) In business since the 1860s, this unchanged corner bar is dark and intriguing, with Modernista decor and a mixed clientele. There are some great original pieces in here, like the marble counter and the cast-iron statue of the muse of the Universal Exposition, held in Barcelona in 1888.

★La Confitería BAR

(Map p236; Carrer de Sant Pau 128; ⊙7.30pm-3am Mon-Thu, 1pm-3am Fri-Sun; MParal·lel) This is a trip into the 19th century. Until the 1980s it was a confectioner's shop, and although the original cabinets are now lined with booze, the look has barely changed in its conversion into a laid-back bar. A quiet enough spot for a house *vermut* (€3; add your own soda) in the early evening, it fills with theatre-goers and local party people later at night.

Bar La Concha BAR, GAY

(Map p236; Carrer de la Guàrdia 14; ⊙5pm-3am daily; MDrassanes) This place is dedicated to worshipping the actress Sara Montiel: the walls groan with over 250 photos of the sultry star. Born in 1928, Montiel bared all on the silver screen in an era that condemned nudity to shameful brazenness – hence 'la concha' (a word commonly used in the Spanish slang) can be read as a sly salute

to the female genitalia. La Concha used to be a largely gay and transvestite haunt, but anyone is welcome and bound to have fun – especially when the drag queens come out to play. Moroccan ownership means you're as likely to see belly dancing nowadays.

Negroni COCKTAIL BAR

(Map p236; www.negronicocktailbar.com; Carrer de Joaquín Costa 46; ⊙7pm-2.30am Mon-Thu, 7pm-3am Fri & Sat; MLiceu) Good things come in small packages and this dark, teeny cocktail bar confirms the rule. The mostly black decor lures in a largely student set to try out the cocktails, among them, of course, the celebrated Negroni, a Florentine invention with one part Campari, one part gin and one part sweet vermouth.

Marmalade BAR

(Map p236; www.marmaladebarcelona.com; Carrer de la Riera Alta 4-6; ⊙6.30pm-2.30am Mon-Wed, 10am-2.30am Thu-Sun; MSant Antoni) The golden hues of this backlit bar and restaurant beckon seductively through the glass facade. There are various distinct spaces, decorated in different but equally sumptuous styles, and a pool table next to the bar. Cocktails are big business here, and a selection of them are €5 all night.

Moog CLUB

(Map p236; www.masimas.com/moog; Carrer de l'Arc del Teatre 3; admission €10; ⊙midnight-5am Mon-Thu & Sun, midnight-6am Fri & Sat; MDrassanes) This fun and minuscule club is a standing favourite with the downtown crowd. In the main dance area, DJs dish out house, techno and electro, while upstairs you can groove to a nice blend of indie and occasional classic-pop throwbacks.

🍷 La Ribera

Mudanzas BAR

(Map p244; ☑93 319 11 37; Carrer de la Vidrieria 15; ⊙9.30am-2.30am Mon-Fri, 5pm-3am Sat & Sun; 🛜; MJaume I) This was one of the first bars to get things into gear in El Born and it still attracts a faithful crowd. It's a straightforward place for a beer, a chat and perhaps a sandwich. Oh, and it has a nice line in rums and malt whiskey.

La Vinya del Senyor WINE BAR

(Map p244; ☑93 310 33 79; www.lavinyadelsenyor.com; Plaça de Santa Maria del Mar 5; ⊙noon-1am Mon-Thu, noon-2am Fri & Sat, noon-midnight Sun; MJaume I) Relax on the *terrassa*, which lies in the shadow of Basílica de Santa Maria del Mar, or crowd inside at the tiny bar. The wine list is as long as *War and Peace* and there's a table upstairs for those who opt to sample by the bottle rather than the glass.

Juanra Falces COCKTAIL BAR
(Map p244; ☏ 93 310 10 27; Carrer del Rec 24; ☺ 8pm-3am, from 10pm Mon & Sun; Ⓜ Jaume I) Transport yourself to a Humphrey Bogart movie in this narrow little bar, formerly (and still, at least among the locals) known as Gimlet. White-jacketed bar staff will whip you up a gimlet, or any other classic cocktail (around €10) your heart desires, with all the appropriate aplomb.

Rubí BAR
(Map p244; ☏ 647 773707; Carrer dels Banys Vells 6; ☺ 7.30pm-2.30am; Ⓜ Jaume I) With its boudoir lighting and cheap mojitos, Rubí is where the Born's cognoscenti head for a nightcap – or several. It's a narrow, cosy space – push through to the back where you might just get one of the coveted tables – with superior bar food, from Vietnamese rolls to more traditional selections of cheese and ham.

Miramelindo BAR
(Map p244; ☏ 93 310 37 27; Passeig del Born 15; ☺ 8pm-2.30am; Ⓜ Jaume I) A spacious tavern in a Gothic building, this remains a classic on Passeig del Born for mixed drinks, while soft jazz and soul sounds float overhead. Try for a comfy seat at a table towards the back before it fills to bursting. A couple of similarly barn-sized places line this side of the *passeig*.

Barceloneta & the Waterfront

The Barcelona beach scene warms up to dance sounds from Easter to early October. In addition to waterfront restaurants and bars (especially on and near Port Olímpic), a string of *chiringuitos* (rustic bars) sets up along the beaches. Most serve food and some turn into miniclubs on the sand from the afternoon until as late as 2am.

Absenta BAR
(Map p248; Carrer de Sant Carles 36; ☺ 7pm-2am Wed-Thu, from 1pm Sat & Sun; Ⓜ Barceloneta) Decorated with old paintings, vintage lamps and curious sculpture (including a dangling butterfly woman and face-painted TVs), this whimsical drinking den takes its liquor seriously. Stop in for the house-made vermouth or try one of the many absinthes on hand. It attracts a hipsterish but easygoing crowd.

THE GREEN FAIRY

Bar Marsella (Map p236; Carrer de Sant Pau 65; ☺ 10pm-2.30am Mon-Wed, 10pm-3am Thu-Sat; Ⓜ Liceu) has been in business since 1820, and has served the likes of Hemingway, who was known to slump here over an *absenta* (absinthe). The bar still specialises in absinthe, a drink to be treated with respect. Your glass comes with a lump of sugar, a fork and a little bottle of mineral water. Hold the sugar on the fork, over your glass, and drip the water onto the sugar so that it dissolves into the absinthe, which turns yellow. The result should give you a warm glow.

CDLC LOUNGE
(Map p248; www.cdlcbarcelona.com; Passeig Marítim de la Barceloneta 32; ☺ noon-4am; Ⓜ Ciutadella Vila Olímpica) Seize the night by the scruff at the Carpe Diem Lounge Club, where you can lounge in Asian-inspired surrounds. Ideal for a slow warm-up before heading to the nearby clubs. You can come for the food (quite good, but pricey) or wait until about midnight, when they roll up the tables and the DJs and dancers take full control.

Ké? BAR
(Map p248; Carrer del Baluard 54; ☺ noon-2am; Ⓜ Barceloneta) An eclectic and happy crowd hangs about this small bohemian bar run by a friendly Dutchman. Pull up a padded 'keg chair' or grab a seat on one of the worn lounges at the back and join in the animated conversation wafting out over the street. Outdoor seating in summer, just a few steps from Barceloneta's market.

L'Eixample

There are three main concentrations for carousers in L'Eixample. The top end of Carrer d'Aribau and the area where it crosses Avinguda Diagonal attract a heterogeneous but mostly local crowd to its many bars and clubs. Carrer de Balmes is lined with clubs for a mostly teen 'n' 20s crowd. The city's gay-and-lesbian circuit is concentrated in 'Gaixample' around Carrer del Consell de Cent.

★ Dry Martini BAR
(Map p250; ☏ 93 217 50 72; www.javierdelasmuelas.com; Carrer d'Aribau 162-166; ☺ 1pm-2.30am Mon-Thu, 6pm-3am Fri & Sat; Ⓜ Diagonal) Waiters with

a discreetly knowing smile will attend to your cocktail needs here. The house drink, taken at the bar or in one of the plush green leather lounges, is a safe bet. The gin and tonic comes in an enormous glass – a couple of these and you're well on the way. Out the back is a restaurant, **Speakeasy** (Map p250; ✆93 217 50 80; www.javierdelasmuelas.com; Carrer d'Aribau 162-166; mains €19-28; ⏰1-4pm & 8pm-midnight Mon-Fri, 8pm-midnight Sat, closed Aug; M Diagonal).

Monvínic
WINE BAR

(Map p250; ✆93 272 61 87; www.monvinic.com; Carrer de la Diputació 249; ⏰wine bar 1.30-11pm Mon-Sat; M Passeig de Gracia) Proclaimed as 'possibly the best wine bar in the world' by the *Wall Street Journal,* and apparently considered unmissable by El Bulli's somme-lier, Monvínic is an ode, a rhapsody even, to wine loving. The interactive wine list sits on the bar for you to browse on a digital tab-let similar to an iPad and boasts more than 3000 varieties.

La Fira
BAR

(Map p250; ✆682 323714; Carrer de Provença 171; admission incl 1 drink €5; ⏰11pm-5am Fri & Sat; ▤FGC Provença) A designer bar with a differ-ence. Wander in past distorting mirrors and ancient fairground attractions from Germa-ny. Put in coins and listen to hens squawk. Speaking of squawking, the music swings wildly from whiffs of house through '90s hits to Spanish pop classics. You can spend the earlier part of the night trying some of the bar's shots – it claims to have 500 varie-ties (but we haven't counted them up).

Les Gens Que J'Aime
BAR

(Map p250; ✆93 215 68 79; www.lesgensquejaime. com; Carrer de València 286; ⏰6pm-2.30am Sun-Thu, 7pm-3am Fri & Sat; M Passeig de Gràcia) This intimate basement relic of the 1960s follows a deceptively simple formula: chilled jazz music in the background, minimal lighting from an assortment of flea-market lamps and a cosy, cramped scattering of red velvet-backed lounges around tiny dark tables.

Milano
COCKTAIL BAR

(Map p250; ✆93 112 71 50; www.camparimilano. com; Ronda de la Universitat 35; ⏰noon-3am; M Catalunya) You don't quite know what to expect when heading downstairs into this cocktail den. Then you are confronted by its vastness and the happily imbibing crowds ensconced at tables or perched at the broad, curving bar to the right.

Gràcia

Viblioteca
WINE BAR

(Map p259; ✆93 284 42 02; www.viblioteca.com; Carrer de Vallfogona 12; ⏰7pm-1am; M Fontana) If the smell of ripe cheese doesn't float your boat, this is not the place for you – a glass cabinet piled high with the stuff assaults your olfactory nerves as you walk into this small, white, cleverly designed space. The real speciality at Viblioteca, however, is wine, and you can choose from 150 mostly local labels, many of them available by the glass.

La Cigale
BAR

(Map p259; ✆93 457 58 23; Carrer de Tordera 50; ⏰6pm-2.30am Mon-Thu, 6pm-3am Fri & Sat; M Joanic) A very civilised place for a cocktail (or, in summer, two for €8 if you order before 10pm) and to hear some poetry read-ings. Prop up the zinc bar, sink into a sec-ondhand lounge chair around a teeny table or head upstairs. Music is chilled, conversa-tion lively, and you're likely to see Charlie Chaplin in action on the silent flat-screen TV. You can also snack on wok-fried dishes.

Raïm
BAR

(Map p259; Carrer del Progrés 48; ⏰7pm-2.30am; M Diagonal) The walls in Raïm are alive with black-and-white photos of Cubans and Cuba. Tired old wooden chairs of another epoch huddle around marble tables, while grand old wood-framed mirrors hang from the walls. They just don't make old Spanish taverns like this any more.

Le Journal
BAR

(Map p259; ✆93 368 41 37; Carrer de Francisco Gin-er 36; ⏰6pm-2.30am Sun-Thu, 6pm-3am Fri & Sat; M Fontana) Students love the conspiratorial basement air of this narrow bar, whose walls and ceiling are plastered with newspapers (hence the name). Read the headlines of yes-teryear while reclining in an old lounge. For a slightly more intimate feel, head upstairs to the rear gallery.

Tibidabo & La Zona Alta

Mirablau
BAR

(Plaça del Doctor Andreu; ⏰11am-4.30am; ▤Avin-guda Tibidabo then ▤tramvia blau) Gaze out over the entire city from this privileged balcony restaurant on the way up to Tibidabo. Wan-der downstairs to join the folk in the tiny dance space. In summer you can step out onto the even smaller terrace for a breather.

Otto Zutz CLUB
(www.ottozutz.com; Carrer de Lincoln 15; admission €10-15; ⊙ midnight-6am Tue-Sat; Ⓡ FGC Gràcia) Beautiful people only need apply for entry to this three-floor dance den. Shake it all up to house on the ground floor, or head upstairs for funk and soul. DJs come from the Ibiza rave mould and the top floor is for VIPs (although at some ill-defined point in the evening the barriers all seem to come down).

Bikini CLUB
(☑ 93 322 08 00; www.bikinibcn.com; Av Diagonal 547; admission €10-20; ⊙ midnight-6am Thu-Sat; ⊟ 6, 7, 33, 34, 63, 67 or 68, Ⓜ Entença) This grand old star of the Barcelona nightlife scene has been keeping the beat since the darkest days of Franco. Every possible kind of music gets a run, from Latin and Brazilian beats to 1980s disco, depending on the night and the space you choose.

Sutton Club CLUB
(www.thesuttonclub.com; Carrer de Tuset 13; admission €15; ⊙ midnight-5am Wed-Thu, midnight-6am Fri & Sat, 10.30pm-4am Sun; Ⓜ Diagonal) A classic disco with mainstream sounds on the dance floor, some hopping house in a side bar and a fair spread of eye candy, this place inevitably attracts just about everyone pouring in and out of the nearby bars at some stage of the evening. The main dance floor is akin to a writhing bear pit. The people are mostly beautiful and the bouncers can be tough.

🍷 Montjuïc, Poble Sec & Sant Antoni

⭐ **La Caseta del Migdia** BAR
(☑ 617 956572; www.lacaseta.org; Mirador del Migdia; ⊙ 8pm-1am Wed & Thu, 8pm-2am Fri, noon-2am Sat, noon-1am Sun, weekends only in winter; Ⓜ Paral·lel, funicular) The effort of getting to what is, for all intents and purposes, a simple *chiringuito* (makeshift cafe-bar) is well worth it. Stare out to sea over a beer or coffee by day. As sunset approaches the atmosphere changes, as lounge music (from samba to funk) wafts out over the hammocks. Walk below the walls of the Castell de Montjuïc along the dirt track or follow Passeig del Migdia – watch out for signs for the Mirador del Migdia.

Tinta Roja BAR
(Map p266; ☑ 93 443 32 43; www.tintaroja.cat; Carrer de la Creu dels Molers 17; ⊙ 8.30pm-1am Wed, to 2am Thu, to 3am Fri & Sat; Ⓜ Poble Sec) A succession of nooks and crannies, dotted with flea

market finds and dimly lit in violets, reds and yellows, makes Tinta Roja an intimate spot for a drink and the occasional show in the back – with anything from actors to acrobats. This was once a *vaqueria* (small dairy farm), where they kept cows out the back and sold fresh milk at the front.

La Terrrazza CLUB
(Map p266; www.laterrrazza.com; Avinguda de Francesc Ferrer i Guàrdia; admission €15-20; ⊙ midnight-5am Thu, to 6am Fri & Sat, closed Oct-Apr; Ⓜ Espanya) One of the city's top summertime dance locations, La Terrrazza attracts squadrons of the beautiful people, locals and foreigners alike, for a full-on night of music and cocktails partly under the stars inside the Poble Espanyol complex.

Bar Calders WINE BAR
(☑ 93 329 93 49; Carrer del Parlament 25; ⊙ 5pm-1.30am Mon-Thu, to 2.30am Fri, 11am-2.30am Sat, 11am-midnight Sun; Ⓜ Sant Antoni) It bills itself as a wine bar, but actually the wine selection at Bar Calders is its weak point. As an all-day cafe and tapas bar, however, it's unbeatable, with a few tables outside on a tiny pedestrian side street, and has become the favoured meeting point for the neighbourhood's boho element.

⭐ Entertainment

To keep up with what's on, pick up a copy of the weekly listings magazine, *Guía del Ocio* (www.guiadelocio.com) from news stands. Newspapers also have listings sections (with an extensive entertainment section on Fridays) and the **Palau de la Virreina** (Map p236) information office can clue you in to present and forthcoming events.

The easiest way to get hold of *entradas* (tickets) for most venues throughout the city is through the Caixa de Catalunya's Tel-Entrada (www.telentrada.com) service or Ticketmaster (www.ticketmaster.es). There's a *venta de localidades* (ticket office) on the ground floor of the Plaça de Catalunya branch of El Corte Inglés and at some of its other branches around town, and at the FNAC store in the El Triangle shopping centre on the same square.

Cinemas

Foreign films, shown with subtitles and their original soundtrack, rather than dubbed, are marked VO *(versión original)* in movie listings. These cinemas show VO films:

★ **Filmoteca de Catalunya**   CINEMA
(Map p236; ☎93 567 10 70; www.filmoteca.cat; Plaça de Salvador Seguí 1-9; adult/concession €4/2; ⏰4-10pm Tue-Sun; Ⓜ Liceu) After almost a decade in the planning, the Filmoteca de Catalunya – Catalonia's national cinema – moved into this modern 6000-sq-metre building in 2012. It's a glass, metal and concrete beast that hulks in the midst of the most louche part of the Raval, but the building's interior shouts revival, with light and space, wall-to-wall windows, skylights and glass panels that let the sun in.

Verdi   CINEMA
(Map p259; ☎93 238 79 90; www.cines-verdi. com; Carrer de Verdi 32; Ⓜ Fontana) A popular original-language movie house in the heart of Gràcia, handy to lots of local eateries and bars for pre- and post-film enjoyment.

Yelmo Cines Icària   CINEMA
(Map p248; ☎90 222 09 22; www.yelmocines. es; Carrer de Salvador Espriú 61; Ⓜ Ciutadella Vila Olímpica) This vast cinema complex screens movies in the original language on 15 screens, making for plenty of choice. Aside from the screens, you'll find several cheerful eateries, bars and the like to keep you occupied before and after the movies.

Live Music

There's a good choice most nights of the week. Many venues double as bars and/or clubs. Starting time is rarely before 10pm. Admission charges range from nothing to €20 or more – the higher prices often include a drink. Note that some of the clubs mentioned, including Razzmatazz and Luz de Gas often stage concerts. Keep an eye on listings.

★ **Palau de la Música Catalana**   CLASSICAL MUSIC
(☎93 295 72 00; www.palaumusica.org; Carrer de Sant Francesc de Paula 2; ⏰box office 9.30am-9pm Mon-Sat; Ⓜ Urquinaona) A feast for the eyes, this Modernista confection is also the city's most traditional venue for classical and choral music, although it has a wide-ranging program, including flamenco, pop and jazz. Just being here for a performance is an experience. Sip a preconcert tipple in the foyer, its tiled pillars all a-glitter. Head up the grand stairway to the main auditorium, a whirlpool of Modernista whimsy.

Jazz Sí Club   LIVE MUSIC
(☎93 329 00 20; www.tallerdemusics.com; Carrer de Requesens 2; admission incl drink €4-9; ⏰8.30-11pm Tue-Sat, 6.30-10pm Sun; Ⓜ Sant Antoni) A cramped little bar run by the Taller de Músics (Musicians' Workshop) serves as the stage for a varied program of jazz jams through to some good flamenco (Friday nights). Thursday night is Cuban night, Tuesday and Sunday are rock, and the rest are devoted to jazz and/or blues sessions. Concerts start around 9pm but the jam sessions can get going earlier.

Harlem Jazz Club   JAZZ
(Map p236; ☎93 310 07 55; www.harlemjazzclub. es; Carrer de la Comtessa de Sobradiel 8; admission around €7-8; ⏰8pm-5am Tue-Sat; Ⓜ Drassanes) This narrow, old-city dive is one of the best spots in town for jazz, as well as funk, Latin, blues and gypsy jazz. It attracts a mixed crowd that maintains a respectful silence during the acts. Most concerts start around 10pm. Get in early if you want a seat in front of the stage.

Razzmatazz   LIVE MUSIC
(☎93 320 82 00; www.salarazzmatazz.com; Carrer de Pamplona 88; admission €12-32; ⏰midnight-3.30am Thu, to 5.30am Fri & Sat; Ⓜ Marina, Bogatell) Bands from far and wide occasionally create scenes of near hysteria in this, one of the city's classic live-music and clubbing venues. Bands can appear throughout the week with different start times. On weekends the live music gives way to club sounds.

Jamboree   LIVE MUSIC
(Map p236; ☎93 319 17 89; www.masimas.com/jamboree; Plaça Reial 17; admission €10-20; ⏰8pm-6am; Ⓜ Liceu) For over half a century, Jamboree has been bringing joy to the jivers of Barcelona, with high-calibre acts featuring jazz trios, blues, Afrobeats, Latin sounds

and big-band sounds. Two concerts are held most nights (at 8pm and 10pm), after which Jamboree morphs into a DJ-spinning club at midnight. WTF jam sessions are held Mondays (entrance a mere €5). Buy tickets online to save a few euros.

Luz de Gas   LIVE MUSIC
(☑ 93 209 77 11; www.luzdegas.com; Carrer de Muntaner 246; admission up to €20; ⊘ Wed-Sun; ▣ 6, 7, 15, 27, 32, 33, 34, 58 or 64, Ⓜ Diagonal) Several nights a week this club, set in a grand former theatre, stages concerts ranging through rock, soul, salsa, jazz and pop. From about 2am, the place turns into a club that attracts a well-dressed crowd with varying musical tastes, depending on the night.

23 Robadors   LIVE MUSIC
(Map p236; Carrer d'en Robador 23; admission varies; ⊘ 8pm-3am daily; Ⓜ Liceu) On what remains a sleazy Raval street, where a hardy band of streetwalkers, junkies and other misfits hang out in spite of all the work being carried out to gentrify the area, a narrow little bar has made a name for itself with its shows and live music. Jazz is the name of the game, but you'll also find live poetry, flamenco and plenty more.

Sidecar Factory Club   LIVE MUSIC
(Map p236; ☑ 93 302 15 86; www.sidecarfactoryclub.com; Plaça Reial 7; admission €8-18; ⊘ 10pm-5am Mon-Sat; Ⓜ Liceu) With its entrance on Plaça Reial, you can come here for a meal before midnight or a few drinks at ground level (which closes by 3am at the latest), or descend into the red-tinged, brick-vaulted bowels for live music most nights. Just about anything goes here, from UK indie through to country punk, but rock and pop lead the way. Most shows start around 10pm. DJs take over at 12.30am to keep things going.

Sala Apolo   LIVE MUSIC
(Map p266; ☑ 93 441 40 01; www.sala-apolo.com; Carrer Nou de la Rambla 113; admission €13-18, concerts vary; ⊘ midnight-5am Sun-Thu, 12.30am-6am Fri & Sat; Ⓜ Paral·lel) This is a fine old theatre, where red velvet dominates

BARCELONA ENTERTAINMENT

GAY & LESBIAN BARCELONA

Although somewhat overshadowed by the beachy gay mecca of Sitges up the coast, Barcelona still has a lively gay scene. Gay bars, clubs and cafes are mostly concentrated around the 'Gaixample', between Carrer de Muntaner and Carrer de Balmes, around Carrer del Consell de Cent.

For information, pick up a copy of *Shanguide* (www.shangay.com), available in many gay bars and shops. Other sources of info include www.60by80.com, www.visitbarcelonagay.com and www.guiagaybarcelona.es.

Arena Madre (Map p250; ☑ 93 487 83 42; www.grupoarena.com; Carrer de Balmes 32; admission Sun-Fri €6, Sat €12; ⊘ 12.30am-5am Sun-Thu, until 5.30am Fri & Sat; Ⓜ Passeig de Gràcia) Popular with a hot young crowd, Arena Madre is one of the top clubs in town for boys seeking boys. Keep an eye out for the striptease shows on Mondays and drag queens on Wednesdays, along with the usual combination of disco and Latin music to get those butts moving. Heteros are welcome but a minority.

Metro (☑ 93 323 52 27; www.metrodiscobcn.com; Carrer de Sepúlveda 185; admission incl 1 drink €19; ⊘ 12.15am-5am Sun & Mon, until 6am Fri & Sat; Ⓜ Universitat) Metro attracts a casual gay crowd with its two dance floors, three bars and very dark room. Keep an eye out for shows and parties, which can range from parades of models to bingo nights (on Thursday nights, with sometimes-interesting prizes). On Wednesday nights there's a live sex show.

Punto Bcn (Map p250; ☑ 93 487 83 42; www.arenadisco.com; Carrer de Muntaner 63-65; ⊘ 6pm-3am; Ⓜ Universitat) It's an oldie but a goody. A big bar over two levels with a crowd ranging from their 20s to their 40s and beyond, this place fills to bursting on Friday and Saturday nights. It's a friendly early stop on a gay night out, and you can shoot a round of pool if you feel so inclined.

Dietrich Gay Teatro Café (Carrer del Consell de Cent 255; ⊘ 10.30pm-3am; Ⓜ Universitat) A classic of the Gaixample, this place hosts some of the best drag in the city in its elegant quarters – all-timber finishing on two levels. Quiet during the week, it goes a little wild with drag shows, acrobats and dancing from Friday on.

and you feel as though you're in a movie-set dancehall scene featuring Eliot Ness. 'Nasty Mondays' and 'Crappy Tuesdays' are aimed at a diehard, we-never-stop-dancing crowd. Earlier in the evening, concerts generally take place, here and in 'La 2', a smaller auditorium downstairs. Tastes are as eclectic as possible, from local bands and burlesque shows to big-name international acts.

Gran Teatre del Liceu   THEATRE, LIVE MUSIC
(Map p236; ☑ 93 485 99 00; www.liceubarcelona. com; La Rambla dels Caputxins 51-59; ☺ box office 1.30-8pm Mon-Fri & 1hr before show Sat & Sun; M Liceu) Barcelona's grand old opera house, restored after a fire in 1994, is one of the most technologically advanced theatres in the world. To take up a seat in the grand auditorium, returned to all its 19th-century glory but with the very latest in acoustic accoutrements, is to be transported to another age. Tickets can cost anything from €9 for a cheap seat behind a pillar to €205 for a well-positioned night at the opera.

Dance

The best chance you have of seeing people dancing the *sardana* (a Catalan folk dance) is at 6.30pm on Saturday or noon on Sunday in front of the Catedral. You can also see the dancers during some of the city's festivals.

SEEING AN FC BARCELONA MATCH

Football in Barcelona has the aura of religion, and for much of the city's population, support of FC Barcelona is an article of faith. FC Barcelona is traditionally associated with the Catalans and even Catalan nationalism. Pride is at an all-time high these days, with FC Barça continually ranked among the world's best teams.

For a pure adrenaline rush, try to see a match at Europe's largest football arena, the massive 99,000-seat Camp Nou (p263). Tickets are available at Camp Nou, as well as online. You can also purchase them at tourist offices and FC Barcelona shops. Tickets cost anything from €20 to €210, depending on the seat and match. If you can't make a match, the high-tech Camp Nou museum is a worthwhile alternative – and a must-see for football fans.

🛍 Shopping

Mainstream fashion and design stores can be found on Plaça de Catalunya as it heads along Passeig de Gràcia, turning left into Avinguda Diagonal.

Fashion does not end in the chic streets of L'Eixample and Avinguda Diagonal. The El Born area in La Ribera, especially on and around Carrer del Rec, is awash with tiny boutiques, especially those purveying young, fun fashion. A bubbling fashion strip is the Barri Gòtic's Carrer d'Avinyó. For secondhand stuff, head for El Raval, especially Carrer de la Riera Baixa. Carrer de Verdi in Gràcia is good for alternative shops too.

The single best-known department store is El Corte Inglés, with branches at Plaça de Catalunya (Map p250; ☑ 93 306 38 00; www. elcorteingles.es; Plaça de Catalunya 14; ☺ 9.30am-9.30pm Mon-Sat; M Catalunya), Plaça de la Reina Maria Cristina (Avinguda Diagonal 617; M Maria Cristina) and other locations around town. FNAC (Map p236; ☑ 93 344 18 00; www. fnac.es; Plaça de Catalunya 4; ☺ 10am-10pm Mon-Sat; M Catalunya), the French book, CD and electronics emporium, has a couple of branches around town. The Maremagnum (Map p236; www.maremagnum.es; Moll d'Espanya 5; ☺ 10am-10pm; M Drassanes) shopping centre can be a diversion when wandering around Port Vell.

Winter sales officially start on or around 10 January and the summer equivalents on or around 5 July.

Empremtes de Catalunya   HANDICRAFTS
(Map p236; ☑ 93 467 46 60; Carrer dels Banys Nous 11; ☺ 10am-8pm Mon-Sat, to 2pm Sun; M Liceu) A celebration of Catalan products, this nicely designed store is a great place to browse for unique gifts. You'll find jewellery with designs inspired by Roman iconography (as well as works that reference Gaudí and Barcelona's Gothic era), plus pottery, wooden toys, silk scarves, notebooks, housewares and more.

Vinçon   HOMEWARES
(Map p250; ☑ 93 215 60 50; www.vincon.com; Passeig de Gràcia 96; ☺ 10am-8.30pm Mon-Fri, 10.30am-9pm Sat; M Diagonal) An icon of the Barcelona design scene, Vinçon has the slickest furniture and household goods (particularly lighting), both local and imported. Not surprising, really, since the building, raised in 1899, belonged to the Modernista artist Ramon Casas. Head upstairs to the furniture area – from the windows and terrace you get close side views of La Pedrera.

L'Arca
VINTAGE, CLOTHING

(Map p236; ☑93 302 15 98; www.larca.es; Carrer dels Banys Nous 20; ⏱11am-2pm & 4.30-8.30pm; Ⓜ Liceu) Step inside this enchanting shop for a glimpse of beautifully crafted apparel from the past, including 18th-century embroidered silk vests, elaborate silk kimonos, and wedding dresses and shawls from the 1920s. Owing to its incredible collection, it has provided clothing for films including *Titanic*, *Talk to Her* and *Perfume*.

Loisaida
CLOTHING, ANTIQUES

(Map p244; ☑93 295 54 92; www.loisaidabcn.com; Carrer dels Flassaders 42; ⏱11am-9pm Mon-Sat, 11am-2pm & 4-8pm Sun; Ⓜ Jaume I) A sight in its own right, housed in what was once the coach house and stables for the Royal Mint, Loisaida (from the Spanglish for 'Lower East Side') is a deceptively large emporium of colourful, retro and somewhat preppy clothing for men and women, costume jewellery, music from the 1940s and '50s and some covetable antiques. There is more womenswear and some very cute children's lines a few doors away at No 32 (Map p244; ☑93 295 54 92; Carrer dels Flassaders 32; ⏱11am-9pm Mon-Sat, 11am-2pm & 4-8pm Sun; Ⓜ Jaume I).

Coquette
FASHION

(Map p244; ☑93 295 42 85; www.coquettebcn.com; Carrer del Rec 65; ⏱11am-3pm & 5-9pm Mon-Fri, 11.30am-9pm Sat; Ⓜ Barceloneta) With its spare, cut-back and designer look, this fashion store is attractive in its own right. Women can browse through casual, feminine wear by such designers as Humanoid, Vanessa Bruno, UKE and Hoss Intropia, and others, with a further collection nearby at Carrer de Bonaire 5 (Map p244; ☑93 310 35 35; Carrer de Bonaire 5; ⏱11am-3pm & 5-9pm Mon-Fri, 11.30am-8.30pm Sat; Ⓜ Barceloneta).

El Bulevard dels Antiquaris
ANTIQUES

(Map p250; ☑93 215 44 99; www.bulevarddelsantiquaris.com; Passeig de Gràcia 55; ⏱9am-6pm Mon-Thu, 9am-2pm Fri & Sat; Ⓜ Passeig de Gràcia) More than 70 stores (most are open from 11am to 2pm and 5pm to 8.30pm) are gathered under one roof (on the floor above the more general Bulevard Rosa arcade) to offer the most varied selection of collector's pieces, ranging from old porcelain dolls through to fine crystal, from Asian antique furniture to old French goods, and from African and other ethnic art to jewellery.

BARCELONA'S MARKETS

The sprawling Els Encants Vells (Fira de Bellcaire; ☑93 246 30 30; www.encantsbcn.com; Plaça de les Glòries Catalanes; ⏱8am-8pm Mon, Wed, Fri & Sat; Ⓜ Glòries) is the city's principal flea market. There is an awful lot of junk, but you can unearth interesting items if you're willing to dig. The Barri Gòtic is enlivened by an art and crafts market (Map p236; Plaça de Sant Josep Oriol; ⏱11am-8.30pm Sat, 10am-3pm Sun; Ⓜ Liceu) on Saturday and Sunday. Just south of La Rambla, the Port Antic (Map p266; Plaça del Portal de la Pau; ⏱10am-8pm Sat & Sun; Ⓜ Drassanes) is a small antique market that's open on weekends.

La Manual Alpargatera
SHOES

(Map p236; ☑93 301 01 72; lamanualalpargatera.es; Carrer d'Avinyó 7; ⏱9.30am-1.30pm & 4.30-8pm; Ⓜ Liceu) Everyone from Salvador Dalí to Jean Paul Gaultier has ordered a pair of *espadrilles* (rope-soled canvas shoes or sandals) from this famous store, which is the birthplace of the iconic footware. The shop was founded just after the Spanish Civil War, though the roots of the simple shoe design date back thousands of years.

Fires, Festes i Tradicions
FOOD, DRINK

(Map p236; ☑93 269 12 61; Carrer de la Dagueria 13; ⏱4-8.30pm Mon, 10am-8.30pm Tue-Sat; Ⓜ Jaume I) Whether assembling a picnic or hoping to bring home a few edible momentos, don't miss this little shop, which stocks a wide range of specialities from Catalunya, including jams, sweets, sausages and cheeses.

Vila Viniteca
DRINK

(Map p236; ☑902 327777; www.vilaviniteca.es; Carrer dels Agullers 7; ⏱8.30am-8.30pm Mon-Sat; Ⓜ Jaume I) One of the best wine stores in Barcelona (and Lord knows, there are a few), this place has been searching out the finest in local and imported wines since 1932. On a couple of November evenings it organises what has by now become an almost riotous wine-tasting event in Carrer dels Agullers and surrounding lanes, at which cellars from around Spain present their young new wines. At No 9 it has another store devoted to gourmet food products.

ⓘ Information

EMERGENCY

Tourists who want to report thefts need to go to the Catalan police, known as the **Mossos d'Esquadra** (☏088; Carrer Nou de la Rambla 80; Ⓜ Paral·lel) or the **Guàrdia Urbana** (Local Police; ☏092; La Rambla 43; Ⓜ Liceu).

Ambulance (☏061)

EU standard emergency number (☏112)

Fire brigade (Bombers; ☏080, 085)

Policía Nacional (National Police; ☏091)

INTERNET ACCESS

A growing number of hotels, restaurants, cafes, bars and other public locations offer wi-fi access.

Bornet (☏93 268 15 07; Carrer Barra de Ferro 3; per 15min/hr €1/2.80; ☺11am-midnight Mon-Thu, to 2.30am Fri-Sun; Ⓜ Jaume I) A cool little internet centre and art gallery.

MEDIA

La Vanguardia and *El Periódico* are the main local Castilian-language dailies.

MEDICAL SERVICES

Call ☏010 to find the nearest late-opening duty pharmacy. There are also several 24-hour pharmacies scattered across town.

Farmàcia Castells Soler (Passeig de Gràcia 90; ☺24hr; Ⓜ Diagonal)

Farmàcia Clapés (La Rambla 98; ☺24hr; Ⓜ Liceu)

Farmàcia Torres (www.farmaciaabierta24h. com; Carrer d'Aribau 62; ☺24hr; Ⓡ FGC Provença)

Hospital Clínic i Provincial (☏93 227 54 00; Carrer de Villarroel 170; Ⓜ Hospital Clínic)

Hospital Dos de Maig (☏93 507 27 00; Carrer del Dos de Maig 301; Ⓜ Sant Pau–Dos de Maig)

MONEY

Banks abound in Barcelona, many with ATMs, including several around Plaça de Catalunya, on La Rambla and on Plaça de Sant Jaume in the Barri Gòtic.

The foreign-exchange offices along La Rambla and elsewhere are open for longer hours than banks but generally offer poorer rates.

POST

The **main post office** (Map p236; Plaça d'Antoni López; ☺8.30am-9.30pm Mon-Fri, to 2pm Sat; Ⓜ Jaume I) is opposite the northeast end of Port Vell. There's a handy **branch** (Map p250; Carrer d'Aragó 282; ☺8.30am-8.30pm Mon-Fri, 9.30am-1pm Sat; Ⓜ Passeig de Gràcia) just off Passeig de Gràcia.

TOURIST INFORMATION

In addition to the following listed tourist offices, information booths operate at Estació Nord bus station, Plaça del Portal de la Pau and at the foot of the Mirador a Colom. At least three others are set up at various points around the city centre in summer.

Oficina d'Informació de Turisme de Barcelona has its **main branch** (Map p250; ☏93 285 38 34; www.barcelonaturisme.com; underground at Plaça de Catalunya 17-S; ☺9.30am-9.30pm; Ⓜ Catalunya) in Plaça de Catalunya. It concentrates on city information and can help book accommodation. The branch in the EU arrivals hall at **Aeroport del Prat** (terminals 1, 2B & 2A; ☺9am-9pm) has information on all of Catalonia; a smaller office at the international arrivals hall opens the same hours. The branch at **Estació Sants** (☺8am-8pm; Ⓡ Estació Sants) has limited city information. There's also a helpful branch near the **town hall** (Plaça Sant Jaume; Map p236; ☏93 285 38 32; Carrer de la Ciutat 2; ☺8.30am-8.30pm Mon-Fri, 9am-7pm Sat, 9am-2pm Sun & holidays; Ⓜ Jaume I).

ⓘ DISCOUNTS

Students generally pay a little over half of adult admission prices, as do children aged under 12 years and senior citizens (aged 65 and over) with appropriate ID. Possession of a Bus Turístic ticket entitles you to discounts to some museums.

Articket (www.articketbcn.org; per person €30) gives you admission to six important art galleries for €30 and is valid for six months. The galleries are the Museu Picasso, Museu Nacional d'Art de Catalunya, Macba (Museu d'Art Contemporani de Barcelona), the Fundació Antoni Tàpies, the Centre de Cultura Contemporània de Barcelona and the Fundació Joan Miró. You can buy the ticket at the museums or at the tourist offices on Plaça de Catalunya, Plaça de Sant Jaume and at Sants train station.

Aficionados of Barcelona's Modernista heritage should consider the **Ruta del Modernisme pack** (www.rutadelmodernisme.com). For €12 you receive a guide to 115 Modernista buildings great and small, a map and discounts of up to 50% on the main Modernista sights in Barcelona, as well as some others around Catalonia. Pick it up at the tourist office at Plaça de Catalunya.

La Rambla Information Booth (Map p236; www.barcelonaturisme.com; La Rambla dels Estudis 115; ⊙8.30am-8.30pm; MLiceu)

Palau Robert Regional Tourist Office (Map p250; ☑93 238 80 91, from outside Catalonia 902 400012; www.gencat.net/probert; Passeig de Gràcia 107; ⊙10am-8pm Mon-Sat, to 2.30pm Sun; MDiagonal) A host of material on Catalonia, audiovisual resources, a bookshop and a branch of Turisme Juvenil de Catalunya (for youth travel).

❶ Getting There & Away

AIR

Aeroport del Prat (☑902 404704; www.aena.es) is 12km southwest of the centre at El Prat de Llobregat. Barcelona is a big international and domestic destination, with direct flights from North America, as well as many European cities.

Several budget airlines, including Ryanair, use Girona-Costa Brava airport, 11km south of Girona and about 80km north of Barcelona. Buses connect with Barcelona's Estació del Nord bus station.

BOAT
Balearic Islands
Regular passenger and vehicular ferries to/from the Balearic Islands, operated by **Acciona Trasmediterránea** (☑902 454645; www.trasmediterranea.es; MDrassanes), dock along both sides of the Moll de Barcelona wharf in Port Vell.

Italy
The Grimaldi group's **Grandi Navi Veloci** (Map p266; ☑in Italy 010 209 4591; www1.gnv.it; MDrassanes) runs high-speed luxury ferries two (sometimes more) days a week between Genoa and Barcelona. The journey takes 19 hours. Ticket prices vary wildly and depend on the season and how far in advance you purchase, but start at about €91 one way for an airline-style seat in summer. They can be bought online or at Acciona Trasmediterránea ticket windows. The same company runs a similar number of ferries between Barcelona and Tangiers, in Morocco (voyage time about 26 hours).

Grimaldi Ferries (Map p266; ☑902 531333, in Italy 081 496 444; www.grimaldi-lines.com; MDrassanes) operates similar services from Barcelona to Civitavecchia (near Rome; 20½ hours, six to seven times a week), Livorno (Tuscany; 19½ hours, three times a week) and Porto Torres (northwest Sardinia; 12 hours, daily). An economy-class airline-style seat costs from €70 in low season to €115 in high season on all routes.

Boats of both lines dock at Moll de Sant Bertran and all vessels take vehicles.

BUS
Long-distance buses for destinations throughout Spain leave from the **Estació del Nord** (☑902 260606; www.barcelonanord.cat; Carrer d'Ali Bei 80; MArc de Triomf). A plethora of companies operate services to different parts of the country, although many come under the umbrella of ALSA (☑902 422242; www.alsa.es). There are frequent services to Madrid, Valencia and Zaragoza (20 or more a day) and several daily departures to such distant destinations as Burgos, Santiago de Compostela and Seville.

Eurolines (www.eurolines.es), in conjunction with local carriers all over Europe, is the main international carrier. It runs services across Europe and to Morocco, departing from Estació del Nord and **Estació d'Autobusos de Sants** (Carrer de Viriat; MEstació Sants), which is next to Estació Sants Barcelona. For information and tickets in Barcelona, contact ALSA. Another carrier is **Linebús** (www.linebus.com).

Within Catalonia, much of the Pyrenees and the entire Costa Brava are served only by buses, as train services are limited to important railheads such as Girona, Figueres, Lleida, Ripoll and Puigcerdà. If there is a train, take it – it's usually more convenient.

Various bus companies operate across the region, mostly from Estació del Nord.

Departures from Estació del Nord include the following (where frequencies vary, the lowest figure is usually for Sunday; fares quoted are one-way and are the lowest available):

TO	FREQUENCY (PER DAY)	DURATION (HR)	COST (€)
Almería	4-5	11¼-14	71
Bilbao	3-5	8-9	48
Burgos	5-6	7½-8½	39
Granada	5-8	12½-14¼	78
Madrid	up to 16	7½-8	32
San Sebastian	3-5	8	33
Seville	1-2	14¾	88
Valencia	9-14	4-4½	29
Zaragoza	17-22	3¾	16

Alsina Graells (☑902 422242; www.alsa.es) A subsidiary of ALSA, it runs buses from Barcelona to destinations west and northwest, such as Vielha, La Seu d'Urgell and Lleida.

Barcelona Bus (☑902 130014; www.barcelonabus.com) Runs direct services between Girona-Costa Brava airport and Estació del Nord bus station in Barcelona (one way/return €14/21, 70 minutes).

Hispano-Igualadina (☑902 292900; www.igualadina.net; Estació Sants) This bus services central and southern Catalonia. It offers a service that runs between Reus airport and Estació

ⓘ WARNING: KEEP AN EYE ON YOUR VALUABLES

Every year aggrieved readers write in with tales of woe from Barcelona. Petty crime and theft, with tourists as the prey of choice, are a problem, so you need to take a few common-sense precautions.

Thieves and pickpockets operate on airport trains and the metro, especially around stops popular with tourists (such as La Sagrada Família). The Old City (Ciutat Vella) is the pickpockets' and bag-snatchers' prime hunting ground. Take special care on and around La Rambla. Prostitutes working the lower (waterfront) end often do a double trade in wallet snatching.

d'Autobusos de Sants to meet flights (€15/26 one-way/return, 2 hours).

Sagalés Bus Company (☑ 902 130014; www. sagales.com)

Sarfa (☑ 902 302025; www.sarfa.com) The main operator on and around the Costa Brava.

TEISA (Map p250; ☑ 93 215 35 66; www.teisa-bus.com; Carrer de Pau Claris 117; Ⓜ Passeig de Gràcia) Covers a large part of the eastern Catalan Pyrenees from Girona and Figueres. From Barcelona, buses head for Camprodon via Ripoll and Olot via Besalú.

CAR & MOTORCYCLE

Autopistas (tollways) head out of Barcelona in most directions, including the C31/C32 to the southern Costa Brava; the C32 to Sitges; the C16 to Manresa (with a turnoff for Montserrat); and the AP7 north to Girona, Figueres and France, and south to Tarragona and Valencia (turn off along the AP2 for Lleida, Zaragoza and Madrid). The toll-free alternatives, such as the A2 north to Girona, Figueres and France, and west to Lleida and beyond, or the A7 to Tarragona, tend to be busy and slow.

Rental

Avis, Europcar, Hertz and several other big companies have desks at the airport, Estació Sants train station and Estació del Nord bus terminus.

Avis (☑ 902 110275; www.avis.com; Carrer de Còrsega 293-295; Ⓜ Diagonal)

Europcar (☑ 93 302 05 43; www.europcar. com; Gran Via de les Corts Catalanes 680; Ⓜ Girona)

Hertz (☑ 902 998707; www.hertz.com; Carrer del Viriat 45; Ⓜ Sants)

MondoRent (☑ 93 295 32 68; www.mondorent. com; Passeig de Joan de Borbó 80-84; Ⓜ Bar-celoneta) Rents scooters (including stylish Vespas) as well as electric bikes.

National/Atesa (☑ 93 323 07 01; www.atesa. es; Carrer de Muntaner 45; Ⓜ Universitat)

TRAIN

The main international and domestic station is **Estació Sants** (Plaça dels Països Catalans; Ⓜ Estació Sants), 2.5km west of La Rambla. Other stops on long-distance lines include Catalunya and Passeig de Gràcia. Information windows operate at Estació Sants and Passeig de Gràcia station. Sants station has a **consigna** (left-luggage lockers; ⊙ 5.30am-11pm), a tourist office, a telephone and fax office, currency-exchange booths and ATMs.

International

One or two daily services connect Montpellier in France with Estació Sants (€47 to €72 each way, three hours). From Estació Sants, there are also two to three high-speed trains direct to Paris (around €112 to €176 each way, 6½ hours).

Domestic

Two dozen high-speed Tren de Alta Velocidad Española (AVE) trains between Madrid and Barcelona run daily in each direction (2½ to 3¼ hours). One-way prices range from €85 to €150. Some popular runs include the following (fares are one-way and represent the range of lowest fares depending on type of train):

TO	FREQUENCY (PER DAY)	DURATION (HR)	COST (€)
Alicante	up to 8	4¾-5¾	52-58
Burgos	4	5½-6½	62-86
Valencia	up to 15	3-4½	35-45
Zaragoza	up to 35	1½-4¼	53-68

ⓘ Getting Around

The metro is the easiest way of getting around and reaches most places you're likely to visit (although not the airport). For some trips you need buses or FGC suburban trains. The tourist office gives out comprehensive transport maps with metro and bus routes.

For public-transport information, call ☑ 010.

TO/FROM THE AIRPORT

The **A1 Aerobús** (Map p266; ☑ 902 100104; www.aerobusbcn.com; one way/return €5.90/10.20) runs from Terminal 1 to Plaça de Catalunya via Plaça d'Espanya, Gran Via de les Corts Catalanes (on the corner of Carrer del Comte d'Urgell) and Plaça de la Universitat (every five to 10 minutes depending on the time of day; 35 minutes) from 6.10am to 1.05am. A2 Aerobús does the same run from Terminal 2, from 6am to 1am. You can buy tickets on the bus.

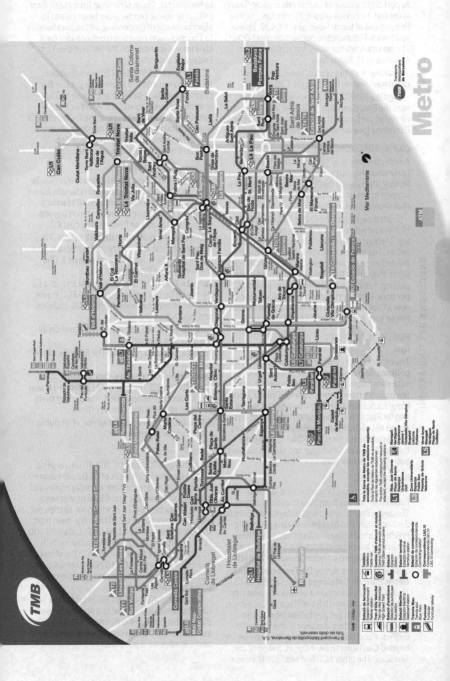

Renfe's R2 Nord train line runs between the airport and Passeig de Gracia (via Estació Sants) in central Barcelona (about 25 minutes), before heading out of town. Tickets cost €4.10, unless you have a T-10 multitrip public-transport ticket. The service from the airport starts at 5.42am and ends at 11.38pm daily.

A taxi to/from the centre, about a half-hour ride depending on traffic, costs €30 to €35.

Sagalés (☏ 902 130014; www.sagales.com) runs the Barcelona Bus (p297) service between Girona airport and Estació del Nord bus station in Barcelona (one way/return €14/21, 70 minutes).

CAR & MOTORCYCLE

An effective one-way system makes traffic flow fairly smoothly, but you'll often find yourself flowing the way you don't want to go, unless you happen to have an adept navigator and a map that shows one-way streets.

Limited parking in the Ciutat Vella is virtually all for residents only, with some metered parking. The narrow streets of Gràcia are not much better. The broad boulevards of L'Eixample are divided into blue and green zones. For nonresidents they mean the same thing: limited meter parking. Fees vary but tend to hover around €3 per hour. Parking stations are also scattered all over L'Eixample, with a few in the old centre too. Prices vary from around €4 to €5 per hour.

PUBLIC TRANSPORT

Bus

The city transport authority, **Transports Metropolitans de Barcelona** (TMB; ☏ 010; www.tmb. net), runs buses along most city routes every few minutes from 5am or 6am to 10pm or 11pm. Many routes pass through Plaça de Catalunya and/or Plaça de la Universitat. After 11pm, a reduced network of yellow *nitbusos* (night buses) runs until 3am or 5am. All *nitbus* routes pass through Plaça de Catalunya and most run about every 30 to 45 minutes.

Metro & FGC

The TMB metro has 11 numbered and colour-coded lines. It runs from 5am to midnight from Sunday to Thursday and on holidays, from 5am to 2am on Friday and days immediately preceding holidays, and 24 hours on Saturday. Line 2 has access for people with disabilities and a growing number of stations on other lines also have lifts.

Suburban trains run by the **Ferrocarrils de la Generalitat de Catalunya** (FGC; ☏ 93 205 15 15; www.fgc.net) include a couple of useful city lines. One heads north from Plaça de Catalunya. A branch of it will get you to Tibidabo and another within spitting distance of the Monestir de Pedralbes. Some trains along this line run beyond Barcelona to Sant Cugat, Sabadell and Terrassa. The other FGC line heads to Manresa

from Plaça d'Espanya and is handy for the trip to Montserrat. These trains run from about 5am (with only one or two services before 6am) to 11pm or midnight (depending on the line) Sunday to Thursday, and from 5am to about 1am (or a little later, depending on the line and stop) on Friday and Saturday.

Three **tram** (☏ 902 193275; www.trambcn. com) lines run into the suburbs of greater Barcelona from Plaça de Francesc Macià and are of limited interest to visitors. Another line (T4) runs from behind the zoo near the Ciutadella Vila Olímpica metro stop to Sant Adrià via Fòrum. The T5 line runs from Glòries to Badalona. All standard transport passes are valid.

Tickets & Targetas

The metro, FGC trains, *rodalies/cercanías* (Renfe-run local trains) and buses come under one zoned fare regime. Single-ride tickets on all standard transport within Zone 1 (which extends beyond the airport), except on Renfe trains, cost €2.

Targetas are multitrip transport tickets. They are sold at most city-centre metro stations. The prices given here are for travel in Zone 1. Children under four travel free.

Targeta T-10 (€10.30) Ten rides (each valid for 1¼ hours) on the metro, buses and FGC trains. You can change between metro, FGC, *rodalies* and buses.

Targeta T-DIA (€7.60) Unlimited travel on all transport for one day.

Targeta T-50/30 (€42.50) For 50 trips within 30 days.

Two-/Three-/Four-/Five-Day Tickets (€14/20/26/31) These provide unlimited travel on all transport except the Aerobús; buy them at metro stations and tourist offices.

T-Mes (€52.75) For unlimited use of all public transport for a month.

TAXI

Taxis charge €2.10 flag fall (€2.40 on weekend nights) plus meter charges of €1.03 per kilometre (€1.30 from 8pm to 8am weekday nights and daytime on weekends, and €1.40 on weekend nights). A further €4.20 is added for all trips to/from the airport (and €2.10 from the main train stations). You can call a **taxi** (☏ Fonotaxi 93 300 11 00, Radiotaxi 93 303 30 33, Radiotaxi BCN 93 225 00 00) or flag them down in the streets. The call-out charge is €3.40 (€4.20 to €4.50 at night and on weekends). In many taxis it is possible to pay with credit card.

Taxi Amic (☏ 93 420 80 88; http://rtljtic.wix. com/taxiamic) is a special taxi service for people with disabilities or difficult situations (such as transport of big objects). Book at least 24 hours in advance if possible.

Catalonia

Best Places to Eat

➡ El Celler de Can Roca (p316)

➡ La Cuina de Can Simon (p305)

➡ El Jardinet (p342)

➡ l'estel de la Mercè (p346)

➡ Cal Ton (p351)

Best Places to Stay

➡ Hotel Platjador (p347)

➡ Hotel El Ciervo (p339)

➡ Mil Estrelles (p319)

➡ Hotel Els Caçadors (p330)

➡ Villa Paulita (p331)

Why Go?

Catalonia packs a lot into its four provinces. The stunning cove beaches of the Costa Brava make it one of Spain's loveliest coasts, backed by the top foodie scene and Jewish history of the medieval city of Girona, and Salvador Dalí's gloriously surreal 'theatre-museum' in Figueres.

For something utterly different head north to where the Pyrenees rise up to mighty 3000m peaks from a series of stunning valleys crisscrossed with numerous hiking trails.

And if that's not enough, there are the flamingo-tinted wetlands of the Delta de l'Ebre (Ebro Delta), the Roman and Greek ruins of Tarragona and Empuriés, and mighty medieval monasteries, gorgeous Romanesque churches and isolated hilltop villages scattered throughout.

Wherever you venture there is the undeniable sense that Catalonia (Catalunya in Catalan, Cataluña in Spanish) is different from the rest of Spain. It's a difference worth celebrating.

When to Go

Tarragona

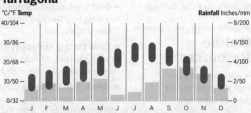

| May Girona blooms for its flower festival and beaches are gorgeous, though the water's chilly. | Sep The Catalan Pyrenees are aflame in autumnal colours and the hiking is perfect. | Oct & Nov The museums and galleries of the Dalí circuit are at their quiet best. |

RODALIES

The network of short-distance rail lines, known as rodalies or cercanías, is a great way to get around the region. Most lines radiate out from Barcelona, though Girona and Tarragona also have networks. Check www20.gencat.cat/portal/site/rodalies for maps and timetables.

Book Ahead For...

➡ Top-end restaurants
➡ Diving in the Illes Medes (p317)
➡ Visits to wineries
➡ Casa Museu Dalí (p320) in Portlligat
➡ Teatre-Museu Dalí (p322) in Figueres

Parks & Reserves

Catalonia boasts numerous parks and nature reserves. For a rundown on all of them, check out www.parcsdecatalunya.net, which is full of useful background information, though in Spanish and Catalan only.

Online Resources

➡ www.gencat.cat – regional government website full of info
➡ www.sarfa.com, www.alsa.es – bus services
➡ www.magrama.gob.es/es/costas/servicios/guia-playas – guide to beaches; in Spanish but self-explanatory

Parles Català?

Get out of Barcelona and away from Costa Brava's beaches and you'll find that *català* (Catalan) is all around you: the menus and street signs are in Catalan and it's pretty much the only language spoken in the villages. Written Catalan resembles both Spanish and French; its roots are in Latin and it's an Occitano-Romance language, stemming from medieval Provençal. It is spoken by over 10 million people in Catalonia (both Spanish and French), Andorra, the Balearic Islands, Valencia (where it's called *valenciano*), Murcia and even Sicily. Though Catalan was severely suppressed under Franco, with books destroyed and the language banned from schools, since his death it has made a strong comeback and become a focus of regional identity.

CATALAN WINE

Looking for local wine? You're in the right region: Greeks and Romans were making it here millennia ago and Catalonia has no fewer than 12 Denominaciones de Origen (DO). The most famous drop is *cava*, a Champagne-style sparkling wine that ranges from ultra-dry *(brut nature)* to sweet. The Penedès region that produces most of it also makes light, fruit-driven whites from macabeo, xarel•lo and other varietals.

Other notable winemaking zones include Priorat, which produces aromatic, full-bodied reds, particularly from *cariñena* (carignan) and *garnacha* (grenache) grapes, and Costers del Segre, which comprises several fairly distinct subregions and produces quality whites and reds from a wide variety of grapes including macabeo, chardonnay, monastrell and cabernet sauvignon. The Raimat subregion is particularly worthy of attention. The general Catalunya appellation includes various quality wines produced in wineries outside of the other regions.

Top Five Food Experiences

➡ **Olot's 'volcanic' cuisine** (p327) Delicious combinations involving fresher-than-fresh ingredients from the region's fertile volcanic soil.
➡ **Cava tasting in Penedès** (p350) Largely a Christmas drink in the rest of Spain, the refreshing sparkling wine is a year-round staple here in its home region.
➡ **Girona's El Celler de Can Roca** (p316) Expect to be wowed by top-drawer molecular gastronomy. Book 11 months ahead or pray for a cancellation.
➡ **Local rice with duck in the Delta de l'Ebre** (p357) This paella-like dish has zero food miles involved – the ducks are hunted on the flooded rice paddies in winter.
➡ **Calçots with romesco sauce** (p307) Highly addictive barbecued leek-like onions. Peel off the blackened outer layer and dip the juicy interior in this nutty sauce. Repeat.

FRANCE

Vielha

Pica d'Estats (3143m)

Espot

Llavorsí

Boí

④ Parc Nacional d'Aigüestortes i Estany de Sant Maurici

Sort

ANDORRA LA VELLA

Puigcerdà
Llívia

Puig Neulós (1256m)

Portbou

Bellver de Cerdanya

La Seu d'Urgell

Ribes de Freser

Beget

Figueres
Roses

Portlligat
Cadaqués

Tremp

Parc Natural Cadí-Moixeró

La Molina

Berga

Olot
Besalú

Castelló d'Empúries

L'Escala

⑨ Illes Medes

Ripoll

Sant Pau

Verges

Àger

CATALONIA

Solsona

Ponts

Sant Joan de les Abadesses

Parc Natural de la Zona Volcànica de la Garrotxa

La Pera

⑥ Girona

Begur
Tamariu

⑦

① Palafrugell
Llafranc

Cardona

Vic

Peratallada

Santa Coloma de Farners

Lloret de Mar

Sant Feliu de Guíxols

Balaguer

Manresa

Monestir de Montserrat

Sant Celoni

Tossa de Mar

Lleida

Reial Monestir de Santa Maria de Vallbona de les Monges

Igualada

Granollers

Blanes

⑤ The Cistercian Route

Reial Monestir de Santes Creus

Terrassa

Mataró

Reial Monestir de Santa Maria de Poblet

Montblanc

Sant Sadurní d'Anoia

Premià de Mar

Vilafranca del Penedès

Barcelona

TARRAGONA

Reus

② Sitges

Móra la Nova

Altafulla

Vilanova i la Geltrú

Castelldefels

Gandesa

Tarragona
PortAventura

Castell de Miravet

MEDITERRANEAN SEA

Tortosa

Deltebre

Amposta

⑧ Delta de l'Ebre

Parc Natural Delta de l'Ebre

Sant Carles de la Ràpita

N ⊕ 0 — 50 km
        0 — 25 miles

Catalonia Highlights

① Chill out on Costa Brava coves and beaches around **Palafrugell** (p306).

② Party on in the pretty, gay-friendly seaside town of **Sitges** (p346).

③ Contemplate Dalí's **theatre of the absurd** (p322) with a visit to Figueres.

④ Hike in **Parc Nacional d'Aigüestortes i Estany de Sant Maurici** (p335).

⑤ Admire the mighty monasteries of the **Cistercian Route** (p345).

⑥ Explore the Jewish heritage of the flower-bedecked medieval city centre of **Girona** (p311).

⑦ Wait till the evening quiet, then pace the lovely medieval village of **Peratallada** (p311).

⑧ See the skies turn pink under flocks of flamingos in the **Delta de l'Ebre** (p356).

⑨ Dive the fish-filled waters of the **Illes Medes** (p317).

COSTA BRAVA

Stretching north to the French border, the Costa Brava, or 'rugged coast', is by far the prettiest and classiest of Spain's three principal holiday coasts. Though you'll find plenty of overdevelopment and English breakfasts, there are also unspoiled coves, charming seaside towns with quality restaurants, spectacular scenery, and some of Spain's best diving around the protected Illes Medes.

Nestling in the hilly backcountry – green and covered in umbrella pine in the south but barer and browner in the north – are charming stone villages and the towering monastery of St Pere de Rodes. A little further inland are the bigger towns of Girona, with its sizeable and strikingly well-preserved medieval centre, and Figueres, famous for its bizarre Teatre-Museu, foremost of a series of sites associated with the famous eccentric surrealist artist Salvador Dalí.

The coastal settlements are very – and we mean *very* – quiet in winter.

❶ Getting There & Away

Direct buses from Barcelona go to most towns on or near the Costa Brava. From Girona and Figueres there are also fairly good bus services to the coast.

The train line between Barcelona and the coastal border town of Portbou runs inland, through Girona and Figueres.

If driving, the AP7 tollway and the NII highway both run from Barcelona via Girona and Figueres to the French border. The C32 *autopista* (tollway) follows the NII up the coast towards Tossa de Mar.

Tossa de Mar

POP 5910

Curving around a boat-speckled bay and guarded by a headland crowned with impressive defensive medieval walls and towers, Tossa de Mar is a picturesque village of crooked, narrow streets onto which tourism has tacked a larger, modern exten-

sion. In July and August it's hard to reach the water's edge without tripping over oily limbs, but out of high season it is still an enchanting place to visit.

Tossa was one of the first places on the Costa Brava to attract foreign visitors – a small colony of artists and writers gravitated towards what painter Marc Chagall dubbed 'Blue Paradise' in the 1930s – and was made famous by Ava Gardner in the 1950 film *Pandora and the Flying Dutchman.*

◉ Sights & Activities

Old Tossa
OLD TOWN

The deep-ochre, fairy-tale walls and towers on the pine-dotted headland, Mont Guardí, at the end of the main beach, were built between the 12th and 14th centuries. The area they girdle is known as the Vila Vella (Old Town), full of steep little cobbled streets and picturesque whitewashed houses, garlanded with flowers.

Far de Tossa
LIGHTHOUSE

(adult/child €3/1.50; ⊙10am-8pm daily Apr-Oct, to 6pm Tue-Sun Nov-Mar) Mont Guardí is crowned with this lighthouse, which has an imaginative, 20-minute walk-through display on the history of lighthouses and life inside them. There's a bar here with a memorable terrace overlooking the steep drop – perfect for an Ava Gardner cocktail. In August, concerts are held on various nights by the light of the lighthouse.

Beaches
BEACHES

The main town beach, golden Platja Gran, tends to be busy. Beyond the headland, at the end of Avinguda de Sant Ramon Penyafort, is the quieter and smaller Platja Mar Menuda, popular with divers. The best beaches, however, are found north and south along the coast, accessible only to those with their own transport, or energetic walkers.

Museu Municipal
MUSEUM

(Plaça de Roig i Soler 1; adult/child €3/free; ⊙9.30am-1.30pm & 3-5pm Tue-Fri, 10am-2pm & 4-6pm Sat, 10am-2pm Sun) In the lower part of Vila Vella, the Museu Municipal, set in the 14th- and 15th-century Palau del Batlle, has mosaics and other finds from a Roman villa, off Avinguda del Pelegrí, and Tossa-related art, including Chagall's *Celestial Violinist.* Opens extended hours in high season.

Glass-Bottomed Boats
BOAT TOUR

(www.fondocristal.com; adult/child 5-12yr €13/9; ⊙Apr-Oct) In season, these trips run hourly

❶ TOURIST TAX

All accommodation in Catalonia is obliged to charge a tourist tax: this is payable by everyone over 16 and ranges from €0.50 per night for most accommodation to €2.50 for five-star establishments. We haven't included this in the prices we list.

or half-hourly to tranquil beaches north-east of Platja Gran, such as Cala Giverola (a pleasant sandy cove with a couple of restaurants and bars).

🛏 Sleeping

Most accommodation is open from Easter to October, with few options outside those months.

Hotel Hermes HOTEL €
(📞972 34 02 96; www.hotelhermes-tossademar.com; Avinguda Ferràn Agulló 6; s/d €43/83; ☉Easter-Oct; @ 🛜 ⛵) This pink concoction a block from the bus station has compact en suites with marble floors, presided over by a friendly *señora*. A bargain for the price, especially with the Jacuzzi on the roof thrown in.

Camping Cala Llevadó CAMPGROUND €
(📞972 34 03 14; www.calallevado.com; tent site incl 2 adults €50; ☉mid-Apr–Sep; P @ 🛜 ⛵ ⛺) This ground stretches back from a cove 4km southwest of Tossa in the settlement of Santa Maria de Llorell. As well as its shady camping spots and prime location with steps leading down to a pretty beach, there are tennis courts, a pool, a restaurant, shops and bars. It also has bungalows from €82.

★ Cap d'Or HOSTAL €€
(📞972 34 00 81; www.hotelcapdor.com; Passeig de la Vila Vella 1; s/d incl breakfast €72/120; ☉Easter-Oct; ❄ 🛜) Rub up against the town's history in this family-run spot right in front of the walls. Rooms are lovingly decorated in sea blues and whites and the best of them look straight onto the beach.

Hotel Diana HOTEL €€€
(📞972 34 18 86; www.hotelesdante.com; Plaça d'Espanya 6; d incl breakfast €150, with sea views €190; ☉Apr-Oct; P ❄ 🛜) Fronting Platja Gran, this artistic 1920s hotel has a Gaudí-built fireplace in the lounge and oozes Modernista decor and stained glass in the central covered courtyard. Half of the spacious, tiled rooms have beach views.

Hotel Delfín HOTEL €€€
(📞972 34 02 50; www.hotelesdante.com; Avinguda Costa Brava 2; r €150-170; ☉Apr-Oct; ❄ 🛜 ⛺) A few paces from the beach and right in the heart of things, this classy four-star has rooms with spacious balconies to catch the sea air and good facilities including a rooftop hot-tub.

🍴 Eating

Look out for *cim i tomba,* a hearty one-pot fish-and-vegetable stew, harking back to Tossa's fishing days. There are plenty of paella-and-sangria restaurant clichés, but a lot of good seafood as well.

★ La Cuina de Can Simon CATALAN €€€
(📞972 34 12 69; www.lacuinadecansimon.com; Carrer del Portal 24; mains €22-35, taster menus €68-98; ☉1-3.30pm & 8-10.30pm Wed-Sat, 1-3.30pm Sun) Tossa's culinary star nestles by the old walls in a former fisherman's stone house and distinguishes itself by the most imaginative creations in town. Taking the *mar i muntanya* (sea and mountain) theme to its logical extreme, it presents stunning combinations of fresh seafood and succulent meat. Even if you're not splurging on the gob-stoppingly good taster menu, try the delicious desserts. Opens daily in summer.

ℹ Information

Tourist Office (📞972 34 01 08; www.info-tossa.com; Avinguda del Pelegrí 25; ☉10am-2pm & 4-7pm Mon-Sat) Next to the bus station. Extended hours in high season.

ℹ Getting There & Away

Sarfa (www.sarfa.com) runs to/from Barcelona's Estació del Nord (€12.15, 1¼ hours, seven daily) and also has direct airport services. The bus station is next to the tourist office.

The C32 *autopista* connects Tossa to Barcelona, while the picturesque GI682 snakes spectacularly 23km north to Sant Feliu de Guíxols.

You can get here by boat from Barcelona and other coastal points in summer; ask at the tourist office.

Sant Feliu de Guíxols

POP 21,960

A snaking road hugs the spectacular ups and downs of the Costa Brava for the 23km from Tossa de Mar to Sant Feliu de Guíxols with – allegedly – a curve for each day of the year.

Sant Feliu itself has an attractive water-side promenade and a handful of curious leftovers from its long past, the most important being the so-called **Porta Ferrada** (Iron Gate): a wall and entrance, which is all that remains of a 10th-century monastery. The gate lends its name to an annual **music festival** held here every July since 1962.

Just north along the coast is **S'agaró**, each of its Modernista houses designed by Gaudí disciple Rafael Masó. Leave your wheels behind and take the Camí de Ronda to Platja Sa Conca – one of the most attractive beaches in the area.

Sarfa buses call in here from Barcelona (€15.40, 1½ hours, seven daily), en route to Palafrugell.

Palafrugell & Around

Halfway up the coast from Barcelona to the French border begins one of the most beautiful stretches of the Costa Brava. The town of Palafrugell, 5km inland, is the main access point for a cluster of enticing beach spots. Calella de Palafrugell, Llafranc and Tamariu, one-time fishing villages squeezed into small bays, are three of the Costa Brava's most charming, low-key resorts.

Begur, 7km northeast of Palafrugell, is a handsomely conserved, castle-topped village with a cluster of less-developed beaches nearby (some of them splendid). Inland, seek out charming Pals and the fabulous village of Peratallada.

Palafrugell

POP 22,940

Palafrugell is the main transport, shopping and service hub for the area. The tourist office (☎972 30 02 28; www.visitpalafrugell.cat; Carrer del Carrilet 2; ⊙9am-9pm Mon-Sat, 10am-1pm Sun) is beside the C66 main road; it opens shorter hours in low season. The bus station (Carrer de Torres Jonama 67-9) is nearby. Sarfa buses run to Barcelona (€18.50, two hours, seven daily) and Girona (€6.50, one hour, at least hourly).

Calella de Palafrugell

POP 780

The low-slung buildings of Calella, the southernmost of Palafrugell's crown jewels, are strung Aegean-style around a bay of rocky points and small, pretty beaches, with a few fishing boats still hauled up on the sand. The seafront is lined with year-round restaurants serving the fruits of the sea.

👁 Sights & Activities

In addition to lingering on one of the beaches, you can stroll along pretty coastal footpaths northeast to Llafranc (20 or 30 minutes) and beyond, or south to Platja del Golfet beach, close to Cap Roig (about 40 minutes).

Jardins de Cap Roig   GARDENS
(adult/child €6/3; ⊙10am-8pm Apr-Sep, to 6pm Oct-Mar, closed Mon-Fri Jan & Feb) Atop Cap Roig, 2.5km from the centre, the Jardí Botànic is a beautiful garden of 500 Mediterranean species, set around the early 20th-century castle-palace of Nikolai Voevodsky. He was a tsarist colonel with expensive tastes, who fell out of grace in his homeland after the Russian Revolution.

🎉 Festivals & Events

Cantada d'Havaneres   MUSIC
(www.havanerescalella.cat) Havaneres are melancholy Caribbean sea shanties that became popular among Costa Brava sailors in the 19th century, when Catalonia maintained busy links with Cuba. These folksy concerts are traditionally accompanied by the drinking of cremat – a rum, coffee, sugar, lemon and cinnamon concoction that you set alight briefly before quaffing. Held in July.

Festival de Cap Roig   MUSIC
(www.caproigfestival.com) Excellent music festival held at the Jardins de Cap Roig around mid-July to late August, with anything from rock to jazz, and featuring big, big names.

🛏 Sleeping & Eating

Camping Moby Dick   CAMPGROUND €
(☎972 61 43 07; www.campingmobydick.com; Carrer de la Costa Verde 16-28; tent & car €13, plus per adult €6; ⊙Apr–mid-Sep; [P][@][🏠][👪]) Set in a pine-and-oak stand about 100m from the seaside, this campground is in an ideal location. It has tennis courts and offers the chance of diving and kayak excursions in the area.

★Hotel Mediterrani   BOUTIQUE HOTEL €€€
(☎972 61 45 00; www.hotelmediterrani.com; Francesc Estrabau 40; s €135, d €160-210; ⊙Apr-Oct; [P][❄][🏠]) Swish, arty rooms decked out in placid creams, with breathtaking views of a hidden sliver of sand and an aquamarine sea from some rooms, make this hotel, at the southern end of town, very hard to beat.

La Croissanteria de Calella   ICE CREAM €
(www.lacroissanteriadecalella.com; Carrer Chopitea 3-5; ice cream €2.50; ⊙10am-5pm; [🏠][👪]) The main reason for stopping by here is the truly exceptional Sandro Desii ice cream (www.sandrodesii.com). The pistachio, canela con café (cinnamon with espresso coffee), or even the humble vanilla will leave you in raptures.

WHAT'S COOKING IN CATALONIA?

Cuina Catalana rivals Basque cuisine as Spain's best, drawing ingredients from *mar i muntanya* (sea and mountain). It's come a long way since medieval recipes for roast cat with garlic: its essence now lies in its sauces for meat and fish. There are five main types: *sofregit*, of fried onion, tomato and garlic; *samfaina*, *sofregit* plus red pepper and aubergine (eggplant) or zucchini (courgette); *picada*, based on ground almonds, usually with garlic, parsley, pine nuts or hazelnuts, and sometimes breadcrumbs; *alioli*, garlic pounded with olive oil and egg yolk to make a mayonnaise; and *romesco*, an almond, tomato, olive oil, garlic and vinegar sauce, also used as a salad dressing.

Calçots, which are a type of long spring onion, are delicious as a starter with *romesco* sauce and are in season in late winter/early spring. This is when Catalans get together for a *calçotada*, the local version of a barbecue.

Catalans seem to live on *pa amb tomàquet*, bread slices rubbed with tomato, olive oil and garlic.

Starters

➡ *escalivada* – red peppers and aubergines (sometimes with onions and tomatoes), grilled, peeled, sliced and served lukewarm dressed with olive oil, salt and garlic

➡ *esqueixada* – salad of shredded salted cod *(bacallà)* with tomato, red pepper, onion, white beans, olives, olive oil and vinegar

Main Dishes

➡ *arròs a la cassola* or *arròs a la catalana* – Catalan paella, cooked in an earthenware pot, without saffron

➡ *arròs negre* – rice cooked in cuttlefish ink, studded with cuttlefish bits

➡ *bacallà a la llauna* – salted cod baked in tomato, garlic, parsley, paprika and wine

➡ *botifarra amb mongetes* – pork sausage with fried white beans

➡ *cargols* – snails; a religion in parts of Catalonia, often eaten in stews

➡ *escudella* – a meat, sausage and vegetable stew

➡ *fideuà* – similar to paella, but using vermicelli noodles as the base, usually cooked with seafood

➡ *mandonguilles amb sipia* – meatballs with cuttlefish

➡ *sarsuela (zarzuela)* – mixed seafood cooked in *sofregit* with various seasonings

➡ *suquet* – a fish-and-potato hotpot, with generous clumps of both drenched in a tomato-based broth

Dessert

➡ *crema catalana* – Catalonia's take on *crème brûlée*

Xabec CATALAN €€
(☎972 61 46 10; Carrer de Lladó 6; mains €12-18; ⏰1-3.30pm & 8-11pm Fri-Wed Easter-Oct) A block back from the beachfront strip, this family-run place offers great-value, quality seafood. Simple grilled fish is great, as are the shellfish and tasty rice dishes. Open daily in summer.

ℹ Information

Tourist Office (☎972 61 44 75; www.visitpalafrugell.cat; Carrer de les Voltes 6; ⏰10am-8pm) By the beachfront strip; opens shorter hours in low season.

ℹ Getting There & Away

Buses from Palafrugell serve Calella and Llafranc (€1.70, 15 minutes, four daily, more in summer).

Llafranc

POP 320

Barely 2km northeast of Calella de Palafrugell, and now merging with it along the roads back from the rocky coast between them, upmarket Llafranc has a smaller bay but a longer, handsome stretch of sand, cupped on either side by pine-dotted craggy coastline.

308

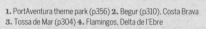

1. PortAventura theme park (p356) **2.** Begur (p310), Costa Brava
3. Tossa de Mar (p304) **4.** Flamingos, Delta de l'Ebre

ALBERTO CASANOVA / GETTY IMAGES ©

Catalonian Beaches

Spain may well be afraid of Catalan independence because it would risk losing some of the nation's most spectacular beaches. Sun, sea, and the Mediterranean: always a winning combination, but there are choices to be made. Secluded cove or endless strand? Fishing village or luxury resort? Over to you.

Costa Brava

Spain's prettiest stretch of coast offers up an endless series of perfect picture-postcard *calas* (coves): small crescents of sand flanked by pine-clad rocky headlands. Some are backed by chic hotels and gourmet restaurants, others have no facilities and can only be reached by boat or poorly signposted rocky paths. The zone around Begur (p310) and Palafrugell (p306) has some of the best, while the coast around Tossa de Mar (p304) has numerous secluded bays. Around Cap de Creus (p321) the sand disappears, but the *calas* have a rugged, remote beauty.

Costa Daurada

If the Costa Brava's boutique coves are for the connoisseur of the artier things in life, the Costa Daurada (p346) is for the no-nonsense, call-a-beach-a-beach types. Long, straight stretches of golden sand are clean and easily accessed; add nearby water parks and the PortAventura theme park (p356) and you have the perfect ingredients for a summer holiday with the kids.

Delta de l'Ebre

The flatlands of the Ebro delta jut out into the sea, marking the end of Catalonia. The beaches here are wild, long and windy, backed by dunes, perfect for a bit of beachcombing or to get away from the crowds. Kitesurfing and wakeboarding are good options. Our favourite beach: Platja de l'Eucaliptus (p357) near Amposta.

◉ Sights & Activities

The GR92 path links Llafranc with the other nearby coastal villages – these are short, spectacular walks. There are also good diving excursions available.

★ **Cap de Sant Sebastià**   HEADLAND

This magical spot up above the east of town offers fabulous views in both directions and out to sea. There's a lighthouse here, as well as a defensive tower and chapel now incorporated into a hotel. There's also the ruins of a pre-Roman Iberian settlement with multilingual explanatory panels. It's a 40-minute walk up: follow the steps from the harbour and the road up to the right. You can continue from here to Tamariu (one hour).

🛏 Sleeping & Eating

Hostal Celimar   HOSTAL €€

(✐972 30 13 74; www.hostalcelimar.com; Carrer de Carudo 12-14; s/d €45/74; ⊙Mar-Oct; 🛜) This vividly painted *hostal* is barely a stumble from the beach and offers bright rooms, with differing colour schemes from room to room, and spotless bathrooms. A good budget deal.

Hotel El Far   HOTEL €€€

(✐972 30 16 39; www.elfar.net; Cap de Sant Sebastià; r €225-300; ⊙mid-Feb–Dec; P❉🛜) A happy marriage of secluded clifftop luxury (each room has its own large balcony and superb sea views) with surprisingly affordable seafood-based cuisine; the rice dishes and the *fideuà* (a paella-like dish made with vermicelli noodles) are particularly good.

Chez Tomás   FRENCH €€

(✐972 30 62 15; Carrer de Lluís Marqués Carbó 2; mains €17-24; ⊙8-11.30pm Jun-Sep, 1-4pm & 8-11.30pm Fri-Sun Mar-May & Oct) As the name hints, the food here has a French flavour. Its strength is the use of fresh market produce to come up with such dishes as *filet de bou amb Torta de Casar trufada* (sirloin steak with a truffle-infused serving of a creamy cheese from Extremadura).

Casamar   CATALAN €€€

(✐972 30 01 04; www.hotelcasamar.net; Carrer del Nero 3; mains €20-26; ⊙1.30-3.30pm & 8.30-10.30pm Tue-Sat, 1.30-3.30pm Sun Apr-Dec) Winningly located on a headland overlooking the bay and harbour, this orangey hotel has a top-notch restaurant, serving classy seafood in a welcomingly cordial atmosphere. There's a value-packed degustation menu for €61.

ⓘ Information

Tourist Office (Passeig Cypsela; ⊙10am-8pm) A kiosk at the western end of the beach; opens shorter hours in low season.

ⓘ Getting There & Away

Buses from Palafrugell serve Llafranc via Calella (€1.90, 15 minutes, four daily, more in summer).

Tamariu

POP 290

Four kilometres north up the coast from Llafranc, quiet Tamariu is a fabulous, small, crescent-shaped cove redolent with the scent of pine. Its beach has some of the most translucent waters on Spain's Mediterranean coast.

🛏 Sleeping

★ **Hotel Es Furió**   HOTEL €€€

(✐972 62 00 36; www.esfurio.com; Carrer del Foraió 5-7; s/d incl breakfast €86/150; ❉🛜) This one-time fishing family's house was converted into a hotel in 1934. Es Furió is set just back from the beach and has spacious, cheerfully decorated rooms, where pale oranges, aqua tints and other seaside hues hold sway.

Hotel Tamariu   HOTEL €€€

(✐972 62 00 31; www.tamariu.com; Passeig del Mar 2; s/d incl breakfast €100/157; ⊙Mar-Oct; ❉🛜) A former fishermen's tavern, the Hotel Tamariu has marine-coloured rooms, stripy bedspreads and decent bathrooms as well as a waterfront restaurant.

ⓘ Getting There & Away

Sarfa buses run to Palafrugell (€1.80, 15 minutes, four daily) from mid-June to mid-September only. Parking in the village is a nightmare in summer.

Begur

POP 4150

Attractive little Begur, 7km northeast of Palafrugell, is dotted with tempting restaurants and cafes. Towering above it is a 10th-century castell (castle), towering above the hill village. It's in much the same state as when it was wrecked by Spanish troops to impede the advance of Napoleon's army in 1810. The Elizabeth Taylor film *Suddenly Last Summer* was shot here in 1959.

The sublime coastline around Begur, with its pocket-sized coves hemmed in by pine trees and subtropical flowers and lapped by azure water, is magical. From Begur, attractive winding roads run down to Aiguablava, Fornells, Sa Tuna and Aiguafreda, the first also reachable via a scenic hilly drive from Tamariu. All four beaches boast exclusive accommodation. A *bus platges* (beach bus) service runs in summer.

🛏 Sleeping & Eating

★ Hotel Classic
HOTEL €€

(☑ 656 906995; www.hotelclassicbegur.com; Carrer de Pi i Ralló 2; d €120-145; ❄ 🖥 🛜) In the heart of the old town, this warmly welcoming year-round spot has beautiful rooms themed on various notable dates in Begur's history. All are spacious and comfortable, with top modern bathrooms. There are endearing details throughout – we liked the fairly priced in-room wine selection. There's a good restaurant – breakfast is praiseworthy – and a downstairs spa zone. A bargain in low season.

Sa Caleta
CATALAN €€

(Carrer de Pi i Ralló 2; mains €10-18; ⏲ 1-4.30pm & 7pm-midnight Thu-Mon) The motherly owner-chef here prefers to let her fresh seafood flavours do the talking: there are few pretensions but plenty of quality. Generously proportioned dishes include several daily fish specials, a selection of delicious carpaccios, and a good-value set menu for €24.50. There are also decent tapas-sized portions to snack on.

ℹ Information

Tourist Office (☑ 972 62 45 20; www.visitbegur.com; Avinguda del Onze de Setembre 7; ⏲ 9am-2pm & 4-9pm Mon-Fri, from 10am Sat & Sun) Helpful. Operates shorter hours in the low season.

ℹ Getting There & Away

Sarfa buses run to Barcelona (€19.50, two to 2¼ hours, four daily) via Palafrugell. There's also a Girona service (€8.35, 1½ hours, one daily on weekdays).

Pals

POP 2740

About 6km inland from Begur (a five-minute ride on the Palafrugell bus, €1.60) is the pretty walled town of Pals. The main monument here is the 15m Torre de les Hores (clock tower) but what makes the trip worthwhile is simply wandering around the uneven lanes and poking your nose into one medieval corner or another. From the Mirador del Pedró you can see northeast across the coastal plains to the sea, with the Illes Medes in the background. There are a number of lodging options in and around town.

Sarfa buses run to Barcelona (€20, 2½ hours, up to four daily on weekdays).

Peratallada

POP 430

The heritage stone streets of Peratallada, one of Catalonia's most gorgeous villages, have made it a favourite day-trip for Catalans. The beautifully preserved narrow lanes, heavy stone arches, 12th-century Romanesque church and 11th-century castle-mansion (now a luxury hotel and restaurant) are supplemented by several enticing places to stay and eat. Though it smells more of essential oils than donkey dung these days, it's still a wonderfully characterful spot, particularly at night.

Colourful rooms with rustic views sit above a tapas-portion restaurant at friendly, charismatic El Cau de Papibou (☑ 972 63 50 30; www.papibou.com; Carrer Major 10; r €130; ⏲ Mar-Jan; 🛜) in the centre of town.

The tourist office (☑ 972 64 55 21; www.forallac.cat; Plaça Castell 3; ⏲ 9am-8pm; @ 🛜) doubles as a cafe.

Two weekday buses run from Palafrugell (€3.35, 30 to 50 minutes) and Begur (€2.25, 25 to 40 minutes) to here, and one from Girona (€5, 55 minutes).

Girona

POP 97,290

A tight huddle of ancient arcaded houses, grand churches, climbing cobbled streets and medieval baths, and Catalonia's most extensive and best-preserved Call (medieval Jewish quarter), all enclosed by defensive walls and the lazy Río Onyar, constitute powerful reasons for visiting northern Catalonia's largest city, Girona.

The Roman town of Gerunda lay on Vía Augusta, the highway from Rome to Cádiz. Taken from the Muslims by the Franks in AD 797, Girona became capital of one of Catalonia's most important counties, falling under the sway of Barcelona in the late 9th century. Its wealth in medieval times produced many fine Romanesque and Gothic buildings that have survived repeated attacks and sieges. Today they combine with fine examples of Modernisme, as well as lively nightlife, a great eating scene and art and music festivals.

Girona

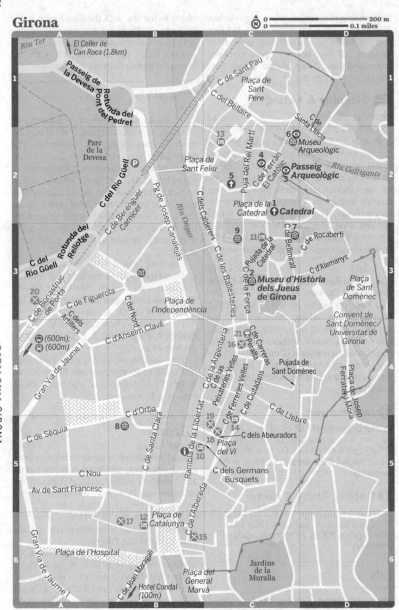

El Celler de
Can Roca (1.8km)

0 ——— 200 m
0 ——— 0.1 miles

Sights

⭐ **Museu d'Història dels
Jueus de Girona**   MUSEUM
(www.girona.cat/call; Carrer de la Força 8; adult/
child €4/free; ⏰10am-8pm Mon-Sat, to 2pm Sun)
Until 1492 Girona was home to Catalonia's

second-most important medieval Jewish
community (after Barcelona), and one of the
finest Jewish quarters in the country. The
Call (Catalan for 'ghetto') was centred on
the narrow Carrer de la Força for 600 years,
until relentless persecution forced the Jews

Girona

out of Spain. This excellent museum shows genuine pride in Girona's Jewish heritage without shying away from the less salubrious aspects, such as persecution by the Inquisition and forced conversions.

Other well-presented displays deal with Girona's Jewish contribution to medieval astronomy and medicine, the synagogue, everyday life, and rituals in the Jewish community and the diaspora. Standout objects include funerary slabs and the original documents ordering the expulsion of Jews from Spain. Opens shorter hours in low season.

★ **Catedral**   CATHEDRAL
(www.catedraldegirona.org; Plaça de la Catedral; adult/student incl Basílica de Sant Feliu €7/5, Sun free; ⊙10am-7.30pm Apr-Oct, 10am-6.30pm Nov-Mar) The billowing baroque facade of the cathedral towers over a flight of 86 steps rising from Plaça de la Catedral. Though the beautiful double-columned Romanesque cloister dates to the 12th century, most of the building is Gothic, with the second-widest nave (23m) in Christendom. The 14th-century gilt-and-silver altarpiece and canopy are memorable, as are the bishop's throne and the museum, which holds the masterly Romanesque *Tapís de la creació* (Tapestry of the Creation) and a Mozarabic illuminated *Beatus* manuscript, dating from 975.

The *Creation* tapestry shows God at the epicentre and in the circle around him the creation of Adam, Eve, the animals, the sky, light and darkness.

Museu d'Art   GALLERY
(www.museuart.com; Plaça de la Catedral 12; admission €2; ⊙10am-7pm Tue-Sat May-Sep, to

6pm Oct-Apr, 10am-2pm Sun) Next door to the cathedral, in the 12th-to-16th-century Palau Episcopal, the art museum collection consists of around 8500 pieces from the Girona region, ranging from Romanesque wood-carvings to Modernist sculptures by Olot-born Miquel Blay and early 20th-century paintings by Francesc Vayreda.

Museu d'Història de Girona   MUSEUM
(www.girona.cat/museuciutat; Carrer de la Força 27; adult/student/child €4/2/free; ⊙10.30am-5.30pm Tue-Sat, to 1.30pm Sun) The engaging and well-presented city history museum does Girona's long and impressive story justice, its displays covering everything from the city's Roman origins, through the siege of the city by Napoleonic troops to the *sardana* (Catalonia's national folk dance) tradition. A separate gallery houses cutting-edge temporary art and photography exhibits.

Banys Àrabs   BATHHOUSE
(www.banysarabs.cat; Carrer de Ferràn el Catòlic; adult/child €2/1; ⊙10am-7pm Mon-Sat, to 2pm Sun Apr-Sep, 10am-2pm daily Oct-Mar) Although modelled on earlier Muslim and Roman bathhouses, the Banys Àrabs are a finely preserved, 12th-century Christian affair in Romanesque style. This is the only public bathhouse discovered from medieval Christian Spain, where, in reaction to the Muslim obsession with water and cleanliness, washing almost came to be regarded as ungodly. The baths contain an *apodyterium* (changing room), followed by a *frigidarium* and *tepidarium* (with respectively cold and warm water) and a *caldarium* (a kind of sauna) heated by an underfloor furnace.

CATALONIA GIRONA

★ **Passeig Arqueològic**   WALLS
(Passeig de la Muralla; ⊙10am-8pm) A walk along Girona's medieval walls is a wonderful way to appreciate the city landscape from above. There are several points of access, the most popular being across the street from the Banys Àrabs, where steps lead up into some heavenly gardens where town and plants merge into one organic masterpiece. The southernmost part of the wall ends right near Plaça de Catalunya.

Basílica de Sant Feliu   CHURCH
(Plaça de Sant Feliu; adult/student incl Catedral €7/5, Sun free; ⊙10am-5.30pm Mon-Sat, 1-5.30pm Sun) Girona's second great church, with its landmark truncated bell tower, is downhill from the cathedral and entered on a combined ticket. The nave is majestic with Gothic ribbed vaulting, while St Narcissus, the patron of the city, is venerated in an enormous marble-and-jasper, late-baroque side chapel. His remains were formerly held in a glorious 14th-century sepulchre displayed alongside. A decent audioguide tour is included with admission.

Monestir de Sant Pere de Galligants   MONASTERY, MUSEUM
(www.mac.cat; Carrer de Santa Llúcia; adult/child €2.30/free; ⊙10.30am-1.30pm & 4-7pm Tue-Sat, 10am-2pm Sun) This beautiful 11th- and 12th-century Romanesque Benedictine monastery has a sublime bell tower and a lovely cloister, featuring otherworldly animals and mythical creatures on the capitals of its double columns. It's also home to the **Museu Arqueològic**, with old-school exhibits that range from prehistoric to Roman times. Opening hours vary.

Museu del Cinema   MUSEUM
(www.museudelcinema.cat; Carrer de Sèquia 1; adult/child €5/free; ⊙10am-6pm Tue-Sat; 🚻) The

---

ⓘ **MUSEUM PASS**

The **GironaMuseus** (www.gironamuseus.cat) covers six Girona museums, including the Museu d'Història dels Jueus de Girona, Museu d'Art, Museu d'Història de Girona, Monestir de Sant Pere de Galligants and the Museu del Cinema. It gives useful savings – you pay the full entrance fee at the first museum you visit and then get a 50% discount at the remainder. It's valid for six months.

Casa de les Aigües houses not only displays tracing the history of cinema from the late 19th-century debut of the Lumiére brothers, but also a parade of hands-on items for indulging in shadow games, optical illusions and the like – it's great for kids. Hours vary check the website.

🛏 **Sleeping**

Equity Point Hostel   HOSTEL €
(📞972 41 78 40; www.equity-point.com; Plaça de Catalunya 23; dm/d incl breakfast €16/48; @ 🛜) Part of an international network of hostels, this friendly, efficient place offers a great location, good social scene and a host of perks – from mounds of tourist info, small guest kitchen, laundry and colourful lounge to great rooftop terrace and spacious rooms equipped with lockers and card-key access. En suite dorms cost a couple of euros more.

Pensió Viladomat   PENSION €
(📞972 20 31 76; www.pensioviladomat.com; Carrer dels Ciutadans 5; s/d without bathroom €23/38, d with bathroom €48; 🛜) This is one of the nicest of the cheaper *pensiones* (small hotels) scattered about the southern end of the old town. It has simple but modernised and well-maintained rooms.

★ **Bells Oficis**   B&B €€
(📞972 22 81 70; www.bellsoficis.com; Carrer dels Germans Busquets 2; r incl breakfast €55-85; ❄ 🛜) A lovingly restored 19th-century flat just by the Rambla in the heart of Girona makes a stylish and ultra-welcoming place to stop. Period details combine with modern styling most effectively – the whole package is immaculate. There are just five beautiful, light rooms: some share bathrooms (those with en suite have no bathroom door) while the largest (€105) has ample room for four people.

Casa Cúndaro   BOUTIQUE HOTEL €€
(📞972 22 35 83; www.casacundaro.com; Pujada de la Catedral 9; s/d €88/110; ❄ 🛜) The understated exterior of this medieval Jewish house hides five sumptuous rooms and four self-catering apartments – all combining original exposed stone walls and antique doors with modern luxuries. You couldn't wish for a more characterful base; the location right next to the cathedral is either a boon or a bane, depending on whether you enjoy the sound of church bells. Reception is at the Hotel Historic a short stroll up the hill.

GIRONA'S JEWS

In its 13th-century heyday, Girona had one of Catalonia's largest Jewish communities, which lived by and large peacefully alongside its Christian neighbours (in fact, the synagogue was originally located next door to the cathedral), gaining in prosperity and contributing to fields as diverse as astronomy and medicine. At its peak, the Jewish quarter (the Call) was known as 'the Mother City of Israel'. Nevertheless, and especially with the later crusades in the 12th and 13th centuries, the Jewish community became a ready target for racist attacks. The Call – a maze of tiny alleys, surrounded by a stone wall – went from refuge to ghetto as Jews were gradually confined to their tiny corner of the town. Things came to a head in 1391, when a mob broke into the ghetto, massacring 40 residents. Since the Jews were still under the king's protection, troops were sent in and the survivors were confined to the Galligants Tower 'for their own safety' for 17 weeks, only to find their houses and possessions destroyed when they came out. Many converted to Christianity in the 15th century, and in 1492 those that remained were expelled from Spain, ending a story that had been over 1500 years in the telling.

Hotel Condal
HOTEL €€

(☑ 972 20 44 62; www.hotelcondalgirona.com; Carrer Joan Maragall 10; s/d €41/69; ❄ 🛜) Handy for bus and train stations and the centre, this is just what you want from a budget city hotel but rarely find: spotless, compact rooms (though the showers are tiny), wi-fi that works throughout, a central location, and friendly staff. Its got a good deal with the car park round the corner (€14 for 24 hours). All in all, a simple but very pleasing package.

★ Hotel Llegendes de Girona Catedral
HOTEL €€€

(☑ 972 22 09 05; www.llegendeshotel.com; Carrer Portal de la Barca 4; d €167-229; 🅿 ❄ 🛜) The rooms at this restored 18th-century building are supremely comfortable, with all manner of high-tech gadgets, and the all-glass bathrooms have huge rain showers. This incongruous but successful blend of modernity and antiquity includes, in the duplex 'Eros' rooms, a tantric sex sofa and instructional video. Some rooms have gorgeous cathedral views.

✖ Eating

+Cub
CAFE €

(www.mescub.cat; Carrer de l'Albereda 15; 3 tapas €10.40; ⏱ 8am-9pm Mon-Thu, 8am-midnight Fri, 9am-midnight Sat; 🛜 🍴) This ubercentral cafe is great at any time of day and distinguished by friendly service, innovative tapas – from black pudding with pistachio to salad with black-fig sorbet – fresh fruit-juice combos, shakes and Girona's own La Moska microbrew. There's a great terrace overlooking Plaça de Catalunya.

Creperie Bretonne
CAFE €

(www.creperiebretonne.com; Cort Reial 14; crêpes €4-9; ⏱ 1-4pm & 8pm-midnight Mon & Wed-Fri, 1pm-midnight Sat & Sun; 🍴 🛜) Your sweet or savoury crêpes are cooked to order inside a small bus and there are coloured pencils and paper provided for kids or the artistically inclined. The lemon-and-sugar crêpe is a standout classic and the ice cream with the signature salted caramel is worth detouring for.

Occi
FUSION €€

(www.restaurantocci.com; Carrer dels Mercaders 3; mains €15-23; ⏱ 1-3.30pm & 8.30-11pm, closed Wed) With elegant contemporary styling and quality glassware and service, this has many elements of a pricier place but remains accessible and welcoming. The menu incorporates Catalan, French and Asian influences, with game dishes featuring in season. Dishes are beautifully presented and delicious. The day it closes can vary.

Nu
CATALAN €€

(☑ 972 22 52 30; www.nurestaurant.cat; Carrer d'Abeuradors 4; mains €16-18, degustation menu €50; ⏱ 1.15-3.45pm & 8.15-10.45pm Tue-Sat, 1.15-3.45pm Mon; 🛜) Sleek and confident, this handsome contemporary old-town spot has innovative, top-notch plates prepared in view by the friendly team. There are always some very interesting flavour combinations, and they work. Great value for this quality.

Txalaka
BASQUE €€

(☑ 972 22 59 75; www.restaurant-txalaka.com; Carrer Bonastruc de Porta 4; mains €12-20, pintxos €2.50-4; ⏱ 1-4pm & 7.30-11.30pm; 🛜) For sensational Basque cooking and *pintxos* (tapas) washed down with *txakoli* (the fizzy white wine from the Basque coast) poured from a great height, don't miss this popular local spot. Just load up your plate with bar-top snacks, make sure to order some hot ones from the kitchen too and pay according to the number of *montadito* sticks/dishes.

L'Alqueria
RICES €€

(☑972 22 18 82; www.restaurantalqueria.com; Carrer de la Ginesta 8; mains €14-20; ⊙1-4pm & 9-11pm Wed-Sat, 1-4pm Tue & Sun) This smart minimalist *arrocería* serves the finest *arròs negre* (rice cooked in cuttlefish ink) and *arròs a la Catalan* in the city, as well as around 20 other superbly executed rice dishes, including paellas. Eat your heart out, Valencia! It's wise to book ahead for dinner.

★ El Celler de Can Roca
CATALAN €€€

(☑972 22 21 57; www.cellercanroca.com; Carrer Can Sunyer 48; degustation menus €150-180; ⊙1-4pm & 8.30-11pm Tue-Sat Sep-Jul) Named best restaurant in the world in 2013 by The World's 50 Best Restaurants, this place, 2km west of central Girona in a refurbished country house, is run by three brothers. The focus is 'emotional cuisine' through ever-changing takes on Catalan dishes. The style is playful and a full range of molecular gastronomy techniques is employed. The voluminous wine list arrives on a trolley. Book online 11 months in advance; if you haven't, you can join a standby list.

🍷 Drinking & Nightlife

Students make the nightlife here, so in summer things calm down. Near the river north of the old town there's a popular string of bars along Carrer de Palafrugell and Ronda de Pedret. For a beer or coffee on a sunny terrace, try Plaça de l'Independència across the river from the old town.

DANCE OF DEATH

If you're in the area on Holy Thursday (Easter), stop by the town of Verges, 15km east of Girona. On that night, the dead (well, people dressed as skeletons) roam the streets, performing the macabre Dansa de la Mort (Dance of Death) and reminding spectators of the brevity of existence as part of a much bigger evening procession enacting Christ's way to Calvary.

Girona–Torroella buses pass through here.

Lola Cafè
BAR

(www.monapartgrup.com; Carrer Bonaventura Carreras Peralta 7; ⊙6pm-3am) Recreating a sultry Latin night in the midst of medieval Girona with regular live salsa and rumba, this bar really hits the spot if you have a weakness for caipirinhas, mojitos and more.

❶ Information

Tourist Office (☑972 22 65 75; www.girona. cat/turisme; Rambla de la Llibertat 1; ⊙9am-8pm Mon-Fri, 9am-2pm & 4-8pm Sat, 9am-2pm Sun) Multilingual and helpful.

❶ Getting There & Away

Girona-Costa Brava airport (www.barcelona-girona-airport.com), a Ryanair hub, is located 11km south of the centre, with **Sagalés** (www. sagales.com) connecting it to Girona's main bus/train station (€2.75, 30 minutes, hourly), as well as Barcelona's Estació del Nord (€16/25 one way/return, 1¼ hours). A taxi (☑872 97 50 00) to central Girona costs around €27/35 day/night. Other direct bus services run to various Costa Brava and other Catalonian destinations.

Teisa (www.teisa-bus.com) runs to Besalú (€4.10 to €4.70, one hour, four to eight daily) and Olot (€7.45 to €8.50, 1¼ hours, seven to 17 daily), while **Sarfa** (www.sarfa.com) serves Cadaqués (€10.80, 1¾ hours, one on weekdays) and other coastal destinations. The bus station is next to the train station.

Girona is on the train line between Barcelona (€8.40 to €15.90, 40 minutes to 1½ hours, up to 36 daily), Figueres (€4.10 to €5.45, 30 minutes), Portbou and the French border, with several through trains to France and beyond.

Torroella de Montgrí

POP 11,470

On the Riu Ter, about 30km northeast of Girona and 15km north of Palafrugell, the agreeable medieval town of Torroella de Montgrí is the gateway to L'Estartit and site of the Festival Internacional de Música (www.festivaldetorroella.cat) – a month of classical music in the plaza in July and August.

Overlooking the town from the top of the 300m limestone Montgrí hills to the north, the impressive shell of Castell de Montgrí was built between 1294 and 1301 for King Jaume II, during his efforts to bring to heel the disobedient counts of Empúries, to the north. There's no road; by foot it's a 40-minute climb from Torroella. Head north from Plaça del Lledoner along Carrer de Fàtima, at the end of which is a sign pointing the way.

DALÍ'S QUEEN OF THE CASTLE

Two kilometres from the village of La Pera, just south of the C66 and 22km northwest of Palafrugell, the Castell de Púbol (www.salvador-dali.org; Plaça de Gala Dalí; adult/concession €8/6; ☉10am-6pm Tue-Sun mid-Mar–early Jan) forms the southernmost point of the 'Salvador Dalí triangle', other elements of which include the Teatre-Museu Dalí in Figueres (p322) and his home in Portlligat (p320).

Having promised to make his wife Gala, his muse and the love of his life, 'queen of the castle', in 1969 Dalí finally found the ideal residence to turn into Gala's refuge, since at the age of 76 she no longer desired Dalí's hectic lifestyle – a semi-dilapidated Gothic and Renaissance stronghold which includes a 14th-century church in the quiet village of Púbol.

The sombre castle, its stone walls covered with creepers, is almost the antithesis to the flamboyance of the Teatre-Museu Dalí or Dalí's seaside home: Gala had it decorated exactly as she wished and received only whom she wished. Legend has it that Dalí himself had to apply for written permission to visit her here.

The interior reflects her tastes, though Dalí touches creep in here and there. In the dining room is a replica of *Cua d'oreneta i violoncels* (Swallow's Tail and Cellos) – his last painting, completed here in 1983 during the two years of mourning following Gala's death.

To get here, catch a bus to Cruïlla de la Pera from Girona (€3, 40 minutes) or Palafrugell, alight at the stop on the C66 and walk the 2km to the castle, or else take a train from Girona to Flaça (€2.50, 12 minutes, hourly) then catch a taxi the last 4km. Opening hours vary; check the website.

Ampsa (www.ampsa.org) runs buses to L'Estartit (€1.70, 10 minutes, eight to 18 daily) and Girona (€5.10 to €5.85, one hour, three to nine daily), while Sarfa serves Barcelona (€21.70, 2¾ hours, three daily).

L'Estartit & Illes Medes

L'Estartit, 6km east of Torroella de Montgrí, has a long, wide beach of fine sand but it's the diving that stands out. The protected Illes Medes, a spectacular group of rocky islets barely 1km offshore, are home to some of the most abundant marine life on Spain's Mediterranean coast.

The range of depths (down to 50m) and underwater cavities and tunnels around the seven islets contribute much to their attraction. On and around rocks near the surface are colourful algae and sponges, as well as octopuses, crabs and various fish. Below 10m to 15m, cavities and caves harbour lobsters, scorpion fish and large conger eels and groupers. Some groupers and perch may feed from your hand. With luck, you'll spot some huge wrasse. If you get down to the sea floor, you may see angler fish, thornback rays or marbled electric rays. Be aware that this area gets pretty busy with divers, especially on summer weekends.

The tourist office (☏972 75 19 10; www.visitestartit.com; Passeig Marítim, L'Estartit; ☉9am-1pm & 3-6pm Mon-Fri, 10am-2pm Sat & Sun), open variable hours through the year, has lists of L'Estartit's scuba diving outfits. If you're a qualified diver, a two-hour trip usually costs around €35 per person. Full gear rental can cost up to €55 a day and night dives are €40 to €45. If you're a novice, do an introductory dive for around €70 or a full, five-day PADI Open Water Diver course for around €400. Glass-hulled boat trips provide an alternative to diving.

Hotel Les Illes (☏972 75 12 39; www.hotel-lesilles.com; Carrer de Les Illes 55, L'Estartit; s/d incl breakfast €68/116; ☉mid-Mar–mid-Nov; ✳☎🖥🅿) is a white, bright, family-friendly divers' hang-out behind the harbour with its own dive shop and tidy rooms with balconies; full board is available. For campers, Les Medes (☏972 75 18 05; www.campinglesmedes.com; Paratge Camp de l'Arbre, L'Estartit; site €21.20 plus per adult €9.30, bungalows from €93.50; 🅿☎✳🅿) is the pick of the eight camping grounds in and around town. It's one of Catalonia's best campsites, open year-round and set in a leafy location about 800m from the seaside, with a sauna, three pools, bike rental and even massages available.

Eateries serving mostly fresh seafood as well as standard Spanish fare are plentiful along the seafront.

L'Estartit is easily reached by bus (€1.70) from Torroella de Montgrí.

L'Escala

POP 10,510

Travel back millennia to the ancient Greco-Roman site of Empúries, set behind a near-virgin beach facing the Mediterranean. Its modern descendant, L'Escala, 11km north of Torroella de Montgrí, is a sunny and pleasant medium-sized resort on the often-windswept southern shore of the Golf de Roses.

◉ Sights

★ Empúries RUINS, MUSEUM

(www.mac.cat; adult/child €3/free; ⊙10am-8pm Jun-Sep, to 6pm Oct-May, closed Mon Nov-Feb) This worthwhile, picturesque two-part site is what remains of an important Greek, and later Roman, trading port, though the site was originally used by Phoenicians. The windswept Greek town, its broken columns fingering the sky, lies in the lower part of the site, closer to the shore. There are fine pieces – including mosaics and a statue found at the Asklepion – in the museum here, which gives good background information.

Above, the less-excavated Roman town has noble buildings and a reconstructed forum.

Points of interest in the Greek ruins include the thick southern defensive walls, the site of the Asklepion (a shrine to the god of medicine) with a copy of his statue found here, and the Agora (town square), with remnants of the early Christian basilica and the Greek stoa (market complex), beside it.

The larger Roman town includes the palatial House 1, source of many of the finest mosaics. Outside the walls are the remains of an oval amphitheatre.

A new visitor centre is slowly being built at the site so expect prices to go up when it's complete. Empúries is 1km northwest of the L'Escala town centre along the coast.

⌘ Sleeping & Eating

L'Escala is famous for its *anchoas* (anchovies) and fresh fish. Numerous mid-priced eateries are scattered along the waterfront parade of Port d'en Perris.

Can Miquel HOTEL €€

(☑972 77 14 52; www.canmiquel.com; Platja de Montgó; s/d incl breakfast €97/122; ⊙Mar-Nov; ⓟ❋⊛⊠⊛) Four kilometres from the centre behind a pretty cove beach, this is an ugly building but it's blessed with excellent modern rooms and top-class staff. There's a good pool area, tennis courts and a popular fish restaurant.

Hostal Spa Empúries BOUTIQUE HOTEL €€€

(☑972 77 02 07; www.hostalempuries.com; Platja del Portitxol; d from €192; ⓟ❋⊛) ✦ A stylish year-round hotel next to the Roman ruins fronting a sandy splash of ocean. Some rooms are beach-coloured and the mosaic bathrooms clearly take their inspiration from the ruins; the rooms in the new wing, with rain showers and enormous beds, are particularly comfortable. The two restaurants specialise in creative Mediterranean and seafood dishes using the freshest local produce. Prices halve in low season.

★ La Gruta FUSION €€

(☑972 77 62 11; www.restaurantlagruta.com; Carrer del Pintor Enric Serra 15; 3-course menu €27; ⊙12.30-3.30pm Mon, 12.30-3.30pm & 8-10.30pm Tue-Sat) This innovative spot with slick service is one of the most interesting places to eat in town: as well as serving catch of the day, it sources top-grade beef fillets and does inventive fusion and pasta dishes. Desserts are delightful.

ⓘ Information

If you arrive by Sarfa bus, you'll alight on Avinguda Girona, just down the street from the **tourist office** (☑972 77 06 03; www.lescala.cat; Plaça de les Escoles 1; ⊙9am-8pm Mon-Sat, 10am-1pm Sun). It opens shorter hours in the low season.

ⓘ Getting There & Away

Sarfa has daily buses from Barcelona (€21.70, three hours, three daily), Girona (€6.40, one hour, two to five daily) and Figueres (€4.95, one hour, two to four daily).

Castelló d'Empúries

POP 11,910

This well-preserved ancient town was once the capital of Empúries, a medieval Catalan county that maintained a large degree of independence up to the 14th century. Today it makes a superb base for birdwatching at the nearby Parc Natural dels Aiguamolls de l'Empordà, as well as a number of wind-blown but peaceful beaches. Away from the feathered treats of the natural park, architectural beauty can be found in the town centre's Església de Santa Maria on Plaça de Jacint Verdaguer. It's a voluminous 13th- and 14th-century Gothic church with a sturdy Romanesque bell tower.

◉ Sights

Parc Natural dels Aiguamolls de l'Empordà
NATURE PARK

(www.parcsdecatalunya.net; parking €2; ⊙ El Cortalet information centre 9.30am-2pm & 3.30-7pm) The remnants of the mighty marshes that once covered the whole coastal plain here are preserved in this natural park, a key site for migrating birds. The March–May and August–October migration periods bring big increases in the numbers of wading birds and even the occasional flamingo, bee eater, glossy ibis, spoonbill or rare black stork. More than 300 species pass through (some 90 nest here). There are enough birds around to make a visit worthwhile at any time of year.

The El Cortalet information centre is 1km east off the Sant Pere Pescador–Castelló d'Empúries road. A weekday bus heads along this road from Castelló in the morning, but doesn't return until the evening. Otherwise, it's a pleasant 6km walk or cycle along a path from Castelló. The centre has information, hires binoculars, and is the trailhead for several paths. Following numbers 1 then 2, each 2km long, leads to a 2km stretch of beach (closed April to June); you could walk along it and loop back to the centre (four to five hours return). Several *aguaits* (hides) offer saltwater-marsh views. Take repellent in spring and summer. Longer circuits are best cycled. The paths are always open, but morning and evening are the best times for birds. The visitor centre is open shorter hours in the low season.

⌭ Sleeping & Eating

There are a couple of great-value places to eat and drink in the town, as well as numerous *casas rurales* (village or farmstead accommodation) in the surrounding countryside and campsites aplenty in nearby Sant Pere Pescador.

★ Hotel Casa Clara
HOTEL €€

(⌨ 972 25 02 15; www.hotelcasaclara.com; Carrer de la Fruita 27; s/d €65/90; ℗❄🛜) The spacious, tiled rooms at this adorable little hotel all feature plenty of natural light, an individual colour scheme and very comfortable beds – some with wrought-iron bedsteads. The attached restaurant features a changing weekly menu of imaginative, beautifully executed dishes, such as courgette-and-hazelnut bake and sea bream with shitake mushrooms (three courses €15).

DON'T MISS

A NIGHT UNDER THE STARS

Stargazers and lovers shouldn't miss **Mil Estrelles** (⌨ 972 59 67 07; www.milestrelles.com; La Bastida, Borgonyà; d incl breakfast €110-179; ℗❄🛜) 🅿, a unique hotel 17km northwest of Girona. Fabulously combining old stone and modern plastic, it offers a noble historic farmhouse with lovably rustic rooms, as well as various cute chambers dotted about the garden in clear plastic bubbles, perfect for spotting constellations from the comfort of your double bed. There might be treehouses by the time you read this too. It's all designed for couples on a romantic break – there are no bathroom doors or children, and relaxation options include a floatarium, massages, sauna and private Jacuzzi. Dinners are available and can be brought to your room. Take the Banyoles road, exit at Borgonyà and follow the signs.

Hotel Canet
HOTEL €€

(⌨ 972 25 03 40; www.hotelcanet.com; Plaça del Joc de la Pilota 2; r €94; ⊙ Mar-Nov; ℗❄🛜🏊) This modernised 17th-century mansion in the town centre has elegant rooms, low-slung stone arches and a sun deck. A soothing swimming pool glistens within the stone walls of the interior courtyard. The decent restaurant (mains €10 to €17) offers Catalan fare cooked mainly from local produce: try the *conill amb cargols* (stewed rabbit with snails).

❶ Getting There & Away

Sarfa runs buses to Figueres (€1.70, 15 minutes, 14 daily on weekdays, one on weekends), Cadaqués (€4.20, 50 minutes, five weekdays, one weekends) and Barcelona's Estació del Nord (€20.75, two hours, one weekdays).

Cadaqués & Around

POP 2940

A whitewashed village around a rocky bay, Cadaqués' narrow, hilly streets are perfect for wandering. The iconic town and its surrounding area have a special magic – a fusion of wind, sea, light and rock – that isn't dissipated even by the throngs of summer visitors.

A portion of that magic owes itself to Salvador Dalí, who spent family holidays here during his youth, and lived much of his later life at nearby Portlligat. Thanks to Dalí and

DON'T MISS

CASA MUSEU DALÍ

Located by a peaceful cove in Portlligat, a tiny fishing settlement a 20-minute walk from Cadaqués, the Casa Museu Dalí (☑ 972 25 10 15; www.salvador-dali.org; adult/child under 9 yr €11/free; ⊗ 10.30am-6pm Tue-Sun, closed Jan–mid-Feb) was the lifelong residence of Salvador Dalí. It started life as a mere fisherman's hut, but was steadily altered and enlarged by Dalí, who lived here with his wife from 1930 to 1982. If the Teatre-Museu Dalí in Figueres is the mask that the showman presented to the world, then this is an intimate glimpse of his actual face. This splendid, bizarre whitewashed structure is a mishmash of cottages and sunny terraces, linked together by narrow labyrinthine corridors and containing an assortment of offbeat furnishings.

From the stuffed-bear umbrella/walking-stick holder in the entry hall and the stuffed swans in the library, to the moving easel in Dalí's study, there's no end to little surprises. Some of the stranger touches include The Oval – the heart of the house built as a sanctuary for Gala; the penis-shaped swimming pool and labial sofa; and the little tower topped with a giant egg, abristle with pitchforks.

Compulsory small-group tours are conducted by multilingual guides; booking a day or three ahead (online or by phone) is essential. It's open longer hours in the high season.

other luminaries, such as his friend Federico García Lorca, Cadaqués pulled in a celebrity crowd and still does. One visit by the poet Paul Éluard and his Russian wife, Gala, in 1929 caused an earthquake in Dalí's life: he ran off to Paris with Gala (who was to become his lifelong obsession and, later, his wife) and joined the surrealist movement.

⊙ Sights

Museu de Cadaqués   MUSEUM

(Carrer de Narcís Monturiol 15; adult/child €4/3; ⊗10.30am-1.30pm & 4-7pm Mon-Sat Apr-Jun & Oct, 10am-8pm daily Jul-Sep) Dalí often features strongly in the temporary exhibitions displayed here, as do his contemporaries also connected to Cadaqués, such as Picasso. It opens roughly Easter to October, but this depends on the yearly exhibition.

🛏 Sleeping

Hostal Vehí   HOSTAL €€

(☑ 972 25 84 70; www.hostalvehi.com; Carrer de l'Església 5; d with bathroom €90; ⊗ Mar-Oct; ✳ 🗑) Near the church in the heart of the old town, this simple spot with clean-as-a-whistle rooms, run by a friendly family, tends to be booked up for July and August. It's a pain to get to if you have a lot of luggage, but it's by far the best budget deal in town. It's a lot cheaper outside high season.

Hotel Llane Petit   HOTEL €€

(☑ 972 25 10 20; www.llanepetit.com; Carrer del Dr Bartomeus 37; r €118-176; ⊗ mid-Mar–Oct; P ✳ 🗑 🐾) This four-storey place overlooks a pocket-sized pebbled beach around the bay from the centre. The location is splendid and most of the 35 rooms have a generous balcony to sit on. Breakfast (€12) and parking (€15) cost extra.

L'Horta d'en Rahola   BOUTIQUE HOTEL €€€

(☑ 972 25 10 49; www.hortacadaques.com; Carrer Sant Vicens 1; d €125-200; P ✳ 🗑) Just by the roundabout at the entrance to the village, this luminous family-run place is a characterful conversion of an old farmhouse, with a restaurant a garden growing vegetables and fruit. The seven rooms, all different, are light and bright with a marine feel. Personal service is excellent and you're made to feel very welcome. Open year-round.

🍴 Eating & Drinking

The seafront is lined with fairly pricey seafood eateries. Cadaqués' signature dish is *suquet* – a hearty traditional potato-based fish-and-shellfish stew. Carrer Miquel Rosset has many hole-in-the-wall bars that get jam-packed on sultry summer nights.

Es Baluard   SEAFOOD €€

(☑ 972 25 81 83; www.esbaluard-cadaques.net; Riba Nemesi Llorens; mains €16-22; ⊗ 1-3.30pm & 8.30-11pm) The family that runs this old-school restaurant that's set into the old sea wall clearly worships at the throne of Poseidon, because the tastiest of his subjects wind up on your plate. Fish dishes drawing on local market produce, such as the *anchoas de Cadaqués* (anchovies from Cadaqués) and *gambitas de Roses* (prawns from Roses), dominate the menu and you shouldn't shy away from the *crema catalana*, either.

Casa Nun
SEAFOOD €€

(☑972 25 88 56; Plaça des Portitxó 6; mains €15-25; ☺1-3.30pm & 8-11pm daily Apr-Oct, Sat & Sun Nov-Mar) Head for the cute upstairs dining area or take one of the few tables outside overlooking the port. Everything is prepared with care, and, you guessed it, seafood predominates.

Pilar
CATALAN €€

(Carrer de la Miranda 4; mains €16-20; ☺1-3.30pm & 8.30-10.30pm Mon-Sat, 1-4pm Sun) This compact, family-run place feels like you're eating in someone's flat. It's where locals come for some of the best rice dishes and *fideuà* in town; the latter arrives crowned with rock lobster and other gifts of the sea.

❶ Information

Tourist Office (☑972 25 83 15; www.visitcadaques.org; Carrer del Cotxe 2; ☺9am-1pm & 3-6pm Mon-Sat) Near where the main road meets the water; open longer hours in the high season.

❶ Getting There & Away

Sarfa buses connect Cadaqués to Barcelona (€24.50, 2¾ hours, one to two weekdays, plus weekends in summer), Figueres (€5.50, one hour, four weekdays) via Castelló d'Empúries, and Girona (€10.80, 1¾ hours, one weekdays).

Cap de Creus

Cap de Creus is the most easterly point of the Spanish mainland and is a place of sublime, rugged beauty, battered by the merciless tramontana wind and reachable by a lonely, 8km-long road that winds its way through the moonscapes. The odd-shaped rocks, barren plateaux and deserted shorelines that litter Dalí's famous paintings were not just a product of his fertile imagination. This is the landscape that inspired the artist:

he described it as a 'grandiose geological delirium'. See if you can find the huge rock that morphed into the subject of his painting *The Great Masturbator*.

With a steep, rocky coastline indented by dozens of turquoise-watered coves, it's an especially wonderful place to be at dawn or sunset. On top of the cape stands a lighthouse featuring a small interpretation centre, and Bar Restaurant Cap de Creus (☑972 19 90 05; restcapdecreus@yahoo.es; mains €15-19; ☺9.30am-8pm Sun-Thu, to midnight Fri & Sat Nov-Apr, 9.30am-midnight daily May-Oct), the world's most unexpected curry house, where you get the likes of *khari gost* as well as local dishes and cheesecake. You can also stay over in one of three apartments that sleep up to four (double/quadruple €90/110); book ahead.

Cadaqués to the French Border

If you want to prolong the journey to France, El Port de la Selva and Llançà are pleasant, low-key spots. The former is a fishing town backed by powerful mountains and filled with bobbing yachts, while the latter boasts a string of strands and coastal walking trails. From El Port de la Selva you can undertake a wild and lonely walk high along the rugged coast. The trail, which is awkward at some points, leads east to Cap de Creus.

Monestir de Sant Pere de Rodes

Combine all-encompassing views of a deep-blue Mediterranean and the (sometimes) snowy peaks of the nearby Pyrenees with a spectacular piece of Romanesque architecture and what you get is the Monestir de Sant Pere de Rodes (adult/ child under 7yr €4.50/free, Tue free; ☺10am-7.30pm Jun-Sep, to

---

THE COSTA BRAVA WAY

The 255km-long stretch of cliffs, coves, rocky promontories and pine groves that make up the signposted Costa Brava Way, stretching from Blanes to Colliure in France, unsurprisingly offers some of the best walks in Catalonia, ranging from gentle rambles to high-octane scrambles (or one long, demanding hike if you want to do the whole thing). For the most part, the trail follows the established GR92, but also includes a number of coastal deviations.

A choice route is Cadaqués to the Cap de Creus Lighthouse (2½ hours), a relatively easy walk from the centre of Cadaqués that passes Portlligat before continuing along windswept, scrub-covered, rocky ground past several isolated beaches before it reaches the lighthouse.

5pm Oct-May, closed Mon), which sits high up in the hills above El Port de la Selva. Founded in the 8th century, it later became the most powerful monastery in the area. Looking at its mighty, brooding exterior, you're transported into the Middle Ages, though the effect is somewhat spoiled by the intensive restoration efforts which fail to blend in with the ruins. It's particularly enjoyable to admire the original stonework inside the great triple-naved, barrel-vaulted basilica, flanked by the square Torre de Sant Miquel bell tower, while ducking in and out of subterranean nooks and crannies will put gamers in mind of *Assassin's Creed*. There's also an information office for the Parc Natural Cap de Creus here.

There are no public buses to the monastery, though it is reachable by road (or a spectacular walk) either from coastal El Port de la Selva (10km) or Vilajuíga, inland.

Figueres

POP 45,120

Twelve kilometres inland, Figueres is a busy town with a French feel and an unmissable attraction: Salvador Dalí. The artist was born in Figueres in 1904 and although his career took him to Madrid, Barcelona, Paris and the USA, he remained true to his roots. In the 1960s and '70s he created here the extraordinary Teatre-Museu Dalí – a monument to surrealism and a legacy that outshines any other Spanish artist, both in terms of popularity and sheer flamboyance. Whatever your feelings about this complex, egocentric man, this museum is worth every cent and minute you can spare.

◉ Sights

★ Teatre-Museu Dalí   MUSEUM
(www.salvador-dali.org; Plaça de Gala i Salvador Dalí 5; admission incl Dalí Joies & Museu de l'Empordà adult/child under 9yr €12/free; ⊙9am-8pm daily Jul-Sep, 9.30am-6pm Tue-Sun Mar-Jun & Oct, 10.30am-6pm Tue-Sun Nov-Feb) The first name that comes into your head when you lay your eyes on this red castle-like building, topped with giant eggs and stylised Oscar-like statues and studded with plaster-covered croissants, is Dalí. An entirely appropriate final resting place for the master of surrealism, its entrance watched over by medieval suits of armour balancing baguettes on their heads, it has assured his immortality. 'Theatre-museum' is an apt label for this trip through the incredibly fertile imagination of one of the great showmen of the 20th century.

Between 1961 and 1974 Salvador Dalí converted Figueres' former municipal theatre, ruined by a fire at the end of the civil war in 1939, into the Teatre-Museu Dalí. It's full of surprises, tricks and illusions, and contains a substantial portion of Dalí's life's work, though you won't find his most famous pieces here: they are scattered around the world.

Even outside, the building aims to surprise, from the collection of bizarre sculptures outside the entrance, on Plaça de Gala

---

DALÍ

One of the 20th century's most recognisable icons, Salvador Dalí (1904–89) could have had the term 'larger-than-life' invented for him. He then would likely have decorated it with pink pineapples.

Born in Figueres, Dalí's surrealist trajectory through the often-serious landscape of 20th-century Spain brought him in contact and collaboration with figures including Pablo Picasso, Luís Buñuel, Federico García Lorca, Franco and a raft of foreign celebrities who flocked to be seen in his extravagant company. He turned his hand to everything from film-making to architecture to literature.

Self-consciously eccentric and a constant source of memorable soundbites, he was nevertheless in some ways a conservative figure and devout Catholic. His long relationship with his Russian wife Gala provided the stable foundation that his whirligig life revolved around.

The celebrity, the extraordinarily prolific output and, let's face it, the comedic moustache tend to pull focus from the fact that this was an artist of the highest calibre. In his paintings, Dalí's surrealism was often far more profound than it seems at first glance. The floppy clocks of his most famous work, *The Persistence of Memory*, are a direct reference to the flexibility of time proposed by Einstein. His *Christ of St John of the Cross* combines expert composition, symbol-laden Renaissance-style imagery and a nostalgic, almost elegiac view of the Catalan coast that he so loved.

i Salvador Dalí, to the pink wall along Pujada del Castell. The Torre Galatea, added in 1983, is where Dalí spent his final years.

Choice exhibits include Taxi Plujós (Rainy Taxi), composed of an early Cadillac, surmounted by statues. Put a coin in the slot and water washes all over the occupant of the car. The Sala de Peixateries (Fish Shop Room) holds a collection of Dalí oils, including the famous Autoretrat Tou amb Tall de Bacon Fregit (Soft Self-Portrait with Fried Bacon) and Retrat de Picasso (Portrait of Picasso). Beneath the former stage of the theatre is the crypt with Dalí's plain tomb, located at 'the spiritual centre of Europe' as Dalí modestly described it.

Gala, Dalí's wife and lifelong muse, is seen throughout – from the Gala Mirando el Mar Mediterráneo (Gala Looking at the Mediterranean Sea) on the 2nd level, which also appears to be a portrait of Abraham Lincoln from afar, to the classic Leda Atómica (Atomic Leda).

After you've seen the more notorious pieces, such as the famous Mae West Room, see if you can find a turtle with a gold coin balanced on its back, the nightmarish El Cavall Feliç (The Happy Horse), and the peepholes into a tiny mysterious room with a mirrored flamingo amidst fake plants.

A separate entrance (same ticket and opening times) leads into Dalí Joies, a collection of 37 jewels, designed by Dalí. He designed these on paper (his first commission was in 1941) and the jewellery was made by specialists in New York. Each piece, ranging from the disconcerting Ull del Temps (Eye of Time) through to the Cor Reial (Royal Heart), is unique.

Museu del Joguet   MUSEUM

(www.mjc.cat; Carrer de Sant Pere 1; adult/child €6/free; ☉10am-6pm Tue-Sat, 11am-2.30pm Sun, closed Jan; 🖐) This museum has more than 3500 toys through the ages – from the earliest board games involving coloured stones and ball-in-a-cup to intricate dolls' houses, 1920s dolls with the creepiest expressions you're ever likely to see, Dinky Toys, and Catalonia- and Valencia-made religious processions of tiny figures. Absolutely mesmerising, and not just for the kids!

Castell de Sant Ferran   FORT

(www.lesfortalesescatalanes.info; adult/child €3/free; ☉10.30am-6pm) This sturdy 18th-century fortress commands the surrounding plains from a low hill 1km northwest of the centre.

ⓘ VISITING THE TEATRE-MUSEU DALÍ

Given that the Teatre-Museu Dalí (p322) is the second-most-visited museum in Spain, it pays to reserve online in advance, and to visit outside the weekends and public holidays. Get here at opening time to avoid the worst of the crowds. In August the museum opens at night (admission €13, 10pm to 12.30am, booking essential); ticket price includes a glass of cava (sparkling wine).

Built in 1750 to repel any French invaders and large enough to house 16,000 men, it nevertheless fell to the Gallic neighbours – both in 1794 and 1808. Spain's Republican government held its final meeting of the civil war (on 8 February 1939) in the dungeons. It's a vast complex: the admission fee includes an audioguide; book ahead for other guided tours (€10 to €15) involving jeeps and boats. Opening hours vary seasonally.

Museu de l'Empordà   MUSEUM

(www.museuemporda.org; La Rambla 2; adult/child €4/free; ☉11am-7pm Tue-Sat, to 2pm Sun) This local museum on the square combines Greek, Roman and medieval archaeological finds with a sizeable collection of art, mainly by Catalan artists, but there are also some works on loan from the Prado in Madrid. Admission is free with a Teatre-Museu Dalí ticket.

🛏 Sleeping & Eating

Most people treat Figueres as a day trip from Barcelona or the coast, but it's worth staying overnight if you want to beat the coachloads of tourists to the Dalí museum. The restaurants closest to the Teatre-Museu Dalí are overpriced, mediocre tourist traps.

Hotel Durán   HOTEL €€

(📞972 50 12 50; www.hotelduran.com; Carrer de Lasauca 5; r €99; P✳🌐) Staying at this mid-19th-century hotel is very much in keeping with the Dalí theme as he and his wife used to frequent the place themselves. Successfully blending old-style elegance with contemporary design, the hotel offers modern, good-value rooms and a restaurant like a royal banquet hall, with smooth service and a fantastic €24 lunch menu which features such expertly prepared delights as seared tuna steak and rabbit loin. Breakfast is cheaper if you book online.

Sidrería Txot's
BASQUE €

(www.sidreriatxots.com; Av Salvadór Dalí 114; dishes €5-11; ⊙ noon-midnight; 🐾) Watch your Basque cider being poured from on high from the barrel – the way it's meant to be – before tucking into *pintxos*, tasty burgers, cured meats, cheeses and salads, as well as dishes such as chorizo in cider and L'Escala anchovies on toast. The kitchen's open all afternoon – handy for a post-Dalí meal.

El Motel
CATALAN €€

(📞 972 50 05 62; www.elmotel.cat; Hotel Empordà, Av Salvador Dalí i Domènech 170; tasting menus €39-60; ⊙ 7.30-11am, 12.45-3.45pm & 9-11pm; 🐾) Jaume Subirós, the chef and owner of this hotel-restaurant on a busy road 1km north of the centre, is a seminal figure in its transition from traditional Catalan home cooking to the polished, innovative affair it is today. Highlights are such dishes as sea urchins

---

THE CHANGING FORTUNES OF CATALONIA

Like many European nations, the kingdom of Spain was cobbled together by a series of conquests and dynastic alliances from what were once separate states. Though the last of these was over 500 years ago, folk on the peninsula still tend to identify more strongly with their ancestral village or local region – the *patria chica* ('small fatherland') – than with the nation as a whole. There are separatist movements in many parts of the peninsula but especially in two regions: the Basque country and Catalonia.

Away from the big cities and Costa Brava, Catalonia feels as if you've entered a separate country. Virtually no Spanish is spoken and the red-and-yellow flag of the region flutters from the balconies. The overall feeling, as expressed by an oft-encountered piece of graffiti, is that 'Catalonia is not Spain'.

The genesis of Catalonia began when the Franks, under Charlemagne, pushed back the Moors in the 8th and 9th centuries. The Catalan golden age began in the early 12th century when Ramon Berenguer III, who already controlled Catalonia and parts of southern France, launched the region's first seagoing fleet. In 1137 his successor, Ramon Berenguer IV, was betrothed to the one-year-old heiress to the Aragonese throne, thereby giving Catalonia sufficient power to expand its empire out into the Mediterranean but joining it to another crown. When Fernando became king of Aragón in 1479 having already married Isabel, Queen of Castilla, Spain was more or less created. Catalonia resented its new subordinate status but could do little to overturn it. After backing the losing side in the War of Spanish Succession (1702–13), Barcelona rose up against the Spanish crown whose armies besieged the city from March 1713 until 11 September 1714. The victorious Felipe V abolished Catalan privileges, built a huge fort (the Ciutadella) to watch over the city, banned writing and teaching in the Catalan language, and farmed out Catalonia's colonies to other European powers.

Trade again flourished from Barcelona in the centuries that followed, and by the late 19th and early 20th centuries there were growing calls for greater self-governance to go with the city's burgeoning economic power. However, after the civil war, pro-republic Catalonia was treated harshly by victorious General Franco. Reprisals and purges resulted in the shootings of at least 35,000 people. Over time, the use of Catalan in public was banned and all street and town names were changed into Spanish, which became the only permitted language in schools and the media. The sense of grievance remains. Self-government was returned, however, in 1977 and Catalan culture has flourished; you'll see this reflected in the reemergence of traditional festivals and dances and the near-universal use of Catalan in public. There is no real sense of ethnic identity in Catalonia: over the centuries everybody and their sister has passed through here. Catalans tend to make their language the key to their identity.

The issue of independence from Spain has been at the forefront of Catalan politics for years, and in recent times has snowballed with regular demonstrations, events, and the 2014 Catalan referendum, declared illegal by Madrid. More prosperous than most of Spain, Catalans often feel their taxes subsidise the rest of the nation, and the tough economic times have exacerbated this feeling. But the fact that it's such a valuable asset makes the central government unwilling to let it go, and, constitutionally at least, a Catalan secession would have to be approved by a nationwide referendum: an unlikely scenario.

from Cadaqués, cod with truffle and calf's cheek in red wine. There are also appealing rooms at your disposal (singles/doubles €94/109).

Mas Pau CATALAN €€€
(☑972 54 61 54; www.maspau.com; Avinyonet de Puigventós; degustation menu €72; ☉1.30-3.30pm & 8.30-10.30pm Wed-Sat, 8.30-10.30pm Tue, 1.30-3.30pm Sun; �) Five kilometres along the road to Besalú, this enchanting 16th-century *masia* (farmhouse), made of rough-hewn stone, offers a dozen-course seasonal menu with an emphasis on fresh local ingredients; some dishes are truly inspired. It closes early January to mid-March and opens Sunday and Monday nights in summer. There are also comfortable rooms (double €102), relaxing gardens and a pool area.

ℹ Information

Tourist Office (☑972 50 31 55; www.visit-figueres.cat; Plaça del Sol; ☉10am-2pm & 4-6pm Tue-Sat, 10am-3pm Sun & Mon) On the main road; open longer hours in high season.

ℹ Getting There & Away

Sarfa buses serve Cadaqués (€5.50, one hour, four weekdays) via Castelló d'Empúries.

There are hourly train connections to Girona (€4.10 to €5.45, 30 minutes) and Barcelona (€12 to €16, 1¾ hours) and to Portbou and into France and beyond.

Besalú

POP 2400

The tall, crooked 11th-century **Pont Fortificat** (Fortified Bridge) over Río Fluvià in medieval Besalú, with its two tower gates and heavy portcullis, is an arresting sight, leading you into the coiled maze of cobbled narrow streets that make up the core of this delightfully well-preserved town. Following a succession of Roman, Visigothic and Muslim rulers, in the 10th and 11th centuries Besalú was the capital of an independent county that stretched as far west as Cerdanya before it came under Barcelona's control in 1111.

◎ Sights

The highlights include the bridge, picturesque **Plaça de la Llibertat**, and the Romanesque churches of **Església de Sant Vicenç**, and **Monestir de Sant Pere**, the latter with an unusual ambulatory (walkway) behind the altar. The churches are normally shut, but you can take a peek by inserting a euro coin for illumination from the doorway.

Miqvé and Synagogue RUINS
(Baixada de Mikwe; guided tours €2.20) Besalú's thriving Jewish community fled the town in 1436 after relentless Christian persecution, leaving behind a **miqvé** – a 12th-century ritual bath – the only survivor of its kind in Spain. It sits down by the river inside a vaulted stone chamber, around which remnants of the ancient **synagogue** were unearthed in excavations in 2005. The *miqvé* itself was sealed when it was discovered in 1964, suggesting that those who left it behind were hoping to return. Access is by guided tour only.

Micromundi MUSEUM
(www.museuminiaturesbesalu.com; Plaça Prat de Sant Pere 15; adult/child €4.90/2.50; ☉10am-7pm daily May-Oct, to 3pm Tue-Fri, to 7pm Sat & Sun Nov-Apr; ⊕) This curious museum is dedicated to painstakingly painted miniatures and micro-miniatures that you can peer at through microscopes. These include the incredibly detailed representation of Pinocchio and Gepetto's workshop (inside a pistachio nut) and Anatoly Konenko's minute camels passing through the eye of a needle.

☞ Tours

Ars Didàctica TOURS
(☑607 453531; www.arsdidactica.com; Carrer Major 2; town/miqvé tours €4.50/2.20; ☉Mar-Dec, groups only Jan-Feb) Runs guided tours of the *miqvé* and the centre of town. Three to four departures daily.

🛏 Sleeping & Eating

There are a couple of inexpensive *pensiones* in Besalú.

Els Jardins de la Martana HOTEL €€
(☑972 59 00 09; www.lamartana.com; Carrer del Pont 2; s/d €70/102; P❄ 🛜 ⊕) This is a charming mansion set on the out-of-town end of the grand old bridge. It has simple rooms with tiled floors, high ceilings and balconies, many offering views across the bridge to the town. There's a beautiful terrace and gardens, a noble library with fireplace, and various family rooms around a dedicated kids' play area. It could do with a spruce-up but is lovable despite that, and very friendly.

3 Arcs
HOTEL €€

(☑972 59 16 78; www.hotel3arcs.com; Carrer Ganganell 15; s/d €60/77; ❀☎) Simple, compact modern rooms in a refurbished historic building in the centre of the old town. Pleasant downstairs cafe and friendly management.

Pont Vell
CATALAN €€

(☑972 59 10 27; www.restaurantpontvell.com; Pont Vell 26; mains €15-24; ⊘1-3.30pm & 8.30-10.30pm Wed-Sun, 1-3.30pm Mon, closed late Dec-late Jan) The views to the old bridge (after which the restaurant is named) are enough to tempt you to take a seat here, even without considering the wide-ranging menu full of locally sourced delights, such as rabbit with prunes.

❶ Information

Tourist Office (☑972 59 12 40; www.besalu. cat; Carrer del Pont 1; ⊘10am-1.30pm & 4-7pm Mon-Sat, 10am-1.30pm Sun) Across the bridge from the centre. Offers audioguides (€4) to the town and can book guided visits.

❶ Getting There & Away

Teisa (www.teisa-bus.com) buses run to Barcelona (€15.40, 1¾ hours, three to four daily), Olot (€3.45, 30 minutes, six to 18 daily), Figueres (€3.45 to €4, 30 minutes, two to three daily) and Girona (€4.10 to €4.70, one hour, four to eight daily).

The N260 road from Figueres to Olot meets the C66 from Girona at Besalú.

THE CATALAN PYRENEES

The Pyrenees in Catalonia encompass some awesomely beautiful mountains and valleys. The Parc Nacional d'Aigüestortes i Estany de Sant Maurici, in the northwest, is a jewel-like area of lakes and dramatic peaks.

As well as the natural beauty of the mountains, and the obvious attractions of walking, skiing and other sports, the Catalan Pyrenees and their foothills have a rich cultural heritage, notably the countless lovely Romanesque churches and monasteries, often tucked away in remote valleys.

When looking for a place to kip, keep an eye out for *casas rurales,* usually set in old village houses and peppered across the Pyrenees. You can browse many of them online at http://establimentsturistics.gencat.cat or pick up the listings booklet at tourist offices throughout Catalonia.

Olot
POP 33,980 / ELEV 443M

Olot is the spread-out capital of La Garrotxa region, with wide, tree-lined walkways (except in its serpentine medieval heart) and plenty of options for rambling in the surrounding countryside, shaped by the ancient activity of the dormant volcanoes of the nearby Parc Natural de la Zona Volcánica de la Garrotxa.

◉ Sights & Activities

Four volcanoes stand sentry on the fringes of Olot; walk up Volcà Montsacopa, 500m north of the centre, or Volcà La Garrinada, 1km northeast of the centre, both of which are volcanic craters.

Museu Comarcal de la Garrotxa MUSEUM
(Carrer de l'Hospici 8; adult/child €3/free; ⊘11am-2pm & 4-7pm Tue-Sat, 11am-2pm Sun) This museum, in the same building as the tourist office – an atmospheric 18th-century hospital – covers Olot's growth and development as an early textile centre, though its star exhibit is the collection of works by local painters and sculptors. Opening hours vary seasonally.

Museu dels Volcans MUSEUM
(Parc Nou, Avinguda de Santa Coloma de Farners; adult/child €3/1.50; ⊘10am-2pm & 3-6pm Tue-Sat, 10am-2pm Sun) Found inside the pleasant Parc Nou, a botanical garden of Olot-area flora, the Museu dels Volcans can teach you everything you ever wanted to know about volcanoes. The interactive section includes an earthquake simulator; other displays cover local flora, fauna and ecosystems. Opens extended hours in summer.

Vol de Coloms BALLOONING
(☑972 68 02 55; www.voldecoloms.cat; adult/child €170/100) Offers memorable hot-air-balloon trips over the volcanic scenery of the natural park. Flights last about 90 minutes and include *cava* and a snack.

🛏 Sleeping & Eating

Torre Malagrida HOSTEL €
(☑972 26 42 00; www.xanascat.cat; Passeig de Barcelona 15; dm under/over 30 years €19/23; @☎) With stone lions guarding the entrance to this marble-columned early 20th-century Modernista building, surrounded by gardens, it's hard to believe this is a youth hostel (HI). The unadorned dorms are comfort-

able without living up to the promise of the exterior; there are meals available, as well as bicycles for rent.

★ Can Blanc
CASA RURAL €€

(☑972 27 60 20; www.canblanc.es; Paratges de la Deu; s/d incl breakfast €62/100; P🌸🌐🚫🎿) This secluded place on the southwestern edge of Olot is surrounded by parkland. Colourful, modern-rustic rooms come in a range of shapes and sizes. The pleasing gardens and pool will put a smile on your face on hot summer days and a great breakfast is thrown in. Ask for the next-door La Deu restaurant, as people are more likely to know it. Don't confuse this with Can Blanc restaurant on the southeastern edge of town.

Hotel l'Estació
HOTEL €€

(☑972 26 10 07; www.hotelolot.com; Avinguda Estació 2; s/d €55/85; 🌸🌐) Run above a bar by a friendly family who'll give plenty of advice on what to do in town, this place has modern, minimalist rooms with comfy beds and stylish bathrooms. You can park easily nearby.

★ La Quinta Justa
CUINA VOLCÀNICA €€

(☑972 27 12 09; www.laquintajusta.cat; Passeig de Barcelona 7; mains €11-20; ☺1-4pm & 8-11pm Mon-Sat, 1-4pm Sun; 🌐) Central, stylish restaurant with excellent service offering plenty of volcanic delights. Anything with local mushrooms or beans in it is bound to be delicious, and the creations with *foie* (liver) are sensational. You might be better dining à la carte than off the various set menus. Very worthwhile.

La Deu
CUINA VOLCÀNICA €€

(☑972 26 10 04; www.ladeu.es; Carretera la Deu; mains €10-23; ☺1-4pm & 8-10.30pm Mon-Sat, 1-4pm Sun; 🌐) Family-run restaurant going back to the 19th century and famous for its takes on the hearty *cuina volcànica*. There's huge variety, including the likes of rabbit stewed with snails (tastier than it sounds!) and *botifarra* sausage with haricot beans. Great atmosphere and picturesque spot.

Les Cols
CUINA VOLCÀNICA €€€

(☑972 26 92 09; www.lescols.com; Carretera de la Canya; degustation menu €85; ☺1-3.30pm Tue, 1-3.30pm & 8.30-10.30pm Wed-Sun) Set in a converted 19th-century farmhouse, Les Cols is 2km northeast of central Olot. Inside, the decor has a 21st-century edge, with iron and glass walls, a chilled-out ambience and gourmet ambitions. Dishes with local products are prepared with a silken touch, from chicken and duck to wild boar.

VOLCANIC CUISINE

In Olot and around, a dedicated group of chefs proudly carries on the *cuina volcànica* culinary tradition, which stems from the exceptionally fertile volcanic soil, responsible for a bounty of locally grown produce that forms the base of this hearty cuisine. Ingredients include black radishes, wild mushrooms, Santa Pau beans, *ratafia* (walnut liquor with aromatic herbs) and *puimoc* (dry pork sausage).

❶ Information

Casal dels Volcans (☑972 26 62 02; www.turismegarrotxa.com; Parc Nou, Avinguda de Santa Coloma de Farners; ☺10am-2pm & 4-6pm Mon-Sat, 10am-2pm Sun) Information about the Parc Natural de la Zona Volcánica de la Garrotxa.

Patronat Municipal de Turisme (☑972 26 01 41; http://areadepromocio.olot.cat; Carrer del Hospici 8; ☺10am-2pm & 4-7pm Mon-Sat, 10am-2pm Sun) Near the bus station; shorter opening hours in low season.

❶ Getting There & Away

Teisa (www.teisa-bus.com) runs buses to/from Barcelona (€13.60 to €18.50, two to 2¾ hours, seven to 11 daily) and Girona via Besalú (€3.90, 45 minutes, seven to 12 daily). The easiest approach by car from Barcelona is by the AP7 and C63.

The Volcano Park

The hills around Olot are volcanic in origin, making up the 120-sq-km Parc Natural de la Zona Volcánica de la Garrotxa. Volcanic activity began here about 350,000 years ago but the last eruption was 11,500 years ago. The park completely surrounds Olot with the most interesting area between Olot and the village of Santa Pau, 10km southeast.

In the park there are about 40 volcanic cones, up to 160m high and 1.5km wide. Together with the lush vegetation, a result of fertile soils and a damp climate, these create a landscape of verdant beauty. Between the woods are crop fields, a few hamlets and scattered old stone farmhouses.

The main park information office is the Casal dels Volcans in Olot, where you can collect helpful hiking maps and information on various trails.

The old part of Santa Pau village, perched on a rocky outcrop, contains a beautiful porticoed plaza, the Romanesque Església de Santa Maria and a locked-up baronial castle. The village has a couple of places to stay, including the great-value Can Menció (☑ 972 68 00 14; www.canmencio.com; Plaça Major 17; d €45; 🖗), a cosy place on the main square.

Several good marked walks, which you can complete in less than a day, allow you to explore the park with ease. There are numerous easy hikes to several of the cones from car parks near Olot and Santa Pau. Enquire at the park information offices about routes.

Ripoll

POP 10,800 / ELEV 691M

One of Spain's finest pieces of Romanesque art is to be found at the medieval heart of this otherwise somewhat shabby industrial town, split down the middle by the Riu Ter and surrounded by hills.

Thirty kilometres west of Olot, Ripoll can claim, with some justice, to be the birthplace of Catalonia. In the 9th century it was the power base from which local strongman Guifré el Pilós (Wilfred the Hairy) succeeded in uniting several counties of the Frankish March along the southern side of the Pyrenees. Guifré went on to become the first *comte* (count) of Barcelona. To encourage repopulation of the Pyrenean valleys, he founded the Monestir de Santa Maria, the most powerful monastery of medieval Catalonia – and was buried there after death.

Sights

Monestir de Santa Maria　MONASTERY
(adult/child €3/1; ⏱ 10am-1pm & 3-7pm Apr-Sep, to 6pm Oct-Mar) Founded in AD 879, the Monestir de Santa Maria was Catalonia's spiritual and cultural heart from the mid-10th to mid-11th centuries. The five-naved basilica was adorned in about 1100 with a stone portal that ranks among the most splendid Romanesque art in Spain. A chart helps decipher the feast of sculpture: a medieval vision of the universe from God to a calendar of rural life. Most interesting in the heavily restored interior is the tomb of Guifré el Pilós.

🛏 Sleeping & Eating

Hostal Ripollès　HOSTAL €
(☑ 972 70 02 15; www.hostaldelripolles.com; Plaça Nova 11; s/d €33/60; 🖗) One of only two lodging options in the town's medieval heart, this friendly family establishment consists of decent en suite rooms above a restaurant mixing pizza and pasta with regional dishes. Good breakfast available for a few extra coins.

El Crocus　CATALAN €
(☑ 972 70 45 57; Carrer Berenguer el Vell 4; mains €12-23, menús €16-27; ⏱ 1-3.15pm Wed-Mon, 8.30-10pm Fri & Sat) Just up the street from the monastery, El crocus combines the elaborate and the simple, with traditional Catalan dishes such as *crema de pésols* (pea soup), *mandonguilles* (meatballs) and a selection of *arroces* (rice dishes) taking their places alongside more ambitious dishes, including occasional Asian plates. Great-value *menú del día* (daily set menu; €10).

DRAGONS, GIANTS & BIG-HEADS

Fire and fireworks play a big part in many Spanish festivals, but Catalonia adds a special twist with the *correfoc* (fire-running), in which devil and dragon figures run through the streets spitting fireworks at the crowds.

Correfocs are often part of the *festa major*, a town or village's main annual festival, which usually takes place in July or August. Part of the *festa major* fun are the *sardana* (Catalonia's national folk dance) and *gegants*, splendidly attired 5m-high giants that parade through the streets or dance in the squares. Giants tend to come in male-and-female pairs, such as a medieval king and queen. Almost every town and village has its own pair, or up to six pairs, of giants. They're accompanied by grotesque 'dwarfs' (known as *capsgrossos*, or 'big-heads').

On La Nit de Sant Joan (23 June), big bonfires burn at crossroads and town squares in a combined midsummer and St John's Eve celebration, and fireworks explode all night. The supreme fire festival is the Patum in Berga, 30km west of Ripoll. An evening of dancing and fireworks-spitting angels, devils, mulelike monsters, dwarfs, giants and men covered in grass culminates in a mass frenzy of fire and smoke. Patum happens on Corpus Christi (the Thursday 60 days after Easter Sunday).

MONESTIR DE SANT JOAN DE LES ABADESSES

Located in Sant Joan de les Abadesses, an attractive little town 10km northeast of Ripoll, the Monestir de Sant Joan de les Abadesses (Plaça de l'Abadia; admission €3; ⊙10am-7pm) is a monastery founded by Guifré el Pilós, which began life as a nunnery – the nuns were expelled in 1017 for alleged licentious conduct. Its elegant 12th-century church contains the marvellous and somewhat unnerving *Santíssim Misteri*, a 13th-century polychrome woodcarving of the descent from the cross, composed of seven life-sized figures. Also remarkable is the Gothic *retablo* (altarpiece) of Santa Maria La Blanca, carved in alabaster. The attached museum charts the town's religious history through a display of sacred art and artefacts. Teisa (www.teisa-bus.com) operates buses more than hourly weekdays and two-hourly at weekends from Ripoll (€1.70, 15 minutes). Monastery opening hours are shorter in low season.

ⓘ Information

Tourist Office (☑972 70 23 51; www.ripoll. cat/turisme; Plaça del Abat Oliba; ⊙9.30am-1.30pm & 4-6pm Tue-Sun) Next door to the Monestir de Santa Maria. Opening hours vary seasonally.

ⓘ Getting There & Away

Daily rodalies trains (line R3) run to Barcelona via Vic (€8.40, two hours, 12 to 16 daily), Ribes de Freser (€2.50, 20 minutes, up to seven daily) and Puigcerdà (€4.90, 1¼ hours, seven daily).

Vall de Ribes & Vall de Núria

North of Ripoll, the pretty Vall de Ribes is the access point for the famous pilgrimage site and ski resort of Núria, nestled high in the mountains and only accessible by foot or train. Bases in the valley below include Ribes de Freser – boasting an excellent hotel-restaurant – and, 6km beyond, the gorgeous stone village of Queralbs (1180m).

The narrow-gauge *cremallera* (rack-and-pinion railway) rises over 1000m on its 12km journey from Ribes de Freser, via Queralbs, up the green, rocky valley of the thundering Riu Núria. It's worth the trip for the scenery alone.

History

Around AD 700, the story goes, Sant Gil came from Nîmes in France to live in an isolated mountain valley 26km north of Ripoll, preaching the gospel to shepherds. Before he fled Visigothic persecution four years later, he concealed a wooden Virgin-and-child image he had carved, a cross, his cooking pot and the bell he had used to summon the shepherds. They stayed hidden until 1079, when an ox led some shepherds to the spot. The statuette, the Mare de Déu de Núria, became the patron of Pyrenean shepherds and Núria's future was assured.

◉ Sights

Queralbs, which formerly made a living from arsenic mining, has a 12th-century church with beautiful Romanesque portico.

★ Santuari de la Mare de Déu   CHURCH (www.valldenuria.cat; Núria; ⊙8am-6.30pm) Sant Gil would recoil in shock if he came back today. The sanctuary (1911) sits incongruously in the centre of a building that looks like a penitentiary but is, in fact, a hotel. The Mare de Déu de Núria sits behind a glass screen above the altar and is in 12th-century Romanesque style, so either Sant Gil was centuries ahead of his time or this isn't his work! The setting, in a green valley surrounded by mountains, is majestic.

The small chapel on the left contains a bell, a cross and a cooking pot (which all date from at least the 15th century). To have your prayer answered, put your head in the pot and ring the bell while you say it. Peek into the chapel with a stained-glass window depicting Sant Bernat, carrying a pair of skis and accompanied by a Bernese mountain dog – he's the patron saint of skiers and hikers. Nearby is a small church (1615) with Sant Gil's symbols etched into the stone at the entrance.

🏃 Activities

In winter, Núria is a small-scale ski resort (☑972 73 20 20; www.valldenuria.cat; day lift pass with/without train €29/19.50; 🎿) with 11 short runs catering to all abilities. There's also a separate area for kids, with tobogganing in winter and pony rides in summer.

There are great marked trails throughout the valley, with one of the best leading down through the gorge from Núria to Queralbs (two hours). From Núria, you can also cap several 2700m to 2900m peaks on the main Pyrenees ridge in about 2½ to four hours' walking (one way) for each. The most popular is Puigmal (2909m).

🛏 Sleeping

Wild camping is banned in the whole Ribes de Freser–Núria area.

Alberg Pic de l'Àliga
HOSTEL €

(☑972 73 20 48; www.xansacat.cat; Núria; dm under/over 30 yr incl breakfast €22/27; ☺ Jan-Sep) The youth hostel is in a spacious lodge in a stunning location at the top of the *telecabina* (cable car) leading up from the Hotel Vall de Núria. Dorm rooms sleep from four to 14. The cable car (€1.50) runs from 9am to 6pm daily (to 7pm mid-July to mid-September).

★Hotel Els Caçadors
HOTEL €€

(☑972 72 70 77; www.cacadors.com; Carrer de Balandrau 24, Ribes de Freser; s/d from €61/82; ☺Dec-Oct; ✳🛜🅿) 🍽 Family-run for several generations, this top-notch place is a Ribes institution and has been completely modernised recently. Excellent rooms come in three grades, mostly differentiated by bathrooms – some have hydromassage tubs – and there's a great top-floor lounge and deck where the Jacuzzi offers great mountain views. The restaurant is brilliant, and a gin and tonic in the bar is quite an experience.

Hostal les Roquetes
HOSTAL €€

(☑972 72 73 69; www.hostalroquetes.com; Carretera de Ribes 5, Queralbs; d €66-76; 🅿🛜) Just above the train station in lovely Queralbs, this cosy place makes a great walking base. There are fantastic views from the sizeable rooms, and some have a little terrace to enjoy them. The restaurant downstairs does filling, hearty meals (set menu €12).

Hotel Vall de Núria
HOTEL €€€

(☑972 73 20 00; www.valldenuria.cat; Núria; half-board d for 2 nights €360, d summer €120; ☺mid-Dec–Easter & Jun-Oct; 🛜🎮) The rather severe grey building surrounding the sanctuary has comfortable, if somewhat overpriced, rooms with bathroom and satellite TV, a cafeteria, a bar and two restaurants. In the exhibition hall you'll find entertaining displays on the history of the *cremallera* in four languages.

ℹ Information

Núria Tourist Office (☑972 73 20 20; www.valldenuria.com; Núria; ☺8.30am-5.45pm) In the sanctuary. Extended hours in high season.

Ribes de Freser Tourist Office (☑972 72 77 28; www.vallderibes.cat; Carretera de Bruguera 2, Ribes de Freser; ☺10am-2pm & 4-6pm Tue-Sat, 10am-2pm Sun) At the southern entrance to town. Opening hours vary seasonally.

OUT & ABOUT IN THE PYRENEES

The Catalan Pyrenees provide magnificent walking and trekking. You can undertake strolls of a few hours, or day walks that can be strung together into treks of several days. Nearly all can be done without camping gear, with nights spent in villages or *refugis* (mountain hostels/shelters).

Most of the *refugis* are run by two Barcelona mountain clubs, the Federació d'Entitats Excursionistes de Catalunya (FEEC; www.feec.org) and the Centre Excursionista de Catalunya (CEC; www.cec.cat), which also provide info on trails. A night in a *refugi* costs from €12.50 to €18. Normally FEEC *refugis* allow you to cook; CEC ones don't. Moderately priced meals (€15 to €20) are often available.

The coast-to-coast GR11 long-distance trail network traverses the entire Pyrenees from Cap de Creus on the Costa Brava to Hondarribia on the Bay of Biscay. The tougher HRP (Haute Randonnée Pyrénéenne), recommended for experienced trekkers only, takes you higher up into the mountains, crossing the Spain–France border several times.

The season for walking in the high Pyrenees is from late June to early October. Always be prepared for fast-changing conditions, no matter when you go.

Local advice from tourist offices, park rangers, mountain *refugis* and other walkers is invaluable. Dedicated hiking maps are essential.

There's boundless scope for climbing – Pedraforca in the Serra del Cadí (p333) offers some of the most exciting ascents.

ⓘ Getting There & Around

Mir (www.autocarsmir.com) runs buses (15 weekdays, nine Saturday, four Sunday) from Ripoll to Ribes de Freser (€2.15, 30 minutes); two continue Monday to Saturday to Queralbs (€3.30, 50 minutes).

There are two train stations in Ribes de Freser: Rebes-Enllaç, just south of town, with connecting trains to Barcelona, and the more centrally located Ribes-Vila. Up to seven trains a day run to Ribes-Enllaç from Ripoll (€2.50, 20 minutes) and Barcelona (€9.10, 2¼ hours).

The **cremallera** (www.valldenuria.cat; Ribes-Núria one way/return adult €13.90/22.30, child €8.35/13.35) runs from Ribes de Freser to Núria via Queralbs six to 12 times a day (35 minutes, 20 from Queralbs), depending on the season.

Cerdanya

Cerdanya, along with French Cerdagne across the border, occupies a low-lying green basin between the higher reaches of the Pyrenees to the east and west. Although Cerdanya and Cerdagne, once a single Catalan county, were divided by the Treaty of the Pyrenees in 1659, Catalan is spoken on both sides of the border and Spain flows seamlessly into France. Cerdanya is particularly popular with hikers and mountain bikers in the summer and skiers in winter.

Puigcerdà

POP 8910 / ELEV 1202M

Just 2km from France, Puigcerdà (puh-cher-da) dates back to the 12th century – not that you'd know it, since it lost most of its historical buildings during the civil war. The town's not much more than a waystation, but it's a jolly one, teeming with hikers in summer and used as a base by skiers during the winter season. A dozen Spanish, Andorran and French ski resorts lie within 45km.

⊙ Sights

Only the tower remains of the 17th-century **Església de Santa Maria** (Plaça de Santa Maria). The 13th-century Gothic **Església de Sant Domènec** (Passeig del 10 d'Abril) was also wrecked but later rebuilt; it contains 14th-century Gothic murals that somehow survived (opening times are erratic). The **estany** (lake) in the north of town is speckled with swans against a backdrop of snow-white mountains. It was created in 1380 for irrigation and is surrounded by turn-of-the-20th-century summer houses, built by wealthy Barcelona families.

ⓘ HIKING IN CERDANYA

Walkers should get a hold of Editorial Alpina's *Cerdanya* map and guide booklet (scaled at 1:50,000). They are available from most bookshops around Catalonia and in some of the larger tourist offices.

⌷ Sleeping

The town and the surrounding area is home to a number of hotels, *pensiones* and *casas rurales*.

Camping Stel   CAMPGROUND €

(☑972 88 23 61; www.stel.es; tent & car €25.60, plus per adult €10; ☉ daily Apr-Sep, Sat & Sun Oct-Mar; P🐾🛜❄) 🐾 Out along the road to Llívia, this is the only nearby camping option, and an action-packed one at that, with a pool, ping-pong hall, indoor climbing wall, basketball court and a football pitch. There are bungalows available and it's much cheaper outside high summer.

Sant Marc   CASA RURAL €€

(☑972 88 00 07; www.santmarc.es; Camí de Sant Marc 34; d/f €100/150; P🐾❄🙌) Extensive tree-lined grounds and down-filled duvets on plush beds greet you at this *casa rural* just outside town. The wood-floored rooms are spacious and decorated in soothing creams, and the stone-walled restaurant (*menú* €20) specialises in dishes that make maximum use of local meats, cheeses and pretty much anything that grows in the area. There are horses to ride here too.

★ **Villa Paulita**   HISTORIC HOTEL €€€

(☑972 88 46 22; www.villapaulitahotel.com; Avinguda Pons i Gasch 15; standard d €150-189; P@🛜❄) The town's most luxurious option has sublime modern rooms in a rusty-red, 19th-century manor house, some with views over the nearby snow-drenched peaks. Rooms in the modern annex lose little by comparison and are slightly cheaper. There's a good spa complex (included), great service, and a really excellent restaurant with vistas over the lake. Open weekends only in March/April and October/November.

✕ Eating

Look out for the local speciality *trinxat*, a warming combination of potato, cabbage and pork.

La Caixeta
TAPAS €

(www.facebook.com/caixetabistro; Carrer Quirol 22; dishes €4-12; ⊙11am-2am Wed-Mon) You're never quite sure which side of the border you're on here. A cheerful cafe-bar with artful hipster decor, this place does cupcakes and cocktails, as well as generous glasses of French wine, and deli-style tapas that run from foie gras and camembert to Catalan charcuterie.

El Caliu
CATALAN €€

(Carrer Alfons Primer 1; mains €8-14; ⊙1-3pm & 8.30-11pm Thu-Mon, 1-3pm Tue) Seasonal dishes, such as meat with wild mushrooms and stewed pig's trotters with Cerdanya turnips, as well as year-round favourites such as chicken casseroled in beer, all make an appearance on the menu of this busy family-run spot, popular with locals.

L'Esperit de Vi
CATALAN €€

(Carrer Major 46; dishes €6-13; ⊙6pm-midnight Wed-Fri, from 1pm Sat & Sun) This cosy, compact corner spot just off the Plaça Santa Maria does a great range of smallish plates of typical Cerdanya fare allied with more adventurous offerings. It's all cooked fresh in front of you in the tiny kitchen. Warm and welcoming.

❶ Information

The bus and train stations are at the foot of the hill. A funicular/lift combo (or 277 steps) takes you to Plaça de l'Ajuntament, off which is the **tourist office** (📞972 88 05 42; Carrer de Querol 1; ⊙9.30am-1.30pm & 4-7.30pm Mon-Fri, 10am-1.30pm & 4-7.30pm Sat, 10am-1pm Sun). There is also a helpful **regional tourist office** (📞972 14 06 65; Carretera Nacional 152; ⊙9am-1pm & 3.30-7pm Mon-Sat, 10am-1pm Sun) by the roundabout on the main road into town.

❶ Getting There & Away

ALSA (📞902 422242; www.alsa.es) buses run to/from Barcelona (€20, three hours, one or two daily) and to/from La Seu d'Urgell (€6.90, one hour, four to six daily).

From Barcelona, the C16 approaches Puigcerdà through the Túnel del Cadí. Puigcerdà is also reachable via the picturesque N152 from Ribes de Freser. The main crossing into France is at Bourg-Madame, immediately east of Puigcerdà.

Rodalies trains run from Barcelona to Puigcerdà (€12, 2½ hours, seven daily) via Vic, Ripoll and Ribes de Freser. Four to five a day continue across the border to Latour-de-Carol, where you can connect to the French network.

Llívia
POP 1630 / ELEV 1224M

Six kilometres northeast of Puigcerdà, across flat farmland, Llívia is a piece of Spain within France. Under the 1659 Treaty of the Pyrenees, Spain ceded 33 villages to France, but Llívia was a 'town' and so, together with the 13 sq km of its municipality, remained a Spanish possession.

Llívia's sights lie in its tiny medieval nucleus, near the top of town. The entertaining modern **Museu Municipal** (www.llivia.org; Carrer dels Forns 4; adult/youth 13-30 yr/child €3/2.50/1; ⊙10am-6pm Tue-Fri, 10am-8pm Sat, 10am-2pm Sun), featuring what's claimed to be Europe's oldest pharmacy, has good multilingual information and an odd 6th-century monkey burial. The 15th-century Gothic **Església de Mara de Déu dels Àngels**, just above the museum (where the key is held), has three defensive towers around it and is particularly lively during the **music festival** in August, held in and around the church. Above is a **ruined castle**.

Plaça Major is the best spot to sample local cuisine; the pick of the restaurants is **Can Ventura** (📞972 89 61 78; www.canventura.com; Plaça Major 1; menú €25, mains €14-20; ⊙1.30-3.30pm & 8.30-10.30pm Wed-Sun), in a venerable building dating from 1791. The food is delightful – traditional Catalan fare, such as slow-cooked local lamb.

Four to eight buses a day run from Puigcerdà to Llívia (€1.70, 15 minutes).

La Molina & Masella

These ski resorts lie either side of **Tosa d'Alp** (2537m), 15km south of Puigcerdà, and are linked by the Alp 2500 lift. The two **resorts** (www.lamolina.cat; day lift pass €44) have a combined total of 117 runs of all grades at altitudes of 1600m to 2537m. Rental equipment and ski schools are available at both resorts; La Molina is better for beginners. Lift passes cover the whole area. In the summer, La Molina caters to adrenalin junkies with its mountain-bike park, quad-biking and more.

🛏 Sleeping

Many skiers stay in Puigcerdà, but there are any number of resort-style hotels and rental apartments around the slopes – all of which are booked solid through the ski season.

WORTH A TRIP

ANDORRA

If you're on the lookout for great hiking or skiing, are keen to stock up on duty-free booze, smokes or electronics, or just want to say you've been in a different country, then the curious nation of Andorra, just 10km north of La Seu d'Urgell, is for you. At only 468 sq km, it's one of Europe's smallest countries and, though it has a democratic parliament, the nominal heads of state are two co-princes: the bishop of Urgell in Spain and the President of France. Catalan is the official tongue, though Spanish, French and, due to a large immigrant workforce, Portuguese, are widely spoken. Regular buses run from La Seu d'Urgell to the busy capital, Andorra la Vella. If driving, make sure to fuel up in Andorra, as it's significantly cheaper. There's rarely any passport control, though you may be stopped by customs on the way back into Spain, so don't go over the duty-free limit.

Alberg Mare de Déu de les Neus   HOSTEL €
(☑ 972 89 20 12; www.xanascat.cat; La Molina; dm under/over 30yr incl breakfast €21/26; ⊘ closed Nov; ⓟ@⍲) At the bottom part of La Molina, near the train station, 5km from the slopes, this handy youth hostel is far and away the cheapest place to stay. Rooms range from twin to eight-bed dorms – there's a small supplement for en suite dorms – and there are meals available and cooking facilities for guests.

Hotel Adserà   HOTEL €€
(☑ 972 89 20 01; www.hoteladsera.com; Carrer Pere Adserà, La Molina; d €120; ⊘ Nov-Easter & Jul-Aug; ⓟ@⍲⌨⍩) With a different feel and attitude to the modern ski-palace hotels, this place is 2.5km below the slopes in a historic stone building with great character and personal service. It's very family-focused, with numerous activities and free equipment. The compact, non-luxurious rooms have views, and the fireplace lounge – not to mention the sauna and Jacuzzi – is great post-ski territory. It's a good base for summer activities too.

❶ Getting There & Away

In the ski season there's a sporadic bus service from Puigcerdà and regular buses from La Molina town (€2) up to the slopes. The easiest driving route from Barcelona is by the C58 toll road and the C16 through the Túnel del Cadí.

La Seu d'Urgell

POP 12,470 / ELEV 691M

The lively valley town of La Seu d'Urgell (la se-u dur-zhey) is Spain's gateway to Andorra, 10km to the north. La Seu has an attractive medieval centre, watched over by an admirable Romanesque cathedral. When the Franks evicted the Muslims from this part of the Pyrenees in the early 9th century, they made La Seu a bishopric and capital of the counts of Urgell; it remains an important market and cathedral town.

◉ Sights

Much of La Seu is dominated by the enormous 19th-century seminary above the cathedral. It still functions, but you can count the students on your fingers.

★ **Catedral de Santa
Maria & Museu Diocesà**   CATHEDRAL, MUSEUM
(adult/child €3/free; ⊘ 10am-1.30pm year-round, plus 4-6pm mid-Mar–May & mid-Sep–Oct, 4-7.30pm Jun–mid-Sep) On the southern side of Plaça dels Oms, the 12th-century Catedral de Santa Maria is one of Catalonia's outstanding Romanesque buildings, with a gorgeous cloister full of characterful carved capitals. The superb attached museum has a wealth of Romanesque frescoes from various churches, as well as a copy of the Beatus de Liébana, king among medieval illustrated manuscripts.

The cathedral is one of more than 100 Romanesque churches lining what has come to be known as the Ruta Románica, from Perpignan (France) to the Urgell district. The fine western facade is decorated in typical Lombard style. The inside is dark and plain but still impressive, with five apses, some murals in the southern transept and a 13th-century Virgin-and-Child sculpture in the central apse.

The fine cloister has pillars held up by monkeys, gargoyles and harpies, and the adjacent 11th-century Romanesque Església de Sant Miquel, rougher hewn and pleasantly free of adornment. The museum includes an audiovisual showing you most of the illustrated pages of the Beatus manuscript.

CATALONIA LA SEU D'URGELL

SERRA DEL CADÍ

The spectacular Serra del Cadí offers a string of picturesque villages and mountains that offer excellent walking for those suitably equipped and experienced. The range's most spectacular peak is Pedraforca ('Stone Pitchfork', 2497m), with the most challenging rock climbing in Catalonia, while the main Cadí range, part of Parc Natural Cadí-Moixeró has a number of staffed refuges in the park for serious multiday hikes.

The villages used as jumping-off points for exploring the area are strung along the picturesque B400, which runs west from the Barcelona-bound C16 from Puigcerdà to La Seu d'Urgell on the C14. These include Saldes, Gósol, picturesque Josa del Cadí, and Tuixent. The valley makes a spectacular drive too; a longer but super-scenic route between Puigcerdà and La Seu d'Urgell.

The main park information centre (☑ 938 24 41 51; Carrer de la Vinya 1; ⊙9am-1pm & 4-7pm Mon-Sat, 9am-1pm Sun) is in Bagà, a quiet village on the C16; it opens shorter hours in low season. If you're tackling Pedraforca, download the Android app of the same name from the Google Play Store. On-demand transport operates in the valley from the main-route town of Guardiola de Berguedà. You need to book by phone before 5pm the day before travel: contact Alsina Graells (☑ 938 21 04 85).

🛏 Sleeping & Eating

There's plenty of accommodation, including a modern *parador* (luxurious state-owned hotel) by the cathedral.

★ **Casa Rural La Vall del Cadí** CASA RURAL €
(☑ 973 35 03 90; www.valldelcadi.com; Carretera de Tuixén; s/d €45/55; P❄🐕) Barely a 1km walk south of the centre and across the Segre River, you are in another, protected, bucolic world in this stone country house on a working family-run farm (and it smells as such!). Cosy rooms, with terracotta floors, iron bedsteads and, in some cases, timber ceiling beams, have a nice winter detail – underfloor heating. Some rooms share bathrooms. The extensive breakfast (€3 or €7.50) features famous Cadí butter and delicious regional cured meats and cheeses.

Els Canonges HOSTAL €
(☑ 973 35 21 78; www.canonges.com; Carrer Canonges 38; s/d €23/39; 🐕) A bargain for spotless, simple heated rooms with bathroom – and some with balcony – in the heart of town.

Hotel Andria HISTORIC HOTEL €€
(☑ 973 35 03 00; www.hotelandria.com; Passeig Joan Brudieu 24; s/d €81/88; P❄🐕) This cordial, characterful hotel has a great front garden and terrace that give it a very distinct feel from the rest of the herd. Rooms vary in size but are all cosy and commodious, with venerable wooden beams. Service is personal and welcoming. There's a good breakfast – served outdoors in summer – with regional products (€5 extra), and a recommended restaurant.

Bodegón Deza TAPAS €
(cnr Carrers Jueus & Estret; dishes €4-11; ⊙11am-4pm & 7.30-11pm Tue-Sat, 11am-4pm Sun) This simple but most agreeable spot is the place to go for straight-up *raciones* (large tapas) of tasty wholesome classics like meatballs, *trinxat* or ham. A crowd of local characters keeps things interesting at the bar.

PKtus CATALAN €€
(☑ 973 35 08 46; www.pktus.com; Carrer de la Creu 14; ⊙8-11pm Mon-Fri, 1-11pm Sat; 🐕) Modern and friendly, this place concentrates on a limited menu of delicious deli produce, with great cheeses, patés, ham and a few well-prepared hot dishes on offer alongside quality wines. They make a big effort to source local ingredients, and the quality is sky-high.

Les Tres Portes SPANISH €€
(Avinguda Joan Garriga i Massó 7; mains €8-19; ⊙1.15-3.30pm & 8.30-10.30pm Thu-Sun) This is a homely spot, where you can chow down on mixed Spanish cuisine in the peaceful garden. Inside, the decor is bright but warm, with orange walls and yellow-and-red table linen. There's a good range of dishes, served with a generous attitude and courteous, your-best-interests service.

ℹ Information

Tourist Office (☑ 973 35 15 11; www.turismeseu.com; Carrer Major 8; ⊙10am-2pm & 4-7pm Mon-Sat, 10am-2pm Sun) Ultra-helpful office across the street from the cathedral has a leaflet on historical walks and a display on city history. Extended hours in high season.

ℹ Getting There & Away

The bus station is on the northern edge of the old town. **ALSA** (www.alsa.es) runs buses to Barcelona (€28.25, three to 3½ hours, five daily), Puigcerdá (€6.90, one hour, four to six daily) and Lleida (€19.25, 2¼ hours, two to three daily).

Vall de la Noguera Pallaresa

The Riu Noguera Pallaresa, running south through a dramatic valley about 50km west of La Seu d'Urgell, is Spain's best-known white-water river. The main centres for white-water sports are the town of Sort and the villages of Rialp and Llavorsí. Outside the March-to-October season it's very quiet.

🏃 Activities

The Riu Noguera Pallaresa's grade IV drops attract a constant stream of white-water fans between mid-March and mid-October. It's usually at its best in May and June.

The best stretch is the 12km from Llavorsí to Rialp, on which the standard raft outing costs around €41 per person for two hours. Longer rides to Sort and beyond will cost more, and Sort is the jumping-off point for the river's tougher grade IV rapids.

In Llavorsí, there are several rafting operators, most of whom offer a full range of summer activities including kayaking, canyoning, horse-riding, rock-climbing and canoeing as well as some winter programs. Operators include Yeti Emotions (📞973 62 22 01; www.yetiemotions.com; Carrer de Borda Era d'Alfons), Roc Roi (📞973 62 20 35; www.rocroi.com; Plaça Biuse 8) and Rafting Llavorsí (📞973 62 21 58; www.raftingllavorsi.com; Camí de Riberies). For rafting, bring your own swimming costume, towel and a change of clothes; other equipment provided.

🛏 Sleeping

Llavorsí is the most pleasant base, more of a mountain village than Rialp or Sort.

Hostal Noguera   HOSTAL €
(📞973 62 20 12; www.hostalnoguera.info; Carretera Vall d'Aran, Llavorsí; s/d €30/58; 🅿🛜) This stone building, on the southern edge of the village, has pleasant rooms overlooking the river, whose cascading noise will lull you to sleep. The downstairs restaurant specialises in regional cuisine and the fresh local fish is particularly good.

Camping Riberies   CAMPGROUND €
(📞973 62 21 51; www.campingriberies.cat; Camí de Riberies, Llavorsí; tent/car/adult €5.50/5.50/5.50; ⊙Easter-Oct; 🅿🛜❄) A decent, fully equipped riverside campground right by the centre of town with numerous activities on offer.

ℹ Information

The main **tourist office** (📞973 62 10 02; www.pallarssobira.info; Camí de la Cabanera, Sort; ⊙10am-2pm Sun-Thu, 10am-2pm & 4-7pm Fri & Sat) for the area is in Sort, with helpful info on the region and a list of the numerous activity operators. Opening hours vary seasonally.

ℹ Getting There & Away

ALSA runs buses to Llavorsí via Sort and Rialp from Barcelona (€36, one daily, five hours) and Lleida (€11.60, four to seven daily, 2¾ hours). On-demand transport runs between La Seu d'Urgell and Sort (€4, twice daily, one hour). Call **Viatges Matí** (📞689 495 777) to book this.

Parc Nacional d'Aigüestortes i Estany de Sant Maurici & Around

Catalonia's only national park (www.gencat.cat/parcs/aiguestortes) extends 20km east to west, and only 9km from north to south. But the rugged terrain within this small area positively sparkles with more than 400 lakes and countless streams and waterfalls, combined with a backdrop of pine and fir forests, and open bush and grassland, bedecked with wildflowers in spring, to create a wilderness of rare splendour.

Created by glacial action over two million years, the park is essentially two east–west valleys at 1600m to 2000m altitudes lined by jagged 2600m to 2900m peaks of granite and slate.

WALKING THE HIGH CIRCUIT

The circular 55km trek between nine of the park's *refugis* (mountain shelters) is a great walk, incorporating the best of the park's scenery. See Carros de Foc (www.carrosdefoc.cat) for details. If you think sleeping's cheating, the gruelling Sky Runner race takes place on the 29th and 30th of August and runners try to do it in one day, getting their card stamped at each *refugi* as they go.

CATALONIA VALL DE LA NOGUERA PALLARESA

Parc Nacional d'Aigüestortes i Estany de Sant Maurici

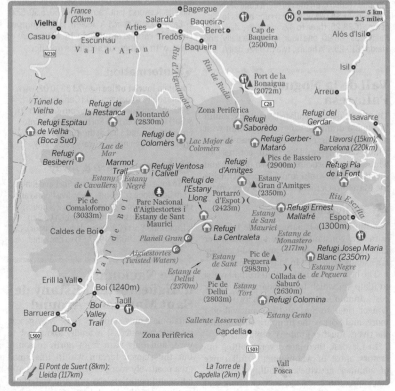

The national park lies at the core of a wider wilderness area. The outer limit is known as the *zona periférica* and includes some magnificent high country to the north and south.

The main approaches are via the village of **Espot**, 4km east of the park's eastern boundary and 8km away from the huge **Estany de Sant Maurici** lake, and **Vall de Boí**, part of its western sector.

◉ Sights

★ Romanesque Churches   CHURCHES

(www.centreromanic.com; 3/6 churches incl interpretation centre €8/10) The Vall de Boí, southwest of Parc Nacional d'Aigüestortes i Estany de Sant Maurici, is dotted with some of Catalonia's loveliest little Romanesque churches – unadorned stone structures sitting in the crisp alpine air, constructed between the 11th and 14th centuries – which together were declared a Unesco World Heritage site in 2000. Two of the finest are at **Taüll**, 3km

east of Boí. Other worthwhile Romanesque churches not mentioned here are at **Barruera** (Sant Feliu) and **Durro** (Nativitat).

➡ Centre d'Interpretació del Romànic

(☑973 69 67 15; www.centreromanic.com; Carrer del Batalló 5, Erill la Vall; admission €2; ⊙9am-2pm & 5-7pm Easter–mid-Oct) This interpretation centre has a small Romanesque art collection; it's also where you can organise guided tours of the churches.

➡ Sant Climent de Taüll

(Taüll; admission €5; ⊙10am-2pm & 4-7pm, closed Mon Nov) At the entrance to Taüll, with its slender six-storey bell tower, this is a gem, not only for its elegant, simple lines but also for the art that once graced its interior. The central apse contains a copy of a famous 1123 mural that now resides in Barcelona's Museu Nacional d'Art de Catalunya. At the church's centre is a Pantocrator (Christ figure), whose rich Mozarabic-influenced colours, and expressive but superhuman features, have become a virtual emblem of Catalan Romanesque art. An audiovisual gives background.

➡ **Santa Maria de Taüll**

(Taüll; ◷ 10am-7pm) `FREE` Up in the old village centre of Taüll and possessing a five-storey tower, this is also well represented in the Barcelona museum. The central fresco is reproduced here.

➡ **Sant Joan de Boí**

(Boí; admission €2; ◷ 10am-2pm & 4-7pm Dec-Oct) Angular structure with excellent fragments of wallpainting. The ones here are copies; the originals are in Barcelona.

➡ **Santa Eulàlia d'Erill la Vall**

(Erill la Vall; admission €2; ◷ 10am-2pm & 4-7pm Dec-Oct) This has a slender six-storey tower and slopes upwards to the altar.

Activities

The park is crisscrossed by paths, ranging from well marked to unmarked, enabling you to pick suitable routes. In winter things are quieter but there's a small ski station (www.skipallars.cat) 2km above Espot.

East–West Traverse

You can walk right across the park in one day. The full Espot–Boí (or vice versa) walk is about 25km and takes nine hours, but you can shorten this by using Jeep-taxis to/from Estany de Sant Maurici or Aigüestortes (3km downstream from Estany Llong) or both. Espot (1300m) to Estany de Sant Maurici (1950m) is 8km (two hours). A path then climbs to the Portarró d'Espot pass (2423m), where there are fine views over both of the park's main valleys. From the pass you descend to Estany Llong and Aigüestortes (1820m; about 3½ hours from Estany de Sant Maurici). Then you have around 3.5km to the park entrance, 4km to the L500 and 2.5km south to Boí (1240m) – a total of about three hours. If attempting this route make sure you have suitable clothing for a high mountain trek.

Shorter Walks

Numerous walks of three to five hours return will take you up into spectacular side valleys from Estany de Sant Maurici or Aigüestortes.

From the eastern end of Estany de Sant Maurici, one path heads south 2.5km up the Monastero valley to Estany de Monastero (2171m), passing Els Encantats on the left. Another goes 3km northwest up by Estany de Ratero to Estany Gran d'Amitges (2350m).

From Planell Gran (1850m), 1km up the Sant Nicolau valley from Aigüestortes, a path climbs 2.5km southeast to Estany de Dellui (2370m). You can descend to Estany Llong (3km); it takes about four hours from Aigüestortes to Estany Llong.

🛏 Sleeping & Eating

There are four similarly priced campground in and around Espot. Serious walkers will want to take advantage of the network of over a dozen *refugis* in and around the park. They tend to be staffed from early or mid-June to September and for some weeks in the first half of the year for skiers. At other times several of them leave a section open where you can stay overnight. The website www.lacentralderefugis.com is the most useful source of information and lets you book them (crucial in summer) online. Most charge €9 to €17 per person.

The villages of Espot, Boí and Taüll have a range of accommodation options. There are *hostales* and *cases de pagés* (rural accommodation) in Barruera, El Pont de Suert, Capdella and La Torre de Capdella. Many sleeping and eating options close in the low season.

🛏 Espot

Pensió Palmira   HOSTAL €

(☑ 973 08 30 20; www.pensiopalmira.com; d €50; ☜) This friendly, family-run place with immaculate rooms on a cobbled street just off the main square is a traveller favourite. It does hearty mountain meals too, with good half- and full-board rates.

Camping Voraparc   CAMPGROUND €

(☑ 973 62 41 08; www.voraparc.com; Prat del Vedat; per tent/car/adult €5.70/5.70/5.70; ◷ Apr-Sep; ℙ☜⛐) This campground is the best in Espot, 1.5km out of town towards the park entrance. It has a pleasant swimming pool, as well as a pool hall, a bar and a minimarket. They've got tents already set up – including posh ones for glamping – if you don't have your own.

★Roca Blanca   HOTEL €€

(☑ 973 62 41 56; www.rocablanca.net; Carrer Església; s/d incl breakfast €77/99; ◷ Dec-Oct; ℙ☜) This great small hotel in the centre of the village looks brand new, it's so well maintained. There's contemporary art on the walls, caring personal service, and lovely rooms with plenty of space. Some have balconies, while

HIKING IN THE VALL DE BOÍ

Tony Capanna, restaurateur and owner of Alberg Taüll in the Vall de Boí, gave us the low-down on hiking in the Parc Nacional d'Aigüestortes i Estany de Sant Maurici.

Best Hike

The Marmot Trail – a round trip of 3½ hours – which begins next to the impressive Cavallers dam and passes a series of waterfalls. The hike ends at Estany Negré (Black Lake), close to this trail's first *refugi* (mountain shelter), Ventosa i Calvell; you spend a half-day amongst the beautiful mountains with breathtaking views of the Vall de Boí. There is also a nice three-hour trail from Taüll that takes in the entire valley and passes through the four villages along the way – Boí, Durro, Barruerra, Boí again, and back to Taüll.

Hiking Tip

If you want to stay in the *refugis* in the national park, they are more comfortable in May, June, September and October than in July and August, when there are 70 people sleeping in the same room.

Favourite Time of Year

It's a tough one! In spring the valley is at its greenest, and the rivers are running the fastest from the snowmelt; in autumn the colours are at their best. Both spring and autumn are great times for hiking as there are not too many visitors.

those on the top floor have a cosy sloping ceiling. There's a gym, sauna and relaxing garden space. Prices are substantially lower outside August.

Restaurant Juquim CATALAN €€
(☑973 62 40 09; Plaça San Martí 1; mains €11-20; ⊕1-3.30pm & 8-11pm, closed Tue mid-Oct–May) This classic on the main square has a varied menu concentrating largely on hearty country fare, with generous winter warmers like *olla pallaresa* (steaming hotpot) or *civet de senglar* (wild boar stew). The adjacent bar (open 8am to 11pm Thursday to Tuesday) does simpler fare and sandwiches.

🛏 Taüll

Three kilometres uphill from Boí, Taüll is by far the most picturesque place to stay on the west side of the park. It has over a dozen hotels and *pensiones,* either in the village itself or in the surrounding area. There's also a small ski resort (www.boitaullresort.com) higher up the valley.

★ **Alberg Taüll** HOSTEL €
(☑973 69 62 52; www.alberguetaull.com; Avenida Feixanes 5; dm/d incl breakfast €25/46; P 🐾) This is everything a hostel should be: the stylish rooms feature large beds with orthopedic mattresses, there's underfloor heating for those crisp mornings and you'll find a large map of the park in the common area to help

you plan your hikes. Families are welcome and there's good walking advice. Sheets and a towel cost an extra €4.50. Cheaper midweek.

Camping Taüll CAMPGROUND €
(☑973 69 61 74; www.campingtaull.com; per tent/car/adult €5.50/5.50/5.50, cabins from €65; ⊕mid-Nov–mid-Oct; P 🐾) Attractive cluster of fully equipped wooden cabins (some with shared bathrooms) by the stream. Campers can pitch their tents here and make use of the facilities.

Santa Maria BOUTIQUE HOTEL €€
(☑973 69 61 70; www.taull.com; Plaça Cap del Riu 3, s/d incl breakfast €75/94; P 🐾) Through a shady entrance a grand stone archway leads into the quiet courtyard of this rambling country haven with rose-draped balcony, run by congenial hosts. The rooms are tastefully furnished and the building, all stonework with a timber-and-slate roof, oozes timeless character.

Sedona INTERNATIONAL €
(☑973 69 62 52; Les Feixes 2; menu €15; ⊕meals 1.30-4pm & 8.30-11pm; 🐾) 🍴 A varied menu of Catalan and international dishes (which may change under prospective new ownership), longer opening hours than anywhere else in the village and use of locally grown organic produce puts this friendly spot ahead of the competition. The bar's a good place to haunt, après-ski or après-hiking, too.

ℹ Information

There are national park information offices in **Espot** (☎ 973 62 40 36; Carrer de Sant Maurici 5; ⊙ 9am-2pm & 3.30-5.45pm Mon-Sat, 9am-2pm Sun) and **Boí** (☎ 973 69 61 89; Carrer de les Graieres 2; ⊙ 9am-2pm & 3.30-5.45pm Mon-Sat, 9am-2pm Sun); both open longer hours in high season. The best map of the park is produced by **Editorial Alpina** (www.editorialalpina.com).

PARK RULES

Private vehicles cannot enter the park. Wild camping is not allowed, nor (sadly!) is swimming or other 'aquatic activities' in the lakes and rivers. Hunting, fishing, mushroom-picking and just about every other kind of potentially harmful activity are banned.

ℹ Getting There & Away

ALSA buses from Barcelona (one daily), Lleida (four to seven daily) and La Pobla de Segur to Esterri d'Àneu stop at the Espot turn-off on the C13. From there it's a 7km uphill walk to Espot. In summer, there's a daily park bus connecting Espot with Boí via Vielha.

Buses between Barcelona/Lleida and Vielha stop at El Pont de Suert year-round. From here a daily bus runs to Boí (€1 to €1.75, 25 minutes), leaving in the afternoon on weekdays and in the morning on weekends.

ℹ Getting Around

The closest you can get to the eastern side of the park is a car park 4km west of Espot. There are more or less continuous Jeep-taxi services between **Espot** (☎ 973 62 41 05; www.taxisespot.com) and Estany de Sant Maurici (€5.10 each way) – with services available to higher lakes and refuges – and between **Boí** (☎ 973 69 63 14; www.taxisvalldeboi.com) and Aigüestortes (€5.10 each way), saving you, respectively, 8km and 10km. Services run from outside the park information offices in Espot and Boí (8am to 7pm July to September, other months 9am to 6pm).

Val d'Aran

It wasn't all that long ago that the verdant Val d'Aran, Catalonia's northernmost outpost, was one of the remotest parts of Spain and its only connection to the outside world was via a small pass leading into France. All this changed with the opening of a tunnel connecting the valley's capital, Vielha, with the rest of the country in the 1950s, which led to a surge of tourism development. The valley is spectacular, like a secret world of cloud-scraping mountain peaks and tumbling slopes dotted with hill villages, many with exquisite Romanesque churches. From Aran's pretty side valleys, walkers can go over the mountains in any direction, notably southward to the Parc Nacional d'Aigüestortes i Estany de Sant Maurici.

Thanks in part to its geography, Aran's native language is not Catalan but Aranese *(aranés)*, which is a dialect of Occitan or the *langue d'oc*, the old Romance language of southern France.

ℹ Getting There & Away

ALSA buses run between Vielha and Barcelona (€34.71, 4¾ to six hours, four to five daily) and Lleida (€13.71, 2¾ hours, four to five daily).

The N230 from Lleida and El Pont de Suert reaches Aran through the 5.25km Túnel de Vielha. From the Vall de la Noguera Pallaresa, the C28 crosses the Port de la Bonaigua pass (2072m) into the upper Aran valley, meeting the N230 Hwy at Vielha.

ℹ Getting Around

ALSA runs regular buses from Vielha up the valley as far as Baqueira.

Vielha

POP 5510 / ELEV 974M

Vielha is Aran's junction capital, a sprawl of holiday housing and apartments straggled along the valley and creeping up the sides, crowded with skiers in winter. The tiny centre retains some charm in the form of the Església de Sant Miquèu, which houses some notable medieval artwork, namely the 12th-century *Crist de Mijaran*. The Muséu dera Val D'Aran (Carrer Major 11; ⊙ 5-8pm Tue, 10am-1pm & 5-8pm Wed-Sat, 10am-1pm Sun) FREE covers Aranese history through a series of black-and-white photos and period furnishings.

🛏 Sleeping & Eating

High season is the ski season (Christmas to February). The local speciality is *olla aranesa* (a hearty stew). There's a great tapas and restaurant scene during the winter months.

★ **Hotel El Ciervo**   BOUTIQUE HOTEL €€
(☎ 973 64 01 65; www.hotelelciervo.net; Plaça de Sant Orenç 3; s/d incl breakfast €48/75; ⊙ closed May–mid-Jun & Nov; P🖥🖨) In the centre of Vielha, this exceptionally welcoming hotel, a real departure from the mundane ski-town norm, feels like an Alpine fairytale, with an exterior covered in paintings of trees and forest creatures and a delightfully cosy

CATALONIA VAL D'ARAN

interior full of decorative touches. Each lovely room varies in style and feel but includes a hydromassage tub, and the breakfast spread is absolutely incredible. Top value, and even better midweek.

Hotel Ço de Pierra
HOTEL €€

(☑ 973 64 13 34; www.hotelpierra.com; Carrèr Major 23; s/d €48/72; 🐾) In Betrén, a timeless village tacked on to the eastern end of Vielha's sprawl, this gorgeous place respects the stone-and-slate pattern of traditional housing and its 10 rooms combine stone, timber and terracotta for warmth.

Restaurant Gustavo (Era Móla)
CATALAN, FRENCH €€

(☑ 973 64 24 19; Carrèr de Marrèc 14; mains €14-19; ⊗8-11pm Mon, Tue, Thu & Fri, 1-3.30pm & 8-11.30pm Sat & Sun Dec-Apr & Jul-Sep) One of the best in town. Expect carefully prepared local cooking with a heavy French hand and savour the *solomillo de cerdo al Calvados* (pork fillet bathed in Calvados).

El Moli
CATALAN €€

(☑ 973 64 17 18; Carrer Sarriulera 26; mains €12-22; ⊗1.30-4.30pm & 8-11.30pm Tue-Sun, 8-11.30pm Mon Dec-Apr & Jun-Oct) In an attractive dining area overlooking the river, El Moli does a great line in steaks cooked over a wood grill, and also excels in creative salads and seasonal set menus. Service is reliably excellent.

ℹ Information

Tourist Office (☑ 973 64 01 10; www.visitvaldaran.com; Carrèr de Sarriulèra 10; ⊗9.30am-1.30pm & 4-8pm) Reduced hours in low season.

Arties

POP 500 / ELEV 1143M

Six kilometres east of Vielha, this village on the southern side of the highway sits astride the confluence of the Garona and Valarties rivers. Among its cheerful stone houses is the Romanesque Església de Santa Maria, with its three-storey belfry and triple apse. Arties has cachet, and is packed with upmarket restaurants and bars.

🛏 Sleeping

The village shuts down virtually completely in May/June and October/November.

Casa Irene
HOTEL €€€

(☑ 973 64 43 64; www.hotelcasairene.com; Carrer Major 22; d incl breakfast €180-235; ⊗Dec-Apr & Jul-Sep; 🅿🌸🐾🏊) Expect exposed wooden

beams, marble bathrooms and colourful throws on the king-sized beds at this luxurious, cosy property. Rooms are huge, suites come with hot tubs and there's a plethora of on-site muscle soothers, from the Turkish hammam to sauna, pool and Jacuzzi. The menu at the gourmet restaurant runs the gamut from Catalan pig's trotters with wild mushrooms to oysters au gratin.

Salardú

POP 580 / ELEV 1267M

Three kilometres east of Arties, Salardú's nucleus of old houses and narrow streets has largely resisted the temptation to sprawl. In the apse of the village's 12th- and 13th-century Sant Andreu church, you can admire the 13th-century *Crist de Salardú* crucifixion carving. Refugi Rosta houses an entertaining private PyrenMuseu (www.pyrenmuseu.com; Plaça Major 3; adult €5; ⊗10.30am-1.30pm & 4.30-7pm) covering the history of tourism in Val d'Aran, with a glass of wine included in the price to enhance your enjoyment. Despite the address, enter via the base of the building on the main road.

The town is a handy base for the Baqueira-Beret ski resort, 3km from here.

🛏 Sleeping

In May/June and October/November absolutely everything in and around Salardú goes into hibernation.

Refugi Rosta
REFUGE €

(☑ 973 64 53 08; www.refugirosta.com; Plaça Major 3; dm/d incl breakfast €26.50/73; 🐾) Pyrenean mountain *refugis* are special, convivial places, and this creaky old building is one of the most characterful. There are no luxuries but plenty of good cheer, and the dormitories, with their typical, side-by-side sleeping, are comfortable enough. Bring a sleeping bag or hire sheets. The restaurant serves a cheap and hearty set menu.

Hotel Seixes
HOTEL €€

(☑ 973 64 54 06; www.seixes.com; Bagergue; s/d incl breakfast €60/80; 🅿@🐾) This hikers' favourite in the village of Bagergue, 2km north of Salardú, has spacious and comfortable rooms, some of which have huge views over the valley and surrounding peaks. While you're tucking into a hearty buffet breakfast with more great vistas the staff will fill you in on all the local trekking routes.

PYRENEAN BACKROADS

As beautiful and dramatic as Vall de la Noguera Pallaresa and Val d'Aran are, they can certainly feel rather overrun in summertime by rafters and hikers, respectively. If you're looking for solitude and adventure off the beaten track, take the B-roads up into the hills northeast of Llavorsí and Esterri d'Àneu, or else north of Vielha, leading to some remote, and in parts tough, mountain-walking country along and across the Andorran and French borders. Highlights include glacial lakes and the ascent of the Pica d'Estats (3143m), the highest peak in Catalonia.

Baqueira-Beret-Bonaigua

Baqueira, 3km east of Salardú, Beret, 8km north of Baqueira, and Bonaigua, at the top of the 2072m pass of the same name, form Catalonia's premier ski resort (www.baqueira. es; day lift pass €47; ☉ late Nov-late Apr), favoured by Spanish celebrities, including the royal family. Its good lift system gives access to 84 varied pistes totalling 120km, amid fine scenery at between 1500m and 2510m.

There's nowhere cheap to stay in Baqueira, and nowhere at all in Beret. Many skiers stay down the valley in Salardú, Arties or Vielha. Out of season everything is closed.

CENTRAL CATALONIA

Away from the beaches and mountains are a host of little-visited gems splashed across the Catalan hinterland. About halfway between Barcelona and the Pyrenees lies the graceful town of Vic, with its grand Plaça Major. Northwest of the capital you can strike out for Montserrat, with its mountain shrine, or Cardona, with its windy castle complex en route to Lleida. An alternative route to Lleida takes you further south through the Conca de Barberà, dotted with majestic medieval monasteries.

Vic

POP 41,650

With its enchanting old quarter crammed with Roman remnants, medieval leftovers, a grand Gothic cloister, an excellent art museum, some hectic markets and a glut of superb restaurants, Vic is one of Catalonia's gems. Despite its resolutely Catalan political outlook, the town is very multicultural. Vic makes for a great day trip from Barcelona, but it's better to stay a little longer and wallow in the town's atmosphere.

◉ Sights

Old Town   OLD TOWN

The largest of Catalonia's central squares, Plaça Major, is lined with medieval, baroque and Modernista mansions. It's still the site of the huge twice-weekly market (Tuesday and Saturday mornings) flogging cheap clothes, fresh local fruit, veg and the town's famous *llonganisa* sausages. Around it swirl the narrow serpentine streets of medieval Vic, lined with mansions, churches, chapels, a Roman temple and a welcoming atmosphere.

★ Museu Episcopal   GALLERY

(www.museuepiscopalvic.com; Plaça del Bisbe Oliba 3; adult/child over 10yr €7/3.50; ☉ 10am-1pm & 3-6pm Tue-Fri, 10am-7pm Sat, 10am-2pm Sun) This museum holds a marvellous collection of Romanesque and Gothic art, second only to the Museu Nacional d'Art de Catalunya in Barcelona.

The Romanesque collection depicts some wonderfully gory images – from saints being beheaded or tortured to the Archangel Michael spearing a devil through his jaw, as well as the vivid *Davallament*, a scene depicting Christ being taken down from the cross.

The Gothic collection contains works by such key figures as Lluís Borrassà and Jaume Huguet. Opens longer hours in high season.

Catedral de Sant Pere   CATHEDRAL

(Plaça de la Catedral; adult/child €2/free; ☉ 10am-1pm & 4-7pm) A neoclassical Goliath with a rather gloomy interior, flanked by a lovely Romanesque bell tower. Highlights of a visit are the Romanesque crypt, the treasury rooms and a wander through the stonelacework splendour of the Gothic cloister. Entrance to the cathedral itself is free – the listed prices and times apply to the cloisters, treasury room and crypt.

✨ Festivals & Events

Mercat del Ram   EASTER MARKET
(www.vicfires.cat) In the week running up to Palm Sunday, Plaça Major hosts the Mercat del Ram (Palm Market, a tradition that goes back to AD 875), selling palms and laurels. The Mercat del Ram is also the excuse for a major gastronomic fiesta, with the Rambla del Carme and Rambla de Passeig along the northern border of the old town filling with stalls selling cured meats, cheeses, *coca* (Easter cake) and other fantastic regional produce.

Mercat de Música Viva   MUSIC
(www.mmvv.net) The town hosts the Mercat de Música Viva, a big if somewhat chaotic event, over several days in September in which Catalan, national and foreign acts of various schools of Latin rock, pop and jazz get together to jam.

🛏 Sleeping & Eating

Browse the old-town lanes for a quality selection of gastrobars, sushi and high-class Catalan cuisine.

Estació del Nord   HOTEL €
(☑935 16 62 92; www.estaciodelnord.com; Plaça de l'Estació 4; s/d €48/61; 🅿 ❄ 🛜) The 14 refurbished rooms of this smart little hotel, well located on the 1st floor of the 1910 train station, are done out in creams and whites and overseen by a friendly family. It's well soundproofed from the trains and busy road.

La Crepería   CRÊPES €
(Pl Sant Felip Neri 9; crêpes €4-6; ⏰7pm-midnight Wed-Mon; 🛜) Popular, colourful and buzzy, this packs out with locals of all ages for its tasty range of crêpes, with lots of appetising vegetarian choices.

★ El Jardinet   CATALAN €€
(☑938 86 28 77; www.eljardinetdevic.com; Carrer de Corretgers 8; menus €19-27, mains €18-23; ⏰1-3.30pm daily, 8.30-11pm Fri & Sat; 🛜) An exceedingly good choice, whose fairly spare interior is enlivened by really warm-hearted service and beautifully prepared traditional dishes, presented with panache. It's the sort of place you'll head back to tomorrow too.

ℹ Information

Tourist Office (☑938 86 20 91; www.victurisme.cat; Carrer de la Ciutat 4; ⏰10am-2pm & 4-8pm Mon-Fri, 10am-2pm & 4-7pm Sat, 10.30am-1.30pm Sun) Just off the square.

ℹ Getting There & Away

Regular rodalies trains (line R3) run from Barcelona (€6.15, one to 1½ hours).

Montserrat

Montserrat, 50km northwest of Barcelona, is a spectacular 1236m-high mountain of strangely rounded rock pillars, shaped by wind, rain and frost. With the historic Benedictine Monestir de Montserrat, one of Catalonia's most important shrines, cradled on its side at 725m, it's the most popular outing from Barcelona. Its caves and many mountain paths offer spectacular rambles, reachable by funiculars.

The monastery throngs with day-trippers, so it's well worth staying overnight to enjoy the stillness and the silence of this remarkable place.

History

The **monastery** (www.abadiamontserrat.net) – Spain's second most important pilgrimage centre after Santiago – was founded in 1025. It commemorates a vision of the Virgin on the mountain, seen by – you've guessed it – shepherds. The Black Virgin icon, allegedly carved by St Luke and hidden by St Peter in the mountains, was discovered thanks to said vision. Wrecked by Napoleon's troops in 1811, then abandoned as a result of anticlerical legislation in the 1830s, the monastery was rebuilt from 1858. Today a community of a few dozen monks lives here. Pilgrims come from far and wide to venerate the Virgen de Montserrat, affectionately known as La Moreneta ('the Little Brown One' or 'the Black Madonna'), a 12th-century Romanesque dark wooden sculpture of a regal-looking Mary with an elongated nose, holding the infant Jesus and a globe which pilgrims come to touch; she has been Catalonia's patron since 1881 and her blessing is particularly sought by newlyweds.

◉ Sights

Basilica   CHURCH
(www.abadiamontserrat.net; ⏰7am-8pm) FREE
The 16th-century church's facade, with carvings of Christ and the Twelve Apostles, dates from 1901, despite its plateresque style. The stairs to the narrow **Cambril de la Mare de Déu** (⏰7-10.30am & 12.15-6.30pm) FREE, housing La Moreneta, are to the right of the main basilica entrance; expect queues.

The room across the courtyard from the basilica entrance is filled with offbeat ex-voto gifts and thank-you messages to the Virgin from people crediting her for all manner of happy events. FC Barcelona dedicate victories to her.

★ **Museu de Montserrat**   MUSEUM
(www.museudemontserrat.com; Plaça de Santa Maria; adult/student €7/6; ☉10am-5.45pm, to 6.45pm Jul-Aug) This museum has an excellent collection, ranging from an Egyptian mummy and Gothic altarpieces to fine canvases by Caravaggio, El Greco, Picasso and several Impressionists as well as a comprehensive collection of 20th-century classic Catalan art and some fantastic Orthodox icons.

Espai Audiovisual   MUSEUM
(adult/child €5/3, with Museu de Montserrat €9; ☉9am-5.45pm Mon-Fri, to 6.45pm Sat & Sun) This walk-through multimedia space (with images and sounds) illustrates the daily life and activities of the monks and the history and spirituality of the monastery. Extended hours in high season.

Santa Cova   CHAPEL
To see the chapel on the spot where the holy image of the Virgin was discovered, you can drop down the Funicular de Santa Cova (one way/return €2.20/3.50; ☉every 20min, closed mid-Jan–Feb), or else it's an easy walk down, followed by a stroll along a precipitous mountain path with fabulous views of the valley below.

Montserrat Mountain   MOUNTAIN
You can explore the mountain above the monastery on a web of paths leading to some of the peaks and to 13 empty and rather dilapidated hermitages. The Funicular de Sant Joan (one way/return €5.85/9; ☉every 20min 10am-6.50pm, closed mid-Jan–Feb) will carry you up the first 250m from the monastery. If you prefer to walk, the road past the funicular's bottom station leads to its top station in about 45 minutes.

From the top station, it's a 20-minute stroll (signposted) to the Sant Joan chapel, with fine westward views. More exciting is the one-hour walk northwest, along a path marked with some blobs of yellow paint, to Montserrat's highest peak, Sant Jeroni, from where there's an awesome sheer drop on the north face. The walk takes you across the upper part of the mountain, with a close-up experience of some of the weird rock pillars, all named.

🛏 Sleeping & Eating

Self-service cafeterias (mains €6 to €10) cater to the masses.

Hotel Abat Cisneros   HOTEL €€
(☎938 77 77 01; www.montserratvisita.com; s/d €63/108; P⑥📶♿) The only hotel in the monastery complex has a super location next to the basilica, and tasteful, spacious rooms, some of which look over Plaça de Santa Maria. There are also inexpensive basic apartments and family packages available. Its restaurant serves imaginative Catalonian dishes (mains €17 to €20).

☆ Entertainment

Escolania de Montserrat   CHORAL MUSIC
(www.escolania.cat; ☉performances 1pm Mon-Fri, noon Sun, 6.45pm Sun-Thu) This famous boys' choir sings in the basilica daily (except school holidays), their clear voices echoing inside the stone walls the way they have done since the 13th century. It is a brief treat; they sing *Virolai*, written by Catalonia's national poet Jacint Verdaguer, and *Salve Regina*. The 40 to 50 *escolanets*, aged between nine and 14, go to boarding school at Montserrat and must endure a two-year selection process to join the choir. See the website for other performances.

🛈 Information

Information Office (☎938 77 77 01; www.montserratvisita.com; ☉9am-5.45pm) Located in the monastery, this place has information on the complex and walking trails. Hours vary substantially through the year.

🛈 Getting There & Away

The R5 line trains operated by **FGC** (www.fgc.net) run hourly from Barcelona's Plaça d'Espanya station, starting at 8.36am (55 minutes). They connect with the AERI **cable car** (☎93 835 00 05; www.aeridemontserrat.com; one way/return €7/10; ☉9.40am-7pm, closed mid-Jan–Feb) at the Montserrat Aeri stop (every 15 minutes, five minutes, operating shorter hours in the low season) and the **cremallera** (☎902 312020; www.cremalleradmontserrat.com; one way/return €5.40/8.60) train at the Monistrol de Montserrat stop. There are various train/cremallera combo tickets available.

By car, take the C16 from Barcelona, then the C58 shortly after Terrassa, followed by the C55 to Monistrol de Montserrat. You can leave the car at the free car park and take the *cremallera* up to the top or drive up and park (cars €5.50).

Cardona

POP 5000

Long before arrival, you spy in the distance the outline of the impregnable 18th-century fortress high above Cardona, which itself lies next to the Muntanya de Sal (Salt Mountain). Until 1990 the salt mine was an important source of income; tours of its interior are available for the non-claustrophobic.

The castle – follow the signs uphill to the Parador Ducs de Cardona (☑ 938 69 12 75; www.parador.es; r €177; P ✱ @ 🛜), a lovely place to stay overnight – was built over an older predecessor. The single-most remarkable element of the buildings is the lofty and spare Romanesque Església de Sant Vicenç (adult/child €3/2; ⊙ 10am-1pm & 3-5pm Tue-Sun, to 7pm Jun-Sep). The bare stone walls were once covered in bright frescoes, some of which can be contemplated in the Museu Nacional d'Art de Catalunya in Barcelona.

Cardona is served by ALSA buses from Barcelona (€12.85, two hours, two to four daily) and Manresa (€4.90, one hour, hourly Monday to Friday, less at weekends).

Lleida

POP 139,810

The hot, dry inland provincial capital of Lleida has forever been squeezed by Spain on one side and France on other like a nut in a vice. It is the place where the battle lines were drawn throughout Catalonia's turbulent history: Lleida has had the misfortune of backing the losing side in just about every battle and much of the old town was reduced to rubble in the early 18th century during the War of the Spanish Succession. The conquerors duly built a citadel to protect their new acquisitions, only for it to be sacked by the French in 1812. However, the mighty fortress-church on top of the hill in the town centre – Lleida's major historical landmark – is one of the most spectacular in Spain and is in itself reason enough to visit. There's a noticeable African migrant presence in the city streets; they are drawn by the intensive fruit-picking seasons in the orchards spread across the plain and make Lleida one of the most multicultural of Spain's cities.

◉ Sights

La Seu Vella   CATHEDRAL
(www.turoseuvella.cat; adult/child €5/free; ⊙ 10am-1.30pm & 3-5.30pm Tue-Fri, 10am-5.30pm Sat, 10am-3pm Sun) Lleida's 'old cathedral', enclosed within a later fortress complex, towers above the city from its commanding hilltop location. The cathedral is a masterpiece of the Transitional style – with sturdy Romanesque pillars and Gothic vaults and arches. The octagonal bell tower rises at the southwest end of the beautiful cloisters, the windows of which are laced with exceptional Gothic tracery and lined with a veritable forest of slender columns with carved capitals. They look over the city and give a wonderful feeling of space and light.

The old town once clustered around the cathedral, but Felipe V razed it in punishment for Lleida's opposition in the War of the Spanish Succession. The main entrance to the complex is from Carrer de Monterey on its western side, but there's also a lift from above Plaça de Sant Joan.

The cathedral opens extended hours in high season. It's free to enter the compound itself, which doesn't close. Above the cathedral are remains of the Islamic fortress and residence of the Muslim governors, known as the Castell del Rei or La Suda, and there are sweeping views of the Urgell Plain from the castle walls.

Museu de Lleida   MUSEUM
(www.museudelleida.cat; Carrer de Sant Crist 1; adult/child €4/free; ⊙ 10am-2pm & 4-6pm Tue-Thu & Sat, 10am-2pm Fri & Sun) This swish museum brings under one roof collections of artefacts that reach back to the Stone Age, pass through a handful of Roman remains and medieval art, and head on to the 19th century.

Castell de Gardeny   CASTLE
(Turó de Gardeny; adult/child €2.60/free; ⊙ 10am-1.30pm & 4.30-7.30pm Tue-Sat, 10am-1.30pm Sun) The Knights Templar built a monastery complex here shortly after Lleida was taken from the Muslims in 1149. It was later expanded as a fortress in the 17th century. Today you can still see the original Romanesque Església de Santa Maria de Gardeny and a hefty tower. An imaginative audiovisual display (in Spanish or Catalan) lends insight into the monastic life of the Knights Templar.

Museu d'Art Jaume Morera   GALLERY
(☑ 973 70 04 19; Carrer Major 31; ⊙ 5-8pm Tue-Fri, noon-2pm & 5-8pm Sat, 11am-2pm Sun) FREE This impressive collection of Catalan art focuses particularly on work by Lleida-associated artists, such as the surrealist sculptures by

THE CISTERCIAN ROUTE

Connecting Tarragona and Lleida, the so-called Cistercian Route (Ruta del Cister; www.larutadelcister.info; combined 3-monastery ticket €9) is a great way to explore inland Catalonia en route between the coast and the mountains. The route links a trio of grand Cistercian monasteries.

Following the AP7 freeway southwest from Vilafranca del Penedès, take the AP2 fork about 18km west, then exit 11 north for the excellent Reial Monestir de Santes Creus (Plaça de Jaume el Just, Santes Creus; adult/senior & student €4.50/free; ◷ 10am-6.30pm Jun-Sep, 10am-5pm Oct-May). Cistercian monks moved in here in 1168 and from then on the monastery developed as a major centre of learning and a launch pad for the repopulation of the surrounding territory. Behind the Romanesque and Gothic facade lies a glorious 14th-century sandstone cloister, austere chapter house, cavernous dormitory and royal apartments where the comtes-reis (count-kings; rulers of the joint state of Catalonia and Aragón) often stayed when they popped by during Holy Week. The church, begun in the 12th century, is a lofty Gothic structure in the French tradition, with a couple of fabulous royal tombs. An audiovisual presentation gives background info.

Back on the AP2, travel another 22km to the medieval town of Montblanc, still surrounded by its defensive walls, and then L'Espluga de Francolí, beyond which you continue 3km to the fortified Reial Monestir de Santa Maria de Poblet (www.poblet. cat; Vimbodí-Poblet; adult/student €7/4; ◷ 10am-12.45pm & 3-6pm Mon-Sat, 10am-12.30pm & 3-5.30pm Sun), a Unesco World Heritage site. Founded in 1151, it became Catalonia's most powerful monastery and the burial place of many of its rulers. Poblet was sacked in 1835 by marauding peasants as payback for the monks' abuse of their feudal powers, which included imprisonment and torture. A community of Cistercian monks moved back in after the Spanish Civil War and did much to restore the monastery to its former glory. High points include the mostly Gothic main cloister and the alabaster sculptural treasures of the Panteón de los Reyes (Kings' Pantheon). The raised alabaster sarcophagi contain eight Catalan kings, such greats as Jaume I (the conqueror of Mallorca and Valencia) and Pere III.

Swinging away north from Montblanc (take the C14 and then branch west along the LP2335), country roads guide you into the low hills of the Serra del Tallat to Reial Monestir de Santa Maria de Vallbona de les Monges (✆ 973 33 02 66; Carrer Major, Vallbona de les Monges; adult/child €4/1; ◷ 10.30am-1.30pm & 4.30-6.45pm Tue-Sat, noon-1.30pm & 4.30-6.45pm Sun Mar-Oct, closes 5.30pm rest of year). It was founded in the 12th century and is where a dozen monges (nuns) still live and pray. You will be taken on an informative guided tour (Spanish or Catalan). The monastery has undergone years of restoration, which has finally cleared up most of the remaining scars of civil war damage and the church marks the clear transition between Romanesque and Gothic architecture.

Leandre Cristòfol, with excellent temporary photography exhibitions held here as well.

🍴 Sleeping & Eating

Lleida's light tourist traffic means few lodging options. Lleida is also Catalonia's capital for *cargol* (snail) eating; especially during the annual Aplec del Cargol (Snail Festival) in early May. Central Lleida is dead at night; the action is around Plaça Ricard Vinyes on the northwest edge of the old town.

Hotel Real HOTEL €
(✆ 973 23 94 05; www.hotelreallleida.com; Avinguda de Blondel 22; r €41-56; P ❄ 🛜) A modern mid-rise place, business-oriented Hotel Real

overlooks the river near the train and bus stations. The rooms are bright and clean; the better ones have generous balconies and all have decent bathrooms. Very good value.

Hostal Mundial HOSTAL €
(✆ 973 24 27 00; www.hostalresidencialmundial. com; Plaça de Sant Joan 4; s/d €24/32, with shared bathroom €21/28; @ 🛜) With a great central location and a friendly welcome, this cheery central spot has compact singles and roomier doubles, all clean and neat.

El Cau de Sant Llorenç CATALAN €€
(Plaça Sant Josep 4; mains €14-19; ◷ 1-3.30pm & 8.30-11pm Wed-Sat, 1-3.30pm Sun & Mon) On a

quiet night, it's all rather hush-hush in this old-town corner. But once you get buzzed in it's as if you've entered a private club: excellent service, elegant contemporary decor and smartly presented modern Catalan cuisine make this a winner.

★ **l'estel de la Mercè** CATALAN €€€
(☏973 28 80 08; www.lesteldelamerce.com; Carrer Cardenal Cisneros 30; mains €16-25; ☺1-4pm & 9-11.30pm Wed-Sat, 1-4pm Tue & Sun) A 10-minute walk from the centre is the new, sleek modern base for this prolific mother-and-son team. They continue to create beautiful fusion dishes using fresh seasonal produce. Feast on the likes of fig 'carpaccio' with foie gras, *risotto de bogavante* (lobster risotto) and cod loin with *butifarra negra* (black pudding) and finish off with strawberries flambéed with pepper.

ℹ Information

Tourist Office (☏973 70 04 02; www.turismedelleida.cat; Carrer Major 31; ☺10am-2pm & 4-7pm Mon-Sat, 10am-1pm Sun) On the main pedestrian street. There's another branch in the cathedral complex.

ℹ Getting There & Away

From the centrally located bus station, regular services include Zaragoza (€11.23, 1¾ to 2½ hours, three to five daily), Barcelona (€21, two to three hours, seven to 14 daily), Vielha (€13, 2¾ hours, four to five daily) and La Seu d'Urgell (€19.25, 2¼ hours, two to three daily).

Numerous trains, ranging from slow rodalies and regionals (€13,50, 2½ to 3½ hours) to high-speed AVEs (€42.60, one hour), run daily to/from Barcelona. Some proceed to Madrid via Zaragoza.

GLIDING AROUND LLEÍDA

Montsec, a hilly range 65km north of Lleida, is the main stage for hang-gliders and microlights in Catalonia. It is also a popular area for walking, caving and climbing. The focal point is the village of Àger, and there are a half-dozen take-off points, including one at the Sant Alís peak (1678m), the highest in the range. Volàger (☏973 32 02 30; www.volager.com; Camí de Castellnou), based in Bellpuig, offers hang-gliding, paragliding and paramotoring here, from single excursions to week-long courses.

COSTA DAURADA & AROUND

South of Barcelona stretches the Costa Daurada (Golden Coast), a series of mostly quiet resorts with unending broad beaches along a mainly flat coast, capped by the delta of the mighty Río Ebre, which protrudes into the Mediterranean. Along the way is the lively gay-friendly beach town of Sitges, followed by the old Roman capital of Tarragona, and the modern extravaganza of PortAventura – Catalonia's answer to Euro-Disney. Inland lies Penedès, Catalonia's prime wine country.

Sitges

POP 29,140

Just 35km along the coast from Barcelona, this lovely fishing-village-turned-pumping-beach-resort town has been a favourite with upper-class Catalans since the late 19th century, as well as a key location for the burgeoning Modernisme movement which paved the way for the likes of Picasso. A famous gay destination, in July and August Sitges turns into one big beach party with a nightlife to rival Ibiza; the beaches are long and sandy, the tapas bars prolific and the Carnaval bacchanalian. It retains plenty of class too, with its pretty centre and fistful of upmarket restaurants. Outside high season it's quiet, but there's enough life to still offer great appeal.

⊙ Sights

The most beautiful part of Sitges is the headland area, where noble Modernista palaces and mansions strike poses in the streets around the striking **Església de Sant Bartomeu i Santa Tecla**, with the blue sea as a backdrop.

Beaches BEACHES
The main beach is flanked by the attractive seafront Passeig Maritim, dotted with *chiringuitos* (beachside bars) and divided into nine sections with different names by a series of breakwaters. The Sant Sebastià, Balmins and D'aiguadolç beaches run east of the headland. Though Bassa Rodona used to be the unofficial 'gay beach', gay sunbathers are now spread out pretty evenly, while Balmins is the sheltered bay favoured by nudists.

Museu Romàntic   MUSEUM

(www.museusdesitges.cat; Carrer de Sant Gaudenci 1; adult/student €3.50/2; ⊙10am-2pm & 3.30-7pm Tue-Sat, 11am-3pm Sun) Housed in a late 18th-century Can Llopis mansion, this faded museum recreates with its furnishings and dioramas the lifestyle of a 19th-century Catalan landowning family, the likes of which would often have made their money in South America, and were commonly dubbed *indianos* on their return. Upstairs is an entertaining collection of several hundred antique dolls, some downright creepy. Hours vary seasonally.

★Fundació Stämpfli Art Contemporani   GALLERY

(www.museusdesitges.cat; Plaça d'Ajuntament; adult/child €3.50/2; ⊙3.30-7pm Fri, 10am-2pm & 3.30-7pm Sat, 11am-3pm Sun) This excellent gallery focuses on 20th-century art from the 1960s onwards. The striking paintings and sculptures by artists from all over the world, spread throughout the two renovated historical buildings, include works by Richard 'Buddy' di Rosa, Oliver Mosset and Takis. Extended hours in high season.

★Museu Cau Ferrat   MUSEUM

(www.museusdesitges.cat; Carrer de Fonollar) Built in the 1890s as a house-cum-studio by artist Santiago Rusiñol – a pioneer of the Modernista movement who organised three groundbreaking art festivals in Sitges in the late 19th century – this whitewashed mansion is full of his own art and that of his contemporaries, including friend Picasso, as well as a couple of El Grecos. The interior, with its exquisitely tiled walls and lofty arches, is enchanting. Under renovation at the time of writing, but due to reopen in 2015.

Museu Maricel del Mar   MUSEUM

(Carrer de Fonollar; adult/child €6.50/4) This spectacular building houses Catalan art, sculpture and handicrafts from the Middle Ages to the 20th century. Under renovation at the time of writing – though it was open Sundays for guided visits at noon and 1pm, and due to reopen in 2015.

⚐ Festivals & Events

Carnaval   CARNIVAL

(www.sitges.com/carnaval) Carnaval in Sitges is a week-long booze-soaked riot made just for the extroverted and exhibitionist, complete with masked balls and capped by extravagant gay parades held on the Sunday and the Tuesday night, featuring flamboyantly dressed drag queens, giant sound systems and a wild all-night party with bars staying open until dawn. Held in February/March; dates change from year to year.

Festa Major   TOWN FIESTA

(Major Festival; www.sitges.cat/festamajor) The town's Festa Major, held over six days in mid-August in honour of Sitges' patron saint, features a huge fireworks display on the 23rd as well as numerous processions, *sardanas* and fire-breathing beasts.

International Film Festival   FILM

(www.sitgesfilmfestival.com) The world's best fantasy-and-horror-film festival is held in early October.

🛏 Sleeping

Sitges has lots of accommodation, but most is closed from around November to April, then is full in July and August, when prices are at their highest and booking is advisable. Most are gay-friendly rather than exclusively so. Gay travellers looking for accommodation in Sitges can try Throb (www.throb.co.uk).

★Hotel Platjador   HOTEL €€

(⌨938 94 50 54; www.hotelsitges.com; Passeig de la Ribera 35; s/d €107/134; ❋@🛜🏊) This seafront hotel is so welcoming that it takes quite a while to get to your room, while staff explain all the thoughtful details, free drinks, and other amenities. Breakfast – delicious – until midday? Here it is. Free afternoon tea, night-time snacks for the party crowd, indoor pool, rooftop bar overlooking the sea, it's all here. The rooms? Fabulous, with enormous plush beds, mountains of pillows and many with balconies. A standout option, and superb value low season.

Sitges Beach Hostel   HOSTEL €€

(⌨938 94 62 74; www.sitgesbeachhostel.com; Calle Anselm Clavé 9; dm incl breakfast €35; ⊙mid-Jan–mid-Dec; ❋🛜) Spotless, bright and modern, this breezy place sits near the beach a 10-minute walk west of the centre. Comfortable dorms are pricey but you get lots for your euro, with cheap meals available, plenty of outdoor terrace and balcony space to relax on, and a sociable lounge.

Parrots Hotel   HOTEL €€

(⌨938 94 13 50; www.parrotshotel.com; Calle de Joan Tarrida 16; s/d from €109/120; ⊙mid-Feb–Oct; ❋@🛜) It's hard to miss this bright-blue gay hotel, right in the heart of the action. The

Sitges

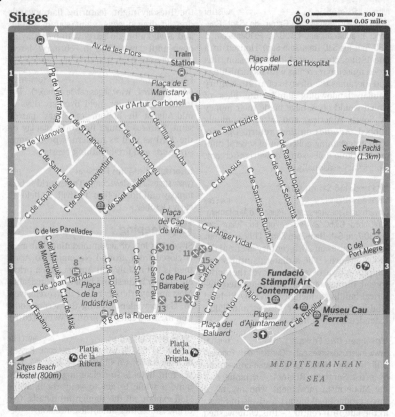

0   100 m
0   0.05 miles

Av de les Flors

Train Station

Plaça del Hospital

C del Hospital

Pg de Vilafranca

Plaça de E Maristany

Av d'Artur Carbonell

C de St Francesc

C de l'Illa de Cuba

C de St Bartomeu

C de Sant Isidre

C de Rafael Llopart

Sweet Pachá (1.3km)

Pg de Vilanova

C de Sant Josep

C de Sant Bonaventura

C de Jesus

C de Sant Sebastià

C de Santiago Rusiñol

C de Espalter

C de Sant Gaudenci

5

Plaça del Cap de Vila

C d'Àngel Vidal

C del Port Alegre

14

C de les Parellades

C del Marquès de Montroig

8

C de Bonaire

C de Sant Pere

C de Sant Pau

10

11 **9**

15

C de la Carreta

C d'en Tacó

C Nou

C Major

Fundació Stämpfli Art Contemporani

1

6

C de Joan Tarrida

C 1er de Maig

Plaça de la Indústria

C de Pau Barrabeig

12

13

Museu Cau Ferrat

4

C de Fonollar

2

C d'Espanya

7

Pg de la Ribera

Plaça del Baluard

Plaça d'Ajuntament

3

Platja de la Ribera

Sitges Beach Hostel (800m)

Platja de la Frigata

MEDITERRANEAN SEA

thoroughly modern rooms come with cable TV and air-con (a godsend in summer), and there are balconies for people-watching and a sauna to get steamy in.

✗ Eating

A couple of local specialities to watch out for are *arròs a la sitgetana* (a brothy rice dish with meat and seafood) and *xató* (a green salad with cod, tuna, anchovies and olives with a dressing containing garlic, almonds, hazelnuts, chilli pepper and more).

La Salseta   CATALAN €€
(☑ 938 11 04 19; www.lasalseta.com; Carrer de Sant Pau 35; mains €12-19; ☺1-4pm daily, 8-11.30pm Wed-Sat) ✔ Solicitous service and a sober, attractive interior set the scene for some delicious dishes in this unobtrusive restaurant. They make an effort to source organic and local products, and always have something

interesting that's in season. A very satisfying experience.

El Pou   TAPAS €€
(www.elpoudesitges.com; Carrer de Sant Pau 5; dishes €4-10; ☺noon-4pm & 8-11.30pm Wed-Mon; 🛜) The tiny Wagyu beef burgers at this friendly gourmet tapas place are an absolute delight, and the rest doesn't lag far behind; the traditional *patatas bravas* (potatoes in a spicy tomato sauce) sit alongside the likes of *mojama* (salted dried tuna) with almonds, fried aubergine and *xató*. The presentation delights the eye as much as the flavours delight the palate.

La Nansa   SEAFOOD €€
(www.restaurantlanansa.com; Carrer de la Carreta 24; mains €14-22; ☺1.30-3.30pm & 8.30-11pm Thu-Sat & Mon, 1.30-3.30pm Sun, closed Jan) Cast just back from the town's waterfront and up a little lane in a fine old house is this seafood specialist, appropriately named after a fish-

Sitges

ing net. It does a great line in paella and other rice dishes, including local speciality, *arròs a la sitgetana*.

El Trull MEDITERRANEAN €€
(☎938 944 705; www.eltrullsitges.com; Carrer Mossèn Fèlix Clarà 3; mains €14-21; ⊗8-11pm Thu-Tue, plus noon-4pm Sat & Sun Nov-Mar, 11am-11pm daily Apr-Oct) Comfortably decorated in seaside villa style, this place offers Spanish ingredients with a few notable French and Italian twists, thanks to the multicultural chef. It's all very tasty without hitting gourmet levels, and the homemade *limoncello* is absolutely scrumptious.

eF & Gi FUSION €€€
(www.efgirestaurant.com; Carrer Major 33; mains €18-25; ⊗1-4pm & 7.30-11.30pm Wed-Mon Mar-Jan; 🐾) Fabio and Greg (eF & Gi) are not afraid to experiment and the results are startlingly good: the mostly Mediterranean menu, with touches of Asian inspiration, throws out such delights as chargrilled beef infused with lemongrass and kaffir lime, and tuna loin encrusted with peanuts and kalamata olives with mango chutney. Don't skip the dessert, either.

🍷 **Drinking & Nightlife**

Much of Sitges' nightlife happens on one short pedestrian strip packed night-long in summer: Carrer 1er de Maig aka Calle del Pecado (Sin Street), Plaça de la Indústria and Carrer del Marquès de Montroig, all in a short line off the seafront, though most bars shut by around 3.30am. All-night revellers are drawn to the clubs just outside of town; the popular ones change name regularly, but you'll soon find out where's trendy this summer.

Sweet Pachá CLUB
(www.sweetpacha.com; Avinguda Port d'Aiguadolç 9; cover incl two drinks €20; ⊗club midnight-6am Fri & Sat, daily in high season) The original Pacha has closed, but this place offers cocktail-fuelled sessions on the dance floor and there's a decent seafood restaurant for those wanting a quieter night. It's located just back from the Aiguadolç marina, a 15-minute walk east from the centre.

Casablanca BAR
(Carrer Pau Barrabeig 5; ⊗8pm-2am Thu-Sat, Tue-Sun in high season) Classier and less loud than some of the central bars, this welcoming spot is tucked away at the bottom of a flight of stairs and makes a more than decent gin and tonic.

★ **Bar Voramar** BAR
(www.pub-voramar.com; Carrer del Port Alegre 55; ⊗4.30pm-1am Thu-Tue) On Platja de Sant Sebastià, this is a fabulous old-time bar decked out like a ship playing flamenco, jazz and more. It does brilliant caipirinhas, mojitos, and more. The chummy booth seating is a Sitges classic.

🛈 **Information**

Main Tourist Office (☎938 94 42 51; www.sitgestur.cat; Plaça de E Maristany 2; ⊗10am-2pm & 4-6.30pm or 8pm Mon-Sat, 10am-2pm Sun) By the train station.

🛈 **Getting There & Away**

From about 6am to 10pm four R2 rodalies trains run every hour to Barcelona's Passeig de Gràcia and Estació Sants (€4.10, 27 to 46 minutes). You can reach Barcelona airport (€3.40) by changing at El Prat de Llobregat. **Buses** (www.monbus.cat) also run to the airport from Passeig de Vilafranca (€6, 35 minutes).

CATALONIA SITGES

Penedès

Some of Spain's finest wines come from the Penedès plains southwest of Barcelona. Sant Sadurní d'Anoia, located about a half-hour train ride west of Barcelona, is the capital of *cava*, a sparkling, Champagne-style wine popular worldwide and drunk in quantity in Spain over Christmas. Vilafranca del Penedès, 12km further down the track, is an attractive historical town and the heart of the Penedès Denominación de Origen (DO; Denomination of Origin) region, which produces noteworthy light whites and some very tasty reds.

ⓘ Getting There & Away

Up to three rodalies trains per hour run from Estació Sants Barcelona to Sant Sadurní (€4.10, 45 minutes) and Vilafranca (€4.90, 55 minutes). By car, take the AP7 and follow the exit signs.

Sant Sadurní d'Anoia

POP 12,600

One hundred or so wineries around Sant Sadurní make it the centre of *cava,* made by the same method as French Champagne. If you happen to be in town in October, you may catch the Mostra de Caves i Gastronomia, a *cava-* and food-tasting fest.

Vilafranca del Penedès

POP 38,930

Vilafranca is larger and more interesting than Sant Sadurní, with appealing narrow streets lined with medieval mansions. The mainly Gothic Basilica de Santa Maria (Plaça de Jaume I) stands at the heart of the old town. Begun in 1285, it has been much restored. There are sunset visits to the bell tower in summer, complete with a glass of *cava;* arrange one at the tourist office.

WINE TASTING IN PENEDÈS

It's easier to get around the wine country if you have your own wheels, though several companies run tours of the wineries from Barcelona. Visitors are welcome to tour several of the region's wineries, though advance booking is essential in most places. The more enthusiastic ones will show you how wines and/or *cava* are made and finish with a glass or two. Tours generally last about 1½ hours and some may only be in Catalan and/or Spanish.

This list should get you started, but browse www.dopenedes.es and www.enoturis-mepenedes.cat for more wine-tourism options.

Codorníu (☑93 891 33 42; www.codorniu.es; Avinguda de Jaume Codorníu, Sant Sadurní d'Anoia; adult/child €9/6; ☺9am-5pm Mon-Fri, to 1pm Sat & Sun) The headquarters of Codorníu are in a beautiful Modernista cellar at the entry to Sant Sadurní d'Anoia when coming by road from Barcelona. Manuel Raventós, head of this firm back in 1872, was the first Spaniard to be successful in producing sparkling wine by the Champagne method.

Freixenet (☑93 891 70 96; www.freixenet.com; Carrer de Joan Sala 2, Sant Sadurní d'Anoia; adult/child 9-17yr €7/4.20; ☺1½hr tours 10am-1pm & 3-4.30pm Mon-Thu, 10am-1pm Fri-Sun) The biggest *cava*-producing company, easily accessible next to the Sant Sadurní train station. Visits include a tour of its 1920s cellar, a spin on the tourist train around the property and samples of its *cava.*

Giró Ribot (☑93 897 40 50; www.giroribot.es; Finca el Pont; tours per person €6; ☺shop 9am-5pm Mon-Fri, 10am-2pm Sat & Sun) The magnificent farm buildings ooze centuries of tradition. This winery uses mostly local grape varieties to produce a limited range of fine *cava* and wines (including muscat). To visit the cellars, call ahead.

Jean León (☑93 899 55 12; www.jeanleon.com; Camí Mas de Rovira, Torrelavit; adult/child €10.25/free; ☺9am-5pm Mon-Fri, 9am-1pm Sat & Sun) Uses cabernet sauvignon and other French varietals to create various high-quality wines. Visits are multilingual and should be booked.

Torres (☑93 817 74 87; www.torres.es; adult/child €6.70/4.70; ☺9am-5pm Mon-Sat, to 1pm Sun & holidays) Just 2km northwest of Vilafranca on the BP2121, this is the area's premier winemaker, with a family wine-making tradition dating from the 17th century. It revolutionised Spanish wine-making in the 1960s by introducing temperature-controlled, stainless-steel technology and French grape varieties. Torres produces an array of reds and whites of all qualities, using many grape varieties.

The basilica faces the Museu de les Cultures del Vi de Catalunya (www.vinseum.cat; Plaça de Jaume I 5; adult/child €7/4; ⊗10am-2pm & 4-7pm Tue-Sat, 10am-2pm Sun) across Plaça de Jaume I. Housed in a fine Gothic building, a combination of museums here covers local archaeology, art, geology and birdlife, along with an excellent section on wine.

A statue on Plaça de Jaume I pays tribute to Vilafranca's *castellers*, who do their thing during Vilafranca's lively Festa Major (main annual festival) at the end of August.

Tours

★ El Molí Tours CYCLING, WINERY
(☑938 97 22 07; www.elmolitours.com; Torreles de Foix) 🍷 This highly recommended tour company, headed by the indomitable Paddy, arranges all manner of tours of the wine country – from luxury gourmet day tours to numerous cycling options, such as half- or full-day guided bike tours which include lunch and *cava* sampling.

Cellar Tours WINERY TOUR
(☑91 143 65 53; www.cellartours.com) One-week all-inclusive or tailor-made luxury tours of the top wineries in Penedés, as well as other parts of Catalonia and Spain. Prices depend on the number of people on the tour and the style of accommodation.

Catalunya Bus Turístic WINERY
(www.catalunyabusturistic.com; Plaça de Catalunya, Barcelona; tours €64) Day tours which include visits to three bodegas, cheese and wine matching and tapas.

Eating

While there is no need to stay in Vilafranca, eating is another story. Cal Ton (☑938 903 741; www.restaurantcalton.com; Carrer Casal 8; mains €16-24; ⊗1-4pm & 8.30-10.30pm Tue-Sat, 1-4pm Sun) is one of several enticing options in town. Hidden away down a narrow side street – go through the archway off the Rambla – it has crisp, modern decor and offers inventive Mediterranean cuisine with a touch of oriental influence, all washed down with local wines.

Information

Tourist Office (☑938 18 12 54; www.turismevilafranca.com; Carrer Hermenegild Clascar 2; ⊗3-6pm Mon, 9.30am-1.30pm & 3-6pm Tue-Sat, 10am-1pm Sun) Can provide tips on visiting some of the smaller wineries in the area. Afternoon opening in summer is 4pm to 7pm.

Tarragona

POP 133,550

The eternally sunny port city of Tarragona is a fascinating mix of Mediterranean beach life, Roman history and medieval alleyways. Spain's second-most important Roman site, Tarragona has a wealth of ruins, including a seaside amphitheatre. The town's medieval heart is one of the most beautifully designed in Spain, its maze of narrow cobbled streets encircled by steep walls and crowned with a splendid cathedral. A lively eating and drinking scene makes for an enticing stop.

History

Tarragona was first occupied by the Romans, who called it Tarraco, in 218 BC; prior to that the area was first settled by Iberians, followed by Carthaginians. Scipio launched his successful military endeavours from here and in 27 BC Augustus made it the capital of his new Tarraconensis province (roughly all modern Spain) and stayed until 25 BC, directing campaigns. During its Roman heyday Tarragona was home to over 200,000 people (more than its current population) and, though abandoned when the Muslims arrived in AD 714, the city was reborn as the seat of a Christian archbishopric in 1089.

◉ Sights

Tarragona has a mediocre town beach separated from town by train tracks, but there are more appealing choices within a short distance.

Museu d'Història de Tarragona RUINS
(MHT; www.museutgn.com; adult/child per site €3.30/free, all sites €11.05/free; ⊗sites 9am-9pm Tue-Sat, 10am-3pm Sun Easter-Sep, 10am-7pm Tue-Sat, 10am-3pm Sun Oct-Easter) The Museu d'Història de Tarragona consists of various separate Unesco World Heritage Roman sites, as well as some other historic buildings around town. Buy a combined ticket and get exploring!

➡ ★ Forùm Provincial Pretori i Circ Romans
(Plaça del Rei) This sizeable complex with two separate entrances includes part of the vaults of the Roman circus, where chariot races were once held, as well as the Pretori tower on Plaça de Rei and part of the provincial forum, the political heart of Tarraconensis province. The circus, 300m long,

Tarragona

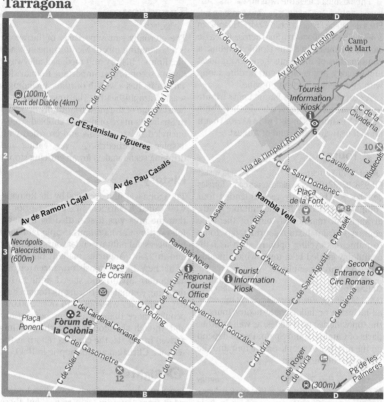

Tarragona

◎ Top Sights

◎ Sights

🛏 Sleeping

⊗ Eating

⊙ Drinking & Nightlife

stretched from here to beyond Plaça de la Font to the west.

➡ **Amfiteatre Romà**

(Plaça d'Arce Ochotorena) Near the beach is this well-preserved amphitheatre, where gladi-

ators hacked away at each other, or wild animals, to the death. In its arena are the remains of 6th- and 12th-century churches built to commemorate the martyrdom of the Christian bishop Fructuosus and two deacons, believed to have been burnt alive

Further down the hill, this local plaza was occupied by a judicial basilica (where legal disputes were settled) among other buildings. Linked to the site by a footbridge is another excavated area, which includes a stretch of Roman street. The discovery of foundations of a temple to Jupiter, Juno and Minerva suggests the forum was bigger and more important than had previously been assumed.

➔ **Pont del Diable**

The so-called Devil's Bridge is actually the **Aqüeducte de les Ferreres**, an engineering marvel left by the Romans. Its most intact section sits 4km away from the centre, just off the AP7 freeway. It is a fine stretch of a two-tiered aqueduct (217m long and 27m high); in its glory days, it delivered water to over 200,000 people from the Ríu Gayo, 32km away. Bus 5 to Sant Salvador from Plaça Imperial de Tàrraco, running every 20 minutes, will take you to the vicinity, or park in one of the lay-bys marked on either side of the AP7, just outside the freeway toll gates.

★ **Museu Nacional Arqueològic de Tarragona** MUSEUM
(www.mnat.cat; Plaça del Rei 5; adult/child €2.40/ free; ⊙ 9.30am-6pm Tue-Sat, 10am-2pm Sun) This excellent museum does justice to the cultural and material wealth of Roman Tarraco. Well-laid-out exhibits include part of the Roman city walls, frescoes, sculpture and pottery. The mosaic collection traces the changing trends – from simple black-and-white designs to complex full-colour creations. A highlight is the large, almost complete *Mosaic de Peixos de la Pineda,* showing fish and sea creatures. It's open extended hours in high season.

Necròpolis Paleocristiana RUINS
(www.mnat.cat; Avinguda de Ramón i Cajal 80; admission €2.40; ⊙ 9.30am-1.30pm & 3-5.30pm Tue-Sat, 10am-2pm Sun) This vast Roman-Christian city of the dead on the western edge of town consists of over 2000 elaborate tombs. It was used from the 3rd century AD onwards, thus attesting to Rome's conversion to Christianity. While you can only look at the tombs through the fence, the museum features curious funereal objects and sarcophagi. Entry is free if you have already purchased a ticket to the Museu Nacional Arqueològic de Tarragona. It opens extended hours in high season.

here in AD 259. Much of the amphitheatre was picked to bits, the stone used to build the port, so what you see now is a partial reconstruction.

➔ **Passeig Arqueològic Muralles**
A peaceful walk takes you around part of the perimeter of the old town between two lines of city walls; the inner ones are mainly Roman and date back to the 3rd century BC, while the outer ones were put up by the British in 1709 during the War of the Spanish Succession. Prepare to be awed by the vast gateways built by the Iberians and clamber up onto the battlements from the doorway to the right of the entrance for all-encompassing views of the city. The walk starts from the **Portal del Roser** on Avinguda Catalunya.

➔ ★ **Fòrum de la Colònia**
(Carrer de Lleida) The main provincial forum occupied most of what is now the old town.

CASTLES OF SOUTHERN CATALONIA

Once the frontline between the Moors and Christians, this part of southern Catalonia is dotted with fortresses. They were originally built to defend the northern frontiers of Al-Andalus, then taken in the Reconquest and used by the Christian kingdom.

The finest is at Miravet (www.mhcat.cat; adult/child €3/2; ⊙ 10am-1.30pm & 3-5.30pm Tue-Sun), 6km off the N420, 60km west and south of Tarragona. Built in the 11th century, it was reconquered then given to the Knights Templar. It's a formidable stronghold, with incredibly solid walls, and it towers above the pretty village that cascades down a hill on the banks of the Ebre. Opening hours vary seasonally.

Tortosa, a dusty town 40km south of Miravet, is watched over by the imposing Castell de la Suda, built in the 10th century but much modified. A small medieval Arab cemetery has been unearthed and in the grounds stands a parador (☎ 977 44 44 50; www.parador.es; r €120; P ❋ 🛜 ☲) offering a stay in luxurious medieval surroundings. Views from the courtyard are great. If you fancy a bite, head straight across the bridge to Xampu-Xampany (www.xampu-xampany.com; Avinguda Catalunya 41; tapas €4-5, mains €11-16; ⊙ noon-4pm & 8pm-midnight Tue-Sat, 8pm-midnight Sun & Mon; 🛜), which does a super range of deli tapas and larger plates, accompanied by excellent wines, *cavas* and Champagne-style wines.

Getting to Miravet by public transport involves getting a train or bus to Móra la Nova from Tarragona or Barcelona, then a taxi the remaining 8km. Tortosa is easier, with regular bus, rodalies and train connections from Tarragona and Barcelona.

★ Catedral   CATHEDRAL

(www.catedraldetarragona.com; Plaça de la Seu; adult/child €5/3; ⊙ 10am-7pm Mon-Sat mid-Mar–Oct, 10am-5pm Mon-Fri, 10am-7pm Sat Nov–mid-Mar) Sitting grandly atop town, Tarragona's cathedral has both Romanesque and Gothic features, as typified by the main facade. The cloister has Gothic vaulting and Romanesque carved capitals, one of which shows rats conducting a cat's funeral...until the cat comes back to life! It's a lesson about passions seemingly lying dormant until they reveal themselves. Chambers off the cloister house the Museu Diocesà, with an extensive collection extending from Roman hairpins to some lovely 12th- to 14th-century polychrome woodcarvings of a breastfeeding Virgin.

🛏 Sleeping

Camping Las Palmeras   CAMPGROUND €

(☎ 977 20 80 81; www.laspalmeras.com; N340, Km 1168; tent site €26-28, plus per adult €9-11; ⊙ late Mar–mid-Oct; P 🛜 ☲ ♿) This cheerful campground lies 3km northeast of Tarragona; perks include a big pool amid leafy parkland just back from the beach and untouched coastal woodland nearby. Windsurfing and kitesurfing classes are also on offer. It's much cheaper outside summer holidays.

Hotel Plaça de la Font   HOTEL €€

(☎ 977 24 61 34; www.hotelpdelafont.com; Plaça de la Font 26; s/d €55/75; ❋ 🛜) Comfortable modern rooms, with photos of Tarragona monuments above the bed, overlook a bustling terrace in a you-can't-get-more-central-than-this location, right on the popular Plaça de la Font. The ones at the front are pretty well soundproofed and have tiny balconies for people-watching.

Hotel Sant Jordi   HOTEL €€

(☎ 977 20 75 15; www.hotelsanjordi.info; Avinguda Vía Auga 185; s/d €67/78; P ❋ 🛜) The daggy '70s decor doesn't inspire much hope as you enter, but this is a great hotel nonetheless. Located 2.5km from central Tarragona, just by the appealing Savinosa beach, this has spotless, comfortable rooms with balcony, and an old-world, caring atmosphere that makes it far more than it appears at first glance.

Hotel Lauria   HOTEL €€

(☎ 977 23 67 12; www.hotel-lauria.com; Rambla Nova 20; s/d incl breakfast €65/77; P ❋ 🛜 ☲) Right on the Rambla Nova near where it ends at a balcony overlooking the sea, this smart hotel offers great-value modern rooms with welcome splashes of colour, large bathrooms and a small swimming pool. The rooms at the back are less exposed to the noise from the Rambla.

Eating

The quintessential Tarragona seafood experience can be had in **Serrallo**, the town's fishing port. About a dozen bars and restaurants here sell the day's catch and, on summer weekends in particular, the place is packed.

AQ
CATALAN €€

(📞977 21 59 54; www.aq-restaurant.com; Carrer de les Coques 7; degustation menu €40-50; ⏱1.30-3.30pm & 8.30-11pm Tue-Sat) This is a bubbly designer haunt alongside the cathedral with stark colour contrasts (black, lemon and cream linen), slick lines and intriguing plays on traditional cooking. One of the two degustation menus is the way to go here, or the weekday lunch *menú* for €18.

Ares
CATALAN, SPANISH €€

(www.aresrestaurant.es; Plaça del Fòrum; mains €11-19; ⏱1-4pm & 8.30-11.30pm Wed-Sun) Amid a riot of colourful, exuberant Modernista decor, the cordial welcome from this husband-and-wife team guarantees good eating. Some classic Catalan dishes take their place alongside quality ingredients from across Spain: Asturian cheeses, Galician seafood, Burgos black pudding. They are complemented by some recreated Roman dishes. Quality and quantity are both praiseworthy.

Barquet
SEAFOOD €€

(📞977 24 00 23; www.restaurantbarquet.com; Carrer del Gasometre 16; mains €11-18; ⏱1-3.30pm & 9-10.30pm Tue-Sat, 1-3.30pm Mon) This popular neighbourhood restaurant is a short downhill stroll from the centre. It's deservedly famous for its excellent rice dishes bursting with maritime flavour, and also has great *raciones* of seafood. Cheerful and good value.

El Palau del Baró
CATALAN €€

(📞977 24 14 64; www.palaudelbaro.com; Carrer de Santa Anna 3; menús €16-27; ⏱1-4pm & 8.30-11pm Mon-Sat, 1-4pm Sun; 🖼) The Baron's Palace provides a romantic, sumptuous 18th-century-mansion setting. Dishes are served with aplomb, and range from paella and *arròs negre* to the likes of the sublime grilled *llom de tonyina fresca* (seared tuna steak).

Arcs Restaurant
CATALAN €€€

(📞977 21 80 40; www.restaurantarcs.com; Carrer Misser Sitges 13; mains €18-22; ⏱1-4pm & 8.30-11pm Tue-Sat) Inside a medieval cavern with bright splashes of colour in the form of contemporary art, you are served some wonderful takes on Mediterranean dishes – with lots of delicious seafood carpaccios and tartars. Ingredients are of the highest quality – the fish of the day is always spectacular.

🍷 Drinking & Nightlife

The bars and clubs along the waterfront at the Port Esportiu (marina), and in some of the streets in front of the train station, such as along Carrer de la Pau del Protectorat, have the main concentration of nightlife.

Sha
CAFE

(Plaça de la Seu; ⏱4pm-midnight Tue-Thu, 4pm-1am Fri & Sat, noon-midnight Sun; 🖼) Part handicraft shop, part bar-cafe, this place has a prime location just below the cathedral, with great outdoor seating. There's a friendly, hippy vibe and tasty salads, hummus, and the like.

El Candil
BAR, CAFE

(Plaça de la Font 13; hot chocolate €3; ⏱11am-3pm & 5pm-midnight; 🖼) Over 30 different hot chocolate combinations are on the menu at this cave-like cafe-bar, as well as a good selection of beers and *cava* for its nocturnal transformation into a cellar-bar.

ℹ Information

There's free wi-fi in most of central Tarragona's major plazas.

REUS – GAUDÍ'S BIRTHPLACE

Reus, 14km west of Tarragona, has no Gaudí buildings, but has the honour of being his birthplace. The superb **Gaudí Centre** (www.gaudicentre.cat; Plaça del Mercadal 3; adult/child €7/4; ⏱10am-2pm & 4-7pm Mon-Sat, 11am-2pm Sun; 🖼) gives you a thorough introduction to the man and his work – from his designs to his influence on architecture around the world – through its engaging multilingual, audiovisual, sensory and hands-on displays. It gives real insights into Gaudí's mindset, and leaves one in no doubt as to his genius.

The museum (open extended hours in high season) doubles as the tourist office, and provides a map guiding you to the 30-odd notable Modernista buildings in Reus. Regular trains and rodalies connect Reus with Tarragona (from €2.50, 15 to 20 minutes).

THE BATTLE FOR CATALONIA

The Spanish Civil War may only have lasted three years (1936–39) but its scars linger well into the present and you'll be hard-pressed to find a family in Catalonia, or indeed Spain, which hasn't been affected by the conflict. The largest battle of the war was fought in the Ebro Valley, leading to the destruction of the town of Corbera, and a crushing defeat of the Republicans. Some 20,000 people lost their lives.

North of Tortosa lies the town of Gandesa, home to the modern **Centre d'Estudis de la Batalla de l'Ebre** (www.usuaris.tinet.cat/cebe; Avinguda Catalunya 3-5; entry by donation; ⊙10am-1.30pm & 4-6.30pm Tue-Sat, 10am-1.30pm Sun), an excellent museum which presents a balanced account of the civil war and the decisive battle in the Ebro Valley through a host of artefacts, photographs and interactive maps. The moving video interviews with those who lived through the horrors of the war are a recent development; the 'pact of forgetfulness' after Franco's death in 1975 meant that the victims of the dictatorship continued to endure past abuses in silence until the last few years, in a country where there has not been any formal postwar reconciliation.

With a car, it's easy to combine a visit to Gandesa with the castles at Miravet and Tortosa (p354).

Tourist Office (☏977 25 07 95; www.tarragonaturisme.es; Carrer Major 39; ⊙10am-2pm & 3-5pm Mon-Fri, to 7pm Sat, 10am-2pm Sun) Good place for booking guided tours of the city. Opens extended hours in high season.

❶ Getting There & Away

Thirteen kilometres from Tarragona, Reus airport is used by Ryanair, with flights to London Stansted and Frankfurt Hahn among others. Buses run from Tarragona's bus station as well as from Barcelona.

The **bus station** (Plaça Imperial Tarraco) is 1.5km northwest of the old town along Rambla Nova. Destinations include Barcelona (€8.70, 1½ hours, 16 daily), Lleida (€10.70, 1¾ hours, five daily) and Valencia (€21.73, 3 to 4½ hours, seven daily).

The local train station is a 10-minute walk from the old town while fast AVE trains arrive at Camp de Tarragona station, a 15-minute taxi ride from the centre. Departures include Barcelona (both normal trains and rodalies on the R14, R15 and R16 lines, €7 to €38.20, 35 minutes to 1½ hours, every 30 minutes), Lleida (€8 to €24, 25 minutes to 1¾ hours, roughly half-hourly) and Valencia (€21.70 to €38, two to 3½ hours, 19 daily).

PortAventura

A massive, blockbuster amusement park, **PortAventura** (www.portaventura.es; adult/child €45/39; ⊙10am-7pm or 8pm, to midnight Jul & Aug; 🎨) lies 7km west of Tarragona. Divided into themed sections, the park has plenty of exhilarating rides and numerous shows to keep all ages happy. Near the entrance, **Furius Baco** is a highlight, giving you a stomach-churning dose of serious acceleration, while **Shambhala** is Europe's highest roller-coaster.

The complex also includes **Costa Caribe Aquatic Park** (adult/child €28/24; ⊙10am-7pm late May–mid-Sep), a water world which includes some fear-inducing water slides.

There are various combined and multiday tickets available, and themed on-site accommodations which are a guaranteed hit with the family.

Rodalies and other trains run to PortAventura's own station, about a 1km walk from the site, several times a day from Tarragona (€2.85, 10 minutes) and Barcelona (€8.80, around 1½ hours). It also opens at Christmas and on weekends in November.

Delta de l'Ebre

The delta of the Río Ebre, formed by silt brought down by the river, sticks out 20km into the Mediterranean near Catalonia's southern border. Dotted with reedy lagoons and fringed by dune-backed beaches, this completely flat and exposed wetland, with **Parc Natural Delta de l'Ebre** comprising 77 sq km, is northern Spain's most important waterbird habitat. The migration season (October and November) sees the bird population peak, but they are also numerous in winter and spring.

Even if you're not a twitcher, a visit here is worthwhile for the surreal landscapes alone. Tiny whitewashed farmhouses seem to float on little islands among green and brown paddy fields which stretch to the horizon. It's completely unlike anywhere else in Catalonia.

The scruffy, sprawling town of Deltebre is at the centre of the delta but push on from here to the smaller villages like Riumar, the coastal village at the delta's easternmost point, or Poblenou del Delta.

◎ Sights

Ecomuseu   MUSEUM
(Carrer de Martí Buera 22, Deltebre; admission €1.50; ⊙10am-2pm & 3-6pm Mon-Sat, 10am-2pm Sun) A fantastic introduction to the strange world of the delta, this museum walks you through the traditional trades, such as fishing and rice cultivation, while the extensive garden shows off a vast array of local plants and the aquarium – the museum's highlight – puts the spotlight on the delta's freshwater denizens. It opens shorter hours in low season.

🏃 Activities

The breezy beach at Riumar is good for kitesurfing, sea kayaking, wakeboarding and more. A couple of beachside operations can set you up with lessons or equipment.

Birdwatching

Good areas include L'Encanyissada and La Tancada lagoons and Punta de la Banya, all in the south of the delta. L'Encanyissada has two observation towers and La Tancada one (others are marked on a map you can pick up at the Centre d'Informació). Almost 2000 greater flamingos nest at the lagoons, and the delta is one of only a handful of places in Europe where they reproduce. Punta de la Banya is joined to the delta by a 5km sand spit with the long, sandy, and often windy and rubbish-splattered, Platja de l'Eucaliptus at its northern end.

Boat Trips

Several companies based in Deltebre and the riverside in Riumar run tourist boat trips (€8 to €11 per person, 1½ hours) to the mouths of the Ebre and the delta's tip. The frequency of departures depends on the season (and whether or not there are enough takers). One operator is Creuers Delta Ebre (☑977 48 01 28; www.creuersdeltaebre.com; Carretera Final Goles de l'Ebre, Riumar; adult/child €8/6.75).

In Poblenou del Delta, visit Mas de la Cuixota (☑977 26 12 25; http://ebre.info/cuixota; Partida de l'Encanyissada). It rents out binocu-

lars for birdwatching and runs organised trips along the delta canals in traditional, pole-propelled *barques de perxar* (shallow-bottom boats).

Cycling

Cycling is an excellent way of exploring the delta, with recommended bike routes (pick up brochures at the tourist information centre) ranging from 7km to 43km. The 26km Lagoon Route is particularly good for birdwatchers, while the 7km Family Route takes in several viewpoints along the river, as well as the rice paddies around Riumar. Bicycles can be rented at Deltebre, Riumar and Poblenou del Delta.

🛌 Sleeping & Eating

Several campgrounds, hotels and *casas rurales* dot the countryside. One of the regional specialities is delta rice with wild duck.

★ Mas del Tancat   CASA RURAL €
(☑656 90 10 14; www.ebreguia.com/masdeltancat; Camí dels Panissos; d/q €55/90; 🅿✱🛜🐾) A converted historic farmhouse, Mas del Tancat has just five rooms with iron bedsteads, terracotta floors and a warm welcome. Sitting by the waters of the delta, with farm animals wandering through the grounds, it is a tranquil escape and excellent home-cooked dinners are available on request. Leave Amposta on the TV3405 towards Sant Jaume and turn right to Els Panissos just after the 3km sign.

CATALONIA'S HUMAN CASTLES

One of the strangest things you'll see in Catalonia are *castells*, or human 'castles' – a sport which originated in Valls, near Tarragona, in the 18th century and which has spread to other parts of Catalonia since. It involves teams of *castellers* standing on each other's shoulders with a death-defying child scrambling up the side of the human tower to perch precariously at the top as the final touch before the whole structure gracefully disassembles itself; towers up to 10 levels high are built. Don't try this at home! For the most spectacular *castells*, pay a visit to Tarragona's Festival de Santa Tecla in mid-September.

Camping L'Aube
CAMPGROUND €

([☎] 977 26 70 66; www.campinglaube.com; mar, Riumar; tent/car/adult €5.30/3.45/4.15; [☺] mid-Mar–mid-Oct; [P][≋]) Near the river mouth, and handy for boat trips and bird-watching, this place has good facilities including a decent restaurant and shop.

L'Algadir del Delta
HOTEL €€

([☎] 977 74 45 59; www.hotelalgadirdelta.com; Ronda dels Pins 27, Poblenou del Delta; s/d incl breakfast €100/120; [☺] Feb-Dec; [P][❋][⌨][≋]) With great birdwatching on the hotel doorstep, this sleek, friendly, modern place in the tranquil village in the heart of the delta makes a top base. Rooms are contemporary, stylish and comfortable; consider the small upgrade to a superior. There's a lovely pool area and it rents bikes to help you explore.

★ Mas Prades
CATALAN €€

([☎] 977 05 90 84; www.masdeprades.cat; Carretera T340, Km 8, Deltebre; mains €12-22, menús €25-35; [☺] 1-3.30pm & 8-11pm Tue-Sun, weekends only Nov-Mar; [⌨]) Gourmets come all the way down from Barcelona to this revamped country house to sample its superb delta cuisine. The five-course gut-busting lunch *menú* is great value for money and allows you to sample the tiny tender local mussels and baby squid, as well as the classic *arròs d'anec al foc de llenya* (delta rice with wild duck), finishing off with the sublime *crema catalana*.

Casa Nuri
SEAFOOD €€

([☎] 977 48 01 28; www.restaurantnuri.com; Final Goles de Ebre, Riumar; mains €13-20; [☺] 10am-10pm Apr-Sep) Locals fill this riverfront place, thanks to its reputation for superb local seafood and rice dishes. Try the signature *arroz á banda* (seafood rice). Opens shorter hours in low season.

ⓘ Information

The main **Centre d'Informació** ([☎] 977 48 96 79; www.turismedeltebre.com; Carrer de Martí Buera 22, Deltebre; [☺] 10am-2pm & 3-6pm Mon-Sat, 10am-2pm Sun) is combined with the Ecomuseu, and opens shorter hours in low season. Pick up maps of the region and brochures on cycle routes here. The **Editorial Alpina** (www.editorialalpina.com) map *E-50* is particularly helpful.

ⓘ Getting There & Away

Weekday **Hife** (www.hife.es) buses head to the delta towns from Tortosa, with connections from Tarragona (€12.64, 1¾ hours).

Aragón

Includes ➡

Best Places to Eat

➡ Tiempo de Ensueño (p394)

➡ La Tasca de Ana (p378)

➡ El Ciclón (p367)

➡ La Tea (p383)

➡ Casa Pardina (p386)

Best Places to Stay

➡ Hostal Un Punto Chic (p387)

➡ Casa del Infanzón (p371)

➡ Hotel Sauce (p366)

➡ La Casa del Tío Americano (p394)

➡ Hotel Barosse (p378)

Why Go?

Landlocked and little known, Aragón is one of Spain's most surprising regions. It's in Aragón that the Pyrenees take on an epic quality, from shapely peaks to deep, deep valleys where quiet rivers meander through forests and past small hamlets that seem unchanged by the passing of time. Stone-built *pueblos* (villages) such as these are an Aragonese speciality: all across Aragón, you'll find numerous candidates for the title of Spain's most beautiful village.

Connections to the past also overflow from the cities, whether in Mudéjar Teruel or in Zaragoza, a city bursting with contemporary vigour yet replete with soaring monuments to Roman, Islamic and Christian Spain. There are also world-class activities – hiking, canyoning and skiing – for those eager to explore the region under their own steam. But Aragón's calling card is its sense of timelessness; it's the sort of place where Old Spain lives and breathes.

When to Go
Zaragoza

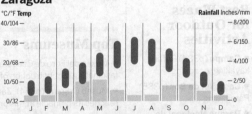

Feb Teruel's Fiesta Medieval returns you to the Middle Ages.	**Mid-Jun–early Sep** The best time to hike the high country of the Aragonese Pyrenees.	**Oct** Zaragoza's Fiestas del Pilar combine the sacred with the city's famed love of revelry.

DON'T MISS

Tasting the locally produced wine. They may not be as well known as the 'two Rs' (Rioja and Ribera del Duero), but there is some seriously good quaffing to be had...

Birds Aplenty

Aragón's diverse landscape of snowcapped mountains, wide river valleys, shallow lagoons and thickly forested woods are home to a rich variety of birdlife. This is one of the best regions in Europe for raptors, and birdwatchers flock here to catch a glimpse of red-and-black kites; Egyptian, griffon, and threatened lammergeier vultures; and, in the highest peaks, that majestic king of all birds: the golden eagle.

By contrast, the natural lake of Gallocanta is the winter home to some 70,000 cranes and other waterfowl, while the forests of pine and beech trees create the perfect habitat for the black woodpeckers who produce a steady drumroll for the honey buzzards that circle lazily overhead. But these are only a handful of the feathered friends to be spied here – more than 360 varieties at latest count. Serious twitchers can check the www.aragonbirding.com website which documents sightings and species in more detail.

Top Five Food Experiences

➡ Picking up a wheel of local Sierra de Albarracín **cheese**

➡ Sampling the local **jamón** (ham) at a Teruel tapas bar

➡ Buying a **chocolate** stiletto shoe at Zaragoza's top choc shop, Fantoba (p368)

➡ Tasting **wine** at a Somontano bodega

➡ Stocking up on local **game pâtés** at village delicatessens

STAYING ACTIVE IN ARAGÓN

The high point, literally, to anyone's experience of Aragón has to be the breathtaking Aragonese Pyrenees, arguably the wildest and most stunning range either side of the Spain–France border. And there are plenty of chances to get up close and personal with the peaks with rock climbing, mountain trails and snowy slopes promising year-round scope for adrenalin-charged outdoor activities.

Serious hikers can also embark on a section of the famous coast-to-coast GR11 trail, while folk who prefer a more gentle Sunday-morning-style stroll can head for the foothills, particularly around the solid stone village of Torla, and the stunning Parque Nacional de Ordesa with its waterfalls, crystal streams and limestone cliffs and canyons. Water-sports junkies can also take the plunge with white-water rafting, kayaking and canoeing in the Ríos Gállego and Ésera, while picturesque stone villages throughout this region ensure that R&R (and refreshments) is never too far away.

Snails

With France just up the road, it's no surprise, perhaps, that *caracoles* are an Aragonese speciality. Try them!

Best Places for Outdoor Activities

➡ **Campo** (p384) Rafting, kayaking, canoeing

➡ **Castejón de Sos** (p385) Paragliding

➡ **Parque Nacional de Ordesa y Monte Perdido** (p379) Hiking, mountain climbing

➡ **Aragonese Pyrenees** (p370) Skiing, snowboarding

Top Museums

➡ Museo del Foro de Caesaraugusta (p364), Zaragoza – fascinating reconstruction of a Roman forum.

➡ Museo Origami (p364), Zaragoza – the art of folding paper reaches its pinnacle at this one-of-a-kind museum.

➡ Museo Diocesano (p375), Jaca – an extraordinary collection of original Romanesque frescoes.

➡ Museo de Juguetes (p393), Albarracín – children (and adults) will enjoy this trip down the memory lane of toys.

➡ Museo de Zaragoza (p365), Zaragoza – superb range of exhibits ranging from Goya paintings to Roman mosaics.

Aragón Highlights

❶ Hike the wilderness in the **Parque Nacional de Ordesa y Monte Perdido** (p379).

❷ Return to the medieval past in the stone-built villages of **Aínsa** (p382) and **Sos del Rey Católico** (p370) in the foothills of the Pyrenees.

❸ Walk with wonder through the cobbled streets of

Albarracín (p393), with its reminders of the Islamic past.

❹ Hit the buzzing streets and bars of **Zaragoza** (p362) by night and visit its glorious monuments by day.

❺ Savour the Mudéjar architecture and wafer-thin perfection of the best *jamón* from **Teruel** (p390).

❻ Go quietly through the beautiful Pyrenean valleys of **Echo and Ansó** (p372).

❼ Plunge down the canyons in **Alquézar** (p385).

❽ Visit the fairy-tale castle of **Castillo de Loarre** (p388) with its sweeping panoramic views.

ZARAGOZA

POP 679,624

Zaragoza (Saragossa) is a vibrant, elegant and fascinating city on the banks of the mighty Río Ebro. The residents comprise over half of Aragón's population and enjoy a lifestyle that revolves around some of the best tapas bars in the province, as well as superb shopping and a vigorous nightlife. But Zaragoza is more than just a good-time city: it also has a host of historical sights spanning all the great civilisations that have left their indelible mark on the Spanish soul.

History

The Romans founded Caesaraugusta (from which 'Zaragoza' is derived) in 14 BC. As many as 25,000 people migrated to the city whose river traffic brought the known world to the banks of the Río Ebro. The city prospered for almost three centuries, but its subsequent decline was confirmed in AD 472 when the city was overrun by the Visigoths. In Islamic times Zaragoza was capital of the Upper March, one of Al-Andalus' frontier territories. In 1118 it fell to Alfonso I, ruler of the expanding Christian kingdom of Aragón, and immediately became its capital. In the centuries that followed, Zaragoza grew to become one of inland Spain's most important economic and cultural hubs and a city popular with Catholic pilgrims. It is now Spain's fifth-largest city.

◉ Sights

The great eras of the city's colourful history – Roman, Islamic and Christian – all left enduring monuments in Zaragoza.

★ Basílica de Nuestra Señora del Pilar   CHURCH

(Plaza del Pilar; lift €3; ⊙7am-9.30pm, lift 10am-1.30pm & 4-6.30pm Tue-Sun) FREE Brace yourself for this great baroque cavern of Catholicism. The faithful believe that it was here on 2 January AD 40 that Santiago saw the Virgin Mary descend atop a marble *pilar* (pillar). A chapel was built around the remaining pillar, followed by a series of ever-more-grandiose churches, culminating in the enormous basilica. A lift whisks you most of the way up the north tower from where you climb to a superb viewpoint over the domes and city.

Originally designed in 1681 by Felipe Sánchez y Herrera, it was greatly modified in the 18th century by the heavier hand of Ventura Rodríguez. The exterior is another story altogether, its splendid main dome lording over a flurry of 10 mini-domes, each encased in chunky blue, green, yellow and white tiles, creating a muscular Byzantine effect.

The legendary pilar is hidden in the lateral passage behind the Capilla Santa. A tiny oval-shaped portion is exposed on the chapel's outer west side and a steady stream of people line up to brush lips with its polished and cracked cheek, which even popes have air-kissed. Parents also line up from 1.30pm to 2pm and from 6.30pm to 7.30pm to have their babies blessed next to the Virgin. More than the architecture, these sacred symbols, and the devotion they inspire, are what makes this cathedral special.

Hung from the northeast column of the Capilla Santa are two wickedly slim shells that were lobbed at the church during the civil war. They failed to explode. A miracle, said the faithful; typical Czech munitions, said the more cynical.

The basilica's finest artwork is a 16th-century alabaster altarpiece by Damián Forment. It stands at the outer west wall of the choir. Goya painted *La Reina de los Mártires* (Mary, Queen of Martyrs) in a cupola above the north aisle, outside the Sacristía de la Virgen.

★ La Seo   CATHEDRAL

(Catedral de San Salvador; Plaza de la Seo; adult/concession €4/3; ⊙10am-6pm Tue-Fri, 10am-noon & 3-6pm Sat, 10-11.30am & 2.30-6pm Sun Jun-Sep, shorter hours Oct-May) Dominating the eastern end of Plaza del Pilar, the La Seo was built between the 12th and 17th centuries and displays a fabulous spread of architectural styles from Romanesque to baroque. The cathedral stands on the site of Islamic Zaragoza's main mosque (which in turn stood upon the temple of the Roman forum). The admission price includes entry to La Seo's Museo de Tapices (Plaza de la Seo; ⊙10am-8.30pm Tue-Sun Jun-Sep, shorter hours Oct-May), an impressive collection of 14th- to 17th-century Flemish and French tapestries.

The northwest facade is a Mudéjar masterpiece, deploying classic dark brickwork and colourful ceramic decoration in complex geometric patterns. The cathedral is also Zaragoza's finest example of Christian architecture: all the chapels are framed by beautiful stonework and ring the changes from the eerie solemnity of the Capilla de San Marcos to the glorious Renaissance facade of the central Christ Chapel and

Zaragoza

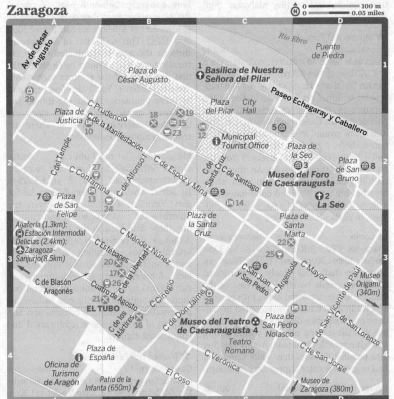

Zaragoza

the exquisite 15th-century alabaster high altarpiece.

★ Museo del Foro de Caesaraugusta
MUSEUM

(Plaza de la Seo 2; adult/concession/child under 8 yr €3/2/free; ⏱ 9am-8.30pm Tue-Sat, 10am-2pm Sun Jun-Sep, shorter hours Oct-May; 🚼) The trapezoidal building on Plaza de la Seo is the entrance to an excellent reconstruction of part of Roman Caesaraugusta's forum, now well below ground level. The remains of porticoes, shops, a great *cloaca* (sewer) system, and a limited collection of artefacts from the 1st century AD are on display. An interesting multilingual 15-minute audiovisual show breathes life into it all and culminates with a clever 'talking head' of a statue which children, in particular, will enjoy.

La Lonja
HISTORIC BUILDING

(Plaza del Pilar; ⏱ 10am-1.30pm & 5-8.30pm Tue-Sat, 10am-1.30pm Sun) FREE Now an exhibition hall, this finely proportioned Renaissance-style building, just east of the basilica, was constructed in the 16th century as a trading exchange. The coloured medallions on its exterior depict kings of Aragón, but it is the soaring columns within (rising to what resemble giant palm fronds merging into petalled flowers) that really stand out. La Lonja has regular temporary exhibitions.

Museo del Puerto Fluvial
MUSEUM

(Plaza de San Bruno 8; adult/concession/child under 8 yr €3/2/free, 1st Sun of month free; ⏱ 9am-8.30pm Tue-Sat, 9am-1.30pm Sun; 🚼) This small museum displays the Roman city's river-port installations, shown beneath glass walkways and comprising several openings which were part of an arched facade linking the docks to the forum. There's a lighthearted 10-minute multilingual audiovisual program every half-hour and a model with explanations at the press of a button.

---

① DISCOUNT TICKET

The four museums dedicated to Zaragoza's Roman past: Museo del Foro de Caesaraugusta, Museo del Teatro de Caesaraugusta, Museo del Puerto Fluvial and Museo de las Termas Públicas form part of what's known as the Ruta de Caesaraugusta; a combined ticket costs €7.

Museo Ibercaja Camón Aznar
MUSEUM

(MICAZ; www.ibercaja.es; Calle de Espoz y Mina 23; ⏱ 10am-2.30pm & 5-9pm Tue-Sat, 10am-2.30pm Sun) FREE This collection of Spanish art through the ages is dominated by an enthralling series of etchings by Goya (on the 2nd floor), one of the premier such collections in existence. You'll also find paintings by other luminaries (including Ribera and Zurbarán) spread over the three storeys of this Renaissance-era mansion. There are regular temporary exhibitions.

Museo de las Termas Públicas
MUSEUM

(Roman Baths; Calle San Juan y San Pedro 3-7; adult/concession/child under 8 yr €3/2/free, 1st Sun of month free; ⏱ 9am-8.30pm Tue-Sat, 9am-1.30pm Sun; 🚼) Roman baths were traditionally the centre of social and cultural life; these date back to the 1st century BC. Although the original complex comprised several rooms, including a gymnasium and changing rooms, all that remains is a large, formerly porticoed swimming pool, surrounded by the remains of several columns. A 10-minute multilingual audiovisual presentation explains the construction and purpose of the baths in a lighthearted and educational manner.

★ Museo del Teatro de Caesaraugusta
RUIN, MUSEUM

(Calle de San Jorge 12; adult/concession/child under 8 yr €4/3/free; ⏱ 9am-8.30pm Tue-Sat, to 1.30pm Sun; 🚼) Discovered during the excavation of a building site in 1972, the ruins of Zaragoza's Teatro Romano (Roman theatre) are the focus of this compelling museum. The theatre once seated 6000 spectators, and great efforts have been made to help visitors reconstruct the edifice's former splendour, including evening projections of a virtual performance (May to October) and an entertaining audiovisual production. The theatre is visible from the surrounding streets and the on-site (and excellent) cafe which may be entered separately.

Museo Origami
MUSEUM

(www.emoz.es; Centro de Historias, Plaza San Agustín 2; adult/concession/child under 12 yr €3/1.50/free; ⏱ 10am-2pm & 5-9pm Tue-Sat, 10am-2.30pm Sun; 🚼) Open since November 2013, this museum devoted to 'the art of folding paper' is the first of its kind in Europe and continues to attract worldwide interest from origami aficionados. Temporary exhibitions covering some six galleries are of a staggeringly high standard. When we visited there was a life-size rhino, a dinosaur skeleton, a virtual aquarium of fish, coral and shells and a group of delicate Degasstyle ballet dancers.

The pieces are labelled with details on how many sheets of paper were used (generally just one). You can also take origami classes (one hour, €6); check the website for more information and to learn about the fascinating historical connection Zaragoza has with origami (dating back to the 1940s).

Museo de Zaragoza MUSEUM
(Plaza de los Sitios 6; ⊘10am-1.45pm & 5-7.45pm Tue-Sat, 10am-1.45pm Sun) FREE Devoted to archaeology and fine arts, the city museum displays artefacts from prehistoric to Islamic times, with some exceptional mosaics from Roman Caesaraugusta. The upper floor contains 15 paintings by Goya and more than two dozen of his etchings. It's 400m south of the Teatro Romano.

Patio de la Infanta GALLERY
(Calle San Ignacio de Loyola 16; ⊘9am-1.30pm & 6-8.30pm Mon-Thu, to 10.30pm Fri, 11am-1.30pm & 6-10.30pm Sat, 11am-1.30pm Sun) FREE This exhibition space houses the Ibercaja bank's collection of paintings, including Goyas, which are displayed in a lovely plateresque (15th- and 16th-century Spanish baroque) courtyard. It's 600m south of Plaza de España.

Museo de Pablo Gargallo GALLERY
(Plaza de San Felipe 3; adult/concession €4/3; ⊘9am-8.30pm Tue-Sat, 9am-1.30pm Sun) Within the wonderfully restored 17th-century Palacio Argillo is a representative display of sculptures by Pablo Gargallo (1881–1934), a friend of Picasso and recognised as Aragón's most gifted artistic son after Goya.

★ **Aljafería** PALACE
(Calle de los Diputados; admission €3, Sun free; ⊘10am-2pm Sat-Wed, plus 4.30-8pm Mon-Wed, Fri & Sat Jul & Aug) The Aljafería is Spain's finest Islamic-era edifice outside Andalucía. Built as a pleasure palace for Zaragoza's Islamic rulers in the 11th century, it underwent its first alterations in 1118 when the city passed into Christian hands. In the 1490s the Catholic Monarchs, Fernando and Isabel, tacked on their own palace, whereafter the Aljafería fell into decay. Twentieth-century restorations brought the building back to life, and in 1987 Aragón's regional parliament was established here. Tours take place throughout the day (multilingual in July and August).

TAKE A RIVERSIDE STROLL

The restoration of the riverbank a few years back has created footpaths on either side of the Río Ebro resulting in an 8km circular route. Take your binoculars as it's superb birdwatching territory with herons, kingfishers, sandpipers, gulls, swallows, swifts, egrets, wagtails and many more species to be spied on or near the water.

Inside the main gate, cross the rather dull introductory courtyard into a second, the Patio de Santa Isabel, once the central courtyard of the Islamic palace. Here you're confronted by the delicate interwoven arches typical of the geometric mastery of Islamic architecture. Opening off the stunning northern porch is a small, octagonal oratorio (prayer room), with a magnificent horseshoe-arched doorway leading into its mihrab (prayer niche indicating the direction of Mecca). The finely chiselled floral motifs, Arabic inscriptions from the Quran and a pleasingly simple cupola are fine examples of Islamic art.

Moving upstairs, you pass through rooms of the Palacio Mudéjar, then to the Catholic Monarchs' palace, which, as though by way of riposte to the Islamic finery below, contains some exquisite Mudéjar coffered ceilings, especially in the lavish Salón del Trono (Throne Room).

🎉 Festivals & Events

Cincomarzada LOCAL FIESTA
Every 5 March, locals commemorate the 1838 ousting of Carlist troops by a feisty populace with concerts, games, and picnics.

Fiestas del Pilar RELIGIOUS
Zaragoza's biggest event is a week of full-on celebrations (religious and otherwise) peaking on 12 October, the Día de Nuestra Señora del Pilar.

🛏️ Sleeping

Hotel Río Arga HOTEL €
(☎976 39 90 65; www.hotelrioarga.es; Calle Contamina 20; s/d €40/45; 🅿 ❄ 🛜) Río Arga offers comfortable spacious rooms with easy-on-the-eye decor and large bathrooms with tubs. The private parking is a real boon given this central city location. Breakfast costs €3.75.

Hostal el Descanso
HOSTAL €

(☑ 976 29 17 41; www.hostaleldescanso.es; Calle de San Lorenzo 2; s/d without bathroom €18/25; ☎) This welcoming family-run place combines a terrific location overlooking a pretty plaza near the Roman theatre with simple, bright rooms with wash basins.

★ Hotel Sauce
BOUTIQUE HOTEL €€

(☑ 976 20 50 50; www.hotelsauce.com; Calle de Espoz y Mina 33; s €48, d €55-66; ✳☎) This chic, small hotel has a great central location and overall light and airy look with white wicker, painted furniture, stripy fabrics and tasteful watercolours on the walls. The superior rooms are well worth the few euros extra. Breakfast (€8) includes homemade cakes and a much-lauded *tortilla de patatas* (potato omelette).

Sabinas
APARTMENT €€

(☑ 976 20 47 10; www.sabinas.es; Calle de Alfonso I 43; d/apt €50/75; ✳☎) These apartments include a contemporary-style kitchen and sitting room. The star performer is the Bayeu Attic (€120), a two-bedroom apartment with fabulous basilica views. There's also standard doubles with microwave and a second location at Calle Francisco Bayeu 4. Reception is at nearby Hotel Sauce.

ℹ CHEAP & EASY ZARAGOZA

Zaragoza Card (☑ 976 20 12 00; www.zaragozacard.com; 24/48/72hr €18/21/24) Free entry to several monuments and museums, travel on the Tourist Bus and discounts on hotels, restaurants, public transport and car hire.

Tourist Bus (Bus Turístico; ☑ 976 20 12 00; www.zaragozaturismo.es; adult/concession/child under 5 yr €8/4.80/free) Hop-on, hop-off sightseeing bus that does two 75-minute city circuits daily in summer.

Guided Tours (www.zaragozaturismo.es; tours €5.50-13; ⏱ 10am & 11am Sat & Sun, daily Jul-Aug) Gastronomic, cultural and architectural walking tours. Book through the tourist office.

BiziZaragoza (☑ 902 319931; www.bizizaragoza.com; 3-day card €5) Public bicycle hire from numerous pick-up and drop-off points around town; first 30 minutes are free and there's a maximum of two hours (€2).

Catalonia El Pilar
HOTEL €€

(☑ 976 20 58 58; www.hoteles-catalonia.com; Calle de la Manifestación 16; s/d €55/80; ✳@☎) A magnificent Modernista building has been artfully renovated to house this eminently comfortable contemporary hotel. Rooms are spacious and decorated in restful muted earthy tones with parquet floors and elegant marble-clad bathrooms. Some of the beds are king-size, a rarity in these parts.

Hotel Las Torres
HOTEL €€

(☑ 976 39 42 50; www.hotellastorres.com; Plaza del Pilar 11; s/d incl breakfast from €75/85; ✳☎) The rooms are seriously white at this central city hotel. So white they are almost clinical (although not many hospital rooms have chandeliers or hydromassage showers, it's true). The public spaces are decorated with whimsical illustrative art work and the views of the basilica are stunning. There's a small spa.

🍴 Eating

Head to the tangle of lanes in El Tubo, north of Plaza de España, for one of Spain's richest gatherings of tapas bars.

Casa Pascualillo
CONTEMPORARY TAPAS €

(Calle de la Libertad 5; tapas from €1.60, mains €5-14; ⏱ noon-4pm & 7-11pm Tue-Sat, noon-4.30pm Sun) When *Metropoli*, the weekend magazine of *El Mundo* newspaper, sought out the best 50 tapas bars in Spain a few years back, it's no surprise that Casa Pascualillo made the final cut. The bar groans under the weight of enticing tapas like El Pascualillo, a 'small' *bocadillo* (filled roll) of *jamón*, oyster mushrooms and onion. There's a more formal restaurant attached.

La Pilara
RACIONES €

(Cuatro de Agosto; raciones €5.50-7; ⏱ 9am-late Mon-Fri, noon-1am Sat & Sun) Ruby-red walls covered with pictures, posters and photos, combined with moody lighting, innovative cuisine and an animated atmosphere make this one of the most popular spots in the *barrio* (district). Thumbs-up choices include *bacalao* (cod), carpaccios, hamburgers, salads and shellfish, duly tarted-up and tasty.

La Miguería
ARAGONESE €

(www.lamigueria.es; Calle Estébanes 4; migas €5-10, raciones €6-19; ⏱ 12.30-4pm & 7.30-11pm Mon-Sat; ♿) Who would have thought you could do so much with *migas* (fried breadcrumbs)... La Miguería serves this filling Aragonese quick-fix food in some 30 ways, including drenched in olive oil, topped with sardines

LOCAL KNOWLEDGE

MARKET TIME

Experience the bustle and atmosphere of Zaragoza's vibrant Mercado Central (Central Market; Avenida de César Augusto; ⊙9am-2pm & 5-8pm Mon-Fri, 9am-2pm Sat). The art-nouveau building dates from 1903, but there has been a market here since the Middle Ages. Some things never change; you can still buy pig heads and unskinned rabbits, or you may prefer admiring the piles of glistening fruit and veg, the smell of fresh bread, the free tastings of olives and nuts, plus coffee, pastries and *churros* aimed at shoppers on the go.

and foie gras and (even) alongside chocolate and orange. It opens for dinner at 7.30pm, which may help those struggling to cope with late Spanish dinner times.

Churrería la Fama   CHURROS €
(Calle Prudencio; chocolate & 4 churros €3.10; ⊙8am-1pm & 5-9.30pm; 🖶) A good spot for *churros* (long, deep-fried doughnuts) and chocolate; if you've been out all night, being here when it opens is a great way to begin (or end) your day.

★ **El Ciclón**   CONTEMPORARY SPANISH €€
(Plaza del Pilar 10; raciones €7-8.50, set menus €15-20; ⊙11am-11.30pm) El Ciclón was opened in November 2013 by three acclaimed Spanish chefs (all with Michelin-star restaurant experience); not surprisingly, the dishes here are superbly prepared. Choose between set menus and tapas and *raciones* (large tapas servings) like the Canary Island favourite, *papas arrugadas* (new potatoes with a spicy coriander sauce), noodles with mussels, and artichokes with *migas* and cauliflower cream.

There is an old fashioned dessert trolly, but there is nothing old fashioned about the industrial-chic decor with its exposed steel pipes, edgy artwork and artistically painted and distressed furniture.

Casa Lac   CONTEMPORARY TAPAS €€
(📞976 29 90 25; Calle de los Mártires 12; 3 tapas €6.50-8, mains from €12; ⊙12.15-4pm & 8.15pm-midnight Mon-Sat, 12.15-8.15pm Sun) The grand old lady of the Zaragoza dining scene, Casa Lac pays homage to the 19th century; it opened in 1825 and is reputedly the oldest licensed restaurant in Spain. The downstairs bar is dedicated to avant-garde tapas like artichoke hearts with foie gras and crispy fried cod in a red-pepper sauce. Reservations recommended for the restaurant.

Tragantua   TAPAS, SEAFOOD €€
(Plaza Santa Marta; tapas from €1.50, mains €9.60-20; ⊙12.30-4pm & 8pm-12.30am) Locals flock here for reputedly the best *croquetas de jamón* (ham croquettes) in town; other popular mini-bites include *bola de bacalao* (breadcrumbed cod) while more substantial tentacle-waving teasers include stewed baby octopus and the sizeable *langostino* (lobster) *de Vinaroz*. The ambience is comfortably traditional.

🍷 Drinking & Nightlife

Calle del Temple, southwest of Plaza del Pilar, is the spiritual home of Zaragoza's roaring nightlife. This is where the city's considerable student population heads out to party, with more bars lined up cheek to jowl than anywhere else in Aragón. Note that nowhere really gets going until well after midnight.

Café Botanico   CAFE
(Calle de Santiago 5; ⊙9am-1pm Mon-Wed, 9am-2am Thu & Fri, 10am-2am Sat, 10am-11pm Sun; 🛜🖶) Café Botanico combines a florist (think plenty of greenery, including fragrant herbs) and a cafe serving great coffee, a tea menu and some truly delicious cakes. It has a real buzz about it. Also runs the contemporary art gallery next door.

Gran Café de Zaragoza   CAFE
(Calle de Alfonso I 25; ⊙8.30am-10pm Sun-Thu, 9am-2.30am Fri & Sat; 🛜🖶) This Zaragoza institution evokes the grand old cafes of Spain's past with a gold-plated facade and an old-style civility in the service. That said, it's a place to be seen by young and old alike and the elegant salon is a good place for morning coffee (along with one of the glorious buttery croissants).

Rock & Blues Café   MUSIC BAR
(www.rockandbluescafe.com; Cuatro de Agosto 5-9; ⊙3pm-2.30am) Rock 'n' roll paraphernalia paying homage to the likes of Jimi Hendrix and Jim Morrison sets the tone for the music and style of this long-standing favourite. There's live pop, rock or blues most Thursdays at 10pm. It's a fascinating and atmospheric spot, open late on weekends.

Tierra Maña LIVE MUSIC
(Calle Contamina 7; ☺noon-3pm & 7pm-midnight Wed-Sun) This evocative bar is set in a medieval building with rooms in the cavernous former cellars and tunnels. There's live Latin American music most nights.

La Casa del Loco LIVE MUSIC
(www.lacasadelloco.com; Calle Mayor 10-12; live music free-€20; ☺9pm-5.30am Thu-Sat) Hugely popular, especially when there's a live band playing. It's mostly rock with a mixed, young-retro crowd. After the bands go home, DJs ensure that things stay lively until late.

🛍 Shopping

Fantoba CHOCOLATES
(www.fantoba.com; Calle de Don Jaime 2, 21; ☺10am-10pm; 🖼) This fabulous shop dates from 1856 and is dedicated to decadent sweet treats, ranging from cream-filled cakes and mini-macarons to wonderfully ornate chocolate stiletto shoes (yes, you read that right), plus handmade chocolates, marzipan fruits and exquisite tins of biscuits.

ⓘ Information

Municipal Tourist Office (☎976 20 12 00; www.zaragozaturismo.es; Plaza del Pilar; ☺9am-9pm mid-Jun–mid-Oct, 10am-8pm mid-

---

WINE (DOC) REGIONS
....

Aragón has a number of Denominación de Origen Calificada (DOC) wine regions:

Somontano The most prestigious wine-producing region (see p386). Produces reds, whites and rosés. Better known labels include Enate and Viñas del Vero.

Calatayud Well known for its big and bold red wine, Calatayud Superior, made from garnacho (grenache) grapes from 50-year-old vines.

Campo de Borja Famed for its powerful aromatic red wines using solely garnacho grapes, as well as its sweet and fruity moscatel.

Pago Aylés Produces two red-wine blends and a popular *rosado* (rosé) made from garnacha and cabernet sauvignon grape varietals.

Cariñena Known for its signature oak-aged reds, dry whites from the maca-beo grapes, fruity *rosados* and sweet moscatel.

Oct–mid-Jun; 🕿) Has branch offices around town, including the train station.
Oficina de Turismo de Aragón (www.turismodearagon.com; Plaza de España; ☺9am-2pm & 5-8pm Mon-Fri, from 10am Sat & Sun; 🕿) Has plenty of brochures on the province.

ⓘ Getting There & Away

AIR
The **Zaragoza-Sanjurjo airport** (☎976 71 23 00; www.zaragoza-airport.com), 8.5km west of the city centre, has direct **Ryanair** (www.ryanair.com) flights to/from London (Stansted), Brussels (Charleroi), Paris (Beauvais), Milan (Bergamo) and Lanzarote (Canary Islands). **Iberia** (www.iberia.es) and **Air Europa** (www.aireuropa.com) also operate a small number of domestic and international routes.

BUS
Dozens of bus lines fan out across Spain from the bus station attached to the Estación Intermodal Delicias train station.
Alosa (☎902 210700; www.alosa.es) Buses to/from Huesca (€7.70, one hour, up to 12 daily) and Jaca (€15.65, 2½ hours, four daily).
ALSA (☎902 422242; www.alsa.es) Frequent daily buses to/from Madrid (from €16.50, 3¾ hours) and Barcelona (€15.50, 3¾ hours).

TRAIN
Zaragoza's futuristic **Estación Intermodal Delicias** (www.renfe.com; Calle Rioja 33) is connected by almost hourly high-speed AVE services to Madrid (€65.50, 1¼ hours) and Barcelona (€71, from 1½ hours). Other destinations include Huesca (from €7, one hour), Jaca (€14.55, 3½ hours) and Teruel (€19.70, 2¼ hours).

ⓘ Getting Around

Airport Buses (☎902 360065; tickets €2) run to/from Paseo María Agustín 7 via the bus/train station every half-hour (hourly on Sunday).

Buses 34 and 51 travel between the city centre and the Estación Intermodal Delicias.

The **C1 tram** (www.urbandezaragoza.es; tickets €1.35) line opened in 2011 running through the centre of town from Plaza de España to Plaza de Bambola due south.

SOUTH OF ZARAGOZA

The A23 south towards Teruel passes through Campo de Cariñena, one of Aragón's premier wine regions. Just off the motorway, the Ermita de la Fuente (Avenida Virgen de la Fuenta; ☺9am-8pm daily) FREE in Muel has some fine paintings of saints by the young Goya. If you take the slower but more tranquil N234 to Cariñena, bodegas (wine cellars) line the main road, and in Cariñena there's a good Museo del Vino (Wine Museum; www.docarinea.com; Camino de la Platera 7; admission €1.50; ⊙10am-2pm & 4-6pm Tue-Sat, 10am-2pm Sun).

Fuendetodos

Located some 23km east of Cariñena along the A220 lies the small village of Fuendetodos where Francisco José de Goya y Lucientes (Goya) was born in 1746.

⊙ Sights

Casa Natal de Goya   MUSEUM
(www.fundacionfuendetodosgoya.org; Calle Zuloaga 3; admission incl Museo del Grabado de Goya €3; ⊙11am-2pm & 4-7pm Tue-Sun) This humble birthplace of Goya stayed in his family until the early 20th century, when it was purchased by Basque painter Ignacio Zuloaga. Destroyed during the civil war, the house was subsequently restored with furniture and exhibits relating to Goya's life and times.

Museo del Grabado de Goya   MUSEUM
(Calle Zuloaga; admission incl Casa Natal de Goya €3; ⊙11am-2pm & 4-7pm Tue-Sun) This museum contains an important collection of the artist's engravings from the series including the famously satirical *Los Caprichos* and the bullfighting-themed *La Tauromaquia*.

⊙ Getting There & Away

Up to four buses daily head to Fuendetodos (€6.75, one hour) from Zaragoza.

WEST OF ZARAGOZA

Tarazona

POP 10,863

The quiet, serpentine streets of Tarazona's old town are an evocative reminder of the layout of a medieval Spanish town and contain some absorbing sights.

⊙ Sights

A signposted walking route takes you around the twisting cobbled ways of the historic 'high part' of town. Meandering through these laneways is undoubtedly the highlight of Tarazona. The medieval *judería* (Jewish quarter) is also exceptionally well preserved.

FOLLOW THE GOYA TRAIL

Francisco José de Goya y Lucientes, better known as the master painter Goya, was born in Aragón and his work can be seen all over his native region.

➡ Casa Natal de Goya, Fuendetodos

➡ Museo del Grabado de Goya, Fuendetodos

➡ Ermita de la Fuente, Muel

➡ Museo Ibercaja Camón Aznar (p364), Zaragoza

➡ Museo de Zaragoza (p365), Zaragoza

➡ Basílica de Nuestra Señora del Pilar (p362), Zaragoza

➡ Museo de Huesca (p387), Huesca

Throughout, the high balconied projections of the 'hanging houses' are remarkable.

Catedral Santa María de la Huerta   CATHEDRAL
(Plaza de la Seo; admission €4; ⊙11am-2pm & 4-6pm Wed-Fri, to 7pm Sat, 11am-2pm Sun) This magnificent cathedral dates from 1158 but was rebuilt in the 15th and 16th centuries. It reopened in 2011 after 30 years of restoration work. Elements from its French-Gothic roots can be observed in the frescoes in the high altar, Mudéjar influences can be seen in the intricate masonry and Renaissance artwork is reflected in the decorative chancel and carved altars. The main portal and retrochoir display paintings from the baroque era.

Palacio Episcopal   PALACE
(Bishop's Palace; Plaza Palacio; ⊙11am-2pm & 4-7pm Sat, 11am-2pm Sun) FREE On the site of an ancient Muslim citadel and, subsequently, the residence of several Aragonese kings, the imposing 16th-century Bishop's Palace took well over a century to construct. Its exterior has a striking series of perfectly proportioned arches while, within, highlights include a series of 16th-century episcopal portraits and a magnificent Mudéjar coffered ceiling (two more are missing – purchased by William Randolph Hearst for his California 'castle' in the early 20th century).

Ayuntamiento   HISTORIC BUILDING
(Town Hall; Plaza de España) The magnificent 16th-century town hall is located in the upper part of town overlooking the river.

The ornate facade has reliefs which show the triumphal procession of Carlos V after his coronation in Bologna.

🛏 Sleeping & Eating

Hostal Santa Agueda HOSTAL €€
(☑ 976 64 00 54; www.santaagueda.com; Calle Visconti 26; s/d incl breakfast from €34/49; ❋ 🛜) Just off Plaza San Francisco, this 200-year-old home has attractive rooms with wooden beams and cheery decor. The little breakfast room is a glorious shrine to local girl Raquel Meller, Aragón's queen of popular song during the early 20th century.

Hotel Condes de Visconti HOTEL €€
(☑ 976 64 49 08; www.condesdevisconti.com; Calle Visconti 15; d €90; P❋@) Beautiful rooms, plus a preserved Renaissance patio, make this 16th-century former palace a fine stopover. It also has a cafe and good old-fashioned service.

Saboya 21 CONTEMPORARY ARAGONESE €€
(☑ 976 64 24 90; www.restaurantesaboya21.com; Calle Marrodán 34; mains €15-28, set menus €15-21.50; ☺ 2-4pm Tue-Sun, 7-11pm Fri & Sat; 🛜) Talented young chef José Tazueco whips up a selection of culinary treats that zap traditional ingredients with a creative flair. Expect artistically presented plates and dishes like *ensalada de pato* (duck salad) *con piña colada* or artichokes stuffed with goose liver pâté. There's a more informal cafe and bar downstairs. Reservations recommended.

ⓘ Information

Tourist Office (☑ 976 64 00 74; www.tarazona.es; Plaza San Francisco 1; city tours €5-9.50; ☺ 9am-1.30pm & 4.30-7pm Mon-Fri,

BORJA'S BUTCHERED ART RESTORATION

The small town of Borja, 45km southeast of Tarazona, attracted worldwide media attention in August 2012 when 81-year-old amateur artist Cecilia Jiménez botched the restoration of a 19th-century religious painting in the local church. The result (subsequently dubbed 'potato Jesus') has, ironically, brought prosperity to the town. Visitors are charged €1 admission to view the 'artwork' and it has become a major tourist attraction. Cecilia is apparently suing for royalties.

from 10am Sat & Sun) Organises guided tours, in Spanish, of the city with an optional extra of the cathedral.

ⓘ Getting There & Away

Up to seven **Therpasa** (☑ 976 64 11 00; www.therpasa.es) buses run daily to/from Zaragoza (€7.50, 1¼ hours) and Soria (€6.10, one hour).

Cistercian Monastery

This one-time Cistercian **Monasterio de Piedra** (☑ 902 196052; www.monasteriopiedra.com; park & monastery adult/child €15/11, monastery €8; ☺ park 9am-8pm, monastery 10.15am-1.15pm & 3-7pm), 28km southwest of Calatayud, dates from the 13th century but was abandoned in the 1830s. Subsequent owners laid out the ground as a formal wooded park full of caves and waterfalls, the latter fed by the Río Piedra. It's a wonderful place for a family day out, although it can get overrun on summer weekends. Incorporated into the complex is the **Hotel Monasterio de Piedra**.

On Tuesday, Thursday, Saturday and Sunday (or daily in summer), Automóviles Zaragoza runs a 9am bus from Zaragoza to the monastery (€14, 2½ hours) via Calatayud, returning at 5pm.

THE ARAGONESE PYRENEES

Leaving behind Zaragoza's parched flatlands, a hint of green tinges the landscape and there's a growing anticipation of very big mountains somewhere up ahead. And they are big. The Aragonese Pyrenees are well over the 3000m mark and among the most dramatic and rewarding peaks of the range. Viewed from the south their crenellated ridges fill the northern horizon wherever you turn and their valleys offer magnificent scenery, stunning stone-built villages, several decent ski resorts and great walking.

Sos del Rey Católico

POP 646 / ELEV 625M

If Sos del Rey Católico were in Tuscany, it would be a world-famous hill town. It's one of Aragón's most beautiful villages and the old medieval town is a glorious maze of twist-

HIKING IN THE PYRENEES

Some 6000km of trails, both long-distance (Grandes Recorridos; GR) and short-distance (Pequeños Recorridos; PR), are marked all across Aragón. The coast-to-coast GR11 traverses the spectacular Aragonese Pyrenees.

The optimum time for walking is mid-June to early September, though the more popular parks and paths can become crowded in midsummer. The weather can be unpredictable, so walkers should always be prepared for extreme conditions.

Dotted throughout the mountains are mountain *refugios* (refuges). Some are staffed and serve meals, while others provide shelter only. At holiday times staffed *refugios* are often full, so unless you've booked ahead, be prepared to camp. The Federación Aragonesa de Montañismo (FAM; p865) in Zaragoza can provide information, and a FAM card will get you substantial discounts on *refugio* stays. To make reservations in *refugios* and *albergues* (refuges), try www.alberguesyrefugiosdearagon.com.

Editorial Alpina (p379) produces excellent maps for walkers.

---

ing, cobbled lanes that wriggle between dark stone houses with deeply overhung eaves.

Sos has historical significance to go with its beauty: half of one of the most formidable double acts in history, Fernando II of Aragón, was born here in 1452. He and his wife, Isabel I of Castilla, became known as the Reyes Católicos (Catholic Monarchs). Together they conquered the last Islamic kingdom of Granada and united Spain.

◉ Sights

Casa Palacio de Seda HISTORIC BUILDING
(Plaza de la Hispanidad; adult/child €2.60/1.50, incl tour of village €4/2; ◷10am-2pm & 4-8pm; 👶) Fernando is said to have been born in this building in 1452. It's an impressive noble mansion, which now contains an interpretative centre, with fine exhibits on the history of Sos and the life of the king. The tourist office, also housed here, runs guided tours of the building.

Iglesia de San Esteban CHURCH
(admission €1; ◷10am-1pm & 3.30-5.30pm) This Gothic church, with a weathered Romanesque portal, has a deliciously gloomy crypt decorated with medieval frescoes.

Castillo de la Peña Feliciano RUIN
The 12th-century watchtower is all that remains of the castle that once guarded the frontier between the two Christian kingdoms of Aragón and Navarra.

Ayuntamiento NOTABLE BUILDING
(◷9.30am-2pm Mon-Fri) Lording it over the central Plaza de la Villa, the Renaissance-era town hall is one of the grandest public buildings in Sos. Duck inside to admire the magnificent central courtyard.

🛏 Sleeping & Eating

Hostal las Coronas HOSTAL €
(☏948 88 84 08; www.hostallascoronas.com; Calle Pons Sorolla 2; s/d incl breakfast €48/65) Run by friendly Fernando, this *hostal* (budget hotel) has modest rustic-style rooms. Request number 3 with its spa shower and balcony overlooking the plaza. The downstairs bar serves tapas (€2 to €6) and *raciones* (from €7).

★ Casa del Infanzón BOUTIQUE HOTEL €€
(☏605 940536; www.casadelinfanzon.com; Calle Coliseo 3; d/ste €59/68; ❋🛜) In the heart of the Jewish quarter, this is a great deal with aesthetically furnished rooms sporting plush fabrics, a soothing colour scheme and spacious bathrooms. Several rooms have small terraces and the ample breakfast (€3.50 to €7.50) includes homemade breads, local *jamón* and eggs prepared to order. There is a cosy salon with a fireplace.

Ruta del Tiempo HOTEL €€
(☏948 88 82 95; www.rutadeltiempo.es; Calle Larraldía 1; s incl breakfast €50, d €70-108; ◷Mar-Oct; ❋🛜) Evocatively located under the arches, rooms on the 1st floor are themed around three Aragonese kings, while the four 2nd-floor rooms have decorations dedicated to four different continents. Spacious 'Asia' and 'Africa' are the best rooms.

Parador de Sos del Rey Católico HOTEL €€€
(☏948 88 80 11; www.parador.es; Calle Arquitecto Sainz de Vicuña 1; r €142; ◷mid-Feb–Dec; 🅿❋🛜) A place that might just have pleased *los reyes* themselves, this grand building blends in perfectly with the stone buildings of Sos. Rooms have terracotta-tiled floors and some have lovely views out over the village or

surrounding plains. The service is faultless and there's a terrific restaurant (set menus €32) serving a changing menu of regional specialities.

Vinacua ARAGONESE €€
(www.vinacua.com; Calle Goya 24; mains €8-16, set menus €12-20; ⊙1-3.30pm & 9-11pm Mon-Fri, 1.30-3.30pm Sat & Sun; 🗟) Hearty local cuisine is served in a contemporary space with raspberry-pink walls and glossy-black furnishings. The menu includes rabbit with snails, garbanzo stew, grilled meats and, for lightweights, some excellent salads with toppings like warm goat's cheese or partridge and pâté.

La Cocina del Principal ARAGONESE €€
(🖉948 88 83 48; www.lacocinadelprincipal.com; Calle Mayor 17; mains €14-17.50; ⊙1.30-3.30pm & 8.30-10.30pm Tue-Sat, noon-4pm Sun) Come here for carefully prepared local cooking that changes with the seasons, including snails and roast suckling pig or a tasty *pochas viudas* (white-bean stew with green peppers, tomatoes and onion).

🛍 Shopping

Morrico Fino DELI
(Calle Mayor 14; ⊙10am-1.30pm & 5-8pm) One of several tiny shops selling regional food products found hidden in Sos' lanes.

ℹ Information

Tourist Office (🖉948 88 85 24; Plaza Hispanidad; ⊙10am-2pm & 4-8pm) Housed in the Casa Palacio de Seda, the tourist office runs twice-daily guided tours (one/two hours €2.60/4) of the village on weekends.

ℹ Getting There & Away

A **Gómez** (🖉976 67 55 29) bus departs from Zaragoza (1½ hours, €10.50) for Sos at 7pm Monday to Friday. It returns from Sos at 7am.

Around Sos del Rey Católico

From just north of Sos, the engaging A1601 begins its 34km-long snaking journey west and then northwest en route to the N240. It passes the pretty villages of Navardún and Urriés, before climbing over the Sierra de Peña Musera and down to the gorgeous abandoned village of Ruesta (medieval murals from the ruined church here can be viewed at Jaca's fine Museo Diocesano,

(p375). The final stretch passes some unusual rock formations and wheat fields with fine views of the hilltop village of Milanos away to the east.

Valles de Echo & Ansó

The verdant Echo and Ansó valleys are mountain magic at its best, beginning with gentle climbs through the valleys and the accumulating charms of old stone villages punctuating slopes of dense mixed woods of beech, pine, rowan, elm and hazel. As the valleys narrow to the north, 2000m-plus peaks rise triumphantly at their heads.

ℹ Getting There & Around

A bus to Jaca leaves Ansó at 6.30am, Siresa at 6.53am and Echo at 7am, Monday to Saturday, returning from Jaca at 6.50pm. A good road links Ansó and Echo, a distance of about 12km.

Echo (Hecho)

POP 630 / ELEV 833M
Lovely Echo, the largest village in the valley, is an attractive warren of solid stone houses with steep roofs and flower-decked balconies.

◉ Sights

Museo de Escultura al Aire Libre y Pinturas Contemporánea SCULPTURE, ART
(www.hecho.es; Carretera Oza; ⊙10am-1.30pm & 5.30-8pm Mon-Sat, 10am-1.30pm Sun) FREE This tiny village is a hub of contemporary art and sculpture thanks, primarily, to a former mayor who helped to initiate an annual sculpture and art symposium back in the 1970s. As well as the artwork exhibited in a downstairs gallery in the tourist office, there are sculptures on permanent display in the village. It opens shorter hours in low season.

Museo Etnológico Casa Mazo MUSEUM
(www.hecho.es; Calle Aire; admission €1.50; ⊙10.30am-1.30pm & 5-8pm; 🖈) At the heart of the village is this endearing museum with a captivating display of photographs of villagers from the 1920s and 1930s. Shorter hours in low season.

🛌 Sleeping & Eating

Casa Blasquico RURAL HOTEL €
(🖉974 37 50 07; www.casablasquico.es; Plaza de la Fuente 1; d €40-53, tr €65; ⊙closed 1st half Sep & Jan; ❄🗟) The best place to stay in town, the charming Casa Blasquico has six rooms

with a mixture of wooden and wrought-iron furnishings.

Camping Valle de Hecho CAMPGROUND €
(📞974 37 53 61; www.campinghecho.com; Carretera Puenta la Reina; sites per adult/tent/car €4.29/4.29/4.29, 4-person bungalow €97; P🛜🏊♿) South of town, this picturesque campground is well kept and has an outstanding range of facilities, from a wi-fi zone to a small supermarket. The bungalows are well equipped and comfortable.

Restaurante Gaby ARAGONESE €€
(📞974 37 50 07; www.casablasquico.es; Plaza de la Fuente 1; mains €9-19; 🕐) This much-lauded restaurant, downstairs in Casa Blasquico, is a delightful place to eat. It has an intimate wood-beamed dining room, plus small outside terrace overlooking the cobbles. There is an extensive wine list and specialities include *crepes de setas* (wild mushroom crepes) and *conejo a la montañesa* (rabbit stew).

ℹ️ Information

Tourist Office (📞974 37 55 05; www.valledehecho.net; Carretera Oza; 🕐10am-1.30pm & 5.30-7pm Fri & Sat, 10am-1pm Sun Jul & Aug, Sat & Sun Sep-Jun)

Siresa

POP 130 / ELEV 850M

A couple of kilometres north of Echo, Siresa is another captivating village.

◉ Sights

Iglesia de San Pedro CHURCH
(admission €1.50; 🕐11am-1pm & 5-7pm Thu-Tue, 11am-1pm Wed) This beautiful 11th-century church is the town's centrepiece; it originally comprised part of one of Aragón's earliest monasteries. The cavernous interior is suitably austere.

🛏️ Sleeping

Hotel Usón RURAL HOTEL €
(📞974 37 53 58; www.hoteluson.com; s/d/apt from €40/53/65; 🕐Easter-Oct; P🛜♿) There's perfect peace in fabulous surroundings at the Hotel Usón, high in the Echo valley, 5km north of Siresa on the road to the Selva de Oza. Popular with birdwatchers and walkers, the restaurant offers home-cooked meals.

Hotel Castillo d'Acher HOTEL €
(📞974 37 53 13; www.castillodacher.com; Plaza Mayor; d €50; 🕐) This hotel has a pleasant mix of rooms, some rather old fashioned,

others pine-clad and modern. The owners also offer a *casa rural* (village accommodation; minimum one week stay). The spacious in-house restaurant does a good *menú del día* (daily set menu; €12).

Selva de Oza

This top end of the Valle de Echo is particularly beautiful, with the road running parallel to the Río Aragón Subordán as it bubbles its way through thick woodlands. Around 7km beyond Siresa, the road squeezes through the Boca del Infierno (Hell's Mouth), while about 14km from Siresa the paved road ends, shortly after it connects with the GR11 path en route between Candanchú and Zuriza. At least half a dozen mountain peaks sit in an arc to the north for strenuous day ascents.

Ansó

POP 480 / ELEV 860M

Ansó takes you even further into a world of high places and harmony. The rough-hewn stone houses here are in grey stone, with red-tiled roofs. Some walls are whitewashed, making a pleasing chequerboard pattern. Forested slopes climb ever upwards from where Ansó straggles along a low escarpment above a partly covered streambed. A grid of narrow streets surrounds the main square, Plaza Mayor.

🛏️ Sleeping & Eating

Posada Magoria RURAL HOTEL €
(📞974 37 00 49; www.posadamagoria.com; Calle Milagros 32; d €55-60; 🕐) Adjoining the lofty rough-walled church, the delightful Posada Magoria is crammed with vintage character and lovingly kept by a family with lots of local knowledge. The kitchen *comedor* (dining room) serves up an excellent €12 *menú* of organically sourced vegetarian dishes (try the nettle soup if it's on offer).

Hostal Kimboa HOSTAL €
(☑974 37 01 84; www.hostalkimboa.com; Paseo Chapitel 24; s/d incl breakfast €45/55) A charming family-owned small hotel in the centre of town with pleasant pine-furnished rooms above a good restaurant (mains €8 to €10) specialising in traditional grilled meats, plus a popular bar with outside terrace.

Maiberal ARAGONESE €€
(☑974 37 01 74; www.restaurantemaiberal.com; Calle Arrigo 1; mains €8-12; ☉11am-4pm Mon, Tue & Thu, 11am-4pm & 7-11pm Fri-Sun) A friendly authentic place serving comfort food like free-range roasted chicken in a creamy mushroom sauce. There are delectable tapas, *tostas* (toasts with toppings) and *raciones*, as well.

❶ Information

Tourist Office (☑974 37 02 25; Plaza Mayor; ☉10am-2pm & 5-8pm daily Jul & Aug, Sat & Sun Sep-Jun) Offers free guided tours of the village.

Valle de Zuriza

This narrow valley, which runs for 15km north of Ansó, follows the Río Jeral and leads high into remote Pyrenean corners where raptors circle above. Where the paved road ends, wonderful walking trails such as the GR11 take over.

Monasterio de San Juan de la Peña

High in a mountain eyrie, 21km southwest of Jaca, Monasterio de San Juan de la Peña is Aragón's most fascinating monastery. Gateway to the monastery is Santa Cruz de la Serós, a pretty village 4km south of the N240.

From Santa Cruz, a winding road climbs the Sierra de la Peña 7km to the stunning Monasterio Viejo (Old Monastery; www.monasteriosanjuan.com; ☉10am-2pm & 3-8pm Jun-Aug, shorter hours Sep-May), tucked under an overhanging lip of rock at a bend in the road.

The rock shelter where the Monasterio Viejo is built, perhaps used by Christian hermits as early as the 8th century, became a monastery in the 10th century, when the Mozarabic lower church was constructed. The monastery emerged as the early spiritual and organisational centre of the medieval kingdom of Aragón. The highlight is the Romanesque cloister, with marvel-

❶ TICKETS & PARKING

Tickets to the two monasteries of Monasterio de San Juan de la Peña and to an audiovisual presentation on the Kingdom of Aragón are sold only at the Monasterio Nuevo. Tickets for one/two/three of these sights cost €7/8.50/12 for adults; students and seniors pay €6/7/10, while children between six and 14 pay €4.50/5/7.

Except in winter, the only permissible parking is up the hill at the Monasterio Nuevo, from where a semiregular bus shuttles down to the Monasterio Viejo and back.

lous carved 12th- and 13th-century capitals depicting Genesis and the life of Christ. The first three kings of Aragón – Ramiro I (1036–64), Sancho Ramírez (1064–94) and Pedro I (1094–1104) – are among those buried here.

A fire in 1675 led the monks to abandon the old monastery and build a new one in brick further up the hill: Monasterio Nuevo (New Monastery; ☉10am-8pm mid-Jul-Aug, shorter hours Sep–mid-Jul). It has a large visitor centre as well as the Monastery Interpretation Centre, which documents the archaeological history of the site, and the Kingdom of Aragón Interpretation Centre, devoted to the kings of Aragón.

Unless you've got a specialist interest, most visitors will be satisfied with the Monasterio Viejo.

🛏 Sleeping

Hostelería Santa Cruz HOSTAL €
(☑974 36 19 75; www.santacruzdelaseros.com; Calle Ordana; s/d from €50.50/62.50; 🐾) Near the church in Santa Cruz de la Serós, this is a beautiful place with friendly service and lovely rooms overlooking the village square. Its restaurant serves a good *menú del día* (€12).

Hospedería Monasterio San Juan de la Peña HISTORIC HOTEL €€
(☑974 37 44 22; www.hospederiasdearagon.es; d from €70; 🌐🐾🏊) Part of the Monasterio Nuevo, this four-star hotel has somewhat bland, if comfortable rooms, a spa complex and a large restaurant that has received mixed reviews from readers.

ⓘ Getting There & Away

There's no public transport to the monastery. For walkers, a stiff 4km marked path (the GR65.3.2) leads up from Santa Cruz to the Monasterio Viejo. With an ascent of 350m, it takes about 1½ hours.

Jaca

POP 13,248 / ELEV 820M

A gateway to the western valleys of the Aragonese Pyrenees, Jaca has a compact and attractive old town dotted with remnants of its past as the capital of the nascent 11th-century Aragón kingdom, including an unusual fortress and a sturdy cathedral. The town also has some great places to eat. On winter weekends, après-ski funsters provide a lively soundtrack.

◎ Sights

★**Catedral de San Pedro**　　CATHEDRAL
(Plaza de la Catedral; ⊘11.30am-1.30pm & 4.15-8pm) **FREE** Jaca's 11th-century cathedral is a formidable building, its imposing facade typical of the sturdy stone architecture of northern Aragón. It was once more gracefully French Romanesque in style, but a Gothic overhaul in the 16th century bequeathed a hybrid look. The interior retains some fine features, in particular the side chapel dedicated to Santa Orosia, the city's patron saint, whose martyrdom is depicted in a series of mysterious murals.

★**Museo Diocesano**　　MUSEUM
(Museum of Sacred Art; www.diocesisdejaca.org; Plaza de la Catedral; adult/concession €6/4.50; ⊘10am-1.30pm & 4-7pm Tue-Sat, 10am-1.30pm Sun) Reopened in 2010 after years of closure, the undoubted highlight here is an extraordinary collection of Romanesque and Gothic frescoes that were rescued from various ruined churches in the region. In the Bagüés gallery, the space has been constructed as an exact replica of the original church where the frescoes were painted; it's the most extensive single Romanesque fresco remaining in Spain.

There are also polychromed carvings, several lipsanotheques (tiny wooden boxes where the relics of a saint were preserved) and 15th-century paintings.

Ciudadela　　FORTRESS
(Citadel; www.ciudadeladejaca.es; Calle del Primer Viernes de Mayo; adult/concession/child under 8 yr €10/5/free; ⊘11am-2pm & 5-8pm Tue-Sun; ⍟) The star-shaped, 16th-century citadel is Spain's only extant pentagonal fortress (the one in Pamplona is not complete) and one of only two in Europe. It now houses an army academy, but visits are permitted, with 40-minute multilingual guided tours. In the citadel the **Museo de Miniaturas Militares** (Museum of Military Miniatures; www.museominiaturasjaca.es) is an extraordinary collection of models and dioramas of battles ancient and otherwise, with more than 32,000 toy soldiers on show. Deer graze in the moat surrounding the citadel. The last tickets are sold at 1pm and 7pm.

Old Town　　HISTORIC SITE
There are some lovely old buildings in the streets of the *casco historico* (old town) that fans out south of the cathedral, including the 15th-century **Torre del Reloj** (clock tower; Plaza del Marqués de la Cadena) and the charming little **Ermita de Sarsa** (Avenida Oroel).

SKIING ARAGÓN

Aragón is one of Spain's premier ski destinations. The following are the major ski stations:

Candanchú (☏974 37 31 94; www.candanchu.com) Around 42km of widely varied pistes, 28km north of Jaca.

Astún (☏974 37 30 88; www.astun.com) Also 42km of pistes, mostly for experienced skiers, 3km east of Candanchú.

Panticosa (☏974 48 72 48; www.panticosa-loslagos.com) At the confluence of two pretty valleys, the runs aren't Aragón's most challenging, though the 2km-long Mazaranuala run is an exception; accessible from the A136 north of Sabiñago.

Formigal (www.formigal.com) A regular host for ski competitions, Formigal has 57km of ski runs and 22 lifts; accessible from the A136 north of Sabiñago.

Cerler & Ampriu (www.cerler.com) Cerler sits at 1500m, 6km southeast of Benasque; Ampriu is at 1900m, 8km beyond Cerler. Together they boast 45 runs totalling 52km.

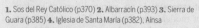

1. Sos del Rey Católico (p370) 2. Albarracín (p393) 3. Sierra de Guara (p385) 4. Iglesia de Santa María (p382), Aínsa

JUANJOFOTOS / GETTY IMAGES ©

Villages of Aragón

Few regions can rival Aragón for its spread of charming villages. Most are built in the sturdy stone typical of the region, with terracotta and slate roofs. And their settings – against a backdrop of Pyrenean peaks or hidden in isolated corners of the south – are as beguiling as the architecture.

Albarracín

One of Spain's most beautiful villages, which would look equally at home in southern Italy, Albarracín combines time-worn streets in shades of ochre and dusky rose with a dramatic setting. The views from the castle or the precipitous walls high on a ridge will stay with you long after you leave.

Aínsa

There's no more beautifully preserved historic centre in Aragón and after the sun sets the crowds go home and silence reigns. Aínsa's stunning laneways, porticoed Plaza Mayor and views of the Pyrenees from the village's hilltop perch are simply wonderful.

Alquézar

A centre for canyoning and other high-octane pursuits, Alquézar's alter ego is a tranquil village that, from above, resembles a Tuscan hill town.

Sos del Rey Católico

Uniformly cobblestoned streets, the whiff of Spanish legend and a perch high above the madding crowd make Sos a memorable stop en route to or from the Pyrenees.

Daroca

Just when you think Aragón's southern badlands have little to offer, Daroca embraces you within its walls, which encircle the town high on the ridgelines.

✷ Festivals & Events

Festividad del Primer Viernes de Mayo   MEDIEVAL
To see displays of medieval archery, visit on the first Friday of May, when Jaca celebrates the Christian victory over the Muslims in 760.

Fiesta de Santa Orosia   RELIGIOUS
Jaca puts on its party gear for the week-long Fiesta de Santa Orosia, which revolves around the saint's day of 25 June.

Festival Folklórico de los Pirineos   FOLKLORE
This folklore festival held in late July and early August (on odd-numbered years), provides 1½ weeks of international music, dance, crafts and theatre.

🛏 Sleeping

It's worth booking ahead at weekends throughout the year, during the skiing season, and in July and August.

Hotel Mur   HOTEL €
(☑ 974 36 01 00; www.hotelmur.com; Calle de Santa Orosia 1; s/d incl breakfast from €50/60; P ⑨) A historic hotel with some atmospheric public hallways and salons decorated accordingly with grainy photos of bygone years, dusty antiques, grim-faced portraits, and the like. The rooms are in keeping, with their quaint painted furniture and custard-coloured walls; several have balconies with Ciudadela views.

Hostal París   HOSTAL €
(☑ 974 36 10 20; www.hostalparisjaca.com; Plaza de San Pedro 5; s/d without bathroom from €30/40; ⑨) Close to the cathedral, this friendly, central option has high ceilings, creaky floorboards, spotless, ample-sized rooms and smart, shared bathrooms (seven bathrooms for 20 rooms). Many rooms overlook the square. Breakfast is available for a minimal extra cost.

★ Hotel Barosse   BOUTIQUE HOTEL €€
(☑ 974 36 05 82; www.barosse.com; incl breakfast s €72-136, d €115-170; ✻ ⑨) In the quiet hamlet of Barós, 2km south of Jaca, Hotel Barosse has six individually styled rooms with lovely attention to detail, from exposed stone walls and splashes of colour to fine bathroom packages of goodies. There's a reading room, garden, on-site Jacuzzi and sauna, and fine views of the Pyrenees. The owner, José, is a wonderful host (and a talented chef – meals are available upon request).

Hotel Jaqués   HOTEL €€
(☑ 974 35 64 24; www.hoteljaques.com; Calle Unión Jaquesa 4; s/d €50/80; ✻ ⑨) A solid midrange choice with Regency-style fabrics, pale-wood decor and smart modern bathrooms.

🍴 Eating

★ La Tasca de Ana   CONTEMPORARY TAPAS €
(Calle de Ramiro I 3; tapas from €3; ⊙ 7-11.30pm Mon-Fri, 12.30-3.30pm & 7-11.30pm Sat & Sun; ⑨) One of Aragón's best tapas bars, La Tasca de Ana has tempting options lined up along the bar, more choices cooked to order and a carefully chosen list of local wines. Check out its *tapas mas solicitados* (most popular orders) listed on the blackboard. Top contenders include the *tostada* (toast) topped with goat's cheese and blueberries.

Crepería El Bretón   CREPERIE €
(☑ 974 35 63 76; Calle de Ferrenal 3; mains €7-12; ⊙ 11am-3.30pm & 7pm-midnight Tue-Sun; ⑭) Serving sweet and salty crêpes and *galettes* that are faithful to old Brittany recipes, this intimate French-run place also serves salads, tapas, Brittany cider (better than the house wine) and an excellent *menú Bretón* for €10.50.

La Casa del Arco   VEGETARIAN €
(☑ 974 36 44 48; www.lacasadelarco.blogspot.com; Calle de San Nicolás 4; mains €5-10, set menu €12; ⑰) A haven of imaginative vegetarian food with a delightfully alternative ambience, La Casa del Arco has an excellent set menu with eight choices of starter and main.

Restaurante El Portón   ARAGONESE €€
(☑ 974 35 58 54; Plaza del Marqués de la Cadena 1; mains €15-28; ⊙ 1.30-4pm & 8.30pm-midnight Thu-Tue) Located in a little tree-shaded plaza, this classy venue serves haute-cuisine versions of Aragonese fare. Foie gras is something of a speciality – try the bison stuffed with foie. Reservations essential.

Gorbea   TAPAS €€
(www.bargorbea.com; Calle Mayor 24; pinchos from €2, miniaturas €5; ⊙ noon-4pm & 7-11.30pm) An

---

ℹ **MOVING ON?**

For tips, recommendations and reviews, head to shop.lonelyplanet.com to purchase a downloadable PDF of the Pyrenees chapter from Lonely Planet's *France* guide.

upbeat contemporary bar with excellent Basque-style *pinchos* (snacks), *miniaturas* (small dishes) like *kokotyas al pil pil* (hake in a chilli-spiced sauce), plus good size *raciones* to share.

🔒 Shopping

Confitería Echeto FOOD
(Plaza de la Catedral 4; ⊙ 9.30am-2.30pm & 4.30-9pm Mon-Sat) This place has been in business since 1890 – take a peek at the original National cash register. The cakes here are unmatched in town. Also sells fancy tins of specialty sweets.

ℹ Information

Tourist Office (☑ 974 36 00 98; Plaza de San Pedro 11-13; ⊙ 9am-1.30pm & 4.30-7.30pm Mon-Sat)

ℹ Getting There & Away

Regular **Alosa** (www.alosa.es) buses go to Huesca (€7.70, 1¼ hours) and Zaragoza (€15.65, 2¼ hours) most days from the central **bus station** (☑ 974 35 50 60; Plaza de Biscós). Twice daily trains go to Huesca (€8.10, two hours) and Zaragoza (€15, two hours).

Valle de Tena

From the regional centre of Biescas, north of Sabiñánigo, the A136 climbs gently towards the French border.

Leading deep into the mountains, a narrow road up the Valle de Tena runs 8km past the ski resort of Panticosa to the Panticosa Resort, a stunning complex that includes the four-star **Hotel Continental** (☑ 974 48 71 61; www.panticosa.com; r from €100; P ✳ 🛜 🛆); three restaurants including the sophisticated **Restaurante del Lago** (meals from €65); bars; a casino; and the **Balneario** (☑ 974 48 71 61; www.balneariodepanticosa.com; baths/massages from €21/40; ⊙ 11am-midnight), a luxurious spa complex designed by star architect Rafael Moneao. The setting is stunning, alongside a lake in the enclosed valley high in the Pyrenees.

Returning to the main A136, **Sallent de Gállego**, 3.5km north of the Panticosa turnoff, is a lovely stone village with a bubbling brook running through it.

From Jaca, one or two daily buses wind over to Panticosa and Formigal (€5.25, two hours). The N260 leaves the valley at Biescas and follows a pretty route to Torla and Aínsa.

Parque Nacional de Ordesa y Monte Perdido

This is where the Spanish Pyrenees really take your breath away. At the heart of it all is a dragon's back of limestone peaks skirting the French border, with a south-eastward spur. Monte Perdido (3348m), the third-highest peak in the Pyrenees, is in the park. Deep valleys slice down from the high ground. Most were carved by glaciers and at their heads lie bowl-like glacial *circos* (cirques) backed by spectacular curtain walls of rock. Chief among the valleys are Pineta (east), Escuaín (southeast), Bellos (south), Ordesa (southwest), Bujaruelo (west) and Gavarnie (north, in France).

ℹ Information

Centro de Visitantes de Torla (☑ 974 48 64 72; Torla; ⊙ 9am-2pm & 4-7pm)
Centro de Visitantes de Tella (☑ 974 48 64 72; Tella; ⊙ 9am-2pm & 3.15-6pm daily Apr-Oct, Sat & Sun Nov-Mar)
Bielsa (☑ 974 50 10 43; Bielsa; ⊙ 9am-2pm & 3.15-6pm daily Apr-Oct, Sat & Sun Nov-Mar; 🛜)
Escalona (☑ 974 50 51 31; Escalona; ⊙ 9am-2pm & 3.15-6pm daily Apr-Oct, Sat & Sun Nov-Mar)

MAPS

If you're keen to traverse the park along the GR11, **Editorial Alpina** (www.editorialalpina.com) produces excellent maps for walkers. Another good reference is the guidebook *Through the Spanish Pyrenees: GR11 – A Trekking Guidebook* by Paul Lucia and available from **Cicerone Press** (www.cicerone.co.uk).

RULES & REGULATIONS

Bivouacing is allowed only above certain altitudes (1800m to 2500m, depending on the sector); ask at one of the information centres for details. Swimming in rivers or lakes, mountain biking, fishing and fires are banned.

ℹ Getting There & Away

The main entry point into the park is **Torla**, 3km south of the southwest corner of the national park.

From **Escalona**, 11km north of Aínsa on the A138, a minor paved road heads northwest across to **Sarvisé**. This road crosses the park's southern tip, with a narrow, sinuous section winding up the dramatic Bellos valley and giving access to walks in the spectacular Cañón de Añisclo (the upper reaches of the Bellos valley).

From **Bielsa** a 12km paved road runs up the Valle de Pineta in the park's northeastern corner.

Parque Nacional de Ordesa y Monte Perdido

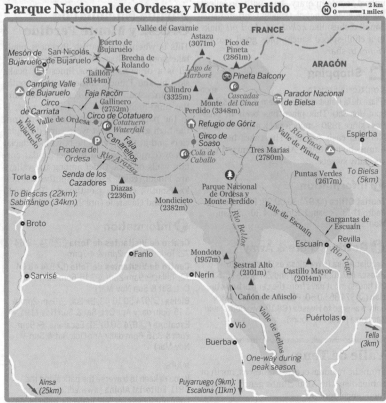

Private vehicles may not drive from Torla to Pradera de Ordesa during Easter week and from July to mid-September. During these periods a shuttle bus (one way/return €3/4.50) runs between Torla's Centro de Visitantes and Pradera de Ordesa. A maximum of 1800 people are allowed in this sector of the park at any one time.

During the same periods, a one-way system is enforced on part of the Escalona–Sarvisé road. From the Puyarruego turn-off, 2km out of Escalona, to a point about 1km after the road diverges from the Bellos valley, only northwestward traffic is allowed. Southeastward traffic uses an alternative, more southerly road.

Torla

POP 320

Torla is a lovely alpine-style village of stone houses with slate roofs, although it does get overrun in July and August. Walkers use Torla as a gateway to the national park, but the setting is also delightful, with the houses clustered above the Río Ara under a backdrop of the national park's mountains. In your ramblings around town, make for the 13th-century Iglesia de San Salvador; there are fine views from the small park on the church's northern side.

🛏 Sleeping

Hotel Villa Russell   HOTEL €€
(☎974 48 67 70; www.hotelvillarussell.com; Calle de Capuvita; s/d/apt €73/90/142; ☺Mar-Nov; ℗🛜) The rooms won't win a style contest, but they're enormous and have sofas, microwaves and hydromassage showers. There's a similarly well-kitted-out, two-bedroom apartment on the top floor. On-site parking costs €6 and there's a Jacuzzi and sauna.

Hotel Villa de Torla   HOTEL €€
(☎974 48 61 56; www.hotelvilladetorla.com; Plaza de Aragón 1; s €35-45, d €52-69; ☺mid-Mar–Dec; 🛁) The rooms here are tidy – some are spacious

HIKING ROUTES

For a range of walking options in Parque Nacional de Ordesa y Monte Perdido (www.senderos.turismodearagon.com), pick up a copy of the *Senderos* maps and route descriptions for the four sectors (Ordesa, Añisclo, Escuaín and Pineta) from any of the information offices. They include maps and route descriptions for the following trails:

Circo de Soaso A classic day walk that follows the Valle de Ordesa to Circo de Soaso, a rocky balcony with the centrepiece Cola de Caballo (Horsetail) waterfall.

Refugio de Góriz & Monte Perdido Fit walkers can climb a series of steep switchbacks (part of the GR11) to Circo de Soaso and up to the Refugio de Góriz, at 2200m. From there, Monte Perdido is a serious undertaking that requires mountaineering skills, crampons and ice axes.

Faja Racón, Circo de Cotatuero & Faja Canarellos This walk takes you along spectacular high-level paths on the north flank of the Valle de Ordesa.

Brecha de Rolando The cool-headed may climb part of the wall of the Circo de Cotatuero by the Clavijas de Cotatuero, a set of 32 iron pegs hammered into the rock. From here you are about 2½ hours' march from the Brecha de Rolando (Roldán; 2807m), a dramatic, breezy gap in the mountain wall on the French frontier.

Puerto de Bujaruelo The GR11 describes a 6km arc up the very pretty Valle de Bujaruelo to San Nicolás de Bujaruelo. From there an east–northeast path leads in about three hours (with a 950m ascent) up to the Puerto de Bujaruelo on the border with France.

Southern Gorges The Cañón de Añisclo is a gaping wound in the earth's fabric. Energetic walkers can start from the Refugio de Góriz and descend the gorge from the north, from where numerous trails fan out into the mountains. The Gargantas de Escuaín is a smaller-scale but still-dramatic gorge on the Río Yaga, further east.

Balcón de Pineta This challenging hike begins close to the Parador Nacional de Bielsa and, after the waterfalls of the Cascadas del Cinca, climbs via a series of steep switchbacks up to the 'Pineta Balcony' for stunning glacier and mountain views.

and stylish, others have floral bedspreads and look a little tired. But the undoubted highlight is the swimming pool and the bar terrace, from where there are lovely views.

Eating

Most of the village's hotels have restaurants with *menús* from €12 to €17.

La Brecha ARAGONESE €
(Calle Francia; mains €8-10; ⊙1.30-4pm & 8-10.30pm) Simple homestyle dishes like *jarretes* (hock of ham) are the speciality of this bustling local bar and restaurant. Don't forget to try the homemade *pacharan* (traditional local liquor said to help with digestion). Open all year – another bonus.

Restaurante el Duende ARAGONESE €€
(☎974 48 60 32; www.elduenderestaurante.com; Calle de la Iglesia; mains €15-22; ⊙1.30-3pm & 8-10pm, Sat & Sun Jan-Apr; ⊛) Best restaurant in town with fine local cuisine, an extensive menu and eclectic decor in a lovely 19th-century building. Typical meaty dishes include wild boar with leeks and mushrooms.

❶ Getting There & Away

One daily bus operated by **Alosa** (☎902 210700; www.alosa.es) connects Torla to Aínsa (€4.30, one hour).

Valle de Bujaruelo

North of Torla and shadowing the eastern boundary of the park, the pretty Valle de Bujaruelo is another good base.

⊨ Sleeping

Camping Valle de Bujaruelo CAMPGROUND €
(☎974 48 63 48; www.campingvalledebujaruelo. com; per person/tent/car €4.50/4.50/4.50, r €40-62; ⊙Easter–mid-Oct; P⊛) This campsite, 3.5km up the Valle de Bujaruelo, features a refuge with bunks, a restaurant and a supermarket. The setting's lovely, the facilities well maintained.

Mesón de Bujaruelo REFUGE €

(☏974 48 64 12; www.mesondebujaruelo.com; dm/d incl breakfast €18.50/52, half-board per person €31.50-39.50; ☺Apr-Oct) This old hostelry provides bunks and meals in a pretty spot by the Puerto de Bujaruelo. Accommodation is mountain basic, but it's all about location here. Approach is via a 6km, or so, dirt track.

Torla to Aínsa

The N260 from Torla to Aínsa runs for 44km through the lovely foothills of the Pyrenees. At around the halfway point, watch for the lookout over the Río Ara to the evocative ruins of Jánovas, a village abandoned in the 1950s. If you want a closer look take the dirt track after around 500m, down to the Rió Ara and cross (by foot) the signposted *puente colgante* (hanging bridge).

🛏 Sleeping

Casa de San Martín HISTORIC HOTEL €€€

(☏974 50 31 05; www.casadesanmartin.com; s/d from €132/165; ☺Apr-Nov; P ✱ 🖥) Along a dirt track 5km off the main Torla–Aínsa road (take the sign for San Martín de la Solana), Casa de San Martín is a stunning rural retreat. The handsome stone house has been beautifully renovated and the rooms are temples to good taste without being overdone. Meals (set menus €38.50) are exceptional and the setting is tranquil and picturesque.

Aínsa

POP 2230

The beautiful hilltop village of medieval Aínsa, which stands above the modern town of the same name, is one of Aragón's gems, a stunning village hewn from uneven stone. From its perch, you'll have panoramic views of the mountains, particularly the great rock bastion of La Peña Montañesa.

◎ Sights

Simply wander down through the village along either Calle de Santa Cruz or Calle Mayor, pausing in the handful of artsy shops en route; note the drain pipes carved into the shape of gargoyles.

Castle CASTLE

(ecomuseum admission €4; ☺ecomuseum 11am-2pm Wed-Fri, 10am-2pm & 4-7pm Sat & Sun Easter-Oct) The castle and fortifications off the western end of the Plaza de San Salvador mostly date from the 1600s, though the main tower is 11th century; there are some reasonable views from the wall. It contains a fascinating ecomuseum on Pyrenean fauna (the focus is on the endangered lammergeier, with some caged birds of prey out the back) and the Espacio del Geoparque de Sobrarbe (www.geoparquepirineos.com; ☺9.30am-2pm & 4-7pm daily) FREE with displays on the region's intriguing geology, as well as good views from the tower.

Iglesia de Santa María CHURCH

(belfry admission €1; ☺belfry 11am-1.30pm & 4-7pm Sat & Sun) This restored Romanesque church lights up when you pop €1 into a box, with five minutes of Gregorian chants thrown in. The crypt and Gothic cloister are charming; you can climb the belfry for glorious views of the mountains to the north and down over the terracotta rooftops of the old town.

⚑ Festivals & Events

Festival Internacional de Música MUSIC

(www.festivalcastillodeainsa.com) In July, Aínsa hosts this month-long festival with predominantly Spanish and a few international music acts in the castle grounds.

WHAT'S COOKING IN ARAGÓN?

The kitchens and tables of Aragón are dominated by meat. The region's cold harsh winds create the ideal conditions for curing *jamón* (ham), a top tapa here; some of the best can be found in no-frills bars like Teruel's Aqui Teruel (p392). Likewise, another meaty favourite, *jarretes* (hock of ham or shanks) is available in simple village restaurants like Torla's La Brecha (p381), while heartier *ternasco* (suckling lamb) is generally served as a steak or ribs with potatoes – try it at Bodegas del Sobrarbe (p383) in Aínsa.

Other popular dishes include *conejo a la montañesa* (rabbit mountain-style) served at Echo's Restaurante Gaby (p373), while (phew!) vegetarians can seek out tasty *pochas viudas* (whitebean stew with peppers, tomatoes and onion), a popular starter at restaurants like La Cocina del Principal (p372) in Sos del Rey Católico.

🛏 Sleeping

Albergue Mora de Nuei   HOSTEL €
(☑974 51 06 14; www.alberguemoradenuei.com;
Calle del Portal de Abajo 2; dm €15-17, d incl breakfast €50-60; 🛜) At the lower end of the old
town, facing onto Plaza de San Salvador,
this fine place is one of Aragón's best hostels. Rooms are colourful, and there's a roof
terrace, an atmospheric basement bar, good
food, and a regular calendar of live music
and other cultural events.

Hotel Sanchez   HOTEL €
(☑974 50 00 14; www.hotelsanchez.com; Avenida
Sobrarbe 10; r €50; 🅿✳@🛜♿) Located in
the new town, this great-value place offers
tidy small rooms with light pine furniture,
cheery blue fabrics and superb high-pressure
showers. There's a popular bar and cafeteria
downstairs mainly frequented by the local
card-playing *pensionistas*.

★ Hotel los Siete Reyes   HOTEL €€
(☑974 50 06 81; www.lossietereyes.com; Plaza
Mayor; d €70-120; ✳🛜) Set in one of the most
charming stone buildings overlooking Plaza
Mayor, this temple of style has stunning
bathrooms, polished floorboards, exposed
stone walls and some lovely period detail
wedded to a contemporary designer look.
The rooms are all spacious and some have
lovely mountain views, while others look
out over the Plaza Mayor. Breakfast (€8) is
served in the former wine cellar.

Posada Real   RURAL HOTEL €€
(☑974 50 09 77; www.posadareal.com; Plaza Mayor
6; d from €70; ✳🛜) A tastefully renovated
noble mansion, this *posada* has large rooms
and exposed wooden beams; some rooms
have four-poster beds and/or good views. It's
a few steps down off Plaza Mayor.

🍴 Eating

★ La Tea   ITALIAN €
(Plaza Mayor 21; pizzas €6.50-8.50; ⊙noon-4pm
& 7pm-midnight; ♿) Justifiably popular, La
Tea offers crispy thin-based pizzas with a
vast range of toppings. Alternative choices
include a handful of superb pasta dishes,
topped *tostadas* and vast salads. Head for
the sprawl of tables and chairs on the plaza.

L'Alfil   TAPAS €
(Calle Traversa; raciones €5.80-18.50; ⊙11am-4pm
& 7pm-midnight Thu-Tue May-Oct, shorter hours
Nov-Apr) This pretty little cafe-bar, with floral
accompaniment to its outside tables, is in a

WORTH A TRIP

SPAIN'S OLDEST MONASTERY

Around 5km northeast of Aínsa, the
quiet and uniformly stone-built hamlet
of El Pueyo de Araguás is home to
the Monasterio de San Victorián;
although it was much modified in the
16th century, its Romanesque origins
ensure that it can lay claim to being the
oldest monastery in Spain. Also in the
village, the Casas Coronas date to
1519 and are among the oldest houses
in the region.

side street along from the church. It has a
heap of *raciones* that are more creative than
you'll find elsewhere, from ostrich chorizo,
snails and deer sausage to wild-boar pâté
and cured duck. Also specialises in local
herbal liquors.

Restaurante Callizo   CONTEMPORARY SPANISH €€
(☑974 50 03 85; Plaza Mayor; set menus €25-42;
⊙1-3pm & 7-11pm Tue-Sat, 1-4pm Sun; ♿) This
place cleverly combines traditional cuisine
with culinary innovation on its constantly
changing menu. The set menus are gastronomic journeys of the highest order; it also
offers a (pricey) children's menu.

Bodegas del Sobrarbe   ARAGONESE €€
(www.bodegasdelsobrarbe.com; Plaza Mayor 2;
mains €15-22; ⊙noon-2pm & 7-11pm Apr-Dec)
This fine longstanding restaurant off the
southeastern corner of Plaza Mayor offers
meaty and traditional Aragonese fare, like
wild boar and roast suckling lamb, as well as
a few fish dishes.

🛍 Shopping

Sabores de Pueblo   FOOD, WINE
(www.saboresdepueblo.com; Plaza Mayor 15;
⊙10am-2pm & 3.30-8pm) Fronting onto the
northeastern corner of Plaza Mayor, this
gourmet food shop has tempting wines,
cheeses and other local goodies.

ℹ Information

Municipal Tourist Office (☑974 50 07 67;
www.ainsasobrarbe.net; Avenida Pirenáica 1;
⊙9am-9pm) Located in the new town down
the hill.
Regional Tourist Office (☑974 50 05 12;
www.turismosobrarbe.com; Plaza del Castillo 1,
Torre Nordeste; ⊙10am-2pm & 4-7pm) Extremely helpful; within the castle walls.

ℹ Getting There & Away

Alosa (☎ 902 210700; www.alosa.es) runs daily buses to/from Barbastro (€5.80, one hour) and Torla (€4.30, one hour).

Benasque

POP 2240 / ELEV 1140M

Aragón's northeastern corner is crammed with the highest and shapeliest peaks in the Pyrenees, and Benasque, a comparatively modern alpine-style town, is perfectly sited to serve as gateway to the high valleys. Even in midsummer these epic mountains can be capped with snow and ice. Northeast of Benasque, the Pyrenees' highest peak, the Pico de Aneto (3404m), towers above the massif.

🏃 Activities

This mostly protected region offers walkers almost limitless options and climbers a wide choice of peaks.

Compañía de Guías Valle de Benasque
ADVENTURE SPORTS

(☎ 974 55 14 25; www.guiasbenasque.com; Avenida de Francia; 🖈) This company has an impressive 20 years of experience and offers a range of activities and courses, including hiking, skiing, snowboarding and rock climbing. It can also supply all the necessary kit and equipment.

Barrabés
ADVENTURE SPORTS

(www.barrabes.com; Avenida de Francia; ⊙ 10.30am-1.30pm & 4.30-9pm; 🖈) This really is the one-stop sports store in town, selling equipment and sportswear for just about every activity you can think of. It also carries a good range of guides and maps and has an online shopping option.

Meridiano Cero
ADVENTURE SPORTS

(www.guiaspirineos.com; 🖈) A local operator which offers guides and courses in every-

---

WHITE-WATER RAFTING

Southwest of Benasque the village of Campo is a major centre for white-water rafting on the Río Ésera. Operators line the main street of town. One good choice is Sin Fronteras (☎ 974 55 01 77; www.sinfronterasadventure.com; Carretera Benasque 1), which also offers kayaking and canoeing.

---

thing from skiing to mountain climbing. Book through the website.

🛏 Sleeping

During the ski season most places offer packages with *media pensión* (half-board).

Hotel Aneto
HOTEL €€

(☎ 974 55 10 61; www.hotelesvalero.com; Avenida de Francia 4; d incl breakfast from €104; ⊙ Jun-Mar; 🖘) A cut above the usual lodge-style accommodation that is a Benasque speciality, Hotel Aneto sports hardwood floors and a contemporary designer look.

Hotel Avenida
HOTEL €€

(☎ 974 55 11 26; www.h-avenida.com; Avenida de los Tilos 14; s/d from €55/70) Rooms here are handsomely furnished and the service is friendly. There's a restaurant attached and there are cheaper room rates for longer stays.

🍴 Eating

The best places are along Avenida de los Tilos and its continuation, Calle Mayor.

La Parrilla
ARAGONESE €€

(☎ 974 55 11 34; Carretera de Francia; mains €12-20; ⊙ 1-4pm & 8.30-11pm; 🖈) A longstanding favourite dating from 1973, the dining room is a cozy clutter of hanging wall plates and family portraits. Although roasted meats are the speciality, the menu is expansive with dishes ranging from ravioli with mushrooms and caramelised apple to grilled frogs' legs (the French border is just up the road).

El Veedor de Viandas
CONTEMPORARY ARAGONESE €€

(www.elveedordeviandas.com; Avenida Los Tilos; pinchos €1.70, mains €8-12; ⊙ noon-2.30pm & 6-11pm Thu-Tue Jun-Sep, shorter hours Oct-May; 🖈) A welcoming informal space combining a gourmet deli, bodega, tapas bar and restaurant. *Pinchos* (snacks) and *tostadas* have innovative toppings like *manzana con foie* (apple and pâté) and oyster mushrooms with bacon and garlic mayonnaise. Plus there are salads, carpaccios, egg-based dishes and belly-filling *cazuelitas* (ministews).

Restaurante el Fogaril
ARAGONESE €€

(☎ 974 55 16 12; Calle Mayor 5; mains €12-20; ⊙ 1-4pm & 8.30-10.30pm) Part of the adjacent and popular Hotel Ciria, this elegant restaurant serves outstanding Aragonese fare. Its specialities include young venison and stuffed partridge, *cozal* (small deer) and freshwater fish.

ℹ Information

Tourist Office (📞974 55 12 89; www.turismo benasque.com; Calle San Sebastián 5; ⏰9.30am-1pm & 4.30-8pm)

ℹ Getting There & Away

Two buses operate Monday to Saturday, and one runs on Sunday, from Huesca (€13.15, 2½ hours).

Castejón de Sos

South of Benasque, the village of Castejón de Sos is a paragliding centre with accommodation. For more information, try www.parapentepirineos.com and www.volarencastejon.com.

Upper Ésera Valley & Maladeta Massif

North of Benasque, the A139 continues paved for about 12km. About 10km from Benasque, a side road leads 6km east along the pretty upper Ésera valley, ending at La Besurta, with a hut selling drinks and some food.

A little under halfway from the A139 to La Besurta, Hospital de Benasque (📞974 55 20 12; www.llanosdelhospital.com; s/d incl breakfast from €80/100; 🅿@🛜) is a large mountain lodge surrounded by handsome peaks. There's a bar, restaurant, spa and wellness centre, and rooms have a comfortable, luxurious feel.

South of La Besurta is the great 3308m Maladeta massif, a superb challenge for experienced climbers culminating in Pico de Aneto (3404m), the highest peak in the Pyrenees.

Alquézar

POP 300 / ELEV 670M

Picturesque Alquézar, 23km northwest of Barbastro, would be worth visiting for its own sake – it's one of Aragón's more handsome villages. But Alquézar also means *descenso de barrancos* (canyoning), which involves following canyons downstream by whatever means available – walking, abseiling, jumping, swimming, even diving.

⬛ WORTH A TRIP

TOP DRIVE: THE SIERRA DE GUARA

North of Alquézar, the A2205 road to Aínsa via Colungo and Arcusa is a delightful drive through pre-Pyrenean canyon country in the Sierra de Guara. There are some fine lookouts, including the spectacular Mirador del Vero (also signposted as Barranca de Portiarcha) – watch for Egyptian vultures, imperial eagles and lammergeiers circling high overhead.

◉ Sights

Colegiata de Santa María CASTLE, MONASTERY (admission €2.50; ⏰11am-1.30pm & 4.30-7.30pm Wed-Mon) Alquézar is crowned by this large castle-monastery. Originally built as an *alcázar* (fortress) by the Arabs in the 9th century, it was subsequently conquered and replaced by an Augustinian monastery in 1099. Remnants are still visible. The columns within its delicate cloister are crowned by carved capitals depicting biblical scenes, and the walls are covered with spellbinding murals. On the upper level is a museum of sacred art.

🏃 Activities

The main canyoning season is mid-June to mid-September and prices, which vary depending on the number of people and the graded difficulty of the trip, generally include gear, guide and insurance – check the websites of the various companies for details. Most of the agencies also offer rafting, trekking, rock climbing and other activities. Recommended places are lined up in a row at the entrance to the village.

Avalancha ADVENTURE SPORTS (📞974 31 82 99; www.avalancha.org; Calle Arrabal) Activities include trekking for €50/80 per half/full day and rock climbing for €120 per half-day.

Guías Boira ADVENTURE SPORTS (📞974 31 89 74; www.guiasboira.com; Calle Arrabal) Offers two-day canyoning packages for €85, plus accommodation.

Vertientes ADVENTURE SPORTS (📞974 31 83 54; www.vertientesaventura.com; Calle San Gregorio 5) Offers rafting from €37, canyoning from €68 and half-day treks from €58.

DON'T MISS

WINE TASTING & TOURS IN SOMONTANO

Somontano is Aragón's most prestigious wine-growing region. Centred on Barbastro, Somontano has more than 30 vineyards producing reds, whites and rosés from 13 different types of foreign and local grape varieties.

The tourist office (☑ 974 30 83 50; turismo@barbastro.org; Avenida de la Merced 64; ☉ 10am-2pm & 4.30-7.30pm Tue-Sat Sep-Jun, daily Jul & Aug) in Barbastro has brochures in Spanish, English and French outlining the various wineries that can be visited for sales, tours and/or tastings. Always ring ahead to arrange a time – the tourist office will help you make the calls if you turn up in person.

Part of the same complex as the tourist office, the Espacio de Vino is an interpretation centre devoted to Somontano wines with audiovisual displays, interactive grape-aroma displays and occasional wine tastings (€10 per person). Attached to the tourist office is also a wine shop. Both places keep the same hours as the tourist office.

Another excellent resource is the website www.rutadelvinosomontano.com, which maps out possible wine itineraries through the region. The website also has details of the Bus del Vino Somontano, a monthly all-day bus tour of selected bodegas from Zaragoza/Huesca (€28/26).

🛏 Sleeping

Albergue Rural de Guara   HOSTEL €
(☑ 974 31 83 96; www.albergueruraldeguara.com; Calle Pilaseras; dm €14.50) This cheerfully run *albergue* is perched up above the village with fine views from the surrounds. Breakfast is available for €5.50 and staff can arrange picnic lunches (€8).

Hotel Maribel   BOUTIQUE HOTEL €€
(☑ 974 31 89 79; www.hotelmaribel.es; Calle Arrabal; d incl breakfast from €130; ☉ Feb-Dec; ❄ 🖐) This boutique hotel has plenty of charm and, while the decor won't be to everyone's taste (following a wine theme and ranging from gorgeous to vaguely kitsch), every room is supremely comfortable. If there's no one at reception, try the nearby Restaurante Casa Gervasio.

Hotel Villa de Alquézar   HOTEL €€
(☑ tel/fax 974 31 84 16; www.villadealquezar.com; Calle Pedro Arenal Cavero 12; d incl breakfast €69-110; 🅿🖐) This is a lovely place with plenty of style in its airy rooms; several sport great views and there are period touches throughout. The most expensive rooms on the top floor are large and have wonderful covered balconies – they're perfect for watching the sun set over town while nursing a bottle of Somontano wine.

🍴 Eating

Restaurants line up along the *mirador* (lookout) section of Calle Arrabal.

⭐ **Casa Pardina**   CONTEMPORARY ARAGONESE €€
(☑ 974 31 84 25; www.casapardina.com; Calle Medio; set menus €27-35; ☉ 1.30-3pm & 8-10pm May-Oct, shorter hours Nov-Apr) A very special restaurant where the food exudes creativity and the setting (in the family home of the owner) is all soothing stone-work, twinkling chandeliers, summer terraces and breathtaking views. The menu is subtle yet classy with dishes such as oxtail with chestnuts, and stewed venison with dates and honey. Reservations recommended.

La Marmita   CONTEMPORARY ARAGONESE €€
(www.lamarmitadeguara.com; Avenida San Hipólito; pinchos from €2, set menu €22.50; ☉ 2-4pm & 7-10pm May-Oct, shorter hours Nov-Apr; 🖐) Located at the entrance to the village, La Marmita has breathtaking views of the Colegiata. Choose between piled-high *pinchos* in the bar or the more expansive *menú del día* in the dining room. A speciality is *caracoles* (snails). If this sounds a mite indigestible, there are also innovative takes on standard favourites like baked cod with potatoes and truffles.

ℹ Information

Tourist Office (☑ 974 31 89 40; www.alquezar.org; Calle Arrabal; ☉ 9.30am-1.30pm & 4.30-8pm daily Jun-Oct, Sat & Sun Nov-May) Runs guided tours (€3.50) three times daily in summer and can arrange audioguides (€4).

❶ Getting There & Away

There's a daily bus to Alquézar from Barbastro (€2.75) Monday to Saturday. Check with the tourist office for times – it doubles as the local school bus and times change during holidays.

Huesca

POP 52,440

Huesca is a provincial capital in more than name, a town that shutters down during the afternoon hours and stirs back into life in the evenings. That said, its old centre retains considerable appeal, it has excellent accommodation and its location in north-central Aragón can serve as a launch pad for the Aragonese high country.

◉ Sights

Catedral de Santa María CATHEDRAL
(Plaza de la Catedral; cathedral free, museum & tower €4; ☉cathedral times vary, museum & tower 10.30am-2pm & 4-8pm Mon-Fri, 10.30am-2pm Sat) This Gothic cathedral is one of Aragón's great surprises. The richly carved main portal dates from 1300; the attached Museo Diocesano contains some extraordinary frescoes and painted altarpieces; and the stately interior features a superb 16th-century alabaster retablo by Damián Forment showing scenes from Christ's crucifixion. To round off your visit, climb the 180 steps of the bell tower for 360-degree views all the way to the Pyrenees.

Museo de Huesca MUSEUM
(Plaza Universidad 1; ☉10am-2pm & 5-8pm Tue-Sat, 10am-2pm Sun) FREE The octagonal city museum contains a well-displayed collection (labels in Spanish only) covering the archaeology and art of Huesca province, including eight works by Goya.

Iglesia de San Pedro El Viejo CHURCH
(Plaza de San Pedro; adult/concession €2.50/1.50; ☉10am-1.30pm & 4-7.30pm Mon-Sat, 11am-noon & 1-1.30pm Sun) The church of San Pedro is 12th-century Romanesque, its cloister adorned with 38 beautifully carved Romanesque capitals.

🛏 Sleeping

★ **Hostal Un Punto Chic** HOSTAL €
(☑974 24 17 74; www.unpuntochic.com; Calle Joaquín Costa 20; s/d €39/49; ❄☎) This stunningly renovated *hostal* is brought to you by the owners of nearby La Posada de la Luna.

There are slick furnishings and cutting-edge decoration (photos take up entire walls), and some rooms even have an exercise machine or a massage chair. Best of all, the hotel quality comes at the price of a *hostal*.

La Posada de la Luna BOUTIQUE HOTEL €€
(☑974 24 08 57; www.posadadelaluna.com; Calle Joaquin Costa 10; s/d €61/69; ᴾ❄☎) This attractive small hotel incorporates some original features of old Huesca architecture with a whimsical but contemporary feel, designer bathrooms and hydromassage showers. It's a comfortable, charming place, although some of the rooms are on the small size.

🍴 Eating

Tatau Bistro TAPAS €
(www.tatau.es; Calle San Lorenzo 4; tapas from €2.80, raciones from €3.80; ☉noon-midnight Tue-Sat, to 4pm Sun) This place has a bright contemporary look with a whiff of a '50s diner about it (or is it the waitresses hair-dos?). Daily tapas and *raciones* are chalked up on a blackboard and range from more ambitious dishes such as steak tartare to the traditional standard *croquetas de jamón* (ham croquettes).

El Origen ARAGONESE €€
(☑974 22 97 45; Plaza del Justicia 4; set menus €15-39.50; ☉1-4pm & 7-11pm Thu-Tue) 🍴 Ignore the inauspicious setting on a somewhat drab modern square – this restaurant is an oasis of elegance and fine dining, with set menus

---

DANCING IN THE DESERT

The rural town of Fraga in the relentless flatlands between Zaragoza and the Mediterranean coast is the unlikely locale for Florida 135 (www.f135.com; Calle Sotet 2; admission €13; ☉from 11.30pm Sat), the temple of Spanish techno. The windowless 3000-sqmetre, graffiti-strewn space is the most recent incarnation of a dance hall that's been going since 1942. Busloads of clubbers arrive for the club's main Saturday-night sessions. In mid-July, Fraga hosts the Monegros Desert Festival (www.monegrosfestival.com; festival pass €70) attracting dozens of Spanish and internationally renowned DJs and bands for 22 hours of nonstop music on five simultaneous stages.

that vary from traditional Aragonese to the more innovative and contemporary. Ecological produce is used as far as possible. Reservations recommended.

❶ Information

Tourist Office (✆974 29 21 70; www.huesca turismo.com; Plaza López Allué 1; ⊙9am-2pm & 4-8pm) Runs daily guided tours of the historic centre (adult/concession €2/1) from mid-June until mid-September, and vintage bus tours (adult/concession/child under 12 €5/2.50/free) during the same period to the Castillo de Loarre, Los Mallos and the Sierra de Guara.

❶ Getting There & Away

Alosa (✆974 21 07 00; www.alosa.es) runs numerous daily buses to/from Zaragoza (€7.70, 1¼ hours), Jaca (€7.70, 1¼ hours) and Barbastro (€4.60, 50 minutes), with a twice-daily service Monday to Saturday to Benasque (€13.15, 2¾ hours), running once on Sunday.

Nine trains a day run to/from Zaragoza (from €7.05, one hour), including two high-speed AVE services (€12.05, 40 minutes). There are also AVE services to/from Madrid (€57, 2¼ hours, one daily), as well as services to Jaca (€8.10, 2¼ hours).

Loarre

The evocative **Castillo de Loarre** (www. castillodeloarre.com; admission with/without tour €5.50/3.90; ⊙10am-2pm & 4-8pm; P⛟) broods above the southern plains across which Islamic raiders once rode. Raised in the 11th century by Sancho III of Navarra and Sancho Ramírez of Aragón, its resemblance to a crusader castle has considerable resonance with those times. Although the dungeons and towers are no longer open to visitors for safety reasons, there is still plenty to see including a Romanesque chapel and crypt.

The castle is a 5km drive or a 2km, one-hour, uphill walk by the PR-HU105 footpath, from the village of Loarre, 35km northwest of Huesca.

Birdwatchers note that this is also an excellent spot to spy griffon and Egyptian vultures and red kites circling overhead.

Just one early-morning daily bus runs to Loarre village from Huesca (€3.50, 40 minutes) Monday to Friday.

Los Mallos

After a rather unexciting patch along the Huesca–Pamplona road, you come to a dramatic area along the Río Gállego north of Ayerbe. On the eastern bank, huge rock towers known as Los Mallos (Mallets) rise up – they wouldn't look out of place in the Grand Canyon and are popular with serious rock climbers – and griffon vultures (who nest here). For a closer look, head for picturesque Riglos. On the approach to town look for the plaque with the sobering list of names, dating from the 1960s, of climbers who have perished climbing the near vertical main rockface.

THE SOUTH

Don't be deceived by the monotony of the vast sweep of countryside that's immediately south of Zaragoza. Head further south or southeast and the landscape takes on a certain drama and shelters some of inland Spain's most intriguing towns and villages.

Daroca

POP 2310

Daroca, a sleepy medieval town, was a onetime Islamic stronghold and, later, a Christian fortress town in the early medieval wars against Castilla. Its well-preserved old quarter is laden with historic references and the crumbling old city walls encircle the hilltops; the walls once boasted 114 military towers.

◉ Sights & Activities

Iglesia Colegiata de Santa María CHURCH (⊙11am-1pm & 5.30-7.30pm Tue-Sat, 5.30-7.30pm Sun) FREE The pretty Plaza de España, at the top of the village, is dominated by this ornate Romanesque Mudéjar Renaissance–style church, which boasts a lavish interior and organ. The 16th-century Gothic Puerta del Perdón rounds out the church's impressive portfolio of European architectural styles. Overall, it's one of Daroca's most appealing (and unexpected) gems.

Iglesia de San Miguel CHURCH Up the hill west of the town centre, this 12th-century church is an austerely beautiful masterpiece of Romanesque architecture, but its greatest treasures are the Gothic frescoes within. Sadly, the church is kept closed, except for guided tours run by the tourist office or for concerts during the town's festivals.

Guided Walks
WALKING TOURS

(guided tours €2-4; ⊙11am & 4.30pm Tue-Sun) The best of the self-guided walks offered by the tourist office is the 45-minute Ruta Monumental, which gives a wonderful feel for the town and is well signposted. The other is the two-hour Ruta del Castillo y Las Murallas, a far more strenuous undertaking that climbs up to and follows the walls. The tourist office also organises fascinating guided tours of the town, each lasting around an hour.

These guided tours are well worth taking, not least because they give you access to the stunning Iglesia de San Miguel as well as other sites, like the Museo de la Pastelería, the production facility of a patisserie dating from 1874, and still in operation today.

🌟 Festivals & Events

Feria Medieval
MEDIEVAL

During the last week of July, Calle Mayor is closed to traffic, locals don their medieval finery and concerts mark the Medieval Festival.

Festival Internacional de Música Antigua
MEDIEVAL

In the first two weeks of August, Daroca hosts the International Festival of Medieval Music in the two main churches.

🛏 Sleeping

La Posada del Almudí
HOTEL €€

(☎976 80 06 06; www.posadadelalmudi.es; Calle Grajera 5; s/d/q incl breakfast €45/65/120; ❄ 🌐) A one-time 16th-century palace, this lovely old place exudes charm. The rooms in the main building have been lovingly restored, retaining the original beams, while across the lane are more contemporary rooms, with stylish black-and-white decor and parquet floors. Rooms on the 3rd floor have great views of the Iglesia de San Miguel.

The restaurant (mains €15 to €18, set menu €12.50) offers good local cuisine and has a delightful terrace overlooking the traditional walled garden. The adjacent tapas bar has an innovative selection of *pinchos* from €1.60.

Hotel Cien Balcones
HOTEL €€

(☎976 54 50 71; www.cienbalcones.com; Calle Mayor 88; s/d incl breakfast from €56/72; ❄❋🌐▦) This contemporary three-star hotel has large designer rooms, modern bathrooms and bold colour schemes. There's an excellent restaurant (mains from €9) and a cafe that serves up cheap *raciones*, *bocadillos* and pizza with outside seating in the attractive central courtyard.

ℹ Information

Tourist Office (☎976 80 01 29; Calle Mayor 44; ⊙10am-2pm & 4-8pm)

ℹ Getting There & Away

Buses stop outside the Mesón Félix bar, at Calle Mayor 104. Four daily buses run to Zaragoza (€11, three hours) and Teruel (€5.45, two hours), Monday to Saturday.

Laguna de Gallocanta

Some 20km south of Daroca, this is Spain's largest natural lake, with an area of about 15 sq km (though it can almost dry up in summer). It's a winter home for tens of thousands of cranes, as well as many other waterfowl – more than 260 bird species have been recorded here. The cranes arrive in mid-October and leave for the return flight to their breeding grounds in Scandinavia in March. Unpaved tracks of 36km in total encircle the lake, passing a series of hides and observation points – the tracks can be driven in normal vehicles except after heavy rain. Take binoculars.

🛏 Sleeping

Allucant
HOSTAL €

(www.allucant.com; Calle San Vicente; dm €13, d with shared/private bathroom from €30/45; ℗🌐▦) Serious twitchers will feel right at home at this simple but well-run birdwatching base in the village of Gallocanta. Meals (€9 to €12) and picnic lunches (€7) can be arranged. The place also acts as an informal cultural centre with regular art exhibitions and courses available, ranging from photography to painting.

ℹ Information

Centro de Interpretación – Bello (⊙10am-2pm & 3-6pm Sat & Sun, daily Oct & Feb) Information and exhibitions, along the Tornos–Bello road near the southeast corner of the lake.

Teruel

POP 35,841 / ELEV 917M

One of Spain's most attractive provincial cities, compact Teruel is an open-air museum of ornate Mudéjar monuments. But this is very much a living museum where the streets are filled with life – a reflection of a city with serious cultural attitude. Be warned, though: in winter Teruel can be one of the coldest places in Spain.

◉ Sights & Activities

Most of Teruel's sights are close to Plaza del Torico, home to two striking Modernista buildings and a lively focus of city life.

★ Catedral de Santa María de Mediavilla
CATHEDRAL

(Plaza de la Catedral; adult/child incl Museo de Arte Sacro €3/2; ◉ 11am-2pm & 4-8pm) Teruel's cathedral is a rich example of the Mudéjar imagination at work with its kaleidoscopic brickwork and colourful ceramic tiles. The superb 13th-century bell tower has hints of the Romanesque in its detail.

Inside, the astounding (and neck craning) Mudéjar ceiling of the nave is covered with paintings that add up to a medieval cosmography – from musical instruments and hunting scenes to coats of arms and Christ's crucifixion. Other highlights include the extraordinary 15th-century Gothic *retablo* in the Capilla de la Coronación.

The adjacent Museo de Arte Sacro housed in the stately Palacio Episcopal has two floors of superb religious paintings and sculptures dating from the 12th century, as well as some ornate 16th-century bishops' vestments. There are also several wood panels from the cathedral's extraordinary Mudéjar ceiling that have been damaged by woodworm (or similar) but which still display their vibrant design.

★ Fundación Amantes
MUSEUM, CHURCH

(www.amantesdeteruel.es; Calle Matías Abad 3; Mausoleo/Iglesia de San Pedro & Torre de San Pedro €4/5, combined ticket €7; ◉ 10am-2pm & 4-8pm Sep-Jul, 10am-8pm Aug) The somewhat curious Mausoleo de los Amantes (Mausoleum of the Lovers) pulls out the stops on the city's famous legend of Isabel and Juan Diego. Here they lie in modern alabaster tombs, sculpted by Juan de Ávalos, with their heads tilted endearingly towards each other. Around this centrepiece has been shaped a predictably sentimental audiovisual exhibition, featuring music and theatre.

Part of the complex is the 14th-century Iglesia de San Pedro, with a stunning ceiling, baroque high altar and simple cloisters, as well as the Torre de San Pedro (Torre Mudéjar) from where there are fine views over Teruel.

Aljibe Fondero
RUIN

(Calle Ramón y Cajal; adult/concession €1.20/0.80; ◉ 11am-2pm & 5-7pm) Off the southeastern corner of Plaza del Torico is the entrance to the Aljibe, a 14th-century underground water-storage facility. In addition to showcasing the remnants of the cisterns, there are audiovisual presentations on medieval Teruel, in Spanish.

Torre de El Salvador
TOWER, MUSEUM

(www.teruelmudejar.com; Calle El Salvador; adult/concession €2.50/1.80; ◉ 11am-2pm & 4.30-7.30pm) The most impressive of Teruel's Mudéjar towers is the Torre de El Salvador, an early 14th-century extravaganza of brick and ceramics built around an older Islamic minaret. You climb the narrow stairways and passageways, and along the way you'll

---

THE LOVERS OF TERUEL

In the early 13th century, Juan Diego de Marcilla and Isabel de Segura fell in love, but, in the manner of other star-crossed historical lovers, there was a catch: Isabel was the only daughter of a wealthy family, while poor old Juan Diego was, well, poor. Juan Diego convinced Isabel's reluctant father to postpone plans for Isabel's marriage to someone more appropriate for five years, during which time Juan Diego would seek his fortune. Not waiting a second longer than the five years, Isabel's father married off his daughter in 1217, only for Juan Diego to return, triumphant, immediately after the wedding. He begged Isabel for a kiss, which she refused, condemning Juan Diego to die of a broken heart. A final twist saw Isabel attend the funeral in mourning, whereupon she gave Juan Diego the kiss he had craved in life. Isabel promptly died and the two lovers were buried together.

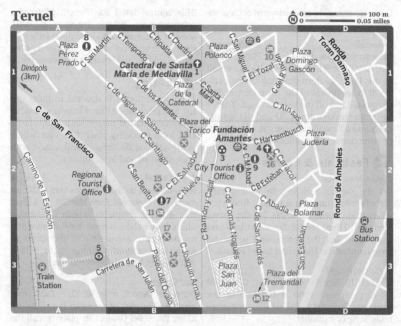

Teruel

find exhibits on Mudéjar art and architecture. The views from the summit are Teruel's best.

La Escalinata STAIRCASE
(Paseo del Óvalo) This grand staircase that connects the Paseo del Óvalo to the train station is a masterpiece of neo-Mudéjar monumental architecture. First built in 1920, it was painstakingly restored in the early 21st century. Along with the redesigned Paseo del Óvalo, La Escalinata has won numerous awards for urban redesign. There's a lift back up to the Paseo.

Torre de San Martín TOWER
(Calle San Martín) Although you can't climb it, Torre de San Martín, the northwestern gate of the old city, is almost as beautiful as the Torre de El Salvador. Completed in 1316, it was incorporated into the city's walls in the 16th century.

Museo Provincial MUSEUM
(Plaza Polanco; ⊙10am-2pm & 4-7pm Tue-Fri, 10am-2pm Sat & Sun) **FREE** Teruel's Museo Provincial is housed in the 16th-century Renaissance Casa de la Comunidad. The archaeological sections are a highlight, and

there are changing exhibitions of contemporary art.

Dinópolis
AMUSEMENT PARK

(www.dinopolis.com; Poligano Los Planos; adult/child €27/21.50; ⊙10am-8pm; ⊕) It's fun for all at this large, modern dinosaur theme park. It's 3km southwest of the town centre, well signposted just off the Valencia road. There's the train through time, 3D and 4D animations and an excellent museum, among other attractions. Ticket office closes 6pm.

★ Festivals & Events

Fiesta Medieval
MEDIEVAL

On the weekend closest to 14 February, Teruel's inhabitants (and visitors from elsewhere) don medieval dress for the Fiesta Medieval. There are medieval markets and food stalls, but the centrepiece is the re-enactment of the Diego and Isabel legend.

Feria del Ángel
LOCAL FIESTA

Held on 10 July, the Día de San Cristóbal (St Christopher's Day) is the hub of the weeklong Feria del Ángel, which commemorates Teruel's founding.

🛌 Sleeping

Fonda del Tozal
HOSTAL €

(☑978 60 21 73; Calle del Rincón 5; s/d €30/40; ☎) Dating from the 16th century, this is one of the oldest inns in Spain; the rooms vary considerably but all have a real sense of the past with beams, solid furniture and ancient floor tiles. In some rooms, the paintwork has been stripped back in places to reveal the original faintly patterned plasterwork beneath.

The cavernous tavern in the inn's former stables has an earthy local feel and is decorated with historic tools.

★ Hotel el Mudayyan
BOUTIQUE HOTEL €€

(☑978 62 30 42; www.elmudayyan.com; Calle Nueva 18; s €55-70, d €70-90; ❋ ☎) A delightful small hotel, El Mudayyan has just eight rooms with polished wood floors, wooden beams and a charming interior design. It also has a tetería (Moroccan-style teahouse) and a fascinating subterranean passage that dates back to the 13th century. An adjacent Modernista building with an additional 20 rooms should be open by the time you read this.

Hotel Sercotel Plaza Boulevard
HOTEL €€

(☑978 60 86 55; www.plazaboulevardhotel.com; Plaza del Tremandal 3; s/d from €49/80; ❋ ☎)

This central hotel has benefitted from a refurbishment. Rooms are spacious, with sofas or armchairs, and have neon-style spot lighting in vivid colours, contemporary tiles, plush bedding and smart new bathrooms.

🍴 Eating

Landlocked Teruel is devoted to meat eating and promotes its local jamón and other embutidos (cured meats) with enthusiasm. One local speciality you'll find everywhere is las delicias de Teruel (local jamón with toasted bread and fresh tomato).

Aqui Teruel
TAPAS €

(Calle de Yagüe de Salas 4; tapas from €3.50, set menu €10; ⊙9am-12.30am Mon-Sat, to 4.30pm Sun; ⊕) This temple to superb jamón also offers better-than-average kids' menus and an inexpensive menú del día, and sports an attractive rustic-style dining space with a wall of jolly, brightly coloured tiles.

Bar Gregori
TAPAS €

(Paseo del Óvalo 6; mains €6-13; ⊙7.30am-midnight; ⊕) The pick of the tapas bars lined up along Paseo del Óvalo, this place has all the local staples, plus outdoor tables and good service.

Los Caprichos
ITALIAN €€

(Calle Caracol 1; pizzas €9-11.50; ⊙1.30-4pm & 8.30-11.30pm Tue-Sun; ⊕) If you've pigged out on jamón and are yearning for something different, the pizzas here are crispy-based and good with over 30 toppings to choose from including genuine buffalo mozzarella (rare in these parts). Pastas are just average and the service a tad shambolic; pizza is definitely the standout here.

La Torre de Salvador
CONTEMPORARY ARAGONESE €€

(☑978 61 73 76; Calle El Salvador; mains €12-19; ⊙1-4pm Tue-Sun, 9-11pm Thu-Sat; ☎) Opposite the Torre de El Salvador, this smart restaurant raises the stakes with its nouveau cuisine aragonesa, with subtle dishes riffing on traditional themes, but plenty of local staples for those eager to get to the heart of Aragonese cooking. Think duck served in a sauce of sparkling wine, wild mushrooms and raisins. The adjacent bar-cafe specialises in pinchos (€1.50 to €2.50).

Mesón Óvalo
ARAGONESE €€

(☑978 61 82 35; Paseo del Óvalo 8; mains €14-19; ⊙1-4pm & 8-11pm Tue-Sat, 1-4pm Sun) There's a strong emphasis on regional Aragonese cui-

WORTH A TRIP

EL MAESTRAZGO

El Maestrazgo, a medieval knightly domain of wonderfully isolated valleys, deep gorges and rocky hills, spills over from Valencia province. Once a thriving centre of agriculture, honey-coloured crumbling farmhouses now dot the countryside. Cantavieja, northeast of Teruel along the A226, is a dramatically sited ridgetop town that was reputedly founded by Hannibal and later became a seat of the Knights Templar. The best-preserved part of town is the porticoed Plaza Cristo Rey. If you're heading for Morella in the Valencian Maestrazgo, follow the A226 northeast of Cantavieja, snaking down past ragged cliffs, and then via Mirambel, a fine example of a gently decaying, walled medieval town.

sine at this pleasant place, with meat and game dishes to the fore. One fine local speciality is *jarretes* (hock of lamb stewed with wild mushrooms), a dish that dates back to the period when Muslims ruled this part of Spain.

ℹ️ Information

City Tourist Office (☎ 978 62 41 05; Plaza de los Amantes 6; ☉ 10am-2pm & 4-8pm Sep-Jul, 10am-8pm Aug) Ask here for audioguides (€2) to the old city, and pick up the *Teruel Ruta Europea del Modernismo* which maps out 17 stunning art-nouveau buildings around town.
Regional Tourist Office (☎ 978 64 14 61; Calle de San Francisco 1; ☉ 9am-2pm & 4.45-7.45pm) Information about the wider Aragón region.

ℹ️ Getting There & Away

From Teruel's **bus station** (☎ 978 61 07 89; www.estacionbus-teruel.com), there are regular buses to/from Zaragoza (€11, two to three hours).

Teruel is on the railway between Zaragoza (€19.70, two hours) and Valencia (€18, 2½ hours).

Albarracín

POP 1100 / ELEV 1180M

Albarracín, 38km west of Teruel, is one of Spain's most beautiful villages, famous for its half-timbered houses with dusky-pink facades, reminiscent of southern Italy. It takes time to get here, but it's worth it for the marvellous sense of timelessness that not even the modern onslaught of summer coach tours can erase. Ragged fortress walls rise up the surrounding slopes and the town's streets retain their maze-like charm.

Built on a steep, rocky outcrop and surrounded by a deep valley carved out by a meander of the Río Guadalaviar, Albarracín was, from 1012 to 1104, the seat of a tiny Islamic state ruled by the Berber Banu Razin dynasty with links to Córdoba. From 1170 to 1285 it was an independent Christian kingdom sandwiched between Castilla and Aragón.

💿 Sights

If you're staying overnight in the village, ask your hotel for *el bono,* which entitles you to small discounts at most sights and some tours.

Muralla   CITY WALL
Albarracín's highest point, the **Torre del Andador** (Walkway Tower) dates from the 9th century; the surrounding walls are more recent and date from the 11th or 12th century. It's a stiff climb to the summit, but worth every gasp for the views down over the town.

Castillo   CASTLE
(Admission €2.50; ☉ guided tours 11am, noon, 1pm, 4.30pm & 5pm Sat-Mon, 1pm & 5.30pm Tue-Fri) Crowning the old town (with stunning views), this fascinating castle, with 11 towers and an area of 3600 sq metres, dates from the 9th century when Albarracín was an important Islamic military post. In private hands until 2005, the archaeological digs have revealed fascinating insights into the town's history. All is explained on the hour-long, Spanish-language tour (buy your tickets at the Museo de Albarracín); contact the Centro de Información to arrange English-language tours.

Museo de Juguetes   MUSEUM
(www.museodejuguetes.com; Calle Medio 2; adult/child €3/1.50; ☉ 11am-2pm & 4-7pm Tue-Sat, 11am-2pm Sun Apr-Oct, Sat & Sun Nov-Mar; 👶) Albarracín's toy museum is a fascinating journey through the historical world of toys – the kids will love it. It's down the hill, around 500m east of the tourist office.

Museo de Albarracín
MUSEUM

(Calle San Juan; admission €2.50; ⊙ 10.30am-1pm & 4.30-6pm Mon-Fri, 10.30am-2pm & 4.30-7.30pm Sat & Sun) In the old city hospital, this interesting museum is devoted to the town's Islamic heritage, with numerous finds from the archaeological digs in the castle. Opposite the museum's entrance, the 17th-century Ermita de San Juan was built on the site of Albarracín's former synagogue.

Catedral del Salvador
CATHEDRAL

With its cupola typical of the Spanish Levant, Albarracín's cathedral is one of the signature monuments of the village skyline; within there is an elaborate gilded altarpiece. Although it is closed for restoration, if you opt for a tour with the Centro de Información, access to the cathedral is included, albeit still restricted.

Museo Diocesano
MUSEUM

(admission €2.50; ⊙ 10.30am-2pm & 4.30-6.30pm Mon-Fri, to 7.30pm Sat & Sun) The Palacio Episcopal (Bishop's Palace), backing onto the cathedral, houses a rich collection of religious art and is a cut above your average church museum. The 15th- to 17th-century tapestries in particular stand out, as does a strange glass salt-holder in the shape of a fish.

Tours

El Andador
WALKING TOUR

(☑ 978 70 03 81; www.elandador.es; Calle de la Catedral 4; tours €3.50) El Andador offers 1½-hour walks through Albarracín two to six times daily.

Centro de Información
WALKING TOUR

(☑ 978 70 40 35; http://fundacionsantamariade albarracin.com; Calle de la Catedral; tours €3.50) Organises 1½-hour guided walks three to four times daily which include access to the cathedral (closed to the general public for restoration).

Sleeping

El Gallo Hotel
HOTEL €

(☑ 978 71 00 32; Calle Los Puentes 1; r €45; ❋ 🛜) Opened in January 2014 at the entrance to the village, this hotel is the result of an aesthetic reforma (restoration) of three traditional village houses. Behind the blush-rose facade are rooms that feel light and contemporary, with wicker furniture, a subtle colour scheme and stunning views. The bathrooms are small but swish with stone-coloured mosaic tiling and hydromassage showers.

Posada del Adarve
HOTEL €

(☑ 978 70 03 04; www.posadadeladarve.com; Calle Portal de Molina 23; s €30, d €50-75; @ 🛜) An Albarracín townhouse by the Portal de Molina (Molina Gateway), this prettily restored hotel has beautifully decorated, if small, rooms, friendly service and a homey intimate feel.

★ La Casa del Tío Americano
HOTEL €€

(☑ 978 71 01 25; www.lacasadeltioamericano.com; Calle Los Palacios 9; s/d incl breakfast €80/100; 🛜) A wonderful small hotel, 'The House of the American Uncle' boasts brightly painted rooms, some with exposed stone walls and friendly, impeccable service. The views of the village from the breakfast terrace (and from rooms 2 and 3) are magnificent. A welcoming glass of cava is a lovely touch, and the generous breakfast features local cheese, honey and ham.

Casa de Santiago
HOTEL €€

(☑ 978 70 03 16; www.casadesantiago.net; Subida a las Torres 11; d/ste €70/95; 🛜) A beautiful place, with lots of exposed wood and tiled floors, and charming service to go with it, the Casa lies at the heart of the old town a few steps up from Plaza Mayor. You step off the street into an immediate comfort zone.

La Casona del Ajimez
HOTEL €€

(☑ 978 71 03 21; www.casonadelajimez.com; Calle de San Juan 2; d €76; 🛜) Like other lovingly restored Albarracín small hotels, this place has warm and charming decor, and fine views from some rooms. It's at the southern end of town, near the cathedral.

Eating

Tapas, raciones and hearty meals are available at all of the bars around town.

La Taberna
TAPAS €

(Plaza Mayor 6; mains €5-15; 📶) A bustling bar right on Plaza Mayor with tables spilling out onto the square in summer, La Taberna does decent food – try the delicias de Teruel (local jamón with bread and tomato).

★ Tiempo de Ensueño
CONTEMPORARY SPANISH €€

(☑ 978 70 40 70; www.tiempodeensuenyo.com; Calle Palacios 1B; mains €19-25; ⊙ 1-4pm & 7-11pm Tue-Sun) This high-class restaurant has a sleek, light-filled dining room, attentive but discreet service, and food that you'll remember long after you've left. Spanish nouvelle cuisine in all its innovative guises makes an appearance here with a changing menu, as well as a book-length wine list, mineral-water menu, choice of olive oils, welcome cocktail and, above all, exquisite tastes.

Rincon del Chorro ARAGONESE €€
(Calle Chorro 5; mains €9-15, degustation menu €24.90; ⏱1-4pm & 8.15-11pm Fri-Sun) Traditional dishes from Albarracín are the show-stoppers here, including heartwarming stews like *jerigota* (a ratatouille-style dish), oxtail and white beans with partridge and wild mushrooms. The comfort-food theme reaches a high note with desserts like chocolate fondant and pumpkin and almond pie.

 Drinking & Nightlife

El Molino del Gato BAR
(www.elgato.arrakis.es; Calle San Antonio 4; ⏱3pm-3am Thu-Tue Sep-Jun, noon-3pm Jul & Aug) Just behind the tourist office, this outstanding bar is the place to drink in Albarracín. Built around a 15th-century mill, it has water gushing beneath a glass panel in the floor and the outdoor tables are fine places to nurse a drink; there are more than 25 types of beer. The bar also hosts regular contemporary art exhibitions.

 Shopping

Sierra de Albarracín FOOD
(www.quesodealbarracin.es; Calle Rubiales 1; ⏱10am-2pm & 4-7pm Mon-Fri, to 8pm Sat & Sun) You'll see the respected local cheeses labelled as Sierra de Albarracín in small shops all over the village, but why not go straight to the source? The owner's shop is around 3km away on the road out of town to Gea de Albarracín, and has the full range of sheep and goat's cheese. You can try most varieties before you buy.

❶ **Information**

Centro de Información (☑978 70 40 35; www.fundacionsantamariadealbarracin. com; Caballerizas del Palacio; ⏱10am-2pm & 4-6.30pm Mon-Fri, to 7.30pm Sat & Sun) Excellent, privately run information office high in the old town.

Tourist Office (☑978 71 02 62; Calle San Antonio; ⏱10am-2pm & 4-7pm Mon-Sat, to 8pm Sun)

❶ **Getting There & Away**

Buses travel once daily between Teruel and Albarracín (€4.40, 45 minutes).

Around Albarracín

Prehistoric Rock Art

The hills around Albarracín conceal some intriguing examples of prehistoric rock art, some of which date back 7000 years. In addition to animal representations (livestock, horses), there are some exceptional human figures.

To get here, follow the signs from the tourist office to *pinturas rupestres* (rock paintings). The main car park (with a picnic area and children's play area) is 4.5km further on, and well-signposted walking trails of between 2.3km and 3km (45 minutes to 1¼ hours) lead out into the hills. Three of the trails leave from here, and a fourth leaves from another car park around 700m back down the road towards Albarracín. A popular trail is the 2.5km Sendero del Arrastradero, which leads to the iconic Abrigo del Arquero de los Callejones (a perfectly rendered human archer seemingly caught in flight) among other drawings and a lookout.

Roman Aqueduct

The road between Gea de Albarracín and Albarracín (18km) is shadowed by traces of an ancient Roman aqueduct. Signs point to the most accessible sections, and there's a Centro de Interpretación in Gea de Albarracín which explains in more depth the history and role of the aqueduct.

Bronchales

Teruel's *jamón* is widely respected throughout Spain, and Jamones Bronchales (☑978 70 13 13; www.jamonesbronchales.com; ⏱10am-2pm & 5-8pm Mon-Sat) **FREE**, in the village of Bronchales, 29km northwest of Albarracín, runs tours (minimum 15 people) of its drying operations and shows how the *jamón* is prepared. You can also buy the end product here.

 ARAGÓN AROUND ALBARRACÍN

Bilbao, the Basque Country & La Rioja

Best Places to Eat

➡ Arzak (p423)

➡ La Cuchara de San Telmo (p424)

➡ Mina Restaurante (p408)

➡ La Fábrica (p424)

➡ La Cocina de Ramon (p448)

Best Places to Stay

➡ Hotel Marqués de Riscal (p452)

➡ Palacio Guendulain (p435)

➡ Pensión Aida (p421)

➡ La Casa de los Arquillos (p432)

➡ Hotel Calle Mayor (p447)

Why Go?

The jade hills and drizzle-filled skies of this pocket of Spain are quite a contrast to the popular image of the country. The Basques, the people who inhabit this corner, also consider themselves different. They claim to be the oldest Europeans and to speak the original European language. Whether or not this is actually the case remains unproven, but what is beyond doubt is that they live in a land of exceptional beauty and diversity. There are mountains watched over by almost-forgotten gods, cultural museums and art galleries, street parties a million people strong, and arguably the best food in Spain.

Leave the rugged north behind and feel the temperature rise as you hit the open, classically Spanish plains south of Pamplona. Here you enter the world of Navarra and La Rioja. It's a region awash with glorious wine, sunburst colours, dreamy landscapes, medieval monasteries and enticing wine towns.

When to Go
Bilbao

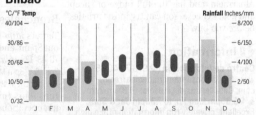

May–Jun Beat the crowds to the art galleries of Bilbao and the *pintxo* bars of San Sebastián.

6–14 Jul Savour the chaos of Pamplona's world-renowned Sanfermines festival.

Sep Hike the high passes of the Navarran Pyrenees and relish the autumnal colours.

Advance Planning

Book accommodation for San Sebastián in high summer and for Pamplona during the Sanfermines at least six months in advance – more if you can. Reserve a table at any of San Sebastián's three-Michelin-star restaurants as far in advance as possible. And buy tickets for the Museo Guggenheim online in advance to save queuing – Bilbao gets very busy over Easter.

FIVE PERFECT DAYS

Day One: Bilbao
Check out the art in the Museo Guggenheim (p399) and the Museo de Bellas Artes (p403), follow our walking tour of the city and peck at some *pintxos* (Basque tapas) in the old town.

Day Two: San Sebastián
Catch some rays on Playa de la Concha (p417), one of the most beautiful urban beaches in Europe. Admire the views from the summit of Monte Igueldo (p417) and dine in one of the city's multi-Michelin-star restaurants.

Day Three: Pyrenees
Drive lazily through Pyrenean foothills (p438) taking in picture-perfect villages like Zugarramurdi, Roncesvalles (p439) and Ochagavía (p440).

Day Four: Southern Navarra
Climb the castle turrets in Olite (p442) and marvel at the desert scenery in the Parque Natural de las Bárdenas Reales (p443).

Day Five: La Rioja
Tour the wine bodegas in La Rioja and visit the Dinastía Vivanco (p451) wine museum.

Top Five Food Experiences

➜ Graze through a plate of *pintxos*, the culinary masterpieces of San Sebastián (p424).

➜ Eat a dinner you'll remember forever in one of the Basque country's three-Michelin-star restaurants (p423).

➜ Sip a glass of wine in La Rioja, home to the best *vino* in the land (p446).

➜ Go on a *pintxo*-making course (p420).

➜ Savour barbecued fish on the seashore in Getaria (p415).

HIKING THE BASQUE COUNTRY & NAVARRA

The Navarran Pyrenees crash into several Basque massifs, making this prime hiking country, with numerous trails winding across the mountain passes. However, finding a suitable place to start walking can be a little confusing. Almost every bookshop in the region stocks hiking guides, but most are in Spanish only. Tourist offices have booklets detailing route descriptions in English.

Best Wine Experiences

➜ Visit the best wine museum in Spain: Dinastía Vivanco (p451).

➜ Make your own bottle of wine with Rioja Trek (p448).

➜ Tour a bodega around Haro (p452).

➜ Learn about the history and culture of the vine in Olite's Museo de la Viña y el Vino de Navarra (p442).

➜ Buy a *bota* from Félix Barbero Botas Rioja (p448).

Historic Spots

➜ See a castle that housed giraffes in Olite (p442).

➜ Walk the streets of the Roman town of Andelos (p445).

➜ Hear the footsteps of pilgrims past and present in Santo Domingo de la Calzada (p441).

BASQUE COUNTRY

No matter where you've just come from, be it the hot, southern plains of Spain or gentle and pristine France, the Basque Country is different. Known to Basques as Euskadi or Euskal Herria ('the land of Basque Speakers') and called El País Vasco in Spanish, this is where mountain peaks reach for the sky and sublime rocky coves are battered by mighty Atlantic swells. It's a place that demands exploration beyond the delightful and cosmopolitan main cities of Bilbao, Vitoria and San Sebastián. You travel through the Basque Country always curious, and always rewarded.

Bilbao, the Basque Country & La Rioja Highlights

❶ Play on a perfect beach, gorge on fabulous *pintxos* (Basque tapas), dance all night and dream of staying forever in stylish **San Sebastián** (p416), the food capital of the planet.

❷ Wish that you too could paint like a genius in the galleries of **Bilbao** (p399).

❸ Get barrelled in the surf at **Mundaka** (p414) and re-create the Guggenheim in sand-castle form on a beautiful Basque beach.

❹ Learn the secrets of a good drop in the museums and vineyards of **La Rioja** (p446).

❺ Roll back the years in the medieval fortress towns of **Olite** (p442) and **Ujué** (p443).

❻ Climb mist-shrouded slopes haunted by witches and vultures in the **Navarran Pyrenees** (p438).

❼ Pretend you're Hemingway during the Sanfermines week of debauchery in **Pamplona** (p433).

History

No one quite knows where the Basque people came from (they have no migration myth in their oral history), but their presence here is believed to predate even the earliest known migrations. The Romans left the hilly Basque Country more or less to itself, but the expansionist Castilian crown gained sovereignty over Basque territories during the Middle Ages (1000–1450), although with considerable difficulty; Navarra constituted a separate kingdom until 1512. Even when they came within the Castilian orbit, Navarra and the three other Basque provinces (Guipúzcoa, Vizcaya and Álava) extracted broad autonomy arrangements, known as the *fueros* (the ancient laws of the Basques).

After the Second Carlist War in 1876, all provinces except Navarra were stripped of their coveted *fueros,* thereby fuelling nascent Basque nationalism. Yet, although the Partido Nacionalista Vasco (PNV; Basque Nationalist Party) was established in 1894, support was never uniform as all Basque provinces included a considerable Castilian contingent.

When the Republican government in Madrid proposed the possibility of home rule (self-government) to the Basques in 1936, both Guipúzcoa and Vizcaya took up the offer. When the Spanish Civil War erupted, conservative rural Navarra and Álava supported Franco, while Vizcaya and Guipúzcoa sided with the Republicans, a decision they paid a high price for in the four decades that followed.

It was during the Franco days that Euskadi Ta Askatasuna (ETA; Basque Homeland and Freedom) was first born. It was originally set up to fight against the Franco regime, which suppressed the Basques through banning the language and almost all forms of Basque culture. After the death of Franco, ETA called for nothing less than total independence and continued its bloody fight against the Spanish government until, in October 2011, the group announced a 'definitive cessation of its armed activity'.

Bilbao

POP 354,200

Bilbao (Bilbo in Basque) had a tough upbringing. Growing up in an environment of heavy industry and industrial wastelands, it was abused for years by those in power and had to work hard to get anywhere. But, like the kid from the estates who made it big, Bilbao's graft paid off when a few wise investments left it with a shimmering titanium fish called the Museo Guggenheim and a horde of arty groupies around the world.

The Botxo (Hole), as it's fondly known to its inhabitants, has now matured into its role of major European art centre. However, in doing so, it hasn't forgotten its past: at heart it remains a hard-working and, physically, rather ugly town, but it's one that has real character. It's this down-to-earth soul, rather than its plethora of art galleries, that is the real attraction of the vital, exciting and cultured city of Bilbao.

History

Bilbao was granted the title of *villa* (city-state) in 1300 and medieval *bilbaínos* went about their business in the bustle of Las Siete Calles, the original seven streets of the old town, and down on the wharves. The conquest of the Americas stimulated trade and Basque fishers, merchants and settlers soon built strong links to cities such as Boston. By the late 19th century the smokestacks of steelworks, shipbuilding yards and chemical plants dominated the area's skyline.

From the Carlist Wars through to the Spanish Civil War, Bilbao was always considered the greatest prize in the north, largely for its industrial value. Franco took the city in the spring of 1937 and reprisals against Basque nationalists were massive and long lasting. Yet during the Franco era, the city prospered as it fed Spanish industrial needs. This was followed by the seemingly terminal economic decline that has been so dynamically reversed in recent years.

◉ Sights

★ **Museo Guggenheim**   ART GALLERY
(www.guggenheim-bilbao.es; Avenida Abandoibarra 2; adult/child €13/free; ⊙10am-8pm, closed Mon Sep-Jun) Opened in September 1997, Bilbao's Museo Guggenheim lifted modern architecture and Bilbao into the 21st century – with sensation. It boosted the city's already inspired regeneration, stimulated further development and placed Bilbao firmly in the world art and tourism spotlight.

Some might say that structure overwhelms function here, and that the Guggenheim is more famous for its architecture than its content. But Canadian architect Frank Gehry's inspired use of flowing canopies, cliffs, promontories, ship shapes, towers and flying fins is irresistible.

Bilbao

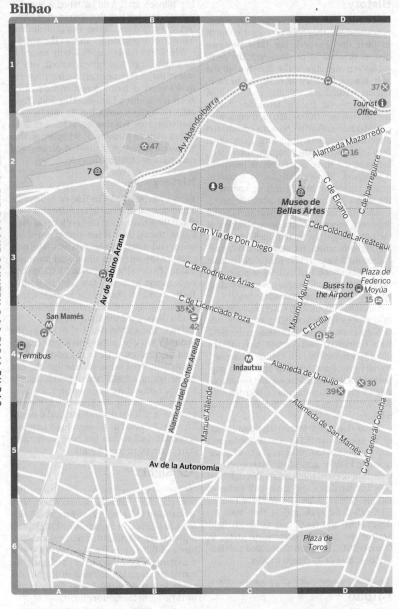

Like all great architects, Gehry designed the Guggenheim with historical and geographical contexts in mind. The site was an industrial wasteland, part of Bilbao's wretched and decaying warehouse district on the banks of Ría de Bilbao. The city's his-torical industries of shipbuilding and fishing reflected Gehry's own interests, not least his engagement with industrial materials in previous works. The gleaming titanium tiles that sheathe most of the building like giant herring scales are said to have been inspired

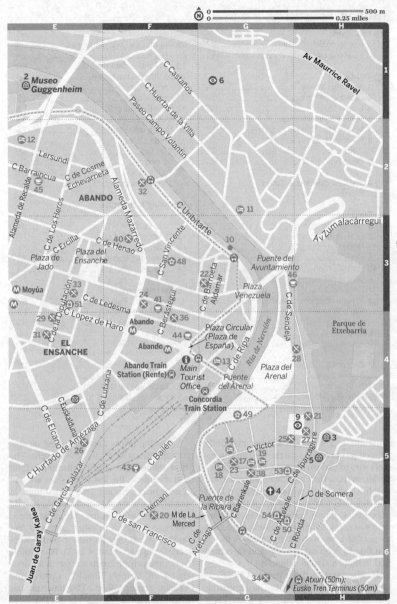

by the architect's childhood fascination with fish.

Other artists have added their touch to the Guggenheim as well. Lying between the glass buttresses of the central atrium and Río Nervión is a simple pool of water that emits at intervals a mist 'sculpture' by Fuyiko Nakaya. Nearby on the riverbank is a sculpture by Louise Bourgeois, a skeletal canopy representing a spider, entitled Maman, said to symbolise a protective embrace. In the open area to the west of the

Bilbao

museum, a fountain sculpture randomly fires off jets of water into the air and youngsters leap to and fro across it. On the Alameda Mazarredo, the city side of the museum, is Jeff Koons' kitsch whimsy Puppy, a 12m-tall Highland terrier made up of thousands of begonias. Bilbao has hung on to 'El Poop', who was supposed to be a passing attraction as part of a world tour. *Bilbaínos* will tell you that El Poop came first – and then they had to build a kennel behind it.

Heading inside, the interior of the Guggenheim is purposely vast. The cathedral-like atrium is more than 45m high. Light pours in through the glass cliffs. Permanent exhibits fill the ground floor and include such wonders as mazes of metal and phrases of light reaching for the skies.

For most people, though, it is the temporary exhibitions that are the main attraction (check the website for upcoming shows).

Admission prices vary depending on special exhibitions and the time of year. The prices quoted here are the maximum (and most common); the last ticket sales are half an hour before closing. Free guided tours in Spanish take place at 11am and 5pm; sign up half an hour before at the information desk. Tours can be given in other languages but you must ask at the information desk beforehand. Groups are limited to 20. It's possible to organise private group tours with advance request in Spanish, English, French and German, among others. The museum has specially adapted magnetic loop PDA video guides for those with hearing impairments. Self-guided audio tours in various languages are free with admission and there is a special children's audio guide. Entry queues can be long, with wet summer days and Easter almost guaranteeing you a wait of over an hour. The museum is wheelchair accessible.

⭐ **Museo de Bellas Artes**   ART GALLERY
(www.museobilbao.com; Plaza del Museo 2; adult/
student/child €7/5/free, Wed free; ⏰10am-8pm
Wed-Mon) The Museo de Bellas Artes houses
a compelling collection that includes everything from Gothic sculptures to 20th-century
pop art. There are three main subcollections:
classical art, with works by Murillo, Zurbarán,
El Greco, Goya and van Dyck; contemporary
art, featuring works by Gauguin, Francis Bacon and Anthony Caro; and Basque art, with
works of the great sculptors Jorge de Oteiza
and Eduardo Chillida, and strong paintings
by the likes of Ignacio Zuloaga and Juan de
Echevarria.

As good as the permanent collection is,
it's the temporary exhibitions that really
draw the crowds. See the website for details
of upcoming exhibitions.

Casco Viejo   OLD TOWN
The compact Casco Viejo, Bilbao's atmospheric old quarter, is full of charming
streets, boisterous bars and plenty of quirky
and independent shops. At the heart of the
casco are Bilbao's original seven streets, **Las
Siete Calles**, which date from the 1400s.

The 14th-century Gothic **Catedral de
Santiago** (Plaza de Santiago; ⏰11am-1pm &
5-7pm Tue-Sat, 11am-noon Sun) has a splendid
Renaissance portico and pretty little cloister. Further north, the 19th-century arcaded **Plaza Nueva** is a rewarding *pintxo*
(Basque tapas) haunt. There's a lively
Sunday-morning **flea market** here, which
is full of secondhand book and record stalls,
and pet 'shops' selling chirpy birds (some
kept in old-fashioned wooden cages), fluffy
mice and tiny baby terrapins. Elsewhere in
the market, children and adults alike swap
and barter football cards and old stamps
from countries you've never heard of; in between weave street performers and waiters
with trays piled high. The market is much
more subdued in winter. A sweeter-smelling
flower market takes place on Sunday mornings in the nearby **Plaza del Arenal**.

Euskal Museoa   MUSEUM
(Museo Vasco; www.euskal-museoa.org/es/hasiera;
Plaza Miguel Unamuno 4; adult/child €3/free, Thu
free; ⏰10am-7pm Tue-Fri, 10am-1.30pm & 4-7pm
Sat, 10am-2pm Sun) This museum is probably
the most complete museum of Basque culture and history in all of Spain. The story
kicks off back in the days of prehistory and
from this murky period the displays bound
rapidly through to the modern age.

The main problem with the museum is
that, unless you speak Spanish (or perhaps
you studied Euskara at school?), it's all a little meaningless as there are no English or
French translations.

The museum is housed in a fine old build-
ing, at the centre of which is a peaceful clois-
ter that was part of an original 17th-century
Jesuit college. In the cloister is the **Mikeldi
Idol**, a powerful pre-Christian, possibly Iron
Age, symbolic figure.

Museo Marítimo Ría de Bilbao   MUSEUM
(www.museomaritimobilbao.org; Muelle Ramón de la
Sota 1; adult/student/child €6/3.50/free; ⏰10am-
8pm Tue-Sun, to 6pm Mon-Fri winter) This space-
age maritime museum, appropriately sited
down on the waterfront, uses bright and
well-thought-out displays to bring the watery
depths of Bilbao and Basque maritime history to life. There's an outdoor section where
children (and nautically inclined grown-ups)
can clamber about a range of boats pretend-
ing to be pirates and sailors.

Arkeologi Museo   MUSEUM
(Calzadas de Mallona 2; adult/student/child
€3/1.50/free, Fri free; ⏰10am-2pm & 4-7.30pm
Tue-Sat, 10.30am-2pm Sun) Through the use
of numerous flashing lights, beeping things
and a fair few spearheads and old pots, this
museum reinforces the point that the inhabitants of this corner of Spain have lived here
for a very long time indeed. Labelling is in
Spanish and Basque only.

Parque de Doña Casilda de Iturrizar   PARK
Floating on waves of peace and quiet just
beyond the Museo de Bellas Artes is another work of fine art – the Parque de Doña
Casilda de Iturrizar. The centrepiece of this
whimsical park is the large pond filled with
ornamental ducks and other waterfowl.

Funicular de Artxanda   FUNICULAR
(Plaza Funicular; adult/child €0.95/0.30; ⏰7.15am-
10pm Mon-Sat, 8.15am-10pm Sun) Bilbao is a
city hemmed by hills and mountains into a
tight valley. For a breathtaking view over the
city, the valley it sits in and the wild Basque

ℹ **ARTEAN PASS**

The Artean Pass is a joint ticket for the
Guggenheim (p399) and the Museo de
Bellas Artes, which, at €14 for adults,
offers significant savings. It's available
from either museum.

CITY TOURS

There are a number of different city tours available. Some are general-interest tours, others focus on specific aspects of the city such as architecture or food. The following are recommended.

Bilbao tourist office (p409) Organises 1½-hour walking tours (€4.50; 10am Saturday and Sunday) covering either the old town or the architecture in the newer parts of town. At busy times tours can run with more frequency.

Bilboats (☑946 42 41 57; www.bilboats.com; Plaza Pío Baroja; adult/child from € 12/7) Runs boat cruises along the Nervión several times a day.

Bilbao Greeters (www.bilbaogreeters.com; adult €12) One of the more original and interesting ways to see the city and get to know a local is through the Bilbao Greeters organisation. Essentially a local person gives you a tour of the city showing you their favourite sights, places to hang out and, of course, *pintxo* (Basque tapas) bars. You need to reserve through the website at least a fortnight in advance.

mountains beyond, take a trip on the funicular railway that has creaked and moaned its way up the steep slope to the summit of Artxanda for nearly a century.

Festivals & Events

Bilbao has a packed festival calendar. The following are just the big daddies.

Carnaval   CARNIVAL
(☉Feb) Carnaval is celebrated with vigour in Bilbao.

**Festival Internacional
de Blues de Getxo**   MUSIC
(Getxo International Blues Festival; ☉early Jul) High-quality blues festival in the seaside suburb of Getxo, 16km north of central Bilbao.

Bilbao BBK Live   MUSIC
(www.bilbaobbklive.com; ☉mid-Jul) Bilbao's biggest musical event is Bilbao BBK Live, which takes place over three days.

Jazz Euskadi   MUSIC
(www.jazzeuskadi.com; ☉Jul) This is one of the region's first major jazz festivals of the summer season. It takes place over five days in Getxo.

Semana Grande   CULTURAL
(☉Aug) Bilbao's grandest fiesta begins on the first Saturday after 15 August. It has a full program of cultural events over 10 days.

**Festival Internacional
de Folk de Getxo**   FOLK MUSIC
(☉Sep) Held in Getxo, this cultural festival promotes regional dance, music and traditions.

Sleeping

Bilbao welcomes quite a lot of tourists and the most popular hotels and guesthouses can get booked up early in high season, so it pays to book as far ahead as possible. The Bilbao tourism authority has a very useful **reservations department** (☑902 877298; www.bilbaoreservas.com).

Pensión Gurea   PENSIÓN €
(☑944 16 32 99; www.hostalgurea.com; Calle de Bidebarrieta 14; s/d from €40/48; ☎) The family-run Gurea has been revamped and has arty, modern rooms with wooden floors and large bathrooms (most of which have bath tubs) and exceptionally friendly staff. Add it all up and you get what is easily one of the best deals in the old town.

Pensión Ladero   PENSIÓN €
(☑944 15 09 32; Calle Lotería 1; s/d without bathroom €22/32; ☎) The no-fuss rooms here (all with shared bathrooms) are as cheap as Bilbao gets and represent good bang for your buck. You could probably get sponsored for clambering up the zillion-odd steps to the 4th storey where this *pensión* is located.

★**Pensión Iturrienea
Ostatua**   BOUTIQUE HOTEL €€
(☑944 16 15 00; www.iturrieneaostatua.com; Calle de Santa María 14; r €50-70; ☎⊕) Easily the most eccentric hotel in Bilbao, it's part farmyard, part old-fashioned toyshop, and a work of art in its own right. The nine rooms here are so full of character that there'll be barely enough room for your own!

There's a lovely breakfast area, and with baby beds and chairs and lots of toys, it's family friendly.

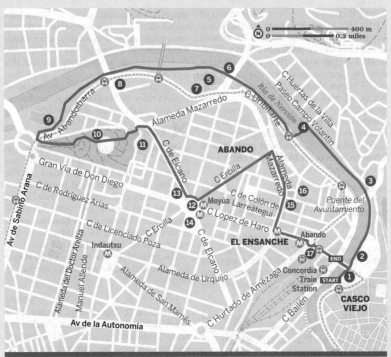

Walking Tour
Architecture & River Views

START TEATRO ARRIAGA
END TEATRO ARRIAGA
LENGTH ABOUT 4KM; THREE HOURS

One of the pleasures of a visit to Bilbao is just walking around admiring its crazy mix of architectural styles and the riverside walkways.

Start at the Baroque ① **Teatro Arriaga** (p409), on the edge of the Casco Viejo, which was built in 1890. Follow the river through the ② **Plaza del Arenal** and pass by the grand ③ **ayuntamiento** (town hall), dating from the late 19th century. Continue upriver along the Paseo Campo Volantin, which is lined with buildings covering a range of styles. Cross over the ④ **Puente Zubizuri**; this wave-like bridge was designed by Santiago Calatrava and is the most striking bridge in the city.

Arriving on the other side of the river, turn right and carry on up the waterfront towards the most famous building in the city, the ⑤ **Museo Guggenheim** (p399). Check out the spider-like ⑥ **Maman** and ⑦ **Puppy**, the sweetest-smelling dog you ever did see.

Continue walking along the river past numerous sculptures. On your left is the ⑧ **Iberdrola tower**, a 165m glass office block, the tallest building in the region. Eventually you arrive at the modern ⑨ **Euskalduna Palace** (p409). Turn left and enjoy the stroll through the whimsical ⑩ **Parque de Doña Casilda de Iturrizar** (p403), pass by the ⑪ **Museo de Bellas Artes** (p403) and head down Calle de Elcano to ⑫ **Plaza de Federico Moyúa**, which marks the centre of the new town. This square is lined by impressive buildings including, on your right, the early-20th-century Flemish-style ⑬ **Palacio de Chávarri** and, opposite, the oh-so-grand ⑭ **Hotel Carlton** (p406). Turn down Calle Ercilla, then right down Alameda Mazarredo until you come to the pretty ⑮ **Jardines Albia**, overlooked by the 16th-century church ⑯ **Iglesia San Vicente Mátir**. Cut down to Calle López de Haro and, passing the art-nouveau facade of the ⑰ **FEVE train station**, cross the Puente del Arenal to arrive back at the start of the walk.

Hostal Begoña
BOUTIQUE HOTEL €€

(944 23 01 34; www.hostalbegona.com; Calle de la Amistad 2; s/d from €57/66; P @) The owners of this outstanding place don't need voguish labels for their very stylish and individual creation. Begoña speaks for itself with colourful rooms decorated with modern artworks, all with funky tiled bathrooms and wrought-iron beds. The common areas have mountains of books, traveller information and a rack of computers for internet usage.

It's probably the best hotel in the city in which to meet other travellers. There's a car park nearby.

Barceló Nervión
HOTEL €€

(944 45 47 00; www.barcelonervion.com; Paseo Campo Volantin 11; d from €90; P) Part of the nationwide chain, the rooms here, which are smart, comfortable and spacious, offer superb value for money, although the hotel charges over the odds for everything else. The location, on the riverfront and equidistant between the old town and the Guggenheim, is ideal.

Miró Hotel
DESIGN HOTEL €€

(946 61 18 80; www.mirohotelbilbao.com; Alameda Mazarredo 77; d from €127; @) This stunning hotel facing Bilbao's most famous designer building has common areas filled with modern photographic art and rooms that are of a slick, minimalist city style. All up, it's a perfect fit with arty Bilbao.

Hotel Bilbao Jardines
BOUTIQUE HOTEL €€

(944 79 42 10; www.hotelbilbaojardines.com; Calle Jardines 9; s €60-65, d €75;) A welcome change from the dusty facades of Casco Viejo, the Jardines has fresh, green decor and rooms that lap up light like a sunbathing lizard. Good value for money.

Gran Hotel Domine
DESIGN HOTEL €€€

(944 25 33 00; www.granhoteldominebilbao.com; Alameda Mazarredo 61; s/d from €170/190; P @) Designer chic all the way, this stellar showpiece of the Silken chain has views of the Guggenheim from some of its pricier rooms, a giant column of rounded beach stones reaching for the heavens and a water feature filled with plates and glasses. Yes, it's a little different. Booking online beforehand can lead to big discounts.

Hotel Carlton
HISTORIC HOTEL €€€

(944 16 22 00; www.hotelcarlton.es; Plaza de Frederico Moyúa 2; s/d €320/329; P @) Style, class and sophistication: the reception area is overpoweringly ornate and the rooms are all classic old-fashioned class (although some might also call this dull!). When James Bond came to Bilbao in *The World Is Not Enough,* you can be absolutely sure that this is where he stayed.

The prices quoted here are maxiumn walk-in rates. By booking online in advance, you may get discounts of 50% to 60%.

Eating

In the world of trade and commerce, the Basques are an outward-looking lot, but when it comes to food they refuse to believe that any other people could possibly match their culinary skills (and they may well have a point). This means that eating out in Bilbao is generally a choice of Basque, Basque or Basque food. Still, life could be worse and there are some terrific places to eat.

The porticoed Plaza Nueva is a good spot for coffee and people-watching, especially in summer.

Rio-Oja
BASQUE €

(944 15 08 71; Calle de Perro 4; mains €7-12; 9am-11pm) An institution that shouldn't be missed. It specialises in light Basque seafood and heavy inland fare, but to most foreigners the snails, sheep brains or squid floating in pools of its own ink are the makings of a culinary adventure story they'll be recounting for years. Don't worry, though: it really does taste much better than it sounds.

La Mary Restaurante
BASQUE €

(www.lamaryrestaurant.com; Plaza de Arriquíbar 3; menú del día €9.90; 1-4pm & 8-11.30pm) From the outside this looks like a swanky place, but in fact it's very relaxed and so exceptionally well priced that to enjoy its bargain lunch menu you must arrive early to avoid joining a queue of locals waiting for a table.

★ Casa Rufo
BASQUE €€

(944 43 21 72; www.casarufo.com; Hurtado de Amézaga 5; mains €10-15; 1.30-4pm & 8.30-11.30pm Mon-Sat) Despite the emergence of numerous glitzy restaurants that are temples to haute cuisine, this resolutely old-fashioned place, with its shelves full of dusty bottles of top-quality olive oil and wine, still stands out as one of the best places to eat traditional Basque food in Bilbao. The restaurant also doubles as a deli and many of the products lining the shelves are for sale.

Advance reservations are a very good idea.

Bascook   CONTEMPORARY BASQUE €€
(☏944 00 99 77; www.bascook.com; Calle de Bar-roeta Aldamar 8; menú del día €23; ☺lunch Mon-Sat, dinner Thu-Sat) The style of this unique place won't appeal to all. The lighting is more nightclub than restaurant and the menu is printed in the form of a newspaper, but even if the decor doesn't appeal the food probably will: an utterly modern and unusual take on Basque classics that's good enough to have locals battling for tables.

Agape Restaurante   BASQUE €€
(☏944 16 05 06; www.restauranteagape.com; Calle de Hernani 13; menus €12-36; ☺1-4pm Sun-Wed,

1-4pm & 8.30-11.30pm Thu-Sat) With a solid reputation among locals for good-value meals that don't sacrifice quality, this place is a great place for a slice of real Bilbao culinary life. It's well away from the standard tourist circuit.

Larruzz Bilbao   MEDITERRANEAN €€
(☏944 23 08 20; www.larruzzbilbao.com; Calle Uribitarte 24; mains €12-17, menú from €17; ☺noon-midnight) Set on the banks of the Nervión, this incredibly popular restaurant (book ahead) has a polished business exterior, but a stone-cottage country interior. Its real speciality is paella, but it also serves various meaty Mediterranean dishes.

BEST PINTXO BARS IN BILBAO

Although it lacks San Sebastián's stellar reputation for *pintxos* (Basque tapas), prices are generally slightly lower here (all charge from around €2.50 per *pintxo*) and the quality is about equal. There are literally hundreds of *pintxo* bars throughout Bilbao, but the Plaza Nueva on the edge of the Casco Viejo offers especially rich pickings, as do Calle de Perro and Calle Jardines. Some of the city's standouts, in no particular order:

Bar Gure Toki (Plaza Nueva 12; pintxos from €2.50) With a subtle but simple line in creative *pintxos* including some made with ostrich.

Café-Bar Bilbao (Plaza Nueva 6; pintxos from €2.50; ☺7am-11pm Mon-Thu, 7am-11.30pm Fri, Sat 9am-11.30pm, Sun 10am-3pm) Cool blue southern tile work and warm northern atmosphere.

Casa Victor Montes (p408) As well known for its *pintxos* as its full meals.

Sorginzulo (Plaza Nueva 12; pintxos from €2.50; ☺9.30am-12.30am) A matchbox-sized bar with an exemplary spread of *pintxos*. The house special is calamari (served on weekends).

Berton Sasibil (Calle Jardines 8; pintxos from €2.50; ☺8.30am-midnight Mon-Sat, 10am-4pm Sun) Here you can watch informative films on the crafting of the same superb *pintxos* that you're munching on.

Claudio: La Feria del Jamón (Calle Iparragirre 9-18; pintxos from €2.50) A creaky old place full of ancient furnishings. As you'll guess from the name and the legs of ham hanging from the ceiling, it's all about pigs. Opposite the bar, it has a shop selling hams.

★**La Viña del Ensanche** (☏944 15 56 15; www.lavinadelensanche.com; Calle de la Diputación 10; pintxos from €2.50; ☺8.30am-11pm Mon-Sat) Hundreds of bottles of wine line the walls of this outstanding *pintxos* bar. And when we say outstanding, we mean that it could well be the best place to eat *pintxos* in the city.

Museo del Vino (Calle de Ledesma 10; pintxos from €2.50; ☺1-5pm & 8-11pm Mon-Fri) Tiled white interior, Gaudíesque windows, delicous octopus *pintxos* and an excellent wine selection (as you'd hope with a name like this). This place makes us smile.

Bitoque de Albia (www.bitoque.net; Alameda Mazarredo 6; pintxos from €2.50; ☺1.30-4pm Mon-Wed, 1.30-4pm & 8.30-11.15pm Thu-Sat) Award-winning modern *pintxos* bar serving such unclassic dishes as miniature red tuna burgers, salmon sushi and clams with wild mushrooms. It also offers a *pintxos* tasting menu (€12).

El Globo (Calle de Diputación 8; pintxos from €2.50; ☺8am-11pm Mon-Thu, till midnight Fri & Sat) An unassuming but popular bar with favourites such as *txangurro gratinado* (spider crab).

Los Candiles (Calle de Diputación 1; pintxos from €2.50; ☺7am-10pm Mon-Sat) A narrow, low-key little bar, with some subtle *pintxos* filled with the taste of the sea.

Mugi (Licenciado Poza 55; pintxos from €2.50; ☺7am-midnight Mon-Sat, noon-midnight Sun) Widely regarded *pintxo* bar. It can get so busy that you might have to stand outside.

BILBAO CAFES

Bilbao has some classic cafes in which to enjoy a caffeine shot and a sweet snack. Styles range from fusty and old fashioned to modern and flash. Here's our pick of the crop.

Café Iruña (www.cafesdebilbao.net; cnr Calles de Colón de Larreátegui & Berástegui; ⊙ 7am-1am Mon-Thu, 7am-2am Fri, 9am-1am Sat, noon-1am Sun) Ornate Moorish style and a century of gossip are the defining characteristics of this grand old dame. It's the perfect place to indulge in a bit of people-watching. Dont miss the delicous *pinchos morunos* (spicy kebabs).

La Granja (www.cafesdebilbao.net; Plaza Circular 3; ⊙ 7.30am-12.30am Mon-Fri, 10.30am-1.30am Sat) With its period furnishings and polished wooden bar top, this place, which first opened its doors in 1926, is another of Bilbao's old time-warp cafes.

Opila (Calle de Sendeja 4) Fantastic patisserie and cafe. Downstairs is all art-deco furnishings and glass display cabinets and upstairs is way more up to the moment.

Mami Lou Cupcake (Calle Barraincua 7; ⊙ 11am-8.30pm Mon-Sat) Relive your childhood at this cute little cafe with 1950s decor and colourful homemade cupcakes.

Casa del Café & Té (Alaveda Doctor Areliza 22; ⊙ 9am-9pm Mon-Fri, 9am-2pm & 5-9pm Sat) This cute little blue teashop sells tea leaves to take away or you can sit and sup your brew in situ.

Casa Victor Montes BASQUE €€

(☏ 944 15 70 67; www.victormontesbilbao.com; Plaza Nueva 8; mains €15, pintxos from €2.50; ⊙ 10.30am-11pm Mon-Thu, 10.30am-midnight Fri-Sun) Part bar, part shop, part restaurant, total work of art, the Victor Montes is quite touristy but locals also appreciate its over-the-top decoration, its good food and the 1000 or so bottles of wine lined up behind the bar. If you're stopping by for a full meal, book in advance and savour the house special, *bacalao* (dried cod).

★ **Mina Restaurante** CONTEMPORARY BASQUE €€€

(☏ 944 79 59 38; www.restaurantemina.es; Muelle Marzana; tasting menu from €60; ⊙ closed Tue & Sun evening & Mon) Offering unexpected sophistication and fine dining in an otherwise fairly grimy neighbourhood, this riverside, and appropriately fish-based, restaurant has some critics citing it as the current *número uno* of Basque cooking. Reservations are essential.

Zortziko Restaurante CONTEMPORARY BASQUE €€€

(☏ 944 23 97 43; www.zortziko.es; Alameda Mazarredo 17; menú from €85, mains €26-38; ⊙ Tue-Sat; ☏) Michelin-starred chef Daniel García presents immaculate modern Basque cuisine in a formal 1920s-style French dining room. The highly inventive menu changes frequently but can include such delicacies as lamb sweetbreads stew with milk and thyme ice cream.

If the food excites your taste buds that much, sign up for one of his occasional cooking courses (€40).

Nerua CONTEMPORARY BASQUE €€€

(☏ 944 00 04 30; www.nerua.com; tasting menu from €72; ⊙ closed Mon & 2 weeks in mid-Jan) The Guggenheim's modernist, chic restaurant, Nerua, is under the direction of multi-award-winning chef Josean Martínez Alija. Needless to say, the *nueva cocina vasca* (Basque nouvelle cuisine) is breathtaking – even the olives are vintage classics: all come from 1000-year-old olive trees!

Reservations are essential. If the gourmet restaurant is too extravagant for you, try El Goog's **Bistro**, which has set menus from €28.

Yandiola CONTEMPORARY BASQUE €€€

(☏ 944 13 36 36; www.yandiola.com; Plaza Alhóndiga 4; menus from €42; ⊙ closed Mon, Sun pm, Easter & early Sep) Inside the Alhóndiga building, Bilbao's new pride and joy, is this outstanding restaurant where chef Ricardo Perez prepares modern Basque and Spanish fare that is also quickly becoming a pride and joy of Bilbao.

The complex houses some cheaper eating options as well.

 Drinking & Entertainment

In the Casco Viejo, around Calles Barrenkale, Ronda and de Somera, there are plenty of terrific hole-in-the-wall, no-nonsense bars with a generally youngish crowd.

Across the river, in the web of streets around Muelle Marzana and Bilbao la Vieja, are scores more little bars and clubs. This is gritty Bilbao as it used to be in the days before the arty makeover. It's both a Basque heartland and the centre of the city's ethnic community. The many bars around here are normally welcoming, but one or two can be a bit seedy. It's not a great idea for a woman to walk here alone at night.

There are plenty of clubs and live-music venues in Bilbao, and the vibe is friendly and generally easygoing. Venues' websites usually have details of upcoming gigs.

Bilbao offers regular performances of dance, opera and drama at the city's principal theatre and the Kafe Antzokia. Check the theatre websites for current information.

El Balcón de la Lola
CLUB

(Calle Bailén 10; admission Fri & Sat €10; ⏰ 11.45pm-6.15am Thu & Fri, noon-3.30pm & 11.45pm-6.15am Sat, noon-4.30pm Sun) One of Bilbao's most popular mixed gay-and-straight clubs, this is the place to come if you're looking for hip industrial decor and a packed Saturday-night disco. It's located under the railway lines.

★ Kafe Antzokia
LIVE MUSIC

(☎944 24 61 07; www.kafeantzokia.com; Calle San Vicente 2) This is the vibrant heart of contemporary Basque Bilbao, featuring international rock bands, blues and reggae, but also the cream of Basque rock-pop. Weekend concerts run from 10pm to 1am, followed by DJs until 5am. Cover charge for concerts can range from about €15 upwards. During the day it's a cafe, restaurant and cultural centre all rolled into one and has frequent exciting events on.

Teatro Arriaga
THEATRE

(☎944 79 20 36; www.teatroarriaga.com; Plaza Arriaga) The baroque facade of this venue commands the open spaces of El Arenal between the Casco Viejo and the river. It stages theatrical performances and classical-music concerts.

Euskalduna Palace
LIVE MUSIC

(☎944 03 50 00; www.euskalduna.net; Avenida Abandoibarra) About 600m downriver from the Guggenheim is another modernist gem, built on the riverbank in a style that echoes the great shipbuilding works of the 19th century. The Euskalduna houses the Bilbao Symphony Orchestra and the Basque Symphony Orchestra.

🔒 Shopping

For major department stores and big-name fashion labels trawl the streets of El Ensanche. For more one-of-a-kind, independent boutiques, Casco Viejo is the place to look (although even here the chain shops are increasingly making their presence felt).

Bilbao is also a great place for food shopping (of course!).

Almacen Coloniales y Bacalao Gregorio Martín
FOOD

(Calle Artekale 32; ⏰ 10am-2pm & 4-8pm Mon-Sat) Specialising in *bacalao* since it first opened some 80 years ago. Today it also sells oils, pulses and hams.

Arrese
FOOD

(Calle Lopez de Haro 24; ⏰ 10am-2pm & 4-8pm Mon-Sat) With 160 years of baking experience behind them, you'd expect the cakes at this little patisserie to taste divine, but frankly they're even better than you'd expect.

Chocolates de Mendaro
FOOD

(www.chocolatesdemendaro.com; Calle de Licenciado Poza 16; ⏰ 10am-2pm & 4-8pm Mon-Sat) This old-time chocolate shop created its first chocolate treats way back in 1850 and is hands down the best place to ruin a diet in Bilbao.

Elkar Megadenda
BOOKS

(Calle de Iparragirre 26; ⏰ 10am-2pm & 4-8pm Mon-Sat) Basque publications are strongly represented here. It also stocks books in Spanish and a few in English, and there's an excellent map and travel section. There are a couple of other branches in the city.

Txorierri
FOOD

(Calle Artekale 19; ⏰ 10am-2pm & 4-8pm Mon-Sat) High-quality deli selling the full tummy-pleasing array of local culinary delicacies.

ℹ️ Information

EMERGENCY

Policía Municipal (☎092, 944 20 50 00; Calle de Luís Briñas 14)

TOURIST INFORMATION

Tourist Office (www.bilbaoturismo.net) main tourist office (☎944 79 57 60; Plaza Circular 1; ⏰ 9am-9pm; @ 🔊); airport (☎944 71 03 01; ⏰ 9am-9pm Mon-Sat, 9am-3pm Sun); Guggenheim (Alameda Mazarredo 66; ⏰ 10am-7pm daily, till 3pm Sun Sep-Jun) Bilbao's friendly tourist-office staffers are extremely helpful, well informed and, above all, enthusiastic about their city. At all offices ask for the free bimonthly *Bilbao Guía*, with its entertainment listings plus tips on restaurants, bars and nightlife.

ℹ TRAVEL PASSES

The **Bilbaocard** (one-/two-/three-day pass €6/10/12) entitles the user to reduced rates on all city transport as well as reductions at many of the sights. It can be purchased from any of the tourist offices. **Creditrans** give significant discounts on the metro, tram and city-bus network. They are available in €5, €10 and €15 denominations from all metro and tram stations.

ℹ Getting There & Away

AIR

Bilbao's **airport** (BIO; ☎ 902 404704; www.aena.es) is near Sondika, to the northeast of the city. A number of European flag carriers serve the city. Of the budget airlines, **EasyJet** (www.easyjet.com) and **Vueling** (www.vueling.com) cover the widest range of destinations.

BUS

Bilbao's main bus station, **Termibus** (☎ 944 39 50 77; Gurtubay 1, San Mamés), is west of the centre. There are regular services to the following destinations:

TO	FARE (€)	DURATION (HR)
Barcelona	48	7-8
Biarritz (France)	198	3
Logroño	13	2¾
Madrid	from 31	4¾
Oñati	6.50	1¼
Pamplona	15	2¾
San Sebastián	6.47	1
Santander	6.60	1¼
Vitoria	6.20	1½

Bizkaibus travels to destinations throughout the rural Basque Country, including coastal communities such as Lekeitio (€3.25) and Guernica (Gernika; €2.45).

TRAIN

The Abando train station is just across the river from Plaza Arriaga and the Casco Viejo. There are frequent trains to the following destinations:

TO	FARE (€)	DURATION (HR)
Barcelona	65	6¾
Burgos	23	3
Madrid	64	5
Valladolid	26	4

Next door is the Concordia train station, with its handsome art-nouveau facade of wrought iron and tiles. It is used by the **FEVE** (www.feve.es), a formerly private rail company that was recently purchased by RENFE. It has trains running west into Cantabria. There are three daily trains to Santander (from €8.75, three hours) where you can change for stations in Asturias.

The Atxuri train station is just upriver from Casco Viejo. From here, **Eusko Tren/Ferrocarril Vasco** (www.euskotren.es) operates services every half-hour to the following:

TO	FARE (€)	DURATION (HR)
Bermeo	3	1½
Guernica	3	1
Mundaka	3	1½

Hourly Eusko Tren trains go to San Sebastián (€5.30, 2¾ hours) via Durango, Zumaia and Zarautz, but the bus is much quicker.

ℹ Getting Around

TO/FROM THE AIRPORT

The **airport bus** (Bizkaibus A3247; tickets €1.40) departs from a stand on the extreme right as you leave arrivals. It runs through the northwestern section of the city, passing the Museo Guggenheim, stopping at Plaza de Federico Moyúa and terminating at the Termibus (bus station). It runs from the airport every 20 minutes in summer and every 30 minutes in winter from 6.20am to midnight. There is also a direct hourly bus from the airport to San Sebastián (€15.70, 1¼ hours). It runs from 7.45am to 11.45pm.

Taxis from the airport to the Casco Viejo cost about €21 to €26, depending on traffic.

METRO

There are metro stations at all the main focal points of El Ensanche and at Casco Viejo. Tickets start at €1.50. The metro runs to the north coast from a number of stations on both sides of the river and makes it easy to get to the beaches closest to Bilbao.

TRAM

Bilbao's Eusko Tren tramline is a boon to locals and visitors alike. It runs to and fro between Basurtu, in the southwest of the city, and the Atxuri train station. Stops include the Termibus station, the Guggenheim and Teatro Arriaga by the Casco Viejo. Tickets cost €1.50 and need to be validated in the machine next to the ticket dispenser before boarding.

Around Bilbao

Guernica

POP 15,600

Guernica (Basque: Gernika) is a state of mind. At a glance it seems no more than a modern and none-too-attractive country town. Apparently, prior to the morning of 26 April 1937, Guernica wasn't quite so ugly, but the horrifying events of that day meant that the town was later reconstructed as fast as possible with little regard for aesthetics.

The reasons Franco wished to destroy Guernica are pretty clear. The Spanish Civil War was raging and World War II was looming on the horizon. Franco's Nationalist troops were advancing across Spain, but the Basques, who had their own autonomous regional government consisting of supporters of the Left and Basque nationalists, stood opposed to Franco and Guernica was the final town between the Nationalists and the capture of Bilbao. What's harder to understand is why Hitler got involved, but it's generally thought that the Nazis wanted to test the concept of 'terror bombing' on civilian targets. So when Franco asked Hitler for some help he was only too happy to oblige.

On that fateful April morning planes from Hitler's Condor Legion flew backwards and forwards over the town demonstrating their newfound concept of saturation bombing. In the space of a few hours, the town was destroyed and many people were left dead or injured. Exactly how many people were killed remains hard to quantify, with figures ranging from a couple of hundred to well over 1000. The Museo de la Paz de Gernika claims that around 250 civilians were killed and several hundred injured. What makes the bombings even more shocking is that it wasn't the first time this had happened. Just days earlier, the nearby town of Durango suffered a similar fate, but that time the world had simply not believed what it was being told.

Aside from blocking the path to Bilbao, Guernica may also have been targeted by Franco because of its symbolic value to the Basques. It's the ancient seat of Basque democracy and the site at which the Basque parliament met beneath the branches of a sacred oak tree from medieval times until 1876. Today the original oak is nothing but a stump, but the Tree of Guernica lives on in the form of a young oak tree.

The tragedy of Guernica gained international resonance with Picasso's iconic painting *Guernica,* which has come to symbolise the violence of the 20th century. A copy of the painting now hangs in the entrance hall of the UN headquarters in New York, while the original hangs in the Centro de Arte Reina Sofía (p89) in Madrid.

Accommodation in Guernica is pretty unremarkable. Most people just come on a day trip from Bilbao.

⊙ Sights

Museo de la Paz de Gernika   MUSEUM

(Guernica Peace Museum; www.peacemuseumgernica.org; Plaza Foru 1; adult/child €5/3; ⊙10am-7pm Tue-Sat, 10am-2pm Sun Mar-Sep, 10am-2pm & 4-6pm Tue-Sat, 10am-2pm Sun Oct-Feb) Guernica's seminal experience is a visit to the museum, where audiovisual displays calmly reveal the horror of war and hatred, both in the Basque Country and around the world. Display panels are in Castilian and Basque, but translations are available. A couple of blocks north, on Calle Allende Salazar, is a ceramic-tile version of Picasso's *Guernica.*

Euskal Herriko Museoa   MUSEUM

(Calle Allende Salazar; adult/child €3/1.50; ⊙10am-2pm & 4-7pm Tue-Sat, 10.30am-2.30pm Sun) Housed in the 18th-century Palacio de Montefuerte, this museum contains a comprehensive exhibition on Basque history and culture, with fine old maps, engravings and a range of other documents and portraits.

Parque de los Pueblos de Europa   PARK, MONUMENT

The pleasant Parque de los Pueblos de Europa contains a couple of typically curvaceous sculptures by Henry Moore and other works by Eduardo Chillida. The park leads to the attractive Casa de Juntas, where the provincial government has met since 1979. Nearby is the famous Tree of Guernica, sheltered by a neoclassical gazebo.

ℹ Information

Tourist Office (☎946 25 58 92; www.gernika-lumo.org; Artekalea 8; ⊙10am-2pm & 4-7pm Mon-Sat, 10am-2pm Sun) This helpful office has friendly multilingual staff.

ℹ Getting There & Away

Guernica is an easy day trip from Bilbao by ET/FV train from Atxuri train station (€2.85, one hour). Trains run every half-hour.

Basque Culture

The Basques are different. They have inhabited their corner of Spain and France seemingly forever. While many aspects of their unique culture are hidden from curious eyes, the following are visible to any visitor.

Pelota

The national sport of the Basque country is *pelota vasca,* and every village in the region has its own court – normally backing up against the village church. Pelota can be played in several different ways: bare-handed, with small wooden rackets, or with a long hand-basket called *chistera,* with which the player can throw the ball at speeds of up to 300km/h. It's possible to see pelota matches throughout the region during summer.

Lauburu

The most visible symbol of Basque culture is *lauburu,* the Basque cross. The meaning of this symbol is lost in the mists of time – some say it represents the four old regions of the Basque Country, others that it represents spirit, life, consciousness and form – but today many regard it as a symbol of prosperity, hence its appearance in modern jewellery and above house doors. It is also used to signify life and death and is found on old headstones.

Traditional Basque Games

Basque sports aren't just limited to pelota: there are also log cutting, stone lifting, bale tossing and tug of war. Most stemmed from the day-to-day activities of the region's farmers and fishers. Although most of these skills are no longer used on a daily basis, the sports are kept alive at numerous fiestas.

Bulls & Fiestas

No other Basque festival is as famous as Sanfermines (p437), with its legendary *encierro* (running of the bulls) in Pamplona. The original purpose of the *encierro* was to transfer bulls from the corrals where they would have spent the night to the bullring where they would fight. Sometime in the 14th century someone worked out that the quickest and 'easiest' way to do this was to chase the bulls out of the corrals and into the ring. It was only a small step from that to the full-blown carnage of Pamplona's Sanfermines.

Traditional Dress

Basque festivals are a good time to see traditional Basque dress and dance. It's said that there are around 400 different Basque dances, many of which have their own special kind of dress.

Basque Language

Victor Hugo described the Basque language as a 'country', and it would be a rare Basque who'd disagree with him. The language, known as Euskara, is the oldest in Europe and has no known connection to any Indo-European languages. Suppressed by Franco, Basque was subsequently recognised as one of Spain's official languages, and it has become the language of choice among a growing number of young Basques.

1. Revellers at Sanfermines, Pamplona 2. Grape Harvest festival, Álava 3. Pelota, Pamplona

WORTH A TRIP

PUENTE COLGANTE

A worthwhile stop en route to the beaches is the Unesco World Heritage–listed Puente Colgante, designed by Alberto Palacio, a disciple of Gustave Eiffel (he of Parisian tower fame). Opening in 1893, it was the world's first transporter bridge and links the suburbs of Getxo and Portugalete. A platform, suspended from the actual bridge high above, is loaded with up to six cars plus foot passengers; it then glides silently over Río Nervión to the other bank. Rides cost €0.35 one way per person. You can also take a lift up to the superstructure at 46m (€7) and walk across the river and back for some great views (not for those prone to vertigo). Another choice is to cross the river by small ferry boat (€0.35). The nearest metro stop from Bilbao is Areeta or Portugalete (both €1.50).

Mundaka

Universally regarded as the home of the best wave in Europe, Mundaka is a name of legend for surfers across the world. The wave breaks on a perfectly tapering sandbar formed by the outflow of the Río Urdaibai and, on a good day, offers heavy, barrelling lefts that can reel off for hundreds of metres. Fantastic for experienced surfers, Mundaka is absolutely not a place for novices to take to the waves.

Despite all the focus being on the waves, Mundaka has done a sterling job of not turning itself into just another 'hey dude' surf town and remains a resolutely Basque port with a pretty main square and harbour area. There's a small tourist office.

Buses and ET/FV trains between Bilbao and Bermeo stop here.

🛏 Sleeping & Eating

Those wishing to stay and practise their tube-riding skills should pull in at one of the following, but be warned prices are high in this popular little town.

For food there are a couple of buzzing bars down by the harbourside selling *pintxos* and more.

Camping Portuondo   CAMPGROUND €
(☎ 946 87 77 01; www.campingportuondo.com; sites per person/tent €8.60/15, bungalows from

€100; 🛜 🏊) Just to the south of town, this campground has pleasant terraced grounds, a pool and a restaurant, but gets overrun in the summer.

Hotel Atalaya   HOTEL €€
(☎ 946 17 70 00; www.atalayahotel.es; Kalea Itxaropena 1; s/d €96/121; 🅿 🛜) This grand hotel is in a lovely old building near the waterfront and has clean and reliable rooms – although, like everywhere in Mundaka, it's a little overpriced.

ℹ Information

Tourist Office (☎ 946 17 72 01; www.mundaka.org; Calle Kepa Deuna; ⊙10.30am-1.30pm & 4-7pm Tue-Sat, 11am-2pm Sun)

The Central Basque Coast

The coast road from Bilbao to San Sebastián is a glorious journey past spectacular seascapes, with cove after cove stretching east and verdant fields suddenly ending where cliffs plunge into the sea. *Casas rurales* (village or farmstead accommodation) and campgrounds are plentiful and well signposted.

Elantxobe

POP 444

The tiny hamlet of Elantxobe, with its colourful houses clasping like geckos to an almost sheer cliff face, is undeniably one of the most attractive spots along the entire coast. The difficulty of building here, and the lack of a beach, has meant that it has been saved from the worst of tourist-related development, but it's a pretty place to explore, and on hot days you can join the local children jumping into the sea off the harbour walls.

Lekeitio

POP 7300

Bustling Lekeitio is gorgeous. The attractive old core is centred on the unnaturally large and slightly out-of-place late-Gothic Iglesia de Santa María de la Asunción and a busy harbour lined by multicoloured, half-timbered old buildings – some of which house fine seafood restaurants and *pintxo* bars. But for most visitors, it's the two beaches that are the main draw. The one just east of the river, with a small rocky mound of an island offshore, is one of the finest beaches in the Basque Country. In many ways the town is like a miniature version of San Sebastián, but for the moment at least, Lekeitio remains a fairly low-key and predominantly Spanish and French holiday town.

The 'highlight' of Lekeitio's annual Fiesta de San Antolín (⊘5 September) involves a tug of war with a goose. The fun and games end when the goose's head falls off (nowadays they use a pre-killed goose).

🛏 Sleeping

Accommodation is fairly scarce and pricey, but the tourist office can point you in the direction of private rooms.

★ Hotel Zubieta   BOUTIQUE HOTEL €€
(📞946 84 30 30; www.hotelzubieta.com; Calle Atea; s/d from €90/108; 🅿🗑) A gorgeous and romantic boutique hotel, five minutes' walk from the centre of town, which is filled with memories of upper-class 18th-century life. It sits within beautiful flower gardens and is surrounded by spring-blossoming cherry trees.

Hotel Palacio Oxangoiti   BOUTIQUE HOTEL €€
(📞944 65 05 55; www.oxangoiti.net; Kalea Gamarra 2; s/d from €88/110; 🗑) This lovely 16th-century 'palace' is now a small boutique hotel. It's filled with the smells of ancient polished wood and elegantly combines old and new to produce a very memorable place to stay. The hotel is right in the centre of town and next to the church, so be prepared for some bell clanging after 8am.

Street noise may be problematic for some on busy summer nights.

Hotel Aisia Zita   HOTEL €€
(📞946 84 26 55; www.aisiahoteles.com; Avenida Santa Elena; s/d from €78/101; 🅿🗑) In a former life this large place, which directly overlooks the beach, was the holiday home of a Hungarian princess, although today its huge rooms with their 1920s period style are looking a little tired. There's an in-house thalassotherapy centre.

🍴 Eating

Lekeitio has some good places to eat, and self-caterers can pick up fish, straight from the boats, from the harbourside stalls.

Bar Lumentza   PINTXOS €
(Calle Buenaventura Zapiran 3; pintxos €2-5) A big hit with the locals, this no-fuss *pintxos* bar is tucked in the sidestreets. Try the octopus cooked on the *plancha* (hot plate).

Oskarbi   SEAFOOD €
(Kaia Txatxo 5; menú del día €12) Pleasing harbourside restaurant with a suitably fishy, and very good value, lunchtime menu.

ℹ Information

Tourist Office (📞946 84 40 17; Plaza Independancia; ⊘10am-2pm & 4-8pm)

ℹ Getting There & Away

Bizkaibus A3513 (€3.25) leaves from Calle Hurtado de Amézaga, by Bilbao's Abando train station, about eight times a day (except Sunday) and goes via Guernica and Elantxobe. Fairly regular buses also run from Lekeitio to San Sebastián. Drivers take note: finding a parking space can be borderline impossible in the summer.

Getaria & Zarautz

POP 2525 & 22,000

The attractive medieval fishing settlement of Getaria is a world away from nearby cosmopolitan San Sebastián and is a much better place to get a feel for coastal Basque culture. The old village tilts gently downhill to a baby-sized harbour, at the end of which is a forested island known as El Ratón (the Mouse), on account of its similarity to a mouse (this similarity is easiest to see after several strong drinks!).

It might have been this giant mouse that first encouraged the town's most famous son, the sailor Juan Sebastián Elcano, to take to the ocean waves. His adventures eventually culminated in him becoming the first man to sail around the world, after the captain of his ship, Magellan, died halfway through the endeavour.

Getaria has a short but very pleasant beach next to the town's busy harbour, which is almost totally sheltered from all but the heaviest Atlantic swells. Its safe bathing makes it an ideal family beach. If you're more a culture vulture than a bronzed god or goddess, get your kicks at the new Cristóbal Balenciaga Museoa (www.cristobalbalenciagamuseoa.com; adult/child over 9yr/child under 9yr €10/8/free; ⊘10am-7pm Jul & Aug, shorter hours Sep-Jun). Local boy Cristóbal became one of the big names in fashion design in the 1950s and '60s and this impressive museum showcases some of his best works.

Just 2km further east, along a coastal road that battles with cliffs, ocean waves and several cavelike tunnels, is Zarautz, which consists of a 2.5km-long soft sand beach backed by a largely modern strip of tower blocks. The town is a popular resort for Spaniards, and in the summer it has a lively atmosphere with plenty of places to eat, drink and stay. The beach, which is one of the longest in the Basque Country, has some of the most consistent surfing conditions in the area, and a number of surf schools will help you 'hang ten'.

🛏 Sleeping & Eating

Despite Zarautz' more energetic atmosphere, Getaria makes for the more attractive base.

We're willing to bet you won't be able walk past one of Getaria's harbour-front restaurants – where the day's catch is barbecued on open fires – without feeling hungry. Wash your lunch down with a glass of crisp, locally produced *txakoli* (white wine).

Getariano Pentsioa   HOTEL €
(☎943 14 05 67; www.pensiongetariano.es; Calle Herrieta 3, Getaria; s €40-50, d €55-70; 🖥) This is a charming, mellow yellow building with flower-filled balconies and comfortable rooms. It's on the edge of the main road through town.

Gran Camping Zarautz   CAMPGROUND €
(☎943 83 12 38; www.grancampingzarautz.com; Zarautz; sites for 2 people, tent & car €24; P🖥📶) In Zarautz, campers will find Gran Camping Zarautz, which has memorable views off the cliffs, at the far eastern end of town.

Hotel Itxas-Gain   HOTEL €€
(☎943 14 10 35; www.hotelitxasgain.com; Roke Devnal, Getaria; s €50, d €70-125; 🖥) The Hotel Itxas-Gain is a very good deal and has a mixture of room types: some have little balconies and whirlpool baths that overlook the whirlpool-like ocean. Weather permitting, breakfast is served in the peaceful gardens.

San Sebastián

POP 183,300

It's said that nothing is impossible. This is wrong. It's impossible to lay eyes on San Sebastián (Basque: Donostia) and not fall madly in love. This stunning city is cool, svelte and flirtatious by night, charming and well mannered by day. It's a city that loves to indulge, and with Michelin stars apparently falling from the heavens onto its resturants and a *pintxo* culture almost unmatched anywhere else in Spain, San Sebastián frequently tops lists of the world's best places to eat.

But just as good as the food is the summer fun in the sun. For its setting, form and attitude, Playa de la Concha is the equal of any city beach in Europe. Then there's Playa de Gros (also known as Playa de la Zurriola), with its surfers and sultry beach-goers. As the sun falls on another sweltering summer's day, you'll sit back with a drink and an artistic *pintxo* and realise that, yes, you too are in love with San Sebastián.

San Sebastián has four main centres of action. The lively Parte Vieja (old town) lies across the neck of Monte Urgull, the bay's eastern headland, and is where the most popular *pintxo* bars and many of the cheap lodgings are to be found. South of the Parte Vieja is the commercial and shopping district, the Centro Romántico, its handsome grid of late-19th-century buildings extending from behind Playa de la Concha to the banks of Río Urumea. On the east side of the river is the district of Gros, a pleasant

---

TOP PICKS FOR KIDS
....

With all those tiring outdoor activities, the Basque Country, Navarra and La Rioja are great places for children. In no particular order, here are our top picks:

➡ Hunting for dinosaurs in Enciso (p451).

➡ Playing dungeons and dragons in the castles of Olite (p442) and Javier (p438).

➡ Gawping at Nemo and Jaws in San Sebastián's aquarium (p417).

➡ Sandcastle-building for the tots and learning to surf for the big boys and girls almost anywhere along the Basque coast.

➡ For older children, playing Jack and Jill went up the (very big) hill in the Pyrenees (p438).

➡ Turning your little sister into a frog with the witches of Zugarramurdi (p438).

➡ Fiesta, fiesta! The daylight hours of almost every fiesta are tailor-made for children.

enclave that, with its relaxed ambience and the surfing beach of Playa de Gros, makes a cheerful alternative to the honeypots on the west side of the river. Right at the opposite, western end of the city is Playa de Ondarreta (essentially a continuation of Playa de la Concha), a very upmarket district known as a millionaires' belt on account of its lavish holiday homes.

History

San Sebastián was for centuries little more than a fishing village, but by 1180 it was granted self-governing status by the kingdom of Navarra, for which the bay was the principal outlet to the sea. Whale and cod fishing were the main occupations, along with the export of Castilian products to European ports and then to the Americas. After years of knockabout trans-European conflicts that included the razing of the city by Anglo-Portuguese forces during the Peninsular War, San Sebastián was hoisted into 19th-century stardom as a fashionable watering hole by Spanish royalty dodging the searing heat of the southern *meseta* (tableland). By the close of the century, the city had been given a superb belle-époque makeover that has left a legacy of elegant art-nouveau buildings and beachfront swagger.

After WWII the city's popularity sagged, but it's now undergoing a major revival, and its overall style and excitement are giving it a growing reputation as an important venue for international cultural and commercial events. The beachfront area now contains some of the most expensive properties in Spain and the city is firmly entrenched on the Spanish tourist trail, which gives it a highly international feel (and, sadly, ever-rising prices).

In 2016 it will share the title of European City of Culture with the Polish city of Wrocław.

◉ Sights

★ Playa de la Concha   BEACH
Fulfilling almost every idea of how a perfect city beach should be formed, Playa de la Concha and its westerly extension, Playa de Ondarreta, are easily among the best city beaches in Europe. Throughout the long summer months a fiesta atmosphere prevails, with thousands of tanned and toned bodies spread across the sands. The swimming is almost always safe.

★ Aquarium   AQUARIUM
(www.aquariumss.com; Plaza Carlos Blasco de Imaz 1; adult/child €13/6.50; ⊙10am-9pm daily Jul & Aug, 10am-8pm Mon-Fri, 10am-9pm Sat & Sun Easter-Jun & Sep, shorter hours rest of year) In the city's excellent aquarium you will fear for your life as huge sharks bear down on you and will get tripped-out by fancy fluoro jellyfish. The highlights of a visit are the cinema-screen-sized deep-ocean and coral-reef exhibits and the long tunnel, around which swim monsters of the deep. The aquarium also contains a maritime museum section. Allow at least 1½ hours for a visit.

Isla de Santa Clara   ISLAND
About 700m from Playa de la Concha, this island is accessible by glass-bottom boats (to the island €3.80, tour the bay €6; ⊙ Jun-Sep) that run every half-hour from the fishing port. At low tide the island gains its own tiny beach.

Playa de Gros   BEACH
(Playa de la Zurriola) Less popular than nearby Playa de la Concha, but just as showy, Playa de Gros, east of Río Urumea, is the city's main surf beach. Though swimming here is more dangerous than at Playa de la Concha, it has more of a local vibe.

Monte Igueldo   VIEWPOINT
The views from the summit of Monte Igueldo, just west of town, will make you feel like a circling hawk staring over the vast panorama of the Bahía de la Concha and the surrounding coastline and mountains. The best way to get there is via the old-world funicular railway (www.monteigueldo.es; return adult/child €3.10/2.30; ⊙10am-9pm Jul, 10am-10pm Aug, shorter hours rest of year) to the Parque de Atracciones (www.monteigueldo.es; admission €2.20; ⊙11.15am-2pm & 4-8pm Mon-Fri, until 8.30pm Sat & Sun Jul-Sep, shorter hours rest of year), a slightly tacky mini theme park at the top

San Sebastián

Mar Cantábrico
(Kantauri Itsasoa)

3

5

8

Plaza de
Zuloaga

36

Plaza de
la Trinidad

29

C de San
Vicente

See Enlargement

PARTE VIEJA

Isla de Santa Clara
(200m)

Aquarium

1

Plaza Carlos
Blasco de Imaz

40

9

6 Paseo del Muelle

Fishing
Port

47

44

Bahía de la Concha
(Kontxako Badia)

Ayuntamiento
(Town Hall)

C de Hernani

Parque
de Alderdi
Eder

0 ——— 50 m

38

18

C de 31 de Agosto

C Juan de Bilbao

C de Iñigo

C de San Juan

C de la Pescadería

25

34

28 33

50

39

C del Puerto

PARTE VIEJA

Plaza de la
Constitución

26

Plaza de
Cervantes

20

23

Nagusia Kalea (C Mayor)

48 C Fermín Calbetón

49

C de San Lorenzo

C San-Jerónimo

C de Esterlines

Plaza
Sarriegi

C del
Campanario

30

C de Embeltrán

19

Alameda del Boulevard

13

C de Arasate

C del Triunfo

Pico
del Loro

C de Zubieta

C de la Marina

C de Manterola

Paseo de la Concha

Playa de Ondarreta (600m);
Monte Igueldo (800m);
Parque de Atracciones (800m)

Playa de
la Concha

2

Paseo de la Concha

12

C San Bartolomé

Cuesta de Aldapeta

of the hill. Individual rides (which include roller coasters, boat rides, carousels and pony rides) cost between €1 and €2.50 extra. Trains on the funicular railway depart every 15 minutes.

San Telmo Museoa   MUSEUM
(www.santelmomuseoa.com; Plaza Zuloaga 1; adult/student/child €5/3/free, Tue free; ⊙ 10am-8pm Tue-Sun) Both the oldest and one of the newest museums in the Basque Country, the San Telmo museum has existed since 1902 – sort

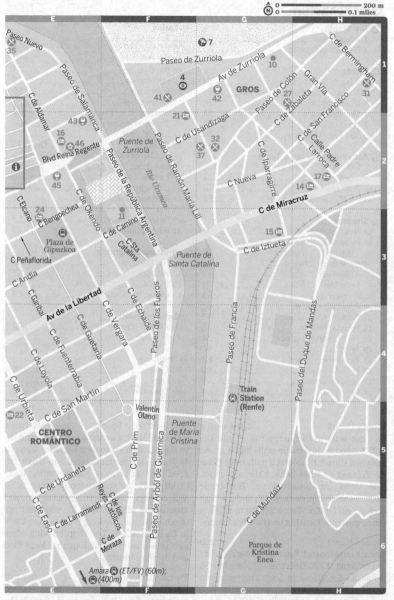

of. It was actually closed for many years but after major renovation work it reopened in 2011 and is now a museum of Basque culture and society. The displays range from historical artifacts to the squiggly lines of modern art, and all the pieces reflect Basque culture and society.

Labelling is in Spanish and Basque, but there are free audio guides available in other languages.

San Sebastián

Top Sights
1 Aquarium B2
2 Playa de la Concha B6

Sights
3 Casa de la Historia B1
4 Kursaal F1
5 Monte Urgull B1
6 Museo Naval B2
7 Playa de Gros G1
8 San Telmo Museoa D1

Activities, Courses & Tours
9 Catamarán Ciudad San Sebastián C2
10 Pukas G1
11 San Sebastián Food F3

Sleeping
12 Hostal Alemana D6
13 Hotel de Londres e Inglaterra D5
14 Hotel Gran Bahia Bernardo H2
Hotel Maria Cristina .... (see 11)
15 Pensión Aida G3
16 Pensión Aldamar E2
17 Pensión Altair H2
18 Pensión Amaiur A3
19 Pensión Artea Narrica C4
20 Pensión Edorta A4
21 Pensión Kursaal F2
22 Pensión Régil E5
23 Pensión Uralde A4
24 Urban House E3

Eating
25 Astelena C3
26 Bar Borda Berri C4
27 Bar Diz G1
28 Bar Goiz-Argi D3
29 Bar Martinez D1
30 Bar Nagusía B5
31 Bergara Bar H1
32 Bodega Donostiarra G2
33 Bodegón Alejandro D3
34 Holly Burger C3
35 Kaskazuri E1
36 La Cuchara de San Telmo D1
La Fábrica .... (see 23)
La Mejíllonera .... (see 20)
37 Ramuntxo Berri G2
38 Restaurante Alberto B3
39 Restaurante Kokotxa A4
40 Restaurante Mariñela C2
41 Restaurante Ni Neu F1

Drinking & Nightlife
42 Bar Ondarra G1
43 Be Bop E2
44 Dioni's D2
45 Museo del Whisky E2

Entertainment
46 Altxerri Jazz Bar E2
47 Etxe Kalte C2

Shopping
48 Elkar B4
49 Elkar C4
50 Kukuxumusu A3

Monte Urgull CASTLE, MUSEUM

You can walk to the summit of Monte Urgull, topped by low castle walls and a grand statue of Christ, by taking a path from Plaza de Zuloaga or from behind the aquarium. The views are breathtaking. The castle houses the well-presented **Mirando a San Sebastián** (10am-2pm & 3-5.30pm) FREE, a small museum focusing on the city's history.

Museo Naval MUSEUM

(www.untzimuseoa.net; Paseo del Muelle 24; adult/student/child €1.20/0.60/free; 10am-2pm & 4-7pm Tue-Sat, 11am-2pm Sun) This museum turns the pages of Basque seafaring and naval history. It's best appreciated by those with at least basic Spanish-language skills.

Courses & Tours

The tourist office runs several different city tours (including a cinema tour) starting at €10.

San Sebastián Food TOUR, COOKING COURSE

(943 42 11 43; www.sansebastianfood.com; Hotel Maria Cristina, Paseo de la República Argentina 4) The highly recommended San Sebastián Food runs an array of *pintxo* tasting tours (from €95), self-guided foodie tours (€75) and cookery courses (from €145) in and around the city, as well as wine tastings (from €45) and day-long wine-tasting tours to La Rioja (€255). The shop/booking office also sells a range of high-quality local food and drink products.

Pintxos Galore FOOD TOUR

(903 443442; www.sansebastianreservas.com; per person €95) Impress your friends by learning how to become a *pintxo* chef yourself on these tourist-board-run tours that show you how to create six differnet *pintxos*. Tours last three hours and there must be at least three people in a group for the tours to run.

Sabores de San Sebastián   TOUR

(Flavours of San Sebastián; 902 443442; www.sansebastianreservas.com; tour €18; 11.30am Tue & Thu Jul & Aug) The tourist office runs the Sabores de San Sebastián, a two-hour tour (in Spanish and English, French tours are available on request) of some of the city's *pintxo* haunts. Tours are held with less frequency outside high season – contact the tourist office for dates.

Pukas   SURFING

(943 32 00 68; www.pukassurf.com; Paseo de Zurriola 24) Playa de Gros, with its generally mellow and easy waves, is a good place for learners to get to grips with surfing. Aspiring surfer wannabes should drop by Pukas, where surf lessons, and board and wetsuit hire are available. Prices vary depending on group size and lesson length, but start at €53 for a weekend course comprising a 1½-hour lesson each day.

Catamarán Ciudad San Sebastián   BOAT TOUR

(www.ciudadsansebastian.com; Paseo del Muelle 14; adult/child €9/5; noon-8pm Jul & Aug, shorter hr Sep-Jun) Boat tours of the bay and out onto the open ocean on a motorised catamaran run hourly (except at 3pm) in the summer.

Festivals & Events

San Sebastián has a busy festival calendar. The main events:

Festividad de San Sebastián   CITY FESTIVAL

(20 Jan) The city's main winter knees-up.

Carnaval   CARNIVAL

(Feb or Mar) Carnaval (dates change) is a big event, but nearby Tolosa goes even more berserk.

Heineken Jazzaldia   JAZZ

(www.heinekenjazzaldia.com; Jul) Big-name acts converge for the San Sebastián jazz festival.

Semana Grande   SUMMER FESTIVAL

(mid-Aug) The big summer festival.

Regatta de Traineras   ROWING

(Sep) The Regatta de Traineras, a boat race in which local teams of rowers race out to sea, takes place on the first two Sundays in September.

Film Festival   FILM

(www.sansebastianfestival.com) The world-renowned, two-week film festival has been an annual fixture in the second half of September since 1957.

Sleeping

Accommodation standards in San Sebastián are generally good, but prices are high and availability in high season is very tight. With the city's increasing popularity, many of the better places are booked up for July and August months in advance. If you do turn up without a booking, head to the tourist office, which keeps a list of available rooms.

Pensión Régil   PENSIÓN €

(943 42 71 43; www.pensionregil.com; Calle de Easo 9; s/d €53/59;) The furnishings might be cheap and the decor a bit pink and floral for our liking, but just look at that price! You won't get a much better deal in San Sebastián in high season. Add in that all rooms have private bathrooms, it's very close to Playa de la Concha and the young owner, Inaki, is a bit of a charmer and you can't go wrong.

Urban House   HOSTEL €

(943 42 81 54; www.enjoyeu.com; Plaza de Gipuzkoa 2; dm €25-26, r from €56;) This busy party house, where summer fun rules supreme, is one of the longest running hostels in town. It's close to all the action and the young, very Anglophone staff (so Anglophone that some don't speak any Spanish) will ensure you have a good time.

They also organise a variety of city tours and surf lessons. The hostel manages the bookings for several cheap and basic places elsewhere in the old town – so if the main building is full, the staff can always find you a bed elsewhere.

★ Pensión Aida   BOUTIQUE HOTEL €€

(943 32 78 00; www.pensionesconencanto.com; Calle de Iztueta 9; s €62, d €84-90, studios €132-152;) The owners of this excellent *pensión* read the rule book on what makes a good hotel and have complied exactly. The rooms are bright and bold, full of exposed stone and everything smells fresh and clean. The communal area, stuffed with soft sofas and mountains of information, is a big plus.

If you need more space then take one of its handful of very slick studios (which come with kitchenettes). For our money, we'd say this one is very hard to beat.

Pensión Amaiur   BOUTIQUE HOTEL €€

(943 42 96 54; www.pensionamaiur.com; Calle de 31 de Agosto 44; s €45, d €90-100;) The young and friendly owners of this top-notch guesthouse, which has a prime old-town location, have really created something different here. The look of the place is 'old-granny

WHAT'S COOKING IN THE BASQUE COUNTRY, NAVARRA AND LA RIOJA

Food and drink is almost the cornerstone of life in this part of Spain. Basque food is generally considered about the best in the country, and the wines of La Rioja are the finest in Spain. Seafood is big on the coast: *bacalao al pil-pil* (salted cod and garlic in an olive-oil emulsion) and *chipirones en su tinta* (baby squid served in its own ink) are both popular. Further into the hills and mountains people tuck into *chuleton de buey* (steaks – never less than massive). Look out also for fine mountain cheese in the Pyrenees and tiny baby elvers on the coast (although nowadays a substitute is often used due to the rarity of elvers).

cottage' with bright floral wallpapers and bathrooms tiled in Andalucian blue and white. The best rooms are those with balconies that overlook the main street. Some rooms share bathrooms. Staff speak English.

Pensión Edorta BOUTIQUE HOTEL €€

(☑ 943 42 37 73; www.pensionedorta.com; Calle del Puerto 15; r €90-100, r without bathroom €65-70; ☎) A fine *pensión* with rooms that are all tarted up in brash modern colours, but with a salute to the past in the stone walls and ceilings. It's very well cared for and well situated. Cheaper rooms share bathrooms.

Pensión Altair PENSIÓN €€

(☑ 943 29 31 33; www.pension-altair.com; Calle Padre Larroca 3; s/d €62/88; ☀ @ ☎) This *pensión* is in a beautifully restored town house, with unusual church-worthy arched windows and modern, minimalist rooms that are a world away from the fusty decor of the old-town *pensiones*. Interior rooms lack the grandiose windows but are much larger. Reception is closed between 1.30pm and 5pm.

Pensión Kursaal BOUTIQUE HOTEL €€

(☑ 943 29 26 66; www.pensionesconencanto.com; Calle de Peña y Goñi 2; d €85-91; ☀ @ ☎) With a rattling 1930s-style lift and massive, wall-sized photos this excellent place, full of light and colour, is a mix of the old and the new. The majestic rooms have a refined edge, which helps the place feel more like a proper hotel than a *pensión*. It's virtually on Playa de Gros.

Pensión Aldamar HOTEL €€

(☑ 943 43 01 43; www.pensionaldamar.com; Calle de Aldamar 2; s €105, d €120-130; ☀ ☎) This smart *pensión* is run on lines more akin to a hotel and offers superb white, modern rooms with stone walls, some of which have little balconies from which to watch the theatre of street life below. It's a big step up in quality from many of the other old-town *pensiones*.

Hostal Alemana BOUTIQUE HOTEL €€

(☑ 943 46 25 44; www.hostalalemana.com; Calle de San Martín 53; s/d from €66/77; P ☎) With a great location just a sandy footstep from the beach, this smart hotel has opted for the white, minimalist look, countered with stylish black-and-white photos, all of which works very well and makes the rooms light and airy.

Pensión Uralde PENSIÓN €€

(☑ 943 42 25 81; www.ur-alde.com; Calle del Puerto 17; s/d €115/120; ☀ ☎) This excellent new *pensión* offers bright colours and quality rooms, all of which differ, but all are fairly in-your-face flamboyant. Try the tartan-coloured Scottish one or the twee, lavender-flavoured Provence one.

Pensión Artea Narrica PENSIÓN €€

(☑ 943 45 51 00; www.pensionartea.com; Calle Narrika 3; s €52-65, d €75; ☀ ☎) Recently renovated, this place doesn't look like much from the outside, but actually offers some of the nicer, and better value, beds in the old town. Rooms have something of a farmhouse look with exposed wooden roof beams and stone walls, but the furnishings are very much city slicker.

Hotel Gran Bahia Bernardo HOTEL €€

(☑ 943 29 80 49; www.hotelgranbahiabernardo. com; Calle Trueba 1; r €137; ☎) This smart, modern hotel in the Gros neighbourhood is dominated by a giant black-and-white picture of a storm-lashed San Sebastián. The rooms themselves are far less storm wracked, although they are rather small.

Breakfast is an outrageous €1. Yes, €1.

Hotel Maria Cristina HISTORIC HOTEL €€€

(☑ 943 43 76 00; www.starwoodhotels.com; Paseo de la República Argentina 4; d from €335, ste from €620; P ☀ @ ☎) In case you're wondering what sort of hotels Lonely Planet authors normally stay in, the absolutely impeccable Maria Cristina, with its huge and luxurious rooms, is not one of them. However, don't be downhearted, because instead of hanging out with us you'll get to mix with royalty and

Hollywood stars, who feel right at home in this palace-like hotel, which dominates the centre of the city. Yes, we know, you're still disappointed.

Hotel de Londres e Inglaterra
HISTORIC HOTEL €€€

(☑ 943 44 07 70; www.hlondres.com; Calle de Zubieta 2; s/d from €214/219; P ✽ ☎) Queen Isabel II set the tone for this hotel well over a century ago, and things have stayed pretty regal ever since. It oozes class and some rooms have stunning views over Playa de la Concha.

✕ Eating

With 16 Michelin stars (including three restaurants with the coveted three stars) and a population of 183,000, San Sebastián stands atop a pedestal as one of the culinary capitals of the planet. As if that weren't enough, the city is overflowing with bars – almost all of which have bar tops weighed down under a mountain of *pintxos* that almost every Spaniard will (sometimes grudgingly) tell you are the best in the country. These statistics alone make San Sebastián's CV pretty impressive. But it's not just us who thinks this: a raft of the world's best chefs, including such luminaries as Catalan super-chef Ferran Adriá, have said San Sebastián is quite possibly the best place on the entire planet to eat.

Restaurante Alberto
SEAFOOD €

(☑ 943 42 88 84; Calle de 31 de Agosto 19; mains €12-15, menú €15; ☺ noon-4pm & 7pm-midnight Thu-Tue) A charming old seafood restaurant with a fishmonger-style window display of the day's catch. It's small and friendly and the pocket-sized dining room feels like it was once someone's living room. The food is earthy (well, OK, salty) and good, and the service swift.

Ramuntxo Berri
BASQUE €

(Calle Peña y Goñi 10; mains €10-14, menú del día €12; ☺ 9am-4.30pm & 7pm-midnight Mon-Sat, 9am-5pm Sun) Anyone else smell a bargain? The well prepared and presented dishes served here, which are largely traditional Basque, would cost double the price if this restaurant were in the old town, and it's so popular with locals at lunchtime you might have to queue for a table. It also has a good array of *pintxos*, of which you shouldn't miss the *foie con manzana* (liver with apple).

Holly Burger
BURGERS €

(Calle de la Pescadería 6; burgers €5-7.50; ☺ 1-4pm & 7.30-11.30pm; ♿) Homemade gourmet burgers with names like Heaven Can Wait (frankly, if you eat too many burgers, it probably won't) and Passion Red. There's also a good strong helping of veggie burgers and even gluten-free ones.

THREE SHINING STARS

The Basque Country seems to be engaged in an eternal battle with Catalonia for the title of the best foodie region in Spain and, just like in Catalonia, the Basque Country is home to an impressive number of restaurants that have been awarded a coveted three Michelin stars, as well as many more with one or two stars. All the three-star places are in and around San Sebastián. Reservations, well in advance, are obligatory at all three restaurants.

★ **Arzak** (☑ 943 27 84 65; www.arzak.info; Avenida Alcalde Jose Elosegui 273; meals €189; ☺ closed Sun-Mon, Nov & late Jun) Acclaimed chef Juan Mari Arzak takes some beating when it comes to *nueva cocina vasca* (Basque nouvelle cuisine) and his restaurant is, not surprisingly, considered one of the best places to eat in Spain. Arzak is now assisted by his daughter Elena, and they never cease to innovate. The restaurant is about 1.5km east of San Sebastián.

Martín Berasategui Restaurant (☑ 943 36 64 71; www.martinberasategui.com; Calle Loidi 4, Lasarte-Oria; tasting menu €195; ☺ closed dinner Sun, Mon, Tue & Dec–mid-Jan) This superlative restaurant, about 9km southwest of San Sebastián, is considered by foodies to be one of the best restaurants in the world. The chef, Martín Berasategui, doesn't approach cooking in the same way as the rest of us. He approaches it as a science, and the results are tastes you never knew existed.

Akelañe (☑ 943 31 12 09; www.akelarre.net; Paseo Padre Orcolaga 56; tasting menu €170; ☺ closed Sun & Mon year-round, & Tue Jan-Jun) This is where chef Pedro Subijana creates cuisine that is a feast for all five senses. As with most of the region's top *nueva cocina vasca* restaurants, the emphasis here is on using fresh, local produce and turning it into something totally unexpected. It's in the suburb of Igeldo just west of the city.

BEST PINTXO BARS IN SAN SEBASTIÁN

Just rolling the word *pintxo* around your tongue defines the essence of this cheerful, cheeky little slice of Basque cuisine. The perfect *pintxo* should have exquisite taste, texture and appearance and should be savoured in two elegant bites. The Basque version of a tapa, the *pintxo* transcends the commonplace by the sheer panache of its culinary campiness. In San Sebastián especially, Basque chefs have refined the *pintxo* to such an art form that many people would say that there's simply no other city in Spain that can beat it.

Many *pintxos* are bedded on small pieces of bread or on tiny half-baguettes, upon which towering creations are constructed and pinned in place by large toothpicks. Some bars specialise in seafood, with much use of marinated anchovies, prawns and strips of squid, all topped with anything from chopped crab to pâté. Others deal in pepper or mushroom delicacies, or simply offer a mix of everything. And the choice isn't normally limited to what's on the bar top in front of you: many of the best *pintxos* are the hot ones you need to order. These are normally chalked up on a blackboard on the wall somewhere.

Locals tend to just eat one or two of the house specials at each bar before moving on somewhere else. When it comes to ordering, tell the bartender what you want first and never just help yourself to a *pintxo* off the counter!

The following *pintxo* bars all charge between €2.50 to €3.50 for one *pintxo*. Not so bad if you just take one, but is one ever enough?

★ **La Cuchara de San Telmo** (www.lacucharadesantelmo.com; Calle de 31 de Agosto 28; pintxos from €2.50; ⊙ 7.30-11pm Tue, noon-3.30pm & 7.30-11pm Wed-Sun) This unfussy, hidden-away (and hard to find) bar offers miniature *nueva cocina vasca* (Basque nouvelle cuisine) from a supremely creative kitchen. Unlike many San Sebastián bars, this one doesn't have *pintxos* laid out on the bar top; instead, order from the blackboard menu behind the counter. Don't miss delights such as *carrílera de ternera al vino tinto* (calf cheeks in red wine), with meat so tender it starts to dissolve almost before it's past your lips.

Bar Borda Berri (Calle Fermín Calbetón 12; ⊙ noon-midnight) At this outstanding little bar, you order freshly made *pintxos* from a blackboard menu. The staff are happy to offer advice on the day's best choice, but the house specials are pigs' ears and delicious calf cheeks.

Bergara Bar (General Artetxe 8; pintxos from €2.50; ⊙ 9am-11pm) The Bergara Bar, which sits on the edge of a busy square, is one of the most highly regarded *pintxo* bars in Gros, a

★ **La Fábrica**　　MODERN BASQUE €€
(☑ 943 98 05 81; Calle del Puerto 17; mains €15-20, menú from €24; ⊙ 1-3.30pm & 8.30-11pm Mon-Sat, 1-3.30pm Sun) The red-brick interior walls and white tablecloths lend an air of class to a restaurant whose modern takes on Basque classics have been making waves with San Sebastián locals over the last couple of years. At just €24, the multidish tasting menu is about the best value deal in the city.

Advance reservations are almost essential.

Bodegón Alejandro　　SEAFOOD €€
(☑ 943 42 71 58; Calle de Fermín Calbetón 4; menú del día from €16, mains €15-18; ⊙ 1-3.30pm Tue & Sun, 1-3.30pm & 8.30-10.30pm Wed-Sat) This highly regarded restaurant, which has a pleasant, casual style, has a menu from which you can select such succulent treats as tripe with veal cheeks, baby tomatoes stuffed with squid or just plain-old baked lobster. Oh, what choices!

Kaskazuri　　SEAFOOD €€
(☑ 943 42 08 94; Paseo de Salamanca 14; menú from €18; ⊙ 1-3.30pm & 8.30-11pm) Upmarket Basque seafood is all the rage in this flash restaurant, which is built on a raised platform allowing views of the former home of your dinner. It cooks up a storm with the €18 *menú del día*.

Restaurante Mariñela　　SEAFOOD €€
(☑ 943 42 73 83; Paseo del Muelle; mains €10-18; ⊙ 1-4pm & 9pm-midnight Tue-Sat, 1-4pm Sun) You pay for the fabulous harbour-front setting, but the location guarantees that the fish is so fresh it may well flop back off your plate and swim away. There are several similar neighbouring places.

Restaurante Ni Neu　CONTEMPORARY BASQUE €€€
(☑ 943 00 31 62; www.restaurantenineu.com; Avenida de Zurriola 1; menú €18-38; ⊙ 10am-8.30pm Sun, Tue & Wed, 10am-11.30pm Thu-Sat) The light, fluffy and utterly modern dishes of the Res-

growing powerhouse in the *pintxo*-bar stakes, and has a mouth-watering array of delights piled onto the bar counter as well as others chalked up on the board.

Astelena (Calle de Iñigo 1; pintxos from €2.50; ⊙1-4.30pm & 8-11pm Tue & Thu-Sat, 1-4.30pm Wed) The *pintxos* draped across the counter in this bar, tucked into the corner of Plaza de la Constitución, stand out. Many of them are a fusion of Basque and Asian inspirations, but the best of all are perhaps the foie-gras-based treats. The great positioning means that prices are slightly elevated.

Bar Goiz-Argi (Calle de Fermín Calbetón 4; pintxos from €2.50) *Gambas a la plancha* (prawns cooked on a hotplate) are the house speciality. Sounds simple, we know, but never have we tasted prawns cooked quite as perfectly as this.

La Mejillonera (Calle del Puerto 15; pintxos from €2.50) If you thought mussels only came with garlic sauce, come here to discover mussels (from €3.50) by the thousand in all their glorious forms. Mussels not for you? Opt for the calamari and *patatas bravas* (fried potatoes with a spicy tomato and mayo sauce). We promise you won't regret it.

Bar Nagusía (Nagusía Kalea 4; pintxos from €2.50) This bar, reminiscent of old San Sebastián, has a counter that groans under the weight of its *pintxos*. You'll be groaning after a few as well – in sheer pleasure.

Bodega Donostiarra (Calle de Peña y Goñi 13; pintxos from €2.50; ⊙9.30am-11pm Mon-Sat) The stone walls, pot plants and window ornaments give this place an old-fashioned French bistro look, but at the same time it feels very modern. It's best regarded for humble *jamón*, chorizo and tortilla. It also has a long wine list (and an attached wine shop).

Bar Martinez (Calle 31 de Agosto 13; pintxos from €2.50; ⊙9.30am-11pm Tue-Sun, Fri & Sat open late) This small bar has won awards for its *morros de bacalao* (slices of cod balanced atop a piece of bread) and is one of the more character-laden places to dip into some *pintxos*.

Bar Diz (Calle Zabaleta 17; pintxos from €2.50) In beach-blessed Gros, tiny Bar Diz has massively good *pintxos* (and the breakfast isn't bad either), and other foreign tourists are rare, so it's a totally local affair. If you're hungry opt for a *ración* (plate).

BILBAO, THE BASQUE COUNTRY & LA RIOJA SAN SEBASTIÁN

taurante Ni Neu will leave you hoping never to eat boring old-fashioned meat and two veg again! Throw in a spectacular setting, inside the Kursaal Centre, with a view straight over Playa de Gros and bargain-priced meals, and you get a place that's hard to beat.

Restaurante Kokotxa MODERN SPANISH €€€
(☑943 42 19 04; www.restaurantekokotxa.com; Calle del Campanario 11; mains €18-20, menú from €30; ⊙1.30-3.30pm & 8.45-11pm Wed-Sat) This Michelin-star restaurant is hidden away down an overlooked alley in the old town, but the food rewards those who search. Although not the cheapest menu offering, most people opt for the *menú de mercado* (€55) and enjoy the flavours of the traders from the busy city market. Hours vary; check website.

 Drinking & Entertainment

It would be hard to imagine a town with more bars than San Sebastián. Most of the city's bars mutate through the day from calm morning-coffee hang-outs to *pintxo*-laden delights, before finally finishing up as noisy bars full of writhing, sweaty bodies. Nights in San Sebastián start late and go on until well into the wee hours.

Museo del Whisky BAR
(Alameda Blvd 5; ⊙3.30pm-3.30am) Appropriately named, this Irish/Scottish-style bar is full of bottles of Scotland's finest (3000 bottles to be exact) as well as a museum's worth of whisky-related knick-knacks – old bottles, tacky mugs and glasses and a nice, dusty, museum-like atmosphere.

Dioni's GAY
(Calle Ijentea 2; ⊙3pm-2.30am Mon-Thu & Sun, 3pm-3.30am Fri & Sat) More a spot for a black coffee in the early hours, this relaxed and very gay-friendly place has an '80s cocktail-bar ambience and is the perfect spot in which to watch the Eurovision Song Contest.

Bar Ondarra
BAR

(Avenida de Zurriola 16) Head over to Gros for this terrific bar, which is just across the road from the beach. There's a great chilled-out mixed crowd, and in the rockin' downstairs bar, every kind of sound gets aired.

Be Bop
BAR, CLUB

(Paseo de Salamanca 3; ⊙8pm-3am) This long-standing bar has recently reinvented itself and is now a snazzy jazz bar with occasional live performances. It attracts a slightly older crowd than some of the old-town bars and on weekends it jams till dawn.

Altxerri Jazz Bar
LIVE MUSIC

(www.altxerri.com; Blvd Reina Regente 2; ⊙4pm-3am) This jazz and blues temple has regular live gigs by local and international stars. Jamming sessions take over on nights with no gig, and there's an in-house art gallery.

Etxe Kalte
JAZZ

(Calle Mari Igentea; ⊙noon-4pm & 6pm-4am Tue, 6pm-4am Wed-Sat, 6pm-midnight Sun) A very-late-night haunt near the harbour, which moves to dance music and grooves to jazz.

🛍 Shopping

The Parte Vieja is awash with independent boutiques, while the Centro Romantíca has brand-name and chain-store favourites.

Elkar
BOOKS

(Calle de Fermín Calbetón 30; ⊙10am-2pm & 4.30-8pm) For a huge range of travel books and guides (including lots of Lonely Planet guides), maps and hiking books in English, Spanish and French, try this specialist travel bookshop. Almost opposite it is a bigger mainstream branch (Calle de Fermín Calbetón 21) dealing in Spanish- and Basque-language books.

Kukuxumusu
CLOTHING

(Nagusía Kalea 15; ⊙10.30am-2.15pm & 4.30-8.15pm Mon & Tue, 10.30am-8.30pm Wed-Sat, 11am-3pm & 4-8pm Sun) The funkiest and best-known Basque clothing label has a whole wardrobe of original T-shirts and other clothing awaiting you here.

MOVING ON?

· ·

For tips, recommendations and reviews, head to shop.lonelyplanet.com to purchase a downloadable PDF of the French Basque Country chapter from Lonely Planet's *France* guide.

ℹ Information

Oficina de Turismo (☎943 48 11 66; www.sansebastianturismo.com; Alameda del Boulevard 8; ⊙9am-8pm Mon-Sat, 10am-7pm Sun) This friendly office offers comprehensive information on the city and the Basque Country in general.

Zarranet (Calle de San Lorenzo 6; per hr €2; ⊙10.30am-10pm Mon-Sat, 4-10pm Sun) One of a handful of places that offer internet access.

ℹ Getting There & Away

AIR

The city's **airport** (☎902 404704; www.aena.es) is 22km out of town, near Hondarribia. There are regular flights to Madrid and Barcelona and occasional charters to other major European cities. Biarritz, just over the border in France, is served by Ryanair and EasyJet, among various other budget airlines, and is generally much cheaper to fly into.

BUS

The main bus station is a 20-minute walk south of the Parte Vieja, between Plaza de Pío XII and the river. Local buses 28 and 26 connect the bus station with Alameda del Boulevard (€1.40, 10 minutes). Construction of a new bus station is currently in progress on Paseo de Francia, next to the Renfe train station. It's possible it might open during the lifetime of this book.

There are daily bus services to the following:

TO	FARE (€)	DURATION (HR)
Biarritz (France)	6.75	1¼
Bilbao	6.74-11.50	1
Bilbao airport	16.50	1¼
Madrid	from 36	5-6
Pamplona	7.68	1
Vitoria	from 6	1½

TRAIN

The main **Renfe train station** (Paseo de Francia) is just across Río Urumea, on a line linking Paris to Madrid. There are several services daily to Madrid (from €47, five hours) and two to Barcelona (from €64, six hours).

For France you must first go to the Spanish/French border town of Irún (or sometimes trains go as far as Hendaye; Renfe from €2.65, 25 minutes), which is also served by **Eusko Tren/Ferrocarril Vasco** (www.euskotren.es), and change there. Trains depart every half-hour from Amara train station, about 1km south of the city centre, and also stop in Pasajes (€1.50, 12 minutes) and Irún/Hendaye (ET/FV €1.70, 25 minutes). Another ET/FV railway line heads west to Bilbao via

Zarautz, Zumaia and Durango, but it's painfully slow, so the bus is a much better plan.

ⓘ Getting Around

Buses to Hondarribia (€2.30, 45 minutes) and the airport (€2.30, 45 minutes) depart from Plaza de Gupúzkoa.

East of San Sebastián

Pasajes

POP 15,885

Pasajes (Basque: Pasaia), where Río Oiartzun meets the Atlantic, is the largest port in the province of Guipúzcoa. The main street and the area immediately around the central square are lined with pretty houses and colourful balconies, and are well worth a half-day's exploration. Highlights are the great seafood restaurants and the spectacular entrance to the port, through a keyhole-like split in the cliff face – even more impressive when a huge container ship passes through it.

Nowadays Pasajes is virtually a suburb of San Sebastián and there are numerous buses plying the route between them. For a much more enjoyable way of getting there, though, you can walk over the cliffs from San Sebastián. The walk takes about 2½ to three hours and passes through patches of forest and past the occasional idyllic beach and strange rock formations covered in seabirds and then descends to Pasajes, which you reach by taking the small ferry boat across the inlet. From Pasajes you could, the following day, continue over the giant whaleback mountain of Jaizkibel (547m), which though not technically very high has views to make you feel you've just conquered a Himalayan peak! This walk takes a full day and is fairly hard going. The tourist office in San Sebastián can supply route details.

Hondarribia

POP 16,518

Lethargic Hondarribia (Castilian: Fuenterrabía), staring across the estuary to France, has a heavy Gallic fragrance, a charming *casco antiguo* (old city) and, in contrast to the quiet old city, a buzzing beach scene.

You enter the *casco* through an archway at the top of Calle San Compostela to reach the pretty Plaza de Gipuzkoa. Head straight on to Calle San Nicolás and go left to reach the bigger Plaza de Armas and the Gothic Iglesia de Santa María de la Asunción.

For La Marina, head the other way from the archway. This is Hondarribia's most picturesque quarter. Its main street, Calle San Pedro, is flanked by typical fishermen's houses, with facades painted bright green or blue and wooden balconies gaily decorated with flower boxes.

The beach is about 1km from the town, and though not exactly attractive, it's lined by bars and restaurants and offers about the calmest waters in the entire region. It's popular with locals, but foreigners rarely come here.

Buses run frequently to nearby Irún and on to San Sebastián; catch them from Sabin Arana.

🛏 Sleeping & Eating

There are some good places to stay in Hondarribia. The main old-city plaza is home to a number of very good *pintxo* bars and restaurants.

Hotel San Nikolás HOTEL €€
(☑943 64 42 78; www.hotelsannikolas.es; Plaza de Armas 6; s €69, d €98-117; 🛜) Inside a cute, wobbly, pink-and-blue old building on the main plaza, this place – which has small, modern rooms painted in arresting colours – is an enjoyable spot to stay for a night or two.

Parador de Hondarribia HISTORIC HOTEL €€€
(☑943 64 55 00; www.parador.es; Plaza de Armas 14; s/d €198/216; 🅿🌣@🛜) It's not every day that the opportunity to sleep in a thousand-year-old fortress guarding the boundaries of Spain arises, so don your suit of armour or princess's ballgown and step into the fantasy that is this sumptuous offering from the Parador chain.

South of San Sebastián

The hills rising to the south between San Sebastián and Bilbao offer a number of appealing towns. There are plenty of *nekazal turismoas* (*casas rurales;* family homes in rural areas with rooms to rent).

Santuario de Loyola

Just outside Azpeitia (12km south of the A8 motorway along the GI631) lies Santuario de Loyola (www.santuarioloyola.org; house adult/child €3/free; ⊙reception centre 8am-2pm & 3.30-7.30pm), dedicated to St Ignatius, the founder of the Jesuit order. From the outside the dark, sooty basilica, laden with grey marble and plenty of carved ornamentation, is monstrous rather than attractive. Inside, however, is much brighter, and smaller, than you'd expect. The house, where the saint was born in 1490, is preserved in one of the two wings of the sanctuary and there's a small museum. The stated opening hours are for the reception centre/ticket office. Individual buildings within the complex have different hours.

Oñati

POP 10,800

With a flurry of magnificent architecture and a number of interesting sites scattered through the surrounding green hills, the small, and resolutely Basque, town of Oñati is a great place to get to know the rural Basque heartland.

There are daily buses to/from San Sebastián, Vitoria and Bilbao.

◉ Sights

Universidad de Sancti Spiritus   HISTORIC BUILDING

Oñati's number-one attraction is the Renaissance treasure of the Universidad de Sancti Spiritus. Built in the 16th century, it was the first university in the Basque Country and, until its closure in 1902, alumni here were schooled in philosophy, law and medicine.

Today it's been taken over as local council offices, but you can still enter the Mudéjar courtyard (⊙9am-2.30pm Mon & Wed, 9am-1pm & 3-4.30pm Tue & Thu, 9am-2pm Fri) and admire its plateresque facade. The tourist office can organise guided tours (from €10) with 24 hours' notice. Although it's something of a hassle organising this in advance, it's well worth doing as you get a much more in-depth look at the building (as well as other sites throughout the town).

Iglesia de San Miguel   CHURCH

This late-Gothic confection has a cloister built over the river. The church faces onto the main square, Foruen Enparantza, dominated by the eye-catching baroque ayuntamiento (town hall).

Bidaurreta Monastery   MONASTERY

(Kalea Lazarraga) Founded in 1510, this monastery contains a beautiful baroque altarpiece. It's at the opposite end of town to the tourist office and Iglesia de San Miguel.

🛏 Sleeping

Oñati doesn't get a lot of tourists staying overnight, a fact that is reflected by the relative dearth of hotels. But the countryside around town is awash in *casas rurales* – ask at the tourist office for a list.

Ongí Hotela   HOTEL €

(☑943 71 82 85; www.hotelongi.com; Calle Zaharra 19; incl breakfast s €32-42, d €44-56; ❉ ❀ ☏) A central place above a bar with sparkling-clean, though unremarkable, rooms with small beds.

ⓘ Information

Tourist Office   TOURIST INFORMATION

(☑943 78 34 53; Calle San Juan 14; ⊙10am-2pm & 3.30-7.30pm Mon-Fri, 10am-2pm & 4-6.30pm Sat, 10am-2pm Sun) The tourist office is just opposite the Universidad de Sancti Spiritus.

Santuario de Arantzazu & Arrikrutz Caves

About 10km south of Oñati is the love-it-or-loathe-it pilgrimage site of Santuario de Arantzazu (www.arantzazukosantutegia.org), a fabulous conflation of piety and avant-garde art. The sanctuary was built in the 1950s on the site where, in 1468, a shepherd found a statue of the Virgin under a hawthorn bush – on which the sanctuary's design is supposed to be based. The overwhelming impression of the building is of spiky towers and hollow halls guarded by 14 strange-looking, chiselled apostles and, in the crypt, a devil-red Christ – all of which caused a bit of a headache for the Vatican.

The road up and the setting are worth the trip in themselves, and the whole area lends itself to excellent walking – the Oñati tourist office has information on routes.

There's a cavern system a couple of kilometres back down the road towards Oñati. The Arrikrutz caves (adult/child €9/6; ⊙10am-2pm & 3-7pm Tue-Sun Jun-Sep, shorter hours Oct-May) have numerous slow-growing stalagmites and stalactites.

Vitoria

POP 235,600 / ELEV 512M

Vitoria (Basque: Gasteiz) has a habit of falling off the radar, yet it's actually the capital of not just the southern Basque province of Álava (Basque: Araba) but also the entire Basque Country. Maybe it was given this honour precisely because it is so forgotten,

Vitoria

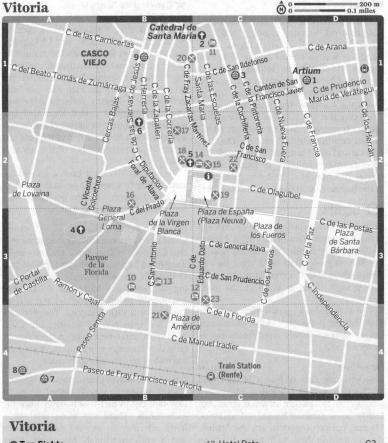

Vitoria

but if that's the case, prepare for a surprise. With an art gallery whose contents frequently surpass those of the more famous Bilbao galleries, a delightful old quarter, dozens of great *pintxo* bars and restaurants, a large student contingent and a friendly local population, you have the makings of a perfect city!

History

Vitoria's name may well derive from the Basque word *beturia,* meaning height, a reference to the hill on which the old town stands. It was so named by the Visigoths. Sancho VI of Navarra settled things by founding a 'New Vitoria' in the 12th century. Thereafter, Vitoria bounced to and fro between the Castilian and Navarran crowns. The economic advances of the late 19th century triggered Vitoria's expansion, which carried over into the 20th century. The city's historic and well-preserved nature made it a good choice for capital of the Basque autonomous government in 1981. The University of the Basque Country also has its base here.

◉ Sights

At the base of Vitoria's medieval Casco Viejo is the delightful Plaza de la Virgen Blanca. It's lorded over by the 14th-century **Iglesia de San Miguel** (Plaza de la Virgen Blanca), whose statue of the Virgen Blanca, the city's patron saint, lends its name to the plaza below.

The 14th-century **Iglesia de San Pedro** (Calle Herrería) is the city's oldest church and has a fabulous Gothic frontispiece on its eastern facade.

★ **Artium** GALLERY
(www.artium.org; Calle de Francia 24; adult/child €6/free, Mon free, Wed by donation; ⊘11am-2pm & 5-8pm Tue-Fri, 11am-9pm Sat & Sun, closed Sep) Unlike some famous Basque art galleries, Vitoria's palace of modern art, the Artium, doesn't need to dress to impress. It knows it's what's on the inside that really counts. It is daring, eccentric and challenging in a way other museums could never get away with.

The large subterranean galleries are filled with engrossing works by Basque, Spanish and international artists, displaying some fairly intense modernist work. Over the years we've seen exhibitions featuring 'art' that many would describe as borderline pornography, children's drawings depicting suicide and even a grainy, and very bloody, video of a woman having her hymen sewn back up to make her a 'virgin' again. Yes, this is art designed to shock. Guided tours, in Spanish, run several times a day. After digesting the art, it's worth digesting some food at the much-praised **Cube Café** (menú del día €15), inside the museum.

★ **Catedral de Santa María** CATHEDRAL
(☑945 25 51 35; www.catedralvitoria.com; tours adult/student/child €8.50/5.50/1; ⊘tours at 10.30am, 1pm, 4.15pm, 5.30pm, 6pm & 6.45pm Apr-Aug, shorter hours Sep-Mar) At the summit of the old town and dominating its skyline is the medieval Catedral de Santa María. For a number of years the cathedral has been undergoing a lengthy restoration project. There are excellent guided tours that give an insight into the excitement of restoration and give you a taste not just of the past and future of the cathedral but of the city as a whole.

Technically you must book a tour in advance either by telephone or via the website, but out of season it's often possible to just turn up and join the next tour.

Museo de Bellas Artes GALLERY
(Paseo de Fray Francisco de Vitoria; adult/student/child €3/1/free; ⊘10am-2pm & 4-6.30pm Tue-Fri, 10am-2pm & 5-8pm Sat, 11am-2pm Sun & holidays) Housed in an astoundingly ornate building, the absorbing Museo de Bellas Artes has Basque paintings and sculpture from the 18th and 19th centuries. The works of local son Fernando de Amaríca are given good space and reflect an engaging romanticism that manages to mix drama with great warmth of colour and composition.

Catedral de María Inmaculada CATHEDRAL
(Cadena y Eleta) Vitoria's cathedral might look old, but in fact it only dates from the early 1970s. There are some impressive, fairly adventurous stained-glass windows and a neck-stretchingly high nave. More interesting, though, is the attached **Museo Diocesano de Arte Sacro** (adult/student/child €3/1/free; ⊘11am-2pm & 4-6.30pm Tue-Fri, 11am-2pm Sat & Sun), which contains some early Christian stone carvings and Basque crosses, detailed paintings of biblical scenes and a glittering ensemble of crucifixes and ceremonial crosses – all of which come from the Basque Country.

Museo de Armería MUSEUM
(Paseo de Fray Francisco de Vitoria; adult/student/child €3/1/free; ⊘10am-2pm & 4-6.30pm Tue-Fri, 10am-2pm Sat & Sun) Any damsels in distress reading this ought to head to this museum where your knight in shining armour awaits. This collection of armour through the ages is surprisingly absorbing and begs the question of how on earth gallant men wearing all this lot even managed to move

let alone rescue damsels from the clutches of fire-breathing dragons.

Museo de Ciencias Naturales MUSEUM
(Calle de las Siervas de Jesús 24; adult/student/child €3/1/free; ☉10am-2pm & 4-6.30pm Tue-Fri, 10am-2pm Sat & Sun) Inside this natural-history museum is a dazzling collection of minerals. You can also marvel at a mantis caught in amber, learn about the local wildlife and stare slack-jawed at a dinosaur jaw.

Bibat MUSEUM
(Calle de la Cuchillería/Aiztogile Kalea 54; adult/student/child €3/1/free; ☉10am-2pm & 4-6.30pm Tue-Fri, 10am-2pm Sat, 11am-2pm Sun) The **Museo de Arqueología** and the **Museo Fournier de Naipes** (☑945 18 19 20) are combined into one museum known as Bibat. The Museo de Arqueología has giant TV screens that bring the dim and distant past to life. The eccentric Museo Fournier de Naipes has an impressive collection of historic presses and playing cards, including some of the oldest European decks.

✨ Festivals & Events

Azkena Rock Festival MUSIC
(www.azkenarockfestival.com; ☉3rd week of Jun) In 2014 headliners included the Black Crowes and Smashing Pumpkins.

Jazz Festival MUSIC
(www.jazzvitoria.com; ☉mid-Jul) Attracts numerous big national and international acts.

Fiestas de la Virgen Blanca CITY FESTIVAL
(☉4-9 Aug) The calm sophistication of Vitoria takes a back seat during the boisterous Fiestas de la Virgen Blanca. Fireworks, bullfights, concerts and street dancing are preceded by the symbolic descent of Celedón, a Basque effigy that flies down on strings from the Iglesia de San Miguel into the plaza below.

🛏 Sleeping

Albergue de la Catedral HOSTEL €
(☑945 27 59 55; www.alberguecatedral.com; Calle de la Cuchillería 87; under 25yr dm €16-18, d €36, over 25yr dm €18-20, d €40; @ 🛜) This hip new hostel is virtually built into the walls of the

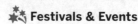

BILBAO, THE BASQUE COUNTRY & LA RIOJA VITORIA

LOCAL KNOWLEDGE

VITORIA'S BEST PINTXO BARS

Vitoria has some superb *pintxo* bars so we asked local journalist, writer and tourism expert Itziar Herrán to give us the low-down on her favourite bars.

Toloño (Calle de San Francisco 3; pintxos from €2; ☉9am-midnight Sun-Thu, 10.30am-4am Fri & Sat) This bar has won awards for its very creative *pintxos*. Mushrooms are the house specials. It's a large bar, so there's normally somewhere to sit down.

Bar la Malquerida (www.lamalquerida.com.es; Calle de la Correría 10; pintxos from €2; ☉10am-10.30pm Mon-Thu, 10am-midnight Fri & Sat) This is a fantastic *pintxo* bar hidden under the shadows of the church spires. The atmosphere is always good and the food even better.

Asador Sagartoki (Calle del Prado 18; pintxos from €2; ☉10am-midnight) A marvellous *pintxo* bar and *sidrería* (cider house) that has one of the most creative menus around and an atmosphere to go with it. The house specials, which have won awards, are the tortilla and the fried-egg *pintxos*. And when it comes to the cider, sit back and marvel as the bar staff, arms flailing like birds' wings, orchestrate jets of cider from the big barrels to the glasses in their outstretched hands.

Usokari (Calle de Eduardo Dato 25; pintxos from €2; ☉7am-midnight Sun-Thu, 8am-1am Fri & Sat) The range of *pintxos* at this discreet and modern bar in the new town is quite small (and it tends to run out quite early on), but the owners know all about the expression 'quality not quantity'. An equally impressive wine selection accompanies the nibbles.

Bar El Tabanco (www.eltabanco.es; Calle de la Correría 46; pintxos from €2; ☉7pm-midnight Thu & Fri, 12.30-3.30pm & 7pm-midnight Sat & Sun) Taking its cue, in terms of both decoration and food, from the steamy southern region of Andalucia, this is another ever busy, ever reliable *pintxo* bar.

Izartza (☑945 23 55 33; Plaza de España 5; pintxos from €2; ☉noon-4pm & 7-11pm Mon-Thu, to 11.30pm Sat & Sun) One of the more sophisticated *pintxo* bars in town. It boasts food and wine to match its upmarket reputation.

cathedral. The shiny white rooms are given added character thanks to the exposed, bendy wooden roof beams. Dorms have anywhere from two to eight beds. It's well-run and offers budget-travel-related services.

Hotel Dato HOTEL €

(☑945 14 72 30; www.hoteldato.com; Calle de Eduardo Dato 28; s €40, d €58-65; ☎) It's hard to know if the extravagant art-deco style, full of semi-naked nymphs, Roman pots and frilly fittings is kitsch or classy (though we'd probably have to go with the first one). Either way, it works well and the whole ensemble produces an exceptionally good value and memorable hotel.

Hotel Dato's annexe is the Hotel Dato 28 on a parallel street.

Abba Jazz Hotel HOTEL €

(☑945 10 13 46; www.abbahotels.com; Calle de la Florida 7; s/d from €55/60; ☎) This confident little hotel has small, searing-white rooms adorned with black-and-white pictures of piano keys, trumpets and other suitably jazzy instruments. Room size varies hugely, so ask to see a few before committing. There's an underground car park nearby.

★ La Casa de los Arquillos B&B €€

(☑945 15 12 59; www.lacasadelosarquillos.com; Paseo Los Arquillos 1; s/d incl breakfast €66/79; ☎) Housed inside a beautiful old building in a prime location above the main square, the eight immaculate rooms here take their young and funky inspiration from the artwork in the Artium. Every room is individually decorated in a highly original style – one has tape measures above the bed and another has a doll sprouting limbs from its head! A hearty breakfast is thrown in. Reception opening hours vary, so call in advance and let them know what time you're arriving.

✕ Eating

Internationally Vitoria might not have the same culinary cachet as San Sebastián, but among in-the-know Spaniards this is a city with serious culinary pedigree. How serious? Well, in 2014 it was awarded the title of *Capital Nacional de la Gastronomia* (National Gastronomic Capital) on account of its stellar array of *pintxo* bars and highly creative chefs. What makes Vitoria even more enticing as a foodie destination is that, unlike San Sebastián, where the price of *pintxos* is starting to get a bit silly, eating out here is very affordable – even more so on Thursday evenings when many bars offer a *pintxo* and drink for €1 to €2.

Querida María Restaurante MODERN BASQUE €

(Plaza de Santa María; mains €12-15, menú €19; ⊙1-4pm & 8-11.30pm Tue-Sat, 1-4pm Sun) Facing the cathedral in the prettiest part of the old town, this is an informal and stylish poppy-red restaurant. For the price, the food is magnificent. The menu focuses on classic Basque dishes, but most have been given a light touch of the unexpected.

Restaurante Xixilu BASQUE €€

(☑945 23 00 68; Plaza de América 2; mains €11-15; ⊙1.30-4pm & 9pm-midnight) Very much a neighbourhood haunt, this traditional-looking restaurant serves high-quality Basque dishes from behind a busy bar that serves equally good *pintxos*. It's on a pedestrianised square with a children's playground, which makes it a hit with families.

Arkupe BASQUE €€€

(☑945 23 00 80; Calle Mateo Benigno de Moraza 13; menú €40-47, mains €15-21; ⊙1.30-3.30pm & 8.30-11pm) For divine and very creative Basque cooking, check out this place. The rough wood exterior belies a formal and slightly chic atmosphere. There's an extensive wine list, with all the offerings racked up against the back wall. Reserve in advance.

❶ Information

Tourist Office (☑945 16 15 98; www.vitoria-gasteiz.org/turismo; Plaza de España 1; ⊙10am-8pm Jul-Sep, shorter hours Oct-Jun) In the central square of the old town. It can organise guided tours of the city, including fascinating tours taking in the city's numerous giant wall murals and tours out to the extensive green spaces and birdwatching sites that fringe the city.

❶ Getting There & Away

There are car parks by the train station, by the Artium and just east of the cathedral.

Vitoria's **bus station** (Calle de los Herrán) has regular services to the following:

TO	FARE (€)	DURATION (HR)
Barcelona	43	7
Bilbao	6.20	1¼
Logroño	9.90	1½
Madrid	27	4½
Pamplona	8.81	1¾
San Sebastián	12	1¼

Trains go to the following:

TO	FARE (€)	DURATION (HR)	FREQUENCY (DAILY)
Barcelona	from 31	5	1
Madrid	from 41	4-6	5
Pamplona	6	1	4
San Sebastián	from 12	1¾	up to 10

NAVARRA

Several Spains intersect in Navarra (Basque: Nafarroa). The soft greens and bracing climate of the Navarran Pyrenees lie like a cool compress across the sun-struck brow of the south, which is all stark plains, cereal crops and vineyards, sliced by high sierras with cockscombs of raw limestone. Navarra is also pilgrim territory: for centuries the faithful have used the pass at Roncesvalles to cross from France on their way to Santiago de Compostela (p503).

Navarra was historically the heartland of the Basques, but dynastic struggles and trimming due to reactionary politics, including Francoism, has left it as a semi-autonomous province, with the north being Basque by nature while the south leans towards Castilian Spain. The centre hangs somewhere in between and Navarra seems intrinsically uncommitted to the vision of a Basque future.

The Navarran capital, Pamplona, tends to grab the headlines with its world-famous running of the bulls, but the region's real charm is in its spectacularly diverse landscapes and its peppering of small towns and villages that seem to melt into the landscape.

Pamplona

POP 195,800 / ELEV 456M

Senses are heightened in Pamplona (Basque: Iruña), capital of the fiercely independent Kingdom of Navarra, alert constantly to the fearful sound of thundering bulls clattering like tanks down cobbled streets and causing mayhem and bloodshed along the way. Of course, visit outside the eight days in July when the legendary festival of Sanfermines takes over the minds and souls of a million people and the closest you'll come to a bloodthirsty bull is in a photograph. For those who do dare venture here outside fi-

esta time, despite the overriding feeling that you're the only one who missed the party, you will find Pamplona a fascinating place. And for those of you who come during fiesta week? Welcome to one of the biggest and most famous festivals in the world – if you hadn't drunk so much, it would have been a week you would remember forever!

History

The Romans called the city Pompaelo, after its founder Pompey the Great. They were succeeded by the Visigoths and then, briefly, by the Muslims. Navarra has been a melting pot of dynastic, political and cultural aspirations and tensions ever since Charlemagne rampaged across the Pyrenees from France in 778. The city achieved great things under Sancho III in the 11th century and its position on the Camino de Santiago ensured its prosperity. Twentieth-century affluence saw an expansion of the city.

◉ Sights

★**Catedral** CATHEDRAL

(www.catedraldepamplona.com; Calle Dormitalería; guided tour per adult/child €5/free; ⏰10.30am-7pm Tue-Sat, 10.30am-2pm Sun) Pamplona's main cathedral stands on a rise just inside the city ramparts amid a dark thicket of narrow streets. The cathedral is a late-medieval Gothic gem spoiled only by its rather dull neoclassical facade, an 18th-century appendage. The vast interior reveals some fine artefacts, including a silver-plated Virgin and the splendid 15th-century tomb of Carlos III of Navarra and his wife Doña Leonor. The real joy is the Gothic cloister, where there is marvellous delicacy in the stonework.

The cathedral tour (which can be conducted in English or French with advance notice) is fascinating. You're taken into the cathedral itself and if, you're on a morning tour, up the bell tower to see (and possibly hear) the second-largest church bell in Spain. You also visit the cloisters and a small museum, which displays religious treasures, the remaining walls of a Roman-era house recently discovered under the cathedral during restoration work, and the tiny skeleton of a seven-month-old baby found inside the house. The museum then turns decidedly pop-art with dramatic lighting, theatre drapes and a room full of virgins! The cathedral itself is open daily for free access outside the stated hours, but you can't access the cloisters or museum.

Pamplona

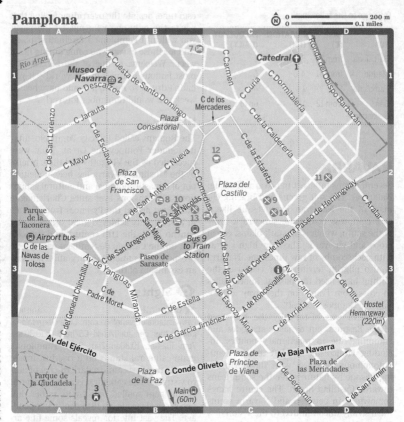

Pamplona

★ **Museo de Navarra**   MUSEUM
(www.cfnavarra.es/cultura/museo; Calle Cuesta de Santo Domingo 47; adult/student/child €2/1/free, Sat afternoon & Sun free; ⊙ 9.30am-2pm & 5-7pm Tue-Sat, 11am-2pm Sun) Housed in a former medieval hospital, this superb museum has an eclectic collection of archaeological finds (including a number of fantastic Roman mosaics unearthed mainly in southern Navarra), as well as a selection of art, including Goya's *Marqués de San Adrián*. Labelling is in Spanish only, but foreign translation leaflets are available.

Ciudadela & Parks   FORTRESS, PARK
(Avenida del Ejército) The walls and bulwarks of the grand fortified citadel, the star-shaped

Ciudadela, lurk amid the grass and trees in what is now a charming park, the portal to three more parks that unfold to the north and lend the city a beautiful green escape.

Museo Oteiza
MUSEUM

(www.museooteiza.org; Calle de la Cuesta 7, Alzuza; adult/student/child €4/2/free, Fri free; ⊙11am-7pm Tue-Sat, to 3pm Sun Jul & Aug, 10am-3pm Tue-Fri, 11am-7pm Sat, 11am-3pm Sun Sep-Jun) Around 9km northeast of Pamplona in the town of Alzuza, this impressive museum contains almost 3000 pieces by the renowned Navarran sculptor Jorge Oteiza. As well as his workshop, this beautifully designed gallery incorporates the artist's former home in a lovely rural setting.

Three buses a day run to Alzuza from Pamplona's bus station. If you're driving, Alzuza is signposted north off the NA150, just east of Huarte.

🛏 Sleeping

During Sanfermines, hotels raise their rates mercilessly – all quadruple their normal rack rates and many increase them fivefold – and it can be near impossible to get a room without reserving between six months and a year in advance. The tourist office maintains a list of private houses with rooms to rent during this period, and touts hang around the bus and train stations offering rooms. With numerous 'San Fermín' buses arriving from all nearby Spanish and French cities, it's actually not a bad idea to stay in a different town altogether and catch a ride on the party buses. Ask local tourist offices for details of departure times and costs.

At any other time of year, Pamplona is packed with good-value accommodation and it's rarely worth booking ahead.

Hostal Arriazu
HOTEL €

(✆948 21 02 02; www.hostalarriazu.com; Calle Comedias 14; s/d €50/55; ⊛) Falling somewhere between a budget *pensión* and a midrange hotel, there is superb value to be found in this former theatre. The rooms are pleasingly old-fashioned, and the bathrooms are as good as you'll find. It has a nice plant-packed glassed-in courtyard and a communal lounge.

Hostel Hemingway
HOSTEL €

(✆948 98 38 84; www.hostelhemingway.com; Calle Amaya 26; dm €17-20, s/d from €35/42; @⊛) Bright, funky colours predominate at this well-run hostel a few minutes' walk from the old town. The dorms have four to six beds and share three bathrooms. It has a TV lounge and a kitchen for guest use. We don't have to tell you what a party it would be staying here during Sanfermines.

It's just off Avenida de Carlos III.

Hostal Bearan
PENSIÓN €

(✆948 22 34 28; www.hostalbearan.es; Calle de San Nicolás 25; s/d €45/50; ⊛) There's real value to be found here, particularly if you bag one of the larger rooms, which are spacious enough for management to have squeezed a sofa in. Sofa or not, make sure you ask for a room away from the noisy street.

Hotel Puerta del Camino
BOUTIQUE HOTEL €€

(✆948 22 66 88; www.hotelpuertadelcamino.com; Calle Dos de Mayo 4; s/d from €72/85; P⊛⊛) A very stylish hotel inside a converted convent (clearly the nuns appreciated the finer things in life!) beside the northern gates to the old city. The rooms are filled with unexpected touches such as bulbous lamps and huge leather bedheads. Some rooms have views across the intricate city walls and beyond to the soaring Pyrenees.

Hotel Castillo de Javier
BOUTIQUE HOTEL €€

(✆948 20 30 40; www.hotelcastillodejavier.com; Calle de San Nicolás 50; s from €45, d €63-69; ⊛⊛) On a street of cheap digs, this slick hotel shows a touch of class. The reception area is modern through and through, and the rooms, though small, represent very good value. Ask to see a few first as some are much more spacious than others.

★ Palacio Guendulain
HISTORIC HOTEL €€€

(✆948 22 55 22; www.palacioguendulain.com; Calle Zapatería 53; s/d incl breakfast from €132/143; P⊛⊛) To call this stunning hotel, inside the converted former home of the viceroy of New Granada, sumptuous is an understatement. On arrival, you're greeted by a museum-piece 17th-century carriage and a collection of classic cars being guarded by the viceroy's private chapel. The rooms contain soft beds, enormous showers and regal armchairs.

🍴 Eating

★ Bar-Restaurante Gaucho
PINTXOS €

(Travesía Espóz y Mina 7; pintxos €2-3; ⊙7am-3pm & 6.30-11pm) This bustling bar serves multi-award-winning *pintxos* that, despite some serious competition, many a local will tell you are the finest in the city – and we tend to agree with them! Try the ones made of sea urchins or the crispy spinach and prawn caramel ones.

DON'T MISS

CAFÉ IRUÑA

Opened on the eve of Sanfermines in 1888, **Café Iruña** (www.cafeiruna.com; Plaza del Castillo 44; ⊙ 8am-midnight Mon-Thu, 9am-midnight Fri-Sun) has a dominant position, a powerful sense of history and a frilly belle-époque decor – all of which make it the most famous and popular watering hole in the city. It's a place nobody should miss. As well as caffeine and alcohol, it has a good range of *pintxos* and light meals.

Baserri   BASQUE €

(☑ 948 22 20 21; Calle de San Nicolás 32; menú del día €14; ⊙ 9.30am-midnight Mon-Thu, 9.30am-1.30am Fri, 11am-4am Sat, 11.30am-midnight Sun) This place has won so many awards for its *pintxo*s that we could fill this entire book listing them. You can taste a selection of *pintxo*s by opting for the €24 tasting menu.

Cafe Con Sal   SPANISH €

(☑ 948 22 79 27; Cuesta de Labrit 29; menú del día €13; ⊙ noon-midnight Mon-Sat) Opposite the bullring, this claret-red local haunt has one of the best-value lunch menus in town, and unlike many other restaurants, there's a long list of choices for each course, almost all of which are tasty and creative.

Casa Otaño   BASQUE €€

(☑ 948 22 50 95; Calle de San Nicolás 5; menú del día €18, mains €15-18; ⊙ 1-4pm & 9-11pm Mon-Sat) A bit pricier than many on this street but worth the extra. Its formal atmosphere is eased by the dazzling array of pink and red flowers spilling off the balcony. Great dishes range from locally caught trout to heavenly duck.

Restaurante Europa   BASQUE, SPANISH €€€

(☑ 948 22 18 00; Hotel Europa, Calle de Espóz y Mina 11; menú €47-62, mains €22-28; ⊙ 1-3.30pm & 9-11pm Mon-Sat) There's fine formal dining to be had in this white-tablecloth establishment (which is part of the rather dull Hotel Europa). Meals consist of very traditional Navarran and Basque dishes and the walls are lined with photos of Spanish celebrities who have eaten here.

ℹ Information

Tourist Office (☑ 848 42 04 20; www.turismo. navarra.es; Avenida da Roncesvalles 4; ⊙ 9am-7pm Mon-Fri , 10am-2pm & 4-7pm Sat, 10am-

2pm Sun) This extremely well-organised office, just opposite the statue of the bulls in the new town, has plenty of information about the city and Navarra. There are a couple of summer-only tourist info booths scattered throughout the city.

ℹ Getting There & Away

AIR

Pamplona's **airport** (☑ 902 40 47 04), about 7km south of the city, has regular flights to Madrid, Barcelona and one or two other Spanish cities. **Bus 16** (€1.35) travels between the city (from the bus station and Calle de las Navas de Tolosa) and the suburb of Noáia, from where it's about a 200m walk to the airport. A taxi costs about €15.

BUS

From the **main bus station** (☑ 902 02 36 51; www.estaciondeautobusesdepamplona.com; Ave de Yanguas y Miranda 2), buses leave for most towns throughout Navarra, although service is restricted on Sunday.

Regular bus services travel to the following places:

TO	FARE (€)	DURATION (HR)
Bilbao	15	2¾
Logroño	8.95	1¾
San Sebastián	7.68	1
Vitoria	7.58-8.35	1¼-2

Regional destinations include the following:

TO	FARE (€)	DURATION (HR)	FREQUENCY (DAILY)
Estella	4.19	1	10
Olite	3.51	¾	16

TRAIN

Pamplona's train station is linked to the city centre by bus 9 from Paseo de Sarasate every 15 minutes. Tickets are also sold at the **Renfe agency** (Calle de Estella 8; ⊙ 9am-1.30pm & 4.30-7.30pm Mon-Fri, 9am-1pm Sat).

Note that it's much quicker to take the bus to San Sebastián. Trains run to/from the following:

TO	FARE (€)	DURATION (HR)	FREQUENCY (DAILY)
Madrid	from 29	3	4
San Sebastián	from 15	2	2
Tudela	from 8.70	1	5
Vitoria	6	1	4

North of Pamplona

Sierra de Aralar

One of Navarra's many natural parks, the scenic Sierra de Aralar offers pleasant walking. There's not much to Lekunberri, the area's main town, except a gaggle of solid Basque farmhouses in the old quarter and an ever-growing estate of soulless modern housing beyond. The tourist office (☑948 50 72 04; www.viaverdeplazaola.org; Calle de Plazaola 21, Lekunberri) here is very helpful and can advise on the numerous fantastic walks the area offers.

Most buses between Pamplona and San Sebastián stop in Lekunberri, but you'll need your own vehicle to explore the sierra.

THE RUNNING OF THE BULLS

Liberated, obsessive or plain mad is how you might describe aficionados who regularly take part in Pamplona's Sanfermines (Fiesta de San Fermín), a nonstop cacophony of music, dance, fireworks and processions – and the small matter of running alongside a handful of agitated, horn-tossing *toros* (bulls) – that takes place from 6 to 14 July each year.

The bullrun is said to have originally developed way back in the 14th century as a way of herding bulls into market, with the seller running alongside the bulls to speed up their movement into the marketplace. In later times the same technique was used to transport bulls from the corrals to the bullring, and essentially that is still the case today. *El encierro*, the running of the bulls from their corrals to the bullring for the afternoon bullfight, takes place in Pamplona every morning during Sanfermines. Six bulls are let loose from the Coralillos de Santo Domingo to charge across the square of the same name. They continue up the street, veering onto Calle de los Mercaderes from Plaza Consistorial, then sweep right onto Calle de la Estafeta for the final charge to the ring. Devotees, known as *mozos* (the brave or foolish, depending on your point of view), race madly with the bulls, aiming to keep close – but not too close. The total course is some 825m long and lasts little more than three minutes.

Participants enter the course before 7.30am from Plaza de Santo Domingo. At 8am two rockets are fired: the first announces that the bulls have been released from the corrals; the second lets participants know they're all out and running. The first danger point is where Calle de los Mercaderes leads into Calle de la Estafeta. Here many of the bulls skid into the barriers because of their headlong speed on the turn. They can become isolated from the herd and are then always dangerous. A very treacherous stretch comes towards the end, where Calle de la Estafeta slopes down into the final turn to Plaza de Toros. A third rocket goes off when all the bulls have made it to the ring and a final one when they have been rounded up in the stalls.

Those who prefer to be spectators rather than action men (and we use the word 'men' on purpose here as, technically, women are forbidden from running, although an increasing number are doing it anyway) bag their spot along the route early. A space doesn't mean an uninterrupted view because a second 'security' fence stands between the spectators and runners, blocking much of the view (only police, medical staff and other authorised people can enter the space between the two fences). Some people rent a space on one of the house balconies overlooking the course. Others watch the runners and bulls race out of the entrance tunnel and into the bullring by buying a ticket for a seat in the ring. Whatever the vantage point, it's all over in a few blurred seconds.

Each evening a traditional bullfight is held. Sanfermines winds up at midnight on 14 July with a candlelit procession, known as the Pobre de Mí (Poor Me), which starts from Plaza Consistorial.

Concern has grown about the high numbers of people taking part in recent *encierros*. Since records began in 1924, 16 people have died during Pamplona's bullrun. The 2008 event resulted in 45 serious injuries (four of them due to gorings), and in 2009 a man was gored to death after a bull became separated from the rest of the herd. The 2013 run will be remembered for the serious pile up of runners in the tunnel leading into the ring, which left dozens injured. For dedicated *encierro* news, check out www.sanfermin.com.

Animal rights groups oppose bullrunning as a cruel tradition.

⊙ Sights

Santuario de San Miguel de Aralar   CHURCH

For most people, the main reason for visiting Lekunberri is to travel the bendy back road NA1510, which leads southwest through a tasty tapestry of mixed deciduous and evergreen forests to culminate (after 21km) at the austere and very bleak 9th-century Santuario de San Miguel de Aralar, which lies in the shadow of Monte Altxueta (1343m).

Despite its attractive naves and 800-year-old altarpiece, it isn't the sort of place you'd want to visit on a moonless night. There are some spectacular views down onto the plains to the south. Opening hours can be very erratic.

🛏 Sleeping & Eating

Hotel Ayestarán II   HISTORIC HOTEL €€

(☑ 948 50 41 27; www.hotelayestaran.com; Calle de Aralar 27, Lekunberri; d €93; P � 🛜 🗷) Sleep with the memory of Hemingway at this beautiful hotel where the writer stayed en route to the Pamplona party. A signed photograph of him standing outside the hotel hangs on the wall. The attached restaurant is equally superb (*menú del día* €15).

East of Pamplona

Javier

POP 80 / ELEV 448M

Tiny Javier (Xavier), 11km northeast of Sangüesa, is a quiet rural village set in gentle green countryside. It's utterly dominated by a childhood-fantasy castle that is so perfectly preserved you half expect the drawbridge to come crashing down and a knight in armour to gallop out on a white steed. As well as being an inspiration for fairy-tale dreams, this is also the birthplace of the patron saint of Navarra, San Francisco Xavier, who was born in the village in 1506. Xavier spent much of his life travelling, preaching, teaching and healing in Asia. Today his body lies in a miraculous state of preservation in a cathedral in Goa, India. The Castillo de Javier (admission €2.75; ⊙ 10am-1.30pm & 3.30-6.30pm) houses a small museum dedicated to the life of the saint.

If you want to stay, the red-brick, ivy-clad Hotel Xabier (☑ 948 88 40 06; www.hotelxabier. com; s/d incl breakfast €50/55; P 🛜) has small rooms, from which you can peer out of your window on a moonlit night and look for ghosts flitting around the castle keep.

Monasterio de Leyre

Totally swamped with visitors on public holidays, the Monasterio de Leyre (www. monasteriodeleyre.com; adult/child €2.75/0.80; ⊙ 10am-7.30pm Jun-Sep, shorter hours Oct-May) is in an attractive setting in the shadow of the Sierra de Leyre, about 4km from Yesa on the N240. The early Romanesque crypt has a three-nave structure with a low roof and the 12th-century main portal of the church is a fine example of Romanesque artistry.

Look down from the monastery, towards the main road, and you won't fail to notice the Embalse de Yesa, an enormous expanse of water that is perfect for swimming.

The Navarran Pyrenees

Awash in greens and often concealed in mists, the rolling hills, ribboned cliffs, clammy forests and snow-plastered mountains that make up the Navarran Pyrenees are a playground for outdoor enthusiasts and pilgrims on the Camino de Santiago. Despite being firmly Basque in history, culture and outlook, there is something of a different feeling to the tiny towns and villages that hug these slopes. Perhaps it's their proximity to France, but in general they seem somehow more prim and proper than many of the lowland towns. This only adds to the charm of exploring what are, without doubt, some of the most delightful and least exploited mountains in western Europe.

Valle del Baztán

This is rural Basque Country at its most typical, a landscape of splotchy reds and greens. Minor roads take you in and out of charming little villages, such as Arraioz, known for the fortified Casa Jaureguizar; and Ziga, with its 16th-century church.

Just beyond Irurita on the N121B is the valley's biggest town, Elizondo, given a distinctly urban air by its tall half-timbered buildings. It's a good base for exploring the area. There's accommodation at the Antxitónea Hostal (☑ 948 58 18 07; www.antxitonea. com; Calle Braulio Iriarte 16; s/d from €62/74; 🛜), which has plain rooms with flower-coated balconies. The attached restaurant is worth frequenting.

Beyond Elizondo, the NA2600 road meanders dreamily amid picturesque farms, villages and hills before climbing sharply to the French border pass of Puerto de

Camino Francés in Navarra & La Rioja

Izpegui, where the world becomes a spectacular collision of crags, peaks and valleys. At the pass, you can stop for a short, sharp hike up to the top of Mt Izpegui. You'll find a good number of *casas rurales* throughout the area.

The N121B continues northwards to the Puerto de Otxondo and the border crossing into France at Dantxarinea. Just before the border, a minor road veers west to the almost overly pretty village of Zugarramurdi, home to the decidedly less pretty Cuevas de Las Brujas (www.turismozugarramurdi.com; adult/child €4/2; ⊙11am-8pm). These caves were once, according to the Inquisition, the scene of evil debauchery. Having established this, the perverse masters of the Inquisition promptly tortured and burned scores of alleged witches. Playing on the flying-broomstick theme is the Museo de las Brujas (www.turismozugarramurdi.com; adult/child €4.50/2; ⊙11am-6.30pm Wed-Fri, 11am-7pm Sat & Sun), a fascinating dip into the mysterious cauldron of witchcraft in the Pyrenees.

Zugarramurdi has plenty of *casas rurales*.

To France via Roncesvalles

As you bear northeast out of Pamplona on the N135 and ascend into the Pyrenees, the yellows, browns and olive greens of lower Navarra begin to give way to more-luxuriant vegetation before the mountains thunder up to great Pyrenean heights. It would be fair to say that this route, which follows the Camino de Santiago, is more culturally attractive than physically attractive in comparison to some mountain areas.

BURGUETE

The main road runs tightly between neat, whitewashed houses with bare cornerstones at Burguete (Basque: Auritz), lending a more sober French air to things. Despite lacking the history, it actually makes a better night's halt than nearby Roncesvalles.

🛏 Sleeping & Eating

There are a sprinkling of *casas rurales* in the surrounding area.

Hotel Loizu HOTEL €€
(☎948 76 00 08; www.hotelloizu.com; Calle de San Nicolás 13; s/d €63/85; ⊙Apr-Dec; 🅿🗻) This is a pleasant country hotel whose upper rooms have attractive beams and exposed stone walls. Downstairs is an excellent restaurant.

RONCESVALLES

History hangs heavily in the air of Roncesvalles (Basque: Orreaga). Legend has it that it was here that the armies of Charlemagne were defeated and Roland, commander of Charlemagne's rearguard, was killed by Basque tribes in 778. This is an event celebrated in the epic 11th-century poem *Chanson de Roland* (Song of Roland) and is still talked about by today's Basques. In addition to violence and bloodshed, though, Roncesvalles has long been a key point on the road to Santiago de Compostela, and today Camino pilgrims continue to give thanks at the famous monastery for a successful crossing of the Pyrenees, one of the hardest parts of the Camino de Santiago.

The main event here is the monastery complex (www.roncesvalles.es; adult/child

€4.30/2.50; ⊙10am-2pm & 3.30-7pm Apr-Oct, shorter hours Nov-Mar), which contains a number of different buildings of interest. The 13th-century Gothic Real Colegiata de Santa María (⊙9am-8.30pm) FREE, houses a much-revered, silver-covered statue of the Virgin beneath a modernist-looking canopy worthy of Frank Gehry. Also of interest is the cloister, which contains the tomb of King Sancho VII (El Fuerte) of Navarra, the apparently 2.25m-tall victor in the Battle of Las Navas de Tolosa, fought against the Muslims in 1212. Nearby is the 12th-century Capilla de Sancti Spiritus.

Sleeping & Eating

If you just can't walk another step, you'll find a couple of places to stay.

Hostal Casa Sabina   HOTEL €
(☑948 76 00 12; www.casasabina.es; Roncesvalles; s/tw €41/51; 🕾) At this small place the rooms have twin beds only – possibly to stop any hanky-panky so close to a monastery? The downstairs bar and restaurant get more lively than the bedrooms.

Casa de Beneficiados   HOTEL €€
(☑948 76 01 05; www.casadebeneficiados.com; Roncesvalles; apt €80; ⊙mid-Mar–Dec; 🕾) In a former life this was an 18th-century monks' residence. Today it's re-born as a far less pious hotel, which is comfortable and utterly modern.

The Roads to Ochagavía

Happy wanderers on wheels can drift around a network of quiet country roads, with pretty villages along the way, in the area east of the main Roncesvalles road. A couple of kilometres south of Burguete, the NA140 branches off east to Garralda. Push on to Arive, a charming hamlet, from where you could continue east to the Valle del Salazar, or go south along Río Irati past the fine Romanesque church near Nagore. Another option is to take a loop northeast through the beautiful Bosque de Irati (car parking €5) forest, with its thousands of beech trees that turn the slopes a flaming orange every autumn and invite exploration on foot (from the parking area several well-marked trails lead off for anything from 2km to 8.2km return). Eventually this route will link you up with the Valle del Salazar at Ochagavía. If you stick to the NA140 between Arive and Ochagavía, Abaurregaina and Jaurrieta

are particularly picturesque. Most villages along the route have *casas rurales*.

Ochagavía

This charming Pyrenean town lying astride narrow Río Zatoya sets itself quite apart from the villages further south. Grey stone, slate and cobblestones dominate the old centre, which straddles a bubbling stream crossed by a pleasant medieval bridge. The town's sober dignity is reinforced by the looming presence of the Iglesia de San Juan Evangelista.

To reach France, take the NA140 northeast from Ochagavía into the Sierra de Abodi and cross at the Puerto de Larrau (1585m), a majestically bleak pass.

Sleeping & Eating

This is a popular base for walkers and even skiers, so there are plenty of *casas rurales* and a campsite in the area. The Hostal Auñamendi (☑948 89 01 89; www.hostalauniamendi.com; Calle Urrutià 23; 🕾), the only official hotel in town, was closed for major renovations at the time of research.

Casa Sario   HOTEL €
(☑948 89 01 87; www.casasario.com; Calle Llana 11, Jaurrieta; s €40-45, d €58-63; 🕾) This sweet little rural hotel, in the heart of the nearby village of Jaurrieta, has simple wood-floored rooms and a busy bar-restaurant downstairs (menús from €16).

Valle del Roncal

Navarra's most spectacular mountain area is around Roncal and this easternmost valley is an alternative route for leaving or entering the Navarran Pyrenees. For details of *casas rurales* in the valley, visit Roncal-Salazar (www.roncal-salazar.com).

BURGUI

The gateway to this part of the Pyrenees is Burgui – an enchanting huddle of stone houses built beside a clear, gushing stream (the Río Esca) bursting with frogs and fish and crossed via a humpbacked Roman bridge. Hostal El Almadiero (☑948 47 70 86; www.almadiero.com; Plaza Mayor; s/d €76/90; 🕾), in the heart of the village, has bright and colourful rooms with 19th-century bathrooms (though with mod cons like hot water and flushing toilets!).

RONCAL

The largest centre along this road, though still firmly a village, Roncal is a place of cobblestone alleyways that twist and turn between dark stone houses and meander down to a river full of trout. Roncal is renowned for its Queso de Roncal, a sheep's-milk cheese that's sold in the village.

ISABA

Lording it over the other villages in the valley, lofty Isaba, lying above the confluence of Ríos Belagua and Uztárroz, is another popular base for walkers and skiers. Heading north out of town towards the French border the scenery becomes ever more spectacular. The road starts off confined between mountain peaks before suddenly opening out into high Alpine pastures with a backdrop of the most majestic mountains in the western Pyrenees. Approaching the French border the road corkscrews up and up to the pass of Roncalia where you'll find a small ski resort. Beyond is France and another, larger ski resort, Pierre St Martin. There are signed walking trails on both sides of the border.

The **tourist office** (☎948 89 32 51; www. vallederoncal.es; ☺10am-2pm & 4-8pm Mon-Sat, 10am-2pm Sun) is up near the church, but it was closed for renovations at the time of research.

🛌 Sleeping & Eating

There are plenty of sleeping places, but many are block-booked during the skiing season.

THE CAMINO IN NAVARRA & LA RIOJA

At the gates of Spain, Navarra is the first Spanish leg of the journey to Santiago de Compostela for walkers on the Camino Francés route. The opening section, which crosses over the Pyrenees, is also one of the most spectacular parts of the entire Camino.

Roncesvalles to Pamplona

From the **Puerto de Ibañeta**, the Camino dramatically enters Spain and drops down to **Roncesvalles**. Dominated by its great, imposing abbey, Roncesvalles admirably sets the tone for this extraordinary route. Inside the heavily restored 13th-century Gothic church, you'll find the first statue of Santiago dressed as a pilgrim (with scallop shells and staff).

Pamplona became an official stop along the Camino in the 11th century, cementing its prosperity. Just inside the cathedral's bland neoclassical facade are the pure, soaring lines of the 14th-century Gothic interior.

Pamplona to Logroño & Beyond

Heading west out of Pamplona via Zariquiegui and the Sierra del Perdón, pilgrims reach **Puente la Reina**, where the Camino Aragonés, coming from the east, joins up with the Camino Francés.

Estella, the next stop, contains exceptional monumental Romanesque architecture: the outstanding portal of the Iglesia de San Miguel; the cloister of the Iglesia de San Pedro de la Rúa; and the Palacio de los Reyes de Navarra.

Outside Estella, evergreen oaks and vineyards fill undulating landscapes until a long, barren stretch leads through the sleepy towns of **Los Arcos**, **Sansol** and **Torres del Río**. In hillside Torres you'll find another remarkably intact eight-sided Romanesque chapel, the Iglesia del Santo Sepulcro.

The great Río Ebro marks the entrance to **Logroño** and explains its wealth and size. The dour Gothic Iglesia de Santiago houses a large Renaissance altarpiece depicting unusual scenes from the saint's life, including run-ins with the wicked necromancer Hermogenes.

Nájera literally grew out of the town's red cliff wall when King Ramiro discovered a miraculous statue of the Virgin in one of the cliff's caves in the 11th century.

Santo Domingo de la Calzada is one of the road's most captivating places. It is named for its energetic 11th-century founder, Santo Domingo, who cleared forests, built roadways, a bridge, a pilgrim's hospice and a church, and performed many wondrous miracles depicted masterfully in Hispano-Flemish paintings in the cathedral.

Hostal Lola
HOTEL €

(☑948 89 30 12; www.hostal-lola.com; Barrio de Mendigatxa 17; d €62; 🛜) This family-run place hidden down a narrow side alley offers probably the best value for money and has rooms loaded with desks, sofas and big beds. There's a nice flower-hemmed terrace and a decent restaurant. The only drawback is that the partition walls are so thin you can pretty much hear everything your neighbours are up to!

Hotel Ezkaurre
HOTEL €

(☑948 89 33 03; www.hotelezkaurre.es; Calle Garagardoia 14; d €60; 🛜) A delightful rainbow-tinged small hotel at the northern edge of the village. While the rooms are quite sober, the common areas are decorated in a style that is half hippy India and half old French village house. Quite the contrast!

South of Pamplona

Take the A15 south of Pamplona and you only have to drive for 15 minutes before you enter an entirely new world. Within the space of just a few kilometres, the deep greens that you will have grown to love in the Basque regions and northern Navarra vanish and are replaced with a lighter and more Mediterranean ochre. As the sunlight becomes more dazzling (and more commonly seen!), the shark's-teeth hills of the north flatten into tranquil lowland plains, while the wet forests become scorched vineyards and olive groves, and even the people change – they're more gregarious and, as the graffiti suggests, sometimes fiercely anti-Basque. For the traveller it feels as though you are finally arriving in the Spain of the clichés.

Olite

POP 3440 / ELEV 365M

The turrets and spires of Olite are filled with stories of kings and queens, brave knights and beautiful princesses – it's as if it has burst off the pages of a fairy tale. Though it might seem a little hard to believe today, this insignificant, honey-coloured village was once the home of the royal families of Navarra, and the walled old quarter is crowded with their memories.

Founded by the Romans (parts of the town wall date back to Roman times), Olite first attracted the attention of royalty in 1276. However, it didn't really take off until it caught the fancy of King Carlos III (Carlos the Noble) in the 15th century, when he embarked on a series of daring building projects.

👁 Sights

Palacio Real
CASTLE

(Castillo de Olite; www.guiartenavarra.com; adult/child €3.50/2; ☉10am-8pm Jul & Aug, 10am-7pm Mon-Fri, 10am-8pm Sat & Sun May-Jun & Sep, shorter hours Oct-Apr) It's Carlos III that we must thank for the exceptional Palacio Real, which towers over the village. Back in Carlos' day, the inhabitants of the castle included not just princes and jesters but also lions, giraffes and other exotic pets, as well as Babylon-inspired hanging gardens. Today, though the princes and lions are sadly missing, some of the hanging gardens remain.

Integrated into the castle is the Iglesia de Santa María la Real, which has a superbly detailed Gothic portal. There are guided tours of both buildings; check with the ticket office for times. Otherwise an audio guide to the castle is €1.

Museo de la Viña y el Vino de Navarra
MUSEUM

(www.guiartenavarra.com; Plaza de los Teobaldos 10; adult/child €3.50/2; ☉10am-2pm & 4-7pm Mon-Sat, 10am-2pm Sun Mar-Oct, shorter hours Nov-Feb) Don't miss this museum, which is a fascinating journey through wine and wine culture. Everything is well labelled and laid out and some fascinating facts are revealed. For instance, did you know that Noah (the one of the Ark fame) was apparently the first human ever to get drunk? It's in the same building as the tourist office.

Galerías Subterráneas
MUSEUM

(Plaza Carlos III; adult/child €1.50/1; ☉11am-1pm Tue-Fri, 11am-2pm & 5-7pm Sat, Sun & public holidays) These underground galleries, whose origin and use remain something of a mystery, contain a small museum explaining the town's medieval life (in Spanish). These basically illustrate that if you had blue blood or were rich then life was one jolly round of wine, food and things that your mother wouldn't approve of, and if you weren't, well, life sucked.

🛏 Sleeping & Eating

★ Principe de Viana
HISTORIC HOTEL €€

(☑948 74 00 00; www.parador.es; Plaza de los Teobaldos 2; r from €120; ✳@) Situated in a wing of the castle (though the cheaper rooms are in a newer extension), this offering from the

Parador chain is in a sumptuous, atmospheric class of its own. Though there might be good rooms available elsewhere in town for considerably fewer euros, they don't come with a castle attached.

Hotel Merindad de Olite　　HISTORIC HOTEL €€
(☑948 74 07 35; www.merindaddeolitehoteles.com; Rúa de la Judería 11; s €58-68, d €68-78; ✳ 🛜)
Built almost into the old town walls, this charming place has small but comfortable rooms and masses of medieval style. Get in fast because it fills quickly.

Hotel el Juglar　　BOUTIQUE HOTEL €€
(☑948 74 18 55; www.merindaddeolitehoteles.com; Rúa Romana 39; s €90-100, d €105-115; 🅿 ✳ 🛜 ▨)
A few minutes' walk into the new suburbs. The handful of rooms here are all slightly different from one another – some have big round whirlpool baths, some old-fashioned stone baths, and others elaborate walk-in showers. All have four-poster beds and lots of fancy decorations, and there's a pool to cool off in on a hot summer day.

Hostal Rural Villa Vieja　　BOUTIQUE HOTEL €€
(☑948 74 17 00; www.hostalvillavieja.com; Calle Villaveija 11; s €50, d €60-80; 🛜) Doing away with all the twee old-world decoration that is so common elsewhere in Olite, the slick rooms in this hotel stick firmly with the 21st century thanks to the ample use of bright colours and pop art.

ℹ Information

Olite has a friendly and helpful **tourist office** (☑948 74 17 03; Plaza de los Teobaldos 10; ⊙10am-2pm & 4-7pm Mon-Sat, 10am-2pm Sun), in the same building as the wine museum.

ℹ Getting There & Away

Up to 16 buses a day run between Olite and Pamplona (€3.51, 45 minutes).

Ujué

Balancing atop a hill criss-crossed with terraced fields, the tiny village of Ujué, some 18km east of Olite and overlooking the plains of southern Navarra, is a perfect example of a fortified medieval village. Today the almost immaculately preserved village is sleepy and pretty, with steep, narrow streets tumbling down the hillside, but what gives it something special is the hybrid Iglesia de Santa María, a fortified church of mixed Romanesque-Gothic style. The church con-

WORTH A TRIP

LAGUNA DE PITILLAS

The lakes and marshes that make up the Laguna de Pitillas are one of the top birding sites in Navarra – a region already renowned for its variety of feathered friends. Now a protected Ramsar wetland site of international importance, the Laguna de Pitillas provides a home for around 160 permanent and migratory species, including marsh harriers, great bitterns and even ospreys. To get there, take the N121 south of Olite and then turn off down the NA5330.

tains a rare statue of the Black Virgin, which is said to have been discovered by a shepherd who was led to the statue by a dove. In addition to the Virgin, the church also contains the heart of Carlos II.

The village plays host to a fascinating *romería* (pilgrimage) on the first Sunday after St Mark's Day (25 April), when hundreds of people walk through the night from Tudela to celebrate Mass in the village church.

Unfortunately, there is no formal accommodation in the village, but it makes a great lunch stop. Mesón las Migas (☑948 73 90 44; Calle Jesús Echauri; mains €12-18, menú del día €26; ⊙closed Mon-Thu Sep–mid-Jul), which serves traditional south Navarran food, is the best place to eat delights such as hunks of meat cooked over an open wood fire, but the house special is *migas de pastor* (fried breadcrumbs with herbs and chorizo).

Monasterio de la Oliva

The 11th-century Monasterio de la Oliva (☑948 72 50 06; guided tours €2; ⊙9am-12.30pm & 3.30-6.15pm Mon-Sat, 9-11.45am & 4-6.15pm Sun), 2km from Carcastillo, which is southeast of Olite, was founded by Cistercian monks and is still functioning as a community. Its austere church gives onto a peaceful Gothic cloister. The monks are dressed in exotic white-hooded robes.

Parque Natural de las Bárdenas Reales

In a region largely dominated by wet mountain slopes, the last thing you'd expect to find is a sunburnt desert, but in the Parque Natural de las Bárdenas Reales a desert is exactly what you'll find. Established as a natural park in 1999 and as a UN Biosphere Reserve in 2000, the Bárdenas Reales is a desiccated landscape of blank tabletop hills, open gravel plains and snakelike gorges covering over 410 sq km of southeastern Navarra. As well as spectacular scenery, the park plays host to numerous birds and animals, including the great bustard, golden eagles, Egyptian and griffon vultures, numerous reptiles, mountain cats and wild boar.

This may look like an almost pristine wilderness, but it is, in fact, totally artificial. Where now there is desert there was once forest, but humans, being quite dumb, chopped it all down, let their livestock eat all the lower growth and suddenly found themselves living in a desert. There are a couple of dirt motor tracks and numerous hiking and cycling trails, all of which are only vaguely signposted. There's a park information office (☑948 83 03 08; www.bardenasreales.es; Km 6 military zone rd; ⊙8am-1hr before sunset) on the main route into the park from Arguedas, which can supply information on driving, cycling and walking routes. Otherwise, the tourist office in Olite has plenty of information.

Sleeping

Hotel Aires de Bárdenas   BOUTIQUE HOTEL €€€
(☑948 11 66 66; www.airedebardenas.com; Ctra de Ejea, Km 1.5, Tudela; d €165-225; P❄🐾🛏) A shipping crate is hardly the most promising of beginnings for a luxury boutique hotel, but here humble crates have been turned into something special. Each one has had it's front cut out to give huge vistas over an expanse of semi-desert, and each is filled with the kind of luxurious fittings that make for a top hotel.

The in-house restaurant (mains €14 to €20) is of the same quality as the rooms, the service is superb and there's a pool. However, some rooms don't have views (it's worth paying extra for one that does), and despite the undoubted quality, we do feel it's a bit overpriced. It's situated several kilometres east of Tudela, just off the NA125.

West of Pamplona

Puente la Reina

POP 2670 / ELEV 421M

The chief calling card of Puente la Reina (Basque: Gares), 22km southwest of Pamplona on the A12, is the spectacular six-arched medieval bridge that dominates the western end of town, but Puente la Reina rewards on many other levels. A key stop on the Camino de Santiago, the town's pretty streets throng with the ghosts of a multitude of pilgrims. Their first stop here was at the late-Romanesque Iglesia del Crucifijo, erected by the Knights Templars and still containing one of the finest Gothic crucifixes in existence. And just a short way out of town is one of the prettiest chapels along the whole Camino. Throw into this mix some fine places to stay and, in the nearby countryside, a ruined Roman city and the result is a fine place to be based for a day or so.

⊙ Sights

Santa María de Eunate   CHURCH
(⊙10am-2pm & 4-7.30pm Tue-Sun) FREE Surrounded by cornfields and brushed by wildflowers, the near perfect octaganal Romanesque chapel of Santa María de Eunate is one of the most picturesque chapels along the whole Camino. Dating from around the 12th century its origins – and the reason why it's located in the middle of nowhere – are something of a mystery.

The chapel is 2km southeast of Muruzábal, which is itself 5km northeast of Puente la Reina.

Sleeping

Hotel Rural El Cerco   BOUTIQUE HOTEL €€
(☑948 34 12 69; www.elcerco.es; Calle Don Rodrigo Ximénez de Rada 36; s €50, d €75-83; 🛏) Of several quality places to stay this one, at the eastern end of the old quarter, has to be our favourite. The owners have taken an old building, stripped it back and turned it into a stylish small boutique hotel with exposed stone walls, wooden roof beams and lime-green walk-in showers.

Estella

POP 14,250 / ELEV 483M

Estella (Basque: Lizarra) was known as 'La Bella' in medieval times because of the splendour of its monuments and buildings, and though the old dear has lost some of its beauty to modern suburbs, it's not without charms. During the 11th century, Estella became a main reception point for the growing flood of pilgrims along the Camino de Santiago. Today most visitors are continuing that same plodding tradition.

REMINDERS OF ROME

The Roman influence in southern Navarra (and neighbouring La Rioja) was strong. There are several key sites that can give an insight into those distant days, and visiting them provides an excuse to explore lightly touristed countryside. Also, don't forget to check out the Roman mosaics in the Museo de Navarra (p434) in Pamplona.

Ciudad Romana de Andelos

The Roman town of **Andelos** (☑948 74 12 73; www.guiartenavarra.com; Mendigorría; adult/child €2/1; ☉10am-2pm & 3-7pm Fri & Sat, 10am-2pm Sun) is very battered, but its remote and peaceful setting gives it a special romance. The town, which reached its peak between the 1st and 2nd centuries AD, is divided into three: the main town, a water reservoir about 300m away from the town, and the tumbledown walls of a dam about 3km from the main site.

In spring and autumn it's a lovely 7km round-trip walk to the dam walls along dusty lanes – take water and a picnic. There's also a small museum with some of the finds from the site just by the entrance. Andelos is close to the village of Mendigorría, which is a short way south of Puente la Reina. Note that hours vary, so check the website.

Villa Romana de las Musas

The good people of Navarra have appreciated the gift of grapes for a very long time, and this magnificent Roman-era nobleman's **villa** (Villa Romana de Arellano; ☑948 74 12 73; www.guiartenavarra.com; Arellano; adult/child €2/1), which dates from between the 1st and 5th centuries, was used to produce wine. Various huge clay wine storage vessels are on display, and there are some impressive mosaics (some are reproductions).

The site is 6km south of Arellano village and sits in the heart of what is still wine-producing country. At the time of research the villa was closed for restoration work.

👁 Sights

Iglesia de San Pedro de la Rúa   CHURCH
This 12th-century church is the most important monument in Estella. Its cloisters are a fine example of Romanesque sculptural work.

Iglesia de San Miguel   CHURCH
Across the river and overlooking the town is the Iglesia de San Miguel, with a fine Romanesque north door.

🎉 Festivals & Events

Feria   FAIR
(☉Jul) From the last Friday in July, Estella hosts a week-long feria with its own *encierro* (running of the bulls).

🛏 Sleeping

Chapitel Hospedería   HOTEL €€
(☑948 55 10 90; www.hospederiachapitel.com; Calle Chapitel 1; s/d from €70/90; P🛜) The town's flashiest rooms are to be found in the Chapitel Hospedería. Although the rooms themselves here are the last word in comfort (in a sterile business kind of way), the bathrooms seem to be an afterthought.

Hotel Tximista   DESIGN HOTEL €€
(☑948 55 58 70; www.sanvirilahoteles.com/tximista; Calle Zaldu 15; s/d €80/90; P❄🛜) This striking modern hotel, built into and out of an old watermill, mixes rusty old industrial cogs and wheels from the mill with poppy-red artwork. Rooms are comfortable, although some suffer from road noise, and there's a nice garden overlooking the gurgling river.

🍴 Eating

Astarriaga Asador   SPANISH €€
(Plaza de Los Fueros 12; mains €10-15; ☉10am-1.30pm & 8pm-midnight Mon-Sat, 10am-1.30pm Sun) On the main square, Astarriaga Asador is a very popular restaurant with Galicia-bound pilgrims on account of its energy-enhancing steak selections – some are almost the size of a cow.

ℹ Getting There & Away

About 10 buses leave from the **bus station** (Plaza Coronación) for Pamplona (€4.19, one hour) Monday to Friday, and six on Saturday and Sunday.

Around Estella

The countryside around Estella is littered with monasteries. One of the best is the **Monasterio de Irache** (⊘ 10am-1.15pm & 4-7pm Wed-Sun, closed 1-17 Jan) FREE, 3km southwest of Estella, near Ayegui. This ancient Benedictine monastery has a lovely 16th-century plateresque cloister and its **Puerta Especiosa** is decorated with delicate sculptures. Those unimpressed by beauty dedicated to God may find the **Fuente de Vino** (Spring of Wine) enough to make you a believer. It's behind the **Bodega de Irache** (www.irache.com; Monasterio de Irache; ⊘ 10am-2pm & 4-7pm Sat), a well-known local wine producer (which is just in front of the church), and yes, it really is a spring of wine, and yes, you really can drink some for free – though only if you're a pilgrim walking to Santiago.

About 10km north of Estella, near Abárzuza, is the **Monasterio de Iranzu** (www.monasterio-iranzu.com; admission €2.50; ⊘ 10am-2pm & 4-8pm). Originally founded way back in the 11th century, but recently restored, this sand-coloured monastery with beautiful cloisters is so calm and tranquil that it could inspire religious meditation in Lucifer himself.

LA RIOJA

Get out the *copas* (glasses) for La Rioja and some of the best red wines produced in the country. Wine goes well with the region's ochre earth and vast blue skies, which seem far more Mediterranean than the Basque greens further north. In fact, it's hard not to feel as if you're in a different country altogether. The bulk of the vineyards line Río Ebro around the town of Haro, but some also extend into neighbouring Navarra and the Basque province of Álava. This diverse region offers more than just the pleasures of the grape, though, and a few days here can see you mixing it up in lively towns and quiet pilgrim churches, and even hunting for the remains of giant reptiles.

Logroño

POP 153,000

Logroño doesn't feel the need to be loud and brash. Instead it's a stately town with a heart of tree-studded squares, narrow streets and hidden corners. There are few monuments here, but there is a monumentally good selection of *pintxos* bars. In fact, Logroño

is quickly gaining a culinary reputation to rival anywhere in Spain. All up, this is the sort of place that you cannot help but feel contented in – and it's not just the wine.

◉ Sights

A stroll around the old town and down to the river is a pleasant diversion.

★ **Museo de la Rioja**   MUSEUM
(Plaza San Agustin 23; ⊘ 10am-2pm & 4-9pm Tue-Sat, 10am-2pm Sun) FREE After being closed for renovations for many years, this superb museum is back in business and, in both Spanish and English, takes you on a wild romp through Riojan history and culture – from the days when our ancestors killed dinner with arrows to recreations of the kitchens your Spanish granny likes to pretend she grew up using.

Catedral de Santa María de la Redonda   CATHEDRAL
(Calle de Portales; ⊘ 8am-1pm & 6-8.45pm Mon-Sat, 9am-2pm & 6.30-8.45pm Sun) The Catedral de Santa María de la Redonda started life as a Gothic church before maturing into a full-blown cathedral in the 16th century.

Iglesia de San Bartolomé   CHURCH
(Calle de Rodríguez Paterna) The impressive main entrance to this 13th-century church has a splendid portico of deeply receding borders and an expressive collection of statuary.

🎭 Festivals & Events

Actual   CULTURE
(⊘ 1st week Jan) A program of cultural, musical and artistic events.

Feast of San Bernabé   FEAST DAY
(⊘ 11 Jun) Commemorates the French siege of Logroño in 1521.

Fiesta de San Mateo   LOCAL FIESTA
(⊘ Sep) Logroño's week-long Fiesta de San Mateo starts on the Saturday before 21 September and doubles as a harvest festival, during which all of La Rioja comes to town to watch the grape-crushing ceremonies in the Espolón and to drink lots of wine.

🛏 Sleeping

Logroño isn't overflowing with hotels, but the ones it has are generally very good value.

Hostal La Numantina   PENSIÓN €
(☎ 941 25 14 11; www.hostalnumantina.com; Calle de Sagasta 4; s/d from €36/59; ☎) This

Logroño

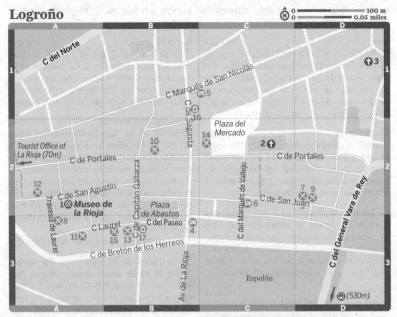

professional operation caters perfectly to the budget traveller's needs. The rooms are comfortable and homely, and some have crazy patterned wardrobes and large baths. The best aspects, though, are the communal TV room and the ample tourist info.

Hotel Marqués de Vallejo   DESIGN HOTEL €€
(☏941 24 83 33; www.hotelmarquesdevallejo.com; Calle del Marqués de Vallejo 8; s/d from €50/75; P ✳ ⑅) From the driftwood art to cow skins, beach pebbles and photographic flashlights, it's clear that a lot of thought and effort has gone into the design of this stylish, modern and very well-priced hotel.

★**Hotel Calle Mayor**   BOUTIQUE HOTEL €€€
(☏941 23 23 68; www.hotelcallemayor.com; Calle Marqués de San Nicolás 71; r incl breakfast €120-160; P ✳ ⑅) This delicious new hotel is *the* place to stay in Logroño. Its huge rooms with cheeky touches like modern lamps atop ancient colomns are bathed in light and ooze class. The staff are highly efficient.

✕ Eating

Logroño is a foodie's delight. There are a number of very good restaurants and then there are the *pintxos* – few cities have such a dense concentration of excellent *pintxo* bars. Most of the action takes place on Calle

Logroño

Laurel and Calle de San Juan. *Pintxos* cost around €2 to €4, and most of the *pintxo* bars are open from about 8pm through to midnight, except on Mondays.

Torrecilla
PINTXOS €

(Calle Laurel 15; pintxos from €2) OK, we're going to stick our necks out here and say that this place serves the best *pintxos* in town. Go for the pyramid of *jamón* or the mini-burgers (which come with mini bottles of ketchup!). In fact, go for anything. It's all good!

Bar Soriano
PINTXOS €

(Travesía de Laurel 2; pintxos from €2) The smell of frying food will suck you into this bar, which has been serving up the same delicious mushroom tapa, topped with a shrimp, for more than 30 years.

La Taberna de Baco
PINTXOS €

(Calle de San Agustín 10; pintxos from €2) This place has a cracking list of around 40 *pintxos*, including *bombitas* (potatoes stuffed with mushrooms) and a delightful mess of toast with pâté, apple, goat cheese and caramel.

La Fontana
PINTXOS €

(Calle Laurel 16; pintxos from €2) Another stellar *pintxo* bar with a welcoming atmosphere. This one's speciality is *sepia fontana*. And when you order this what emerges from the kitchen? A pile of egg, mushroom, aubergine and foie gras. The octopus isn't bad either.

Bar Vinissimo
PINTXOS €

(Calle de San Juan 23; pintxos from €2; ⊙ closed all Wed & lunch Thu) The speciality of this cramped little locals' bar is *foie fresco a la plancha* (fresh liver cooked on the *plancha*). It also has a very good wine selection.

La Taberna del Laurel
PINTXOS €

(Calle Laurel 7) The speciality here is *patatas bravas* (potatoes in a spicy tomato sauce).

MAKE YOUR OWN WINE

Based in the small village of Fuenmayor (10 minutes west of Logroño), **Rioja Trek** (☑ 941 58 73 54; www.riojatrek.com) offers three-hour wine 'experiences' where you visit a vineyard and bodega and participate in the process of actually making wine yourself (and keeping the bottle afterwards). The same people also run well-priced wine-tasting courses, family-friendly wine-related activities and, as the name would suggest, guided hikes along some of La Rioja's fabulous mountain trails.

They're not just good, they're damn near divine.

Bar A Tu Gusto
PINTXOS €

(Calle de San Juan 21; pintxos from €2; ⊙ closed Wed) Serves delicious seafood *pintxos* in an Andalucian-flavoured bar and has an impressive wine list. The special is the *crepe de ajoarriero con gulas* (cod and elver crêpe).

Marinée Restaurante
SEAFOOD €€

(☑ 941 24 39 10; Plaza de Mercardo 2-3; mains €15-20; ⊙ 1.45-3.45pm Tue & Wed, 1.45-3.45pm & 9-11.30pm Thu-Sun) It's the seafood that really garners all the attention at this resturant on the main square, and that's no surprise: the prawns, cod, seabass and shellfish are all perfectly executed. But don't limit yourself to the fruits of the sea: the landlubber dishes are decent too.

The €22 lunch menu is the deal of the day.

★ La Cocina de Ramon
SPANISH €€€

(☑ 941 28 98 08; www.lacocinaderamon.es; Calle de Portales 30; menú €28-37; ⊙ 1-4pm & 8-11pm Tue-Sat, 1-4pm Sun) It looks unassuming from the outside, but Ramon's mixture of high-quality, largely locally grown market-fresh produce and tried-and-tested family recipes gives this place a lot of fans. But it's not just the food that makes it so popular: the service is outstanding, and Ramon likes to come and explain the dishes to each and every guest.

Shopping

Félix Barbero Botas Rioja
WINE

(http://botasrioja.artesaniadelarioja.org; Calle de Sagasta 8; ⊙ 10am-2pm & 4-8pm Mon-Sat) Maintaining a dying craft, Félix Barbero handmakes the classic Spanish animal skin wine carriers in which farmers carried their daily rations of wine while working in the fields. Expect to pay from €20.

Vinos El Peso
WINE

(Calle del Peso 1; ⊙ 9am-9pm Mon-Fri, 9am-4pm Sat, 9am-2pm Sun) There are countless wine outlets in town, but this one is excellent.

ℹ Information

Tourist Office of La Rioja (☑ 941 29 12 60; www.lariojaturismo.com; Calle de Portales 50; ⊙ 9am-2pm & 5-8pm Mon-Fri, 10am-2pm & 5-8pm Sat, 10am-2pm & 5-7pm Sun Jul-Sep, shorter hours Oct-Jun) This office can provide lots of information on both the city and La Rioja in general.

ℹ Getting There & Away

If you arrive at the train or **bus station** (☎ 941 23 59 83; Avenida de España 1), first head up Avenida de España and then Calle del General Vara de Rey until you reach the Espolón, a large, park-like square lavished with plane trees (and with an underground car park). The Casco Viejo starts just to the north.

Buses bounce off to the following:

TO	FARE (€)	DURATION (HR)
Bilbao	13	2¾
Burgos	6	2¼
Haro	3.26	1
Pamplona	8.95	1¾
Santo Domingo de la Calzada	3.05	¾

By train, Logroño is regularly connected to the following:

TO	FARE (€)	DURATION (HR)
Bilbao	from 16	2½
Burgos	from 13	1¾
Madrid	from 29	3¼
Zaragoza	from 13	2½

West of Logroño

San Millán de Cogolla

POP 270 / ELEV 733M

About 16km southwest of Nájera, in the hamlet of San Millán de Cogolla, are two remarkable monasteries, which between them helped give birth to the Castilian language. On account of their linguistic heritage and artistic beauty, they have been recognised by Unesco as World Heritage sites.

The Monasterio de Yuso (☎ 941 37 30 49; www.monasteriodeyuso.org; adult/child €6/2; ⊙ 10am-1.30pm & 4-6.30pm Tue-Sun), sometimes presumptuously called El Escorial de La Rioja, contains numerous treasures in its museum. You can only visit as part of a guided tour (in Spanish only; non-Spanish speakers will be given an information sheet in English and French). Tours last 50 minutes and run every half-hour or so. In August it's also open on Mondays.

A short distance away is the Monasterio de Suso (☎ 941 37 30 82; admission €3; ⊙ 9.30am-1.30pm & 3.30-6.30pm Tue-Sun). Built above the caves where San Millán once lived,

it was consecrated in the 10th century. It's believed that in the 13th century a monk named Gonzalo de Berceo wrote the first Castilian words here. Again, it can only be visited on a guided tour. Tickets, which must be bought in advance and include a short bus ride up to the monastery, can be reserved by phone or can be picked up at the helpful tourist office at the Monasterio de Yuso.

Santo Domingo de la Calzada

POP 6260 / ELEV 630M

Santo Domingo is small-town Spain at its very best. A large number of the inhabitants live in the partially walled old quarter, a labyrinth of medieval streets where the past is alive and the sense of community is strong. It's the kind of place where you can be certain the baker knows all his customers by name and that everyone will turn up for María's christening. Santiago-bound pilgrims have long been a part of the fabric of this town, and that tradition continues to this day, with most visitors being foot-weary pilgrims. All this helps to make Santo Domingo one of the most enjoyable places in La Rioja.

◉ Sights

Catedral de Santo Domingo de la Calzada   CATHEDRAL
(www.catedralsantodomingo.es; Plaza del Santo 4; adult/student/child €4/3/free; ⊙ 10am-8.30pm Mon-Fri, 9am-7.10pm Sat, 9am-12.20pm & 1.45-7.10pm Sun Apr-Oct, shorter hr Nov-Mar) The morose, monumental cathedral and its attached museum glitter with the gold that attests to the great wealth the Camino has bestowed on otherwise backwater towns. An audio guide to the cathedral and its treasures is €1. Guided tours, including a nighttime tour, are also available.

The cathedral's most eccentric feature is the white rooster and hen that forage in a glass-fronted cage opposite the entrance to the crypt (look up!). Their presence celebrates a long-standing legend, the Miracle of the Rooster, which tells of a young man who was unfairly executed only to recover miraculously, while the broiled cock and hen on the plate of his judge suddenly leapt up and chickened off, fully fledged.

🛏 Sleeping & Eating

There are some very good places to stay in Santo Domingo. For food, however, things aren't quite as exciting. There are a few lacklustre cafes and bars in the modern centre of town by the bus stop, and some posher, but not necessarily better, ones near the cathedral.

Hospedería Sta Teresita
HOTEL €

(☑941 34 07 00; www.cister-lacalzada.com; Calle Pinar 2; s/d €39/58; 🖸) If your idea of a religious-run hotel includes lumpy beds, 5am prayers and severe sisters, then forget it, because the Hospedería Sta Teresita is much more about elevators, swipe cards and comfortable rooms.

Hostal R Pedro
HOTEL €

(☑941 34 11 60; www.hostalpedroprimero.es; Calle San Roque 9; s/d €48/59; 🖸) This carefully renovated town house, which has terracotta-coloured rooms with wooden roof beams and entirely modern bathrooms, is a terrific deal.

Parador Santo Domingo
HISTORIC HOTEL €€

(☑941 34 03 00; www.parador.es; Plaza del Santo 3; r from €105; 🅿🖸🍴) The Parador Santo Domingo is the antithesis of the town's general air of piety. Occupying a 12th-century former hospital, opposite the cathedral, this palatial hotel offers anything but a frugal medieval-like existence. The in-house restaurant is reliably good.

Parador Santo Domingo Bernado de Fresneda
HOTEL €€

(☑941 34 11 50; www.parador.es; Plaza de San Francisco 1; r from €90; 🅿🖸) Just on the edge of the old town is the Parador Santo Domingo Bernado de Fresneda, which occupies a former convent and pilgrim hostel, although quite honestly, with its divine beds and rooms that gush luxury, you probably wouldn't describe it as a 'hostel' any more.

ℹ Getting There & Away

Buses run to Logroño (€3.05, one hour via Nájera, up to 13 daily on weekdays, fewer on weekends).

La Rioja's Wine Region

La Rioja wine rolls on and off the tongue with ease, by name as well as by taste. All wine fanciers know the famous wines of La Rioja, where the vine has been cultivated since Roman times. The region is classic vine country and vineyards cover the hinterland of Río Ebro. On the river's north bank, the region is part of the Basque Country and is known as La Rioja Alavesa.

Haro

POP 11,500 / ELEV 426M

Despite its fame in the wine world, there's not much of a heady bouquet to Haro, the capital of La Rioja's wine-producing region. But the town has a cheerful pace and the compact old quarter, leading off Plaza de la Paz, has some intriguing alleyways with bars and wine shops aplenty.

There are plenty of wine bodegas in the vicinity of the town, some of which are open to visitors (almost always with advance reservation). The tourist office keeps a full list.

👉 Tours

Bodegas Muga
WINERY TOUR

(☑941 30 60 60; www.bodegasmuga.com; Barrio de la Estación; winery tour €8) Just after the railway bridge on the way out of town, this bodega is one of the most receptive to visitors and gives daily guided tours (except Sunday) and tastings in Spanish, and although technically you should book in advance in high season, you can often just turn up and tack onto the back of a tour.

For an English-language tour, it's essential to book several days ahead.

🎊 Festivals & Events

Batalla del Vino
WINE FESTIVAL

(🕙29 Jun) The otherwise mild-mannered citizens of Haro go temporarily berserk during the Batalla del Vino (Wine Battle), squirting and chucking wine all over each other in the name of San Juan, San Felices and San Pedro. Plenty of it goes down the right way, too.

🛏 Sleeping & Eating

There are plenty of cafes and bars around Plaza de la Paz and the surrounding streets.

Los Agustinos
HISTORIC HOTEL €€

(☑941 31 13 08; www.aranzazu-hoteles.com; Calle San Agín 2; s/d from €72/87, restaurant menú from €39; 🅿✴🖸) History hangs in the air of this stately hotel. And, although the rooms are lovely, it's the stunning covered courtyard of this former monastery that steals the show. The attached restaurant, with its fabulous setting, is highly recommended.

Hotel Arrope
HOTEL €€

(☑941 30 40 25; www.hotelarrope.com; Calle Vega 31; d from €76; ✴🖸) This town-centre hotel has a young-and-cool attitude, which is quite unexpected in conservative Haro. Closer

HUNTING FOR DINOSAURS

For those with their own transport, heading south of Logroño towards Soria via Arnedo and Arnedillo leads through some stunning semi-desert countryside riven by red-tinged gorges. Today eagles and vultures are commonly seen prowling the skies. But if you had been travelling around these parts some 120 million years ago, it wouldn't have been prowling vultures you'd need to keep an eye out for but prowling tyrannosauruses. Perhaps a little disappointingly, the dinosaurs are long gone. But if you know where to look, you can still find clues to their passing.

A short way south of Arnedillo is the small and pretty hill village of Enciso, which is the centre of Jurassic activity in these parts. The El Barranco Perdido (☑941 39 60 80; www.barrancoperdido.com; over 12yr/4-12yr €24/18; ☉11am-8pm), is a dino theme park containing a museum with complete dinosaur skeletons, various climbing frames, zip-wire slides and an outdoor swimming-pool complex. The real highlight of a visit to Enciso though is the chance to see some real-life dinosaur footprints scattered across former mudflats (now rock slopes) in the surrounding countryside. The nearest prints can be found just a kilometre or so east of El Barranco Perdido and the village – look for the terrifying T-Rex and dippy diplodocus on the hillside and you're in the right place.

Further dinosaur footprints can be found throughout the region – get hold of a map indicating sites from any nearby tourist office.

Accommodation is rather limited around here, but in Enciso itself is the cheery Casa Rural La Tahona (☑941 39 60 66; www.casatahona.es; d incl breakfast €45; ☒), which has large, bright rooms, some of which are family rooms. Rare for these parts, it's open year round (but call ahead in winter).

inspection reveals that the furnishings and fittings are quite plasticky. The attached bar-cafe is a very pleasant place for a drink and some tapas.

ℹ Information

Tourist Office (☑941 30 35 80; www.haro-turismo.org; Plaza de Florentino Rodríguez; ☉10am-2pm & 4-7pm Mon-Sat, 10am-2pm Sun mid-Jun–Sep, 10am-2pm Mon-Fri, 10am-2pm & 4-6pm Sat Oct–mid-Jun) A couple of hundred metres along the road from Plaza de la Paz.

ℹ Getting There & Away

Regular trains connect Haro with Logroño (from €5.95, 40 minutes). Buses additionally serve Logroño, Vitoria, Bilbao, Santo Domingo de la Calzada and Laguardia.

Briones

POP 900 / ELEV 501M

One man's dream has put the small, obscenely quaint village of Briones firmly on the Spanish wine and tourism map. The sunset-gold village crawls gently up a hillside and offers commanding views over the surrounding vine-carpeted plains. It's on these plains where you will find the fantastic Dinastía Vivanco (Museo de la Cultura del Vino; www.dinastiavivanco.com; adult/child €8/

free; ☉10am-8pm Tue-Sat, 11am-6pm Sun Jul-Sep, shorter hours Oct-Jun). Over several floors and numerous rooms, you will learn all about the history and culture of wine and the various processes that go into its production. All of this is done through interesting displays brought to life with the latest in computer technology.

The treasures on display include Picasso-designed wine jugs; Roman and Byzantine mosaics; gold-draped, wine-inspired religious artefacts; and the world's largest collection of corkscrews – and yes, they do have some in the shape of amusingly large penises. At the end of the tour, you can enjoy some wine tasting, and by booking in advance, you can join a tour of the winery (€6.50 or €12 including museum entry; in Spanish only).

🛌 Sleeping & Eating

Los Calaos de Briones   HOTEL €
(☑941 32 21 31; www.loscalaosdebriones.com; Calle San Juan 13; r €58; ☎) Currently the only place to rest wine-heavy heads is Los Calaos de Briones, which has delicious rooms with subtle colour schemes. Some have suitably romantic four-poster beds. The attached restaurant, in an old wine cellar, is stuffed with excellent locally inspired cuisine (mains €12 to €15).

Laguardia

POP 1490 / ELEV 557M

It's easy to spin back the wheels of time in the medieval fortress town of Laguardia, or the 'Guard of Navarra' as it was once appropriately known, sitting proudly on its rocky hilltop. The walled old quarter, which makes up most of the town, is virtually traffic-free

EXPERIENCE THE WEALTH OF THE GRAPE

The humble grape has created great wealth for some of the villages around La Rioja. Proof of this are some of the extravagant bodegas and hotels that have sprung up in recent years in what otherwise appear to be backwater farming communities. Visit the following to see what we mean.

When the owner of the Bodegas Marqués de Riscal, in the village of Elciego, decided he wanted to create something special, he didn't hold back. The result is the spectacular Frank Gehry–designed Hotel Marqués de Riscal (945 18 08 80; www.starwoodhotels. com/luxury; Calle Torrea 1; r from €304; P✳️🛜). Costing around €85 million, the building is a flamboyant wave of multicoloured titanium sheets that stands in utter contrast to the village behind. The building is having a radical effect on the surrounding countryside and has led to more tourists, more jobs, more wine sales and more money appearing in the hands of locals.

Casual visitors are not, however, welcome at the hotel. If you want a closer look, you have three options. The easiest is to join one of the bodega's wine tours (945 18 08 88; www.marquesderiscal.com; tour €11) – there's at least one English language tour a day, but it's best to book in advance. You won't get inside the building, but you will get to see its exterior from some distance. A much closer look can be obtained by reserving a table at one of the two superb in-house restaurants: the Michelin-approved Restaurante Marqués de Riscal (945 18 08 80; menu from €70) or the Bistró 1860 (945 18 08 80; menu from €49). But for the most intimate look at the building, you'll need to reserve a room for the night, but be prepared to part with some serious cash!

Just a couple of kilometres to the north of Laguardia is the Bodegas Ysios (www. ysios.com; Camino de la Hoya, Laguardia). Designed by Santiago Calatrava as a 'temple dedicated to wine', its wave-like roof made of aluminium and cedar wood matches the flow of the rocky mountains behind it. However, it looks its best at night when pools of light flow out of it. Daily tours (902 239773; per person €12; ⏰tours 11am, 1pm & 4pm Mon-Fri, 10am, 11am, 1pm & 4pm Sat, 11am & 1pm Sun) of the bodega are an excellent introduction to wine production. The 4pm tour on Saturdays is in English.

The Hotel Viura (945 60 90 00; www.hotelviura.com; Calle Mayor; d from €125; P✳️🛜), which at first glance appears to be dozens of multi-coloured boxes piled haphazardly atop one another, is an architecturally challenging building that is a shocking contrast to the honey-coloured village of Villabuena de Álava in which it sits.

There are several other, somewhat less confronting, wine cellars around Laguardia that can be visited, often with advance notice only – contact the tourist office in Laguardia for details. Bodegas Palacio (945 60 01 51; www.bodegaspalacio.com; Carretera de Elciego; tour €5; ⏰tours 11am & 1pm Mon, 4.30pm Tue-Fri, 11.30am & 1pm Sat, 1.30pm Sun, closed pm Jul & Aug) is only 1km from Laguardia on the Elciego road; reservations are not essential but are a good idea (especially out of season). The same bodega also runs excellent wine courses. The beginners' wine-tasting course (€30) runs monthly throughout the year, except August and January. Advance reservations are essential. There's also a hotel (945 62 11 95; s €73-78, d €83-90; 🛜) attached to the complex, but compared to options in Laguardia, it lacks character.

Also just outside Laguardia is the Centro Temático del Vino Villa Lucia (945 60 00 32; www.villa-lucia.com; Carretera de Logroño; museum €11; ⏰11am-6.30pm Tue-Fri, 10.15am-6.30pm Sat, 11am-12.30pm Sun), a wine museum and shop selling high-quality wine from a variety of small, local producers. Museum visits are by guided tour only and finish with a 4D film and wine tasting.

It's worth noting that buried under the houses of Laguardia are numerous small wine bodegas, some of which are open to the public. Ask at the tourist office for details.

and is a sheer joy to wander around. As well as memories of long-lost yesterdays, the town further entices visitors with its wine-producing present.

◉ Sights

Maybe the most impressive feature of the town is the castle-like Puerta de San Juan, one of the most stunning city gates in Spain.

It is also possible to visit some of the many bodegas in the area (including some in the old town itself), as well as a wine museum.

Iglesia de Santa María de los Reyes   CHURCH
(guided tours €2) The impressive Iglesia de Santa María de los Reyes has a breathtaking late-14th-century Gothic doorway, thronged with beautiful sculptures of the disciples and other motifs. If the church doors are locked, pop down to the tourist office where you can get a key.

🛏 Sleeping & Eating

Laguardia is an increasingly popular weekend-break destination with Spaniards and French visitors. In season it may be wise to book ahead.

Posada Mayor de Migueloa   HISTORIC HOTEL €€
(✆945 62 11 75; www.mayordemigueloa.com; Calle Mayor 20; d from €80; ❄🐾) For the ultimate in gracious La Rioja living, this old mansion-hotel with its rickety rooms full of polished wood is irresistible. The in-house restaurant (meals from €20), which is open to non-guests, is recommended and offers original twists on local cuisine. Under the hotel is a small wine bodega (guided visits for non-guests €5).

Castillo el Collado   HISTORIC HOTEL €€€
(✆945 62 12 00; www.hotelcollado.com; Paseo el Collado 1; d €125-185; 🐾) Like a whimsical Disney dream castle this place, which from the outside is all sturdy turrets and pretty flower gardens, is a truly unique place to stay. The half-dozen rooms are all different but combine quirky style with luxury living. The open-to-all restaurant (tasting menú €49) is also excellent.

Hospedería de los Parajes   HISTORIC HOTEL €€€
(✆945 62 11 30; www.hospederiadelosparajes.com; Calle Mayor 46-48; s/d from €121/132; ❄@🐾) Extraordinarily plush rooms that combine a bit of today with a dollop of yesteryear. Rooms are stuffed with antiques, cow-skin rugs and ever-glaring statues. The beds are divinely comfortably, the showers have rustic stone floors and the service is top-notch.

★Restaurante Amelibia   SPANISH €€
(✆945 62 12 07; Barbacana 14; menú del día €17; ⊙1-3.30pm Sun, Mon, Wed & Thu, 1-3.30pm & 9-10.30pm Fri & Sat) There are few things we like doing more in Laguardia than sitting back in this classy restaurant, staring out the windows at a view over the scorched plains and distant mountain ridges and dining on sublime traditional Spanish dishes – the meat dishes in particular are of exquisitely high quality.

ℹ Information

Tourist Office (✆945 60 08 45; www.laguardia-alava.com; Calle Mayor 52; ⊙10am-2pm & 4-7pm Mon-Fri, 10am-2pm & 5-7pm Sat, 10.45am-2pm Sun) Has a list of local bodegas that can be visited.

ℹ Getting There & Away

Several slow daily buses connecting Vitoria and Logroño pass through Laguardia.

Cantabria & Asturias

Includes ➡

Best Places to Eat

Best Places to Stay

Why Go?

You can traverse either of these two regions from north to south in little more than an hour. But don't. The coastline is a sequence of sheer cliffs, beautiful beaches and small fishing ports. Behind it, gorgeously green river valleys dotted with stone-built villages rise to the 2000m-plus mountain wall of the Cordillera Cantábrica, which reaches majestic heights in the Picos de Europa. The beauty is endless and ever-changing. The damp climate makes sure that you'll eat and drink well too: on offer are quality meat, local cheeses, and cider from Asturias' apple orchards, as well as the fruits of the sea. And travellers with a feel for history will be in their element: early humans painted some of the world's most magnificent prehistoric art at Altamira and elsewhere, and it was at Covadonga in Asturias that the seed of the Spanish nation first sprouted 1300 years ago.

When to Go
Oviedo

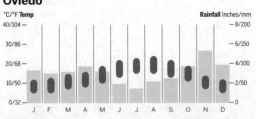

May, Jun & Sep Best time: temperatures are up, rainfall and prices are down, crowds are away.	**Aug** Descenso Internacional del Sella – kayak mania from Arriondas to Ribadesella.	**Late Aug** Join thousands of tipplers at Gijón's Fiesta de la Sidra Natural (Natural Cider Festival).

Cave Art

The scattered caves of Cantabria and Asturias are home to some of the oldest and most superlative prehistoric art in the world, painted by early humankind between around 39,000 and 10,000 BC. Most of the images depict wild animals such as horses, deer, bison and mammoths, and in the best examples the fluidity of the drawing, the skilful employment of colour and relief, and the lifelike animal representations attain the level of artistic genius. Getting a close-up view of this work, created by hunter-gatherers living an arduous existence during the last Ice Age – probably as some form of homage or worship – is truly awe-inspiring.

The world-famous bison and other beasts of the Cueva de Altamira (p468) have been on the World Heritage List since 1985, but there's plenty more. In 2008 a further 17 Palaeolithic art caves in northern Spain were added to the list, including Ribadesella's Cueva de Tito Bustillo (p487) and Cantabria's Cueva de Covalanas (p464), whose intricately designed deer depictions are true artistic masterpieces. In 2012, a red symbol at Puente Viesgo's Cueva de El Castillo (p462) was named the oldest cave art in the world.

ITINERARIES

Five Days
Get friendly with Santander for a day, then make your way along the west coast of Cantabria, taking in medieval Santillana del Mar, the Cueva de Altamira, and Modernista Comillas. Wander the Picos de Europa for a day or two and wrap up with civilised Oviedo.

Ten Days
Follow the five-day itinerary and explore further into the Picos before heading west to Oviedo. Cycle the Senda del Oso and finish off with Gijón and Asturias' west coast towns.

Top Five Food Experiences

➡ **El bulevar de la sidra** (p475) Teeming with dozens of overflowing cider bars, Oviedo's Calle de la Gascona is the epicentre of Asturias' cider scene.

➡ **La Conveniente** (p461) One of Santander's finest bodegas, cavernous and packed out, with huge *tablas* (platters) of fantastic cheeses, meats and pâtés.

➡ **Picos de Europa blue cheeses** (p463) Venture into the pungent world of *queso Picón* and *queso de Cabrales,* where every bite has its kick.

➡ **Mercado La Esperanza** (p460) Santander's colourful food market bursts with fresh seafood, meat, cheese and fruit.

➡ **Sensational seafood** Fresh from the Bay of Biscay, everywhere along the coast.

BEAR FACTS

Nearly all of Spain's estimated 240 surviving brown bears live in Asturias or Cantabria (p487).

Best Beaches

➡ Playa del Silencio (p485)

➡ Playa de Rodiles (p479)

➡ Playa de Torimbia (p481)

➡ Playa del Sardinero (p459)

➡ Playa de Merón (p470)

Best Picos de Europa Walks

➡ Teleférico de Fuente Dé to Collado de Horcados Rojos (p498)

➡ Garganta del Cares (p494)

➡ Sotres to Vega de Urriello, via the Collado de Pandébano (p495)

➡ Lago de la Ercina to Vega de Ario (p492)

➡ Sotres to Urdón, via the Desfiladero de la Hermida (p495)

Top Festivals

➡ Fiesta de la Sidra Natural (p477)

➡ Festival Internacional de Santander (p460)

➡ Descenso Internacional del Sella (p480)

➡ Fiesta del Orujo (p496)

➡ Semana Grande (p460)

Cantabria & Asturias Highlights

1 Marvel at the prehistoric artistic genius of **Altamira** (p468), Puente Viesgo's **Cueva de El Castillo** (p462) and Ribadesella's **Cueva de Tito Bustillo** (p487).

2 Walk the dramatic gorge of **Garganta del Cares** (p494).

3 Sidle up for cider in Asturias' convivial **sidrerías** (cider bars; p476).

4 Let medieval **Santillana del Mar** (p466) bewitch you with its charms.

5 Ride the scary **Teleférico de Fuente Dé** (p498) to the superb heights of the Picos de Europa.

6 Cycle the **Senda del Oso** (p486) and meet its bears.

7 Delight in the grace of Oviedo's **pre-Romanesque buildings** (p471).

8 Bathe at spectacular, secluded **Playa del Silencio** (p485) or **Playa de Torimbia** (p481).

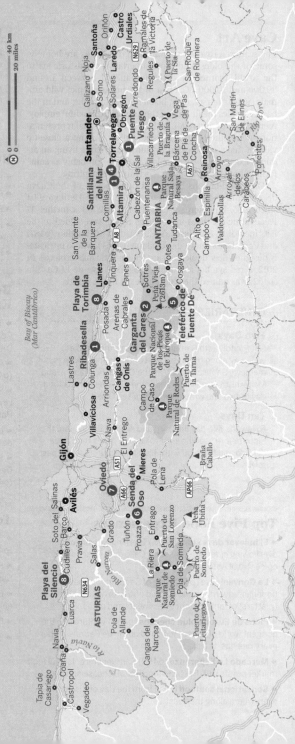

CANTABRIA

It's no wonder both Romans and Visigoths had a hard time subduing the Cantabrian clans. The lushness of the vegetation belies the complexity of much of Cantabria's terrain, which is sliced up by deep, multibranched mountain valleys connected only by steep passes. For the modern traveller, Cantabria offers a little of everything. Some pretty beaches make summer seaside days quite possible (unreliable weather permitting), while the inland valleys, sprinkled with sleepy towns and villages, are a feast for the eyes, whether you choose to drive the country roads or walk the trails. The rugged ranges culminate in the abrupt mountain walls of the Picos de Europa in the west.

The capital, Santander, provides a slice of urban seaside life, with bustling bodegas and beaches. Santillana del Mar and Comillas entice with their medieval and Modernista trappings. The prehistoric art of the Cuevas de Altamira, El Castillo and Covalanas is some of the oldest and very best in the world.

The Romans finally carried the day against the proud Cantabrians and pacified the region by around 19 BC. The Visigoths only managed to secure the area shortly before they were themselves eclipsed by the Moors in AD 711, after which Cantabria quickly became part of the nascent Christian Kingdom of Asturias. In later centuries, Cantabria was long regarded simply as Castilla's gateway to the Bay of Biscay, before becoming a separate region under Spain's 1978 constitution. Cantabrians are known as *montañeses* because Castilians thought of them as hailing from the mountains of the Cordillera Cantábrica.

Santander

POP 134,700

The belle-époque elegance of El Sardinero aside, modern Santander is not the most beautiful of cities. A huge fire raged through the centre back in 1941, leaving little that's old or quaint. But Cantabria's capital makes the most of its setting along the northern side of the handsome Bahía de Santander, and it's a lively place to spend a day or two, with good city beaches, bustling shopping streets, a heaving bar and restaurant scene, and a few cultural attractions. It's a popular summer holiday resort for Spaniards.

The parklands of the Península de la Magdalena mark the eastern end of the bay. North of the peninsula, Playa del Sardinero, the main beach, faces the open sea.

History

Founded by the Romans as Portus Victoriae (Victory Harbour) in 21 BC, Santander prospered as a trading and fishing port from the 12th century, and emerged as Cantabria's main city in the 18th century. Its heyday came in the early 20th century when King Alfonso XIII made a habit of spending summer here and turned Santander, especially the Sardinero area, into the fashionable seaside resort it is today.

◉ Sights

Península de la Magdalena PARK

(◷8am-10pm) These parklands are perfect for a stroll and popular with picnickers. Kids will enjoy the seals and penguins and the little train that choo-choos around the headland.

➡ **Palacio de la Magdalena**

(☑942203084;www.centenariopalaciomagdalena. com; tours €3; ◷tours 11am, noon & 5pm Mon-Fri, hourly 10am-1pm Sat & Sun late Sep–mid-Jun) The palace crowning the Península de la Magdalena was built between 1908 and 1912 as a gift from the city to the royal family, which used it every summer until 1930. It's an eclectically styled building which you can visit by 50-minute guided tours, except in summer when the palace hosts the **Universidad Internacional Menéndez Pelayo** (www.uimp.es), a global get-together for specialists in all sorts of disciplines.

Museo Marítimo del Cantábrico MUSEUM

(www.museosdecantabria.es; Calle de San Martín de Bajamar; adult/child €8/5; ◷10am-7.30pm, closed Mon) If seafaring is your thing, visit the maritime museum 800m east of the Puerto Chico marina. The four floors cover all facets of Cantabria's relationship with the sea, and include an aquarium. With its fine ship models, the maritime history section is perhaps the most interesting. The 60-tonne whale skeleton is a star attraction.

Jardines & Paseo de Pereda PARK, PROMENADE

The pretty Jardines de Pereda (Pereda's Gardens) are named after the Cantabrian writer José María de Pereda, whose seminal work, *Escenas Montañesas,* is illustrated in bronze and stone here.

Santander

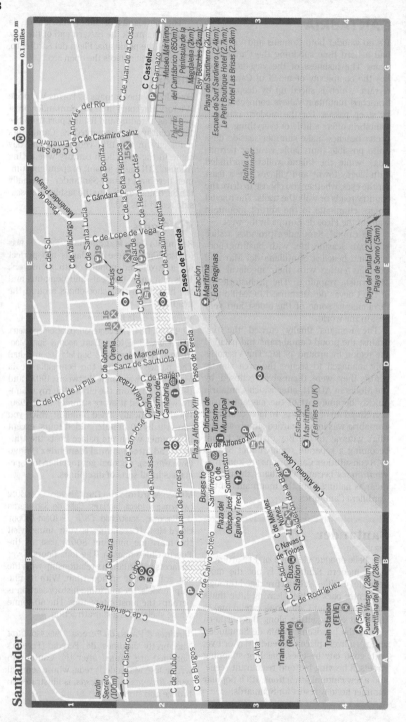

0 — 200 m
0 — 0.1 miles

C de Cisneros
Jardín Secreto (100m)
C de Rubio
C de Burgos
C Alta
C de Cervantes
C de Guevara
C Cubo
9 5
Av de Calvo Sotelo
C de Juan de Herrera
C de Rualasal
10
C de San José
Plaza Alfonso XIII
Oficina de Turismo Cantabria
6
C del Río de la Pila
C de Gómez Oreña
18 16
1
C de Marcelino Sanz de Sautuola
Paseo de Pereda
Plaza del Obispo José Eguino y Trecu
Buses to Sardinero C de Somorrostro
Oficina de Turismo Municipal
Av de Alfonso XIII
12
4
2
C de Méndez Núñez
C Navas de Tolosa
C de Cádiz
11 17
Calderón de la Barca
Bus Station
C de Rodríguez
C de Antonio López
Estación Marítima (Ferries to UK)
Train Station (Renfe)
Train Station (FEVE)
(5km); Puente Viesgo (28km); Santillana del Mar (28km)
3
Bahía de Santander
Paseo de Pereda
Estación Marítima Los Reginas
Playa del Puntal (2.5km); Playa de Somo (5km)
7
P Jesús R G
8
13
14 20
19
C de Ataúlfo Argenta
C de Daoíz y Velarde
C del Sol
C de Valliciergo
C de Santa Lucía
C de Lope de Vega
E
C Gándara
C de la Peña Herbosa
15
C de Bonifaz
C de Casimiro Sainz
C de Andrés del Río
C de San Emeterio
Paseo de Menéndez Pelayo
C de Hernán Cortés
C de Juan de la Cosa
C Castelar
C Garnazo
Museo Marítimo del Cantábrico (850m); Península de la Magdalena (2km); Bay Beaches (2km)
Puerto Chico
Playa del Sardinero (2km); Escuela de Surf Sardinero (2.4km); Le Petit Boutique Hotel (2.7km); Hotel Las Brisas (2.8km)

Santander

The bayfront promenade fronting the Jardines de Pereda continues east to the Puerto Chico (Little Port) marina. Half the city seems to stroll here on summer evenings. Both Paseo de Pereda and Calle Castelar, opposite Puerto Chico, are dotted with lively cafes and lined with grand buildings characterised by their glassed-in balconies.

You can't miss the 1875 Banco Santander building, with the arch in the middle, across the street from the Jardines de Pereda. The Santander is now one of the world's biggest banks, so the architectural grandiloquence is not entirely misplaced.

Centro Botín
ARTS CENTRE

(www.centrobotin.org) Italian architect Renzo Piano is behind the distinctly contemporary concept of this ambitious arts and cultural centre – social hub, local learning centre and international art gallery all rolled into one – which is being constructed amid the Jardines de Pereda, overlooking the Bahía de Santander. At the time of writing, it was due to open in late 2014.

Museo de Prehistoria y Arqueología de Cantabria
MUSEUM

(www.museosdecantabria.es; Calle de Bailén; adult/child €5/2; ⊙10.30am-2pm & 5-8pm Wed-Sun) Reopened in 2013 after a six-year closure, the prehistory and archaeology museum showcases Cantabria's archaeological wealth, with explanatory matter in French, English and Spanish. The excellent multimedia displays range from early hominid remains to giant steles (stone disks) carved by the pre-Roman Cantabrians, Roman culture and the medieval Spanish kingdoms of Asturias and León. Free Sunday afternoon.

Catedral de la Asunción
CATHEDRAL

(Plaza del Obispo José Eguino y Trecu; ⊙upper church 10am-1pm & 4.30-7.30pm, Iglesia del Santísimo Cristo 8.30am-1pm & 5-8pm) Santander's cathedral is composed of two Gothic churches, one above the other. The 14th-century upper church, off which is a 15th-century cloister, was extensively rebuilt after a 1941 fire. In the lower, 13th-century Iglesia del Santísimo Cristo, glass floors reveal excavated bits of Roman Santander. Displayed nearby are silver vessels containing the skulls of the early Christian martyrs San Emeterio and San Celedonio, Santander's patron saints.

🏖 Beaches

The glorious 1.25km sweep of the ocean-facing Playa del Sardinero sits 3km east of the city centre, but Santander has plenty of other stunning beaches, plus a vibrant surf scene.

Playa del Sardinero
BEACH

Surfers emerge in force along Sardinero when the waves are right, mainly in autumn and winter, when they can reach 1.5m. Sardinero is backed by some of Santander's most expensive real estate, including emblematic early 20th-century creations such as the Gran Casino. Buses 1, 2 and 3 (€1.30) run east to Sardinero from Avenida de Calvo Sotelo beside the main post office.

Playa del Puntal
BEACH

A finger of sand jutting out across the bay toward Santander, roughly opposite the Península de la Magdalena, El Puntal is idyllic on calm days (but beware the currents). Weather permitting, passenger ferries (€3.80 return) sail there about every 30 minutes from 10.30am to 7.30pm, May to October, from the Estación Marítima Los Reginas (www.losreginas.com; Paseo Marítimo).

Playa de Somo
BEACH

Just beyond Playa del Puntal (p459) across the bay from Santander, Playa de Somo is another sandy beach with, usually, pretty good surf. A year-round ferry (one way/return €2.60/4.65, every 30 or 60 minutes from 9.30am to 7.30pm) runs to Somo from the Estación Marítima Los Reginas.

Escuela de Surf Sardinero
SURFING

(942 27 03 01; www.escueladesurfsardinero.com; Balneario de la Primera Playa del Sardinero; per person 2hr group class incl board, wetsuit & transport €30, board/wetsuit rental per half-day €15/7; ⏰10.30am-12.30pm & 4-6pm, closed afternoons Oct-May) This well-organised surf school and shop, perfectly placed in the middle of Playa del Sardinero, offers classes in Spanish, English and French. Depending on conditions, sessions might run in Liencres, 10km west. You'll find several other surf outfits in Sardinero and across the bay in Somo.

🎉 Festivals & Events

Baños de Ola
SUMMER FESTIVAL

Several days of events are held during the first half of July at Playa del Sardinero, commemorating the arrival of the first seabathing tourists there in the 19th century.

Semana Grande
SUMMER FESTIVAL

Santander's big summer fiesta, a week of fun around 25 July.

Festival Internacional de Santander
MUSIC

(www.festivalsantander.com) In August, Santander's sweeping musical season covers everything from jazz to ballet.

PLAZAS

The streets of central Santander open out into several pretty plazas. The stately Plaza Porticada, surrounded by 64 porticoes, was created after the disastrous fire of 1941. A short walk east are the more spacious Plaza de Pombo and lively Plaza de Cañadío, which brims with bars and can get quite rowdy at night. To the west, Plaza La Esperanza, behind the city hall, is home to the Mercado La Esperanza (Plaza la Esperanza; ⏰8am-2pm Mon-Sat), a colourful, bustling food market.

🛏 Sleeping

The city centre, where most of the action is, has options in all price ranges. There are also some good midrange and top-end digs over by Playa del Sardinero, though some close from about October to mid-May. Most rates dip sharply outside the high season (typically July and August).

Hostel BBB
HOSTEL €

(942 22 78 17; www.hostelsantander.com; 1st fl, Calle de Méndez Núñez 6; dm incl breakfast €23; 📶) Cosy, colourful, super-clean dorms and a friendly, on-the-ball welcome make this hostel a top budget choice and a great spot to meet other travellers. It's handy for the train and bus stations, and the bright common area overlooks the bay.

Jardín Secreto
BOUTIQUE HOTEL €€

(942 07 07 14; www.jardinsecretosantander.com; Calle de Cisneros 37; s/d €60/75; 📶) Named for its tiny, tranquil back garden, this is a charming little six-room world of its own in a 200-year-old house near the city centre. It's run by an engaging brother-and-sister team, and comfortably designed by their mother in a stylish, contemporary blend of silvers and greys with exposed stone, brick and wood. The free morning coffee hits the spot.

Hotel Las Brisas
BOUTIQUE HOTEL €€

(942 27 01 11; www.hotellasbrisas-santander. com; Calle La Braña 14; s/d incl breakfast €94/104; ⏰closed Jan; @📶) Almost as much gallery as hotel, century-old Las Brisas is a three-storey belle-époque Sardinero villa decked out with art and crafts. The 13 comfy characterful rooms feature coffee- and tea-makers and recently updated bathrooms with huge shower heads. Some enjoy beach views, as does the front terrace. For longer stays consider its nearby apartments.

Le Petit Boutique Hotel
BOUTIQUE HOTEL €€

(942 07 57 68; www.lepetithotelsantander. com; Avenida de los Castros 10; s/d incl breakfast €79/128; ❇📶) Seven smart, individually styled rooms make for attractive, if slightly snug, lodgings at this ultramodern, efficiently run new Sardinero arrival. Each room takes its inspiration from a different city around the world, with thematic touches like teak furniture or oriental wall art; all have warm, tasteful decor, comfy beds and spotless bathrooms with hairdryers.

Plaza Pombo B&B B&B €€

(☑ 942 21 29 50; www.plazapombo.com; 3rd fl, Calle de Hernán Cortés 25; r incl breakfast with/without bathroom €80/62; 🛜) A long-established, central *pensión* (small private hotel), run by keen new owners. The eight high-ceilinged rooms are light and airy, with good beds, and some boast balconies overlooking Plaza de Pombo.

Hotel Bahía HOTEL €€€

(☑ 902 570627; www.hotelbahiasantander.com; Avenida de Alfonso XIII 6; s €167, d €177-197; P ✱ ☒ @ 🛜) Central Santander's top hotel, opposite the UK ferry port, offers large, very comfortable rooms with thick carpets and solid wood furnishings. Many have sea views. The hotel sports an elegant restaurant and cafe.

✗ Eating

Central Santander throngs with great food options. You can push in for scrumptious snacks in a tapas bar, dig into hearty local food in a no-nonsense bodega or head upmarket in any number of restaurants. And do sample the beloved local Regma ice cream, sold in immense scoops around town.

★ La Conveniente TAPAS, TABLAS €€

(Calle de Gómez Oreña 9; raciones & tablas €6-20; ☺ 7pm-midnight Mon-Sat) This cavernous bodega has high stone walls, wooden pillars and more wine bottles than you may ever have seen in one place. Squeeze into the tramlike enclosure at the front, line up for the cave-like dining room or just snack at the bar. The food offerings are straightforward – *tablas* (platters) of cheese, *embutidos* (sausages), ham, pâtés – and servings are generous.

★ Asubio Gastrobar CONTEMPORARY CANTABRIAN €€

(www.asubiogastrobar.com; Calle de Daoíz y Velarde 23; pinchos €2-4, mains €14-20; ☺ noon-4pm & 8pm-midnight) Creatively prepared, prize-winning *pinchos* (snacks) infused with

Cantabrian flavours and colourfully chalked up on a blackboard are the order of the day here. Try baked octopus with potato mousse or a local *pasiego* cheese bake, along with one of the 50 wines on display, and finish off with a tangy *pizarra de quesucos regionales* (platter of local cheeses).

El Machichaco SEAFOOD, BREAKFAST €€

(www.elmachi.es; Calle de Calderón de la Barca 9; mains €12-25; ☺ 8am-midnight) A welcoming, good-value seafood spot convenient to all transport terminals and the city centre. Go for tapas such as the Santander speciality *rabas* (deep-fried squid or potato strips) or heartier choices such as baked fish of the day with crunchy potatoes. It's also good for breakfast – even bacon and eggs!

Cañadío CONTEMPORARY CANTABRIAN €€€

(☑ 942 31 41 49; www.restaurantecanadio.com; Calle de Gómez Oreña 15; mains €19-26; ☺ 11am-midnight Mon-Sat) A tastefully contemporary place with art on the red walls, comfy booths and timber floors, Cañadío offers top-notch creative cooking with local inspiration. Hake is prepared every which way. Or you can join the crowds in the front bar for tempting tapas.

Bar Del Puerto SEAFOOD €€€

(☑ 942 21 30 01; www.bardelpuerto.com; Calle de Hernán Cortés 63; mains €18-45; ☺ 1.30-4pm & 8.30pm-midnight, closed Sun dinner & Mon Oct-Jun) With its grand windows looking out towards the Puerto Chico waterfront, the upstairs restaurant here is a perfect spot for top-class seafood. It offers a huge selection: you might try curious northern Spain specialities like *centollos* (spider crabs) and *percebes* (goose barnacles), and fish of the day is never a bad choice. The €46 lunch and dinner menu makes some of your decisions.

⚫ Drinking & Nightlife

Plaza de Cañadío and Calles de Daoíz y Velarde and Hernán Cortés are home to plenty of popular *bares de copas* (drinks bars), where you can chill over beer, cocktails, spirits and wine, inside or out, until the early hours. The neighbourhood of Calle de Santa Lucía, Calle del Sol and, in particular, Calle del Río de la Pila teems with a more bohemian bevy of bars, and crowds spill out onto the streets until at least 3am or 4am.

Rocambole   CLUB
(www.salarocambole.com; Calle de Hernán Cortés 35; ☉10.30pm-6am) Party until dawn at this long-standing bar-cum-nightclub, where DJs spin everything from rock to reggae.

Malaspina   MUSIC BAR
(Pasaje de Jesús Revaque Garea; ☉11.30pm-4.30am Thu-Sat) Named after an Italian explorer, jam-packed Malaspina has a semi-nautical theme, and attracts a more mature crowd. It's just off Calle de Santa Lucía.

ⓘ Information

Oficina de Turismo Municipal (☎942 20 30 00; www.ayto-santander.es; Jardines de Pereda; ☉9am-9pm) A summer branch operates at El Sardinero.

Oficina de Turismo de Cantabria (☎901 111112, 942 31 07 08; www.turismodecantabria. com; Calle de Hernán Cortés 4; ☉9am-9pm) Inside the Mercado del Este.

ⓘ Getting There & Around

AIR
The airport is 5km south of town at Parayas. Buses run to/from Santander bus station (€2.20) every 30 minutes, 6.30am to 11pm daily.
    Airlines and destinations:

Iberia (www.iberia.com) Madrid

Ryanair (www.ryanair.com) London (Stansted), Dublin, Edinburgh, Madrid, Barcelona, Brussels (Charleroi), Frankfurt (Hahn), Málaga, Paris (Beauvais-Tillé), Rome (Ciampino), Seville and Valencia

Vueling (www.vueling.com) Barcelona

BOAT
Brittany Ferries (www.brittany-ferries.co.uk) runs three weekly car ferries (including one no-frills service) from Portsmouth, UK (24 to 28 hours), and one from Plymouth, UK (20 hours). Fares vary enormously. A standard return trip for two adults and a car, with two-berth interior cabins, booked in February, might cost UK£1000 for July/August travel or UK£550 for October, from either UK port. Taking the no-frills Portsmouth ferry, a similar deal (with reclining seats) costs approximately £500 for July and £350 for October.

LD Lines (ldlines.com) operates one weekly car ferry from Poole, UK (25 hours). A return cabin trip for two adults and a car, booked in February, could cost between UK£500 and UK£700 for July and about UK£400 for October.

BUSES FROM SANTANDER
Transporte de Cantabria (www.transportede-cantabria.es) is a useful schedule source. **ALSA** (www.alsa.es) is the major company operating from the **bus station** (☎942 21 19 95; Calle Navas de Tolosa).
Buses run to the following destinations:
Bilbao (€6.60 to €15, 1¼-two hours, at least 22 daily)
Madrid (€31 to €43, 5¼-six hours, at least six daily)
Oviedo (€13 to €27, 2¼-3¼ hours, at least eight daily)
San Sebastián (€13 to €29, 2½-3¾ hours, at least eight daily)

TRAIN
There are two train stations, beside each other on Calle de Rodríguez: **FEVE** (☎985 98 23 81; www. renfe.com/viajeros/feve) serves destinations along Spain's north coast, while **Renfe** (www. renfe.com) serves destinations to the south.
Bilbao (€8.60, 2¾ hours, three FEVE trains daily)
Madrid (€52, 4½ hours, two or three long-distance Renfe trains daily) Via Palencia and Valladolid.
Oviedo (€16, 4½ hours, two FEVE trains daily) Via San Vicente de la Barquera, Llanes, Ribadesella and Arriondas.
Valladolid (€23, 3½ hours, three daily regional Renfe trains)

Around Santander

Cuevas de Monte Castillo

The valley town of Puente Viesgo, 25km south of Santander, lies at the foot of the conical Monte Castillo. About 2km up this hill are the Cuevas de Monte Castillo, a series of caves frequented by humans since 150,000 years ago. Four or more daily buses run to Puente Viesgo from Santander (€2.25, 40 minutes).

Cuevas de El Castillo y Las Monedas   CAVE
(☎942 59 84 25; http://cuevas.culturadecantabria.com; per cave adult/child €3/1.50; ☉9.30am-2.30pm & 3.30-7.30pm Tue-Sun, reduced hours & closed Tue mid-Sep-mid-Jun) Two of the four World Heritage-listed Cuevas de Monte Castillo – El Castillo and Las Monedas – are open for 45-minute guided visits. Booking

WHAT'S COOKING IN CANTABRIA & ASTURIAS?

The most traditional Cantabrian and Asturian food is simple peasant fare, fuelled by the surrounding mountains and sea. Green mountain pastures yield not only good meats but a whole array of tasty cheeses, while fresh seafood abounds in the Bay of Biscay. Meat-eaters will be in their element, although vegetarians might struggle.

Cocido montañés Inland Cantabria's dish par excellence: a filling stew of white beans, cabbage, potato, chorizo, black pudding and sometimes port. The Hotel del Oso (p498) in Cosgaya has been pleasing the public with its excellent *cocido montañés* and its local variation, *cocido lebaniego,* for over 30 years.

Fabada asturiana No dish better represents Asturias' taste for simplicity than the humble *fabada,* a hearty bean dish jazzed up with meat and sausage. For a taste of this classic favourite head to El Molín de la Pedrera (p492) in Cangas de Onís or El Corral del Indianu (p490) in Arriondas.

Ultra-tangy blue cheeses from the Picos de Europa King of Asturian cheeses is the powerful – but surprisingly moreish – bluey-green *queso de Cabrales,* made with untreated cow's-milk cheese and matured in mountain caves. In Cantabria, seek out the super-pungent *queso picón* (from a mix of cow's, sheep's and goat's milk) made in Tresviso and Bejes. To best sample local cheeses, order a *tabla de quesos* (platter of cheeses) at an elegant city eatery, like La Corrada del Obispo (p475) in Oviedo or Santander's Asubio Gastrobar (p461).

Seafood There is a wealth of fresh seafood in Cantabria and Asturias, while inland rivers provide trout, salmon and eels. You can go with good old, top-quality traditional fish preparations or explore a world of 'new concept' seafood at the Real Balneario de Salinas (p484), near Avilés.

Cachopo Asturias' *cachopo* (breaded veal stuffed with ham, cheese and vegetables) is a carnivore's dream, with vegetables to boot! Dig in at Restaurante Cares (p494), in Arenas de Cabrales.

ahead is highly advisable, especially for the more spectacular El Castillo, which contains the oldest cave art in the world. Here, you penetrate 500m into the cave where the art is almost as breathtaking as Altamira's – and unlike at Altamira, this is the genuine article rather than a replica.

The 275 paintings and engravings of deer, bison, horses, goats, aurochs, mammoths, handprints and mysterious symbols found within El Castillo date from 39,000 to 11,000 BC. Las Monedas has less art (black animal outlines, from around 10,000 BC) but contains an astounding labyrinth of stalactites and stalagmites.

Parque de Cabárceno

An open-air zoo, **Parque de la Naturaleza Cabárceno** (📞 942 56 37 36; www.parquede cabarceno.com; adult/child €25/15; ⊙ 9.30am-6pm; P), 17km south of Santander, is a curious but successful experiment, a free-range home on the site of former open-cut mines for everything from rhinos to wallabies and gorillas to dromedaries. You need a car

and about three hours to tour its 14km of roadways. From Santander, take the N623 towards Burgos and exit onto the CA144 towards Guarnizo; you'll soon see signs to the park, which is another 5km away.

Langre

The wild beaches of Langre are backed by cliffs topped with green fields, and often have surfable waves. Most people head for **Langre Grande**, although adjacent **Langre Pequeña** is more protected. It's about a 25km drive from Santander: round the bay to Somo, then east on the CA141 for a couple of kilometres, then turn left to Langre.

Eastern Cantabria

The 95km stretch of coast between Santander and Bilbao offers citizens of both cities several seaside escapes. While the towns are less attractive than those on Cantabria's western coast, some of the beaches are top-drawer.

WORTH A TRIP

EXPLORING CANTABRIA'S EASTERN VALLEYS

Rich in unspoiled rural splendour, the little-visited valleys of eastern Cantabria are ripe for exploration. The following route could be taken after a visit to the Cuevas de Monte Castillo. Do check weather conditions before setting off.

From El Soto, just off the N623 shortly south of Puente Viesgo, take the CA270 and CA262 southeast towards Vega de Pas, the 'capital' of the Valles Pasiegos (the Pas, Pisueña and Miera valleys; www.vallespasiegos.org), one of Cantabria's most traditional rural areas. The views from the Puerto de la Braguía pass are stunning. From Vega de Pas continue southeast on the CA631 into Castilla y León, before turning north again near Las Nieves to follow the BU571 up over the Puerto de la Sía pass towards Arredondo in Cantabria's southeastern Alto Asón district (www.citason.com). The road is full of switchbacks, has a couple of mountain passes and takes you past the 50m waterfall that constitutes the Nacimiento (Source) del Río Asón.

Alto Asón claims more than half of the 9000 known caves in Cantabria, and from Arredondo you can go east to Ramales de la Victoria, a valley town with two outstanding visitable caves. The Cueva de Cullalvera (☎ 942 59 84 25; http://cuevas.culturadecantabria.com; adult/child €3/1.50; ⊙ 9.30am-2.30pm & 3.30-7.30pm Tue-Sun, reduced hours & closed Tue-Thu mid-Oct–mid-Apr) is an impressively vast cavity with some signs of prehistoric art. The Cueva de Covalanas (☎ 942 59 84 25; http://cuevas.culturadecantabria.com; adult/child €3/1.50; ⊙ 9.30am-2.30pm & 3.30-7.30pm Tue-Sun, reduced hours & closed Tue-Thu mid-Oct–mid-Apr), 3km up the N629 south from Ramales, then 650m up a footpath, is World Heritage listed for its numerous excellent animal paintings from around 18,000 BC, done in an unusual dot-painting technique. Guided visits to either cave last 45 minutes and it's best to book ahead.

In a lovely, tranquil spot beside the Río Gándara in Regules, 10km southwest of Ramales, stands La Casa del Puente (☎ 942 63 90 20; www.lacasadelpuente.com; r €90-145; P ⊛ ⊟), a beautifully restored *casa de indianos* (mansion built by a returned emigrant from Latin America or the Caribbean). Rooms follow a funky-coloured, modern-rustic style, with exposed stonework, floral finishes and, for some, private Jacuzzis. You can enjoy good Cantabrian cooking in the glassed-in restaurant, and helpful, efficient owner Emilio is a fountain of local knowledge.

South of Ramales the N629 climbs to the panoramic Alto de los Tornos lookout at 920m, before continuing towards Burgos in Castilla y León.

Santoña

POP 11,100

The fishing port of Santoña is famed for its anchovies, which are bottled or tinned here with olive oil to preserve them. Santoña is dominated by two fortresses, the Fuerte de San Martín and, further east, the abandoned Fuerte de San Carlos. You can take a pleasant walk around both, or take the shuttle ferry (€1.70; March to November) across the estuary to the western end of Laredo beach. Or head off for a hike in the Parque Cultural Monte Buciero, which occupies the hill-cum-headland rising northeast of the town. The helpful tourist office (☎ 942 66 00 66; www.turismosantona.com; Calle Santander 5; ⊙ 10am-2pm & 5-8pm daily Jun-Sep, 10am-5pm Mon-Fri & 10am-2pm Sat & Sun Oct-May) offers free, one-day bicycle loans in July and August. Otherwise, go north along the

C141 to Playa Berria, a magnificent sweep of sand and surf on the open sea, linked to Santoña by frequent buses (€1.45). Here, Hotel Juan de la Cosa (☎ 942 66 12 38; www.hoteljuandelacosa.com; Playa de Berria 14; s €65-95, d €65-125; ⊙ closed Nov-Mar; P ⊛ @ ⊛ ⊠) may be in an unsympathetic-looking building, but about two-thirds of its spacious, blue-hued rooms have beach views, and it has a good seafood restaurant too.

Thirteen buses run Monday to Saturday (seven on Sunday) to Santoña from Santander (€4.20, one hour). From June to September there's also a two-hourly passenger ferry to central Laredo (€6).

Laredo

POP 11,200

Laredo's long, sandy beach, across the bay from Santoña, is backed by ugly 20th-century blocks. But at the east end of town the cobbled streets of the old Puebla Vieja slope down from the impressive 13th-century Iglesia de Santa María, with the remains of the 16th-century Fuerte del Rastrillar fortress on La Atalaya hill above. The Puebla Vieja has a lively food and drinks scene: for tasty creative tapas such as *lubina con mojo de cilantro y tallarines de calamares* (sea bass with a coriander sauce and squid noodles), head to Somera (Rua Mayor 17-19; tapas €1.80-4; ⊗12.30-3.30pm & 8-11.30pm, closed Nov & Mon Sep-Jun).

Plenty of buses from Santander (€4.15, 40 minutes) call in here.

Playas de Oriñón & Sonabia

The broad sandy strip of Playa de Oriñón, just off the *autovía* (toll-free highway) 14km east of Laredo, is set deep behind protective headlands, making the water calm and *comparatively* warm. The settlement here consists of drab holiday flats and caravan parks. Continue 1.7km past Oriñón to the smaller but wilder Playa de Sonabia, set in a rock-lined inlet beneath high crags. An up-and-down 10km walking trail links Oriñón with Laredo via Playa de Sonabia and the even more isolated Playa de San Julián.

Castro Urdiales

POP 25,500

The haughty Gothic jumble that is the Iglesia de Santa María de la Asunción (⊗10am-1pm & 4-6pm Mon-Sat) stands out above the harbour and the tangle of narrow lanes that make up the medieval centre of Castro Urdiales. The church shares its little headland with the ruins of the town's old defensive bastion, now supporting a lighthouse.

Of Castro's two beaches, the northern Playa de Ostende is the more attractive.

🛏 Sleeping & Eating

Traditional fare, such as *sopa de pescado* (fish soup) and *pudín de cabracho* (scorpion-fish pâté), abounds in *mesones* (old-style eateries) and *tabernas* (taverns) along Calle de la Mar and Calle de Ardigales, and on Plaza del Ayuntamiento in front of the fishing boats.

Ardigales 11   HOTEL €€
(☑942 78 16 16; www.pensionardigales11.com; Calle de Ardigales 11; s/d €56/78; 🖭) Behind a solid stone exterior in the old town centre hides this somewhat futuristic hotel, with

11 slick modern rooms decked out in blacks and whites.

ℹ Information

Tourist Office (☑942 87 15 12; www.turismo castrourdiales.net; Parque Amestoy; ⊗9am-9pm Jul-Aug, 9.30am-1.30pm & 4-7pm Sep-Jun) On the seafront.

ℹ Getting There & Away

ALSA (www.alsa.es; Calle de Leonardo Rucabado 42) runs at least nine buses daily to Santander (€6.20, one hour). Buses to Bilbao (€2.72, 45 minutes) go every half-hour until 10pm, making various stops including at La Barrera flower shop at Calle La Ronda 52, half a block from the seafront.

Southern Cantabria

Fine panoramas of high peaks and deep river valleys flanked by verdant patchwork quilts await the traveller penetrating the Cantabrian interior. Every imaginable shade of green seems to have been employed to set this stage, strewn with warm stone villages and held together by a network of narrow country roads.

Reinosa

POP 11,200 / ELEV 851M

Southern Cantabria's main town is an unexceptional place, but its tourist office (☑942 75 52 15; Avenida del Puente de Carlos III 23; ⊗9.30am-2.30pm & 4.30-7.30pm Mon-Fri, 9.30am-2.30pm Sat, closed afternoons Oct-Jun) can inform you about plenty of curiosities nearby. These include the Colegiata de San Pedro in Cervatos, 5km south, one of Cantabria's finest Romanesque churches, with rare erotic carvings on its corbels; the Yacimiento Arqueológico de Camesa Rebolledo (☑942 59 84 25; http://centros.culturadecantabria.com; adult/child €3/1.50; ⊗9.30am-2.30pm & 3.30-6.30pm, closed afternoons Mon-Fri Nov-Mar), the fascinating triple-epoch excavation site of a Roman villa buried beneath a Visigothic necropolis and a medieval graveyard just outside Mataporquera, 20km south; and the remains of Cantabria's most significant Roman town, Julióbriga (☑942 59 84 25; http://centros.culturadecantabria.com; adult/child €3/1.50; ⊗9.30am-2.30pm & 3.30-6.30pm Tue-Sun Apr-Oct, 9.30am-2.30pm Wed-Sun Nov-Mar; 🅿), at Retortillo, 5km east. The guided visit at Julióbriga includes the Museo Domus, a full-scale recreation of a Roman house.

TOURING THE EBRO'S ROCK-CUT CHURCHES

Spain's most voluminous river, the Ebro, rises at Fontibre about 6km west of Reinosa, fills the Embalse del Ebro reservoir to the east, and then meanders south and east into Castilla y León. Its course is strung with some fascinating and picturesque stops. You can follow it on the GR99 long-distance footpath or on minor roads out of Reinosa.

Head first east along the CA730 (visiting Roman Julióbriga en route if you like) to Arroyo, where you turn south and follow signs to the Monasterio de Montesclaros, which has a fine site overlooking the Ebro valley and a history going back to at least the 12th century. From here follow the CA741 down to Arroyal de los Carabeos, then head south on the CA272 to a roundabout where it meets the CA273. Nine kilometres west on the CA273 is the remarkable Iglesia Rupestre de Santa María de Valverde. This beautiful, multi-arched church, hewn from the living rock, is the most impressive of several *iglesias rupestres* (rock-cut churches) in this area, dating from probably the 7th to 10th centuries, the early days of Christianity in the region. Santa María church itself is often locked outside July and August, but you can arrange visits in advance through the tourist office (☑ 942 77 61 46; www.valderredible.es; Avenida Cantabria; ⏱ 10am-2pm & 5-8pm Tue-Sat, 11am-2pm Sun) in Polientes, the area's biggest village. Next to the church, the Centro de Interpretación del Rupestre (☑ 605 828380; adult/child €1/free; ⏱ 10am-6pm Tue-Sun mid-Jun–mid-Sep, 10am-2pm & 4-6.30pm Sat & Sun Mar–mid-Jun, 10am-3.30pm Sat & Sun mid-Sep–Feb) tells the story of the area's curious rock-church phenomenon through photos, maps, video and multimedia – well worth a visit even if you don't understand Spanish – and can provide plenty of useful information. From here head back east and continue to Polientes, which has a bank, petrol station (self-service with credit cards only) and four places to stay, of which the pick is Posada El Cuartelillo Viejo (☑ 942 77 61 51; www.elcuartelilloviejo.com; Carretera General 31; r incl breakfast €50-64; ⏱ closed Dec-Mar).

East of Polientes you'll find the best of the area's other rock-cut churches. The church at Arroyuelos is a two-level affair: ask for keys at the nearest whitewashed house. Across the Ebro from Arroyuelos, San Martín de Elines is well worth a detour for its lovely Romanesque church (key available at the priest's house). The small but wonderfully sited El Tobazo cave-church is part of a small group of caves towards the top of the Ebro gorge east of Arroyuelos. To find it, cross the bridge into Villaescusa del Ebro, turn immediately left and follow the track for 900m to a grassy clearing on the right. From here you have a 700m uphill walk, starting from the far corner of the clearing. A waterfall (appearing as a moss-covered, cave-pocked cliff after prolonged dry weather) comes into view about halfway up, with the cave-church just above it to the right.

From Villaescusa the CA275 continues along the Ebro gorge to picturesque Orbaneja del Castillo in Castilla y León.

Reinosa has a half-dozen sleeping options. Set in a charmingly restored, century-old Modernista building, Villa Rosa (☑ 942 75 47 47; www.villarosa.com; Calle de los Héroes de la Guardia Civil 4; r incl breakfast €70; @ 🛜) 🅿 looks more like something you'd expect in central Europe and most of its 12 very comfy rooms have an inviting period feel. It's handily close to the train and bus stations.

Nine Renfe *cercanías* (suburban trains; €5.05, 1¾ hours) and at least six buses (€6.30, 1¼ hours) head from Santander to Reinosa daily. A few daily trains and buses head south to Palencia, Valladolid, Salamanca and Madrid.

Western Cantabria

Santillana del Mar

POP 1020

They say this is the town of the three lies, since it is not *santi* (holy), *llana* (flat) or *del mar* (by the sea)! This medieval jewel is in such a perfect state of preservation, with its bright cobbled streets and tanned stone and brick buildings huddling in a muddle of centuries of history, that it seems too good to be true. Surely it's a film set! Well, no. People still live here, passing their precious houses down from generation to generation.

Strict town planning rules were introduced back in 1575, and today they include the stipulation that only residents or guests in hotels with garages may bring vehicles into the old heart of town. Other hotel guests may drive to unload luggage and must then return to the car park at the town entrance.

Santillana is a gem in its own right, but also makes an obvious base for visiting nearby Altamira.

⊙ Sights

Colegiata de Santa Juliana CHURCH
(admission €3; ⊙10am-1.30pm & 4-7.30pm, closed Mon Oct-Jun) A stroll along Santillana's cobbled main street, past solemn nobles' houses from the 15th to 18th centuries, leads you to this lovely 12th-century Romanesque ex-monastery. The big drawcard is the cloister, a formidable storehouse of Romanesque handiwork, with the capitals of its columns carved into a huge variety of figures. The monastery originally grew up around the relics of Santa Juliana, a 3rd-century Christian martyr from Turkey (and the real source of the name Santillana), whose sepulchre stands in the centre of the church.

Museo de Tortura MUSEUM
(Calle del Escultor Jesús Otero 1; adult/student/child €3.60/2.40/free; ⊙10am-9pm) This exhibition displays more than 70 grim instruments of torture and capital punishment used by the Inquisition and elsewhere in Europe. You might want to leave the kids outside even though their entry is free!

🛏 Sleeping

There are dozens of places to stay, many of them in converted atmospheric historic buildings. They are scattered about the old part of town, around Campo del Revolgo south of the main road, and along the roads towards Altamira, Comillas and Santander. Rates at most places drop outside August. Many close for varying periods in winter.

Posada de la Abadía GUESTHOUSE €
(☏942 84 03 04; www.posadadelabadia.com; Calle de Revolgo 26; s/d incl breakfast €50/59; P🐾) A small family-run place in a traditional Cantabrian-style house, 200m south of the main road. It's clean and friendly, with a decent breakfast, and the 10 pretty, if not exactly inspired, rooms all have a bathtub.

Casa del Organista HOTEL €€
(☏942 84 03 52; www.casadelorganista.com; Calle de Los Hornos 4; s/d €77/93; ⊙closed Jan; P@🐾) The 14 rooms at this elegant 18th-century house, once home to the organist of the Colegiata de Santa Juliana, are particularly attractive, with plush rugs, antique furniture and plenty of exposed oak beams and stonework. Some have balconies looking across fields towards the *colegiata*. The welcome is warm and helpful, and an excellent breakfast costs €5.85. There are three or four similarly styled places up the street.

La Casona de Revolgo HOTEL €€
(☏942 81 82 77; www.lacasonaderevolgo.com; Campo del Revolgo 3; s/d €80/120; ⊙closed Sun-Thu Dec–mid-Mar; P🐾) There's a majestic, old-fashioned air about this place, but in fact it's a fairly contemporary creation, built from the burnt-down ruins of a 17th-century coaching inn 100m south of the main road. All 14 rooms are large and richly decorated, with heavy wood beams and plenty of pillows. The friendly owners also run the cheaper but still charming Posada Santa Juliana (☏648 26 24 20; www.santillanadelmar.com; Calle Carrera 19; r €54; ⊙Fri & Sat only Nov-Mar).

Casa del Marqués HISTORIC HOTEL €€€
(☏942 81 88 88; www.hotelcasadelmarques.com; Calle del Cantón 24; r €187-226; ⊙Mar-early Dec; P🐾@🐾) Feel like the lord or lady of the manor in this 15th-century Gothic mansion, once home to the Marqués de Santillana. Exposed timber beams, thick stone walls and cool terracotta floors contribute to the atmosphere of the 14 all-different rooms. The owners are proud of their banister, 700 years old and made from a single tree.

🍴 Eating

Santillana has many humdrum eateries catering to the tourist trade, and you should be able to get a full meal for about €25. A few options stand out from the crowd.

Restaurante Gran Duque CANTABRIAN €€
(www.granduque.com; Calle del Escultor Jesús Otero 7; mains €15-19; ⊙1-4pm & 8-11pm, closed Sun dinner & Mon lunch mid-Sep–mid-Jun, closed mid-Jan–mid-Feb) The food is high-quality local fare and what sets it apart is the setting, a grand stone house with noble trappings and nice decorative touches such as exposed brick and beams. There is a reasonable balance of surf or turf options including *mariscadas* (seafood feasts) for two at €50 to €90

CANTABRIA & ASTURIAS WESTERN CANTABRIA

and a decent €19 *menú del día* (daily set menu), available for lunch and dinner.

Los Blasones
CANTABRIAN €€

(Plaza La Gándara; mains €16-24; ⊘1-3.30pm & 8-10.30pm, closed dinner & Fri Nov-Feb) Set in a warm yellow dining room lined with chestnut wood, Los Blasones has been proudly dishing up the usual Cantabrian selection since 1970. Hearty offerings from the open-plan kitchen include *cocido montañés* (white bean, potato, chorizo and black pudding stew) and fresh fish of the day, as well as a €14 *menú del día*.

ℹ Information

Oficina Regional de Turismo (☑942 81 88 12; Calle del Escultor Jesús Otero; ⊘9am-9pm)

ℹ Getting There & Away

Autobuses La Cantábrica (☑942 72 08 22; www.lacantabrica.net) runs three or more daily buses from Santander to Santillana (€2.55, 40 minutes), and on to Comillas and San Vicente de la Barquera. They stop by Campo del Revolgo.

Altamira

Spain's finest prehistoric art, the wonderful paintings of bison, horses and other animals in the Cueva de Altamira, 2km southwest of Santillana del Mar, was discovered in 1879 by Cantabrian historian and scientist Marcelino Sanz de Sautuola and his eight-year-old daughter María Justina. By 2002 Altamira had attracted so many visitors that the cave was closed to prevent deterioration of the art, but a replica cave in the museum here now enables everyone to appreciate the inspired, 13,000- to 35,000-year-old paintings. In 2014 the Altamira authorities began trialling an experimental program whereby on one day each week five visitors to the museum will be randomly selected to visit the real Altamira cave on the same day. People entering the museum on the selected days will be offered an application form if interested. This is the first time that the general public has been allowed into the original cave since 2002.

★ Museo de Altamira
MUSEUM

(http://museodealtamira.mcu.es; adult/EU senior or student/child €3/1.50/free, Sun & from 2pm Sat free; ⊘9.30am-8pm Tue-Sat, to 3pm Sun & holidays; P) The museum's highlight is the Neocueva, a dazzling, full-sized recreation of the real cave's most interesting chamber, the Sala de Polícromos (Polychrome Hall). Other excellent displays, in English and Spanish, cover prehistoric humanity and cave art around the world, from Altamira to Australia. The museum is incredibly popular (around 240,000 visitors a year), so it's best to reserve tickets in advance, especially for Easter week, July, August and September.

You can book tickets at any branch of Banco Santander in Spain or online via the Altamira website – although, oddly enough, the final stages for online payment are available in Spanish only. Advance tickets cost €3 for everybody (children, students and seniors included), and are not available for Saturday afternoon or Sunday. Same-day tickets are sold only at the museum ticket office. With all tickets you are assigned an exact time for entering the Neocueva. During busy periods this might involve a wait of several hours if you have not reserved in advance.

Those without vehicles must walk or take a taxi to Altamira from Santillana del Mar.

Comillas

POP 1900

Sixteen kilometres west from Santillana through verdant countryside, Comillas has a lovely golden beach and a tiny fishing port, but there is more: a pleasant, cobbled old centre, and hilltops crowned by some of the most original buildings in Cantabria. For the latter, Comillas is indebted to the first Marqués de Comillas, who was born here as plain Antonio López, made a fortune in Cuba as a tobacco planter, shipowner, banker and slave trader, and then returned to commission leading Catalan Modernista architects to jazz up his home town in the late 19th century. This in turn prompted the construction of other quirky mansions here.

◎ Sights

Capricho de Gaudí
ARCHITECTURE

(www.elcaprichodegaudi.com; Barrio de Sobrellano; adult/child €5/2.50; ⊘10.30am-9pm, to 5.30pm Nov-Feb) Antoni Gaudí left few reminders of his genius beyond Catalonia, but of those that he did, the 1885 Gaudí Caprice in Comillas is easily the most flamboyant. The brick building, one of Gaudí's earliest works and originally a summer play pad for the Marqués de Comillas' sister-in-law's brother, is liberally striped on the outside with ceramic bands of alternating green leaves and sunflowers. Its interior is comparatively restrained but still has quirky touches like *artesonado* ceilings (patterns of timber beams inset with decorative panels).

It's worth watching the video in the greenhouse/conservatory before you go round the interior.

Palacio de Sobrellano MANSION
(942 72 03 39; adult/child €3/1.50; 9.40am-2.30pm & 3.30-7.20pm Tue-Sun, reduced hours mid-Oct–mid-Apr) In hillside parklands stands the Marqués de Comillas' wonderful neo-Gothic Palacio de Sobrellano. With this building, Modernista architect Joan Martorell truly managed to out-Gothic real Gothic. Martorell also designed the marquis' ornate family tomb, the **Capilla Panteón de Sobrellano** (adult/child €3/1.50), next door. Visits to both buildings are by 20-minute guided tour in Spanish; entry to the grounds is free.

Town Centre SQUARE, CHURCH
Comillas' compact medieval centre is built around several cobbled plazas, with a vernacular architecture of solid sandstone houses with wooden balconies or glassed-in galleries. The main church, the **Iglesia de San Cristóbal**, was built in the 17th century from the townspeople's own pockets after they took offence at the Duque de Infantado's retinue refusing to share a pew with common folk in the old church.

Seminario Mayor ARCHITECTURE
(Calle de Manuel Noriega; adult/child €3.50/free, car €2; 10am-1pm & 5-8pm, closed afternoons Oct-May; P) Modernista architects Joan Martorell and Lluís Domènech i Montaner both had a hand in this large, elaborate, former seminary, with Domènech i Montaner contributing its medieval flavour. It's now an international Spanish-language-and-culture study centre, the **Centro Internacional de Estudios Superiores de Español** (www. fundacioncomillas.es). Visits inside the building are guided in Spanish; from June to September a daily 6pm tour runs in English. You can visit the grounds for free (unless you take a car in).

🛏 Sleeping

Hotel Marina de Campíos BOUTIQUE HOTEL €€
(942 72 27 54; www.marinadecampios.com; Calle del General Piélagos 14; s/d €105/120; Jun-Sep; ❄@🛜) This 19th-century house, a few steps from the central plaza, Corro de Campíos, has been revamped into a classy modern hotel

with 19 boldly styled rooms, most sporting curtained beds. There's a lovely inner patio, with a piano bar opening onto it.

Hostal Esmeralda HOSTAL €€
(942 72 00 97; www.hostalesmeralda.com; Calle de Antonio López 7; s/d €60/80; 🛜) A short distance east of the town centre, Esmeralda is a handsomely restored 1874 stone building with large, old-fashioned but comfy rooms, good beds, dashes of colourful decor and plenty of character. It's well run by the fourth generation of the family that built it. Rates dive outside August.

🍴 Eating

Plenty of restaurants and cafes around the central squares provide straightforward seafood and meat *raciones* (large tapas servings; €6 to €15), *menús* (€10 to €12) and *platos combinados* (seafood/meat/omelette with chips and vegies; €7 to €9).

Restaurante Gurea CANTABRIAN, BASQUE €
(Calle Ignacio Fernández de Castro 11; mains €8-12; 1-4pm & 8-11pm, closed Tue) This elegant restaurant, hidden in a small street a few blocks from the town centre, dishes up Basque and Cantabrian fare, and can throw together an excellent salad. The €50 menu for two, available for lunch or dinner, is a good bet.

ℹ Information

Tourist Office (942 72 25 91; www.comillas. es; Plaza de Joaquín del Piélago; 9am-9pm daily Jun-Sep, 9am-2pm & 4-6pm Mon-Sat & 9am-2pm Sun Oct-May)

ℹ Getting There & Away

Comillas is served by the same buses (€3.90, one hour from Santander) as Santillana del Mar. The main stop is on Calle del Marqués de Comillas, close to the town centre.

San Vicente de la Barquera & Around

POP (SAN VICENTE) 3300

The last town on the Cantabrian coast before you enter Asturias, San Vicente de la Barquera sits handsomely on a point of land between two long inlets, backed by dramatic Picos de Europa mountainscapes. The eastern inlet, the estuary of the Río Escudo, is spanned by the low-slung, 15th-century Puente de la Maza. San Vicente was one of the Cuatro Villas de la Costa, a federation of four dominant medieval ports that was converted into the province of Cantabria in 1779 (along with Santander, Laredo and Castro Urdiales). The long beaches east of town make San Vicente quite a busy summer spot.

◉ Sights

Iglesia de Nuestra Señora de los Ángeles
CHURCH

(admission €1.50; ⊙10am-2pm & 3-9pm Jul-mid-Sep, 10am-1pm & 4-6pm mid-Sep–Jun) The outstanding monument in the old part of town is the Iglesia de Nuestra Señora de los Ángeles, commissioned by Alfonso VIII in 1210. Although Gothic, it sports a pair of impressive Romanesque doorways. Inside, the eerily lifelike statue of 16th-century Inquisitor Antonio del Corro (reclining on one elbow, reading) is deemed one of the best pieces of Renaissance funerary art in Spain.

Castillo del Rey
CASTLE

(adult/child €1.40/0.70; ⊙10.30am-1.30pm & 5-9pm, closed Mon mid-Sep–Jun) This 13th-century medieval castle, one of Cantabria's best preserved, tops the old part of town.

Playa El Rosal & Playa de Merón
BEACH

Along the coast east of town, these two beaches are basically one broad, 4km-long golden strand. Merón gets some surf and you should heed the warning flags: red means don't swim; yellow means take care.

El Soplao
CAVE

(☎902 820282; www.elsoplao.es; adult/senior, student & child €12/9.50; ⊙10am-7pm Jul & Aug, 10am-2pm & 3-6pm Sep-Jun, closed Mon Oct-Jun; P) This extensive cave system full of stalactites and stalagmites, and a lead and zinc mine before 1979, makes for a popular outing inland from San Vicente de la Barquera. The one-hour visit goes 400m into the cave in a mine train then continues on foot. Booking ahead is highly recommended. A separate adventure tour travelling 3km in (€32, 2½ hours) opens up an extraordinary subterranean world. It's about 30km southwest of San Vicente: turn east off the CA181 at Rábago and climb 7km.

🍽 Sleeping & Eating

Hotel Luzón
HOTEL €€

(☎942 71 00 50; www.hotelluzon.net; Avenida Miramar 1; s/d €45/70; ⊙closed Jan; 🤶) The centrally positioned Luzón is a stately looking, century-old town house still possessing an air of older times, with its high ceilings, long corridors and quiet drawing rooms. Rooms are plain and simple but mostly spacious. Ask for a front room with broad views over town and water.

Hotel Azul de Galimar
HOTEL €€

(☎942 71 50 20; www.hotelazuldegalimar.es; Camino Alto Santiago 11; s/d €90/107; ⊙closed Dec-Feb; P🤶) This modern hotel, with a small lawned garden, is set in an excellent high position on the east side of town and has just 16 airy, attractive rooms in shades of pastel. Many have balconies or terraces overlooking the Escudo estuary. It's signposted from the Puente de la Maza.

Boga-Boga
SEAFOOD €€

(www.restaurantebogaboga.es; Plaza José Antonio 9; mains €16.50-22; ⊙1-4pm & 8-11pm, closed Mon dinner & Tue Oct-Jun) Despite its less than stunning exterior, this popular seafood spot has a warm, maritime feel, its walls decked out with Spanish warship insignia. The Boga-Boga hake comes cooked in a clay pot with oil and garlic, or you might try the speciality *marmita de bogavante* (seafood stew with European lobster). Several other seafood-dominated restaurants line Avenida del Generalísimo, leading off Plaza de José Antonio.

❶ Getting There & Away

San Vicente's **bus station** (Avenida Miramar), near the Puente de la Maza, is served by at least six daily buses to Santander (€5, 1¼ hours, some via Comillas and Santillana del Mar), five to Oviedo (€9.02, two hours, some via Llanes, Ribadesella and Arriondas) and two to Potes (€3.70, 1¼ hours).

Two FEVE trains stop en route between Santander and Oviedo at La Acebosa, 3km south of town.

ASTURIAS

'Ser español es un orgullo', the saying goes, *'ser asturiano es un título'*. 'If being Spanish is a matter of pride, to be Asturian is a title', or so some of the locals would have you think. Asturias, they claim, is the real Spain; the rest is simply *tierra de reconquista* (reconquered land). Like neighbouring Galicia, Asturias was Celtic territory before the Romans arrived (and is bagpipe territory today!). It's also the sole patch of Spain never completely conquered by the Muslims. A Visigothic chieftain, Pelayo, warded them off in the Battle of Covadonga in AD 722, laying

the foundations of the Kingdom of Asturias from which modern Spain grew.

Asturias has many similarities with neighbouring Cantabria and its scenic beauty is, if anything, even greater. The coast is wilder and more dramatic, and strung with even more beaches (over 200), always with rolling green countryside behind. Inland, the mountains are higher, the valleys deeper (though equally green) and the villages a tad more rustic. Much of the Picos de Europa are on Asturian territory. For the architecture buff, Asturias is the land of the pre-Romanesque – modest but unique survivors from early medieval times. The region's cultured capital, Oviedo, is both historic and coolly contemporary. Asturias also has its gritty industrial side. The Oviedo–Gijón–Avilés triangle is the heart of industrial Asturias and, despite its slow decline, the mining industry still operates, especially in the southwest.

The Reconquista's southward progress left Asturias increasingly a backwater. As a concession, Juan I of Castilla y León made Asturias a *principado* (principality) in 1388, and to this day the heir to the Spanish throne holds the title Príncipe de Asturias (Prince of Asturias). Awards handed out by the prince to personalities of distinction in Oviedo's Teatro Campoamor every October are Spain's equivalent of the Nobel prizes.

Oviedo

POP 210,000 / ELEV 232M

The compact but characterful and historic *casco antiguo* (Old Town) of Asturias' civilised capital is agreeably offset by elegant parks and busy, modern shopping streets to its west and north. Out on the periphery, the hum and heave of factories is a strong reminder that Oviedo is a major producer of textiles, weapons and food.

History

When Asturian king Alfonso II El Casto (the Chaste; AD 791–842) defeated a Muslim detachment that had practically razed the settlement of Oviedo, he was sufficiently impressed by the site to move his court there from Pravia. Oviedo remained the Asturian kingdom's capital until 910, when León replaced it and the kingdom became the Kingdom of León. Oviedo's university was founded in 1608, and industry took off in the 19th century. The 1934 miners' revolt and a

ⓘ ASTURIAS WEBSITES

www.turismoasturias.es Excellent, comprehensive site of Asturias' regional tourism office.

www.casasdealdea.com Over 200 *casas rurales* (village or farmstead accommodations) across Asturias.

www.casonasasturianas.com Fifty top country-house hotels.

nasty siege at the beginning of the Spanish Civil War destroyed much of the Old Town, but now restored it's a fascinating place to explore.

⊙ Sights

★ **Catedral de San Salvador**   CATHEDRAL
The cathedral's origins and main interest lie in the Cámara Santa, a pre-Romanesque chapel built by Alfonso II to house holy relics. The chapel now contains several key symbols of medieval Spanish Christianity and is a small part of a much bigger complex that was built piecemeal over many years, chiefly in Gothic and baroque styles between the 13th and 18th centuries.

In the northwest corner of the Capilla del Rey Casto, a baroque chapel entered from the cathedral's north transept, the **Panteón Real** is believed to hold the tombs of most of the Asturian monarchs, including Alfonso II himself.

You enter the **Cámara Santa** (admission €3, incl museum & cloister €5, Thu afternoon free; ⊙10am-2pm & 4-8pm Mon-Fri, to 6pm Sat & Nov-Feb), cloister and museum from the southern transept. Inside the Cámara Santa you'll find a collection of important sacred medieval artefacts, including two jewel-encrusted gold crosses: Alfonso II presented the central Cruz de los Ángeles (Cross of the Angels) to the cathedral in 808, and it's still Oviedo's city emblem. A century later Alfonso III donated the Cruz de la Victoria (Cross of Victory), which in turn became the sign of Asturias. The Cámara Santa also contains the Santo Sudario, a cloth said to have covered Christ's face. These items are viewed from the Sala Apostolar, whose remarkable Romanesque sculptures of the 12 apostles are in the style of Maestro Mateo, creator of Santiago de Compostela's Pórtico de la Gloria. Turning to leave, you'll see three heads sculpted from a single block of stone above

Oviedo

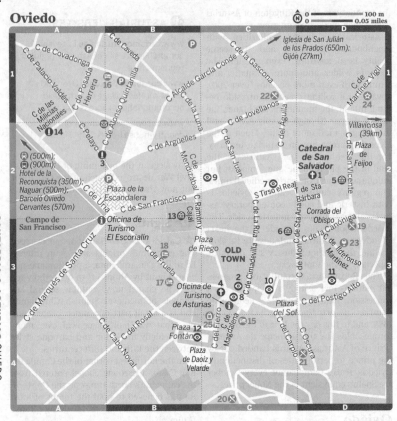

Oviedo

PLAZAS & STATUES

A key pleasure of Oviedo is exploring the Old Town's nooks and crannies. Plaza de Alfonso II, in front of the cathedral, and neighbouring Plaza de Porlier are fronted by elegant 17th- and 18th-century mansions. Plaza de la Constitución occupies a barely perceptible rise close to the heart of old Oviedo, capped at one end by the Iglesia de San Isidoro, and lined by the 17th-century ayuntamiento (town hall). Past the colourful Mercado El Fontán (⊙8am-8pm Mon-Fri, 8am-3.30pm Sat) food market, arcaded Plaza Fontán is equipped with a couple of *sidrerías* (cider bars) and has passages leading in under pretty houses from surrounding streets.

Other cute squares include Plaza de Trascorrales and Plaza del Paraguas. The latter got its name from its inverted-umbrella design, which once accommodated an open-air market. Today it sports a big concrete umbrella to protect people from the elements.

Wandering around central Oviedo, you'll run into an array of striking modern open-air sculptures, such as Eduardo Úrculo's Culis Monumentalibus (Calle Pelayo), which is a pair of legs topped by a pair of large buttocks, and a statue of Woody Allen. Allen expressed a particular affection for Oviedo when filming here for his 2008 flick *Vicky Cristina Barcelona*.

the doorway. This strikingly simple work depicts, from left to right, the Virgin Mary, Christ and St John on Calvary. Their bodies were originally painted on the wall below.

The cloister is pure 14th-century Gothic, rare enough in Asturias. The pre-Romanesque Torre Vieja (Old Tower), from the late 9th century, rises above its northwestern corner (best viewed from the street Tránsito de Santa Bárbara).

The Cámara Santa and museum were closed for restoration work at the time of research. The cathedral's ticketing and admission arrangements may change once works are complete.

Museo Arqueológico de Asturias   MUSEUM
(www.museoarqueologicodeasturias.com; Calle de San Vicente 3; ⊙9.30am-8pm Wed-Fri, 9.30am-2pm & 5-8pm Sat, 9.30am-3pm Sun) FREE Partly within a restored 16th-century monastery, Asturias' archaeology museum makes the most of the region's archaeological riches through video as well as informative displays of artefacts. Subject matter ranges from prehistoric cave art to *castro* (pre-Roman fortified village) culture, Roman times and the medieval Kingdom of Asturias. Explanatory details are in Spanish, but staff will lend you a guide booklet in English or French.

Museo de Bellas Artes
de Asturias   MUSEUM
(www.museobbaa.com; Calle de Santa Ana 1; ⊙10.30am-2pm & 4.30-8.30pm Tue-Sat, 10.30am-2.30pm Sun) FREE The Fine Arts Museum, housed in two of Oviedo's finest urban palaces, has a large and rewarding collection, including paintings by Spanish and European greats such as Goya, Zurbarán, Picasso, Titian and Brueghel the Elder, and plenty by Asturians, such as Evaristo Valle.

Universidad de Oviedo   HISTORIC BUILDING
(www.uniovi.es; Calle de San Francisco 3; ⊙8am-8pm Mon-Fri, 9am-2pm Sat & Aug) This elegant 17th-century building, set around two superposed cloisters, was originally home to the University of Oviedo's schools of Arts, Theology and Law. Nowadays it's an administrative house, but well worth a wander. In the centre sits the majestic statue of Fernando de Valdés Salas, the university's founder, while the cloister's columns still bear bullet holes from the civil war.

⭐ Festivals & Events

Oviedo's biggest fiesta is that of San Mateo, celebrated in the third week of September and climaxing around 21 September.

🛏 Sleeping

There's only a handful of places actually in the Old Town, but plenty of others are scattered around its periphery.

Hostal Arcos   HOSTAL €
(☏985 21 47 73; www.hostal-arcos.com; Calle de Magdalena 3; s €35-40, d €48-55; 🖭) One of the few lodgings actually in the Old Town is this modern brick building with a friendly welcome and 10 simple, clean rooms, all quite

DON'T MISS

PRE-ROMANESQUE OVIEDO

Largely cut off from the rest of Christian Europe by the Muslim invasion, the tough and tiny kingdom that emerged in 8th-century Asturias gave rise to a unique style of art and architecture known as pre-Romanesque.

The 15 buildings, mostly churches (and collectively a World Heritage site), that survive from the two centuries of the Asturian kingdom take some inspiration from Roman, Visigothic and possibly Carolingian French buildings, but have no real siblings. They are typified by straight-line profiles, semicircular Roman-style arches, and a triple-naved plan for the churches. In many cases the bases and capitals of columns, with their Corinthian or floral motifs, were simply cannibalised from earlier structures. The use of lattice windows as a design effect owes something to developments in Muslim Spain.

Some of the best of the genre are found in and near Oviedo, including the cathedral's Cámara Santa (p471). The **Iglesia de San Julián de los Prados** (Iglesia de Santullano; adult/child €1.20/0.60, Mon free; ☺ 10am-12.30pm Mon, 10am-12.30pm & 4-5.30pm Tue-Fri, 9.30am-noon & 3.30-5pm Sat, closed afternoons Oct-Apr), 1km northeast of the town centre, just above the highway to Gijón, is the largest remaining pre-Romanesque church, and one of the oldest, built in the early 9th century under Alfonso II. It is flanked by two porches – another Asturian touch – and the inside is covered with frescoes. On the slopes of Monte Naranco, 3km northwest of central Oviedo, the tall, narrow **Palacio de Santa María del Naranco** (adult/child incl Iglesia de San Miguel de Lillo €3/2, Mon free; ☺ 9.30am-1pm & 3.30-7pm Tue-Sat, 9.30am-1pm Sun & Mon, shorter hours Oct-Mar) and the **Iglesia de San Miguel de Lillo** (☺ 9.30am-1pm & 3.30-7pm Tue-Sat, 9.30am-1pm Sun & Mon, shorter hours Oct-Mar) were built by Ramiro I (842–50), and mark an advance in Asturian art. An outstanding decorative feature of the beautifully proportioned Santa María (which may have been a royal hunting lodge) is the *sogueado*, the sculptural motif imitating rope used in its columns. Some of the medallions are copies of ancient Iranian motifs, known here through Roman contact. Of the original San Miguel, only about one-third remains – the rest collapsed centuries ago – but what's left has a singularly pleasing form. Also here, the **Centro de Interpretación del Prerrománico** (☎ 902 306600; ☺ 10am-1.30pm & 3.30-6pm or later, closed Mon & Tue Sep-Jun, closed Jan) **FREE** has informative displays in English, Spanish and French. Take bus 10 (€1.05), hourly from 9am to 9pm, northwest from the Uría Norte stop at the north end of Calle de Uría near the train station.

Visits to San Julián, Santa María and San Miguel are guided (in Spanish) except on Monday.

cheery and colourful. Note that there's no lift.

Hotel City Express Covadonga HOTEL €
(☎ 985 20 32 32; www.hotelcityexpresscovadonga.
es; Calle de Covadonga 7; s/d €40/45) Basic but well-kept rooms, mostly in sky-blues and yellows, in a central location.

Hotel Fruela HOTEL €€
(☎ 985 20 81 20; www.hotelfruela.com; Calle de Fruela 3; r €75-79; P ❄ ☎) With a pleasing contemporary style and a touch of original art, plus professional yet friendly service, the 28-room Fruela achieves a cosy, almost intimate feel and is easily the top midrange option in central Oviedo. Rooms are bright and welcoming, with plenty of easily accessible plugs. Breakfast, tapas and other meals are available in its cafe-restaurant.

Munia Princesa Hotel & Spa BOUTIQUE HOTEL €€
(☎ 984 28 55 80; www.hotelprincesamunia.com;
Calle de Fruela 6; r €85-109; P ☎) On the fringe of the Old Town, the sparkling Munia is all contemporary design and feminine chic, with funky fire features and an on-site spa. Service is warm and efficient and the 23 sleek, modern rooms, in whites and creams, offer big, comfy beds and rain-effect showers.

Barceló Oviedo Cervantes HOTEL €€
(☎ 985 25 50 00; www.barcelo.com; Calle de Cervantes 13; r €99-129; P ❄ @ ☎) Comprising a revamped century-old mansion and two modern smoked-glass wings, the Barceló is just a couple of blocks northwest of the central Campo de San Francisco. Impeccably contemporary style runs right through it,

from the shiny lobby bar with its club-like decor to the 72 spacious, luxurious rooms and their glass-partitioned bathrooms.

Hotel de la Reconquista HISTORIC HOTEL €€
(✆985 24 11 00; www.hoteldelareconquista.com; Calle de Gil de Jaz 16; r €125-155; P✶@🖨) The city's fanciest lodgings, two blocks northwest of the Campo de San Francisco, started life as an 18th-century hospice. Rooms, set around two patios, in all shapes and sizes, strike just the right note between tradition and comfort, with timber furniture and floor-to-ceiling windows. Spanish royalty and other luminaries hang out here during the annual Príncipe de Asturias prizes jamboree.

Eating

It's customary to serve good food at reasonable prices in Oviedo's *sidrerías* (cider bars). For the experience, head to Calle de la Gascona – *el bulevar de la sidra* (the boulevard of cider) – which is lined with boisterous *sidrerías*, most serving *raciones* from €8 to €18. *La ruta de los vinos* (the wine route), on Calles Manuel Pedregal and Campoamor near the train station, is a good bet for tapas. Elsewhere, Oviedo boasts some of northern Spain's most sophisticated eateries.

Naguar TAPAS, FUSION €€
(www.naguar.es; Avenida de Galicia 14; raciones €10-19; ⊙11am-midnight) Under the watch of acclaimed Asturian chef Pedro Martino, Naguar oozes cool. It's an incredibly popular spot for top-notch creative, contemporary tapas, often with an Asian touch, such as teriyaki sesame chicken with seaweed. Head past the open-plan kitchen to the dining area or just pull up a stool in the orange-lit bar with everyone else. It's 200m west of the Campo de San Francisco.

Tierra Astur SIDRERÍA, ASTURIAN €€
(✆985 20 25 02; www.tierra-astur.com; Calle de la Gascona 1; mains €9-24; ⊙9am-2am) A particularly atmospheric *sidrería*-restaurant, Tierra Astur is famed for its grilled meats and prize-winning cider. People queue for tables, or give up and settle for tapas at the bar. Some just buy local products in the shop area to the right and go home. The €9.80 *menú del día*, available for lunch Monday to Friday, is excellent value.

La Puerta Nueva SPANISH €€
(✆985 22 52 27; www.lapuertanueva.com; Calle de Leopoldo Alas 2; mains €14-26; ⊙1.30-4pm & 9pm-midnight Fri & Sat) Despite its limited opening times, this is a gourmet experience worth seeking out. The weekly market-based menu mixes northern Spanish with Mediterranean cuisine in a welcoming atmosphere; the €35 set menu (with wine) is probably your best option.

Sidrería El Fartuquín ASTURIAN €€
(www.restauranteelfartuquin.es; Calle del Carpio 19; mains €12-22; ⊙1-4pm & 7.30pm-midnight, closed Sun) The Fartuquín's busy little dining room offers an excellent range of Asturian meat, fish and seafood, and its good-value €14 set menu, including wine, is available for dinner as well as lunch Monday to Friday. Locals pack into the front bar for tapas in the evenings.

★**La Corrada del Obispo** ASTURIAN €€€
(✆985 22 00 48; www.lacorradadelobispo.com; Calle de la Canóniga 18; mains €19-24; ⊙1-4pm & 8pm-midnight, closed Sun & dinner Mon Dec-Feb) Modern decor combines with the open stone walls of this 18th-century house to provide a welcoming setting for quality local meat and fish in inventive, expertly executed preparations, like sea bass in a buttery citrus sauce. You might be able to snag a romantic petal-strewn table in the outer gallery. Woody Allen shot some scenes for *Vicky Cristina Barcelona* here.

Drinking & Entertainment

For *sidrerías* head to Calle de la Gascona. The Old Town's narrow pedestrian streets are thronged with people having a great time inside and outside dozens of bars on weekends. The main axis is Calle de Mon, with wall-to-wall bars, and its extension

> **WORTH A TRIP**
>
> ### PARQUE NATURAL DE REDES
>
> Drivers looking for a treat should head southeast from Oviedo, along the AS117 up the Nalón valley towards the 1490m Puerto de la Tarna pass on the Castilla y León border. The latter part of the route is a paradise of green, crossing the Parque Natural de Redes, with plenty of walking routes, a range of accommodation, and a **Centro de Interpretación** (✆985 60 80 22; www.parquenaturalderedes.es; ⊙9am-2pm & 4-7pm, closed Mon & Sun afternoon Oct-May; P) at Campo de Caso.

THE ART OF CIDER DRINKING

Ancient documents show Asturians were glugging cider as far back as the 8th century!

Cider is served *escanciada*, that is, poured from a bottle held high overhead into a glass held low, which gives it some fizz. Don't worry, you don't have to do this yourself – in fact, bar staff probably won't even let you try. They will show off their own skills by not even looking at the glass or bottle as they pour, in all likelihood chatting to somebody else over their shoulder at the same time. A shot of cider, about one-fifth of a glass, is known as a *culete* or *culín* and should be immediately knocked back in one (leaving a tiny bit in the glass) before the fizz dissipates.

Asturias churns out 80% of Spanish cider: anything up to 30 million litres a year, depending on the apple harvest. Apples are reaped in autumn and crushed to a pulp (about three-quarters of which winds up as apple juice). The cider is fermented in *pipes* (barrels) kept in *llagares* (the places where the cider is made) over winter. It takes about 800kg of apples to fill a 450L *pipa*, which makes 600 bottles. Traditionally, the *pipes* were transported to *chigres* (cider taverns) and drinkers would be served direct from the *pipa*. The *chigre* is dying out, though, and most cider now comes in bottles in *sidrerías* (cider bars).

Every Asturian town has plenty of *sidrerías* and the epicentre of the scene is Oviedo's *el bulevar de la sidra* (p475), lined with a dozen jam-packed *sidrerías*.

The main cider-producing region is east of Oviedo: find out more at **Comarca de la Sidra** (www.lacomarcadelasidra.com).

Calle Oscura, as well as adjacent Calle del Carpio and Plaza del Sol. During the week, these bars generally stay open until 1am and can be quiet. On Friday and Saturday they're packed out until about 3am.

Salsipuedes CLUB
(www.salsipuedes.es; Calle de Ildefonso Martínez 7; ⏲1-6am Thu, 1-7.30am Fri & Sat; 🛜) If you fancy partying on around 3am, hit this three-floor drinks and dance spot inside an Old Town house, where the spin is a mix of house, '80s and mainstream hits.

Ca Beleño LIVE MUSIC
(www.facebook.com/cabeleno; Calle de Martínez Vigil 4; ⏲5pm-3.30am) This small pub is a well-established venue for Celtic music, whether of Asturian, Galician or Irish extraction. Live jams usually get going around 11pm on Thursday.

🛈 Information

Oficina de Turismo de Asturias (☑984 49 37 85; www.turismoasturias.es; Plaza de la Constitución 4; ⏲9.30am-7pm, closed Sun mid-Sep–mid-Jun)

Oficina de Turismo El Escorialín (☑985 22 75 86; www.turismoasturias.es; Calle del Marqués de Santa Cruz 1; ⏲9.30am-3.30pm Mon-Fri, 10am-6pm Sat & Sun) At the Campo de San Francisco.

🛈 Getting There & Around

AIR

The **Aeropuerto de Asturias** (☑902 404704) is at Santiago del Monte, 47km northwest of Oviedo and 40km west of Gijón. Buses run hourly from Oviedo's bus station (€8, 40 minutes) from 6am to 8pm, plus 10pm, returning hourly from 7am to 9.20pm, plus 11.20pm.

Airlines and destinations:

Air Berlin (www.airberlin.com) Destinations in Germany, via Madrid and Palma de Mallorca

EasyJet (www.easyjet.com) London (Stansted) and Geneva

Iberia (www.iberia.com) Barcelona, Madrid and Valencia

Volotea (www.volotea.com) Málaga and Valencia

Vueling Airlines (www.vueling.com) Barcelona, Paris, Málaga and Seville

BUS

From the **bus station** (☑985 96 96 96; www.estaciondeautobusesdeoviedo.com; Avenida de Pepe Cosmen), 700m north of the central Campo de San Francisco, direct services head up the motorway to Gijón (€2.45, 30 minutes) every 10 or 15 minutes from 6.30am to 10.30pm. Buses run to the following destinations:

Cangas de Onís (€6.95, 1½ hours, at least seven daily)

Madrid (€34 to €56, 5¼ to 6½ hours, at least 15 daily)

Ribadesella (€8, 1¼ to 1¾ hours, at least six daily)

Santander (€3 to €27, 2¼ to 3¼ hours, at least seven daily)

Santiago de Compostela (€30 to €42, 4¾ to 6¾ hours, at least four daily)

TRAIN

One **train station** (Avenida de Santander; 🛜) serves both train companies: **Renfe** (www.renfe.com), for destinations to the south; and **FEVE** (☑ 985 98 23 81; www.renfe.com/viajeros/feve), on the upper level, for destinations along Spain's north coast.

Cudillero (€3.25, 1¼ hours, three direct FEVE trains daily)

Gijón (€3.35, 33 minutes, up to three hourly Renfe *cercanías* until 10.45pm)

León (€9.80 to €21, two hours, five or more Renfe trains daily)

Llanes (€8.35, 2½ hours, two to four FEVE trains daily) via Arriondas (€5.05, 1½ hours) and Ribadesella (€6.55, two hours), with two continuing to Santander (€16, 4¾ hours)

Luarca (€7.25, 2¼ hours, two FEVE trains daily), continuing into Galicia as far as Ferrol

Madrid (€52, five hours, four Renfe trains daily)

Gijón

POP 261,000

Bigger, grittier and gutsier than Oviedo, Gijón (khi-*hon*) produces iron, steel and chemicals, and is the main loading terminal for Asturian coal. But Gijón has emerged like a phoenix from its industrial roots, having given itself a facelift with pedestrianised streets, parks, seafront walks, cultural attractions and a lively food and drinks scene. It's a surprisingly engaging city, and a party and beach hot spot too, with endless summer entertainment. It's no quaint Asturian fishing port, but Gijón sure knows how to live.

The ancient core of Gijón is concentrated on the headland known as Cimadevilla. The harmonious, porticoed Plaza Mayor marks the southern end of the promontory. To the west stretches the Puerto Deportivo (marina) and the broad Playa de Poniente, while to the south is the more modern, 19th- to 20th-century city centre bounded on its east side by the Playa de San Lorenzo.

◉ Sights

Parque del Cerro Santa Catalina   PARK
At the top of Cimadevilla, this grassy parkland includes Gijón's Elogio del Horizonte, a brutal concrete sculpture by Basque artist Eduardo Chillida that has become a symbol of the city.

Plaza de Jovellanos   SQUARE
Wrapped around the landward side of Cimadevilla is an enticing web of narrow lanes and small squares. Plaza de Jovellanos is dominated by the home of Gijón's most celebrated scion, the 18th-century Enlightenment politician Gaspar Melchor de Jovellanos. It is now the Museo Casa Natal de Jovellanos (☑ 985 18 51 52; http://museos.gijon.es; ⏱ 10am-2pm & 5-7.30pm Tue-Sun) **FREE**. A section of Gijón's Roman walls and towers has been reconstructed stretching west from the plaza.

Museo del Ferrocarril de Asturias   MUSEUM
(☑ 985 18 17 77; http://museos.gijon.es; Plaza de la Estación del Norte; adult/senior & student/child €2.50/1.40/free, Sun free; ⏱ 10am-7pm Tue-Sun) Gijón's excellent railway museum explores the important role of trains in Asturian history, with 50 locomotives and carriages, and plenty of railway paraphernalia. It's housed in the 19th-century Renfe train station, 1km west of Cimadevilla.

Acuario   AQUARIUM
(☑ 958 18 52 20; http://acuario.gijon.es; adult/senior & student/child €14/10/7; ⏱ 10am-7pm or later) On Playa de Poniente, 1.5km west from Cimadevilla, this aquarium houses 4000 specimens, from otters to sharks and penguins, in 12 separate underwater environments, including tropical oceans and an Asturian river.

✦ Festivals & Events

Throughout summer Gijón finds some excuse for a fiesta almost every week, all accompanied by varied musical programs and plenty of partying.

Semana Grande   SUMMER FESTIVAL
Held in August, this is the biggest of all Gijón fiestas.

Fiesta de la Sidra Natural   DRINK
Gijón's Natural Cider Festival, held in late August, includes an annual attempt at the world record number of people simultaneously pouring cider (8601 in 2013).

⌸ Sleeping

Finding a room in August can be a challenge, so try to book ahead. Prices tumble outside summer, but overall Gijón's hotels aren't particularly great value for money.

Hotel Pasaje HOTEL €€

(☑985 34 49 15; www.hotelpasaje.es; Calle del Marqués de San Esteban 3; s/d €50/85; ☻) A pleasant, friendly, family-owned hotel with good, clean, bright rooms, many enjoying sea views. It's conveniently and centrally located facing the Puerto Deportivo and staff are a wonderful source of local information.

Hotel Asturias HOTEL €€

(☑985 35 06 00; www.hotelasturiasgijon.es; Plaza Mayor 11; s €77, d €110-132, incl breakfast; ❉☻) The Asturias' rooms are plain but spacious and quite comfy, and some have sea glimpses and glassed-in galleries. The location is ultra-central, overlooking Cimadevilla's main square.

Hotel Central HOTEL €€

(☑985 09 86 51; www.hotelcentrogijon.es; Plaza del Humedal 4; s/d €55/70; ☻) The welcoming, family-run Central, opened in 2013, may feel a little dated here and there, but it's certainly one of Gijón's most characterful hotels, tucked away in its own fluffy-cushioned world 900m south of Cimadevilla near the bus station. There are just nine smallish but homey rooms, in a minimalist boutique style with soft white and cream decor.

✖ Eating

The most atmospheric area is Cimadevilla, though the newer city centre also offers plenty of choice.

La Galana SIDRERÍA, ASTURIAN €€

(www.restauranteasturianolagalana.es; Plaza Mayor 10; mains & raciones €15-24; ☉1.30-4pm & 8pm-midnight; ☑) The front bar is a boisterous *sidrería* where you can snack on tapas (€9 to €15) accompanied by torrents of cider. Up a few steps at the back is a spacious, colourful dining room. Fish, such as *pixín* (anglerfish) with clams or wild sea bass, is the strong suit. It also does excellent vegetarian adaptations of dishes on request, including beautifully prepared salads.

Restaurante Ciudadela ASTURIAN €€

(ciudadela@grupogravia.com; Calle de Capua 7; mains & raciones €15-25; ☉1.30-4pm & 9pm-midnight, closed Sun dinner & Mon) Like many Gijón eateries, the Ciudadela has a front bar for nibbling tapas backed by a dining room, in this case combined with a unique cave-like basement that attempts to recreate a Castilian bodega of yesteryear. The carefully concocted dishes range over the best of Asturian offerings, from daily *pucheros* (casse-

roles/stews) to excellent seafood and meat, and even a low-calorie selection.

It's half a block back from the western end of Playa de San Lorenzo.

Tierra Astur SIDRERÍA, ASTURIAN €€

(☑985 327 448; www.tierra-astur.com; Playa de Poniente; mains €15-25; ☉11am-2am) Brave the ugly apartment-block exterior and jump in line at this buzzing *sidrería*-restaurant, a favourite among locals and tourists alike where slurping cider is practically compulsory. The focus is on sizzling meats and grilled seafood, but platters of cheese, sausage or ham are a good bet too. There's a great-value €9.80 weekday lunch *menú*. Book ahead for seats inside a cider barrel.

Casa Gerardo ASTURIAN €€€

(☑985 88 77 97; www.restaurantecasagerardo.com; Carretera AS19, Prendes; mains €19-27; ☉1-3.45pm Tue-Sun, 9-10.45pm Fri & Sat) About 12km west of Gijón, this stone-fronted, neo-rustic house has been serving top-quality local cooking since 1882. Five generations of the Morán family have refined their art to the point of snagging a Michelin star. The fish and shellfish are delectable, but to best sample the Morán blend of tradition and innovation go for one of the set menus (€55 to €88).

♥ Drinking & Entertainment

In theory, normal bars shut down around 1.30am Sunday to Thursday and 3.30am on Friday and Saturday, while those licensed to have bands and DJs (many fall into this category) can stay open another two hours. But Gijón takes everything with a pinch of salt and night-time antics tend to go on well into the next morning.

The *sidrerías* in Cimadevilla and around town are a fun way to start the night (and inject some food), and further up in Cimadevilla a young, studenty scene flourishes around Plaza Corrada. South of Cimadevilla, lively bars abound along *la ruta de los vinos*, centred around Calles del Buen Suceso and Santa Rosa. The Naútico area near Playa de San Lorenzo and the busy Fomento area running parallel to Playa de Poniente host a whole assortment of locales, from funky little cocktail hang-outs to live-music venues and all-night dance clubs.

Café Dam BAR

(www.facebook.com/cafedamgijon; Calle de San Agustín 14; ☉5.30pm-1am Sun-Thu, 5.30pm-5.30am Fri & Sat; ☻) Amsterdam-inspired Café

Dam is a gallery, chill bar and a great den for varied live music, which kicks off in the basement bar around 9pm on Friday and Saturday; from midnight DJs take over with electronica, funk and reggae beats.

La Bodeguita del Medio MUSIC BAR
(Calle de Rodríguez San Pedro 43; ⊘ 8pm-4am, to 6.30am Fri & Sat) A popular, friendly little salsa bar near the marina, with a more mature crowd than Cimadevilla's bars.

❶ Information

Gijón Turismo (☑ 985 34 17 71; www.gijon.info; Espigón Central de Fomento; ⊘ 10am-9pm, reduced hours Nov-Apr) The main tourist office, on a pier of the Puerto Deportivo, is very helpful; a summer information booth opens at Playa de San Lorenzo.

❶ Getting There & Around

BOAT

LD Lines (www.ldlines.com) runs three weekly car ferries from Saint-Nazaire in northwest France (15 hours), one from Poole, UK (25 hours), and one from Rosslare in Ireland (39 to 48 hours, via Saint-Nazaire). Fares vary: a July return trip for two adults plus car could cost anywhere between UK£550 and UK£750 from Poole, and from about UK£900 from Rosslare. Ferries dock at Puerto de El Musel, 5km west of Gijón centre.

BUS

Buses fan out across Asturias and beyond from the **ALSA bus station** (☑ 902 422242; www. alsa.es; Calle de Magnus Blikstad), including the following:

Asturias airport (€8, 45 minutes, hourly 6am to 8pm, plus 10pm)

Oviedo (€2.45, 30 minutes, every 10 to 20 minutes from 6.30am to 10.30pm)

Santander (€14 to €30, 2¾ to 3¾ hours, nine or more daily)

TRAIN

All **Renfe** (☑ 902 320320; www.renfe.com) and **FEVE** (☑ 985 98 23 81; www.renfe.com/via-jeros/feve) trains use the temporary **Estación Sanz Crespo** (Calle de Sanz Crespo), 1km west of the city centre, while work on underground lines proceeds. Destinations include the following:

Cudillero (€3.25, 1¾ hours, five to 12 direct FEVE *cercanías* daily)

Oviedo (€3.35, 33 minutes, up to three Renfe *cercanías* hourly)

Renfe also has several daily trains to León and Madrid. Change at Pravia or Oviedo for most other FEVE destinations.

City bus 16 (€1.25) links the station with the city centre.

East Coast

Mostly Spanish holidaymakers seek out a summer spot on the beaches and coves along the coast east of Gijón, backed by the Picos de Europa, which rise only 15km inland.

Villaviciosa & Around

POP (VILLAVICIOSA) 6400

Villaviciosa rivals Nava as Asturias' cider capital. Apart from the Romanesque Iglesia de Santa María, its pretty little town centre is mostly a child of the 18th century.

◉ Sights & Activities

Iglesia de San Salvador de Valdediós CHURCH
(☑ 670 242372; adult/child €1.50/1.25; ⊘ 11am-1.30pm & 4.30-7pm Tue-Sun, closed afternoons Oct-Mar) The area surrounding Villaviciosa is sprinkled with ancient churches. Don't miss this triple-naved pre-Romanesque church, built in AD 893 as part of a palace complex for Alfonso III. It's 9km southwest of Villaviciosa, off the AS267 to Pola de Siero.

Playa de Rodiles BEACH
The beautiful, broad golden sands of 1km-long Playa de Rodiles front the sea at the mouth of the Ría de Villaviciosa, 11km north of Villaviciosa. Surfers might catch a wave here in late summer.

Museo del Jurásico de Asturias MUSEUM
(MUJA; www.museojurasicoasturias.com; Rasa de San Telmo; adult/senior & child €7.10/4.60, Wed free; ⊘ 10.30am-8pm, shorter hours & closed Mon & Tue Sep-Jun, closed Jan; 🅿) Located in Colunga, 18km east of Villaviciosa, Asturias' popular Jurassic museum takes you through 4.5 billion years of prehistory with dinosaur footprints, fossils and bones (which are plentiful along this part of the Asturian coast) and 20 giant dinosaur replicas. The pair of mating tyrannosaurus is over 12m high.

El Gaitero BREWERY TOUR
(☑ 985 89 01 00; www.gaitero.com; La Espuncia; ⊘ 10am-1.20pm & 4-6.20pm Mon-Fri, 10am-1.20pm Sat mid-May–mid-Sep, 10am-12.30pm & 4-6.30pm Thu-Sun mid-Sep–mid-Jun) FREE For the full

cider experience, tour the El Gaitero cider-brewing bodegas, 2km from the centre of Villaviciosa on the N632; visits include a free tasting session. The museum (June to mid-September only) costs an extra €1.50.

Sleeping & Eating

Villaviciosa has plenty of *sidrerías,* a few restaurants, and a dozen hotels and *pensiones* (small private hotels).

★ La Casona de Amandi — COUNTRY HOUSE €€
(985 89 01 30; www.lacasonadeamandi.com; Calle de San Juan 6, Amandi; s/d incl breakfast €90/100; closed Jan-Mar;) The most attractive lodgings in the Villaviciosa area are at this exquisite, British-run, 19th-century farmhouse in Amandi, 1.5km south of Villaviciosa. Rooms, all of which ooze their own character and vary in size, contain antique beds and hand-painted furnishings, and floors are original chestnut. Dinner is on offer throughout July and August, served outside in the tranquil lawned gardens.

❶ Getting There & Away

ALSA (www.alsa.es) provides eight or more buses daily to Oviedo (€4.25, 35 minutes to one hour) and Ribadesella (€3.85, 35 minutes to one hour), and 13 or more to Gijón (€2.95, 30 minutes to 1¼ hours).

Ribadesella
POP 2900

Unless you've booked ahead, it's best to stay away from Ribadesella on the first weekend of August, when the place goes mad for the Descenso Internacional del Sella (International Descent of the River Sella; www.descensodelsella.com), a kayaking festival. Otherwise, Ribadesella is a low-key fishing town and resort. Its two halves, split by the Río Sella's estuary, are joined by the long, low Sella bridge. The western half (where most hotels are) has a good beach, Playa de Santa Marina, while the older part of town and fishing harbour are on the eastern side.

◉ Sights

★ Cueva de Tito Bustillo — CAVE
(985 86 12 55, reservations 902 306600; www.centrotitobustillo.com; incl Centro de Arte Rupestre adult/senior, student & child €7.20/5.20, Wed free; 10.15am-5pm Wed-Sun Apr-Oct;) To see some of Spain's best cave art, including superb horse paintings probably done around 13,000 to 12,000 BC, visit this World Heritage–listed cave, a short distance south of the western end of the Sella bridge. Daily visitor numbers are limited so online or telephone reservations are essential. Even if you miss the cave itself, the Centro de Arte Rupestre Tito Bustillo (adult/senior, student & child €5.20/3.10, Wed free; 10am-7pm Wed-Sun Jul-mid-Sep, 10am-2.30pm & 4-6pm or 7pm Wed-Sun mid-Sep-Jun, closed Jan), 200m along the road, is well worth a visit for its displays, video and replicas.

The one-hour visit (guided in Spanish) to the Cueva de Tito Bustillo includes some slippery stretches, and children under seven years are not admitted. Visits to La Cuevona, a separate, impressively large cave (though without art), are free with the Centro de Arte Rupestre ticket: up to 15 groups of 20 are taken in each day when the Centro is open. Enquire upon arrival at the Centro.

Sleeping

Rates everywhere decline dramatically outside the August peak season.

Hotel Covadonga — HOTEL €€
(985 86 01 10; www.hotelcovadongaribadesella.com; Calle de Manuel Caso de la Villa 6; r €65-75; closed Nov-Apr;) About 100m back from the port in the old part of town, the Covadonga is a step back in time, full of character and generally booked out in August.

Villa Rosario — HISTORIC HOTEL €€€
(985 86 00 90; www.hotelvillarosario.com; Calle de Dionisio Ruisánchez 6; r incl breakfast €185-270;) This luxurious hotel, fronting Playa de Santa Marina, is a classic century-old *casa de indianos* (house built by a returned colonist), eclectically styled with rich-coloured carpets, cherry wood and marble, although rooms are contemporary with a nod to minimalism. Go for a room in the original *palacete.*

✖ Eating

The lively waterfront *sidrerías* located on the eastern side of the river are a good bet for seafood.

Casa Gaspar — ASTURIAN €€
(Calle de López Muñiz 6; dishes €9-18; 1-4.30pm & 8pm-midnight, closed Jan-Mar) For a break from seafood you could go for grilled meats, *sartenes* (frying pans) of eggs, chorizo and bacon, or other *raciones,* and cider in copious quantities, at busy little Casa Gaspar, in the heart of the Old Town.

ℹ Information

Tourist Office (☑985 86 00 38; www.ribadesella.es; Paseo Princesa Letizia; ⊙10am-2pm & 4-8pm, shorter hours & closed Mon Sep-Jun) At the eastern end of the Sella bridge.

ℹ Getting There & Away

FEVE trains run at least three times daily to Llanes, Arriondas and Oviedo, and twice to Santander. The **bus station** (Avenida del Palacio Valdés) is 300m south of the Sella bridge, east of the river.

Buses go from Ribadesella to the following destinations:

Gijón (€6.80, 1½ hours, at least six daily)

Llanes (€2.75, 35 minutes, at least seven daily)

Oviedo (€8, 1 to 1¾ hours, at least five daily)

Santander (€8, 1½ to 2½ hours, at least two daily)

Ribadesella to Llanes

More than 20 sandy beaches and pretty coves await discovery between Ribadesella and Llanes. About 12km west of Llanes, Playa de San Antolín is a vast, unprotected beach where surfers might pick up the odd wave.

Playa de Torimbia, a beautiful golden crescent bounded by rocky headlands and a bowl of green hills, is truly spectacular. It's also a particularly popular nudist beach. Turn off the AS263 at Posada to reach Niembro (2km), from where it's a further 2km to the beach – follow *Playa* signs through Niembro's narrow streets. You have to walk the last kilometre or so, which keeps the crowds down too. Playa de Toranda, only 500m from Niembro and backed by fields and a forested headland, is also pretty striking.

Llanes

POP 5200

Inhabited since ancient times, Llanes was for a long time an independent-minded town and whaling port with its own charter awarded by Alfonso IX of León in 1206. Today, with a small medieval core and bustling harbour, it's one of northern Spain's more popular holiday destinations – a handy base for the Asturias coast, with the Picos de Europa close at hand.

◉ Sights & Activities

Strewn alongside the far end of the pier like a set of children's blocks are the Cubes of Memory, painter Agustín Ibarrola's playful public artwork using the port's breakwater as his canvas. La Basílica, the town's main, mostly Gothic church, begun in 1240, is worth a quick inspection if you find it open. Of the three town beaches, Playa de Toró to the east, its limpid waters dotted with jutting pillars of rock, is easily the prettiest.

The tourist office (☑985 40 01 64; www.llanes.com; Calle de Posada Herrera; ⊙10am-2pm & 5-9pm, shorter hours & closed Sun afternoon mid-Sep–mid-Jun) can tell you about plenty of good walking routes in the area, including the E9 coastal path, which passes through here on its journey from Russia to Portugal, and the Camino de Santiago del Norte heading towards Santiago de Compostela in Galicia.

🛏 Sleeping & Eating

Llanes and its surrounding area have plenty of accommodation, but do book ahead for June to mid-September.

★ **La Posada de Babel**   RURAL HOTEL €€
(☑985 25 25; www.laposadadebabel.com; s/d €100/124; ⊙closed mid-Dec–Mar; P🅿🛈) 🅿 In La Pereda, 4km south of Llanes, this unique spot combines striking modern architecture and design with lovely, large lawns and a relaxed yet civilised vibe, all inspired by its owners' extended travels in Asia. The 12 rooms are installed in four contrasting buildings, including one in a typical Asturian *hórreo* (grain store) on stone stilts. The kitchen emphasises market-fresh and organic food.

Hotel Arpa de Hierba   RURAL HOTEL €€
(☑985 40 34 56; www.arpadehierba.com; s/d incl breakfast €103/122; ⊙closed mid-Dec–Feb; P🛈) The immaculate, six-year-old Arpa is a homey, welcoming world of pastels and florals, set amid peaceful gardens in La Pereda, 4km south of Llanes. Delightfully stylish cosiness runs through the eight individually furnished rooms, which have lovely beds, tiled floors and, in some cases, mountain views.

Pensión La Guía   PENSIÓN €€
(☑985 40 25 77; www.pensionlaguia.com; Plaza de Parres Sobrino 1; s/d €60/65; 🛈) This good-value, spick-and-span spot, in a 300-year-old house, is a charming web of dark timber beams and terracotta floors. Rooms are plain but welcoming, with glassed-in balconies overlooking a central plaza.

ARGUALE / GETTY IMAGES ©

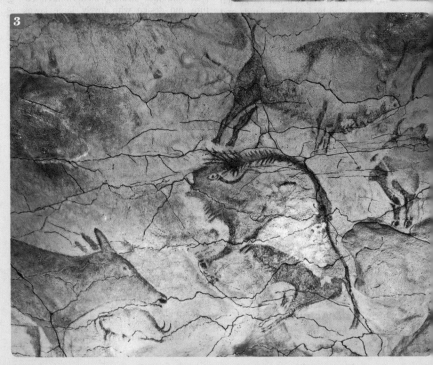

1. Pouring cider **2.** Playa del Silencio (p485), Cudillero **3.** Rock paintings at Cueva de Altamira (p468) **4.** Picos de Europa (p489)

Surprises of the North

The small northern regions of Cantabria and Asturias are a delightful discovery. Green valleys stretch down from snow-topped peaks to beautiful beaches. Locals drink cider and eat fantastic seafood and cheese, and the region's fascinating history begins with some of the world's most outstanding cave art.

Spectacular Peaks

Rising majestically only 15km inland, the Picos de Europa mark the greatest, most dramatic heights of the Cordillera Cantábrica, with enough awe-inspiring mountainscapes to make them arguably the finest hill-walking country in Spain. You can ramble past high-level lakes, peer over kilometre-high precipices or traverse the magnificent Garganta del Cares gorge (p494).

Legendary Cider Bars

In a region that rolls out 80% of Spanish cider, Asturias' boisterous, fabulously fun *sidrerías* (cider bars) are a way of local life. There's no greater pleasure than knocking back a fizzing *culín* (cider shot), expertly poured from high above into a low-held glass (p476).

Ancient Cave Art

Humanity's first accomplished art was painted, drawn and engraved on the walls of European caves by Stone Age hunter-gatherers between about 39,000 and 10,000 BC, and reached some of its greatest artistic genius at the World Heritage–listed caves of Altamira (p468), El Castillo (p462) and Covalanas (p464) in Cantabria.

Glorious Beaches

Wild, rugged and unspoilt, the hundreds of secluded sandy stretches and mysterious coves that line the 550km-long Cantabrian and Asturian coast are some of Spain's most beautiful and breathtaking beaches, and when the waves are up, the region's surf scene comes alive.

Restaurante Siete Puertas SEAFOOD €€€
(Calle de Manuel Cué 7; mains €18-30, menús €22-30; ☺1-4pm & 8pm-midnight, closed Mon-Thu & Sun dinner Nov-Mar) Plenty of lively *marisquerías* (seafood eateries) and *sidrerías* line Calles Mayor and Manuel Cué, so tucking into sea critters and washing them down with cascades of cider is no problem. The Siete Puertas is a cut above the average, with neat white tablecloths, efficient service and well-prepared local dishes. Fish and home-made desserts are its fortes.

❶ Getting There & Away

Four daily **ALSA** (www.alsa.es) buses head to Gijón (€8.65, 1¾ to two hours), six to Santander (€5.91, 1¼ to two hours) and at least 11 to Oviedo (€11, 1¼ to 2¼ hours). Three or four FEVE trains arrive daily from Oviedo, Arriondas and Riba-desella, two of them continuing to Santander.

East of Llanes

The 350m-long Playa La Ballota is a particularly attractive beach a few kilometres east of Llanes, hemmed in by green cliffs and signposted down a dirt track from the Cué–Andrín road.

From Puertas de Vidiago, 6km east of Llanes on the N634, signs past the church lead you 2km to Los Bufones de Arenillas, a dozen geyser-style jets of seawater, which are pumped up through holes in the earth by the pressure of seawater. When heavy seas are running, some jets can spurt 20m high and are quite a spectacle (and it's also dangerous to get too close). With calm seas, you'll just hear the eerie sound of air and water whooshing through the tunnels below.

Playa de la Franca, further towards Cantabria, is another nice beach, with a summer campground. Two kilometres from Pimiango (past a spectacular coastal lookout), the World Heritage–listed Cueva del Pindal (☑608 175284; adult/senior & child €3.10/1.60; ☺10am-5pm Wed-Sun) contains 31 Palaeolithic paintings and engravings of animals, including rare depictions of a mammoth and a fish. It's not in the same league as the Altamira or Tito Bustillo caves, but it was the first cave with prehistoric art to be discovered in Asturias; with its setting among wooded sea-cliffs and with a 16th-century chapel, ruined Romanesque monastery and interpretation centre nearby, it's an appealing visit. Booking ahead by phone is strongly recommended; a maximum of six groups of 20 can enter each day and chidren under seven are not admitted.

West Coast

The cliffs of Cabo Peñas, 20km northwest of Gijón, mark the start of the western half of Asturias' coast as well as its most northerly and highest (almost 100m) points.

Avilés

POP 77,300

You might visit this old estuary port and steel-making town to attend one of the innovative, independent Spanish and global music, theatre, cinema or art events at the Centro Cultural Internacional Oscar Niemeyer (Centro Niemeyer; ☑984 83 50 31; www.niemeyercenter.org; ☺10am-10pm Sun-Thu, 10am-midnight Fri & Sat) FREE. The Niemeyer arts centre, founded in 2011, was designed by Brazilian architect Oscar Niemeyer (the creator of Brasília) as a gift to Asturias and as a cultural nexus between the Iberian Peninsula and Latin America. While you're here, the Old Town's attractive colonnaded streets and central Plaza de España, fronted by two elegant 17th-century buildings, make for a lovely stroll.

Serious food lovers should head to Salinas, a coastal suburb, and the Real Balneario de Salinas (☑985 51 86 13; www.realbalneario.com; Avenida de Juan Sitges 3; mains €28-34; ☺1-4pm & 8pm-midnight, closed Sun dinner, Mon & early Jan-early Feb). Opened as a bathing centre right on the beach by King Alfonso XIII in 1916, it's a top seafood restaurant today, where you can choose from a range of traditional or creative 'new concept' fish preparations, as well as some very tempting desserts.

ALSA (www.alsa.es) buses run frequently from Avilés to Oviedo (€2.50, 30 to 60 minutes) and Gijón (€2.40, 30 minutes). FEVE trains head to both cities too.

Cudillero

POP 1490

Cudillero is the most picturesque fishing village on the Asturian coast, and it knows it. The houses, painted in varying pastel shades, cascade down to a tiny port on a narrow inlet. Despite its touristy feel, Cudillero is cute and reasonably relaxed, even in mid-August when almost every room in town is taken.

The main activity in town is watching the fishing boats come in (between 5pm and 8pm) and unload their catch, then sampling fish, molluscs and urchins at the *sidrerías*. You can also head out along well-made paths to several lookouts, including La Garita La Atalaya perched high above the harbour.

The coast around here is an appealing sequence of cliffs and beaches. The nearest beach is the fine, sandy Playa de Aguilar, a 3km drive or walk east.

Playa del Silencio is one of Spain's most beautiful beaches: a long sandy cove backed by a natural rock amphitheatre. It's 15km west of Cudillero: head to Castañeras on the N632 and follow the signs through the village. The last 500m down to the beach is on foot.

🛏 Sleeping & Eating

Accommodation in Cudillero is limited, especially during the low season, when many places shut down. The cheaper digs are back up the main street, away from the port. Plenty of hotels, *casas de aldea* (village houses), *pensiones* and apartments are scattered around the countryside within a few kilometres. There's no shortage of eateries down towards the port. A meal with drinks is likely to cost you €25 to €35 in most places.

La Casona de Pío   HOTEL €€
(📋985 59 15 12; www.lacasonadepio.com; Calle del Ríofrío; s/d €73/92; ⊘closed mid Jan–mid Feb; 🐾) Tucked away just behind the port is this charming hotel in a 200-year-old stone building, featuring 11 very comfortable rooms with a rustic touch and hydromassage baths. It serves a terrific €7 breakfast.

Hotel Casa Prendes   HOTEL €€
(📋985 59 15 00; www.hotelcasaprendes.com; Calle San José 4; r €83; 🐾) A nicely maintained hotel near the harbour with nine comfy, stone-walled rooms and a small private cafe. Rates drop dramatically outside August. The owners also rent apartments nearby.

El Faro   SEAFOOD €€
(Calle del Ríofrío; mains €12-21; ⊘10am-4.30pm & 7-11pm) An attractive eatery hidden one street back from the port. Stone, timber and cool cream decor create a welcoming atmosphere in which to dig into fish of the day, a *parrillada de marisco* (mixed grilled shellfish) or an *arroz caldoso* (seafood and rice stew).

ℹ Getting There & Away

From the bus station, at the top of the hill 800m from the port, three or more daily buses go to Gijón (€5.55, 1¼ hours) and Avilés (€3.15, 45 minutes), where you can connect for Oviedo. The FEVE train station is 1km further inland: trains to Gijón (€3.25, 1¾ to two hours) run about hourly until 6pm (fewer on weekends); for Oviedo (€3.25, 1¼ hours) you usually change at Pravia.

Luarca
POP 5180

Marginally less picturesque than Cudillero, Luarca has a similar setting in a deep valley running down to a larger harbour full of fishing boats. It's a base for some good nearby beaches.

◎ Sights & Activities

Atalaya Lookout   LOOKOUT
Find your way up to the town's Atalaya lookout, with its small church, surprisingly elaborate cemetery and dramatic coastal vistas. Luarca's mariners' guild met for centuries at the nearby Mesa de Mareantes, where the town's history is now told in colourful tiles.

Playa de Cueva   BEACH
Sandy, 600m-long Playa de Cueva, 7km east of Luarca on the old coast road (N634), is one of the best beaches in the district, with cliffs, caves, a river and occasional decent surf.

Cabo Busto   CAPE
Twelve kilometres east of Luarca, Cabo Busto will give you some sense of the Asturian coast's wildness as waves crash onto the jagged, rocky cliffs.

Playa de Barayo   BEACH
West of Luarca, Playa de Barayo is part of a protected natural reserve, with a good sandy beach in a pretty bay at the mouth of a river winding through wetlands and dunes. Turn off the N634 11km from central Luarca onto the NV2 towards Puerto de Vega, then after 800m turn right towards Vigo (1.5km) and follow signs. From the car park, the beach is accessible by a well-marked 30-minute nature hike.

🛏 Sleeping & Eating

At least seven hotels and *hostales* (budget hotels) are on or just off the central Plaza de Alfonso X, including three cheapies in Calle Crucero. Seafood eateries dot the waterfront.

Hotel 3 Cabos
RURAL HOTEL €€

(☑ 985 92 42 52; www.hotelrural3cabos.com; Carretera de El Vallín, Km 4; s €90, d €105-125, incl breakfast; ☉ closed Jan & Nov; P @ ☎ ♨) A beautiful contemporary conversion of a 120-year-old farmhouse, 3 Cabos enjoys fabulous vistas from its elevated inland site, and provides six well-designed, well-equipped rooms with stone walls, original timber beams, wide, comfy beds and good-sized bathrooms. There's a lovely panoramic bar-restaurant for breakfast and dinner (mains €16 to €22, focused on fresh local fish and meat), and a grassy garden with play area.

You can borrow bikes for free. Take the El Vallín turnoff from the N634 about 4km southwest of central Luarca and go 4.5km – it's well signed.

Hotel La Colmena
HOTEL €€

(☑ 985 64 02 78; www.lacolmena.com; Calle de Uría 2; s/d €45/65; ☎) Rooms are a tad more comfortable than the dour exterior facing Plaza de Alfonso X suggests. It has some nice touches, like the dark parquet floors, high ceilings and tall windows, though the showers are a bit of a squeeze.

Restaurante Sport
SEAFOOD €€€

(Calle de Rivero 9; mains €20-30; ☉ 11am-5pm & 8pm-midnight, closed early Jan-early Feb) ✦ This seafood restaurant, facing the river a few steps back from the harbour, has been pleasing customers with its daily-changing menu of local fish and shellfish since the early 1950s. Choose from the tasty tapas menu (€6 to €8) or slurp a half-dozen oysters (€9) as a starter. Anything 'del pincho' has been caught with a rod and line.

The rollo de bonito al estilo de Luarca (delicious patties of northern tuna mixed with vegetables, drowned in fresh tomato sauce) is a traditional local dish. Percebes, a northwest Spain delicacy, are sold at €6 per 100g when available.

ⓘ Information

Tourist Office (☑ 985 64 00 83; www.turismoluarca.com; Plaza de Alfonso X; ☉ 10.30am-1.45pm & 4-7.15pm)

ⓘ Getting There & Away

At least four daily ALSA buses run east to Oviedo (€9.85, 1¼ to two hours) and west to Ribadeo (€6.90, 1½ hours) in Galicia. The FEVE train station is 800m south of the town centre. Two trains run daily east to Cudillero and Oviedo, and west to Ribadeo and as far as Ferrol (Galicia).

Coaña

The small town of Coaña lies about 4km inland of the port of Navia, west of Luarca. A couple of kilometres beyond is the Castro de Coaña (☑ 985 97 84 01; adult/senior & child €3.10/1.60, Wed free; ☉ 10.30am-5.30pm Wed-Sun, to 3.30pm Oct-Mar), one of northern Spain's best-preserved Celtic settlements and well worth visiting.

Inland Western Asturias

There's some gorgeous country in southwest Asturias. Even just driving through on alternative routes into Castilla y León can be rewarding, such as the AS228 via the 1587m Puerto Ventana, the AS227 via the beautiful 1486m Puerto de Somiedo or the AS213 via the 1525m Puerto de Leitariegos.

Senda del Oso

The Senda del Oso (Path of the Bear) is a 20km cycling and walking track along the course of a former mine railway between the villages of Tuñón and Entrago, southwest of Oviedo. With easy gradients, it runs through increasingly spectacular valley scenery into deep, narrow canyons, with several bridges and tunnels. It also offers the high probability of seeing Cantabrian brown bears in a large enclosure, and is a fun outing with (or without) the kids. A more recently opened branch track southeast to Santa Marina in the Valle de Quirós has increased the total rideable track to 31km. There are many casas rurales and village hotels in the area, and a good source of further information (including on numerous walking trails) is www.caminrealdelamesa.es.

You can rent mountain or city bikes for €9 to €12 per day at several places along the route, typically open daily in July and August, and on Saturday and Sunday in April, May, June, September and October:

Centro BTT Valle del Oso (☑ 985 76 11 77, 659 209383; www.vallesdeloso.es; ♨) At Tuñón.

Deporventura (☑ 666 557630, 985 24 52 67; www.deporventura.es; ♨) At the Área Recreativa Buyera, beside the AS228 road about 5km south of Tuñón. Open year-round; by reservation only on weekdays from October to June.

La Cabaña del Oso Goloso (☑ 985 76 10 29; www.osogoloso.blogspot.com.es; ♨) At

THERE'S A BEAR IN THERE

The wild mountain area of southwest Asturias and northwestern Castilla y León, including Parque Natural de Somiedo, is the main stronghold of Spain's biggest animal, the brown bear *(oso pardo)*. Bear numbers in the Cordillera Cantábrica have climbed to over 200 from as low as 70 in the mid-1990s, including a smaller population of about 30 in a separate easterly area straddling southeast Asturias, southwest Cantabria and northern Castilla y León. Killing bears has been illegal in Spain since 1973 but only since the 1990s have concerted plans for bear recovery been carried out. The year 2012 saw a record 62 new cubs in the Cordillera Cantábrica, 56 of them in the western area. Experts are further heartened by the fact that there has been at least one recent case of interbreeding between the western and eastern groups.

This lumbering beast can reach 250kg and live 25 to 30 years, and has traditionally been disliked by farmers even though it is almost entirely vegetarian. Public support has played a big part in its recent recovery in the Cordillera Cantábrica, which owes a lot to the celebrated bears of Asturias' Senda del Oso. Experts warn that the bear is not yet completely out of the woods – illegal snares set for wild boar and poisoned bait put out for wolves continue to pose serious threats, as do forest fires, new roads and ski stations, which reduce the bears' habitat and mobility, while poaching has claimed the lives of at least two bears in the last few years.

You can see bears in semi-liberty at the Cercado Osero on the Senda del Oso. For a chance of finding bears in the wild, the **Fundación Oso Pardo** (☑ 985 76 34 06; www. fundacionosopardo.org) 🖉 organises bear-themed hikes (half-/full day adult €11/19, child €3/6) in the Parque Natural de Somiedo (p488), which has about 80 bears. The walks are not specifically aimed at spotting bears, but you might get lucky. The Fundación's **Centro de Interpretación 'Somiedo y El Oso'** (☑ 985 76 34 06; adult/senior & child €2/1; ⊙ 11am-2pm & 5-9pm Jun-Sep), in Pola de Somiedo, is a good place to learn bear facts.

Proaza, 2km south of the Área Recreativa Buyera.

TeverAstur (☑ 985 76 46 23; www.sendadelosoaventura.com; 🚲) At Entrago.

It's highly advisable to reserve bikes one or two days ahead. All of the outfits we've listed offer assorted options such as baby seats, trailers for small children, electric bikes or Segways. Some also offer activities like caving, canyoning and guided mountain-bike trips elsewhere in the area. One option with TeverAstur is a one-way ride from Entrago to Tuñón, with a drive back to Entrago afterwards, so that you only do the route downhill (Entrago is 380m higher than Tuñón).

👁 Sights

★ **Cercado Osero**   NATURE PARK
🖉 **FREE** About 5.5km south of Tuñón (or a 1.1km walk from the Área Recreativa Buyera), the Senda del Oso reaches the Cercado Osero, a 40,000-sq-metre hillside compound home to three female Cantabrian brown bears, Paca, Tola and Molinera. The two older bears, Paca and Tola, were orphaned as cubs by a hunter in 1989. Since 2008 they have spent much of their time in a second enclosure just below the path at the same spot.

A fourth (male) bear, Furaco, was brought in from Cantabria's Parque de la Naturaleza Cabárceno with hopes of breeding with Paca and Tola, and may still be found in the same enclosure when you read this. Hopes that baby bears might ensue were abandoned in 2011, but Paca, Tola and Furaco were joined in December 2013 by one-year-old Molinera, who failed to integrate back into the wild after being treated for various life-threatening injuries and is now generally kept out of sight. There is talk of returning the three female bears to the original upper compound, where Paca and Tola used to be fed around noon and 4.30pm daily (outside their December-to-February hibernation) at a spot beside the path.

Casa del Oso   INTERPRETATION CENTRE
(☑ 985 96 30 60; www.osodeasturias.es; ⊙ 10am-2pm & 4-6pm) **FREE** The Casa del Oso, in Proaza, is the headquarters of the Fundación Oso de Asturias, which runs the Paca-Tola bear conservation project, and has exhibits on Spanish brown bears.

Parque de la Prehistoria INTERPRETATION CENTRE
(☎902 306600; www.parquedelaprehistoria.es; Hwy AS228; adult/senior & child €6/3.50; ⊙10am-2.30pm & 4-8pm Jul & Aug, 10am-2.30pm & 4-6pm Wed-Sun Sep-Jun, closed Jan, closed Wed Feb & Dec; P) Four kilometres south of Entrago, the Parque de la Prehistoria is well worth a visit for its excellent introduction to Spanish and European cave art. It includes replicas of Asturias' World Heritage–listed Tito Bustillo and Candamo caves and France's Niaux cave (visitable by guided tour in Spanish), and has a good museum-gallery that explains much of the what, when, who, how and why of Europe's Palaeolithic cave-art phenomenon.

ⓘ Getting There & Away

Pullmans Llaneza (☎985 46 58 78) runs three or four daily buses from Oviedo bus station to Tuñón, Proaza and Entrago (45 minutes), terminating at San Martín, 1km beyond Entrago and 3km before the Parque de la Prehistoria.

Parque Natural de Somiedo

If you fancy exploring beautiful mountain country that few foreigners reach, head for this 292-sq-km Unesco-listed biosphere reserve on the northern flank of the Cordillera Cantábrica. Composed chiefly of five valleys descending from the cordillera's 2000m-plus heights, the park combines thick woodlands, rocky mountains and high pastures dotted with *brañas* (groups of now largely abandoned *cabanas de teito* – thatched herders' shelters). It's also a key stronghold of Spain's bear population (487).

Each valley has a number of marked walking trails, which you can find out about at the park's Centro de Recepción (☎985 76 37 58; www.parquenaturalsomiedo.es; ⊙10am-2pm & 4-8pm, to 6pm & closed Sun afternoon & Mon Oct–mid-Jun) in plain Pola de Somiedo. Pola also has a bank, an ATM and a supermarket.

One of the best (and most popular) walking areas is the Valle de Lago, whose upper reaches contain glacial lakes and high summer pastures. You must leave vehicles in Valle de Lago village, a wonderful 8km drive southeast of Pola de Somiedo that winds and climbs to about 1300m. Other good walks include the route from La Peral to Villar de Vildas in the upper Pigüeña valley (13km, approximately five hours, one-way), which passes one of the largest and best-preserved *brañas*, La Pornacal, and the ascent of El

Cornón (2194m), the park's highest peak (14km, approximately nine hours, return).

🛏 Sleeping & Eating

Pola de Somiedo has around 12 places to stay and there are several more in Valle de Lago village.

Palacio de Florez Estrada HISTORIC HOTEL €€
(☎616 170018; www.hotelflorezestrada.com; s/d incl breakfast €80/110, apt €80; ⊙closed Nov-Mar; P🐕☎🏊) A gorgeous old-world riverside mansion in lovely gardens just off the road to Valle de Lago, on the east side of Pola de Somiedo. The four two-person apartments, on the same pretty site, are open year-round.

Hotel Castillo del Alba HOTEL €€
(☎985 76 39 96; www.hotelcastillodelalba.es; Calle de Florez Estrada; s/d incl breakfast €55/70; ⊙closed late Jan-early Mar; 🐕🏊) Two emblematic bear statues welcome guests at the door of this friendly Pola de Somiedo hotel, which features 15 bright, contemporary-style rooms. If you're travelling with children, ask for one of the rooms with a sofa bed that neatly converts into a pair of bunks. There's also a decent restaurant serving local dishes (mains €10 to €20).

Braña La Code CABIN €€
(☎661 431209, 985 76 37 76; www.campinglagosdesomiedo.com; cabins for 1 or 2 €88, each extra person €15; P🏊) This quirky spot in Valle de Lago village offers accommodation in *cabanas de teito*, built with traditional materials but with more comfort than the real thing (including bathrooms and kitchenettes)! Adjoining is the agreeably rustic Camping Lagos de Somiedo (☎985 76 37 76; www.campinglagosdesomiedo.com; sites per 2 people, car & tent €23; ⊙Easter-Sep; P). The two share a bar-restaurant serving simple meals.

ⓘ Getting There & Away

An ALSA bus departs Oviedo bus station for Pola de Somiedo (€8.60, two hours) at 5pm Monday to Friday and 10am on weekends, returning from Pola at 6.30am (5.30pm on weekends).

From the Senda del Oso area, with your own wheels, you can approach Somiedo by the spectacular AS265 west from San Martín to La Riera, via the Puerto de San Lorenzo pass (1347m, often snowed under in winter). At the pass the road crosses the Camín Real de la Mesa, an ancient track linking Astorga (Castilla y León) with the Asturian coast, that is now a long-distance footpath, the GR101.

PICOS DE EUROPA

These jagged, deeply fissured mountains straddling southeast Asturias, southwest Cantabria and northern Castilla y León amount to some of the finest walking country – indeed, some of the most spectacular country of any kind – in Spain. The Picos comprise three limestone massifs: the eastern Macizo Ándara, with a summit of 2444m; the western Macizo El Cornión, rising to 2596m; and the particularly rocky Macizo Central or Macizo Los Urrieles, reaching 2648m. The 647-sq-km Parque Nacional de los Picos de Europa covers all three massifs.

Virtually deserted in winter, the area bursts with visitors in August, when it's always best to book ahead, whether you are heading for a hotel or a mountain refuge. July is not far behind. June and September are quieter and just as likely to be sunny as August.

ℹ Information

The national park has three main information centres:

Centro de Información Casa Dago (☎985 84 86 14; Avenida de Covadonga 43, Cangas de Onís; ☉8am-2.30pm & 4-6pm Jul–mid-Sep, 8am-2.30pm Mon-Fri mid-Sep–Jun & Sun Oct-Jun)

Centro de Visitantes Sotama (☎942 73 81 09; ☉9am-6pm) On the N621 in Tama, 2km north of Potes, with interesting exhibitions on Picos geology, rivers and wildlife.

Oficina de Información Posada de Valdeón (☎987 74 05 49; El Ferial, Posada de Valdeón; ☉9am-2pm Mon-Fri)

Other information points open at strategic places around the national park from 1 July to 15 September and during other major national holidays. Local tourist offices provide information too.

Cangas de Onís and Potes are the best places to buy outdoor equipment. Wild camping is not permitted within the national park except for overnight bivouacking above 1600m.

MAPS

The best maps of the Picos, sold in shops in Cangas de Onís, Potes and elsewhere for €4 to €5 each, are Adrados Ediciones' *Picos de Europa* (1:80,000), *Picos de Europa Macizos Central y Oriental* (1:25,000) and *Picos de Europa Macizo Occidental* (1:25,000).

ℹ Getting There & Around

The main access towns for the Picos are Cangas de Onís in the northwest, Arenas de Cabrales in the central north, Potes in the southeast and Posada de Valdeón in the south. Paved roads lead from Cangas southeast up to Covadonga and the Lagos de Covadonga; from Arenas south up to Poncebos then east up to Sotres and Tresviso; from Potes west to Fuente Dé, and from Posada de Valdeón north to Caín. This last is extremely narrow in parts.

Only a few bus services (mostly summer only) will get you into the hills from the access towns. An alternative to buses is taxis.

BUS & TRAIN

Details of the following services change from time to time, but their broad outlines are fairly reliable.

Cangas de Onís to Arenas de Cabrales Two to four buses daily run between Cangas and Arenas (€2.95, 35 minutes).

Cangas de Onís to Covadonga and Lagos de Covadonga Three or more ALSA buses daily run from Cangas to Covadonga (€1.50, 15 minutes). To avoid traffic chaos from late July to early September and during some other major holidays, private vehicles cannot drive up from Covadonga to the Lagos de Covadonga from about 8.30am to 8pm. During these times a shuttle-bus service (day ticket adult/child €8/3.50) operates to Covadonga and the lakes from four car parks (€2 per vehicle) in Cangas de Onís (beside the bus station) and along the road between there and Covadonga. Private vehicles *can* drive up to the lakes before 8.30am or after 8pm and, once up, can drive down any time.

Cangas de Onís to Garganta del Cares From mid-July to early September, ALSA buses depart Cangas de Onís at 8am and 10am for Caín (2¼ hours, €7.90), starting back from Caín to Cangas at 1pm and 4pm; and depart Cangas for Poncebos (€4.45, 45 minutes) at 3.15pm and 6.15pm, starting back from Poncebos to Cangas at 4.15pm and 7.15pm. This enables you to take a bus from Cangas to Caín, walk the Garganta del Cares north from Caín to Poncebos, and get a bus back from there to Cangas, all in one day.

Oviedo to Arriondas and Cangas de Onís From Oviedo, ALSA runs at least seven buses daily to Arriondas (€6.20, one to 1¼ hours) and Cangas de Onís (€6.95, 1½ hours). Arriondas

CANTABRIA & ASTURIAS PICOS DE EUROPA

ℹ **PICOS WEBSITES**

www.magrama.gob.es/es/red-parques-nacionales The official national parks site.

www.picosdeeuropa.com

www.liebanaypicosdeeuropa.com For the eastern Picos.

is also on the FEVE railway between Oviedo, Ribadesella, Llanes and Santander.

Ribadesella and Llanes to Arriondas and Arenas de Cabrales Arriondas is linked with the two coastal towns by four or more buses (€1.80, 25 minutes from Ribadesella; €4.50, one hour from Llanes) and three or four FEVE trains daily. Two buses daily, Monday to Friday only, link Arenas with Llanes (€3.40, one hour, or €6.40, two hours).

Santander to Eastern Picos From Santander, **Autobuses Palomera** (☑ 942 88 06 11; www. autobusespalomera.com) travels via San Vicente de la Barquera and Panes to Potes (€8.05, 2½ hours), and returns, two or three times daily. From July to September there is service once or twice daily between Potes and Fuente Dé (30 minutes, €1.70).

TAXI

As well as regular taxis that stick to the better roads, such as **Taxitur** (☑ 689 143881; www.taxi tur.com) in Cangas, there are 4WD taxi services that can manage some of the mountain tracks. Several of these offer 4WD day trips in the Picos for typically €50 per person. A regular taxi costs €30 from Cangas de Onís to the Lagos de Covadonga, about €20 from Arenas de Cabrales to Sotres, and about €25 from Potes to Fuente Dé.

Western Picos

Arriondas

POP 2500 / ELEV 85M

The ordinary little town of Arriondas is the starting point for highly popular and fun kayak trips down the pretty Río Sella to various end points between Toraño and Llovio (7km to 16km). A dozen agencies in town will rent you a kayak, paddle, life jacket and waterproof container, show you how to paddle and bring you back to Arriondas at the end. This stretch of the Sella has a few entertaining minor rapids, but it isn't a serious white-water affair, and anyone from about

---

> ### ⓘ WARNING
>
> Picos weather is notoriously changeable, and mist, rain, cold and snow are common problems. When the summer sun shines, you need protection from that too. Higher up, few trails are marked and water sources are rare. Paying insufficient attention to these details has cost several lives over the years.

---

eight years old can enjoy the outing. The standard charge, including a picnic lunch, is €25 per person. Starting time is normally from 11am to 1pm. Bring a change of clothes. Agencies in Cangas de Onís and nearby coastal towns offer much the same deal, including transport to Arriondas and return.

Arriondas is mayhem on the first weekend in August when tens of thousands of people converge for the Descenso Internacional del Sella (p480), an international kayaking event that involves about 1500 serious kayakers starting off downriver to Ribadesella at noon on the Saturday, followed by many more fun paddlers later on.

🛏 Sleeping & Eating

⭐ **Posada del Valle**　　RURAL HOTEL €€
(☑ 985 84 11 57; www.posadadelvalle.com; r €64-79; ⊙ Apr-Oct; P 🛜 🐾) 🕊 This remarkable place, run by an English family and set in a beautiful valley 3km north of Arriondas, just past Collía village, is not only a charming rural retreat and a wonderful walking base, but also a multifaceted sustainable-living experience. About 35% of food served comes fresh from the hotel's own organic farm (managed partly for wildflower conservation), and there's always a vegetarian option.

Design and decor emphasise local art and artistry, and the 12 rooms all have valley views. Self-guided walking information is provided for the Picos de Europa and Asturias coast as well as the local area. Also on offer are various courses and workshops, including organic vegetarian cooking, Spanish conversation, felt-making and retreats focused on sustainable living.

El Corral del Indianu　　CONTEMPORARY ASTURIAN €€€
(☑ 985 84 10 72; www.elcorraldelindianu.com; Avenida de Europa 14; mains €26-33; ⊙ 1.30-3.30pm & 9-11pm, closed Wed & Sun dinner, Thu) Putting a gourmet spin on traditional Asturian cooking, this is the most original place for a feed. If you don't fancy the highly creative (and extensive) €77 tasting menu, you might go for a hearty Asturian *fabada* (bean, meat and sausage stew) or *tortos de maíz* (maize cakes) and guacamole, followed by baked monkfish in oyster-and-octopus sauce.

Cangas de Onís

POP 4600 / ELEV 84M

Good King Pelayo, after his victory at Covadonga, moved about 12km down the hill

Picos de Europa

to settle the base of his nascent Asturian kingdom at Cangas in AD 722. Cangas' big moment in history lasted 70 years or so, until the capital was moved to Pravia. Its second boom time arrived in the late 20th century with the invasion of Picos de Europa tourists. In August, especially, the largely modern and rather unremarkable town is bursting with trekkers, campers and holidaymakers.

Sights

Puente Romano BRIDGE

Arching like a cat in fright, the so-called Roman Bridge that spans the Río Sella was actually built in the 13th century, but is no less beautiful for the mistaken identity. From it hangs a copy of the Cruz de la Victoria, the symbol of Asturias that resides in Oviedo's cathedral.

Capilla de Santa Cruz CHAPEL

(Avenida Contranquil; admission €2; ⊙11am-2pm & 5-7pm Thu-Tue, reduced hours mid-Sep–mid-Jun) This tiny chapel was built in 1943 to replace its 8th-century predecessor (erected by Pelayo's son Favila), which was destroyed during the Spanish Civil War. The 1940s rebuilders discovered that the mound the chapel sits on was an artificial one containing a megalithic tomb 6000 years old, now visible beneath the chapel's floor. Visits are guided in Spanish, English or French.

Activities

Many agencies, including Los Cauces (☑985 94 73 18; www.loscauces.com; Avenida Covadonga 6) and the ubiquitous Cangas Aventura (☑985 84 92 61; www.cangasaventura.com; Avenida de Covadonga 17), offer a whole range of activities, including canoeing down the Río Sella from Arriondas (€25 per person), horse riding (€18/30 per one/two hours), canyoning (€40 for three hours) and caving (€25 for two hours).

Sleeping

Cangas has loads of hotels and a few *pensiones,* many of which almost halve their high-season rates from about mid-September to June. There are plenty more places, including numerous *casas rurales,* in nearby villages such as Soto de Cangas, Mestas de Con and Benia de Onís, all along the road towards Arenas de Cabrales.

Hotel Los Robles HOSTAL €

(☑985 94 70 52; www.losrobleshotel.com; Calle de San Pelayo 8; s €32-45, d €52-77, incl breakfast, apt for 4 €70-90; ☜) Clean, simple rooms – some with balconies, mostly in shades of red and blue – and five decent apartments for up to four people, in a restored 19th-century building handily located in the town centre.

Hotel Nochendi
HOTEL €€

(☑ 985 84 95 13; www.hotelnochendi.com; Calle de Constantino González 4; r €110; ☎) Occupying one sparkling floor of a modern apartment block beside the Río Güeña, this is a lovely surprise and easy to feel at home in. The 12 spacious, spotless, bright, white rooms feature good beds, spot lighting and a touch of modern art, and most have river views.

Parador de Cangas de Onís
HISTORIC HOTEL €€€

(☑ 985 84 94 02; www.parador.es; r €130-169; P ✳ ☎) Cangas' *parador* (luxurious state-owned hotel) stands by the Río Sella in Villanueva, 3km northwest of Cangas towards Arriondas. The main building was originally a monastery, built between the 12th and 18th centuries on the site of early Asturian king Favila's palace. Rooms have a very comfortable, classical style, and some are former monks' cells, though suitably upgraded! Check the website for offers.

Even if you don't stay here, the *parador* makes for a fascinating (free) visit. The adjoining monastery church, the Iglesia de San Pedro, is embellished with very unusual medieval carvings depicting sins and the story of Favila's death.

✗ Eating

★ El Molín de la Pedrera
CONTEMPORARY ASTURIAN €€

(☑ 985 84 91 09; www.elmolin.com; Calle del Río Güeña 2; dishes €10-23; ☉ 1.30-4pm & 9-11pm, closed Tue & Sun dinner & Wed Oct-May, closed mid-Dec—early Feb) This stone-and-brick-walled, family-run eatery wins with both its traditional Asturian dishes like *fabada* (bean, meat and sausage stew) or *tortos de maíz* (maize cakes), and more creative efforts like the Cabrales cheese and hazelnut filo parcels starter, or the delicious homemade desserts. The meat dishes are generally excellent, and welcoming service and good wines complete a top dining experience.

Los Arcos
ASTURIAN €€

(☑ 985 84 92 77; www.restaurantelosarcos.es; Jardines del Ayuntamiento 3; raciones & mains €7-20; ☉ 7am-midnight) Half elegant restaurant, half bustling *sidrería*, slow-food-focused Los Arcos pulls a lot of its punters in with its ex-cellent-value €12 *menú*, available for lunch and dinner. It also offers a good range of *raciones* of local meats, seafood and cheeses, as well as a few gourmet items and plenty of gluten-free choices.

ℹ Information

Tourist Office (☑ 985 84 80 05; www.cangas-deonis.com; Avenida de Covadonga 1; ☉ 10am-2pm & 4-7pm)

Covadonga
POP 70 / ELEV 260M

The importance of Covadonga, 12km southeast of Cangas de Onís, lies in what it represents rather than what it is. Somewhere hereabouts, in approximately AD 722, the Muslims received their first defeat in Spain, at the hands of the Visigothic nobleman Pelayo – an event considered to mark the beginning of the 800-year Reconquista.

The place is an object of pilgrimage, for in a cave here, the Santa Cueva, the Virgin supposedly appeared to Pelayo's warriors before the battle. On weekends and in summer long queues of the faithful and curious line up to enter the cave, now with a chapel installed. The two tombs in the cave claim to be those of Pelayo himself, his daughter Hermesinda and her husband Alfonso I. The Fuente de Siete Caños spring, by the pool below the cave, supposedly ensures marriage within one year to women who drink from it.

Landslides destroyed much of Covadonga in the 19th century and the main church, the Basílica de Covadonga, is a neo-Romanesque affair built between 1877 and 1901. Nearby is the extensive Museo de Covadonga (☑ 985 84 60 96; adult/senior & child €2.50/1.50; ☉ 10.30am-2pm & 4-6.30pm Wed-Mon), devoted to Covadonga history and gifts from the faithful.

Lagos de Covadonga

Don't let summer crowds deter you from continuing 10km uphill past Covadonga to these two beautiful little lakes. Most of the trippers don't get past patting a few cows' noses near the lakes, so walking here is as nice as anywhere else in the Picos. At peak visitor periods, private vehicles may only drive up to the lakes before 8.30am or after 8pm, but can drive back down at any time. A shuttle bus runs from Cangas de Onís (p489).

Lago de Enol is the first lake you reach, with the main car park just past it. It's linked to Lago de la Ercina, 1km away, not only by the paved road but also by a footpath via the Centro de Visitantes Pedro Pidal (⊙ 10am-6pm mid-Jul–mid-Sep), which has displays on Picos flora and fauna. There are rustic restaurants near both lakes, closed in winter.

When mist descends, the lakes, surrounded by the green pastures and bald rock that characterise this part of the Picos, take on an eerie appearance.

🏃 Activities

A marked circuit walk, the Ruta de los Lagos (PRPNPE2; 5.7km, about 2½ hours), takes in the two lakes, the visitors centre and an old mine, the Minas de Buferrera. About 400m south of Lago de Enol, the route passes the Refugio Vega de Enol (☑ 985 94 28 28, 622 203897; www.elrefugio vegadeenol.com; dm €12; ⊙ year-round), whose 10 bunks are the nearest accommodation to the lakes. It has hot showers, serves basic meals (€7 to €15), and is reachable by vehicle.

Two other relatively easy trails will take you a bit further afield. The PRPNPE4 leads 7.6km southeast from Lago de la Ercina, with an ascent of 600m, to the Vega de Ario, where the Refugio Vega de Ario (Refugio Marqués de Villaviciosa; ☑ 984 09 20 00, 656 843095; www.refugiovegadeario.es; dm €12; ⊙ Jun-Oct; 🕾) has bunks for 34 people, plus meal service. The reward for about three hours' effort in getting there is magnificent views across the Garganta del Cares to the Picos' Macizo Central.

The PRPNPE5 takes you roughly south from Lago de Enol to the 68-place Refugio de Vegarredonda (☑ 626 343366, 985 92 29 52; www.vegarredonda.com; dm €12; ⊙ Mar-Nov), with meal service, and on to the Mirador de Ordiales, a lookout point over a 1km sheer drop into the Valle de Angón. It's a 10km (about a 3½-hour) walk each way – relatively easy along a mule track as far as the *refugio,* then a little more challenging on up to the mirador. Track conditions permitting, drivers can save about 40 minutes by driving as far as the Pandecarmen car park, 2km from Lago de Enol.

South from Cangas de Onís

The N625 south from Cangas de Onís follows the Río Sella upstream through one of the most extraordinary defiles in Europe. The road through the Desfiladero de los Beyos gorge is a remarkable feat of engineering. Towards the southern end of the defile, you cross from Asturias into Castilla y León.

Central Picos

A star attraction of the Picos' central massif is the gorge that divides it from the western Macizo El Cornión. The popular Garganta del Cares (Cares Gorge) trail can be busy in summer, but the walk is always an exciting experience. This part of the Picos also has plenty of less heavily tramped paths and climbing challenges. Arenas de Cabrales is a popular base with a lot of accommodation, but Poncebos, Sotres, Bulnes and Caín also have sleeping options.

Arenas de Cabrales

POP 830 / ELEV 135M

Arenas lies at the confluence of the bubbling Ríos Cares and Casaño, 30km east of Cangas de Onís. The busy main road is lined with hotels, restaurants and bars, and just off it lies a little tangle of quiet squares and back lanes. You can learn all about and sample the fine smelly Cabrales cheese at Arenas' Cueva-Exposición Cabrales (☑ 985 84 67 02; www.fundacioncabrales.com; adult/child €4.50/3; ⊙ 10.15am-1.15pm & 4.15-7.15pm, reduced hours Oct-Mar), a cheese-cave museum 500m from the centre on the Poncebos road, with 45-minute guided visits in Spanish.

Buses stop in front of the tourist office (☑ 985 84 64 84; www.cabralesturismo.com; ⊙ 10am-2pm & 4-7pm Tue-Sun Easter & Jun-Sep), in the middle of town opposite the junction of the Poncebos road.

🛏 Sleeping & Eating

The large number of places to stay and eat here keeps prices healthily competitive.

La Portiella del Llosu   CASA RURAL €
(☑ 646 866780; www.llosu.es; r incl breakfast €60; 🕾) Set against magnificent valley and Picos panoramas in tiny, peaceful Pandiello, 10km northwest of Arenas, this is a delightfully rustic restoration of a 16th-century home. The five warm-coloured rooms have lovely bathrooms and come furnished with family heirlooms and other antiques, such as hand-painted cupboards, all spruced up by the hospitable owners. It's 2km from the Pandiello turnoff just east of Ortiguero.

Hotel Rural El Torrejón
HOTEL €

(985 84 64 28; www.hotelruraleltorrejon.com; s/d incl breakfast €30/57; closed mid-Dec–mid-Jan;) This friendly, family-run country house welcomes the weary traveller with tastefully decorated rooms in a rural style and some original colour schemes. It's good value and the setting is idyllic, in a pretty garden beside the Río Casaño, just outside the village centre.

Hotel Rural El Ardinal
HOTEL €

(985 84 64 34; www.ardinal.com; Barriu del Riu; r incl breakfast €60; closed Dec & Jan;) In a lovely tranquil spot with good views, the cosy little Ardinal offers eight smallish rooms with a cottagey feel (plenty of wood, wrought iron and flowery prints) and a warm sitting-room-cum-bar with a fireplace. It's on the north edge of Arenas, 400m up a lane opposite the central Restaurante Cares.

Restaurante Cares
ASTURIAN €€

(985 84 66 28; mains €14-22, menús €15; 8am-midnight, closed Mon Oct-Jun, closed Jan-Mar) Beside the Poncebos junction on the main road, this is one of the best-value restaurants for miles around. It does great-value *menús* for both lunch and dinner, as well as *platos combinados* and à la carte fish and meat dishes. Dig into a hearty *cachopo* (veal steak stuffed with ham and cheese) and finish with *delicias de limón* (between lemon mousse and yoghurt).

Garganta del Cares

Ten kilometres of well-maintained path (the PRPNPE3) high above the Río Cares between Poncebos and Caín constitute, perhaps unfortunately, the most popular mountain walk in Spain; in August the experience can feel like Saturday morning on London's Oxford St. But the walk is still a spectacular and at times vertiginous excursion along the gorge separating the Picos' western and central massifs. If you're feeling fit (or need to get back to your car), it's quite possible to walk the whole 10km and return in one (somewhat tiring) day's outing; it takes six to seven hours plus stops. A number of agencies in Picos towns will transport you to either end of the walk and pick you up at the other end, usually for around €115 for up to four people.

PONCEBOS

Poncebos, a tiny straggle of buildings at the northern end of the Cares gorge, is set amid already spectacular scenery. A side road uphill from here leads 1.5km to the hamlet of Camarmeña, where there's a lookout with views to El Naranjo de Bulnes in the Macizo Central.

Poncebos' 11-room Hotel Garganta del Cares (985 84 64 63; www.hotelgargantadel-cares.com; Calle de Poncebos; s/d incl breakfast €38/62; closed Dec & Jan;) offers the closest beds and meals (*menú del día* €10) to the Garganta del Cares trail. Rooms are simple, clean and comfy, with twin beds.

GARGANTA DEL CARES WALK

By doing the walk from north to south, you save the best till last. Follow the 'Ruta de Cares' sign pointing uphill about 700m along the road from the top end of Poncebos. The beginning involves a steady climb in the wide and mostly bare early stages of the gorge. After about 3km you'll reach some abandoned houses. A little further and you're over the highest point of the walk.

As you approach the regional boundary with Castilla y León, the gorge becomes narrower and its walls thick with vegetation, creating greater contrast with the alpine heights above. The last stages of the walk are possibly the prettiest, and as you descend nearer the valley floor, you pass through a series of low, wet tunnels to emerge at the end of the gorge among the meadows of Caín.

CAÍN

If you're coming from the south, the trailhead of the Cares walk is at the hamlet of Caín, where the narrow (and picturesque) road from Posada de Valdeón comes to an end. There's a handful of simple places to stay – Hostal La Ruta (987 74 27 02; s/d incl breakfast €37/50;), with clean, reasonably sized rooms, is closest to the gorge and one of the best – plus two small supermarkets and several restaurants offering very similar lunch menus for €11. More lodgings are in the villages south of Caín, including Cordiñanes and the rather drab Posada de Valdeón.

Bulnes

POP 22 / ELEV 647M

The hamlet of Bulnes, inaccessible by road, sits high up a side valley off the Cares Gorge, south of Poncebos. You can get there by a quite strenuous 5km uphill walk (about two hours) or aboard the Funicular de Bulnes

(☑985 84 68 00; one-way/return adult €17/22, child €4.20/6.50; ☉10am-8pm Easter & mid-Jun–mid-Sep, 10am-12.30pm & 2-6pm rest of year), a tunnel railway that climbs steeply for 2km up inside the mountain from its lower station just below Poncebos. The funicular makes the seven-minute trip every half-hour in both directions. At the top of this thrill-inducing ride, tiny Bulnes sits in a pretty, secluded valley surrounded on all sides by towering rocky peaks.

Bulnes is divided into two parts, the upper Barrio del Castillo and the lower La Villa. All amenities are in La Villa, including an attractive six-room *casa rural*, La Casa del Chiflón (☑985 84 59 43; www.casadelchiflon.com; s/d/tr incl breakfast €45/60/75; ☉closed Oct-Easter; 🐾), and Bar Bulnes (☑985 84 59 34; raciones €5-11; ☉10am-8pm Easter & Jul-Sep, 10am-6pm rest of year, closed Mon-Fri Jan & Feb), with good home cooking.

You can also approach Bulnes from the east by walking about 2.5km (one hour) down from the Collado de Pandébano.

Sotres

POP 130 / ELEV 1045M

A side road heads up 11km from Poncebos to Sotres, the highest village in the Picos and the starting point for a number of good walks.

🏃 Activities

A popular walking route goes east to the village of Tresviso and on down to Urdón, on the Potes–Panes road. As far as Tresviso (10km) it's a paved road, but the final 7km is a dramatic walking trail, the Ruta de Tresviso (PRPNPE30), snaking 850m down to the Desfiladero de la Hermida gorge. Doing this in the upward direction, starting from Urdón, is at least as popular.

Many walkers head west from Sotres to the Collado de Pandébano, a 4km or one to 1½ hours' walk away on the far side of the Duje valley. At Pandébano the 2519m rock finger called El Naranjo de Bulnes (Pico Urriello) comes into view – an emblem of the Picos de Europa and a classic challenge for climbers. Few walkers can resist the temptation to get even closer to El Naranjo. From Pandébano it's 5km (about three hours), with 700m of ascent, up the PRPNPE21 trail to the Vega de Urriello, at the foot of the mountain. Here the 96-bunk Refugio Vega de Urriello (☑650 780381, 984 09 09 81; www.refugiodeurriellu.com; dm €12; ☉mid-Mar–mid-

SPOTTING PICOS WILDLIFE

Although a few wolves survive in the Picos and the odd brown bear might wander through, you stand a much better chance of spotting the *rebeco* (chamois), some 6000 of which skip around the rocks and steep slopes. Deer, badgers, wild boar, squirrels and martens, in various quantities, inhabit wooded areas.

Eagles, hawks and other raptors soar in the Picos' skies. Keep your eyes peeled for the majestic *águila real* (golden eagle) and the huge scavenging *buitre leonado* (griffon vulture). Choughs, with their unmistakable caws, accompany walkers at high altitudes.

Dec) is attended, with meal service, nine months of the year.

Otherwise, you can descend 2.5km (about one hour) west from Pandébano to Bulnes.

🛏 Sleeping & Eating

There are half a dozen places to stay, most with their own restaurants.

Casa Cipriano   HOTEL €
(☑985 94 50 24; www.casacipriano.com; s/d incl breakfast €35/50; ☉closed mid-Dec–Jan; 🐾) Casa Cipriano is a long-time haunt of mountain aficionados. Aside from 16 plain but cheerful rooms, it offers a professional mountain-and-caving guide service and a simple restaurant.

Hotel Sotres   HOTEL €€
(☑985 94 50 48; www.hotelsotres.com; s/d incl breakfast €51/77; ☉closed early Jan-Feb; 🅿🐾) Hotel Sotres has 12 straightforward, good-sized rooms, all quite comfy and pleasant with big, decent beds, and a restaurant serving mostly meaty mountain fare.

Eastern Picos

The AS114 east from Cangas and Arenas meets the N621, running south from the coast, at the humdrum town of Panes. South of Panes, the N621 to Potes follows the Río Deva upstream through the impressive Desfiladero de la Hermida gorge. You cross into Cantabria at Urdón, 2km before the hamlet of La Hermida, which has a couple of hotels.

Lebeña

About 8.5km south of La Hermida, 600m east off the N621 and just outside the village of Lebeña, stands the fascinating little **Iglesia de Santa María de Lebeña** (admission €1.50; ⊙10am-1.30pm & 4-7.30pm Tue-Sun; **P**), built in the 9th or 10th century. The horseshoe arches in the church are a telltale sign of its Mozarabic style – rarely seen this far north in Spain. The floral motifs on the columns are Visigothic, while below the main *retablo* (altarpiece) stands a Celtic stone engraving. They say the yew tree outside (finally reduced to a sad stump by a storm in 2007) was planted 1000 years ago.

Potes

POP 1440 / ELEV 291M

Overrun in peak periods, but with a little charm in the Old Town centre, Potes is a popular staging post on the southeastern edge of the Picos, with the Macizo Ándara rising close at hand. Potes is effectively the 'capital' of Liébana, a beautifully verdant and historic valley area lying between the Picos and the main spine of the Cordillera Cantábrica.

◉ Sights

The heart of town is a cluster of bridges, towers and quaint back streets restored in traditional slate, wood and red tile after considerable damage during the civil war. The Centro de Visitantes Sotama (p489), in Tama, 2km north of Potes, has interest-ing displays on Picos de Europa wildlife and geology, as well as on Beato de Liébana and Romanesque architecture.

Monasterio de Santo Toribio de Liébana MONASTERY
(santotoribiodeliebana.org; ⊙10am-1pm & 4-7pm; **P**) **FREE** Christian refugees, fleeing from Muslim-occupied Spain to Liébana in the 8th century, brought with them the **Lígnum Crucis**, purportedly the single biggest chunk of Christ's cross and featuring the hole made by the nail that passed through Christ's left hand. The Santo Toribio monastery, 3km west of Potes, has housed this holy relic ever since. The monastery is also famous for being the home of medieval monk and theologian Beato de Liébana, celebrated around Europe for his *Commentary on the Apocalypse.*

Illuminated manuscripts of Beato's work were distributed throughout Europe and came to be known as Beatos. Around 25 survive today and the monastery's cloister is lined with replicas, but the original text was lost. The Lígnum Crucis is kept inside a crucifix of gold-plated silver in a lavish 18th-century baroque chapel off the monastery's austere Gothic church and is an extraordinary magnet for the faithful.

You can drive 500m past the monastery to the tiny **Ermita de San Miguel**, a chapel with great valley and Picos views.

Torre del Infantado TOWER
(adult/child €3/1.50; ⊙10am-2pm & 4-6pm, closed Mon Oct-May) Beside the medieval San Cayetano bridge, the squat Torre del Infantado, with an amazingly modern interior inside its 15th-century shell, now houses an intriguing exhibition on the life and works of local historical figure, theologian and monk Beato de Liébana.

🛏 Sleeping & Eating

Potes' dozen or so sleeping options are mostly straightforward, simple places.

Casa Cayo HOSTAL €
(☑942 73 01 50; www.casacayo.com; Calle Cántabra 6; s/d €35/50; ⊙closed late Dec–mid-Mar; 🛜) Easily the best value in Potes, with friendly service and attractive, comfy, timber-beamed rooms. Ask for room 206, 207 or 305 to look down on the burbling river below. You can eat well in the restaurant (mains €8 to €18), which has particularly good meat like *solo-millo* (sirloin) with blue Tresviso cheese or

---

POTES FIREWATER

The potent liquor *orujo,* made from grape pressings, is drunk throughout northern Spain and is something of a Potes speciality. People here like to drink it as an after-dinner aperitif as part of a herbal tea called *té de roca* or *té de puerto.* Plenty of shops around town sell *orujo,* including varieties flavoured with honey, fruits and herbs, and many will offer you tastings if you're thinking of buying. Potes' jolly **Fiesta del Orujo** (www.fiestadelorujo. es) kicks off on the second weekend in November, and involves practically every bar in town setting up a stall selling *orujo* shots for a few cents, the proceeds of which go to charity.

POTES TO POSADA DE VALDEÓN

Drivers will be well rewarded by a trip around the southern approaches to the Picos, and there are a couple of great places to stay off the N621 as it winds through verdant Liébana not far south of Potes. They can provide info on local walks and make good bases for the eastern and southern Picos.

A turn-off 5km from Potes leads 4.5km up a winding road to the pretty hamlet of Tudes, where you'll find the superb, English-owned La Casa de las Chimeneas (☎942 73 63 00; www.lacasadelaschimeneas.es; 2-bedroom apt per week late Jul-Aug €1085, rest of year per night €80-140; P 🛜 🌐 👪), an old farmstead converted into eight very comfy, well equipped and characterful apartments. Each apartment follows its own theme, detailed by beautifully intricate hand-painted wall and ceiling murals. Most are on two or three levels and several have balconies. Enjoy the curved infinity pool, fabulous views, and drinks and light meals in the equally original Taberna del Inglés (dishes €5-15; ⏲11am-11pm, closed Mon-Thu Nov-Apr) across the street.

Posada de Cucayo (☎942 73 62 46; www.laposadadecucayo.com; s €46, d €57-66, incl breakfast; ⏲closed mid-Jan–mid-Feb; P 🛜 👪) sits at an altitude of more than 900m in little Cucayo village, at the top of a lovely 12km drive up from the crossroads hamlet of La Vega de Liébana, 9km south of Potes. Around you are scarred mountain peaks and green fields below. Eleven of the 12 spacious, tasteful and colourful rooms at this marvellous little family-run hotel enjoy sweeping views. The family's next-door farm provides a lot of the meat, eggs or vegetables you'll eat in their good-value restaurant (mains €5 to €10) and you can help milk the cows if you want a true taste of rural bliss!

From La Vega de Liébana, the N621 southwest rises to the Puerto de San Glorio pass (1609m), where you enter Castilla y León. In clear weather the 2km detour to the panoramic Mirador de Llesba is very worthwhile. The N621 drops down quickly on the Castilian side of the frontier. From Portilla de la Reina, follow signposts towards the Picos de Europa and take the narrow and pretty LE2703 northwest across the Puerto de Pandetrave (1562m) to Santa Marina de Valdeón and Posada de Valdeón, where you are at the southern gateway to the Picos.

the local speciality *lechazo asado* (roast young lamb or kid).

Hostería La Antigua
HOSTAL €

(☎942 73 00 37; hosterialaantigua@hotmail.com; Calle Cántabra 9; s/d €30/50; ⏲closed Jan & Feb; ❄🛜) In the heart of town, this helpful, English-and-French-speaking, family-run *hostal* (budget hotel) offers 13 small, basic but well-kept rooms in cosy yellows and creams. Room 202 has a cute little terrace, and from top-floor rooms you'll get Picos views. Enquire at the shop below.

Asador Llorente
CANTABRIAN €€

(Calle de San Roque; mains €8-18; ⏲1-4pm & 8.30-11.30pm, closed Tue Sep-Jul) For super-generous helpings of high-quality, fresh local food, head upstairs to this warm, wood-beamed loft-like space. Carnivores are in for a treat: try the Liébana speciality *cocido lebaniego* (a filling stew of chickpeas, potato, greens, chorizo, black pudding, bacon and beef) or tuck into a half-kilogram *chuletón* (giant beef chop). The lovely, crisp salads are good too.

ℹ Information

Tourist Office (☎942 73 07 87; Plaza de la Independencia; ⏲10am-2pm & 4-6pm) In the deconsecrated 14th-century, rustic Gothic Iglesia de San Vicente.

Potes to Fuente Dé

The CA185 from Potes to Fuente Dé is a beautiful 23km trip, and is dotted with several attractive rural hotels, *hostales* and campgrounds.

Hostal Remoña
HOSTAL €

(☎942 73 66 96; www.turismoruralremona.es; s/d €33/55, apt for 2/4 €60/100; ⏲closed Wed Oct-May; P @🛜) The family-run Remoña in Espinama, 3.5km southeast of Fuente Dé, is a homey little place with a very on-the-ball welcome and cosy rooms. Next door are seven fully equipped apartments for two to eight people. The *hostal* also runs walking excursions into the Picos and the restaurant (mains €10-16; ⏲1-4pm & 8.30-10.30pm, closed Wed Oct-May) serves home-cooked local dishes made with beef from the owners' farm.

★ Hotel del Oso
HOTEL €€

(☎942 73 30 18; www.hoteldeloso.com; s/d €68/85; ⊙ closed Jan–mid-Feb; P 🅿 🛇 ≋) In Cosgaya, 13km southwest of Potes, Hotel del Oso comprises majestic twin stone houses facing each other across the Río Deva and the road. Spacious rooms with timber floors and finishings are very inviting; the restaurant (mains €13 to €22, *menú* €20) is one of the area's best, with top-quality meat and desserts, and there's a lovely big outdoor pool.

Posada San Pelayo
COUNTRY HOUSE €€

(☎942 73 32 10; www.posadasanpelayo.com; s/d €61/83; P 🅿 🛇 ≋) In San Pelayo, 5km west of Potes, this is a beautiful, welcoming, family-run *casa rural,* of recent construction but in traditional country style. The spacious rooms come in cheerful colours, many with big timber terraces, and there are ample common areas and a lovely garden and pool with great mountain views. For €6.60 you'll enjoy a very good breakfast.

Fuente Dé & the Teleférico

At 1078m, Fuente Dé lies at the foot of the stark southern wall of the Macizo Central. In four minutes the dramatic Teleférico de Fuente Dé (☎942 73 66 10; www.cantur.com; adult/child return €16/6; ⊙ 9am–8pm Easter & Jul–mid-Sep, 10am–6pm rest of year, closed 2nd half Jan) cable car whisks people 753m up to the top of that wall, from where walkers and climbers can make their way deeper into the central massif.

Be warned that during the high season (especially August) you can wait an hour or more for a place in the cable car, going up or down.

⊙ Sights & Activities

It's an easy 3.5km, one-hour walk from the top of the *teleférico* to the Hotel Áliva, where you can get refreshments. From the hotel two 4WD tracks descend into the valley that separates the central massif from its

eastern cousin. One heads north to Sotres via Vegas de Sotres (about 9km or two hours' walking). The other winds 7km south down to Espinama on the CA185 (about 2½ hours' walking); the PRPNPE24 footpath branches off this about halfway down to return to Fuente Dé (11km, about 3¼ hours, from the hotel).

Other possibilities for the suitably prepared include making your way across the massif to El Naranjo de Bulnes or climbing Peña Vieja (2613m). These require proper equipment and experience – Peña Vieja has claimed more lives than any other mountain in the Picos. Less exacting is the PRPNPE23, a route of about 5km northwest from the Teleférico de Fuente Dé, passing below Peña Vieja to the Collado de Horcados Rojos pass, which opens up spectacular panoramas including El Naranjo de Bulnes, with an ascent of 500m. It takes about four hours there and back.

In Fuente Dé, the Casa del Oso (☎942 23 49 00; www.fundacionosopardo.org; adult/child €3/1; ⊙ 11am–8pm Apr-Nov, closed Mon & Tue Apr & May) is run by the Fundación Oso Pardo and has interactive exhibits and documentaries on Cantabrian brown bears.

🛏 Sleeping & Eating

Hotel Rebeco
HOTEL €€

(☎942 73 66 01; www.hotelrebeco.com; s/d €55/71; ⊙ closed Jan; P 🅿 🛇 ♿) Many of the 30 rooms in this handsome stone lodge at Fuente Dé have mountain views, and 11 include loft levels suitable for kids. It has a good, reasonably priced restaurant (mains €11 to €20) and you can't help but admire owner Conchi Cuesta's tapestries!

Hotel Áliva
HOTEL €€

(☎942 73 09 99; www.cantur.com; s/d €50/80; ⊙ mid-Jun–mid-Oct) At an altitude of 1700m, this 27-room mountain lodge features a cafe and restaurant as well as a sun deck. It's linked by 4WD tracks to the top of the *teleférico* (which is operated by the same company, Cantur) and to Espinama and Sotres. Packages including transport and meals are offered.

Santiago de Compostela & Galicia

Includes →

Best Places to Stay

Best Scenery

Why Go?

Santiago de Compostela, goal of 200,000 people who set out every year on the storied Camino de Santiago pilgrim trail, is one of Spain's most beautiful and magical cities, and an exceptionally good reason for any traveller, pilgrim or not, to make their way to Spain's northwestern corner.

But Galicia, a unique region with its own language and distinctive culture, is much more than Santiago. The wild coastline is frayed up and down its 1200km length by majestic *rías* (inlets), and strung with cliffs, beaches, islands, and fishing ports that bring in indisputably the best seafood in Spain. Then there's the interior, a labyrinth of deep-green valleys and hills, speckled with stone-built villages, aged monasteries, vineyards and farms that put top-quality meat on Galician tables. Nor is Santiago Galicia's only exciting city: A Coruña, Vigo and Lugo are all contemporary cultural hubs with heady nocturnal scenes.

When to Go
Santiago de Compostela

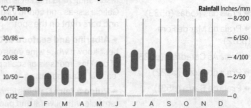

Jun & Sep No peak-season crowds or prices but (hopefully) decent weather.

Jul Dance a jig at the Festival Ortigueira, Spain's biggest Celtic music festival.

24 Jul Spectacular fireworks launch Santiago de Compostela's celebration of the Día de Santiago.

HIT THE ROOF

Following the success of Santiago de Compostela's exciting cathedral-rooftop visits (p505), Lugo (p541) and Tui (p535) cathedrals are following suit. These visits don't just give you fine city panoramas but also unique angles on the cathedrals' interiors.

Top Day Walks

➜ Ruta del Litoral (p514)

➜ Camelle–Laxe (p513)

➜ Ruta Monte Faro (p533)

➜ Camiño Real (p538)

➜ Mosteiro de Caaveiro walk (p521)

Bring Your Umbrella

Swept by one rainy front after another from the Atlantic, Galicia has, overall, twice as much rain as the Spanish national average. June to August are the least rainy months.

Best Beaches

➜ Praia das Rodas (p533)

➜ Praia da Mar de Fora (p512)

➜ Praia As Catedrais (p523)

➜ Praia do Picón (p522)

➜ Praia da Barra (p531)

Living the History of the Camino

Travellers from all over Europe have been beating paths to Santiago de Compostela ever since the discovery of what were accredited as the Apostle James' remains there 12 centuries ago. In few cities is the aura of past centuries so intense. Santiago's magnificent cathedral, its monasteries and churches and its ancient stone-paved streets are thick with reminders that the city has been the goal of millions of pilgrims over 1200 years. The sense of millenarian tradition is even stronger when travelling the Camino de Santiago itself, strung with time-honoured landmarks, inns, churches and monuments by which pilgrims have always measured their progress.

The Camino de Santiago is not just one Camino. About 70% of people arrive by the Camino Francés (French Route), which starts in the Pyrenees. But many also reach Santiago by other traditional routes, from A Coruña, Portugal, Cantabria, Asturias or Andalucía. All over Galicia you will encounter the blue signs with a yellow scallop-shell emblem that tell you you're on one of the many Caminos de Santiago.

ITINERARIES

One Week

Santiago de Compostela is Galicia's number-one destination and will keep you happy for at least two days. Then travel round the beautiful Costa da Morte to A Coruña and, if time allows, on round the spectacular Rías Altas.

Two Weeks

Add parts of the Rías Baixas and their islands, plus inland Lugo, Ourense or the Ribeira Sacra, to the one-week itinerary.

Top Five Food Experiences

➜ **Mercado de Abastos** (p508) Santiago de Compostela's fascinating food market is piled with fine produce from Galicia's seas and countryside, and there are lively eateries and bars right on the spot.

➜ **Albariño and seafood at Cambados** (p525) Galicia's best-known white wine goes down perfectly with a plate of cockles, mussels or scallops in the taverns of albariño's 'capital', Cambados.

➜ **Pulpo á feira** Galicia's iconic octopus dish: tender slices of tentacle with olive oil and paprika, delicious everywhere.

➜ **Eirado da Leña** (p529) This cute little Pontevedra restaurant serves up the best of creative contemporary Galician cuisine, and with a smile.

➜ **Rúa Pescadería** (p532) Buy oysters from the shuckers in this Vigo street and enjoy them with a glass of wine at neighbouring bars.

Santiago de Compostela & Galicia Highlights

1 Soak up the unique atmosphere and history of **Santiago de Compostela** (p502).

2 Gaze towards America at Spain's 'Land's End', **Cabo Fisterra** (p511).

3 Feast on freshly caught seafood with good Galician wines overlooking the fishing ports at **A Guarda** (p534), **O Grove** (p526) or **O Barqueiro** (p522).

4 Seek out remote beaches on dramatic coasts, such as **Area de Trece** (p514) or **Praia do Picón** (p522).

5 Stand atop southern Europe's highest sea cliffs at the **Garita de Herbeira** (p521).

6 Sail out to the pristine beaches and walking trails of the spectacular, traffic-free **Illas Cíes** (p533).

7 Follow the Camino de Santiago down from the heights of **O Cebreiro** (p541) to the monastery at **Samos** (p541).

History

Early Civilisations

Early Galicians built numerous dolmens (megalithic tombs) and Iron Age *castros* (protected settlements of circular stone huts). Many such monuments can be visited today. Most Galicians say the *castro*-builders were Celts, though sceptics claim that supposed Celtic origins are an invention by romantic Galician nationalists. The Romans pacified 'Gallaecia' in the 1st century BC, founding cities like Lucus Augusti (Lugo).

Middle Ages

After the Muslim invasion in 711, the Iberian Peninsula's sole surviving Christian kingdom, Asturias, soon drew Galicia into its ambit. Galicia remained within the Asturian kingdom and its successors, León and Castilla, thereafter, apart from brief independent spells in the 10th and 11th centuries.

The supposed grave of Santiago Apóstol (St James the Apostle), discovered in about 814 at what became Santiago de Compostela, grew into a rallying symbol for the Christian Reconquista of Spain, and pilgrims from all over Europe began trekking to Santiago. But by the time the Reconquista was completed in 1492, Galicia had become an impoverished backwater, where Spain's Catholic Monarchs, Isabel and Fernando, had already begun to supplant the local tongue and traditions with Castilian culture.

Modern Galicia

The Rexurdimento, an awakening of Galician identity, surfaced late in the 19th century, but suffered a 40-year interruption during the Franco era. In the 19th and 20th centuries, hundreds of thousands of impoverished Galicians departed on transatlantic ships in search of better lives in Latin America.

Things looked up after democracy returned to Spain in the 1970s. Galicia today

---

> ### ⓘ GALEGO
>
> Most Galicians speak both Spanish (Castilian) and the separate Galician language (*galego* or, in Castilian, *gallego*). Galician is a Romance language, close to Portuguese and slightly less so to Castilian. In this chapter we use the place names you're most likely to encounter during your travels. By and large, these are Galician.

---

is an important fishing, shipbuilding and agricultural region, with more ports than any other region of the EU. The labyrinthine coastline, incidentally, is a major European entry point for South American cocaine.

SANTIAGO DE COMPOSTELA

POP 80,000 / ELEV 260M

Locals say the arcaded, stone streets of Santiago de Compostela are at their most beautiful in the rain, when the old city glistens. Most would agree, however, that it's hard to catch Santiago in a bad pose. Whether you're wandering the medieval streets of the old city, nibbling on tapas in the taverns, or gazing down at the rooftops from atop the cathedral, Santiago seduces.

The faithful believe that Santiago Apóstol (St James the Apostle) preached in Galicia and, after his death in Palestine, was brought back by stone boat and buried here. The tomb was supposedly rediscovered in about 814 by a religious hermit, Pelayo, following a guiding star (hence, it's thought, 'Compostela' – from the Latin *campus stellae,* field of the star). Asturian king Alfonso II had a church erected above the holy remains, pilgrims began flocking to it, and by the 11th century the pilgrimage along the Camino de Santiago was a major European phenomenon, bringing a flood of funds into the city. Bishop Gelmírez obtained archbishopric status for Santiago in 1100 and added numerous churches in the 12th century. The following centuries, however, were marked by squabbling between rival nobles, and Santiago gradually slipped into the background.

Only since the 1980s, as capital of the autonomous region of Galicia and a rediscovered tourist and pilgrimage destination, has the city been revitalised. Today some 200,000 pilgrims and countless thousands of other visitors journey here each year. The biggest numbers hit the city in July and August, but Santiago has a festive atmosphere throughout the warmer half of the year. If you'd like to enjoy the place less than jam-packed, May, June and September are good months to come.

The Old Town, a roughly oval-shaped area bounded by the line of the medieval city walls, is where almost everything of interest is found. Praza de Galicia marks the boundary between the Old Town and the Ensanche

(Extension), the 20th-century shopping and residential area to its south.

◉ Sights

The magnificent cathedral and Praza do Obradoiro are the natural starting points and focus for exploring Santiago. The old city's stone-paved streets radiating out from here are a delight to wander, with plenty of cafes, bars and restaurants to drop in on as you go.

★ Catedral de Santiago de Compostela   CATHEDRAL

(www.catedraldesantiago.es; Praza do Obradoiro; ⏱ 7am-8.30pm) The grand heart of Santiago, the cathedral soars above the city centre in a splendid jumble of moss-covered spires and statues. Built piecemeal over several centuries, its beauty is a mix of the original Romanesque structure (built between 1075 and 1211) and later Gothic and baroque flourishes. The tomb of Santiago beneath the main altar is a magnet for all who come to the cathedral. The artistic high point is the Pórtico de la Gloria inside the west entrance, featuring 200 masterly Romanesque sculptures.

What we see today is actually the fourth church to stand on this spot. It has a traditional Latin-cross layout and three naves. The lavish baroque facade facing Praza do Obradoiro was erected in the 18th century, replacing the weather-damaged Romanesque one. This is the cathedral's main entrance, but owing to repair work on the towers and interior, it's likely to be closed until about 2021. In the meantime, most people enter through the south door on Praza das Praterías (beneath the only facade that conserves its original Romanesque structure).

The artistically unparalleled Pórtico de la Gloria (Galician: Porta da Gloria), just inside the Obradoiro entrance, features 200 Romanesque sculptures by Maestro Mateo, who was placed in charge of the cathedral-building program in the late 12th century. These detailed and inspired sculptures add up to a comprehensive review of major figures from the Bible, with the Old Testament on the left (looking from the Obradoiro doorway), the New Testament on the right, and glory and resurrection depicted in the central archway. The restoration work means, unfortunately, that you may find the portico partly obscured by scaffolding.

The main figure in the portico's central archway is a throned, resurrected Christ, surrounded by the four Evangelists plus angels and symbols of Jesus' passion. In an arc above are the 24 musicians said in Revelations to sit around the heavenly throne. Below Christ's feet is Santiago, and below him Hercules (holding open the mouths of two lions). On the other side of the central pillar is Maestro Mateo. For centuries, tradition called for visitors to bump heads with the maestro to acquire some of his genius. But countless knocks led to Mateo's notably flat nose, and he is now blocked off behind a metal barrier. Another tradition called for a brief prayer as visitors placed their fingers in five holes in the pillar above Hercules' head, created by the repetition of this very act by millions of faithful over the centuries. Hercules too is now blocked off.

The large, remarkably lifelike figures on the right-hand pillars of the portico are apostles; those on the left are Old Testament prophets. The very bright smile on the prophet Daniel's face is, in popular

---

SEEING THE BOTAFUMEIRO FLY

The use of a large censer or *botafumeiro* (loosely 'smoke spitter') in Santiago's cathedral dates from the 13th century, a time when masking the odours of road-weary pilgrims who slept and cooked inside the cathedral was more than a mere ceremonial act. Today the cathedral has two *botafumeiros*, one made in 1851 of silver-plated brass, the other a 1971 silver replica, which is the more commonly swung. Each weighs up to 100kg when filled with coal and incense, and attains a speed of 68km/h as it swings high over the centre of the cathedral, reaching an angle of 82 degrees from vertical.

In recent years the *botafumeiro* has flown during the 7.30pm Mass every Friday, by agreement between the cathedral and Santiago's city hall and tourism organisations, but whether this will continue indefinitely is uncertain. Traditionally it flies only on certain religious feast days (listed at www.peregrinossantiago.es), or at the end of the noon pilgrims' Mass if a pilgrimage group donates €300. When the *botafumeiros* are not in action, you can see them in the Museo da Catedral.

Santiago de Compostela

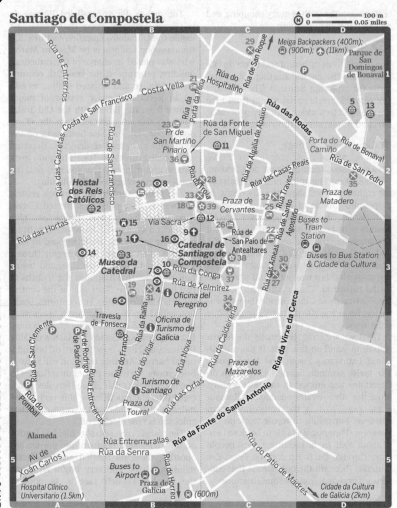

belief, caused by the tightly dressed figure of Queen Esther on the pillar opposite him. Local lore also has it that Esther's stone breasts were originally much larger, but were filed down on orders of a disapproving bishop – to which townspeople responded by inventing Galicia's cone-shaped *tetilla* (nipple) cheese in Esther's honour.

Towards the far (west) end of the cathedral's main nave, to the right of the fantastically elaborate, Churrigueresque Altar Mayor (Main Altar), a small staircase leads up to a statue of Santiago, which has watched over the cathedral since its con-

secration in 1211. The faithful queue up to kiss or embrace the statue. From here you emerge on the left side, then descend some steps into the Cripta Apostólica, where we are assured Santiago's remains lie, inside a large 19th-century silver casket. Behind the Altar Mayor is the Puerta Santa (Holy Door), which opens onto Praza da Quintana and is cracked open only in holy years (next in 2021).

A special pilgrims' Mass is usually celebrated at noon daily, with other Masses usually at 9.30am or 10am daily, 1.15pm Sunday, 6pm Saturday and Sunday, and 7.30pm

Santiago de Compostela

daily. Touristic visits are discouraged during these services.

➜ Cathedral Rooftop Tour

(📞902 557812; www.catedraldesantiago.es; adult/senior, pilgrim, unemployed & student/child €12/10/free, combined ticket with Museo da Catedral €15/12/free; ⊙tours hourly 10am-1pm & 4-7pm, to 6pm Nov-Mar) For unforgettable bird's-eye views of the cathedral interior from its upper storeys, and of the city from the cathedral roof, take the rooftop tour, which starts in the visitor reception centre beneath the Obradoiro facade. The tours are popular, so go beforehand to book a time, or book online. One of the afternoon tours is usually given in English; the rest are in Spanish. The guides provide a good insight into Santiago's history.

The visit includes the Pazo de Xelmírez, the 12th-century bishop's palace, where the main banquet hall is adorned with exquisite little wall busts depicting feasters, musicians, kings and jugglers.

★Museo da Catedral   MUSEUM

(Colección Permanente; www.catedraldesantiago.es; Praza do Obradoiro; adult/senior, pilgrim, unemployed & student/child €6/4/free; ⊙9am-8pm Apr-Oct, 10am-8pm Nov-Mar) The Cathedral Museum spreads over four floors and includes the cathedral's large, 16th-century, Gothic/plateresque cloister. You'll see a sizeable section of Maestro Mateo's original carved stone choir (destroyed in 1604 but recently pieced back together), an impressive collection of religious art (including the *botafumeiros,* in the 2nd-floor library), the lavishly decorated 18th-century *sala capitular* (chapter house) and, off the cloister, the Panteón de Reyes, with tombs of kings of medieval León.

Museo das Peregrinacións e de Santiago   MUSEUM

(www.mdperegrinacions.com; Praza das Praterías; adult/senior, pilgrim & student/child €2.50/1.50/free; ⊙10am-2pm & 5-8pm Tue-Sat, 11am-2pm Sun) The recently converted building on Praza das Praterías stages changing exhibitions on the themes of pilgrimage and Santiago

EXPLORING AROUND THE CATHEDRAL

The cathedral is surrounded by handsome plazas that invite you to wander through them.

Praza do Obradoiro

The grand square in front of the cathedral's west facade earned its name from the workshops set up there while the cathedral was being built. It's free of both traffic and cafes and has a unique atmosphere.

At its northern end, the Hostal dos Reis Católicos (admission €3; ⊘noon-2pm & 4-6pm Sun-Fri) was built in the early 16th century by order of the Catholic Monarchs, Isabel and Fernando, as a refuge for pilgrims. Today it's a *parador* (luxurious state-owned hotel) and shelters well-heeled travellers instead, but its four courtyards and some other areas are open to visitors. Along the western side of the *praza* is the elegant 18th-century Pazo de Raxoi, now Santiago's city hall.

Praza de Fonseca

South of the cathedral, stop in cafe-lined Praza de Fonseca to look into the Colexio de Fonseca (⊘9am-9pm Mon-Fri, 10am-8.30pm Sat) FREE with its beautiful Renaissance courtyard; this was the original seat of Santiago's university (founded in 1495) and now houses the university's main library. Its Gothic chapel and Salón Artesonado, either side of the entrance, house assorted temporary exhibitions.

Praza das Praterías

'Silversmiths' Square' is marked by the Fuente de los Caballos fountain (1829), a popular photo op, with the cathedral's south entrance at the top of the steps. Curiously, the Casa do Cabildo, on the lower side of the square, is no more than a 3m-deep facade, erected in 1758 to embellish the plaza.

Praza da Quintana

At the cathedral's east end, Praza da Quintana is lined by the long, stark wall of the Mosteiro de San Paio de Antealtares, founded 11 centuries ago for the monks who looked after Santiago's relics. Its Museo de Arte Sacra (Vía Sacra 5; admission €1.50; ⊘10.30am-1.30pm & 4-7pm Mon-Sat, 4-7pm Sun) contains the original altar raised over those relics.

Praza da Inmaculada

Praza da Inmaculada, on the cathedral's north side, is where most pilgrims arriving in Santiago first set eyes on the cathedral. Opposite looms the huge, austerely baroque Mosteiro de San Martiño Pinario, now a seminary.

(man and city), and affords close-up views of some of the cathedral's towers from its 3rd-floor windows. The museum's permanent collection – an extensive and interesting assemblage of art, artefacts, models and memorabilia – resides in its original building (www.mdperegrinacions.com; Rúa de San Miguel 4; ⊘10am-8pm Tue-Fri, 10.30am-1.30pm & 5-8pm Sat, 10.30am-1.30pm Sun) FREE 300m away, though there are plans to eventually move it to the new site.

Museo do Pobo Galego   MUSEUM
(Galician Folk Museum; www.museodopobo.es; Rúa San Domingos de Bonaval; adult/senior & student/child €3/1/free, Sun free; ⊘10.30am-2pm & 4-7.30pm Tue-Sat, 11am-2pm Sun) A short walk northeast of the Old Town, this former convent houses large and interesting exhibits on Galician life and arts ranging from fishing boats and bagpipes to traditional costumes and antique printing presses.

Centro Galego de Arte
Contemporánea   GALLERY
(☎981 54 66 19; www.cgac.org; Rúa de Ramón del Valle-Inclán; ⊘11am-8pm Tue-Sun) FREE The Contemporary Art Centre presents excellent exhibitions of modern art (including film and video) from Galicia and the rest of the world, in spacious, well-lit halls.

Cidade da Cultura
de Galicia   CULTURAL CENTRE
(www.cidadedacultura.org; ⊘8am-11pm; P) FREE Much reviled by Galicians as a gigantic

waste of public money, work on this vast prestige project on Monte Gaiás, 1.5km southeast of the Old Town, was stopped in 2013 after a decade of delays, rethinks and budget blowouts. Four of the six main buildings are open, but there's little inside them to see or do unless your visit happens to coincide with a worthwhile event. If you're curious, the City of Culture merits a visit for its dramatic 21st-century architecture and as a monument to Spain's boom-gone-bust.

Get there on bus 9 (hourly Monday to Friday until 10.35pm and Saturday until 1.35pm), northbound on Rúa da Virxe da Cerca.

✹ Festivals & Events

Fiestas del
Apóstol Santiago　　　　CULTURAL, RELIGIOUS

(Fiestas of the Apostle St James; ⊙2nd half Jul) Two weeks of music, parades and other festivities surround the Día de Santiago (Feast of Santiago; 25 July), which is simultaneously Galicia's 'national' day. Celebrations peak in a truly spectacular lights-and-fireworks display, the Fuegos del Apóstol, on Praza do Obradoiro on the night of 24 July.

🛏 Sleeping

From *hostales* (budget hotels) and hostels to chic hotels, Santiago has hundreds of lodgings at all price levels. Even so, the best-value and most central places can fill up weeks ahead in summer, especially July and August. Book ahead if you can.

Meiga Backpackers　　　　HOSTEL €

(☑981 57 08 46; www.meiga-backpackers.es; Rúa dos Basquiños 67; dm incl breakfast €15; ⊙Mar-Nov; @☎) Clean, colourful, sociable and handily placed between the bus station and city centre, Meiga has spacious bunk dorms, a good big kitchen and lounge, and a long garden. A great choice if you're on the budget backpacking trail.

Albergue Azabache　　　　HOSTEL €

(☑981 07 12 54; www.azabache-santiago.com; Rúa Acibechería 15; dm €15-18; ☎) This small, friendly hostel is less than 100m from the cathedral. The two top-floor dorms are the pick for their terraces with views. Kitchen and sitting room are a bit of a squeeze but well equipped.

The Last Stamp　　　　HOSTEL €

(El Último Sello; ☑981 56 35 25; www.thelaststamp. com; Rúa Preguntoiro 10; dm €18; ⊙closed approx mid-Dec–mid-Jan; @☎) A recently opened, purpose-designed hostel, Last Stamp occupies a 300-year-old five-storey house (with lift) in the heart of the Old Town. The cleverly designed dorms feature semi-private modules with ultra-solid bunks, good mattresses and individual reading lights. Some rooms enjoy cathedral views. Bathrooms and kitchen are good and big – and Camino-themed murals add a bit of fun.

Pensión da Estrela　　　　PENSIÓN €

(☑981 57 69 24; www.pensiondaestrela.com; Praza de San Martíño Pinario 5; s/d €35/45; ☎) There are just six smallish rooms here but they're bright, colourful and clean, and four overlook a quiet plaza. The welcome is warm, with nice touches like neatly rolled towels and a bag of sweets, and there's a small kitchen with free tea and coffee.

★Hotel Costa Vella　　　　BOUTIQUE HOTEL €€

(☑981 56 95 30; www.costavella.com; Rúa da Porta da Pena 17; s €59, d €81-97; ❋☎) Tranquil, thoughtfully designed rooms – some with typically Galician *galerías* (glassed-in balconies) – a friendly welcome and a lovely garden cafe make this old stone house a wonderful option, and the €6 breakfast is substantial. Even if you don't stay, it's an ideal spot for breakfast or coffee. Book ahead from May to September.

Hotel Pazo de Altamira　　　　BOUTIQUE HOTEL €€

(☑981 55 85 42; www.pazodealtamira.com; Rúa Altamira 18; r €65-90; ❋☎) A former noble mansion just steps from the bustling Mercado de Abastos, the Altamira provides 18 very appealing, bright, white rooms with real wood floors, comfy beds, bathtubs and, in many cases, their own *galerías*. The hotel is also home to the **Café de Altamira** (Rúa das Ameas 9; mains €13-18, lunch menú Mon-Fri €14; ⊙1.30-3.45pm & 8.30-11.30pm Mon-Sat, closed Tue evening), with two long shared tables and a short but good menu of seasonal Galician dishes.

San Francisco Hotel
Monumento　　　　HISTORIC HOTEL €€

(☑981 58 16 34; www.sanfranciscohm.com; Campillo San Francisco 3; s €110, d €137-165; 🅿❋@☎⊠) The courtyards and the low-lit hallways with their stone door frames recall the hotel's former life as a Franciscan monastery. But the rooms, minimalist, modern and spacious, are all about contemporary comfort, and there's a great indoor pool. This is luxury in historic surroundings at prices much lower than Santiago's more famous *parador*.

Smart Hotel Boutique Literario San Bieito
BOUTIQUE HOTEL €€

(☑981 57 28 90; www.hotelsanbieito.com; Cantón de San Bieito 1; s/d incl breakfast €80/95; ❊@❋) An excellent conversion of a 16th-century building with 20 bright, comfortable and reasonably spacious rooms in fashionable greys and whites, all with exterior windows and individually controlled air-con.

It's 'smart' for its tech gadgetry (like smart TVs and tablets in rooms) and 'literary' for its Galician writing and culture theme and the fact that the husband of Galicia's 'national poet' Rosalía de Castro once lived here.

Barbantes Libredón
HOSTAL €€

(☑981 57 65 20; www.libredonbarbantes.com; Praza de Fonseca; s €49, d €59-69; ⊘closed mid-Dec–Mar; @❋) This is actually two *hostales* under the same management on opposite sides of the same lively little square. Rooms in both are simple but bright and fresh-feeling, though bathrooms are a bit cramped and there are no lifts. The Barbantes, on the south side of the square, has a touch more contemporary pizazz. Reception for both is in the Libredón.

Hospedería Seminario Mayor
MONASTERY €€

(☑981 56 02 82; www.sanmartinpinario.eu; Praza da Inmaculada 3; s/d incl breakfast €50/70; ❋) This establishment offers the rare experi-

ence of staying inside a centuries-old monastery (San Martiño Pinario), one wing of which has been upgraded into a hotel. With 81 rooms, it often has vacancies when other places don't. The rooms are spartan in decor, with massively thick stone walls, but have comfy beds with wrought-iron bedheads, and glassed-in showers.

Parador Hostal dos Reis Católicos
HISTORIC HOTEL €€€

(☑981 58 22 00; www.parador.es; Praza do Obradoiro 1; s/d incl breakfast from €175/190; ℗❊@❋) Opened in 1509 as a pilgrims' hostel, and with a claim to be the world's oldest hotel, this palatial *parador,* steps from the cathedral, is Santiago's top hotel, with regal (if rather staid) rooms. If you're not staying, stop in for a look round (p506) and coffee and cakes at the elegant cafe.

Eating

Central Santiago is packed with eateries and most do their job pretty well. Rúa do Franco (named for pilgrims arriving by the Camino Francés) is full of them, but you'll find many enticing options elsewhere. Don't leave Santiago without trying a *tarta de Santiago,* the city's famed almond cake.

Mercado de Abastos
MARKET €

(www.mercadodeabastosdesantiago.com; Rúa das Ameas 5-8; ⊘7am-2pm Mon-Sat) ✔ Santiago's food market is a fascinating, always lively

---

WHAT'S COOKING IN GALICIA

With the produce of the ocean (p512), coastline and rich inland pastures all readily to hand, Galician food bursts with exceptional variety and freshness.

Pulpo á feira Galicia's signature dish (known as *pulpo a la gallega* elsewhere in Spain): tender slices of octopus tentacle sprinkled with olive oil and paprika. It's available almost everywhere that serves food, but most Galicians agree that the best *pulpo á feira* is cooked in the inland town of O Carballiño, 30km northwest of Ourense. Cooks here invented the recipe in the Middle Ages, when the local monastery received copious supplies of octopus from tenants on its coastal properties. Around 70,000 people pile into O Carballiño on the second Sunday of August for the Festa do Pulpo de O Carballiño.

Percebes (goose barnacles) Galicia's favourite shellfish delicacy, pulled off coastal rocks at low tide and looking like miniature dragon claws. Cedeira is famed for its rich *percebes* and Taberna Praza do Peixe (p521) is one of the best spots to try them.

Chuletón A giant beef chop that can weigh 1kg or more – perfect at A Coruña's Pablo Gallego (p518).

Queso tetilla Cone-shaped 'nipple cheese', made from Galician cow's milk, is gentler on the taste buds than many Spanish cheeses. Browse the varieties at Santiago de Compostela's Mercado de Abastos (p508).

Tortilla de Betanzos Spain's beloved potato omelette is taken to new levels of gooey deliciousness in the taverns of Betanzos, such as O Pote (p520).

scene, very clean and with masses of fresh produce from the seas and countryside attractively displayed at 300-odd stalls. Stock up on *tetilla* cheese, cured meats, sausage, fruit and *empanada* (pastry pie) for a picnic – or buy seafood or meat and have it cooked up on the spot for €4 per person at hugely popular **Mariscomanía 10%** (stall 81, Mercado de Abastos; ⊙ 9am-3pm or later Tue-Sat, closed Tue-Fri Jan).

One vendor in the central alley sells wooden plates of *pulpo á feira* (octopus dish), which you can take to any nearby bar and enjoy with a drink.

O Beiro TAPAS, RACIONES €
(Rúa da Raíña 3; raciones €5-10; ⊙ 10am-1am Tue-Sun Mar-Dec) The house speciality is *tablas* (trays) of delectable cheeses and sausages, but there are plenty of other tapas and *raciones* (large tapas servings) at this friendly two-level wine bar. It has a terrific range of Galician wines and the fiery local grape-based liquors *orujo* and *aguardiente*.

★ **O Curro da Parra** CONTEMPORARY GALICIAN €€
(www.ocurrodaparra.com; Rúa do Curro da Parra 7; mains €17-23, tapas €4-8; ⊙ 1.30-3.30pm & 8.30-11.30pm Tue-Sat, 1.30-3.30pm Sun) With a neat little stone-walled dining room upstairs and a narrow tapas and wine bar below, O Curro da Parra serves up a broad range of thoughtfully created, market-fresh fare. You might go for pork cheeks with apple purée and spinach – or just ask what the fish and seafood of the day are. On weekday lunchtimes there's a good-value €12 *menú mercado* (market menu).

Abastos 2.0 CONTEMPORARY GALICIAN €€
(☑ 981 57 61 45; www.abastosdouspuntocero.es; Rúa das Ameas 3; dishes €1-10, menú €21; ⊙ noon-3pm & 8-11pm Tue-Sat) This highly original and incredibly popular marketside eatery offers new dishes concocted daily from the market's offerings. You can go for small individual items, or plates to share, or a six-item *menú* that adds up to a meal for €21. The seafood is generally fantastic, but whatever you order you're likely to love the great tastes and delicate presentation – if you can get a seat!

La Bodeguilla de San Roque SPANISH €€
(☑ 981 56 43 79; www.labodeguilladesanroque. com; Rúa de San Roque 13; raciones & mains €5-16; ⊙ 9am-12.30am Mon-Fri, 10.30am-4pm & 7pm-12.30am Sat & Sun) A busy two-storey restaurant-cum-wine-bar just northeast of

the Old Town, the Bodeguilla serves an eclectic range of excellent dishes ranging from salads to casseroles of shrimp, mushroom and seaweed, Galician beef sirloin in port, or plates of cheeses, sausages or ham.

Bierzo de Enxebre LEONESE €€
(www.bierzoenxebre.es; Rúa da Troia 10; raciones €9-17; ⊙ 1-4pm & 8-11.30pm) The cuisine at this busy spot is that of El Bierzo, a rural area of northwest Castilla y León, meaning excellent grilled and cured meats, but also cheeses, pies and vegetables. There are two small, stone-walled, wood-beamed dining rooms and a few prized outside tables.

O Piorno GALICIAN €€
(www.opiorno.com; Rúa Caldeirería 24; dishes €7-15; ⊙ 8.30am-midnight Mon-Sat) Generous servings of uncomplicated Galician fare at good prices are Piorno's recipe for success. Options range from *revueltos* (scrambled-egg dishes) and *tixolas* (stir-fries) to grilled turbot or sirloin in mushroom sauce.

Restaurante Ó Dezaseis GALICIAN €€
(☑ 981 56 48 80; www.dezaseis.com; Rúa de San Pedro 16; mains €13-15; ⊙ 2-4pm & 8.30pm-midnight Mon-Sat) This cellar eatery just outside the Old Town has an invitingly rustic air. It's a hearty rather than gourmet experience, but extremely popular with visitors and locals of all types, tucking into the Monday-to-Friday lunch menu (€12) or specialities like *lacón con grelos* (ham with greens), grilled octopus or entrecôte steak.

O Filandón TAPAS, RACIONES €€
(Rúa Acibechería 6; raciones €14-20, media raciones €10-12; ⊙ 12.30-4pm & 8.30pm-1am) Squeeze past the cheese-shop counter into the thin, cellar-like bar area behind, where you'll receive exceedingly generous free *pinchos* (snacks) with drinks, and can order plates of ham, sausage, cured meats, cheese or peppers. Thousands of notes and words of wisdom scribbled by past clients dangle from the walls.

🍷 Drinking & Entertainment

On summer evenings every streetside nook in the Old Town is filled with people relaxing over tapas and drinks. The liveliest bar area lies east of Praza da Quintana. Santiago's large student population comes out in full force approaching midnight, Thursday to Saturday. Later, people gravitate towards clubs along Rúas da República Arxentina and Nova de Abaixo, in the new town.

A busy agenda of concerts, theatre and exhibitions goes on year-round. Pick up a program at Turismo de Santiago or check the cultural guide on its website, or visit www.quehacerensantiago.com.

Atlántico
BAR

(☏ 981 57 21 52; Rúa da Fonte de San Miguel 9; ⏰ 7pm-3am or later) This multilevel bar pulls in a hip 20s and 30s artsy clientele with cocktails and a soundtrack ranging from Cajun blues to Spanish indie.

Modus Vivendi
PUB

(www.pubmodusvivendi.net; Praza de Feixóo 1; ⏰ 6pm-3am or 4am) In the stables of an 18th-century mansion, Modus Vivendi attracts all types and hosts regular varied live music, DJs and exhibitions. It's reckoned to be Galicia's oldest 'pub' (since 1972).

★ Casa das Crechas
LIVE MUSIC

(www.casadascrechas.com; Vía Sacra 3; ⏰ 4.30pm-late) There's no better place for Celtic and other folk music. Head to the tightly packed downstairs bar about 10.30pm most Wednesdays from September to mid-June for terrific Galician jam sessions (admission €1). Visiting artists from Portugal, Brazil and elsewhere also play here regularly (about three nights a week in summer), and there are DJ sessions on Friday and Saturday.

Borriquita de Belém
MUSIC BAR

(www.borriquitadebelem.blogspot.com.es; Rúa de San Paio de Antealtares 22; ⏰ 10pm-2.30am or later Tue-Sat) The tightly packed 'Little Donkey' serves mojitos and wine from the barrel and has live or DJ-spun reggae, jazz, flamenco or blues several nights a week.

Shopping

The Old Town is littered with enticing boutiques and other shops purveying Santiago's traditional jet jewellery, books, original art, Galician wine and *tetilla* cheese, and Galician craft specialities such as Camariñas lace and Sargadelos pottery.

ℹ Information

Hospital Clínico Universitario (☏ 981 95 00 00; chusantiago.sergas.es; Travesa da Choupana) Southwest of the Old Town; has emergency service.

Oficina del Peregrino (Pilgrims' Office; ☏ 981 56 88 46; peregrinosantiago.es; Rúa do Vilar 3; ⏰ 9am-9pm May-Oct, 10am-7pm Nov-Apr) People who have covered at least the last 100km of the Camino de Santiago on foot or horseback, or the last 200km by bicycle, can obtain their 'Compostela' certificate here to prove it. The website has a good deal of useful Camino info.

Oficina de Turismo de Galicia (www.turgalicia.es; Rúa do Vilar 30-32; ⏰ 10am-8pm Mon-Fri, 11am-2pm & 5-7pm Sat, 11am-2pm Sun) The scoop on all things Galicia.

Turismo de Santiago (☏ 981 55 51 29; www.santiagoturismo.com; Rúa do Vilar 63; ⏰ 9am-9pm, to 7pm approx Nov-Mar) The efficient main municipal tourist office.

ℹ Getting There & Away

AIR

Santiago's **Lavacolla airport** (☏ 981 54 75 00; www.aena-aeropuertos.es) is 11km east of the city. Direct flights (some only operating during variable summer months):

Aer Lingus (www.aerlingus.com) Dublin.

EasyJet (www.easyjet.com) Basel-Mulhouse, Geneva, London (Gatwick).

BUSES & TRAINS FROM SANTIAGO DE COMPOSTELA

DESTINATION	BUS	TRAIN
A Coruña	€6; 1-1¼hr; 14 or more daily	€6-7.50; 30-40min; 21 or more daily
León	€30; 6hr; 1 or more daily	
Lugo	€9.15; 2hr; 6 or more daily	
Madrid	€47-68; 8-10hr; 5 or more daily	€34-54; 5½-9½hr; 4 or more daily
Ourense	€9; 2hr; 4 or more daily	€10-20; 40min-1¾hr; 9 or more daily
Oviedo	€30-42; 5-7hr; 3 or more daily	
Pontevedra	€5.85; 1hr; 14 or more daily	€6-7.20; 1hr; 13 or more daily
Porto (Portugal)	€31; 4hr; 2 or more daily	
Santander	€42-62; 8-10hr; 4 or more daily	
Vigo		€9.10-11; 1½hr; 13 or more daily

Iberia (www.iberia.com) Madrid, Barcelona, Bilbao.

Ryanair (www.ryanair.com) Alicante, Barcelona, Frankfurt (Hahn), London (Stansted), Madrid, Málaga, Milan, Seville, Valencia.

Vueling Airlines (www.vueling.com) Barcelona, Brussels, Málaga, Paris, Rome, Zurich.

The **bus station** (☏981 54 24 16; Praza de Camilo Díaz Baliño; ⊙) is about a 20-minute walk northeast of the city centre. **Castromil-Monbus** (☏902 292900; www.monbus.es) runs to many places in Galicia; **ALSA** (☏902 422242; www.alsa.es) operates further afield.

The **train station** (☏981 59 18 59; Rúa do Hórreo) is about a 15-minute walk south from the Old Town. All trains are run by **Renfe** (☏902 320320; www.renfe.com).

ℹ Getting Around

Santiago is walkable, although it's a bit of a hike from the train and bus stations to the city centre. Private vehicles are barred from the Old Town from about 10am to dusk for most of the summer. Underground car parks around its fringes generally charge about €16 per 24 hours.

Empresa Freire (www.empresafreire.com) runs buses (€3, 35 minutes) to Lavacolla airport from Praza de Galicia every half-hour from 6am to midnight, via the train and bus stations. Taxis charge around €20.

City bus 6 runs every 20 to 30 minutes from Rúa do Hórreo near the train station to Rúa da Virxe da Cerca on the eastern edge of the Old Town. Bus 5 runs every 15 to 30 minutes between the bus station, Rúa da Virxe da Cerca and Praza de Galicia. Tickets cost €1.

COSTA DA MORTE

Rocky headlands, winding inlets, small fishing towns, narrow coves, wide sweeping bays and many a remote, sandy beach – this is the eerily beautiful 'Coast of Death'. For some the most enchanting part of Galicia, this relatively isolated and unspoilt shore runs from Muros, at the mouth of the Ría de Muros, around to Caión, just before A Coruña. It's a coast of legends, like the one about villagers who used to put out lamps to lure passing ships on to deadly rocks. This treacherous coast has certainly seen a lot of shipwrecks, and the idyllic landscape can undergo a rapid transformation when ocean mists blow in.

Some appealing rural hotels make great bases for exploring the region. Many are listed at the useful www.turismocostadamorte.com.

Public transport on the area's sinuous country roads is limited, so having your own wheels makes it far easier to get around.

Carnota & O Pindo

The Costa da Morte starts just past Muros (p524). At Monte Louro, the coast turns north and you immediately encounter a series of long, sweeping, sandy beaches facing the open Atlantic, most notably the spectacular but exposed 7km curve of Praia de Carnota. Carnota village is renowned as home to Galicia's largest *hórreo* (traditional stone grain store) – 34.5m long and constructed in an 18th-century *hórreo*-building contest with nearby Lira.

O Pindo, 14km further on, is a starting point for walks in the coastal hills here, which are covered in weirdly eroded granite rock formations dubbed El Olimpo Celta (Celtic Olympus). The classic, quite steep route climbs 627m to the top of Monte Pindo (5.4km one-way). O Pindo has several *hostales* with restaurants on the main road, including friendly Pensión Sol e Mar (☏981 76 02 98; s/d €35/45; ⊙), where eight of the plain, clean, decent-sized rooms have beach views. If you're not up for hill-walking, you can still enjoy spectacular vistas from the Mirador do Ézaro, 4.5km north of O Pindo. The main road continues around the beautiful Ría de Corcubión towards Fisterra.

Fisterra & Around

POP (FISTERRA) 2930

★Cabo Fisterra (Castilian: Cabo Finisterre) is the western edge of Spain, at least in popular imagination. The real westernmost point is Cabo da Nave, 5km north, but that doesn't stop throngs of people from heading out to this beautiful, windswept cape, which is also the end-point of an 86km extension of the Camino de Santiago. Pilgrims ending their journeys here ritually burn smelly socks, T-shirts etc on the rocks just past the lighthouse.

The cape is a 3.5km drive past the town of Fisterra. On the edge of town you pass the 12th-century Igrexa de Santa María das Areas. Some 600m past the church, a track up to the right to Monte Facho and

LOCAL KNOWLEDGE

GALICIA SEAFOOD TIPS

Galician seafood is plentiful and fresh, and may well be the best you have ever tasted. Almost every restaurant and bar has several seafood specialities on the menu. Shellfish fans will delight over the variety of *ameixas* (clams), *mexillons* (mussels), *vieiras* and *zamburiñas* (both types of scallop), *berberechos* (cockles) and *navajas* (razor clams). But Galicia's ultimate shellfish delicacy is the much-prized *percebes* (goose barnacles), which bear a disconcerting resemblance to fingernails or claws: to eat them you hold the 'claw' end, twist off the other end and eat the soft, succulent bit inside!

Other delicacies include various crabs, from little *nécoras* and *santiaguiños* to huge *centollos* (spider crabs) and the enormous *buey del mar* ('ox of the sea'), and the *bogavante* or *lubrigante* (European lobster), with two enormous claws.

Shellfish in restaurants are often priced by weight and are not particularly cheap: *percebes* can cost anywhere from €60 to over €250 per kg, depending on size and season.

While mussels, oysters and some fish are farmed, most crabs are caught wild. Look for 'salvaje' (wild) or 'del pincho' (rod-caught) on menus to identify nonfarmed fish.

Monte de San Guillerme provides a longer (by 2.5km) and more challenging but even more scenic alternative walking route to the cape. These hilltops were once a site of pagan fertility rites, and they say childless couples used to come up here to improve their chances of conception.

Fisterra itself is a fishing port with a picturesque harbour, and a tourist destination growing ever more popular among Camino pilgrims. The spectacular beach **Praia da Mar de Fora**, over on the ocean side of the promontory, is reachable via an 800m walk. For a view of Cabo Fisterra from the ocean, take a one-hour cruise with **Cruceros Fisterra** (607 198095; www.crucerosfisterra.com; adult/child €12/6).

🛌 Sleeping

There are two dozen places to stay, about half of which are hostels that have opened in the last few years. Some of the latter close for long periods each year and/or only admit people with Camino stamps.

Albergue Cabo da Vila HOSTEL €
(981 74 04 54; www.alberguecabodavila.com; Rúa Coruña 13; dm incl breakfast €12; ⊙closed Feb; @🛜) Open to everyone, this is a typically simple, but welcoming, hostel with 24 bunk places in one big dorm, plus kitchen, laundry facilities and an ample sitting area.

★ Hotel Mar da Ardora DESIGN HOTEL €€
(981 74 05 90; www.hotelmardaardora.com; Rúa Atalaia 15; s/d incl breakfast €99/110; P🛜❄️♿) 🌿 This delightful little family-run hotel sits at the top of town with fantastic westward ocean views from the big windows and ter-

races of its six rooms. Everything is in impeccably contemporary but comfortable style, from the cubist architecture to the soothing white/grey/silver colour schemes.

A new pool, spa and jacuzzi add to the appeal, and prices include not just a good buffet breakfast but also free bicycles and (from about May to November) products from the hotel's organic garden.

Hotel Rústico Spa Finisterrae RURAL HOTEL €€
(981 71 22 11; www.hotelspafinisterrae.com; Lugar da Insua 128; r €69-109; P🛜❄️) A characterful converted farmhouse with panoramic views, 700m up from the harbour, the Finisterrae provides spacious, bright rooms with brass beds, fresh white linen and stone walls.

🍴 Eating

You can choose from about a dozen eateries facing the harbour.

Mesón A Cantina GALICIAN €
(Paseo de Calafiguera 1; raciones & mains €6-15; ⊙1-4pm & 8-11pm) Multitasking as a hang-out for fishermen, pilgrims, tourists and everyone else, busy A Cantina is an always-sound bet for *bocadillos* (long-bread sandwiches) and burgers, as well as octopus, squid and fish, and meat mains.

★ O Fragón CONTEMPORARY GALICIAN €€
(659 077320; Praza da Cerca 8; mains €9-20, menú €30; ⊙1.15-3.30pm & 8-10.45pm May-Sep, 1.15-3.30pm Oct & Dec-Apr, closed Tue Sep-Jun, last week Jun, Carnaval week) Neat O Fragón prepares original, tasty dishes from locally available ingredients. The *menú gastronómico*, available for all meals, is a diverse feast that includes fish, shellfish and meat dishes and

a starter and dessert (drinks are extra). It's just round the corner, past the main restaurant strip.

ℹ️ Getting There & Away

Monbus (www.monbus.es) runs four or five daily buses to/from Santiago de Compostela (€13, 2½ to three hours) via Noia, Muros and Carnota. **Autocares Vázquez** (www.autocaresvazquez. net) runs up to five buses to/from A Coruña (€14, two hours). You may be able to reach Muxía and Camariñas with a transfer at Cee, but schedules are changeable.

Muxía & Around

POP (MUXÍA) 1600

The route north from Fisterra to Muxía passes along enchanting lanes through thick woodlands; along the way is a nice detour to Cabo Touriñán, a very picturesque spot for a breezy walk. Just south of Muxía, Praia de Lourido is an unspoilt stretch of sand in a sheltered bay perfect for a sunny day.

Muxía itself is a photogenic little fishing port with a handful of cosy bars. Follow signs to the Santuario da Virxe da Barca to reach one of Galicia's most beloved pilgrimage points. This church marks the spot where (legend attests) the Virgin Mary arrived in a stone boat and appeared to Santiago (St James) while he was preaching here. Two of the rocks strewn before the chapel are, supposedly, the boat's sail and tiller. A lightning-sparked fire on Christmas Day 2013 gutted the church's interior: it was hoped the church would reopen by the end of 2014.

Heading on from Muxía towards Camariñas, take the pretty road via the inviting beach Praia do Lago, the *hórreo*-studded hamlet Leis and the riverside village of Cereixo.

🛏️ Sleeping & Eating

⭐ **Casa de Trillo** COUNTRY HOUSE €€
(☑981 72 77 78; www.casadetrillo.com; Santa Mariña; s €60-74, d €75-92, apt for 2 €95, all incl breakfast; ⊗closed 7 Jan-7 Feb; 🅿@🛜) 🏊 Deep in typically Galician countryside at Santa Mariña, about 8km south of Muxía, this charming and hospitable 16th-century manor house has a lot of history, lovely gardens, cosy, well-appointed rooms and home-grown food. It's a marvellous base for exploring the area.

A de Loló HOTEL €€
(☑981 74 24 22; www.hoteladelolo.com; Rua Virxe da Barca 37, Muxía; s €55-60, d €70-75, incl breakfast; 🛜) The thinnest of street frontages conceals eight sizeable, attractively contemporary rooms with some cute maritime decorative details and good bathrooms. The restaurant (mains €9-19; ⊗noon-5pm & 7-11pm Mar-Dec) is one of Muxía's best, with a focus on seafood.

ℹ️ Getting There & Away

Between one and three buses daily link Muxía with Camariñas and A Coruña (with Autocares Vázquez) and Santiago (with Hefe SL).

Camariñas & Around

POP (CAMARIÑAS) 2700

The fishing village of Camariñas is known for its fine traditional lacework, with several specialist shops and the interesting Museo do Encaixe (Lace Museum; Praza Insuela; admission €2; ⊗11am-2pm & 5-8pm Tue-Sun mid-Jun–Aug, noon-2pm & 6-8pm Wed-Sat Oct–mid-Jun).

The rugged coast between Camariñas and Camelle, to the northeast (p514), is one of the most beautiful stretches of the Costa da Morte. Camelle has no outstanding charm, but it does have the so-called Museo do Alemán (⊗24hr) FREE, beside the pier, a quirky and touching open-air sculpture garden made from rocks and ocean bric-a-brac by 'Man' (Manfred Gnädinger), an eccentric long-time German resident who died in 2002. Praia de Traba, a little-frequented 2.5km stretch of sand with dunes and a lagoon, is a lovely 4km walk east along the coast, and from there footpath PRG114 continues 8km to Laxe.

🛏️ Sleeping & Eating

Hotel Puerto Arnela HOTEL €
(☑981 70 54 77; www.hotelpuertoarnela.es; Plaza del Carmen 20, Camariñas; s/d incl breakfast €30/55; 🛜) A stone manor house facing the harbour with appealing country-style rooms and a restaurant (mains €6-15; ⊗1-3.30pm & 9-11.30pm) serving good, uncomplicated shellfish, fish and meat.

Apartamentos Molinera APARTMENT €
(☑609 349114, 981 71 03 28; Rúa Principal 79, Camelle; apt €42; 🛜) Four good-value upstairs apartments in Camelle for up to four people each. The entrance is next door to

OFF THE BEATEN TRACK

RUTA DEL LITORAL

You can walk, bike or drive this scenic coastal route (part paved, part potholed dirt/gravel) from Camariñas 5km northwest to the Cabo Vilán lighthouse (with a cafe and an exhibition on shipwrecks and lighthouses), then east to Camelle, a further 21km. The route winds past secluded beaches like Area de Trece – a picturesque set of short sandy strands divided by groups of boulders – across windswept hillsides and past weathered rock formations, and there are many places to stop along the way, such as the Cementerio dos Ingleses (English Cemetery), the sad burial ground from an 1890 shipwreck that took the lives of 172 British naval cadets. Signposting after the cemetery is almost nonexistent: go left at forks after 2km and 3km, straight on at the junction after 5.7km, and left at the fork after 8.5km.

A Molinera cafe: ask for the owner, Lola, along the street at Rúa Principal 44.

★Lugar do Cotariño   RURAL HOTEL €€
(☑639 638634; www.docotarino.com; r incl breakfast €90-105; ⊙closed late Dec-late Jan; P@奎) A labour of love for its owners, this beautifully reconstructed 400-year-old farmstead sits in verdant countryside 1km out of Camariñas. The seven rooms are homey and pretty in perfect country style, the two 'specials' in the main house being especially large and appealing. The lovely garden includes two ancient *hórreos*.

Dinner (€20) is available for guests in the stone-walled dining room. To find Cotariño, turn right opposite the Boya cannery as you enter Camariñas from Ponte do Porto, right again at Stella del Mare cafe after 300m, and go 1.3km.

ⓘ Getting There & Away

At least two daily Autocares Vázquez buses run to/from A Coruña. Monday to Friday, there are two buses to/from Muxía.

Laxe & Around

POP (LAXE) 1830

A sweeping bay beach runs right along the lively waterfront of Laxe, and the 15th-century Gothic church of Santa María da Atalaia stands guard over the harbour. Much of this area's appeal lies beyond the town. Laxe's tourist office (☑981 70 69 65; www.concellodelaxe.com/turismo; Avenida Cesáreo Pondal 26; ⊙10am-2pm Mon-Fri) and its website have information on walks in the area, including the 8km coastal walk west to Praia de Traba via the surf beach Praia de Soesto.

For a fascinating archaeological outing, drive inland past Canduas, then 2.4km south on the AC430 to find the turn-off for the Castro A Cidá de Borneiro, a pre-Roman *castro* amid thick woodlands. One kilometre further along the AC430, turn right and go 1km to the Dolmen de Dombate (⊙9am-8pm or dusk, whichever earlier) FREE, a large 3700 BC megalithic tomb recently encased in a protective pavilion. A full-size replica, which (unlike the real thing) you can go inside, stands in the adjacent visitors centre.

🍴 Sleeping & Eating

There are several inviting places for tapas and drinks along the main beachfront street, Rúa Rosalía de Castro.

Hostal Bahía   HOSTAL €
(☑981 72 83 04, 630 160317; www.bahialaxe.com; Avenida Besugueira 24; s €42, d €50-70; 奎) Hostal Bahía, 150m up past Laxe's Santa María church, has good-value rooms in shades of orange and yellow, most with sea views. Owner Manolo is only too keen to supply information on places to go on the Costa da Morte. From September to June, call first as you enter Laxe at his Cafe Bar Bahía (Rúa Rosalía de Castro 9; raciones €4-12; ⊙8am-midnight).

Playa de Laxe Hotel   HOTEL €€
(☑981 73 90 00; www.playadelaxe.com; Avenida Cesáreo Pondal 27; s €76, d €87-108; ⊙closed Nov-Mar; P❄@奎) Just off the beach towards the south end of town, this hotel is modern, spick and span, comfortable and bland. Best views are from the top-floor 'special' rooms.

Mesón O Salvavidas   GALICIAN €€
(Avenida Cesáreo Pondal 27; mains €12-21; ⊙1-4pm & 8-11pm Fri-Wed; 奎) For a proper meal head to the Salvavidas, towards the south end of town, which offers appetising grilled meats and seafood.

ⓘ Getting There & Away

Laxe is linked to A Coruña by two or more daily Vázquez buses (€8.65, two hours).

A CORUÑA & THE RÍAS ALTAS

In few places do land and sea meet in such abrupt beauty. The untamed beaches, towering cliffs and powerful waves of the Rías Altas (the eastern half of Galicia's north coast) are certainly more dramatic than the landscapes of the Rías Baixas. They're also far less touristic, and make an ideal destination for travellers yearning to get off the heavily beaten path. Add in the allure of cultured, maritime A Coruña and the lively little towns further along the shores, and you'll wonder why more visitors don't journey north.

A Coruña

POP 217,000

A Coruña (Castilian: La Coruña) is a port city, beachy hot spot and cruise-ship stop; a busy commercial centre and a cultural enclave; a historic city and a modern metropolis with a buzzing nightlife – all in all, an intriguing place to discover.

Britain looms large on A Coruña's horizon. In 1588 the ill-fated Spanish Armada weighed anchor here. The following year Sir Francis Drake tried to occupy the city but was seen off by María Pita, a heroine whose name lives on in the city's main square. In 1809 a British army helping Spain resist the invading French was forced into a Dunkirk-style evacuation here, losing its leader Sir John Moore in the process. In the 19th and 20th centuries, A Coruña's port was the gateway through which hundreds of thousands of Galicians emigrated to new lives in the Americas.

The city occupies a particularly contorted corner of the Galician coast. The centre sits on an isthmus straddled by the port on its southeast side and the main ocean beaches on the northwest. An irregularly shaped peninsula extends 2km north out to the city's World Heritage–listed Roman lighthouse, the Torre de Hércules. The Paseo Marítimo, a wonderful 13km walkway and bike path, runs all the way from the port, around the peninsula, along the ocean beaches and on out to the west.

◉ Sights

★ **Torre de Hércules**   LIGHTHOUSE
(www.torredeherculesacoruna.com; Avenida de Navarra; adult/senior & child €3/1.50, Mon free;

⊘10am-9pm Jun-Sep, 10am-6pm Oct-May; P)
The 'Tower of Hercules' sits near the windy northern tip of the city. Legend attributes its construction to one of the labours of Hercules, but it was actually the Romans who orginally built this lighthouse in the 1st century AD – a beacon on what was then the furthest edge of the civilised world. Climb the 234 steps for great panoramas of the city, coast and the surrounding **Parque Escultórico** (Sculpture Park).

The exterior facing of the 59m-high stone tower was added in 1788–90, but the inside, apart from the staircase and cupola, is all original Roman. Buses 3 and 5 run here from Paseo de la Dársena near Plaza de María Pita.

Aquarium Finisterrae   AQUARIUM
(☑981 18 98 42; www.mc2coruna.org/aquarium; Paseo Marítimo 34; adult/senior & child €10/4; ⊘10am-9pm, shorter hours Sep-Jun; ♠) Kids love the seal colony and the underwater Nautilus room (surrounded by sharks and 50 other fish species) at this excellent aquarium on the city's northern headland.

Ciudad Vieja   OLD CITY
Shady plazas, charming old churches, hilly cobbled lanes and a good smattering of cafes and bars fill A Coruña's compact old city. Start your explorations at stately **Plaza de María Pita**, rimmed with cafes and dominated by the early-20th-century **Ayuntamiento** (Town Hall) and a monument to the eponymous heroine, and make your way through the labyrinth towards the **Castillo de San Antón**, the 16th-century fort proudly guarding the entrance to the port.

The fort houses the eclectic **Museo Arqueológico e Histórico** (☑981 18 98 50; Paseo Marítimo; adult/senior & child €2/1, Sat free; ⊘10am-9pm Tue-Sat, 10am-3pm Sun), ranging widely over the area's prehistory and history. The British general Sir John Moore (killed in the nearby Battle of Elviña in 1809) lies buried in the nearby **Xardín de San Carlos** (Calle de San Francisco), where Charles Wolfe's famous poem on Moore's burial is inscribed on a plaque.

The 12th-century **Iglesia de Santiago** (Calle de Santiago), with three Romanesque apses backing on to pretty little Plaza de la Constitución, is the city's oldest church.

Galerías   ARCHITECTURE
The expanse of classic late-19th-century Galician *galerías* (glassed-in balconies) fronting Avenidas de Montoto and Marina is

A Coruña

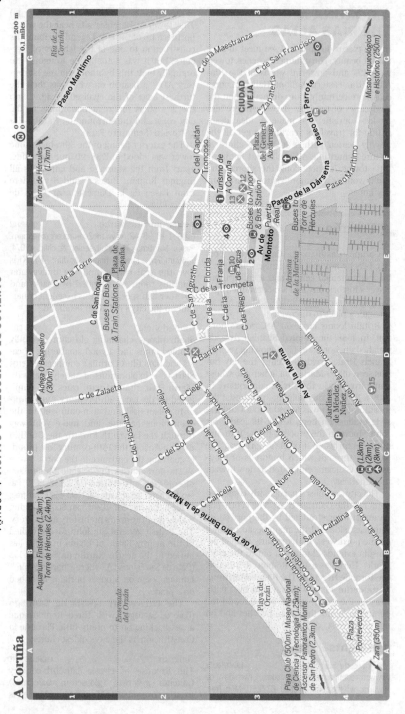

200 m
0.1 miles

Ría de A Coruña

Paseo Marítimo

Torre de Hércules (1.7km)

C de la Maestranza

C de San Francisco

CIUDAD VIEJA

C Zapatería

5

C del Capitán Troncoso

Turismo de A Coruña

13

12

Plaza del General Azcárraga

3

Paseo del Parrote

6

Buses to Airport & Bus Station

Museo Arqueológico e Histórico (250m)

Puerta Real

Paseo de la Dársena

1

4

2

10

Av de Montoto

Buses to Torre de Hércules

Paseo Marítimo

C del Capitán

Plaza de España

C de San Agustín

C de la Florida

C de la Franja

C de Riego de Agua

C de la Trompeta

Dársena de la Marina

C de la Torre

Buses to Bus & Train Stations

C de San Roque

Plaza de España

Adega O Bebedeiro (300m)

C de Zalaeta

14

C Barrera

C Ciega

11

Av de la Marina

Av del Alférez Provisional

15

C Cantón Pequeño

C Cantón Grande

Jardines de Méndez Núñez

C del Hospital

C Cañalelo

C del Sol

C del Orzán

C de San Andrés

8

C de la Galera

C Real

C Olmos

C de General Mola

C Estrella

R Nueva

C Cancela

(1.8km); (2km); (8km)

Playa del Orzán

Ensenada del Orzán

Av de Pedro Barrié de la Maza

Playa Club (500m); Museo Nacional de Ciencia y Tecnología (1.25km); Ascensor Panorámico Monte de San Pedro (2.3km)

Aquarium Finisterrae (1.3km); Torre de Hércules (2.4km)

C Cordelería

C Panaderas

C Cordelería Fontanes

Santa Catalina

Durán Loriga

9

7

Plaza Pontevedra

Zara (350m)

A Coruña

an emblematic A Coruña sight and the origin of its label 'the city of glass'.

Beach BEACH
A Coruña's city beach is a glorious, 1.4km-long, protected sweep of sand. Named **Playa del Orzán** at its east end and **Playa de Riazor** at the west, it gets pretty busy on warm summer days.

Monte de San Pedro PARK
(🅿🚻) This hilltop park 2km northwest of the city centre provides exceptional views over the city and coast, and contains the **Cúpula Atlántica** (adult/senior & child €2/1; ⊙11am-9pm), an observation dome with displays on A Coruña, as well as a maze, cafe, restaurant and two very large 1920s guns. Part of the fun is getting up there in the **Ascensor Panorámico** (Panoramic Lift; 1-way €3; ⊙every 30min 11.45am-8.45pm Tue-Sun, to 7.15pm Oct-May; 🅿), a large glass ball that slowly ascends the steep hillside from the Paseo Marítimo.

🛏 Sleeping

Central lodging options are mostly straightforward business hotels or modest *hostales,* but a few places escape the mould. Prices dip, often sharply, outside August.

Hotel Nido HOTEL €
(☑981 21 32 01; www.hotel-nido-coruna.com; Calle de San Andrés 146; s/d incl breakfast €40/60; 🛜) Welcoming and clean, the Nido is an excellent, well-run budget choice with 47 medium-sized rooms. There's a good little cafe for breakfast, and rooms overlooking the busy street are double-glazed for effective noise exclusion.

Pensión Alborán HOSTAL €
(☑981 22 65 79; www.hostalalboran.es; Calle de Riego de Agua 14; s/d €30/50; ✳🛜) Just steps

from Plaza de María Pita, efficiently run Alborán boasts a shiny new reception/cafe area and lift, and three spiffy modernised rooms in contemporary white, black and grey. The other 27 rooms are of an older vintage but are still clean and quite bright.

Hotel Zenit Coruña HOTEL €€
(☑981 21 84 84; www.zenithoteles.com; Calle Comandante Fontanes 19; s €76-110, d €80-115; 🅿✳@🛜) The sunny, stylishly minimalist rooms – all with outside views – have glass wardrobe doors and washbasins, big bathroom mirrors, tasteful modern art and a menu of pillows, and there's a creative but not overpriced restaurant. And it's just a block from Playa del Orzán.

Hotel Hesperia Finisterre HOTEL €€
(☑981 20 54 00; www.hesperia-finisterre.com; Paseo del Parrote 2-4; r €120-125; 🅿✳@🛜🏊) This elder statesman of A Coruña hotels has a bright, traditional-meets-contemporary ambience. All rooms enjoy sea views and soft furnishings, and the hotel's impressive sports complex includes a beautiful big outdoor heated pool and two gyms.

Hotel Sol HOTEL €€
(☑981 21 03 62; www.hotelsolcoruna.com; Calle del Sol 10; r €77; 🅿🛜) A friendly, family-run place with eight large, modernised rooms and 31 older but still comfortable ones. The Sol is a good deal, especially with its free parking. The street can get noisy on weekend nights, so request an inside room if you bed down early.

🍴 Eating

For tapas, *raciones,* wine and cheap lunch menus, hit the narrow lanes west of Plaza de María Pita. Along and near Calle de la Franja you'll find plenty of lively *mesones* (old-style eateries) and *tabernas* (taverns). A bit further west, Calles Barrera, Galera, Olmos and Estrella are strung with more contemporary tapas bars, attracting a mainly 20s and 30s crowd.

Tapa Negra
CONTEMPORARY TAPAS €

(Calle de Barrera 32; tapas €1.80-2.70, raciones €6-13; ⊙1-4pm & 7pm-midnight Sun-Thu, to 3am Fri & Sat) Tapa Negra's black, white and red decor suggests a little creativity, and this popular spot delivers with tasty combinations like croquettes of Cabrales cheese or *revuelto de pulpo, grelos y langostinos* (scrambled eggs with octopus, greens and prawns).

★ Adega O Bebedeiro
GALICIAN €€

(☑981 21 06 09; www.adegaobebedeiro.com; Calle de Ángel Rebollo 34; mains €13-25; ⊙1.30-4pm & 8pm-midnight Tue-Sat, 1.30-4pm Sun) It's in a humble street on the northern headland and it looks a dump from outside, but the inside is rustically neat with a conversation-inspiring assortment of Galician bric-a-brac. The food is classic home-style cooking with some inventive touches, like scallop-stuffed sea bass in puff pastry, or spiced venison with chestnuts, all in generous quantities. Packed on weekends.

Pablo Gallego
CONTEMPORARY GALICIAN €€

(☑981 20 88 88; www.pablogallego.com; Calle del Capitán Troncoso 4; mains €12-22; ⊙1-4pm & 9pm-midnight) This fine restaurant prepares artful

NATIONAL SCIENCE & TECHNOLOGY MUSEUM

Not just for nerds, A Coruña's innovative, recently opened Museo Nacional de Ciencia y Tecnología (www.muncyt.es; Plaza del Museo Nacional 1; ⊙11am-3pm & 5-8pm Tue-Sat, 11am-3pm Sun, shorter hours mid-Oct–Jun, closed mid-Sep–mid-Oct; 👶) FREE will engage everybody. You'll see the first computer used in Spain (a monstrous IBM 650 bought by the railway company Renfe in 1959) and the entire front section of a Boeing 747. But perhaps most fascinating is the room displaying innovations from every year of the 20th century – a Fender Stratocaster guitar (1964), a Sony PlayStation (1994) and much more.

21st-century dishes with traditional Galician market ingredients. Try the speciality carpaccio of crayfish, or hake with green pil-pil and cockles, or their perfect *chuletón* (giant beef chop).

Taberna Da Penela
GALICIAN €€

(☑981 20 19 69; www.lapenela.com; Plaza de María Pita 9; mains €11-22; ⊙1.30-4pm & 8.30pm-midnight Tue-Sun) Get tasty Galician favourites like octopus, *caldo gallego* (a soup of potatoes, other vegetables and bits of meat and/or sausage) and roast veal at this popular plaza-side spot. It does a great *tortilla de Betanzos* (a gooey potato omelette), too, and has a long wine list.

Coral Restaurante
GALICIAN €€€

(Callejón de la Estacada 9, off Avenida de la Marina; ⊙1-4pm & 8.30-11.30pm Mon-Sat) With its long white tablecloths and gleaming wine glasses, Coral is a little more formal than most and a top place for quality Galician classics like ocean fish in albariño wine sauce.

🍺 Drinking & Entertainment

At night, A Coruña buzzes with taverns, bars and clubs. Before midnight, head to Plaza de María Pita for low-key drinks or navigate the taverns and tapas bars in the lanes to its west. The lounge 'pubs' on the top floor of the shopping centre Los Cantones Village (Avenida del Alférez Provisional) have terraces overlooking the port and develop quite a party/club scene from around midnight, Thursday to Saturday. Dozens of pubs and music bars on Calle del Sol, Calle de Canalejo and other streets behind Playa del Orzán party on till 3am or 4am on weekends.

Playa Club
CLUB

(www.playaclub.net; Playa de Riazor; admission incl 1 drink €7; ⊙sessions from 3am Thu-Sat) As the pubs close, the clubs start to fill. This ever-popular beachside spot with three different zones boasts views across the bay and a dance-inducing mix of alternative pop, funk, soul-jazz, disco and electronica.

❶ Information

Turismo de A Coruña (☑981 92 30 93; www.turismocoruna.com; Plaza de María Pita 6; ⊙9am-8.30pm Mon-Fri, 10am-2pm & 4-8pm Sat, 10am-7pm Sun) The helpful main city tourist office, with information in several languages.

TRAINS FROM A CORUÑA

DESTINATION	FARE (€)	DURATION (HR)	MINIMUM DAILY FREQUENCY
Ferrol	4.60-6	1¼-2	5
León	20-23	5-6	4
Lugo	10-18	1½-2	4
Madrid	37-56	6-10	5
Pontevedra	13-16	1½	13
Santiago de Compostela	7.20-16	30-40min	21

❶ Getting There & Away

AIR

From A Coruña's **Alvedro airport** (☎981 18 72 00), 8km south of the centre, **Iberia** (www. iberia.com) and **Air Europa** (www.aireuropa. com) fly daily to Madrid; **Vueling Airlines** (www. vueling.com) flies daily to London (Heathrow), Barcelona, Seville and Bilbao; and **TAP Portugal** (www.flytap.com) flies daily to Lisbon.

BUS

From the **bus station** (☎981 18 43 35; Calle de Caballeros), 2km south of the city centre, Castromil-Monbus heads south to Santiago de Compostela (€6, one to 1½ hours, 14 or more daily) and beyond. **Arriva** (☎981 31 12 13; www. arriva.es) serves Ferrol, the Rías Altas, Lugo and Ourense; Autocares Vázquez serves the Costa da Morte; and ALSA heads to Madrid and towns along Spain's north coast.

TRAIN

The **train station** (Plaza de San Cristóbal) is 2km south of the city centre.

Trains along Spain's north coast are operated by **FEVE** (www.renfe.com/viajeros/feve) and start from Ferrol.

❶ Getting Around

Buses (€1.45) run every half-hour (hourly on Saturdays and Sundays) from about 7.15am to 9.45pm between the airport and Puerta Real in the city centre.

Local bus 5 runs from the train station to Avenida de la Marina in the centre, and back to the station from Plaza de España. Buses 1, 1A and 4 run from the bus station to the city centre; returning, take the 1 or 1A from Puerta Real or 4 from Plaza de España. Rides cost €1.30.

Rías Altas

If you're seeking dramatic scenery, look no further than the Rías Altas. Here, towering forests open to views of sheer sea cliffs, sweeping beaches and vivid green fields studded with farmhouses. Add in medieval towns like Betanzos and Pontedeume, a scattering of quaint fishing ports, and the constant roar of the Atlantic, and it's easy to argue that the Rías Altas form Galicia's most beautiful area.

Betanzos

POP 10,600

Once a thriving estuary port rivalling A Coruña, Betanzos has a well-preserved medieval Old Town and is renowned for its welcoming taverns with local wines and good food.

⊙ Sights

Praza dos Irmáns García Naveira SQUARE
The sprawling main square is named after two Betanzos brothers who made a fortune in Argentina then returned home to do good works in the late 19th century. Around 50,000 people cram into the square at midnight on 16 August to witness the release of an enormous paper hot-air balloon during the **Fiestas de San Roque**. Around the corner, the **Museo das Mariñas** (☎981 77 19 46; Rúa Emilio Romay 1; admission €1.30; ⊙10am-2pm & 4-8pm Mon-Fri, 10.30am-1pm Sat, closed afternoons Jul & Aug) peers into traditional Galician life with exhibits ranging from the mundane (old coffee mugs) to the culturally significant (typical costumes), plus archaeology and art.

Old Town OLD TOWN
Take Rúa Castro up into the oldest part of town. Handsome Praza da Constitución is flanked by a couple of appealing cafes along with the Romanesque/Gothic **Igrexa de Santiago**, whose main portico inspired Santiago de Compostela's Pórtico de la Gloria. A short stroll northeast, two beautiful Gothic churches, **Santa María do Azougue** and **San Francisco**, stand almost side by side. The latter is full of particularly fine stone carving, including many sepulchres of 14th- and 15th-century Galician nobility.

Don't miss the sepulchre of Fernán Pérez de Andrade 'O Boo' (The Good), the local strongman who had all three of these medieval churches built. It rests on a stone bear and boar (the latter being the Andrade family emblem).

Sleeping & Eating

Hotel Garelos (981 77 59 30; www.hotelgarelos.com; Calle Alfonso IX 8; s/d incl breakfast €61/83; P❋🖥), 150m down from Praza dos Irmáns García Naveira, has spick-and-span rooms with comfy beds, parquet floors and original watercolours, and rates include a generous buffet breakfast.

A string of cafes flanks the main square. Amid the pavement tables dart two narrow alleyways, Venela Campo and Travesía do Progreso, lined with popular taverns for drinks, tapas and *raciones*. Be sure to try *tortilla de Betanzos*, a gooey potato omelette for which the town is famed. The terrific *menú del día* (set lunch) at **O Pote** (www.mesonopote.com; Travesía do Progreso 9; raciones €8-12, menú del día €16; 1-4pm & 8-11.30pm Wed-Mon) includes said tortilla.

Getting There & Away

Arriva buses to/from A Coruña (€2.15, 40 minutes, at least hourly 8am to 10pm) stop in Praza dos Irmáns García Naveira. Four or more Arriva buses head to Pontedeume (€2.20, 30 minutes) and a few to Ferrol, Lugo, Viveiro and Ribadeo.

Betanzos Cidade train station is northwest of the town centre, across the Río Mendo. At least five trains go daily to/from A Coruña (€3.95, 40 minutes) and Pontedeume (€2.20, 15 minutes).

Pontedeume

POP 4600

This hillside town overlooks the Eume estuary, where fishing boats bob. The Old Town is an appealing combination of handsome galleried houses, narrow cobbled streets and occasional open plazas, liberally sprinkled with taverns and tapas bars. Several parallel narrow streets climb up from the main road, the central one being the porticoed Rúa Real.

The area's most enticing sleeping options are rural hotels like the **Casa do Castelo de Andrade** (981 43 38 39; www.casteloandrade.com; Lugar Castelo de Andrade; r €103-130 late Jul-early Sep, €78-112 rest of year; closed Dec & Jan; P🖥), 7km southeast of town and close to the Parque Natural Fragas do Eume.

It's a pretty stone farmhouse in enormous grounds, with 10 immaculate, all different, olde-worlde-style rooms. The owner is a mine of helpful information about the area.

You'll find some of the town's best eats in the small, wood-panelled bar **Zas** (Travesía Real 2; tapas €2.50-8, raciones €5-16; 12.15-4.30pm & 7.30-11pm Wed-Mon), in a street off Rúa Real, cooking up simple but perfect Galician classics like *pulpo á feira*, steamed cockles or *percebes* (goose barnacles), and *raxo* and *zorza* (both bite-sized chunks of marinated pork).

Cedeira & Around

POP (CEDEIRA) 4700

Heading north from Pontedeume, the coast is studded with small maritime towns and pretty beaches. The naval port of **Ferrol**, 17km from Pontedeume, is the Rías Altas' largest hub and the western terminus of the FEVE railway to the Basque Country, but has little to detain you. Continuing north, you reach Valdoviño, with the beautiful **Praia Frouxeira**, and just beyond Valdoviño, **Praia de Roda** at Pantín has a great right-hander for surfers. In late August or early September it hosts the **Pantín Classic** (www.pantinclassic.com), an international pro surfers' contest.

Some 38km from Ferrol is the fishing port and very low-key resort of Cedeira. The cute little old town sits on the west bank of the Río Condomiñas, while **Praia da Magdalena** fronts the modern, eastern side of town. Around the headland to the south (a 7km drive) is the much more appealing **Praia de Vilarrube**, a long, sandy beach with shallow waters between two river mouths, in a protected dunes and wetlands area.

For a nice stroll of an hour or two, walk along the waterfront to the fishing port, climb up beside the old fort above it and walk out to **Punta Sarridal**, overlooking the mouth of the Ría de Cedeira. The rocky coast around here produces rich harvests of *percebes* (goose barnacles), a much-coveted seafood delicacy.

Sleeping & Eating

Cedeira has a fair supply of *hostales* and small hotels, but two places in Cordobelas, just off the main road 1km before Cedeira as you approach from the south, stand out. The town is full of bars and cafes, especially around the river mouth.

PARQUE NATURAL FRAGAS DO EUME

East of Pontedeume, the Eume valley is home to Europe's best-preserved Atlantic coastal forest, with mixed deciduous woodlands and several species of rare relict ferns that have survived here for many millions of years. The Centro de Interpretación (981 43 25 28; 10am-2pm & 4-8pm, closed afternoons Mon-Fri approx mid-Sep–mid-Jun) of the 91-sq-km park is 6km from Pontedeume on the Caaveiro road (no public transport comes here). Next door, Restaurante Andarubel (981 43 39 69; www.andarubel.com; mains €8-21; 1-4.30pm & 8.30pm-midnight Tue-Sun May-Oct, Sat & Sun Nov-Apr) is an excellent lunch spot, and rents bikes (€5/8/12 per one/two/four hours) and kayaks (€6 per person per hour). You can cycle or drive a paved road along the thickly forested valley for 7.5km from here to a stone footbridge, where a 500m path leads up to the Mosteiro de Caaveiro. This monastery dates back to the 9th century and occupies a lovely, scenic outcrop among the woods. Walkers can cross to a footpath on the bank opposite the road for the final 5km to the monastery.

Over Easter and from mid-June to the end of September, the road is closed to cars from La Alameda, 1km past the Centro de Interpretación, but is covered by an hourly free bus. Another easy option during these periods is the electric bicycles of Tour e-bike (www.tour-ebike.com; 1/1½/2hr €7/11/15; 🚲), available for rent at La Alameda.

With time and a vehicle it's well worth venturing into the less frequented eastern part of the park: the A Capela-Monfero road gives access to several marked walking trails of a few kilometres each – particularly scenic is the 6.5km Camiño dos Cerqueiros loop.

⭐ Hotel Herbeira
DESIGN HOTEL €€

(981 49 21 67; www.hotelherbeira.com; Cordobelas; s/d €83/110; closed 22 Dec-12 Jan; 🅿✳@🛜🚲🚲) As sleek as Galicia gets, this welcoming, family-run hotel boasts 16 contemporary rooms with large, glassed-in galleries, stunning views over the *ría* (estuary) and all sorts of pleasing design touches. There's a beautiful pool at the front and a nice, bright cafe for breakfast.

Hospedería Cordobelas
COUNTRY HOUSE €€

(981 48 06 07; www.cordobelas.com; Cordobelas; s/d €50/66; closed mid-Dec–mid-Jan; 🅿🛜) A charming stone-built property comprising four converted century-old village houses with comfortable, spacious, rustic-style rooms, and a lovely garden.

Taberna Praza do Peixe
SEAFOOD €

(Rúa do Mariñeiro 1; raciones €6-12; 10.30am-4pm & 7.30-11pm) This bar popular with locals, just west of the river, is one of the best places in town for servings of fish and seafood. Savour Cedeira's famous *percebes,* or its tasty version of the local speciality *rape a cedeiresa* (breaded monkfish in a tomato-and-white-wine sauce).

ℹ Information

Tourist Office (981 48 21 87; Avenida de Castelao 18; 10.30am-2pm & 5-8pm Mon-Fri, 11am-2pm Sat) A helpful place on the main road in the new part of town.

ℹ Getting There & Away

By bus from the south, you'll need to get to Ferrol, then take a **Rialsa** (www.monbus.es) bus from Praza de Galicia to Cedeira (€3, one hour, five daily Monday to Friday, two daily Saturday and Sunday). Arriva runs two daily buses, Monday to Friday, from Cedeira to Cariño (€2.85, 50 minutes). Cedeira's bus station is on Rúa Deportes, just off the main road, Avenida Castelao, 700m southeast of the Río Condomiñas.

Cabo Ortegal & Around

The wild, rugged coastline for which the Rías Altas are famous begins above Cedeira. If you have a vehicle (and, even better, time for some walks), Galicia's northwestern corner is a spectacular place to explore, with lush forests, vertigo-inducing cliffs, stunning oceanscapes and horses roaming free over the hills.

Busloads of tourists descend on San Andrés de Teixido (12km past Cedeira), a jumble of stone houses in a beautiful fold of the coastal hills renowned for its sanctuary of relics of St Andrew. A spectacular 5km stretch of the Ruta dos Peiraos walking path runs along the clifftops from Chao do Monte lookout, 4km back up the road towards Cedeira (or a steep 1km walk from San Andrés), to the Boca de Tarroiba lookout. Cedeira's tourist office has route leaflets, but on the ground the trail is haphazardly signed.

Drivers should head on from San Andrés up the winding CP2205 across the Serra da Capelada towards Cariño for incredible views. Six kilometres beyond San Andrés is the must-see Garita de Herbeira lookout, 600m above sea level and the best place to be wowed over southern Europe's highest sea cliffs.

Four kilometres north of the workaday town of Cariño looms the mother of Spanish capes, Cabo Ortegal, where the Atlantic Ocean meets the Bay of Biscay. Great stone shafts drop sheer into the ocean from such a height that the waves crashing on the rocks below seem pitifully benign. Os Tres Aguillóns, three islets, provide a home to hundreds of marine birds, and with binoculars you might spot dolphins or whales.

On the road from Cariño, you can stop at the first mirador to take the well-marked cliff-top trail to the San Xiao de Trebo chapel (1.6km). The path traverses a forest, crosses the Río Soutullo and affords grand views. From the chapel you can continue along the road to Cabo Ortegal (1.5km).

Rural hotels are the way to go in the area. Charming Muiño das Cañotas (☑ 981 42 01 81; www.muinodascanotas.com; A Ortigueira 10; r incl breakfast €65-80; P🔊), in a pretty little valley 200m off the DP6121, 2km south of Cariño, has five beautiful rooms in a converted 14th-century watermill.

Bares Peninsula

East of Cabo Ortegal, the Bares Peninsula offers further marvellous scenery, several good walking trails and a few delightfully low-key spots to stay over.

En route from the Ortegal area, some of Spain's most dramatic and least-known beaches are strung along the foot of the spectacular Acantilados de Loiba cliffs. Easiest to reach is Praia do Picón, 2km from Loiba FEVE station. By road, turn off the AC862 at Km 63 and follow the DP6104 to Picón village, where a sharp left turn leads to a small picnic area and a path down to the beach.

A few kilometres further along the AC862, O Barqueiro, on the Ría del Barqueiro, is a storybook Galician fishing village where slate-roofed, white houses cascade down to the port. There's little to do but stroll around the harbour and watch the day's catch come in. Overlooking the harbour, O Forno (☑ 981 41 41 24; www.hostaloforno.com; Porto do Barqueiro; s/d €35/50; ⊙ closed Jan-Easter; 🔊) offers

15 spick-and-span, medium-sized rooms, and a neat restaurant (mains €7-16; ⊙ 9am-11pm Easter-Dec) serving good local fish and shellfish. A few daily FEVE trains, and Arriva buses on Ferrol–Viveiro routes, serve O Barqueiro.

For an even quieter base, push north to tiny Porto de Bares, on a lovely crescent of sand lapped by the ría's waters. The only accommodation is the 18 smallish, clean and cosy rooms (half of them sea-facing) at Hospedaxe Porto Mar (☑ 981 41 40 23; www.portomar.eu; Calle Feliciano Armada; r €30-45; 🔊), whose amiable owners also run one of the three seafood-focused eateries by the beach. For a treat, book a room in the maritime-signalling-station-turned-contemporary-hotel Semáforo de Bares (☑ 699 943 584, 981 41 71 47; www.hotelsemaforodebares.com; s €51, d €66-120, ste €180; P🔊), with six rooms (the best are quite indulgent), sitting 3km above the village on a wonderfully panoramic hilltop.

From the lighthouse near the peninsula's tip, a 500m trail follows the spine of a rock outcrop to the Punta da Estaca de Bares, Spain's most northerly point, with awe-inspiring cliffs and fabulous panoramas.

Viveiro

POP 7400

This town at the mouth of the Río Landro has a well-preserved historic quarter of stone buildings and stone-paved streets, where outward appearances haven't changed a great deal since Viveiro was rebuilt after a 1540 fire. It's famous for its elaborate Easter-week celebrations, when the town fills with processions and decorations. Check out the Gothic Igrexa de Santiago (Rúa de Cervantes; ⊙ 11.30am-1.30pm & 7-8.30pm) and the 13th-century Romanesque Igrexa de Santa María do Campo (Rúa de Felipe Prieto; ⊙ variable) – and the bizarre Gruta de Lourdes behind the latter, festooned with plastic limbs and dolls. The 4km drive up to Mirador San Roque rewards with expansive panoramas.

If you feel like staying over, the excellent, contemporary-style Hotel Ego (☑ 982 56 09 87; www.hotelego.es; Playa de Area; s €110, d €110-165; P✻@🔊) is 4km north on the Ribadeo road, overlooking Playa de Area beach. Most of its 45 rooms have sea views and balconies, and the adjacent Restaurante Nito (mains €12-25; ⊙ 1-4pm & 8pm-midnight) is one of the coast's best eateries, providing quality meat, fish and shellfish and fine vistas.

FEVE trains between Ferrol and Oviedo stop at Viveiro, and a few Arriva buses fan out to Lugo and along the Rías Altas as far as A Coruña and Ribadeo. The bus station is on the waterfront street Avenida Ramón Canosa, just north of the old town.

Ribadeo

POP 6700

This lively port town on the Ría de Ribadeo, which separates Galicia from Asturias, is a sun-seeker magnet in summer. The old town between Praza de España and the port is an attractive mix of handsome old galleried and stone houses. For a beach you'll have to head out of town, but you won't be disappointed with Praia As Catedrais (Cathedrals Beach), 10km west. This 1.5km sandy stretch is home to awesome Gothic-looking rock arches, creations best seen at low tide.

🛏 Sleeping & Eating

This area has plenty of camping grounds, beachy *hostales* and appealing hotels. There's a handful of budget and lower mid-range places along Rúa de San Francisco, just off Praza de España.

Hotel Rolle　　　　　　　　　　HOTEL **€€**
(🖉982 12 06 70; www.hotelrolle.com; Rúa de Ingeniero Schulz 6; r incl breakfast €90; 🕸 @ 🛜) Just two blocks from Praza de España, the Rolle has spacious, attractive rooms in a rustically modern style, with nice, up-to-date bathrooms and plenty of exposed stone and wood. The owner is keen to tell you about things to see and do in the area.

Parador de Ribadeo　　　LUXURY HOTEL **€€€**
(🖉982 12 88 25; www.parador.es; Rúa de Amador Fernández 7; s €120-192, d €135-208, incl breakfast; 🅿🛜) For views, you can't beat the *parador*, where most of the 47 fairly formal rooms have their own *galerías* with *ría* vistas.

La Botellería　　　　MODERN SPANISH **€€**
(Rúa de San Francisco 24; mains €8-16; ⊙11am-midnight) Head to this convivial bar and small restaurant near Praza de España for good wine and tempting dishes like hake-and-prawn casserole or banana-and-chorizo croquettes with mint sauce.

❶ Getting There & Away

Multistop FEVE trains operate to/from Oviedo (€12.20, 3½ hours, two daily) and Ferrol (€10.95, three hours, four daily). At least four daily buses head to Luarca, Oviedo and (Monday to Friday only) Viveiro, and two to Lugo. The bus station is on Avenida Rosalía de Castro, about 500m north of Praza de España.

RÍAS BAIXAS

Wide beaches and relatively calm waters have made the Rías Baixas (Castilian: Rías Bajas) Galicia's most popular holiday destination. It boasts way more towns, villages, hotels and restaurants than other stretches of the Galician coast, which obscures some of its natural beauty. Still, the mix of pretty villages, sandy beaches and good eating options keep most people happy. Throw in the Illas Cíes, lovely old Pontevedra and lively Vigo, and you have a very tempting travel cocktail.

The following sections start at the inland end of each *ría* and work outwards, but if you have a vehicle and plenty of time you could simply follow the coast around all four *rías*. That would be some 250km from Muros to Nigrán – a straight-line distance of just 72km.

It's a great idea to book accommodation ahead for the second half of July or August. At other times room prices often dip dramatically. There's lots of information about the area at www.riasbaixas.depo.es.

Ría de Muros y Noia

Noia

POP 8400

This beachless town was Santiago de Compostela's de facto port for centuries. Stop for a look at the Gothic Igrexa de San Martiño, dominating Praza do Tapal, and the Igrexa de Santa María A Nova (Carreiriña do Escultor Ferreiro; ⊙10.30am-1.30pm & 4-6pm, closed Sat & Sun afternoon), both classics of so-called Galician sailors' Gothic church architecture, typified by a single very wide nave. San Martiño's western facade is adorned with wonderful sculptures of the apostles, Christ and archangels. Santa María contains a curious collection of tombstones from its graveyard, including those of medieval guild members showing tools of their trades such as an anchor, butcher's knives or tailor's scissors.

Noia's lively tapas scene centres on the old stone streets near San Martiño. For a fuller meal head to the neat, stone-walled dining room of Restaurante Ferrador (Rúa Costa do

Rías Baixas

N ▲ 0 —— 10 km
0 —— 5 miles

Ferrador 11; mains €9-15, 3-course lunch menú €10; ⊙1-5pm & 8.30-11.30pm, closed evenings Mon-Fri; 🛈), which specialises in local seafood.

Muros

POP 4300

Muros, near the far end of the *ría's* north shore, is an agreeable halt en route to the Costa da Morte. Behind the bustling seafront extends a web of stone-paved lanes dotted with taverns and lined with dignified stone houses. The 14th-century Igrexa de San Pedro is a fine example of Galician sailors' Gothic architecture. Stop by Licores Luisa (Praza de Galicia 2; ⊙9.30am-2pm & 4.30-7pm Mon-Sat) to sample homemade *orujo* (a firewater made from grape pressings) or liqueurs with an amazing variety of flavours from coffee to banana.

Casa Petra (Avenida Castelao 31; dishes €5-13; ⊙noon-3.30pm & 7.30-11.30pm) is a good,

---

informal spot to fill up on local octopus prepared half a dozen ways.

South Shore

The coast here isn't completely unspoilt, but it's pleasantly low-key. In Porto do Son, a fishing port, a small beach and a diminutive Old Town jumble together by the *ría*. Hotel Villa del Son (☑981 85 30 49; www.hotelvilladelson.es; Rúa de Trincherpe 11; s €42, d €49-60; 🅿 🛈) has tidy rooms with cool tile floors, sparkling bathrooms and cheery country-cottage-type decor. The neatly set little dining area at Restaurante Porto Nadelas (Avenida de Galicia 39; mains €8-18; ⊙1-4pm & 9pm-midnight Wed-Mon) is one of the best in town for seafood or rice dishes.

Four kilometres past Porto do Son is the turn-off for the Castro de Baroña, Galicia's most spectacularly sited prehistoric settlement. Park near the cafe and take the rocky 600m path down to the ruins. The settlement, abandoned in the first century BC, is poised majestically on a wind-blasted headland overlooking the crashing Atlantic waves. Stretching south from the *castro,* Praia Area Longa is a nudist beach and also the first of a small string of surfing beaches down this side of the *ría*.

Drivers can continue to the Dolmen de Axeitos, a well-preserved megalithic monument, signposted between Xuño and Ribeira, and Corrubedo at the tip of the peninsula, with beaches either side of town and a few relaxed bars around its small harbour.

Ría de Arousa

Cambados

POP 6700

The capital of the albariño wine country, famed for its fruity whites, the pretty little *ría*-side town of Cambados makes a pleasant base for touring the Rías Baixas. Its compact core of old streets is lined by stone architecture dotted with inviting taverns and eateries.

⊙ Sights & Activities

Cambados has four museums (joint admission adult/senior & child €3.20/1.60; ⊙10am-2pm & 5-8pm Tue-Sat, 10am-2pm Sun), three of them covering wine, fishing and local culture and one preserving a quaint old tide-operated cereal mill. You can visit and taste at more than 30 wineries in the district: Cambados' tourist office and www.rutadelvinoriasbaixas.com have detailed information.

Pazo de Fefiñáns MANSION, WINERY
The most easily visited wineries are two small establishments in the Pazo de Fefiñáns, a handsome 16th-century mansion on broad Praza de Fefiñáns: **Bodegas del Palacio de Fefiñanes** (www.fefinanes.com; visits incl tasting per person €4-9, minimum per group €24-50; ☉10am-1pm & 4-7pm Mon-Fri Mar-Dec) and **Gil Armada** (www.bodegagilarmada.com; house tour & tasting €7; ☉1hr tour noon & 7pm Mon-Sat Jun-Sep, noon & 5.30pm Mon-Sat Oct-May). Visits to the latter include a house tour.

Igrexa de Santa Mariña Dozo CHURCH
(Rúa do Castro) Pay a visit to this ruined 15th-century church, which is now roofless but still has its four semicircular roof arches intact. It's surrounded by a well-kept cemetery with elaborate graves – quite spooky at dusk! Just beyond, **Monte de A Pastora** park provides expansive views over the Ría de Arousa.

Martín Códax WINERY
(☎986 52 60 40; www.martincodax.com; Rúa Burgáns 91, Vilariño; admission incl tasting €3; ☉11am-1pm & 5-7pm Mon-Fri) Galicia's best-known winery is only a short drive from Cambados: 45-minute tours are available hourly during visiting hours. For English, book three days ahead.

✦ Festivals & Events

Concerts, fireworks and exhibitions accompany the consumption of huge quantities of wine and tapas during the **Fiesta del Albariño**, on the first Sunday of August and the four preceding days.

🛏 Sleeping

Hotel O Lagar HOTEL €
(☎986 52 08 07; www.hotelolagar.com; Rúa Pontevedra 14; s €40, d €50-60; 🅿🤶) A good budget choice, Hotel O Lagar has 16 good-sized, sparkling clean rooms, all with bathtubs, and its own cafe. Try for rooms 107, 108, 207 or 208, which look out on a pretty little plaza and church.

Pazo A Capitana COUNTRY HOUSE €€
(☎986 52 05 13; www.pazoacapitana.com; Rúa Sabugueiro 46; s/d incl breakfast €70/90; ☉closed mid-Dec–end Jan; 🅿✳🤶) This 17th-century country house on the edge of town is a lovely sleeping option, with stately rooms, beautiful, expansive gardens and an on-site winery with four century-old stone presses.

Hotel Real Ribadomar BOUTIQUE HOTEL €€
(☎986 52 44 04; www.hotelrealribadomar.com; Rúa Real 8; r incl breakfast €80-125; ✳🤶) A charmingly renovated central townhouse with pretty, wallpapered rooms, fresh white linen on soft beds, and gleaming, up-to-date bathrooms.

🍴 Eating

Pedestrian-friendly Rúa Príncipe, Rúa Real and Praza de Fefiñáns have plenty of eateries that may look touristic but mostly offer decent food at decent prices.

Rincón del Tío Paco GALICIAN €
(Rúa San Gregorio 2; tapas & raciones €3-11; ☉9am-midnight) This welcoming bar at the entrance to Rúa Príncipe serves up quality grilled meats as well as straightforward but tasty seafood and fish.

★**Restaurante Ribadomar** GALICIAN €€
(www.ribadomar.es; Rúa Valle Inclán 17; mains €13-18; ☉1.30-4pm & 9-11.30pm, closed Sun-Thu evenings Oct-Jun) For something more upscale than taverns, you can get a great traditional Galician meal at family-run Restaurante Ribadomar, with dishes such as sole with scallops or *chuletón de ternera* (a giant beef chop), amid original paintings and sculptures.

A Casa de Miguel GALICIAN €€
(Rúa Real 14A; tapas & raciones €3.25-12, mains €9-18; ☉noon-midnight) Miguel's is celebrated for the generous and tasty free tapas it serves with drinks, but portions are equally generous when you order from the menu. For a filling snack, try a *tosta de pulpo y tetilla* (toasted baguette covered in octopus and melted cheese), or *zamburiñas* (bay scallops) in albariño.

ℹ Information

Tourist Office (☎986 52 07 86; www.cambados.es; Paseo da Calzada; ☉10am-2pm & 5-8pm, closed Sun afternoon & Mon Oct-May) Helpful office between the bus station and old town.

ℹ Getting There & Away

Several daily buses head to/from Santiago de Compostela, Pontevedra and O Grove. The bus station is on Avenida de Galicia, 300m south of the old town.

GALICIAN WINES

There's no better accompaniment to Galician food than Galician wines, which have a character all their own. Best known are the fruity whites from the albariño grape, which constitute over 90% of the wine produced in the Rías Baixas Denominación de Origen (DO), located near Galicia's southwestern coast and along the lower Río Miño. Albariño's surge in popularity in the last couple of decades has, to some palates, yielded some wines that are *too* sweet and fruity. A good traditional albariño should have the aroma of a green apple and a slightly sour taste.

Encouraged by albariño's success, vintners elsewhere in Galicia are innovating, expanding, and reviving native Galician grapes that almost disappeared in the 19th-century phylloxera plague – among them the white godello and the red brancellao and merenzao.

Galicia's other DOs:

Ribeiro – from the Ribadavia area in southern Galicia, Ribeiro produces some very good whites, mostly from the treixadura grape.

Ribeira Sacra – in the southeast, yielding rich reds from mencía grapes grown on the amazingly steep hillsides above the Río Sil.

Monterrei – in the warmest, driest part of southeast Galicia, bordering Portugal, Monterrei turns out both reds and whites: Crego e Monaguillo produces very drinkable mencía reds and fruity godello whites.

Valdeorras – this southeastern region bordering Castilla y León produces, among others, godello whites and mencía and brancellao reds.

O Grove

POP 7300

More than two dozen sandy beaches make this seaside town and the relatively unspoilt peninsula surrounding it a buzzing summer destination.

Sights & Activities

★ **Praia A Lanzada**   BEACH

(👪) Dune-backed Praia A Lanzada sweeps a spectacular 2.3km along the west side of the isthmus leading to O Grove. It's enticingly natural, but not exactly deserted, as the mammoth car parks attest.

Illa A Toxa   ISLAND

Approaching O Grove town, you could cross the bridge for a look around Illa A Toxa (Castilian: Isla La Toja), a manicured island known for its golf course, expensive holiday homes, upmarket hotels and the Capilla de las Conchas, a chapel completely plastered with scallop shells.

Illa de Sálvora   ISLAND

This interesting small island, part of the Islas Atlánticas national park, has a mainly rocky coast, a lighthouse, an abandoned village, and an old fish-salting-plant-cum-mansion.

Daily four-hour trips (adult/child €20/10) from O Grove from July to mid-September with Cruceros Rías Baixas (www.crucerosriasbaixas.com) or Cruceros do Ulla (☎986 73 18 18; www.crucerosdoulla.com) include a guided walk and a little beach time.

Acuario de O Grove   AQUARIUM

(www.acuariodeogrove.es; adult/senior & child €10/8; ⊙10.30am-8.30pm, earlier closing & closed Mon & Tue mid-Oct–mid-Jun; 👪) About 100 mostly Galician marine species, including several types of shark, are showcased in the aquarium at Punta Moreiras.

Ría Cruises   BOAT TOUR

(incl mussel tasting & drink adult/child €13/6; 👪) In fine weather from April to November, several boat companies depart from the *estación de catamaranes* (behind the bus station) for 75-minute *ría* cruises, chiefly to look at the *bateas* – platforms where shellfish are cultivated.

Sleeping & Eating

There are plenty of hotels for all budgets in town and elsewhere on the peninsula. O Grove is famous for its shellfish and in early or mid-October it stages the 10-day Festa do Marisco seafood festival.

Norat Marina Hotel & Spa HOTEL €€

(✆ 986 73 33 99; www.hotelesnorat.com; Rúa Peralto A 32; s €80-110, d €90-160; P ✳ 🛜 🛋) The four-star, family-run Norat Marina offers appealing, contemporary-style, soundproofed rooms and a very good, modern spa/gym. It shares the building with the older but attractively modernised three-star **Norat Hotel & Spa** (Avenida Luis Casáis 22; s €51-75, d €60-90; P ✳ 🛜 🛋). Also here is the popular restaurant and tapas and wine bar **El Rincón de Norat** (mains €15-30; ⊙ 10am-midnight).

Check the website for good-value packages, and big discounts outside the summer peak.

Beiramar SEAFOOD €€

(Avenida Beiramar 30; mains €15-22; ⊙ 1-4pm & 8-11.30pm Tue-Sat, 1-4pm Sun, closed Nov) Among the slew of eateries facing the seafront, the Beiramar is a superior option with its big white tablecloths and classy but contemporary feel. It specialises in quality fish and seafood but also does good Galician beef grills.

ⓘ Getting There & Away

The **bus station** (Avenida Beiramar) is by the port. Monbus runs at least nine buses daily to Pontevedra (€4.15, one hour) via Sanxenxo, and two or more to Santiago de Compostela (€7.30, two hours) via Cambados.

Pontevedra

POP 62,100

Back in the 16th century Pontevedra was Galicia's biggest city and an important port, where Columbus' flagship, the *Santa María*, was built. Today it's an inviting, small, riverside city that combines history, culture and style into a lively base for exploring the Rías Baixas. The interlocking lanes and plazas of the compact Old Town are abuzz with shops, markets, cafes and tapas bars.

⊙ Sights

More than a dozen plazas dot the mainly pedestrianised old quarter. **Praza da Leña** is a particularly quaint nook, partly colonnaded and with a *cruceiro* (stone crucifix; a traditional Galician art form) in the middle.

Museo de Pontevedra MUSEUM

(✆ 986 80 41 00; www.museo.depo.es; ⊙ 10am-9pm Tue-Sat, 11am-2pm Sun) FREE Pontevedra's eclectic museum is scattered over five city-centre buildings. If time is limited, head for the bright new **Sexto Edificio** (Rúa de Padre Amoedo) and the adjoining ★ **Edificio Sarmiento** (Rúa Sarmiento) in a renovated 18th-century Jesuit college.

The Sexto Edificio has three floors of Galician and Spanish art from the 14th to 20th centuries, though you won't find any really big names. The Edificio Sarmiento houses an absorbing collection ranging over Galician Sargadelos ceramics, modern art (including a few works by Picasso, Miró, Dalí and Tapiès), statues of prophets from the original facade of Santiago de Compostela cathedral, and prehistoric Galician gold jewellery, petroglyphs and carvings.

Displays in the **Edificio Castro Monteagudo** (Rúa da Pasantería) and adjoining **Edificio García Florez** (Rúa da Pasantería) run from Spanish Renaissance art to the captain's saloon of a 19th-century warship. The **Ruínas de San Domingos** (Gran Vía de Montero Ríos) harbour an intriguing assemblage of heraldic shields, sepulchres and other medieval carvings in a ruined 14th-century church.

Basílica de Santa María a Maior CHURCH

(Praza de Alonso de Fonseca; ⊙ 10am-1.30pm & 5-9pm, except during Mass) Pontevedra's most impressive church is a mainly Gothic affair with a whiff of plateresque and Portuguese Manueline influences. It was built by Pontevedra's sailors' guild. Busts of Christopher Columbus and that other great empire-builder Hernán Cortés flank the rosette window on the western facade.

Praza da Ferrería SQUARE

Praza da Ferrería has the best selection of cafes (as opposed to bars) in town. It's overlooked by the 14th-century **Igrexa de San Francisco**, said to have been founded by St Francis of Assisi when on pilgrimage to Santiago. Just off the plaza, you can't miss the distinctive curved facade of the **Santuario da Virxe Peregrina** (Praza da Peregrina), an almost circular 18th-century caprice with a distinctly Portuguese flavour.

⚘ Festivals & Events

The **Festas da Peregrina**, throughout the second week of August, feature a big funfair on the Alameda, street parades and nightly free concerts in the Old Town.

Pontevedra

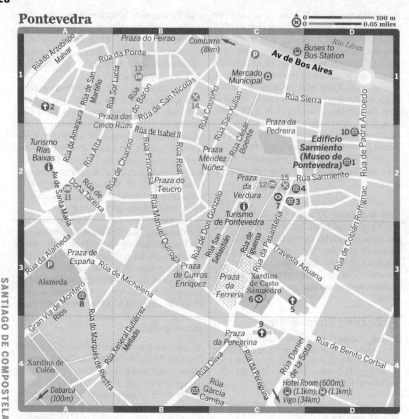

🛏 Sleeping

Casa Maruja PENSIÓN €

(☎986 85 49 01; www.facebook.com/pension.casa-maruja; Avenida de Santa María 12; s €30-35, d €40; 🛜) A clean, friendly budget option with several bright rooms looking over a quiet Old Town plaza.

Hotel Rúas HOTEL €

(☎986 84 64 16; www.hotelruas.net; Rúa de Figueroa 35; s/d €44/61; ❄@🛜) The rooms are attractive, with shiny wooden floors, unfussy furnishings and large bathrooms, and some have nice plaza views – excellent value for this absolutely central location. The cafe is one of the town's most popular breakfast spots.

Dabarca HOTEL €€

(☎986 86 97 23; www.hoteldabarca.com; Calle de los Palamios 2; apt s/d €102/107; P❄🛜🍴) Run

like a hotel but offering spacious apartments instead of standard rooms, this pleasant spot on the fringe of the Old Town is ideal for families. Apartments are fitted with a kitchenette, washing machine and beige, Ikea-inspired furniture. Check the website for big off-peak discounts.

Hotel Room HOTEL €€

(☎986 86 95 50; www.hotelroompontevedra.com; Rúa Filgueira Valverde 10; s/d €50/70; P❄🛜) Midway between the stations and the Old Town (walking distance from all), the Room's rooms have light wood tones, bathtubs and a clean, bright feel.

Parador Casa del Barón HISTORIC HOTEL €€€

(☎986 85 58 00; www.parador.es; Rúa do Barón 19; r €130-178; P❄🛜) This elegant refurbished 17th-century palace is equipped throughout with antique-style furniture and historical art, and has a lovely little garden.

Pontevedra

◎ **Top Sights**

  1 Edificio Sarmiento (Museo de
      Pontevedra).. D2

◎ **Sights**

  2 Basílica de Santa María a Maior............ A1
  3 Edificio Castro Monteagudo
      (Museo de Pontevedra)..................... C2
  4 Edificio García Florez (Museo de
      Pontevedra).. C2
  5 Igrexa de San Francisco......................... C3
  6 Praza da Ferrería C3
  7 Praza da Leña.. C2
  8 Ruínas de San Domingos (Museo
      de Pontevedra) A3

  9 Santuario da Virxe Peregrina................. C4
 10 Sexto Edificio (Museo de
      Pontevedra) D2

😴 **Sleeping**

 11 Casa Maruja.. A2
 12 Hotel Rúas... C2
 13 Parador Casa del Barón B1

❌ **Eating**

 14 Casa Verdún... B1
      Eirado da Leña............................... (see 7)
      La Casa de las 5 Puertas .... (see 11)
 15 Loaira Enoteca.. C2

Eating

Virtually all the Old Town's plazas, and streets like Rúas Real and Princesa, are lined with restaurants and bars doing good-value set lunches by day and tapas and *raciones* by evening.

Casa Verdún　　　　　　　TAPAS, RACIONES €€
(www.casaverdun.com; Rúa Real 46; raciones €8-19; ⊗7pm-midnight Mon-Sat) A superior tapas-and-*raciones* spot with an interior patio as well as a busy bar area. Multifarious tempting options range from monkfish-and-prawn brochette to inventive salads or entrecôte steak in Arzúa cheese.

Loaira Enoteca　　　　　　　　　GALICIAN €€
(Praza da Leña 2; raciones €8-17; ⊗noon-4pm & 7.30pm-midnight Mon-Sat, noon-4pm Sun) With tables out on the lovely little plaza and in the upstairs dining room, this is a fine spot for Galician specialities with a creative touch such as tempura of prawns, wild mushrooms and organic vegetables. Local lamb, fish and good Galician wines too.

La Casa de las 5 Puertas　　　　GALICIAN €€
(www.5puertas.com; Avenida de Santa María 8; mains €13-19; ⊗noon-4pm & 8pm-midnight Mon-Sat, noon-4pm Sun) The 5 Puertas serves up the best of Galician fare from *ría*-caught fish to steaks in mushroom sauce, along with homemade desserts and a big choice of Spanish wines, in three attractive dining areas.

★ **Eirado da Leña**　　　GALICIAN, FUSION €€€
(⊘986 86 02 25; www.eiradoeventos.com; Praza da Leña 3; mains €18-25; ⊗1.30-4pm & 9-11.30pm Wed-Sat, 1.30-4pm Mon & Tue) A deliciously creative culinary experience in an intimate little stone-walled restaurant, tastefully set with white linen and fresh flowers. The €24 set menu, available at lunchtime and in the evening, comprises four beautifully presented courses, served with a smile and some curious little surprises!

🍷 Drinking & Nightlife

It's hard to find a bar-less street in the Old Town. For laid-back drinks and people-watching, you have several atmospheric squares to choose from, like Prazas da Verdura, do Teucro or da Leña, or the tapas bars along Rúa Real. From there you can head to the pocket of bars on Rúa do Barón and then, for some heftier *marcha* (action), down the street to the thumping music bars of Rúa de Charino.

ℹ Information

Turismo de Pontevedra (⊘986 09 08 90; www.visit-pontevedra.com; Praza da Verdura; ⊗9.30am-2pm & 4.30-8.30pm Mon-Sat, 10am-2pm Sun) The helpful city tourist office has a convenient central location.

Turismo Rías Baixas (⊘886 21 17 10; www.riasbaixas.depo.es; Praza de Santa María; ⊗9am-9pm Mon-Fri, 10am-2.30pm & 4.30-8pm Sat & Sun) Information on all of Pontevedra province.

ℹ Getting There & Around

The **bus station** (⊘986 85 24 08; www.autobusespontevedra.com; Rúa da Estación) is about 1.5km southeast of the Old Town. Castromil-Monbus goes at least 17 times daily to Vigo (€2.50, 30 minutes), 10 times to Santiago (€5.85, one hour) and five times to Ourense (€11, two hours). Buses also run to Sanxenxo, O Grove, Cambados, Tui and Lugo.

WORTH A TRIP

VISITING ILLA DE ONS

In summer you can hop on a boat to vehicle-free Illa de Ons, part of the Islas Atlánticas national park. The island is 5.6km long with sandy beaches, cliffs, ruins, walking trails and rich bird life. You can stay in simple accommodation (reservations advised) at Casa Acuña (☑986 68 76 99; www.isladeons.net; s €40, d €60-75, apt for 4/6 €150/180; ☺May-Sep), whose restaurant serves prize-winning *pulpo á feira,* or camp for free at the camping area (reserve through www.iatlanticas.es).

Weather permitting, Naviera Mar de Ons (www.mardeons.com) and Cruceros Rías Baixas (www.crucerosriasbaixas.com) sail to Ons (45 minutes) several times daily from Sanxenxo and nearby Portonovo, from July to mid-September (round-trip adult/child €14/7).

Pontevedra's **train station** (☑986 85 13 13), across the street from the bus station, has almost hourly services to Santiago de Compostela, A Coruña and Vigo.

City buses (€1.40) run between the bus station (platform 14) and Avenida de Bos Aires, on the north edge of the Old Town, every half-hour.

Ría de Pontevedra

Combarro

POP 1350

Near Pontevedra on the *ría's* north shore, Combarro's postcard-perfect old quarter unfurls around a tidy bay and looks like it was plucked straight out of the Middle Ages. With a jumble of seaside *hórreos* and crooked lanes (some of them hewn directly out of the rock bed) dotted with *cruceiros,* and a smattering of waterside restaurants, this is some people's favourite stop in the Rías Baixas. It can get extremely busy in high summer. The main activity here is eating: a good place to savour excellent fish, rice and meat dishes is Taberna O Peirao (Rúa do Mar 6; mains €14-23; ☺noon-10pm or later), which features a waterside terrace among the *hórreos.*

Sanxenxo

POP 2330

Sanxenxo (Castilian: Sangenjo) has been dubbed the 'Marbella of Galicia' and it does have a thing or two in common with Spain's Mediterranean resorts in the summer season: a busy leisure port, a long buzzing waterfront, and streets packed with eateries and tourist accommodation. The tourism here, however, is almost exclusively Spanish. Praia de Silgar is a fine, sandy and busy beach.

Stylish and comfortable Hotel Rotilio (☑986 72 02 00; www.hotelrotilio.com; Avenida do Porto 7; s €60-75, d €100-172; ☺closed mid-Oct–mid-Mar; ﹡☎), run by the third generation of the same family, overlooks both Praia de Silgar and the marina. The 39 all-sea-view rooms are bright and pretty, with unusual silk paintings by local fine-arts students. There's a five-night minimum stay from mid-July to end-August. Its restaurant, La Taberna de Rotilio (mains €15-27; ☺2-4pm & 9-11.30pm Tue-Sat, 2-4pm Sun, closed mid-Oct–mid-Mar), serves up terrific Galician seafood and meat with a creative touch, and also has an innovative downstairs *'gastroteca',* where you can enjoy tasty smaller creations like spider-crab cannelloni with good albariño wine.

Buses between Pontevedra and O Grove (over 20 a day in summer) stop in Sanxenxo.

South Shore

Zip past the sprawl surrounding Marín to discover the quiet appeal of the *ría's* southern shore, where you can stop at beaches like wide Praia de Lapamán or in maritime towns like Bueu, with its busy waterfront. Venture past the fishing hamlet of Beluso towards Cabo de Udra, where the jagged shoreline has a backdrop of the Illa de Ons and there are several secluded (though not secret) beaches, such as clear-watered Praia Mourisca.

Ría de Vigo

The far end of the *ría's* north shore is one of the least populated and most scenic parts of the Rías Baixas. The peaceful village of Hío draws visitors for a look at Galicia's most famous cruceiro, a small but elaborate 19th-century cross standing outside the

San Andrés de Hío church. Sculpted from a single block of stone, its delicate carvings narrate key passages of Christian teaching, from Adam and Eve to the taking down of Christ from the cross. Several sandy beaches are signposted in the area, including 800m-long **Praia Areabrava**, 3km north of Hío.

From Hío continue through the hamlet of Donón to windswept **Cabo de Home**, a rocky cape with walking trails, three lighthouses and great views of the Illas Cíes. The partly excavated Iron Age *castro* **Berobriga** sits atop panoramic Monte Facho nearby. Between Hío and Donón a 1.6km side road leads down to sandy, 1.3km-long **Praia da Barra**, widely agreed to be Galicia's most beautiful nudist beach.

🛏 Sleeping & Eating

A Casa de Aldán   RURAL HOTEL €€
(☎986 32 87 32; www.apartamentosardora.com; Avenida José Graña 20, Aldán; s €71-88, d €110-143, incl breakfast; ☒) This clever, bright conversion of a 19th-century fish-salting plant overlooks the fishing harbour in Aldán. Thick stone walls combine with contemporary cedar furnishings and good, modern bathrooms in 13 sizeable rooms, and there's a lovely walled garden.

The owners also run the attractive waterside **O Conde Aldán** (mains €10-14; ⊙1-4pm & 8.30-11pm) a few steps away, serving market-fresh fish daily.

Hotel Doade   HOTEL €€
(☎986 32 83 02; www.hoteldoade.com; Bajada Praia de Arneles 1, Hío; s €60, d €70-90, incl breakfast; ⊙closed Nov; ☒☒☒) Friendly, sparkling clean Doade has eight snug, spacious rooms with fresh, white linen, and a good **restaurant** (mains €9-31; ⊙1-4.30pm & 8.30-11.30pm Tue-Sun, closed Nov) focusing on *ría*-fresh seafood, with baked fish the speciality.

Vigo

POP 207,000

Depending on where you point your lens, Vigo is a historic and cultured city or a gritty industrial port. Home to Europe's largest fishing fleet, this is an axis of commerce in northern Spain. Yet its centre is walkable, compact and full of intriguing nooks, and it's the main gateway to the beautiful Illas Cíes.

The Casco Vello (Old Town) climbs uphill from the cruise-ship port; the heart of the modern city spreads east from here, with Praza de Compostela a welcome green space in its midst.

◉ Sights

Casco Vello   OLD TOWN
At the heart of the Old Town's jumbled lanes is elegant **Praza da Constitución**, a perfect spot for a drink. Head down **Rúa dos Cesteiros**, with its quaint wicker shops, and you'll come upon the **Igrexa de Santa María**, built in 1816 – long after its Romanesque predecessor had been burnt down by Sir Francis Drake.

Parque do Castro   PARK
Head directly south (and uphill) from the Old Town for a wander in this verdant park with nearly 100 camellia trees. You can inspect the partly reconstructed **Castro de Vigo** (⊙11am-1pm & 5-7pm Tue-Sat) FREE dating back to the 3rd century BC, and poke around the hilltop **Castelo do Castro**, which formed part of Vigo's defences built under Felipe IV.

Museo de Arte Contemporánea de Vigo   MUSEUM
(Marco; www.marcovigo.com; Rúa do Príncipe 54; ⊙11am-2.30pm & 5-9pm Tue-Sat, 11am-2.30pm Sun) FREE Vigo is something of a modern art centre, with several museums and galleries to prove it. The Contemporary Art Museum is the number-one venue for exhibitions ranging from painting and sculpture to fashion and design.

Centro de Visitantes Illas Atlánticas   INTERPRETATION CENTRE
(Rúa da Palma 4; ⊙10am-2pm & 4.30-7.30pm Tue-Sat, 11am-2pm Sun) FREE An attractive audiovisual display and photos and information on the nature and history of the Illas Cíes and the Ons, Sálvora and Cortegada archipelagos further north, which together comprise the Parque Nacional de las Islas Atlánticas de Galicia (p533).

🛏 Sleeping

Hotel Compostela   HOTEL €
(☎986 22 82 27; www.hcompostela.com; Rúa García Olloqui 5; s/d €48/60; ☒☒) Solidly comfy, spotlessly clean and reasonably spacious rooms make this efficient hotel near Praza de Compostela a sound choice. The cafe is handy for breakfast.

SANTIAGO DE COMPOSTELA & GALICIA VIGO

Hotel Náutico HOTEL €

(☑986 12 24 40; www.hotelnautico.net; Rúa de Luis Taboada 28; s/d incl breakfast €30/45; 🛜) A friendly budget hotel near Praza de Compostela, with clean, crisp style and a pleasant nautical look. Rooms are small but cosy.

★**Nagari** LUXURY HOTEL €€

(☑986 21 11 11; www.granhotelnagari.com; Praza de Compostela 21; s/d incl breakfast from €109/121; P ❄ 🛜 ⊠) Luxurious Nagari has a welcome personal feel to its contemporary design and service. Rooms boast giant-headed showers, remote-controlled colour-changing lighting, coffee-makers and big-screen smart TVs, and there's a rooftop heated pool and terrace with fabulous views.

Hotel América HOTEL €€

(☑986 43 89 22; www.hoteles-silken.com; Rúa de Pablo Morillo 6; s €79-87, d €85-95, incl breakfast; P ❄ @ 🛜) The América gets a big thumbs-up for its well-equipped, spacious rooms with tasteful modern art and elegantly muted colour schemes, its friendly, efficient staff and its quiet side-street location near the waterfront. Nearly all the 45 rooms are exterior, and the breakfast is a good buffet-style affair, served on the roof terrace in summer.

🍴 Eating

For tapas bars and informal cafes, head to the narrow lanes of the Old Town, especially around Praza da Constitución.

★**Rúa Pescadería** SEAFOOD €

Short Rúa Pescadería, in the lower part of the Old Town, is jammed with people tucking into fresh seafood. From about 9.30am until 3.30pm you can buy oysters for €12 to €15 per dozen from the *ostreras* (shuckers) here, and sit down to eat them with a drink at one of the restaurants. Oysters and albariño wine are Vigo's traditional Sunday-morning hangover cure.

★**Suppo** GALICIAN, FUSION €€

(www.suppobar.com; Praza de Compostela 29; mains €16-19; ⊙1.15-4pm & 8.30-11.45pm) Excellent fusion fare amid contemporary black-white-and-grey decor with picture windows overlooking the leafy park. The speciality is oven-baked market-fresh whole fish for two, which the staff will debone for you immediately before serving. There's a huge and impressive list of Spanish wines, from €11 a bottle, and the ground-floor lounge-bar and terrace are lively spots for evening tapas and *raciones*.

Taverna da Curuxa CONTEMPORARY GALICIAN €€

(☑986 43 88 57; Rúa dos Cesteiros 7; menú €9, mains €10-12; ⊙12.30-4pm & 8.30pm-midnight Wed-Mon, closed approx 10-31 Jan) This atmospheric stone tavern just off Praza da Constitución mixes the traditional and contemporary in decor and menu. Try Galician favourites like *arroces* (rice dishes) and fish *cazolas* (casseroles), or opt for a creative salad or seafood tapas. The lunch menu (Monday and Wednesday to Friday) is a terrific deal. Worth booking for dinner.

Estrella Galicia Vigo GALICIAN €€

(Praza de Compostela 17; mains €7-20; ⊙noon-midnight, kitchen closed 4-8pm Mon-Thu) This modern beer hall run by the brewers of Galicia's excellent Estrella beer is good both for *cerveza de bodega* (non-pasteurised beer) and for tapas or more substantial meals such as the excellent *codillo braseado* (braised pork knuckles).

🍷 Drinking & Entertainment

Vigo's nightlife is hopping. Start off at one of several enticing Old Town bars around Praza da Constitución such as rock-music den **Bar Princesa** (Praza da Constitución; ⊙9am-midnight Mon-Thu, 9am-2am Fri, 11am-2am Sat) or wine bar **Buqué Enoteca** (Rúa da Palma 9; ⊙11am-3pm & 6.30-10.30pm Tue-Sat, 11am-3pm Sun). The outdoor tables of bars on Praza de Compostela and Rúa de Montero Ríos (opposite the waterfront) are also enticing in nice weather. From around 10pm or 11pm the action moves a little further east, to the fashionable music bars along Rúa de Areal such as US-themed **20th Century Rock** (Rúa de Areal 18; ⊙7pm-2am Sun-Thu, 7pm-3.30am Fri & Sat) and the pubs along Rúa de Rosalía de Castro like **Van Gogh Café** (Rúa de Rosalía de Castro 28; ⊙9am-1am Sun-Tue, 9am-4am Thu-Sat).

The more alternative *zona de marcha* (party area), after about midnight, is the Churruca district about 1km southeast of the Old Town. Reggae, rock, indie and electronic music abounds and here you'll find two of northern Spain's top live-band venues: **La Iguana Club** (www.facebook.com/laiguanaclub; Rúa da Churruca 14; ⊙10.30pm-4.30am Thu-Sat) and **La Fábrica de Chocolate Club** (www.fabricadechocolateclub.com; Rúa de Rogelio Abalde 22; ⊙10.30pm-4.30am Thu-Sat), both hosting two or three live bands or guest DJs weekly.

ILLAS CÍES

The Illas Cíes, three spectacular islands that form a beautiful bird sanctuary and are home to some of Galicia's most privileged beaches, are a 45-minute, 14km ferry ride from Vigo. This small archipelago forms a 6km breakwater that protects the Ría de Vigo from the Atlantic's fury and is the main attraction of the **Parque Nacional de las Islas Atlánticas de Galicia** (Atlantic Islands of Galicia National Park; www.iatlanticas.es) 🍃 .

This is an ideal spot for lolling on pristine sandy beaches such as the 1km-long, lagoon-backed crescent of **Praia das Rodas** (🏖), on the sandy isthmus joining Illa de Monteagudo and Illa do Faro, or nudist **Praia das Figueiras**. Walking trails skirt the shores and climb up to spectacular high lookouts, like the **Ruta Monte Faro**.

Public boats to the Cíes (round-trip adult/child €19/6) normally only sail during Semana Santa (Holy Week), on weekends and holidays in May, daily from June to late September, and on the first two weekends of October. They are operated, weather permitting, by three companies. **Naviera Mar de Ons** (📞 986 22 52 72; www.mardeons.com) runs at least five daily trips from Vigo's Estación Marítima de Ría, six from Cangas, and four from Baiona; **Nabia Naviera** (www.piratasdenabia.com) does four or five trips a day from both Vigo and Cangas; and **Cruceros Rías Baixas** (www.crucerosriasbaixas.com) runs up to three daily trips from Vigo.

To stay overnight you must camp at **Camping Islas Cíes** (📞 986 68 76 30; www.campingislascies.com; sites per person €10, 2-person tent rental per night €46 with 2-night minimum), and from June to September you must book this in advance, either online or at the **camping office** (📞 986 43 83 58; ⏱ 8.30am-1.30pm & 3.30-7.30pm) in Vigo's Estación Marítima de Ría. The camping ground has a restaurant and supermarket, and a capacity of about 800 people – often filled in August.

ℹ Information

Centro de Interpretación de Vigo y su Ría (📞 986 22 47 57; www.turismodevigo.org; Estación Marítima de Ría, Rúa Cánovas del Castillo 3; ⏱ 10am-5pm Apr-Oct, 8am-3pm Tue-Sat Nov-Mar) Helpful tourist office, in the Illas Cíes ferry terminal.

ℹ Getting There & Away

AIR

Vigo's Peinador airport, 9km east of the city centre, has direct flights to/from Paris (Air France), Madrid (Iberia and Air Europa), Barcelona (Vueling) and Bilbao (Air Nostrum).

BUS

The **bus station** (📞 986 37 34 11; Avenida de Madrid 57) is 2km southeast of the Old Town. Castromil-Monbus makes several trips daily to all major Galician cities, including Pontevedra (€2.80, 30 minutes), Santiago de Compostela (€8, 1½ hours) and Ourense (€11.20, 1½ hours), and the coastal resorts. **Autna** (www.autna.com) runs at least twice daily to/from Porto, Portugal (€12, 2½ hours), with connections there for Lisbon.

TRAIN

All trains use Vigo-Guixar station, 1km east of the Old Town, while the main station on Praza da Estación, 1km southeast of the Old Town, is un-

der reconstruction (probably till 2015 or 2016). Trains run at least 13 times daily to Pontevedra (€3.15 to €3.60, 30 minutes), Santiago de Compostela (€9.10 to €11, 1½ hours) and Ourense (€12 to €24, 1½ to three hours).

ℹ Getting Around

Vitrasa (📞 986 29 16 00; www.vitrasa.es) runs city buses (€1.32 per ride). Bus C9A runs between the central Rúa Policarpo Sanz and the airport; the bus station is linked to the centre by buses C2 (to/from Porta do Sol) and C4C, 12A and 12B (to/from Rúa Policarpo Sanz).

THE SOUTHWEST

Galicia's southwest corner is home to three towns that all make enjoyable stops on a circuit of the region or a journey to or from Portugal – the historic port/resort Baiona, the pretty fishing town A Guarda, and riverside Tui.

Baiona

POP 2900

Baiona (Castilian: Bayona) is a popular resort with its own little place in history: the shining moment came on 1 March 1493, when one of Columbus' small fleet, the *Pinta,* stopped in for supplies, bearing the remarkable news that the explorer had made it to the (West) Indies. Today you can visit a replica of the Pinta (admission €2; ⊙10am-8pm; ⓘ) in Baiona's harbour.

You can't miss the pine-covered promontory Monte Boi, dominated by the Fortaleza de Monterreal (pedestrian/car €1/5; ⊙10am-10pm). The fortress, erected between the 11th and 17th centuries, is protected by a 3km circle of walls, and an enjoyable 40-minute walking trail loops round the promontory's rocky shoreline, which is broken up by a few small beaches. Also within the precinct today is a *parador* – have a drink on its cafe terrace, with fabulous views across the bay.

A tangle of inviting lanes, with a handful of 16th- and 17th-century houses and chapels, makes up Baiona's casco histórico (historic centre), behind the harbourfront road, Rúa Elduayen. Four kilometres east of town is the magnificent sweep of Praia América at Nigrán.

Sleeping & Eating

Many of Baiona's hotels face the harbourfront road, and the cobbled lanes of the old centre are full of restaurants, tapas bars and watering holes.

Hotel Cais HOTEL €€
(☏986 35 56 43; hotelr.cais@gmail.com; Rúa Alférez Barreiro 3; s €40-65, d €50-75; 🛜) Little Cais overlooks the harbour but rooms at the side or back are likely to be quieter than front ones. All have bright white bedding and paintwork. There's a cafe downstairs.

Parador de Baiona LUXURY HOTEL €€€
(☏986 35 50 00; www.parador.es; s €160-308, d €175-328, incl breakfast; 🅿❄🛜🏊) This privileged *parador,* inside Monte Boi's fortress enclosure, is suitably grandiose. Suits of armour stand in the lobby, while the best rooms boast canopied beds and wonderful views. Check the website for discounts.

Pazo de Mendoza GALICIAN €€
(Rúa Elduayen 1; mains €10-24; ⊙1.30-4pm & 8.30-11pm, closed Sun evening) The stone-walled dining room here is a cut above most other harbour-facing eateries, with efficient service and big windows. Maritime fare like the grilled sea bass with vegies is a solid choice, but you could equally go for products of inland Galicia like wild boar with apple sauce.

ⓘ Information

Tourist Office (☏986 68 70 67; www.baiona.org; Paseo da Ribeira; ⊙10am-2pm & 4-7pm) On the approach to the Monte Boi promontory.

ⓘ Getting There & Away

ATSA buses run to and from Vigo (€2.55) every 30 or 60 minutes till 9pm. Just a couple a day go south to A Guarda. Catch buses at stops on the harbourfront road, Rúa Elduayen.

A Guarda

POP 6300

A fishing port just north of where the Río Miño spills into the Atlantic, A Guarda (Castilian: La Guardia) has a pretty harbour and good seafood restaurants, but its unique draw is beautiful Monte de Santa Trega (adult/child in vehicle Tue-Sun Feb-Dec €1/0.50, other times free), whose summit is a 4km drive or 2km uphill walk (the PRG122) from town. On the way up, poke around the partly restored Iron Age Castro de Santa Trega. At the top, you'll find a 16th-century chapel, an interesting small archaeological museum (⊙10am-8pm Tue-Sun) FREE on *castro* culture, a couple of cafes and souvenir stalls – and majestic panoramas up the Miño, across to Portugal and out over the Atlantic. It's also nice to take the 3km walking path south from A Guarda's harbour along the coast to the heads of the Miño.

Sleeping & Eating

A real treat, Hotel Convento de San Benito (☏986 61 11 66; www.hotelsanbenito.es; Praza de San Bieito; s €55-58, d €65-96; ⊙closed Jan; 🅿❄🛜) is housed in a 16th-century convent down by the harbour. Its 33 elegant rooms are romantic and individually decorated, with period furniture and plenty of exposed stone walls.

A Guarda is famed for its *arroz con bogavante* (rice with European lobster). A dozen seafood eateries line up facing the harbour. The relatively upscale Bitadorna (☏986 61 19 70; www.bitadorna.com; Rúa do Porto 30; mains €18-26, menú for 2 €55-78; ⊙11am-4.30pm & 7.30-11.30pm, closed Sun-Tue evenings Sep-Jun) offers both traditional and creative treatments of whatever comes in fresh from the local fishing boats. A good plan is to go for one of its daily menús of up to five courses including wine.

ℹ Getting There & Away

ATSA buses run to/from Vigo (€5.80, 80 minutes) approximately half-hourly until 7pm (fewer on weekends). Most go via Tui, but a few go via Baiona. A **ferry** (🕿 986 61 15 26; car & driver €3, passenger €1; ⊙ about hourly 9.30am-1.30pm & 3.30-7.30pm Tue-Sun, 1st sailing 11.30am Sat & Sun, daily to 9.15pm late Jul-Aug) crosses the Miño from Camposancos, 2km south of A Guarda, to Caminha, Portugal. Buses stop on the main street running through the town centre, Avenida de Galicia.

Tui

POP 6000

Sitting above the broad Río Miño 25m inland, the border town of Tui (Castilian: Tuy) draws Portuguese and Spanish day trippers with its lively bar scene, tightly packed medieval centre and magnificent cathedral. Just across the Gustave Eiffel–designed bridge is Portugal's equally appealing Valença.

◉ Sights

The highlight of the Old Town is the fortress-like Catedral de Santa Maria (adult/child €3/ free; ⊙ 10.30am-2pm & 4-9pm May-Oct, 10.30am-1pm & 4-7pm Nov-Apr), which reigns over Praza de San Fernando. Begun in the 12th century, it reflects a stoic Romanesque style in most of its construction, although the ornate main portal is reckoned the earliest work of Gothic sculpture on the Iberian Peninsula. You can visit the main nave and chapels for free, but it's well worth the ticket price to see the lovely Gothic cloister, the 15th-century tower and the gardens with views over the river. Rooftop tours in Spanish (€6) are available from May to November.

⌂ Sleeping & Eating

On Friday to Sunday nights, Entrefornos and other quaint cobbled streets in the Old Town are the scene of some major partying.

O Novo Cabalo Furado   HOSTAL €
(🕿 986 60 44 45; www.cabalofurado.com; Rúa Seijas 3; s/d/apt €40/60/80; 🛜) The rooms and apartments at this superior Old Town *hostal* are simple but inviting, with all-wood furnishings and sparkling bathrooms.

Hotel A Torre do Xudeu   HISTORIC HOTEL €€
(🕿 986 60 35 35; www.atorredoxudeu.es; Rúa Tide 3; r incl breakfast €59-75; 🅿🛜) A lovely 1746 mansion with thick stone walls and a pretty garden, the atmospheric 'Jew's Tower' has

just seven beautifully looked-after rooms in a fairly formal style, with large bathrooms. Several rooms look across the Miño to Portugal.

O Novo Cabalo Furado   GALICIAN €€
(Praza do Concello; mains €9-21, tapas €6.50-9; ⊙ 1-3.30pm & 8.30-11pm Tue-Sat, 1-3.30pm Sun & Mon, closed Sun Jul-Sep) A couple of doors from the cathedral, this restaurant is very strong on fish, shellfish and heaping plates of lamb chops – but also tapas delicacies like quail eggs with *chistorra* sausage.

★ El Silabario   CONTEMPORARY GALICIAN €€€
(www.restaurantesilabario.com; Rúa Colón 11; mains €23-36, menú €29-75; ⊙ 1.30-4pm & 9-11.30pm Tue-Sat, 1.30-4pm Sun) Silabario converts market-fresh ingredients into delicious and original flavour combinations – the likes of spit-roast venison with a mushroom carpaccio and pesto, or spider crab with lightly cooked egg. An enormous wine list and picture windows looking across to Portugal enhance the experience. You can sample Silabario creativity on a budget at the adjoining gastrobar La Pizarra del Silabario (mains €8-17, lunch menú Mon-Fri €9-14; ⊙ 1.30-4pm & 8.30-11pm Mon-Fri, 9-11.30pm Sat).

ℹ Getting There & Away

ATSA buses to both Vigo and A Guarda (both €3.70, 40 minutes, approximately half-hourly until 7.30pm, fewer on weekends) stop on Paseo de Calvo Sotelo, in front of Hostal Generosa.

THE EAST

Although often overshadowed by Galicia's glorious coastline and the better-known attractions of Santiago de Compostela, eastern Galicia is a treasure trove of enticing provincial cities, lovely landscapes and old-fashioned rural enclaves – perfect territory for travellers who like digging out their own gems.

Ourense

POP 100,500

Galicia's third-largest city has a spruced-up labyrinth of a historic quarter, a lively tapas scene and tempting thermal baths. An oddly beguiling place, Ourense (Castilian: Orense) first came into its own as a trading centre in the 11th century. The broad Río Miño runs east–west across the city, crossed by several bridges, including the medieval Ponte Vella. The central area, including the compact Old Town, rises south of the river.

Sights

Old Town   OLD TOWN

The Old Town unfolds around the 12th-century Catedral de San Martiño (Rúa de Juan de Austria; ☺11.30am-1.30pm & 4-7.30pm Mon-Sat, 4.30-7.30pm Sun), whose artistic highlight is the gilded Santo Cristo chapel, inside the northern entrance. At the west end of the dark interior is the Pórtico do Paraíso, a less inspired Gothic copy of Santiago de Compostela's Pórtico de la Gloria.

Around the cathedral is a maze of narrow streets and small plazas that are a pleasure to wander. The largest square is sloping Praza Maior, rimmed by cafes and with the Casa do Concello (City Hall) at its foot.

The capitals of the 63 arches of the lovely 14th-century Claustro de San Francisco (Rúa Emilia Pardo Bazán; ☺11.30am-1.30pm & 6.30-9.30pm Tue-Sat, 11.30am-1.30pm Sun, afternoons 5-8pm approx mid-Oct–May) FREE are carved with a fascinating collection of people, animals, imaginary creatures and Galician plants – well worth a visit, and the attendant may give you a free tour. Next door is a small but good exhibition of sculptures (Escolma Escultura; ☺9am-10pm Tue-Sat, 9.30am-3pm Sun) FREE from Ourense's temporarily closed (since 2002!) archaeological museum.

Sleeping

Hotel Irixo   HOTEL €

(☑988 25 46 20; www.hotelirixo.es; Rúa dos Irmans Villar 15; s/d €35/50; 🛜) On a small Old Town square, the Irixo provides neat, clean, recently renovated rooms, though only a few look out on the street. Singles can be tight but have ample bathrooms.

Hotel Cardenal Quevedo   HOTEL €€

(☑988 37 55 23; www.carrishoteles.com; Rúa Cardenal Quevedo 28; r €69-79; 🅿✳@🛜) Aimed at both leisure and business travellers, the Cardenal Quevedo offers bright and pleasing rooms with contemporary lines, and professional service. It's a 600m walk north from the heart of the Old Town.

Eating

Ir de tapeo ('going for tapas') is a way of life in Ourense, and central streets like Fornos, Paz, Lepanto, Viriato, San Miguel and Praza do Ferro brim with taverns where having to push and shove your way to the bar is a sign of quality. Tapas start at €1 and are nearly always washed down with a glass of local wine.

★ Mesón Porta da Aira   TAPAS, RACIONES €

(Rúa dos Fornos 2; tapas €2-16, raciones & dishes €5-25; ☺1-4pm & 8pm-midnight Tue-Sat, 1-4pm Sun, closed 2nd half Sep) This narrow bar has locals flocking in for its generous platters of *huevos rotos:* broken fried eggs over a bed of thinly sliced potatoes, to which you can add various sausages and meats. It offers an impressive range of wines too.

A Taberna   GALICIAN €€

(Rúa Julio Prieto 32; mains €13-21; ☺1-4pm & 9pm-midnight Mon-Sat, closed last 3 weeks Aug & Mon Sep-Jun) Reminiscent of a countryside inn with its wood beams and shelves of decorative crockery, A Taberna serves up first-class traditional Galician seafood and meat dishes with a few tasty twists such as its grilled scallops with sea-urchin caviar. It's 500m south of the cathedral.

Drinking & Entertainment

Ourense is packed with intimate pubs and tapas bars that easily make the transition into night-time. Stroll the streets around the cathedral for a host of options.

Café Latino   LIVE MUSIC

(Praza Eufemia 7; ☺7.30am-3am) Classy Café Latino has a fabulous corner stage that hosts a jazz festival in May and occasional jazz gigs through the year. It's a good breakfast spot too.

Information

Oficina Municipal de Turismo (☑988 36 60 64; www.ourense.travel; Calle Isabel La Católica 2; ☺9am-2pm & 4-8pm Mon-Fri, 11am-2pm Sat & Sun) A very helpful place underneath the Xardinillos Padre Feijóo park, just off pedestrianised Rúa do Paseo.

Getting There & Away

From Ourense's **bus station** (☑988 21 60 27; Carretera de Vigo 1), 2km northwest of the city centre, Monbus runs to Santiago (€9, two hours, five or more daily), Vigo (€11, 1½ hours, six or more daily) and Lugo (€8, 1¾ hours, two or more daily). **Avanza** (www.avanzabus.com) journeys to Madrid (€36 to €49, six to seven hours, five or more daily).

TAKING A DIP IN OURENSE'S THERMAL POOLS

Ourense's original raison d'être was its hot springs. As Burgas springs (Rúa As Burgas), a short walk southwest of Praza Maior, gush out 67°C waters reputedly with therapeutic properties and have been used since Roman times. People still fill containers with steaming water from spouts at the foot of the plaza here.

The city's various thermal pools, attractively modernised a few years ago, enable everyone to take a reviving and enjoyable dip in the waters, even in the depths of winter. Estación Termal das Burgas (Rúa As Burgas; ⊙10am-1pm & 5-9pm Tue-Sun) FREE is a nice enough spot right in the city centre, with indoor changing rooms, but more fun are the hot pools along a nicely landscaped 4km stretch of the north bank of the Miño. Here are four sets of open-air pools (termalismo.ourense.es; ⊙9am-9pm) FREE and two privately run sets of partly indoor pools. Closest to the centre are the A Chavasqueira open pools, on the riverbank, and the Japanese-style Termas Chavasqueira (www. termaschavasqueira.com; admission €4; ⊙9am-11.30pm or later Tue-Sun), with four hot pools and one cold one, plus two saunas and a cafe. You can walk to these from the Old Town in 20 to 30 minutes.

The other pools, of which open-air Muiño da Vega is the most enticing, are a further 3km to 3.5km west along the riverside path – most easily reached by the Tren das Termas (tickets €0.85; ⊙hourly 10am-1pm & 4-8pm, reduced frequency approx Oct-May), a minitrain from Praza Maior that goes to all the pools.

Take swimming gear, a towel and flip-flops (thongs) to any of the pools, and remember that their waters are hot and mineral-laden, so don't stay in them longer than about 10 minutes without a break.

The **train station** (Rúa de Eulogio Gómez Franqueira) is 500m north of the Río Miño. Renfe runs to Santiago (€9.80 to €20, 40 minutes to 1¾ hours, nine or more daily), Vigo (€12 to €24, 1½ to three hours, 14 or more daily), León (€25 to €49, four to five hours, four daily) and elsewhere.

🛈 Getting Around

Local buses 1, 3 and 6A (€0.85) run between the train station and the central Parque de San Lázaro. Buses 6A, 6B and 12 connect the bus station with Parque de San Lázaro.

Ribadavia & Around

POP (RIBADAVIA) 3200

The headquarters of the Ribeiro DO, which produces some of Galicia's best white wines, Ribadavia sits on the Río Avia in a verdant valley. Its little historic centre is an enticing maze of narrow streets lined with heavy stone arcades and broken up by diminutive plazas; within this in medieval times was Galicia's largest Jewish quarter, centred on Rúa Merelles Caulla.

🔘 Sights & Activities

Some 25 wineries in the area are open for visits. Most require a phone call in advance: Ribadavia's tourist office can help arrange visits. For further information on

the Ribeiro wine area, check out www. rutadelvinoribeiro.com.

Castelo do Sarmento   CASTLE
(Rúa Progreso; admission €2; ⊙9.30am-2.30pm & 4-8pm, closed Sun afternoon) The large, chiefly 15th-century castle of the Counts of Ribadavia is one of Galicia's biggest medieval castles. Tickets are sold at the tourist office.

Centro de Información
Xudía de Galicia   MUSEUM
(Praza Maior 7; admission €2; ⊙9am-2.30pm & 4-8pm, closed Sun afternoon) Above the tourist office on the lovely main square, this centre has exhibits, in Galician, on the Jews of Galicia since their expulsion from Spain in 1492.

Bodega Castro Rei   WINERY TOUR
(☑615 323221, 988 47 09 00; www.bodegacastrorei. com; 1hr tour €2; ⊙tours 12.30pm Thu-Sun Easter-early Dec, 8pm Thu-Sun Jul & Aug, 12.30pm Fri & Sun early Dec-Easter) Castro Rei offers visits to its pretty, walled vineyard, just a 500m walk from the town centre, without prior booking. Meet at Ribeiro e Xamón shop on Praza Maior a few minutes before the start time.

Paseo Fluvial   WALKING
Relax with a stroll along this 4km riverside path by the Ríos Avia and Miño; you can access it by steps down from Praza Buxán, next to Praza Madalena.

Viña Costeira
WINERY TOUR

(☑988 47 72 10; www.vinoribeiro.com; Valdepereira; tour €2; ⊙noon & 5pm Mon-Fri, noon Sat, mid-Jun–Aug) One of Ribeiro's biggest wineries, Costeira does summer tours without prior booking at its installations 3km northeast of Ribadavia.

🎉 Festivals & Events

Feria del Vino Ribeiro
WINE FESTIVAL

Ribadavia parties on the first weekend in May with this big wine festival.

🛏 Sleeping & Eating

Lodgings in town are limited but there are some wonderful rural hotels in the area. The central Praza Maior is ringed by cafes and restaurants.

Viña Meín
COUNTRY HOUSE €€

(☑617 326385; www.vinamein.com; Meín, San Clodio; d incl breakfast €55; ⊙closed mid-Dec–Jan; P🖥🛜🏊) Viña Meín, in a beautiful part of the Avia valley about 10km north of Ribadavia, is a delightful country guesthouse run by a friendly family, with a small on-site winery (☑617 326248; visits free; ⊙9am-1pm & 3.30-6.30pm Mon-Fri, by reservation).

Hostal Plaza
HOSTAL €

(☑988 47 05 76; www.hostalplazaribadavia.com; Praza Maior 15; s/d €28/38; 🛜) Hostal Plaza has 11 neat, well-kept rooms, and its Restaurante Plaza (Praza Maior 15; menú €10, mains €7-14; ⊙1-4pm & 8.30-11.30pm) serves uncomplicated seafood and meat in generous quantities.

⭐ Casal de Armán
COUNTRY HOUSE €€

(☑699 060464; www.casaldearman.net; O Cotiño, San Andrés; r incl breakfast €75-90; P🖥) A 5km drive east of Ribadavia, you can kill several birds with one stone at Casal de Armán, a dignified country house with six cosy rooms overlooking the countryside, a rustic-chic restaurant (☑988 49 18 09; meals €30-45; ⊙1-3.30pm & 8.30-11pm Tue-Sun, closed 10 Jan-10 Feb & dinner Tue-Thu & Sun Nov-May) serving excellent traditional Galician fare, and a winery (☑638 043335; admission incl tasting €5; ⊙visits by reservation 1pm, 6pm & 8pm Tue-Sun, closed 20 Sep-31 Oct) too.

ℹ Information

Tourist Office (☑988 47 12 75; www.turismoribadavia.com; Praza Maior 7; ⊙9.30am-2.30pm & 4-8pm, closed Sun afternoon)

Helpful office in the Counts of Ribadavia's old mansion on the lovely main square.

ℹ Getting There & Away

At least three buses and four trains run daily to Ourense and Vigo from stations in the east of town, just over the Río Avia.

Ribeira Sacra & Cañón do Sil

Northeast of Ourense, along the Ríos Sil and Miño, unfolds the unique natural beauty and cultural heritage of the Ribeira Sacra (Sacred Riverbank), so called because at least 18 monasteries grew up here in medieval times, after early Christian hermits and monks were drawn to this remote area. Today the Ribeira Sacra gives its name to one of Galicia's five wine DOs.

The area is poorly served by public transport, but it makes for a marvellous road trip with your own vehicle. The following sections outline a possible one- or two-day driving route along country roads, focusing on the magnificent Cañón do Sil (Sil Canyon). For more information, see www.ribeirasacra.org.

◉ Sights & Activities

◉ Ourense to Parada de Sil

Leave Ourense eastward by the OU536 highway. At Tarreirigo, 500m past the Km 15 post, turn left on to the OU0509 and follow lanes 4km through the forests to the Mosteiro de San Pedro de Rocas (⊙10.30am-1.45pm & 4-7.45pm, closed Mon Oct-Mar) **FREE**. Founded in AD 573, this enchanting mini-monastery contains three cave chapels carved out of the rock of the hillside. The adjacent interpretation centre has interesting displays on the Ribeira Sacra. You can also take a beautiful walk round the Camiño Real (PRG4), a 9km circuit that loops through this area of dense woods and rocky crags.

Back on the OU0509, continue north to Luintra then head east following signs to the mammoth Mosteiro de Santo Estevo (⊙Mar-Nov) **FREE**, on the steep valley side above the Río Sil. This monastery dates to the 12th century and has three magnificent cloisters (one Romanesque/Gothic, two Renaissance), an originally Romanesque church and an 18th-century baroque facade.

It's now a *parador*, but nonguests are free to wander round the main monumental parts and eat in the cafe or restaurant. The monastery is also nexus of marked walking trails, including the Ruta Ermida San Xoan de Cahón, which descends steeply 2.5km to the riverbank road, and the GR56 leading 19km southeast to Parada de Sil.

From Santo Estevo continue east along the OU0508 through moss-drenched forests and along a ridge high above the gorge to Parada de Sil, where a side road leads 4km down to the little Mosteiro de Santa Cristina de Ribas de Sil, with a 12th-century Romanesque church, hidden romantically among trees above the canyon. The spectacular Balcón de Madrid lookout is 1km from the village, and the PRG98 walking trail from Parada heads to the monastery via the lookout.

◉ Castro Caldelas & Around

From Parada de Sil the road continues east as the OU0605, passing waterfalls, impossibly steep vineyards, stone villages and occasional jaw-dropping vistas of the gorge below. After 14km turn left into lost-in-time Cristosende and continue 2km to A Teixeira, then follow the signs 10km to Castro Caldelas. This delightful village of 700 people, with the requisite cobbled streets, Galician *galerías* and well-tended flower boxes, is an ideal spot to spend the night. Explore the old quarter at the top of the village, crowned by an imposing 14th-century castle (admission €2; ⊙10am-2pm & 4-7pm), which contains the local tourist office (☑988 20 33 58; ⊙10am-2pm & 4-7pm) and affords great views from its tower.

From Castro Caldelas, the OU903 winds down towards the Sil Canyon. Six kilometres below the village, you can tour the interesting winery Ponte da Boga (☑988 20 33 06; www.pontedaboga.es; ⊙11am-2.30pm & 4-8pm Easter-Oct, 9am-1.30pm & 2.30-6pm Mon-Fri Nov-Easter) FREE, which dates back to 1898. From the bridge over the Sil the Diputación de Lugo (☑982 26 01 96; www.lugoterra.com; adult/senior & child €9/5; ⊙11.30am, 5pm & 7pm Jun-Sep, 11.30am & 4pm Wed-Sun Oct-May; ♿) operates two-hour river cruises in 50- and 100-passenger boats, while the 16-passenger Brandán (☑982 41 02 99; www.adegaalgueira.com; tickets €15; ⊙11am, 12.30pm, 5pm & 6.30pm Apr-Oct, noon & 4pm Nov-Mar; ♿) includes wine-tasting in its appealing 1½-hour trips

and offers free visits to the owners' winery at nearby Doade.

The road becomes the LU903 climbing the north side of the gorge, cutting across almost vertical vineyards. At Doade, a few kilometres up the hill towards Monforte de Lemos, you can visit, taste and dine at the relatively large winery Regina Viarum (☑619 009777; www.reginaviarum.es; tour incl tasting €1-3; ⊙tours 11am, noon, 1pm, 1.45pm, 4.15pm, 5pm, 6pm & 7.15pm Jun-Oct, 11am, noon, 1pm, 1.45pm, 4.30pm, 5.30pm & 6.15pm Thu-Sun Nov-May) and the smaller Adega Algueira (☑629 208917; www.adegaalgueira.com; tour incl tasting €3; ⊙11am-2pm & 4.30-7pm Apr-Oct, noon-2pm & 4-8pm Nov-Mar). It's recommended to call ahead, especially if you want a tour in English.

◉ Monforte de Lemos

This historic crossroads town of 16,700 people is neither as compact nor as pristine as other stops on the route. The Centro do Viño da Ribeira Sacra (☑982 10 53 03; www.centrovino-ribeirasacra.com; Rúa Comercio 6; incl glass of wine €2.50; ⊙11am-2pm & 5-9pm Tue-Sun) has displays on the region's wine, culture and history, brought to life in enjoyable 45-minute guided visits, usually scheduled for 11.30am, 12.30pm, 5pm and 6.30pm Tuesday to Saturday; call the day before for English or French. The centre doubles as Monforte's tourist office and has a good, reasonably priced cafe-restaurant, A Tapería (raciones and mains €6-14; ⊙8am-midnight, kitchen 1-4pm & 8.30-10.15pm Mon-Sat), and loads of Ribeira Sacra wine for sale. Rising above the town is the Monte de San Vicente, where the Pazo Condal, formerly the residence of the counts of Lemos, is now a *parador*. Beside the *pazo* looms the medieval Torre da Homenaxe (admission €1.55; ⊙11am-1pm & 5-8pm Jun-Sep), the last vestige of the counts' castle.

🛏 Sleeping

Hotel Casa de Caldelas   HOTEL €
(☑988 20 31 97; www.hotelcasadecaldelas.com; Praza do Prado 5, Castro Caldelas; s €30-40, d €40-55, incl breakfast; 🖤) Snug, up-to-date rooms in a handsome 18th-century stone house on the village's main square make this recently opened hotel an exceptional find. A wine and crafts shop in the bright reception area adds to the interest. Bathrooms are smallish but have good contemporary fittings.

Camino Francés in Galicia

Pazo Molinos de Antero   HOTEL, APARTMENT €
(☎676 573563; www.pazomolinosdeantero.com;
Carretera de Malvarón, Monforte de Lemos; r/apt
€62/112; P🛇) Monforte's best-value lodgings are the cosy, modern rooms and apartments (three of each) at this 18th-century
manor house on the east side of town. Converted from former stables, they're adorned
with quirky colour schemes and curious art.
Guided tours of the house, still in the hands
of its original family, add to the interest of
staying here.

⭐**Parador de
Santo Estevo**   HISTORIC HOTEL €€
(☎988 01 01 10; www.parador.es; Nogueira de
Ramuín; r €110-144; ⊘closed Dec-Feb; P❄🛇)
The Ribeira Sacra's best-known monastery
(p538) is also an indulgent hotel with all the
comforts, including a panoramic spa, and
a wonderful setting among thick woods in
the Sil canyon. *Superior* rooms are twice the
size of the standards and brighter, for not a
great many more euros.

❶ Getting There & Away

From Monforte, the N120 Hwy zips back to Ourense. Renfe trains (€5 to €14, 40 minutes, 11 or
more daily) link the two places. Trains between
León and Vigo also stop here. There's bus service to Lugo, Santiago de Compostela, Ourense,
Oviedo and León.

Monbus runs twice daily Monday to Friday and
once on Sunday from Ourense to Castro Caldelas (€5.25, one hour), and once to Santo Estevo
and Parada de Sil Monday to Friday.

Lugo

POP 90,200 / ELEV 475M

The grand Roman walls encircling old Lugo
are considered the best preserved of their
kind in the world and are the number-one
reason visitors land here. Within the fortress
is a beautifully preserved labyrinth of streets
and squares, most of them traffic-free and
ideal for strolling. Lucus Augusti was a major town of Roman Gallaecia and modern
Lugo is a quiet but very engaging city, with
a good number of other Roman remains besides the walls.

◎ Sights

⭐**Roman Walls**   WALLS
(⊘24hr; ♿) FREE The path running right
round the top of the World Heritage–listed
Roman walls is to Lugo what a maritime
promenade is to a seaside resort: a place
to jog, take an evening stroll, see and be
seen. The walls, erected in the 3rd century
AD, make a 2.2km loop around the old city,
rise 15m high and are studded with 85 stout
towers. Until well into the 19th century tolls
were charged to bring goods into the walled
city, and its gates were closed at night.

The **Centro de Interpretación de la Muralla** (Praza do Campo 11; adult/senior, student &
child €2/1; ⊘11am-1.30pm & 5-7.30pm Mon-Sat,
11am-2pm Sun, 4-6pm afternoons mid-Oct–mid-
Jun), a block north of Lugo's cathedral, gives
interesting background on the Roman walls,
with videos and free audio guides, all available in English.

★**Catedral de Santa María**   CATHEDRAL
(☎982 23 10 38; Praza Pio XII; ⊙8.15am-8.45pm)
The cathedral, inspired by Santiago's, was begun in 1129, though work continued for centuries, yielding an aesthetic mix of styles ranging from Romanesque (as in the transepts) to neoclassical (the main facade). It's a serene building that merits a close look.

The superb original main altarpiece, carved with scenes from the life of Christ by Cornelis de Holanda in the 1530s, now stands in two parts in the two transepts. Behind the ultra-baroque high altar, an ornate chapel houses the beautiful Gothic image of Nosa Señora dos Ollos Grandes (Our Lady of the Big Eyes), Lugo's Christian patron. Outside, just above the north doorway, the sculpture of Christ in majesty is a masterpiece of Spanish Romanesque stone carving. Fascinating Spanish-language tours of the upper levels of the cathedral (€5 per person), including the balconies of the west facade and south tower, take place at 11am and noon, except Sundays; reserve by phone or emailing exposicionscatedraldelugo@gmail.com.

Museo Provincial   MUSEUM
(www.museolugo.org; Praza da Soidade; ⊙9am-9pm Mon-Fri, 10.30am-2pm & 4.30-8pm Sat, 11am-2pm Sun) FREE Lugo's main museum includes parts of the Gothic Convento de San Francisco and is one of Galicia's best

---

CAMINOS OF GALICIA

All of the Caminos de Santiago converge in Galicia, their shared goal. About 70% of pilgrims arrive by the Camino Francés from the Pyrenees, breasting the hills on the border of Castilla y León, then striding west for the final 154km across welcome green countryside to Santiago de Compostela. But many also reach Santiago by the Camino Portugués (entering Galicia at Tui or A Guarda), Camino del Norte (from the Basque Country through Cantabria and Asturias), Vía de la Plata (from Andalucía), Camino Primitivo (from Oviedo) or Camino Inglés (from A Coruña).

Tiny O Cebreiro, where the Camino Francés enters Galicia, is 1300m high and marks the top of the route's longest, hardest climb. About half the buildings here are bars (many offering cheap set menus) or pilgrims' hostels: the nicest accommodation is the five wood-beamed, stone-walled rooms in the main building of Hotel Cebreiro (☎982 36 71 82; www.hotelcebreiro.com; s/d €40/50; ⊛), where reservations are advised for summer).

In Triacastela, 19km downhill from O Cebreiro, the camino divides, with both paths reuniting later in Sarria. The longer (25km) southern route passes through Samos, a village built around the very fine Benedictine Mosteiro de Samos (www.abadiadesamos.com; tour €3; ⊙tours every 30min 10am-12.30pm Mon-Sat, 12.45-1.30pm Sun, 4.30-6.30pm daily). This monastery has two beautiful big cloisters (one Gothic, with distinctly unmonastic Greek nymphs adorning its fountain, the other neoclassical and filled with roses). Samos has plenty of cheap lodgings, but nicest is the welcoming Casa de Díaz (☎982 54 70 70; www.casadediaz.com; d €29-42; ⊙closed early Dec-Mar; P@⊛≋), an 18th-century farmhouse turned rural hotel at Vilachá, 3.5km beyond Samos. It has 12 comfy rooms in olde-worlde style.

People undertaking just the last 100km of the camino usually start in Sarria, from which the camino winds through village after village, across forests and fields, then descends steeply to Portomarín, above the Río Miño. After a tough 25km stretch to Palas de Rei, the next 15km to Melide follows some lovely rural lanes. From Melide, 53km remain through woodlands, villages, countryside and, at the end, city streets. The camino approaches central Santiago along Rúa de San Pedro and arrives in Praza da Inmaculada on the northern side of the cathedral. Most pilgrims take a few more steps down through an archway to emerge on magnificent Praza do Obradoiro, before the cathedral's famous western facade.

If you're touring Galicia rather than pilgriming it, the 30km from O Cebreiro to Samos make a marvellous side trip. Drivers entering Galicia along the A6 from Astorga can turn off into Pedrafita do Cebreiro, then follow the LU633 4km south up to O Cebreiro. The road from there to Samos winds down through green countryside with great long-distance views, frequently criss-crossing the camino.

and biggest museums. Collections range from pre-Roman gold jewellery and Roman mosaics to Galician Sargadelos ceramics and art from the 15th to 20th centuries.

Domus do Mitreo   ARCHAEOLOGICAL SITE
(Praza Pio XII; ⊙11am-2pm Mon & Thu-Sat, 4-7pm Wed) FREE Just outside the cathedral's west doors are the subterranean remains of a Roman temple dedicated to mysterious god Mithras and of a Roman house with parts of mosaics and murals.

🛏 Sleeping

Hotel Méndez Núñez   HOTEL €
(✆982 23 07 11; www.hotelmendeznunez.com; Rúa da Raíña 1; r €60; 🅿 @ 🛜) The Méndez Núñez offers bright, spacious quarters with good beds, gleaming bathrooms and parquet floors. With a great old-town location and discounts on nearby parking, it's a good deal. The wi-fi signal can be very feeble on the upper floors.

Pensión San Roque   PENSIÓN €
(✆982 22 27 00; Plaza de Comandante Manso 11; s €24-28, d €30-38, incl breakfast) Just outside the Roman walls and 200m from the bus station, well-run San Roque provides 25 bare, clean, modern rooms, all with windows. Cable internet is available in some. There are at least three other *pensiones* or *hostales* within 150m.

Orbán e Sangro   BOUTIQUE HOTEL €€
(✆982 24 02 17; www.pazodeorban.es; Travesía do Miño; r €66-198; 🅿 🅿 🛜) The 12 rooms of this welcoming hotel, in an 18th-century mansion just inside the city walls, are regal, with rich linen, antique furnishings, designer bathrooms and huge 2.15m beds with latex mattresses. It serves a €10 'ecological' breakfast and has its own tavern in a highly original early-20th-century style.

🍴 Eating

The Old Town is liberally endowed with bars-cum-restaurants serving both tapas and main dishes. Rúa da Cruz, Rúa Nova and Praza do Campo, north of the cathedral, are especially packed with inviting options. Many of them offer two free tapas with a drink: one will be offered to you on a plate, and you have to try to pick the other from a list recited by bar staff at high speed.

Mesón de Alberto   GALICIAN €€
(✆982 22 83 10; www.mesondealberto.es; Rúa da Cruz 4; mains €16-26; ⊙1-4pm & 8.30-11.30pm, closed Sun & Tue evenings) Alberto serves very well-prepared traditional meat, fish and shellfish – meals in the main dining room upstairs, tapas downstairs. The €15 tapas tasting menu (three dishes and wine) is a good bet.

A Nosa Terra   TAPAS, RACIONES €€
(Rúa Nova 8; mains €7-18; ⊙1-4pm & 9pm-midnight) An inviting classic on the Rúa Nova tapas trail, with a long by-the-glass wine list. Stand in the narrow bar area for tapas and drinks, or sit at tables in the back for seafood salads, *raciones* of scallops or main dishes like pork sirloin in blue-cheese sauce.

Café del Centro   SPANISH €€
(Praza Maior 9; dishes €6-14; ⊙7am-2am; 🛜) Old-timey Café del Centro is a great spot for breakfast, coffee or filling *platos combinados* like its *sartén* (frying pan) of *huevos rotos* (broken fried eggs) with ham, bacon or sausage.

🍷 Drinking & Nightlife

Weekend nights, things get lively in the Old Town. Start with tapas and drinks along Rúa Nova, Praza do Campo or Rúa da Cruz, then hit the music bars around Campo Castelo or the cathedral if you're in the mood for partying on.

ℹ Information

Oficina Municipal de Turismo (✆982 25 16 58; www.lugoturismo.com; Praza do Campo 11; ⊙11am-1.30pm & 5-7.30pm Mon-Sat, 11am-2pm Sun, 4-6pm afternoons mid-Oct–mid-Jun) In the Centro de Interpretación de la Muralla.

ℹ Getting There & Away

From the **bus station** (✆982 22 39 85; Praza da Constitución), just outside the southern walls, Empresa Freire runs to Santiago de Compostela (€9.10, 1½ to two hours, five or more daily), and Arriva heads to A Coruña (€11, 1¼ to two hours, six or more daily). Other services head to Monforte de Lemos, Ourense, Pontevedra, Viveiro, Ponferrada, León, Madrid, and Asturias and beyond.

Renfe trains head at least three times daily to A Coruña (€9.30 to €18, 1½ to two hours), Monforte de Lemos (€6 to €15, one hour) and Madrid (€26 to €54, seven to nine hours).

Extremadura

Best Places to Eat

→ Atrio (p549)

→ Restaurante Torre de Sande (p549)

→ La Finca (p558)

→ Tábula Calda (p565)

→ Casa Juan (p556)

Best Places to Stay

→ Hotel Casa Don Fernando (p548)

→ La Flor de Al-Andalus (p564)

→ Hospedería del Real Monasterio (p555)

→ Posada dos Orillas (p553)

→ Haldón Country (p557)

Why Go?

Visiting Extremadura is a journey into the heart of old Spain, from the country's finest Roman ruins to beautiful medieval cities and villages. Mérida, Cáceres and Trujillo rank among the country's best-preserved historical settlements, while *extremeño* hamlets have a timeless charm, from the remote hills of the north to beguiling Zafra on the cusp of Andalucía in the south.

Relatively few foreign travellers make it this far. Spaniards, however, know it as a place to sample some of inland Spain's finest food, especially roasted meats, the pungent and creamy Torta del Casar cheese and the finest *jamón* from Monesterio. If food is your thing, you'll love it here.

And this is a region of big skies and vast swathes of sparsely populated land with isolated farmhouses. Wooded sierras rise along the region's northern, eastern and southern fringes, while the raptor-rich Parque Nacional de Monfragüe is arguably Extremadura's most dramatic corner.

When to Go
Cáceres

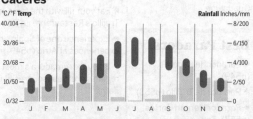

Apr The Valle del Jerte becomes a spectacular white sea of cherry blossom.

Jul–Aug Mérida's 2000-year-old Roman theatre hosts the Festival del Teatro Clásico.

Sep Good weather and few tourists make this a prime time to visit.

NATURAL EXTREMADURA

The crown jewel in Extremadura's natural spaces is the Parque Nacional de Monfragüe (p561). Both the Ruta de Isabel La Católica (p555) and Vía de la Plata have sacred roots. Other fine trails include the PR40 (p560) and the Ruta del Emperador (p558).

Best Festivals

➡ Festival del Teatro Clásico (p564), Mérida, July and August

➡ Los Empalaos (p558), Valverde de la Vera, Good Friday

➡ Womad (p548), Cáceres, May

➡ Fiestas de Trujillo (p553), September

Unesco World Heritage Sites

➡ Ciudad Monumental (p544), Cáceres

➡ Roman Ruins (p562), Mérida

➡ Real Monasterio de Santa María de Guadalupe (p554), Guadalupe

Best Paradors

➡ Parador de Cáceres (p549)

➡ Parador de Trujillo (p553)

➡ Parador Hernán Cortés (p567), Zafra

➡ Parador de Plasencia (p556)

➡ Parador Vía de la Plata (p565), Mérida

To Drive or Not to Drive

If you plan on only visiting the major population centres, a car can be an inconvenience – the old centres of Cáceres, Mérida, Plasencia, Badajoz and, to a lesser extent, Trujillo and Zafra can be extremely difficult to navigate if you're driving. All of these towns are well connected with each other and cities further afield by train and bus. If, on the other hand, you want to get off the beaten track to places like Guadalupe, the Parque Nacional de Monfragüe, Alcántara and Monesterio, you'll have no choice but to rent a car.

VÍA DE LA PLATA

The name of this ancient highway (aka Ruta de la Plata) probably derives not from the word for 'silver', but the Arabic *bilath,* meaning tiled or paved. But it was the Romans in the 1st century who laid this artery that originally linked Mérida with Astorga and was later extended to the Asturian coast. Along its length moved goods, troops, travellers and traders. Later, it served as a pilgrim route for the faithful walking from Andalucía to Santiago de Compostela and it's now increasingly a rival to the much more crowded Camino de Santiago. From Seville, it's a 1000km walk or cycle to Santiago or a similar distance to Gijón. Entering Extremadura south of Zafra, the well-marked route passes through Mérida, Cáceres and Plasencia, then heads for Salamanca in Castilla y León. Take a look at www.rutadelaplata.com or pick up the guide (€3) from tourist offices on the route.

Top Five Food Experiences

➡ Visit the Museo del Jamón (p570) in Monesterio and then sample the region's best *jamón*.

➡ Track down one of Spain's most celebrated cheeses, the Torta del Casar, in Casar de Cáceres (p549).

➡ Eat your fill with the famously epic portions served up at Trujillo's Restaurante La Troya (p554).

➡ Experience one of Spain's most celebrated fine-dining experiences at Atrio (p549) in Cáceres.

➡ Enjoy Extremadura's most creative tapas on one of the region's prettiest squares at Gastro-Bar Baraka (p567) in Zafra.

Extremadura Highlights

❶ Stroll the Ciudad Monumental's evocative cobbled streets in **Cáceres**.

❷ Clamber over Spain's finest Roman ruins in **Mérida** (p562).

❸ Travel to **Trujillo** (p551), medieval home town of some of Latin America's most infamous conquistadors.

❹ Spot majestic birds of prey as they wheel over the **Parque Nacional de Monfragüe** (p561).

❺ Enjoy tapas beneath palm trees in Plaza Grande then sleep in a castle in **Zafra** (p566).

❻ Check out the mighty impressive Roman bridge over the Tajo in peaceful **Alcántara** (p551).

❼ Admire the fabulous art collection in the extraordinary **monastery** (p554) of Guadalupe.

❽ Explore the half-timbered villages of **La Vera** (p557) and marvel at the cherry blossom of adjacent **Valle del Jerte** (p558).

❾ Pace the quiet lanes of the restored historic museum village of **Granadilla** (p560).

❿ Learn all about Spain's favourite food at the **Museo del Jamón** (p570) in Monesterio.

Cáceres

POP 95,925

The Ciudad Monumental (Old Town) of Cáceres is truly extraordinary. Narrow cobbled streets twist and climb among ancient stone walls lined with palaces and mansions, while the skyline is decorated with turrets, spires, gargoyles and enormous storks' nests. Protected by defensive

Cáceres

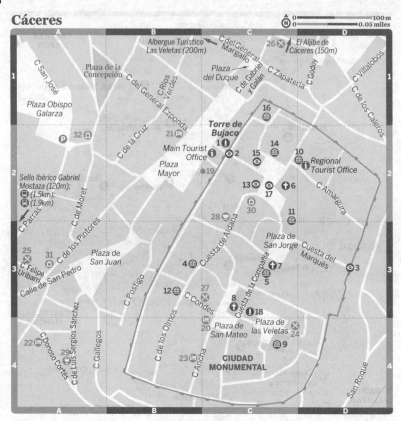

Albergue Turístico
Las Veletas (200m)
C del General Margallo
26 ⊗ El Aljibe de
Cáceres (150m)
C San José
Plaza de la Concepción
C del General Ezponda
C Ríos Verdes
Plaza del Duque
C de Gabriel y Galán
C Zapatería
Godoy
C Villalobos
C de los Caleros
Plaza Obispo Galarza
C de la Cruz
16
Torre de Bujaco
Sello Ibérico Gabriel Mostaza (120m);
(1.5km);
(1.9km)
32
21
1
Main Tourist Office
2
15
14
10
Regional Tourist Office
C Amargura
C Parras
C de Moret
Plaza Mayor
19
13
17
6
30
11
28
C de los Pintores
Plaza de San Juan
Cuesta de Aldana
Plaza de San Jorge
Cuesta del Marqués
3
25
31
C de los Pintores
C Felipe Uribarri
Calle de San Pedro
4
7
5
C Postigo
12
27
C Condes
8
18
Cuesta de la Compañía
C de Luis Sergios Sánchez
C de los Olmos
20
Plaza de San Mateo
Plaza de las Veletas
24
22
C Donoso Cortés
29
C Gallegos
23
C Aricha
9
CIUDAD MONUMENTAL
San Roque

EXTREMADURA CÁCERES

walls, it has survived almost intact from its 16th-century heyday. At dusk or after dark, when the crowds have gone, you'll feel like you've stepped back into the Middle Ages. Stretching at its feet, the lively and arcaded Plaza Mayor is one of Spain's finest public squares.

⊙ Sights

Ciudad Monumental's name captures it all. The churches, palaces and towers are hugely impressive although few people actually live here and there are just a handful of bars and restaurants. If you're lucky (as we always seem to be), a flamenco singer might be busking in one of the squares, which only adds to the magic.

Sights in Cáceres open and close one hour earlier in the afternoon from October to April.

★ **Torre de Bujaco**   TOWER
(Plaza Mayor; adult/child €2/free; ⊙10am-2pm & 5.30-8.30pm Mon-Sat, 10am-2pm Sun) As you climb up the steps to the Ciudad Monumental from the Plaza Mayor, turn left to climb the 12th-century Torre de Bujaco, home to an interpretative display. From the top there's a fine stork's-eye view of the Plaza Mayor.

⊙ Plaza de Santa María & Around

As the closest square to the Plaza Mayor, Plaza de Santa María and the surrounding tangle of lanes is most people's introduction to the Ciudad Monumental. It's also arguably the most impressive of the Old Town's three main squares with medieval palaces and public buildings at every turn.

Cáceres

Pass beneath the 18th-century Arco de la Estrella, built wide for the passage of carriages, and on to the Plaza de Santa Marta.

Notable facades on the plaza include the Palacio Episcopal (Bishop's Palace), the Palacio de Mayoralgo and the Palacio de Ovando, all in 16th-century Renaissance style. As you move deeper into the Ciudad Monumental to the southeast, you'll also pass the Renaissance-style Palacio de la Diputación.

Concatedral de Santa María   CATHEDRAL
(Plaza de Santa María; admission €1; ⊙ 10am-2pm & 5.30-9pm Mon-Sat, 9.30-11.50am & 5.30-7.15pm Sun) The Concatedral de Santa María, a 15th-century Gothic cathedral, creates an impressive opening scene on the Plaza de Santa María. At its southwestern corner is a modern statue of San Pedro de Alcántara, a 16th-century extremeño ascetic (his toes are worn shiny by the hands and lips of the faithful). Inside, there's a magnificent carved 16th-century cedar altarpiece, several fine noble tombs and chapels, and a small ecclesiastical museum. Climb the bell tower for views over the old town.

Palacio Carvajal   HISTORIC BUILDING
(Calle Amargura 1; ⊙ 9am-9pm Mon-Fri, 10am-2pm & 5-8pm Sat, 10am-2pm Sun) FREE Just off the northeastern corner of the Plaza de Santa María is this late 15th-century mansion.

There's a modern display on the province's attractions and the regional tourist office (p550).

Palacio Toledo-Moctezuma   HISTORIC BUILDING
Just to the west of the Plaza de Santa María lies the domed Palacio Toledo-Moctezuma, once home of a daughter of the Aztec emperor Moctezuma, brought to Cáceres as a conquistador's bride. The palace now houses the municipal archives.

◎ Plaza de San Jorge

Plaza de San Jorge lies southeast of Plaza de Santa María, while due east of here is the Arco del Cristo, a Roman gate.

Iglesia de San Francisco Javier   CHURCH
(Iglesia de la Preciosa Sangre; Plaza de San Jorge; adult/child €1/free; ⊙ 10am-2pm & 5.30-8.30pm) An 18th-century Jesuit church that rises above the Plaza de San Jorge.

Centro Divulgación Semana Santa   GALLERY
(Cuesta de la Compañía; ⊙ 10am-2pm & 5.30-8.30pm) FREE This gallery has exhibits on Easter celebrations in Cáceres atop 18th-century cisterns.

◎ Plaza de San Mateo & Around

From Plaza de San Jorge, Cuesta de la Compañía climbs to Plaza de San Mateo, which occupies the summit of the Ciudad Monumental. Generally quieter than the lower squares, it, too, has some fine old buildings in the vicinity. Much of it spills over into the neighbouring Plaza de las Veletas.

Iglesia de San Mateo
CHURCH

Dominating the plaza is the Iglesia de San Mateo, traditionally the church of the landowning nobility and built on the site of the town's mosque. If you're lucky enough to find it open, the soaring wooden altarpiece is an impressive sight at the end of the single nave with its high Gothic vaulting.

Torre de las Cigüeñas
TOWER

(Tower of the Storks) This was the only Cáceres tower to retain its battlements when the rest were lopped off in the late 15th century. It houses occasional art exhibitions.

Museo de Cáceres
MUSEUM

(Plaza de las Veletas 1; non-EU/EU citizens €1.20/free; ⊙ 9am-2.30pm & 5-8.15pm Tue-Sat, 10.15am-2.30pm Sun) The excellent Museo de Cáceres in a 16th-century mansion, built over an evocative 12th-century *aljibe* (cistern), is the only surviving element of Cáceres' Muslim castle. It has an impressive archaeological section and an excellent fine-arts display (open only in the mornings), with works by Picasso, Miró, Tàpies and other renowned artists.

Palacio de los Golfines de Arriba
HISTORIC BUILDING

(Calle de los Olmos 2) This is where Franco was declared head of state in 1936.

Casa Mudéjar
HISTORIC BUILDING

(Cuesta de Aldana 14) The Casa Mudéjar still reflects its Islamic influence in its brickwork and 1st-floor window arches.

🏃 Activities

El Aljibe de Cáceres
HAMMAM

(☎ 927 22 32 56; www.elaljibedecaceres.com; Calle de Peña 5; ⊙ 10am-2pm & 6-10pm Tue-Thu & Sun, to midnight Fri & Sat) This beautifully indulgent re-creation of an Arab-style bath experience combines soothing architecture and a range of treatments. The basic thermal bath with aromatherapy starts from €18; throw in a massage and you'll pay €25.

☞ Tours

★ Cuentatrovas del Cordel
WALKING TOUR

(☎ 666 836332, 667 283187; www.cuentatrovas.com; adult €10, child over/under 11 €5/free) Guides

and actors dress up in period dress and take you on a tour with a difference through the Ciudad Monumental. It's fun and informative (if you understand Spanish) and very much recommended. Times vary, with after-dark tours their speciality.

Asociación de Guías Turísticas
WALKING TOUR

(Tourist Guides Association; ☎ 927 21 72 37; Plaza Mayor 2) These guides lead 1½- to two-hour tours (€5) in Spanish around the Ciudad Monumental at least three times daily, with only morning tours on Sunday. Tours start from the office on Plaza Mayor, and tours in English can be arranged with advance notice.

🎉 Festivals & Events

Womad
WORLD MUSIC

(World of Music, Arts and Dance; www.womadcaceres.com) For three fiesta-fuelled days in mid-May, Cáceres stages a long-running edition of Womad, with international bands playing in the Old Town's squares.

Fiesta de San Jorge
LOCAL FIESTA

From 21 to 23 April the town celebrates the Fiesta de San Jorge in honour of its patron saint.

🛏 Sleeping

Hotel Don Carlos
HOTEL €

(☎ 927 22 55 27; www.hoteldoncarloscaceres.com; Calle Donoso Cortés 15; s/d from €33/42; 🅿️ 🕸 @ 🛜) Rooms are tastefully decorated with bare brick and stone at this welcoming small hotel, sensitively created from a long-abandoned, early-19th-century house. There are two artists among the owner's family, hence plenty of original artwork.

Albergue Turístico Las Veletas
HOSTEL €

(☎ 927 21 12 10; www.alberguelasveletas.com; Calle del General Margallo 36; per person €30; 🕸 🛜) This modern hostel, with its homey rear garden with flowers, offers agreeable accommodation in rooms with three to six beds. Reserve in advance, since it works primarily with groups. Meals are available.

★ Hotel Casa Don Fernando
BOUTIQUE HOTEL €€

(☎ 927 21 42 79; www.casadonfernando.com; Plaza Mayor 30; d €50-150; 🅿️ 🕸 🛜 ♿) The classiest midrange choice in Cáceres, this boutique hotel sits on Plaza Mayor directly opposite the Arco de la Estrella. Spread over four floors, the designer rooms and bathrooms

EXTREMADURA'S HOME OF CHEESE

Extremadura may be well-known for its *jamón* but one of its cheeses is equally celebrated in Spanish culinary circles. The Torta del Casar is a pungent, creamy cheese that's aged for 40 days and eaten most often as a spread on *tostas* (open sandwiches) or even with a steak.

Casar de Cáceres (pop 4576), around 12km north of Cáceres and well-signposted off the N630 to Plasencia, is where the Torta del Casar was born and its main street is lined with shops selling it. There's even the small Museo de Queso (Calle Barrionuevo Bajo 7, Casar de Cáceres; ☉10am-2pm Tue-Sat) FREE dedicated to the cheese.

If you don't have your own wheels, eight buses run daily between Casar de Cáceres and the bus station in Cáceres (€0.80, 20 minutes).

are tastefully chic; superior rooms (€30 more than the standards) have the best plaza views (although nights can be noisy, especially on weekends). Attic-style top-floor rooms are good for families.

Atrio BOUTIQUE HOTEL €€€
(☎927 24 29 28; www.restauranteatrio.com; Plaza de San Mateo 1; d without/with dinner €240/450; P❋⊛⊚⊠) Impeccable modern styling and some serious pieces of original contemporary art characterise this excellent fusion of five-star boutique hotel and one of Spain's most garlanded restaurants. The location in the heart of the Old Town is impressive, and neither the sleek rooms nor the solicitous personal service will disappoint.

Parador de Cáceres HOTEL €€€
(☎927 21 17 59; www.parador.es; Calle Ancha 6; r €95-280; P❋@⊚) A substantial makeover has given this 14th-century Gothic palace in the Old Town a swish modern look to its interiors, with bedrooms and bathrooms exhibiting a distinctively non-medieval level of style and comfort.

✗ Eating

From the restaurants and cafes flanking the Plaza Mayor, you can watch the swallows and storks swoop and glide among the turrets of the Old Town. Stick to a drink and tapas, however, as the food here tends to be overpriced and indifferent. There's a better-quality tapas scene around nearby Plaza de San Juan.

★ **Restaurante Torre de Sande** FUSION €€
(☎927 21 11 47; www.torredesande.com; Calle Condes 3; set menus €25-35; ☉1-4pm & 7pm-midnight Tue-Sat, 1-4pm Sun) Dine in the pretty courtyard on dishes like *salmorejo de cerezas del Jerte con queso de cabra* (cherry-based cold soup with goat's cheese) at this elegant

gourmet restaurant in the heart of the Ciudad Monumental. More modestly, stop for a drink and a tapa at the interconnecting *tapería* (tapas bar).

El Racó de Sanguino SPANISH €€
(☎927 22 76 82; www.racodesanguino.es; Plaza de las Veletas 4; tapas €4.50, mains €14-20; ☉noon-4pm & 8-11pm Tue-Sat, noon-4pm Sun; ⊕) 🥗 Tables and wicker chairs spread beneath the sloping, timber ceiling within, while romantics can head for the candlelit tables outside. Carlos Sanguino has created a traditional *extremeño* menu with the focus on locally produced ingredients of quality.

Madruelo MODERN SPANISH €€
(☎927 24 36 76; www.madruelo.com; Calle Camberos 2; mains €13-21, set menus €30-51; ☉1.30-4pm & 9.15-11.30pm Wed-Sat, 1.30-4pm Sun-Tue) This intimate and soberly decorated restaurant is where *cacereños* in the know go for high-class modern Spanish cuisine at a fair price. Excellent grilled meats are complemented by rices, a range of foie gras dishes and the odd dish from elsewhere in the Mediterranean like moussaka.

La Tahona TAPAS, SPANISH €€
(☎927 21 20 73; Calle Felipe Uribarri 4; tapas from €3.75, mains €16-36, set menus €19-23; ☉12.30-4pm & 8pm-midnight Mon-Sat, 12.30-4pm Sun) This appealing side-street choice has an upmarket yet casual feel. Succulent meats (such as *cochinillo* – suckling pig) cooked in a wood oven are the speciality here, but there's a wide choice of creative tapas as well. The tapas tasting menu (€19) is especially good value.

★ **Atrio** MODERN SPANISH €€€
(☎927 24 29 28; www.restauranteatrio.com; Plaza de San Mateo 1; menú €99-119; ☉2-4pm & 8.30-11.30pm) With a stunning location in the

WHAT'S COOKING IN EXTREMADURA

➡ *migas extremeñas* (breadcrumbs fried with garlic, peppers and pork), Restaurante La Troya (p554)

➡ *caldereta de cabrito* (stewed goat kid), La Finca (p558)

➡ *cochinillo asado* (roast suckling pig), La Tahona (p549)

➡ Torta del Casar (a strong, creamy cheese served on toast), La Bodeguilla (p565)

➡ *jamón ibérico* (Iberian ham), anywhere, but especially the bars of Monesterio (p570)

heart of old Cáceres, Extremadura's best restaurant goes from strength to strength. Service that manages to be both formal and friendly backs up the wonderful culinary creations. The focus is on local produce of the highest quality; there's a degustation menu chosen by the chef or you can pick from a selection of daily specials to make up your own menu.

Drinking & Nightlife

Just beyond the walls on the southern side of the Ciudad Monumental, around Calles Pizarro and Luis Sergios Sánchez, is a zone of popular nocturnal hang-outs, staying open until around 3am.

El Corral de las Cigüeñas CAFE
(☎927 21 64 25; www.elcorralcc.com; Cuesta de Aldana 6; ☺7.30am-1pm Mon-Wed, 7am-late Thu & Fri, 5pm-late Sat) The secluded courtyard with its lofty palm trees and ivy-covered walls just inside the Ciudad Monumental is the perfect spot for a quiet drink in relaxing surroundings. There's often live music on Saturdays around 6pm for the cost of a drink.

La Traviata BAR
(Calle de Luis Sergios Sánchez 8; ☺4pm-4am) With floral wallpaper, original tiles, arches, great music and a terrace, this is the pick of the places in this area.

Shopping

Sello Ibérico Gabriel Mostaza FOOD
(☎927 24 28 81; www.gabrielmostazo.com; Calle de San Antón 6; ☺9.30am-2pm & 5-8.30pm Mon-

Sat, 10am-2pm Sun) One of the best delis in town with plenty of fresh and tinned local products.

Degusta San Juan FOOD, DRINK
(☎927 24 54 93; Plaza de San Juan; ☺10am-11pm) Part gourmet delicatessen and part tasting *salón*, this fabulous place allows you to buy and/or try the usual *jamón*, cheeses and wine, as well as (unusually for Spain) some artisan beers from the Extremadura region. Three euros will get you started on the tasting.

Sierra de Montánchez FOOD, WINE
(☎927 21 20 25; www.sierrademontanchez.es; Calle de Moret; ☺10am-2pm & 5-8pm Mon-Sat, 10am-2pm Sun) This place stocks a range of local *extremeño* products, but the speciality is premium *jamón* from the Montánchez region southeast of Cáceres.

Centro de Artesanía Casa Moraga HANDICRAFTS
(Plaza de Santa María; ☺10am-2pm & 4.30-7.30pm) This government-run emporium showcases local *extremeño* handicrafts, including leather and woodcarving.

ℹ Information

Main Tourist Office (☎927 01 08 34; www.turismoextremadura.com; Plaza Mayor 3; ☺8.30am-2.30pm & 4-6pm Mon-Fri, 10am-2pm Sat & Sun) Opens later in the afternoon in summer.

Regional Tourist Office (☎927 25 55 97; www.turismocaceres.org; Palacio Carvajal, Calle Amargura 1; ☺8am-8.45pm Mon-Fri, 10am-1.45pm & 5-7.45pm Sat, 10am-1.45pm Sun) Covers Cáceres province and city.

ℹ Getting There & Away

The **bus station** (☎927 23 25 50; www.estacionautobuses.es; Calle Túnez 1) has services to Madrid (normal/express €25/32, 3¾ to 5½ hours, seven daily), Trujillo (€4.63, 40 minutes, six daily), Plasencia (€5.15, 1¼ hours, up to five daily) and Mérida (€5.63, one hour, two daily).

Up to five trains per day run to/from Madrid (€27 to €32, four to five hours), Plasencia (€5.10, one hour) and Mérida (€6, one hour).

ℹ Getting Around

Bus L1 from outside the train station – close to the bus station – heads to central Plaza Obispo Galarza.

Valencia de Alcántara

POP 5957

This pretty town is 7km from the Portuguese border and its well-preserved old centre is a curious labyrinth of whitewashed houses and mansions. One side of the old town is watched over by the ruins of a medieval castle and the 17th-century Iglesia de Rocamador.

The surrounding countryside is known for its cork industry and some 50 ancient dolmens (stone circles of prehistoric monoliths).

Two buses run Monday to Friday from Cáceres (€5.75, 1½ hours).

Alcántara

POP 1588

Alcántara is Arabic for 'the Bridge', and sure enough, below this remote Extremaduran town, a magnificent Roman bridge – 204m long, 61m high and much reinforced over the centuries – spans the Río Tajo below a huge dam retaining the Embalse de Alcántara. From the bridge, a beautiful 20km circuit follows the river then loops up into the hills via a village and a prehistoric menhir. Spot rare birds of prey and black storks along the way.

The town retains old walls, a ruined castle, several imposing mansions and the enormous Renaissance Convento de San Benito (www.fundacionsanbenito.com; Calle Trajano; ⏰10.30am-1.30pm & 5-7pm Wed-Sat, 10.30am-1.30pm Sun) FREE. This was built in the 16th century to house the Orden de Alcántara, an order of Reconquista knights, part-monks part-soldiers, who ruled much of western Extremadura as a kind of private fiefdom. The highlights of the down-at-heel monastery include the Gothic cloister and the perfectly proportioned three-tier loggia. Admission is by free hourly guided visits.

Just outside town, the Hospedería Conventual de Alcántara (☎927 39 06 38; www.hospederiasdeextremadura.es; Carretera del Poblado Iberdrola; r €63-105; P❄@🛜🐕) is a comfortable and stylish modern hotel that enjoys a marvellous setting in an old monastery.

Four buses run Monday to Friday to/from Cáceres (€6.20, 1½ hours).

Trujillo

POP 9085

The core of Trujillo is one of the best-preserved medieval towns in Spain. It begins in the Plaza Mayor and the splendour continues up the hillside with a labyrinth of mansions, leafy courtyards, fruit gardens, churches and convents all enclosed within 900m of walls circling the upper town and dating back to the 16th century when Trujillo's favourite sons returned home as wealthy conquistadors. Whether bathed in the warm light of a summer sunset or shrouded in the mists of winter, Trujillo can feel like a magical place.

◉ Sights

In summer, sights stay open longer in the afternoons (from 5pm to 8.30pm).

Plaza Mayor   SQUARE

Trujillo's main square is one of Spain's most spectacular plazas, surrounded as it is by baroque and Renaissance stone buildings topped with a skyline of towers, turrets, cupolas, crenellations and nesting storks.

In the plaza's northeastern corner is a large equestrian statue of the conquistador Francisco Pizarro, by American Charles Rumsey. But all is not as it seems. Apparently, Rumsey originally sculpted it as a statue of Hernán Cortés to present to Mexico, but Mexico, which takes a dim view of Cortés, declined it, so it was given to Trujillo as Pizarro instead.

On the south side of the plaza, carved images of Pizarro and his lover Inés Yupanqui (sister of the Inca emperor Atahualpa) decorate the corner of the 16th-century Palacio de la Conquista. To the right is their daughter Francisca Pizarro Yupanqui with her husband (and uncle), Hernando

---

WORTH A TRIP

GARROVILLAS

If you're driving between Alcántara and Cáceres or Plasencia, make sure that you stop in the small town of Garrovillas (pop 2237), which lies along the EX302, 11km west of the N630. The otherwise unremarkable town is distinguished by a truly remarkable Plaza Mayor, which is surrounded by arched porticoes and is one of the prettiest in Extremadura.

Pizarro. The mansion was built in the 1560s for Hernando and Francisca after Hernando – the only Pizarro brother not to die a bloody death in Peru – emerged from 20 years in jail for murder.

Off the plaza's northeastern corner is the 16th-century **Palacio de los Duques de San Carlos**, which serves as a convent for the Jerónimo order. The distinctive brick chimneys were built in Mudéjar style.

Iglesia de San Martín   CHURCH
(adult/child €1.40/free; ⊘10am-2pm & 4-6.30pm) Overlooking the Plaza Mayor is the 16th-century Iglesia de San Martín, with delicate Gothic ceiling tracing in its single nave, stunning stained-glass windows and a grand 18th-century organ (climb up to the choir loft for the best view).

Torre del Alfiler   TOWER, INTERPRETATION CENTRE
(Calle Ballesteros; admission €1.40; ⊘10am-2pm & 4-7pm) Once part of the defensive walls guarding the fortress, this tower later became a fortified aristocratic dwelling. It holds an interpretative display about Trujillo and Extremadura history, and offers fine views over the Plaza Mayor.

Iglesia de Santiago   CHURCH
(adult/child €1.40/free; ⊘10am-2pm & 4-7pm) Coming up from the Plaza Mayor, you pass through the **Puerta de Santiago**. To its right is the Iglesia de Santiago, the oldest church in Trujillo, founded in the 13th century by the Knights of Santiago (look for their scallop-shell emblem).

The nave is studded with coats of arms and has a modest 14th-century altarpiece and the locally revered (and utterly compelling) sculpture of **Cristo de las Aguas**. Check out the recreated sacristan's room, the small bell tower and the permanent nativity scene in the choir.

Iglesia de Santa María la Mayor   CHURCH
(Plaza de Santa María; adult/child €1.50/free; ⊘10am-2pm & 4-6.30pm) This 13th-century church is our favourite church in Trujillo. It has a mainly Gothic nave and a Roman-

---

EXTREMADURA & THE AMERICAS

Extremeños jumped at the opportunities opened up by Columbus' discovery of the Americas in 1492, which is hardly surprising given that this was one of Spain's poorest regions.

In 1501 Fray Nicolás de Ovando from Cáceres was named governor of all the Indies. Among the 2500 followers who joined him in his capital of Santo Domingo, many were from Extremadura, including Francisco Pizarro, illegitimate son of a minor noble family from Trujillo. In 1504 Hernán Cortés, from a similar family in Medellín, arrived in Santo Domingo.

Both young men prospered. Cortés took part in the conquest of Cuba in 1511 and settled there. Pizarro, in 1513, accompanied Vasco Núñez de Balboa (from Jerez de los Caballeros) to Darién (Panama), where they 'discovered' the Pacific Ocean. In 1519 Cortés led a small expedition to what's now Mexico, a place that was rumoured to be full of gold and silver. By 1524, with combined fortitude, cunning, luck and ruthlessness, Cortés and his band had subdued the Aztec empire.

Pizarro returned to Spain and, before returning to the New World, visited Trujillo, where he received a hero's welcome and collected his four half-brothers, as well as other relatives and friends. Their expedition set off from present-day Panama in 1531, with just 180 men and 37 horses, and managed to capture the Inca emperor Atahualpa, despite the 30,000-strong Inca army. Pizarro demanded an enormous ransom, which was paid, but Trujillo's finest went ahead and executed Atahualpa anyway. The Inca empire, with its capital in Cuzco and extending from present-day Colombia to Chile, soon fell to a combination of casual brutality, broken alliances, cynical realpolitik and civil war between Pizarro and his longtime ally, Diego de Almagro. Pizarro was eventually assassinated by the executed Almagro's son and is buried in the cathedral of Lima, Peru.

About 600 people of Trujillo made their way to the Americas in the 16th century, so it's no surprise that there are several other Trujillo towns in Central and South America. Conquistadors and colonists from all over Spain also took with them the cult of the Virgen de Guadalupe in eastern Extremadura; it remains widespread throughout Latin America.

esque tower that you can ascend for fabulous views to all four corners of the compass. The church's magnificent altarpiece includes 25 brilliantly coloured 15th-century paintings in the Flemish style, depicting scenes from the lives of Mary and Christ.

The church also contains the tombs of leading Trujillo families from the Middle Ages, including that of Diego García de Paredes (1466–1530), a warrior of legendary strength who, according to Cervantes, could stop a mill wheel with one finger.

Alcazaba   CASTLE
(adult/child €1.40/free; ⊙ 10am-2pm & 4.30-7pm) Occupying the town's summit, Trujillo's storybook castle is of 10th-century Islamic origin (note the horseshoe arch just inside the entrance) and was later strengthened by the Christians. Patrol the battlements for magnificent sweeping views, visit the derelict *aljibe* (cisterns) and climb to the hermitage of Our Lady of the Victory, Trujillo's patron; a 50-cent coin in a slot makes her spin around in her alcove.

Casa-Museo
de Pizarro   MUSEUM, HISTORIC BUILDING
(Calle del Convento de las Jéronimos; adult/child €1.40/free; ⊙ 10am-2pm & 4-7pm) High in the upper town, and signposted from the Puerta de Santiago, this small museum occupies one of the former homes of the Pizarro family. It includes period furniture and various knick-knacks from the Pizarro boys' conquests.

⚜ Festivals & Events

Fiestas de Trujillo   LOCAL FIESTA
The town's annual Fiestas de Trujillo, with music, theatre and plenty of partying, are spread over a few days around the first Saturday in September.

Feria del Queso   FOOD
(Cheese Fair; www.feriadelquesotrujillo.es) The last weekend in April or first weekend in May is a pungent period as cheesemakers from all over Spain converge on Trujillo for the Feria del Queso.

🛏 Sleeping

El Mirador de las Monjas   HOTEL €
(☑ 927 65 92 23; www.elmiradordelasmonjas.com; Plaza de Santiago 2; d from €50; ❄ 🛜) High in the old town, this six-room *hostería* (small hotel) attached to a quality restaurant has spotless, light, modern rooms decorated in

ℹ GUIDED TOURS
Two-hour guided tours of Trujillo (in Spanish) leave from the tourist office (p554) daily at 11am and 5pm (4.30pm in winter). Tickets cost €7 and take in the Alcazaba, Iglesia de Santa María la Mayor, Casa-Museo de Pizarro, Iglesia de Santiago and the Plaza Mayor. The ticket also entitles you to free entry into the Iglesia de San Martín and Torre del Alfiler.

minimalist style. The upstairs ones with sloping ceilings and pleasant vistas are slightly better than the ones below, but all are outrageously good value and feature excellent bathrooms.

Hostal Nuria   HOSTAL €
(☑ 927 32 09 07; www.hostal-nuria.com; Plaza Mayor; s/d €30/45, apt €60-90; ❄🛜) Rooms here are modern and comfortable; there are no frills, but the location on Plaza Mayor is hard to beat. You'll spend most of your time looking out the window onto the plaza if you're in rooms 204 or 205. There's a busy downstairs bar-restaurant.

★ Posada dos Orillas   HISTORIC HOTEL €€
(☑ 927 65 90 79; www.dosorillas.com; Calle de Cambrones 6; d €50-70; ❄🛜) This tastefully renovated 16th-century mansion is in a great location in the walled town. Rooms replicate Spanish colonial taste and are named for the countries in which towns called Trujillo are found. Personal service from the owners is excellent here, and the nights are as quiet as can be.

NH Palacio de Santa Marta   HOTEL €€
(☑ 927 65 91 90; www.nh-hoteles.es; Calle Ballesteros 6; d standard/premium from €60/90; 🅿❄@🛜🌊) Just above the Plaza Mayor, this hotel occupies a 16th-century palace and combines slick modern chambers with beautiful original features such as exposed stone walls and high ceilings. There's a summer-only pool with views across the rooftops; if you want the prime vistas over the square, upgrade to a deluxe or premium room – room 208 with its little balcony is stunning.

Parador de Trujillo   HISTORIC HOTEL €€€
(☑ 927 32 13 50; www.parador.es; Calle Santa Beatriz de Silva 1; r €75-130; 🅿❄@🛜🌊) No surprise that this *parador* (luxury state-owned hotel) is also a former 16th-century convent;

there's an agreeable overdose in this town. Rooms are large with terracotta-tiled floors and understated historical touches. It's in the winding backstreets of the old town, east of the Plaza Mayor.

Eating

★ **Restaurante La Troya** TRADITIONAL SPANISH €
(Plaza Mayor 10; menú €15; ☺1-4pm & 8.30-11pm) Famed across Spain for its copious servings of no-frills *comida casera* (home-style cooking), Troya enjoys a prime location on the main town square. On entering, you'll be directed to one of several dining areas, to be presented with plates of tortilla and chorizo and a lettuce-and-tomato salad. And that's even before you've ordered your three-course *menú* (set menu). It's all about quantity, and queues stretch out the door on weekends.

Restaurante Corral del Rey SPANISH €€
(☑927 32 30 71; www.corraldelreytrujillo.com; Plazuela Corral del Rey 2; mains €15-28, set menus from €21; ☺1.30-4pm & 9pm-midnight Mon-Sat) This classic restaurant has four intimate dining rooms. Settle for the *menú del día* (€21) or choose from a tempting range of grills, roasts and fish dishes, the latter speciality being *bacalao Corral del Rey* (grilled cod with a courgette and roasted garlic sauce). Closed Wednesday night in winter.

Mesón Alberca TRADITIONAL SPANISH €€
(Calle de Cambrones 8; mains €11-18; ☺1-4pm & 8.30-11pm Thu-Sun) A pretty ivy-clad terrace, or dark-timber tables laid with gingham tablecloths create a choice of warm atmospheres for sampling classic *extremeño* cooking. The specialities here are oven roasts and local cheeses. The regional set menu is excellent value at €24.50.

❶ Information

Tourist Office (☑927 32 26 77; www.turismotrujillo.com; Plaza Mayor; ☺10am-2pm & 4.30-7.30pm) Right on Plaza Mayor.

❶ Getting There & Away

The **bus station** (☑927 32 12 02; Avenida de Miajadas) is 750m south of Plaza Mayor. There are services to/from Madrid (normal/express €22/34, 3¼/2¾ hours, five daily), Cáceres (€4.63, 40 minutes, five daily) and Mérida (€9.85, 1½ hours, three daily), among other destinations.

Guadalupe

POP 2004

Centred on its palatial monastery, a treasure trove of art, architecture and history, this sparkling white village is a popular pilgrimage centre and a worthy destination in its own right, a bright jewel set in the green crown of the surrounding ranges and ridges of the Sierra de Villuercas. There are thick woods of chestnut, oak and cork meshed with olive groves and vineyards, offering plenty of good walking options.

◉ Sights

While the monastery is the obvious highlight, take some time to wander the picturesque streets off the Plaza Mayor.

★ **Real Monasterio de Santa María de Guadalupe** MONASTERY, CHURCH
(☑927 36 70 00; www.monasterioguadalupe.com; Plaza de Santa María de Guadalupe; church free, monastery by guided tour adult/child €5/2; ☺church 8.30am-9pm, monastery 9.30am-1pm & 3.30-6.30pm) Guadalupe's renowned monastery is located, according to legend, on the spot where a shepherd found an effigy of the Virgin, hidden years earlier by Christians fleeing the Muslims. A sumptuous church-monastery was built on the site and ever since then has drawn pilgrims from across the world. Now cared for by Franciscan monks, this is still one of Spain's most important pilgrimage sites, especially for South American and Filipino Catholics.

The church received royal patronage from Alfonso XI and became an Hieronymite monastery in the late 14th century. The figure of the Virgin, a black Madonna made from cedar wood, was so revered in the 16th century that she was made patron of all Spain's New World territories. Columbus was particularly devoted to her and, after his fragile fleet survived a terrible tempest on his first voyage, made a pilgrimage of thanks here shortly after returning.

Hurried **guided tours** of the monastery (in Spanish only, one hour) leave on the half hour. At the complex's centre is a lovely late-14th-century Mudéjar cloister decorated with paintings telling the history of the Virgin and miracles she wrought. In one of the three **museums** spaced around it is a gallery that includes three paintings by El Greco (St Andrew, the Assumption, and St Peter), a sombre late Goya *(Confession* *in Prison)*, a fine Ecce Homo by Pedro de Mena, a handful of monks by Francisco de Zurbarán and a beautiful little ivory crucifixion attributed to Michelangelo.

In the majestic sacristía (sacristy) hangs a series of superb canvases (1638–47) by Zurbarán. There are some exalted works here, none better than the *Temptation of St Jerome*, the stern ascetic saint seemingly at odds with the elaborate baroque decoration of this chamber. The Relicario-Tesoro holds spooky relics of martyr saints and a rather vulgar display of treasure, including a 200,000-pearl cape for the Virgin. The camarín, a chamber behind the altarpiece, has an image of the Virgin that is revolved for the faithful to kiss a fragment of her mantle; you can elect to do this when your tour ends.

Inside the church, the black Virgin's image occupies the place of honour lit up within the soaring *retablo* (altarpiece), separated from the main body of the nave by a fine plateresque *reja* (grille). The fantastic walnut choir is an 18th-century work with an immense lectern, while the fabulous baroque organs are visited on the tour.

Activities

Ruta de Isabel la Católica   HIKING
One splendid walking option is to take any Miajadas- or Cáceres-bound bus to the village of Cañamero, southwest of Guadalupe, and hike back along a well-signed 15km trail that retraces the steps of pilgrims coming to Guadalupe from the south – including Reyes Católicos (the Catholic Monarchs) Isabel and Fernando, after the fall of Moorish Granada.

Sleeping

Cerezo II   HOSTAL €
(☑ 927 15 41 77; www.hostalcerezo2meson.com; Plaza Mayor 23; s/d Sun-Thu from €31/45, Fri & Sat from €38/52; ✸) On the main square, Cerezo II has attractive if fairly standard *hostal* (budget hotel) rooms, decorated in earthy colours with thick quilts.

★ Hospedería del Real Monasterio   HISTORIC HOTEL €€
(☑ 927 36 70 00; www.monasterioguadalupe.com; Plaza Juan Carlos I; s/d €50/72; ☉ closed Jan & Feb; P✸🛜) Centred on the Real Monasterio's beautiful Gothic cloister, this old-fashioned hotel gives you the chance to live it up in a national monument without having to pay *parador*-style prices. There's a sumptuous patio just off the lobby, and a palpable historical ambience. High-ceilinged rooms are darkish and venerable but comfortable.

Parador de Guadalupe   HISTORIC HOTEL €€€
(☑ 927 36 70 75; www.parador.es; Calle Marqués de la Romana 12; r €80-115; ☉ closed Jan–mid-Feb; P✸🛜❄) This place occupies a converted 15th-century hospital and 16th-century religious school opposite the Guadalupe monastery. Spacious rooms are tastefully decorated and the cobbled courtyard is delightful, with its lemon and orange trees surrounded by a cloister-like colonnade with arches.

Eating

Cheap restaurants around the Plaza Mayor offer no-frills Extremadura cooking at low prices. The Parador de Guadalupe has a terrific restaurant.

Hospedería del Real Monasterio   SPANISH €€
(☑ 927 36 70 00; www.monasterioguadalupe.com; Plaza Juan Carlos I; mains €11-24; ☉ 2-4pm & 9pm-midnight, closed Jan-Feb) Dine grandly under the arches of the magnificent Gothic cloister or in the dining halls, rich with 17th-century timber furnishings and antique ceramics. There's a competent range of both meat and fish dishes, and most of the desserts are homemade. Set meals are €22 if you're staying.

Information

Tourist Office (☑ 927 15 41 28; www.turismoextremadura.com; Plaza de Santa María de Guadalupe; ☉ 10am-2pm & 4-7pm Wed-Mon) On the square below the monastery.

Getting There & Away

Buses stop on Avenida Conde de Barcelona near the town hall, a two-minute walk from Plaza Mayor. **Mirat** (☑ 927 23 48 63; www.mirat.net) runs two services Monday to Friday (and one on Sunday) to/from Cáceres (€12, 2¼ hours) via Trujillo. **Samar** (☑ 902 257025; www.samar. es) has one to three daily buses to/from Madrid (€18, four hours).

Plasencia
POP 41,047

This pleasant, bustling town is the natural hub of northern Extremadura. Rising above a bend of the Río Jerte, it retains long sections of its defensive walls. It has an earthy and attractive old quarter of narrow streets, Romanesque churches and stately stone palaces.

Sights

Catedral
CATHEDRAL

(Plaza de la Catedral; Catedral Nueva free, Catedral Vieja €2; ⊙ 9am-1pm & 5-7pm Mon-Sat, 9am-1pm Sun) Plasencia's cathedral is actually two-in-one. The 16th-century **Catedral Nueva** is a Gothic-Renaissance blend with a handsome plateresque facade, soaring *retablo* (altarpiece) and intricately carved choir stalls. Within the Romanesque **Catedral Vieja** are classic 13th-century cloisters surrounding a trickling fountain and lemon trees. Also on view is the soaring octagonal **Capilla de San Pablo** with a dramatic 1569 Caravaggio painting of John the Baptist.

Plaza Mayor
SQUARE

In Plasencia life flows through the lively, arcaded Plaza Mayor, meeting place of 10 streets and scene of a Tuesday farmers market since the 12th century. The jaunty fellow striking the hour atop the Gothic **town hall** is El Abuelo Mayorga, a 1970s replica of the 13th-century original and the unofficial symbol of the town.

Centro de Interpretación de la Ciudad Medieval
INTERPRETATION CENTRE

(Plaza de Torre Lucía; ⊙ 10am-2pm & 5-8pm Tue-Sat Jun-Sep, 10am-2pm & 4-7pm Oct-May) **FREE** The best-preserved defensive tower of the old city wall, located at the top of the old town, tells the history of medieval Plasencia through video, models and artefacts, and provides access to a walkable chunk of the wall.

Sleeping

Hotel Rincón Extremeño
HOTEL €

(☑ 927 41 11 50; www.hotelrincon.com; Calle Vidrieras 6; s/d from €25/35; ❄ 🖤) This friendly and unpretentious hotel on a narrow street just off Plaza Mayor has a great location and clean, if unmemorable, rooms above a popular local restaurant. This is the heart of Plasencia's eating zone, with many good choices within a few minutes' walk.

★ Palacio Carvajal Girón
HOTEL €€

(☑ 927 42 63 26; www.palaciocarvajalgiron.com; Plaza Ansano 1; r €85-155; P ❄ 🖤 🖳) A mightily impressive conversion job on a formerly ruined palace in the heart of the old town has resulted in this chic Plasencia address. Rooms have modern fittings with crisp white linen juxtaposed with original features of the building – a most successful combination.

Parador de Plasencia
HISTORIC HOTEL €€€

(☑ 927 42 58 70; www.parador.es; Plaza San Vicente Ferrer; r €100-165; P ❄ 🖤) This *parador* is a classic – still oozing the atmosphere and austerity of its 15th-century convent roots, with massive stone columns, soaring ceilings and a traditional Renaissance cloister. The rooms are far from monastic, being luxuriously furnished with rugs and rich fabrics.

Eating

At lunchtime and sunset, the bars and terraces surrounding Plaza Mayor fill up with eager punters downing the local *pitarra* red wine and munching complimentary *pinchos* (tapas). Narrow Calle Vidrieras running off it has lots of bars and restaurants worth investigating.

★ Casa Juan
SPANISH €€

(☑ 927 42 40 42; www.restaurantecasajuan.com; Calle Arenillas 5; mains €13-28; ⊙ Fri-Wed, closed Jan) Tucked down a quiet lane, French-owned Casa Juan does well-prepared *extremeño* meat dishes, such as shoulder of lamb and suckling pig. Try the homemade melt-in-the-mouth foie gras or the expertly hung local *retinto* beef. Fairly priced wines from all around Spain seal the deal.

Information

Municipal Tourist Office (☑ 927 42 38 43; www.plasencia.es; Calle Santa Clara 4; ⊙ 7.45am-3.15pm & 4-7pm Mon-Fri, 9.30am-2pm & 4-7pm Sat & Sun) Information on the town.

Regional Tourist Office (☑ 927 01 78 40; www.turismoextremadura.com; Calle Torre Lucía; ⊙ 8am-3pm Mon-Fri, 10am-2pm Sat & Sun mid-Jun–mid-Sep, 8.30am-2.30pm & 4-6pm Mon-Fri, 10am-noon Sat & Sun rest of year) Information on the wider Extremadura region.

Getting There & Away

The **bus station** (☑ 927 41 45 50; Calle de Tornavacas 2) is about 750m east of Plaza Mayor. The train station is off the Cáceres road, about 1km southwest of town.

Up to five buses daily run to/from Cáceres (€5.15, 50 minutes), Madrid (€18, 3½ hours) and Salamanca (€9.60, 1¾ to 2½ hours). Others serve smaller destinations around northern Extremadura.

Trains depart three to four times daily from Plasencia to Madrid (from €23, 2¾ hours), Cáceres (from €5.10, one hour) and Mérida (from €12, two hours).

La Vera

Surrounded by mountains often still capped with snow as late as May, the fertile La Vera region produces raspberries, asparagus and, above all, *pimentón* (paprika), sold in charming old-fashioned tins and with a distinctive smoky flavour. Typical, too, are half-timbered houses leaning at odd angles, their overhanging upper storeys supported by timber or stone pillars. La Vera makes a great driving tour from Plasencia (p555).

◎ Sights & Activities

Monasterio de Yuste   MONASTERY
(www.patrimonionacional.es; Cuacos de Yuste; adult/child €9/4, audio guide €6; ☺ 10am-8pm Apr-Sep, to 6pm Oct-Mar) In a lovely setting 2km above the village of Cuacos de Yuste, this monastery is where Carlos I of Spain (also known as Carlos V of Austria) came in 1557 to prepare for death after abdicating his emperorship over much of Western and Central Europe. It's a soulful, evocative place amid the forested hills and a tranquil counterpoint to the grandeur of so many formerly royal buildings elsewhere in Spain.

If you have an interest in Spanish history, it's fascinating to see the royal apartments, including the bedroom where he died in September 1558. A doorway allowed this religious monarch to see, from his deathbed, the Hieronymite monks giving Mass in the single-naved church alongside. Carlos was buried behind the high altar, but his son Felipe (Philip) II later had him moved to El Escorial. Two cloisters and a collection of religious art (as well as copies of Titians that Carlos brought with him) are other features. In 2013, it became a working monastery again after a community of Polish monks took up residence. The monastery is free for EU citizens for the last three hours on Wednesday and Thursday.

Walking   HIKING
There are many marked trails winding between various villages in La Vera. One of them is the 10km section of the **Ruta del Emperador**, which leads from Jarandilla to the Yuste monastery.

⌂ Sleeping & Eating

Most villages have well-signposted camping grounds and *casas rurales* (rural homes) with rooms to let. Local dishes include *caldereta de cabrito* (stewed kid) and *migas* (breadcrumbs fried with garlic, peppers and pork).

La Vera de Yuste   CASA RURAL €
(☎ 927 17 22 89; www.laveradeyuste.com; Calle Teodoro Perianes 17, Cuacos de Yuste; s/d €45/65; ❄) This real gem is set in two typical 18th-century village houses near the Plaza Mayor. The beamed rooms have chunky rustic furniture and the garden is a delight, surrounded by rose bushes with a small courtyard and vegetable patch. Dinner available.

★ **Haldón Country**   RURAL HOTEL €€
(☎ 927 57 10 04; www.hotelhaldoncountry.com; Finca El Haldón, Robledillo de la Vera; s incl breakfast €62-78, d €92-125; P ❄ ☎ ❄) This exquisite rural hotel, which is just off the main road between Jarandilla and Villanueva, is a haven of peace and relaxation. Set in extensive grounds, it has airy, light modern rooms (as well as a few older-style rooms) decorated with original art. The atrium holds a heated pool, there's a small spa, and a warm welcome from the hosts. Prices drop midweek.

EXTREMADURA LA VERA

LA VERA ITINERARY

La Vera is famous for its *pimentón* (paprika) and has lovely traditional architecture dignifying its string of villages. Begin in **Plasencia**, stopping first in prettily situated **Pasarón**, with its fine 16th-century palace of the Condes de Osorno. Next is **Jaraíz**, the *pimentón* HQ. Tracking northeast, **Cuacos de Yuste** is rich in typical half-timbered houses and lovely plazas, with a fine royal monastery not far away. Beyond, **Jarandilla** is one of the most appealing stops. Its castle-like church was built by the Templars and features an ancient font brought from the Holy Land. After Jarandilla, explore **Valverde** – home of the Easter ritual of Los Empalaos – whose lovely Plaza de España is lined with timber balconies. Double back to **Garganta La Olla**, a picturesque, steeply pitched village with overhanging balconies on the main street and centuries-old inscriptions above the doors. From here it's a spectacular drive over the **Puerto de Piornal** pass (Piornal is famous for its *jamón*) and down into the **Valle del Jerte**.

Parador de Jarandilla HISTORIC HOTEL €€
(☑ 927 56 01 17; www.parador.es; Avenida de García Prieto 1, Jarandilla de la Vera; r €80-120; P ✳ 🕾 🌫) Be king of the castle for the night at this 15th-century castle-turned-hotel. Carlos I stayed here for a few months while waiting for his monastery digs to be completed. Within the stout walls and turrets are period-furnished rooms, plus a classic courtyard where you can dine royally from the restaurant menu.

La Casa de Pasarón CASA RURAL €€
(☑ 927 46 94 07; www.pasaron.com; Calle de la Magdalena 18, Pasarón de la Vera; r €80-95; P ✳ 🕾) Follow the signs to this handsome family house, where the ground floor dates from 1890. Rooms are bathed in light with terracotta tiles and lashings of white linen and paintwork. Pretty attic rooms with sloping ceilings cost a little more. The restaurant is excellent, but only opens if there are enough people.

★**La Finca** SPANISH €€
(☑ 927 66 51 50; www.villaxarahiz.com; Ctra 203, Km 32.8, Jaraíz de la Vera; mains €14-20; ⊘ Tue-Sun; 🕾) Offering spectacular sierra views from the terrace and the upmarket dining room, this hotel restaurant just below Jaraíz is one of La Vera's best bets for smart regional food, featuring local peppers, *caldereta de*

EASTER SUFFERING

At midnight on the eve of Good Friday, Valverde de la Vera is the scene of one of the more bizarre of Spain's religious festivities, Los Empalaos (literally 'the Impaled'). Several penitent locals strap their arms to a beam (from a plough) while their near-naked bodies are wrapped tight with cords from waist to fingertips. Barefoot, veiled, with two swords strapped to their backs and wearing a crown of thorns, these 'walking crucifixes' follow a painful Way of the Cross. Iron chains hanging from the timber clank sinisterly as the penitents make painful progress through the crowds. Guided by *cirineos* (who pick them up should they fall), the *empalaos* occasionally cross paths. When this happens, they kneel and rise again to continue their laborious journey. Doctors stay on hand, as being so tightly strapped does nothing for blood circulation.

cabrito and other quality Extremadura produce. There's also a bar with an amazing array of gin-and-tonic choices.

❶ Information

Browse www.aturive.com and www.comarcadelavera.com, two useful websites.
Tourist Office (☑ 927 56 04 60; www.jarandilla.com; Avenida Soledad Vega Ortiz, Jarandilla de la Vera; ⊘ 10am-2pm & 4.30-7.30pm Tue-Sat, 10am-2pm Sun) One of a number of tourist offices dotted around La Vera.

❶ Getting There & Away

Three buses run Monday to Friday from Plasencia to Jarandilla via lower La Vera villages (€6.50, one hour), and one on Sunday. Some continue further up the valley.

Valle del Jerte

This valley, separated from La Vera by the Sierra de Tormantos, grows half of Spain's cherries and is a sea of white blossom in early spring. Visit in May and every second house is busy boxing the ripe fruit.

🏃 Activities

Walking Routes HIKING
There are excellent walks for all levels in the Valle del Jerte, some along the pretty gorge, Garganta de los Infiernos. The main trailhead is at the Centro de Interpretación de la Naturaleza (☑ 927 01 49 36; ⊘ 9am-2pm & 4-6pm), 2.5km from central Jerte; it begins the easy stroll to the natural pools of Los Pilones (two hours return from Jerte itself). From Los Pilones, you can head on to Cabezuela (four hours). Further up the valley, Tornavacas is the launch pad for the seven- to nine-hour, 28km Ruta del Emperador hike over the sierra to Jarandilla in La Vera via the Yuste monastery. The abdicated Emperor Carlos I was carried to Yuste via this route in the mid-16th century.

🛏 Sleeping & Eating

Antigua Posada CASA RURAL €
(☑ 927 17 70 19; www.antiguaposada.com; Calle Real de Abajo 32, Tornavacas; s/d incl breakfast €45/62; 🖷) Occupying a lovely old 18th-century dwelling in the heart of Tornavacas, this exceptionally welcoming house offers great value for well-kept rooms, a home-from-home feel and great sightseeing and walking advice on the surrounding area.

El Cerezal de los Sotos CASA RURAL €€

(🖉927 47 04 29; www.elcerezaldelossotos.net; Calle de las Vegas, Jerte; s/d incl breakfast €63/79; P❄☎❄) The valley is known for *casas rurales* like this one. It is a quiet, homey stone house dating from 1890, with beams, an open fireplace and spacious attractive rooms set amid cherry orchards and sweeping lawns above the river. Follow the signs over the bridge from Jerte. There's a two-night minimum stay and dinner is available.

Valle del Jerte SPANISH €€

(🖉927 47 04 48; www.donbellota.com; Gargantilla 16, Jerte; mains €13-19; ⊙1.30-3.30pm & 8.30-10.30pm Tue-Sat, 1.30-3.30pm Sun) This warmly decorated restaurant near the main plaza serves local specialities such as trout and *cabrito* (kid). Service is on the fussy side, but the excellent wine selection and delicious desserts make up for it.

ℹ Information

Jerte Tourist Office (🖉927 47 04 53; www.jerte.es; Avenida Ramón y Cajal, Jerte; ⊙10am-2pm & 6-8pm Mon-Sat, 10.30am-1.30pm Sun) Along the main road.

ℹ Getting There & Away

One to four buses daily from Plasencia serve Jerte and other valley towns, some going on to Madrid.

Valle del Ambroz

This broader valley west of the Valle del Jerte is split by the Vía de la Plata and the A66 motorway.

Hervás

POP 4193

Hervás is a lively and handsome town with a picturesque old quarter. It makes a great base for exploring the area.

◉ Sights

Hervás has Extremadura's best surviving barrio judío (Jewish quarter); it thrived until the 1492 expulsion of the Jews, when most families fled to Portugal. Seek out Calles Rabilero and Cuestecilla, then, for a fine view, climb up to the Iglesia de Santa María, on the site of a ruined Templar castle.

Museo Pérez Comendador-Leroux GALLERY

(🖉927 48 16 55; http://mpcl.net; Calle Asensio Neila; admission €1.20, Sun free; ⊙5-8pm Tue,

11am-2pm & 5-8pm Wed-Fri, 10.30am-2pm Sat & Sun) Within an impressive 18th-century mansion, the Museo Pérez Comendador-Leroux houses works by Hervás-born, 20th-century sculptor Enrique Pérez Comendador and his wife, the French painter Magdalena Leroux.

Museo de la Moto Clásica MUSEUM

(www.museomotoclasica.com; Carretera de la Garganta; adult/child €10/free; ⊙10.30am-1.30pm & 5-9pm Mon-Fri, 10.30am-9pm Sat & Sun Jul-Sep, shorter hours & closed Mon Oct-Jun) Set in distinctive conical-roofed buildings 200m north of the river, this museum offers great views, a fabulous collection of more than 300 classic motorcycles, as well as cars and horse-drawn carriages.

🛏 Sleeping & Eating

Albergue de la Vía de la Plata HOSTEL €

(🖉927 47 34 70; www.alberguesviaplata.es; Paseo de la Estación; dm incl breakfast €20; P@❄) Owner Carlos runs this delightful hostel with warmth and enthusiasm. The setting is an evocative converted train station overlooking the disused tracks. Rooms and the communal areas are brightly furnished and there's a bar and kitchen.

★**El Jardín del Convento** HOTEL €€

(🖉927 48 11 61; www.eljardindelconvento.com; Plaza del Convento 22; r €65-100, cottage €115; ❄☎) On the edge of the Jewish quarter, with a fabulous garden – all roses, vegetables and tranquil seating space – that makes for very rural relaxation, this is a wonderful place to stay. The rooms are all different and full of character, with wooden floors, exposed stone walls and period furniture.

La Tapería del Convento TAPAS €

(www.lataperiadelconvento.es; Calle Convento 45; raciones €5-10; ⊙noon-midnight Thu-Tue) This small bar is a great destination for no-frills but extremely tasty dishes at low prices and in huge quantities. You get a decent free tapa with your glass of wine too. Local cheeses feature heavily, and are also available for sale.

ℹ Information

Tourist Office (🖉927 47 36 18; www.turismodehervas.com; Calle Braulio Navas 6; ⊙10am-2pm & 5-8pm Tue-Sun) Good for information on the town and Valle del Ambroz.

SIERRA DE GATA & LAS HURDES

The Sierra de Gata and Las Hurdes in Extremadura's far north form one of Spain's most remote corners. The prettiest villages in the Sierra de Gata include Hoyos and San Martín de Trevejo, where people speak their own isolated dialect, a unique mix of Spanish and Portuguese. In Valverde del Fresno, A Velha Fábrica (☑927 51 19 33; www.avelhafabrica.com; Calle Carrasco 24, Valverde del Fresno; s/d/f incl breakfast €60/90/140; Ⓟ🕸🛜🖳) is a great small hotel set in a former textile mill.

The Las Hurdes region has taken nearly a century to shake off its image of poverty, disease, and chilling tales of witchcraft and even cannibalism. In 1922 the miserable existence of the *hurdanos* prompted Alfonso XIII to declare during a horseback tour, 'I can bear to see no more'. Head for villages like Casares and Ladrillar, with traditional stone, slate-roofed houses huddled in clusters, while the PR40 is a near-circular 28km route from Casares that follows ancient shepherd trails.

ⓘ Getting There & Away

One to four buses a day run between Cáceres, Plasencia and Salamanca via the Valle del Ambroz, calling by Hervás (€3.15 from Plasencia).

Granadilla

About 25km west of Hervás, the ghost village of Granadilla (⊙10am-1pm & 4-8pm Tue-Sun Apr-Oct, to 6pm Nov-Mar) FREE is a beguiling reminder of how Extremadura's villages must have looked before the rush to modernisation. Founded by the Moors in the 10th century but abandoned in the 1960s when the nearby dam was built, the village's traditional architecture has been painstakingly restored as part of a government educational project.

You enter the village through the narrow Puerta de Villa, overlooked by the sturdy castle. From here, the cobblestone Calle Mayor climbs up to the delightfully rustic Plaza Mayor. Some buildings function as craft workshops or exhibition centres in summer; make sure also to walk your way along the top of the Almohad walls, with evocative views of village, lake and pinewoods.

Coria

POP 13,010

This pretty, small market town lies south of the Sierra de Gata and is a good gateway to it. Massive and largely intact protective walls, marked by four gates, enclose the historic quarter of town. The Romans called the place Caurium; after a period of decay, its splendour was revived under the Moors, when it was briefly the capital of a small Islamic state.

◉ Sights & Activities

Catedral
CATHEDRAL

(Plaza de la Catedral; museum €2; ⊙10am-2pm & 5-8pm Mon-Sat, 10am-2pm Sun) FREE The primarily Gothic cathedral has intricate plateresque decoration around its north portal. It occupies a well-used sacred site: there was a Visigothic cathedral here, then the main mosque, then a Romanesque cathedral before this one was built. The interior highlight is a high sober gold altarpiece. On the plain below is a fine stone bridge, abandoned in the 17th century by Río Alagón, which now takes a more southerly course.

Museo de la Cárcel Real
MUSEUM

(Calle de las Monjas 2; ⊙10am-2pm & 5.30-8.30pm) FREE Once the town prison, this building houses Coria's tiny two-storey archaeological museum. Step inside the dark, poky *celda del castigo* (punishment cell), then see how the cushy 1st-floor cells differed from the plebs' prison below.

Convento de la Madre de Dios
CONVENT

(Calle de las Monjas; admission €1.50; ⊙10am-12.15pm & 4-6.15pm) The Convento de la Madre de Dios is a thriving 15th-century convent with an elegant cloister. The sisters sell a variety of delicious homemade sweets and pastries.

🛏 Sleeping & Eating

Palacio Coria
HOTEL €€

(☑927 50 64 49; Plaza de la Catedral; s/d incl breakfast €75/95; Ⓟ🕸🛜) In a 17th-century former bishop's palace next to the cathedral, this sumptuous accommodation successfully couples modern comfort and convenience with heady palatial surrounds. There are excellent weekend deals.

El Bobo de Coria SPANISH €€
(☎ 927 50 07 95; www.elbobodecoria.com; Calle de las Monjas 6; mains €10-16; ⊘ noon-4.30pm & 8pm-midnight Tue-Sun) Particularly strong on local mushrooms in season, 'the Idiot of Coria' (named after a Velázquez painting), with its eclectically rustic decor, is also rich in traditional Extremadura dishes.

ℹ Information

Tourist Office (☎ 927 50 80 00; http://turismo.coria.org; Plaza de San Pedro 1; ⊘ 9.30am-2pm & 5-9pm Mon-Fri, 10am-2pm Sat & Sun) Local town information.

ℹ Getting There & Away

The **bus station** (☎ 927 50 01 10; Calle de Chile) is in the new part of town. Buses run to/from Plasencia (€6.50, 50 minutes, four Monday to Friday, one Sunday) and Cáceres (€8.75, one hour, two Monday to Friday and one Sunday).

Parque Nacional de Monfragüe

Spain's 14th and newest national park is a hilly paradise for birdwatchers. Straddling the Tajo valley, it's home to spectacular colonies of raptors and more than 75% of Spain's protected species. Among some 175 feathered varieties are around 300 pairs of black vultures (the largest concentration of Europe's biggest bird of prey) and populations of two other rare large birds: the Spanish imperial eagle and the black stork. The best time to visit is between March and October, since many bird species winter in Africa.

Signed walking trails criss-cross the park. The best base is the pretty hamlet of Villareal de San Carlos, from where most trails leave. The EX208 road also traverses the park and you can drive to several of the hides and lookout points. The hilltop Castillo de Monfragüe, a ruined 9th-century Islamic fort, has sweeping views; the castle can also be reached via an attractive 1½-hour walk from Villareal. Arguably the best spot is the Mirador del Salto del Gitano, a lookout point along the main road. From here, there are stunning views across the river gorge to the Peña Falcón crag.

☞ Tours

The Centro de Visitantes in Villareal de San Carlos runs free guided walks at weekends; prior reservations by telephone are required.

Other private organisations offer a range of tours.

Birding in Extremadura BIRDWATCHING
(☎ 927 31 93 49; www.birdingextremadura.com) Run by British ornithologist Martin Kelsey.

Iberian Nature BIRDWATCHING
(☎ 676 784221; www.extremadurabirds.net) Birdwatching experts with guided hikes.

Monfragüe Natural BIRDWATCHING
(☎ 638 520891; www.monfraguenatural.com) A variety of excursions, including wildlife-watching, horseriding and kayaking.

🛏 Sleeping

Camping Monfragüe CAMPGROUND €
(☎ 927 45 92 33; www.campingmonfrague.com; sites per adult/tent/car €4.20/4.20/3.80, 2-/4-person bungalows €50/90; P 🐾) Precisely 14km north of Villareal on the EX208 is this shady camping ground, with a restaurant, shop and pool, plus homey bungalows complete with front porches.

Casa Rural Monfragüe CASA RURAL €
(☎ 927 19 90 02; www.monfraguerural.com; Calle de Villareal 15, Villareal de San Carlos; s/d incl breakfast €39/55; 🐾 🛜) This light-filled *casa rural* has large, brightly painted rooms in a lovely stone building directly opposite the park's information centre. There's an attractive bar-restaurant downstairs serving solid Extremadura fare. The owners rent bikes and binoculars and can arrange tours.

Hospedería Parque de Monfragüe HOTEL €€
(☎ 927 45 52 78; www.hospederiasdeextremadura.es; Km 39; d incl breakfast €63-120; P 🐾 @ 🛜 🐾 🐾) This tranquil four-star hotel on the northern edge of Torrejón el Rubio looks out across the plains to the national park, with pretty views all around. Spacious slate-walled rooms come with squeaky floors and a TV with internet. Duplexes are good for families, and there's a decent restaurant (mains €16 to €25). Prices can halve in the low season.

ℹ Information

Centro de Visitantes (☎ 927 19 91 34; www.porticodemonfrague.es; Villareal de San Carlos; adult/child €2/1; ⊘ noon-1pm Tue-Thu, 10am-1pm & 5-8pm Fri-Sun) This place offers the perfect introduction to the park. You can reserve free guided visits to cave paintings near the Castillo de Monfragüe here.

ℹ Getting There & Away

Public transport through the park is restricted to one bus each way Monday to Friday between Plasencia and Torrejón el Rubio; it stops in Villareal de San Carlos. The nearest train station is at Monfragüe, 18km north of Villareal de San Carlos.

Mérida

POP 59,049

Mérida, capital of Extremadura, was once also capital of the Roman province of Lusitania and it's still home to the most impressive and extensive Roman ruins in all Spain. The ruins lie sprinkled around the town, often appearing in the most unlikely corners, and one can only wonder what still lies buried beneath the modern city.

◉ Sights

★ Teatro Romano   RUIN
(Paseo Álvarez Sáez de Buruaga; entry by combined ticket adult/concession/child €12/6/free; ◷ 9am-9pm Apr-Sep, 9.30am-2pm & 4-6.30pm Mon-Fri, 9am-6.30pm Sat & Sun Oct-Mar) Mérida's most spectacular Roman monument, and the only one to once again fulfil its original function – the theatre hosts performances during the Festival del Teatro Clásico (p564) in summer – the Teatro Romano is the highlight of any visit to the town. It was built around 15 BC to seat 6000 spectators. The adjoining Anfiteatro opened in 8 BC for gladiatorial contests (the gladiator-versus-lion fresco in the Museo Nacional de Arte Romano was taken from here) and held 14,000.

The centrepiece of the theatre is the dramatic and well-preserved two-tier stage

---

ℹ COMBINED TICKET

Admission to most of Mérida's Roman sites is via a combined ticket, which costs €12 for adults, €6 for students and pensioners, and is free for children under 12. It includes entry to the Teatro Romano and Anfiteatro, Casa del Anfiteatro (when it reopens), Los Columbarios, Casa del Mitreo, Alcazaba, Circo Romano, Basílica de Santa Eulalia and the Zona Arqueológica de Morería. The Museo Nacional de Arte Romano is not included. The ticket has no time limit and can be bought from any of the sights.

---

building of Corinthian columns; the stage's facade (scaenae frons) was inaugurated in AD 105. Outside the main gate, the Casa del Anfiteatro (entry by combined ticket adult/concession/child €12/6/free), a 3rd-century mansion, has some reasonable floor mosaics but was closed for restoration works when we visited.

★ Museo Nacional de Arte
Romano   MUSEUM
(http://museoarteromano.mcu.es; Calle de José Ramón Mélida; adult/child €3/free, EU seniors & students free, all free after 2pm Sat & all day Sun; ◷ 9.30am-8pm Tue-Sat, 10am-3pm Sun Apr-Sep, 9.30am-6.30pm Tue-Sat, 10am-3pm Sun Oct-Mar) On no account should you miss this fabulous museum, which has a superb collection of statues, mosaics, frescoes, coins and other Roman artefacts, all beautifully displayed. Designed by the architect Rafael Moneo, the soaring brick structure makes a remarkable home for the collection.

Circo Romano   RUIN
(Avenida Juan Carlos; entry by combined ticket adult/concession/child €12/6/free; ◷ 9am-9pm Apr-Sep, 9.30am-2pm & 4-6.30pm Mon-Fri, 9am-6.30pm Sat & Sun Oct-Mar) The remains of the 1st-century Circo Romano, which could accommodate 30,000 spectators, represent the only surviving hippodrome of its kind in Spain. Inside you can see brief footage in Spanish about Diocles, a champion auriga (chariot racer) who served his apprenticeship in Mérida before going on to the big league in Rome.

Los Columbarios   RUIN
(Calle del Ensanche; entry by combined ticket adult/concession/child €12/6/free; ◷ 9am-9pm Apr-Sep, 9.30am-2pm & 4-6.30pm Mon-Fri, 9am-6.30pm Sat & Sun Oct-Mar) This Roman funeral site is well documented in Spanish and illustrated. A footpath connects it with the Casa del Mitreo (Calle Oviedo; entry by combined ticket adult/concession/child €12/6/free; ◷ 9am-9pm Apr-Sep, 9.30am-2pm & 4-6.30pm Mon-Fri, 9am-6.30pm Sat & Sun Oct-Mar), a 2nd-century Roman house with several intricate mosaics (especially the partial but beautiful remains of the mosaico cosmológico, with its allegories and bright colours) and a well-preserved fresco.

Templo de Diana   RUIN
(Calle de Sagasta) Inaccurately named, for it's now known to have been dedicated to the Imperial cult, this temple stood in the mu-

Mérida

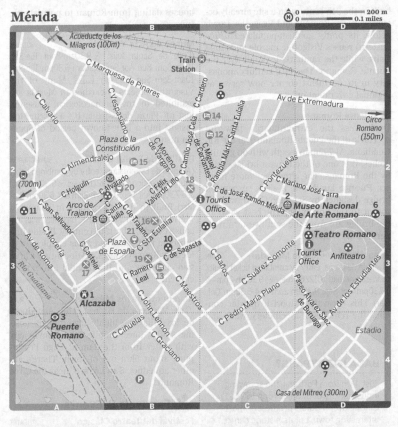

Mérida

⊙ Top Sights
1 Alcazaba	A3
2 Museo Nacional de Arte Romano	C2
3 Puente Romano	A4
4 Teatro Romano	D3

⊙ Sights
5 Basílica de Santa Eulalia	C1
6 Casa del Anfiteatro	D2
7 Los Columbarios	D4
8 Museo de Arte Visigodo	A3
9 Pórtico del Foro	C3
10 Templo de Diana	B3
11 Zona Arqueológica de Morería	A2

⊛ Sleeping
12 Capitolio	C2
13 Hotel Adealba	B3
14 La Flor de al-Andalus	C1
15 Parador Vía de la Plata	B2

⊗ Eating
16 Casa Benito	B3
17 Casa Nano	A3
18 La Bodeguilla	B2
19 Tábula Calda	B3

⊙ Drinking & Nightlife
20 Jazz Bar	B2
21 La Moett	B3

nicipal forum, where the city government was based. Parts were incorporated into a 16th-century mansion built within it. The forum's restored **Pórtico del Foro** (Calle de Sagasta) is just along the road.

★**Alcazaba** FORTRESS
(Calle Graciano; entry by combined ticket adult/concession/child €12/6/free; ⏰ 9am-9pm Apr-Sep, 9.30am-2pm & 4-6.30pm Mon-Fri, 9am-6.30pm Sat & Sun Oct-Mar) This large Islamic fort was

EXTREMADURA MÉRIDA

built in the 9th century on a site already occupied by the Romans and Visigoths. Down below, its pretty goldfish-populated *aljibe* (cistern) reuses Visigothic marble and stone slabs, while the ramparts look out over the Puente Romano. The 15th-century monastery in its northeast corner now serves as regional goverment offices.

★ **Puente Romano** BRIDGE
Don't miss the extraordinarily powerful spectacle of the Puente Romano over the Río Guadiana. At 792m in length with 60 granite arches, it is one of the longest bridges built by the Romans. The altogether more modern **Puente Lusitania**, a sleek suspension bridge designed by Santiago Calatrava, mirrors it to the northwest. The best views of the bridge are from the southwestern ramparts of the Alcazaba.

Zona Arqueológica de Morería RUIN
(Avenida de Roma; entry by combined ticket adult/concession/child €12/6/free; ☺9.30am-2pm & 5-7.30pm Apr-Sep, 9.30am-2pm & 4-6.30pm Oct-Mar) This excavated Moorish quarter contains the remains of a cemetery, walls and houses dating from Roman to post-Islamic times.

Museo de Arte Visigodo MUSEUM
(Calle de Santa Julia; ☺9.30am-8pm Tue-Sat, 10am-3pm Sun Apr-Sep, 9.30am-6.30pm Tue-Sat, 10am-3pm Sun Oct-Mar) **FREE** Many of the Visigothic objects unearthed in Mérida are exhibited in this archaeological museum, just off Plaza de España. It's a fascinating insight into a little-known period of Spanish history.

Basílica de Santa Eulalia RUIN, CHURCH
(Avenida de Extremadura; entry by combined ticket adult/concession/child €12/6/free; ☺9.30am-2pm & 5-7.30pm Apr-Sep, 9.30am-2pm & 4-6.30pm Oct-Mar) Built in the 5th century in honour of Mérida's patron saint, the basilica was reconstructed in the 13th century. Beside it, a museum and excavated areas enable you to identify Roman houses, a 4th-century Christian cemetery and the original 5th-century church.

Acueducto de los Milagros RUIN
(Calle Marquesa de Pinares) The Acueducto de los Milagros, highly favoured by nesting storks, once supplied the Roman city with water from the dam at Lago Proserpina, about 5km out of town. There's another aqueduct, **San Lázaro**, near the Circo Romano.

✯ Festivals & Events

Festival del Teatro Clásico THEATRE
(www.festivaldemerida.es; admission €15-45) This prestigious summer festival, held at the Roman theatre and amphitheatre, features Greek and more recent drama classics, plus music and dance. It starts around 11pm most nights in July and August.

🛌 Sleeping

★ **La Flor de Al-Andalus** HOSTAL €
(☏924 31 33 56; www.laflordeal-andalus.es; Avenida de Extremadura 6; s/d/tr €33/45/54; ✳@) If only all *hostales* were this good. Describing itself as a 'boutique *hostal*', La Flor de Al-Andalus has rooms beautifully decorated in Andalucían style, friendly service and a good location within walking distance of all the main sites. This is hotel standard at a great price. Try to avoid the rooms on the ground floor by the reception. Breakfast is available for €3.

BADAJOZ BYPASS?

Just 4km from Portugal, the sprawling industrial city of Badajoz (pop 150,621) is not Extremadura's prettiest or most interesting town, but its historic centre is worth a visit if you're in the area.

Highlights include the unusual **Plaza Alta** (1681) beneath the imposing **Alcazaba**. On the square itelf, **La Casona Alta** (☏924 24 73 95; www.tabernalacasona.com; Plaza Alta; tapas €2-4, mains €9-16; ☺1-4pm & 8pm-midnight Mon-Sat, 1-4pm Sun) is good for a meal. Elsewhere, the **Museo de Bellas Artes** (☏924 21 24 69; www.dip-badajoz.es/cultura/museo; Calle del Duque de San Germán 3; ☺10am-2pm & 4-6pm Tue-Sat, 10am-2pm Sun) **FREE** has works by Zurbarán, Picasso and Dalí, while the **Museo Extremeño e Iberoamericano de Arte Contemporáneo** (MEIAC; www.meiac.es; Calle Museo 2; ☺10am-1.30pm & 5-8pm Tue-Sat, 10am-1.30pm Sun) **FREE** houses contemporary art.

Most people visit on a day trip by bus from Mérida (€5.60, one hour, five to nine daily) or Zafra (€6.07, 1¼ hours).

Capitolio APARTMENT €

(924 30 31 63; www.capitolio.es; Travesia de Cervantes 2; s/d from €50/60) These beautifully decorated mini-apartments in a good central location have kitchens, plenty of space and a colour scheme that alternates between sober and minimalist and exuberantly colourful with wall-high photographs of flowers. Whichever version you choose, it's outrageously good value.

Hotel Adealba HOTEL €€

(924 38 83 08; www.hoteladealba.com; Calle Romero Leal 18; s €50-80, d €60-90; P ❄ ⊛) This chic but cordial hotel occupies a 19th-century townhouse close to the Templo de Diana and does so with a classy, contemporary look. Although some of the installations are starting to show their age, the beds are super comfy and the bigger the room, the better the deal. There's a compact on-site spa complex. Valet parking (€18) is available.

Parador Vía de la Plata HISTORIC HOTEL €€€

(924 31 38 00; www.parador.es; Plaza de la Constitución 3; r €70-145; P ❄ ⊛ ☲) You're sleeping on the site of a Roman temple in a building that started life as a convent; the lounge was a former chapel, then served as both hospital and prison. In the gardens, the assembled hunks of Roman, Visigothic and Mudéjar artefacts give a brief canter through Mérida's architectural history. Rear-room balconies look onto a quiet garden with fountains.

Eating

Tábula Calda SPANISH €€

(www.tabulacalda.com; Calle Romero Leal 11; mains €10-18, set menu €13.50-27; 1-4pm & 8pm-midnight Mon-Sat, 1-4pm Sun) This inviting space, with tilework and abundant greenery, serves up well-priced meals that cover most Spanish staples. Everything either comes from its garden or is sourced from within 100km of the kitchen. Before your food arrives, you'll be plied with a complimentary tapa, house salad (orange, sugar and olive oil, reflecting the family's Jewish roots) and olives. Manuel is a warm and welcoming host.

La Bodeguilla SPANISH €€

(924 31 88 54; Calle Moreno de Vargas 2; mains €9-18, set menu from €10) A local favourite, La Bodeguilla ticks all the right boxes – friendly service, well-priced food and a varied menu that spans the full range of *extremeño* and wider specialities (grilled meats, creative sal-

MOVING ON?

For tips, recommendations and reviews, head to shop.lonelyplanet.com to purchase a downloadable PDF of the Alentejo chapter from Lonely Planet's *Portugal* guide.

ads, rice dishes and everything from snails to local Torta del Casar cheese on toast). Emilio, the owner, keeps things ticking over. Don't turn up at lunchtime without a reservation.

Casa Benito SPANISH €€

(Calle San Francisco 3; tapas from €3.75, mains €13-26) Squeeze onto a tiny stool in the wood-panelled dining room, prop up the bar or relax on the sunny terrace for tapas at this bullfighting enthusiasts' hang-out, with walls plastered with photos, posters and memorabilia from the ring. The tapas are original and tasty; the upstairs restaurant specialises in roasts and is also a fine choice.

Casa Nano SPANISH €€

(casanano.es/restaurante; Calle Castelar 3; mains €9-16, set menus €12-16; 1-4pm & 8-11.30pm Mon-Sat) Tucked behind Plaza de España, the *simpático* staff here serve up hearty traditional dishes such as *cordero a la ciruela* (lamb with plums) and tasty *patatas al rebujón* (fried potatoes with garlic and ham). We also recommend the three-course *menú extremeño* (€16).

Drinking & Nightlife

The best place to enjoy an early-evening drink is at one of the kiosk-bars on Plaza de España. You'll find a more diverse selection of bars in and around Plaza de la Constitución.

La Moett BAR

(www.lamoett.com; Plaza de España 2; 4pm-late) Under the arches of the *ayuntamiento* (town hall) on the Plaza de España's northeastern side, La Moett is a classy option for a coffee or after-dinner *copa* (glass), with tables on the square.

Jazz Bar BAR, LIVE MUSIC

(Calle Alvarado 10; 4pm-2am Tue-Sat; ☲) This jazz stalwart has a sophisticated scene with regular exhibitions, and live jazz once or twice a week at 10pm.

EXTREMADURA MÉRIDA

ℹ️ Information

Tourist Office (☑924 33 07 22; www.turismo merida.org; Paseo Álvarez Sáez de Buruaga; ☺9.30am-2pm & 4.30-7.30pm) Next to the Teatro Romano.

Tourist Office (☑924 38 01 90; www.turismo merida.org; Calle Santa Eulalia; ☺9.30am-2pm & 5-8pm Mon-Sat) At the top of the main shopping street.

ℹ️ Getting There & Around

From the **bus station** (☑924 37 14 04; Avenida de la Libertad), across the river via the Puente Lusitania, destinations include Badajoz (€5.60, one hour, five to nine daily), Seville (€4.75, 2½ hours, six daily), Cáceres (€5.63, one hour, two daily), Trujillo (€9.85, 1½ hours, three daily) and Madrid (normal/express €28/41, five/four hours, eight daily).

There are trains to Madrid (€31 to €46, 4½ to eight hours, five daily), Cáceres (from €6, one hour, six daily) and Seville (€20, 3¾ hours, one daily) via Zafra (from €6, 50 minutes, three daily).

Alburquerque

POP 5544

Looming large above this small town, 38km north of Badajoz, is the intact Castillo de la Luna (☺11am-2pm & 4-6pm Tue-Sun) FREE. The centrepiece of a complex frontier defence system of forts, the castle was built on the site of its Islamic antecedent in the 13th century and subsequently expanded. From the top, views take in the Portuguese frontier (the Portuguese actually took the town for a few years in the early 18th century). Among many curiosities is a hole set in the wall of one of its towers. It was used by the castle's masters as a toilet – sending an unpleasant message to hostile forces below when under siege.

Alburquerque is served by two to five buses Monday to Saturday from Badajoz (€3.75).

Olivenza

POP 12,043

Pretty Olivenza, 24km south of Badajoz, clings to its Portuguese heritage – it has only been Spanish since 1801. The cobbled centre is distinctive for its whitewashed houses, typical turreted defensive walls and penchant for blue-and-white ceramic tile work.

Smack-bang in its centre is the 14th-century castle, dominated by the Torre del Homenaje, 36m-high, from which there are fine views. The castle houses an ethnographic museum (☑924 49 02 22; www.elmuseodeolivenza.com; adult/child €2/1; ☺10.30am-2pm & 5-8pm Tue-Fri, 10am-2pm & 5-8pm Sat, 10am-2pm Sun), with a collection of toy cars on the 1st floor. The most impressive section of the original defensive walls is around the 18th-century Puerta del Calvario, on the western side of town. There's a small tourist office on the same square.

Hotel Palacio de Arteaga (☑924 49 11 29; www.palacioarteaga.com; Calle Moreno Nieto 5; s/d €75/85; ℗❄🛜) is a historic conversion in the heart of town and features spacious modern rooms around a pretty patio. Friendly Casa Maila (www.casamaila.com; Calle Colón 3; mains €11-18) is great for delicious free tapas or more elaborate restaurant mains.

Buses to Badajoz (€2, 30 minutes) run almost hourly during the week.

Zafra

POP 16,762

Looking for all the world like an Andalucían *pueblo blanco*, gleaming-white Zafra is a serene, attractive stop between Seville and Mérida. Originally a Muslim settlement, Zafra's narrow streets are lined with baroque churches, old-fashioned shops and traditional houses decorated by brilliant red splashes of geraniums.

👁️ Sights

Zafra's 15th-century castle, a blend of Gothic, Mudéjar and Renaissance architecture, is now a *parador* and dominates the town. Plaza Grande and the adjoining Plaza Chica, arcaded and bordered by bars, are the places to see Zafra life. The southern end of the Plaza Grande, with its palm trees, is one of Extremadura's prettiest spots.

Convento de Santa Clara   CONVENT
(www.museozafra.es; Calle Sevilla 30; ☺11am-2pm & 5-6.30pm Tue-Sun) FREE Just off the main shopping street, this imposing 15th-century Mudéjar convent was originally designed as a holy resting place for the remains of the powerful local Feria dynasty. It's still a working convent with cloistered nuns; the museum has a gilded chapel and there are interesting insights (in Spanish) into the lives of these sisters, who also sell pastries.

Iglesia de la Candelaria CHURCH
(Calle Tetuán; ⊙ 11am-2pm & 4-7pm Tue-Thu & Sat, 11am-2pm Fri) **FREE** This 16th-century church is worth a look for its fine altarpieces.

Sleeping

★ **Hotel Plaza Grande** HOTEL €
(☎ 924 56 31 63; www.hotelplazagrande.com; Calle Pasteleros 2; s/d incl breakfast €28/45; ❋ ⏶) The genial owner has created a gem of a hotel here, right on Plaza Grande and quite a bargain. Go for room 108, with its corner balconies overlooking the plaza (room 208 is the same but with windows instead of balconies). Decor is terracotta accentuated by cream paintwork and muted earth colours. The downstairs restaurant and bar are reliably good.

Hotel Huerta Honda HOTEL €€
(☎ 924 55 41 00; www.hotelhuertahonda.com; Calle López Asme 1; s/d/superior/ste €55/65/85/120; ▣ ❋ ⏶ ⏷) There are two grades of rooms here: standards are contemporary, stylish and supremely comfortable, with lots of browns and beiges, while 'Gran Clase' are sumptuous, with four-poster beds, timber ceilings and antiques. Whichever you choose, this place is outstanding. Ask for a room overlooking the bougainvillea-draped courtyard and the castle next door.

Parador Hernán Cortés HOTEL €€
(☎ 924 55 45 40; www.parador.es; Plaza Corazón de María 7; r €80-125; ▣ ❋ ⏶ ⏷) They say a person's home is their castle: here it's the reverse. The large rooms are richly decorated with burgundy-coloured fabrics and antiques. The marble-pillared courtyard is truly magnificent, while the secluded pool is surrounded by ivy and turrets. The restaurant is excellent.

Eating

Gastro-Bar Baraka TAPAS €
(Plaza Grande 20; tapas from €3.50, raciones €7-13; ⊙ 7pm-midnight Mon-Wed, 7pm-3am Thu, 1pm-3am Fri-Sun) Gastro-Bar Baraka adds a touch of sophistication to Plaza Grande's charm. The food here ranges from creative *tostas* (€3 to €4) to outstandng tapas and on to more substantial *raciones*. Enjoy these dishes on a balmy summer's evening with a glass of red in the lamplit square – bliss. Downstairs, there's a groovy bar (open Thursday to Sunday) inhabiting the 15th-century cisterns.

> ### WINE REGION: RIBERA DEL GUADIANA
>
> Extremadura is not known for its wines, but it does have one recognised wine region, the Ribera del Guadiana, which produces whites, reds and moscatel. Spread across the provinces of Badajoz and Cáceres, there are six sub-zones, one of which centres on the mountain hamlet of Montánchez, which is also known for its first-rate *jamón*.

El Dropo INTERNATIONAL €€
(☎ 657 783301; www.eldropo.com; Plaza Grande 16; mains €12-17; ⊙ noon-4pm & 9pm-midnight) With cuisines that range from Mexico to Italy via Asia (with an occasional nod to Spanish staples such as *salmorejo cordobés*, a cold tomato-based soup from Córdoba), El Dropo is quite a surprise in provincial little Zafra. There are cocktails as well as tapas and a fine perch overlooking our favourite square. What more could you want?

La Rebotica SPANISH €€
(☎ 924 55 42 89; Calle Boticas 12; mains €15-21; ⊙ 1-4pm & 8.30-11.30pm Tue-Sat, 1-4pm Sun) This restaurant in the heart of the old town offers a traditional meaty menu, including *rabo de toro* (oxtail stew) and five different pork fillet dishes, subtly prepared by Dutch chef Rudy Koster. Reservations recommended.

Shopping

Iberllota FOOD
(☎ 924 55 59 95; www.iberllota.com; Avenida López Asme 36; ⊙ 10am-2pm & 5-8pm Mon-Sat, 10am-2pm Sun) Specialising in the finest cured meats, Iberllota is perfect for a picnic or if you're looking for gifts for friends back home. It also sells €1 *pulgitas* (mini-bocadillos or filled rolls) with *jamón* inside.

Joaquín Luna FOOD
(☎ 924 55 02 45; www.joaquinluna.com; Plaza de España 10) An outlet for one of Extremadura's well-respected producers of *jamón* and other cured meats, as well as cheeses.

Information

Municipal Tourist Office (☎ 924 55 10 36; Plaza de España 8A; ⊙ 10am-2pm & 6-7.30pm Mon-Fri, 11am-2pm Sat & Sun) On the main square.

Jamón: a Primer

There's no more iconic presence on the Spanish table than cured ham from the high plateau and the sight of *jamónes* hanging from the ceiling is one of Spain's most enduring images.

Types of Jamón

Spanish *jamón* is, unlike Italian prosciutto, a bold, deep red and well marbled with buttery fat. At its best it smells like meat, the forest and the field.

Like wines and olive oil, Spanish *jamón* is subject to a strict series of classifications. *Jamón serrano* refers to *jamón* made from white-coated pigs introduced to Spain in the 1950s. Once salted and semidried by the cold, dry winds of the Spanish sierra, most now go through a similar process of curing and drying in a climate-controlled shed for around a year. *Jamón serrano* accounts for about 90% of cured ham in Spain.

Jamón ibérico – more expensive and generally regarded as the elite of Spanish hams – comes from a black-coated pig indigenous to the Iberian Peninsula and a descendant of the wild boar. Gastronomically, its star appeal is its ability to infiltrate fat into the muscle tissue, thus producing an especially well-marbled meat. If the pig gains at least 50% of its body weight during the acorn-eating season, it can be classified as *jamón ibérico de bellota*, the most sought-after designation for *jamón*.

Jamón Regions

There's something about sampling *jamón* close to its source, and these are the most famous *jamón*-producing villages:

KRZYSZTOF DYDYNSKI / GETTY IMAGES ©

RAFAEL CAMPILLO / GETTY IMAGES ©

1. *Jamón* stall, Mercat de la Boqueria (p280) 2. *Pintxos* (tapas)

Guijelo (Castilla y León) South of Salamanca.

Monasterio (Extremadura) South of Zafra; also has Spain's best *jamón* museum (p570).

Montánchez (Extremadura) Southwest of Cáceres.

Jabugo (Andalucía) Northwest of Sevilla.

Teruel province (Aragón) Southern Aragón. Check out www.jamondeteruel.com.

Eating Jamón

The best-quality *jamón* is most commonly eaten as a starter or a *ración* (large tapa) – on menus it's usually called a *tabla de jamón ibérico* (or *ibérico de bellota*). Cutting it is an art form and it should be sliced so wafer-thin as to be almost transparent. Spaniards almost always eat it with bread.

Cheaper types of *jamón* appear in a *bocadillo de jamón* (roll filled with *jamón*) or in small pieces in everything from *salmorejo cordobés* (a cold tomato-based soup from Córdoba) to *huevos rotos* (eggs and potatoes).

Another local version in Aragón is *las delicias de Teruel* (*jamón* served with toasted bread and fresh tomato).

THE ORIGINS OF JAMÓN?

The recipe for cured meats such as *jamón* is most often attributed to a noble Roman, Cato the Elder, who changed the course of Spanish culinary history with his tome *De Re Rustica*.

DON'T MISS

MONESTERIO – HOME OF JAMÓN

Since the completion of the A66 motorway, many bypassed towns have disappeared into quiet obscurity, but not Monesterio because this is one of Spain's (and certainly Extremadura's) most celebrated sources of *jamón*. Occupying pride of place at the southern end of the town is the outstanding **Museo del Jamón** (⬚924 51 67 37; www.museodeljamondemonesterio.com; Paseo de Extremadura 314, Monasterio; ⊙9.30am-2pm & 6-8pm Mon-Sat, 10am-2pm Sun), arguably the best of its kind in Spain. Opened in September 2012, its video, displays and interactive exhibits take visitors through the process of *jamón* production, from ideal pig habitats, to the *matanza* (killing of the pigs) and right through to the finished product. To round out the experience, they give you a voucher for a €1 tapa of *jamón ibérico* in one of eight bars or restaurants in town, and a 5% discount when buying *jamón* and related products in five *jamón* delicatessens in Monesterio.

❶ Getting There & Away

Zafra is on the main bus routes linking Seville (€11.34, 1¾ hours, six daily) to the south with Mérida (from €5.23, 1¼ hours, eight daily) and Badajoz (€6.60, 1¼ hours, up to nine daily). Trains also pass through.

Around Zafra

Roads through the rolling Sierra Aracena into Andalucía head southwest into northern Huelva province, and southeast into the Parque Natural Sierra Norte.

In **Fregenal de la Sierra**, highlights include the 13th-century **castle** (Plaza Constitución; ⊙10.15am-2.45pm & 5.15-7.15pm Wed-Sun) **FREE** – enter through the adjacent tourist office – which houses a bullring, and nearby **Santa María church**. On Tuesday and Friday mornings there's a lively market in the main square.

Walled and hilly **Jerez de los Caballeros**, 42km west of Zafra, was a cradle of conquistadors. It has a 13th-century **castle** that was built by the Templars. They refused to lay down arms when the order was suppressed and came to a sticky end. You can wander around at will, but it's basically just the impressive walls that are preserved. There are several handsome **churches**, three with towers emulating the Giralda in Seville.

Quiet **Burguillos del Cerro**, southwest of Zafra, is overlooked by a 15th-century **castle** atop a grassy hill.

One weekday bus runs between Zafra and Fregenal de la Sierra (€3.10, 1½ hours), and one Monday to Saturday to Jerez de los Caballeros (€3.45, one hour) via Burguillos.

Seville & Andalucía's Hill Towns

Best Places to See Flamenco

➡ Casa de la Memoria (p595)

➡ Peña Flamenca La Perla (p613)

➡ Museo del Baile Flamenco (p584)

➡ Peña Flamenca Tomás El Nitri (p616)

➡ Damajuana (p624)

Best Tapas

➡ La Brunilda (p592)

➡ Vinería San Telmo (p592)

➡ El Aljibe (p612)

➡ Casa Balbino (p618)

Why Go?

A parched region fertile with culture, a conquered land that went on to conquer, a fiercely traditional place that has accepted rapid modernisation: western Andalucía has multiple faces. Here, in the cradle of quintessential Spain, the questions are often as intriguing as the answers. Who first concocted flamenco? How did tapas become a national obsession? Could Cádiz be Europe's oldest settlement? Are those *really* Christopher Columbus' bones inside Seville cathedral? And where on earth did the audacious builders of Córdoba's Mezquita get their divine inspiration from? Putting together the missing pieces of the puzzle is what makes travel in the region the glorious adventure that it is.

Seville is western Andalucía's Holy Grail, Córdoba deserves more than a day trip, while the white towns will lure you into quieter rural areas and perhaps inspire you to visit the region's only national park amid the bird-rich wetlands of Doñana.

When to Go
Seville

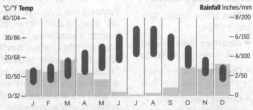

Apr Sombre	May Relatively	Late Sep The
Semana Santa processions are followed by the exuberance of the spring fairs.	cool weather. Many towns and villages celebrate *romerías* (pilgrimages).	heat diminishes, the crowds go home – but it's still warm enough for the beach.

Top Five Food Experiences

➜ Digging into seafood in Sanlúcar de Barrameda (p618).

➜ Visiting a sherry bodega in Jerez de la Frontera (p621).

➜ Sampling nouveau tapas in Seville (p591).

➜ Taking a language and cooking course in Vejer de la Frontera (p632).

➜ Tasting raw sea urchins in Cádiz (p612).

Best Places to Stay

➜ Palacio San Bartolomé (p615)

➜ Hotel Casa 1800 (p590)

➜ V... (p632)

➜ Bed and Be (p645)

Bus Companies

➜ **Alsa** Serves Andalucía's major cities.

➜ **Amarillos** Links smaller towns in western Andalucía.

➜ **Dumas** Primarily serves Huelva province.

➜ **Comes** Covers Cádiz province including many white towns.

➜ **Carrera** Serves Cordoba province.

➜ **Portillo** Links Costa del Sol resorts.

Wine Regions

Western Andalucía has four *Denominaciónes de Origen* (DO).

Jerez-Xerez-Sherry The legendary sherry region was Spain's first DO in 1933 and uses mainly palomino grapes to make some of the world's oldest wines. Varietals span from dry *fino seco* to sweet Pedro Ximénez.

Manzanilla Sanlúcar de Barrameda Although it uses the same grapes as Jerez, Sanlúcar's coastal microclimate produces a more delicate, suave sherry with a faint salty essence known as manzanilla.

Condado de Huelva The white wines in this understated DO are primarily made from zalema grapes, which produce fresh, light, if unspectacular, wines that go well with seafood.

Montilla-Moriles This DO in southern Córdoba province centers on the town of Montilla and produces sweet dessert wines closely related to sherry using Pedro Ximénez and moscatel (muscat) grapes.

SPAIN'S FINEST RAILWAY

The most spectacular train ride in Spain? The Ronda–Algeciras line is certainly a contender. Opened in 1892 to allow bored British military personnel bivouacked in Gibraltar access to the (then) hidden wonders of Spain, the line was engineered and financed by a couple of wealthy Brits who furnished the towns at each end with two magnificent Victorian hotels: the Reina Victoria (Ronda) and the Reina Cristina (Algeciras). Still running on single track, the line traverses some of Andalucía's finest scenery including cork oak forest, Moorish white towns, boulder-strewn mountainscapes and diminutive *Thomas the Tank Engine* stations. Trains run three times a day in either direction.

Learning Spanish

Privately run language schools are scattered all over Spain and many of them are excellent. But, with most courses requiring a minimum of one week's study, it's important to find the right location. **Seville** is a beautiful city in which to linger for a week or two and has an abundance of top-notch language schools. If you'd prefer a slightly smaller city with instant access to history and beaches, **Cádiz** has a couple of good schools located in the old quarter. For a more rural experience in a diminutive hilltop town close to the coast, you can't beat **Vejer de la Frontera.**

Best schools:

➜ CLIC (p588) in Seville.

➜ K2 Internacional (p611) in Cádiz.

➜ La Janda (p632) in Vejer de la Frontera.

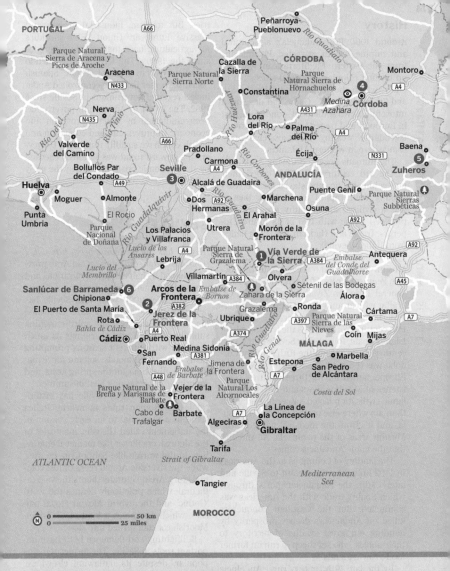

Seville & Andalucía's Hill Towns Highlights

1 Seeing griffon vultures nesting on high crags on the **Vía Verde de la Sierra** (p631).

2 Watching a spontaneous flamenco performance in a backstreet bar in **Jerez de la Frontera** (p618).

3 Riding a bicycle on a sultry summer's evening through **Seville** (p574) and unearthing the latest creative tapas bars.

4 Tackling the tangle of Moorish streets in the **Córdoba** *judería* (p644).

5 Following the kilometre markers along the Vía Verde de la Subbética to the spectacular white town of **Zuheros** (p649).

6 Realising you quite like sherry if it's accompanied by fresh-from-the-ocean seafood in **Sanlúcar de Barrameda's** Bajo de Guía (p618).

History

Around 1000 BC, Andalucía's agricultural and mining wealth attracted Phoenicians from the eastern Mediterranean who set up trading colonies at coastal sites such as Cádiz, which they called Gadir. By the 8th and 7th centuries BC, Gadir had developed into a full-blown settlement – one of the first in Europe – and traded with the mysterious, legendarily wealthy Tartessos civilisation somewhere in western Andalucía.

The Romans began occupying Andalucía in the 3rd century BC. They called their new colony Baetica and stayed for 700 years making their capital in Córdoba. Baetica was a civilised and wealthy province that provided Rome with two of its future Emperors, Trajan and Hadrian, who both hailed from Itálica (Seville).

Andalucía was the obvious base for the Muslim invaders who surged onto the Iberian Peninsula from Africa in 711 under Arab general Tariq ibn Ziyad, who landed at Gibraltar with around 10,000 men, mostly Berbers (indigenous North Africans). Until the 11th century, Córdoba was the leading city of Islamic Spain, followed by Seville in the 13th century. At its peak in the 10th century, Córdoba was the most dazzling city in Western Europe, famed for its 'three cultures' coexistence of Muslims, Jews and Christians. Islamic civilisation lasted longer in Andalucía than anywhere else on the Iberian Peninsula, and it's from the medieval name for the Muslim areas of the peninsula, Al-Andalus, that the name Andalucía comes.

The landing of Columbus in the Americas in 1492 brought great wealth to Seville and later Cádiz, the Andalucian ports through which Spain's trade with the Americas was conducted. But the Castilian conquerors killed off Andalucía's deeper prosperity by handing out great swaths of territory to their nobles, who set sheep to run on former food-growing lands.

By the late 19th century rural Andalucía was a hotbed of anarchist unrest. During the civil war Andalucía split along class lines and savage atrocities were committed by both sides. Most of western Andalucía, including Seville, Cádiz and Córdoba fell quickly into Nationalist hands.

Spain's post-war 'hungry years' were particularly hungry in the south, and between 1950 and 1970 some 1.5 million Andalucians left to find work in the industrial cities of northern Spain and in other European coun-tries. But tourism, industrial growth and massive European Union (EU) subsidies for agriculture have made a big difference since the 1960s. The left-of-centre Partido Socialista Obrero Español (PSOE; Spanish Socialist Worker Party) has controlled Andalucía's regional government in Seville since 1982. The worst of Andalucian poverty has been eradicated by welfare provision and economic improvement, and education and health care have steadily improved. However, this upward trend was seriously checked by the economic crisis that hit in the early 2010s.

SEVILLE

POP 703,000

He who has not at Seville been, has not, I trow, a wonder seen, goes an old Arab proverb. Shaped by half a dozen civilisations and reborn in numerous incarnations since its founding over 2000 years ago, Seville has never lost its capacity to amaze. Drenched for most of the year in spirit-enriching sunlight, this is a city of feelings as much as sights with different seasons prompting vastly contrasting moods: solemn for Semana Santa, flirtatious for the spring fiesta, and soporific for the gasping heat of summer.

Like all great cities, Seville has historical layers. Roman ruins at nearby Itálica stand as a memorial to an early version of the settlement called Hispalis, memories of the Moorish era flicker like medieval engravings in the warren-like Santa Cruz quarter, while the riverside Arenal reeks of lost colonial glory. Architecturally there's the vast cathedral, which practically defines the word 'Gothic', and the hybrid Alcázar (royal palace), which resembles a kind of Christian-Moorish cocktail turned into stone.

Bullfighting and flamenco both have important roots in Seville. The former remains popular, despite its outlawing elsewhere; the latter is undergoing something of a renaissance with new venues opening all the time. Then there are the legends, romantic stories filled with larger-than-life characters that provided rich pickings for 19th-century aesthetes such as Rossini and Mozart. Don Juan, the womaniser; Carmen, the seductress; the Barber of Seville; and the Marriage of Figaro.

One of the most remarkable things about modern Seville is its ability to adapt and etch fresh new brush strokes onto an ancient canvas. Nowhere is this better exemplified than in the Metropol Parasol, a daring futuristic public building in the middle of the historic city centre that sits directly on top of well-preserved Roman ruins unearthed during its construction.

History

Roman Seville, named Hispalis, was a significant port on the Río Guadalquivir, which is navigable to the Atlantic Ocean 100km away. Muslim Seville, called Ishbiliya, became the most powerful of the *taifas* (small kingdoms) into which Islamic Spain split after the Córdoba caliphate collapsed in 1031. In the 12th century a strict Islamic sect from Morocco, the Almohads, took over Muslim Spain and made Seville capital of their whole realm, building a great mosque where the cathedral now stands. Almohad power eventually crumbled and Seville fell to Fernando III (El Santo, the Saint) of Castilla in 1248.

By the 14th century, Seville was the most important Castilian city, and was in sole control of trade with the American colonies from 1503. It rapidly became one of the most cosmopolitan cities on earth. However, over the next 300 years, both plague and the silting up of the river contributed to Seville's long decline. Seville fell very quickly to the Nationalists at the start of the Spanish Civil War in 1936. Things looked up a few decades later in the 1980s when Seville was named capital of the new autonomous Andalucía within democratic Spain, and *sevillano* Felipe González became Spain's prime minister. The Expo 92 international exhibition in 1992 brought to the city millions of visitors, eight new bridges across the Guadalquivir, and the speedy AVE rail link to Madrid. And in the new century, where less is more, Seville is already experimenting with green initiatives, including trams, a metro and bikes that glide quietly alongside antique monuments to past glory.

◎ Sights & Activities

◉ Cathedral & Around

Catedral & Giralda CHURCH
(www.catedraldesevilla.es; adult/child €8/free; ⊘11am-3.30pm Mon, 11am-5pm Tue-Sat, 2.30-6pm Sun Sep-Jun, 9.30am-2.30pm Mon, 9.30am-4pm Tue-Sat, 2.30-6pm Sun Jul & Aug) After Seville fell to the Christians in 1248 the existing

mosque was used as a church until 1402. Then, in view of its decaying state, the church authorities decided to knock it down and start again. Let's 'construct a church so large, future generations will think we were mad', they purportedly said. When it was completed in 1502 after one hundred years of hard labour, the **Catedral de Santa María de la Sede**, as it is officially known, was (and remains) the largest cathedral in the world by volume and pretty much defines the word 'Gothic'. It is also a veritable art gallery replete with notable works by Zurbarán, Murillo, Goya and others.

➡ **Sala del Pabellón**

Selected treasures from the cathedral's art collection are exhibited in this room, the first after the ticket office. Much of what's displayed here, as elsewhere in the cathedral, is the work of masters from Seville's 17th-century artistic golden age.

➡ **Southern & Northern Chapels**

The chapels along the southern and northern sides of the cathedral hold riches of sculpture and painting. Near the western end of the northern side is the **Capilla de San Antonio**, housing Murillo's 1666 canvas depicting the vision of St Anthony of Padua; thieves cut out the kneeling saint in 1874 but he was later found in New York and put back.

➡ **Tomb of Columbus**

Inside the **Puerta de los Príncipes** (Door of the Princes) stands the monumental tomb of Christopher Columbus (Cristóbal Colón in Spanish) – the subject of a continuous riddle – containing what were long believed to be the great explorer's bones, brought here from Cuba in 1898.

Columbus died in 1506 in Valladolid, in northern Spain. His remains lay at La Cartuja monastery in Seville before being moved to Hispaniola in 1536. Even though there were suggestions that the bones kept in Seville's cathedral were possibly those of his son Diego (who was buried with his father in Santo Domingo, Hispaniola), recent DNA tests seemed to finally prove that it really is Christopher Columbus lying in that box. Yet unfortunately, to confuse matters further, the researchers also say that the bones in Santo Domingo could also be real, since Columbus' body was moved several times after his death. It seems that even death couldn't dampen the great explorer's urge to travel.

Seville

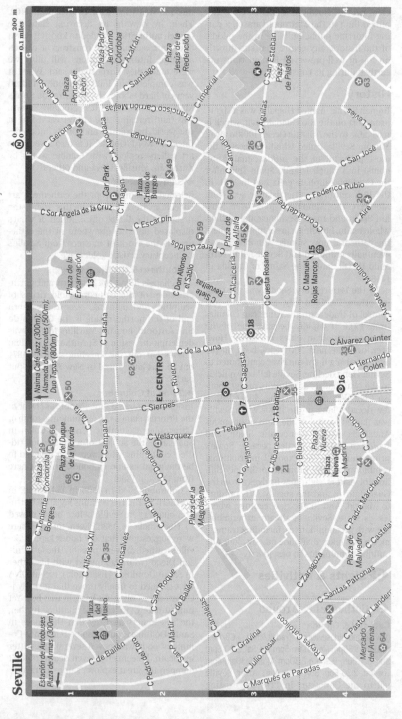

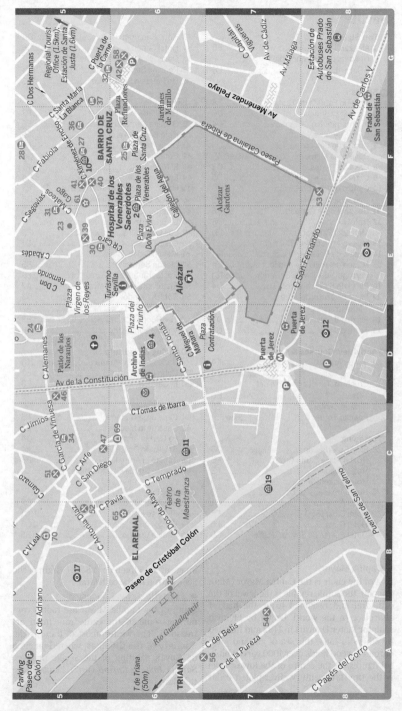

Seville

➡ **Capilla Mayor**

East of the choir is the Capilla Mayor (Main Chapel). Its Gothic retable is the jewel of the cathedral and reckoned to be the biggest altarpiece in the world. Begun by Flemish sculptor Pieter Dancart in 1482 and finished by others in 1564, this sea of gilt and polychromed wood holds over 1000 carved biblical figures. At the centre of the lowest level is the tiny 13th-century silver-plated cedar image of the Virgen de la Sede (Virgin of the See), patron of the cathedral.

➡ **Sacristía de los Cálices**

South of the Capilla Mayor are rooms containing some of the cathedral's main art treasures. The westernmost of these is the Sacristy of the Chalices, where Francisco de Goya's painting of the Seville martyrs, *Santas Justa y Rufina* (1817), hangs above the altar.

➡ Sacristía Mayor

This large room with a finely carved stone dome was created between 1528 and 1547: the arch over its portal has carvings of 16th-century foods. Pedro de Campaña's 1547 *Descendimiento* (Descent from the Cross) above the central altar at the southern end, and Francisco de Zurbarán's *Santa Teresa,* to its right, are two of the cathedral's most precious paintings. The room's centrepiece is the Custodia de Juan de Arfe, a huge 475kg silver monstrance made in the 1580s by Renaissance metalsmith Juan de Arfe.

➡ Cabildo

The beautifully domed chapter house, also called the Sala Capitular, in the southeastern corner, was originally built between 1558 and 1592 as a venue for meetings of the cathedral hierarchy. Hanging high above the archbishop's throne at the southern end is a Murillo masterpiece, *La Inmaculada.*

➡ Giralda

In the northeastern corner of the cathedral you'll find the passage for the climb up to the belfry of the Giralda. The ascent is quite easy, as a series of ramps goes all the way up to the top, built so the guards could ride up on horseback. The decorative brick tower that stands 104m tall was the minaret of the mosque, built between 1184 and 1198 at the height of Almohad power. Its proportions, its delicate brick-pattern decoration, and its colour, which changes with the light, make it perhaps Spain's most perfect Islamic building. The top-most parts of the Giralda – from the bell level up – were added in the 16th century, when Spanish Christians were busy 'improving on' surviving Islamic buildings. Right at the very top is El Giraldillo, a 16th-century bronze weathervane representing 'faith', which has become a symbol of Seville.

➡ Patio de los Naranjos

Outside the cathedral's northern side, this patio was originally the courtyard of the mosque. It's planted with 66 *naranjos* (orange trees), and a Visigothic fountain sits in the centre. Hanging from the ceiling in the patio's southeastern corner is a replica stuffed crocodile – the original was a gift to Alfonso X from the Sultan of Egypt.

★ Alcázar   CASTLE

(www.alcazarsevilla.org; adult/child €9.50/free; ⏱ 9.30am-7pm Apr-Sep, to 5pm Oct-Mar) If heaven really *does* exist, then let's hope that it looks a little bit like the inside of Seville's Alcázar. Built primarily in the 1300s during the so-called 'Dark Ages' in Europe, the architecture is anything but dark. Indeed, compared to our modern-day shopping malls and throwaway apartment blocks it could be argued that the Alcázar marked one of history's architectural high points. Unesco agreed, making it a World Heritage site in 1987.

Originally founded as a fort for the Cordoban governors of Seville in 913, the Alcázar has been expanded or reconstructed many times in its 11 centuries of existence. In the 11th century, Seville's prosperous Muslim *taifa* (small kingdom) rulers developed the original fort by building a palace called Al-Muwarak (the Blessed) in what's now the western part of the Alcázar. The 12th-century Almohad rulers added another palace east of this, around what's now the Patio del Crucero. Christian Fernando III moved into the Alcázar when he captured Seville in 1248, and later Christian monarchs used it as their main residence. Fernando's son Alfonso X replaced much of the Almohad palace with a Gothic one. Between 1364 and 1366 Pedro I created the Alcázar's crown jewel, the sumptuous Mudéjar Palacio de Don Pedro.

➡ Patio del León

From the ticket office inside the Puerta del León (Lion Gate) you emerge into the Patio del León (Lion Patio), which was the garrison yard of the original Al-Muwarak palace. Just off here is the Sala de la Justicia (Hall of Justice), with beautiful Mudéjar plasterwork and an *artesonado* (ceiling of interlaced beams with decorative insertions); this room was built in the 1340s by Christian king Alfonso XI, who disported here with one of his mistresses, Leonor de Guzmán, reputedly the most beautiful woman in Spain.

The room leads on to the pretty Patio del Yeso, part of the 12th-century Almohad palace reconstructed in the 19th century.

➡ Patio de la Montería

The rooms on the western side of this patio were part of the Casa de la Contratación (Contracting House) founded by the Catholic Monarchs in 1503 to control trade with Spain's American colonies. The Salón del Almirante (Admiral's Hall) houses 19th- and 20th-century paintings showing historical events and personages associated with Seville; the room off its northern end has an international collection of beautiful, elaborate fans. The Sala de Audiencias

Seville Cathedral

'We're going to construct a church so large future generations will think we were mad,' declared the inspired architects of Seville in 1402 at the beginning of one of the most grandiose building projects in medieval history. Just over a century later their madness was triumphantly confirmed.

WHAT TO LOOK FOR

To avoid getting lost, orient yourself by the main highlights. Directly inside the southern (main) entrance is the grand **tomb of Columbus** ❶. Turn right here and head into the southeastern corner to uncover some major art treasures: a Goya in the Sacristía de los Cálices, a Zurbarán in the **Sacristía Mayor** ❷, and Murillo's shining Immaculada in the Sala Capitular. Skirt the cathedral's eastern wall taking a look inside the **Capilla Real** ❸ with its important royal tombs. By now it's impossible to avoid the lure of **Capilla Mayor** ❹ with its fantastical altarpiece. Hidden over in the northwest corner is the **Capilla de San Antonio** ❺ with a legendary Murillo. That huge doorway almost in front of you is the rarely opened **Puerta de la Asunción** ❻. Make for the **Giralda** ❼ next, stealing admiring looks at the high, vaulted ceiling on the way. After looking down on the cathedral's immense footprint, descend and depart via the **Patio de los Naranjos** ❽.

Capilla Mayor
Behold! The cathedral's main focal point contains its greatest treasure, a magnificent gold-plated altarpiece depicting various scenes in the life of Christ. It constitutes the life's work of one man, Flemish artist Pieter Dancart.

Patio de los Naranjos
Inhale the perfume of 60 Sevillan orange trees in a cool patio bordered by fortress-like walls – a surviving remnant of the original 12th-century mosque. Exit is gained via the horseshoe-shaped Puerta del Perdón.

Puerta del Perdón

8

5

6

Iglesia del Sagrario

Puerta del Bautismo

Puerta de la Asunción
Located on the western side of the cathedral and also known as the Puerta Mayor, these huge, rarely opened doors are pushed back during Semana Santa to allow solemn processions of Catholic *hermanadades* (brotherhoods) to pass through.

TOP TIPS

» **Pace yourself** Don't visit the Alcazar and Cathedral on the same day. There is far too much to take in.

» **Viewpoints** Take time to admire the cathedral from the outside. It's particularly stunning at night from the Plaza Virgen de los Reyes, and from across the river in Triana.

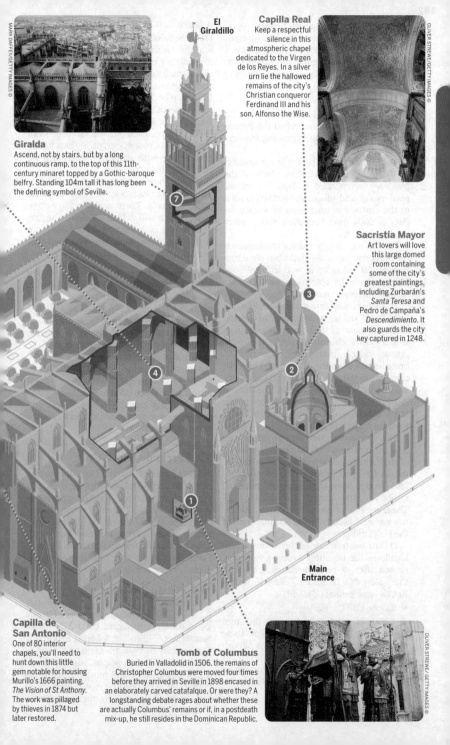

El Giraldillo

Capilla Real
Keep a respectful silence in this atmospheric chapel dedicated to the Virgen de los Reyes. In a silver urn lie the hallowed remains of the city's Christian conqueror Ferdinand III and his son, Alfonso the Wise.

Giralda
Ascend, not by stairs, but by a long continuous ramp, to the top of this 11th-century minaret topped by a Gothic-baroque belfry. Standing 104m tall it has long been the defining symbol of Seville.

Sacristía Mayor
Art lovers will love this large domed room containing some of the city's greatest paintings, including Zurbarán's *Santa Teresa* and Pedro de Campaña's *Descendimiento*. It also guards the city key captured in 1248.

Capilla de San Antonio
One of 80 interior chapels, you'll need to hunt down this little gem notable for housing Murillo's 1666 painting, *The Vision of St Anthony*. The work was pillaged by thieves in 1874 but later restored.

Tomb of Columbus
Buried in Valladolid in 1506, the remains of Christopher Columbus were moved four times before they arrived in Seville in 1898 encased in an elaborately carved catafalque. Or were they? A longstanding debate rages about whether these are actually Columbus' remains or if, in a postdeath mix-up, he still resides in the Dominican Republic.

Main Entrance

(Audience Hall) is hung with tapestry representations of the shields of Spanish admirals and Alejo Fernández' 1530s painting *Virgen de los Mareantes* (Virgin of the Sailors), the earliest known painting about the discovery of the Americas.

➜ Palacio de Don Pedro

Posterity owes Pedro I a big thank you for creating this palace (also called the Palacio Mudéjar), the single most stunning architectural feature in Seville.

At the heart of the palace is the wonderful Patio de las Doncellas (Patio of the Maidens), surrounded by beautiful arches, plasterwork and tiling. The sunken garden in the centre was uncovered by archaeologists in 2004 from beneath a 16th-century marble covering.

The Cámara Regia (King's Quarters), on the northern side of the patio, has stunningly beautiful ceilings and wonderful plaster- and tile-work. Its rear room was probably the monarch's summer bedroom.

From here you can move west into the little Patio de las Muñecas (Patio of the Dolls), the heart of the palace's private quarters, featuring delicate Granada-style decoration; indeed, plasterwork was actually brought here from the Alhambra in the 19th century when the mezzanine and top gallery were added for Queen Isabel II. The Cuarto del Príncipe (Prince's Room), to its north, has a superb wooden cupola ceiling trying to recreate a starlit night sky.

The spectacular Salón de Embajadores (Hall of Ambassadors), at the western end of the Patio de las Doncellas, was the throne room of Pedro I's palace. The room's fabulous wooden dome of multiple star patterns, symbolising the universe, was added in 1427. The dome's shape gives the room its alternative name, Sala de la Media Naranja (Hall of the Half Orange).

On the western side of the Salón de Embajadores the beautiful Arco de Pavones, named after its peacock motifs, leads into the Salón del Techo de Felipe II, with a Renaissance ceiling (1589–91).

➜ Salones de Carlos V

Reached via a staircase at the southeastern corner of the Patio de las Doncellas, these are the much-remodelled rooms of Alfonso X's 13th-century Gothic palace. The rooms are now named after the 16th-century Spanish king Carlos I, using his title as Holy Roman Emperor, Charles V.

➜ Gardens & Exit

From the Salones de Carlos V you can go out into the Alcázar's large and sleepy gardens. Immediately in front of the building is a series of small linked gardens, some with pools and fountains. From one, the Jardín de las Danzas (Garden of the Dances), a passage runs beneath the Salones de Carlos V to the Baños de Doña María de Padilla (María de Padilla Baths). These are the vaults beneath the Patio del Crucero – originally that patio's lower level – with a grotto that replaced the patio's original pool.

Concerts are sometimes held in the gardens during summer; see www.actidea. com for details. There is also a fun hedge maze, which will delight children. The gardens to the east, beyond a long wall, are 20th-century creations, but don't hold that against them – they are heavenly indeed.

Archivo de Indias   MUSEUM

(Calle Santo Tomás; ⊘9.30am-5pm Mon-Sat, 10am-2pm Sun) FREE On the western side of Plaza del Triunfo, the Archivo de Indias is the main archive on Spain's American empire, with 80 million pages of documents dating from 1492 through to the end of the empire in the 19th century: a most effective statement of Spain's power and influence during its Golden Age. The building was refurbished between 2003 and 2005.

A short film inside tells its full story and there are some fascinating original colonial maps and documents.

◎ Barrio de Santa Cruz

Seville's medieval *judería* (Jewish quarter), east of the cathedral and Alcázar, is today a tangle of atmospheric, winding streets and lovely plant-decked plazas perfumed with orange blossom. Among its most characteristic plazas is Plaza de Santa Cruz, which gives the *barrio* (district) its name. Plaza de Doña Elvira is another romantic perch, especially in the evening.

★ Hospital de los Venerables
Sacerdotes   ART GALLERY

(☑954 56 26 96; www.focus.abengoa.es; Plaza de los Venerables 8; adult/child €5.50/2.75, Sun afternoon free; ⊘10am-2pm & 4-8pm) Inside this 17th-century baroque mansion once used as a hospice for ageing priests, you'll find one of Seville's greatest and most admirable art collections. The on-site Centro Velázquez was founded in 2007 by the local Focus-

Abengoa Foundation with the intention of reviving Seville's erstwhile artistic glory. Its collection of a dozen masterpieces anchored by Diego Velázquez' *Santa Rufina* is perhaps the best and most concise art lesson the city has to offer.

Pick up an audio-commentary and learn how medieval darkness morphed into inspirational Velázquezian realism.

The 'Hospital' also guards what is perhaps the city's most typical *sevillano* patio – intimate, plant-embellished and spirit-reviving – plus a chapel adorned with more golden-age paintings.

**Centro de Interpretación
Judería de Sevilla**   MUSEUM
(954 04 70 89; www.juderiadesevilla.es; Calle Ximenez de Enciso; admission €6.50; 10.30am-

3.30pm & 5-8pm Mon-Sat, 10.30am-6.30pm Sun) A reinterpretation of Seville's weighty Jewish history has been long overdue and what better place to start than in the city's former Jewish quarter. This new museum is encased in an old Sephardic Jewish house in the higgledy-piggledy Santa Cruz quarter, the one-time Jewish neighbourhood that never recovered from a brutal pogrom and massacre carried out in 1391.

The events of the pogrom and other historical happenings are catalogued inside along with a few surviving mementoes, including documents, costumes and books. It's small but poignant.

Guided walks of the Jewish sites of Seville are offered daily for €22 and there's a small shop on the premises that sells lovely Sephardic ceramics.

A NEW START FOR SEVILLE'S ART

For a golden 50 years, starting in the 1620s, Seville's painters defined world art. The so-called 'Seville School' that came together in the wake of Spain's New World discoveries was spearheaded by a trio of homegrown baroque masters: the light, easy-on-the-eye Bartolomé Murillo; the sober, moody Francisco de Zurbarán; and the dramatically realistic Diego Velázquez. Between them, these three Andalucian artists redrew the rules of painting in the 17th century with their subtle use of colour and vivid religious-themed canvases.

The great maestro, Velázquez, is often referred to as 'the artist's artist' for the profound influence he had on other painters – including Picasso, who made over 40 abstract reinterpretations of Las Meninas, Velázquez' greatest work. Murillo was a painter of polished skills, known for his multiple renderings of the Immaculate Conception, who went on to found Spain's first art academy in Seville in 1660. Zurbarán, though born in Extremadura, spent most of his career in Seville, where he toiled for monastic orders producing darkly serious religious works.

Affected adversely by Spain's yo-yoing international fortunes, Seville's artistic glory was ephemeral. When the city lost its trading monopoly with the American colonies in the late 1600s, political power and influence migrated north to Spain's new capital in Madrid, taking many great artists with it. Other catastrophes further dented its prestige. In 1800, a yellow fever epidemic wiped out one third of Seville's population, and in 1810 the armies of Napoleon arrived and pillaged the city of some of its finest masterpieces. By the early 1900s, Spain's best art was being displayed in big galleries in Madrid, London or New York while former Seville giants such as Murillo were being derided for being vacuous and overly sentimental.

In recent years, local efforts to reclaim Seville's art have put the city back in the international reckoning. At the same time, the art world has re-evaluated its opinions of erstwhile *sevillano* greats such as Murillo whose reputation was deservedly revived in the 1980s. Meanwhile, Diego Velázquez, whose work has been strangely absent in his native city since his time at the royal court in Madrid in the 1650s, spiritually returned home in July 2007 when a local cultural foundation, Focus-Abengoa, bought one of his early paintings, *Santa Rufina*, for a record €12.4 million.

The painting is currently on display, along with 15 other important canvases by Seville artists such as Murillo, Zurbarán and Francisco Pacheco, in the Centro Velázquez, an art gallery encased in the Hospital de los Venerables Sacerdotes. Set up in 2007 to demonstrate the key role that Seville played in revolutionising Spanish and global painting in the 17th century, this centre and others have ushered in a new era for the city's art.

Baños Árabes HAMMAM

(📞955 01 00 25; www.airedesevilla.com; Calle Aire 15; bath/bath with massage €26/37; ⊘every 2hr from 10am-midnight) Seville's Moorish bath experience wins prizes for its tranquil atmosphere, historic setting (in the Barrio de Santa Cruz), and Moroccan riad-style decor – living proof that the Moors knew a thing or two about how to relax. For an excellent post-bath pick-me-up, hit the on-site *tetería* (tea house, p594) for a silver pot of mint tea.

👁 El Centro

The real centre of Seville is the densely packed zone of narrow pedestrianised streets north of the cathedral that melds imperceptibly with the Santa Cruz quarter.

⭐**Casa de la Memoria** CULTURAL CENTRE

(📞954 56 06 70; www.casadelamemoria.es; Calle Cuna 6; admission €3; ⊘10.30am-6.30pm) Lucid memories will be hard to shake off after visiting the Casa de la Memoria, especially if you stay for an evening flamenco show. This flamenco cultural centre, recently relocated from the Santa Cruz quarter, has expanded to include a suite of exposition rooms with revolving flamenco exhibits. An exposé of Seville's Cafe Cantantes was showing at last visit. It is the only centre of its kind in Seville.

⭐**Museo del Baile Flamenco** MUSEUM

(www.museoflamenco.com; Calle Manuel Rojas Marcos 3; adult/senior & student €10/8; ⊘10am-7pm) The brainchild of *sevillana* flamenco dancer Cristina Hoyos, this museum, spread over three floors of an 18th-century palace, makes a noble effort to showcase the mysterious art, although at €10 a pop it is a little pricey. Exhibits include sketches, paintings, photos of erstwhile and contemporary flamenco greats, plus a collection of dresses and shawls.

Classes, workshops and fantastic nightly concerts (7pm, €20) are regular occurrences here, and there's the obligatory shop.

Plaza de San Francisco SQUARE

Plaza de San Francisco has been Seville's main public square since the 16th century. The southern end of its decorative **ayuntamiento** (town hall; Plaza de San Francisco) is encrusted with lovely Renaissance carving from the 1520s and '30s.

Calle Sierpes STREET

Pedestrianised Calle Sierpes, heading north from the Plaza de San Francisco, and the parallel Calle Tetuán/Velázquez are the hub of Seville's fanciest shopping zone. Between the two streets is the 18th-century **Capilla de San José** (Calle Jovellanos; ⊘8am-12.30pm & 6.30-8.30pm), with breathtakingly intense baroque ornamentation.

Plaza del Salvador SQUARE

This plaza, which has a few popular bars, was once the forum of Roman Hispalis. It's dominated by the **Parroquia del Divino Salvador** (Plaza Salvador; ⊘11am-5.30pm & 7.30-9pm Mon-Sat, noon-1.30pm & 3-9pm Sun), a big baroque church built between 1674 and 1712 on the site of Muslim Ishbiliya's main mosque. The interior reveals a fantastic richness of carving and gilding. At sunset, colour from stained-glass windows plays on the carvings to enhance their surreal beauty.

Casa de Pilatos PALACE, MUSEUM

(📞954 22 52 98; www.fundacionmedinaceli.org; Plaza de Pilatos; admission ground fl only €5, whole house €8; ⊘9am-7pm Apr-Oct, to 6pm Nov-Mar) The haunting Casa de Pilatos, which is still occupied by the ducal Medinaceli family, is one of the city's most glorious mansions. It's a mixture of Mudéjar, Gothic and Renaissance styles, with some beautiful tile work and *artesonado*. The overall effect is like a mini-Alcázar.

The staircase to the upper floor has the most magnificent tiles in the building, and a great golden *artesonado* dome above. Visits to the upper floor itself, still partly inhabited by the Medinacelis, are guided. Of interest are the several centuries' worth of Medinaceli portraits and a small Goya bullfighting painting.

Museo de Bellas Artes ART GALLERY

(Fine Arts Museum; Plaza del Museo 9; admission €1.50, EU citizens free; ☉10am-8.30pm Tue-Sat, 10am-5pm Sun; 🛜) Housed in the beautiful former Convento de la Merced, Seville's Museo de Bellas Artes does partial justice to Seville's leading role in Spain's 17th-century artistic golden age (Velázquez is conspicuous by his absence). Much of the work here is of the dark, brooding religious type.

The most visually startling room is that of the convent church, which is hung with paintings by masters of *sevillano* baroque, above all Murillo and his rendering of the *Inmaculada Concepción*.

Metropol Parasol MUSEUM, LANDMARK

(www.metropolsevilla.com; Plaza de la Encarnación) Smarting with the audacity of a modern-day Eiffel Tower, the opinion-dividing Metropol Parasol, which opened in March 2011 in the Plaza de la Encarnación, claims to be the largest wooden building in the world. Its undulating honeycombed roof is held up by five giant mushroom-like pillars, earning it the local nickname *Las Setas de la Encarnación* (Encarnación's mushrooms).

Six years in the making, the construction covers a former dead zone in Seville's central district once filled with an ugly car park. Roman ruins discovered during the building's conception have been cleverly incorporated into the foundations at the Museo Antiquarium (Plaza de la Encarnación; admission €2; ☉10am-8pm Tue-Sat, 10am-2pm Sun), while upstairs on level 2 you can (for €1.35) stroll along a surreal panoramic walkway with killer city views. The Metropol also houses the plaza's former market, a restaurant and a concert space. Though costly and controversial, architect Jürgen Mayer-Hermann's daring creation has slotted into Seville's ancient core with a weird kind of harmony, turning (and tilting) the heads of all who pass.

Club Piragüismo Triana KAYAKING

(☎954 28 25 26; www.clubpiraguismotriana.com; Instalaciones Deportivas Municipales Arjona; ☉10.30am-8.30pm Mon-Fri, 10.30am-1.30pm Sat & Sun) The River Guadalquivir is rarely without a rower or two cutting through its calm waters in pursuit of leisure or sport. Several riverside clubs rent out kayaks (€20 per person per day), incuding this one close to the Plaza de Armas bus station.

◉ El Arenal & Triana

Colonising *caballeros* made rich on New World gold once stalked the streets of El Arenal on the banks of the Río Guadalquivir watched over by Spanish galleons offloading their American booty. There's no port here today, but the compact quarter retains plenty of rambunctious bars and a seafaring spirit.

Triana, the one-time Roma quarter, faces El Arenal across the river.

Torre del Oro MUSEUM

(Paseo de Cristóbal Colón; admission €3; ☉9.30am-6.45pm) This 13th-century Almohad watchtower by the river supposedly had a dome covered in golden tiles, hence its name, 'Tower of Gold'. It was also once used to store the booty siphoned off the colonial coffers by the returning conquistadors from Mexico and Peru. Since then, it has become one of the most recognisable architectural symbols of Seville. Inside is a small maritime museum spead over two floors and a rooftop viewing platform.

Hospital de la Caridad ART GALLERY

(Calle Temprado 3; admission €5; ☉9.30am-1pm & 3.30-7pm Mon-Sat, 9am-12.30pm Sun) The Hospital de la Caridad, a large sturdy building one block east of the river, was once a hospice for the elderly founded by Miguel de Mañara, by legend a notorious libertine who changed his ways after seeing a vision of his own funeral procession. Its main setpiece inside is its gilded chapel decorated profusely by several golden-age painters and sculptors, most notably Murillo and Roldán.

The hospital was notoriously pillaged by Napoleon's troops in 1811 when a kleptomaniac French officer named General Soult stole several of the Murillo paintings that adorned the chapel's walls. The paintings were never returned (they later ended up in the British Museum and St Petersburg's Hermitage Museum), though copies were made and hung up in place of the originals in 2008. See if you can spot the 'fakes'.

Plaza de Toros de la Real Maestranza
BULLRING, MUSEUM

(☑954 22 45 77; www.realmaestranza.com; Paseo de Cristóbal Colón 12; tours adult/child €7/3; ☺ half-hourly 9.30am-8pm, 9.30am-3pm bullfight days) In the world of bullfighting, Seville's bullring is the Old Trafford and Camp Nou. In other words, if you're selected to fight here then you've pretty much made it. In addition to being regarded as a building of almost religious significance to fans, it's also the oldest ring in Spain (building began in 1758). Slightly robotic guided visits, in English and Spanish, take you into the ring and its museum.

Castillo de San Jorge
MUSEUM

(☑954 33 22 40; Plaza del Altozano; ☺9am-1.30pm & 3.30-8pm Mon-Fri, 10am-2pm Sat & Sun) FREE 'Nobody' expects the Spanish Inquisition!' Monty Python once quipped, but in Seville it's not so easy to escape the trauma. After all, this is where the Inquisition Court held its first ever council, in the infamous Castillo de San Jorge in 1481, an act that ignited 325 years of fear and terror. When the Inquisition fires were finally doused in the early 1800s, the castle was destroyed and a market built over the top, but its foundations were rediscovered in 1990.

A modern museum overlays the castle's foundations and takes viewers on a journey around the ruins juxtaposing details of each room's function with macabre stories of the cruelty dished out inside them. It's sometimes gruesome reading.

The Castillo is in Triana adjacent to the San Telmo bridge.

⊙ South of the Centre

South of Santa Cruz and El Centro, the city opens out into expansive parks and broad streets recently reclaimed by trams, bikes and couples on romantic strolls.

Antigua Fábrica de Tabacos
UNIVERSITY

(Calle San Fernando; ☺8am-9.30pm Mon-Fri, to 2pm Sat) FREE Seville's massive former tobacco factory – workplace of Bizet's passionate operatic heroine, Carmen – was built in the 18th century and is the second-largest building in Spain after El Escorial. It's now the university and is wheelchair accessible.

Hotel Alfonso XIII
LANDMARK

(Calle San Fernando 2) As much a monument as an accommodation option, and certainly more affordable if you come for a cup of coffee as opposed to a room, this striking hotel – conceived as the most luxurious in Europe when it was built in 1928 – was constructed in tandem with the Plaza de España for the 1929 world fair.

The style is classic neo-Mudéjar with glazed tiles and terracotta bricks.

Parque de María Luisa & Plaza de España
PARK

(☺8am-10pm) A large area south of Antigua Fábrica de Tabacos was transformed for Seville's 1929 international fair, the Exposición Iberoamericana, when architects adorned it with fantastical buildings, many of them harking back to Seville's past glory or imitating the native styles of Spain's former colonies. In its midst you'll find the large Parque de María Luisa, a living expression of Seville's Moorish and Christian past. Entrance to the park is from the corner of Avenida del Cid and Avenida de Portugal at the southeastern corner of the university (former tobacco factory), about 800m southeast from the cathedral.

Plaza de España, one of the city's favourite relaxation spots, faces the park across Avenida de Isabel la Católica. Around it is the most grandiose of the 1929 buildings, a semicircular brick-and-tile confection featuring Seville tile work at its gaudiest.

On Plaza de América, at the southern end of the park, is Seville's Museo Arqueológico (admission €1.50, EU citizens free; ☺10am-8.30pm Tue-Sat, 10am-5pm Sun), with plenty to interest. Facing it is the Museo de Artes y Costumbres Populares (☑954 23 25 76; admission €1.50, EU citizens free; ☺10am-8.30pm Tue-Sat, 10am-5pm Sun), which contains art, furniture, embroidery and the like. Both are wheelchair accessible.

⊙ North of the Centre

North of El Centro lies the youthful Alameda de Hércules, a long rectangular plaza, and the adjacent Maracena district centred on its famous church. Facing it across the river is Isla Cartuja, site of the 1992 Expo.

Centro de la Interpretación Mudéjar
MUSEUM

(Plaza Calderón de la Barca; ☺8am-2pm & 5-8pm Mon-Fri, 8am-2pm Sat) FREE The architectural

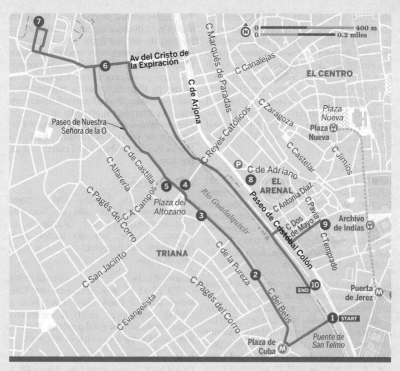

City Walk
Seville's River & Bridges

START PUENTE DE SAN TELMO
END TORRE DEL ORO
LENGTH 4KM; 90 MINUTES

Taking its name from the Arabic *al-wadi al-kabir* ('great river'), the Río Guadalquiver has long defined Seville. Start this walk on the east side of the **1 Puente de San Telmo**, built in 1931 as a lift-up bridge, but converted into a fixed structure in 1968. The bridge links central Seville with the neighbourhoods of Los Remedios and Triana, and thousands of revelers cross it during April and May on their way to the Spring Fair. On the Triana side, take the riverside walk known as **2 Calle del Betis** (Betis was the name given to the river by the Phoenicians). The street is known for its nightlife and tapas restaurants. If you have time, stop for a drink in **3 Café de la Prensa** and admire the unrivalled views of the cathedral across the river. The **4 Puente de Isabel II** is Seville's oldest bridge and was the first permanent one to ford the river when it was completed in 1852. On its northern side

lies Triana Market, underneath which lie the ruins of the **5 Castillo de San Jorge**, seat of the Inquisition Council from 1481 until 1785. Cut through the market and back down to the river walkway. The **6 Puente del Cristo de la Expiración**, with its distinctive white awnings, was built in 1991 just before the Expo. Close by, on the Isla de la Cartuja, it's impossible to miss the 180m-high **7 Torre Cajasol**, Seville's first skyscraper, which rose up amid much controversy in 2013–14. Cross the bridge and join the pedestrian walkway heading south on the opposite side. Passing back under the Puente de Isabel II, you'll enter **8 El Arenal**, the one-time port and ship-building quarter from which galleons once sailed for the New World. In the late 1600s the Guadalquivir silted up and ships began docking in Cádiz instead, but the **9 Atarazanas Reales** (Royal Shipyards), built in Gothic-Mudéjar style in the 13th century, can still be seen. Finish this walk by the **10 Torre del Oro**, a Muslim-era watchtower, which has guarded the river and the city for 800 years.

style that long defined Seville has recently acquired a shrine to its importance encased in one of Seville's textbook Mudéjar buildings, the **Palacio de Los Marqueses de la Algaba** (Plaza Calderón de la Barca). The small on-site museum with collected Mudéjar relics from the 12th to the 20th centuries gets a little lost in the large wonderfully restored mansion with its dreamy courtyard, but the captions (in Spanish and English) do a good job of explaining the nuances of the complex Mudéjar style.

Isla Mágica   THEME PARK
(☏902 16 17 16; www.islamagica.es; adult/child €29/20; ⊙high season around 11am-10pm, closed Dec-Mar; ⊕) This Disney-goes-Spanish-colonial amusement park provides a great if expensive day out for kids and all lovers of white-knuckle rides. Confirm times before going; hours vary by season. Both buses C1 and C2 run to Isla Mágica.

El Pabellon de la Navegación   MUSEUM
(www.pabellondelanavegacion.es; Camino de los Descubrimientos 2; adult/child €4.90/3.50; ⊙11am-7.30pm Tue-Sat, 11am-3pm Sun; ⊕) This sleek pavilion on the banks of the Guadalquivir River opened in 2012 and revived a previous navigation museum that lasted from the 1992 Expo until 1999. Its permanent collection is split into four parts – navigation, mariners, shipboard life and historical views of Seville. Although its exhibits are interactive and kid-friendly, for an adult it might be a bit underwhelming. The ticket includes a ride up the adjacent **Torre Schindler**.

**Conjunto Monumental de la
Cartuja**   MONASTERY, ART
(Cartuja Monastery; ☏955 03 70 70; www.caac.es; admission complete visit/monument or temporary exhibitions €3/1.80, free 7-9pm Tue-Fri & all day Sat; ⊙11am-9pm Tue-Sat, 11am-3pm Sun) You couldn't have invented this historic but off-beat art gallery, which was once a monastery and then a ceramics factory, but today is home to the **Centro Andaluz de Arte Contemporáneo**. Founded in 1399, the Conjunto Monumental de la Cartuja became the favourite *sevillano* lodging place for Columbus, who prayed in its chapel before his trip to the Americas and whose remains lay here for more than two decades in the 1530s and '40s.

In 1839 the complex was bought by an enterprising Englishman, Charles Pickman, who turned it into a porcelain factory, building the tall bottle-shaped kilns that stand rather incongruously beside the monastery.

The factory ceased production in the 1980s and in 1992 the building served as the Royal Pavilion during the Expo. It has since become Seville's shrine to modern art with temporary expos revolving around some truly bizarre permanent pieces. You can't miss *Alicia,* by Cristina Lucas, a massive head and arm poking through two old monastery windows that was supposedly inspired by Alice in Wonderland; though you could be forgiven for walking obliviously past Pedro Mora's *Bus Stop,* which looks exactly like...a bus stop.

Courses

Seville has many flamenco and language schools; tourist offices and *El Giraldillo* (www.elegirhoy.com) have information on options. The best language schools offer both short- and long-term courses at a variety of levels.

Giralda Center   LANGUAGE COURSE
(☏954 22 13 46; www.giraldacenter.com; Calle Mateos Gago 17; 1-week course €170) Has a friendly atmosphere, plenty of excursions and a reputation for good teaching. You can join any Monday for as little as one week.

CLIC   LANGUAGE COURSE
(☏954 50 21 31; www.clic.es; Calle Albareda 19) A well-established language centre headquartered in a pleasant house with a good social scene and an adjacent library. Courses for children, adults and seniors. Prices are approximately €125 for 10 lessons. It also has a branch in Cádiz.

Tours

Horse-drawn carriages wait near the cathedral, Plaza de España and Puerta de Jerez, charging a hefty €50 for up to four people for a one-hour trot around the Barrio de Santa Cruz and Parque de María Luisa areas.

★**Pancho Tours**   CULTURAL TOUR
(☏664 64 29 04; www.panchotours.com) FREE The best walking tours in the city? Join in and see – they're free, although you're welcome to tip the hardworking guide who'll furnish you with an encyclopedia's worth of anecdotes, stories, myths and theories about Seville's fascinating past. Tours kick off daily, normally at 11am – check the website for exact details. Pancho also offers bike tours (€15, Friday and Saturday 10am and 6pm) and nightlife tours (€10 to €15, daily).

FLAMENCO IMMERSION – LEARNING THE ART

For the devout follower of flamenco, mere listening isn't enough – it is necessary to participate. Seville is probably the best place in Andalucía to arrange classes in flamenco's four main disciplines – singing, dancing, guitar, and percussion/handclaps. For long-term options, the **Fundación Cristina Heeren de Arte Flamenco** (☑ 954 21 70 58; www.flamencoheeren.com; Avenida de Jerez 2) is Seville's best-known school, running annual courses in all the flamenco arts, though you can sign up for as little as one month if you partake in one of its intensive summer courses available in both Seville and Málaga.

People on shorter itineraries should check out **Taller Flamenco** (☑ 954 56 42 34; www.tallerflamenco.com; Calle Peral 49), which offers one-week packages with the possibility of being taught in groups or on a one-to-one basis. It also offers Spanish language classes. A third option is the prestigious Museo del Baile Flamenco (p584), which has an attached *escuela* (school) that offers workshops, classes and courses in all areas of flamenco. You can pay per class starting at approximately €60 per hour for private lessons, or €200 for 10 hours of group lessons spread over a week. Check the website for the latest details.

Cruceros Turísticos Torre del Oro
BOAT TOUR

(☑ 954 56 16 92; www.crucerostorredeloro.com; adult/child under 14yr €16/free) One-hour sightseeing river cruises every half-hour from 11am, departing from the river bank by the Torre del Oro. Last departure can range from 6pm in winter to 10pm in summer.

✴ Festivals & Events

Seville's Semana Santa processions and its Feria de Abril a week or two later are worth travelling a long way for, as is the Bienal de Flamenco.

Semana Santa
HOLY WEEK

(www.semana-santa.org) Every day from Palm Sunday to Easter Sunday, large, life-sized *pasos* (sculptural representations of events from Christ's Passion) are carried from Seville's churches through the streets to the cathedral, accompanied by processions that may take more than an hour to pass. The processions are organised by over 50 different *hermandades* or *cofradías* (brotherhoods, some of which include women).

The climax of the week is the *madrugada* (early hours) of Good Friday, when some of the most-respected brotherhoods file through the city. The costume worn by the marching penitents consists of a full robe and a conical hat with slits cut for the eyes. The regalia was incongruously copied by America's Ku Klux Klan.

Procession schedules are widely available during Semana Santa, or see the Semana Santa website. Arrive near the cathedral in the early evening for a better view.

Feria de Abril
SPRING FAIR

The April Fair, held in the second half of the month (sometimes edging into May), is the jolly counterpart to the sombre Semana Santa. The biggest and most colourful of all Andalucía's ferias is less invasive (and also less inclusive) than the Easter celebration – it takes place on El Real de la Feria, in the Los Remedios area west of the Guadalquivir.

The ceremonial lighting-up of the fairgrounds on the opening Monday night is the starting gun for six nights of *sevillanos*' favourite activities: eating, drinking, dressing up and dancing till dawn.

Bienal de Flamenco
FLAMENCO

(www.labienal.com; ☉ Sep) Most of the big names of the flamenco world participate in this major flamenco festival. Held in the September of even-numbered years.

🛏 Sleeping

There's a good range of places to stay in all three of the most attractive areas – Barrio de Santa Cruz (within walking distance of Prado de San Sebastián bus station), El Arenal and El Centro (both convenient for Plaza de Armas bus station).

Room rates are for each establishment's high season – typically from March to June and again in September and October. During Semana Santa and the Feria de Abril rates are doubled – at least! – and sell out completely. Book well ahead at this time.

Renting a tourist apartment here can be good value: typically costing under €100 a night for four people, or between €30 and €70 for two. Try **Apartamentos Embrujo** de Sevilla (⏧627 569919; www.embrujodesevilla.com), which specialises in historic townmansion apartments, or Sevilla5.com (⏧954 22 62 87, 637 011091; www.sevilla5.com).

🛏 Barrio de Santa Cruz

This old Jewish labyrinth is stuffed with majestic mansions, hidden patios and some very atmospheric accommodation.

Hotel Puerta de Sevilla HOTEL €
(⏧954 98 72 70; www.hotelpuertadesevilla.com; Calle Puerta de la Carne 2; r from €45; 🅿 🌐 @ 🛜) In a fantastic position, this superfriendly hotel is a great mix of chintz and style. There's an indoor water feature in the lobby, which is lined with superb Seville tile work. The rooms are all flower-pattern textiles, wrought-iron beds and pastel wallpaper.

Hotel Goya HOTEL €
(⏧954 21 11 70; www.hotelgoyasevilla.com; Calle Mateos Gago 31; s/d €40/60; 🌐 @ 🛜) The gleaming Goya, close to the cathedral, remains a popular draw and accepts pets. It's clean, and good value considering its location.

Pensión San Pancracio PENSIÓN €
(⏧954 41 31 04; Plaza de las Cruces 9; d €50, s/d without bathroom €25/35) An ideal budget option in Santa Cruz, this old rambling family house has plenty of different room options (all cheap) and a pleasant flower-bedizened patio/lobby. Friendliness makes up for the lack of luxury.

⭐Hotel Amadeus HOTEL €€
(⏧954 50 14 43; www.hotelamadeussevilla.com; Calle Farnesio 6; s/d €100/114; 🅿 🌐 🛜) Just when you thought you could never find hotels with pianos in the rooms any more, along came Hotel Amadeus. It's run by an engaging musical family in the old *judería*, and several of its astutely decorated rooms come complete with soundproofed walls and upright pianos, ensuring you don't miss out on your daily practice.

Other perks include in-room classical CDs, wall-mounted violins, and a rooftop terrace with a jacuzzi. Composers and Mozart lovers, look no further.

Un Patio en Santa Cruz HOTEL €€
(⏧954 53 94 13; www.patiosantacruz.com; Calle Doncellas 15; s €65-85, d €65-120; 🌐 🛜) Feeling more like an art gallery than a hotel, the Patio has starched-white walls coated in loud works of art, strange sculptures and preserved plants. The rooms are immensely comfortable, staff are friendly and there's a cool rooftop terrace with mosaic Moroccan tables. It's easily one of the hippest and best-value hotels in town.

Hotel Alcántara HOTEL €€
(⏧954 50 05 95; www.hotelalcantara.net; Calle Ximénez de Enciso 28; s/d €39/75; 🌐 🛜; 🚉1, C3, C4, 21, 23) This small, friendly hotel on a pedestrian street punches above its weight with sparkling modern bathrooms, windows onto the hotel's patio, and pretty floral curtains. It's next door to a flamenco venue.

Hostal Plaza Santa Cruz HOTEL €€
(⏧954 22 88 08; www.hostalplazasantacruz. com; Calle Santa Teresa 15; d/ste €67/95; 🌐 🛜) A new accommodation in the old quarter, this place has two options: a small hotel with unflashy creamy-white rooms just off Plaza Santa Cruz, or some more upmarket suites enhanced with deluxe touches such as tiles, art and heavy wooden furniture a block away.

⭐Hotel Casa 1800 LUXURY HOTEL €€€
(⏧954 56 18 00; www.hotelcasa1800sevilla.com; Calle Rodrigo Caro 6; d €147-210; 🌐 @ 🛜) Reigning as number one in Seville's 'favourite hotel' charts is this relatively new Santa Cruz jewel where the word *'casa'* (house) is taken seriously. This really is your home away from home (albeit a posh one!), with charming staff catering for your every need. Historic highlights include a sweet afternoon tea buffet, plus a quartet of penthouse garden suites with Giralda views.

It's also one of the only places in the city that doesn't hike up its Semana Santa rates to ridiculous levels.

🛏 El Arenal & Triana

A central location and a good mix of accommodation make this riverside neighbourhood worth contemplating as a base.

Hotel Simón HOTEL €€
(⏧954 22 66 60; www.hotelsimonsevilla.com; Calle García de Vinuesa 19; s/d €55/75; 🌐 @) A typically grand 18th-century Sevillian house in the Arenal, with an ornate patio and smaller slightly less ornate rooms, this place gleams way above its two-star rating. Some of the rooms are embellished with rich *azulejos* tile work.

Hotel Adriano
HOTEL €€

(954 29 38 00; www.adrianohotel.com; Calle Adriano 12; s/d €75/96; P) A solid Arenal option with great staff, rooms with attractive *sevillano* features, and a lovely little cafe out front.

El Centro

Handily situated for everywhere, El Centro mixes hotel glitter with some real bargains.

★ Oasis Backpackers' Hostel
HOSTEL €

(955 26 26 96; www.oasissevilla.com; Calle Almirante Ulloa 1; dm/d incl breakfast €15/50;) It's not often you get to backpack in a palace. A veritable oasis in the busy city-centre district, this place is a friendly welcoming hostel set in a palatial 19th-century mansion with some private room options, a cafe-bar, and a rooftop deck with a small pool.

You can organise tons of activities here and meet plenty of multilingual fellow travellers in an atmosphere that's sociable but never over-the-top noisy. Oasis has another branch near the Metropol Parasol.

Hotel Abanico
HOTEL €€

(954 21 32 07; www.hotelabanico.com; Calle Águilas 17; r from €120;) If you want to wake up and know instantly that you're in Seville, book into this central gem where the colourful tile work, wrought-iron balconies and radiant religious art have 'Sevilla' written all over them.

Hotel América
HOTEL €€

(954 22 09 51; www.hotelamericasevilla.com; Plaza del Duque de la Victoria 9; s/d €69/89;) If you like no fuss, then head for the Hotel América, a well-located, professionally run hotel with a business-like sheen that won't offer you fancy tile work or carnations on your pillow, but *will* give you all you need to set up a decent sightseeing base.

Hotel San Francisco
HOTEL €€

(954 50 15 41; www.sanfranciscoh.com; Calle Álvarez Quintero 38; s/d €55/68;) A well-positioned place on a pedestrianised street, the San Francisco is definitely one-star territory, with laissez-faire service, dark but clean rooms and slightly temperamental wi-fi. The hotel is closed in August.

EME Catedral Hotel
LUXURY HOTEL €€€

(954 56 00 00; www.emecatedralhotel.com; Calle de los Alemanes 27; d €187-348;) Take 14 fine old Sevillan houses and knock them into one. Bring in a top designer and a decorated Spanish chef. Carve out a hammam-like spa, rooftop pool, seven restaurants and slick, striking rooms with red colour accents. Then stick it all nose-to-nose with the largest Gothic cathedral in the world.

The result: EME Catedral Hotel, a self-styled avant-garde boutique accommodation where ancient Seville has been fused with something a bit more cutting edge. Does it work? Cough up the €200-plus a night and find out.

North of the Centre

As this area is a little peripheral to the main sights, you'll need to find somewhere special to justify staying here. Here are two contenders.

Hotel Sacristía de Santa Ana
BOUTIQUE HOTEL €€

(954 91 57 22; www.hotelsacristia.com; Alameda de Hércules 22; d from €79;) Possibly the best deal in Seville, this utterly delightful hotel is located on the Alameda. It's great for visiting the neighbouring bars and restaurants and the hotel itself is a heavenly place with a small fountain surrounded by bonsai trees greeting you in the central courtyard.

Away from the courtyard there are old-fashioned rooms with big arty bedheads, circular baths and cascading showers. Service is equally excellent.

Hotel San Gil
HOTEL €€

(954 90 68 11; www.hotelsangil.com; Calle Parras 28; d/ste from €80/120;) Shoehorned at the northern end of the Macarena neighbourhood, San Gil's slightly out-of-the-way location is balanced by its proximity to the nightlife of the Alameda de Hercules. A beautifully opulent lobby fronts more modern rooms that have large beds and ample space. Worth the walk.

✗ Eating

In the competition to produce Andalucía's most inventive tapas, Seville wins – hands down. Many tapas bars have adjoining restaurants where you can choose from an à la carte menu.

For a sit-down meal, restaurants preparing Spanish food open late: ie at 9pm, or nearer 10pm in summer. But with a surfeit of tourists, Seville has plenty of options for earlier dining.

✖ Barrio de Santa Cruz

Good tapas bars are everywhere in this compact quarter. Wander the narrow streets and allow the atmosphere to draw you in.

Casa Plácido   TAPAS €

(Calle Mesón del Morro 15; tapas €2.50; ⊙12.30-4pm & 8pm-midnight Mon-Thu, to 1am Fri-Sun) A tight-fitting, time-worn bar that hasn't changed much since 1870-something where you can enjoy traditional tapas banged down on the table quicker than you can say *dos cervezas, por favor*. Wasn't that what you came to Seville for?

Café Bar Las Teresas   TAPAS €

(Calle Santa Teresa 2; tapas €3; ⊙10am-midnight) The hanging hams look as ancient as the bar itself, a sinuous wraparound affair with just enough room for two stout waiters to pass carrying precariously balanced tapas plates. The atmosphere is dark but not dingy, the food highly traditional, and the crowd an integrated mix of tourists and Santa Cruz locals.

Bodega Santa Cruz   TAPAS €

(Calle Mateos Gago; tapas €2; ⊙11.30am-midnight) This forever crowded bodega is where eating tapas becomes a physical contact sport. Watch out for flying elbows and admire those dexterous waiters who bob and weave like prizefighters amid the chaos. The fiercely traditional tapas are best enjoyed alfresco with a cold beer as you watch marching armies of Santa Cruz tourists go squeezing past.

★ Vinería San Telmo   TAPAS, FUSION €€

(✆954 41 06 00; www.vineriasantelmo.com; Paseo Catalina de Ribera 4; tapas €3.50, media raciones €10; ⊙1-4.30pm & 8pm-midnight) San Telmo invented the *rascocielo* (skyscraper) tapa, an 'Empire State' of tomatoes, aubergine, goat's cheese and smoked salmon. If this and other creations – such as foie gras with quail's eggs and lychees, or exquisitely cooked bricks of tuna – don't make you drool with expectation, then you're probably dead.

Catalina   TAPAS €€

(Paseo Catalina de Ribera 4; raciones €10; ⊙9am-1am) If your view of tapas is 'glorified bar snacks', then get ready to have your ideas blown out of the water with a creative mix of just about every ingredient known to Iberian cooking. Start with the cheese, aubergine and paprika special. The equally wonderful Vinería San Telmo is next door. Tough choice! Toss a coin.

Restaurante Egaña
Oriza   CONTEMPORARY SPANISH €€€

(www.restauranteoriza.com; Calle San Fernando 41; mains €22-32; ⊙1.30-4pm & 8.30-11.30pm Mon-Fri, 8.30-11.30pm Sat) Say Basque and you've got a byword for fine-dining these days, so it's not surprising that Basque-run Egaña Oriza is regarded as one of the city's standout restaurants. Situated opposite the bus station, this could be your first (and best) culinary treat in Seville. There's an equally posh tapas spot on the ground floor.

✖ El Arenal

Surprisingly lively at night, El Arenal has some good small tapas places that force half the clientele to congregate in the street.

Mesón Serranito   TAPAS, ANDALUCIAN €

(✆954 21 12 43; Calle Antonia Díaz 11; media raciones €7; ⊙9am-midnight) Vegetarians steer clear: this place is dangerously close to the bullring and has *rabo de toro* (bull's tail) on the menu to go with the bulls' heads hanging on the wall – next to pictures of the final few seconds of their lives.

It also specialises in the *serranito*, a Spanish gastronomic institution consisting of a slice of toasted bread heaped with a pork fillet, roasted pepper, a nice bit of *jamón* and garlic.

★ La Brunilda   TAPAS, FUSION €€

(✆954 22 04 81; Calle Galera 5; tapas €3.50-6.50; ⊙1-4pm & 8.30-11.30pm Tue-Sat, 1-4pm Sun) Seville's crown as Andalucía's tapas capital is regularly attacked by well-armed rivals from the provinces, meaning it constantly has to reinvent itself and offer up fresh competition. Enter Brunilda, a new temple of fusion tapas sandwiched into an inconspicuous backstreet in the Arenal quarter where everything – including the food, staff and clientele – is pretty.

If you have an unlimited appetite, try the whole menu. For those with smaller bellies, the creamy risotto is unmissable.

Mesón Cinco Jotas   TAPAS €€

(www.mesoncincojotas.com; Calle Castelar 1; media raciones €10; ⊙9am-midnight Mon-Sat, noon-midnight Sun) In the world of *jamón*-making, if you are awarded 'Cinco Jotas' (Five Js) for your *jamón*, it's like getting an Oscar. The owner of this place, Sánchez Romero Carvajal, is the biggest producer of Jabugo ham, and is clearly the Tom Hanks of his field.

Infanta
ANDALUCIAN €€€

(📞954 56 15 54; www.infantasevilla.es; Calle Arfe 34-36; mains €16-24; ⏰12.30-5pm & 8pm-midnight Mon-Sat, 12.30-5pm Sun) A one-time spit-and-sawdust Arenal tapas bar that recently moved around the corner and re-invented itself as something a little slicker and 'nouveau'. Nonetheless the bright interior includes some beautiful throwback architectural features and the food never strays far from local ingredients. For a break from tapas, try the on-site sit-down restaurant with a full à la carte menu.

Enrique Becerra
ANDALUCIAN €€€

(📞954 21 30 49; www.enriquebecerra.com; Calle Gamazo 2; mains €17-25; ⏰1-4.30pm & 8pm-midnight Mon-Sat, 1-4.30pm Sun) Squeeze in with the locals at lunchtime and enjoy some hearty Andalucian dishes. The lamb drenched in honey sauce and stuffed with spinach and pine nuts (€22) is just one of many delectable offerings, but be warned – the restaurant charges a whopping €2.50 for bread and olives!

✖ El Centro

Plaza de la Alfalfa wears many hats. It is the hub of the tapas scene in the day, a stopping-off point for boisterous families in the early evening, and a hive of late-night bars and clubs after darkness falls. There are a couple of decent Italian restaurants on or around the square if you need a break from the usual Spanish suspects.

★ Redhouse Art & Food
INTERNATIONAL €

(📞661 61 56 46; www.redhousespace.com; Calle Amor de Dios 7; snacks from €4; ⏰11.30am-12.30am Tue-Sun; 🛜) It's hard to classify Redhouse. With its mismatched chairs and abstract wall art, it's clearly flirting with hipster affiliations, yet inside you'll find families, seniors, college geeks, and the obviously not-so-hip enjoying a whole variety of food from casual coffee to romantic meals. Whatever you opt for, save room for the best homemade cakes in Andalucía.

Fashion shows, art expos, poetry readings and music all happen here.

The Room
FUSION €

(📞619 20 09 46; www.theroomartcuisine.com; Calle Cuesta del Rosario 15; tapas €2.75-5; ⏰8.30am-1am Mon-Fri, 1pm-1am Sat, 1-6pm Sun; 🛜) Another new 'art cuisine' place, the Room sticks its succinct menu on a blackboard and offers everything from British-style fish and chips to tasty *tortas*. Open all day, it's a good place to while away the quiet siesta hours with a glass of wine and something good to read, such as – ahem – this book.

Horno de San Buenaventura
CAFE, SNACKS €

(www.hornosanbuenaventura.com; Avenida de la Constitución; pastries from €1; ⏰9am-9pm) There are two of these gilded pastry/coffee/snack bars in Seville, one here in Avenida de la Constitución opposite the cathedral and the other (inferior one) in the Plaza de Alfalfa (⏰9am-9pm). All kinds of fare are on show, though it's probably best enjoyed for its lazy continental breakfasts (yes, the service can be slow) or a spontaneous early evening cake fix.

Bar Alfalfa
TAPAS €

(cnr Calles Alfalfa & Candilejo; tapas €3; ⏰9am-midnight) It's amazing how many people, hams, wine bottles and other knick-knacks you can stuff into a space barely large enough to swing a small cat. No matter: order through the window when the going gets crowded – you won't forget the tomato-tinged magnificence of the Italy-meets-Iberia *salmorejo* (thick gazpacho) bruschetta.

★ Los Coloniales
CONTEMPORARY ANDALUCIAN €€

(www.tabernacoloniales.es; cnr Calle Dormitorio & Plaza Cristo de Burgos; mains €10-12; ⏰12.30pm-12.15am) The quiet ones are always the best. It might not look like much from the outside, but take it on trust: Los Coloniales is something very special. The quality plates line up like models on a catwalk: *chorizo a la Asturiana* (a divine spicy sausage in an onion sauce served on a bed of lightly fried potato), aubergines in honey and pork tenderloin *al whisky*.

La Azotea
FUSION, ANDALUCIAN €€

(📞955 11 67 48; Jesús del Gran Poder 31; raciones €10; ⏰1.30-4.30pm & 8.30pm-midnght Thu-Mon) The latest word in '*nueva cocina*' comes from Azotea whose proliferating empire – there are now four branches – testifies to a growing legend. The decor is Ikea-friendly, staff wear black, and the raciones, which are sweetened and spiced with panache, arrive like pieces of art in a variety of plates, dishes and boxes.

Luso Tapas
TAPAS, PORTUGUESE €€

(☑955 09 75 53; Calle Javier Lasso de la Vega 9; tapas €4-6.50; ⊙noon-5pm & 8-11.30pm Tue-Sun) Save on a day trip to Lisbon and decamp to Luso for a Portuguese take on tapas. New in 2013, the boys from across the border treat their Iberian cousins to some impressive bites of Iberian flavour – the fish is a highlight – and they're *muito bom* (very good) as they say on the other side of the frontier.

Robles Laredo
CONTEMPORARY SPANISH €€

(www.casa-robles.com; Plaza de San Francisco; raciones €9-12; ⊙11am-1am Sat-Wed, 11am-2am Thu & Fri) This small Italianate cafe-restaurant is fairly dwarfed by its two huge chandeliers and a vast collection of delicate desserts displayed in glass cases. The tapas are equally refined. Try the foie gras, beef burgers with truffle sauce, or oysters and whitebait.

El Rinconcillo
TAPAS, ANDALUCIAN €€

(☑954 22 31 83; www.elrinconcillo.es; Calle Gerona 40; tapas €3, raciones €12; ⊙1pm-1.30am) Some say the Rinconcillo is resting on its laurels. Maybe so; but, with over 345 years of history, there are a lot to rest on. Seville's oldest bar first opened in 1670, when the Inquisition was raging and tapas were still just tops you screwed on bottles.

Come here for the sense of history rather than for the food, but stay for the *ortiguillas fritas* (fried sea anemones) and a saucerful of the biggest olives you've ever seen.

🍴 Alameda de Hércules

Seville's trendiest nightlife quarter also has some decent eating places overlooking the main pedestrianised park.

★ Bar-Restaurante Eslava
FUSION, ANDALUCIAN €€

(www.espacioeslava.com; Calle Eslava 3; media raciones €9-13; ⊙12.30pm-midnight Tue-Sat, 12.30-4.30pm Sun) A legend in its own dinnertime, Eslava shirks the traditional tile work and bullfighting posters of tapa-bar lore and delivers where it matters: fine food backed up with equally fine service.

There's a 'nouvelle' tinge to the memorable *costillas a la miel* (pork ribs in a honey and rosemary glaze) and vegetable strudel in a cheese sauce, but there's nothing snobby about the atmosphere, which is local and pretty fanatical after 9pm. The restaurant overlooks the Plaza de San Lorenzo just off the southwestern corner of the Alameda de Hércules.

Duo Tapas
TAPAS, FUSION €€

(Calle Calatrava 10; tapas €3-4.50, media raciones €9-12; ⊙12.30-4.30pm & 8.30pm-midnight) Missed by the masses who rarely wander north from the Alameda de Hércules, Duo Tapas is 'new school'. But what it lacks in *azulejos* tiles and illustrious past patrons, it makes up for in inventive tapas with an Asian twist. Alameda trendies swear by its green chicken with rice and spicy noodles.

🍴 Triana

In Triana, look no further than riverside Calle del Betis. The restaurants here are at their best around 11pm. Sit outside and enjoy fried seafood with the Torre del Oro reflecting on the river.

Ristorante Cosa Nostra
ITALIAN €€

(☑954 27 07 52; Calle del Betis 52; pizzas €8.50-12; ⊙1.30-4.30pm & 8.30pm-12.30am Tue-Sun; 🎵) Forget the Mafiosi nameplate; this is the best Italian food in Seville and well worth crossing the river for. The pizzas are spun in front of your eyes and the rich creamy risottos ought to have every paella chef in the city looking over their shoulder.

T de Triana
ANDALUCIAN €€

(☑954 33 12 03; Calle del Betis 20; ⊙8pm-2am) The 'T' is Triana in a nutshell: simple fish-biased tapas, walls full of history, *fútbol* on the big screen whenever local boys Sevilla or Real Betis are playing, and live gutsy flamenco every Friday night at 10pm.

🍷 Drinking

Bars usually open 6pm to 2am weekdays and 8pm to 3am at the weekend. Drinking and partying really get going around midnight on Friday and Saturday (daily when it's hot). In summer, dozens of open-air late-night bars (*terrazas de verano*) spring up along both banks of the river. Ideal bar-hopping neighbourhoods include the Barrio de Santa Cruz and the web of streets around Plaza de Alfalfa. The Alameda de Hércules is the centre of gay Seville.

Baños Árabes Tetería
TEAHOUSE

(Calle Aire 15; ⊙4pm-midnight) Seville doesn't have an abundance of *teterías* like Granada and Málaga, making this one encased in the hear-a-pin-drop tranquillity of the Baños Árabes (p584) in Santa Cruz all the more precious. An intellectual atmosphere is generated within by edgy art and murmuring students discussing Almodóvar movies.

El Garlochi
BAR

(Calle Boteros 4; ☺10pm-6am) Dedicated entirely to the religious iconography of Semana Santa, the ubercamp El Garlochi is a true marvel. Taste the rather revolting-sounding cocktail Sangre de Cristo (Blood of Christ), and pray more bars like this are opened.

Bulebar Café
BAR, CAFE

(☏954 90 19 54; Alameda de Hércules 83; ☺4pm-late) This place gets pretty *caliente* (hot) at night, but is pleasantly chilled in the early evening, with friendly staff. And don't write off its spirit-reviving alfresco breakfasts, which pitch together early-birds and up-all-nighters. The cafe is on the eastern side of the Alameda de Hércules.

Habanilla
BAR, CAFE

(☏954 90 27 18; Alameda de Hércules 63; ☺8am-2am) Habanilla's subversive charm is encapsulated in the cheeky beer-bottle chandelier that dominates the room.

Cabo Loco
BAR

(Calle Pérez Galdós 26; ☺5pm-1am Tue & Wed, 5pm-3am Thu-Sat, 5pm-midnight Sun) Two really is a crowd in this Alfalfa district dive bar, hole-in-the-wall, cheap shot heaven... call it whatever you like. It's a good stop on any elongated bar crawl, if you don't mind standing – alfresco.

☆ Entertainment

Seville is reborn after dark, with live music, experimental theatre and exciting flamenco.

Teatro Duque La Imperdible
THEATRE

(☏954 38 82 19; www.imperdible.org; Plaza del Duque de la Victoria; adult/child €12/5) This epicentre of experimental arts stages lots of contemporary dance, theatre and flamenco, usually around 9pm. The bar here also hosts varied music events from around 11pm Thursday to Saturday.

Sevilla de Ópera
THEATRE

(☏955 29 46 61; www.sevilladeopera.com; Mercado del Arenal; ☺shows 9pm Fri & Sat) Seville has served as the fictional setting for countless operas, so it made sense when in 2012 a group of opera singers and enthusiasts decided to initiate the Sevilla de Ópera club. Located in Arenal market the club functions like an 'Opera *tablao*', staging shows designed to make the music more accessible.

You can come for either drinks and/or dinner and enjoy renditions of pieces from the likes of *Carmen, The Marriage of Figaro* and *The Barber of Seville.*

Naima Café Jazz
JAZZ

(☏954 38 24 85; Calle Trajano 47; ☺live performances from 11pm Sat & Sun) If you need a break from the intensity of flamenco, then you can find respite at this intimate bar, which sways to the sound of mellow live jazz at weekends.

FLAMENCO

Soleares, Flamenco's truest *cante jondo* (deep song), was first concocted in Triana; head there to find some of the more authentic clubs. Elsewhere, the city puts on nightly *tablaos* (flamenco shows aimed mainly at tourists) at about half-a-dozen venues.

Tablao El Arenal
FLAMENCO

(www.tablaoelarenal.com; Calle Rodo 7; admission with 1 drink €37, with dinner €72; ☺restaurant from 7pm, shows 8pm & 10pm) Of the three places in Seville that offer flamenco dinner shows, this is the best – ask any local. A smaller seating capacity (100 compared to 500 at the Palacio Andaluz) offers greater intimacy, although, as a big venue, it still lacks the grit and – invariably – *duende* (flamenco spirit) of the *peñas* (small flamenco clubs).

Casa de la Memoria
FLAMENCO

(☏954 56 06 70; www.casadelamemoria.es; Calle Cuna 6; admission €18; ☺shows 7.30pm & 9pm) Neither a *tablao* nor a private *peña*, this cultural centre – recently relocated from Santa Cruz to El Centro, where it is accommodated in the old stables of the Palacio de la Lebrija – offers what are, without doubt, the most intimate and authentic nightly flamenco shows in Seville.

It's perennially popular and space is limited to 100, so reserve tickets a day or so in advance by calling or visiting the venue.

Casa de la Guitarra
FLAMENCO

(☏954 22 40 93; Calle Mesón del Moro 12; adult/child €17/10; ☺shows 7.30pm & 9pm) Tiny new flamenco-only venue in Santa Cruz (no food or drinks served) where a miscued step from the performing dancers would land them in the front row of the audience. Glass display cases filled with guitars of erstwhile flamenco greats adorn the walls.

La Carbonería
FLAMENCO

(Calle Levíes 18; ⊙8pm-4am) During the day there is no indication that this happening place is anything but a large garage. But come after 8pm and this converted coal yard in the Barrio de Santa Cruz reveals two large bars, and nightly live flamenco (11pm and midnight) for no extra charge.

Casa Anselma
FLAMENCO

(Calle Pagés del Corro 49; ⊙midnight-late Mon-Sat) If you can squeeze in past the forbidding form of Anselma (a celebrated Triana flamenco dancer) at the door, you'll quickly realise that anything can happen in here. Casa Anselma (beware: there's no sign, just a doorway embellished with *azulejos* tiles) is the antithesis of a tourist *tablao,* with cheek-to-jowl crowds, thick cigarette smoke, zero amplification and spontaneous outbreaks of dexterous dancing. Pure magic.

Anselma is in Triana on the corner of Calle Alfarería, about 200m from the western end of the Puente de Isabel.

 Shopping

The craft shops in the Barrio de Santa Cruz are inevitably tourist oriented, but many sell attractive ceramic tiles and poster art.

Shoe fetishists beware: Seville has possibly the densest quota of shoe shops on the planet, primarily focused in El Centro around the pedestrianised shopping streets of Calles Sierpes, de la Cuna, Velázquez and Tetuán. **El Corte Inglés** (Plaza del Duque de la Victoria 8; ⊙10am-10pm Mon-Sat) department store occupies four separate buildings a little west, on Plaza de la Magdalena and Plaza del Duque de la Victoria. Further north, Calle Amor de Dios and Calle Doctor Letamendi have more alternative shops.

Cerámica Santa Ana
CERAMICS

(☑954 33 39 90; www.ceramicasantaana.com; Calle San Jorge 31; ⊙9.30am-1.30pm & 5-8.30pm Mon-Fri, 10am-2pm Sat) Seville specialises in distinctive ceramic tiles or *azulejos* and they are best seen in Triana. Cerámica Santa Ana has been around for over 50 years and the shop itself almost qualifies as a tourist attraction. There are a dozen more tile-making shops and workshops on the same street.

El Postigo
MARKET

(cnr Calles Arfe & Dos de Mayo; ⊙11am-2pm & 4-8pm) This covered arts-and-crafts market in the Arenal houses a few shops selling everything from pottery and textiles to silverware.

Padilla Crespo
CLOTHING

(☑954 21 29 88; Calle Adriano 18B; ⊙10am-8.30pm Mon-Sat) If you're really immersing yourself in the culture, you can pick up your wide-brimmed hat and riding outfit for the Spring Feria right here.

Casa del Libro
BOOKS

(www.casadellibro.com; Calle Velázquez 8; ⊙9.30am-9.30pm Mon-Sat) Part of Spain's oldest bookshop chain, this branch is spread over four floors and stocks plenty of multilingual fiction and guidebooks (including this one).

ℹ Information

EMERGENCY

Ambulance (☑061)
Emergency (☑112)
Policía Local (☑092)
Policía Nacional (☑091)

MEDICAL SERVICES

Centro de Salud El Porvenir (☑954 71 23 23; cnr Avenidas Menéndez y Pelayo & de Cádiz) Public clinic with emergency services.
Hospital Virgen del Rocío (☑955 01 20 00; Avenida de Manuel Siurot) The main general hospital, 1km south of Parque de María Luisa.

MONEY

There's no shortage of banks and ATMs in the central area. Santa Justa train station, the airport and both bus stations have ATMs.

POST

Post Office (Avenida de la Constitución 32; ⊙8.30am-9.30pm Mon-Fri, 8.30am-2pm Sat)

TOURIST INFORMATION

Tourist Office (Avenida de la Constitución 21B; ⊙9am-8pm Mon-Fri, 10am-2pm Sat & Sun, closed holidays) City tourist info. The staff here are well informed but often very busy.
Turismo Sevilla (www.turismosevilla.org; Plaza del Triunfo 1; ⊙10.30am-7pm Mon-Fri) Information on all Sevilla province.

ℹ Getting There & Away

AIR

Seville's Aeropuerto San Pablo has a fair range of international and domestic flights. **Iberia** (www.iberia.com) flies direct to Barcelona, Madrid and Toulouse. Air Europa (p878) connects to the Canary Islands and low-cost Vueling

CYCLING SEVILLE

Since the inauguration of the Sevici (☎902 01 10 32; www.sevici.es; ⏰7am-9pm) bike-sharing scheme in April 2007, Seville has logged a phenomenal 1300% increase in daily cycling usage and become a blueprint for urban cycling planning everywhere. Sevici was the second bike-sharing initiative in Spain (there are now dozens), opening a couple of weeks after Barcelona's *Bicing* program. Despite newer competition, it remains the ninth-largest scheme of its kind in Europe with 2500 bikes. Grab a two-wheeled machine from any one of 250 docking stations and you'll quickly discover that cycling rather suits this flat, balmy metropolis, which was seemingly designed with outdoor experiences in mind.

Most of Sevici's 70,000-plus daily users are locals, but visitors can take advantage of the sharing system by purchasing a seven-day pass online for €12.30 (plus a €150 returnable deposit). Proceed to the nearest docking station, punch in the number from your coded receipt, and hey presto. The first 30 minutes of usage are free. Beyond that, it's €1 for the first hour and €2 an hour thereafter. Seville has 130km of city bike lanes (all painted green and equipped with their own traffic signals).

Another way of taking advantage of the new cycling infrastructure is to take a bike tour around the city's main sights. Pancho Tours (p588) organises 2½-hour rides on Fridays and Saturdays for €15 including bike hire.

(p878) links to Barcelona, Paris and (seasonally) Amsterdam and Rome.

From the British Isles there are flights with **EasyJet** (www.easyjet.com) from London-Gatwick, and **Ryanair** (www.ryanair.com) from London-Gatwick and London-Stansted. Ryanair also flies to Barcelona, Brussels, Rome, various Italian destinations and Marrakech. **Transavia** (www.transavia.com) comes from Paris and (seasonally) Lyon and Nantes. Carrier and schedule information changes frequently, so it's best to check with specific airlines or major online bookers.

BUS

Seville has two bus stations. From the **Estación de Autobuses Plaza de Armas** (www.autobusesplazadearmas.es; Avenida del Cristo de la Expiración) the bus company **Alsa** (www.alsa.es) runs buses to Córdoba (€12, two hours, seven daily), Granada (€23, three hours, 10 daily) and Málaga (€18, 2¾ hours, eight daily), while Damas serves Huelva (€8.67, 1¼ hours, 18 daily). This is also the main station for **Eurolines** (www.eurolines.es) and international services to Germany, Belgium, France and beyond. **Comes** (www.tgcomes.es) runs buses from the **Estación de Autobuses Prado de San Sebastián** (Plaza San Sebastián) to Cádiz (€13, 1¾ hours, eight daily) and Jerez de la Frontera (€8.90, 1¼ hours, seven daily).

TRAIN

Seville's **Estación Santa Justa** (☎902 43 23 43; Avenida Kansas City) is 1.5km northeast of the centre. Trains go to/from Madrid (€76, 2½ hours, 20 daily), Cádiz (€16, 1¾ hours, 15 daily),

Córdoba (€30, 42 minutes, 30 daily), Huelva (€12, 1½ hours, three daily), Granada (€30, three hours, four daily) and Málaga (€43, two hours, 11 daily).

❶ Getting Around

TO/FROM THE AIRPORT

The airport is 7km east of the city centre on the A4 Córdoba road. A special airport bus marked *Especial Aeropuerto* runs between the airport and the Plaza de Armas bus station (€4, every 15 minutes, 5.45am to 12.45am, less frequent on Sundays). It stops, among other places, beside the Torre del Oro in the city centre. A taxi costs about €22.

BUS

Run by Seville's urban transport authority, **Tussam** (www.tussam.es), buses C1, C2, C3 and C4 do useful circular routes linking the main transport terminals and the city centre. The standard ticket is €1.40 but a range of passes are available (from stations and kiosks next to stops) if you're likely to use public transport a lot.

CAR & MOTORCYCLE

Central Seville is a nightmare to drive in. Avoid it if you can. Hotels with parking usually charge you €12 to €18 a day for the privilege – no cheaper than some public car parks but at least your vehicle will be close to hand. **Parking Paseo de Colón** (cnr Paseo de Cristóbal Colón & Calle Adriano; per hr up to 10hr €1.20, 10-24hr €13.50) is a relatively inexpensive underground car park.

DON'T MISS

ITÁLICA

Situated in the suburban settlement of Santiponce, 8km northwest of Seville, Itálica ([phone] 955 62 22 66; www.juntadeandalucia.es/cultura/italica; Avenida de Extremadura 2; admission €1.50, EU citizens free; ⊙ 8.30am-9pm Tue-Sat, 9am-3pm Sun & holidays Apr-Sep, 9am-6.30pm Tue-Sat, 10am-4pm Sun & holidays Oct-Mar) was the first Roman town in Spain. Founded in 206 BC, it was also the birthplace and home of the 2nd-century-AD Roman emperors Trajan and Hadrian. The partly reconstructed ruins include one of the biggest of all the Roman amphitheatres, broad paved streets, the ruins of several houses with beautiful mosaics, and a theatre.

Buses run to Santiponce (€1.40, 40 minutes) from Seville's Plaza de Armas bus station at least twice an hour from 6.35am to 11pm Monday to Friday, and a little less often at weekends. They stop right outside the Itálica entrance.

METRO

Seville's first metro line opened in April 2009 and connects Ciudad Expo with Olivar de Quinto (this line isn't particularly useful for visitors). Three more lines are due for completion by 2017. The standard ticket is €1.40. A one-day travelcard is €4.50.

TRAM

Tranvia (www.tussam.es) is the city's sleek tram service, first introduced in 2007. Two parallel lines run in pollution-free bliss between Plaza Nueva, Avenida de la Constitucíon, Puerta de Jerez, San Sebastián and San Bernardo. The standard ticket is €1.40, but a range of passes is available if you're likely to use it a lot.

SEVILLE PROVINCE

Seville province invites day trips. You'll find Andalucía's best Roman ruins at Itálica, while east of Seville on the rolling agricultural plains known as La Campiña, fascinating old towns such as Carmona, Osuna and Écija bespeak many epochs of history.

Carmona

POP 27,950 / ELEV 250M

Perched on a low hill overlooking wonderful *vega* (farmland) that sizzles in the summer heat, and dotted with old palaces and impressive monuments, Carmona comes as an unexpected highlight of western Andalucía.

⊙ Sights

The tourist office in the Puerta de Sevilla, the impressive fortified main gate of the old town, sells tickets (adults/students and seniors €2/1) for the gate's interesting upper levels.

Iglesia Prioral de Santa María CHURCH
([phone] 954 19 14 82; Plaza Marqués de las Torres; admission €3; ⊙ 9am-2pm & 5.30-7.30pm Mon-Fri, 9am-2pm Sat) This splendid church was built mainly in the 15th and 16th centuries on the site of the former main mosque. The Patio de los Naranjos by which you enter has a Visigothic calendar carved into one of its pillars. Inside, the plateresque altar is detailed to an almost perverse degree, with 20 panels of biblical scenes framed by gilt-scrolled columns.

Roman Necropolis CEMETERY, RUINS
([phone] 954 14 08 11; Avenida de Jorge Bonsor; ⊙ 9am-2pm Tue-Sat 15 Jun–14 Sep, closed holidays & 1 Jul–31 Aug) **FREE** Just over 1km southwest of the Puerta de Sevilla is Carmona's impressive Roman Necropolis. You can look down into a dozen family tombs, hewn from the rock.

Museo de la Ciudad MUSEUM
(City History Museum; [phone] 954 14 01 28; www.museociudad.carmona.org; Calle San Ildefonso 1; adult/child €3/free, Tue free; ⊙ 11am-7pm Tue-Sun, 11am-2pm Mon) An interesting background to the town can be explored at the city museum, housed in a centuries-old palace, with pieces dating back to Paleolithic times. The sections on the Tartessos and their Roman successors are highlights: the former includes a unique collection of large earthenware vessels with Middle Eastern decorative motifs, the latter several excellent mosaics.

Puerta de Córdoba GATE
(Calle de Dolores Quintanilla; admission €2; ⊙ tours min 8 people 11.30am, 12.30pm & 1.30pm Tue, Sat & Sun) The Roman gate that controlled access to the city from the east is in marvellous repair, framing the fertile countryside outside it like a precious, faded rug.

Alcázar
LANDMARK

(Calle Alcázar) The stark, ruined Alcázar was an Almohad fort that Pedro I turned into a country palace. It was brought down by earthquakes in 1504 and 1755, and part of it is now the site of a *parador* (luxury state-owned hotel).

🛏 Sleeping & Eating

The tourist office publish a 'tapas trail' of the best local drinking and eating places.

Hostal Comercio
HOSTAL €

(📞 954 14 00 18; hostalcomercio@hotmail.com; Calle Torre del Oro 56; r €50-70; ❄ 🛜) Just inside the Puerta de Sevilla, this old-fashioned inn provides 14 spiffy, simple rooms around a plant-filled patio with Mudéjar-style arches. The unpretentious decor is matched by the cordial service, cultivated over generations.

Posada San Fernando
BOUTIQUE HOTEL €€

(📞 954 14 14 08; Plaza de San Fernando 6; r €71-82; ❄ 🛜) This excellent-value hotel stands on Carmona's liveliest square. Each room in the 16th-century structure is uniquely appointed, with thoughtfully chosen furniture, fittings and wallpaper, down to the hand-painted tiles in the bathrooms, some with claw-foot tubs.

Parador Alcázar del Rey Don Pedro
HISTORIC HOTEL €€€

(📞 954 14 10 10; www.parador.es; Calle Alcázar; s/d €150/188; 🅿 ❄ @ 🛜 🏊) Carmona's luxuriously equipped *parador* feels even more luxurious for the ruined Alcázar in its grounds. The beautiful dining room (*menú del día* – daily set menu – €32) overlooks a jaw-dropping view of the surrounding *vega* roasting under the Sevillian sun.

Casa Curro Montoya
TAPAS €€

(Calle Santa María de Gracia 13; tapas €2.50; ⏱ 1.15-5pm & 8.45pm-12.30am Wed-Mon) This friendly, family-run joint occupies a narrow hall littered with memorabilia. Long-standing family traditions find expression in such items as fresh tuna in a luscious onion sauce, foie gras–stuffed eggplant and fried *pizcotas* (small sardinelike fish).

ℹ Information

Tourist Office (www.turismo.carmona.org; Alcázar de la Puerta de Sevilla; ⏱ 10am-6pm Mon-Sat, 10am-3pm Sun & holidays) This helpful tourist office is inside the Puerta de Sevilla.

ℹ Getting There & Away

Monday to Friday, **Casal** (www.autocarescasal. com) runs hourly buses to Seville (€2.65, one hour) from the stop on Paseo del Estatuto, but less often on weekends. Two or three buses a day go to Córdoba via Écija from the car park next to the Puerta de Sevilla.

Écija

POP 40,000 / ELEV 110M

A city of baroque church towers, suffocating summer heat, and an unpronounceable name if you're a non-Spanish speaker, Écija (*eth*-ee-ha) is a hardworking Andaluícian settlement where tourism is an afterthought and history can be peeled off in layers, starting with the Romans. Archaeological treasures lie like discarded jewels all over (and under) the city centre, barely seen by the bulk of Andalucía's 7.5 million annual visitors. Should you drop by – easily done as a journey-breaker between Córdoba and Seville – try to avoid July and August when Écija lives up to its nickname, *la sartén de Andalucía* (the frying pan of Andalucía). The barometer has been known to hit 50°C.

◎ Sights & Activities

The centre of life in Écija is the cafe-lined Plaza de España, locally referred to as El Salón (the parlor); before you dive into the old quarter that surrounds this square, you'd be wise to drop by for a drink and a spot of people-watching.

Churches
CHURCH

Écija's spire-studded townscape is evidence of its prosperous past, though some structures toppled as a result of Lisbon's great quake in 1755. One of the finest towers belongs to the Iglesia de Santa María (Plaza Santa María; ⏱ 9.30am-1pm & 6-9pm), just off Plaza de España, while that of the Iglesia de San Juan (Plaza San Juan) rises like a frosted wedding cake a few blocks south. The tower of the Iglesia de San Pablo-Santo Domingo (Plaza de Santo Domingo), east of the square, is startlingly strung with a gigantic set of rosary beads.

The Parroquia Mayor de Santa Cruz (Plazuela de Nuestra Señora del Valle; ⏱ 9am-1pm & 5-8.30pm Mon-Sat, 10am-1pm & 6-8pm Sun May-Sep, 9am-1pm & 6-8pm Mon-Sat, 10am-1pm & 6-9pm Sun Oct-Apr) FREE was once the town's principal mosque and still has traces of Islamic features and some Arabic inscriptions.

Beyond a roofless atrium is an interior crammed with sacred paraphernalia and baroque silverwork. A sarcophagus in front of the altar dates from the early Christian period, with a chiseled likeness of Daniel flanked by a pair of lions.

Museo Histórico Municipal MUSEUM
(http://museo.ecija.es; Plaza de la Constitución 1; ⊙10am-1.30pm & 4.30-6.30pm Tue-Sat, 10am-3pm Sun) FREE The 18th-century Palacio de Benamejí houses the city's history museum. Pride of place goes to the best Roman finds from the area, including a sculpture of an Amazon (legendary female warrior). The upper level features a hall devoted to six fantastically preserved Roman mosaics, some unearthed beneath Écija's central square, with one tableau depicting the 'birth' of wine.

🛏 Sleeping & Eating

Hotel Palacio de los Granados HISTORIC HOTEL €€
(☑955 90 53 44; www.palaciogranados.com; Calle Emilio Castelar 42; s/d/ste €55/65/75; P❄🐾🅿) This small palace has been carefully restored by its architect owner, with lavishly furnished chambers of varying design around a small patio. Check out the fantastic Écija frescoes on the front facade.

Hispania TAPAS €€
(www.hispaniacafe.com; Pasaje Virgen de Soterraño; tapas €2, mains €10-14; ⊙noon-3am Tue-Sun) Hip, friendly and invariably packed with locals, this side-street operation has a bold colour scheme that matches its exuberant kitchen. The innovative chefs keep coming up with new creations that give classic Spanish fare a contemporary zing, whether they're doing tapas, *bocatas* (sandwiches) or desserts. Leave room for the white-chocolate soup.

❶ Information

Tourist Office (www.turismoecija.com; Calle Elvira 1; ⊙9.30am-3pm Mon-Fri) On weekends, get information at the Museo Histórico Municipal next door. In an adjacent hall, the office shows a 15-minute video about Écija's deep-rooted equestrian traditions.

❶ Getting There & Away

Alsa buses depart from the bus station on Avenida del Genil for Córdoba (€4.82, one hour, five daily) and Seville (€7.32, 1¼ hours, three daily).

HUELVA PROVINCE

To fixed-itinerary travellers, Huelva province is that nodule of land 'on the way to Portugal'. To those willing to drag their heels a little, it's home to the region's best cured ham, its most evocative fandangos, and Spain's largest and most ebullient *romería* (pilgrimage). Throw in some British-influenced mining heritage, Christopher Columbus memorabilia, and what is possibly Spain's most revered national park, and you've got the makings of an Andalucian break well outside the standard mould.

Huelva

POP 149,000

Blemished by factories and with its historical heritage smashed to pieces in the 1755 Lisbon earthquake (and not rebuilt), Huelva is never going to win any beauty contests. If you're passing through, there's a clutch of journeyman hotels, and some low-key but poignant Columbus memorabilia to ponder (yes, the great explorer first sailed from here). Alternatively, you can tackle Huelva province's sights on day trips from Seville or from the more salubrious small town of Aracena 100km to the north.

◉ Sights

Huelva's sights barely merit a plural, but will cost you *nada*.

Museo De Huelva MUSEUM
(www.museosdeandalucia.es/cultura/museos/MHU; Alameda Sundheim 13; ⊙9am-3.30pm Tue-Sat, 10am-5pm Sun) FREE Standing on the Alameda, domain of the early-20th-century bourgeoisie, the town museum is stuffed to the gills with art and history. The permanent exhibition concentrates on the province's impressive archaeological pedigree, with interesting items culled from its Roman and mining history. Upstairs, changing exhibits delve into the museum's substantial art collection, going back to the 16th century.

Embarcadero de Mineral de Río Tinto HISTORIC SITE
FREE An odd legacy of the area's mining history, this impressive iron pier curves out into the Odiel estuary about 500m south of the port. It was built for the Río Tinto company in the 1870s. Equipped with boardwalks on the upper and lower levels, it makes for a delightful stroll to admire the harbour and

ships. It's about 1km southwest of the Plaza de las Monjas.

Sleeping & Eating

Hotel Familia Conde   BUSINESS HOTEL €
(☎959 28 24 00; www.hotelfamiliaconde.com; Alameda Sundheim 14; r without/with breakfast €52/65; P ❄ @ ☎) True, it's housed in a rather soulless block, but this business-class operation is efficiently run with cordial service, and the fresh-smelling rooms have plenty of space and gleaming orange-toned bathrooms. It's a short stroll from the cafe-lined Gran Vía.

Albergue Juvenil de Huelva   HOSTEL €
(☎959 65 00 10; www.inturjoven.com; Avenida Marena Colombo 14; dm/d €26/52; ❄ @ ☎ ♿; ▣6) This is a good, modern youth hostel, with 53 rooms around a bright and pleasant courtyard. There are two to six beds per room, all with bathroom. Bike rentals are available. It's 2km north of the bus station: city bus 6 from the bus station stops just around the corner from the hostel, on Calle JS Elcano.

★El Picoteo   TAPAS €
(Avenida Pablo Rada 5; raciones €9.50; ⊙12.30-4pm & 7pm-midnight) On the north side of Pablo Rada is this casual tapas joint for gourmands in the know. It's usually packed, but the kitchen can handle any size crowd. *Bacalao* (codfish) is prepared in many ways (in lobster or Pedro Ximénez wine sauce, for example) and there are plenty of vegetarian items, such as eggplant tart stuffed with Gouda cheese.

Ciquitrake   TAPAS €
(www.ciquitrake.com; Calle Rascón 21; tapas €2.50, raciones €7.50; ⊙8.30am-midnight Mon-Sat) 'To know how to eat is to know how to live' is the motto of this innovative tapas maker, which specialises in novel variations on Huelva mainstays, attractively presented in cool minimalist surroundings (with a glossary of Huelva slang as wallpaper).

Try the *salmorejo* (thick, garlicky, tomato-based version of gazpacho, garnished with bits of ham and crumbled egg), croquettes and cuttlefish balls, or ask what's new on the ever-expanding menu.

❶ Information

Regional Tourist Office (www.turismohuelva.org; Ave Jesús Nazareno 21; ⊙9am-7.30pm Mon-Fri, 9.30am-3pm Sat & Sun) Information on the whole province.

❶ Getting There & Away

BUS

Most buses from the **bus station** (☎959 25 69 00; Calle Doctor Rubio) are operated by **Damas** (www.damas-sa.es), with services to such destinations as Seville, Aracena, Isla Cristina, Moguer, Matalascañas and Faro (Portugal). Socibus runs at least two buses a day to Madrid (€24, 7¼ hours).

TRAIN

Three services daily run to Seville (€12, 1½ hours). One service a day goes to Córdoba (€38, four hours) and Madrid (€72, four hours) from the **train station** (☎902 43 23 43; www.renfe.com; Avenida de Italia).

Lugares Colombinos

The Lugares Colombinos (Columbus Sites) are the three townships of La Rábida, Palos de la Frontera and Moguer, along the eastern bank of the Tinto estuary east of Huelva. All three played key roles in the discovery of the Americas and can be combined in a single day trip from Huelva, the Doñana area or the nearby coast.

La Rábida
POP 600

In this pretty and peaceful town, don't miss the 14th-century **Monasterio de La Rábida** (☎959 35 04 11; Paraje de La Rábida; admission €3; ⊙10am-1pm & 4-7pm Tue-Sun), visited several times by Columbus before his great voyage of discovery. On the waterfront below the monastery is the **Muelle de las Carabelas** (Wharf of the Caravels; admission €3.55; ⊙10am-2pm & 5-9pm Tue-Fri, 11am-8pm Sat & Sun Jun-Aug, 9.30am-8.30pm Tue-Sun Sep-May), where you can board replicas of Columbus' tiny three-ship fleet, crewed by ludicrous mannequins.

Palos de la Frontera
POP 8500

In La Rábida's neighbouring town you'll find the **Casa Museo Martín Alonso Pinzón** (☎959 10 00 41; Calle Colón 24; admission €1; ⊙10am-2pm Mon-Fri), once the home of the *Pinta*'s captain. Further along Calle Colón is the 15th-century **Iglesia de San Jorge**, where Columbus and his men took communion before embarking on their great voyage.

If you can't face staying in Huelva itself, try the **Hotel La Pinta** (☎959 53 05 11; www.hotellapinta.com; Calle Rábida 79; s/d €39/63), which has a big bar, a restaurant and decent-sized clean rooms. Stop to take on supplies yourself at El Bodegón (959 53 11 05; Calle Rábida 46; mains €10-23; noon-4pm & 9pm-midnight Mon-Sat), a noisy, atmospheric cavern of a restaurant that cooks up fish and meat on wood-fired grills.

Moguer

POP 16,300

Sleepy Moguer provided many of Columbus' crew. The 14th-century Monasterio de Santa Clara (959 37 01 07; www.monasteriodesantaclara.com; Plaza de las Monjas; guided tour €3; 10am-1.30pm & 4.30-8pm Tue-Sat, 10am-1.30pm Sun) is where Columbus kept a prayerful vigil the night after returning from his first voyage, in March 1493.

Right across the plaza from the monastery, Barola (Plaza de las Monjas; 8am-midnight Wed-Mon) is a cool, stylish tapas bar in a cavernous reconstructed building with Moorish arches.

There's a helpful tourist office (959 37 18 98; Calle Castillo; 10am-2pm & 5-7pm Tue-Sat, 10am-3pm Sun) a couple of blocks south of the central Plaza del Cabildo, in Moguer's castillo, a dramatic, bare-walled enclosure of Almohad origin, expanded in the 14th century.

❶ Getting There & Away

At least 10 buses a day leave Huelva for La Rábida (15 minutes), with half of them continuing to Palos de la Frontera (20 minutes) and Moguer (30 minutes). The others go on to Mazagón.

Parque Nacional de Doñana

Spain's most celebrated and in many ways most important wildlife refuge, the Doñana National Park, created in 1969, is one of Europe's last remaining great wetlands. Covering 542 sq km in the southeast of Huelva province and neighbouring Seville province, this World Heritage site is a vital refuge for such endangered species as the Spanish imperial eagle and the Iberian lynx (p56). It offers a unique combination of ecosystems and is a place of haunting beauty that is well worth a day of nature-viewing.

To visit the national park you must take a tour with one of three licensed companies. Cooperativa Marismas del Rocío and Doñana Reservas operate land-based tours departing from the northwestern side of the park from either the Centro de Visitantes El Acebuche or the village of El Rocío. A third company, Visitas Doñana (p617), runs boat/jeep trips out of Sanlúcar de Barrameda on the south side of the park.

Half the park consists of *marismas* (wetlands) of the Guadalquivir delta, the largest area of wetlands in Europe. Almost dry from July to October, in autumn the *marismas* fill with water, attracting hundreds of thousands of wintering waterbirds from the north. As the waters sink in spring, other birds – greater flamingos, spoonbills, storks – arrive, many to nest. The park also has a 28km Atlantic beach, separated from the *marismas* by a band of sand dunes up to 5km wide; and 144 sq km of *coto* (woodland and scrub), which harbours many mammals, including deer, wild boar and semiwild horses. The beach is the only part of the park you are allowed to access without a guide.

Surrounding the national park is the similarly sized Parque Natural de Doñana, a less heavily protected buffer zone comprising four distinct areas. Various private companies offer trips into this area to engage in activities such as horseriding, mountain biking and birdwatching.

National Park Tours

Trips in 20-person all-terrain vehicles from El Acebuche are the only way for ordinary folk to get into the interior of the national park from the western side. Book ahead through Cooperativa Marismas del Rocío (959 43 04 32; www.donanavisitas.es; Centro de Visitantes El Acebuche; 4hr tour per person €29.50) or Doñana Reservas (959 44 24 74; www.donanareservas.com; Avenida La Canaliega, El Rocío; 4hr trip per person €28-38). During spring, summer and holidays, book at least a month ahead, but otherwise a week is usually plenty of notice. Bring binoculars if you can, drinking water in summer, and mosquito protection, except in winter. Most guides speak Spanish only. The tour normally starts with a long beach drive, before moving inland. You can be pretty certain of seeing deer and boar, but ornithologists may be disappointed by the limited bird-observation opportunities.

For trips into the *natural* park, try one of the following private operators.

Doñana Nature   OUTDOORS, NATURE

(959 44 21 60; www.donana-nature.com; Calle Las Carretas 10; 3½hr trip per person €26) Half-

day trips, at 8am and 3.30pm daily, are general interest, though specialised ornithological and photographic trips are also offered; English- and French-speaking guides are available.

Doñana Ecuestre HORSERIDING
(📞 959 44 24 74; www.donanaecuestre.com; Avenida de la Canaliega; per 1hr/2hr/half-day €20/30/60) This branch of the licensed Doñana Reservas offers enjoyable guided horse rides through the woodlands west of El Rocío, some led by qualified biologists.

ℹ Information

The park has five visitior centres. The best three are listed below.

Centro de Visitantes El Acebuche (📞 959 43 96 29; ⊙ 8am-9pm Apr-Sep, to 7pm Oct-Mar) Twelve kilometres south of El Rocío on the A483, then 1.6km west, El Acebuche is the national park's main visitor centre. It has an interactive exhibit on the park and paths to birdwatching hides, plus a film about Iberian lynxes – probably the closest visitors can get to them.

Centro de Visitantes de Doñana 'La Rocina' (📞 959 43 95 69; ⊙ 9am-7pm Mon-Fri year-round, 9am-3pm Sun 15 Jun–15 Sep) Located an easy 1km walk south of the village of El Rocío on the A483, this centre has a staffed national park information office plus a small exhibit on the history of the Romería del Rocío (p604). A 3.8km hiking path, Charco de la Boca, leads off through pinewoods and marsh to several bird hides.

Centro de Visitantes El Acebrón (📞 671 59 31 38; ⊙ 9am-3pm & 4-7pm) Located 6km along a paved back road west from La Rocina, this centre has an ethnographic exhibition on the park inside a palatial residence.

El Rocío

POP 1200

The ethereal village of El Rocío overlooks a beautiful section of the Doñana *marismas* (wetlands) at the park's northwestern corner. The village's sandy streets bear as many hoof prints as tyre marks, and they are lined with rows of verandahed buildings that are empty most of the time. But this is no ghost town: most of the houses belong to the 90-odd *hermandades* (brotherhoods) of pilgrim-revellers and their families, who converge on El Rocío every year in the extraordinary Romería del Rocío (p604). In fact, a party atmosphere pervades the village

at most weekends as *hermandades* arrive to carry out lesser ceremonial acts.

⊙ Sights & Activities

The marshlands in front of El Rocío have water almost year-round and thus offer some of the best bird- and beast-watching in the entire Doñana region – no 4WD required! Deer and horses graze in the shallows and you may be lucky enough to see a flock of flamingos wheeling through the sky in a big pink cloud. Pack a pair of binoculars and stroll the wonderful waterfront promenade.

Ermita del Rocío CHURCH
(⊙ 8am-10.30pm Apr-Sep, 8.30am-8pm Oct-Mar) FREE Rising like a heavenly apparition over the marshes, the Ermita del Rocío was built in its present form in 1964. This is the permanent home of the venerated **Nuestra Señora del Rocío** (Our Lady of El Rocío), a small wooden image of the Virgin dressed in long, jewelled robes, which normally stands above the main altar.

People arrive to see the Virgin every day of the year and especially on weekends, when the brotherhoods of El Rocío often gather for colourful celebrations.

Francisco Bernis Birdwatching Centre BIRDWATCHING
(📞 959 44 23 72; ⊙ 9am-2pm & 4-6pm Tue-Sun) FREE About 800m east of the Ermita along the waterfront, this small facility backs onto the marsh, and flamingos, glossy ibis, spoonbills etc can be observed through the rear windows or from the observation deck with high-powered binoculars provided free of charge. The on-site ornithologists can help you identify species and inform you about which migratory birds are visiting and where to see them.

🍽 Sleeping & Eating

Don't bother even trying for a room at Romería del Rocío time.

Hotel Toruño HOTEL €€
(📞 959 44 23 23; www.toruno.es; Plaza Acebuchal 22; s/d incl breakfast €59/80; 🅿 ❄ 🖥) An attractive villa overlooking the wetlands, Toruño has 30 well-appointed rooms. Some have marsh views, so you can see the spoonbills having their breakfast when you wake. Across the road, the restaurant (mains €12 to €22) dishes up generous portions of well-prepared country and coastal fare.

Hotel La Malvasía HOTEL €€
(☑ 959 44 38 70; www.lamalvasiahotel.com; Calle
Sanlúcar 38; s/d incl breakfast €75/90; [P] [❄] [🖥])
Overlooking the marshes, this idyllic hotel is
located inside a truly magisterial building.
Rooms are crushed with character, including rustic tiled floors, vintage photos of the
town and iron bedsteads in floral designs.
Top-level units make great bird-viewing
perches.

Restaurante El Real ANDALUCIAN €
(Calle Real 7; set lunch €9; ☺ 8am-7pm Tue-Sun)
Opposite the shrine, this may be a tourist-
oriented place but it's one that seems to relish serving outsiders. The food is homemade
and there's a pleasant terrace. Be sure to try
the *salmorejo* and for dessert the 'heavenly
bacon' (flan with pine nuts).

❶ Information

Tourist Office (www.turismodedonana.com;
Calle Muñoz Pavon; ☺ 9.30am-2pm Mon-Fri)
Inside the town hall *(ayuntamiento)*, beside
where the Seville bus stops.

❶ Getting There & Away

Damas (www.damas-sa.es) buses run from
Seville to El Rocío and on to Matalascañas
(€6.36, 1½ hours, two daily). From Huelva, take
a Damas bus to Almonte, and catch another to El
Rocío (10 daily).

Minas de Riotinto
POP 4100 / ELEV 420M

Tucked away on the southern fringe of the
sierra is one of the world's oldest mining
districts, so old that even King Solomon of
faraway Jerusalem is said to have mined
gold here for his famous temple. Though the
miners clocked off for the last time in 2001,
it's still a fascinating place to explore, with a
superb museum and the opportunity to visit
the old mines and ride the mine railway.

Minas de Riotinto is the area's hub.
The Río Tinto itself rises a few kilometres
northeast of town, its name ('Red River')
stemming from the deep red-brown hue
produced by the reaction of its acidic waters
with the abundant iron and copper ores.

◉ Sights & Activities

A joint ticket for all three of the following
sights costs a more economical adult/child
€17/14.

Museo Minero MUSEUM
(☑ 959 59 00 25; www.parquemineroderiot-
into.com; Plaza Ernest Lluch; adult/child €4/3;
☺ 10.30am-3pm & 4-8pm) This mining museum is a figurative goldmine for devotees of
industrial archaeology, taking you through
the area's unique history from the mega-

ROMERÍA DEL ROCÍO

Every Pentecost (Whitsuntide), the seventh weekend after Easter, El Rocío is inundated
with up to a million pilgrim-revellers from all corners of Spain in the Romería del Rocío
(Pilgrimage to El Rocío). This vast cult festivity revolves around the tiny image of Nuestra
Señora del Rocío, which was found here in a tree by a hunter from Almonte back in the
13th century. Carrying it home, the hunter stopped for a rest and the statue miraculously made its own way back to the tree. Before long a chapel was built where the tree
had stood (now El Rocío) and pilgrims were making for it.

Today 106 *hermandades* (brotherhoods) from around and beyond Andalucía, some
comprising several thousand men and women, travel to El Rocío each year on foot,
on horseback and in gaily decorated covered wagons pulled by cattle or horses, using
cross-country tracks.

Solemn is the last word you'd apply to this quintessentially Andalucian event. The
'pilgrims' dress in bright Andalucian costume and sing, dance, drink and romance their
way to El Rocío.

Things reach an ecstatic climax in the early hours of the Monday. Members of the
hermandad of Almonte, which claims the Virgin for its own, barge into the church and
bear her out on a float. Chaotic struggles ensue as others battle with the Almonte lads
for the honour of carrying La Blanca Paloma, but somehow good humour survives and
the Virgin is carried round to each of the brotherhood buildings, finally returning to the
Ermita in the afternoon.

The first Sunday in February is another big day when El Rocío is overwhelmed by visitors – it's when the Virgin's cloak is brought out for children to kiss.

lithic tombs of the 3rd millennium BC to the Roman and British colonial eras and finally the closure of the mines in 2001. The tour includes an elaborate 200m-long recreation of a Roman mine.

The museum also features a big display on the railways that served the mines. Pride of place goes to the Vagón del Maharajah, a luxurious carriage built in 1892 for a tour of India by Britain's Queen Victoria, though she never actually rode in it.

Peña de Hierro
MINE

(adult/child €8/7; ⊙noon-1.30pm & 5.30-7pm) These are old copper and sulphur mines 3km north of Nerva. Here you see the source of Río Tinto and a 65m-deep opencast mine, and are taken into a 200m-long underground mine gallery. It's essential to book ahead (online at the Museo Minero website, www.parquemineroderiotinto.com), and schedules may change.

Ferrocarril Turístico-Minero
TOUR

(⊘959 59 00 25; www.parquemineroderiotinto.com; adult/child €10/9; ⊙1pm Mon-Fri, 4.30pm Sat & Sun Mar–mid-Jun, Oct & Nov, 1.30pm & 5.30pm daily mid-Jul–Sep) A fun way to see the area (especially with children) is to ride the old mining train, running 22km (round trip) through the surreal landscape in restored early-20th-century carriages.

Trips start at the old railway repair workshops 4km east of Minas de Riotinto off the road to Nerva. Commentary is in Spanish. It's mandatory to book ahead. Tickets may be purchased either at the museum or the railway station.

❶ Getting There & Away

From Monday to Friday, **Damas** (www.damas-sa.es) runs five buses between Minas de Riotinto and Huelva (€6.30, 1¾ hours), with three on weekends. There is no public transport to the Ferrocarril Turístico-Minero.

Aracena & Around

POP 7800 / ELEV 730M

Who knew? The gently folded uplands of northern Huelva province offer yet another nuance to rural *andaluz* culture: pastoral, flower-bedecked hills and sheltered valleys replete with gnarly oak trees and foraging pigs that produce what many consider to be the finest cured ham in Spain – the legendary *jamón ibérico*. You can dump your car here; the region's sleepy, half-forgotten vil-

lages are all linked by good footpaths that thread out from the regional nexus of Aracena, a whitewashed market town that is markedly different in character to the traditional *pueblos blancos* (white towns) further east. The 1840-sq-km Parque Natural Sierra de Aracena y Picos de Aroche comprises Andalucía's second-largest protected area.

⊙ Sights & Activities

The Cerro del Castillo is where the old town originated. Climb to the top of the hill to view the 13th-century Portuguese-built castillo and the adjacent Iglesia Prioral (⊙9.30am-7pm). A little lower down in Plaza Alta there's an interesting Centro de Visitantes (⊘959 12 95 53; Plaza Alta; ⊙10am-2pm & 4-6pm Tue-Sun), which showcases the highlights of Parque Natural Sierra de Aracena y Picos de Aroche.

Gruta de las Maravillas
CAVE

(Cave of Marvels; ⊘663 93 78 76; Calle Pozo de la Nieve; tour adult/child €8.50/6; ⊙10am-1.30pm & 3-6.30pm, tours every hour; ⊕) Beneath the castle hill is a web of caves and tunnels carved from the karstic topography. An extraordinary 1km route takes you through 12 chambers and past six underground lakes, all beautifully illuminated and filled with weird and wonderful rock formations that provided a backdrop for the film *Journey to the Centre of the Earth*.

Tours are in Spanish, but audio guides are available. You're not allowed to take photos but a photographer is on hand on the way in for that obligatory portrait.

Linares de la Sierra
HIKING

Hikes in the Aracena area are legion and the trails are rarely crowded. If you're on a day trip from Seville, try the undulating route to Linares de la Sierra and – time and energy permitting – continue onto Alájar (there's a return bus from Alájar to Aracena that leaves at 4pm connecting with the 5pm Aracena–Seville service). The signposted path is easy to find on the southwest side of Aracena approximately 500m past the municipal swimming pool.

Follow the wide bucolic track as far as Linares (6km), a soporific village renowned for its *llanos* (front-patio mosaics). From here the path narrows and becomes a little trickier to navigate, though you'll spot plenty of snorting pigs and eye-catching wildflowers along the way. Just before the hamlet of Los Madroñeros, fork right on the

'Caracol' trail (signposted), which traverses an oak-sprinkled hillside into Alájar (total distance 12km).

You can stay over in Alájar at **La Posada** (☑959 12 57 12; www.posadasalajar.com; Calle Médico Emilio González 2; s/d €35/55), a very cosy inn whose English-speaking owners are keen walkers. Shop around in the village for the excellent local ham. Another walking path heads northwest to the next village, Castaño de Robledo.

🛏 Sleeping & Eating

Hospedería Reina de los Ángeles HOTEL **€**
(☑959 12 83 67; www.hospederiareinadelosange-les.com; Avenida Reina de los Ángeles, Aracena; s/d incl breakfast €26/43; P ⏏) On the west edge of town, this uncharacteristically hulking structure has an institutional vibe left over from its former role as a student residence hall. Nonetheless, the 90 utilitarian rooms with TV and phone are spotless and surround a placid courtyard. It has a convivial cafe-bar and, for those inclined, a full-on chapel. Staff members are extremely friendly and helpful.

Molino del Bombo BOUTIQUE HOTEL **€**
(☑959 12 84 78; www.molinodelbombo.com; Calle Ancha 4, Aracena; s/d €36/60; ✳⏏) Though of recent vintage, this lodging at the top of the town has a rustic style that blends in with Aracena's time-worn architecture. Bright rooms feature frescoes and exposed stone and brick work as design features, and bathrooms are done up as picturesque grottoes. You'll likely want to linger in the salon or the courtyard with its trickling fountain.

★Rincón de Juan TAPAS **€**
(☑627 33 47 66; Calle José Nogales; tapas €1.80, raciones €7-10; ⏱7am-4pm & 6.30pm-midnight Mon-Fri, 8am-midnight Sat) It's standing room only at this wedge-shaped, stone-walled corner bar, indisputably the finest tapas joint in town. Iberian ham is certainly the star attraction and forms the basis for a variety of *montaditos* (little sandwiches) and *rebana-das* (sliced loaves that feed several people). The homemade sausage, sweet or spicy, is always a good bet.

Café-Bar Manzano TAPAS
(☑959 12 75 13; Calle Campito 9; raciones €9-14; ⏱9am-4.30pm & 8pm-midnight Wed-Mon) This classy terrace cafe on the main plaza is a fine spot from which to watch Aracena go by while you enjoy varied tapas and *raciones* that celebrate wild mushrooms and other regional fare. Even out of season, it serves up such tempting fungi as *tentullos, gurumelos* and *tanas*, sautéd or in enticing scrambles.

ℹ Information

Municipal Tourist Office (www.aracena.es; Calle Pozo de la Nieve; ⏱10am-2pm & 4-6pm) Faces the entrance to the Gruta de las Maravillas and sells some maps of the area.

ℹ Getting There & Away

The **bus station** (Avenida de Sevilla) is 700m southeast of the Plaza del Marqués de Aracena, on the Seville road. **Damas** (www.damas-sa.es) runs one morning and two afternoon buses from Seville (€7.46, 1¼ hours), continuing on to Cortegana via Alájar or Jabugo. From Huelva, there are two afternoon departures daily (€10, three hours). There is also local service between Aracena and Cortegana via Linares, Alájar and Almonaster La Real.

NORTHERN CÁDIZ PROVINCE

If you had to break off one part of Andalucía to demonstrate to aliens what it looked like, you'd probably choose Cádiz province. Emblematic regional highlights are part of the furniture here: thrillingly sited white towns, craggy mountains, endless olives trees, flamenco in its purist incarnation, the original (and best) fortified sherry, the cradle of Andalucian horse culture, and festivals galore. Stuffed in among all of this condensed culture are two expansive natural parks that cover an unbroken tract of land that runs from Olvera in the north to Algeciras in the south. The same line once marked the blurred frontier between Christian Spain and Moorish Granada, and the ancient border is flecked with huddled white towns, many of them given a 'de la Frontera' suffix testifying to their volatile but fascinating history.

Cádiz

POP 125,000

You could write several weighty university theses about Cádiz and still fall a mile short of nailing its essence. Old age accounts for much of the complexity. Cádiz is generally considered to be the oldest continuously inhabited settlement in Europe.

Now well into its fourth millennium, the ancient centre, surrounded almost entirely by water, is a romantic hodgepodge of sinuous streets where Atlantic waves crash against eroded sea walls, municipal beaches stretch for miles, and rambunctious taverns echo with the sounds of cawing gulls and frying fish.

Over its long history, Cádiz has also proven to be influential. Spain's first liberal constitution was signed here in 1812, while the city's distinctive urban model went on to provide an identikit for fortified Spanish colonial cities in the Americas. Indeed, the port – with its crenellated sea walls and chunky forts – is heavily reminiscent of Havana in Cuba, or San Juan in Puerto Rico.

Enamoured return visitors talk fondly of its seafood, surfing, and cache of intriguing churches and museums, which inflict little, if any, damage on your wallet. More importantly, they wax lyrical about the *gaditanos*, an upfront and gregarious populace whose Carnaval is an exercise in ironic humour and whose upbeat flamenco songs (known as *alegrías*) will bring warmth to your heart.

History

Cádiz is probably the oldest city in Europe. Historians date its founding to the arrival of Phoenician traders in 800 BC.

In less-distant times, Cádiz began to boom after Columbus' trips to the Americas. He sailed from here on his second and fourth voyages. Cádiz attracted Spain's enemies too: in 1587 England's Sir Francis Drake 'singed the king of Spain's beard' with a raid on the harbour, delaying the imminent Spanish Armada. In 1596, Anglo-Dutch attackers burnt almost the entire city.

Cádiz' golden age was the 18th century, when it enjoyed 75% of Spanish trade with the Americas. It grew into the richest and most cosmopolitan city in Spain and gave birth to the country's first progressive, liberal middle class. During the Napoleonic Wars, Cádiz held out under French siege from 1810 to 1812, when a national parliament meeting here adopted Spain's liberal 1812 constitution, proclaiming sovereignty of the people.

The loss of the American colonies in the 19th century plunged Cádiz into a decline from which it is only today recovering, with increased tourism playing a significant role.

The year 2012 was a big one for Cádiz, with the city dolling itself up for the 200th anniversary of La Pepa, Spain's (and the world's) first liberal constitution. As a result, visitors will find that many of its streets, squares and sights have been recently spruced up.

◉ Sights & Activities

To understand Cádiz you need to first become acquainted with its *barrios*. The old city can be split into classic quarters: **Barrio del Pópulo**, home of the cathedral, and nexus of the once prosperous medieval settlement; **Barrio de Santa María**, the old Roma quarter and an important fount of flamenco; **Barrio de la Viña**, a former vineyard that became the city's main fishing quarter; and **Barrio del Mentidero**, centre of Cádiz' modern nightlife and bar scene.

Plaza San Juan de Dios   SQUARE
Broad Plaza San Juan de Dios, recently spruced up for the 200th anniversary of the 1812 constitution, is lined with cafes, fountains and statues, and is dominated by the imposing neoclassical **ayuntamiento**, built around 1800. Between here and the cathedral is the Barrio del Pópulo, the kernel of medieval Cádiz. Nearby is the **Roman Theatre** (Campo del Sur; ⊘10am-2.30pm & 5-7pm Wed-Mon) **FREE**, discovered by chance in 1980, where you can walk along a gallery beneath the tiers of seating.

★**Casa del Obispo**   MUSEUM
(Plaza de Fray Félix 5; admission €5, combined ticket with Torre de Poniente €7; ⊘10am-6pm, to 8pm mid-Jun–mid-Sep) Outside Cádiz cathedral's eastern exterior wall, this expansive museum of glass walkways over 1500 sq metres of excavated ruins takes you through Cádiz' eventful history, from the 8th century BC to the 18th century.

It served as a Phoenician funerary complex, Roman temple and the city's mosque, before becoming the city's Episcopal Palace in the 16th century. There are four free guided tours in Spanish daily.

Catedral   CATHEDRAL
(Plaza de la Catedral; adult/student €5/3, 11am-12.30pm Sun free; ⊘10am-6pm Mon-Sat, 11am-12.30pm & 1.30-6pm Sun) Cádiz' gorgeous yellow-domed cathedral is arguably Andalucía's most attractive when the sun catches it in an ethereal evening light. An impressively proportioned baroque-neoclassical

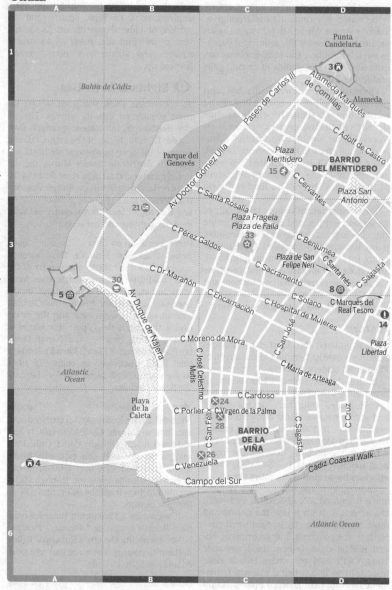

construction, it fronts a broad, traffic-free plaza where the cathedral's ground-plan is picked out in the paving stones. The decision to build the cathedral was taken in 1716 but the project wasn't finished until 1838, by which time neoclassical elements, such as the dome, towers and main facade, had diluted Vicente Acero's original baroque plan.

You can usually climb one of the cathedral's towers, the Torre de Poniente for marvellous vistas, though it was temporarily closed at our last visit.

Museo de las Cortes de Cádiz MUSEUM
(Calle Santa Inés 9; ☉ 9am-6pm Tue-Fri, to 2pm Sat & Sun) FREE The remodelled Museo de las Cortes de Cádiz is full of memorabilia of the revolutionary 1812 Cádiz parliament. One exhibit jumps out at you: the huge, marvellously detailed model of 18th-century Cádiz, made in mahogany and ivory by Alfonso Ximénez in 1777–79.

The plush new overhanging viewing gallery decorated with old city maps allows a bird's-eye perspective of the model.

Cádiz

Puerta de Tierra   GATE
FREE This imposing gateway guarding the thin isthmus that provides the only land entry to the old town hosts a couple of museums: the mildly interesting Museo Taller Litográfico (⊙ 9am-6pm Tue-Fri, 9am-2pm Sat & Sun) **FREE**, which exhibits lithographs, and Museo del Títere (⊙ 10am-7pm Tue-Sat, 10am-3pm Sun) **FREE**, which exhibits puppets. However, in 2013, the upper fortifications and defense tower were opened to visitors for the first time, with interpretative panels explaining both the broad views and the evolution of Cadiz' complex system of fortifications.

Museo de Cádiz   MUSEUM
(Plaza de Mina; admission €1.50; ⊙ 2.30-8.30pm Tue, 9am-8.30pm Wed-Sat, 9.30am-2.30pm Sun) The Museo de Cádiz, despite being a little dusty and grubby in places, is the best museum in the province. The most amazing of many important relics are two Phoenician marble sarcophagi carved into human likenesses. Supporting them is a statue of Roman Emperor Trajan, from the ruins of Baelo Claudia, and an excellent fine-arts collection, including a group of 18 superb canvases of saints, angels and monks by Francisco de Zurbarán.

Equally important is the painting that cost Murillo his life, the beautifully composed altarpiece from the chapel of Cádiz' Convento de Capuchinas. The artist died in 1682 after falling from the scaffolding. His fatal fall has been immortalised in art in the same room in Manuel Cabral Aguado's 1862 painting entitled, *La Caída Mortal de Murillo* (Murillo's fatal fall).

Torre Tavira   TOWER
(Calle Marqués del Real Tesoro 10; admission €6; ⊙ 10am-6pm mid-Sep–mid-Jun, to 8pm mid-Jun–mid-Sep) Northwest of Plaza de Topete, the Torre Tavira has another dramatic panorama of Cádiz with a camera obscura that projects live, moving images of the city onto a screen (sessions start every half-hour).

Castillo de San Sebastián   FORT, MUSEUM
(admission €2; ⊙ 11am-7.30pm) After centuries as a military installation, this polygonic fort built in 1706 on a small islet joined by a stone walkway to Playa de la Caleta has finally opened its doors to the public. It will ultimately house a permanent show of exhibits due to open in Spring 2014 called *Americadiz* focusing on the relationship between Cádiz and Spain's erstwhile Latin American colonies.

Equally visit-worthy are the fort's chunky fortified walls and walkways replete with city views. Turn your back to the sea and you can admire a 41m-high lighthouse that was installed in 1908 on the site of an old Moorish watchtower.

Playa de la Victoria
BEACH

Normally overshadowed by its rich historical booty, Cádiz' beaches are Copacabana-like in their size and vitality. This lovely, wide strip of fine Atlantic sand stretches about 4km along the peninsula from its beginning at the Puerta de Tierra. At weekends in summer the whole city seems to be out here.

Bus 1 (Plaza España–Cortadura) from Plaza de España will get you there or you can walk – or jog – along the promenade from Barrio de Santa María.

Coastal Walk
WALKING

This airy 4.5km walk takes at least 1¼ hours. Go north from Plaza de Mina to the city's northern seafront, with views across the Bahía de Cádiz. Head west along the Alameda gardens to the Baluarte de la Candelaria, then turn southwest to the Parque del Genovés, a semitropical garden with waterfalls and quirkily clipped trees. Continue to the Castillo de Santa Catalina (956 22 63 33; 11am-8.30pm Mar-Oct, to 7.30pm Nov-Feb) FREE, built after the 1596 sacking; inside you'll find an interesting historical exhibit on Cádiz and the sea, and a gallery for exhibitions. Sandy Playa de la Caleta (very crowded in summer) separates Santa Catalina from the 18th-century Castillo de San Sebastián, which is accessible via a breezy 750m causeway. Finally, follow the broad promenade along Campo del Sur to the cathedral.

Festivals & Events

Carnaval
CARNIVAL

(Feb) No other Spanish city celebrates Carnaval with the verve, dedication and humour of Cádiz, where it turns into a 10-day singing, dancing and drinking fancy-dress party spanning two weekends in February. The fun, abetted by huge quantities of alcohol, is irresistible.

Costumed groups called *murgas* tour the city on foot or on floats, dancing, singing satirical ditties or performing sketches (most of their famed verbal wit will be lost on all but fluent Spanish speakers). In addition to the 300-or-so officially recognised *murgas*, who are judged by a panel in the Gran Teatro Falla, there are also the *ilegales* – any group that fancies taking to the streets and trying to play or sing.

Some of the liveliest and most drunken scenes are in the working-class Barrio de la Viña, between the Mercado Central and Playa de la Caleta, and along Calle Ancha and around Plaza de Topete, where *ilegales* tend to congregate.

If you plan to be here during Carnaval, book accommodation months in advance.

Courses

Cádiz is a great city in which to linger and learn some Spanish. There's a good cross-section of language schools, including K2 Internacional (956 21 26 46; www.k2inter-nacional.com; Plaza Mentidero 19) and Melkart Centro Internacional de Idiomas (956 22 22 13; www.centromelkart.com; Calle General Menacho 7), both based in the Barrio del Mentidero. The latter has special courses for people over 50 years old.

Sleeping

Casa Caracol
HOSTEL €

(956 26 11 66; www.caracolcasa.com; Calle Suárez de Salazar 4; dm/hammock incl breakfast €16/10;) Casa Caracol is the only backpacker hostel in the old town. Friendly, as only Cádiz can be, it has bunk dorms for four and eight, a communal kitchen and a roof terrace with hammocks. Green initiatives include recycling, water-efficiency measures and plans for solar panels. It's advisable to book through www.hostelworld.com or www.hostelbookers.com as the hostel often fills up.

★ Parador de Cádiz
HOTEL €€

(956 54 79 79; www.parador.es; Avenida Duque de Nájera 9; s/d €110/137) Reopened in late 2012 after a massive rebuilding campaign, the so-called Parador Atlántico contrasts with the rest of Andalucía's *paradors* in that it's super-modern and built from scratch. It's right next to Playa de la Caleta and its famous sunsets. This is luxury fit for James Bond.

Hotel Argantonio
HOTEL €€

(956 21 16 40; www.hotelargantonio.com; Calle Argantonio 3; d/ste incl breakfast €119/222;) Welcome to another characterful small-is-beautiful hotel in Cádiz' old quarter. The stand-out features here are the hand-painted doors, the beautifully tiled floors that adorn bedrooms and bathrooms, and the intricate Moorish arch in the lobby.

The hotel has three themes: the 1st floor is Mudéjar, the 2nd floor is colonial, and the 3rd floor is a mix.

Hotel Convento
HOTEL €€

(956 20 07 38; www.hotelconventocadiz.com; Calle Santo Domingo 2; d/ste €67/91; ❄🌐) Rest assured: you won't be living like a nun here. A new hotel in an old convent, this place has huge rooms with comfortable modern decor and some unexpected bonuses, including a small on-site gym.

Hotel Patagonia Sur
HOTEL €€

(856 17 46 47; www.hotelpatagoniasur.es; Calle Cobos 11; d €85-105; ❄@🌐) A relative new-comer to Cádiz' old town, this sleek gem offers clean-lined modernity just steps from the 18th-century cathedral. Bonuses include a glass-fronted minimalist cafeteria at street level and sun-filled attic rooms on the 5th floor with cathedral views.

Eating

Cádiz' hallowed seafood street is Calle Virgen de la Palma in the Viña quarter. Good fish restaurants are legion here. In and around Plaza de San Juan de Díos is another good place to dine.

Café Royalty
CAFE €

(956 07 80 65; www.caferoyalty.com; Plaza de la Candelaria; snacks €7-10; ⏰11am-11pm) Origi-nally opened in 1912 on the centenary of the 1812 constitution, the Royalty was once a discussion corner for the intellectuals of the day, including the composer and Cádiz native Manuel de Falla. The cafe closed in the 1940s, but thanks to an inspired renova-tion project overseen by a local *gaditano* it reopened in 2012, 100 years after its initial inauguration.

The frescoed, mirrored, intricately carved interior is – no word of a lie – breathtaking. A fantastic spot for brunch or a *merienda*.

Freiduría Las Flores
SEAFOOD €

(956 22 61 12; Plaza de Topete 4; seafood per 250g €3-8; ⏰9am-4pm & 8pm-midnight) You have to dive in, almost literally, to this glo-rious local fish fryer and digest the two op-tions: 1) fight for a small, rarely available table, or 2) order takeaway. The takeaway is the slightly less chaotic choice as there is a queueing system (grab a numbered ticket). You order by weight (250g is the usual order).

If you're finding it hard to choose, or-der a *surtido* (a mixed fry-up). There'll be

some heads, tails and tentacles thrown into your skilfully wrapped paper cone, but who cares? It's all good!

Casa Manteca
TAPAS €

(956 21 36 03; Calle Corralón de los Carros 66; tapas €1.50-2; ⏰noon-midnight Tue-Sat, noon-4.30pm Sun) No one knows the colour of the walls in Casa Manteca, as every inch of them is covered in flamenco, bullfighting and Carnaval memorabilia. Welcome to a Viña district classic that serves mussels the size of muscles and myriad fish tapas plonked down on wax paper in front of you alongside your Cruzcampo beer.

★ El Aljibe
TAPAS €€

(www.pablogrosso.com; Calle Plocia 25; tapas €2-3.50, mains €12-20; ⏰1-5pm & 8pm-midnight) Opt for tapas at El Aljibe and you'll feel like one of the judges on *Iron Chef* having a cornucopia of superbly creative dishes slid in front of you. The cuisine developed by *gaditano* chef Pablo Grosso is a delicious combination of the traditional and the adventurous – goat's cheese on nut bread with blueberry sauce, spinach and prawn lasagna...you get the drift?

Arrocería La Pepa
SPANISH €€

(956 26 38 21; www.restaurantelapepa.es; Paseo Maritimo 14; paella per person €12-17; ⏰noon-5pm & 8pm-midnight) To get a decent paella you have to leave the old town behind and head a few kilometres southeast along Playa de la Victoria – a pleasant, appetite-inducing oceanside walk along a popular jogging route or a quick ride on bus 1. Either method is worth it.

The fish in La Pepa's seafood paella tastes as if it's just jumped the 100m or so from the Atlantic onto your plate.

Atxuri
BASQUE, ANDALUCIAN €€

(956 25 36 13; www.atxuri.es; Calle Plocia 7; mains from €12; ⏰1-4.30pm daily & 9-11pm Thu-Sat) One of Cádiz' most decorated and long-standing restaurants, Atxuri fuses Basque and Anda-lucian influences, and the result is a sophis-ticated range of flavours. *Bacalao* (cod) and high-quality steaks are recurring themes, as you'd expect in a place with Basque roots.

Mesón Criollo
SEAFOOD €€

(www.mesoncriollo.com; cnr Calles Virgen de la Palma & Lubet; raciones €10-12; ⏰12.30-4.30pm & 8.30pm-midnight) In the plethora of Barrio de la Viña's fish joints, this one stands out for its prawns, fish bruschettas and individual paella (no sharing or half-hour waits here). Sit out in the street at tapas time and you'll feel as if there's a permanent carnival going on in what is Cadiz' primary Carnaval quarter.

El Faro SEAFOOD €€€
(www.elfarodecadiz.com; Calle San Félix 15; mains €15-25; ⊙1-4pm & 8pm-midnight) Ask many *gaditanos* for their favourite Cádiz restaurant and there's a fair chance they'll choose El Faro. Close to the Playa de la Caleta, this place is at once a crammed-to-the-rafters tapas bar and an upmarket restaurant decorated with pretty ceramics. Seafood is why people come here, although the *rabo de toro* (bull's tail stew) has its devotees.

🍷 Drinking & Nightlife

In the old city, the Plaza de Mina–Plaza San Francisco–Plaza de España area is the main hub of the nocturnal bar scene; things get moving around midnight at most places, but can be quiet in the first half of the week.

The second hot spot is down Playa de la Victoria, along Paseo Marítimo and nearby in the Hotel Playa Victoria area, about 2.5km from the Puerta de Tierra.

Head out late, Thursday to Saturday nights, to Punta de San Felipe (known as La Punta) on the northern side of the harbour, where there's a line of disco bars packed with an 18-to-25 crowd from about 3am to 6am.

Quilla CAFE
(www.quilla.es; Playa de la Caleta; ⊙10am-2am; 🛜) A bookish coffee bar encased in what appears to be the rusty hulk of an old ship overlooking Playa de la Caleta, with pastries, tapas, wine, art expos and free wi-fi – to say nothing of the gratis sunsets.

Nahu BAR, CAFE
(www.nahucadiz.es; Calle Beato Diego 8; ⊙4pm-3am Sun-Thu, to 4am Fri & Sat; 🛜) Trendy bar with mood lighting, worn-wood finishes and a chill-out zone with sofas out front. It's best for drinking cocktails while posing on a bar stool, although if you ask for coffee, cheesecake and the wi-fi password, staff will happily oblige.

Tetería El Oasis TEAHOUSE
(Calle San José 6; ⊙3pm-1am Mon-Wed, 4pm-2am Thu-Sat, 4pm-midnight Sun) Find dark nooks under the red and orange lace curtains and sip discreetly on a Darjeeling in a state of contemplative meditation – until the belly dancers arrive!

Sala Anfiteátro CLUB
(Paseo Pascual Pery; admission €6-8; ⊙1am-close Thu-Sun) On the *punta* (Punta de San Felipe) on the northern side of the harbour, this big club is packed with a young crowd from around 3am to 6am.

☆ Entertainment

★Peña Flamenca La Perla FLAMENCO
(☑956 25 91 01; www.laperladecadiz.es; Calle Carlos Ollero) Andalucía's friendliest *peña* is set romantically next to the crashing Atlantic surf in the Barrio de Santa María and hosts flamenco nights at 10pm most Fridays, more so in spring and summer. Entry is free and the audience is stuffed with aficionados. It's an unforgettable experience.

Gran Teatro Falla THEATRE
(☑956 22 08 34; Plaza de Falla) The beautifully sculpted Gran Teatro Falla hosts busy and varied programs of theatre, dance and music.

La Cava FLAMENCO
(www.flamencolacava.com; Calle António López 16; admission €22, with tapas €39) La Cava is Cadiz' nominal flamenco *tablao* offering dinner and a show on Fridays at 10pm.

ℹ Information

You'll find plenty of banks and ATMs along Calle Nueva and the parallel Avenida Ramón de Carranza. The main post office is in Plaza de Topete next to the central market.

Hospital Puerta del Mar (☑956 00 21 00; Avenida Ana de Viya 21) The main general hospital, 2km southeast of Puerta de Tierra.

Municipal Tourist Office (Paseo de Canalejas; ⊙8.30am-6pm Mon-Fri, 9am-5pm Sat & Sun) Handily close to the bus and train stations.

Regional Tourist Office (Avenida Ramón de Carranza; ⊙9am-7.30pm Mon-Fri, 10am-2pm Sat, Sun & holidays)

ℹ Getting There & Around

BICYCLE

Urban Bike (www.urbanbikecadiz.es; Calle Marques de Valderñigo 4; ⊙10am-2pm & 5.30-9pm Mon-Fri, 10am-2pm Sat) rents bikes for €12 per day. There's a partial bike path along the *malecón* (sea wall).

BOAT

Catamarans (www.cmtbc.es) leave from the **Terminal Marítima Metropolitana** for El Puerto de Santa María (€2.35), with 18 daily departures

Monday to Friday, but just six on Saturdays and five on Sundays.

BUS

Comes (☎ 956 80 70 59; www.tgcomes.es; Plaza de la Hispanidad) has regular departures from the **bus station** (☎ 956 80 70 59; Plaza Sevilla) to Arcos de la Frontera (€6.48, 1½ hours, four daily), El Puerto de Santa María (€1.56, 45 minutes), Granada (€33, 5½ hours), Jerez de la Frontera (€1.72, one hour), Málaga (€25, four hours), Ronda (€15, two hours), Seville (€8.68, 1¾ hours), Tarifa (€8.60, 1½ hours) and Vejer de la Frontera (€5.95, 80 minutes). In addition to some of the above destinations, **Los Amarillos** (www.losamarillos.es) also runs buses to El Bosque, Sanlúcar de Barrameda and Ubrique from the southern end of Avenida Ramón de Carranza. Buses M050 and M051, run by the **Consorcio de Transportes Bahía de Cádiz** (☎ 956 01 21 00; www.cmtbc.com), travel from Jerez de la Frontera airport to Cádiz' Comes bus station, via Jerez city and El Puerto de Santa María.

CAR & MOTORCYCLE

The AP4 motorway from Seville to Puerto Real on the eastern side of the Bahía de Cádiz carries a €6.30 toll. The toll-free A4 is slower.

There's a handily placed underground **car park** (Paseo de Canalejas; per 24hr €9) near the port area.

TRAIN

From the **train station** (☎ 902 240202), plenty of trains run daily to/from El Puerto de Santa María (€4.95, 30 minutes, 15 daily), Jerez de la Frontera (€5.95, 35 minutes, 15 daily), Seville (€16, 1¾ hours, 15 daily) and Madrid (€74, 4½ hours, three daily).

El Puerto de Santa María
POP 89,000

When you're surrounded by such cultural luminaries as Cádiz, Jerez and Seville, it's easy to get lost in the small print; such is the fate of El Puerto de Santa María, a strange oversight considering its stash of well-known cultural icons. Osborne with its famous bull logo (which has become the national symbol of Spain) was founded and retains its HQ here, as do half a dozen other sherry bodegas. El Puerto also claims one of Spain's great bullrings and a weighty bullfighting legacy to go with it. Gastronomy is its other forte. There are more decent tapas bars per head than almost anywhere else in Spain. Review your itinerary and try to squeeze El Puerto in.

◉ Sights & Activities

The four-spouted **Fuente de las Galeras Reales** (Fountain of the Royal Galleys; Plaza de las Galeras Reales), by the Muelle del Vapor, once supplied water to America-bound ships.

The nearest beach is pine-flanked **Playa de la Puntilla**, a half-hour walk from the centre – or take bus 26 (€1) along Avenida Aramburu de Mora. In high summer the beaches furthest out, such as Playa Fuenterrabía, reached by bus 35 from the centre, are least hectic.

Castillo de San Marcos   CASTLE
(☎ 956 85 17 51; Plaza Alfonso X El Sabio; admission €6, Tues free; ⊙ tours 11.30am, 12.30pm & 1.30pm Tue, 10am-2pm hourly Wed-Sat) The castle is open for half-hour guided tours, with a sampling of Caballero sherry included (the company owns the castle). The highlight is the pre-13th-century mosque (now a church) preserved inside.

Fundación Rafael Alberti   MUSEUM
(☎ 956 85 07 11; www.rafaelalberti.es; Calle Santo Domingo 25; admission €4; ⊙ 10am-2pm Tue-Sun) A few blocks inland from Castillo de San Marcos, this place has interesting exhibits on Rafael Alberti (1902–99), one of the great poets of Spain's 'Generation of 27', who grew up here. The exhibits are well displayed and audio guides (€1) in English, German or Spanish are available.

Plaza de Toros   BULLRING
(Plaza Elías Ahuja; ⊙ 11am-1.30pm & 6-7.30pm Tue-Sun May-Sep, 11am-1.30pm & 5.30-7pm Tue-Sun Oct-Apr) FREE Four blocks southwest from Plaza de España is El Puerto's grand Plaza de Toros, which was built in 1880 and remains one of Andalucía's most beautiful and important bullrings, with room for 15,000 spectators. It's closed on days before and after bullfights. Entry to the bullring is from Calle Valdés.

Bodegas Osborne   WINERY
(☎ 956 86 91 00; www.osborne.es; Calle Los Moros 7; tours €8; ⊙ tours 10.30am, noon & 12.30pm) Creator of the legendary black bull logo still exhibited on life-sized billboards all over Spain (though without the name advertised these days), Osborne, the best known of El Puerto's seven sherry wineries, was set up by an Englishman, Thomas Osborne Mann (from Exeter) in 1772. It remains one of Spain's oldest companies run continuously by the same family.

The gorgeous whitewashed bodega offers weekday tours (in English, Spanish and German) and sometimes adds extra tours, including on Saturday, in summer. It is best to phone ahead.

📇 Sleeping

The tourist office's accommodation list and website helpfully highlight places with wheelchair access.

El Baobab Hostel HOSTEL €
(📞956 54 21 23; www.casabaobab.es; Calle Pagador 37; s/d incl breakfast €30/55, dm €22.50; P ✳ 🛜) Just across from the Plaza de Toros in a converted 19th-century building, this small, six-room hostel is the best budget choice in El Puerto, with a homely friendly feel. The interior renovations are tastefully done and the shared bathrooms are spotless.

Hotel Monasterio San Miguel HOTEL €€
(📞956 54 04 40; www.sanmiguelhotelmonasterio. com; Calle Virgen de los Milagros 27; r from €112; P ✳ @ 🛜 ➰) A gourmet restaurant, a pool in a semitropical garden, and classically elegant rooms await your pleasure at this luxurious converted 18th-century monastery. The on-site restaurant is gourmet and the cafeteria is equally tempting.

Casa del Regidor Hotel BOUTIQUE HOTEL €€
(📞956 87 73 33; www.hotelcasadelregidor.com; Ribera del Río 30; s/d €60/98; ✳ @ 🛜) 🏖 A converted 18th-century mansion with its original patio. The excellent rooms have all the mod cons and solar-heated hot water.

★Palacio San Bartolomé LUXURY HOTEL €€€
(📞956 85 09 46; www.palaciosanbartolome.com; Calle San Bartolomé 21; r €80-175; ✳ @ 🛜 ➰) Every now and again along comes a hotel that blows even the most jaded hotel reviewer out of the water. Fancy a room with its own mini swimming pool, sauna, jacuzzi, towelling bathrobes and deckchairs? It's all yours for €175 at the deftly designed San Bart, opened in a former palace in 2010.

If you don't bag the pool room, the others are equally luxurious. Count on four-poster beds, giant showers and a shared on-site gym and spa.

🍴 Eating

El Puerto has one of the best collections of tapas bars of any town of its size in Andalucía. The main streets to look in are the central Calle Luna; Calles Misericordia and Ribera del Marisco to the north; and Avenidas Bajamar and Aramburu de Mora to the south. Seafood is the speciality.

Romerijo SEAFOOD €
(📞956 54 12 54; Plaza de la Herrería; seafood per 250g from €4.50; ⏱11am-12.30am) A huge, always busy El Puerto institution, Romerijo has two buildings, one boiling seafood, the other frying it. Purchase by the quarter-kilogram from the displays, and eat from paper cones at the formica tables.

★Mesón del Asador SPANISH, GRILL €€
(www.mesondelasador.com; Calle Misericordia 2; tapas €2.20, mains €12-20; ⏱1-5pm & 8pm-midnight) It's a measure of El Puerto's gastronomic nous that, in such a seafood-oriented town,

WHAT'S COOKING IN SEVILLE & ANDALUCÍA'S HILL TOWNS?

Pescaíto Frito The nose doesn't lie and you'll need it in Cádiz to lead you to the best fried fish. There's an abundance of good seafood restaurants in the city, but the best – if you follow the crowds – is Freiduría Las Flores (p612), where take-out cones of assorted battered fish are scooped fresh out of the fryer.

Solomillo al Whisky This rich tapa – pork tenderloin cooked in a garlic, lemon and whisky sauce – is a speciality in Seville. Try it in Bodega Santa Cruz (p592) or Los Coloniales (p593).

Salmorejo Córdoba's take on cold gazpacho soup is rich, orange in colour and – unlike gazpacho – too thick to drink. To pick out its nuances proceed to Salmorejería Umami (p646) in Córdoba, a unique new restaurant where it comes in a variety of unconventional flavours from green tea to avocado.

Jamón Ibérico The champagne of Spain's cured meats is produced from black Iberian pigs that roam freely in the Sierra de Aracena in Huelva province feeding mainly on acorns. Sweeter and nuttier than the more ubiquitous *jamón serrano*, it is served in its highest grading (*cinco jotas* – five stars) at Mesón Cinco Jotas (p592) in Seville.

there exists a meat restaurant that could compete with any steakhouse in Buenos Aires. The power of the Mesón's delivery is in the smell that hits you as soon as you open the door – char-grilled beef and pork sizzling away on mini-barbecues that are brought to your table.

Try the chorizo, and don't miss the chicken or pork bruschettas.

Aponiente SEAFOOD, FUSION €€€
(☑956 85 18 70; www.aponiente.com; Puerto Escondido 6; 12-course tasting menu €95; ☺1.30-4pm & 9-11.30pm Tue-Sat, closed late Nov–mid-Mar) Audacious is the word for the bold experimentation of leading Spanish chef Angel León, whose seafood-biased *nueva cocina* menu has won a cavalcade of unusual awards, including a Michelin star and a 2011 plug from the *New York Times* citing it as one of 10 restaurants in the world 'worth a plane ride' (not particularly eco-friendly, but you get the idea).

The restaurant splits local opinion in traditional El Puerto. Some snort at its prices and pretension; others salivate at the thought of tripe stew, yeast-fermented mackerel and creamy rice with microseaweeds.

🍷 Drinking & Entertainment

Bodega Obregón BAR
(Calle Zarza 51; ☺9am-2pm & 6-9pm Mon-Fri, 10am-3pm Sat) Think sherry is just a drink for grandmas? Come and have your illusions blown out of the water at this spit-and-sawdust-style bar where the sweet stuff is siphoned from woody barrels. Flamenco is supposed to happen Sundays between 12.30pm and 3pm.

★Peña Flamenca Tomás El Nitri FLAMENCO
(☑956 54 32 37; Diego Niño 1) Good honest *peña* with the air of a foot-stomping, 19th-century flamenco bar that showcases some truly amazing guitarists, singers and dancers in a club full of regular aficionados. Platefuls of tasty food appear miraculously out of a tiny back kitchen.

ℹ Information

Tourist Office (☑956 54 24 13; www.turismoelpuerto.com; Plaza de Alfonso X El Sabio 9; ☺10am-2pm & 6-8pm May-Sep) The excellent tourist office sits right next to the Castillo de San Marcos.

ℹ Getting There & Away

BOAT
Catamarans (www.cmtbc.es) leave from in front of the Hotel Santa María bound for Cádiz' Terminal Marítima Metropolitana (€2.35, 30 minutes), with 18 daily departures Monday to Friday and six/five on Saturdays/Sundays.

BUS
Make a note: El Puerto de Santa María has two bus departure points. Buses to Cádiz (€1.56, 45 minutes), Jerez de la Frontera (€1.60, 20 minutes) and Sanlúcar de Barrameda (€1.67, 15 minutes) generally leave from a stop outside the Plaza de Toros. Buses to Seville go daily from outside the train station.

TRAIN
Daily trains go to/from Jerez de la Frontera (€2.65, 10 minutes, 15 daily), Cádiz (€4.95, 30 minutes, 15 daily) and Seville (€13, 80 minutes, 15 daily).

Sanlúcar de Barrameda
POP 67,000

Sanlúcar is one of those lesser-known Andalucian cities that you'd do well to shoehorn into your itinerary. The reasons? Firstly, there's gastronomy. Sanlúcar cooks up some of the best seafood in the region on a hallowed waterside strip called Bajo de Guía. Secondly, Sanlúcar sits at the northern tip of the esteemed sherry triangle and the bodegas here, nestled in the somnolent old town, retain a less commercial, earthier quality. Thirdly, situated at the mouth of the Guadalquivir estuary, the city provides a quieter, less trammelled entry point into the ethereal Parque Nacional de Doñana, preferably via boat.

As if that wasn't enough, Sanlúcar harbours a proud nautical history: both Columbus (on his third sojourn) and Portuguese mariner Ferdinand Magellan struck out from here on their voyages of discovery.

With excellent transport links, Sanlúcar makes for an easy day trip from Cádiz or Jerez.

◉ Sights

Palacio de Orleans y Borbon PALACE
(cnr Cuesta de Belén & Calle Caballero; ☺book at tourist office) **FREE** From Plaza del Cabildo, cross Calle Ancha to Plaza San Roque and head up Calle Bretones, which becomes Calle Cuesta de Belén. Then dog-leg up to this beautiful neo-Mudéjar palace in the old

town. It was built as a summer home for the aristocratic Montpensier family in the 19th century and is now Sanlúcar's town hall.

Iglesia de Nuestra Señora de la O   CHURCH
(Plaza de la Paz; ☉ Mass 7.30pm Mon-Fri, 9am, noon & 7.30pm Sun) On Calle Caballeros, this medieval church stands out among Sanlúcar's churches for its beautiful Gothic Mudéjar main portal, created in the 1360s, and the richness of its interior decoration, including the Mudéjar *artesonado* ceilings.

Palacio de los Duques de Medina Sidonia   PALACE, MUSEUM
(☑ 956 36 01 61; www.fcmedinasidonia.com; Plaza Condes de Niebla 1; adult/concession €5/2; ☉ tours 12.30pm Mon-Sat, 11.30am & 12.30pm Sun) Next door to the Iglesia de Nuestra Señora de la O, this was the rambling home of the aristocratic family that once owned more of Spain than anyone else. The house, mostly dating to the 17th century, bursts with antiques and paintings by Goya, Zurbarán and other famous Spanish artists.

Castillo de Santiago   CASTLE
(☑ 956 08 83 29; www.castillodesantiago.com; Plaza del Castillo de Santiago; adult/concession €5/3; ☉ 10am-2.30pm Tue-Sun) Located amid buildings of the Barbadillo sherry company, this restored 15th-century castle has great views from its hexagonal Torre del Homenaje (Keep). Entry to the Patio de Armas and its restaurant is free.

☞ Tours

Sanlúcar's Bajo de Guía is another potential entry point to Parque Nacional de Doñana, which glimmers across the Río Guadalquivir. Trips here are run by Visitas Doñana (☑ 956 36 38 13; www.visitasdonana.com; Bajo de Guía; tours €30), whose boat, the *Real Fernando*, chugs up the river for wildlife viewing. Two trips are offered: one is a boat/jeep combo, the other is a boat trip plus a short hike. The boat departs from Bajo de Guía, 750m northeast of La Calzada. You can book, reserve or gain more park info at the Centro de Visitantes Fábrica de Hielo (☑ 956 38 16 35; Bajo de Guía; ☉ 9am-7pm) in an old ice factory on the water's edge.

Sanlúcar produces a distinctive sherry-like wine called manzanilla that uses the same grapes as the bodegas in Jerez and El Puerto de Santa María, but has a smoother taste due to Sanlúcar's maritime microclimate. Barbadillo and Pedro Romero bodegas give tours, for which you don't need to book ahead.

★ Barbadillo Bodega   WINERY TOUR
(☑ 956 38 55 00; www.museobarbadillo.com; Calle Luis de Eguilaz 11; tour €5, museum free; ☉ tours noon & 1pm Tue-Sat, in English 11am Tue-Sat, Museo de Manzanilla 10am-3pm Tue-Sat) Near the castle, Barbadillo is the oldest and biggest manzanilla firm. There's also a good manzanilla museum here, which you can visit independently of the tour.

✯✯ Festivals & Events

The Sanlúcar summer gets going with the Feria de la Manzanilla in late May or early June, and blossoms in July and August with jazz, flamenco and classical-music festivals, one-off concerts by top Spanish bands, and Sanlúcar's unique horse races, the Carreras de Caballo (www.carrerassanlucar.es), in which thoroughbred racehorses thunder along the beach during two three-day evening meetings in August.

🛏 Sleeping

Book well ahead at holiday times.

Hotel Barrameda   HOTEL €
(☑ 956 38 58 78; www.hotelbarrameda.com; Calle Ancha 10; d incl breakfast €47-58; ❀ ☎) Looking out over the tapas bar action of Plaza Cabildo, this 30-room central hotel has added some stylish modern rooms to its newer wing, with no big price hikes. Throw in a ground-floor patio, marble floors, decent art and a roof terrace, and you've nabbed a bargain.

★ Hostal Alcoba   HOTEL €€
(☑ 956 38 31 09; www.hostalalcoba.com; Calle Alcoba 26; s/d €70/75; ❀) This wonderfully funky small hotel with a slick, modernist courtyard complete with loungers, pool, hammocks and a deck looks like something that Frank Lloyd Wright might have conceived. Skilfully put together (and run), it manages to be functional, attractive and comfortable all at the same time.

Hotel Posada de Palacio   HISTORIC HOTEL €€
(☑ 956 36 48 40; www.posadadepalacio.com; Calle Caballeros 11; d/ste from €93/131; 🅿 ❀ @ ☎) Plant-filled patios, gracious historical charm and 18th-century luxury add up to one of the best places to stay in this part of Andalucía. There's antique furniture, but it's rarely overdone and never weighs heavily on the

surrounds thanks to the high ceilings and abundance of light.

Eating

Spain holds few dreamier dining experiences than tucking into ocean-fresh seafood while watching the sun go down over the Guadalquivir at Bajo de Guía, a strip of high-quality but easygoing fish restaurants overlooking the river estuary about 750m northeast of the town centre.

★ Casa Balbino   Tapas, Seafood €

(www.casabalbino.com; Plaza del Cabildo 11; tapas €3; ⊙noon-5pm & 7pm-midnight) What, no waiters? Perennially packed Casa Balbino is like a British pub; you must elbow your way to the bar, shout your order to a staff member and then wait for them to bring it back to you so you can carry it to your chosen corner. Very un-Spanish!

The *tortillas de camarones* (crisp shrimp fritters) and *langostinos a la plancha* (grilled king prawns) here are legendary.

Helados Artesanos Toni   ICE CREAM €

(www.heladostoni.com; Plaza de Cabildo 2; ⊙noon-midnight Mar-Oct) For some of the best ice cream in Andalucía don't miss Helados Artesanos Toni, family-run since 1896, with videos demonstrating the fine art of making ice cream playing behind the counter.

Cafetería Guzmán El Bueno   CAFE, DESSERTS €

(Plaza Condes de Niebla 1; dishes €3-8; ⊙9am-8pm Tue-Sun, 8.30am-1pm & 4-8pm Mon) Sink into plump cushions surrounded by antique furnishings at the cafe in the Palacio de los Duques de Medina Sidonia (p617). Fare is simple – omelettes, cheese, ham – but the setting is uniquely atmospheric.

★ Poma   SEAFOOD €€

(www.restaurantepoma.com; Avenida de Bajo de Guía 6; mains €12-18; ⊙noon-5pm & 8pm-midnight) You could kick a football on the Bajo de Guía and guarantee it'd land on a decent plate of fish, but the Messis among us usually aim for Poma, where the *plato variado* comes with about five different varieties of lightly fried species freshly plucked out of the nearby sea and river.

Casa Bigote   SEAFOOD €€€

(www.restaurantecasabigote.com; Avenida Bajo de Guía 10; fish mains €20; ⊙1-4pm & 8.30-11.30pm Mon-Sat) The most renowned of the Bajo de Guía restaurants is Casa Bigote, which has a classier air than most places and serves only fish and seafood. Its tapas bar across the small lane is always packed.

☆ Entertainment

There are some lively music bars on and around Calzada del Ejército and Plaza del Cabildo, and lots of concerts in summer.

❶ Information

Tourist Office (www.turismosanlucar.com; Calzada Duquesa Isabel; ⊙10am-2pm & 6-8pm Wed-Sun, 8.30am-2.30pm Mon & Tue) Multilingual and very helpful staff.

❶ Getting There & Away

Los Amarillos (☑956 38 50 60; www.losamarillos.es) runs hourly buses to/from El Puerto de Santa María (€1.87, 15 minutes), Cádiz (€4.55, one hour) and Seville (€8.04, 1½ hours) from the bus station on Avenida de la Estación. **Linesur** (☑956 34 10 63) has hourly buses to/from Jerez de la Frontera.

Jerez de la Frontera

POP 211,000

Stand down all other claimants. Jerez, as most savvy Spain-o-philes know, *is* Andalucía. It just doesn't broadcast the fact in the way that Seville and Granada do. As a result, few people plan their trip around a visit here, preferring instead to jump-cut to the glories of the Giralda and the Alhambra. If only they knew. Jerez is the capital of *andaluz* horse culture, stop one on the famed sherry triangle and – cue the protestations from Cádiz and Seville – the cradle of Spanish flamenco. The *bulería* (flamenco style), Jerez' jokey, tongue-in-cheek antidote to Seville's tragic *soleá*, was first concocted in the legendary Roma *barrios* of Santiago and San Miguel. If you really want to unveil the eternal riddle that is Andalucía, start here.

◉ Sights

Alcázar   FORTRESS

(☑956 14 99 55; Alameda Vieja; admission excl/incl camera obscura €5/7; ⊙9.30am-7.30pm Mon-Fri, to 2.30pm Sat & Sun; closes 2.30pm Nov-Feb) Jerez' muscular yet refined 11th- or 12th-century fortress is one of the best preserved Almohad-era (1140s–1212) relics left in Andalucía. It's noted for its octagonal tower, a classic example of Almohad defensive forts.

You enter the Alcázar via the **Patio de Armas**. On the left is the beautiful *mezquita* (mosque), which was converted to a chapel by Alfonso X in 1264. Beyond the Patio de Armas, the lovely gardens recreate the ambience of Islamic times with their geometrical plant beds and tinkling fountains, while the domed Baños Árabes (Arab Baths) with their shafts of light are another highlight. Back on the Patio de Armas, the 18th-century Palacio Villavicencio, built over the ruins of the old Islamic palace, contains works of art, but is best known for its bird's-eye view of Jerez from the summit; the palace's tower also contains a camera obscura, which provides a picturesque live panorama of Jerez.

★ Catedral de San Salvador   CATHEDRAL
(Plaza de la Encarnación; admission €5; ⊙10am-6.30pm Mon-Sat, Mass 11am Sun) Echoes of Seville colour Jerez' wonderful cathedral, a surprisingly harmonious mix of baroque, neoclassical and Gothic styles. Stand-out features are its broad flying buttresses and its intricately decorated stone ceilings. In 2012 the cathedral opened as a museum showing off its art (including works by Zurbarán and Pacheco), religious garments and silverware in a series of rooms and chapels behind the main altar.

You can also enjoy an orange tree–lined patio (the church was built on the site of an old mosque) and a 'secret staircase' to nowhere. Named for San Salvador, the building only officially became a cathedral in 1980.

A couple of blocks northeast of the cathedral is Plaza de la Asunción, with the handsome 16th-century Antiguo Cabildo (Old Town Hall) and lovely 15th-century Mudéjar Iglesia de San Dionisio.

Real Escuela Andaluza del Arte Ecuestre   EQUESTRIAN SHOW
(☑956 31 80 08; www.realescuela.org; Avenida Duque de Abrantes; training sessions adult/child €11/6.50, exhibición adult/child €21/13; ⊙training sessions 11am-1pm Mon, Wed & Fri, noon Tue & Thu Sep-Jul, Mon & Wed Aug, exhibición noon Tue & Thu Oct-Jul, Tue, Thu & Fri Aug & Sep) The famed Royal Andalucian School of Equestrian Art trains horses and riders in equestrian skills, and you can watch them going through their paces in training sessions and visit the Horse Carriage Museum, which includes an 18th-century Binder Hunting Break. The highlight for most is the official exhibición (show) where the handsome white horses show off their tricks to classical music. You can book tickets online for this – advisable for the official shows, which can sell out.

Museo Arqueológico   MUSEUM
(☑956 35 01 33; Plaza del Mercado; admission €5; ⊙10am-2pm & 4-7pm Tue-Fri, 10am-2pm Sat & Sun) In the Santiago quarter, Jerez' archaeology museum reopened in 2012 after almost a decade of renovations. It contains, among

SEVILLE & ANDALUCÍA'S HILL TOWNS   JEREZ DE LA FRONTERA

SHERRY & FOOD PAIRINGS

Wine neophytes are in luck. Sherry, aside from being one of the world's most unappreciated wines, is also one of its most versatile, particularly the *fino* and manzanilla varietals, so you don't need a degree in oenology to pair it. Here are some pointers:

TYPE OF SHERRY	SERVING TEMPERATURE	QUALITIES	FOOD PAIRINGS
Manzanilla	well-chilled	dry, fresh, delicate, slightly salty essence	tapas, almonds, sushi, olives
Fino	chilled	very dry & pale	aperitif, tapas, soup, white fish, shellfish, prawns, oysters, a counterpoint for cheeses
Amontillado	cool, but not chilled	off dry	aperitif, blue cheeses, chicken and white meat, cured cheese, foie gras, organs, rabbit, consommé
Oloroso	cool, but not chilled	dry, nutty, dark	red meat and game, cheese sauces
Pale Cream	room temperature	sweetened *fino*	fresh fruit, blue cheese
Cream	room temperature	sweet	dried fruit, cheesecake
Pedro Ximénez	room temperature	very sweet	dark chocolate, biscotti

Jerez de la Frontera

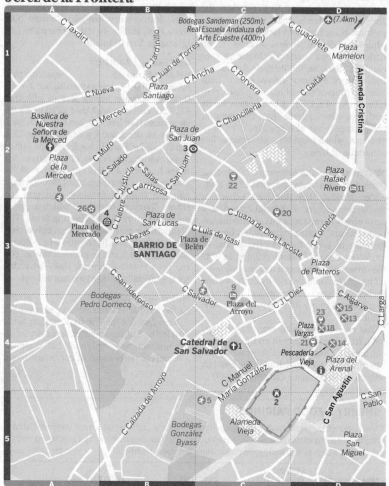

other relics, a 7th-century-BC Greek helmet found in the Río Guadalete.

Centro Andaluz de Flamenco   ARTS CENTRE
(Andalucian Flamenco Centre; ☏856 81 41 32; www.centroandaluzdeflamenco.es; Plaza de San Juan 1; ☉9am-2pm Mon-Fri) **FREE** At once architecturally interesting (note the original 15th-century Mudéjar *artesonado* in the entrance and the Andalucian baroque courtyard) and a fantastic flamenco resource, this unique centre has print and music libraries holding thousands of works.

Flamenco videos are screened at 10am, 11am, noon and 1pm, and staff can provide you with a list of 17 local *peñas*, as well as information on flamenco dance and singing classes in Jerez.

🏃 Activities

Hammam Andalusi   HAMMAM
(Arabic baths; ☏956 34 90 66; www.hammam-mandalusi.com; Calle Salvador 6; baths €24, with 15/30min massage €34/53; ☉10am-midnight) Jerez is replete with echoes of the city's Islamic past, but there is none more evocative than the Hammam Andalusi. As soon

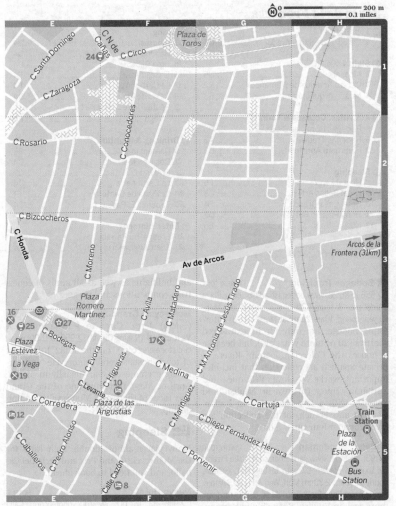

as you enter, you're greeted by the wafting scent of incense and essential oils, and the soothing sound of tinkling water and Arab music. Inside there are the usual three pools (hot, tepid or cold) and even an option for a chocolate bath (€90). Reserve beforehand.

Tours

Jerez is home to around 20 sherry bodegas and most are open to visitors, but they're scattered around town and many of them require you to call ahead. The tourist office has up-to-date information.

Bodegas González Byass   WINERY TOUR
(Bodegas Tio Pepe; ☏ 956 35 70 16; www.bodegastiopepe.com; Calle Manuel María González 12; tours €12.50, with tapas €16; ☺ tours in English & Spanish hourly 11am-6pm Mon-Sat, to 2pm Sun Oct-Apr) This is the home of the Tio Pepe brand and one of the biggest sherry houses, handily located just west of the Alcázar. Six or seven tours each are given daily in English and Spanish, and a few in German and French. Reservations can be made online.

Jerez de la Frontera

★ **Bodegas Tradición** WINERY TOUR
(☑ 956 16 86 28; www.bodegastradicion.com; Plaza Cordobeses 3; tours €20; ⊙ 9.30am-6.30pm Mon-Fri year-round, 10am-2pm Sat Mar-Jun) An interesting bodega, not only for its extra-aged sherries (20 or more years old), but because it houses the Colección Joaquín Rivera, a private Spanish art collection that includes important works by Goya, Velázquez and Zurbarán. Tours (mainly in English and Spanish, with a few conducted in Italian, German and French) of the collection are given three or four times a day.

Bodegas Sandeman WINERY TOUR
(☑ 956 15 17 11; www.sandeman.com; Calle Pizarro 10; tours in English €7, with tasting €14; ⊙ tours hourly 11.30am-2.30pm Mon, Wed & Fri, 10.30am & hourly noon-3pm Tue & Thu) Has three or four tours each in English, Spanish and German, and one in French.

★ Festivals & Events

Jerez has a comprehensive calendar of festive events. These are the biggest highlights:

Festival de Jerez FLAMENCO
(www.festivaldejerez.com; ⊙ Feb-Mar) Jerez' biggest celebration of flamenco, held in late February/early March.

Feria del Caballo HORSES
(Horse Fair) Jerez' week-long Horse Fair in late April or the first half of May is one of Andalucía's grandest festivals, with music, dance and bullfights as well as all kinds of equestrian competitions and parades.

Motorcycle Grand Prix MOTORCYCLES
(⊙ May) Jerez' **Circuito Permanente de Velocidad** (Racing Circuit; ☑ 956 15 11 00; www.circuitodejerez.com), on the A382 10km east of town, hosts several motorcycle- and car-racing events each year (usually in March, April or May), including one of the Grand Prix races of the World Motorcycle Championship.

🛏 Sleeping

Many places almost double their rates for the Motorcycle Grand Prix and Feria del Caballo, and you need to book ahead.

Nuevo Hotel HOTEL €
(☑ 956 33 16 00; www.nuevohotel.com; Calle Caballeros 23; s/d/tr incl breakfast €30/42/57; ❄@🔊🚺) One of the most pleasant family-run hotels in Andalucía, the Nuevo's comfortable rooms are complemented by spectacular *habitación* (room) 208, replete with Islamic-style stuccowork and *azulejos* tiles. You'll wake up thinking you've taken up residence in the Alhambra – for €42!

Hostal Fenix HOSTAL €
(☑ 956 34 52 91; www.hostalfenix.com; Calle Cazón 7; d incl breakfast from €30; ❄🔊) There's nothing flash about the Fenix, which is part of its charm. Simple rooms are well-maintained by ultrafriendly owners who'll bring you breakfast (included in the price) on a tray

to your room. The impressive art adorning the walls is painted by the *dueña* (owner) and her cousin.

Hotel Palacio Garvey
HOTEL €€

(☑956 32 67 00; www.sferahoteles.net; Calle Tornería 24; d/ste €70/100; P✸@🛜🏊) Jerez' nominal posh hotel is a sensational 19th-century neoclassical palace conversion, with part of the ancient city wall visible from the lift and more of it in the gardens. The public areas sport animal prints, large, colourful paintings and Japanese-inspired bowls on low-slung tables, while subtle colours and luxurious leather furniture feature in the 16 individually decorated rooms.

Hotel Casa Grande
HOTEL €€

(☑956 34 50 70; www.casagrande.com.es; Plaza de las Angustias 3; r €85-105, ste €115-125; P✸🛜@) This brilliant hotel occupies a carefully restored 1920s mansion. Rooms are spread over three floors and set around a patio, or beside the roof terrace, which has views of Jerez' roof line. All is overseen by the congenial Monika Schroeder, a mine of information about Jerez.

Hotel Bellas Artes
HOTEL €€

(☑956 34 84 30; www.hotelbellasartes.com; Plaza del Arroyo 45; d €69-99; ✸@🛜) A top-notch palace conversion, the Bellas Artes overlooks the cathedral from its main terrace and suites. An exquisite carved stone corner pillar graces the sand-coloured neoclassical exterior. Strong interior colours contrast with white marble floors. Free-standing bathtubs further contribute to an old-world ambience, though rooms have all the mod cons.

Eating

The sherry trade has introduced English and French accents into the local cuisine. Jerez also prizes its cured and grilled meats, and fish. Central Jerez is littered with great tapas bars. The pedestrian streets just north of Plaza del Arenal are a fine place to start.

Bar Juanito
TAPAS €

(www.bar-juanito.com; Calle Pescadería Vieja 8-10; tapas from €2.20, media raciones €5-7) One of the best tapas bars in Jerez, 70-year-old Bar Juanito, with its outdoor tables and chequered tablecloths, is like a slice of village Andalucía in the heart of the city. Its *alcachofas* (artichokes) are a past winner of the National Tapa Competition, but there's so much local cuisine to choose from here and it's all served up with the best local wines.

Cruz Blanca
TAPAS €

(www.lacruzblanca.com; Plaza de la Yerva; tapas €1.80-3; ☺8am-midnight) The Cruz whips up good seafood, egg, meat and salad offerings and has tables on a quiet little plaza. The marinated fish in a pesto-flecked sauce could steal the crown for Jerez' best meal.

Restaurante Cafetería La Vega
CAFE €

(☑956 33 77 48; Plaza Estevez; snacks €3-7; ☺8.30am-11pm) Crowd into this totally down-to-earth nook at 5pm with what looks like the whole of Jerez' over-55 population for churros and coffee dispatched from a special churros counter.

Albores
ANDALUCIAN €

(☑956 32 02 66; Calle Consistorio 12; mains €8-15; ☺noon-midnight) Pitching itself among the old favourites in the city centre, Albores has added a new edge. Opened in 2013 its tapas and meals provide ideal pairings for the locally concocted sherries. If there's a speciality, it's probably the fish, in particular the tuna *escabeche* (marinated and poached). It stays open all day and the homemade cakes are divine.

El Gallo Azul
SPANISH €€

(Calle Larga 2; raciones from €12; ☺11.30am-midnight Tue-Sun) Housed in what has become Jerez' signature building, a circular facade emblazoned with a sherry logo, El Gallo Azul (the blue cockerel) has a restaurant upstairs and tapas at street level. It's also an excellent perch at which to enjoy an afternoon coffee and a slice of cake as the city springs back to life after the siesta.

La Carboná
ANDALUCIAN €€

(☑956 34 74 75; www.lacarbona.com; Calle San Francisco de Paula 2; mains €12.50-16.50; ☺1-4pm & 8pm-midnight Wed-Mon) This popular, cavernous restaurant with an eccentric menu occupies an old bodega with a hanging fireplace. It's cosy in winter. Specialities include grilled meats and fresh fish, and the quirky quail with foie gras and rose petals.

Reino de León
CONTEMPORARY ANDALUCIAN €€€

(☑956 32 29 15; www.reinodeleongastrobar.com; Calle Latorre 8; mains €17-27; ☺8am-1am Mon-Fri, noon-1am Sat & Sun) Styling itself as a gastrobar, this place is a bit more 'nouveau' than other Jerez institutions, taking the region's basic ingredients – sherry, tuna, cured ham, etc – and dousing them with creative sauces and embellishments. Think tuna cooked with dry sherry and peppers, or chicken with parsley mayonnaise. It's created quite a local buzz.

🍷 Drinking & Nightlife

A few bars in the narrow streets north of Plaza del Arenal can get lively with an under-30 crowd: try beer bar **Dos Deditos** (Plaza Vargas 1; ⊙ noon-3.30pm & 7.30pm-2am Mon-Fri, 4pm-4am Sat & Sun) and wine bar **La Carbonería** (Calle Letrados 7; ⊙ 4.40pm-late Tue-Sun). Northeast of the centre, **La Plaza de Canterbury** (cnr Calles Zaragoza & N de Cañas; ⊙ 8.15am-2.30am Mon-Wed, 8.15am-4am Thu-Sat, 4pm-4am Sun) has a couple of pubs (one English and one Irish) around a central courtyard that attract a 20s clientele, while music bars northeast on Avenida de Méjico are the late-night headquarters for the 18-to-25 crowd.

Tabanco El Pasaje   BAR
(☑ 956 33 33 59; Calle Santa María 8; ⊙ 11am-3.30pm & 7.30-10.30pm Sun-Thu, to 11.30pm Fri & Sat) One of six famous old *tabancos* (Jerez-style taverns that serve sherry from the barrel) listed by the town hall, this 90-year-old drinking house sells plenty of the local plonk (ie sherry), which it serves up with suitably raw flamenco on weekend evenings.

☆ Entertainment

★ El Lagá Tío Parrilla   FLAMENCO
(Plaza del Mercado; show & 2 drinks €25; ⊙ 10.30pm Mon-Sat) Jerez' regular *tablao*

puts on gutsy shows that rarely end without rousing renditions of that old Jerez stalwart – the *bulería*.

Teatro Villamarta   THEATRE
(☑ 956 35 02 72; www.villamarta.com; Plaza Romero Martínez) Stages a busy program where you can pick up Bizet, Verdi, Mozart and – of course – a dash of flamenco.

ℹ️ Information

Municipal Tourist Office (☑ 956 33 88 74; www.turismojerez.com; Plaza del Arenal; ⊙ 9am-3pm & 5-7pm Mon-Fri, 9.30am-2.30pm Sat & Sun)

ℹ️ Getting There & Around

AIR

Jerez airport (☑ 956 15 00 00; www.aena.es), the only one serving Cádiz province, is 7km northeast of town on the Carretera de Sevilla (N-IV). It has a small selection of mainly seasonal sevices. **Ryanair** (www.ryanair.com) flies from Barcelona and London-Stansted (seasonal), **Air-Berlin** (www.airberlin.com) from Mallorca and Düsseldorf (seasonal), and **Iberia** (www.iberia.com) daily to/from Madrid. Taxis from the airport start at €14. The local airport buses M050 and M051 (€1, 30 minutes) run roughly 12 times daily.

BUS

The **bus station** (☑ 956 33 96 66; Plaza de la Estación) is 1.3km southeast of the centre. Destinations include Seville (€8.90, 1¼ hours, seven daily), Sanlúcar de Barrameda (€1.68, 30 minutes, seven or more daily), El Puerto de Santa María (€1.60, 20 minutes, 15 or more daily),

---

JEREZ' FERTILE FLAMENCO SCENE

Jerez' moniker as the 'cradle of flamenco' is regularly challenged by aficionados in Cádiz and Seville, but the claim has merit. This surprisingly untouristed city harbours not just one but *two* Roma quarters, **Santiago** and **San Miguel**, which, between them, have produced a glut of renowned artists, including Roma singers Manuel Torre and António Chacón. Like its rival cities to the north and west, Jerez has also concocted its own flamenco *palo*, the intensely popular *bulería*, a fast rhythmic musical style with the same *compás* (accented beat) as the *soleá*.

Explorations of Jerez' flamenco scene ought to start at the Centro Andaluz de Flamenco (p620), Spain's only bona fide flamenco library, where you can pick up information on clubs, performances and singing/dance/guitar lessons. From here you can stroll down **Calle Francos** and visit legendary flamenco bars such as **Damajuana** (www.damajuanacafebar.com; Calle Francos 18; ⊙ 4.30pm-3am Tue-Sun) and **El Arriate** (Calle Francos 41; ⊙ 8am-midnight), where singers and dancers still congregate. To the north, in the Santiago quarter, you'll find dozens of *peñas* (small private clubs) all known for their accessibility and intimacy; entrance is normally free if you buy a drink at the bar. The *peña* scene is particularly fertile during the February flamenco festival, which is arguably Andalucía's finest.

Cádiz (€1.72, one hour, nine or more daily), Arcos de la Frontera (€3.11, 35 minutes, four daily), and Ronda (€13, 2½ hours, two daily).

TRAIN

Jerez **train station** (☑ 956 34 23 19; Plaza de la Estación) is an extravagantly tiled architectural creation. It's right beside the bus station. Regular trains go to El Puerto de Santa María (€2.65, 10 minutes, 15 daily) and Cádiz (€5.95, 40 minutes, 15 daily), and 10 or more go to Seville (€10.90, 1¼ hours, 15 daily).

Arcos de la Frontera

POP 31,500 / ELEV 185M

Choosing your favourite *pueblo blanco* (white town) is like choosing your favourite Beatles album; they're all so damned good it's hard to make a definitive decision. When pressured for an answer, many people single out Arcos de la Frontera as their 'Sergeant Pepper.' This is a larger-than-average white town thrillingly sited on a high ridge with sheer precipices plummeting away on both sides. With the Sierra de Grazalema as a distant backdrop, Arcos possesses all the classic white-town calling cards: spectacular location, soporific old town, fancy *parador* (luxury state-owned hotel) and volatile frontier history. The odd tour bus and foreign-owned homestay do little to dampen the drama.

For a brief period during the 11th century, Arcos was an independent Berber-ruled *taifa* (kingdom). In 1255 it was claimed by Christian King Alfonso X for Seville.

◉ Sights

Along the streets east of Plaza del Cabildo, take time to seek out lovely buildings such as the Iglesia de San Pedro (Calle Núñez de Prado; admission €1; ⊙ 10.30am-2pm & 5-7pm Mon-Fri, 11am-2pm Sat; 🅿), a Gothic-baroque confection sporting what is perhaps one of the most magnificent small-church interiors in Andalucía – and it's not depressingly dark, either.

Plaza del Cabildo   SQUARE

The old town captures multiple historical eras evoking the ebb and flow of the once-disputed Christian-Moorish frontier. Plaza del Cabildo is the centre of this quarter. Close your eyes to the modern car park and focus instead on the fine surrounding buildings (all old) and a vertiginous mjrador (lookout) with views over Río Guadalete.

The 11th-century Castillo de los Duques is firmly closed to the public, but its outer walls frame classic Arcos views. On the plaza's northern side is the Gothic-cum-baroque Basíllica-Parroquia de Santa María sporting beautiful stone choir stalls and Isabelline ceiling tracery. On the eastern side, the Parador Casa del Corregidor hotel is a reconstruction of a 16th-century magistrate's house. If you think you've already seen every possible jaw-dropping vista in Andalucía, drink this one in – preferably over a *café con leche* and accompanying *torta* (piece of cake).

☞ Tours

One-hour guided tours of the old town's monuments and pretty patios start from the tourist office at 11am Monday to Friday.

⚘ Festivals & Events

Semana Santa   HOLY WEEK

Holy Week processions through the narrow old streets are dramatic; on Easter Sunday there's a hair-raising running of the bulls.

Fiesta de la Virgen de las Nieves   FLAMENCO
(⊙ early Aug) This three-day festival includes a top-class flamenco night in Plaza del Cabildo.

Feria de San Miguel   RELIGIOUS

Arcos celebrates its patron saint with a four-day fair; held around 29 September.

⏗ Sleeping

Casa Campana   GUESTHOUSE €
(☑ 956 70 47 87; www.casacampana.com; Calle Nuñez de Prado 4; d/apt from €35/65; ✳ @ 🛜 🛗) In the heart of old Arcos, and run by the superfriendly Emma and Jim who are extremely knowledgeable about the local area, Casa Campana has two simple doubles and a massive apartment that's filled with character. There's a typical Andalucian patio and the quiet roof terrace is a fine place to relax with good views and a real sense of privacy.

Hotel Marques de Torresoto   HOTEL €
(☑ 956 70 07 17; www.torresoto.es; Calle Marqués de Torresoto 4; s/d €35/50) The deal of the season is waiting in the jungle-like inner courtyard of this Arcos gem. Beyond the grand entry, the 15 rooms are a little plain with an odd layout, but at this price who's complaining?

Seeing Flamenco

The intensity and spontaneity of flamenco have never translated well onto CDs or studio recordings. Instead, to raise the goose-bumps and inspire the powerful emotional spirit known to aficionados as '*duende*', you have to be there at a performance, stamping your feet and passionately yelling óle.

Peñas

Peñas are private local clubs run by aficionados determined to preserve the art in its traditional form. Tourist offices don't always advertise *peñas* as they seldom post regular show schedules, although the clubs themselves are invariably happy to welcome interested outsiders. To find a *peña* ask around in flamenco bars, check posters on noticeboards (or lampposts!), and follow any interesting sounds you might hear in the street. Not surprisingly, *peñas* present some of the most authentic and passionate shows in Spain and incorporate flamenco's vital fourth element: the *jaleo*, or audience participation.

Tablaos

Tablaos are grand and well-rehearsed flamenco performances that showcase the art in a professional and choreographed way. Unlike *peñas*, *tablao* shows are held in theatre-like venues where drinks and sometimes dinner are included in the price of your ticket. While the artistic talent at these events is of a high standard, *tablaos* are sometimes derided by aficionados for lacking the spit and sawdust that makes the music so unique. *Tablaos* are usually more expensive than other flamenco shows. One of the largest, Seville's Palacio Andaluz, is a 500-seat theatre and costs around €70 for a ticket (dinner included).

Bars

Local bars are your best bet to see flamenco on the cheap, although the music and dancing in these places is sometimes more akin to mad jamming sessions than authentic *cante jondo*, which is flamenco in its purest form. Entry to a flamenco bar is usually free as long as you buy a drink. Well-known flamenco neighbourhoods such as Triana in Seville or Santiago in Jerez have a multitude of bars close to each other and are known as places where dancers and musicians come together to talk, drink and, if you're lucky, perform.

Cultural Centres

A varied stash of cultural centres in Andalucía's bigger cities offer a more authentic and intimate alternative to *tablao* shows. Particularly notable is the Casa de la Memoria (p595) in Seville which has recently relocated to El Centro and added a small exposition space. Flamenco museums such as Seville's Museo del Baile Flamenco (p584) and Cordoba's Centro Flamenco Fosforito (p645) also organise regular concerts. Cultural centres usually attract more knowledgeable audiences than *tablaos*, and they'll shout encouraging '*óles*' from the sidelines to will the show to a soulful climax.

For more on flamenco, see p856.

1. Flamenco performers, Barrio de Santa Cruz, Seville
2. Flamenco dancing, Seville 3. Flamenco dancer and singers

Hotel El Convento
HOTEL €€

(☑956 70 23 33; www.hotelelconvento.es; Calle Maldonado 2; r incl breakfast from €65) The nuns who used to live in this beautiful, former 17th-century convent obviously appreciated a good view. Now it's been turned into a slightly chintzy hotel.

Hotel Real de Veas
HOTEL €€

(☑956 71 73 70; www.hotelrealdeveas.com; Calle Corredera 12; s/d incl breakfast €55/70) A superb option inside a lovingly restored building. The dozen or so rooms are arranged around a glass-covered patio and are cool and comfortable. It's one of the few places that has easy car access.

★Parador Casa del Corregidor
HISTORIC HOTEL €€€

(☑956 70 05 00; www.parador.es; Plaza del Cabildo; r from €155; ❄@🛜) This rebuilt 16th-century magistrate's residence combines typical *parador* luxury with a magnificent cliff-side setting. Eight of the 24 rooms have balconies with sweeping cliff-top views. Otherwise, most of the rest of the rooms look out onto the pretty Plaza del Cabildo.

🍴 Eating

Taberna Jóvenes Flamencos
ANDALUCIAN €

(☑657 13 35 52; www.tabernajovenesflamencos. blogspot.com; Calle Dean Espinosa; raciones €6; ☉noon-late Thu-Tue) You've got to hand it to this new place, which opened up successfully in 2012 in the middle of a recession. It has wonderful flamenco/bullfighting decor and an easy-to-navigate menu split in to meat, fish, bread, vegetarian and scramble sections – all delicious. Service is impeccable and there are regular outbreaks of music and dance.

Restaurante-Café Babel
MOROCCAN, FUSION €€

(Calle Corredera 11; dishes €8-12; ☉8am-11pm Tue-Sun) Arcos' new Moorish fusion spot has some tasteful decor (the ornate stools were shipped in from Casablanca) and some equally tasty dishes: count on tagines and couscous, or the full Arabic tea treatment with silver pots and sweet pastries.

ℹ Information

The **tourist office** (☑956 70 22 64; Calle Cuesta de Belén 5; ☉9.30am-2pm & 3-7.30pm Mon-Sat, 10am-2pm Sun) doubles as a Centro de Interpretación relaying the history of Arcos and including an excellent 1:800 scale model of the present-day town.

Banks and ATMs are along Calle Debajo del Corral and Calle Corredera.

ℹ Getting There & Away

From the **bus station** (☑956 70 49 77; Calle Los Alcaldes), **Los Amarillos** (www.losamarillos. es) and/or **Comes** (www.tgcomes.es) have daily buses (fewer on weekends) to Cádiz (€5.11, one hour, eight daily), Olvera (€5.81, 1½ hours, three daily), Jerez de la Frontera (€2.64, 45 minutes, 19 daily), Málaga (€16.85, 3½ hours, two daily) and Ronda (€8.75, two hours, two daily).

Parque Natural Sierra de Grazalema & Around

Of all Andalucía's protected areas, Parque Natural Sierra de Grazalema is the most accessible and best set up for lung-stretching sorties into the countryside. Though not as lofty as the Sierra Nevada, the park's rugged pillarlike peaks nonetheless rise abruptly off the plains northeast of Cádiz, revealing precipitous gorges, wild orchids and hefty rainfall – stand aside Galicia and Cantabria, this is the wettest part of Spain, logging an average 2000mm annually. Grazalema is also fine walking country (the best months are May, June, September and October). For the more intrepid there are opportunities for climbing, caving, canyoning, kayaking and paragliding.

The park extends into northwestern Málaga province, where it includes the Cueva de la Pileta. The **Centro de Visitantes** (☑956 70 97 33; Calle Federico García Lorca 1; ☉9am-2pm & 4-6pm Mon-Sat, 9am-2pm Sun), with limited displays and information, is situated in the village of El Bosque, 20km east of Grazalema village.

Grazalema

POP 2200 / ELEV 825M

A true mountain 'white town', Grazalema looks like it has been dropped from a passing spaceship onto the steep rocky slopes of its eponymous mountain range. Few *pueblos blancos* are as generically perfect as this one, with its spotless whitewashed houses sporting rust-tiled roofs and wrought-iron window bars. Grazalema embraces the great outdoors with hikes fanning out in all directions, but it's also an age-old producer of blankets, honey, meat-filled stews and an adrenalin-filled bullrunning festival. There's an artisan textile factory in the town that still employs traditional weaving methods.

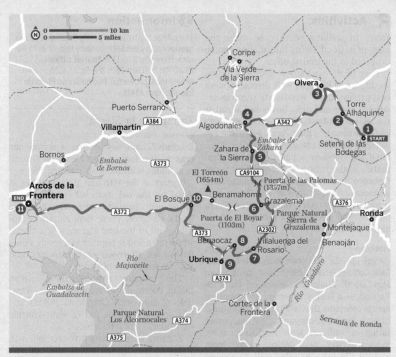

Driving Tour
White Towns

START SETENIL DE LAS BODEGAS
END ARCOS DE LA FRONTERA
LENGTH 131KM; ONE TO TWO DAYS

Rev up in ① **Setenil de las Bodegas**, close to the border with Málaga province. The town is recognisable for its cave houses once used for storing wine and today offering a shady antidote to the summer heat. Winding north on CA9120 you'll pass ② **Torre Alháquime**, a white town with a 13th-century Moorish castle. CA9106 takes you into ③ **Olvera**, visible for miles around thanks to its lofty neo-Renaissance church and Almohad castle, but also known for its high-quality olive oil and *vía verde* cycle path. The N342 threads west from here passing Europe's largest griffon vulture colony at Peñon de Zaframagón on its way to the cusp of Parque Natural Sierra de Grazalema and ④ **Algodonales**, a white town known for its guitar-making workshop and hang-gliding/paragliding obsession. In the lee of the Grazalema Mountains above a glassy reservoir, ⑤ **Zahara de la Sierra** is a quintessential white town with a huddle of

houses stretched around the skirts of a rocky crag. Count the switchbacks on steep CA9104 as you climb up to the view-splayed Puerta de las Palomas and, beyond, the village of ⑥ **Grazalema**, a red-roofed park-activity nexus also famous for its blanket-making and homemade honey. Plying the craggy western face of the Sierra on A2302 brings you to tiny ⑦ **Villaluenga del Rosario** with its artisan cheese museum. Further on is equally diminutive ⑧ **Benaocaz**, a start/finish point for numerous Grazalema park hikes and guardian of a historical museum. ⑨ **Ubrique**, close to the borders of the Grazalema and Alcornocales Natural Parks, is a leather-making centre. Browse its specialist shops for bargains, then motor on to ⑩ **El Bosque**, the western gateway to Cádiz province's high country and location of the natural park's main information centre. Though the mountains melt away as you track further west on A372, the drama returns at ⑪ **Arcos de la Frontera**, a Roman-turned-Moorish-turned-Christian citadel perched atop a steep sandstone cliff.

🏃 Activities

You're in walking country, so make the most of it. Good hiking information can be procured at the tourist office.

Four of the park's best hikes (including the 12.5km El Pinsapar walk through Spain's best-preserved fir woodland) traverse restricted areas and must be booked ahead at the visitor centre (☑956 72 70 29; Calle Federico García Lorca 1; ⊙10am-2pm & 5-7pm Mon-Sat, 9am-2pm Sun) in El Bosque.

Of the free-access paths, the most dramatic is the 7.2km Sendero Salto del Cabrero between Grazalema village and Benaocaz via the Puerto del Boyar that traverses the western flanks of the Sierra del Endrinal. Look out for rare wild orchids along the way.

Horizon   ADVENTURE SPORTS
(☑956 13 23 63; www.horizonaventura.com; Calle Corrales Terceros 29; ⊙10am-2pm & 5-8pm Mon-Sat) 🖉 Horizon, a block off Plaza de España, is a highly experienced adventure sports company that will take you climbing, bungee jumping, canyoning, caving, paragliding or walking, with English-speaking guides. Prices per person range from around €14 for a half-day walk to around €60 for the 4km underground wetsuit adventure from the Cueva del Hundidero near Montejaque to the Cueva del Gato near Benaoján.

Note that minimum group sizes apply for some activities.

🛏 Sleeping & Eating

Casa de las Piedras   RURAL HOTEL €
(☑956 13 20 14; www.casadelaspiedras.net; Calle de las Piedras 32; s/d/apt €42/48/65; ❄🌐) 🖉
Mountain airs and a homely feel go together like Fernando and Isabel in the Casa de la Piedras, a 16-room rural hotel with a cosy downstairs lounge and bags of information on park activities. The blankets in the simple but clean rooms are made in Grazalema village.

Restaurante El Torreón   ANDALUCIAN €€
(www.restauranteeltorreongrazalema.com; Calle Agua 44; mains €8-12; ⊙11am-4pm & 7-11pm) This friendly mountain restaurant is where you can take a break from the Cádiz fish monopoly with local chorizo, spinach, soups and the menu speciality, partridge. There's pasta for kids.

ℹ️ Information

The village centre is the pretty Plaza de España, overlooked by the 18th-century Iglesia de la Aurora. Here you'll find the **tourist office** (☑956 13 20 73; ⊙10am-2pm & 4-9pm), with a shop selling local products. Two banks on Plaza de España have ATMs.

Zahara de la Sierra

POP 1500 / ELEV 550M

Rugged Zahara, set around a vertiginous crag at the foot of the Sierra de Grazalema, hums with Moorish mystery. For over 150 years in the 14th and 15th centuries, it stood on the old medieval frontier facing off against Christian Olvera, clearly visible in the distance. These days Zahara encapsulates all of the best elements of a classic white town and is popular as a result. Come during the afternoon siesta, however, and you can still hear a pin drop.

The precipitous road over the ultrasteep 1331m Puerto de los Palomas (Doves' Pass) links Zahara with Grazalema (18km) and is a spectacular ride full of white-knuckle switchbacks (try it on a bike!).

Zahara's streets invite investigation, with vistas framed by tall palms and hot-pink bougainvillea. To climb to the 12th-century castle keep, take the path almost opposite the Hotel Arco de la Villa – it's a steady 10- to 15-minute climb. The castle's recapture from the Christians by Abu al-Hasan of Granada, in a night raid in 1481, provoked the Catholic Monarchs to launch the last phase of the Reconquista, which ended with the fall of Granada.

For accommodation choose one of the 17 rooms at Hotel Arco de la Villa (☑956 12 32 30; www.tugasa.com; Paseo Nazarí; s/d €36/60; 🅿❄🌐), which is partially built into the rock face. All rooms have jaw-dropping views, but little rural character.

Zahara sports the usual consortium of bars. For something with a more contemporary slant head to the foot of the village where, overlooking the lake, Al Lago (☑956 12 30 32; www.al-lago.es; Calle Félix Rodríguez de la Fuente; 6-course tasting menu €42; ⊙12.30-4.30pm & 8-10.30pm) serves a six-course tasting menu. It also rents rooms: €68 to €98 for a double.

Zahara village centres on Calle San Juan, where you'll find the natural park's helpful Punto de Información Zahara de la Sierra (☑956 12 31 14; Plaza de Zahara 3; ⊙9am-2pm & 4-7pm).

VÍA VERDE DE LA SIERRA

Regularly touted as the finest of Spain's *vía verdes* (greenways that have transformed old railway lines into traffic-free thoroughfares for bikers, hikers and horseriders), the Vía Verde de la Sierra between Olvera and Puerto Serrano is one of 17 such schemes in Andalucía. Aside from its wild, rugged scenery, the greenway is notable for four spectacular viaducts, 30 tunnels (with sensor-activated lighting), and three stations-turned-hotels/restaurants that are spread over a 36km route. Ironically, the train line that the greenway follows was never actually completed. Constructed in the 1920s as part of the abortive Jerez to Almargen railway, the project's private backers went bankrupt during the Great Depression and the line wasn't used. After languishing for decades, it was restored in the early 2000s.

The unique Hotel/Restaurante Estación Verde (☑ 661 463207; Olvera; s/d/apt €30/50/130) just outside Olvera is the official start of the route. You can hire a multitude of bikes here including tandems, kids' bikes and chariots, from €10 a day. Bike hire is also available at Coripe and Puerto Serrano stations. Other facilities include a kids' playground, exercise machines and the Patrulla Verde, a helpful staff of bike experts who dole out info and can help with mechanical issues.

A highlight of the Vía Verde is the Peñon de Zaframagón, a distinctive crag that acts as a prime breeding ground for griffon vultures. The Centro de Interpretación y Observatorio Ornitologico (adult/child €2/1; ⊙ 10am-4pm) encased in the former Zaframagón station building 16km west of Olvera allows close up observations activated directly from a high-definition camera placed up on the crag.

The Vía Verde de la Sierra is open 365 days a year. Devotee cyclists like to tackle it on hot summer nights under a full moon with head torches.

Setenil de las Bodegas

While most white towns sought protective status atop lofty crags, the people of Setenil did the opposite and burrowed into the dark caves beneath the steep cliffs of the River Trejo. The strategy clearly worked. It took the Christian armies a 15-day siege to dislodge the Moors from their well-defended positions in 1484. Many of the original cavehouses remain and some have been converted into bars and restaurants. Further afield, you can hike along a 6km path (the Ruta de los Molinos) past ancient mills to the next village of Alcalá del Valle.

The tourist office (Calle Villa; ⊙ 10am-4pm Tue-Sun) is near the top of the town in the 16th-century Casa Consistorial, which exhibits a rare wooden Mudéjar ceiling. A little higher up is the 12th-century castle (opening hours are sporadic; check at the tourist office), captured by the Christians just eight years before the fall of Granada.

Setenil has some great tapas bars, which are an ideal pit stop while you study its unique urban framework. Start in Restaurante Palermo in Plaza de Andalucía at the top of town and work your way down.

Olvera

A bandit refuge until the mid-19th century, Olvera has come in from the cold and now supports more family-run farming co-ops than anywhere else in Spain. A white town par excellence, it is also renowned for its olive oil and Renaissance church, and for its roller-coaster history, which started with the Romans.

Built on top of an older church, the neoclassical Iglesia Parroquial Nuestra Señora de la Encarnación (Plaza de la Iglesia; ⊙ Mass Sun) was commissioned by the Dukes of Osuna and completed in 1843. Perched above it is the 12th-century Nasrid Castillo Árabe (Arab Castle; admission incl Museo Histórico €3; ⊙ 10am-2pm & 6-9pm). Next door in La Cilla (⊙ 10.30am-2pm & 4-6pm Tue-Sun, to 7pm May-Sep), an old grain store of the Dukes of Osuna, you'll find the fascinating Museo 'La Frontera y los Castillos', the Vía Verde de la Sierra Interpretive Centre relating the natural history of the nearby bike path, and the tourist office. All share the same opening times.

For accommodation try the excellent Hotel Sierra y Cal (☑ 956 13 03 03; www.tugasa. com; s/d €36/60; P❋🖥🏊). Bars and restaurants line Avenida Julian Besteiro, including the wonderfully 'local' Bodega La Pitarra (www.bodegalapitarra.com; Julián Besteiro 44; media raciones €8-10; ⊗12.30-4pm & 7.30-11pm).

ⓘ Getting There & Around

Los Amarillos (☑ 902 21 03 17; www.losamarillos.es) and **Comes** (☑ 902 19 92 08; www.tgcomes.es) run daily buses from Jerez de la Frontera via Arcos de la Frontera to Olvera (€8.22, 2¼ hours, three daily) and Setenil de las Bodegas (€8.88, 2½ hours, three daily). Two of these buses carry on to Málaga (€11, 2¼ hours).

Los Amarillos runs twice-daily buses either way between Zahara de la Sierra and Ronda (€3, one hour). Grazalema has buses to/from Ronda (€2.63, 45 minutes, twice daily); El Bosque (€2.35, 30 minutes, one daily), where you can change for Arcos; and Ubrique/Benaocaz (€2.13, 40 minutes, two daily).

Southern Costa de la Luz

Arriving on the Costa de la Luz from the Costa del Sol is like opening the window in a crowded room and gasping in the early-morning sunlight. Bereft of tacky resorts and unplanned development, suddenly you can breathe again. More to the point, you're unequivocally back in Spain – a world of flat-capped farmers and clacking dominoes, grazing cows and Sunday Mass followed by a furtive slug of dry sherry. Don't ask why these wide yellow sandy beaches and spectacularly located white towns are so deserted. Just get out and enjoy them while you still can.

Vejer de la Frontera

POP 12,800 / ELEV 190M

Vejer – the jaw drops, the eyes blink, the eloquent adjectives dry up. Looming moodily atop a rocky hill above the busy N340, 50km south of Cádiz, this placid and compact white town is something very special. Yes, there's a cool labyrinth of twisting streets, some serendipitous viewpoints and a ruined castle. But Vejer possesses something else – soulfulness, an air of mystery, an imperceptible touch of *duende* (spirit).

◉ Sights

Plaza de España has a fantastical Seville-style terracotta-and-tile fountain and is surrounded by some amazing eating nooks.

Castle   CASTLE
(Calle del Castillo; ⊗approx 10am-9pm Jun-Sep) **FREE** Vejer's much-reworked castle has great views from its battlements. Its small museum (with erratic opening hours) preserves one of the black cloaks that Vejer women wore until just a couple of decades ago (covering everything but the eyes).

Casa del Mayorazgo   HOUSE
(Callejón de La Villa; admission by donation) If the door is open, as it often is, this 15th-century house has a pretty patio and one of just three original towers that kept watch over the city – the views from here, including down onto Plaza de España, are worth the short climb.

⚑ Courses

La Janda   LANGUAGE COURSE
(☑956 44 70 60; www.lajanda.org) Who wouldn't want to study Spanish in Vejer, with its winding streets, authentic bars and proximity to countryside and coast? La Janda's courses stress cultural immersion, integrating everything from cooking classes to Almodóvar movie nights in a lovely old mansion in the village. Prices start at €180 per week (20 lessons).

⌂ Sleeping & Eating

Here are three more reasons to come to Vejer.

Hotel La Casa del Califa   HOTEL €€
(☑956 44 77 30; www.lacasadelcalifa.com; Plaza de España 16; s/d €80/98; ▣@☎) Rambling over several floors, this gorgeous hotel oozes character. Rooms are peaceful and very comfortable, with Islamic decorative touches. Special 'Emir' service (€43) also bags you fresh flowers, chocolates and champagne. Downstairs there's a superb Middle Eastern restaurant, El Jardín del Califa (mains €8-16; ⊗1-4pm & 7.30-11pm; ✎).

★ V...   BOUTIQUE HOTEL €€€
(☑956 45 17 57; www.hotelv-vejer.com; Calle Rosario 11-13; d €219-274; ▣@) V... (that's V for Vejer not V for five, and, yes, the three dots are part of the name) is one of Andalucía's most exquisite creations, an old-world boutique hotel where trendy modern design features (bathtubs in the middle of the room) mix with antique artefacts (doors).

The 12 fine rooms all require double takes, and the communal areas include

DON'T MISS

BAELO CLAUDIA

In the tiny village of Bolonia hidden on a beautiful bay about 20km up the coast from Tarifa (p700), you'll find the ruins of the most complete Roman town yet uncovered in Spain, Baelo Claudia (956 10 67 97; admission €1.50, EU citizens free; 9am-7pm Tue-Sat Mar-May & Oct, to 8pm Tue-Sat Jun-Sep, to 6pm Tue-Sat Nov-Feb, to 2pm Sun year-round).

Baelo Claudia's zenith was in the 1st century AD during the reign of Emperor Claudius (AD 41–54).The site – which affords fine views across the water to Africa – includes a theatre where plays are still sometimes staged, a market, forum, temples, and workshops that turned out the products that made Baelo Claudia famous in the Roman world: salted fish and garum, a prized condiment made from fish entrails. There's a good recently opened museum too.

A hilly 7km side road to Bolonia runs west off the N340, 15km from Tarifa. A couple of local buses run daily from Tarifa to Bolonia in July and August only.

comfy sofas in interesting nooks and a waterfall – wait for it – on a vista-laden roof terrace next to a bubbling jacuzzi.

La Vera Cruz CONTEMPORARY ANDALUCIAN €€
(956 45 16 83; www.restaurantelaveracruz.es; Calle Shelly 1; mains €12-18; noon-4pm Sun-Wed, noon-4pm & 8pm-midnight Thu-Sat) Situated in an old convent with slightly limited opening hours, the 'True Cross' specialises in gourmet tapas such as cold anchovy lasagne and glazed ribs with wasabi purée. Local buzz suggests it's the best in town.

☆ Entertainment

Peña Cultural Flamenca 'El Aguilar de Vejer' FLAMENCO
(Calle Rosario 29; cover charge €3) Part of Vejer's magic is its genuine small-town flamenco scene, which is best observed in this atmospheric old-town bar/performance space. Singing and guitar lessons are offered on Thursday nights. Ask at the tourist office about concerts.

ℹ Information

Buses stop beside the **tourist office** (956 45 17 36; Avenida Los Remedios 2; 10am-2pm daily, 6-8pm Mon-Sat approx May-Oct), about 500m below the town centre. Also here is a large, convenient, free car park.

ℹ Getting There & Away

Comes (902 19 92 08; www.tgcomes.es) buses leave from Avenida Los Remedios. Buses run to Cádiz (one hour) and Barbate (15 minutes) five or six times a day. Buses for Tarifa (45 minutes, 10 daily), Algeciras (1¼ hours, 10 daily), Jerez de la Frontera (1½ hours, two daily), Málaga (2¾ hours, two daily) and Seville (2¼ hours, four

daily) stop at La Barca de Vejer, on the N340 at the bottom of the hill. It's a steep 20-minute walk up to town from here or an equally steep €6 in a taxi.

Los Caños de Meca
POP 300

The 'chilled' beach village of Los Caños straggles along a series of spectacular open beaches southwest of Vejer. Once a hippie hideaway, Los Caños still has a highly alternative, hedonistic scene, especially in summer with its nudist beaches and a strong gay following. Windsurfing, kitesurfing, surfing, horse riding and hikes in the nearby Parque Natural de la Breña y Marismas de Barbate are all among the activities you can pursue here.

◎ Sights & Activities

At the western end of Los Caños a side road, often half-covered in sand, leads out to a lighthouse and the ruins of a watchtower built on a crag or *tómbolo* linked to the mainland by a sand-spit. This is Cabo de Trafalgar, the nearest land-point to the site of the eponymous battle where Admiral Nelson saw off the Spanish and French in 1805. The beach under the cliffs here – Playa del Faro – is a popular nudist spot.

Some 5km along the coast northwest of Los Caños, the long beach at El Palmar has Andalucía's best board-surfing waves from about October to May.

★Parque Natural de la Breña y Marismas de Barbate WALKING
This small coastal park protects important coastal marshes and pine forest from Costa del Sol–type development. Its prime entry

JIMENA DE LA FRONTERA

Tucked away in crinkled hills on the cusp of the Parque Natural Los Alcornocales, Jimena sits in prime cork oak country. Its blanched houses and crumbled castle look out towards Gibraltar and Africa, both magnificently visible from its Nasrid-era citadel. Property-seeking Brits have discovered the town, though it has, so far, managed to keep a Spanish village feel. The walking trails here are very special and include treks along the cross-continental E4 (GR7) path, which bisects the town, and forays out to Bronze Age cave paintings at Laja Alta. Another rare find is Restaurante El Anón (www.hostalanon.com; Consuelo 34; mains €10-15; ⏰1-3.30pm & 8-11.30pm Thu-Tue), a rambling house full of interesting nooks and even more interesting fusion food. It also rents rooms.

The best way to arrive in Jimena is on one of Spain's most delightfully scenic railway lines from Ronda (€7.20, one hour, three daily) and Algeciras (€4.95, 40 minutes, three daily). The station is in the village of Los Ángeles (1km from Jimena).

point is the 7.2km Sendero de Acantilado hike between Los Caños de Meca and Barbate along cliff-tops that rival Cabo de Gata in their serendipity.

The high point of the hike is the Torre de Tajo with its tranquil mirador (lookout) perched above the Atlantic. The path starts just behind Hotel La Breña at the far eastern end of Los Caños de Meca and comes out by Barbate's fishing port.

Escuela de Surf 9 Pies
SURFING

(☏620 10 42 41; www.9piesescueladesurf.com; Avenida de la Playa, El Palmar; board & wetsuit rental per 2/4hr €12/18, classes 1/2 days €28/55) Rents out boards and gives surfing classes and is open all year. It's towards the north end of the beach at El Palmar.

Trafalgar Surf
SURFING

(☏657 88 56 65; www.trafalgarsurf.com; Carretera de la Florida 43, Conil de la Frontera; beginners' classes from €35) Offers classes in English on the beach in Conil de la Frontera, 8km north of Caños.

🛏 Sleeping & Eating

For further accommodation options check www.playasdetrafalgar.com or www.placerdetrafalgar.com.

Hostal Mini-Golf
HOTEL €€

(☏956 43 70 83; www.hostalminigolf.com; Avenida Trafalgar 251; s €35-60, d €45-70; P🅿❄🌐🐕) If you can get past the misleading name (there's no golf or even mini-golf here), this well-positioned hotel with an on-site restaurant where the road forks to Cabo Trafalgar is probably Caños' best midrange crash pad. Kitesurfing central is just 400m down the road.

Las Dunas
CAFE, BAR

(Carretera del Faro de Trafalgar; 📶) Say hola to the ultimate relaxation spot, at least during the day when kiteboarding dudes kick back between white-knuckle sorties launched from the beach outside. There's free wi-fi, sweet tortas and a laid-back, beach-shack feel.

ℹ Getting There & Away

Monday to Friday, there are two Comes buses between Los Caños de Meca and Cádiz (1¼ hours), also stopping in Palmar (15 minutes). There's also one morning bus, Monday to Friday, running between both places. There may be extra services from Cádiz and even Seville from mid-June to early September.

RONDA

POP 37,000 / ELEV 744M

For Ronda, read 'rugged'. The largest of the official white towns enjoys a brawny mountain setting perched spectacularly above the sheer cliffs of the Tajo gorge in the Serranía de Ronda. Supposedly one of Spain's oldest settlements, Ronda has an embattled history infested with bandits, smugglers, warriors and other colourful characters who have all helped promote its romantic image. The stories were not lost on the likes of such writers as Alexandre Dumas, Rainer Maria Rilke, Ernest Hemingway and Orson Welles, who passed through in the 19th and 20th centuries and stoked the image further. Ronda's other forte is bullfighting. The town claims one of Spain's greatest bullfighting legacies enshrined in the tale of two pugnacious local families – the hard-bitten Romero and Ordóñez clans.

These days Ronda, thanks to its proximity to the Costa del Sol, is firmly on the tourist circuit; in summer it turns into a bit of a theme park with buses rolling in from dawn till dusk. However, if you stay around after the last bus has departed you'll get a fleeting sense of the old mountain-inspired magic.

◉ Sights & Activities

Ronda has an abundance of museums for a small town covering subjects as varied as hunting, wine and banditry. Ask at the tourist office about the €10 *Bono Turístico* card.

Plaza de España   SQUARE
Directly across the Puente Nuevo is the main square, Plaza de España, made famous by Hemingway in his novel *For Whom the Bell Tolls*. Chapter 10 tells how early in the Civil War the 'fascists' of a small town were rounded up in the *ayuntamiento,* clubbed and made to walk the gauntlet between two lines of townspeople before being thrown off the cliff.

The episode is based on events that took place here in Plaza de España. What was the *ayuntamiento* is now Ronda's *parador.*

La Ciudad   NEIGHBOURHOOD
Straddling the dramatic gorge and the Río Guadalevín (Deep River) is Ronda's most recognisable sight, the towering Puente Nuevo, best viewed from the Camino de los Molinos, which runs along the bottom of the gorge. The bridge separates the old and new towns. You can learn about its construction at the Centro de Interpretación Puente Nuevo (admission €2; ☺10am-6pm Mon-Fri, 10am-3pm Sat & Sun).

The old town is surrounded by massive fortress walls pierced by two ancient gates: the Islamic Puerta de Almocábar, which in the 13th century was the main gateway to the castle; and the 16th-century Puerta de Carlos V. Inside, the Islamic layout remains intact, and its maze of narrow streets now takes its character from the Renaissance mansions of powerful families whose predecessors accompanied Fernando el Católico in the taking of the city in 1485.

Plaza de Toros   BULLRING
(Calle Virgen de la Paz; admission €6.50; ☺10am-8pm) Ronda's Plaza de Toros is a mecca for bullfighting aficionados. In existence for more than 200 years, it is one of the oldest and most revered bullrings in Spain and has also been the site of some of the most important events in bullfighting history.

Built by Martín Aldehuela, the bullring is universally admired for its soft sandstone hues and galleried arches. At 66m in diameter it is also the largest and, therefore, most dangerous bullring, yet it only seats 5000 spectators – a tiny number compared with the huge 50,000-seater bullring in Mexico City. In July the ring is used for a series of fabulous concerts, and opera.

The on-site Museo Taurino is crammed with memorabilia such as blood-spattered costumes worn by Pedro Romero and 1990s star Jesulín de Ubrique. It also includes photos of famous fans such as Orson Welles and Ernest Hemingway, whose novel *Death in the Afternoon* provides in-depth insight into the fear and tension of the bullring.

Behind the Plaza de Toros, spectacular cliff-top views open out from Paseo de Blas Infante and the nearby Alameda del Tajo park.

Museo Lara   MUSEUM
(www.museolara.org; Calle de Armiñán 29; adult/child €4/2; ☺11am-8pm; ▣) Juan António Lara Jurado has been a collector since the age of 10. Now in his 70s, he still lives above this museum, but his living space is set to shrink as he wants to expand still further. You name it, it is here: priceless, historic collections of clocks, weapons, radios, gramophones, sewing machines, telephones, opera glasses, Spanish fans, scales, cameras and way, way more.

Walks   WALKING TOUR
The tourist office publishes a series of brochures (€5) highlighting eight easy hikes around Ronda, all of which start in the town. Distances range from 2.5km to 9.1km and the walks visit viewpoints, old hermitages and parks. One of the best is the 4.6km SL-A38, which starts at Plaza Campillos near the Palacio de Mondragón before tracking down below the gorge (for the classic bridge photo). After winding past some old mills, it loops back uphill into the New Town.

✦ Festivals & Events

During the first two weeks of September, Ronda's Feria de Pedro Romero (an orgy of partying, including the important Festival de Cante Grande, a flamenco festival) takes place. It culminates in the Corridas Goyesca (bullfights in honour of legendary bullfighter Pedro Romero).

Ronda

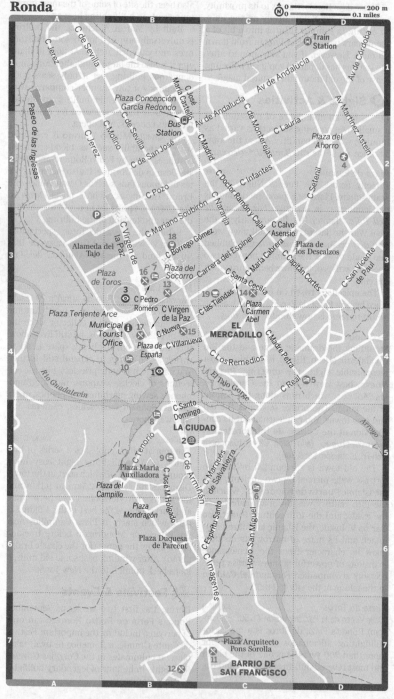

Ronda

🛏 Sleeping

Hotel Hermanos Macias HOTEL €
(☑ 952 87 42 38; www.hermanosmacias.com; Calle Pedro Romero 3; s/d €35/48; P ❄) Located above a popular restaurant and bar, the rooms here are excellent value. Rustic-style and simply furnished, several overlook the bustling pedestrian street.

★**Enfrente Arte** HOTEL €€
(☑ 952 87 90 88; www.enfrentearte.com; Calle Real 40; r incl breakfast €80-90; ❄ @ ☀) On an old cobblestoned street, Belgian-owned Enfrente offers a huge range of facilities and funky modern/Eastern decor. It has a bar, pool, sauna, recreation room, flowery patio with black bamboo, film room and fantastic views out to the Sierra de las Nieves. What's more, the room price includes all drinks, to which you help yourself, and a buffet breakfast.

Hotel San Gabriel HOTEL €€
(☑ 952 19 03 92; www.hotelsangabriel.com; Calle José M Holgado 19; s/d incl breakfast €72/96; ❄ 🛜) This charming hotel is filled with antiques and photographs that offer insight into Ronda's history – bullfighting, celebrities and all. Ferns hang down the huge mahogany staircase, there is a billiard room, a cosy living room stacked with books and a DVD screening room with 10 velvet-covered seats rescued from Ronda's theatre and autographed photos of Bob Hoskins and Isabella Rossellini.

Hotel Alavera de los Baños HOTEL €€
(☑ 952 87 91 43; www.alaveradelosbanos.com; Hoyo San Miguel; s/d incl breakfast €72/97; ❄ 🛜 ☀) Taking its cue from the Arab baths next door, the Alavera de los Baños continues the Hispano-Islamic theme throughout, with Eastern decor and tasty North African–inspired cuisine using predominantly organic foods. Ask for a room on the terrace, as these open out onto a small, lush garden.

Parador de Ronda HOTEL €€€
(☑ 952 87 75 00; www.parador.es; Plaza de España; r €160-171; P ❄ @ 🛜 ☀) Acres of shining marble and deep-cushioned furniture give this modern *parador* a certain appeal. The terrace is a wonderful place to drink in views of the gorge with your coffee or wine, especially at night.

Hotel Montelirio HOTEL €€€
(☑ 952 87 38 55; www.hotelmontelirio.com; Calle Tenorio 8; s/d €100/150; ❄ ☀) Hugging El Tajo gorge, the Montelirio has magical views. The converted *palacio* has been sensitively refurbished, with sumptuous suites. The lounge retains its gorgeous Mudéjar ceiling and opens out onto a terrace complete with plunge pool. The restaurant is similarly excellent.

🍴 Eating

Traditional Ronda food is hearty mountain fare that's big on stews; trout; game such as rabbit, partridge and quail; and, of course, oxtail. The largest concentration of restaurants is situated in the grid east of Plaza de España, though there are some less-heralded gems just south of the old town in the Barrio San Francisco.

★**Bodega San Francisco** TAPAS €
(www.bodegasanfrancisco.com; Calle Ruedo Alameda; raciones €6-10; ⊙1.30-5pm & 8pm-1am Wed-Mon) With three dining rooms and

tables spilling out onto the narrow pedestrian street, this may well be Ronda's top tapas bar. The menu is vast – including nine-plus salad choices – and should suit the fussiest of families. Try the *revuelto de patatas* (scrambled eggs with potatoes and peppers). House wine is good.

Bar Restaurant Almocábar   ANDALUCIAN €
(Calle Ruedo Alameda 5; tapas €1.50, mains €10; ⏱ 1.30-5pm & 8pm-1am Wed-Mon) Almocábar is little touched by the tourist hordes at the top of town. But the tapas are so good that this spot is normally superpacked, and finding a place at the bar can be a challenge. If that's the case, try reserving in the restaurant section *comedor* (dining room).

Faustino   ANDALUCIAN €
(Calle Santa Cecilia; tapas €1.50, raciones €6-8; ⏱ 11.30am-midnight Tue-Sun) This is the real deal, a lively atmospheric tapas bar with plenty of seating space in the open traditional atrium decorated with plants, feria posters and bullfighting and religious pictures. Tapas and *raciones* are generous. Go with the recommendations like *champingnones a la plancha* (grilled mushrooms with lashings of garlic).

The only downside is the uncomfortable, if pretty, rustic-style painted chairs. Ouch!

Nonno Peppe   ITALIAN €
(Calle Nueva 18; pasta dishes from €6; ⏱ 11am-midnight) If you're on a long haul and need a break from tapas, you can't go wrong with the genuine Italian fare served up in this economical place run by a couple from Salerno, near Naples. There's great *spaghetti alla vongole* (with clams), pesto and pizzas, along with homey Italian-style service.

Chocolat   CAFE €
(☑ 952 87 69 84; Carrera de Espinel 9; breakfasts from €2.20; ⏱ 8am-10pm) A funky modern cafe where you can choose from a long list of teas, coffees, breakfasts and a boggling array of cakes and pastries. Prices are refreshingly reasonable.

Restaurante Pedro Romero   ANDALUCIAN €€
(☑ 952 87 11 10; www.rpedroromero.com; Calle Virgen de la Paz 18; menú €16, mains €15-18; ⏱ noon-4.30pm & 7.30-11pm) Opposite the bullring, this celebrated eatery dedicated to bullfighting turns out classic *rondeño* dishes (dishes from Ronda). This is a good place to try the *rabo de toro*, a tender meat dish made from bull's tail. Vegetarians will doubtless prefer

the fried goat-cheese starter served with apple sauce.

Restaurante Tragabuches   CONTEMPORARY SPANISH €€€
(☑ 952 19 02 91; www.tragabuches.com; Calle José Aparício 1; menú €59-87; ⏱ 1.30-3.30pm & 8-10.30pm Tue-Sat) Ronda's best and most famous restaurant is a 180-degree turn away from the ubiquitous 'rustic' look and cuisine. Michelin-starred in 1998, Tragabuches is modern and sleek with an innovative menu to match. Choose from three set menus. People flock here from miles away to taste the food, prepared by its creative chef.

 Drinking

New Baco   BAR
(⏱ 7pm-4am) Get here too early and you may be greeted by football on the big screen, but later on, and most definitely at weekends, there are hot DJs and plenty of dancing from midnight.

Tetería Al Zahra   TEAHOUSE
(Calle las Tiendas 17; ⏱ 4.30pm-midnight) Come here and try a pot of herbal, Moroccan, Pakistani or a host of other teas, all served in pretty Moroccan ceramic teapots and cups and saucers. There are hookahs for smoking, too, and you can settle in for a few hours of sipping, puffing and gossiping.

ⓘ Information

Banks and ATMs are mainly on Calle Virgen de la Paz and Plaza Carmen Abela.
Municipal Tourist Office (www.turismoderonda.es; Paseo de Blas Infante; ⏱ 10am-7.30pm Mon-Fri, 10.15am-2pm & 3.30-6.30pm Sat, Sun & holidays) Helpful and friendly staff with a wealth of information on the town and region.

ⓘ Getting There & Away

BUS

The bus station is at Plaza Concepción García Redondo 2. **Comes** (www.tgcomes.es) has buses to Arcos de la Frontera (€8.75, two hours, two daily), Jerez de la Frontera (€12, three hours, three daily) and Cádiz (€15, two hours, three daily). **Los Amarillos** (www.losamarillos.es) goes to Seville via Algodonales, Grazalema, and to Málaga via Ardales.

TRAIN

Ronda's **train station** (☑ 952 87 16 73; Avenida de Andalucía) is on the line between Bobadilla and Algeciras. Trains run to Algeciras (€10.90,

---

LOCAL KNOWLEDGE

CYCLING THE WHITE TOWNS

One answer to the white town transportation conundrum, where bus services are sketchy and car rental often expensive, is to hire a bicycle. Ronda makes a good base for single or multi-day bicycle excursions thanks to its well-developed tourist infrastructure, geographic location, and ample eating and sleeping options. Locally based Cycle Ronda (☑ 952 87 78 14; www.cycleronda.com; Calle Serrato 3; ⊙ 9.30am-2pm & 5-7pm Mon-Fri) hires bikes for as little as €15 a day and can also provide detailed maps, itineraries, route suggestions and baggage transfers. The white villages of Setenil de las Bodegas, Olvera, Zahara de la Sierra and Grazalema are all reachable in a day from Ronda, though with some long hills and hot summer weather, you might want to take your time and plot a multi-day bike tour.

1¾ hours, three daily) via Gaucín and Jimena de la Frontera. This train ride is incredibly scenic and worth taking just for the views. Other trains depart for Málaga (€9.80, 2¼ hours, three daily), Córdoba (€26, two hours, five daily) and Madrid (€76, four hours, three daily). For Seville and Granada change at Antequera.

ℹ Getting Around

Minibuses operate every 30 minutes to Plaza de España from Avenida Martínez Astein, across the road from the train station.

AROUND RONDA

Ronda is more than just a destination in itself. Surrounded by beautiful mountains, it acts as an ideal launching pad for trips into the parks and white towns of Málaga and Cádiz provinces. Hire a car or, even better, a bike, and strike out in earnest.

This area has many traditional houses converted into gorgeous rural accommodation. For information try Ronda's municipal tourist office or www.serraniaronda.org.

Cueva de la Pileta

Palaeolithic paintings of horses, goats, fish and even a seal, dating from 20,000 to 25,000 years ago, are preserved in this large cave (☑ 952 16 73 43; www.cuevadelapileta.org; Benaoján; adult/child €8/4; ⊙ hourly tours 10am-1pm & 4-6pm; 🅿) 20km southwest of Ronda. You'll be guided by kerosene lamp and one of the knowledgeable Bullón family from the farm in the valley below. A family member found the paintings in 1905. The Cueva de la Pileta is 250m (signposted) off the Benaoján–Cortes de la Frontera road, 4km from Benaoján. Guides speak a little English. If it's busy, you may have to wait, but

you can phone ahead to book a particular time.

Parque Natural Sierra de las Nieves

This precious area of rare natural diversity, a Unesco Biosphere Reserve, also has an unusual history of human endeavour. For hundreds of years before refrigeration, the snow sellers of the region would gather at the end of the winter to shovel tonnes of snow into containers and transport it to huge pits, where it was pressed and compacted to form ice, and tightly covered until summer. Mule teams would then transport huge blocks of ice into neighbouring towns to sell at astronomical prices. Today, this 180-sq-km protected area, southeast of Ronda, offers some excellent walks. Torrecilla (1910m), the highest peak in the western half of Andalucía, is a five- to six-hour (return) walk from Área Recreativa Los Quejigales, which is 10km east by unpaved road from the A376 Ronda–San Pedro de Alcántara road.

Cerro de Hijar (☑ 952 11 21 11; www.cerrodehijar.com/eng; Carretera del Balneario; d/ste €80/90; 🅿 ✴ @ 🛜 🐾), just above the dazzling white village of Tolox and just within the park, sits at 650m above sea level. This tastefully decorated hotel is generous with its room sizes, decoration, sweeping views and the range of activities it cheerfully organises for guests, including mountain biking, guided walks and 4WD excursions.

CÓRDOBA PROVINCE

Ascending over the Sierra Morena from La Mancha, the window into northern Andalucía is Córdoba province, a largely rural area renowned for its olive oil, wine and historic Roman-founded city that, at its zenith, was the capital of Al-Andalus and home to the glittering court of Abd ar-Rahman III.

Córdoba

POP 328,000 / ELEV 110M

Picture a city 500,000-strong, embellished with fine architecture and fuelled by a prosperous and diverse economy. Picture universities and libraries filled with erudite artists and wise philosophers. Picture an Islamic caliphate more advanced and civilised than anything else the world had ever known. Picture Córdoba c AD 975.

OK, so this slightly grainy image may be over 1000 years old now, but enough of ancient Córdoba remains to place it in the contemporary top three drawcards of Andalucía. The centrepiece is the gigantic Mezquita, an architectural anomaly and one of the only places in the world where you can worship Mass in a mosque. Surrounding it is an intricate web of winding streets, geranium-sprouting flower boxes and cool intimate patios that are at their most beguiling in late spring.

Córdoba

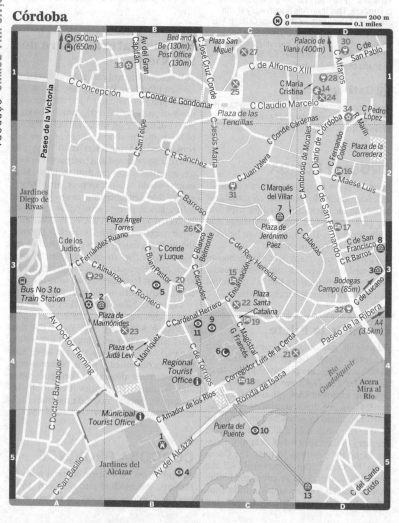

History

The Roman colony of Corduba, founded in 152 BC, became capital of Baetica province, covering most of today's Andalucía. In 711 Córdoba fell to Muslim invaders and became the Islamic capital on the Iberian Peninsula. It was here in 756 that Abd ar-Rahman I set himself up as emir of Al-Andalus.

Córdoba's heyday came under Abd ar-Rahman III (r 912–61). The biggest city in Western Europe had dazzling mosques, libraries, observatories and aqueducts, a university and highly skilled artisans in leather, metal, textiles and glazed tiles. And the multicultural court was frequented by Jewish, Arabian and Christian scholars.

Towards the end of the 10th century, Al-Mansour (Almanzor), a fearsome general, took the reins of power and struck terror into Christian Spain with over 50 *razzias* (raids).

Córdoba's intellectual traditions, however, lived on. Twelfth-century Córdoba produced two of the most celebrated of all Al-Andalus scholars: the Muslim Averroës (Ibn Rushd) and the Jewish Maimonides. These polymaths are best remembered for their philosophical efforts to harmonise religious faith with reason.

In 1236 Córdoba was captured by Fernando III of Castilla and became a provincial town of shrinking importance. The decline began to be reversed only with the arrival of industry in the late 19th century. In common with other Andalucian cities in recent years, the culture, artefacts and traditions of Al-Andalus have enjoyed a growing revival of scholarly and popular interest.

Córdoba, along with 14 other Spanish cities (including Málaga), is aspiring to be the 2016 European Capital of Culture. You can check the campaign's status at www.cordoba2016.es.

◉ Sights & Activities

Opening hours for Córdoba's sights change frequently, so check with the tourist offices for updated times. Most places (except the Mezquita) close on Monday. Closing times are generally an hour or two earlier in winter than summer.

Mezquita MOSQUE
(Mosque; ☎957 47 05 12; www.mezquitadecordoba.org; Calle Cardenal Herrero; adult/child €8/4, 8.30-9.20am Mon-Sat free; ◷8.30am-7pm Mon-Sat, 8.30-10am & 2-7pm Sun Mar-Oct, 8.30am-6pm Mon-Sat, 8.30-1.30am & 3-6pm Sun Nov-Feb) Founded in 785, Córdoba's gigantic mosque is a wonderful architectural hybrid with delicate horseshoe arches making this unlike anywhere else in Spain. The main entrance is the **Puerta del Perdón**, a 14th-century

Córdoba

Mezquita

TIMELINE

600 Foundation of the Christian Visigothic church of St Vincent on the site of the present Mezquita.

785 Salvaging Visigoth and Roman ruins, Emir Abd ar-Rahman I converts the Mezquita into a mosque.

822–5 Mosque enlarged in reign of Abd ar-Rahman II.

912–961 A new minaret is ordered by Abd ar-Rahman III.

961–6 Mosque enlarged by Al-Hakam II who also enriches the **mihrab** ❶.

987 Mosque enlarged for the last time by Al-Mansur Ibn Abi Aamir. With the addition of the **Patio de los Naranjos** ❷, the building reaches its current dimensions.

1236 Mosque reconverted into a Christian church after Córdoba is recaptured by Ferdinand III of Castile.

1271 Instead of destroying the mosque, the overawed Christians elect to modify it. Alfonso X orders the construction of the **Capilla de Villaviciosa** ❸ and **Capilla Real** ❹.

1300s Original minaret is replaced by the baroque **Torre del Alminar** ❺.

1520s A Renaissance-style cathedral nave is added by Charles V. 'I have destroyed something unique to the world,' he laments on seeing the finished work.

2004 Spanish Muslims petition to be able to worship in the Mezquita again. The Vatican doesn't consent.

TOP TIPS

» **Among the oranges** The Patio de los Naranjos can be enjoyed free of charge at any time.

» **Early birds** Entry to the rest of the Mezquita is offered free every morning except Sunday between 8.30am and 9.30am.

» **Quiet time** Group visits are prohibited before 10am, meaning the building is quieter and more atmospheric in the early morning.

The mihrab
Everything leads to the mosque's greatest treasure – a scallop-shell-shaped prayer niche facing Mecca that was added in the 10th century. Cast your eyes over the gold mosaic cubes crafted by imported Byzantium sculptors.

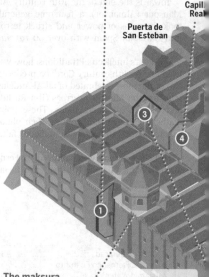

Puerta de San Esteban

Capilla Real

The maksura
Guiding you towards the mihrab, the maksura is a former royal enclosure where the caliphs and their retinues prayed. Its lavish, elaborate arches were designed to draw the eye of worshippers towards the mihrab and Mecca.

The cathedral choir

Few ignore the impressive *coro* (choir): a late-Christian addition dating from the 1750s. Once you've admired the skilfully carved mahogany choir stalls depicting scenes from the Bible, look up at the impressive baroque ceiling.

Torre del Alminar

This is the Mezquita's cheapest sight because you don't have to pay to see it. Rising 93m and viewable from much of the city, the baroque-style bell tower was built over the mosque's original minaret.

The Mezquita arches

No, you're not hallucinating. The Mezquita's most defining characteristic is its unique terracotta-and-white striped arches that support 856 pillars salvaged from Roman and Visigoth ruins. Glimpsed through the dull light they're at once spooky and striking.

Puerta del Perdón

Patio de los Naranjos

Abandon architectural preconceptions all ye who enter here. The ablutions area of the former mosque is a shady courtyard embellished with orange trees that acts as the Mezquita's main entry point.

Capilla Mayor

A Christian monument inside an Islamic mosque sounds beautifully ironic, yet here it is: a Gothic church commissioned by Charles V in the 16th century and planted in the middle of the world's third largest mosque.

Capilla de Villaviciosa

Sift through the building's numerous chapels till you find this gem, an early Christian modification added in 1277 which fused existing Moorish features with Gothic arches and pillars. It served as the Capilla Mayor until the 1520s.

Mudéjar gateway, with the ticket office immediately inside. Also inside the gateway is the aptly named Patio de los Naranjos (Courtyard of the Orange Trees).

Once inside, you can see straight ahead to the mihrab, the prayer niche in the mosque's qibla (the wall indicating the direction of Mecca) that was the focus of prayer. The first 12 transverse aisles inside the entrance, a forest of pillars and arches, comprise the original 8th-century mosque.

In the centre of the building is the Christian cathedral. Just past the cathedral's western end, the approach to the mihrab begins, marked by heavier, more elaborate arches. Immediately in front of the mihrab is the maksura, the royal prayer enclosure (today enclosed by railings) with its intricately interwoven arches and lavishly decorated domes created by Caliph Al-Hakam II in the 960s. The decoration of the mihrab portal incorporates 1600kg of gold mosaic cubes, a gift from the Christian emperor of Byzantium, Nicephoras II Phocas. The mosaics give this part of the Mezquita the aura of a Byzantine church.

After the Christians captured Córdoba, the Mezquita was used as a church. In the 16th century the centre of the building was torn out to allow construction of a cathedral comprising the Capilla Mayor, now adorned with a rich 17th-century jasper and marble *retablo* (altarpiece), and the coro (choir), with fine 18th-century carved mahogany stalls.

Judería   HISTORIC NEIGHBOURHOOD

Jews were among the most dynamic and prominent citizens of Islamic Córdoba. The medieval *judería*, extending northwest from the Mezquita almost to Avenida del Gran Capitán, is today a maze of narrow streets and whitewashed buildings with flowery window boxes.

The beautiful little 14th-century Sinagoga (Calle de los Judíos 20; ⊙9.30am-2pm & 3.30-5.30pm Tue-Sat, 9.30am-1.30pm Sun) FREE is one of only three surviving medieval synagogues in Spain and the only one in Andalucía. In the late 1400s it became a hospital for hydrophobics. Translated Hebrew inscriptions eroded in mid-sentence seem like poignant echoes of a silenced society.

In the heart of the *judería*, and once connected by an underground tunnel to the Sinagoga, is the 14th-century Casa de Sefarad (www.casadesefarad.es; cnr Calles de los Judíos & Averroes; adult/concession €4/3;

⊙11am-6pm Mon-Sat, 11am-2pm Sun). Opened in 2008 on the corner of Calles de los Judíos and Averroes, this small, beautiful museum is devoted to reviving interest in the Sephardic-Judaic-Spanish tradition. There is a refreshing focus on music, domestic traditions and on the women intellectuals (poets, singers and thinkers) of Al-Andalus. A specialist library of Sephardic history is housed here, and there's also a well-stocked shop. A program of live-music recitals and storytelling events runs most of the year.

Alcázar de los Reyes Cristianos   CASTLE

(Castle of the Christian Monarchs; Campo Santo de Los Mártires; admission €4.50, Fri free; ⊙8.30am-8.45pm Tue-Fri, 8.30am-4.30pm Sat, 8.30am-2.30pm Sun; 🖼) Built by Alfonso XI in the 14th century on the remains of Roman and Arab predecessors, the castle began life as a palace. It hosted both Fernando and Isabel, who made their first acquaintance with Columbus here in 1486. Its terraced gardens – full of fish ponds, fountains, orange trees, flowers and topiary – are a pleasure to stroll and a joy to behold from the tower.

A hall here displays some remarkable Roman mosaics, dug up from the Plaza de la Corredera in the 1950s. Most notable is a portrait of mythical couple Polyphemus and Galatea, whose story was later retold by Spanish poet Luis de Góngora.

Puente Romano   BRIDGE

The much-restored Puente Romano (Roman Bridge) crosses the Guadalquivir just south of the Mezquita. Not far downstream, near the northern bank, is a restored Islamic water wheel.

At the southern end of the bridge is the Torre de la Calahorra (☑957 29 39 29; Puente Romano; adult/child €4.50/3; ⊙10am-6pm Oct-Apr, 10am-2pm & 4.30-8.30pm May-Sep), a 14th-century tower with the curious Museo Vivo de Al-Andalus highlighting the intellectual achievements of Islamic Córdoba.

Palacio de Viana   MUSEUM

(www.palaciodeviana.com; Plaza de Don Gome 2; admission whole house/patios only €8/5; ⊙10am-7pm Tue-Sat, 10am-3pm Sun Sep-Jun, 9am-3pm Tue-Sun Jul & Aug) This stunning Renaissance palace is set around 12 beautiful patios that are a pleasure to visit in the spring. Occupied by the Marqueses de Viana until a few decades ago, the 6500-sq-metre building is packed with art and antiques. The whole-house fee covers a one-hour guided tour of the rooms and access to the patios and garden.

Museo Arqueológico   MUSEUM

(Archaeological Museum; Plaza de Jerónimo Páez 7; admission €1.50, EU citizens free; ⊘10am-8.30pm Tue-Sat, 10am-5pm Sun) Calling on the city's Roman and early Moorish roots, Córdoba's recently refurbished archaeology museum brilliantly covers the city's illustrious history with an overriding theme of cultural interchange. The building stands upon an archaeological site, the Roman theatre of Colonia Patricia, and the basement level features a walkway through the ruins.

Museo Julio Romero de Torres   ART GALLERY

(Plaza del Potro 1; admission €4.50, Fri free; ⊘8.30am-8.45pm Tue-Fri, 8.30am-4.30pm Sat, 8.30am-2.30pm Sun) A former hospital houses what is, surprisingly enough, Córdoba's most visited museum, the Museo Julio Romero de Torres, devoted to revered local painter Julio Romero de Torres (1873–1930). Romero de Torres specialised in sensual yet sympathetic portraits of Cordoban women.

In the same building you'll find the **Museo de Bellas Artes** (Plaza del Potro 1; admission €1.50, EU citizens free; ⊘10am-8.30pm Tue-Sat, 10am-5pm Sun), a small collection of works by mainly Córdoban artists.

Centro Flamenco Fosforito   MUSEUM

(✆957 48 50 39; www.centroflamencofosforito.cordoba.es; Plaza del Potro; admission €2; ⊘8.30am-7.30pm Tue-Fri, 8.30am-2.30pm Sat, 9.30am-2.30pm Sun) Possibly the best flamenco museum in Andalucía – which is saying something – this new place benefits from a fantastic location inside the ancient **Posada del Potro**, an inn named-checked by Cervantes in his novel, *Don Quixote*. Touch-screens, rare archive footage and arty displays meticulously explain the building blocks of flamenco and its history, along with the singers, guitarists and dancers who defined it. You'll walk out both enthused *and* wiser.

✿ Festivals & Events

May to July are the chief festival times in Córdoba.

Festival de Los Patios Cordobeses   PATIOS

(Córdoba Courtyard Festival; ⊘May) A 'best patio' competition with many private courtyards open for public viewing till 10pm nightly (till midnight Friday and Saturday). A concurrent cultural program has flamenco concerts set appropriately in the city's grandest patios, gardens and plazas. The tourist office provides a list of the contestants along with a program of events.

Festival Internacional de la Guitarra   MUSIC

(International Guitar Festival; www.guitarracordoba.org; ⊘Jun-Jul) A two-week celebration of the guitar, with live performances of classical, flamenco, rock, blues and more; top names play in the city's concert halls and plazas. Held in the first half of July.

🛏 Sleeping

There is plenty of budget accommodation in Córdoba, though finding single rooms for a decent price is not easy. Booking ahead is wise from March to October and essential during the main festivals.

★ Bed and Be   HOSTEL €

(✆661 42 07 33; www.bedandbe.com; Calle Cruz Conde 22; dm/d with shared bathroom €19/60; ❄🖥🛜) ⬤ A hugely engaging new accommodation option thanks in part to the foresight of owner, José who also runs free evening bike tours around the city. There's an assortment of double and dorm rooms, all super-clean and as gleaming white as a *pueblo blanco*.

Extra value is added with a communal kitchen, lounge area and roof terrace plus various special events regularly organised by José.

Hostal La Fuente   HOTEL €

(✆957 48 78 27; www.hostallafuente.com; Calle San Fernando 51; s/d €35/50; ❄@🛜) A journeyman hotel, though in Córdoba this means you get an airy patio, *azulejos* tiles, exposed brick and interesting architectural details. The rooms are clean and comfortable and the staff quietly helpful. There's some street noise, but it all adds to the brew.

Séneca Hostel   HOSTEL €

(✆957 47 32 34; www.cordoba-hostalseneca.com; Calle Conde y Luque 7; dm/s/d incl breakfast from €18/45/57; 🛜) An upgraded version of a long-time backpackers' haunt, the Séneca occupies a rambling house with typical Moorish elements. A small cafe-bar supplies breakfast and drinks on a marvellous pebbled patio that's filled with greenery, and there's a kitchen available for guest use. Rooms vary widely – some share a bathroom – so have a look around before checking in.

Hotel Mezquita
HOTEL €€

(☑957 47 55 85; www.hotelmezquita.com; Plaza Santa Catalina 1; s/d €42/74; ❄🐾) One of the best deals in town, the Hotel Mezquita stands right opposite its namesake monument, amid the bric-a-brac of the tourism zone. The 16th-century mansion has large, elegant rooms with marble floors, tall doors and balconies, some affording views of the great mosque.

Hotel Hacienda Posada de Vallina
HOTEL €€

(☑957 49 87 50; www.hhposadadevallinacordoba. com; Calle del Corregidor Luís de la Cerda 83; r from €99; P❄@🐾) In an enviable nook on the quiet side of the Mezquita, this cleverly renovated hotel uses portraits and period furniture to enhance a plush and modern interior. There are two levels overlooking a salubrious patio, and the rooms make you feel comfortable but in-period (ie medieval Córdoba). Columbus allegedly once stayed here.

Casa de los Azulejos
HOTEL €€

(☑957 47 00 00; www.casadelosazulejos.com; Calle Fernando Colón 5; s/d incl breakfast from €85/107; ❄@🐾) Mexican and Andalucian styles converge in this stylish hotel, where the patio is all banana trees, ferns and potted palms bathed in sunlight. Colonial-style rooms feature tall antique doors, massive beds, walls in lilac and sky blues, and floors adorned with the beautiful old *azulejos* that give the place its name.

Balcón de Córdoba
BOUTIQUE HOTEL €€€

(☑957 49 84 78; www.balcondecordoba.com; Calle Encarnación 8; r from €197; ❄🐾) Offering top-end boutique luxury, the 10-room Balcón is a riveting place with the obligatory *cordobés* patio and roof terrace, plus slick rooms, antique doorways, and ancient stone relics dotted around as if it was a wing of the nearby archeological museum. Service doesn't miss a beat and there's a substantial breakfast served as a fruity buffet.

✗ Eating

Córdoba has its share of signature food including *salmorejo,* a very thick tomato-based gazpacho (cold vegetable soup), and *rabo de toro* (oxtail). Some restaurants feature recipes from Al-Andalus, such as garlic soup with raisins, honeyed lamb, or meat stuffed with dates and nuts. The local tipple is wine from the nearby regions of Montilla and Moriles; it is similar to sherry but unfortified.

There are lots of places to eat right by the Mezquita, but beware the inflated prices and uninspired food.

Bar Santos
TAPAS €

(Calle Magistral González Francés 3; tortilla €2.50; ⊙2pm-1.30am) Never frequent a restaurant overlooking the Mezquita; they're too touristy. Unless, of course, it's the legendary Santos, which serves the best *tortilla de patata* (potato omelette) in town. Thick wedges are deftly removed from giant wheels of the stuff and customarily served with plastic forks on paper plates to take outside and gaze at the great church/mosque.

La Tortuga
CAFE, BAR €

(☑957 48 19 56; www.latortugacordoba.com; Plaza Marmol de Bañuelos 1; cakes from €1.50; ⊙8am-midnight, to 2am Fri & Sat) Open all hours, but best for breakfast, afternoon tea and cake, or a late-evening tipple, Tortuga is a hip abode amid a cluster of other hip abodes near the Plaza de las Tendillas, the evening meeting point for everyone who matters on Córdoba's social scene.

La Caña de España
INTERNATIONAL €

(☑957 47 04 88; www.lacanadespana.com; Calle Claudio Marcelo 2; mains €6.50; ⊙noon-2am) Recession-busting prices (all dishes are €6.50) and huge portions mean this fast, casual restaurant is always busy, primarily with young Millennials filling up on simple Spanish-international cross-over food.

★ Salmorejería Umami
MODERN ANDALUCIAN €€

(☑957 48 23 47; www.grupoumami.com; Calle Blanco Belmonte 6; mains €14-22; ⊙1-4pm & 8-11.30pm Mon-Sat, 1-4pm Sun) It's new, it's good and it's celebrating what is probably Córdoba's favourite dish: the locally concocted *salmorejo,* a tomato-y version of gazpacho soup that's too thick to drink. The trick ('cos there's always a trick) is that Umami does a good dozen versions of the recipe including avocado, Thai and green-tea flavours. The main dishes are equally imaginative.

Casa Mazal
JEWISH €€

(☑957 94 18 88; www.casamazal.com; Calle Tomás Conde 3; mains €12-15; ⊙12.30-4pm & 7.30-11pm) A meal here makes a fine complement to the nearby Casa de Sefarad museum, as it brings the Sephardic (Judeo-Spanish) tradition to the table. A sort of culinary diaspora,

Sephardic dishes contain elements of Andalucian, Turkish, Italian and North African cuisine, with such varied items as Syrian lentil salad, honeyed eggplant fritters and *minas* (a vegetarian lasagna) on the menu.

Taberna San Miguel El Pisto TAPAS €€
(www.casaelpisto.com/en; Plaza San Miguel 1; tapas €3, media raciones €5-10; ☺noon-4pm & 8pm-midnight) Brimming with local character, El Pisto is one of Córdoba's best *tabernas* (taverns), both in terms of atmosphere and food. Traditional tapas and *media raciones* are done perfectly, and inexpensive Moriles wine is ready in jugs on the bar. Be sure to try the namesake item, a sort of ratatouille topped with a fried egg.

Bodegas Campos ANDALUCIAN €€
(☎957 49 75 00; www.bodegascampos.com; Calle de Lineros 32; tapas €5, mains €13-21; ☺1.30-4.30pm & 8-11.30pm Mon-Sat, 1.30-4.30pm Sun) One of Córdoba's most atmospheric and famous wine cellar-restaurants, this sprawling hall features dozens of rooms and patios, with oak barrels signed by local and international celebrities stacked up alongside. The bodega produces its own house Montilla, and the restaurant, frequented by swankily dressed *cordobeses* (residents of Córdoba), serves up a delicious array of meals.

Amaltea ORGANIC €€
(☎957 49 19 68; Ronda de Isasa 10; mains €10-16; ☺1-4pm & 8pm-late Mon-Sat, 1-4pm Sun; 🍴) This intimate riverside spot specialises in organic food and wine, with a serious Middle Eastern influence (Lebanese-style tabbouleh, couscous). There's a good range of vegetarian fare.

Drinking & Entertainment

Córdoba's liveliest bars are mostly scattered around the newer parts of town and ignite around 11pm to midnight at weekends. Most bars in the medieval centre close around midnight.

★ Cervezas Califa BREWPUB
(Calle Juan Valera 3; ☺12.30-3.30pm & 7.30pm-late) It was probably only a matter of time before the Andalucians came up with their own microbrewery, and here it is. Challenging the hegemony of big-brand *cerveza* brewers, Cruzcampo, these enterprising lads from Córdoba have opened what they're saying is the region's first microbrewery.

In fact, it's more accurately described as a brewpub as they concoct the stuff on the premises. Slide by and try the Rubia, Morena, IPA and Sultana Stout varieties.

La Bicicleta BAR, CAFE
(☎666 54 46 90; Cardenal González 1; ☺10am-late) Supporting Córdoba's effort to enhance its bike-friendliness, this new bar welcomes cyclists (and anyone else who's thirsty) with an array of drinks, snacks and – best of all – large fruity smoothies.

Bodega Guzmán BAR
(Calle de los Judíos 7; ☺noon-4pm & 8pm-midnight Fri-Wed) This atmospheric drinking spot bedecked with bullfighting memorabilia is frequented by both locals and tourists. Montilla wine is dispensed from three giant barrels behind the bar; don't leave without trying some *amargoso* (bitter).

Café Bar Automático MUSIC BAR
(Calle Alfaros 4; ☺4pm-late) This is a low-key spot specialising in wacky cocktails and fruit shakes, with alternative rock over a good sound system.

Bar-Cafetería Soul MUSIC
(Calle de Alfonso XIII 3; ☺9am-3am Mon-Fri, 10am-4am Sat & Sun, closed Aug; 🔊) Quirkily furnished with music to match, this DJ bar gets hotter and busier as the evening progresses. The vibe is friendly and funky.

Gran Teatro de Córdoba THEATRE
(☎957 48 02 37; www.teatrocordoba.com; Avenida del Gran Capitán 3) This theatre hosts a busy program of concerts, theatre, dance and film, mostly geared to popular Spanish tastes.

Jazz Café LIVE MUSIC
(Calle Espartería; ☺8am-late) Not just for jazzbos, this long-standing club is as likely to stage electric blues or belly dancing as Dave Brubeck, attracting a varied crowd until the small hours. Tuesday nights are reserved for jazz jam sessions.

Shopping

Córdoba is known for its *cuero repujado* (embossed leather) goods, silver jewellery (particularly filigree) and attractive pottery. Craft shops congregate around the Mezquita.

Information

Most banks and ATMs are around Plaza de las Tendillas and Avenida del Gran Capitán. The bus and train stations have ATMs.

MEDINA AZAHARA

Even in the cicada-shrill heat and stillness of a summer afternoon, the Medina Azahara (Madinat al-Zahra; admission €1.50, EU citizens free; ⊙ 10am-6.30pm Tue-Sat, to 8.30pm May–mid-Sep, to 2pm Sun) whispers of the power and vision of its founder, Abd ar-Rahman III. The self-proclaimed caliph began the construction of a magnificent new capital 8km west of Córdoba around 936, and took up full residence around 945. Medina Azahara was a resounding declaration of his status, a magnificent trapping of power.

The new capital was amazingly short-lived. Between 1010 and 1013, during the caliphate's collapse, Medina Azahara was wrecked by Berber soldiers. Today, less than a tenth of it has been excavated, and only about a quarter of that is open to visitors.

A new museum on the foundation of one of the excavated buildings blends seamlessly with its surroundings and takes you through the history of the city, with beautifully displayed pieces taken from the site and some amazing interactive displays.

Medina Azahara is signposted on Avenida de Medina Azahara, which leads west out of Córdoba onto the A431.

A taxi costs €37 for the return trip, with one hour to view the site, or you can book a three-hour coach tour for €8.50 online at www.turismodecordoba.org.

Hospital Reina Sofia (☑957 21 70 00; Avenida de Menéndez Pidal) Located 1.5km southwest of the Mezquita.

Municipal Tourist Office (☑902 201774; www.turismodecordoba.org; ⊙9am-2pm & 5-7pm) Opposite the Alcázar de los Reyes Cristianos.

Policía Nacional (☑091; Avenida Doctor Fleming 2) The main police station.

Post Office (Calle José Cruz Conde 15; ⊙8.30am-9.30pm Mon-Fri, 8.30am-2pm Sat)

Regional Tourist Office (Calle de Torrijos 10; ⊙9am-7.30pm Mon-Fri, 9.30am-3pm Sat, Sun & holidays) Inside the Palacio Episcopal.

ⓘ Getting There & Away

BUS

The bus station is next to the train station. Each bus company has its own terminal. **Alsa** (www.alsa.es) runs services to Seville (€12, 1¾ hours, seven daily), Granada (€15, 2¾ hours, eight daily), Málaga (€15, 2¾ hours, four daily) and Baeza (€11, 2½ hours, two daily). **Secorbus** (☑902 22 92 92; www.socibus.es) operates buses to Madrid (€16, 4½ hours, six daily). **Empresa Carrera** (www.autocarescarrera.es) heads south, with several daily buses to Priego de Córdoba, Cabra, Zuheros and Iznájar.

TRAIN

Córdoba's **train station** (☑957 40 02 02; Glorieta de las Tres Culturas) is on the high-speed AVE line between Madrid and Seville. Rail destinations include Seville (€30, 45 minutes, every 30 minutes), Madrid (€62, 1¾, every 30 minutes), Málaga (€27, one hour, 16 daily) and Barcelona (€115, 4½ hours, seven daily). For Granada, change at Bobadilla.

ⓘ Getting Around

Bus 3 (€1.20), from the street between the train and bus stations, runs to Plaza de las Tendillas and down Calle de San Fernando, east of the Mezquita. For the return trip, you can pick it up on Ronda de Isasa, just south of the Mezquita.

Taxis from the bus or train station to the Mezquita cost around €7.

For drivers, Córdoba's one-way system is nightmarish, but routes to many hotels and *hostales* are fairly well signposted with a 'P' if they have parking (€12 to €18 per day).

Bicycle Córdoba has installed bicycle lanes throughout town, though they're still little used. Bike rentals are available from **Solobici** (☑957 48 57 66; www.solobici.net; María Cristina 5; per day €15; ⊙10am-4pm Tue-Sun), which also offers regional bike tours.

Parque Natural Sierras Subbéticas

Verde que te quiero verde (Green, how I love you green). You could be forgiven for breaking into poetic stanzas from Lorca as you walk, cycle or horseride your way through the emerald Subbéticas Natural Park, a cluster of craggy uplands in southern Córdoba province speckled with lakes, wild olive trees and quintessential white villages.

Despite being one of Andalucía's least-visited parks, the Subbéticas is not lacking in trails, many of which emanate from the spectacular white town of Zuheros. The park's easiest and best-marked path is the Vía Verde de la Subbética (www.viasverdes. com), a greenway that follows an old railway line and skirts the northern border of the park. Aside from utilising old bridges, tunnels and viaducts, the Vía Verde boasts novel cafes located in old station buildings and is equipped with bike-hire outlets, kilometre markers and numerous informative mapboards. It's impossible to get lost.

For a nature-discovering day-trip from Córdoba, take a bus to the village of Cabra and hike the Vía Verde 16km east to Zuheros, where you can catch a bus back to Córdoba.

For the more adventurous, the Vía Verde de la Subbética – which measures 58km in its entirety – connects with the adjacent Vía Verde del Aceite to form a 112km unbroken path between Jaén and Puente Genil, the longest in Andalucía.

Zuheros

POP 746 / ELEV 625M

Rising above the low-lying *campiña* (countryside) south of the CO241, Zuheros sits in a dramatic location, crouching in the lee of a craggy mountain. It's approached via a steep road through a series of hairpin bends and provides a beautiful base for exploring the northern portion of the Parque Natural Sierras Subbéticas. Zuheros is also renowned for its local organic cheeses.

◉ Sights & Activities

Zuheros has a delightfully relaxed atmosphere. All around the western escarpment on which it perches are miradors (lookouts) with exhilarating views of the dramatic limestone crags that tower over the village and create such a powerful backdrop for Zuheros' castle.

Museo Arqueológico   MUSEUM
(Plaza de la Paz 2; admission €2; ⊙ 10am-2pm & 5-9pm Tue-Fri) Though tiny, the local museum still manages to cough up some crumbling Bronze-Age artefacts unearthed in the nearby Cueva de los Murciélagos (Cave of the Bats), plus a couple of Roman relics. Admission also includes entry to the Castillo de Zuheros and its panoramic views. The museum doubles as a tourist office.

Cueva de los Murciélagos   CAVE
(Cave of the Bats; ☑ 957 69 45 45; www.cuevadelos-murcielagos.com; adult/child €5/4; ⊙ guided tours 11am, 12.30pm & 2pm year-round, 5pm & 6.30pm Apr-Sep, 4pm & 5.30pm Oct-Mar) Carved out of the limestone massif some 4km above the village is this extraordinary cave. From the vast hall at the start of the tour, it's an almost 500m hike through a series of corridors filled with fantastic rock formations. Traces of rock paintings showing abstract figures of goats dating from the Neolithic period can be admired along the way.

Visits to the cave are by guided tour only and can be reserved by phone or via the website.

🛏 Sleeping & Eating

Hotel Zuhayra   HOTEL €€
(☑ 957 69 46 93; www.zercahoteles.com; Calle Mirador 10; s/d €55/70; ❄ 🖭) A short distance below Zuheros' castle, this hotel holds a privileged perch with breathtaking views of the countryside from every room. Featuring a good restaurant, it makes an excellent base for exploring the cliffs and caves.

The friendly proprietors, the Ábalos brothers (who speak English), offer copious information on walking routes and can set you up with a local guide.

Asador Los Palancos   ANDALUCIAN €€
(☑ 957 69 45 38; Plaza La Paz 1; mains €10-20; ⊙ noon-11pm) Cut into the cliff with astounding views of tens of thousands of olive trees, this place is a little pricey, but good for a drink and a taste of the local goats' cheese best served smeared over a salad. The walls are covered with photos of former guests, football players David Beckham, Xabi Alonso and Zinedine Zidane among them.

ⓘ Getting There & Away

Buses depart from opposite Museo de Costumbres y Artes Populares, on the northeast side of the village.

Empresa Carrera (☑ 957 50 03 02) runs two to four daily buses to/from Córdoba (€5.75, two hours).

Granada & South Coast Andalucía

Includes ➡

Best Places to Stay

➡ Hotel Hospes Palacio de Los Patos (p669)

➡ Carmen de la Alcubilla del Caracol (p666)

➡ Hotel Real de Poqueira (p679)

➡ Hotel Misiana (p701)

Best Places for Churros

➡ Gran Café Bib-Rambla (p671)

➡ Casa Aranda (p687)

➡ Café Colón (p719)

➡ Café Futbol (p669)

Why Go?

From sprawling coastal condo complexes where Spanish is the second or third language to mountain villages barely changed since Federico Lorca penned his rural trilogy, eastern and southern Andalucía harbour microcosms of Spain, both antediluvian and super-modern. There's the Afro-European cross-fertilisation of Moorish Granada, the fiercely traditional port city of Málaga, sun-kissed tomato-growing Almería, and the shamelessly unsubtle resorts of the Costa del Sol.

Incorporating the four provinces of Málaga, Granada, Jaén and Almería, this region leaves no one uncatered for. Golf fanatics: pack your clubs. Nightclub-loving beach bums: commandeer the sun lounger. Solitude-seeking outdoor types: pack a day bag and find a natural park to get lost in. Attracting all types, half of this part of Andalucía is worryingly overdeveloped; the other half remains innately Spanish and largely ignored by unknowing outsiders. Weave carefully between the two and find your own Spanish spirit.

When to Go
Granada

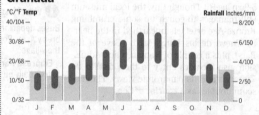

Mar–Apr A time of festivals and processions, but prices go up. Book ahead.

May–Jun The weather's bearable; there are plenty of activities if you don't mind the crowds.

Nov–Feb Mild winter weather. Accommodation prices fall. Go skiing in the Sierra Nevada.

Wine Regions

Eastern Andalucía has two *Dominiaciónes de Origen* (DO), Málaga and Sierras de Málaga, and a long wine-making tradition that has had its peaks and troughs, but is currently enjoying something of a renaissance. The region is known for its sweet dessert wines made from moscatel and Pedro Ximénez grapes. With a high sugar content, the wines are dark, full-bodied and pair well with dried fruit, chocolate and local pâtés.

FEDERICO GARCÍA LORCA

It is debatable whether you can truly understand modern Andalucía without some knowledge of Spain's greatest poet and playwright, Federico García Lorca (1898–1936). Lorca epitomised many of Andalucía's potent hallmarks – passion, ambiguity, exuberance and innovation – and brought them skilfully to life in a litany of precocious works. Early popularity was found with *El romancero gitano* (Gypsy Ballads), a 1928 collection of verses on Roma themes, full of startling metaphors yet crafted with the simplicity of a flamenco song. Between 1933 and 1936 he wrote the three tragic plays for which he is best known: *Bodas de sangre* (Blood Wedding), *Yerma* (Barren) and *La casa de Bernarda Alba* (The House of Bernarda Alba) – brooding and dark but dramatic works dealing with themes of entrapment and liberation. Granada produced, inspired and ultimately destroyed Lorca (he was executed by Nationalists there in 1936), and this is the city where his legacy remains most evident.

Churros

Supposedly invented by Spanish shepherds centuries ago, churros are long thin doughnut-like strips that are deep-fried in olive oil and then eaten as a snack dipped in coffee or – even better – thick hot chocolate. In Andalucía churros are enjoyed for breakfast or during the early evening *merienda* (afternoon snack). Good churros cafes or *churrerías* are ubiquitous in the region, although Granada is often held up as the churros capital, in particular Plaza Bib-Rambla and its eponymous cafe (p671). Casa Aranda (p687) in Málaga is another legendary churros spot. The *tejerngo* is a distinctively Andalucían version of the churro, a lighter, fluffier doughnut strip rolled into a large wheel.

OLIVE OIL

Jaén province's 40 million olive trees provide about half of Andalucía's olive oil, one-third of Spain's and 10% of that used in the entire world.

GRANADA & SOUTH COAST ANDALUCÍA

Wild Andalucía

➜ Wildlife-watching in Parque Natural de las Sierras de Cazorla, Segura y Las Villas (p715).

➜ Diving in La Herradura (p680).

➜ Rock climbing in the El Chorro gorge (p695).

➜ Hiking the GR-7 in Las Alpujarras (p677).

Top Five Food Experiences

➜ Enjoying churros dipped in hot chocolate in Granada.

➜ Eating sardines straight off the grill at a *chiringuito* (beach bar) in Málaga.

➜ Dipping your bread in fruity, green, extra-virgin olive oil in Jaén.

➜ Tasting Arabic sweets in a Granada *tetería* (teahouse).

➜ Going in search of free tapas in Granada.

Best Hikes

➜ Mediterranean Steps (p706)

➜ El Chorro-Bobastro (p695)

➜ San José-Isleta del Moro (p723)

➜ Río Borosa (p716)

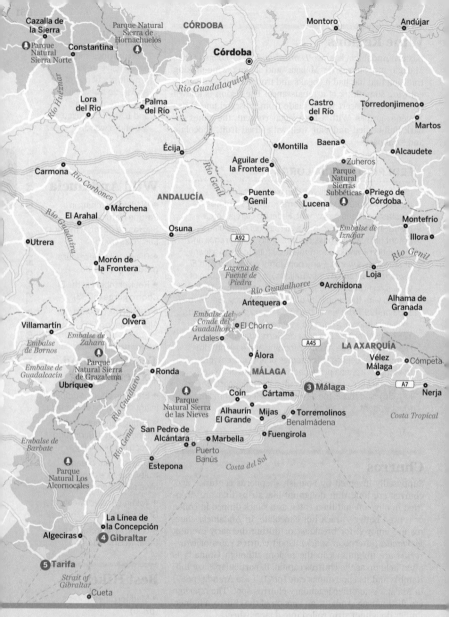

Granada & Andalucía's South Coast Highlights

1 Following the masses and making a pilgrimage to Alhambra in **Granada** (p654), then joining 300 others in the Plaza Bib-Rambla for churros dipped in hot chocolate.

2 Going long-distance hiking along the coast in **Cabo de Gata** (p721).

3 Sifting through the array of art galleries and museums in the city of **Málaga** (p681).

4 Climbing the Mediterranean Steps in **Gibraltar** (p703) and gazing out at Africa, the jaws of the Mediterranean and huge flocks of gliding seabirds.

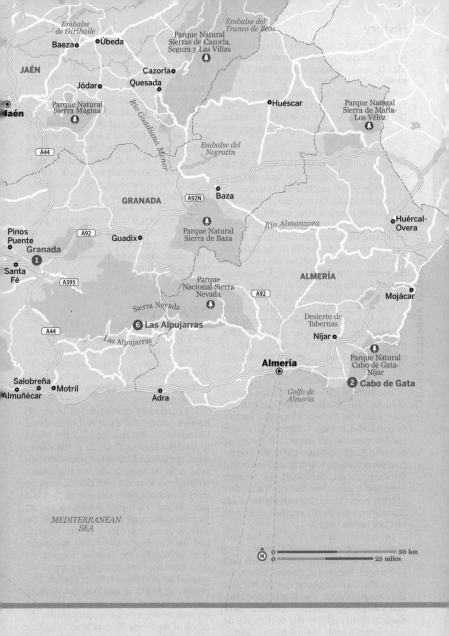

Embalse de Giribaile

Baeza • Úbeda •

JAÉN

Parque Natural
Sierras de Cazorla,
Segura y Las Villas

Embalse del
Tranco de Beas

Jódar •
Cazorla •
Quesada •

Jaén •

Parque Natural
Sierra Mágina

Huéscar •

Parque Natural
Sierra de María-
Los Vélez

Río Guadiana Menor

Embalse del
Negratín

A44

GRANADA

A92N

Baza •

Parque Natural
Sierra de Baza

Río Almanzora

Huércal-
Overa •

Pinos
Puente •

A92

Guadix •

1 Granada

Santa
Fé •

A395

Sierra Nevada

Parque
Nacional Sierra
Nevada

ALMERÍA

Mojácar •

A44

Las Alpujarras

6 Las Alpujarras

A92

Desierto de
Tabernas

Níjar •

Almería

Parque Natural
Cabo de Gata-
Níjar

Salobreña •
Almuñécar •

Motril •

Adra •

Golfo de
Almería

2 Cabo de Gata

MEDITERRANEAN
SEA

N 0 ————————————— 50 km
   0 ————————————— 25 miles

5 Trying your hand
windsurfing, diving, whale-
watching or horse-riding
in adventure nexus **Tarifa**
(p700).

6 Going shopping for local
handicrafts in the lofty villages
of **Las Alpujarras** (p677).

History

Cave paintings found in the Cueva de Nerja on Andalucía's southern coast date back 25,000 years, making them some of the world's oldest. Indeed, Nerja's caves were occupied by our prehistoric ancestors for thousands of years and remains found there illustrate a trajectory of human evolution from simple hunter-gatherers to Bronze Age potters and weavers.

Phoenician traders settled along Andalucía's coastline between the 10th and 7th centuries BC founding the settlements of Sexi (Almuñécar) and Malaka (Málaga).

Eastern Andalucía was quickly conquered by Muslim invaders who surged onto the Iberian Peninsula from Africa in 711. Córdoba became the leading city of Islamic Spain, but was replaced by Seville in the 13th century. Nasrid Muslim culture enjoyed a late flowering in the independent Kingdom of Granada in the 14th and 15th centuries, during which time the Alhambra was built.

While the province of Jaén fell early to the Christian forces soon after they triumphed at the Battle of Navas de Tolosa in 1212, much of southern and eastern Andalucía stayed under Muslim rule for another 250 years. Málaga remained Moorish until 1478, while Almería fell in 1489.

The Emirate of Granada, the last bastion of Al-Andalus (Muslim-controlled Spain), finally fell to the Catholic Monarchs, Fernando and Isabel, in 1492. Columbus' landing in the Americas the same year shifted regional power to Seville and later Cádiz, the Andalucian ports through which Spain's trade with the Americas was conducted, and Granada went into a long, slow decline. Spain's final Muslim enclaves, in the mountains of Las Alpujarras, were finally crushed during the Morisca revolts in 1568-71.

During the civil war (1936–39), the traditionally conservative city of Granada along with most of Western Andalucía fell early to Franco's Nationalist forces. Málaga was taken after heavy fighting in 1937, but eastern Andalucía along with Madrid, Barcelona and Valencia remained in Republican hands until 1939. Indeed, the city of Almería, despite being heavily shelled by the German Navy, was one of the last cities in Spain to surrender to the Fascists.

After Spain's 'hungry years' in the 1950s and '60s when huge numbers of Andalucians moved north or emigrated, Andalucía's coastline became the focus of the new tourist boom. Former fishing villages along the Costa del Sol were turned into massive tourist resorts, a development that brought big economic benefits but posed questions about sustainability, urbanisation and cultural authenticity.

After Spain's entry into the EU in 1986, many of the original tourists put down roots, investing in houses and apartments mainly on the Costa del Sol. As a result, the number of Andalucía's foreign residents grew eightfold between the mid-1990s and the early 2010s to over 700,000, the vast bulk of them living in the provinces of Jaén, Granada, Málaga and Almería.

Andalucía has been hit hard by Spain's recent recession, with unemployment peaking at 33% and nudging up to 58% among the region's youth. The financial squeeze has also caused some of the region's expats to up sticks and go home.

GRANADA

POP 258,000 / ELEV 685M

Read up on your Nasrid history, slip a copy of Federico Lorca's *Gypsy Ballads* into your bag, and acquire a working knowledge of Andalucía's splendid Moorish architectural heritage; Granada is calling and its allure is hard to ignore.

Internationally revered for its lavish Alhambra palace, and enshrined in medieval history as the last stronghold of the Moors in Western Europe, Granada is the darker more complicated cousin of sunny, exuberant Seville. Humming with a feisty cosmopolitanism and awash with riddles, question marks, contradictions and myths, this is a place to put down your guidebook and let your intuition lead the way – through the narrow ascending streets of the Albayzín and the tumbling white-walled house gardens of the Realejo quarter. Elegant yet edgy, grandiose but gritty, monumental but marked by pockets of stirring graffiti, 21st-century Granada is anything but straightforward. Instead, this sometimes stunning, sometimes ugly city set spectacularly in the crook of the Sierra Nevada is an enigmatic place where – if the mood is right – you sense you might find something that you've long been looking for. A free tapa, perhaps? An inspirational piece of street art? A flamenco performance that finally unmasks the intangible spirit of *duende*?

Endowed with relics from various epochs of history, there's lots to do and plenty to admire in Granada: the mausoleum of the Catholic Monarchs, old-school bars selling generous tapas, bohemian *teterías* where Arabic youths smoke *cachimbas* (shisha pipes), and an exciting nightlife that bristles with the creative aura of the counterculture. Make no mistake, you'll fall in love here, but you'll spend days and weeks trying to work out why. Best idea – don't bother. Instead, immerse yourself in the splendour, and leave the poetic stanzas to the aesthetes. 'Your elegy, Granada, is spoken by the stars which from the heavens perforate your black heart', wrote Lorca, Granada's most famous man of letters. It's the perfect coda.

History

Granada's history reads like a thriller. Granada began life as an Iberian settlement in the Albayzín district. Muslim forces took over from the Visigoths in 711, with the aid of the Jewish community around the foot of the Alhambra hill in what was called Garnata al Jahud, from which the name Granada derives; *granada* also happens to be Spanish for pomegranate, the fruit on the city's coat of arms.

After the fall of Córdoba (1236) and Seville (1248), Muslims sought refuge in Granada, where Mohammed ibn Yusuf ibn Nasr had set up an independent emirate. Stretching from the Strait of Gibraltar to east of Almería, this 'Nasrid' emirate became the final remnant of Al-Andalus, ruled from the increasingly lavish Alhambra palace for 250 years. Granada became one of the richest cities in medieval Europe.

However, in the 15th century the economy stagnated and violent rivalry developed over the succession. One faction supported the emir, Abu al-Hasan, and his harem favourite, Zoraya. The other faction backed Boabdil, Abu al-Hasan's son by his wife Aixa. In 1482 Boabdil rebelled, setting off a confused civil war. The Christian armies invading the emirate took advantage, besieging towns and devastating the countryside, and in 1491 they finally laid siege to Granada. After eight months, Boabdil agreed to surrender the city in return for the Alpujarras and 30,000 gold coins, plus political and religious freedom for his subjects. On 2 January 1492 the conquering Catholic Monarchs, Fernando and Isabel, entered Granada ceremonially in Muslim dress. They set up court in the Alhambra for several years.

Jews and Muslims were steadily persecuted, and both groups were expelled by the 17th century. Granada sank into a deep decline until the Romantics revived interest in its Islamic heritage during the 1830s, when tourism took hold.

When the Nationalists took over Granada at the start of the civil war, an estimated 4000 *granadinos* (residents of Granada) with left or liberal connections were killed, among them Federico García Lorca. Granada has a reputation for political conservatism.

◉ Sights & Activities

Most major sights are within walking distance of the city centre, though there are buses to save you walking uphill.

◉ Alhambra & Realejo

★**Alhambra**   PALACE
(☏902 441221; www.alhambra-tickets.es; adult/child under 12yr €14/free, Generalife only €7; ⏲8.30am-8pm 15 Mar-14 Oct, to 6pm 15 Oct-14 Mar, night visits 10-11.30pm Tue-Sat Mar-Oct, 8-9.30pm Fri & Sat Oct-Mar) The Alhambra, Andalucian poet Federico Lorca once declared, is where the water from the Sierra Nevada's bubbling streams 'lies down to die' and where Granada's air is 'so beautiful, it is almost thought'. Part palace, part fort, part World Heritage site, part lesson in medieval architecture, the Alhambra has long enchanted a never-ending line of expectant visitors. As a historic monument, it is unlikely it will ever be surpassed – at least not in the lifetime of anyone reading this book.

As a tourist sight, it is an essential pilgrimage and, as a result, predictably crowded. At the height of summer, some 6000 visitors tramp through daily, making it difficult to pause to inspect a pretty detail, much less mentally transport yourself to the 14th century. Schedule a visit in quieter months, if possible; if not, then book in advance for the very earliest or latest time slot.

The Alhambra takes its name from the Arabic *al-qala'a al-hamra* (Red Castle). The first palace on the site was built by Samuel Ha-Nagid, the Jewish grand vizier of one of Granada's 11th-century Zirid sultans. In the 13th and 14th centuries the Nasrid emirs turned the area into a fortress-palace complex, adjoined by a village, of which only ruins remain. After the Reconquista (Christian reconquest), the Alhambra's mosque

Granada

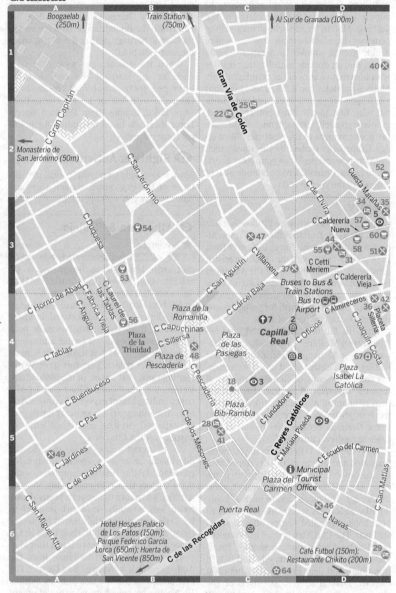

was replaced with a church, and the Convento de San Francisco (now the Parador de Granada) was built. Carlos I (also known as the Habsburg emperor Charles V), grandson of the Catholic Monarchs, had a wing of the palaces destroyed to make space for his huge Renaissance work, the Palacio de Carlos V. During the Napoleonic occupation, the Alhambra was used as a barracks and nearly blown up. What you see today has been heavily but respectfully restored.

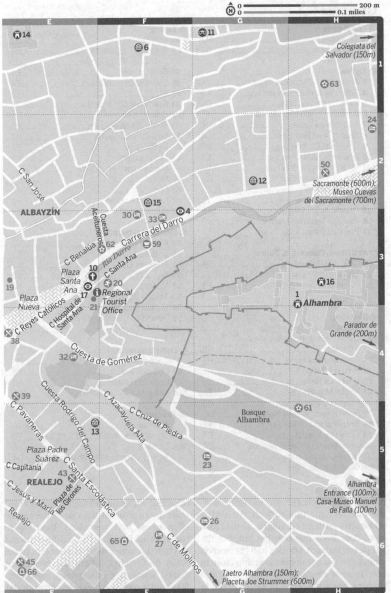

⇒ Palacios Nazaríes

The central palace complex is the pinnacle of the Alhambra's design.

Entrance is through the 14th-century **Mexuar**, perhaps an antechamber for those awaiting audiences with the emir. Two cen-turies later, it was converted into a chapel, with a prayer room at the far end. Look up here and elsewhere to appreciate the geo-metrically carved wood ceilings. From the Mexuar, you pass into the **Patio del Cuarto Dorado**. It appears to be a forecourt to the

Granada

◎ Top Sights

◎ Sights

◎ Activities, Courses & Tours

◎ Sleeping

◎ Eating

◎ Drinking & Nightlife

◎ Entertainment

◎ Shopping

main palace, with the symmetrical doorways to the right, framed with glazed tiles and stucco, setting a cunning trap: the right-hand door leads nowhere but out, but the left passes through a dogleg hall (a common strategy in Islamic domestic architecture to keep interior rooms private) into the **Patio de Arrayanes**, the centre of a palace built in the mid-14th century as Emir Yusuf I's private residence.

Rooms (probably used for lounging and sleeping) look onto the rectangular pool edged in myrtles, and traces of cobalt blue paint cling to the *muqarnas* (honeycomb vaulting) in the side niches on the north end. Originally, all the walls were lavishly coloured; with paint on the stucco-trimmed walls in the adjacent **Sala de la Barca**, the effect would have resembled flocked wallpaper. Yusuf I's visitors would have passed through this annex room to meet him in the Salón de Comares, where the marvellous domed marquetry ceiling uses more than 8000 cedar pieces to create its intricate star pattern representing the seven heavens.

Adjacent is the **Patio de los Leones** (Courtyard of the Lions), built in the second half of the 14th century under Muhammad V at the political and artistic peak of Granada's emirate. But the centrepiece, a fountain that channelled water through the mouths of 12 marble lions, dates from the 11th century. The courtyard layout, using the proportions of the golden ratio, demonstrates the complexity of Islamic geometric design – the varied columns are placed in such a way that they are symmetrical on numerous axes.

Walking counterclockwise around the patio, you first pass the Sala de Abencerrajes. The Abencerraje family supported the young Boabdil in a palace power struggle between him and his own father, the reigning sultan. Legend has it that the sultan had the traitors killed in this room, and the rusty stains in the fountain are the victims' indelible blood. But the multicoloured tiles on the walls and the great octagonal ceiling are far more eye-catching. In the Sala de los Reyes (Hall of the Kings) at the east end of the patio, the painted leather ceilings depict 10 Nasrid emirs.

On the patio's north side, doors once covered the entrance to the Sala de Dos Hermanas (Hall of Two Sisters). The walls are adorned with local flora – pine cones and acorns – and the band of calligraphy at eye level, just above the tiles, is a poem praising Muhammad V for his victory in Algeciras in 1369, a rare triumph this late in the Islamic game. The dizzying ceiling is a fantastic *muqarnas* dome with some 5000 tiny cells. The carved wood screens in the upper level enabled women (and perhaps others involved in palace intrigue) to peer down from hallways above without being seen. At the far end, the tile-trimmed Mirador de Lindaraja was a lovely place for palace denizens to look onto the garden below. Traces of paint still cling to the window frames, and a few panels of coloured glass set in the wood ceiling cast a warm glow.

From the Sala de Dos Hermanas a passageway leads past the domed roofs of the baths on the level below and into rooms built for Carlos I in the 1520s and later used by Washington Irving. From here you descend to the pretty Jardin de Lindaraja. In the southwest corner is the bathhouse – you can't enter, but you can peer in at the rooms lit by star-shaped skylights.

You emerge into an area of terraced gardens created in the early 20th century, and the reflecting pool in front of the small Palacio del Partal (Palace of the Portico), the oldest surviving palace in the Alhambra, from the time of Mohammed III (r 1302–09). You can leave the gardens by a gate facing the Palacio de Carlos V or continue along a path to the Generalife.

GRANADA & SOUTH COAST ANDALUCÍA GRANADA

ℹ ALHAMBRA ADMISSION

Some areas of the Alhambra can be visited at any time free of charge, but the highlight areas can be entered only with a ticket. Up to 6600 tickets are available for each day. About one third of these are sold at the ticket office on the day, but they sell out early, especially in high season (March to October) when you need to start queuing by 7am to be reasonably sure of getting one.

It's highly advisable to book in advance (€1.40 extra per ticket). You have a choice of booking online, by phone, via a cash machine, or in person:

Alhambra Advance Booking (☑ 902 888001, for international calls 0034 934 92 37 50; www.alhambra-tickets.es; ⊙ 9am-8pm) Book online or by phone up to three months in advance.

Servicaixa (www.servicaixa.com) Buy tickets in advance from Servicaixa cash machines.

Tienda Librería de la Alhambra (p673) Buy tickets in advance at this friendly shop near Plaza Nueva.

For internet or phone bookings you need a Visa card, MasterCard or Eurocard. You receive a reference number, which you must show, along with your passport, national identity card or credit card, at the Alhambra ticket office when you pick up the ticket on the day of your visit.

The Palacio Nazaríes is also open for night visits (⊙ 10-11.30pm Tue-Sat Mar-Oct, 8-9.30pm Fri & Sat Nov-Feb). Tickets cost the same as daytime tickets: the ticket office opens 30 minutes before the palace's opening time, closing 30 minutes after it, or you can book online.

Buses 30 and 32 (€1.20) both run between Plaza Nueva and the Alhambra ticket office every five to nine minutes from 7.15am to 11pm, or it's an easy and pleasant walk up the Cuesta de Gomérez from Plaza Nueva.

Alhambra

TIMELINE

900 The first reference to al-qala'at al-hamra (red castle) atop Granada's Sabika Hill.

1237 Founder of the Nasrid dynasty, Muhammad I, moves his court to Granada. Threatened by belligerent Christian armies he builds a new defensive fort, the **Alcazaba** ❶.

1302–09 Designed as a summer palace-cum-country estate for Granada's foppish rulers, the bucolic **Generalife** ❷ is begun by Muhammad III.

1333–54 Yusuf I initiates the construction of the **Palacio Nazaríes** ❸, still considered the highpoint of Islamic culture in Europe.

1350–60 Up goes the **Palacio de Comares** ❹, taking Nasrid lavishness to a whole new level.

1362–91 The second coming of Muhammad V ushers in even greater architectural brilliance exemplified by the construction of the **Patio de los Leones** ❺.

1527 The Christians add the **Palacio de Carlos V** ❻. Inspired Renaissance palace or incongruous crime against Moorish art? You decide.

1829 The languishing, half-forgotten Alhambra is 'rediscovered' by American writer Washington Irving during a protracted sleep-over.

1954 The Generalife gardens are extended southwards to accommodate an outdoor theatre.

TOP TIPS

» **Queue-dodger** Reserve tickets in advance online at www.alhambra-tickets.es

» **Money-saver** You can visit the general areas of the palace free of charge any time by entering through the Puerta de Justica.

» **Stay over** Two fine hotels are encased in the grounds: Parador de Granada (expensive) and Hotel América (more economical).

Sala de la Barca
Throw your head back in the anteroom to the Comares Palace where the gilded ceiling is shaped like an up-turned boat. Destroyed by fire in the 1890s, it has been painstakingly restored.

Mexuar

Patio de Machuca

Palacio de Carlos V
It's easy to miss the stylistic merits of this Renaissance palace added in 1527. Check out the ground floor Museo de la Alhambra with artefacts directly related to the palace's history.

Palacio Nazaríes

Detail

Puerta de Justica

Alcazaba
Find time to explore the towers of the original citadel, the most important of which – the Torre de la Vela – takes you, via a winding staircase, to the Alhambra's best viewpoint.

Patio de Arrayanes

If only you could linger longer beside the rows of *arrayanes* (myrtle bushes) that border this calming rectangular pool. Shaded porticos with seven harmonious arches invite further contemplation.

Palacio de Comares

The neck-ache continues in the largest room in the Comares Palace renowned for its rich geometric ceiling. A negotiating room for the emirs, the Salón de los Embajadores is a masterpiece of Moorish design.

Sala de Dos Hermanas

Focus on the *dos hermanas* – two marble slabs either side of the fountain – before enjoying the intricate cupola embellished with 5000 tiny moulded stalactites. Poetic calligraphy decorates the walls.

Torre de Comares

Baños Reales

Washington Irving Apartments

Patio de Arrayanes

(4)

Jardín de Lindaraja

(5)

Palacio del Partal

Sala de los Abencerrajes

Jardines del Partal

Patio de los Leones

Count the 12 lions sculpted from marble, holding up a gurgling fountain. Then pan back and take in the delicate columns and arches built to signify an Islamic vision of paradise.

Generalife

A coda to most people's visits, the 'architect's garden' is no afterthought. While Nasrid in origin, the horticulture is relatively new: the pools and arcades were added in the early 20th century.

→ **Alcazaba, Christian Buildings & Museums**

The west end of the Alhambra grounds are the remnants of the **Alcazaba**, chiefly its ramparts and several towers. The **Torre de la Vela**, with a narrow staircase leading to the top terrace, is where the cross and banners of the Reconquista were raised in January 1492.

By the Palacios Nazaríes, the hulking **Palacio de Carlos V** clashes spectacularly with its surroundings. In a different setting its merits might be more readily appreciated.

Inside, the **Museo de la Alhambra** (⊙ 8.30am-8pm Wed-Sat, 8.30am-2.30pm Tue) **FREE**. has a collection of Alhambra artefacts, including the door from the Sala de Dos Hermanas, and the **Museo de Bellas Artes** (Fine Arts Museum; non-EU/EU citizen €1.50/free; ⊙ 2.30-8pm Tue, 9am-8pm Wed-Sat, 9am-2.30pm Sun) displays paintings and sculptures from Granada's Christian history.

Further along, the 16th-century **Iglesia de Santa María de la Alhambra** sits on the site of the palace mosque. At the crest of the hill, the Convento de San Francisco, now the Parador de Granada hotel, is where Isabel and Fernando were laid to rest while their tombs in the Capilla Real were being built.

→ **Generalife**

From the Arabic *jinan al-'arif* (the overseer's gardens), the Generalife is a soothing arrangement of pathways, patios, pools, fountains, tall trees and, in season, flowers of every imaginable hue. To reach the complex you must pass through the Alhambra walls on the east side, then head back northwest. At the north end is the emirs' **summer palace**, a whitewashed structure on the hillside facing the Alhambra. The courtyards here are particularly graceful; in the second courtyard, the trunk of a 700-year-old cypress tree suggests what delicate shade once graced the patio.

Casa-Museo Manuel de Falla   MUSEUM
(✆ 958 22 21 88; www.museomanueldefalla.com; Paseo de los Mártires; adult/concession €3/1; ⊙ 9am-2.30pm & 3.30-7pm Tue-Fri, 9am-2.30pm Sat & Sun) Arguably Spain's greatest classical composer and a friend of Lorca, Manuel de Falla (1876–1946) was born in Cádiz, but spent the key years of his life in Granada until the Civil War forced him into exile. Find out all about the man at this attractive *carmen* where he lived and composed, and which has been preserved pretty much as he left it. Tours are guided and intimate.

Museo Sefardi   MUSEUM
(✆ 958 22 05 78; www.museosefardidegranada.es; Placeta Berrocal 5; admission €5; ⊙ 10am-2pm & 5-9pm) Since being expelled en masse in 1492, there are very few Sephardi Jews left living in Granada today. But this didn't stop one enterprising couple from opening up a museum to their memory in 2013, the year the Spanish government began offering Spanish citizenship to any Sephardi Jew who could prove their Iberian ancestry. The museum is tiny, but the selected artefacts make excellent props to the passionate and fascinating historical portrayal related by the owners.

◉ Near Plaza Nueva

Plaza de Santa Ana   SQUARE
Plaza Nueva extends northeast into Plaza de Santa Ana, where the **Iglesia de Santa Ana** (Plaza Santa Ana) incorporates a mosque's minaret in its bell tower. Along narrow Carrera del Darro is a 11th-century Muslim bathhouse, the **Baños Árabes El Bañuelo** (Carrera del Darro 31; ⊙ 10am-2pm Tue-Sat) **FREE**. Further along is the **Museo Arqueológico** (Archaeological Museum; ✆ 58 57 54 08; Carrera del Darro 43; non-EU/EU citizens €1.50/free), which was closed for renovations at last visit.

Hammams de Al Andalus   HAMMAM
(✆ 902 333334; www.granada.hammamalandalus.com; Calle Santa Ana 16; bath/bath & massage €24/36; ⊙ 10am-midnight) With three pools of different temperatures, plus a steam room and the option of a proper skin-scrubbing massage (*masaje tradicional;* €39), this is your best option in town.

◉ Albayzín

On the hill facing the Alhambra across the Darro valley, Granada's old Muslim quarter (the Albayzín) is an open-air museum in which you can lose yourself for a whole morning. The cobblestone streets are lined with gorgeous *carmenes* (large mansions with walled gardens, from the Arabic *karm* for garden). It survived as the Muslim quarter for several decades after the Christian conquest in 1492.

Buses 31 and 32 both run circular routes from Plaza Nueva around the Albayzín about every seven to nine minutes from 7.30am to 11pm.

Palacio de Dar-al-Horra   PALACE
(Callejón de las Monjas) Close to the Placeta de San Miguel Bajo, off Callejón del Gallo and

GRANADA ON A SHOESTRING

Here are a few tips on how to have a high time in Granada on a low budget.

➡ To the surprise of many, large parts of the Alhambra (p655) including the evocative Plaza de los Aljibes can be accessed free of charge. Just walk in and stroll around.

➡ Once inside the Alhambra grounds, the Museo de la Alhambra and the Museo de Bellas Artes, in the renaissance Palacio de Carlos V have free entry (the latter is €1.50 to non-EU citizens).

➡ Several other museums in Granada are free, including the Centro Jose Guerrero (p664) art gallery and the beautiful Carmen Museo Max Moreau in the Albayzín.

➡ The Albayzín is a veritable open-air museum where you can stroll at will admiring churches and *carmenes* before finishing at the view-laden Mirador San Nicolás.

➡ The Huerta de San Vicente (p665), Federico Lorca's erstwhile summer house, has free entry on Wednesdays, while Catedral de Granada (p664) can be accessed for Mass on Sundays at 10am, 11am and 12.30pm.

➡ Like many Spanish cities, Granada offers some great free walking tours. Granatours (www.granatours.com) FREE meets daily beside the fountain in Plaza Nueva at 11am.

➡ Granada's finest savings come when you hit the city's bars. The city is famous for its generous free tapas. Have dinner by crawling Calle de Elvira or Calle Navas, dropping in for a drink and a free tapa in two or three bars. Churros are another cheap treat. Gran Café Bib-Rambla (p671) pipes out some of the best churros in Spain for the price of a bag of crisps.

➡ Round off the evening by squeezing into the cave-like Le Chien Andalou (p673) for a rousing flamenco show. Price: only €6!

down a short lane, is the 15th-century Palacio de Dar-al-Horra, a romantically dishevelled mini-Alhambra that was home to the mother of Boabdil, Granada's last Muslim ruler.

Calle Calderería Nueva STREET
Linking the upper and lower parts of the Albayzín, Calle Calderería Nueva is a narrow street famous for its *teterías*, but also a good place to shop for slippers, hookahs, jewellery and North African pottery from an eclectic cache of shops redolent of a Moroccan souk.

Colegiata del Salvador CHURCH
(Plaza del Salvador; admission €0.60; ◷10am-1pm & 4.30-6.30pm) Plaza del Salvador, near the top of the Albayzín, is dominated by the Colegiata del Salvador, a 16th-century church on the site of the Albayzín's former main mosque, the patio of which still survives at the church's western end.

Mirador San Nicolás LOOKOUT
(Callejón de San Cecilio) Callejón de San Cecilio leads to the Mirador San Nicolás, a lookout with unbeatable views of the Alhambra and Sierra Nevada. Come back later for sunset (you can't miss the trail then!). At any time of day take care: skilful, well-organised wallet-lifters and bag-snatchers operate here. Don't

be put off: it boasts a terrific atmosphere, with buskers, jugglers and students intermingling with camera-toting tourists.

Palacio de los Olvidados MUSEUM
(☑655 55 33 40; www.palaciodelosolvidados.com; Cuesta de Santa Inés 6; admission €5; ◷10am-7pm) Lest we forget, the Jews played a vital role in the glorious Nasrid Emirate of Granada that reigned from the 1200s to 1492 built on peaceful Christian, Muslim and Jewish coexistence. The aptly named 'palace of the forgotten', which opened in January 2014 in the Albayzín, revisits this oft-ignored Jewish legacy. It's the second and best of Granada's new Jewish-related museums with seven rooms filled with attractively displayed relics (scrolls, costumes and ceremonial artifacts) amassed from around Spain.

A well-versed guide takes you round the exhibits.

Carmen Museo Max Moreau MUSEUM
(☑958 29 33 10; Camino Nuevo de San Nicolás 12; ◷10.30am-1.30pm & 4-6pm Tue-Sat) FREE
Most of the Albayzín's *carmenes* are true to their original concept – quiet private houses with high walls that hide beautiful terraced gardens. But you can get a rare (and free)

GRAFFITI ART

While the UK has Banksy, Granada has El Niño de las Pinturas, real name, Raúl Ruíz, a street artist whose creative graffiti has become a defining symbol of a city where the grandiose and the gritty often sit side by side. Larger-than-life, lucid and thought-provoking, El Nino's giant-sized murals, the majority of which adorn the Realejo neighbourhood, juxtapose vivid close-ups of the human countenance with short poetic stanzas written in highly stylized lettering.

Over the past two decades, El Niño has become a famous underground personality in Granada and has sometimes been known to give live painting demonstrations at the university. Although he risks criticism and occasional fines for his work, most *granadinos* agree that his street art brings creative splashes of colour to their ancient city, ensuring it remains forward-thinking and edgy. You can see some of El Niño's best work while walking around the city (p666).

glimpse of one of these secret domains at the former home of Belgium-born portrait painter and composer Max Moreau. His attractive house has been made into a museum showing his former living quarters and work space along with a gallery that showcases his best portraits.

◉ Plaza Bib-Rambla & Around

Catedral de Granada   CATHEDRAL
(☏958 22 29 59; www.catedraldegranada.com; Gran Vía de Colón 5; admission €4; ⊙10am-1.15pm & 4-7.45pm Mon-Sat, 2-6pm Sun) Too boxed in by other buildings to manifest its full glory to observers at ground level, Granada's cavernous cathedral is, nonetheless, a hulking classic that sprang from the fertile imagination of the 17th-century painter-cum-sculptor-cum-architect Alonso Cano. Although commissioned by the Catholic Monarchs in the early 1500s, construction began only after Isabella's death, and didn't finish until 1704.

The result is a mishmash of styles: baroque outside, courtesy of Cano, and Renaissance inside, where the Spanish pioneer in this style, Diego de Siloé, directed operations to construct huge piers, white as meringue, a black-and-white tile floor and the gilded and painted chapel. Even more odd, the roof vaults are distinctly Gothic.

★ Capilla Real   HISTORIC BUILDING
(www.capillarealgranada.com; Calle Oficios; admission €4; ⊙10.15am-1.30pm & 3.30-6.30pm Mon-Sat, 11am-1.30pm Sun) Here they lie, Spain's notorious Catholic Monarchs, entombed in a chapel adjoining Granada's cathedral, far more peaceful in death than their tumultuous lives would have suggested. Isabel and Fernando commissioned the elaborate Isabelline-Gothic-style mausoleum that was to house them, but it was not completed until 1521, hence their temporary interment in the Alhambra's Convento de San Francisco.

The monarchs lie in simple lead coffins in the crypt beneath their marble monuments in the chancel, enclosed by a stunning gilded wrought-iron screen created in 1520 by Bartolomé de Jaén. Also here are the coffins of Isabel and Fernando's unfortunate daughter, Juana the Mad, and her husband, Philip of Flanders.

The sacristy contains a small but impressive *museum* with Fernando's sword and Isabel's sceptre, silver crown and personal art collection, which is mainly Flemish but also includes Botticelli's *Prayer in the Garden of Olives*. Felipe de Vigarni's two fine early-16th-century statues of the Catholic Monarchs at prayer are also here.

Alcaicería & Plaza Bib-Rambla   SQUARE
Just south of the Capilla Real, the Alcaicería was the Muslim silk exchange, but what you see now is a restoration after a 19th-century fire, filled with tourist shops. Just southwest of the Alcaicería is the large and picturesque Plaza Bib-Rambla. Nearby, the handsome, horseshoe-arched 14th-century Corral del Carbón (Calle Mariana Pineda; ⊙10am-8pm) was once an inn for coal dealers (hence its modern name, meaning Coal Yard). It houses a government-run crafts shop, Artespaña.

Centro José Guerrero   ART GALLERY
(☏958 22 51 85; www.centroguerrero.org; Calle Oficios 8; ⊙10.30am-2pm & 4.30-9pm Tue-Sat, 10.30am-2pm Sun) FREE An art gallery named for the Granada-born abstract painter (1914–91) who went to live in the US. Exhibitions are temporary and with a modernist bent,

though the gallery keeps half a dozen of Guerrero's characteristically vibrant works in a permanent collection.

◎ Outside the Centre

Monasterio de San Jerónimo — MONASTERY
(Calle Rector López Argüeta 9; admission €4; ⊙10am-1.30pm & 4-8pm Mon-Fri, 10am-2.30pm & 4-7.30pm Sat & Sun) One of the most stunning Catholic buildings in Granada is a little out of the centre. At the 16th-century Monasterio de San Jerónimo, where nuns still sing vespers, every surface of the church has been painted – the stained glass literally pales in comparison.

Gonzalo Fernández de Córdoba, known as El Gran Capitán and the Catholic Monarchs' military man, is entombed here, at the foot of the steps, and figures of him and his wife stand on either side of the enormous gilt retable, which rises eight levels. Almond cookies, baked by the nuns, are for sale at the front desk, to stop your head from spinning.

Museo Cuevas del Sacromonte — MUSEUM
(www.sacromontegranada.com; Barranco de los Negros; admission €5; ⊙10am-2pm & 5-9pm Tue-Sun) This wide-ranging ethnographic and environmental museum and arts centre in the Roma neighbourhood northeast of the Albayzín is set in large herb gardens and hosts art exhibitions, as well as flamenco and films at 10pm on Wednesday and Friday from June to September.

Huerta de San Vicente — MUSEUM
(☎958 25 84 66; Calle Virgen Blanca; admission only by guided tour in Spanish €3, Wed free; ⊙9.15am-1.30pm & 5-7.30pm Tue-Sun) This house, where Federico García Lorca spent summers and wrote some of his best-known works, is only 1.5km south of the city centre, but still retains the evocative aura of an early-20th-century country villa. Today the modern but handsome Parque Federico García Lorca separates it from whizzing traffic.

To get here, head 700m down Calle de las Recogidas from Puerta Real.

Monasterio de la Cartuja — MONASTERY
(Paseo de la Cartuja; admission €4; ⊙10am-1pm & 4-8pm Mon-Sat) Built between the 16th and 18th centuries by the Carthusian monks themselves, this monastery has an imposing sand-coloured stone exterior, but it is the lavish baroque monastery church that people come to see, especially the *sagrario* (sanctuary) behind the main altar, a confec-tion of red, black, white and grey-blue marble, columns with golden capitals, profuse sculpture and a beautiful frescoed cupola.

☞ Tours

Cicerone Cultura y Ocio — WALKING TOUR
(☎958 56 18 10; www.cicecronegranada.com; tour €15) Informative walking tours of central Granada and the Albayzín leave daily from its Plaza Bib-Rambla kiosk at 10.30am and 5pm (11am and 4pm in the winter).

Secret Granada — WALKING TOUR
(☎958 20 19 39; www.granadaunderground. blogspot.com.es; tours €15-30; ⊙9.30am-noon & 4-6.30pm) Explore the tunnels and dungeons that lie under the city (including the Alhambra), dug out by the Moors or by Christian prisoners (no one is certain). Reserve via the website.

Play Granada — CULTURAL
(segway tour €30) 𝄞 The make or break of a good tour is the tour guide, and Play Granada's are truly fantastic. Even if you don't do a tour, you'll see the congenial guides buzzing around Plaza Nueva on their Segways, stopping to chat with anyone and everyone.

Highly recommended is the Segway Tour, which lasts one hour 45 minutes and covers 8km. You'll cover twice the distance in the same time period if you partake in the electric bike tour instead.

☞ Courses

Escuela Delengua — LANGUAGE
(☎958 20 45 35; www.delengua.es; Calderería Vieja 20; 2-week course €260) With a massive student population, Granada is an ideal place to learn Spanish. This school in the heart of the Albayzín starts courses every Monday and offers loads of extra-curricular activities, including free cooking demonstrations.

☞ Festivals & Events

Feria del Corpus Cristi — RELIGIOUS
(Corpus Christi Fair) The big annual fair, which starts 60 days after Easter Sunday, is a week of bullfights, dancing and street puppets; most of the action is at the fairgrounds by the bus station.

Festival Internacional de Música y Danza — MUSIC
(www.granadafestival.org; ⊙Jun & Jul) For three weeks first-class classical and modern performance takes over the Alhambra and other historic sites.

🛏 Sleeping

Granada's strong Moorish bent is reflected in its hotels, many of which have taken old medieval mansions and converted them into Moroccan-style riads. Most of these establishments reside in the Albayzín quarter. Equally beguiling is Granada's handful of restored *cármenes*.

As in all Andalucian cities, it's worthwhile booking ahead during Semana Santa and Christmas.

🛏 Alhambra & Realejo

Hostal La Ninfa   HOSTAL $
(☑958 22 79 85; Plaza Campo Príncipe; s/d €45/50; ❊ 🛜) The show-stopping facade of this hotel, its walls covered with ceramic plaques, sets the scene for the interior, which is artistically cluttered and charming. The rooms are brightly painted (think turquoise-painted beams) with tiled bedheads and pretty tiled bathrooms. It's on the edge of the Realejo's main square.

★ Carmen de la Alcubilla del Caracol   HISTORIC HOTEL $$
(☑958 21 55 51; www.alcubilladelcaracol.com; Calle del Aire Alta 12; s/d €100/120; ❊ @ 🛜) Hidden behind white walls in the lee of the Alhambra hill, this heavenly *carmen* strikes an eloquent balance between history, romance and modern comfort – and it's backed up by attentive personal service by host, Manuel. The rooms perch over a flowery terraced garden, and an open deck hosts leisurely breakfasts that involve far more than just *tostadas* and coffee.

Hostal Molinos   HOTEL $$
(☑958 22 73 67; www.hotelmolinos.es; Calle de Molinos 12; s/d/tr €53/85/115; ❊ 🛜) Don't let the 'narrowest hotel in the world' moniker put you off (and yes, it actually is – and has a certificate from the *Guinness Book of Records* to prove it), there's plenty of space in Molinos' nine recently boutique-ised rooms, and warm hospitality in its information-stacked lobby. Situated at the foot of the Realejo, it makes an economical central option.

Hotel Palacio de Los Navas   HISTORIC HOTEL $$
(☑958 21 57 60; www.palaciodelosnavas.com; Calle Navas 1; s/d €102/135; ❊ 🛜) Lovely 16th-century building with individually furnished rooms featuring lots of cool creams and whites, original columns and doors, desks and terracotta-tiled floors. The rooms surround a traditional columned patio.

🏃 City Walk
Graffiti & Street Art

START BAR ÍZARO
END CUESTA ESCORIAZA
LENGTH 2.5KM; ONE HOUR

Seville has Velázquez and Málaga has Picasso, while Granada has a mélange of modern street art painted, etched and sprayed by various 'underground' graffiti artists, the most notable being El Niño de las Pinturas (p664). This easy walk guides you through the city's ever-changing outdoor art gallery, incorporating the best of its thought-provoking graffiti. In the process, you'll pass through two of the Granada's most definitive neighbourhoods.

The walk starts near the Puerta de Elvira, the city's old Moorish entry gate. Providing a spectacular welcome to Granada's famous tapas street, Calle de Elvira, is an astonishing mural by El Niño de las Pinturas detailing the outline of three rowers in a sunset emblazoned over two perpendicular walls of ❶ **Bar Ízaro**. It is highlighted with the words *El mundo es oscuro, ilumina su parte* (The world is dark, light up your part). Inside the bar, the (free) tapas match the colourful artwork.

Continue along Calle de Elvira, resisting or yielding to the lure of plenty more tapas bars. At the junction with ❷ **Calle Calderería Nueva**, take time to slip up the so-called 'Calle de las Teterías' with its numerous Arabic-style tearooms. If you're here before the shops open, you'll be able to see the art that decorates the metal shutters of some of the closed businesses – a common feature in Granada. The Tienda de la Solidaridad at No 4 has a particularly striking mural. If it's already late afternoon, drop into a *tetería* for a reviving brew.

Cross Plaza Nueva, turn right into Plaza Isabel La Católica and then left into Calle Pavaneras and the Realejo quarter, where Granada's street art is most abundant.

It is not uncommon for cafes or shops to ask street artists to liven up their premises in Granada. The most colourful example of this can be seen at ❸ **Hicuri Art Restaurant**, a vegan restaurant which has been decorated inside and out by El Niño de las Pinturas. Across the street,

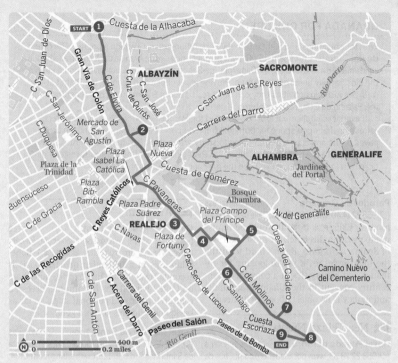

similar treatment has been given to Bar Candela, where a striking painting of a group of flamenco dancers appears on the side wall courtesy of guess who? Both bars are worth a stop if you're hungry or thirsty.

Follow the main road through Plaza del Realejo into Calle de Molinos, where you'll find, next to **4 Hotel Molinos**, one of El Niño de las Pinturas' largest and most prominent murals: a huge study of Rodin's 'thinker' with the words *Cansado de no encontrar repuestas, decidi cambiar mis preguntas* (Tired of not finding answers, I decided to change my questions) written in his stylised, instantly recognisable handwriting. The next street on the left will take you into Plaza Campo del Príncipe, the Realejo's main square. Just off the northeastern corner behind the **5 Iglesia de San Cecilio** is a multicoloured graffiti wall on the rise that leads up towards the Alhambra.

Rejoin Calle de Molinos and a block or so further on you'll spot a **6 painting of an owl** and a boy blowing bubbles with more inspired poetry scrawled underneath.

The long bleached wall on **7 Cuesta del Caidero** that protects the Colegio Santo Domingo has been turned into a kind of free art space that stretches right up the street. Various artists and *grafiteros* have pitched in here, although it's the distinctive images of El Niño de las Pinturas that jump out at you. Notable are his paintings of an old man playing a violin, a close-up of American jazz trumpeter, Louis Armstrong, and a study of a girl's face next to the figure of a woman playing a violin entitled *El silencio*.

Rejoin the main street, now called Calle Vistillas de los Ángeles, and proceed southeast for a few hundred metres. The small plaza with six trees that appears on your right is **8 Placeta Joe Strummer**, named after the late singer of British rock band the Clash. The *placeta* was dedicated in 2013, and on a wall on the south side is a painting of the singer/guitarist wearing a trademark punk sneer by El Niño de las Pinturas. Walk a few metres below the square into **9 Cuesta Escoriaza** and, right there in front of you, the whole facade of an otherwise boring beige tenement building has been given the artistic treatment. It's stunning and rather psychedelic display that – like all the street art in this feisty city – can turn a grey day into a sunny one.

GRANADA FOR CHILDREN

With four buildings and eight interactive exhibition areas, Granada's popular **Parque de las Ciencias** (🖉 958 13 19 00; www.parqueciencias.com; Avenida del Mediterráneo; adult/child under 18yr €6.50/5.50; ⊙ 10am-7pm Tue-Sat, 10am-3pm Sun & holidays) should keep the kids happily absorbed for hours. Playing giant chess or threading the Plant Labyrinth are just two activities they can do here. It's about 900m south of the centre, near the Palacio de Congresos conference centre.

If even less intellectual exertion is called for, Parque Federico García Lorca offers refreshing, flat open space for both children and parents. The park abounds in broad paved paths and is also a great place to study *granadinos* (Granada residents) at leisure. To get to the park, follow Calle de las Recogidas for 800m in a southwesterly direction from Puerta Real until you see the greenery on your right.

Parador de Granada HISTORIC HOTEL $$$

(🖉 958 22 14 40; www.parador.es; Calle Real de la Alhambra; r €315; P❄@🛜) It would be remiss not to mention this hotel, the most luxurious of Spain's *paradores*. But it's hard to justify the high price. Yet if you're looking for romance and history (it's in a converted 15th-century convent in the Alhambra grounds) and money is no object...book well ahead.

🛏 Near Plaza Nueva

Hotel Posada del Toro BOUTIQUE HOTEL $

(🖉 958 22 73 33; www.posadadeltoro.com; Calle de Elvira 25; r from €54; ❄🛜) A lovely small hotel with rooms set around a tranquil central patio. Walls are washed in a delectable combination of pale pistachio, peach and cream, and the rooms are similarly enticing with parquet floors, Alhambra-style stucco detailing, rustic furniture, and bathrooms with double sinks and hydromassage showers.

The restaurant offers Spanish dishes such as Galician octopus, plus pastas and pizza.

Hotel Zaguán del Darro HISTORIC HOTEL $$

(🖉 958 21 57 30; www.hotelzaguan.com; Carrera del Darro 23; s/d €55/70; ❄@) This place offers excellent value for the Albayzín. The 16th-century house has been tastefully restored, with sparing use of antiques. Its 13 rooms are all different; some look out over the Río Darro. There's a good bar-restaurant below, and the main street in front means easy taxi access – but also a bit of evening noise.

Hotel Puerta de las Granadas HOTEL $$

(🖉 958 21 62 30; www.hotelpuertadelasgranadas.com; Cuesta de Gomérez 14; s/d €68/73; ❄@🛜) This small hotel has a prime location just off the Plaza Nueva and halfway up the hill to the Alhambra. Rooms overlook either a back garden (quiet) or the street (a little larger).

🛏 Albayzín

Oasis Backpackers' Hostel HOSTEL $

(🖉 958 21 58 48; www.oasisgranada.com; Placeta Correo Viejo 3; dm from €13; ❄@🛜❄) Bohemian digs in a bohemian quarter, Oasis is seconds away from the *teterías* and bars on Calle Elvira. It has free internet access, a rooftop terrace and personal safes. As far as backpacker hostels go, it's a gem.

Hotel Palacio de Santa Inés HOTEL $$

(🖉 958 22 63 80; www.palaciosantaines.es; Cuesta de Santa Inés 9; d €95-125, r with sitting room €184; ❄🛜) A Moorish-era house, extended in the 16th and 17th centuries, with an interesting double patio around which rooms are arranged on three levels. The interior resembles a coaching inn, though the furniture is more up-to-date and functional.

Casa Morisca Hotel HISTORIC HOTEL $$$

(🖉 958 22 11 00; www.hotelcasamorisca.com; Cuesta de la Victoria 9; d/ste €167/220; ❄@🛜) Fall asleep in 21st-century Granada and wake up thinking you've been teleported to 19th-century Marrakech. Casa Morisca lays on the Moorish nostalgia thickly, but it works. Of Granada's plethora of historic hotels, this late-15th-century mansion is arguably the best. There are heavy wooden doors, lofty ceilings, fluffy white beds and flat-weave rugs over brick floors.

🛏 Plaza Bib-Rambla & Around

Hostal Arteaga HOSTAL $

(🖉 958 20 88 41; www.hostalarteaga.es; Calle Arteaga 3; s/d €40/49; ❄@🛜) A charming bargain option off the Gran Vía de Colón, just inching into the Albayzín. The rooms are spruced up with lavender walls, striped bedspreads and chequered blue bathroom tiles, for a tidy, modern feel. Stay three nights and you get a free session at the adjacent Baños de Elvira spa.

Hotel Los Tilos
HOTEL **$$**

(☑ 958 26 67 12; www.hotellostilos.com; Plaza Bib-Rambla 4; s/d €55/80; ❄) The spacious rooms, clean and regularly renovated, overlook Plaza Bib-Rambla, and there are double-glazed windows to shut out the hubbub at night. There's a small but panoramic roof terrace if you don't get your own Alhambra view from your room.

★ Hotel Hospes Palacio de Los Patos
LUXURY HOTEL **$$$**

(☑ 958 53 57 90; www.hospes.com; Solarillo de Gracia 1; r €180-220; 🅿❄@🛜🛝) Put simply, the best hotel in Granada – if you can afford it – offering lucky guests sharp modernity and exemplary service in a palatial Unesco-protected building. You could write a novella about its many memorable features: the grand staircase, the post-modern chandeliers, the Arabian garden, the Roman Emperor spa, the carnations they leave on your bed in the afternoon…

AC Palacio de Santa Paula
LUXURY HOTEL **$$$**

(☑ 902 292293; www.ac-hotels.com; Gran Vía de Colón; r from €200; 🅿❄@🛝) As if all the rest wasn't enough, Granada hits five stars with this inspired fusion of neoclassical traditionalism and modern-industrial. The hotel's princely price tag brings you a spa, a snazzy restaurant, lush gardens, a pool, numerous fancy soaps and a red carnation on your bed when you return for an afternoon siesta.

✗ Eating

Aside from its free tapas, Granada also serves some of Andalucía's best Moroccan and Middle Eastern food, particularly in the Albayzín. *Teterías* are becoming increasingly popular and many new ones have opened in the last few years. Most serve light desserts – others offer fuller menus.

✗ Alhambra & Realejo

Café Futbol
CAFE **$**

(www.cafefutbol.com; Plaza de Mariana Pineda 6; churros €2; ☺6am-1am; 🚻) More about chocolate and ice cream than football this three-storey cafe, with its butter-coloured walls and gaudy chandeliers, dates from 1910 and is generally packed with coiffured *señoras*, foreign students and families. Elderly white-

shirted waiters attend to the Sunday afternoon rush when everyone in Granada seemingly turns up for hot chocolate and churros.

Hicuri Art Restaurant
VEGAN **$**

(Plaza de los Girones 3; mains €7-12; ☺10am-10pm Mon-Sat; ✍) Granada's leading graffiti artist, El Niño de las Pinturas, has been let loose on the walls of Hicuri and the results are positively psychedelic. The food used to be vegetarian with a few dishes for diehard carnivores, but it recently went full-on vegan.

Tofu and seitan are liberally used in the food, and classic Spanish puds are given the eco treatment with soy milk.

★ La Botillería
TAPAS, FUSION **$$**

(☑ 958 22 49 28; Calle Varela 10; mains €13-20; ☺1pm-1am Wed-Sun, 1-8pm Mon) Establishing a good reputation for nouveau tapas, La Botillería is just around the corner from the legeandary La Tana bar, to which it has family connections. It's a more streamlined modern place than its cousin, where you can *tapear* (eat tapas) at the bar or sit down for the full monty, Andalucian style. The *solomillo* (pork tenderloin) comes in a rich, wine-laden sauce.

Carmela Restaurante
TAPAS, ANDALUCIAN **$$**

(☑ 958 22 57 94; www.restaurantecarmela.com; Calle Colcha 13; tapas €5-10; ☺12.30pm-midnight) Long a bastion of traditional tapas, Granada has taken a leaf out of Seville's book and come up with something a little more out-of-the-box at this new streamlined restaurant, guarded by the statue of Jewish philosopher Yehuba ibn Tibon at the jaws of the Realejo quarter. The best of Carmela's creative offerings is the made-to-order tortilla and cured-ham croquettes the size of tennis balls.

Los Diamantes
SEAFOOD **$$**

(www.barlosdiamantes.com; Calle Navas 26; racionés €8-10; ☺noon-6pm & 8pm-2am Mon-Fri, 11am-1am Sat & Sun) Granada's great tapas institution has two central outlets: this old-school scruffy joint in tapas-bar-lined Calle Navas, and a newer, hipper, Ikea-esque version in Plaza Nueva. What doesn't change is the tapas speciality – fish, which you'll smell sizzling in the fryer as soon as you open the door.

Restaurante Chikito
ANDALUCIAN **$$**

(☑ 958 22 33 64; www.restaurantechikito.com; Plaza Campillo Bajo 9; mains €17-20; ☺12.30-3.30pm & 7.30-11.30pm Thu-Tue) One of the city's most historic restaurants, Chikito was apparently a favourite of Lorca's (his table is in the corner) and remains perennially popular with the smart local set. The tapas bar speciality is snails (€5). The adjacent restaurant concentrates on hearty dishes like oxtail stew and pork medallions, which it has spent many years getting right. The walls are plastered with local celeb pics. Reservations recommended.

Parador de Granada INTERNATIONAL **$$$**
(☑ 958 22 14 40; Calle Real de la Alhambra; mains €19-22; ☺ 1-4pm & 8.30-11pm) On one side, the Parador de Granada is a hushed, swanky dinner experience, with a Moroccan-Spanish-French menu that also features local goat and venison. On the other, it's a stylish little canteen for sightseers, where even your *bocadillo de jamón* (ham-filled roll) tastes special – and it ought to, considering its €12 price tag. Overall, a bit inflated, but a lovely treat for the location.

🗶 Near Plaza Nueva

Plaza Nueva is rimmed with restaurants, most with alfresco seating. The more obvious places can be a little touristy. For the better nooks, hunt around the backstreets or head up Carrera del Darro.

For fresh fruit and veg, head for the large covered **Mercado Central San Agustín** (Calle San Agustín; ☺ closed Sun), a block north of the cathedral.

La Bella y La Bestia ANDALUCIAN, TAPAS **$**
(☑ 958 22 51 87; www.bodegaslabellaylabestia.com; Calle Carcel Baja 14; tapas €2-3; ☺ noon-midnight) Lots of beauty, but no real beast; this place wins the prize for Granada's most generous free tapas: a huge plate of bagels, chips and pasta arrives with your first drink. There are four branches, though this one is particularly well-placed just off Calle de Elvira.

Bodegas Castañeda TAPAS **$**
(Calle Almireceros; tapas €2-3, raciónes €6-8; ☺ 11.30am-4.30pm & 7.30pm-1.30am) A much-loved relic among locals and tourists alike, the buzzing Castañeda is the Granada tapas bar to trump all others. Don't expect any fancy new stuff here, but do expect lightning-fast service, booze from big casks mounted on the walls, and eating as a physical contact sport.

Yes, it gets crowded, with customers overflowing into its sister bar, Antigua Bodega Castañeda, around the corner.

Café Lisboa CAFE, BREAKFAST **$**
(cnr Calle Reyes Catolicos & Plaza Nueva; breakfast €3-7; ☺ 7.30am-11pm) Tourists trip over locals in the Lisboa in Plaza Nueva, which is good for breakfasts (including the fried English variety), *meriendas* (afternoon snacks) and people who can't wait until 9pm for dinner.

Greens & Berries INTERNATIONAL **$**
(Plaza Nueva 1; snacks from €2.50; ☺ 10am-11.30pm; ⓐ) Close to public benches in the square, this is a great choice if you want to pick up something healthy, fast and filling. Sandwiches include tasty choices like salmon, avocado and lemon, and goats' cheese and caramelised onion, plus there are soups of the day, fresh fruit smoothies and a wickedly delicious New York cheesecake.

Ruta del Azafrán FUSION **$$**
(☑ 958 22 68 82; www.rutadelazafran.es; Paseo del Padre Manjón 1; mains €13-20; ☺ 1-4pm & 8-11pm) Like a lot of 'fusion' restaurants, La Ruta tries a lot of different tricks with differing results, some of them successful. The menu is a pot luck of Asian-inspired tempuras, broccoli-based pesto, lamb couscous and roasted pork. The setting, however, is unquestionable, especially after dark with the glowing hulk of the Alhambra perched up above you.

🗶 Albayzín

The labyrinthine Albayzín holds a wealth of eateries all tucked away in its narrow streets. Calle Calderería Nueva is a fascinating muddle of *teterías,* leather shops and Arabic-influenced takeaways.

★ Arrayanes MOROCCAN **$$**
(☑ 958 22 84 01; www.rest-arrayanes.com; Cuesta Marañas 4; mains €15; ☺ 1.30-4.30pm & 7.30-11.30pm; ✍) The best Moroccan food in a city that is well known for its Moorish throwbacks? Recline on lavish patterned seating, try the rich, fruity tagine casseroles and make your decision. Note that Arrayanes does not serve alcohol.

El Ají MODERN SPANISH **$$**
(☑ 958 29 29 30; Plaza San Miguel Bajo 9; mains €12-20; ☺ 1-11pm; ✍) Up in the Albayzín, this chic but cosy neighbourhood restaurant is no bigger than a shoebox but serves from breakfast right through to the evening. Chatty staff at the tiny marble bar can point out some of the highlights of the creative menu (such as prawns with tequila and honey).

FREE TAPAS

Granada – bless its generous heart – is one of the last bastions of that fantastic practice of free tapas with every drink. Place your drink order at the bar and, hey presto, a plate will magically appear with a generous portion of something delicious-looking on it. Order another drink and another plate will materialise. The process is repeated with every round you buy – and each time the tapa gets better. As Spanish bars serve only small glasses of beer (*cañas* measure just 250ml), it is perfectly easy to fill up on free tapas over an enjoyable evening without getting totally inebriated. Indeed, some people 'crawl' from bar to bar getting a drink and free tapa in each place and call it 'dinner'. Packed shoulder to shoulder with tapas institutions, Calle de Elvira and Calle Navas are good places for bar crawls. If you're super-hungry, you can always order an extra plate or two to soak up the *cervezas*.

The free tapa practice is carried on throughout most of Granada province and also extends into Almería, where bars will even allow you to choose which tapas you wish to try.

It's a good place to get out of the sun and rest up, especially if you are hiking up from Plaza Nueva.

Samarkanda LEBANESE $$
(Calle Calderería Vieja 3; mains €8-12; ⏱1-4.30pm & 7.30-11.30pm Thu-Tue; 🍴) For a night off tapas, this longstanding Lebanese restaurant is a sound choice, particularly if you've had your fill of cured hams swinging above your head. The lentil soup spiked with lemon and cumin is delicious, along with mainstays hummus, *mutabal* (aubergine-and-tahini-based dip) and falafel.

🍴 Plaza Bib-Rambla & Around

In the heart of modern Granada, the plaza and its surrounding network of streets cater to a range of tastes and pockets from student to executive. Don't miss the excellent ice cream and churros.

★Gran Café Bib-Rambla CAFE $
(Plaza Bib-Rambla 3; chocolate & churros €4; ⏱8am-11pm; 👶) It's 5pm, you've just traipsed around five vaguely interesting churches and hypoglycaemia is rapidly setting in. Time to hit Plaza Bib-Rambla, where Granada's best churros are served in a no-nonsense 1907-vintage cafe. Check their freshness by watching Mr Churro-maker lower them into the fryer behind the bar and then enjoy them dipped in cups of ulta-thick hot chocolate.

Poë TAPAS, FUSION $
(www.barpoe.com; Calle Paz; media-raciones €3; ⏱8pm-late) British-Angolan Poë offers Brazilian favourites such as *feijoada* or chicken stew with polenta, and a trendy multicultur-al vibe. Doesn't look much from the outside, but like Dr Who's Tardis, it's a whole different world once you push open the door.

Café Gran Vía de Colón CAFE, BREAKFAST $
(Gran Vía 13; breakfast €3-5; ⏱8am-11pm) Stand at the bar with working stiffs knocking back mega-strong coffee and wolfing down *molletes* (toast and crushed tomatoes) and thank your lucky stars you don't have to rush off to the office – at least for today.

Oliver SEAFOOD $$
(📞958 26 22 00; www.restauranteoliver.com; Calle Pescadería 12; mains €12-18; ⏱1-4pm & 8pm-midnight Mon-Sat) An Oliver that's got nothing to do with celeb chef Jamie, this restaurant on Calle Pescadería (fish street) is a temple to fish – and the *granadinos* love it. Sleek business types pack in alongside street-sweepers to devour *raciones* of garlicky fried treats at the mobbed lunch-time bar, which can be ankle deep in crumpled napkins and shrimp shells come 4pm.

🍷 Drinking

The best street for drinking is the rather scruffy Calle de Elvira, but other chilled bars line Río Darro at the base of the Albayzín. Just north of Plaza de Trinidad are a bunch of cool hipster-ish bars.

Old stalwarts on the drinking/tapas scene are Los Diamontes (two branches), Bodega La Bella y la Bestia (four branches including one in Calle de Elvira) and the eternal classic Bodegas Castañeda.

★Botánico BAR
(www.botanicocafe.es; Calle Málaga 3; ⏱1pm-1am) A haven for cool dudes with designer beards, students finishing off their Lorca

LOCAL KNOWLEDGE

GRANADA'S BEST TETERÍAS

Granada's *teterías* (tea rooms) have proliferated in recent years, but there's still something exotic and dandyish about their dark, atmospheric interiors stuffed with lace veils, stucco, low cushioned seating and an invariably bohemian clientele. Most offer a long list of aromatic teas accompanied by sticky Arabic sweets. Some serve up music and more substantial snacks. Many still permit their customers to indulge in the *cachimba* (shisha pipe). Narrow Calle Calderería Nueva is Granada's best '*tetería* street', but there are plenty of other nooks dotted around.

Albayzín Abaco Té (958 22 19 35; Calle Alamo de Marqués 5;) Hidden high up in the Albayzin maze, Abaco's Arabian-minimalist interior allows you to enjoy Alhambra views from a comfy-ish floor mat. Health freaks hog the carrot juice; sweet tooths bag the excellent cakes.

Tetería Dar Ziryab (655 44 67 75; Calle Calderería Nueva 11) A warm stove and regular live music provide two reasons to duck into the Arabian Nights interior of Dar Ziryab, where amorous undergraduates share *chicambas*. Then there are the 40+ teas, sweet milkshakes and lovely white-chocolate tarts.

Tetería Kasbah (Calle Calderería Nueva 4; mains €8-12) Savoury food, ample student-watching potential and amazing stucco make up for the sometimes slow service in Calle Calderería Nuevo's biggest and busiest *tetería*.

Tetería La Cueva de Ali Baba (Puente de Epinosa 15) Slightly more refined *tetería*, where you can sip wine and pick at gratis tapas overlooking the Río Darro.

Tetería Nazarí (Calle Calderería Nueva 13) Snuggle down on the misshapen pouffes with flamenco singers, art students and the winner of last year's Che Guevara look-a-like contest.

dissertations and anyone else with arty inclinations, Botánico is a casual snack restaurant by day, a cafe at *merienda* time (5pm to 7pm) and a bar and club come dusk with DJs or live music emphasising jazz and blues.

Al Sur de Granada BAR
(958 27 02 45; www.alsurdegranada.net; Calle de Elvira 150; 10.30am-3.30pm & 6.30-11.30pm) This delicatessen, dedicated to the best food and wine from around Granada province, doubles as a bar. Get a sampler cheese platter, and try some of the various mountain liqueurs. It's also a great place to pick up some local products to take home.

El Bar de Eric BAR
(Calle Escuelas 8; 8am-2am) Imagine Keith Moon reincarnated as a punk rocker and put in charge of a modern tapas restaurant. Eric's is the brainchild of Spanish rock 'n' roll drummer Eric Jiménez, of Los Planetas, but in this new bastion of rock chic things aren't as chaotic as you might think.

Indulge in some fusion tapas served with cocktails and admire photo art that highlights band shoots and old rock-gig posters. Don't try throwing any TVs out of the window.

Mundra BAR
(Plaza de la Trinidad; platters €10; 8.30pm-2am Mon-Thu, 8.30pm-3am Fri & Sat) Overlooking the urban greenery of Plaza de la Trinidad, Mundra has a global-chic feel with its black barrel tables, Buddha statues and chill-out soundracks. There are platters to share including fresh prawns (which come from Motril) and provolone cheese (which doesn't).

Granada 10 CLUB
(646 81 96 00; www.granada10.com; Calle Carcel Baja 11; admission €10; from midnight) A glittery converted cinema is now Granada's top club for the glam crowd, who recline on the gold sofas and get hip swivelling to cheesy Spanish pop tunes.

☆ Entertainment

A population that is 25% student during term-time ensures that Granada has a youthful and edgy nightlife.

Peña de la Platería FLAMENCO
(www.laplateria.org.es; Placeta de Toqueros 7) Buried in the Albayzín warren, Peña de la Platería claims to be the oldest flamenco aficionados' club in Spain, founded in 1949. Unlike other more private *peñas*, it regularly opens its doors to nonmembers

for performances on Thursday nights (and sometimes Saturdays) at 10.30pm.

Casa del Arte Flamenco   FLAMENCO
(958 56 57 67; www.casadelarteflamenco.com; Cuesta de Gomerez 11; tickets €18; shows 7.30pm & 9pm) Just what Granada needed: a new small flamenco venue that is neither *tablao* (tourist show) nor *peña* (private club), but something in between. The peformers are invariably top-notch while the atmosphere depends largely on the tourist-local make-up of the audience.

Le Chien Andalou   FLAMENCO
(www.lechienandalou.com; Carrera del Darro 7; admission €6; shows 9.30pm & 11.30pm) Small cavernous bar that was once a well but now hosts two nightly flamenco shows for half the price of the bigger places. Performances can be hit or miss, but at this price, it's probably worth the gamble.

Boogaclub   DJ
(www.boogaclub.com; Calle Santa Barbara 3; 2am-6pm Mon-Thu, 11pm-7am Fri-Sun) Chill to soulful house, funk, electro and Chicago house then kick up your (high) heels to the international DJs hitting the decks with funk, soul, reggae and tribute sessions (to Amy Winehouse and the like). Karaoke nights, jam sessions and live music. Check the website for the current line-up.

Teatro Alhambra   THEATRE
(958 22 04 47; Calle de Molinos 56) Both Teatro Alhambra and the more central **Teatro Isabel La Católica** (958 22 15 14; Acera del Casino) have ongoing programs of theatre and concerts (sometimes flamenco); you may pick up a Lorca play here.

 Shopping

Granadino crafts include embossed leather, *taracea* (marquetry), blue-and-white glazed pots, handmade guitars, wrought iron, brass and copper ware, basket weaving and textiles. Look out for these in the Alcaicería and Albayzín, on Cuesta de Gomérez and in the government-run Artespaña in Corral del Carbón (p664).

The Plaza Nueva area is awash with jewellery vendors, selling from rugs laid out on the pavement, and ethnic-clothing shops.

For general shopping try pedestrianised Calle de los Mesones or expensive department store El Corte Inglés in Calle Acera del Darro, 400m southeast of Puerta Real.

La Oliva   FOOD
(Calle Rosario 9; 11am-2.30pm & 7-10pm Mon-Sat) Sells a superb range of quality deli items with an emphasis on fine wines and olive oil.

Daniel Gil de Avalle   MUSIC
(www.gildeavalle.com; Plaza del Realejo 15; 10am-1pm & 5-8pm) This longstanding music store specialises in exquisite handmade guitars. Step inside and you may well see the *guitarrero* (guitar maker) at work. It also offers guitar lessons.

Alcaicería   SOUVENIRS
(Calle Alcaicería) Formerly a grand Moorish bazaar where silk was made and sold, the stalls are now taken up with souvenir shops. The setting is still very reminiscent of the past, however, especially in the early morning, before the coach tours descend.

Tienda Librería de la Alhambra   SOUVENIRS
(Calle Reyes Católicos 40; 9.30am-8.30pm) *The* place for Alhambra aficionados with a tasteful selection of quality gifts including excellent coffee table-style tomes, children's art books, hand-painted fans and arty stationery. You can buy Alhambra tickets from an automatic machine inside.

 Information

EMERGENCY
Policía Nacional (958 80 80 00; Plaza de los Campos) The most central police station.

MEDICAL SERVICES
Hospital Ruiz de Alda (958 02 00 09, 958 24 11 00; Avenida de la Constitución 100) Central, with good emergency facilities.

MONEY
There are plenty of banks and ATMs on Gran Vía de Colón, Plaza Isabel La Católica and Calle Reyes Católicos.

POST
Post Office (Puerta Real; 8.30am-8.30pm Mon-Fri, 9.30am-2pm Sat) Often has long queues.

TOURIST INFORMATION
Municipal Tourist Office (www.granadatur. com; Plaza del Carmen; 10am-7pm Mon-Sat, 10am-2pm Sun) New digs in the town hall.
Regional Tourist Office (958 22 10 22; Calle Santa Ana 1; 9am-7pm Mon-Sat, 10am-2pm Sun & holidays) You best bet for information on all of Granada province.

❶ Getting There & Away

AIR

Iberia (☏ 902 400500; www.iberia.com) flies daily to/from Madrid from **Aeropuerto Federico García Lorca** (www.aena.es), 17km west of the city. There are also flights to Barcelona, Mallorca and London City Airport – the latter with **British Airways** (www.ba.com).

BUS

Granada's bus station is inconveniently situated 3km northwest of the city centre. Fortunately, city buses 3 and 33 run from Gran Vía de Colón to and from the bus station every 15 minutes. A taxi costs €7 to €9. **Alsa** (www.alsa.es) handles buses in the province and across the region, plus a night bus direct to Madrid's Barajas airport (€33, five hours). Other destinations include Córdoba (€15, 2¾ hours direct, eight daily), Seville (€23, three hours direct, 10 daily), Málaga (€14, 1¾ hours direct, hourly) and Las Alpujarras (p679).

CAR

Car rental is expensive. **ATA** (☏ 958 22 40 04; Plaza Cuchilleros 1) has small cars (eg Renault Clio) for approximately €75/48/36 per day for one/two/seven days. You would be better advised to take a taxi to the airport (€18 to €22), where four or five good car-hire operators have offices.

TRAIN

The **train station** (☏ 958 24 02 02; Avenida de Andaluces) is 1.5km west of the centre, off Avenida de la Constitución. Four trains run daily to/from Seville (€30, three hours) and Almería (€20, 2¼ hours) via Guadix, and six daily to/from Antequera (€11, 1½ hours). Three go to Ronda (€20, three hours) and Algeciras (€30, 4½ hours). For Málaga (€17, 2½ hours) or Córdoba (€36, 2½ hours) take an Algeciras train and change at Bobadilla. One or two trains go to each of Madrid (€68, four to five hours), Valencia (€32, 7½ to eight hours) and Barcelona (€70, 12 hours).

❶ Getting Around

TO/FROM THE AIRPORT

The airport is 17km west of the city on the A92. **Autocares J González** (www.autocaresjose gonzalez.com) runs buses between the airport and a stop near the Palacio de Congresos (€3, five daily), with a stop in the city centre on Gran Vía de Colón, where a schedule is posted opposite the cathedral, and at the entrance to the bus station. A taxi costs €18 to €22 depending on traffic conditions and pick-up point.

BUS

Individual tickets are €1.20, or pay €2 for a refillable pass card, then add at least €5, for rides as low as €0.80. Both can be bought with notes or coins from the bus driver. Most lines stop on Gran Vía de Colón; the tourist office dispenses maps and schedules.

METRO

Stalled by the economic crisis, Granada's long-awaited new metro secured a loan from the European Bank in 2012 and is finally on the road to completion. It should open sometime in 2014. The 16km route, which will run between Albolote in the north and Amarilla in the southwest, includes 26 stations and will take 45 minutes to ride in its entirety. As only 2.5km of the route in central Granada will travel beneath the ground, the metro is better described as a light-rail link.

CAR & MOTORCYCLE

Vehicle access to the Plaza Nueva area is restricted by red lights and little black posts known as *pilonas*, which block certain streets during certain times of the day. If you are going to stay at a hotel near Plaza Nueva, press the button next to your hotel's name beside the *pilonas* to contact reception, which will be able to lower the *pilonas* for you.

TAXI

If you're after a taxi, head for Plaza Nueva, where they line up. Most fares within the city cost between €4.50 and €8.50.

GRANADA PROVINCE

Beyond the eponymous city, Granada Province offers plenty of surprises: skiing and climbing in the snowy Sierra Nevada; walking in the amazing Las Alpujarras; and swimming, sunbathing and diving on the Costa Tropical on Granada's Mediterranean coastline.

Around Granada

Granada is surrounded by a fertile plain called La Vega, planted with poplar groves and crops ranging from melons to tobacco. The Vega was an inspiration to Federico García Lorca, who was born and died here. The Parque Federico García Lorca, between the villages of Víznar and Alfacar (about 2.5km apart), marks the site where Lorca and hundreds, possibly thousands, of others are believed to have been shot and buried by the Nationalists at the start of the civil war. His remains have never been found.

Fuente Vaqueros

The touchingly modest house where Lorca was born in 1898, in this otherwise unremarkable suburb 17km west of Granada, is now the Casa Museo Federico García Lorca (☑958 51 64 53; www.patronatogarcialorca. org; Calle Poeta Federico García Lorca 4; admission €1.80; ⊙guided visits hourly 10am-2pm & 5-7pm Tue-Sat). The place brings his spirit to life, with numerous charming photos, posters and costumes from his plays, and paintings illustrating his poems. A short video captures him in action with the touring Teatro Barraca.

Ureña (☑958 45 41 54) buses to Fuente Vaqueros (€1.55, 20 minutes) leave from Avenida de Andaluces in front of Granada train station, roughly once an hour from 9am during the week, and at 9am, 11am, 1pm and 5pm on weekends and holidays.

Sierra Nevada

True to their name, Spain's highest mountains rise like icy sentinels behind the city of Granada, culminating in the rugged summit of Mulhacén (3479m), mainland Spain's highest peak. But the snowcapped mountains you see shimmering in the background of all those scenic Alhambra postcards are just the tip of the iceberg. The Sierra Nevada proper stretches 75km west to east from Granada into Almería province. The upper reaches of the range form the 862-sq-km Parque Nacional Sierra Nevada, Spain's biggest national park, with a rare high-altitude environment that is home to about 2100 of Spain's 7000 plant species. Andalucía's largest ibex population (about 5000) is here too. Surrounding the national park at lower altitudes is the 848-sq-km Parque Natural Sierra Nevada. The mountains and Las Alpujarras valleys comprise one of the most spectacular areas in Spain, and the area offers wonderful opportunities for walking, horse riding, climbing, mountain biking and, in winter, good skiing and snowboarding.

Estación de Esquí Sierra Nevada

The ski station Sierra Nevada Ski (☑902 70 80 90; www.sierranevadaski.com), at Pradollano, 33km from Granada on the A395, often has better snow conditions and weather than northern Spanish ski resorts, so it can get very crowded on weekends and holidays in season. A few of the 85 marked runs start almost at the top of 3395m Veleta. There are cross-country routes, too, and a dedicated snowboard area, plus a whole raft of other activities for nonskiers. In summer you can mountain bike, ride horses and more.

In winter Tocina (☑958 46 50 22) operates three daily buses (four on the weekends) to the resort from Granada's bus station (€5/8 one way/return, one hour). Outside the ski season there's just one daily bus (9am from Granada, 5pm from the ski station). A taxi from Granada costs about €50.

ⓘ Information

The Centro de Visitantes El Dornajo (☑958 34 06 25; ⊙9.30am-2.30pm & 4.30-7.30pm), about 23km from Granada, on the A395 towards the ski station, has plenty of information on the Sierra Nevada. Knowledgeable, English-speaking staff are happy to help.

Mulhacén & Veleta

The Sierra Nevada's two highest peaks are Mulhacén (3479m) and Veleta (3395m). Two of three known as Los Tresmiles (because they rise above 3000m), they're on the western end of the range, close to Granada. From Pradollano on the mountains' north flank, a road climbs up and over to Capileira, the highest village in the Barranco de Poqueira in the Alpujarras on the south side, but it's closed to motor vehicles on the highest stretch. From late June to the end of October, the national park operates two shuttle buses to give walkers access to the upper reaches of the range – or just a scenic guided drive.

One bus runs up from 3km above the ski station, starting at the national park information post at Hoya de la Mora (⊙during bus-service season approx 8.30am-2.30pm & 3.30-7.30pm). The other leaves from the town of Capileira in Las Alpujarras. Tickets cost €5 one way or €9 return.

From the end of the bus route on the north side, it's about 4km up Veleta, an ascent of about 370m; or 14km to the top of Mulhacén. From the Mirador de Trevélez (the end stop on the Capileira side), it's 6km to the top of Mulhacén (800m ascent).

If you want to make it an overnight trip, you can bunk down for the night at the Refugio Poqueira (☑958 34 33 49; Mulhacén, Sierra Nevada; per person €17). The refuge is open year-round.

Western Sierra Nevada & Las Alpujarras

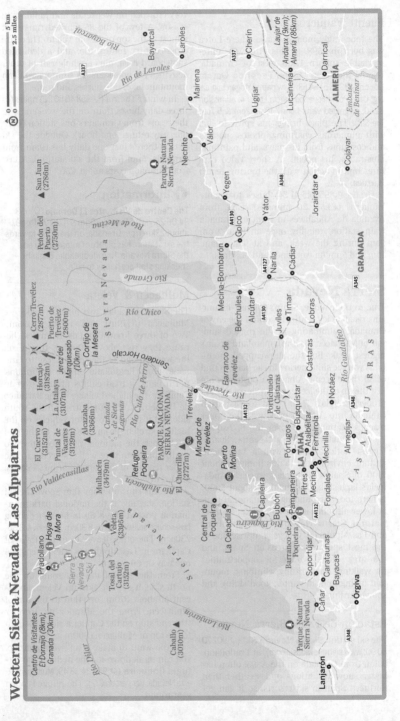

Las Alpujarras

Below the southern flank of the Sierra Nevada lies the 70km-long jumble of valleys known as Las Alpujarras. Arid hillsides split by deep ravines alternate with oasislike white villages set beside rapid streams and surrounded by gardens, orchards and woodlands. Las Alpujarras was the last part of Spain to retain a strong Muslim population. After the fall of Granada in 1492, Moors who refused to convert took to these hills where they held out until the failed Morisco Rebellion of 1568.

Many good walking routes link valley villages and head up into the Sierra Nevada: the best times to visit are between April and mid-June, and mid-September and early November.

A recent surge in tourism and New Age and foreign (mainly British) settlers have given the area a new dimension.

History

In the 10th and 11th centuries Las Alpujarras, settled by Berbers, was a great silkworm farm for the workshops of Almería. But after Granada fell to Fernando and Isabel in 1492, the industry languished and many villages were abandoned. Following the Morisco Rebellion of 1568, the Alpujarra villages were resettled by Christians imported from northern Spain.

South from Granada by Gerald Brenan, an Englishman who lived in Las Alpujarras village of Yegen in the 1920s and '30s, gives a fascinating picture of what was then a very isolated, superstitious corner of Spain. Another Englishman, Chris Stewart, settled here more recently, as a sheep farmer near Órgiva. His entertaining and best-selling *Driving over Lemons* tells of life as a foreigner in Las Alpujarras in the '90s.

Lanjarón

Known as 'the gateway to the Alpujarras', Lanjarón's heyday was during the late 19th and early 20th centuries, when it was a fashionable *balneario* (spa). Today, although Lanjarón water is sold all over Spain, the balneario (958 77 00 137; www.balneario delanjaron.com; Avenida de la Constitución; baths from €18) is visited largely by elderly Spanish cure-seekers. Yet the town has authentic charms. Traditional family life is lived along its main streets, Avenida de la Alpujarra and Avenida Andalucía.

Of the long-distance footpaths that traverse Las Alpujarras, the GR-7 (which runs all the way to Greece) follows the most scenic route; you could walk it from Lanjarón to Pampaneira (20km) in a long day. The path is signposted at the far eastern end of the town, just across the bridge over the Río Lanjarón.

There are plenty of hotels. Hotel Andalucía (958 77 01 36; www.hotelandalucia.com; Avenida de la Alpujarra 15-17; s/d €42/52; ✱🛜💲) close to the *balneario,* is a good budget option, with clean if bland rooms and an outdoor pool. Eat at seafood restaurant Los Mariscos (Avenida de la Alpujarra 6; mains €8-12; 9am-midnight Wed-Sun), where everything is cooked with fresh ingredients.

The tourist office (Avenida de Madrid; 10am-2pm & 4.30-8.30pm), opposite the *balneario,* provides comprehensive information on outdoor activities and accommodation for the entire Alpujarras region.

Órgiva

POP 6500 / ELEV 725M

The western Alpujarras' main town, Órgiva, is a scruffy but bustling place with a big hippie/New Age element. Stay at Casa Rural Jazmín (958 78 47 95; www.casaruraljazmin.com; Calle Ladera de la Ermita; r €53-70; ✱🛜), a French-run house with four rooms, each decorated in a different style (Asian and Alpujarran rooms are smaller; French and African, larger). Good places to eat include Teteria Baraka (www.teteria-baraka.com; Calle Estación 12; mains €10-13; noon-10.30pm Sat-Wed, 9am-4.30pm Thu), located beside the municipal car park in the upper part of town; it has an eclectic menu that includes Moroccan dishes, tofu burgers, shwarmas, delicious brownies and natural juices. Mesón Casa Santiago (Plaza García Moreno; mains €6-12; Mon-Sat) is the best of the bar-restaurants on the plaza, with outside tables and a bricks-and-beams rustic interior.

Pampaneira, Bubión & Capileira

POP 1270 / ELEV 1200-1440M

These small white villages clinging to the side of the deep Barranco de Poqueira gorge, 14km to 20km northeast of Órgiva, are stacked up on top of one another like mini glaciers. Communally they are revered for their dramatic setting, flat-roofed

Moroccan-style houses and high-quality local handicrafts produced since ancient times. They are also used as major bases for sorties into the Sierra Nevada.

Pampaneira, the lowest and smallest village, is known for its coarsely woven rugs and blankets. Bubión, the quiet middle village, has a small museum and is bisected by the GR-7 cross-continental footpath. Capileira, the highest, largest and – arguably – the prettiest village, sports the best restaurants and accommodation options, and has a long tradition for producing top-quality leather goods. It is also significant for its old flat-roofed houses reminiscent of Berber houses in Southern Morocco.

The villages are a sometimes terrifying two-hour bus ride from Granada and are thus possible to incorporate into a long day trip. Serious hikers usually stay over and enjoy the clear mountain air and ambience.

Sights & Activities

All three villages have solid 16th-century Mudéjar churches. They also have small weaving workshops, descendants of a textile tradition that goes back to Islamic times, and plentiful craft shops. In Bubión you'll get a marvellous glimpse of bygone Alpujarras life at the excellent little folk museum Casa Alpujarreña (Calle Real; admission €2; ⊙11am-2pm Sun-Thu, 11am-2pm & 5-7pm Sat & holidays), beside the church.

Eight walking trails, ranging from 4km to 23km (two to eight hours), are marked out in the beautiful Barranco de Poqueira with little colour-coded posts. Their starting points can be hard to find, but they are

ARTISAN CRAFTS OF THE ALPUJARRAS

Firecely traditional despite the recent influx of foreign residents, the Alpujarras villages remain bastions of age-old artisan crafts. While this might not look like a typical shopping destination (there's not a shopping mall for miles around), you might just get lucky. Here are some pointers:

Pampaneira

Though it's more famous for the colourful rugs that seem to hang from every wall, the lowest of the Barranco de Poqueira villages is a place for unexpected treats in Abuela Ili Chocolates (www.abuelailichocolate.com; Plaza de la Libertad 1; ⊙10am-1.30pm & 5-8pm Mon-Fri, 10am-1.30pm Sat), where fabulous chocolate is made on-site, including wonderful and unusual sweet and savoury flavours ranging from mango to mustard. There's a small museum explaining the process.

Bubión

For a glimpse of the past, visit the French-owned weaving workshop Nade Taller del Telar (www.tallerdeltelar.com; Calle Trinidad 11; ⊙11am-2.30pm & 5-8.30pm), with its historic enormous looms that come from the Albayzín in Granada. The shawls, sofa throws and blankets made using only natural fabrics are beautiful. Prices start at €65.

Capileira

Leatherwork is a speciality in the highest Poqueira village. J Brown (www.jbrowntaller depiel.com; Calle Doctor Castilla 7; ⊙10am-1.30pm & 5-8pm Mon-Fri, 10am-1.30pm Sat) – who, despite the name, is Spanish – makes excellent bags, belts and Western-style hats, all by hand. You can watch him at work at the back of the shop.

Pitres & La Tahá

Like the rest of Las Alpujarras region, La Tahá attracts plenty of artists and craftsmen (and women). For exquisite handmade tiles with a definite Moorish influence, check out Alizares Fatima (☑958 76 61 07; www.alizares.es; Calle Paseo Marítimo 19; ⊙10am-1.30pm & 5-8pm Mon-Fri, 10am-1.30pm Sat) on the edge of Pitres, which does beautiful work.

Trevélez

Spain's highest village is famous all over Spain for its cured ham. Jamones González (www.jamonescanogonzalez.com; Calle Nueva; ⊙10am-1.30pm & 5-8pm Mon-Fri, 10am-1.30pm Sat) is the place to come if you fancy taking some home. It also sells other local gourmet products.

marked and described on Editorial Alpina's *Sierra Nevada, La Alpujarra* map. **Nevadensis** (☑ 958 76 31 27; www.nevadensis.com), at the information office in Pampaneira, offers hikes and treks, 4WD trips, horse riding, mountain biking, climbing and canyoning, all with knowledgeable guides.

🛏 Sleeping & Eating

Book ahead for rooms around Easter and from July to September. Many villages have apartments and houses for rent; ask in tourist offices or check websites such as **Turgranada** (www.turgranada.es) or **Rustic Blue** (www.rusticblue.com).

PAMPANEIRA

Opened in 2010, **Estrella de las Nieves** (☑ 958 76 39 81; www.estrelladelasnieves.com; Calle Huerto 21, Pampaneira; s/d €54/70; P 🛜 ☒), just above the town, has airy, light and modern rooms with terraces overlooking the rooftops and mountains. **Restaurante Casa Diego** (Plaza de la Libertad 3; menú €9, mains €6.50-14; ⊙ 10am-5pm & 7pm-midnight), across from the church, has a pleasant upstairs terrace and serves local trout and ham.

BUBIÓN

Las Terrazas de la Alpujarra (☑ 958 76 30 34; www.terrazasalpujarra.com; Plaza del Sol 7; s/d €26/36, 2-/4-/6-person apt €45/55/72) is located below the main road and near the car park with a mix of hotel rooms and apartments. Traditional **Teide Restaurant** (☑ 958 76 30 37; Carretera de Sierra Nevada 2; menús €10; ⊙ 10am-10.30pm Wed-Mon) on the main road has a good *menú del dia*, while **Estación 4** (Calle Estación 4; mains €7-12; ⊙ 6-11pm Tue-Fri, 1-4pm & 6.30-11pm Sat & Sun; ☑) inhabits an old village house.

CAPILEIRA

A gorgeous modern makeover of an ancient building opposite the church, **Hotel Real de Poqueira** (☑ 958 76 39 02; www.hotel poqueira.com; Doctor Castillas 11; d €60-70; ☒ 🛜 ☒) is a rare newcomer to the village's hotel fold and the winner of plenty of early plaudits. It joins the ever-popular **Finca Los Llanos** (☑ 958 76 30 71; www.hotelfincalosllanos. com; Carretera de Sierra Nevada; s/d €50/66; ☒), which has tasteful rooms, a pool, a restaurant, and an office that serves as an official Sierra Nevada information point. **Bar El Tilo** (Plaza Calvario; raciones €8; ⊙ 11.30am-11pm), Capileira's village tavern, enjoys prime position on a lovely whitewashed square with a

---

🛈 LAS ALPUJARRAS BY BUS

Alsa (☑ 958 18 54 80) runs three daily buses from Granada right through the Alpujarras region. Buses leave Granada at 10am, noon and 4.30pm and call at Lanjarón (€4.27, one hour), Órgiva (€5.11, 1¼ hours), Pampaneira (€6, two hours), Bubión (€6.08, 2¼ hours), Capileira (€6.12, 2½ hours), Pitres (€6.79, 2¾ hours) and Trevélez (€7.97, 3¼ hours). Three buses make the return leg leaving Trevélez at 6.15am, 4pm and 5.30pm.

---

terrace. You can't go wrong with the *plato alpujarreño,* a medley of the local nosh, including cured ham, blood sausage, peppers and eggs. **El Corral del Castaño** (Plaza del Calvario 16; menú €10, mains €8.50-14; ⊙ 9am-11pm Thu-Tue) has an Italian menu and does a local take on gastronomic dishes.

🛈 Information

You'll find ATMs outside the car-park entrance in Pampaneira, and in Capileira at La General (Calle Doctor Castilla).

Punto de Información Parque Nacional de Sierra Nevada (www.nevadensis.com; Plaza de la Libertad; ⊙ 10am-2pm & 4-6pm Tue-Sat, to 3pm Sun & Mon Oct-Mar) Plenty of information about Las Alpujarras and Sierra Nevada; outdoor gear, maps and books for sale. Located in Pampaneira.

Servicio de Interpretación de Altos Cumbres (☑ 671 56 44 06, 958 76 34 86; picapileira@ oapn.mma.es; ⊙ about 9am-2pm & 4.30-7.30pm) Next to where the bus stops in Capileira; information mainly about the national park, but also on Las Alpujarras in general.

Pitres & La Taha

POP 800 / ELEV 1245M

Pitres is a break from the tourism and souvenirs in the Poqueira Gorge villages, although not quite as pretty. The beautiful valley below it, with five tranquil hamlets (Mecina, Mecinilla, Fondales, Ferreirola and Atalbéitar), all grouped with Pitres in the municipio called La Taha, is particularly fascinating to explore. Its ancient pathways are a walker's delight.

Above Pitres in the tiny hamlet of Capilerilla (and on the E4 footpath) lies **Hotel Maravedi** (☑ 958 76 62 92; www.hotelmaravedi. com; r €60-70), rustic but with all the home comforts plus satellite TV and a private bar-restaurant for guests. In nearby Mecina, welcoming French-run guesthouse **L'Atelier** (☎958 85 75 01; www.atelier-mecina.com; Calle Alberca 21; s/d incl breakfast €38/50; ⊙Mar-Nov), situated in an ancient village house, also serves gourmet vegetarian/vegan meals (lunch Saturday and Sunday, dinner Wednesday to Monday). In peaceful Ferreirola, **Sierra y Mar** (☎958 76 61 71; www.sierraymar.com; Calle Albaicín; s/d incl breakfast €42/62; P 📶) has just nine rooms, set around patios and gardens. It is closed in January and February.

Trevélez

POP 1150 / ELEV 1476M

To gastronomes Trevélez equals ham – or *jamón serrano* to be more precise, one of Spain's finest cured hams. To hikers it means a cobweb of high mountain trails including easy access to Mulhacén, mainland Spain's highest peak. To statisticians it is the second-highest village in Spain after Valdelinares in Aragón.

The village, sited at 1486m on the almost treeless slopes of the Barranco de Trevélez, is divided into *alto* (high) and *bajo* (low) sections. The Alpujarra bus generally stops in both. The *alto* section is older and more labyrinthine, while *bajo* has the bulk of the tourist facilities.

On a leafy, terraced hillside 1km west of Trevélez, **Camping Trevélez** (☎tel/fax 958 85 87 35; www.campingtrevelez.net; Carretera Trevélez-Órgiva, Km 1; sites per adult/tent/car/cabin €4.75/5.25/4/26; ⊙closed Jan–mid Feb; 📶) has ecologically minded owners and a good-value restaurant. Walkers' favourite **Hotel La Fragua I** (☎958 85 86 26; www.hotellafragua.com; Calle San Antonio 4; s/d/tr €35/48/65) provides pine-furnished rooms, with a more upmarket annex at **La Fragua II** (d/tr €55/72). La Fragua is closed early January to early February. Its restaurant, **Mesón La Fragua** (mains €7.50-13; ⊙1-4pm & 8-11pm), a few doors away, is one of the best in town and worth the steep climb to the upper town. In **Mesón Joaquín** (☎958 85 85 60; Calle Puente; mains €9-14; ⊙10am-11pm), white-coated *jamón* technicians slice up transparent sheets of the local product, and the trout comes from the wholesaler just behind. Rest assured, every restaurant in town serves the delicate mountain-air-cured ham.

A good hike from Trevélez follows the **Sendero Horcajo** up the Trevélez river valley from the top of town. The ultimate goal is the Cortijo de la Meseta, a *refugio* where you can stay overnight. The full walk one-way is 8.7km.

Costa Tropical

Granada's cliff-lined, 80km-long coast has a hint of Italy's Amalfi about it, although it is definitively Spanish when you get down to the nitty-gritty, with Moorish relics, old-school tapas joints and some damn fine churros. Its warm climate – there's no real winter to speak of – gives rise to its name: Costa Tropical. A sprinkling of attractive beach towns less colonised by expats than those on the Costa del Sol is linked by several daily buses to Granada, Málaga and Almería.

WORTH A TRIP

WATER SPORTS IN LA HERRADURA

If you're craving a more remote beach scene than Almuñécar, or more activity, consider heading 7km west to the small, horseshoe-shaped bay at La Herradura, where a younger demographic of windsurfers and paragliders congregate. **Windsurf La Herradura** (☎958 64 01 43; www.windsurflaherradura.com; Paseo Andrés Segovia 34) is one good operator for these, as well as for less-extreme water sports, including kayaking.

While the western Mediterranean, with its shallow, sandy coastal waters, is of limited interest for aspiring divers, the eastern Med, more specifically the Costa Tropical around La Herradura, is a different kettle of fish. Here you'll find a varied seabed of sea grass, sand and rock flecked with caves, crevices and passages. Local dive operator **Open Water La Herradura** (☎644 44 43 14; www.openwater.es; Paseo Andrés Segovia; 1/5 dives €27/120, open-water course €360) keeps a boat moored at the marina from where its a five- to 10-minute journey out to various dive sites.

When you return, you can enjoy the seafood in one of the many *chiringuitos* on La Herradura's beach.

Almuñécar

POP 27,000

More interesting and certainly more Spanish than anything on the Costa del Sol, Almuñécar is well worth a day's diversion. There's easy access from either Granada or Málaga. The attractive old town, which hugs the coast amid small coves and precipitous cliffs, huddles around the 16th-century Castillo de San Miguel (Santa Adela Explanada; adult/child €2.35/1.60; ☺10am-1.30pm & 4-6.30pm Tue-Sat, 10.30am-1pm Sun) and the adjoining Museo Arqueológico (Calle San Joaquín; adult/child €2.35/1.60; ☺10am-1.30pm & 4-6.30pm Tue-Sat, 10.30am-1pm Sun), situated in the basement of an old Roman construction. The castle has an excellent interactive museum.

The breezy seafront is an excellent place to *dar un paseo* (go for a slow evening stroll). Make for the Peñon del Santo, a steep, pointed headland that divides the town's two beaches.

Just behind Playa de San Cristóbal is a tropical-bird aviary, Parque Ornitológico Loro-Sexi (adult/child €4/2; ☺11am-2pm & 6-9pm; ⊞).

You can paraglide, windsurf, dive, sail, ride a horse or descend canyons in and around Almuñécar and nearby La Herradura. The tourist office and its website have plenty of information.

🛏 Sleeping & Eating

Hotel Casablanca   HOTEL $
(☎958 63 55 75; www.hotelcasablancaalmunecar. com; Plaza de San Cristóbal 4; s/d €50/64) In town, the distinctive terracotta arches of the Hotel Casablanca really could have sprung from Casablanca. The place is furnished in distinctive Al-Andalus style, with sea views from some rooms.

La Italiana Cafe   CAFE, ITALIAN $
(☎958 88 23 12; www.laitaliancafe.com; Hurtado de Mendoza 5; pizza & pasta €8-9; ☺8am-10pm; ☜) Weirdly, considering its name and pizza/ pasta menu, La Italiana is *the* place to go for local Almuñécar pastries such as *torta de alhajú* and *cazuela mohina*. Enjoy them with a cappuccino surrounded by ceiling frescoes and elaborately gilded pillars and mirrors.

Pepe Dígame   SEAFOOD $$
(☎958 34 93 15; Plaza San Cristóbal; mains €9.50-15; ☺8am-10pm) One of those beachfront, fish-biased restaurants where you can loll around all afternoon with a bottle of wine as the kids build sandcastles and the fishermen sail back from a hard day at the office.

ⓘ Information

The **main tourist office** (www.almunecar.info; Avenida Europa; ☺10am-2pm & 6-9pm) is 1km southwest of the town centre, just back from Playa de San Cristóbal, in the rose-pink neo-Moorish Palacete La Najarra, which has lovely gardens and is a tourist sight in its own right.

ⓘ Getting There & Away

The **Almuñécar bus station** (☎958 63 01 40; Avenida Juan Carlos I 1) is just south of the N340. At least six buses a day go to Almería (€10, two hours) and Málaga (€6.50, 1¾ hours), with eight to Granada (€7.50, 1½ hours), 11 to La Herradura (€1, 10 minutes), and 13 to Nerja (€2.50, 30 minutes). A bus goes to Órgiva (€4, 1¼ hours) at 4.30pm Monday to Saturday.

MÁLAGA PROVINCE

Misty-eyed old men on park benches reminisce about whitewashed fishing villages as blue-eyed invaders from the north pick up the keys to their new Costa del Sol condominiums. Málaga province is where Spain's great tourist experiment went viral, leaving a once-tranquil coastline covered in concrete and a local populace fighting to maintain a semblance of its traditional culture. Odd snippets of the old way of life still exist. The provincial capital, Málaga, is an oasis of old-fashioned Spanishness while, further inland, outside encroachments have been kept to a minimum in eye-catching towns such as Antequera, and in equally spectacular natural features such as the Garganta del Chorro (Chorro Gorge).

Málaga

POP 558,000

The Costa del Sol can seem wholly soulless until you fall, gasping for a shred of culture, into Málaga, an unmistakably Spanish metropolis curiously ignored by the lion's share of the millions of tourists who land annually at Pablo Ruíz Picasso International Airport before getting carted off to the golf courses and beaches of 'Torrie' and Fuengirola. Their loss could be your gain.

Stubborn and stalwart, Málaga's history is storied and its feisty populace could

Málaga

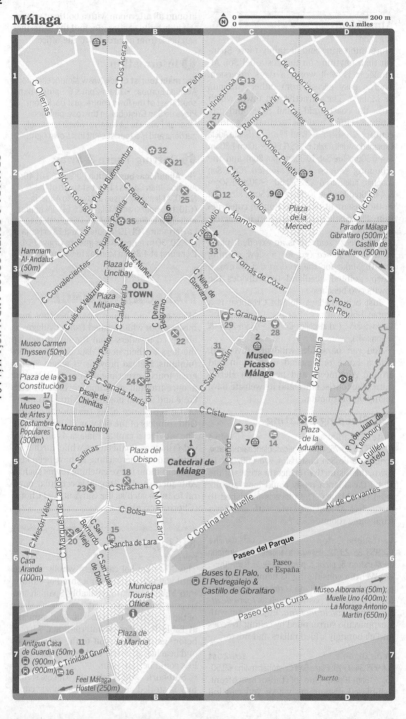

Málaga

challenge *sevillanos* as 24-hour party people. Not known for their timidity in battle, the *malagueños* (residents of Málaga) held out until 1487 against the invading Christian armies and employed equal tenacity when Franco's fascists came knocking in the Spanish Civil War. More recently, Málaga has fought off the less-attractive effects of mass tourism and opened a cache of culturally relevant museums, many of them art-orientated. Renovations have recently been completed on its once weathered port area.

Málaga endowed the world with another priceless gift – Pablo Picasso, the 20th century's most ground-breaking artist, who was born in a small house in Plaza de Merced in 1881. A couple of excellent museums guard his gigantic legacy.

History

Probably founded by Phoenicians, Málaga has long had a commercial vocation. It flourished in the Islamic era, especially as the chief port of the Emirate of Granada, later reasserting itself as an entrepreneurial centre in the 19th century when a dynamic middle class founded textile factories, sugar and steel mills, and shipyards. Málaga dessert wine ('mountain sack') was popular in Victorian England. During the civil war, Málaga was initially a Republican stronghold.

Hundreds of Nationalist sympathisers were killed before the city fell in February 1937 after being bombed by Italian planes. Vicious reprisals followed.

Málaga has enjoyed a steadily increasing economic spin-off from the mass tourism launched on the nearby Costa del Sol in the 1950s. In recent years, the city has become an important destination in itself.

◎ Sights & Activities

★ **Museo Picasso Málaga**   MUSEUM
(☏902 443377; www.museopicassomalaga.org; Calle San Agustín 8; permanent/temporary collection €6/4.50, combined ticket €8; ◷10am-8pm Tue-Thu & Sun, to 9pm Fri & Sat) Granted, there are probably better Picasso museums in Paris and Barcelona, but nowhere can claim the poignancy of this impressive collection encased in a palatial building in the city that created the 20th century's most influential and enigmatic artist.

Well-endowed with 204 Picasso works, 155 donated and 49 loaned to the museum by Christine Ruiz-Picasso (wife of Paul, Picasso's eldest son) and Bernard Ruiz-Picasso (his grandson), the museum includes some wonderful paintings of the family, including the heartfelt *Paulo con gorro blanco*, a portrait of Picasso's eldest son painted in the 1920s.

MÁLAGA'S MUSEUMS – BEST OF THE REST

After polishing off Málaga's not-to-be-missed sights, visitors with more time on their hands can go in search of the city's more esoteric museums – time-permitting. Here is a 'greatest hits' of Málaga's second-tier attractions.

Museo de Artes y Costumbres Populares (Museum of Popular Arts & Customs; ☑952 21 71 37; www.museoartespopulares.com; Pasillo de Santa Isabel 10; adult/child under 14yr €2/ free; ☉10am-5pm Mon-Fri, 10am-2pm Sat) Located in a 17th-century inn, this museum displays *barros* (painted clay figures) of characters from Málaga folklore.

Museo del Vidrio y Cristal (Museum of Glass & Crystal; ☑952 22 02 71; www.museo-vidrioycristalmalaga.com; Plazuela Santísimo Cristo de la Sangre 2; adult/concession €5/3; ☉11am-7pm Tue-Sun) More interesting than it sounds, the privately owned museum of glass has a whole range of antique furniture with an obvious bias towards glass objects.

Museo Interactivo de la Música Málaga (☑952 21 04 40; www.mimma.es; Calle Beatas 15; adult/concession €4/3; ☉10am-2pm Mon, 10am-2pm & 4-8pm Tue-Sun) Play drums, strum lyres and partake in various other interactive experiences at this recently relocated and refurbished music museum.

Museo Revello de Toro (☑952 06 20 69; www.museorevellodetoro.net; Calle Afligidos 5; admission €2.50; ☉10am-2pm & 5-8pm Tue-Sat, 10am-2pm Sun) Showcases the work of 20th-century *malagueño* artist Félix Revello de Toro in a 17th-century mansion that was once the workshop of religious sculptor Pedro de Mena.

★**Catedral de Málaga** CATHEDRAL
(☑952 21 59 17; Calle Molina Lario; cathedral & museum €3.50; ☉10am-6pm Mon-Sat, closed holidays) Containing what is possibly the finest church interior in Andalucía, Málaga cathedral's beauty is overshadowed by the fact that – rather like Beethoven's Ninth Symphony – it was never finished. Started in the 16th century, building continued for 200 years before it ran out of funds and was stopped, a victim of over-ambition. A series of five architects was eventually used to transform the one-time mosque into the beautiful, if incomplete, church we see today.

Inside, it is easy to see why the epic project took three lifetimes to enact. The fabulous domed ceiling soars 40m into the air, while the vast colonnaded nave houses an enormous cedar-wood choir. Aisles give access to 15 chapels with gorgeous retables and a stash of 18th-century religious art. Such was the project's cost that by 1782 it was decided that work would stop. One of the two bell towers was left incomplete, hence the cathedral's well-worn nickname, La Manquita (the one-armed lady). The cathedral entrance is on Calle Císter. There's a small museum inside displaying religious items and sacred art, plus a diminutive courtyard of orange trees and the ablutions fountain from the original mosque.

Museo de Arte Flamenco MUSEUM
(☑952 22 13 80; www.museoflamencojuanbreva.com; Calle Juan Franquelo 4; suggested donation €1; ☉10am-2pm Tue-Sun) Fabulously laid-out over two floors in the HQ of Málaga's oldest and most prestigious *peña* (private flamenco club), this collection of fans, costumes, posters and other flamenco paraphernalia is testimony to the city's illustrious flamenco scene.

★**Alcazaba** CASTLE
(Calle Alcazabilla; admission €2.10, incl Castillo de Gibralfaro €3.40; ☉9.30am-8pm Tue-Sun Apr-Oct) No time to visit Granada's Alhambra? Fear not. Málaga's Alcazaba can provide a taster. The entrance is next to the Roman amphitheatre, from where a meandering path climbs amid lush greenery: crimson bougainvillea, lofty palms, fragrant jasmine bushes and rows of orange trees.

Extensively restored, this palace-fortress dates from the 11th-century Moorish period, and the caliphal horseshoe arches, courtyards and bubbling fountains are evocative of this influential period in Málaga's history.

Don't miss the small archaeological museum located within the former servants' quarters of the Nazari palace, with its exhibits of Moorish ceramics and pottery.

Roman Amphitheatre LANDMARK, MUSEUM
(☑951 50 11 15; Calle Alcazabilla 8) Uncovered in 1951, this Roman theatre slap-bang in the

city centre had lain hidden for hundreds of years. It was built in the time of Augustus (1st century AD) and remains relatively well-preserved. An adjacent interpretive centre has touch screens and some artifacts dug up from the site. The theatre is particularly evocative at night with the shadowy Alcazaba illuminated behind it.

Castillo de Gibralfaro CASTLE
(admission €2.10; ⊙ 9am-9pm Apr-Sep, to 6pm Oct-Mar) One remnant of Málaga's Islamic past is the craggy ramparts of the Castillo de Gibralfaro, spectacularly located high on the hill overlooking the city. Built by Abd ar-Rahman I, the 8th-century Cordoban emir, and later rebuilt in the 14th century when Málaga was the main port for the emirate of Granada, the castle originally acted as a lighthouse and military barracks.

Nothing much is original in the castle's interior, but the airy walkway around the ramparts affords the best views over Málaga. There is also a military museum, which includes a small-scale model of the entire castle complex and the lower residence, the Alcazaba. The model clearly shows the 14th-century curtain wall that connected the two sites and which has been recently restored.

The best way to reach the castle on foot is via the scenic Paseo Don Juan de Temboury, to the south of the Alcazaba. Alternatively, you can drive up the Camino de Gibralfaro or take bus 35 from Avenida de Cervantes.

★ Museo Carmen Thyssen MUSEUM
(www.carmenthyssenmalaga.org; Calle Compañia 10; adult/child €6/free; ⊙10am-7.30pm Tue-Sun) Málaga's art is about a lot more than Picasso, as this aesthetically impressive museum, set in a renovated 16th-century palace, proves. The permanent collection concentrates on 19th-century Spanish and Andalucian art and its compelling if cliched images of Roma people, bandits, bullfighters and Carmen-like seductresses. Exceptional painters are represented, including Joaquín Sorolla y Bastida, Ignacio Zuloaga and Francisco de Zurbarán.

Casa Natal de Picasso MUSEUM
(www.fundacionpicasso.malaga.eu; Plaza de la Merced 15; admission €3; ⊙9.30am-8pm) For an insight into Picasso's early childhood, head to the house where he was born in 1881, which now acts as a study foundation. The house has a replica 19th-century artist's studio and small quarterly exhibitions of Picas-so-related work. Family memorabilia make up part of the display, but more interesting are the paintings by his father, who was also an accomplished artist.

Across the square, in another house, is the Sala de Exposiciones (Plaza de la Merced 13; ⊙9.30am-8pm) where you can view more temporary art displays on the same ticket.

Muelle Uno PORT
The city's long-beleaguered port area underwent a radical rethink in 2011–13 and was redesigned to cater for the increase in cruise passengers to the city. Wide quayside walkways now embellish Muelle 1 and Muelle 2 lined by palm trees and backed by shops, restaurants, bars and a small kid-orientated aquarium, the so-called Museo Alborania (✓ 951 60 01 08; www.museoalborania.com; Palmeral de las Sopresas, Muelle 2; adult/child €7/5; ⊙11am-2pm & 5pm-midnight July-15 Sep, 10.30am-2.30pm & 4.30-6:30pm Sep 15-Jun; ⊕).

Still growing into itself, the port is slowly trying to prise the socialising masses away from the far more vibrant old town. Suffice to say, Rome wasn't built in a day.

Hammam Al-Andalus HAMMAM
(✓ 952 21 50 18; www.hammamalandalus.com; Plaza de los Mártires 5; admission €30; ⊙10am-midnight) These new Moorish-style baths opened in the historic centre in 2013 to allow *malagueños* access to the same relaxation benefits as those offered by similar facilties in Granada and Córdoba. Massages are also available.

Beaches BEACHES
Sandy city beaches stretch several kilometres in each direction from the port. Playa de la Malagueta, handy to the city centre, has some excellent bars and restaurants close by. Playa de Pedregalejo and Playa del Palo, about 4km east of the centre, are popular and reachable by bus 11 from Paseo del Parque.

🐾 Courses

There are many private language schools in Málaga; try the Instituto Picasso (✓ 952 21 39 32; www.instituto-picasso.com; Plaza de la Merced 20), which runs two-/three-/four-week courses for €310/440/560 starting every fortnight on a Monday. There are four 50-minute lessons a day and the price includes access to cultural activities such as flamenco and cookery courses. Accommodation is also available.

⚐ Tours

Malaga Bike Tours CYCLING
(☑606 978513; www.malagabiketours.eu; Calle Trinidad Grund 1; tours €25) Málaga is robustly promoting bike culture with a new residents-only bike-sharing scheme, and while the city can't yet match Seville for bike friendliness, things are definitely improving. Bike tours are an excellent way to see the sights and you can't do better than Malaga Bike Tours, which runs daily tours leaving from outside the municipal tourist office in Plaza de la Marina at 10am. Reservations are required. Book at least 24 hours ahead.

Alternatively, you can rent your own bike from them for €10 a day.

⚔ Festivals & Events

Semana Santa HOLY WEEK
Each night from Palm Sunday to Good Friday, six or seven *cofradías* (brotherhoods) bear their holy images for several hours through the city, watched by large crowds.

Feria de Málaga FAIR
(☉Aug) Málaga's nine-day *feria* launched by a huge fireworks display on the opening Friday in mid-August, is the most ebullient of Andalucía's summer *ferias*. It resembles an exuberant Rio-style street party with plenty of flamenco and *fino* (sherry). Head for the city centre to be in the thick of it.

⎆ Sleeping

Hotel Carlos V HOTEL $
(☑952 21 51 20; www.hotel-carlosvmalaga.com; Calle Císter 10; s/d €36/59; P ✳ @) Close to the cathedral and Picasso museum, the Carlos V is enduringly popular. Benefiting from regular renovations, bathrooms sparkle in a uniform of cream-and-white tiles. Excellent standard for the price plus helpful staff make this hotel a bargain.

Hotel Sur HOTEL $
(☑952 22 48 03; www.hotel-sur.com; Calle Trinidad Grund 13; s/d €42/55; P ✳ ⧖) A good no-frills budget option located a Messi volley away from the Plaza de la Marina, the Sur is plain but pristine in the cleanliness department. Upping its score are friendly, polite staff and dedicated parking.

Feel Málaga Hostel HOSTEL $
(☑952 22 28 32; www.feelmalagahostel.com; Calle Vendeja 25; d with/without bathroom €35/45,, shared rooms per person from €16; @ ⧖) One of two sparkling-new Feel hostels in Má-

laga, this one is located within a suitcase trundle of the city-centre train station in a neighbourhood recently given the moniker Soho. The accommodation is clean and well equipped with a choice of doubles and shared rooms. Bathrooms sport classy mosaic tiles and the top-floor kitchen has all the essentials.

Room Mate Larios HOTEL $$
(☑952 22 22 00; www.room-matehotels.com; Calle Marqués de Larios 2; s/d €80/100; ✳ @ ⧖) Located on the central Plaza de la Constitución, this hotel is housed in a 19th-century building that has been elegantly restored. Rooms are luxuriously furnished with carpeting throughout and king-sized beds; several rooms have balconies overlooking the sophisticated strut of shops and boutiques along Calle Marqués de Larios.

The roof terrace bar is separately owned but easily accessible and boasts stunning views of the cathedral.

El Hotel del Pintor BOUTIQUE HOTEL $$
(☑952 06 09 81; www.hoteldelpintor.com; Calle Álamos 27; s/d €54/69; ✳ @ ⧖) The red, black and white colour scheme of this friendly small hotel echoes the abstract artwork of *malagueño* artist Pepe Bornov, whose paintings are on permanent display throughout the public areas and rooms. The Pintor is convenient for most of the city's main sights. The rooms in the front can be noisy, especially on a Saturday night.

El Riad Andaluz GUESTHOUSE $$
(☑952 21 36 40; www.elriadandaluz.com; Calle Hinestrosa 24; s/d/tr €62/89/119; ✳ @ ⧖) A French-run guesthouse near the Teatro Cervantes with eight rooms set around the kind of atmospheric patio that's known as a *riad* in Morocco. Not surprisingly, the decor has a heavy Moroccan influence with each room decorated differently, though all have colourful tiled bathrooms. Breakfast is available.

Hotel Don Curro HOTEL $$
(☑952 22 72 00; www.hoteldoncurro.com; Calle Sancha de Lara 7; s/d €63/74; P ✳ @ ⧖) Big, busy Don Curro is efficient, comfortable and central, with well-appointed, spacious rooms and substantial breakfasts just a few steps away at its own Café Moka.

Parador Málaga Gibralfaro HISTORIC HOTEL $$$
(☑952 22 19 02; www.parador.es; Castillo de Gibralfaro; r €160-171; P ✳ ⧖ ⧖) With an unbeat-

able location perched on the pine-forested Gibralfaro, Málaga's stone-built Parador is a popular choice, although the rooms are fairly standard. Most have spectacular views from their terraces, however, and you can dine at the excellent terrace restaurant even if you are not a hotel guest.

✗ Eating

Málaga's restaurants are well priced and of a good standard due to the largely local clientele. A speciality here is fish fried quickly in olive oil. *Fritura malagueña* consists of fried fish, anchovies and squid. Most of the best eating places are sandwiched in the narrow eating streets between Calle Marqués de Larios and the cathedral.

Casa Aranda
CAFE $

(www.casa-aranda.net; Calle Herrería del Rey; churro from €1; ♿) Casa Aranda is in a narrow alleyway next to the market and, since 1932, has been *the* place in town to enjoy chocolate and churros. The cafe has taken over the whole street with several outlets all overseen by a team of mainly elderly white-shirted waiters who welcome everyone like an old friend (most are).

El Piyayo
TAPAS $

(☏ 952 22 90 57; www.entreplatos.es; Calle Granada 36; raciones €6-10; ⊙ 12.30pm-midnight) A popular traditionally tiled bar and restaurant, famed for its *pescaitos fritos* (fried fish) and typical local tapas, including wedges of crumbly Manchego cheese, the ideal accompaniment to a glass of hearty Rioja wine. The *berenjenas con miel de caña* (aubergine with molasses) is also good.

Noviembre
BREAKFAST, CAFE $

(☏ 952 22 26 54; Calle Álamos 18; breakfast €3.50-6.50; ⊙ 9am-1am Sun-Thu, 9am-2am Fri & Sat; ☏☏) ✐ With its purposefully aged mood, mismatched furniture, and bearded young men who somehow make facial hair look trendy, Noviembre has the word 'hipster' written all over it. No matter, the excellent breakfast choices are made with organic eggs and the big apple burger provides a good lunch filler. The later you linger, the trendier the clientele becomes.

Café Lepanto
CAFE, SNACKS $

(Calle Marqués de Larios 7; ⊙ 8.30am-10pm) Old-fashioned pastry shop and cafe on pedestrianised Calle Marqués de Larios with bow-tied waiters and fancy glass display cases. As Málaga's poshest *confitería* (sweet

shop), Lepanto serves up a whole host of delicate *pasteles* (pastries and cakes), plus good ice cream, sweets, chocolates, coffees, teas and other drinks.

Café Central
CAFE $

(www.cafecentralmalaga.com; Plaza de la Constitución; mains €5-12; ⊙ 8.30am-11.30pm) Come here for your morning tomato on toast, best enjoyed alfresco so that you can admire Málaga's main pedestrianised square as it shrugs off the previous night's hangover.

★ El Mesón de Cervantes
TAPAS, ARGENTINIAN $$

(☏ 952 21 62 74; www.elmesondecervantes.com; Calle Álamos 11; mains €13-16; ⊙ 7pm-midnight Wed-Mon) Once a secret, then a whisper, now a loud shout, Cervantes has been declared Málaga's *numero uno* restaurant by a growing number of impressed bloggers, tweeters and anyone else with tastebuds and an internet connection.

It started as a humble tapas bar run by expat Argentinian Gabriel Spatz (the original bar is still operating around the corner), but has now expanded into plush new digs with an open kitchen, fantastic family-style service and – no surprises – incredible meat dishes.

Restaurante Garum
ANDALUCIAN $$

(☏ 952 21 84 08; www.garum.com.es; Calle Alcazabilla 1; mains €12-18; ⊙ noon-5pm & 8pm-midnight Tue-Sun) Despite its location next to the ancient Roman ampitheatre, Garum specialises in refreshing new-age food, dousing Málaga's signature seafood in some rich and inventive sauces, marinades and side dishes. You can get your tuna presented multiple ways, or settle for your sardines done simply and covered in the best extra-virgin olive oil.

La Rebaná
TAPAS $$

(www.larebana.com; Calle Molina Lario 5; raciones €7-12; ⊙ 12.30-5pm & 7.30pm-midnight Mon-Fri, 12.30pm-1am Sat & Sun) A great, noisy tapas bar near the Picasso museum and the cathedral. Dark wood, tall windows and exposed-brick walls create a modern, minimal, laid-back space. Try the unique foie gras with salted nougat tapa.

Vino Mio
INTERNATIONAL $$

(www.restaurantevinomio.com/en; Plaza Jeronimo Cuervo 2; mains €10-15; ⊙ 1pm-2am) This Dutch-owned restaurant is a jack of all trades and a master of, well, some. There are kangaroo steaks, vegetable stir fries, duck breast with sweet chilli, pasta, innovative salads...you get the drift? The atmosphere is contemporary chic with nightly flamenco that may or may not rouse you from your kangeroo steak.

Gorki
TAPAS $$

(www.grupogorki.com; Calle Strachan 6; platos combinados €7.50-16; ⏰12.30pm-midnight) A popular upmarket tapas bar with pavement tables and an interior full of wine-barrel tables and stools, Gorki serves tangy cheeses and an extensive list of Spanish wines. Try the belly-warming *alubias con cordoniz* (white-bean stew with partridge) or the cold *ajoblanco* white soup using almonds.

It's recently opened a second branch on Muelle Uno.

Alumbre
CONTEMPORARY ANDALUCIAN $$

(www.alumbrebar.com; Calle Strachan 11; mains €12-17; ⏰noon-midnight) Located on a pedestrian street flanked by classy bars and restaurants, Alumbre dishes up arty plates of innovative Andalucian-inspired cooking with its roots in traditional 16th-century dishes. Surprises on the menu include snail croquettes, while more conservative palates may prefer the cuttlefish steak.

La Moraga
Antonio Martín
CONTEMPORARY ANDALUCIAN $$$

(☑952 22 41 53; www.lamoraga.com; Plaza Malagueta 4; tapas from €5, mains from €20; ⏰1-4pm & 8-11.30pm) This is one of two La Moraga restaurants by Michelin-star chef Dani Garcia in Málaga (the other is in the airport). The concept is based on traditional tapas given the nouvelle treatment – like cherry gazpacho garnished with fresh cheese, anchovies and basil; king prawns wrapped in fried basil leaves; and mini-burgers created from oxtail.

Drinking

On weekend nights, the web of narrow old streets north of Plaza de la Constitución comes alive. There are also lines of well-used bars along the north side of Plaza de la Merced and – more recently – on Muelle Uno.

Antigua Casa de Guardia
BAR

(www.antiguacasadeguardia.net; Alameda Principal 18; ⏰11am-midnight) Not just old, but positively antediluvian, this atmospheric tavern dates back to 1840 and is the oldest bar in Málaga. The peeling custard-coloured paintwork, black-and-white photographs of local boy Picasso and elderly bar staff look fittingly antique. The dark brown, sherrylike Málaga wine and romantically named *lagrima trañañejo* (very old tear) come straight from the barrel with zero ceremony.

Bodegas El Pimpi
BAR

(www.bodegabarelpimpi.com; Calle Granada 62; ⏰11am-2am) This rambling bar is a warren of rooms with a central courtyard, elongated bar and large open terrace overlooking the Roman amphitheatre. Walls are decorated with historic *feria* posters and photos of celeb-style visitors like Tony Blair. The clientele mixes silver-haired *malagueños* with lippy young Brits on stag weekends.

La Tetería
TEAHOUSE, CAFE

(Calle San Agustín 9; ⏰3-10pm Sun-Wed, to 1am Thu-Sat; 🖥) Before Andalucía's *teterías* became the new Starbucks, this place was knocking out herbal infusions, coffees, juices and teas ranging from peppermint to 'anti-depresivo' from a pretty pitch near the Picasso museum. Less ornate than some of the other Granada-style tearooms, it has more of a cafe feel, with tourists, students and a few laptop users intermingling.

Casa Lola
BAR

(Calle Granada 46; ⏰11am-4pm & 7pm-midnight) It might look historic, but Lola only opened in 2010. Fronted by traditional blue-and-white tiles, it offers sophisticated small bites to support its specialist tipple: vermouth on tap, served ice cold and costing just a couple of euros.

El Jardín
CAFE, BAR

(☑952 22 04 19; Calle Cañón 1; mains €13; ⏰9am-midnight Mon-Thu, 9am-2pm & 5pm-midnight Fri & Sat, 5pm-midnight Sun) A beautiful Viennese-style cafe next to palm-filled gardens behind the cathedral, El Jardín attracts young flamencologists and ancient *malagueños*, plus the odd inebriated Picasso lookalike. Art nouveau flourishes and old photographs evoke a pleasant ambience, but not great food. Instead, come for wine or coffee and listen to some young-at-heart septuagenarian pound away on the upright piano.

☆ Entertainment

Málaga's substantial flamenco heritage has its nexus to the northwest of Plaza de la Merced. Venues include **Kelipe** (☑692 82 98 85; www.kelipe.net; Calle Pena 11; admission €20-35; ⏰show 9pm Thu-Sat), a flamenco centre that puts on performances Thursday to Saturday at 9.30pm; entry includes one drink and tapa – reserve ahead. Kelipe also runs intensive weekend courses in guitar and dance. Vino Mio (www.restaurantevinomio.com; Calle Alamos) is a small restaurant with an international menu where musicians and dancers fill the wait for the food.

Peña Juan Breva   FLAMENCO
(Calle Juan Franquelo 4) You'll feel like a gate-crasher at someone else's party at this private *peña*, but persevere; the flamenco is *muy puro*. Watch guitarists who play like they've got 24 fingers and listen to singers who bellow forth as if their heart had been broken the previous night. There's no set schedule. Ask about dates when/if you visit the onsite Museo de Arte Flamenco (p684).

Teatro Cervantes   THEATRE
(www.teatrocervantes.com; Calle Ramos Marín; ☺ closed mid-Jul–Aug) The handsome art deco Cervantes has a fine program of music, theatre and dance, including some well-known names on the concert circuit, such as Rufus Wainwright, who called Cervantes 'the most beautiful theatre in Europe'.

Velvet Club   LIVE MUSIC
(www.velvetclub.es; Calle de Juan de Padilla 22; ☺ 11pm-4am) Small bar/club with no cover that has DJs during the week and live bands at weekends playing indie, pop-rock and electronica.

🛍 Shopping
Central Calle Marqués de Larios and nearby streets have glitzy boutiques and shoe shops in handsomely restored old buildings.

ℹ Information
There are plenty of banks with ATMs on Calle Puerta del Mar and Calle Marqués de Larios, and ATMs in the airport arrivals hall.

In addition to the **municipal tourist office** (Plaza de la Marina; ☺ 9am-8pm Mar-Sep, 9am-6pm Oct-Feb) there are also information booths at the main train station, the Alcazaba, the Plaza de la Merced, the main post office and on the eastern beaches.

Hospital Carlos Haya (☏ 951 03 01 00; Avenida de Carlos Haya) The main hospital, 2km west of the centre.

Policía Local (☏ 952 12 65 00; Avenida de la Rosaleda 19)

Post Office (Avenida de Andalucía 1; ☺ 8.30am-8.30pm Mon-Fri, 9.30am-2pm Sat)

ℹ Getting There & Away

AIR
Málaga-Costa del Sol Airport (www.aena.es), the main international gateway to Andalucía, is 9km southwest of the city centre. It is a major hub in southern Spain serving close to 13 million passengers annually. Budget airlines Ryanair (www.ryanair.com), EasyJet (www.easyjet.com) and Vueling (www.vueling.com) link to multiple European destinations. Air Transat fly to Montreal and Toronto, and Delta Air Lines fly seasonally to New York-JFK. These are also numerous charter airlines.

BOAT
Trasmediterránea (☏ 952 06 12 18, 902 454645; www.trasmediterranea.com; Estación Marítima, Local E1) operates a ferry (7½ hours) daily year-round to/from Melilla, the Spanish enclave in North Africa (passenger/car one way €38/100).

BUS
Málaga's **bus station** (☏ 952 35 00 61; www.estabus.emtsam.es; Paseo de los Tilos) is just 1km southwest of the city centre. Frequent Alsa (p674) buses travel to Seville (€18, 2½ hours, six daily), Granada (€11, 1¾ hours, hourly), Córdoba (€15, three hours, four daily), Antequera (€5.73, one hour, hourly) and Ronda (€9.50, 2½ hours, nine or more daily). Five buses also run daily to Madrid Airport (€25, six hours). Buses west along the Costa del Sol are handled by **Portillo** (☏ 952 87 22 62; www.portillo.avanzabus.com). There are services to France, Germany, Holland, Portugal and Morocco, too.

CAR
Numerous local and international agencies (including Avis and Hertz) have desks at the airport.

TRAIN
The super-modern **Málaga María Zambrano train station** (www.renfe.es; Explanada de la Estación) – the best in Andalucía – is adjacent to the bus station. Destinations include Córdoba (€41, one hour, 18 daily), Seville (€43, two hours, 11 daily) and Madrid (€80, 2½ hours, 10 daily).

ℹ Getting Around
To/From the Airport
Train From the airport cheap trains (€1.75) run every 20 minutes from 6.50am to 11.54pm to the María Zambrano station and Málaga-Centro station beside the Río Guadalmedina. Departures from the city to the airport are every 20 minutes from 5.30am to 10.30pm.

Taxi A taxi from the airport to the city centre costs around €16.

Legacy of the Moors

Between 711 and 1492, Andalucía spent nearly eight centuries under North African influence and exotic reminders flicker on every street, from the palatial Alhambra to the tearooms and bathhouses of Córdoba and Málaga.

Teterías

Andalucía's caffeine lovers hang around in exotic *teterías*, Moorish-style tearooms that carry a whiff of Marrakech or even Cairo in their ornate interiors. Calle Calderería Nueva in Granada's Albayzín is where the best stash are buried, but they have proliferated in recent years; now even Torremolinos has one! Look out for dimly lit, cushion-filled, fit-for-a-sultan cafes where pots of herbal tea accompanied by plates of Arabic sweets arrive at your table on a silver salver.

Andalucian Bathhouses

Sitting somewhere between a Western spa and a Moroccan hammam, Andalucía's bathhouses retain enough old-fashioned elegance to satisfy a latter-day emir with a penchant for Moorish-era opulence. You can recline in candlelit subterranean bliss sipping mint tea, and experience the same kind of bathing ritual – successive immersions in cold, tepid and hot bathwater – as the Moors did. Seville, Granada, Almería, Córdoba and Málaga all have excellent Arabic-style bathhouses, with massages also available.

Architecture

The Alhambra was undoubtedly the pinnacle of Moorish architectural achievement in Andalucía, but there are many other buildings in the region that draw inspiration from the rulers of

1. Puerta del Vino, Alhambra (p655) **2.** Arabic sweets

Al-Andalus. Sometimes the influences are obvious. At others, hybrid buildings constructed in Mudéjar or neo-Moorish styles drop mere hints of former Nasrid glories: an ornate wooden ceiling, some geometric tile patterns, or an eruption of stucco. Granada is the first stop for Moorish relics, closely followed by Málaga, Córdoba, Almería and Las Alpujarras.

Cuisine

Andalucía's and Spain's cuisine draws heavily upon the food of North Africa where sweet spicy meat and starchy couscous are melded with Mediterranean ingredients. The Moors introduced many key ingredients into Spanish cooking: saffron, used in paella; almonds, used in Spanish desserts; and aubergines, present in the popular Andalucian tapa, *berenjenas con miel de caña* (aubergines

with molasses). If you'd prefer the real thing, there are plenty of pure Moroccan restaurants in Andalucía, especially in Granada and Tarifa.

MOORISH HIGHLIGHTS

Granada Alhambra (p655), Albayzín (p662)

Córdoba Mezquita (p641), Medina Azahara (p648)

Seville Giralda (p575), Torre del Oro (p585)

Málaga Alcazaba (p684), Castillo de Gibralfaro (p685)

Almería Alcazaba (p718)

Las Alpujarras Berber-style houses in the village of Capileira (p678)

Bus

Bus 34 goes to the eastern beaches including El Pedregalejo; bus 35 climbs up to Castillo de Gibralfaro. Both depart from Paseo del Parque.

Costa del Sol

Splaying from Nerja in the east to Gibraltar in the west in an almost unbroken ribbon of urban (over)development, the Costa del Sol is despised as much as it is loved. Among culture-seeking purists fresh out of Seville or Granada, you'll hear it described as tacky, obnoxious, overdeveloped, unsubtle and soulless. To the millions of tourists who have been coming here yearly since the 1960s, and to the hundreds of thousands of foreigners who now call it home, it is a Mediterranean paradise with a famously mild climate, limitless beaches and a spectacular mountain backdrop. Irrespective of your viewpoint, what you won't find here is an atmosphere that is inherently Spanish. With 20% of the Costa's population now made up of expats (mainly Brits, Germans and Scandinavians), the coast's five main resorts are awash with Irish pubs, fish-and-chip shops, Swedish hairdressers, golf courses, theme parks, Spanglish-speaking waiters and the occasional throwback-to-the-old-days tapas bar.

However, in among the gated communities and nonstop beachside frolics, even the Costa del Sol has its nuances. Torremolinos is a big gay resort, Fuengirola attracts families, Marbella is swanky, Puerto Banús is swankier still, while Estepona remains vaguely down-to-earth with a pleasant old town that hasn't been completely buried by ugly breeze-block apartments and karaoke bars – yet.

A convenient train service links Málaga's Renfe and Aeropuerto stations with Torremolinos (€1.75), Benalmádena/Arroyo de la Miel (€2) and Fuengirola (€3.55). Buses from Málaga link all the resorts, and services to places such as Ronda, Cádiz, Seville and Granada go from the main resorts.

Torremolinos & Benalmádena

POP 68,000 & 59,000

Like an overexposed film star with a fame addiction, Torremolinos' reputation precedes it. Think T-shirt suntans and Union Jack swimming trunks, beer over fish and chips and permanently inebriated 18 to 30 year olds on elongated stag weekends. Yet, despite being the butt of everything from Monty Python jokes to hysterical tabloid holiday exposés, 'Terrible Torrie' refuses to die. Reinvention is its perennial hallmark. Dogged by a lager-loutish reputation in the 1990s, the resort has successfully embraced its kitsch side and started attracting an older demographic backed up by a strong gay following. Make no mistake, the town of towers (torres) and windmills (molinos) has life in it yet.

Benalmádena, 5km west of Torremolinos, offers more of the same with a youthful nightlife, large family-orientated theme parks and a penchant for a style of architecture best described as Gaudí meets Mr Whippy. The 59,000-strong town can be split into three parts. Benalmádena Pueblo is set inland and retains a semblance of its pre-tourist-era self. Arroyo de Miel, where the train stops, has developed as the tightly packed town centre. Benalmádena Costa is the busy beach area well known for its swanky port and happening nightlife.

⊙ Sights & Activities

Playa La Carihuela, between Benalmádena marina and the Punta de Torremolinos, is by far the best beach in the area. For a fine seaside walk get off at Benalmádena train station, head down to the water and then walk east for 5km along the lovely Paseo Marítimo to Torremolinos where you can get back on the train. There are hundreds of eating/drinking options along the way.

Buddhist Stupa   MUSEUM, MONUMENT
(Benalmádena Pueblo; ⊙10am-2pm & 3.30-6.30pm Tue-Sat, 10am-7.30pm Sun) FREE The largest Buddhist stupa in Europe is in Benalmádena Pueblo. It rises up, majestically out of place, on the outskirts of the village, surrounded by new housing and with sweeping coastal views. The stupa is open to visitors. Nearby you'll find the mildly diverting Museo Benalmádena (www.benalmadena.com; Benalmádena Pueblo; ⊙10am-6pm Mon-Fri) FREE.

Tivoli World   AMUSEMENT PARK
(www.tivoli.es; Avenida de Tivoli; admission €7.95; ⊙6pm-1am) Just five minutes' walk from Benalmádena–Arroyo de la Miel train station, this is the biggest amusement park on the costa. The Supertivolino ticket (€14) includes the admission price and gives unlimited access to more than 35 rides.

🛏 Sleeping & Eating

Torremolinos alone lists 55 hotels in its tourist-office brochures, and in addition to British breakfasts and beer, it has no shortage of good seafood places to eat. Many of these so-called *chiringuitos* line the Paseo Marítimo in La Carihuela.

Hotel Tropicana   HOTEL $$
(📞952 38 66 00; www.hoteltropicana.es; Calle Tropico 6, La Carihuela; s/d €95/120; 🅿❄🛜♿📶) A thong's throw from La Carihuela beach, this pleasant low-rise hotel has attractive homey rooms with warm colour schemes and dazzling white fabrics, a garden of lofty palms and a decent restaurant. It is also perfectly positioned for strolling along the promenade that links Benalmádena port with Torremolinos.

⭐ La Alternativa   TAPAS $
(Avenida de la Constitución, Arroyo de la Miel; tapas from €2.50) Looking more real Spain than faux resort, this tiny traditionally tiled place next to Benalmádena train station has a year-round *feria* atmosphere with its walls papered with flamenco posters, matador pics and the occasional Virgin. It's always packed and the tapas are superb. There is an array of similar places in the same covered mall.

ℹ Information

Tourist Office (www.pmdt.es; Plaza de la Independencia; ⊙9.30am-1.30pm Mon-Fri) There are also offices on Playa Bajondillo (⊙10am-2pm) and Playa Carihuela (⊙10am-2pm).

Fuengirola

POP 71,800

Fuengirola is a genuine Spanish working town, as well as being firmly on the tourist circuit. It attracts mainly Northern European visitors and also has a large foreign resident population, many of who arrived here in the '60s – and stayed after their ponytails went grey. The beach stretches for a mighty 7km, encompassing the former fishing quarter of Los Boliches.

Biopark (📞952 66 63 01; www.bioparc fuengirola.es; Avenida Camilo José Cela; adult/child €17.90/12.50; ⊙from 10am, times vary; ♿) is the Costa's best zoo and treats its animals very well with no cages or bars, but rather spacious enclosures, conservation and breeding programs, plus educational activities. There is no space for elephants or giraffes but you can enjoy big cats, gorillas and a range of other species. It also has a bat cave, a reptile enclosure, cafes for refreshments and a large gift shop.

For eating, in among the chippies and British boozers, there's **Charolais** (www. bodegacharolais.com; Calle Larga 14; mains €12-20; ⊙1-4pm & 7.30-11.30pm), a modern tapas bar with a terrace and a rustic-style restaurant emphasising expertly prepared meat dishes.

The **tourist office** (📞952 46 74 57; Avenida Jesús Santos Rein 6; ⊙9.30am-2pm & 5-7pm Mon-Fri, 10am-1pm Sat) is about a block from the **train station** (Avenida Jesús Santos Rein), which runs half-hourly trains to Torremolinos, Málaga airport and Málaga city.

GAY TORRIE

Torremolinos is the most gay-friendly town in Andalucía with rainbow flags dotted everywhere from the moment you exit the subterranean train station in pedestrianised Plaza de la Nogalera, a rectangular square whose south side is a nexus for the Costa del Sol's gay bar and nightclub scene. This being Spain, most of the clubs don't open until 11pm at the earliest and start to fill up from 3am onwards. Don't miss your siesta, as nights can be long. Clubbers usually call it a night (morning?) at 7am, though after-parties can entertain endurance freaks until the afternoon. The current favourite dancing spot is **Parthenon** (www.parthenondisco.com; La Nogalera 716; ⊙midnight-7am), but in the fickle world of nightclubs, tastes change quickly. Ask around.

For some day-time action hit Torrie's best-known gay-friendly bar/restaurant, the durable **El Gato Lounge** (📞951 25 15 09; www.elgatolounge.com; Paseo Marítimo 1; mains €5-10; ⊙9am-1am) on Playa Beirola (sometimes known as 'El Gato Beach' or 'Gay Beach') tucked just east of the rocky headland known as Punta de Torremolinos. El Gato has been in business since 2006 and serves Spanish-International cuisine in a relaxed environment that welcomes people of all persuasions.

For more information on Torrie's gay life visit www.gaytorremolinos.eu. There's also a Torremolinos Gay Map published twice a year and available at many businesses in town.

Marbella

POP 136,000

Marbella is the Costa del Sol's classiest, and most expensive, resort. This wealth glitters most brightly along the Golden Mile, a tiara of star-studded clubs, restaurants and hotels that stretches from Marbella to Puerto Banús, the flashiest marina on the Costa del Sol, where black-tinted Mercs slide along a quayside of luxury yachts. Marbella has a magnificent natural setting, sheltered by the beautiful Sierra Blanca mountains, as well as a surprisingly attractive casco antiguo (old town) replete with narrow lanes and well-tended flower boxes.

Sights & Activities

Pretty Plaza de los Naranjos, with its 16th-century town hall, is at the heart of the largely pedestrianised old town. Puerto Banús, the Costa del Sol's flashiest marina, is 6km west of Marbella and has a slew of glamorous boutiques and busy restaurants strung along the waterfront.

There are good walks in the Sierra Blanca, starting from the Refugio de Juanar, a 17km drive north of Marbella. Alternatively, you can walk along the seafront and sniff the money. This is about as close as Andalucía comes to a Californian experience.

Museo Ralli MUSEUM

(Urbanización Coral Beach; ☉10am-2pm Tue-Sat) FREE This superb private art museum – part of a nonprofit foundation – exhibits paintings by primarily Latin American and European artists in bright, well-lit galleries. Exhibits include sculptures by Henry Moore and Salvador Dalí, and vibrant contemporary paintings by Argentinian surrealist painter Alicia Carletti and Cuban Wilfredo Lam, plus works by Joan Miró, Chagall and Chirico.

Museo del Grabado Español MUSEUM

(Calle Hospital Bazán; admission €3; ☉10am-2pm & 5.30-8.30pm) This small art museum in the old town includes works by some of the great masters, including Picasso, Joan Miró and Salvador Dalí, among other, primarily Spanish, painters.

Sleeping & Eating

Hotel Lima HOTEL $$

(☑952 77 05 00; www.hotellimamarbella.com; Avenida Antonio Belón, Marbella; s/d €60/75; ❄ ☎) Although this hotel does not have a lot of character, it provides a good central base near the beach. The rooms have dark-wood furnishings and floral bedspreads, and several have balconies overlooking the leafy street.

★ Claude BOUTIQUE HOTEL $$$

(☑952 90 08 40; www.hotelclaudemarbella.com; Calle San Francisco 5, Marbella; d/ste €280/330; ❄ ☎) Situated in the quieter upper part of town, this beautiful hotel is housed in a 17th-century mansion of some historical significance – it was the former summer home of Napoleon's third wife. The decor successfully marries contemporary flourishes with the original architecture, while claw-foot tubs and crystal chandeliers add to the classic historical feel. There are superb views from the rooftop terrace.

El Estrecho TAPAS $$

(Calle San Lázaro; raciones €5-8; ☉noon-midnight) Elbow your way through the always-crammed El Estrecho to a space in the small back dining room and order from a massive menu that includes tapas such as salmorejo (Córdoba-style thick gazpacho). This is one of several great tapas bars on Calle San Lázaro, a street so narrow you'd better make sure you don't eat too much.

Skina MODERN, FUSION $$$

(☑952 76 52 77; www.restauranteskina.com; Calle de Aduar 12; tasting menu €79; ☉1-3.30pm & 7-11pm Tue-Fri, 7-11pm Sat) A tiny Michelin-starred restaurant with small portions of unconventional dishes (lobster and strawberries, carrot ice cream) aimed at people who like to call themselves 'foodies'.

Drinking & Entertainment

The busiest nightlife zone in the Marbella area is at Puerto Banús, where dozens of pubs and varied dance clubs cluster along a couple of narrow lanes behind the marina.

Information

Tourist office (www.marbella.es; Glorieta de la Fontanilla; ☉8.30am-8.30pm Mon-Fri, 10am-2pm Sat) Has plenty of leaflets and a good town map.

Getting There & Around

Portillo (p689) runs hourly buses to Fuengirola (€4.29, one hour), Málaga (€6.34, 1½ hours) and Estepona (€4.23, one hour) from the **bus station** (☑952 76 44 00; Avenida Trapiche), located 1.2km north of Plaza de los Naranjos.

Marbella's streets are notoriously traffic-clogged. Fortunately there are a number of pay carparks where you can take refuge on arrival.

Estepona

POP 66,500

Of the big five resorts on the Costa del Sol, Estepona is the most Spanish in flavor. You don't need a particularly discerning eye to identify the historic old town here, an attractive tangle of narrow whitewashed streets embellished by well-tended pots of geraniums.

That said, Estepona is primarily a resort. Its wide promenade, not unlike Fuengirola or Torremolinos, overlooks the sandy Playa de la Rada beach. The Puerto Deportivo is the heart and soul of the nightlife, especially at weekends, and is also excellent for water sports, as well as for bars and restaurants.

If you tire of the beach, there are a couple of modest museums in and around the aptly named Plaza de las Flores. Colección Arte Garó (Plaza de las Flores; ⊙ 9am-3.30pm Mon-Fri, 10am-2pm Sat) FREE shares digs with the tourist office and spreads six centuries of art over three well-laid-out floors. The Museo Arqueológico (Plaza Blas Infante 1; ⊙ 8am-3pm Mon, 8am-8pm Tue-Fri, 10am-2pm & 4-8.30pm Sat) FREE testifies to Estepona's 4th-century AD roots with many of the displayed pieces dug out of offshore shipwrecks, often by local divers and fishermen.

Talking of fish, Estepona specialises in them. The freshest catch usually ends up in La Escollera (Puerto Pesquero; mains €6-9; ⊙ 1-4.30pm & 8-11.30pm Tue-Sat, 1-4.30pm Sun), a no-nonsense restaurant right on the port where the locals arrive in shoals. For a non-generic tourist hotel drop your suitcase in tiled Hostal El Pilar (☑ 952 80 00 18; www.hostalelpilar.es; Plaza de las Flores 10; s/d €35/50; ✳) on pretty Plaza de las Flores.

Portillo (p689) runs hourly buses from Estepona to Marbella (€4.23, one hour), and Málaga (€9.91, two hours) in the east and La Línea de la Concepción (€5.52, one hour) in the west. Buses stop on Avenida Juan Carlos I in the city centre.

El Chorro & Bobastro

POP (EL CHORRO) 100

Fifty kilometres northwest of Málaga, Río Guadalhorce and the main railway in and out of Málaga both pass through the awe-inspiring Garganta del Chorro, a mas-sive natural fissure that is 4km long, up to 400m deep and as little as 10m wide. The gorge is a magnet for rock climbers, with hundreds of varied routes of almost every grade of difficulty. Anyone can view the gorge by walking along the railway from the tiny El Chorro village (ask locally for directions). The view provides an adrenalin rush all by itself.

◎ Sights & Activities

There's a strong white-knuckle climbing fraternity in El Chorro, but more-grounded hikers can take advantage of a network of fine trails. The GR-7 cross-continental path passes through the village. Follow it east on the Sendero de Haza del Río or west to Bobastro. Both are doable day hikes that start from the train station.

If you have a car, it is worth driving 9km northwest to the Restaurante El Mirador (☑ 952 11 98 09; Parque Ardales; mains €12-16; ⊙ 9am-11pm) that overlooks the calming reservoir, Embalse del Conde del Guadalhorce. A couple of easy circular hikes start here, including the 5km Sendero del Gaitanejo.

Swiss-owned Finca La Campana, 2km outside the tiny village of El Chorro, is the best place for organised adventure activities. Come here for climbing courses (€45), caving (€180 for a group of up to four people), kayaking (€20 per person) and mountain-bike rentals (€15 to €18 per day).

Camino del Rey
LANDMARK

The gorge is particularly famous for the Camino del Rey, a 1m-wide white-knuckle path similar to an Italian *via ferrata* that contours across the sheer rock-face on a ledge 100m above the ground. Initially built in 1905 and traversed by King Alfonso XIII in 1921 (hence the name 'Path of the King'), the path had fallen into severe disrepair by the late 1990s. In 2006, €7 million was ear-marked by the Andalucian government to restore it. The work is still pending.

Currently the path is only tackled by well-equipped climbers.

Bobastro
RUIN

(⊙ guided tours 10am-2pm Fri-Sun) FREE Bobastro was the hilltop redoubt of 9th-century rebel Omar ibn Hafsun, a sort of Islamic Robin Hood, who led a prolonged revolt against Cordoban rule. Ibn Hafsun at one stage controlled territory from Carta-gena to the Strait of Gibraltar. It's thought that Ibn Hafsun converted from Islam to

Christianity (thus becoming a Mozarab) before his death in 917 and was buried here. When Córdoba finally conquered Bobastro in 927, the poor chap's remains were taken for grisly posthumous crucifixion outside Córdoba's Mezquita.

At the top of the hill, 2.5km further up the road and with unbelievable views, are faint traces of Ibn Hafsun's rectangular *alcázar* (Muslim-era fortress).

From El Chorro village, follow the road up the far (western) side of the valley and after 3km take the signed Bobastro turnoff. Nearly 3km up here, an 'Iglesia Mozárabe' sign indicates a 500m path to the remains of a remarkable little Mozarabic church cut from the rock, the shape so blurred by time that it appears to have been shaped by the wind alone.

You can hike 4km to Bobastro from El Chorro village. Take the road downhill from the station, cross the dam and turn left after 400m at the GR-7 trail signpost. The first 2km are steep uphill then it's flat and slightly downhill. The views of El Chorro are stunning.

📐 Sleeping

Finca La Campana HOSTEL, HOTEL **$**
(📞 626 96 39 42; www.fincalacampana.com; dm/d €12/29, 23/4 person cottages €42/52/64; P 🔋 🛏) A 2km uphill hike from the train station, but worth it ('cos that's what you came here for), La Campana is a favourite with outdoor types, especially climbers. There are various sleeping configurations – including dorms, doubles and cottages – plus a pool, a kitchen and even a small climbing wall.

Complejo Turístico Rural La Garganta HOTEL **$$**
(📞 952 49 50 00; www.lagarganta.com; r/half-board €92/161; P ❄ @ 🛜 🛏) Amazing what you can make out of an old flour mill. La Garganta sits right next to El Chorro station, its former milling installations now hosting a pleasant rural hotel with pool, restaurant and comfortable rooms.

ℹ️ Getting There & Away

Two daily trains run to El Chorro from Málaga (€5.95, 40 minutes), Ronda (€9.35, 70 minutes) and Seville (€20, two hours). No buses run to El Chorro. Drivers can get there via Álora (south of El Chorro) or Ardales (west of El Chorro).

Antequera

POP 45,000 / ELEV 575M

Antequera is a fascinating town, both architecturally and historically, yet has somehow managed to avoid being on the coach-tour circuit – which only serves to add to its charms. The three major influences in the region – Roman, Islamic and Spanish – have left the town with a rich tapestry of architectural gems. The highlight is the opulent Spanish baroque style that gives the town its character and which the civic authorities have worked hard to restore and maintain. There is also an astonishing number of churches here – over 30, many with wonderfully ornate interiors.

🎯 Sights

Alcazaba & Around FORTRESS
The main approach to the Alcazaba (adult/child incl Colegiata de Santa María la Mayor €6/3; ⏱10.30am-2pm & 6-8.30pm Tue-Sun) passes through the Arco de los Gigantes, built in 1585 and incorporating stones with Roman inscriptions. What remains of the Alcazaba affords great views. The audioguide does its best to enliven your trajectory through its gardens, walls and two accessible towers. Just below the Alcazaba is the Colegiata de Santa María la Mayor (Plaza Santa María; adult/child incl Alcazaba €6/3; ⏱10am-2pm & 6-8.30pm), a 16th-century church with a beautiful Renaissance facade and plainer interior.

Museo Municipal MUSEUM
(Plaza del Coso Viejo; compulsory guided tour €3; ⏱10am-1.30pm & 4.30-6.30pm Tue-Fri, 10am-1.30pm Sat, 11am-1.30pm Sun) The pride of the Museo Municipal is the elegant and athletic 1.4m bronze statue of a boy, *Efebo*. Discovered on a local farm in the 1950s, it is possibly the finest example of Roman sculpture found in Spain.

The museum, located in the town centre, also displays some pieces from a Roman villa in Antequera, where a superb group of mosaics was discovered in 1998.

Museo Conventual de las Descalzas MUSEUM
(Plaza de las Descalzas; compulsory guided tour €3.30; ⏱10.30am-1.30pm & 5-6.30pm Tue-Fri, 10am-noon & 5-6.30pm Sat, 10am-noon Sun) Situated in the 17th-century convent of the Carmelitas Descalzas (barefoot Carmelites), approximately 150m east of town's Museo

Municipal, the Museo Conventual de las Descalzas displays highlights of Antequera's rich religious-art heritage. Outstanding works include a painting by Lucas Giordano of St Teresa of Ávila (the 16th-century founder of the Carmelitas Descalzas), a bust of the Dolorosa by Pedro de Mena and a *Virgen de Belén* sculpture by La Roldana.

Dolmens ARCHAEOLOGICAL SITE

(Cerro Romeral; ⊘ 9am-6pm Tue-Sat, 9.30am-2.30pm Sun) FREE Two ancient burial sites, the Dolmen de Viera and the Dolmen de Menga, are situated 1km from the city centre, on the road leading northeast to the A45. The Viera dates from about 2500 BC or 2000 BC and was made by local folk who managed to transport dozens of huge rocks from nearby hills to construct these earth-covered tombs for their chieftains. The Dolmen de Menga is even older. In 2006 it was dated to 3790 BC. There is a third burial site, the Dolmen de Romeral, 3km to the north.

🛏 Sleeping & Eating

Hotel Coso Viejo HOTEL $$

(☑ 952 70 50 45; www.hotelcosoviejo.es; Calle Encarnación 9, Antequera; s/d incl breakfast €62/78; P ✸) This converted 17th-century neoclassical palace is right in the heart of Antequera, opposite Plaza Coso Viejo and the town museum. The comfortable, simply furnished rooms are set around a handsome patio with a fountain, and it has an excellent tapas bar and restaurant.

Parador de Antequera HISTORIC HOTEL $$$

(☑ 952 84 02 61; www.parador.es; Paseo García del Olmo, Antequera; s/d €120/145; P ✸ 🛜 ☒) The Parador is in quiet parkland north of the bullring and near the bus station. It's comfortably furnished and set in pleasant gardens with wonderful views, especially at sunset.

★ Arte de Cozina ANDALUCIAN $

(www.artedecozina.com; Calle Calzada 27-29; mains €7-13, tapas €2.50; ⊘1-11pm) The *simpática* (friendly) owner of this hotel restaurant has her own garden that provides fresh ingredients for her dishes. Meat, fish, Antequeran specialities, traditional Spanish egg dishes and salads await you. On Thursday and Friday evenings classical musicians provide entertainment.

The adjacent tapas bar serves unusual light bites like a *sartén de pisto con huevo* (ratatouille topped with a fried egg).

Capella Cafe y Tapas ANDALUCIAN, CAFE $

(☑ 951 23 58 06; Calle Infanta Don Fernando 20; tapas, pastries €1; ⊘8am-11pm, to midnight Fri & Sat; 🛜) A thoroughly pleasant place to come for any number of options: coffee, wine, tapas, *meriendas* and wi-fi. It's made doubly interesting by the onsite Maqueta de Antequera (www.maquetadeantequera.es; admission €1; ⊘8am-11pm, to midnight Fri & Sat), a huge scale model of the city in the 18th century unveiled in 2013. It is said to be the largest model of its kind in Spain.

Rincon de Lola TAPAS $

(www.rincondelola.net; Calle Encarnación 7; tapas €2, raciones €7; ⊘noon-11.30pm Tue-Sun) A great place to come for inexpensive varied tapas that can give you a taster of local dishes, like *cochinillo* (suckling pig), or more unusual dishes (for these parts), like sushi.

ℹ Information

Municipal Tourist Office (☑ 952 70 25 05; www.antequera.es; Plaza de San Sebastián 7; ⊘11am-2pm & 5-8pm Mon-Sat, 11am-2pm Sun)

ℹ Getting There & Away

The **bus station** (Paseo Garcí de Olmo) is found 1km north of the centre. **Alsa** (www.alsa.es) runs buses to Seville (€14, 2½ hours, five daily), Granada (€8.79, 1½ hours, five daily), Córdoba (€11, 3¼ hours, one daily), Almería (€23, six hours, one daily) and Málaga (€5.73, one hour, nine daily).

Beware. Antequera has two train stations: Antequera **train station** (Avenida de la Estación) is 1.5km north of the centre and handles regional services; Antequera-Santa Ana station is 18km away and handles AVE high-speed trains to Málaga, Córdoba, Madrid and Barcelona. Six trains a day run to/from Granada (€11, 1½ hours, nine daily), and there are daily services to Seville (€38, 1½ hours).

El Torcal

Sixteen kilometres south of Antequera, nature has sculpted this 1336m mountain into some of the weirdest, most wonderful rock formations you'll see anywhere. Its 12 sq km of gnarled, pillared and deeply fissured limestone began life as seabed about 150 million years ago.

An impressive Centro de Vistantes is situated 16km south of Antequera near the village of Villanueva de la Concepción. Two marked walking trails, the 1.5km 'Ruta Verde' (Green Route) and the 3km 'Ruta

Amarilla' (Yellow Route), start and end near here.

See www.torcaldeantequera for more information.

East of Málaga

The coast east of Málaga, sometimes called the Costa del Sol Oriental, is less developed than the coast to the west, although there's an unnerving feeling that the bulldozers are never too far away.

Behind the coast, La Axarquía, a region dotted with white villages (of Islamic origin) linked by snaking mountain roads, climbs to the sierras along the border of Granada province. There's good walking here (best in April and May, and from mid-September to late October). Once impoverished and forgotten, La Axarquía has experienced a surge of tourism and an influx of expat residents in recent years.

Nerja

POP 22,000

Nerja, 56km east of Málaga, is where the Costa del Sol becomes a little easier on the eye, with more precipitous topography and prettier vistas allowing a peek into the Spain that once was. Though locals like to distance themselves from the gaudy resorts further west, Nerja has been similarly inundated by (mainly British) tourists in recent years. Those seeking solitude might want to look elsewhere.

The town's pièce de résistance, right in the centre, is the spectacular **Balcón de Europa**, a palm-shaded walkway that protrudes out into the ocean. The new **Museo de Nerja** (✉ 952 52 72 24; Plaza de España; adult/child €4/2; ⊙ 10am-2pm & 4-6.30pm Tue-Sun, to 10pm Jul & Aug) traces Nerja's history from cave dwellers to tourist boom and acts as an ideal prelude to a visit to the enormous Cueva de Nerja, 3km north of town.

🛏 Sleeping & Eating

Rooms in the better hotels get booked up well in advance for the summer period.

Hotel Carabeo   HOTEL $$
(✉ 952 52 54 44; www.hotelcarabeo.com; Calle Carabeo 34; d/ste incl breakfast €85/180; ❄@🛜🏊) Full of stylish antiques, this small, family-run, seafront hotel is set above manicured terraced gardens. There's also a good restaurant and the pool is on a terrace overlooking the sea. The building, an old school house, is on one of the prettiest pedestrian streets in town, festooned with colourful bougainvillea. The hotel is open from April through to October.

Oliva   MODERN EUROPEAN $$
(✉ 952 52 14 29; www.restauranteoliva.com; Calle Pintada 7; mains €15-19; ⊙ 1-4pm & 7-11pm) Think single orchids, a drum and bass soundtrack and a charcoal-and-green colour scheme. In short, this place has class. The menu is reassuringly brief and changes regularly according to what is fresh in season; typical dishes are grilled scallops in a beetroot sauce and sea bass with wasabi, soy and ginger.

Merendero Ayo   SEAFOOD $$
(www.ayonerja.com; Playa Burriana; mains €9-13; ⊙ 9am-midnight) At this open-air place you can enjoy a plate of paella cooked on the spot in great sizzling pans over an open fire – and even go back for a free second helping. It's run by Ayo, a delightful local character famed for the discovery of the Cueva de Nerja complex, who throws the rice on the *paellera* (paella dish) in a very spectacular fashion, amusing all his guests.

ℹ Information

Municipal Tourist Office (✉ 952 52 15 31; www.nerja.org; Calle Carmen 1; ⊙ 10am-2pm & 3-6.45pm Mon-Fri, 10am-2pm Sat & Sun) Downstairs in the *ayuntamiento* (town hall).

ℹ Getting There & Away

From the N340 near the top of Calle Pintada, **Alsa** (www.alsa.es) runs regular buses to/from Málaga (€4.52, 1¼ hours, every 30 minutes), Marbella (€11, 2½ hours, one daily) and Antequera (€9, 2¼ hours, three daily). There are also buses to Almería and Granada.

AROUND NERJA

The big tourist attraction is the **Cueva de Nerja** (www.cuevadenerja.es; adult/child €9/5; ⊙ 10am-1pm & 4-6.30pm, to 10pm Jul & Aug), just off the N340, 3km east of town on the slopes of the Sierra Almijara. The enormous 4km-long cave complex, hollowed out by water around five million years ago and once inhabited by Stone Age hunters, is a theatrical wonderland of extraordinary rock formations, subtle shifting colours and stalactites and stalagmites. Large-scale performances including ballet and flamenco are staged here throughout the summer. About 14 buses run daily from Málaga and Nerja, except on Sunday. The whole site is very well organised for large-scale tourism and has a huge restaurant and car park. A full tour of the caves takes about 45 minutes.

Cómpeta & La Axarquía

POP 3800

The Axarquía region, east of Málaga, is riven by deep valleys lined with terraces and irrigation channels that date back to Islamic times. Nearly all the villages dotting the hillsides – planted with olives, almonds and vines – date from that era. The wild inaccessible landscapes, especially around the Sierra de Tejeda, made it a stronghold of *bandoleros* (bandits), who roamed the mountains without fear or favour. Nowadays, its chief attractions include fantastic scenery; pretty white villages; strong, sweet, local wine made from sun-dried grapes; and good walking in spring and autumn.

A good base for hiking and other similar adrenalin-fuelled activities is Cómpeta, a picturesque village with panoramic views, steep winding streets and a central, bar-lined plaza, overlooking a 16th-century church. Organised walking groups often base themselves here.

Sights & Activities

Cómpeta has some of the area's best local wine, and the popular Noche del Vino (Night of the Wine) on 15 August features a program of flamenco and *sevillana* music and dance in the central and pretty Plaza Almijara, and limitless free wine.

Keeping the local heritage alive and worth a peep at the end of a hike, the Museo de Artes y Costumbres ([phone] 952 51 60 06; Calle Hornos; [clock] 10am-3pm Tue-Sun) FREE showcases local beekeeping and wine-making techniques, and has a mock-up of an old blacksmith's forge.

El Lucero   WALKING
An exhilarating long walk from Cómpeta is up the dramatically peaked El Lucero (1779m), from whose summit, on a clear day, you can see both Granada and Morocco. This is a demanding full-day return walk from Cómpeta, but it's possible to drive as far up as Puerto Blanquillo pass (1200m) via a slightly hairy mountain track from Canillas de Albaida. From Puerto Blanquillo a path climbs 200m to another pass, the Puerto de Cómpeta.

One kilometre down from there, past a quarry, the summit path (1½ hours), marked by a signboard, diverges to the right across a stream bed.

Sleeping & Eating

Hotel Balcón de Cómpeta   HOTEL $$
([phone] 952 55 35 35; www.hotel-competa.com; Calle San Antonio 75; r €77; [icons]) Cómpeta's only centrally located hotel has comfortable rooms with balconies, a good restaurant, a bar, a big pool and a tennis court. Views stretch to Morocco on a clear day.

Taberna-Tetería
Hierbabuena   MOROCCAN, INTERNATIONAL $$
([phone] 951 70 76 38; www.tabernateteriahierbabuena. com; Ave de la Constitución 35; mains €7-12; [clock] 9am-late Mon-Sat, 1.30pm-late Sun, closed Mon in winter) Not your average *tetería*, the Hierbabuena offers English breakfasts and 'curry nights' as well as the obligatory tagines and teas. It seems to satisfy the food urges of its largely expat clientele.

Museo del Vino   ANDALUCIAN $$
(Avenida Constitución; mains €9.50-17; [clock] 1-4pm & 7.30-10.30pm) Exuding rustic warmth with exposed bricks and beams, this long-time tourist favourite serves excellent ham, cheese and sausage *raciones* and wine from the barrel.

Information

Tourist Office ([phone] 952 55 36 85; Avenida de la Constitución; [clock] 10am-3pm Mon-Sat, 10am-2pm Sun) By the bus stop at the foot of the village. Pick up local walking maps here.

Getting There & Away

Three or four buses run daily from Málaga (€4, 1½ hours) via Torre del Mar. They stop in the lower village next to the tourist office.

SOUTHERN CÁDIZ PROVINCE & GIBRALTAR

The southern tip of Cádiz province is called the Campo de Gibraltar and is the southernmost part of Europe. Stretching from Tarifa in the west to San Roque in the east, it's famous for its wind farms and as a desembarkation point for Morocco clearly visible across the Strait of Gibraltar.

Tarifa

POP 17,900

Tarifa's tip-of-Spain location has given it a different climate and a different personality to the rest of Andalucía. Stiff Atlantic winds draw in surfers, windsurfers and kitesurfers, who lend this ancient, yet deceptively small settlement a laidback internationalist image that is noticeably (some would say, refreshingly) at odds with the commercialism of the nearby Costa del Sol. While the town acts as the last stop in Spain before Morocco, it also serves as a taste of things to come. Moroccan fusion food is par for the course here, and the walled old town with its narrow whitewashed streets and ceaseless winds could pass for Chefchaouen or Essaouira.

Tarifa may be as old as Phoenician Cádiz and was definitely a Roman settlement, but it takes its name from Tarif ibn Malik, who led a Muslim raid in AD 710, the year before the main Islamic invasion of the peninsula.

Sights

Old Town   OLD TOWN

A wander round the old town's narrow streets, which are of mainly Islamic origin, is an appetiser for Morocco. The Mudéjar **Puerta de Jerez** was built after the Reconquista. Look in at the small but action-packed **market** (Calle Colón) before wending your way to the mainly 15th-century **Iglesia de San Mateo** (Calle Sancho IV El Bravo; ◷ 9am-1pm & 5.30-8.30pm). South of the church, the **Miramar**, a lookout atop part of the castle walls, has spectacular views across to Africa, located only 14km away.

Castillo de Guzmán   CASTLE

(Calle Guzmán El Bueno; admission €2; ◷ 11am-4pm) Originally built in AD 960 on the orders of Cordoban caliph Abd ar-Rahman III, this fortress is named after Reconquista hero Guzmán El Bueno. In 1294, when threatened with the death of his captured son unless he surrendered the castle to attacking Islamic forces, El Bueno threw down his own dagger for the deed to be done.

Guzmán's descendants later became the Duques de Medina Sidonia, one of Spain's most powerful families. You'll need to buy tickets for the fortress at the tourist office.

Beaches   BEACHES

On the isthmus leading out to Isla de las Palomas, tiny **Playa Chica** lives up to its name. Spectacular **Playa de los Lances** is a different matter, stretching northwest for 10km to the huge sand dune at **Ensenada de Valdevaqueros**.

The low dunes behind Playa de los Lances are a natural park and you can hike across them on a raised boardwalk from the end of Tarifa's concrete promenade.

⚓ Activities

Diving

Diving is generally done from boats around the Isla de las Palomas where shipwrecks, corals, dolphins and octopuses await. Of the handful of dive companies in Tarifa, try **Aventura Marina** (☑ 956 05 46 26; www.aventuramarina.org; Avenida de Andalucía 1), which offers 'Discover Scuba Diving' courses (€75, three hours). One-tank dives with equipment rental and guide cost €50.

Horse Riding

Contemplating Tarifa's wind-lashed coastline (or heading off into the hilly hinterland) on horseback is a terrific way to pass an afternoon or even longer. A one-hour beach ride along Playa de los Lances costs €30, a two-hour beach-and-mountain ride costs €50, while three-/five-hour rides start at €70/80. One recommended place, with excellent English-speaking guides, is **Aventura Ecuestre** (☑ 956 23 66 32; www.aventuraecuestre.com; Hotel Dos Mares, N340 Km 79.5), which organises mainly five-day riding courses (€300) and accommodates children. **Molino El Mastral** (☑ 956 10 63 10; www.mastral.com; Carretera Sanctuario de la Luz), 5km northwest of Tarifa, is also excellent.

Whale-Watching

The waters off Tarifa are one of the best places in Europe to see whales and dolphins as they swim between the Atlantic and the Mediterranean between April and October; sightings of some description are almost guaranteed between these months. In addition to striped and bottlenose dolphins, and long-finned pilot whales, orcas (killer whales) and sperm whales, you may also, if you're lucky, see endangered fin whales and the misleadingly named common dolphin. The best months for orcas are July and August, while sperm whales are present in the Strait of Gibraltar from April to July. Of the dozens of whale-watching outfits, not-for-profit **FIRMM** (☑ 956 62 70 08; www.firmm.org; Calle Pedro Cortés 4; tours €30; ◷ Apr-Oct) is a good bet, not least because its primary purpose is to study the whales, record data and encourage environmentally sensitive tours.

Windsurfing & Kitesurfing

Occupying the spot where the Atlantic meets the Mediterranean, Tarifa's legendary winds have turned the city into one of Europe's premier windsurfing and kitesurfing destinations. The most popular strip is along the coast between Tarifa and Punta Paloma, 10km to the northwest, but you'll see kitesurfers on Tarifa's town beach as well (it's a rather good spectator sport).

Over 30 places offer windsurfing equipment rental and classes (from beginners to experts, young and old). Recommended are Club Mistral (www.club-mistral.com; Hurricane Hotel N340) and Spin Out (☑956 23 63 52; www.tarifaspinout.com; El Porro Beach, N340 Km 75), both of which are signposted off the N340 northwest of town. Kitesurfing rental and classes are available from the same places as for windsurfing, or from Hot Stick Kite School (☑647 155516; www.hotsticktarifa. com; Calle Batalla del Salado 41; 1 day course €50).

Price-wise, for kitesurfing you're looking at €70 for a three-hour 'baptism', €135 for a six-hour 'initiation', and €180 for a nine-hour 'total course'. To rent equipment is €60 per day. You can also train in windsurfing, surfing and paddle-boarding (all €50 for two hours).

🛏 Sleeping

High season is typically from the beginning of July to mid-September, and it's essential to phone ahead in August.

Melting Pot HOSTEL **$**
(☑956 68 29 06; www.meltingpothostels.com; Calle Turriano Gracil 5; dm/d incl breakfast from €13/35; P @ 🛜) The Melting Pot is a friendly, well-equipped hostel just off the Alameda. The five dorms, for five to eight people, have bunks, and there's one for women only. A good kitchen adjoins the cosy bar-lounge, and all guests get their own keys.

Hostal Africa HOSTAL **$**
(☑956 68 02 20; www.hostalafrica.com; Calle María Antonia Toledo 12; s/d €50/65, with shared bathroom €35/50; 🛜) This revamped 19th-century house close to the Puerta de Jerez is one of the best *hostales* along the coast. The owners are hospitable and the rooms sparkle with bright and attractive colours and plenty of space. There's a lovely, expansive roof terrace with an exotic cabana and

views of Africa. The *hostal* is open from late December to late January.

★ Hotel Misiana HOTEL **$$**
(☑956 62 70 83; www.misiana.com; Calle Sancho IV de Bravo 16; d/ste €95/200; 🌼 🛜) Extensively and skilfully refurbished in 2012, Misiana is the best place to stay in Tarifa if you've got the money, courtesy of its exquisite penthouse suite with private roof terrace and Africa views. Talk about taking it to a higher level! With their Tarifa whiteness and driftwood decor, the double rooms aren't bad either.

La Casa de la Favorita HOTEL, APARTMENT **$$**
(☑690 180253; www.lacasadelafavorita.com; Plaza de San Hiscio 4; d €60-125; 🌼 🛜 🛗) A quick internet search will reveal that La Favorita has become a lot of people's favourite recently. It must be something to do with creamy furnishings, the surgical indoor cleanliness, the kitchenettes in every room, the small library, the roof terrace, and the dynamic colorful art.

Posada La Sacristía BOUTIQUE HOTEL **$$**
(☑956 68 17 59; www.lasacristia.net; Calle San Donato 8, Tarifa; r incl breakfast €115-135; 🌼 @ 🛜) Tarifa's most elegant boutique accommodation is in a beautifully renovated 17th-century town house. Attention to detail is impeccable with 10 stylish rooms, tasteful colour schemes, large comfortable beds and rooms on several levels around a central courtyard. Best of all, it maintains the same prices year-round. Its restaurant is similarly excellent.

🍴 Eating

Tarifa has some excellent breakfast joints and a couple of good Moroccan-Arabic–inspired restaurants. The most populous 'eat street' is Paseo de la Alameda, leading northwest from the port.

★ Café Azul Bar BREAKFAST **$**
(Calle Batalla del Salado 8; breakfast €3.50-8; ⊙9am-3pm, closed Wed winter) This little Italian-owned place packs 'em in every day

MOVING ON?

For tips, recommendations and reviews, head to shop.lonelyplanet.com to purchase a downloadable PDF of Lonely Planet's *Morocco* guide.

for Tarifa's best breakfasts. The muesli, fruit salad and yoghurt is large and tasty, or choose one of the excellent crêpes. It has good coffee, juices and shakes, plus *bocadillos* (filled rolls) and cakes.

Mandrágora MOROCCAN, ARABIC $$
(☑956 68 12 91; www.mandragoratarifa.com; Calle Independencia 3; mains €12-18; ⏱from 8pm Mon-Sat) Behind Iglesia de San Mateo, this intimate place serves Andalucian-Arabic food and does so terrifically well. It's hard to know where to start, but the options for mains include lamb with plums and almonds, prawns with *ñora* (Andalucian sweet pepper) sauce, or monkfish in a wild mushroom and sea-urchin sauce.

Bar-Restaurante Morilla TAPAS, ANDALUCIAN $$
(☑956 68 17 57; Calle Sancho IV El Bravo 2; mains from €10; ⏱8am-11pm) One of numerous places lying in wait along Calle Sancho IV El Bravo in the heart of the old town, Morilla attracts more locals than other places. They come here for the high-quality tapas and lamb dishes, and an outstanding *cazuela de pescados y mariscos* (fish-and-seafood stew). Witty waiters scurry between the tables.

La Oca da Sergio ITALIAN $$
(www.la-oca-da-sergio.artesur.eu; Calle General Copons 6; mains €10-16; ⏱1-4pm & 8pm-midnight) Italians rule in Tarifa, at least on the food scene. The amiable Sergio, who roams the tables Italian-style, armed dexterously with loaded plates and amusing stories, presides over genuine home-country fare. Bank on homemade pasta, wood-oven thin-crust pizzas, cappuccinos and post-dinner offers of limoncello.

 Drinking & Entertainment

A large ever-changing contingent of surfing and kiteboarding dudes ensures that Tarifa has a decent bar scene focused primarily on narrow Calle Santísima Trinidad and Calle San Francisco, just east of the Alameda. Don't even bother going out before 11pm. The real dancing starts around 2.30am and ultimate endurance freaks keep bopping until 8am. Many places close on Sunday. Several bars and clubs line the southern end of the Alameda. There are further bar and club possibilities on Playa de los Lances and outside town. Follow the noise.

Bar Almedina BAR, FLAMENCO
(Calle Almedina; ⏱11am-4pm & 11pm-2am Tue-Sun) Built into the old city walls, this place has a cavernous feel and squeezes a flamenco ensemble into its clamorous confines every Thursday at 11pm. DJs spin on Fridays.

Bear House BAR
(Calle Sancho IV El Bravo 26; ⏱2pm-2am) A sort of wine bar meets surf bar, the slick new Bear House has low, cushioned, 'chill-out' sofas, a variety of cocktails, football on the big screen, but no bears.

La Ruina CLUB
(Calle Santísima Trinidad 2; ⏱1am-4am) Try La Ruina, with good electro dance music, or its downstairs warm-up zone El Pósito (Calle Santísima Trinidad 9; ⏱9am-2am), open all day but best for the cocktail hour.

ℹ Information

Centro de Salud (Health Centre; ☑956 02 70 00; Calle Amador de los Ríos; ⏱8am-8pm) Has emergency service.

Policía Local (☑956 61 41 86; Plaza de Santa María) Local police.

Tourist Office (☑956 68 09 93; www.ayto tarifa.com; Paseo de la Alameda; ⏱10am-2pm daily, 6-8pm Mon-Fri Jun-Sep) Near the top end of the palm-lined Paseo de la Alameda.

ℹ Getting There & Around

Boat FRS (☑956 68 18 30; www.frs.es; Avenida Andalucía 16) runs a fast (35-minute) ferry between Tarifa and Tangier in Morocco (one way per adult/child/car €35/18/94) up to eight times daily. All passengers need a passport. There's also now a new ferry company, **Inter Shipping** (www.intershipping.es; Recinto Portuario, Local 4), offering similar service and prices.

Bus Comes (☑956 68 40 38; www.tgcomes. es; Calle Batalla del Salado 13) operates from the small bus station at the north end of Calle Batalla del Salado. It has regular departures to Cádiz, Jerez de la Frontera, La Línea de La Concepción (for Gibraltar), Málaga, Seville and Zahara de los Atunes.

La Línea de la Concepción

La Línea, 20km east of Algeciras, is the stepping stone to Gibraltar. A left turn as you exit the bus station brings you onto Avenida 20 de Abril, which runs the 300m or so from the main square, Plaza de la Constitución, to the Gibraltar border. The municipal tourist office (Avenida Príncipe Felipe; ⏱8am-8pm Mon-Fri, 9am-2pm Sat) faces the border.

Comes (☑956 17 00 93; www.tgcomes.es) buses run every 30 minutes to/from Alge-

ALGECIRAS – GATEWAY TO MOROCCO

The major port linking Spain with Africa is an ugly industrial town and fishing port notable for producing the greatest flamenco guitarist of the modern era, Paco de Lucía, who was born here in 1947. New arrivals usually make a quick departure by catching a ferry to Morocco, or a bus to Tarifa or Gibraltar.

The bus station is on Calle San Bernardo. **Comes** (☑ 956 65 34 56; www.tgcomes.es) has buses for La Línea (€2.65, 30 minutes) every half-hour, Tarifa (30 minutes, 13 daily), Cádiz (2½ hours, 13 daily) and Seville (2½ hours, six daily).

The adjacent **train station** (☑ 956 63 10 05) runs services to/from Madrid (€72, five hours and 20 minutes, two daily) and Granada (€30, 4¼ hours, three daily).

The four-times-a-day ferry crossing to Tangier with FRS (p702) is cheaper than Tarifa but deposits you in Tangier Med, 40km east of the main city. The cost per adult/car one way is €22/93 and the journey takes 1½ hours. As Morocco isn't in the EU, you'll need a passport. Remember to put your watch back one hour when you land.

There are also five daily crossings to the Spanish Moroccan enclave of Ceuta (adult/car one way €37/85, two hours). To get from the Algeciras bus station to the port, walk approximately 600m east along Calle San Bernardo.

ciras (€2, 30 minutes). Portillo (p689) serves Málaga (€16, three hours, four daily) via the Costa del Sol.

To save queuing at the border, many visitors to Gibraltar park in La Línea, then walk across. The underground Parking Fo Cona, just off Avenida 20 de Abril, is the safest place to leave your wheels.

Gibraltar

POP 30,000

Red pillar boxes, fish-and-chip shops, bobbies on the beat, and creaky seaside hotels with 1970s furnishings; Gibraltar – as British writer Laurie Lee once opined – is a piece of Portsmouth sliced off and towed 500 miles south. As with many colonial outposts, 'the Rock', as it's invariably known, tends to overstate its underlying Britishness, a bonus for lovers of pub grub and afternoon tea, but a confusing double-take for modern Brits who thought that their country had moved on since the days of stuffy naval prints and Lord Nelson memorabilia.

Stuck strategically at the jaws of Europe and Africa, Gibraltar's Palladian architecture and camera-hogging Barbary apes make an interesting break from the tapas bars and white towns of Cádiz province. Playing an admirable supporting role is its swashbuckling local history; lest we forget, the Rock has been British longer than the United States has been American.

History

In 711 Tariq ibn Ziyad, the Muslim governor of Tangier, landed at Gibraltar to launch the Islamic invasion of the Iberian Peninsula. The name Gibraltar is derived from Jebel Tariq (Tariq's Mountain).

Castilla wrested the Rock from the Muslims in 1462. Then in 1704 an Anglo-Dutch fleet captured Gibraltar during the War of the Spanish Succession. Spain ceded the Rock to Britain in 1713, but didn't abandon military attempts to regain it until the failure of the Great Siege of 1779–83. Britain developed it into an important naval base (bringing in a community of Genoese ship repairers). During the Franco period, Gibraltar was an extremely sore point between Britain and Spain: the border was closed from 1967 to 1985. In 1969 Gibraltarians voted – 12,138 to 44 – in favour of British rather than Spanish sovereignty, and a new constitution gave Gibraltar domestic self-government. In 2002 the UK and Spain held talks about a possible future sharing of sovereignty over Gibraltar, but Gibraltarians expressed *their* feelings in a referendum (not recognised by Britain or Spain), which voted resoundingly against any such idea.

In December 2005 the governments of the UK, Spain and Gibraltar set up a new, trilateral process of dialogue. The three parties reached agreement on some issues but tricky topics remain, not least Britain's military installations and 'ownership' of Gibraltar airport. Gibraltarians want self-determination

Gibraltar

⊙ Sights
1 Alameda Botanical Gardens..............B6
2 Gibraltar Museum................................A4
3 Trafalgar Cemetery............................B5

⊟ Sleeping
4 Bristol Hotel...A4
5 Rock Hotel B6

⊗ Eating
6 Bistro Madeleine..................................A4
7 Clipper...A2
8 House of Sacarello.............................A2
9 Star Bar...A2

munications on the Rock, Gibraltar airport and other issues, but not sovereignty. Gibraltar airport is currently being expanded, and flights from Spanish cities and other European destinations direct to Gibraltar airport were re-introduced in 2006 (though they had been suspended at the time of writing due to lack of demand). In December 2009 a ferry link to mainland Algeciras was reactivated after lying dormant for 40 years.

The mainstays of Gibraltar's economy are tourism, the port and financial services. Investment on the Rock continues apace with a huge luxury waterfront development on its western side. Much of the demand for space is being met through extensive land reclamation (reclaimed land currently comprises approximately 10% of the territory's total area).

⊙ Sights & Activities

Gibraltar's biggest sight is the Rock itself, a massive limestone crag spectacularly cited at the jaws of the Mediterranean. Coming a close second is its history, a swashbuckling tale of battles and sieges, with the Rock changing hands with the frequency of a well-used library book until it was ultimately nabbed by the British in 1703.

⊙ The Town

Pedestrianised Main St has a typically British appearance, including pubs, imperial statues and familiar British shops, though you'll catch Spanish inflections in the shuttered windows, narrow winding side streets and bilingual locals who have a tendency to start their sentences in English and finish them in Spanish. Most Spanish and Islamic buildings on Gibraltar were destroyed in

and to retain British citizenship, making joint sovereignty improbable. Few foresee a change in the status quo but at least relations are less strained these days. On 18 September 2006 a three-way deal was signed by Spain, Gibraltar and Britain relating to telecom-

18th-century sieges, but the Rock bristles with British fortifications, gates and gun emplacements.

Gibraltar Museum
MUSEUM

(www.gibmuseum.gi; Bomb House Lane; adult/child £2/1; ⊙10am-6pm Mon-Fri, to 2pm Sat) Gibraltar's history is tumultuous to say the least and it quickly unfolds in this fine museum – comprising a labyrinth of rooms large and small – from Neanderthal to medieval to the infamous 18th-century siege. Don't miss the well-preserved Muslim bathhouse and an intricately painted 7th-century-BC Egyptian mummy that washed up here in the late 1800s.

Trafalgar Cemetery
CEMETERY

(Prince Edward's Road; ⊙8.30am-sunset) The Rock's cemetery gives a very poignant history lesson, with its graves of British sailors who died at Gibraltar after the Battle of Trafalgar in 1805.

Alameda Botanical Gardens
PARK

(Europa Rd; ⊙8am-sunset) These lush gardens make a refreshing break from Gibraltar's inexplicably manic traffic.

⊙ The Rock

★ Upper Rock
Nature Reserve
NATURE RESERVE

(adult/child incl attractions £10/5, vehicle £2, pedestrian excl attractions £0.50; ⊙9am-6.15pm, last entry 5.45pm) Most of the upper parts of the Rock (but not the main lookouts) come within the Upper Rock Nature Reserve; entry tickets include admission to St Michael's Cave, the Apes' Den, the Great Siege Tunnels, the Moorish castle, the Military Heritage Centre, the 100-tonne supergun and the 'Gibraltar: A City Under Siege' exhibition. The upper Rock is home to 600 plant species and is the perfect vantage point for observing the migrations of birds between Europe and Africa.

The Rock's most famous inhabitants are the tailless Barbary macaques. Some of the 200 apes hang around the top cable-car station, while others are found at the Apes' Den (near the middle cable-car station) and the Great Siege Tunnels. Legend has it that when the apes (which may have been introduced from North Africa in the 18th century) disappear from Gibraltar, so will the British. Summer is the ideal time to see newborn apes, but keep a safe distance to avoid the sharp teeth and short tempers for which they're well known.

About 15 minutes' walk south down St Michael's Rd from the top cable-car station, O'Hara's Rd leads up to the left to O'Hara's Battery, an emplacement of big guns on the Rock's summit. A few minutes further down is the extraordinary St Michael's Cave, a spectacular natural grotto full of stalagmites and stalactites. In the past, people thought the cave was a possible subterranean link with Africa. Today, apart from attracting tourists in droves, it's used for concerts, plays and even fashion shows. For a more extensive look at the cave system, the Lower St Michael's Cave Tour (ticket £8; ⊙6pm Wed, 2.30pm Sat) is a three-hour guided adventure into the lower cave area. Wear appropriate footwear. Children must be over 10 years old. Contact the tourist office to arrange a guide.

About 30 minutes' walk north (downhill) from the top cable-car station is Princess Caroline's Battery, housing the Military Heritage Centre. From here one road leads down to the Princess Royal Battery – more gun emplacements – while another leads up to the Great Siege Tunnels, a complex defence system hewn out of the Rock by the British during the siege of 1779–83 to provide gun emplacements. The WWII tunnels (adult/child £8/free; ⊙10am-5pm Mon-Fri), where the Allied invasion of North Africa was planned, can also be visited, but this isn't included on your nature reserve ticket. Even combined, these tunnels constitute

GRANADA & SOUTH COAST ANDALUCÍA GIBRALTAR

ⓘ CABLE CAR–NATURE RESERVE COMBO

You can ascend to the Upper Rock and Nature Reserve, weather permitting, by Gibraltar's spectacular cable car (Red Sands Rd; one way/return £10/12; ⊙9.30am-7.15pm, last cable down 7.45pm Apr-Oct, 9.30am-5.15pm, last cable down 5.45pm Nov-Mar). For the Apes' Den, disembark at the middle station.

To save climbing lots of steep hills, the best idea is to take the cable car one way and stop off at all the Nature Reserve sights on the way down. You can buy a Cable Car–Nature Reserve one-way combo ticket for this purpose for adult/child £22/14.

For more information, see www.gibraltarinfo.gi.

DOLPHIN-WATCHING

The Bahía de Algeciras has a sizeable year-round population of dolphins and at least three companies run excellent dolphin-watching trips. From about April to September most outfits make two or more daily trips; at other times of the year they make at least one trip daily. Most of the boats go from Watergardens Quay or the adjacent Marina Bay. Trips last from 1½ to 2½ hours. **Dolphin Safari** (☑20071914; www.dolphinsafari.gi; Marina Bay; adult/child £22.50/13.50) has been running trips since 1969. Advance bookings are essential.

only a tiny proportion of the more than 70km of tunnels and galleries in the Rock, most of which are off limits to the public.

On Willis's Rd, the way down to the town from Princess Caroline's Battery, you'll find the **'Gibraltar: A City Under Siege'** exhibition, in the first British building on the Rock, and the **Moorish Castle** (Tower of Homage), the remains of Gibraltar's Islamic castle built in 1333.

★**Mediterranean Steps**   HIKE
Not the most well-known 'sight' in Gibraltar, but surely the most spectacular, this narrow, ancient path with steep steps – many of them hewn out of the limestone – starts at the park entrance by Jew's Gate and traverses the south end of Gibraltar before steeply climbing the crag on the eastern escarpment. It comes out on the upper ridge, meaning you can descend via the road.

The views along the way are stupendous and ornithologists won't know where to look with birds soaring above, below and around your head. The 1.5km trail is steep and mildly exposed.

🛏 Sleeping

Bristol Hotel   HOTEL $$
(☑20076800; www.bristolhotel.gi; 10 Cathedral Sq; s/d/tr £63/81/93; P✴🛜🅿) Where else can you stay in a retro 1970s hotel that isn't even trying to be retro? The been-around-forever Bristol has creaky floorboards, heavy red patterned carpets and front desk staff who have the endearing habit of calling you 'love' or 'darling'. Harking back to a bygone era, it's

great if you're British, nostalgic and remember the days of kipper ties and flares.

Caleta Hotel   HOTEL $$$
(☑20076501; www.caletahotel.gi; Sir Herbert Miles Rd; d with/without sea view £150/110;🅿) An alternative to the town centre, the mildly luxurious Caleta overlooks Catalan Bay, on the east side of the Rock, five minutes from town by bus. Its cascading terraces have panoramic sea views, and it also has a gym, spa, pool and restaurant. Bedrooms are large and bright.

Rock Hotel   HOTEL $$$
(☑20073000; www.rockhotelgibraltar.com; 3 Europa Rd; d/ste £160/195; P✴@🛜🅿) As Gibraltan as the famous wild monkeys, the Rock is more grand dame than chic young newcomer these days, though it's not lacking in facilities. Tick off sea-view rooms, gym, pool, welcome drink, bathrobes and that all-important trouser press you'll never use. Sit on the terrace with the yachties and retired naval captains and rekindle the empire spirit.

🍴 Eating

Goodbye tapas, hello fish and chips. Gibraltar's food is unashamedly British. The staples are pub grub, beer and sandwiches, chippies and stodgy desserts. Grand Casemates Sq has a profusion of cooler, more modern Euro-cafes, while trendier sit-down restaurants, many with an international bent, can be found waterside at Queensway Quay or in Marina Bay's Ocean Village.

Bistro Madeleine   CAFE, BISTRO $
(256 Main St; cakes from £3; ⏰9am-11pm; 🛜🍴) If you've just polished off steak-and-ale pie in the local pub, come here for your dessert. In this refined, smoke-free bistro, Illy coffee is served with big chunks of British-inspired cakes. The toffee and date cake is outstanding.

★**Clipper**   BRITISH $$
(78B Irish Town; mains £3.50-9; ⏰8.30am-10pm; 🍴) Ask five...10....20 people in Gibraltar to name their favourite pub, and chances are, they'll say the Clipper – at least for the food. Recipient of a recent modernising refurb that has cleared out some of the stuffy naval decor, the Clipper offers real pub grub in traditionally large portions.

Try the chicken tikka masala and don't leave without a dollop of sticky toffee pudding.

Star Bar
PUB **$$**

(12 Parliament Lane; breakfast £3.50-5, mains £5-11; ◷8am-11pm) Not just another pub, Star Bar is Gibraltar's oldest boozer and none the worse for it. Squeeze inside for lamb chops, Irish fillet, hake in a Spanish-style green sauce, and – of course – a pint.

House of Sacarello
INTERNATIONAL **$$**

(57 Irish Town; daily specials £7-12; ◷9am-7.30pm Mon-Fri, to 3pm Sat, closed Sun; ✐) Located in an old coffee warehouse, House of Sacarello serves a good range of vegetarian options and some tasty homemade soups, alongside pastas, salads and a few pub-style dishes; check out its daily specials. You can linger over afternoon tea (£3.50) between 3pm and 7.30pm.

Shopping

Gibraltar has lots of British high-street stores, such as Next, Marks & Spencer, Monsoon and Mothercare (all on or just off Main St), and a huge Morrisons supermarket in Europort at the northern end of the main harbour. No siesta here. Shops are normally open 9am to 7.30pm weekdays, and until 1pm Saturday.

Information

ELECTRICITY
Electric current is the same as in Britain: 220V or 240V, with plugs of three flat pins. You'll thus need an adaptor to use your Spanish plug lead, available for £3 to £4 from numerous electronics shops in Main St.

EMERGENCY
Emergency (✐199) For police or ambulance.
Police Station (120 Irish Town) Just off Main St with an old-fashioned blue lamp hung outside.

MEDICAL SERVICES
St Bernard's Hospital (✐20079700; Europort) With 24-hour emergency facilities.

MONEY
The currencies are the Gibraltar pound (£) and pound sterling, which are interchangeable. You can spend euros (except in payphones and post offices), but conversion rates are poor. Change unspent Gibraltar currency before leaving. Banks are generally open from 9am to 3.30pm weekdays; there are several on Main St.

POST
Post Office (104 Main St; ◷9am-4.30pm Mon-Fri, 10am-1pm Sat, closes at 2.15pm Mon-Fri mid-Jun–mid-Sep)

TELEPHONE
To dial Gibraltar from Spain, you now precede the five-digit local number with the code 00350; from other countries, dial the international access code, then the Gibraltar country code 350 and the local number. To phone Spain from Gibraltar, just dial the nine-digit Spanish number.

TOURIST INFORMATION
Tourist Office (Grand Casemates Sq; ◷9am-5.30pm Mon-Fri, 10am-3pm Sat, to 1pm Sun & holidays) Several information desks provide all the information you need about Gibraltar. There are plenty of pleasant cafes in the same square where you can read through it all at leisure. There are information booths at the airport (✐20073026; ◷mornings only, Mon-Fri) and Customs House (✐20050762;◷9am-4.30pm Mon-Fri, 10am-1pm Sat).

VISAS
To enter Gibraltar, you need a passport or EU national identity card. EU, USA, Canadian, Australian, New Zealand and South African passport holders are among those who do not need visas for Gibraltar. For further information contact Gibraltar's **Immigration Department** (✐20072500; Joshua Hassan House; ◷9am-12.45pm Mon-Fri).

ⓘ Getting There & Away

AIR
EasyJet (www.easyjet.com) flies daily to/from London-Gatwick and three times a week from Liverpool, while **Monarch Airlines** (www.monarch.co.uk) flies daily to/from London-Luton, Birmingham and Manchester. **British Airways** (www.ba.com) flies seven times a week from London-Heathrow. Gibraltar's airport has a brand new terminal right next to the border.

BUS
There are no regular buses to Gibraltar, but La Línea de la Concepción bus station is only a five-minute walk from the border.

CAR & MOTORCYCLE
Snaking vehicle queues at the 24-hour border and congested traffic in Gibraltar often make it easier to park in La Línea and walk across the border. To take a car into Gibraltar (free) you need an insurance certificate, registration document, nationality plate and driving licence.

FERRY
One **ferry** (www.frs.es) a week sails between Gibraltar and Tangier in Morocco (one way/return £38/68, 70 minutes) on Fridays at 6pm. Buy tickets at **Turner & Co** (✐20072006; 5/67 Irish Town).

ℹ Getting Around

Bus 5 goes from the border into town (and back) every 15 minutes on weekdays, and every 30 minutes on weekends. The standard fare is £1.50 or £2.25 for a day pass. Bus 2 goes to Europa Point; buses 4 and 8 serve Caleta Beach.

JAÉN PROVINCE

Jaén province is rarely included in standard Andalucía itineraries, a crying shame for lovers of olive oil, Renaissance architecture, and rugged mountain scenery strafed with rare flora and fauna. The architecture is courtesy of the historic towns of Baeza and Úbeda, and the nature is encased in the expansive Parque Natural de Cazorla (Spain's largest single protected area), while the olive oil is everywhere you look; indeed, it is doubtful if there's a vista in Jaén that doesn't include at least one neat patchwork of olive plantations. The province *alone* accounts for about 10% of the world's olive-oil production.

Jaén

POP 116,000 / ELEV 575M

You don't need to be a genius to deduce the pillar of Jaén's economy. With olive plantations pushing right up against the city limits, the health-enhancing 'liquid gold' has long filled the coffers of the local economy and provided rich topping for one of the most dynamic (and least heralded) tapas strips in Andalucía. In the skirts of a sentinel-like castle lies Jaén's magnificent Renaissance cathedral, a building worthy of a city twice the size, from which emanate narrow alleys, smoky bars, cavernous *tabernas* and *mucha alegría* (joy). Welcome to Andalucía at its gritty and understated best.

◎ Sights

Catedral de la Asunción de Jaén CATHEDRAL
(Plaza de Santa María; adult/child €5/1.50; ◎10am-6pm Mon-Sat, 10am-noon Sun) The size and opulence of Jaén cathedral, built on the site of an old mosque, dominate and dwarf the entire city. The southwestern facade, set back on Plaza de Santa María, was not completed until the 18th century, and it owes more to the late baroque tradition than to the Renaissance, thanks to its host of statuary by Seville's Pedro Roldán.

However, overall, the Renaissance aesthetic is dominant, a fact particularly evident in the overall size and solidity of the internal and external structures, with huge, rounded arches and clusters of Corinthian columns that lend it great visual strength.

The cathedral entry fee comes with an audioguide and is well worth the entry fee. There's an art museum in the vaults.

Palacio de Villardompardo PALACE
(Plaza de Santa Luisa de Marillac; ◎9am-8pm Tue-Fri, 9.30am-2.30pm Sat & Sun) FREE When renovations are complete in mid-2014, this Renaissance palace will have three excellent attractions: the huge 11th-century Baños Árabes (Arab Baths; Palacio de Villardompardo) the largest of their kind in Spain, with a transparent walkway for viewing the excavated baths; the Museo de Artes y Costumbres Populares (Museum of Popular Art & Customs; Palacio de Villardompardo), devoted to the artefacts of the harsh rural lifestyle of pre-industrial Jaén province; and the Museo Internacional de Arte Naïf (International Museum of Naïve Art; Palacio de Villardompardo), with a large international collection of colourful and witty Naive art.

Castillo de Santa Catalina CASTLE
(Cerro de Santa Catalina; admission €3; ◎10am-2pm & 5-9pm Tue-Sun) Watching the city from atop the cliff-girt Cerro de Santa Catalina is the former Islamic fortress, Castillo de Santa Catalina, which has been undergoing renovations for some time. Past the castle at the end of the ridge stands a large cross, from where there are magnificent views over the city and the olive groves beyond.

🛏 Sleeping

Hotel Xauen HOTEL $
(☎953 24 07 89; www.hotelxauenjaen.com; Plaza del Deán Mazas; s/d incl breakfast €50/60; P✳🕸) This hotel has a good position in the centre of the historic quarter. Communal areas are decorated with large photos of colourful local scenes, while the rooms are a study in beige but good sized. The rooftop bar and solarium have stunning cathedral views.

Parador Castillo de Santa Catalina HISTORIC HOTEL $$$
(☎953 23 00 00; www.parador.es; Cerro de Santa Catalina; r incl breakfast €142; P✳@🕸▦) Next to the castle at the top of the Cerro de Santa Catalina, this hotel is handy for views, but

less handy for late-night bar crawls. Rooms are luxuriously dignified with plush furnishings; some have four-poster beds.

It also has an excellent restaurant and a bar with terrace seating to maximise views, from which you can sit and count the olive trees. 26,001, 26,002...

✖ Eating

The Jaén tapas trail is full of pleasant surprises, especially along tiny Calle del Cerón and Arco del Consuelo.

★ El Gorrión ANDALUCIAN $
(Calle Arco del Consuelo 7; tapas from €1.50; ⊙ 1.30-4pm Tue-Thu & Sun, 1.30-4pm & 8.30pm-12.30am Fri & Sat) Lazy jazz plays on the stereo, old newspaper cuttings are glued to the walls, and paintings of bizarre landscapes hang lopsidedly next to oval oak barrels. It feels as though local punters have been propping up the bar for centuries (or at least since 1888, when it opened).

The tapas are simple and traditional, and are best enjoyed with the sherry and wine on offer.

Taberna La Manchega ANDALUCIAN $
(www.tabernalamanchegadejaen.com; Calle Bernardo López 12; platos combinados €4-10; ⊙ 10am-5pm & 8pm-1am Wed-Mon) This place has been in action since the 1880s. Apart from enjoying the great, simple tapas, you can drink wine and watch the local, characterful clientele. La Manchega has entrances on both Calle Arco del Consuelo and Calle Bernardo López.

🍺 Drinking

Cool drinking spots include Deán (Plaza del Deán Mazas; ⊙ 11am-late), which has a pulsating late-night vibe with its exposed industrial steel piping and pumping music. At Columbia 50 (Calle del Cerón 6; ⊙ 10am-9pm) global coffees and hot chocolates are spiked with everything from Irish whisky to honey and cream.

❶ Information

There's no shortage of banks or ATMs around Plaza de la Constitución.

Tourist Office (www.andalucia.org; Calle de la Maestra 8A; ⊙ 9am-7.30pm Mon-Fri, 9.30am-3pm Sat & Sun) Has helpful, multilingual staff and plenty of information about the city and province.

❶ Getting There & Away

From the **bus station** (☑ 953 25 01 06; Plaza de Coca de la Piñera), **Alsa** (www.alsa.es) runs buses to Granada (€8.88, 1¼ hours, 12 daily), Baeza (€4.46, 45 minutes, eight daily), Úbeda (€5.36, one hour, 10 daily) and Cazorla (€9.24, two hours, three daily). The Ureña line travels up to Córdoba and Seville. Other buses head for Málaga and Almería.

Jaén's **train station** (☑ 953 27 02 02; www.renfe.com; Paseo de la Estación) is at the end of a branch line. Trains leave for Córdoba (€14, 1¾ hours, four daily) and Seville (€28, three hours, four daily). There are also trains to Madrid (€35, four hours, four daily).

Baeza

POP 17,000 / ELEV 790M

If the Jaén region is known for anything apart from olives, it's the twin towns of Baeza (pronounced 'ba-eh-thah') and Úbeda, two shining examples of Renaissance beauty. Smaller Baeza makes a good day trip from Úbeda, some 9km away. It has a richness of architecture that defies the notion that there is little of architectural interest in Andalucía apart from Moorish buildings. Here a handful of wealthy, fractious families, made rich by the wool trade, left a staggering catalogue of perfectly preserved Renaissance churches and civic buildings.

◉ Sights

Opening times of some buildings are unpredictable.

In the centre of beautiful Plaza del Pópulo is the Fuente de los Leones (Fountain of the Lions), topped by an ancient statue believed to represent Imilce, a local Iberian princess who was married to Hannibal. On the southern side of the plaza is the plateresque Casa del Pópulo, from about 1540 (housing Baeza's helpful tourist office).

Catedral de Baeza CATHEDRAL
(Plaza de Santa María; donations welcome; ⊙ 10.30am-1pm & 4-6pm Oct-Mar, 10.30am-1pm & 5-7pm Apr-Sep) FREE Baeza's eclectic cathedral is chiefly in 16th-century Renaissance style, with an interior designed by Andrés de Vandelvira and Jerónimo del Prado. One chapel displays a life-sized Last Supper, with finely detailed wax figures and Mary in Victorian flounces of cream lace and pearls.

WHAT'S COOKING IN GRANADA & ANDALUCÍA'S SOUTH COAST?

Ajoblanco A cold white soup that's similar to gazpacho, but uses almonds rather than tomatoes, *ajoblanco* is a classic dish in Andalucía's eastern provinces. Try it in Málaga's Gorki (p688), where it's served topped with grapes.

Berenjenas con miel de caña For an alternative to meat that *isn't* tortilla, try lightly fried aubergines covered in molasses. This sweet-savoury vegetarian delight is served all over Andalucía, but it's especially good in Málaga in El Piyayo (p687).

Paté de Perdiz Game is a popular product in Jaén province. Partridge pâté highlights many menus in the town of Úbeda, where it is served at Restaurante Antique (p714) doused in the local olive oil.

Plato Alpujarreño A hearty mountain dish of blood sausage, fried potatoes, peppers, fried egg and the best Trevélez *jamón serrano*, Plato Alpujarreño is best enjoyed in – where else? – Las Alpujarras. Bar El Tilo (p679) in the village of Capileira does an outstanding version.

Antigua Universidad   HISTORIC BUILDING
(Old University; Calle del Beato Juan de Ávila; ⊙10am-2pm & 4-7pm Wed-Sun) FREE Baeza's historic university was founded in 1538 and became a fount of progressive ideas that generally conflicted with the conservatism of Baeza's dominant families, often causing scuffles between the highbrows and the well-heeled. It closed in 1824, and since 1875 the building has housed an *instituto de bachillerato* (high school).

The main patio, with its elegant Renaissance arches, is open to the public, as is the classroom of poet Antonio Machado, who taught French at the high school from 1912 to 1919.

Palacio de Jabalquinto   PALACE
(Plaza de Santa Cruz; admission free; ⊙9am-2pm Mon-Fri) FREE Baeza's most extraordinary palace was probably built in the early 16th century for one of the Benavides clan. It has a spectacularly flamboyant facade with pyramidal stone studs typical of Isabelline Gothic style, and a patio with Renaissance marble columns, two-tiered arches and an elegant fountain. A magnificent carved baroque stairway ascends from one side.

Ayuntamiento   HISTORIC BUILDING
(Town Hall; Pasaje del Cardenal Benavides 9) A block north of the Paseo de la Constitución is the *ayuntamiento* with its marvellous plateresque facade. The four finely carved balcony portals on the upper storey are separated by the coats of arms of the town, Felipe II (in the middle) and the magistrate Juan de Borja, who had the place built. The building was originally a courthouse and, conveniently, a prison.

Torre de los Aliatares   TOWER
(Tower of the Aliatares; Plaza de España) FREE The lonely Torre de los Aliatares is one of the few remnants of Muslim Bayyasa (as the town was called by the Muslims), having miraculously survived the destructive Isabel la Católica's 1476 order to demolish the town's fortifications.

🛏 Sleeping & Eating

With such a wealth of building heritage, there are several beautifully restored hotel conversions to choose from in Baeza. Eatingwise, Paseo de la Constitucíon is a good place to start, though there are a few gems hidden in the old town.

⭐**La Casona del Arco**   BOUTIQUE HOTEL $$
(☑953 74 72 08; www.lacasonadelarco.com; Calle Sacramento 3; r €70; ❊ 🛜 🏊) A tastefully renovated 16th-century palace in the historic centre with modern comforts, including a spa, and delightful rooms with parquet floors, pale stonework, ochre-washed walls and pitched ceilings (or beams). There's a large garden, plus a small pool, and the whole place has a tasteful exclusive feel – at an unexclusive price.

Palacio de los Salcedo   HOTEL $$
(☑953 74 72 00; www.palaciodelossalcedo.com; Calle San Pablo 8; r from €65; ❊ 🛜) The only part of this 16th-century palace that is genuine is the facade; the rest is authentic-looking faux, ranging from the intricate carved and painted ceilings to murals, columns and arches. The '80s-style rag-rolled paintwork looks dated and some of the gilt furniture is

pretty kitsch, but overall the atmosphere is fittingly historic.

Nuevo Casino de Baeza   ANDALUCIAN **$$**
(www.casinobaeza.es; Calle San Pablo 22; menú €12, mains €10; ⊘ 10am-2pm & 5-8pm Mon-Fri) Dine in the courtyard of the 16th-century Palacio Sánchez Valenzuela, although don't get too excited – the chairs are metal and there is no shade. The setting is still pretty impressive, however, while the food is simple local fare with a well-priced daily menu.

Mesón Restaurante
La Góndola   ANDALUCIAN **$$**
(www.asadorlagondola.com; Portales Carbonería 13, Paseo de la Constitución; mains €8-16; ⊘ 11am-4pm & 8pm-midnight) A terrific and atmospheric local restaurant, helped along by the glowing, wood-burning grill behind the bar, cheerful service and good food. Try *patatas baezanas,* a vegetarian delight that mixes a huge helping of sautéed potatoes with mushrooms.

🍷 Drinking

⭐**Café Teatro Central**   BAR
(www.cafeteatrocentral.com; Calle Obispo Narváez 19; ⊘ 4pm-3am) Well worth a visit, except possibly on Wednesday – karaoke night. Owner Rafael has put a lot of love into creating a virtual museum piece with his display of family-owned historic instruments, and eclectic decorations ranging from giant stone Buddhas to his own abstract paintings. Once inside, don't miss the open lift with flashing lights.

❶ Information

Tourist Office (☑ 953 77 99 83, 953 77 99 82; www.andalucia.org; Plaza del Pópulo; ⊘ 9am-7.30pm Mon-Fri, 9.30am-3pm Sat, Sun & holidays Apr-Sep) Situated just southwest of Paseo de la Constitución in the 16th-century plateresque Casa del Pópulo, a former courthouse.

❶ Getting There & Away

Alsa (www.alsa.es) runs to Jaén (€4.46, 45 minutes, eight daily), Úbeda (€1.16, 15 minutes, every 30 minutes) and Granada (€13, two to three hours, nine daily). There are also buses to Cazorla (€4.84, one hour, four daily), Córdoba (€11, 2½ hours, two daily) and Seville (€23, 4½ hours, two daily).

The nearest train station is **Linares-Baeza** (☑ 953 65 02 02; www.renfe.es), 13km northwest of town, where a few trains a day leave for Granada (€14, 2½ hours, one daily), Córdoba

(€20, 1½ hours, one daily), Málaga (€50, 2¾ hours, one daily), and Almería (€28, 3¼ hours, three daily). Buses connect with most trains from Monday to Saturday. A taxi to the train station costs €15.

Úbeda

POP 36,000 / ELEV 760M

Úbeda is where Andalucía enters a different realm. Bereft of Moorish relics, the city's architecture celebrates the Renaissance. The reason: Úbeda fell to the Christians in 1233, earlier than any other city in Andalucía. Then, in the early 16th century it benefited from the extensive patronage of local-boy-made-good Francisco de los Cobos, who rose to become a chief adviser to King Carlos I. Los Cobos hired a skilled Jaén architect, Andrés de Vandelvira to design most of Úbeda's strapping Renaissance buildings. As a result, the town, along with its smaller neighbour, Baeza, is often seen as a textbook example of the Spanish Renaissance. Were it not for the tapas bars and the '*buenos dias*' greetings, you could easily imagine you were in Italy.

Architecture aside, Úbeda, makes a good base for exploring Jaén province. The town has some excellent tapas bars, a handful of opulent hotels and a fine ceramics tradition.

◉ Sights

Sacra Capilla del Salvador   CHAPEL
(Plaza Vázquez de Molina; adult/child €3/1.50; ⊘ 10am-2pm & 4-7.30pm Mon-Sat, 11.15am-2pm & 5-8pm Sun) The purity of Renaissance lines is best expressed in this famous chapel, the first of many works executed in Úbeda by celebrated architect Andrés de Vandelvira. A pre-eminent example of the plateresque style, the chapel's main facade is modelled on Diego de Siloé's Puerta del Perdón at Granada's cathedral.

The classic portal is topped by a carving of the transfiguration of Christ, flanked by statues of St Peter and St Paul. The underside of the arch is an orgy of classical sculpture, executed by French sculptor Esteban Jamete, depicting the Greek gods – a Renaissance touch that would have been inconceivable a few decades earlier.

Next door to the *capilla* stands the **Palacio del Condestable Dávalos**. Partly remodelled in the 17th century, the mansion is now Úbeda's luxurious *parador* (state-owned hotel).

REDISCOVERING ANDALUCÍA'S JEWISH HERITAGE

It's been a long time coming, but there are signs that Andalucía may finally be ready to re-evaluate its ambiguous Jewish history, a legacy that has haunted it since the Jews were ruthlessly expelled en masse from Spain soon after the fall of Granada in 1492.

In 2012, a new Jewish Interpretation Centre opened in Seville's Santa Cruz quarter, a largely Jewish neighbourhood until the 15th century. The following year, Granada inaugurated the Museo Sefardi (the word Sepharad translates as 'Iberia' in Hebrew) to highlight the city's Jewish past. The museums were accompanied by an announcement from the Spanish government that promised to grant Spanish citizenship to any Sephardic Jew who could prove his or her Spanish ancestry. The law is still awaiting ratification.

Some testimonies claim the first Jews arrived on the Iberian Peninsula in the sixth century BC. Already well-established by the time of the Roman occupation, Jewish fortunes fluctuated up until the arrival of the Moors in AD 711 when their conditions improved markedly. The Sephardic Jews enjoyed a 'golden age' after the accession of the enlightened emir, Abd ar-Rahman III in 912 when they thrived economically and politically, most famously in Córdoba, capital of Al-Andalus, where the three Abrahamic faiths lived in relative harmony for over a century. But the honeymoon came to an abrupt end in 1066 when over 1500 Jews were massacred by a Muslim mob in Granada following the assassination of a top Jewish government advisor amid an atmosphere of jealousy and suspicion.

Thereafter, Jewish fortunes in Al-Andalus were never quite the same, ebbing and flowing with the whims of successive Moorish dynasties. The finest Jewish philosopher of the medieval period, Maimonides, was forced out of Córdoba in 1148 by the Almohads, fundamentalist Muslims who forced all Jews to convert to Islam or die. Intermittent pogroms became uncomfortably common in the Middle Ages culminating in the Jewish massacres of 1391, which started in Seville's Santa Cruz quarter, but quickly spread across Christian Spain.

Plaza del 1° de Mayo   HISTORIC SITE

This imposing plaza was originally the town's market square and bullring. It was also the grisly site of Inquisition burnings, which local worthies used to watch from the gallery of the Antiguo Ayuntamiento (Old Town Hall) in the southwestern corner. Leaving no doubt about their political persuasion, locals renamed this square from the former (fascist) Plaza del Generalissimo several years ago.

Sinagoga del Agua   MUSEUM

(Calle Roqas 2; admission €4; ⊗10am-8.30pm) Úbeda's Jewish community dates back to the 10th century when it cohabited peacefully with the considerably larger Muslim population. However, it was not until 2006 when this synagogue and former Rabbi's house was discovered by a refreshingly ethical realtor who bought the property to knock down and build apartments – only to discover that every swing of the pickaxe revealed some tantalising archaeological piece of a puzzle. The result is this, the city's latest museum, a sensitive re-creation of a centuries-old synagogue and Rabbi's house using original masonry whenever possible, some still bearing Jewish symbols, and including capitals, caliphs and arches. A separate women's gallery was discovered in the excavation, as well as a bodega, with the giant urns still in place.

Hospital de Santiago   CULTURAL CENTRE

(Calle Obispo Cobos; ⊗8am-3pm & 4-10pm Mon-Fri, 11am-3pm & 6-10pm Sat & Sun) FREE Vandelvira's last architectural project is here, the Hospital de Santiago. Completed in 1575, it has often been dubbed the Escorial of Andalucía – a reference to a famous old monastery outside Madrid, which was a precursor to the kind of baroque architecture employed by Vandelvira. It now acts as Úbeda's cultural centre, housing a library, municipal dance school and exhibition hall.

★ Casa Museo Arte Andalusí   MUSEUM

(☑953 75 40 14; Calle Narvaez 11; admission €2; ⊗11am-2pm & 5-8pm) The Casa Museo Arte Andalusí is a fascinating private museum and the venue for regular flamenco performances. Behind the heavy original 16th-century carved door, Paco Castro has lovingly restored this former palace without detracting from its crumbling charm. A Star of David is etched into one of the original columns in the central patio and above are

Realistically 1391, not 1492, was the turning point for Sephardic Jews in Spain. Those that were spared death were forced to convert to Christianity and traditional Jewish neighbourhoods, along with their synagogues and trades, quickly lost their identities. The Inquisition was set up in 1478 largely to police *conversos*, Jews who had, under duress, converted to Christianity. Not surprisingly, many of them continued to practice their old faith in secret. The only place where Jews remained well treated was in the Nasrid emirate of Granada. All that ended on 31 March 1492 when, following the defeat of the Moors in Granada, the Catholic Monarchs signed the Alhambra decree giving all Jews the choice to either convert to Christianity or leave Spain within four months – on pain of death. Amid extreme hardships, the Sephardic Jews were exiled across Europe and beyond where they often faced further persecution. Many took the keys of their Spanish homes with them – keys that some families retain to this day.

Although they lack many contemporary Jewish residents, Seville, Granada, Córdoba and Úbeda are the cities where Andalucía's Jewish heritage still has some resonance. Despite being savagely burnt in 1391, Córdoba's Judería (Jewish quarter) remains relatively intact and retains Andalucía's only surviving medieval synagogue. Úbeda, meanwhile, opened up a fascinating museum in an old Jewish house in 2011.

Santa Cruz, Seville's old Judería was once the second biggest in Spain after Toledo, but it fell into rapid decline after the 1391 massacre. Plaques to commemorate old synagogues were put up in 2003.

Granada's Jewish population lived in what was known as the Garnata-al-Yahud (Granada of the Jews) peacefully until 1492. After the re-conquest, the district was renamed El Realejo and many homes were demolished. Save for the new Sephardic museum and a statue of the poet Yehuba ibn Tibbon, there is little to betray a Jewish past today.

the balconies and painted Mudéjar-style ceiling and eaves. It is the ideal faded-grandeur setting for Paco's fascinating collection of antiques, which include 19th-century ceramics, a 14th-century well, stained glass, ancient millstones, painted tiles, tapestries, and intricately carved wooden chests. Depending on the time of year, there is a flamenco show at 9.30pm on Saturday (€18, includes a drink). Book in advance.

🛏 Sleeping

Hotel Postigo　　　　　　　　HOTEL **$**
(☏ 953 75 00 00; www.hotelelpostigo.com; Calle Postigo 5; d/ste €50/70; ☷☷) This appealing small hotel is situated on a cobbled backstreet with plenty of nearby parking. The rooms are spacious and modern with parquet floors and shiny black furnishings. There is a pleasant outside terrace and a large sitting room with a log fire for winter.

Afán de Rivera　　　　　　　HOTEL **$$**
(☏ 953 79 19 87; www.hotelafanderivera.com; Calle Afán de Rivera 4; s/d €96/128; ☷☷) This incredible small hotel lies inside one of Úbeda's oldest buildings, predating the Renaissance. Expertly maintained and run by the amiable Jorge, it has beautifully historic common areas and conmfortable rooms that offer far more than is normal at this price: shaving kits, personal toothbrushes and fancy shampoos. Breakfast – should you opt for it – is a locally sourced feast.

⭐ **Palacio de la Rambla**　　HISTORIC HOTEL **$$**
(☏ 953 75 01 96; www.palaciodelarambla.com; Plaza del Marqués de la Rambla 1; d/ste incl breakfast €96/120; ☷☷) Úbeda's loveliest converted palace has eight gorgeous rooms in the home of the Marquesa de la Rambla. It's not an overstatement to call this one of Andalucía's most stunning places to stay. The ivy-clad patio is wonderfully romantic and each room is clad in precious antiques and has its own salon, so that you feel like you're staying with aristocratic friends. Breakfast can be enjoyed in the former bodega or served in your room. This hotel is closed for part of July and August.

**Parador Condestable
Dávalos**　　　　　　　　HISTORIC HOTEL **$$$**
(☏ 953 75 03 45; www.parador.es; Plaza Vázquez de Molina; r €132-154; ☷☷) One of Spain's original *paradors* (opened 1930) and an inspiration for a lot of what was to follow, this plush hotel occupies one of Úbeda's

prime spot, looking out over the wonderful Plaza Vázquez de Molina. It's housed inside a historic monument, the Palacio del Deán Ortega, which has, of course, been comfortably modernised and is appropriately luxurious. It also has the poshest restaurant in town.

✗ Eating

La Taberna ANDALUCIAN $
(Calle Real 7; mains €6-10; ⊘ noon-3.30pm & 7.30pm-midnight; 🍴) Simple menu, quick service, tasty food, a wide variety of clientele and usually some football on the big screen, La Taberna is an oasis of solid reliability in a town where food can sometimes be a little on the expensive side.

Zeitúm EUROPEAN $$
(www.zeitum.com; Calle San Juán de la Cruz 10; mains €14-20; ⊘ 1.30-4pm & 8pm-midnight Tue-Sat, 1.30-4pm Sun) This restaurant is housed in a headily historic building, dating from the 14th century, in a former Jewish quarter. Ask the owner to show you the original well and stonework and beams bearing Jewish symbols. Olive-oil tastings are taken seriously here, along with the superb preparation of diverse dishes like steak tartare and a local favourite: partridge salad.

Taberna La Imprenta CONTEMPORARY ANDALUCIAN $$
(www.restaurantelaimprenta.com; Plaza del Doctor Quesada 1; mains €10-19; ⊘ 1.30-4pm & 8.30pm-midnight) This wonderful old print shop, done stylishly and frequented by Úbeda's posh noshers, provides a delicate free tapa with your drink. You can also sit down and eat lobster salad, excellent meat dishes, and saucy little desserts like green apple sorbet with gin on crushed ice.

★ Restaurante Antique CONTEMPORARY ANDALUCIAN $$$
(☑ 953 75 76 18; www.restauranteantique.com; Calle Real 25; mains €12-26; ⊘ 1-4pm & 8-11.30pm Mon-Sat) A restaurant with a penchant for irony. Antique is not at all 'antique'. Indeed, the interior is modern minimalist and the food puts a big twist on traditional recipes producing high-quality cuisine such as partridge pâté with quinoa and olive-oil marmalade or wild salmon with a creamy leek sauce. The fruity green olive oil is practically drinkable it's so good.

🛍 Shopping

The typical green glaze on Úbeda's attractive pottery dates back to Islamic times. Several workshops on Cuesta de la Merced and Calle Valencia in the Barrio San Millán, the potters' quarter northeast of the old town, sell their wares on the spot, and the potters are often willing to explain some of the ancient techniques they still use. **Alfarería Tito** (Plaza del Ayuntamiento 12; ⊘ 8am-2pm & 4-8pm Mon-Sat, 10am-2pm Sun) has a large selection too. Tito's intricately made blue-and-cream ware is particularly covetable.

ℹ Information

Regional Tourist Office (☑ 953 75 08 97; otubeda@andalucia.org; Calle Baja del Marqués 4; ⊘ 9am-2.45pm & 4-7pm Mon-Fri, 10am-2pm Sat) In the 18th-century Palacio Marqués de Contadero in the old town.

ℹ Getting There & Away

The scruffy **bus station** (☑ 953 75 21 57; Calle San José 6) is located to the northwest in the new part of town. **Alsa** (www.alsa.es) runs to Baeza (€1.16, 15 minutes, every 30 minutes), Jaén (€5.36, one hour, 10 daily), Cazorla (€4.20, one hour, four daily), Granada (€13, two to three hours, seven daily) and Córdoba (€12, 2½ hours, four daily).

Cazorla

POP 8100 / ELEV 885M

Cazorla, 45km east of Úbeda, is a gorgeous foot-of-the-mountains village with a hunting obsession. It acts as a gateway to Spain's largest protected park, which starts – quite literally – on the edge of town.

👁 Sights & Activities

At one end of lovely Plaza de Santa María is the large shell of the Iglesia de Santa María. It was built by Andrés de Vandelvira in the 16th century but was wrecked by Napoleonic troops. A 3.5km round-trip hike starts here to the Ermita San Sebastión via a mirador. Look out for the many species of birds along the route. Alternatively, you can pitch further into the park on a path to the fancy *parador* hotel known as 'Adelantado' 8.5km away. This route follows the cross-continental GR-7 path for some of its duration and makes a doable out-and-back day-hike with lunch at the *parador*. The tourist office has maps.

Castillo de la Yedra
CASTLE, MUSEUM

(Castle of the Ivy; admission €1.50; ⊙2.30-8pm Tue, 9am-8pm Wed-Sat, 9am-2pm Sun) The dramatic Castle of the Ivy is of Roman origin, though it was largely built by the Muslims, then restored in the 15th century after the Reconquista. Much money has been spent on a modern restoration. There are superb panoramic views from here. The castle is home to the Museo del alto Guadalquivir, containing intricate models of old olive oil mills and an armaments collection.

Centro Temático Frondosa Naturalesa
GUIDED TOUR

(☑953 72 17 91; Camino del Ángel 7; admission €3; ⊙10:30am-1:30pm & 6-9pm) If you're pressed for time, this guided tour takes you through a little of Cazorla's natural and physical history visiting the ruined Santa María church, an old restored flour mill and a small info centre/museum. The guides really bring it to life.

🛏 Sleeping & Eating

Check out some new and wonderful tapas, including *rin-ran* (mixed salted cod, potatoes and red peppers), *talarines* (pasta), *gachamiga* (a kind of Spanish polenta), *carne de monte* (meat – usually venison), and Sierra de Cazorla's memorable olive oil – fresh, fruity and slightly bitter.

Hotel Ciudad de Cazorla
HOTEL $$

(☑953 72 17 00; Plaza de la Corredera 9; s/d incl breakfast €61/70; ❄️🌐🏊) This modern structure on mansion-ruled Plaza de Corredera has faced some resistance from tradition-minded locals, but it sort of blends in. Modern facilities include spacious rooms, a restaurant and an outdoor pool.

Hotel Guadalquivir
HOTEL $$

(☑953 72 02 68; www.hguadalquivir.com; Calle Nueva 6; r €70; ❄️🌐) Cheerful and family-run, the Guadalquivir has comfortable, blue-hued rooms with pine furniture, TV and heating, though no memorable views. The singles can be a bit cramped, but the hotel is in a central location and equals good value for money.

Bar Las Vegas
TAPAS $

(Plaza de la Corredera 17; raciones €6; ⊙noon-4pm & 8-11pm) The best of Cazorla's bars with barrel tables outside (but little atmosphere within). You can try tasty prawn-and-capsicum *revuelto* (scrambled eggs), as well as the town's top breakfast, *tostadas* (toasted bread) with various toppings, including the classic crushed tomatoes with garlic and olive oil.

Mesón Don Chema
ANDALUCIAN $$

(Calle Escaleras; mains €10-17; ⊙1-4pm & 8.30-11.30pm) Dine under the mounted antlers on game, pork and a variety of meaty mains, as well as such sizzling local fare as *huevos cazorleña* (a mixed stew of sliced boiled eggs and chorizo with vegetables).

ℹ Information

Oficina de Turismo Municipal (☑953 72 08 75; Plaza de Santa María; ⊙10am-1pm & 5-7.30pm) The tourist office is located inside the half-restored Iglesia de Santa María on the north side of the eponymous plaza. It has useful information on the Parque Natural de las Sierras de Cazorla, Segura y Las Villas, as well as Cazorla town.

ℹ Getting There & Away

Alsa (www.alsa.es) runs buses to Úbeda (€4.20, one hour, four daily), Jaén (€9.24, two hours, four daily) and Granada (€18, 3¾ hours, two daily). The main stop in Cazorla is Plaza de la Constitución. A few buses run from Cazorla to Coto Ríos in the Parque Natural de las Sierras de Cazorla, Segura y Las Villas, with stops at Arroyo Frío and Torre del Vinagre.

Parque Natural de las Sierras de Cazorla, Segura y Las Villas

Filling almost all the eastern side of Jaén province, the Parque Natural de las Sierras de Cazorla, Segura y Las Villas is a stunning region of rugged mountain ranges divided by high plains and deep, forested valleys, and it's one of the best places in Spain for spotting wildlife. At 2143 sq km, it's also the biggest protected area in the country. Walkers stand a good chance of seeing wild boar, red and fallow deer, ibex and mouflon (a large wild sheep). The park also supports 2300 plant species.

The Guadalquivir, Andalucía's longest river, rises in the south of the park and flows north into the Embalse del Tranco de Beas reservoir, then west towards the Atlantic.

Admittedly, you do need wheels to reach some of the most spectacular areas and walks. The best times to visit are between late April and June, and September and October, when the vegetation flourishes and the weather is at its best. In spring, the flowers are magnificent. Peak visitor periods are Semana Santa, July and August.

The park starts just a few hundred metres up the hill east of Cazorla town.

Sights & Activities

The tourist office in the village of Cazorla has maps and descriptions of six park hikes (from 8km to 23km) and seven drives.

Río Borosa Walk

Though it gets busy on weekends and holidays, this walk of about seven hours return (plus stops) is the park's most popular for good reason. It follows the course of Río Borosa upstream to two beautiful mountain lakes: an ascent of 500m in the course of 12km from Torre del Vinagre. Using the bus to Torre del Vinagre, you can do it as a day trip from Cazorla (but confirm bus schedules before setting off). You can top up your water bottle at good, drinkable springs along the walk; the last is at the Central Eléctrica hydroelectric station.

A road signed 'Central Eléctrica', opposite Torre del Vinagre, soon crosses the Guadalquivir and, within 1km, reaches the marked start of the walk, on your right beside Río Borosa. The first section is an unpaved road, crisscrossing the tumbling river on bridges. After 4km, where the road starts climbing to the left, take a path forking right. This takes you through a beautiful 1.5km section, where the valley narrows to a gorge, Cerrada de Elías, and the path takes you to a wooden walkway to save you from swimming. Rejoining the main track, continue for 3km to the Central Eléctrica hydroelectric station. Just past this, a sign points you on up towards the Laguna de Valdeazores. This path will lead you, via some dramatic mountain scenery and two tunnels supplying water to the power station (there's room to stay dry as you go through), to reservoir Laguna de Aguas Negras, then the natural Laguna de Valdeazores.

Hornos & El Yelmo

The small village of Hornos sits atop a high rocky outcrop with a romantic ruined castle and panoramic views over the northern end of the Embalse del Tranco. The southern approach is awe-inspiring. About 10km northeast of Hornos is the Puerto de Horno de Peguera pass and junction. One kilometre north from here, a dirt road turns left to the top of El Yelmo (1809m), one of the most distinctive mountains in the north of the park. It's 5km to the top, an ascent of 360m – driveable, but better as a walk, with superb views and griffon vultures wheeling around the skies (plus paragliders and hanggliders on weekends). At a fork after 1.75km, go right.

Segura de la Sierra

The most spectacular village inside the park, Segura sits 20km north of Hornos, perched on an 1100m hill crowned by a castle. When taken in 1214 by the Knights of Santiago, Segura was one of the very first Christian conquests in Andalucía.

As you reach the upper part of the village, there's a tourist office (Calle Cortijos Nuevos; ⊘10.30am-2pm & 6.30-8.30pm) beside the Puerta Nueva arch. Segura's two main monuments are normally left open all day, every day, but you should check this before proceeding.

The Baño Moro (Calle Baños Moro 1; ⊘10.30am-2pm Wed-Sun) FREE, built about 1150, has three elegant rooms (for cold, tepid and hot baths) with horseshoe arches and barrel vaults studded with skylights. The castle, at the top of the village, has Islamic (or maybe even earlier) origins. From its three-storey keep there are great views across to El Yelmo and far to the west.

Tours

A number of operators offer trips to some of the park's less accessible areas, plus other activities. Hotels and campgrounds in the park can often arrange for them to pick you up.

Tierraventura ADVENTURE TOURS
(☑953 71 00 73, 953 72 20 11; www.aventura cazorla.com; Calle Ximénez de Rada 17; ⊘10am-8pm Mon-Sat, 10am-2pm Sun) Multiadventure activities including canoeing, hiking, canyon descents and rock climbing.

Sleeping & Eating

There's plenty of accommodation in the park, much of it dotted along the A319 north of Empalme del Valle. At peak times it's worth booking ahead. Most restaurants in the park are part of hotels or *hostales*.

Camping is not allowed outside the organised campgrounds.

Los Abedules
APARTMENT **$**

([☎]953 12 43 08; www.losabedules-cazorla.com; Los Peralejos, Aptdo 44, Parque Natural de las Sierras de Cazorla, Segura y Las Villas; 2-/4-person apt €60/70; [P][❄]) Surrounded by olive groves, this is an ideal spot for walkers; it offers fully furnished, comfortable apartments and a salt-water pool for cooling down after a long day's hike. It's run by an English couple; Diane is a qualified therapist in a number of alternative therapies, including reflexology and Reiki. Pets welcome.

Hotel Noguera de la Sierpe
RURAL HOTEL **$$**

([☎]953 71 30 21; www.hotelnogueracazorla.com; Carretera del Tranco Km 44.5, Parque Natural de las Sierras de Cazorla, Segura y Las Villas; s/d €60/95, 4-person chalet €120; [P][❄][❄]) A paradise for hunting aficionados, this hotel is run by an equally fanatical proprietor who has decorated the place with stuffed animals and photos of his exploits. The hotel is housed in a converted *cortijo* (farmhouse) and overlooks a picturesque lake. You can arrange riding sessions at the hotel's stables.

ⓘ Information

The main information centre is the **Centro de Interpretación Torre del Vinagre** ([⊙]10am-2pm & 4-7pm), 16km north of Empalme del Valle on the A319. Kids will enjoy the interactive AV exhibits about the park's flora and fauna. The **Museo de Caza** (Hunting Museum), with stuffed park wildlife, is in an adjoining building; a more cheerful **botanic garden** is just along the road.

Editorial Alpina's 1:40,000 *Sierra de Cazorla*, which covers the south of the park and is available in English, and *Sierra de Segura*, which covers the north, are the best maps, showing selected walks that are described in accompanying booklets. You may be able to get the maps locally, but don't count on it.

ⓘ Getting There & Away

Carcesa ([☎]953 72 11 42; www.autocares carcesa.net) runs two buses daily (except Sunday) from Cazorla's Plaza de la Constitución to Empalme del Valle, Arroyo Frío, Torre del Vinagre and Coto Ríos. Pick up the latest timetable from the tourist office. No buses link the northern part of the park with the centre or south, and there are no buses to Segura de la Sierra or Hornos. **Alsa** (www.alsa.es) runs two daily buses from Jaén, via Baeza and Úbeda, to La Puerta de Segura (€13, 3¼ hours).

ALMERÍA PROVINCE

Way out east, the gritty working port of Almería and its arid hinterland lie half-forgotten on Andalucía's most unblemished stretch of coastline. Defiantly Spanish with a strong Moorish history, the Costa del Sol–style tourist juggernaut has yet to arrive in this neck of the woods, although Clint Eastwood dropped by in the 1960s to make his trilogy of spaghetti westerns amid scenery as reminiscent of the Wild West as it is of southern Spain. Lying in the rain shadow of the Sierra Nevada, Almería is the Iberian Peninsula's sunniest and driest region, and the site of Europe's only desert. Modern greenhouse farming techniques have recently turned its parched landscapes into a horticultural powerhouse and a huge centre for immigrant labour.

Almería
POP 190,000

Don't underestimate sun-baked Almería, a tough waterside city with an illustrious history and a handful of important historical monuments to prove it. While the queues bulge outside Granada's Alhambra, mere trickles of savvy travellers head for Almería's equally hefty Alcazaba fortress, which lords it over a city that once served as chief sea outlet for the 10th-century Córdoba caliphate.

No Andalucian city has proved as stubborn or resolute as Almería. During the Reconquista, it remained Moorish until 1489 whereupon it fell to the Christian invaders just three years before Granada, and it was the last city in Andalucía to surrender to Franco's Fascist forces during the Civil War.

Today Almería is an increasingly prosperous port with a thriving agribusiness sector (count the greenhouses) and a strong flamenco tradition enshrined in its distinctive *tarantos*.

ⓞ Sights & Activities

Almería's old Moorish quarter lies in the skirts of the Alcazaba hill and hasn't been spruced up for the tourist hordes, meaning it is scruffy, but very real.

In central Plaza de las Flores, there's a statue of John Lennon strumming a guitar on a bench. Why? Lennon spent a month in Almería in 1966 making the film *How I Won the War*. It was here that he wrote the song *Strawberry Fields Forever*.

Alcazaba   FORTRESS
(Calle Almanzor; adult/EU citizen €1.50/free; ⊙9am-8.30pm Tue-Sat, 10am-5pm Sun Apr-Oct, to 6.30pm Tue-Sun Nov-Mar) A looming fortification with great curtain-like walls rising from the cliffs, the Alcazaba was built in the 10th century by Abd ar-Rahman III, the greatest caliphate of Al-Andalus, and was the most powerful Moorish fortress in Spain. It lacks the intricate decoration of the Alhambra, but it is nonetheless a compelling monument.

The interior is divided into three distinct sections. The lowest area, the Primer Recinto, was the civic centre, with houses, baths and other necessities – now replaced by lush gardens and water channels. From the battlements you can see the Muralla de Jayrán, a fortified wall built in the 11th century.

In the Segundo Recinto you'll find the ruins of the Muslim rulers' palace, built by Almotacín (r 1051–91), under whom medieval Almería reached its peak. Within the compound is a chapel, the Ermita de San Juan, once a mosque.

The highest part, the Tercer Recinto, is a fortress added by the Catholic Monarchs. Its keep is used as a gallery for painting and photography (and similar) exhibitions (9am to 8.30pm Tuesday to Sunday).

Catedral de la Encarnación   CATHEDRAL
(Plaza de la Catedral; admission €5; ⊙10am-1.30pm & 4-5pm Mon-Fri, 10am-1.30pm Sat) Cathedral or fortress? Almería's unusually weighty cathedral in the heart of the old part of the city below the Alcazaba is a little bit both. Begun in 1524, it took on its fortress-like appearance, with six towers, due to the prevalence of pirate raids from North Africa during this era.

The interior has a Gothic ribbed ceiling and is trimmed with jasper and local marble. The chapel behind the main altar contains the tomb of Bishop Diego Villalán, the cathedral's founder, whose broken-nosed image is the work of Juan de Orea, who also created the Sacristía Mayor with its fine carved stonework.

★ Museo de la Guitarra   MUSEUM
(☑950 27 43 58; Ronda del Beato Diego Ventaja; ⊙10am-1pm Tue-Fri & Sun, 5-8pm Fri & Sat) FREE It's worth establishing two important facts before you enter this fantastic new interactive museum (opened December 2013). First: the word 'guitar' is derived from the Andalucían-Arabic word qitara, hinting at its Spanish roots. Second: all modern acoustic guitars owe a huge debt to Almerian guitar-maker Antonio de Torres (1817–92), to whom this museum is dedicated. The museum itself is a minor masterpiece that pays homage to the history of the guitar and Torres' part in it.

An interactive zone allows you to strum electric and acoustic instruments, quizzes test your musical knowledge, and a fascinating film shows how guitars are made.

Centro Andaluz de Fotografía   GALLERY
(Andalucian Photographic Centre; ☑950 26 96 80; Calle Pintor Diaz Molina, 9; ⊙11am-2pm & 5.30-9.30pm) FREE Revolving temporary photo exhibits are showcased in a fine old building. The collections are invariably modern and edgy.

Museo de Almería   MUSEUM
(Carretera de Ronda 91; ⊙10am-8.30pm Tue-Sat, 10am-5pm Sun) FREE Almería's fantastic modern Museo Arqueológico presents finds from Los Millares and other ancient settlements in the region, as well as Roman and Islamic traces. Even if pot shards and bone fragments normally make you yawn, don't skip this – it's a rare example of multimedia technology deployed to excellent effect, touched with a uniquely Spanish flair for the macabre.

Aljibes de Jayrán   HISTORIC SITE
(☑950 27 30 39; Calle Tenor Iribarne; ⊙10am-2pm & 5-8pm Tue-Sat) FREE North of Plaza de las Flores, the Aljibes de Jayrán were built in the early 11th century to supply the city's water. These subterranean aqueducts are well preserved, and are the venue for regular exhibitions, and for the Peña El Taranto flamenco club.

Hammam Aíre de Almería   HAMMAM
(www.airedealmeria.com; Plaza de la Constitución 5; baths €21; ⊙10am-10pm) Opened in 2011, this new hammam occupies a wonderful setting on the Plaza de la Constitución, a 17th-century arcaded square that was once the city's main Arab souq. It offers the usual trio of cold, tepid and hot baths, as well as a range of aromatherapy massages. The hammam also incorporates a hotel and a bar.

🛏 Sleeping

★ Hotel Nuevo Torreluz   HOTEL $
(☑950 23 43 99; www.torreluz.com; Plaza de las flores 10; r €54; P ✳ 🕸) Reopened in 2012 this reformed four-star enjoys a superb position on a small square in the heart of the historic centre. Rooms are slick and modern if not luxurious and well equipped and comfort-

able with warm colour schemes. The hotel runs a trio of cafe/restaurants all in the surrounding square.

Hotel Costasol
HOTEL $

(☏950 23 40 11; www.hotelcostasol.com; Paseo de Almería 58; r €50; P❄@🖭) This sensible hotel has a few hip details, such as round red rugs and jaunty wall lamps, but the real perks are firm beds, spotless floors, vast bathrooms and some tiny balconies (with a sea view, way down the boulevard). Parking (€10) is in a city lot, half a block away. There's a cafe below the lobby.

Hotel Sevilla
HOTEL $

(☏950 23 00 09; www.hotelsevillaalmeria.es; Calle de Granada 23; s/d €32/40; ❄🖭) This cheapest hotel deal is a cheerful and efficient place that offers clean rooms and a good central location. Bathrooms are minuscule but modern.

Plaza Vieja Hotel & Lounge
HOTEL $$

(☏950 28 20 96; www.plazaviejahl.com; Plaza de la Constitución 5; d/ste €109/129; P❄🖭) Part of the plush Hammam Aíre de Almería, the rooms here are spacious and modern with high ceilings, lots of glass and shiny wood, soft natural colours and vast photo-friezes of local sights like the Cabo de Gato.

Hotel Catedral
HOTEL $$

(☏950 27 81 78; www.hotelcatedral.net; Plaza de la Catedral 8; d €65-120; ❄@🖭) Cosied up to the cathedral and built with the same warm honey-coloured stone, the building dates from 1850 and has been sensitively restored. Rooms are large with luxury touches, and the sun terrace has heady cathedral views.

✗ Eating

Almería seems to specialise in crowded, standing-room-only tapas bars with bullfighting posters and noisy posses of loyal regulars who are so regular they barely have to mouth their orders. The best of them lie in the triangle between Plaza Pablo Cazard, Puerta de Putchería and the cathedral.

Café Colón
CAFE $

(Plaza Marqués de Heredia; churros from €1.50; ⊙8am-11pm) A much-loved cafe in a recently renovated square. It's good for televised football matches and wickedly scrumptious churros, preferably enjoyed together.

Habana Cristal
CAFE $

(Calle Altamira 6; cocktails €3.80; ⊙7am-10pm) Senior señoras with *mucho* hairspray

crowd into Almería's most emblematic and well-known cafe, where everyone ought to come for a slice of cake and an exotic coffee, including the winter-warming Habana Negra with Swiss chocolate, Tia Maria and Cointreau.

Casa Puga
TAPAS $

(www.barcasapuga.es; Calle Jovellanos 7; drink & tapa €2.20; ⊙noon-4pm & 8pm-midnight Mon-Sat) Shelves of ancient wine bottles are the backdrop for a tiny cooking station that churns out small saucers of stews, griddled goodies such as mushrooms, and savoury *hueva de maruca* (smoked fish roe).

Lamarca
ANDALUCIAN, DELI $

(☏950 08 66 25; www.grupolamarca.com; Calle San Francisco de Asís; tapas €3-6; ⊙9am-midnight Mon-Sat, 10am-midnight Sun) What started as a humble Almería ham shop has now morphed into a funky eco-market-cum-restaurant that resembles Italy's famous *Eataly* chain. This new Lamarca, which opened in late 2013, sells top-quality produce and deli goods downstairs adjacent to a trendy open-plan tapas bar. Upstairs is an even trendier sit-down restaurant.

★ Tetería Almedina
TEAHOUSE $$

(www.restauranteteteriaalmedina.com; Calle Paz 2, off Calle de la Almedina; teas €3, mains €8-12; ⊙11am-11pm Tue-Sun; 🖉) Way more than your average tea-room, this lovely little place in the old city serves as a cafe, restaurant (with good Moroccan food) and bona fide cutural centre. It's run by a group dedicated to restoring and revitalising the old city; they regularly put on art shows, live music and the like.

Casa Joaquín
SEAFOOD $$

(☏950 264 359; Calle Real 111; mains €14-21; ⊙noon-4pm & 8.30pm-midnight Mon-Fri, noon-4pm Sat) Reserve one of the few tables for lunch if you're really serious about your seafood. If you don't mind standing, you can jostle at the bar for platters of baby clams swimming in garlic, delicately fried pieces of monkfish liver and other briny treats. There is no menu.

🍷 Drinking & Nightlife

Burana
BAR

(Paseo de Almería 56; ⊙9am-4am) Bar-cafe in the front portals of the neoclassical Teatro Cervantes with a trendy vibe and live music on Fridays. Not a bad pew for morning coffee as well.

C Bar

BAR

(www.hotelcatedral.net; Plaza de la Catedral 8; ⊙noon-midnight) Part of the Hotel Catedral, this slick bar has a young fashionable audience with its giant blackboards, minimalist furniture and innovative tapas like raspberry, gin and basil sorbet.

☆ Entertainment

Almería's flamenco scene is generally restricted to private *peñas* that may or may not open their doors to interested outsiders. The leading light is Peña El Taranto (www.eltaranto.net), where local guitar star Tomatito has been known to strum. On the northern edge of town Peña Flamenco El Morato (☑ 950 25 09 14; www.elmorato.com; Calle Manuel Vicente; ⊙10pm-late) is scooped out of a cave and about as local as it gets.

Teatro Apolo

THEATRE

(☑ 950 26 92 68; www.almeriacultura.com; Rambla del Obispo Orbera 25) This relatively new theatre adds a welcome injection of culture into Almería's predominant and animated bar scene.

ℹ Information

There are numerous banks on Paseo de Almería.

Main Post Office (behind Plaza Ecuador; ⊙8.30am-9.30pm Mon-Fri, 8.30am-2pm Sat)

Municipal Tourist Office (Ayuntamiento, Plaza de la Constitución 1; ⊙9am-3pm) Also opens from 6pm to 8pm in July and August.

Policía Local (Local Police; ☑950 62 12 06; Calle Santos Zárate 11)

Regional Tourist Office (Parque de Nicolás Salmerón; ⊙9am-7pm Mon-Fri, 10am-2pm Sat & Sun) Provides more free leaflets and brochures.

ℹ Getting There & Away

AIR

Almería **airport** (☑ 950 21 37 00; www.aena.es), 10km east of the city centre, receives flights from several European countries. **EasyJet** (www.easyjet.com) flies from London-Gatwick, **Ryanair** (www.ryanair.com) seasonally from Stansted, East Midlands (UK) and Dublin, **Thomas Cook Airlines** (www.thomascook airlines.co.uk) from Manchester and London-Gatwick (seasonally), and **Monarch Airlines** (www.flymonarch.com) from Birmingham (seasonally). **Air-Berlin** (www.airberlin.com) flies from Mallorca and **Transavia** (www.transavia.com) from Amsterdam (seasonally). **Iberia** (www.iberia.com) flies direct to/from Madrid and Seville.

BOAT

For Morocco, **Acciona Trasmediterránea** (☑ 902 454645; www.trasmediterranea.es) sails from the passenger port to Melilla, Nador (Morocco) and Ghazaouet (Algeria). Prices are €38, €48 and €88 respectively for a one-way adult fare.

BUS

From the clean, efficient **bus station** (☑ 950 26 20 98) the company **Alsa** (☑ 902 422242; www.alsa.es) run services to Granada (€14, 2¼ hours, eight daily), Málaga (€19, three to four hours, seven daily), Murcia (€20, 2½ hours, seven daily), Madrid (€28, seven hours, eight daily) and Valencia (€41, seven to nine hours, five daily).

TRAIN

Almería's train station shares digs with the bus station. Direct trains run to/from Granada (€20, 2¼ hours, four daily), Seville (€40, 5½ hours, four daily) and Madrid (€46, 6¼ hours, two daily).

ℹ Getting Around

Almería is pretty walkable. City bus 20 (€1, 30 minutes) runs to the centre, near Avenida de Federico García Lorca, on weekdays approximately every 50 minutes; less often at weekends.

Desierto de Tabernas

Beyond Benahadux, north of Almería, the landscape becomes a series of canyons and rocky wastes that look like they're straight out of the Arizona badlands, and in the 1960s and '70s movie-makers shot around 150 westerns here.

The movie industry has left behind two Wild West town sets that are open as tourist attractions. Oasys/Mini Hollywood (www.oasysparquetematico.com; adult/child €22/12.50; ⊙10am-9pm May-Sep, weekends only Oct-Apr; 🖶), the best known and best preserved of these, is 25km from Almería on the N340 Tabernas road. Parts of more than 100 movies, including *A Fistful of Dollars* and *The Good, the Bad and the Ugly*, were filmed here. Twice a day a hammed-up bank hold-up and shootout is staged in the town followed by a ritzy can-can dance in the saloon bar. The set has modest cinema and stagecoach museums plus a bar/restaurant. The ticket also includes entry to an adjoining Reserva Zoológica with lions, tigers and hippos. It's kitschy, but fun, especially if you have kids. Fort Bravo (www.fort-bravo.com; adult/child €17.90/9.90; ⊙10am-10pm, weekends only Oct-Apr), 4km further on, is a slightly more grown-up theme park with stagecoach rides and horse-riding treks.

An Alsa bus from Almería (€1.80, 40 minutes, three daily) can drop you at both places. You'll have to flag the bus down for the return leg.

Cabo de Gata

If you can find anyone old enough to remember the Costa del Sol before the bulldozers arrived, they'd probably say it looked a bit like Cabo de Gata. Some of Spain's most beautiful and least-crowded beaches are strung between the grand cliffs and capes east of Almería city, where dark volcanic hills tumble into a sparkling turquoise sea. Though Cabo de Gata is not undiscovered, it still has a wild, elemental feel and its scattered fishing villages (remember them?) remain low-key. You can walk along, or not far from, the coast right round from Retamar in the northwest to Agua Amarga in the northeast (61km), but beware – the sun can be intense and there's often little shade. The area is also one of the best places in Andalucía for diving.

It's worth calling ahead for accommodation over Easter and in July and August.

Parque Natural de Cabo de Gata-Níjar covers Cabo de Gata's 60km coast plus a slice of hinterland. The park's main information centre is the **Centro de Interpretación Las Amoladeras** (☑ 950 16 04 35; ☻ 10am-2pm & 5.30-9pm mid-Jul–mid-Sep, to 3pm Tue-Sun mid-Sep–mid-Jul), located 2.5km west of Ruescas with displays on neolithic human settlements and the park's ecosystems.

San Miguel de Cabo de Gata

Fronted by a long straight beach, this scruffy village isn't the best introduction to the park. It's composed largely of holiday houses and apartments (deserted out of season), and resembles a detached suburb of Almería. Press on to the Faro (lighthouse), or start hiking in San José and use this as your finishing point.

South of the village stretch the **Salinas de Cabo de Gata**, which are salt-extraction lagoons. In spring many migrating greater flamingos and other birds call in here: by late August there can be a thousand flamingos. An 11km trail circumnavigates the *salinas*, equipped with strategically placed viewing hides. You should see a good variety of birds from here except in winter, when the *salinas* are drained, but you really need binoculars to appreciate the scene.

Cabo de Gata

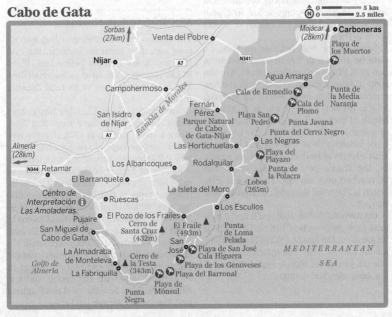

San José is a better place to stay unless you want to camp at the extremely well-run Camping Cabo de Gata (☎ 950 16 04 43; www.campingcabodegata.com; sites per adult, caravan, car & power supply €20, bungalow €71-112), 1km from the beach; it has all the necessary amenities, including a restaurant. It's 2.5km north of the village by dirt roads.

Faro de Cabo de Gata & Around

Beyond the Salinas de Cabo de Gata, a narrow road winds 4km round the cliffs to the Faro de Cabo de Gata, the lighthouse at the promontory's tip. A turnoff by Café Bar El Faro, just before the lighthouse, leads to the Torre Vigía Vela Blanca, an 18th-century watchtower atop 200m cliffs, with awesome views. Here the road ends, but a walking and cycling track continues down to Playa de Mónsul (one hour on foot).

San José

POP 550

San José, spreading round a bay on the eastern side of Cabo de Gata, is a mildly chic resort in summer, but it remains a small, pleasant, low-rise place and is a base for both watery and land-bound activities. Out of season you may have the place almost to yourself.

The road from the north becomes San José's main street, Avenida de San José, with the beach and harbour a couple of blocks down to the left.

Some of the best beaches on Cabo de Gata lie along a dirt road southwest from San José. Playa de los Genoveses, a broad strip of sand about 1km long with shallow waters, is 4.5km away. Playa de Mónsul, 2.5km further from town, is a shorter length of grey sand, backed by huge lumps of volcanic rock. Away from the road, the coast between these two beaches is strung with a series of isolated, sandy, cove beaches, the Calas del Barronal, which can be reached only on foot. The largest cove beach is Playa del Barronal, a popular nudist spot.

On Avenida de San José you'll find a natural park information office (☎ 950 38 02 99; Avenida de San José 27; ◷ 10am-2pm & 5-8pm), a bank and an ATM. The information office can tell you about bicycle rental, horse riding, boat trips and diving.

🍽 Sleeping & Eating

Hostal Aloha HOSTAL $
(☎ 950 38 04 61; www.hostalaloha.com; Calle Cala Higuera; r €55; ❄ ≋) White walls, firm beds and gleaming bathrooms make this an appealing budget hotel to start with. Throw in the enormous pool on the back terrace, and it's one of the best deals in San José. It's a few blocks back from the beach; to reach it, turn left off the main street at the tourist office.

MC San José HOTEL $$
(☎ 950 61 11 11; www.hotelesmcsanjose.com; Carretera El Faro; d incl breakfast €139; ❄ @ ≋ ≋) The MC is the best of both hotel worlds: chic boutique design, with just 32 rooms and plenty of stylish details, but with the kind of hospitality that only comes from a local family. Open all year-round, with a reasonable Chinese restaurant on the ground floor.

Casa Miguel SEAFOOD $$
(☎ 950 38 03 29; www.restaurantecasamiguel.es; Avenida de San José 43-45; mains €18-22) The best seafood restaurant in San José has pavement seating and good service. Skip the pallid paella, however, in favour of the rich *arroz negro* (mixed seafood and rice, black from squid ink). Or pick and mix with the daily fish specials. The bar does good tapas. Reservations recommended at weekends.

San José to Las Negras

The rugged coast northeast of San José allows only two small settlements, the odd fort and a few beaches before the village of Las Negras, 17km away as the crow flies. The road spends most of its time ducking inland.

The hamlet of Los Escullos has a short beach. You can walk here from San José, along a track starting at Cala Higuera bay. One kilometre beyond Los Escullos, La Isleta del Moro is a tiny village with a beach, a medley of fishing boats and a couple of salt-of-the-sea restaurants offering about 20 different types of fish. You can arrange diving here with Buceo Almería (☎ 950 38 95 26; www.buceoalmeria.com; Calle Cala Chumba 1). Casa Café de la Loma (☎ 950 38 98 31; www.degata.com/laloma; s/d €40/60), on a small hill above the village and five minutes from the beach, is a 200-year-old house restored in Al-Andalus style with airy rooms and terrific views. From here the road heads inland past the spooky former gold-mining village

HIKING CABO DE GATA'S COAST

Hiking along an uninhabited slice of Andalucian coastline is a rare joy these days, so make the most of Cabo de Gata, where you can sometimes walk for an hour or so off-season without seeing a soul. For good day hikes, start in the village of San José, accessible by bus from Almería. The coastal path that swings south around the headland and then heads northwest to San Miguel de Cabo de Gata passes secluded beaches, crashing surf, a lighthouse and bird-filled salt pans. The full distance from San José to San Miguel de Cabo de Gata, where you can catch a bus back to Almería, is 16km.

If you head in the other direction (northeast), you'll climb the precipitous cliffs of the ancient Los Frailes volcanoes and be deposited on the lovely beach of Los Escullos fronted by the Batería San Felipe, an 18th-century fort restored in the 1990s. The fit can soldier on another 1km to the village of La Isleta del Moro for lunch in a waterside fish restaurant. Due to poor bus connections, you'll need to retrace your steps back to San José, a 16km out-and-back hike.

At the time of writing the last weekday bus from San José to Almería was leaving at 8pm.

of Rodalquilar, which is worth a detour. About 1km past Rodalquilar is the turnoff to Playa del Playazo, a good beach between two headlands, 2km along a level track. From here you can walk near the coast to the village of Las Negras, which is set on a pebbly beach and is largely given over to seasonal tourism.

On Las Negras' main street, Hostal Arrecife (☑950 38 81 40; www.hostalelarrecife.es; Calle Bahía 6; s/d €28/40) has cool, quiet, well-maintained rooms, some with sea views from their balconies. Camping La Caleta (☑950 52 52 37; www.campinglacaleta.com; sites per adult/tent €6.40/12; bungalows €98; P🐕🛜🏊) lies in a separate cove 1km south of Las Negras. It can be fiercely hot in summer, but there is a good pool. Other accommodation in Las Negras is mostly holiday apartments and houses to let. Restaurante La Palma (☑950 38 80 42; www.restaurantelapalma.com; mains €12-26; ☺9am-11.30pm), overlooking the beach, plays good music and serves a huge array of fish dishes.

Las Negras to Agua Amarga

There's no road along this secluded, cliff-lined stretch of coast, but walkers can take an up-and-down path of about 11km, giving access to several beaches. Playa San Pedro, one hour from Las Negras, is the site of a ruined hamlet (with castle), inhabited erratically by hippies and naturists. It's another 4km to Cala del Plomo beach, with another tiny village, then 3km further to Agua Amarga.

Drivers must head inland from Las Negras through Las Hortichuelas. A mostly unsealed road heads northeast, cross-country from the bus shelter in Fernán Pérez. Keep to the main track at all turnings, and after 10km you'll reach a sealed road running down from the N341 to Agua Amarga, a chic and expensive but still low-key former fishing village on a straight sandy beach.

Breezy beachfront Hostal Restaurante La Palmera (☑950 13 82 08; www.hostal restaurantelapalmera.com; Calle Aguada; d €60-90) has 10 bright rooms all with sea views, and its restaurant (mains €11 to €19) is Agua Amarga's most popular lunch spot.

Stylish, slick MiKasa Suites & Spa (☑950 13 80 73; www.mikasasuites.com; Carretera Carboneras, Agua Amarga; d/ste incl breakfast €90/110; ❄🛜🏊) is an elegant, comfortable, romantic hideaway for the long-weekend crowd. It has a poolside restaurant, a beach bar, and more expensive food (by the sound of it) in the on-site spa – ever heard of caviar facials or algae wraps?

Top spot for food on the beach is Costamarga (Playa de Aguamarga, Agua Amarga; mains €11-16; ☺noon-4pm & 8-11pm; 🅿), which does fish, of course, but also has a considerable menu section devoted to seasonal vegetables, such as artichoke hearts with ham.

❶ Getting There & Away

Alsa (☑902 422242; www.alsa.es) connects Almería to San Miguel de Cabo de Gata (€3, one hour, six daily) and Las Negras (€5, 1¼ hours, one daily Monday to Saturday). Autocares Bernardo (www.autocaresbernardo.com) runs buses from Almería to San José (€2.65,

1¼ hours, four Monday to Saturday, two Sunday). It also runs one bus to La Isleta del Moro (€2.65, 1¼ hours) on Mondays and Saturdays. **Autocares Frahermar** (www.frahermar.com) in Almería runs to/from Agua Amarga (€5.50, 1¼ hours) once on Monday, Wednesday, Friday, Saturday and Sunday; service increases to daily in July and August. There is no bus service connecting towns within the park.

Mojácar

POP 7745

Tucked away in an isolated corner of one of Spain's most traditional regions lies Mojácar, a town that was almost abandoned in the mid-20th century until a foresighted local mayor started luring artists and others with giveaway property offers. Although the tourists have arrived, Mojácar has retained its essence.

There are actually two towns here: old Mojácar Pueblo, a jumble of white, cube-shaped houses on a hilltop 2km inland, and Mojácar Playa, a modern beach resort.

◉ Sights & Activities

Exploring Mojácar Pueblo is mainly a matter of wandering the mazelike streets, with their bougainvillea-swathed balconies, stopping off at craft shops, galleries and boutiques. **El Mirador del Castillo** (⊙11am-11pm or later), at the topmost point, provides magnificent views. The fortress-style **Iglesia de Santa María** (Calle Iglesia) dates from 1560 and may have once been a mosque.

The most touching spot is the **Fuente Mora** (Moorish Fountain) in the lower part of the old town. Though remodelled in modern times, it maintains the medieval Islamic tradition of making art out of flowing water.

South of Mojácar Playa, the beaches are quieter, and once you get to the fringes of town, there are a number of more secluded areas. Several beyond the **Torre de Macenas**, an 18th-century fortification right on the sand, are naturist beaches.

🛏 Sleeping & Eating

El Mirador del Castillo　　　HOSTAL **$$**
(☑950 47 30 22; www.elcastillomojacar.com; El Mirador del Castillo; d €87, with shared bathroom €69; ❋ 🗟 ⊠) Up at the top of Mojácar's hill, this laid-back *hostal* is part of a larger art centre and retreat, with a cafe-bar as well. The atmosphere is resolutely bohemian, but even with some peeling paint, it manages to stay just the right side of characterful, with richly coloured walls and art books on the bedside tables.

La Taberna　　　TAPAS **$**
(Plaza del Caño 1, Mojácar Pueblo; tapas & platos combinados from €4; ⊙1-4pm & 8pm-midnight; ▯) Good tapas and tasty vegetarian bites get everyone cramming into this thriving little restaurant inside a warren of intimate rooms, full of chatter and belly-full diners. Located next to an evocative 11th-century Moorish arch. To get here, head downhill and pass through the old city gate – just on the right, you'll see the tiny tapas *plancha* (griddle) in action.

ⓘ Information

Tourist Office (☑950 61 50 25; www.mojacar.es; Calle Glorieta 1; ⊙10am-2pm & 5-7.30pm Mon-Fri, 10.30am-1.30pm Sat) Very helpful tourist office just off Mojácar Pueblo's Plaza Nueva.

ⓘ Getting There & Around

There is a bus stop at the foot of Mojácar Pueblo and another at the Parque Comercial in Mojácar Playa. **Alsa** (www.alsa.es) runs buses to/from Almería (€7.59, 1¼ hours, four on weekdays, two on weekends), Granada (€21, 4¼ hours, two daily) and Madrid (€40, eight hours, two daily). Buses to Alicante, Valencia and Barcelona go from Vera, 16km north, which is served by several daily buses from Mojácar (€1.50, 50 minutes, nine daily).

Valencia & Murcia

Includes ➡

Why Go?

Principal settlement in the region and an utterly addictive city, Valencia exudes confidence. Its sophisticated cultural scene, kicking nightlife, quality museums, great restaurants, understated beach and stunning Modernista and contemporary architecture make it one of the peninsula's real jewels.

Throughout this sun-bathed coastal pleasure-ground, a wealth of festivals awaits you, whether you fancy top-notch rock music at Benicàssim, hooded processions and friendly rivalry at Lorca's Semana Santa, reenactments of Reconquista battles in the numerous Moros y Cristianos festivals or one of the world's biggest food fights at La Tomatina.

While some of the coastal resorts – hello Benidorm! – are notoriously overdeveloped, there are plenty of places to explore that aren't. The ancient port of Cartagena has a magnificent array of Roman and Carthaginian ruins, while Murcia is a buzzy regional capital where there's not a fried breakfast in sight.

Best Places to Eat

➡ Carosel (p738)

➡ Delicat (p739)

➡ Daluan (p752)

➡ Cervecería Sento (p759)

➡ El Granaino (p765)

Best Places to Stay

➡ Caro Hotel (p738)

➡ Cases Noves (p763)

➡ Hotel Chamarel (p754)

➡ Villa Venecia (p756)

➡ Mont Sant (p762)

When to Go
Valencia City

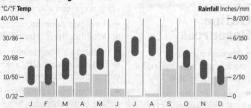

Mar Las Fallas, Valencia's wild spring festival, brings some two million visitors to town.	**Aug** Paint the town red at Buñol's tomato fight, then hit the coast's lively nightlife scene.	**Oct** The sea's still just about swimmable; there's decent weather but far fewer people.

CERCANÍA TRAINS

The *cercanía* short-distance trains run by Renfe are good ways to get around the region. One network radiates out from Valencia, another from Alicante and Murcia. Trains are cheap and leave regularly.

Top Festivals

➔ Las Fallas (p745), Valencia, mid-March

➔ Semana Santa (p774), Lorca, Easter

➔ Moros y Cristianos (p762), Alcoy, late April

➔ Festival Internacional de Benicàssim (p748), mid-July

➔ La Tomatina (p748), Buñol, late August

Off the Beaten Track

In summer the coast is packed. Though quieter corners exist, if you want to explore away from crowds, head inland, where valleys and hill towns offer a more relaxed experience.

Online Resources

➔ www.comunitat valenciana.com – regional government website

➔ www.murciaturistica. es – the equivalent for the Murcia region

➔ www.magrama.gob. es/es/costas/servicios/ guia-playas – guide to beaches; in Spanish, but self-explanatory

Street Names

Though many locals don't like to see it as such, for a traveller's purposes, the regional language Valenciano is a form of Catalan. There's a constant to-and-fro here as councils replace Spanish (Castilian) street names with the Valenciano/Catalan equivalents, then their successors change them back. The result is a little chaotic: some streets have a different name at each end. While the difference between the two versions is often minimal, this can sometimes be confusing for visitors. Occasionally we use the Valenciano form where it's clearly the dominant one. But since Spanish is the version the majority uses, we've elected to stick with it in most cases.

WINE REGIONS

The Valencia region has a long winemaking tradition dating back to Phoenicians, Greeks and Romans, and several unusual local grape varieties to taste and quaff. The Alicante and Valencia denominations both cover a wide variety of areas, from coastal plains to mountain valleys, so the range of wines produced is broad, including reds, rosés and whites, as well as sweet wines. Utiel-Requena is an inland region and produces very distinctive reds from the indigenous bobal grape. In Murcia, Jumilla is the zone with the highest average quality; the hot climate produces powerful, full-bodied reds, mostly from the monastrell grape, known in France as mourvèdre. The zone, which also has reasonable whites from Airén, crosses into Castilla-La Mancha. The other Murcian Denominación de Origens (DOs), Yecla and Bullas, also focus primarily on monastrell, though a number of other white and red varietals are used.

Top Five Food Experiences

➔ Denia's gourmet dining options – this lively port (p754) has one of Spain's most renowned restaurants as well as several intriguing tapas and seafood options.

➔ The region's enormous variety of rice dishes – you could be here for months just trying them all (p739).

➔ Valencia's embarrassing wealth of restaurants – the city (p738) is surrounded by a rich horticultural zone, locals love eating out, and there's a quality option on nearly every street.

➔ The most interesting town for wine-tasting is Requena (p747), in the Valencian hills – the local bobal wines are distinctive and delicious.

➔ Murcia's kicking deli-tapas scene – (p768) the city has loads of delis where you can stock up on charcuterie or fish preserves, and also sample them with a glass of wine in hand.

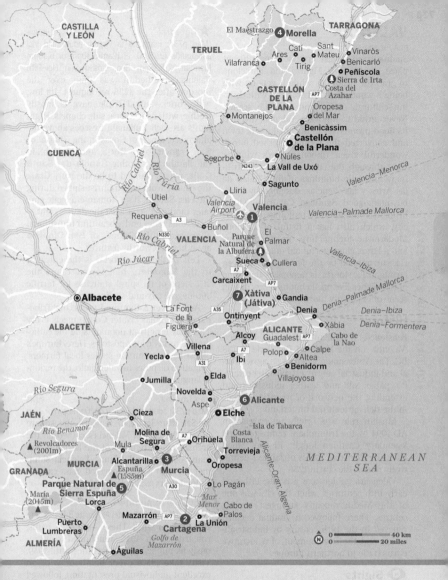

Valencia & Murcia Highlights

1 Gasp at the daring architecture of the **Ciudad de las Artes y las Ciencias** (p729) in Valencia; if you're here in mid-March, fling fireworks and suffer serious sleep deprivation at **Las Fallas** (p745).

2 Explore Cartagena's fascinating **Roman and Carthaginian sites** (p770).

3 Sip a drink at sundown in Plaza del Cardenal Belluga, **Murcia** (p765), overlooked by the magnificent cathedral.

4 Savour your first glimpse of the medieval fortress town of **Morella** (p751) from afar.

5 Lace up those hiking boots and explore the unspoilt beauty of the **Parque Natural de Sierra Espuña** (p775).

6 Kick on through the night with the great tapas and bar scene in **Alicante** (p760).

7 Trudge up to Xàtiva's magnificent **castle** (p762) and chow down on a picnic at the top.

VALENCIA

POP 792,300

Spain's third-largest city is a magnificent place, content for Madrid and Barcelona to grab the headlines while it gets on with being a wonderfully liveable city with thriving cultural, eating and nightlife scenes. Never afraid to innovate, Valencia diverted its flood-prone river to the outskirts of town and converted the former riverbed into a wonderful green ribbon of park winding right through the city. On it are the strikingly futuristic buildings of the Ciudad de las Artes y las Ciencias, designed by local-boy-made-good Santiago Calatrava. Other brilliant contemporary buildings grace the city, which also has a fistful of fabulous Modernista architecture, great museums and a large, characterful old quarter. Valencia, surrounded by the fertile fruit-and-veg farmland La Huerta, is famous as the home of rice dishes like paella but its buzzy dining scene offers plenty more besides.

History

Pensioned-off Roman legionaries founded 'Valentia' on the banks of Río Turia in 138 BC. The Arabs made Valencia an agricultural and industrial centre, establishing ceramics, paper, silk and leather industries and extending the network of irrigation canals in the rich agricultural hinterland.

Muslim rule was briefly interrupted in AD 1094 by the triumphant rampage of the legendary Castilian knight El Cid. Much later, the Christian forces of Jaime I definitively retook the city in 1238.

Valencia's golden age was the 15th and early 16th centuries, when the city was one of the Mediterranean's strongest trading centres. There followed a gradual decline, relieved in the 19th century by industrialisation and the development of a lucrative citrus trade to northern Europe.

Sights

Plaza de la Virgen & Around

Busy Plaza de la Virgen, ringed by cafes and imposing public buildings, was once the forum of Roman Valencia. The reclining figure in its central fountain represents Río Turia, while the eight maidens with their gushing pots symbolise the main irrigation canals flowing from it.

★ Catedral
CATHEDRAL

(Map p734; Plaza de la Virgen; adult/child incl audioguide €5/3.50; ⊙ 10am-5.30pm or 6.30pm Mon-Sat, 2-5.30pm Sun, closed Sun Nov-Feb) Valencia's cathedral was built over the mosque after the 1238 reconquest. Its low, wide, brick-vaulted triple nave is mostly Gothic, with neoclassical side chapels. Highlights are rich Italianate frescoes above the altarpiece, a pair of Goyas in the Chapel of San Francisco de Borja, and...da-dah...in the flamboyant Gothic Capilla del Santo Cáliz, what's claimed to be the Holy Grail, the chalice from which Christ sipped during the Last Supper. It's a Roman-era agate cup, later modified, so at least the date is right.

Various relics and a beautiful transitional altarpiece in the Chapel of San Dionisio are other noteworthy features.

Left of the main portal is the entrance to the Miguelete bell tower. Climb the 207 steps of its spiral staircase for terrific 360-degree city-and-skyline views.

As for over a thousand years, the Tribunal de las Aguas (Water Court) meets every Thursday exactly at noon outside the cathedral's Puerta de los Apóstoles. Here, Europe's oldest legal institution settles local farmers' irrigation disputes in Valenciano, the regional language.

La Almoina
RUINS

(Map p734; adult/child €2/1; ⊙ 10am-6pm or 7pm Tue-Sat, 10am-3pm Sun) Beneath the square just to the east of Valencia's cathedral, the archaeological remains of the kernel of Roman, Visigoth and Islamic Valencia shimmer through a water-covered glass canopy. Guided tours available for a little extra.

Baños del Almirante
BATHHOUSE

(Map p734; Calle Baños del Almirante 3-5; ⊙ 11am-2pm Tue-Sun) FREE These Arab-style baths, constructed in 1313, functioned continuously as public bathing facilities until 1959. Visits take place every half-hour with an excellent audiovisual presentation, followed by a short guided tour.

Plaza del Mercado

Facing each other across Plaza del Mercado are two emblematic buildings, each a masterpiece of its era.

★ La Lonja
HISTORIC BUILDING

(Map p734; Calle de la Lonja; adult/child €2/1; ⊙ 10am-6pm or 7pm Tue-Sat, to 3pm Sun) This splendid late 15th-century building, a

CIUDAD DE LAS ARTES Y LAS CIENCIAS

The aesthetically stunning Ciudad de las Artes y las Ciencias (City of Arts & Sciences; Map p730; www.cac.es; combined ticket for Oceanogràfic, Hemisfèric & Museo de las Ciencias Príncipe Felipe adult/child €36.25/27.55) occupies a massive 350,000-sq-metre swathe of the old Turia riverbed. It's mostly the work of world-famous, locally born architect Santiago Calatrava. He's a controversial figure for many Valencians, who complain about the expense, and various design flaws that have necessitated major repairs. Nevertheless, if your taxes weren't involved, it's awe-inspiring stuff, and pleasingly family-oriented.

Take bus 35 (among several others) from Plaza del Ayuntamiento. A number of chain hotels cluster near the complex.

Oceanogràfic (Map p730; www.cac.es/oceanografic; adult/child €27.90/21; ☉10am-6pm Oct-Jun, 10-8pm Jul & Sep, 10am-midnight Aug; ☑) For most families with children this indoor-outdoor aquarium is the highlight of a visit to Valencia's City of Arts & Sciences. There are polar zones, a dolphinarium, a Red Sea aquarium, a Mediterranean seascape and a couple of underwater tunnels, one 70m long, where the fish have the chance to gawp back at visitors. Opening hours here are approximate; check the website by date. It opens later on Saturday.

Museo de las Ciencias Príncipe Felipe (Map p730; www.cac.es; adult/child €8/6.20; ☉10am-6pm Mon-Thu, 10am-7pm Fri-Sun mid-Oct–mid-Apr, 10am-7pm mid-Apr–Jun & mid-Sep–mid-Oct, 10am-9pm Jul–mid-Sep; ☑) This interactive science museum, stretching like a giant whale skeleton within the City of Arts & Sciences, has plenty of touchy-feely things for children, and machines and displays for all ages. Each section has a pamphlet in English summarising its contents.

Hemisfèric (Map p730; www.cac.es; sessions €8.80) The unblinking heavy-lidded eye of the Hemisfèric is at once planetarium, IMAX cinema and laser show. Optional English soundtrack for all films. Sessions are roughly hourly, with a break at lunchtime.

Palau de les Arts Reina Sofía (Map p730; www.lesarts.com) Brooding over the riverbed like a giant beetle, its shell shimmering with translucent mosaic tiles – the cause of quite a few problems – this ultramodern arts complex (p745), grafted onto the City of Arts & Sciences, has four auditoriums.

Unesco World Heritage site, was originally Valencia's silk and commodity exchange. Highlights are the colonnaded hall with its twisted Gothic pillars and the 1st-floor Consulado del Mar with its stunning coffered ceiling.

★ Mercado Central   MARKET
(Map p734; www.mercadocentralvalencia.es; Plaza del Mercado; ☉8am-2.30pm Mon-Sat) Valencia's vast Modernista covered market, constructed in 1928, is a swirl of smells, movement and colour. Don't miss the fish, seafood and offal annexe. A tapas bar in the middle of the market lets you sip a wine and enjoy the atmosphere.

Plaza Redonda   SQUARE
(Map p734) Again trim and smart, though over-tourist-oriented after an elaborate makeover, this small, circular 19th-century space – once the abattoir of Valencia's Mercado Central – is ringed by stalls.

◉ Central Valencia

Torres de Serranos   GATE
(Map p734; Plaza de los Fueros; adult/child €2/1, Sun free; ☉10am-6pm or 7pm Tue-Sat, 10am-3pm Sun) Once the main exit to Barcelona and the north, the imposing 14th-century Torres de Serranos overlook the former bed of Río Turia. Together with the Torres de Quart, they are all that remain of Valencia's old city walls. Climb to the top for a great overview of the Barrio del Carmen and riverbed.

★ Jardines del Turia   PARK
(☑) Stretching the length of Río Turia's former course, this 9km-long lung of green is a fabulous mix of playing fields, cycling, jogging and walking paths, lawns and playgrounds. As it curves around the eastern part of the city, it's also a pleasant way of getting around. See Lilliputian kids scrambling over a magnificent, ever-patient Gulliver (Map p730; Jardines del Turia; ☉10am-8pm

Valencia City

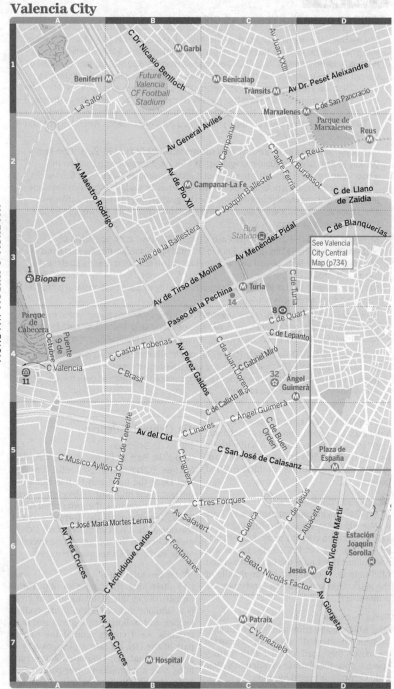

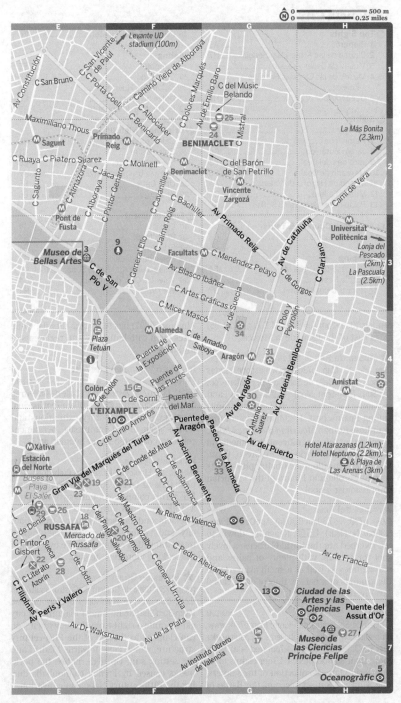

0
0

500 m
0.25 miles

Levante UD
stadium (100m)

La Más Bonita
(2.3km)

Av Constitución
C San Bruno
San Vicente
de Paúl
C Porta Coeli
Camino Viejo de Alboraya
C del Músic
Belando
C del Emilio Baró
Maximiliano Thous
M Sagunt
C Ruaya C Piatero Suárez
C Sagunto
C Albocàcer
C Benicarló
C Molinell
Prímado
Reig
C Dolores Marqués
C Mistral
25
24
BENIMACLET

M Benimaclet
C del Barón
de San Petrillo
Vincente
Zargozá

M Pont de
Fusta
C Alboraya
C Atmazora
C Jaca
C Pintor Genaro
C Cavanilles
C Bachiller
C Jaime Roig
Av Primado Reig
Av de Cataluña

Universitat
Politècnica
Lonja del
Pescado
(2km);
La Pascuala
(2.5km)

Museo de
Bellas Artes
3
C de San
Pío V
9
C General Elío
Facultats
C Menéndez Pelayo
Av Blasco Ibáñez
C Artes Gráficas
C Micer Mascó
C de Suecia
C de Gorgos
C Clariano

16
Plaza Tetuán
i
M Alameda
C de Amadeo
Saboya
Aragón M
C Polo y
Peyrolón
34
31
Amistat
35

Colón
15
C de Colón
C de Sorní
L'EIXAMPLE
10
C de Cirilo Amorós
Puente de
la Exposición
Puente de
las Flores
Puente
del Mar
Puente de
Aragón
30
Av de Aragón
C Antonio
Suárez
Av Cardenal Benlloch

M Xàtiva
Estación
del Norte
Buses to
Playa
El Saler
Gran Vía del Marqués del Turia
19
23
21
C de Conde del Altea
C de Dr Císcar
C de Salamanca
Av Jacinto Benavente
Paseo de la Alameda
Av del Puerto
33
Hotel Atarazanas (1.2km);
Hotel Neptuno (2.2km);
& Playa de
Las Arenas (3km)

29
26
18
RUSSAFA
Mercado de
Russafa
20
C del Maestro Gozalbo
C del Pintor
C de Dr Sumsi
Av Reino de Valencia
6

C de Denia
C Pintor
Gisbert
C Sueca
C Literato
Azorín
22
28
C de Cádiz
C Salvador
C Pedro Aleixandre
C General Urrutia
12
13
Av de Francia

C Filipinas
Av Peris y Valero
Av Dr Waksman
Av de la Plata
17
Ciudad de las
Artes y las
Ciencias
7
2
4
27
Museo de
las Ciencias
Príncipe Felipe
Puente del
Assut d'Or

Av Instituto Obrero
de Valencia
5
Oceanogràfic

Camí de Vera

Valencia City

Sep-Jun, 10am-2pm & 5-9pm Jul & Aug; 📖 19, 95) **FREE** east of the Palau de la Música.

★ **Museo de Bellas Artes**   GALLERY
(San Pío V; Map p730; www.museobellasartes
valencia.gva.es; Calle de San Pío V 9; ⊙10am-7pm Tue-Sun, 11am-5pm Mon) **FREE** Bright and spacious, the Museo de Bellas Artes ranks among Spain's best. Highlights include the grandiose Roman *Mosaic of the Nine Muses,* a collection of magnificent late-medieval altarpieces, and works by El Greco, Goya, Velázquez, Murillo and Ribalta, plus artists such as Sorolla and Pinazo of the Valencian Impressionist school.

Jardines del Real   PARK
(Map p730; ⊙7.30am-9.30pm Apr-Oct, 7.30am-8.30pm Nov-Mar) **FREE** Reaching down to the riverbed are the Royal Gardens, a lovely spot for a stroll, with plenty of palms and orange trees as well as a small aviary. Once the grounds of a palace, they're often called Los Viveros.

L'Iber   MUSEUM
(Museo de Soldaditos de Plomo; Map p734; www. museoliber.org; Calle de Caballeros 22; adult/under 27yr €5/3; ⊙11am-2pm & 4-7pm Wed-Sun) With more than 85,000 pieces, L'Iber claims to be the world's largest collection of toy soldiers. The 4.7m x 2.8m set piece of the Battle of

Almansa (1707) has 9000 combatants, while cases teem with battalions and regiments of toy soldiers.

Instituto Valenciano de Arte Moderno   GALLERY
(IVAM; Map p734; www.ivam.es; Calle de Guillem de Castro 118; adult/child €2/1; ⊙10am-7pm Tue-Sun) Hosts excellent temporary exhibitions and houses a small but impressive permanent collection of 20th-century Spanish art.

La Beneficència   MUSEUM
(Museo de Etnología, Museo de Prehistoria; Map p734; Calle de Corona 36; ⊙10am-8pm Tue-Sun) **FREE** This complex contains two museums: a **folk museum** displaying photographs, artefacts and household items from both city and region, and an **archaeological museum** with a comprehensive overview of the region's more remote past.

★ **Torres de Quart**   GATE
(Map p734; Calle de Guillem de Castro; adult/child €2/1, Sun free; ⊙10am-6pm or 7pm Tue-Sat, 10am-3pm Sun) Spain's most magnificent city gate is quite a sight from the new town. You can clamber to the top of the 15th-century structure, which faces towards Madrid and the setting sun. Up high, notice the pockmarks caused by French cannonballs during the 19th-century Napoleonic invasion.

Jardín Botánico
GARDENS

(Map p730; www.jardibotanic.org; Calle de Quart 80; adult/child €2/1; ⊙10am-dusk) Established in 1802, this was Spain's first botanic garden. With mature trees and plants, an extensive cactus garden and a wary colony of feral cats, it's a shady, tranquil place to relax.

Palacio del Marqués de Dos Aguas
PALACE

(Map p734; Calle del Poeta Querol 2) A pair of wonderfully extravagant rococo caryatids (columns in the shape of female figures) curl around the main entrance of this over-the-top palace. Inside, the **Museo Nacional de Cerámica** (Map p734; adult/child €3/free, Sat afternoon & Sun free; ⊙10am-2pm & 4-8pm Tue-Sat, 10am-2pm Sun) displays ceramics from around the world – and especially from the renowned local production centres of Manises, Alcora and Paterna.

Museo del Patriarca
GALLERY

(Map p734; Calle la Nave 1; admission €2; ⊙11am-1.30pm) This bijou gallery is a must if you're interested in ecclesiastical art. It's particularly strong on Spanish and Flemish Renaissance painting, with several canvases by Juan de Juanes, Ribalta and El Greco. The adjacent **church** has a soberly handsome cloister, some high-quality Renaissance frescoes, and a stuffed cayman with some history in the anteroom.

Mercado de Colón
MARKET

(Map p730; www.mercadocolon.es; Calle de Cirilo Amorós; ⊙8am-1.30am) This magnificent Modernista building, now colonised by boutiques and cafes, was formerly a market, built in 1916 to serve the rising bourgeoisie of the new suburb of L'Eixample. It's a good place to try *horchata* (a sugary drink made from tiger nuts) and Sundays are nice, with free midday concerts.

Museo Fallero
MUSEUM

(Map p730; Plaza Monteolivete 4; adult/child €2/1; ⊙10am-6pm or 7pm Tue-Sat, 10am-3pm Sun) Each Fallas festival (p745), only one of the thousands of *ninots,* the figurines that pose at the base of each *falla* (huge statues of papier mâché and polystyrene), is saved from the flames by popular vote. Those reprieved over the years are displayed here.

⊙ Western Valencia

For both the Bioparc and Museo de Historia de Valencia, take bus 3, 81 or 95 or get off at the Nou d'Octubre metro stop.

★Bioparc
ZOO

(Map p730; www.bioparcvalencia.es; Avenida Pio Baroja 3; adult/child €24/18; ⊙10am-dusk; 🛝) 🐾 'Zoo' is far too old-fashioned and inept a term for this wonderful, innovative, eco-friendly and gently educational space. Wild animals apparently (fear not: only apparently) roam free as you wander from savannah to equatorial Africa and Madagascar, where large-eyed lemurs gambol around your ankles.

Museo de Historia de Valencia
MUSEUM

(Map p730; Calle Valencia 42; adult/child €2/1; ⊙10am-6pm or 7pm Tue-Sat, 10am-3pm Sun) This museum, very hands-on and with plenty of film and video, plots more than 2000 years of the city's history. Grab the informative folder in English.

⊙ The Coast

At the coastal end of the tram line, 3km from the centre, Playa de las Arenas runs north into Playa de la Malvarrosa and Playa de la Patacona forming a wide strip of sand some 4km long. It's bordered by the Paseo Marítimo promenade and a string of restaurants and cafes. One block back, lively bars and discos thump out the beat in summer.

Playa El Salér, 10km south, can be reached by bike/footpath and is backed by shady pine woods. There are campsites here, and plenty of good rice restaurants. Autocares Herca (☑96 349 12 50; www.autocaresherca.com) buses run between Valencia and Perelló hourly (half-hourly in summer), calling by El Salér village. They stop at the junction of Gran Vía de las Germanias and Calle de Sueca, beside Plaza de Cánovas and in front of the Oceanogràfic.

☞ Tours

Numerous operators offer multilingual walking tours, bike tours, tapas tours and other options.

VALENCIA & MURCIA VALENCIA

Valencia City Central

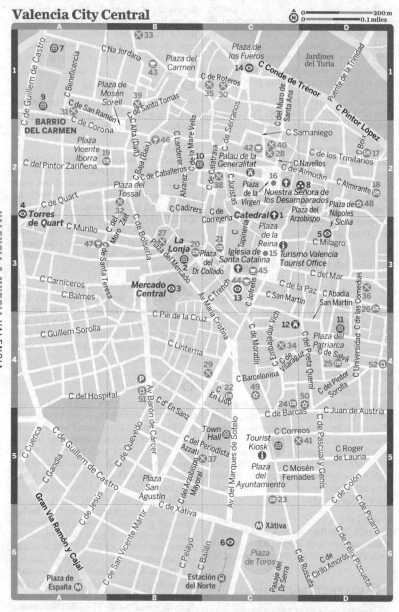

Carriage Rides

CARRIAGE RIDES

(Map p734) Hire a horse-drawn carriage in Plaza de la Reina and clip-clop around the Centro Histórico, lording it over the pedestrians. Prices are a little negotiable but think €30 for 40 minutes (seats up to five).

Liber Tours

WALKING TOUR

(Map p734; ☎978 11 88 88; www.libertours. com; adult/child €16/8; ☺10.30am Mon-Sat) Recommended 2¼-hour walking tours of the centre leaving from Plaza de la Virgen.

Valencia City Central

Separate English and Spanish tours (with other languages bookable).

Valencia Guías BICYCLE TOUR
(Map p730; ☑963 85 17 40; www.valenciaguias. com; Paseo de la Pechina 32) Daily three-hour guided bicycle tours in English, Dutch and German (€25 including rental and snack; minimum two people).

🎊 Festivals & Events

Fiesta de San Vicente Ferrer FIESTA
Colourful parades and miracle plays are performed around town on the Sunday after Easter.

Día de San Juan MIDSUMMER
On the night of 23 June, *valencianos* in their thousands celebrate Midsummer's Day, the longest day of the year, with bonfires on the beach.

Feria de Julio FIESTA
(www.feriadejulio.com) Performing arts, brass-band competitions, bullfights, fireworks and a 'battle of the flowers' in the second half of July.

Día de la Comunidad LOCAL FIESTA
Commemorates every 9 October the city's 1238 liberation from the Moors.

🛏 Sleeping

As Valencia is a business centre, big hotels struggle to fill rooms outside the working week. Most offer fat weekend and high-summer discounts.

Home Youth Hostel HOSTEL €
(Map p734; ☑963 91 62 29; www.homehostels valencia.com; Calle de la Lonja 4; dm €15-17, tw €40-46; @🖃) Offering location, facilities and plenty more, this sits right opposite the Lonja, a few steps from the central market. The rooms have happy retro decor

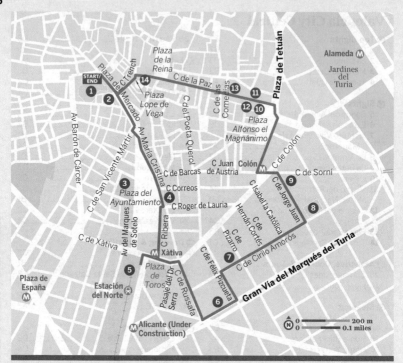

City Walk
Modernisme Meander

START MERCADO CENTRAL
END MERCADO CENTRAL
LENGTH 3.25KM; 1½ HOURS

This walk takes in Valencia's main Modernista buildings. After sniffing around **❶ Mercado Central** (p729) take in the elaborate stucco facade – with neo-Gothic pilasters above allegories of Valencia's fertility – of **❷ Calle Ramilletes 1**. Follow Avenida María Cristina to Plaza del Ayuntamiento, site of the sober **❸ town hall** and resplendent **❹ central post office**, a neoclassical affair with 1920s flourishes.

At the end of Calle Ribera, detour to **❺ Estación del Norte**, with its original Modernista booking area of dark wood, and adjacent hall with elaborate tilework. Take Calle de Russafa, then turn left for **❻ Casa Ortega** (Gran Vía 9), with its ornate floral decoration and balcony, supported by a pair of caryatids. Go left along Calle de Félix Pizcueta, then take the first right onto Calle de Cirilo Amorós. From here onwards, look up to

appreciate each building's original structure. Pause by **❼ Casa Ferrer** (No 29), garlanded with stucco roses and ceramic tiling. Continue northwards to the resplendent **❽ Mercado de Colón** (p733), a chic spot for a drink, then head northwest to **❾ Casa del Dragón** (Calle de Jorge Juan 3), named for its dragon motifs.

Cross Calle de Colón, turn right along Calle Poeta Quintana and pass the mounted statue of King Jaime I to join Calle de la Paz. In the 19th century, **❿ Hotel Vincci Palace** was known as the Palace Hotel, in its time Valencia's finest. Both it and **⓫ No 31**, opposite, have elaborate, decorated miradors (corner balconies), while **⓬ Red Nest Hostel** (No 36) has delicate, leafy iron railings. Opposite, on the corner of Calle Comedias, **⓭ No 21 & 23** has characteristically magnificent window and balcony work, and a columned mirador.

At the end of Calle de la Paz, continue straight – maybe calling in for a *horchata* at **⓮ Horchatería de Santa Catalina** (p744). Then, at Plaza Lope de Vega, turn left into Calle Trench to return to the Mercado Central.

and proper beds with decent sheets, with a minimum of roommates. A kitchen, film library and cheery staff make this a top budget spot. There's **another location** (Map p734; ☑ 96 391 37 97; Calle Santa Cristina) in the Barrio del Carmen, though it's closed in winter.

Russafa Youth Hostel HOSTEL €

(Map p730; ☑ 963 28 94 60; www.russafayouthhostel.com; Calle Padre Perera 5; dm/d incl breakfast €20/44; @ ☎) You'll feel instantly at home in this super-welcoming, cute hostel set over various floors of a venerable building in the heart of vibrant Russafa. It's all beds, rather than bunks, and with a maximum of three to a room, there's no crowding. Sweet rooms and spotless bathrooms make for a mighty easy stay.

Pensión París HOSTEL €

(Map p734; ☑ 963 52 67 66; www.pensionparis.com; Calle de Salvà 12; s €24, d €32-44; ☎) Welcoming, with spotless rooms – most with shared bathrooms, some with private facilities – this family-run option on a quiet street is the antithesis of the crowded, pack-'em-in *hostal*. The best of the rooms have balconies and original features from this stately old building.

Purple Nest HOSTEL €

(Map p730; ☑ 963 53 25 61; www.purplenesthostel.com; Plaza Tetuan 5; dm €17-20, tw €45-50; ✳ @ ☎) Well equipped and with plenty of events to help your Valencian social life along, this makes a pleasing base. There's a bar, kitchen and deck, and spacious, colourful rooms sleeping four to 10. There's a sister hostel, **Red Nest** (Map p734; ☑ 963 42 71 68; www.nesthostelsvalencia.com; Calle Paz 36; ☼ Mar-Oct), a couple of streets away.

Ad Hoc Monumental HOTEL €€

(Map p734; ☑ 963 91 91 40; www.adhochoteles.com; Calle Boix 4; s/d €72/84; ✳ ☎) Friendly Ad Hoc offers comfort and charm deep within the old quarter and also runs a splendid small restaurant (open for dinner Monday to Saturday). The late 19th-century building has been restored to its former splendour with great sensitivity, revealing original ceilings, mellow brickwork and solid wooden beams.

Lotelito HOTEL €€

(Map p734; ☑ 962 06 09 30; www.lotelitovalencia.com; Calle de las Barcas 13; s/d/q €80/100/120; ✳ ☎) Behind a lively, latest-thing bar-restaurant these modern rooms and apartments are small but svelte, with modern white floorboards and good facilities. It makes a stylish, fashionable Valencian base and offers decent value.

Hotel Sorolla Centro HOTEL €€

(Map p734; ☑ 963 52 33 92; www.hotelsorollacentro.com; Calle Convento Santa Clara 5; s/d €66/77; ✳ ☎) Neat and contemporary but without any flashy design gimmicks, this offers very solid value for comfortable, well-thought-out modern rooms with powerful showers and plenty of facilities. Staff are extremely helpful and the location on a pedestrian street between the train station and main square, is fab.

Hostal Venecia HOSTAL €€

(Map p734; ☑ 963 52 42 67; www.hotelvenecia.com; Plaza del Ayuntamiento 3; s/d €60/70; ✳ @ ☎) Right on the city's main square, this sumptuous building's functional interior doesn't give many hints of the noble exterior but it offers compact modern rooms, many with small balcony, at a sharp price. Excellent value, its strong points are exceptionally friendly service and its prime location.

Rooms Deluxe Hostel HOSTAL €€

(Map p730; ☑ 963 81 53 39; www.roomsdeluxe.com; Avenida Instituto Obrero de Valencia 20; d/q €70/91; Ⓟ ✳ ☎) A mosaic tile's throw from the Ciudad de las Artes y las Ciencias, this spot is pushing it a bit calling itself a hostel. The private rooms all have en suites and are thematically decorated with great style and flair. Low-season prices can be excellent.

Hotel Neptuno HOTEL €€

(☑ 963 56 77 77; www.hotelneptunovalencia.com; Paseo de Neptuno 2; s/d from €125/136; Ⓟ ✳ @ ☎) Modern, welcoming Neptuno overlooks the leisure port and beach of Las Arenas. It's ideal for mixing cultural tourism with a little beach frolicking. Upgrade to a room with a view (an extra €22) or head

---

ⓘ APARTMENTS

For independence and your own accommodation, from one night to a long stay, consult these websites:

➜ www.valenciaflats.com

➜ www.valencialuxury.com

➜ www.accommodation-valencia.com

➜ www.bedandbikevalencia.com

upstairs to the roof terrace for views, sunshine and a hot tub. The hotel restaurant, Tridente, is very good.

Hostal Antigua Morellana
HOSTAL €€

(Map p734; ✆ 963 91 57 73; www.hostalam.com; Calle En Bou 2; s/d €55/65; ❉ ❀) The friendly, family-run, 18-room spot is tucked away near the Mercado Central. It occupies a renovated 18th-century *posada* (where wealthier merchants bringing their produce to the nearby food market would spend the night) and has cosy, good-sized rooms, most with balconies. It's kept very shipshape by the rightly house-proud owners. Higher floors have more natural light. Good value.

Hotel Atarazanas
HOTEL €€

(✆ 963 20 30 10; www.hotelatarazanas.com; Plaza Tribunal de las Aguas 5; r €107; ⓟ ❉ ❀) In an interesting, non-touristy zone handy for both beach and port, this has a breezy rooftop terrace with a magnificent wraparound view of sea and city. The cream walls and fabrics of each bedroom contrast with the dark, stained woodwork. Sybaritic bathrooms have deep tubs with hydromassage and the broad shower head is as big as a discus. It's an extra-good deal in the low season.

★ Caro Hotel
HOTEL €€€

(Map p734; ✆ 963 05 90 00; www.carohotel.com; Calle Almirante 14; r €143-214; ⓟ ❉ ❀) Housed in a sumptuous 19th-century mansion, this sits atop some 2000 years of Valencian history, with restoration revealing a hefty hunk of the Arab wall, Roman column bases and Gothic arches. Each room is furnished in soothing dark shades, with a great king-sized bed and varnished cement floors. Bathrooms are tops. For that very special occasion, reserve the 1st-floor grand suite, once the ballroom. Savour, too, its excellent restaurant Alma del Temple.

Hospes Palau de la Mar
HOTEL €€€

(Map p730; ✆ 963 16 28 84; www.hospes.es; Calle Navarro Reverter 14; r €179-214; ⓟ ❉ ❀) Created by the merging of two elegant 19th-century mansions (plus 18 very similar modern rooms surrounding a tranquil internal garden), this boutique hotel, all black, white, soft fuscous and beige, is cool and contemporary. There's a sauna, a Jacuzzi – and a pool scarcely bigger than your bathtub.

Eating

Valencia is surrounded by La Huerta, a fertile coastal agricultural plain that supplies the city with delightfully fresh fruit and vegetables. The number of restaurants has to be seen to be believed: it seriously spoils you for choice. At weekends, heading to the waterside suburb of Pinedo, south of the port, or beyond to Albufera villages like El Palmar to eat rice dishes is a local tradition.

✖ Central Valencia

★ Carosel
VALENCIAN €

(Map p734; ✆ 961 13 28 73; www.carosel.es; Calle Taula de Canvis 6; mains €7-16, menu €15; ⏱ 1-4pm & 9-11pm Tue-Sat, 1-4pm Sun) Jordi and his partner, Carol, run this delightful small restaurant with outdoor seating on a square. The freshest of produce from the nearby market is blended with Alicante and Valencia traditions to create salads, *cocas*, rices and other delicious titbits. Top value and warmly recommended.

La Tastaolletes
VEGETARIAN €

(Map p734; ✆ 963 92 18 62; www.latastaolletes.es; Calle de Salvador Giner 6; mains €8-12; ⏱ 1.30-4pm & 8.30pm-midnight Tue-Sat, 1.30-4pm Sun; ❀ ✐) La Tastaolletes does a creative range of vegetarian tapas and mains. Pleasantly informal, it does good, wholesome food created from quality prime ingredients. Salads are large and leafy and desserts (indulge in the cheesecake with stewed fruits) are a dream.

La Pilareta
TAPAS €

(Bar Pilar; Map p734; Calle del Moro Zeit 13; dishes €5-9; ⏱ noon-midnight, closed Tue mid-Oct–Feb) Cramped, earthy La Pilareta is great for hearty tapas and *clóchinas* (small, juicy local mussels), available between May and August. For the rest of the year it serves *mejillones* (mussels), altogether fatter if less tasty. Ask for an *entero,* a platterful in a spicy broth that you scoop up with a spare shell. At the bar, etiquette demands that you dump your empty shells in the plastic trough at your feet.

La Utielana
VALENCIAN €

(Map p734; Carrer de Sant Andreu 3; mains €5-12; ⏱ 1-4pm & 9pm-midnight Mon-Fri, 1-4pm Sat) Not the easiest to track down, tucked-away La Utielana well merits a minute or two of sleuthing. Very Valencian, it packs in the crowds, drawn by the wholesome fare and exceptional value for money. Arrive early

WHAT'S COOKING IN VALENCIA? RICE!

Joan Francesc Peris García, Green party spokesperson, teacher and judge of *paella-fideuà* competitions, gives us the low-down on Valencia's rice.

Valencian Rice Dishes

Rice is a whole world! Paella is a dry rice, the liquid evaporates. There are *caldoso* (soupy) rices, with broth. There are winter rices and rices made with summer produce. Rices with meat, with fish, with vegetables, with almost anything!

Best Dishes to Try

Paellas are typical of the Valencian coast. Meat paellas normally have chicken and rabbit and then we'd add green beans and other vegetables in summer, or fava beans and artichokes in winter.

That's the most typical of Valencia, but then you've got fish ones, soupy with calamari or cuttlefish for the flavour and prawns or langoustines for decoration. You can also add prawns to a meat paella to make a *paella mixta*. Another one on the coast is *arroz negro* (black rice) that's made with squid ink and fish stock. There are other great winter ones too: what about one with cauliflower and salt cod? Delicious!

In the interior, they make heavier rices. In Alcoy and Xàtiva, rices are baked in the oven and might have pork, sausage, beans and black pudding. In Alicante's interior they do a tasty one with snails, rabbit and chickpeas, while around Orihuela it's *arroz con costra* (crusty rice), made in the oven with a crust of beaten egg on top. There are so many!

The Secret of Good Fideuà

Fideuà is similar to paella, but made with fine pasta. The secret is a good fish stock with fresh rockfish. Noodles cook quicker than rice so it's ready faster.

Where Locals Go for Great Rice

Mostly to houses of friends or family. The best paella is always grandma's! That's because it's a question of experience, when you've made so many you know how to judge the perfect quantity of rice to add. My mother-in-law let me make rice in her kitchen. That's a real achievement!

as it doesn't take reservations – if you have to wait, grab a numbered ticket from the dispenser.

La Lluna　　　　　　　VEGETARIAN €
(Map p734; www.facebook.com/restaurantelalluna; Calle de San Ramón 23; mains €6-12; ⊙9am-4pm & 8pm-midnight Mon-Sat; 🕾🍃) Friendly and full of regulars, with walls of clashing tilework, La Lluna has been serving quality, reasonably priced vegetarian fare (including a superb-value, four-course lunch menu at €8) for over 30 years. You can check what's cooking that day on the Facebook page.

★ **Delicat**　　　　　TAPAS, FUSION €€
(Map p734; ☑963 92 33 57; Calle Conde Almodóvar 4; mains €9-14; ⊙1-4pm & 8.30-11.30pm Tue-Sat, 1-4pm Sun) At this particularly friendly, intimate option (there are only nine tables, plus the terrace in summer), Catina, up front, and her partner, Paco, on full view in the kitchen, offer an unbeatable-value, five-course menu

of samplers for lunch and a range of truly innovative tapas anytime.

Mood Food　　　　　　　FUSION €€
(Map p734; ☑963 15 48 90; www.moodfoodvalencia.com; Calle de las Comedias 5; light meals €6-10; ⊙1-3.30pm & 8-11.30pm Mon & Wed-Sat, 1-3.30pm Tue; 🕾) This intimate space is so tiny that you wonder how the two-man team manage to prepare anything more elaborate than a fried egg. But find room, as wonders emerge from the open kitchen, bursting with taste and freshness. Salads, open sandwiches and a selection of more elaborate plates set the scene for a stellar eating experience.

El Encuentro　　　　　　SPANISH €€
(Map p734; ☑963 94 36 12; www.restauranteelencuentro.com; Calle de San Vicente Mártir 28; mains €10-18; ⊙1.30-4.30pm & 8.30pm-12.30am Mon-Sat; 🕾) There's a likeable old-fashioned feel about this place, which offers stalwart Spanish cuisine at fair prices. Expect plenty of stew-type dishes like beans and chorizo;

The Perfect Paella

There's something life-affirming about a proper Spanish paella, cheerily yellow like the sun and bursting with intriguing morsels. It seems to promise warm days and fine company. But there's more to this most Valencian of dishes than meets the eye. Here we give you the inside scoop.

Origins

Originally domesticated in China some 10,000 years ago, rice was brought to Spain by the Moors in the 8th century AD. The low-lying wetlands of the Valencian coast were perfect for its cultivation but it was viewed with suspicion by the Catholic reconquerors, due to outbreaks of malaria in rice-growing regions.

Secrets of the Rice

Traditional Valencian rice dishes can have almost any ingredients, varying by region and season. The base always includes short-grain rice, garlic, olive oil and saffron; see p739 for the lowdown. The best rice is bomba, which opens accordion-like when cooked, allowing for maximum absorption while remaining firm. Paella should be cooked in a large shallow pan to enable the maximum amount of rice to touch the bottom of the pan and thus absorb the flavour. And for the final touch of authenticity, the grains on the bottom (and only those) should have a crunchy, savoury crust known as the *socarrat*.

Fiesta Rices

Paella competitions are a common feature of fiestas in Valencia. Judges look for taste, colour, perfectly done rice, distribution of ingredients and quality of *socarrat*. Also common are giant paellas made in

1. Seafood paella **2.** Serving paella

huge pans. Feeding the 5000 was nothing compared to some of these monsters – the largest fed 110,000 people out of a pan 21m wide and weighing 23 tons.

Tips on Ordering

Rice dishes are traditional in Catalonia, Valencia and Andalucía, so that's where they are best eaten. Check out the clientele first. No locals? Walk on by.

Restaurants should take around 20 minutes or more to prepare a rice dish – beware if they don't – so expect to wait. You can pre-order so it's ready sooner. Though rice dishes are usually for a minimum of two, many places will do one for a solo diner if asked.

Paella has all the liquid evaporated, *meloso* rices are wet, and *caldoso* rices come with a brothy liquid.

TRY THIS AT HOME

➡ Brown the meat or seafood with olive oil in the pan over high heat, brown the garlic, then add the vegetables – more equals more flavour – and fry lightly on lower heat.

➡ Add water or stock, about three parts liquid to one part rice. It's better to err on the side of less liquid so as not to overcook the rice. When the meat and vegetables are cooked, add the rice, spread out thinly across the pan.

➡ Rice cooks in about 15 minutes; the first nine minutes on high heat, then the last few on low.

➡ Add saffron and/or colouring towards the end and garnish.

the meat and fish plates are also reliable. Browse the wines on your way in so you don't have to get up again.

Navarro
VALENCIAN €€

(Map p734; ☑963 52 96 23; www.restaurantenavarro.com; Calle del Arzobispo Mayoral 5; rices €14-18, set menu €22; ☺1.15-4pm daily, 8.30-11pm Sat; 🐭) A byword in the city for decades for its quality rice dishes, Navarro is run by the grandkids of the original founders and offers plenty of choice, outdoor seating and a set menu including one of the rices as a main.

Refugio
FUSION €€

(Map p734; ☑963 91 77 54; www.refugiorestaurante.com; Calle Alta 42; mains €12-16, set menu €12-15; ☺2-3.30pm & 9-11.30pm; 🐭) Named for the civil-war hideout opposite and simply decorated in whitewashed brick, Refugio preserves some of the Barrio del Carmen's former revolutionary spirit. Excellent Med-fusion cuisine is presented in lunchtime menus of surprising quality: there are some stellar plates on show, though the veggie options aren't always quite as flavoursome.

Mattilda
FUSION €€

(Map p734; ☑963 92 31 68; www.mattilda.es; Calle de Roteros 21; set menu €12, mains €11-17; ☺2-4pm Mon & Tue, 2-4pm & 9-11.45pm Wed-Sat; 🐭) The decor is stylish, modern and unpretentious – just like Francisco Borell and his cheery young team, who offer friendly service, an imaginative à la carte selection and a particularly good-value lunch menu.

El Tap
TAPAS €€

(Map p734; ☑963 91 26 27; www.restaurantevalenciaeltap.es; Calle de Roteros 9; tapas €5-12; ☺7.30pm-midnight; 🐭) El Tap is one of Barrio del Carmen's rich selection of small, characterful restaurants. Tapas are original and delightfully prepared, and there's a carefully selected choice of both wines and boutique beers. Excellent value.

Vuelve Carolina
MEDITERRANEAN €€

(Map p734; ☑963 21 86 86; www.vuelvecarolina.com; Calle Correos 8; mains €14-25; ☺1.30-4.30pm & 8.30-11.30pm Mon-Sat; 🐭) Overseen from a distance by three-star Michelin chef Quique Dacosta, this trendy and upbeat bar-restaurant offers style – those clothes-horse bar stools could be more comfy though – and an inspiring selection of tapas and fuller plates. Service is solicitous.

Pepita Pulgarcita
TAPAS €€

(Map p734; ☑963 91 46 08; Calle de Caballeros 19; tapas €4-10; ☺noon-5pm & 7pm-2am Thu-Sun, 7pm-midnight Mon-Wed; 🐭🖉) With wines stacked high behind the bar and subtle, inventive tapas, tastefully presented, tiny Pepita Pulgarcita is great for a snack, meal or simply a *copa* (glass).

Seu Xerea
FUSION €€€

(Map p734; ☑963 92 40 00; www.seuxerea.com; Calle Conde Almodóvar 4; mains €17-25; ☺1.30-3.30pm & 8.30-11pm Mon-Sat) Welcoming and popular, Seu Xerea has a creative, regularly changing, rock-reliable, à la carte menu featuring dishes both international and deep-rooted in Spain. Wines, selected by the owner, a qualified sommelier, are uniformly excellent. Degustation and tapas menus are on-hand for trying lots of morsels.

🍴 Russafa & Around

The trendy boho-bourgeois district of Russafa (Spanish: Ruzafa) has a particularly vibrant restaurant and cafe scene, with new places constantly popping up.

Dulce de Leche
CAFE €

(Map p730; Calle Pintor Gisbert 2; brunch €5; ☺9am-9pm Mon & Wed-Fri, 9.30am-9pm Sat & Sun; 🐭) Delicious sweet and savoury snacks with an Argentine twist are the stock-in-trade of this delicately decorated corner cafe in Russafa. The weekend brunch is well priced and tasty but you might have to bring out your Mr Hyde to bag a street table.

Appetite
FUSION €€

(Map p730; ☑961 10 56 60; www.appetite.es; Calle Pintor Salvador Abril 7; 6-/8-course menu €26/32; ☺9-11pm Thu-Mon, 2-3.30pm Sat & Sun) 'Multi-cultural cuisine' is how Bonnie from Australia and her partner, Arantxa, as Valencian as they come, describe their fusion delights with an Asian slant, reflecting Bonnie's Singaporean origins. Sit back and let her compose your menu for you. Each dish is freshly prepared, delightfully presented and enticingly described. Across the road is their lower-budget **La Cantina de Appetite** (Map p730; Calle Pintor Salvador Abril 6; menus €12-22; ☺1.30-4pm daily, 8.30-11pm Mon-Sat), with a good-value, if small-portioned, lunch *menú* for €12.

Coloniales Huerta
TAPAS €€

(Map p730; ☑963 34 80 09; www.vinosdeautor.com; Calle del Maestro Gozalbo 13; dishes €8-19;

⏲10am-1am Mon-Sat, 11am-4pm Sun) Occupying a classic centenarian Valencian delicatessen turned wine shop, this offers tables among the bottle shelves and an air of benign clutter and unhurried pace. Tapas range from the classic – top-notch charcuterie – to the innovative. There's a worthwhile lunch *menú* for €16.

Ca Mandó
FUSION €€

(Map p730; ☑662 024000; www.ca-mando.com; Calle Pedro III el Grande 12; dishes €6-10; ⏲8pm-1am Tue-Sat; 🗐🖋) Quality tatakis, carpaccios, salads and toasts dominate the blackboard specials – all in Valencian, but happily translated by the cheerful staff – in this friendly neighbourhood tapas spot. Food is fresh, sourced at the nearby market. It's all carefully prepared to order, so be prepared to wait.

✖ The Coast

On weekends locals head for Las Arenas, on the beach near the port, where a long line of restaurants overlooking the beach all serve up rice dishes and seafood.

La Pascuala
TAPAS €

(Calle de Eugenia Viñes 177; rolls €4-5; ⏲9am-3.30pm Mon-Sat) A block back from the beach, this neighbourhood bar has barely changed since the 1920s and is legendary for its *bocadillos* (filled rolls) that come absolutely stuffed with fillings. Half of Valencia seems to be in here around 11am for a mid-morning bite. It couldn't be more authentic. Try the super horse burger.

La Más Bonita
CAFE €€

(www.lamasbonita.es; Paseo Marítimo de la Patacona; pastries €3-7, light meals €6-15; ⏲8am-1.30am; 🗐) Pretty in turquoise and white, this beachfront place has comfy outdoor seating, a hipster vibe, and a big interior and patio. It's a charming venue for breakfast in the sun, or for muffins, cheesecakes or other delicacies at any time of day. The savoury meals are of lesser quality.

Lonja del Pescado
FISH €€

(www.restaurantelalonjapescadovalencia.com; Calle de Eugenia Viñes 243; dishes €8-15; ⏲1-3.30pm Sat & Sun, 8-11.30pm Tue-Sun Mar-Oct, 1-3.30pm Fri-Sun, 8-11.30pm Fri & Sat Nov-Feb) One block back from the beach at Malvarrosa, this busy, informal place has plenty of atmosphere and offers unbeatable value for fresh fish. Grab an order form as you enter and fill it in at your table. The tram stops outside.

🍸 Drinking & Nightlife

Russafa has the best bar scene, with a huge range of everything from family-friendly cultural cafes to megaclubs. The Barrio del Carmen is also nightlife territory: on weekends, Calle de Caballeros, the main street, seethes with punters. The university area, especially around Avenidas de Aragón and Blasco Ibáñez, has enough bars and *discotecas* to keep you busy all night. In summer the port area and Malvarrosa leap to life.

Agua de Valencia couldn't be further from water, mixing *cava* (sparkling wine), orange juice, gin and vodka.

🍸 Central Valencia

Café de las Horas
CAFE, BAR

(Map p734; www.cafedelashoras.com; Calle Conde de Almodóvar 1; ⏲10am-2am; 🗐) Offers high baroque, tapestries, music of all genres, candelabras, bouquets of fresh flowers and a long list of exotic cocktails. Also does themed Sunday brunches (11am to 4pm).

Jimmy Glass
MUSIC BAR

(Map p734; www.jimmyglassjazz.net; Calle Baja 28; ⏲8pm-2.30am Mon-Thu, 8pm-3.30am Fri & Sat) Playing jazz from the owner's vast CD collection, Jimmy Glass also sometimes has

LOCAL KNOWLEDGE

SAMPLING HORCHATA

A summer delight across Spain, *horchata* (Valenciano: *orxata*), a Valencian speciality, is an opaque sugary drink made from pressed *chufas* (tiger nuts), into which you dip large finger-shaped buns called – no sniggering – *fartóns*. Two great traditional places to sample *horchata* in the heart of town are **Horchatería de Santa Catalina** (Map p734; www.horchateriasantacatalina.com; Plaza de Santa Catalina 6; horchata €2.70; ⊙8am-9pm) and **Horchatería el Siglo** (Map p734; Plaza de Santa Catalina 11; horchata €2.10; ⊙8am-9pm), facing each other in eternal rivalry on Plaza de Santa Catalina.

live performances. It's just what a jazz bar should be – dim and serving jumbo measures of high-octane cocktails.

Café Museu CAFE
(Map p734; Calle Museo 7; ⊙9am-11pm Mon-Thu, 9am-1.30am Fri, 11am-1.30am Sat, 11am-11pm Sun; 🛜) A real forum for bohemian souls in the Carmen district, this grungy, edgy spot has an impressive cultural program including English/Spanish conversation sessions, regular live music, theatre and more. The terrace is a popular place to knock back a few beers.

Radio City CLUB
(Map p734; www.radiocityvalencia.es; Calle de Santa Teresa 19; ⊙10.30pm-3.30am Tue-Sun) Almost as much minicultural centre as club, Radio City, always seething, pulls in the punters with activities including cinema, flamenco and dancing to an eclectic mix. Pick up a flyer here for its younger sister, Music Box, also in the Centro Histórico, which stays open until dawn.

Terraza Umbracle/Mya BAR, CLUB
(Map p730; www.umbracleterraza.com; ⊙midnight-8am Thu-Sat May–mid-Oct) At the southern end of the Umbracle walkway within the Ciudad de las Artes y las Ciencias, this a cool, sophisticated spot to spend a hot summer night. Catch the evening breeze under the stars on the terrace, then drop below to Mya, a top-of-the-line club with an awesome sound system that's open year-round. Admission covers both venues.

📍 Russafa

Slaughterhouse CAFE, BAR
(Map p730; www.slaughterhouse.es; Calle de Denia 22; ⊙6pm-1.30am; 🛜) Once a butcher's shop (hence its title, also inspired by the Kurt Vonnegut novel of the same name), Slaughterhouse abounds in books (even in the toilets), new, old, for sale and simply for browsing. There's a limited menu of burgers, salads, cheeses, where every dish (€5 to €9) has a literary reference.

Ubik Café CAFE, BAR
(Map p730; http://ubikcafe.blogspot.com.es; Calle Literato Azorín 13; ⊙5pm-1am Mon & Tue, noon-1am Wed-Sun; 🛜🍴) This child-friendly Russafa cafe, bar and bookshop is a comfy place to lounge and browse. It has a short, well-selected list of wines and serves cheese and cold-meat platters, salads and plenty of Italian specialities.

Xtra Lrge BAR, CLUB
(Map p730; www.xlxtralrge.com; Gran Vía de las Germanias 21; ⊙11pm-4am Thu-Sat) Spread over 600 sq metres, this underground club merits its outsize name. All soft pastel colours on brute metal and concrete, it offers live DJs. Sip something special at the Spanglishly named Gintonería-Coktelería, then dance away until late.

☆ Entertainment

Live Music

Black Note LIVE MUSIC
(Map p730; www.blacknoteclub.com; Calle Polo y Peyrolón 15; ⊙9pm-3.30am Mon-Sat) Valencia's most active venue for jazz, boogaloo, funk and soul, Black Note has live music around midnight most nights and good canned sounds. Admission, including first drink, ranges from free to €15, depending on who's grooving.

Wah Wah LIVE MUSIC
(Map p730; www.wahwahclub.es; Calle Campoamor 52; ⊙10pm-3am Thu-Sat) For many clubbers, Wah Wah remains Valencia's hottest venue for live music, especially underground and international indie.

El Loco LIVE MUSIC
(Map p730; www.lococlub.org; Calle Erudito Orellena 12; ⊙10.30pm-3am) This popular, long-established venue puts on groups and solo

acts, usually between Thursday and Saturday. Entry, depending upon the band of the day, is €5 to €20.

Football

Valencia Club de Fútbol   FOOTBALL
(Map p730; www.valenciacf.com; Estadio de Mestalla) The city's principal team, and a major player in Spanish football, with famously demanding fans.

Levante Unión Deportiva   FOOTBALL
(www.levanteud.com) The city's second team, who at time of research were punching above their weight in the top division.

Cinemas

Filmoteca   CINEMA
(Map p734; www.ivac.gva.es; Plaza del Ayuntamiento; admission €2) This cinema, on the 4th floor of the Teatro Rialto building, screens undubbed classic and art-house films for a pittance.

Babel   CINEMA
(Map p730; www.cinesalbatrosbabel.com; Calle Vicente Sancho Tello 10; admission €8.20) Multiscreen Babel shows exclusively undubbed films and runs a pleasant cafe. Admission prices are lower on Monday and Wednesday.

Theatre & Opera

Espacio Inestable   DANCE
(Map p734; 963 91 95 50; www.espacioinestable.com; Calle de Aparisi y Guijarro 7; tickets €8-10; 8pm Thu-Sun) This edgy space presents innovative movement and dance of sometimes spectacular quality. It's a notable reference point of Valencia's alternative cultural scene.

Teatro Principal   THEATRE
(Map p734; tickets 902 48 84 88; www.teatres.gva.es; Calle de Barcas 15) One of Valencia's main venues for theatre.

Palau de la Música   CONCERT HALL
(Map p730; 963 37 50 20; www.palaudevalencia.com; Paseo de la Alameda 30) A sizeable 'riverside' venue hosting mainly classical music recitals.

Palau de les Arts Reina Sofía   OPERA
(Map p730; 902 20 23 83; www.lesarts.com; Avenida Profesor López Piñero) A spectacular arts venue offering mostly opera.

Shopping

Librería Patagonia   BOOKS
(Map p734; www.libreriapatagonia.com; Calle del Hospital 1; 10am-2pm & 4.30-8.30pm Mon-Fri, 10.30am-2pm & 5.30-8.30pm Sat) An excellent travel bookshop and travel agency with some guides in English and lots of Lonely Planet titles.

Valencia Club de Fútbol Shop   SOUVENIRS
(Map p734; Calle del Pintor Sorolla 24; 10am-9pm Mon-Sat) Souvenirs, scarfs, woolly hats and many a memento more for the city's major football club.

Information

Regional Tourist Office
(Map p730; 963 98 64 22; www.comunitatvalenciana.com; Calle de la Paz 48; 10am-6pm Mon-Fri, to 2pm Sat) A fount of information about the Valencia region.

Turismo Valencia Tourist Office
(VLC; Map p734; 963 15 39 31; www.turisvalencia.es; Plaza de la Reina 19; 9am-7pm Mon-Sat,

---

LAS FALLAS

The exuberant, anarchic swirl of **Las Fallas de San José** (www.fallas.es) – fireworks, music, festive bonfires and all-night partying – is a must if you're visiting Spain in mid-March.

The *fallas* themselves are huge sculptures of papier mâché on wood built by teams of local artists. Each neighbourhood sponsors its own *falla*, and when the town wakes after the *plantà* (overnight construction of the *fallas*) on the morning of 16 March, more than 350 have sprung up. Reaching up to 15m in height, with the most expensive costing hundreds of thousands of euros, these grotesque, colourful effigies satirise celebrities, current affairs and local customs.

Around-the-clock festivities include street parties, paella-cooking competitions, parades, open-air concerts, bullfights and free firework displays. Valencia considers itself the pyrotechnic capital of the world and each day at 2pm from 1 to 19 March a *mascletà* (over five minutes of deafening thumps and explosions) shakes the window panes of Plaza del Ayuntamiento.

After midnight on the final day each *falla* goes up in flames – backed by yet more fireworks.

10am-2pm Sun) Has several other branches around town, including Plaza del Ayuntamiento (Map p734; ⊗9am-7pm Mon-Sat, 10am-2pm Sun), the AVE station and airport arrivals area.

ⓘ Getting There & Away

AIR

Valencia's **airport** (VLC; ☏902 40 47 04) is 10km west of the city centre along the A3, towards Madrid. Budget flights serve major European cities including London, Paris and Berlin.

BUS

Valencia's **bus station** (Map p730; ☏96 346 62 66; Avenida Menéndez Pidal) is beside the riverbed. Bus 8 connects it to Plaza del Ayuntamiento.

ALSA (www.alsa.es) Has up to 10 daily buses to/from Barcelona (€29 to €35, four to five hours) and over 10 to Alicante (€20.60 to €25, two to five hours), most via Benidorm.

Avanza (www.avanzabus.com) Operates hourly bus services to/from Madrid (€29.40, four hours).

TRAIN

From Valencia's **Estación del Norte** (Map p734; Calle Xàtiva; ⊚), major destinations include the following:

TO	PRICE (€)	DURATION (HR)	FREQUENCY (PER DAY)
Alicante	17-30	1½-2	11-13
Barcelona	40-44	3-4¼	14-18
Madrid	27-73	1¾-6½	13-20

ⓘ Getting Around

Valencia has an integrated bus, tram and metro network. Tourist offices sell the **Valencia Tourist Card** (www.valenciatouristcard.com; 24/48/72hr €15/20/25), entitling you to free urban travel and discounts at participating sights, shops and restaurants.

TO/FROM THE AIRPORT

Metro lines 3 and 5 connect the airport, central Valencia and the port. A taxi into the city centre costs around €18 (including a supplement for journeys originating at the airport).

BICYCLE & SCOOTER

Cycling is a great way to get around: the riverbed park gives you easy access to most of the city and there are several other bike lanes. There are numerous hire places, and most accommodation can organise it. **Valenbisi** (www.valenbisi. es) is the city-bike scheme – sign up for a short-term contract (€13) at machines at the bike racks.

Cooltra (☏963 39 47 51; www.cooltra. com; Carrer Ribalta 6; per day/24hr/week €29/33/169; ⊗9.30am-2pm & 4.30-8.30pm) Scooter hire with several pick-up points.

Do You Bike (☏963 15 55 51; www.doyou-bike.com; Calle del Mar 14; per day €10-15; ⊗9.30am-2pm & 5-8.15pm) Has a couple of other offices in town. It's cheaper midweek.

Solution Bike (☏961 10 36 95; www.solution-bike.com; Calle Embajador Vich 13; per day €10-15; ⊗9am-2pm & 5-8pm or 9pm)

CAR & MOTORCYCLE

Street parking is a pain. Underground car parks are signposted throughout the centre. The cheapest central one is at the corner of Calles Barón de Cárcer and Hospital.

Numerous car rental firms, both local and international, operate from the airport and centre.

PUBLIC TRANSPORT

Most buses run until about 10pm, with various night services continuing until around 1am. Buy a **Bonobús Plus** (€8 for 10 journeys) at major metro stations, most tobacconists and some newspaper kiosks or pay as you get on (€1.50). One-/two-/three-day travel cards valid for the bus, metro and tram cost €4/6.70/9.70.

The tram is a pleasant way to get to the beach and port. Pick it up at Pont de Fusta or where it intersects with the metro at Benimaclet.

Metro (www.metrovalencia.es) lines (five with a sixth on the way) cross town and serve the

---

BOATS FROM VALENCIA

Balearia (www.balearia.com) runs to Mallorca (passenger/car €60/165, six to seven weekly)
Trasmediterránea (☏902 45 46 45; www.trasmediterranea.es) operates car and passenger ferries to Ibiza, Mallorca and Menorca. Prices are for one way in the high season:

DESTINATION	PASSENGER FARE (€)	CAR FARE (€)	DURATION (HR)	FREQUENCY
Ibiza	75	150	3-6½	up to 2 daily
Mallorca	77	165	8	almost daily
Menorca	60	150	15	1 weekly

REQUENA

Requena, 65km west of Valencia, grew rich from silk; today it's primarily wine and livestock country, producing robust reds – try the local bobal grape – *cavas* (sparkling wines), rich sausages and spicy meats. From its heart rears La Villa, the medieval nucleus, with its twisting streets and blind alleys. It's great to explore, atmospheric without being dolled up for tourism. Check out the guard tower, the lovely Gothic facades, and the narrow lanes of the one-time Jewish quarter.

Two venues for wine lovers are Museo del Vino (Carrer Somera 13; adult/child €4/3; ⊙11am-2pm Tue-Sun), a wine museum within the handsome 15th-century Palacio del Cid, and Ferevin (www.ferevin.com; Cuesta de las Carnicerías; tastings €3; ⊙11am-2pm Tue-Sun, plus 4-7pm Fri & 5-7pm Sat) FREE, a showroom for local wine producers. There's a wine festival at the end of August. A useful website is www.rutavino.com.

Within the intestines of Plaza Albornoz – around which are several accommodation options – is a network of interlinked cellars, once used as storerooms and, during strife, hideouts. Guided visits (adult/child €4/3; ⊙2-7 times daily Tue-Sun) meet outside No 6. Ask at the tourist office (☑962 30 38 51; www.requena.es; Calle García Montés; ⊙10am-2pm Tue-Sun, plus 4-7pm Fri-Sun) for times; it's below the main entrance to the old town.

Requena is right beside the Valencia–Madrid motorway. There are regular buses (€4.85, one hour) and *cercanía* trains (one way/return €5.70/8.60, 1½ hours) to/from Valencia. There are also fast AVE/Avant trains that take only 25 minutes but are significantly pricier, and arrive at a different station (Requena Utiel), 6km from town.

outer suburbs. The closest stations to the city centre are Ángel Guimerá, Xàtiva (for the train station), Colón and Pont de Fusta.

TAXI

Radio-Taxi (☑963 70 33 33; www.radiotaxi valencia.es)

AROUND VALENCIA CITY

La Albufera

About 15km south of Valencia, La Albufera is a huge freshwater lagoon separated from the sea by a narrow strip of pine-forested sand dunes. Birdwatchers flock to Parque Natural de la Albufera (http://parquesnaturales.gva.es) FREE, where around 90 species regularly nest and more than 250 others use it as a migratory staging post.

Sunsets can be spectacular here. You can take a boat trip out on the lagoon, joining the local fisherfolk, who use flat-bottomed boats and nets to harvest fish and eels from the shallow waters.

Surrounded by rice fields, La Albufera was the birthplace of paella. Every second house in the villages hereabouts is a rice restaurant. One of the nicest villages is El Palmar, which has easily arranged boat trips. At the end of the main street here

the luminous dining room at El Sequer de Tonica (☑961 62 02 24; www.elsequerdetonica.com; Carrer Redolins 85; rices per person €10-17; ⊙10am-10.30pm Mon-Sat, to 4pm Sun) is highly esteemed by Valencians for its rice, which includes one with duck: the ducks are hunted on the water-filled rice paddies in winter.

Autocares Herca buses for Playa El Salér (Map p730) are also good for La Albufera, and go on to either El Palmar (minimum five daily) or El Perello (hourly or half-hourly), further down the coast. The area is also great to explore by bike.

Sagunto

POP 65,190

The port town of Sagunto (Valenciano: Sagunt), 25km north of Valencia, primarily offers spectacular panoramas of the coast, Balearics and sea of orange groves from its hilltop castle complex. It's an easy half-day excursion from Valencia.

Sagunto was once a thriving Iberian community (called – infelicitously, with hindsight – Arse) that traded with Greeks and Phoenicians. In 219 BC Hannibal besieged and destroyed the town, sparking the Second Punic War between Carthage and Rome. Rome won, named the town Saguntum and set about rebuilding it.

From the train station, an uphill walk brings you first to the over-restored Roman

LA TOMATINA

The last or penultimate Wednesday in August (the date varies) marks Spain's messiest festival. Held in Buñol, 40km west of Valencia City, La Tomatina is a tomato-throwing orgy that attracts more than 20,000 visitors to a town of just 9000 inhabitants.

At precisely 11am, over 100 tonnes of squishy tomatoes are tipped from trucks to the waiting crowd. For precisely one hour everyone joins in a cheerful, anarchic tomato battle. After being pounded with pulp, expect to be sluiced down with hoses by the local fire brigade.

Participation costs €10; if you want to be pouring them off the truck you'll have to fork out €750. Don't forget a set of fresh clothes and perhaps a pair of goggles to protect the eyes. For more background, visit www.latomatina.info.

theatre. Above it, the stone walls of the castle complex (⊙10am-6pm or 8pm Tue-Sat, to 2pm Sun) FREE girdle the hilltop for almost 1km. Mostly in ruins, it's great for a stroll with views. Its seven rambling sections each speak of a different period in Sagunto's long history.

The best option from Valencia to Sagunto are the *cercanía* trains on lines C5 and C6 (one way/return €3.65/5.50, 30 minutes, very regular).

COSTA DEL AZAHAR & EL MAESTRAZGO

All along the Costa del Azahar (Blossom Coast) spread citrus groves, from whose headily scented flowers the region takes its name. The busy, developed – not always harmoniously – seaside resorts are enticing if you're after sun and sand. By contrast, the high hinterland, especially the wild, sparsely populated lands of the Maestrazgo, offer great walking solitude and hearty mountain cooking.

Benicàssim

POP 18,990

Benicàssim, scarcely a couple of blocks wide, stretches for 6km along the coast. It has been a popular resort since the 19th century, when wealthy Valencian families built summer residences here.

◉ Sights & Activities

Those 6km of broad beach are the main attraction. Bordering the promenade at the northeastern end are Las Villas, exuberant, sometimes frivolous holiday homes built by wealthy *valencianos* at the end of the 19th

century and into the 20th. Ask for the tourist office leaflet, *The Las Villas Path*.

Desierto de les Palmes   HILL
The twisting, climbing CV147 leads after about 6km to this inland range – cooler than the coast, on occasion misty – with a Carmelite monastery and first-class restaurant at its heart. Nowadays it's a nature reserve and far from being a desert (for the monks it meant a place for mystic withdrawal), it's a green, outdoor activities area. From Monte Bartolo (728m), its highest point, there are staggering views. The tourist office hands out an excellent booklet listing a range of different walks in the hills.

Aquarama   AMUSEMENT PARK
(www.aquarama.net; adult/child day ticket €25/19; ⊙11am-7pm mid-Jun–early Sep) This vast water park is just south of town, off the N340.

✦✦ Festivals & Events

Festival Internacional de Benicàssim   MUSIC
(FIB; www.fiberfib.com) Fans by the tens of thousands gather in mid-July for this annual four-day bash, one of Europe's major outdoor music festivals. Top acts in recent years have included Bob Dylan, the Killers and Oasis.

🛏 Sleeping & Eating

Benicàssim's five campgrounds are all within walking distance of the beaches. Plenty of economical restaurants line Calles de Santo Tomás and Castellón, the old town's main street.

Rooms Boutique Benicàssim   HOSTAL €
(☎632 813480; www.hotelbenicassim.net; Calle San Antonio 13; s/d €45/59; 🛜) Full of summertime colour and flair, this is a stylish budget option on the edge of the town centre.

Rooms are comfortable and the decor upbeat; expect to be left to your own devices. Minimum stays apply in summer.

Camping Azahar
CAMPGROUND €

(📞 964 30 31 96; www.campingazahar.es; adult/tent/car €5/17/5; 🅿 🛜 🏊) Extensive sites are shaded by mature mulberry trees. The beach is a minute's walk, and there's a restaurant, large pool, and toilet blocks that are kept scrupulously clean.

Hotel Voramar
HOTEL €€

(📞 964 30 01 50; www.voramar.net; Paseo Pilar Coloma 1; s/d incl breakfast €107/114, with sea view €122/144; 🅿 ❄ 🛜) Venerable (it's been run by the same family for four generations) and blooded in battle (it functioned as a hospital in the Spanish Civil War), this place has character and is spectacularly located right at the very northern edge of the beach. The rooms – which are much cheaper outside of high summer – could do with a touch-up but those with balcony (and hammock) have utterly magnificent sea views and sounds. The first-class restaurant also has great perspectives. Bikes and kayaks can be hired.

Restaurante Desierto de las Palmas
RESTAURANT €€

(📞 964 30 09 47; www.restaurantedesierto.com; CV147, Km 9; mains €12-19; ⏱ 9.30am-5.30pm Wed-Mon Mar-Dec, plus 5.30pm-midnight late Jun-early Sep; 🚗) Families flock from miles around to this popular venue, famed for its rice and seafood dishes. Lively, noisy and very Spanish, it sits on a spur close to the Carmelite monastery and offers heart-stopping views from its broad windows.

ℹ Information

Tourist Office (📞 964 30 01 02; www.turismobenicassim.com; Calle Santo Tomás 74; ⏱ 9am-2pm & 4-7pm Mon-Fri, 10.30am-1.30pm & 4-7pm Sat, 10.30am-1.30pm Sun Oct-May, 9am-2pm & 5-8pm Mon-Fri, 10.30am-1.30pm & 5-8pm Sat & Sun Jun-Sep) Inland, in the centre of town.

ℹ Getting There & Away

There are 10 daily trains from Benicàssim to Valencia (€8 to €19, one hour), and services north to Tortosa, Tarragona and Barcelona. Buses run every quarter-hour to the provincial capital Castellón de la Plana, from where there are more connections.

Peñíscola
POP 8180

Peñíscola's old town, all cobbled streets and whitewashed houses, huddles within stone walls that protect the rocky promontory jutting into the sea. It's pretty as a postcard – and just as commercial, with ranks of souvenir and ceramics shops (one prominent item: a pot with – oh dear – a penis for a spout, a tourist-oriented pun on the town name). By contrast, the highrises sprouting northwards along the coast are mostly leaden and charmless. But the **Paseo Marítimo** promenade makes pleasant walking, and the beach, which extends as far as neighbouring Benicarló, is superb, sandy and over 5km long. Peñíscola is quiet off-season but there's enough on to not make it spooky – and you'll have the old town to yourself.

⊙ Sights & Activities

Castle
CASTLE

(adult/child under 10yr €3.50/free; ⏱ 10.30am-5.30pm mid-Oct–Easter, 9.30am-9.30pm Easter–mid-Oct) The rambling 14th-century castle was built by the Knights Templar on Arab foundations and later became home to Pedro de Luna ('Papa Luna', the deposed Pope Benedict XIII). There are various exhibits relating to the history of the castle and town.

Sierra de Irta
PARK

To escape the summer crowds, seek solitude in the Sierra de Irta. Running south from Peñíscola, it's both nature park and protected marine reserve, best explored on foot or by mountain bike. You can attack the full 26km of the circular PR V-194 trail or slip in one or more shorter loops. Ask at the tourist office for a trail map.

🛏 Sleeping & Eating

Chiki
PENSIÓN €

(📞 964 48 02 84; www.restaurantechiki.com; Calle Mayor 3-5; d with/without bathroom €55/50; 🛜) Right in the old town, this has seven spotless, modern rooms with views and a genuine welcome. The nearby church chimes tinnily from 8am. From March to October, it runs an attractive restaurant (mains from €9; closed Tuesday) with a great-value three-course menu. Hours are unreliable, so ring in advance.

Tio Pepe HOTEL €€

(☑964 48 06 40; www.hotelrestaurantetiopepe. com; Avenida España 32; s/d €67/98; ❄ ☎) Offering noteworthy value outside of high summer, half a block from the beach, this upbeat place has correct rooms at the right price. The downstairs restaurant is overlit and lacks atmosphere but does tasty meals, with a drink-less set menu for €18.50. Check current specials for the best on offer.

Rojo Picota TAPAS €€

(www.rojopicota.es; Avenida Papa Luna 1; mains €9-18; ☺11am-11pm; ☎) Open year-round (till later in summer) and a favourite with locals as well as visitors, this offers a range of excellent wines by the glass, and wallet-friendly Basque-style *pintxos* (tapas) at the bar. A range of tasty plates prepared in the open kitchen, home-macerated vermouth and well-mixed gin and tonics make it an all-round star.

❶ Information

Main Tourist Office (☑964 48 02 08; www. peniscola.es; Paseo Marítimo; ☺9am-8pm Mon-Fri, 10am-1pm & 4.30-8pm Sat & Sun Apr-Sep, 9.30am-5.30pm Mon-Sat, 9.30am-2pm Sun Oct-Mar) At the southern end of Paseo Marítimo. Pick up or download info on town.

❶ Getting There & Around

Buses run at least half-hourly between Peñíscola, Benicarló and Vinaròs, from where you can connect to Valencia or Castellón. From July to mid-September there's an hourly run to Peñíscola/Benicarló train station, 7km from town.

El Maestrazgo

Straddling northwestern Valencia and southeast Aragón, El Maestrazgo (Valenciano: El Maestrat) is a mountainous land, a world away from the coastal strip. Here spectacular ancient *pueblos* (villages) huddle on rocky outcrops and ridges. The Maestrazgo is great, wild, on-your-own trekking territory.

Sant Mateu

POP 2070 / ELEV 325M

Not as picturesque as the hilltop villages further into the region, Sant Mateu, once capital of the Maestrazgo, is an appealing spot nonetheless, whose solid mansions and elaborate facades recall the town's more illustrious past and former wool-based wealth.

◉ Sights & Activities

Ask at the tourist office for details of the medieval dungeons and paleontological museum. A small street from the Jewish quarter is preserved just off the square.

Radiating from the village are three signed circular walking trails of between 2½ and five hours that lead through the surrounding hills. Ask for the free tourist office pamphlet 'Senderos de Sant Mateu' (in Spanish).

Iglesia Arciprestal CHURCH, MUSEUM

(Calle Santo Domingo; admission €1.50; ☺10am-2pm & 4-7pm Tue-Sun Jun-Sep) The Gothic village church can be admired through a glass screen at any time. The visit – free or guided in summer, guided only in winter – includes a museum of religious art.

Ermita de la Mare de Déu dels Àngels CHURCH

(☺11am-7pm Sat & Sun) FREE Follow signs from Plaza Mayor to this chapel perched on a rocky hillside, a 2.5km drive or somewhat shorter walk away. It was a monastery until the Spanish Civil War and preserves a cherub-infested baroque chapel. The views are great, and there's an excellent restaurant. The monastery guesthouse is gradually being refurbished too. It's open weekends and usually on weekdays as well.

🛏 Sleeping & Eating

La Perdi HOSTAL €

(☑964 41 60 82; laperdicb@hotmail.com; Carrer Historiador Betí 9; s/d €20/40; ☎) Family-run (see the photos of its three generations around the tiled dining room), this is a bargain with five plain, comfortable rooms and a restaurant that does an equally good-value *menú del día* (set menu; €9.50 or €12).

L'hostal de Cabrit HOSTAL €€

(☑964 41 66 21; www.hostaldecabrit.com; Pla Mare de Deu de la Font 19; s/d/ste incl breakfast €30/60/115; ❄ ☎) Decent value is to be had at this good-looking spot on a central plaza. Rooms vary in size but are cute, equipped with safe and fridge, and commodious. The suite has a king-sized bed and an in-room shower. The stone-faced restaurant does a nice line in rices and other plates (mains €12 to €15).

Farga

VALENCIAN €€

(📞 663 909586; www.fargarestaurant.com; Er-mita de la Mare de Déu dels Àngels; set menu €25; ⊙ noon-4pm Sun & Tue-Thu, noon-11pm Fri & Sat) This quality restaurant at a former monas-tery perched on a hill 2.5km from town of-fers incomparable views of the surrounding plain.

ℹ Information

Tourist Office (📞 964 41 66 58; www.sant mateu.com; Carrer Historiador Betí 13; ⊙ 10am-2pm & 4-6pm Tue-Sat, 10am-2pm Sun) Very helpful. Just off the main square, in Pala-cio Borrull, a stalwart 15th-century building.

ℹ Getting There & Away

Autos Mediterráneo (📞 964 22 00 54; www. autosmediterraneo.com) buses link Sant Mateu with the following destinations:

TO	PRICE (€)	DURATION (HR)	FREQUENCY
Castellón	5	1½	3 Mon-Fri, 1 Sat
Morella	3.20	¾	2 Mon-Fri, 1 Sat
Vinaròs	2.60	1	4 Mon-Fri

Morella

POP 2720 / ELEV 1000M

Bitingly cold in winter and refreshingly cool in summer, striking Morella is the Val-encian Maestrazgo's principal town. This outstanding example of a medieval fortress town is perched on a hilltop, crowned by a castle and girdled by an intact rampart wall over 2km long. It's the ancient capital of Els Ports, the 'Mountain Passes', a rugged region offering some outstanding scenic drives and strenuous cycling excursions, plus excellent possibilities for walkers.

⊙ Sights

Morella is a compact jumble of narrow streets, alleys and steep steps. Its main street, running between Puerta San Miguel and Puerta de los Estudios, is bordered by shops selling mountain honey, perfumes, cheeses, pickles, pâtés, sausages and fat hams.

On the outskirts of town stretch the arches of a handsome 13th-century aque-duct. You can also get a guard's-eye view of the town by climbing up onto the city walls

OFF THE BEATEN TRACK

PREHISTORIC PAINTING

Museo de Valltorta (📞 964 33 60 10; www.valltorta.com; Tirig; ⊙ 10am-2pm & 4-7pm or 5-8pm Tue-Sun) **FREE** is an informative museum 2km from Tirig, 10km southwest of Sant Mateu. It presents (info in various languages available) a detailed overview of pre-historic art and El Maestrazgo's World Heritage ensemble of rock paintings. There's a reproduction of the most interesting piece, a hunting scene. From here free guided walks to the painting sites leave a few times daily.

and into a guard tower. Ask at the tourist office for the key.

Combined entrance tickets can save you euros here.

Castle

CASTLE

(adult/child €3.50/2.50; ⊙ 11am-6pm Oct-Apr, to 7pm May-Sep) Though badly knocked about, Morella's castle well merits the long wiggly ascent to savour breathtaking views of the town and surrounding countryside. Built by the Moors, it was regularly remodelled and saw action in the Napoleonic and Carlist wars of the 19th century. Carlists took it in 1838 by climbing up through the long-drop toilet. At its base is the bare church and cloister of the Convento de San Francisco. Last entry is one hour before closing.

Basílica de Santa María la Mayor

CHURCH

(Plaza Arciprestal; ⊙ 10.30am-2pm & 3-5.30pm or 6.30pm Mon-Sat, 10.30-11.30am & 1-5pm or 6pm Sun) This imposing Gothic basilica has two elaborately sculpted doorways on its south-ern facade. A richly carved polychrome stone staircase leads to the elaborate over-head choir, while cherubs clamber and peek all over the gilded altarpiece. Its ecclesias-tical treasure is kept within the Museo Ar-ciprestal (admission €1.50).

Museo Tiempo de Dinosaurios

MUSEUM

(adult/child €2/1.50; ⊙ 11am-2pm & 4-6pm or 7pm Tue-Sun; 👶) Opposite the tourist office, this museum, which is full of dinosaur bones and fossils, is one for children, children at heart and cavemen. The Maestrazgo's remote hills have been a treasure trove for palaeontolo-gists. The film is in Spanish only.

OFF THE BEATEN TRACK

MAESTRAZGO VILLAGES

Blazing your own trails across the Maestrazgo on foot, by bike or by car is most appealing. There are numerous lonely landscapes and lovely villages to discover. Ares, 30km south of Morella, is one of the most spectacular, hanging over a cliff. Thirteen kilometres from here, Vilafranca (del Cid) has a museum that explores its dry-stone wall tradition, the excellent Museo de Pedra en Sec (964 44 14 32; admission by donation; ☉10am-1.30pm & 4-7pm Fri-Sat, 10.30am-1.30pm Sun). Get keys from the tourist office opposite. And don't miss the stunning spots over the border in Teruel province!

⚝ Festivals & Events

Sexenni FIESTA

Morella's major festival is the Sexenni, held during August every six years without interruption since 1673 (the next is in 2018) in honour of the town's patron, the Virgen de Vallivana.

🛏 Sleeping & Eating

Hotel Cardenal Ram HOTEL €€

(964 16 00 46; www.hotelcardenalram.com; Cuesta Suñer 1; s/d €50/75; P ❋ �🛜) Bang in the heart of old Morella, this noble Renaissance palace has been completely refurbished and offers a tantalising blend of historical feel and modern amenities. Half the rooms have splendid views, those without are generally very spacious. There's also a handsome restaurant and midweek discounts.

Hotel del Pastor HOTEL €€

(964 16 10 16; www.hoteldelpastor.com; Carrer San Julián 12; s/d incl breakfast €56/74; P ❋ �🛜) This is an excellent deal, with slightly old-fashioned rooms – some with vistas – spread over four floors (there's no lift but that's the only downside of this option). Rooms are traditionally furnished and come in warm ochre colours with plenty of polished wood. Bathrooms have marble washstands, bathtubs and large mirrors.

Casa Masoveret DELI €

(www.casamasoveret.com; Segura Barreda 9; deli plates €5-12; ☉10am-9pm Tue-Sun; 🍴) At this exceptionally friendly family place, perch on a wooden bench and enjoy a glass of choice wine while nibbling on tapas of mountain cheeses and ham or scoffing a well-filled *bocadillo*. Many of the pork products come from their own pigs. Scan the shelves too for gourmet produce.

★ Daluan FUSION €€

(964 16 00 71; www.daluan.es; Carreró de la Presó 6; mains €14-20, degustation menu €35; ☉1.30-3.30pm Sun-Wed, 1.30-3.30pm & 9-11pm Fri & Sat) Run by Avelino Ramón, a cookery teacher by trade, and his wife, Jovita, Daluan offers friendly service and a hugely creative menu that changes regularly with the seasons. The small interior is satisfyingly contemporary, and its terrace, beside a quiet alley, is equally relaxing.

Mesón del Pastor SPANISH €€

(964 16 02 49; www.mesondelpastor.com; Cuesta Jovaní 5; mains €7-17; ☉1-4pm Thu-Tue, 9-11pm Fri & Sat) Within the dining room, bedecked with the restaurant's trophies and diplomas, this place is all about robust mountain cuisine: thick stews in winter, rabbit, juicy sausages, partridge, wild boar and goat. It's located a short walk from the hotel of the same name.

ℹ Information

Tourist Office (964 17 30 32; www.morella turistica.com; Plaza San Miguel 3; ☉10am-2pm & 4-6pm or 7pm Mon-Sat, 10am-2pm Sun daily Apr-Oct, closed Mon Nov-Mar) The tourist office is just behind Torres de San Miguel, twin 14th-century towers flanking the main entrance gate.

ℹ Getting There & Around

Morella is best reached via Castellón, which has good train connections. Two daily weekday buses (€9.40, 2¼ hours) and one Saturday service with Autos Mediterráneo run to/from Castellón's train station. There are also weekday buses to Vinaròs on the coast and Alcañiz in Teruel province.

COSTA BLANCA

The long stripe of the Costa Blanca (White Coast) is one of Europe's most heavily visited areas. If you're after a secluded midsummer strand, stay away – or head inland to enjoy traditional villages and towns. Then again, if you're looking for a lively social scene, good beaches and a suntan...

It isn't all concrete and package deals. Although the original fishing villages have long been engulfed by the sprawl of resorts, a few old-town kernels, such as those of Xàbia (Jávea) and Altea, still survive.

Gandia

POP 78,540

Gandia's main town, once home to a branch of the Borja dynasty (more familiar as the infamous Borgias), is a prosperous commercial centre with a lively atmosphere. The other side of the coin is the fun-in-the-sun beach town and port, a 6km drive away.

◉ Sights & Activities

Palacio Ducal de los Borja   PALACE
(www.palauducal.com; Calle Duc Alfons el Vell 1; adult/child €6/5; ⊙10am-1.30pm & 3-6.30pm or 4-7.30pm Mon-Sat, 10am-1.30pm Sun) Gandia's magnificent palace was the 15th-century home of Duque Francisco de Borja. Highlights include its finely carved *artesonado* ceilings and rich ceramic work – look out for the vivid *mapa universal* floor composition. Guided tours (in Spanish, with an English leaflet) leave regularly and cost a euro more.

Playa de Gandia   BEACH
Six kilometres from the centre, Playa de Gandia is a long, broad beach of fine sand, groomed daily by a fleet of tractors. It's a popular resort, if a little tacky, with a good summer and weekend scene.

⊨ Sleeping & Eating

Mediocre eating choices line the beachfront strip. There are better options in the centre and around the port.

Hostal El Nido   HOSTAL €€
(☑962 84 46 40; www.hostalelnidogandia.com; Calle Alcoy 22; s/d €50/70; 🛜) This homey place is the mirror opposite of all the giant resort hotels that line the beach and the rooms are as cheerful as the owners. It's a block back from the beach. Between June and September it also runs a small bar for guests.

Hotel Riviera   HOTEL €€€
(☑962 84 50 42; www.hotelesrh.com; Paseo Neptuno 28; s/d incl breakfast €99/164; ⊙Mar-Oct; 🅿⊛@🛜⊛) This is one of Gandia's oldest seaside hotels, but rooms are up to date and luxurious in a way that is unexpected for a three-star hotel. Much cheaper off-season. The same chain has three other options in the beach zone.

❶ Information

Playa de Gandia Tourist Office (☑962 84 24 07; www.gandiaturismo.com; Paseo de Neptuna 45; ⊙9.30am-1.30pm, 4-7pm Mon-Fri, 9.30am-1.30pm Sat & Sun) Opens extended hours in summer.

Town Tourist Office (☑962 87 77 88; www.gandiaturismo.com; ⊙9.30am-1.30pm & 3.30-7.30pm Mon-Fri, 9.30am-1.30pm Sat) Opposite the bus and train station. Opens extended hours in summer.

❶ Getting There & Around

Trains run between Gandia and Valencia (€5.70, one hour) every 30 minutes (hourly on weekends). The combined bus and train station is opposite the town tourist office. Stopping beside the office, La Marina Gandiense buses for Playa de Gandia run every 20 minutes.

Denia

POP 44,450

A major passenger port for the fairly nearby Balearic Islands, Denia is a cheery place that lives for more than just tourism. The old town snuggles up against a small hill mounted by a tumbledown castle and the town's streets buzz with life. The beaches of La Marina, to its north, are good and sandy, while southwards the fretted coastline of Las Rotas and beyond offers less-frequented rocky coves.

◉ Sights & Activities

Castillo   CASTLE
(adult/child €3/2; ⊙10am-1pm or 1.30pm & 5-8.30pm) From Plaza de la Constitución, steps lead up to the ruins of Denia's castle from where there's a great overview of the town and coast. The castle grounds contain the **Museo Arqueològic de Denia**: a collection of pot shards illustrating the town's long history. Outside high summer the castle opens earlier in the afternoon and closes around dusk.

Mundo Marino   BOAT TOUR
(☑966 42 30 66; www.mundomarino.es; Explanada Cervantes; ⊙May–mid-Sep) To catch the sea breezes, sign on with Mundo Marino, which runs a whole array of different boat trips including 'mini cruises' to/from Xàbia.

⊨ Sleeping

Hostal L'Anfora   HOSTAL €
(☑966 43 01 01; www.hostallanfora.com; Explanada Cervantes 8; s/d €40/60; ⊛🛜) The genial

boss here is rightly proud of this top *hostal* on the waterfront strip. Rooms are compact but new in feel, with colourful bedcovers, faultless bathrooms and not a speck of dust or dirt. Prices are very fair: a budget gem.

★ **Hotel Chamarel** BOUTIQUE HOTEL €€
(☑966 43 50 07; www.hotelchamarel.com; Calle Cavallers 13; d/ste incl breakfast €85/115; P ❋ ☎) This delightful hotel, tastefully furnished in period style, occupies a lovably attractive, 19th-century bourgeois mansion. The rooms surround a tranquil patio and are all different, with space and so much character; bathrooms artfully combine modern fittings with venerable floor tiles. The internal salon with marble-topped bar is equally relaxing. The whole place is a capacious gallery for the paintings of the artist owner. Prices drop significantly off-season.

El Raset HOTEL €€€
(☑965 78 65 64; www.hotelelraset.com; Calle Bellavista 1; s/d incl breakfast €118/143; ❋ @ ☎) This modern designer hotel overlooks the port with spotlit rooms, colourful bedspreads and art on the walls. There's a buzzy vibe and very friendly service. A row of house restaurants alongside give you doorstep eating options.

Posada del Mar HOTEL €€€
(☑966 43 29 66; www.laposadadelmar.com; Plaza Drassanes 2; s/d incl breakfast €165/180; P ❋ @ ☎) Sensitively renovated, this hotel occupies a 13th-century building that last functioned as Denia's customs house. Each of its 25 rooms is individually decorated with a nautical theme and light streams through large windows that overlook the harbour.

✗ Eating

Denia has a vibrant eating scene and is famous for its pricey *gambas rayadas* (striped prawns). Restaurants run along the waterfront. Pedestrianised Calle Loreto, a 10-minute stroll back from the beach, is the main tapas zone and a great spot.

El Baret de Miquel Ruiz TAPAS €€
(Carrer Historiador Palau 1; tapas €3-12; ⊙1.30-3.30pm & 8-10.30pm Wed-Sat, 1.30-3.30pm Sun & Mon) This haven of good service and stellar cuisine is a real find for gastronauts. Delicious, exquisitely presented morsels of market produce are almost too pretty to eat. Take the plunge, though, for they are taste sensations. The simple, retro-casual vibe of the front room of an old house adds

to the impression. Book a week ahead for weekends.

Quique Dacosta MODERN SPANISH €€€
(☑965 78 41 79; www.quiquedacosta.es; Carretera Las Marinas Km 3, El Poblet; degustation menu €182, wine flight €77-99; ⊙1.30-3pm & 8.30-10.30pm Wed-Sun Feb-Nov, daily Jul & Aug) In sleek white minimalist premises near the beach 3km west of Denia, this coolly handsome place is one of the peninsula's temples to modern gastronomy. The eponymous chef employs molecular and other contemporary techniques to create a constantly surprising cornucopia of flavours and textures.

ⓘ Information

Tourist Office (☑966 42 23 67; www.denia. net; Calle Dr Manuel Lattur 1; ⊙9am-2pm & 4-7.30pm Mon-Fri, 10am-2pm Sat Nov-Feb, plus 10am-2pm Sun Mar-May & Oct, 9am-2pm & 4-8pm daily Jun-Sep) Near the waterfront and ferry and opposite the train station.

ⓘ Getting There & Away

Balearia Lines (☑902 160 180, from overseas 966 428 700; www.balearia.com) runs ferries year-round to/from Mallorca (passenger €50 to €60, car €70 to €110) and Ibiza (passenger €55 to €75, car €80 to €90), and direct to Formentera (passenger €55 to €75, car €80 to €90) from mid-May to mid-September.

Hourly light-rail services follow the scenic route southwards via Calpe and Altea to Benidorm, connecting with the tram for Alicante.

ALSA (www.alsa.es) buses run around a dozen times daily to Valencia (€10.90, 1½ to two hours) and Alicante (€11.25, 1½ to three hours); there are also Benidorm services.

Xàbia

POP 33,150

With a high expat resident population, Xàbia (Spanish: Jávea) is a gentle, family-oriented place that has largely resisted the high-rise tourist developments that blight so much of the Costa Blanca. Pleasant, relaxed and picturesque, it comes in three flavours: the small old town 2km inland; El Puerto (the port), directly east of the old town; and the beach zone of El Arenal, a couple of kilometres south.

◉ Sights & Activities

In addition to El Arenal's broad beach, the old town, with quiet plazas and boutique shops, well merits a wander. Tourist offices sell *Xàbia: Nature Areas Network* (€1), containing five brochures, each describing a waymarked route in the area, including an ascent of Montgó, the craggy mountain that looms over the town.

🛏 Sleeping

⭐ Hotel Triskel   BOUTIQUE HOTEL €€

(☎966 46 21 91; www.hotel-triskel.com; Calle Sor María Gallard 3; d €100; 🅿❄🛜) 🐾 By the market in the old town, this cordially run place is a standout. The five lovely rooms are subtly and beautifully decorated according to themes, with thoughtful details, objets d'art and pleasing handmade wooden furniture. Everything is done with a warm personal touch and the cosy bar downstairs does a cracking gin and tonic. Pets welcome and prices halve off-season.

Hotel Miramar   HOTEL €€

(☎965 79 01 00; www.hotelmiramar.com.es; Plaza Almirante Bastarreche 12; s/d €43/73; ❄🛜) You'll be that close to the sea that you might want to sleep in your swimming things in this faded, but comfy enough, year-round hotel right beside the port. Rooms overlooking the bay carry a €15 supplement. There's a bar and restaurant, too.

🍴 Eating

The old town has several enticing tapas bars, while restaurants and bars flank Avenida de la Marina Española, the pedestrianised promenade south of the port. In El Arenal, cafes and restaurants hug the rim of beachside Paseo Marítimo.

La Renda   VALENCIAN €€

(☎965 79 37 63; www.larenda.es; Calle Cristo del Mar 12; mains €9-19; ⏱1-4pm & 7-11pm Tue-Sat, 1-4pm Sun) There's more than you think to a paella, and this well-priced but classy, welcoming place at the port has 14 different rice dishes. The house special, though, is *arroz de renda* (creamy rice with snails). For most dishes a minimum of two people are required but there's a set menu with a rice option always available.

Embruix   TAPAS €€

(☎966 46 20 73; www.embruix.es; Carrer Major 17; tapas €4-9, mains €12-18; ⏱1-4pm & 8-11pm Tue-Sat, 1-4pm Sun; 🛜) In the heart of the old town, this convivial spot does handsomely presented tapas portions, particularly of seafood. They are bursting with flavour and backed up by some decent à la carte meat dishes.

ℹ Information

Tourist Offices (www.xabia.org; ⏱9am-1.30pm & 4-7.30pm or 4.30-8pm Mon-Fri, 10am-1.30pm Sat) El Arenal (☎966 46 06 05; Carretera Cabo de la Nao); Old Town (☎965 79 43 56; Plaza de la Iglesia); Port (☎965 79 07 36; Plaza Almirante Bastareche 11). The Port office is also open Saturday afternoon and Sunday morning.

ℹ Getting There & Around

Alsa (www.alsa.es) run at least six buses daily to both Valencia (€11.85, two to three hours) and Alicante (€10, 2¼ to 2¾ hours). They stop on Avenida Óndara, at Rotonda del Olivo, with a large olive tree at its heart.

You can rent a bicycle at **Xàbia's Bike** (www.xabiasbike.com; Avenida Lepanto 5; per day/week €10/49; ⏱9.30am-1.30pm & 4.30-8.30pm Mon-Fri, 10am-2pm Sat) in the port area. It also does guided bike tours. The tourist office has a booklet of cycling excursions.

Calpe

POP 29,440

The striking Gibraltaresque Peñon de Ifach, a giant limestone molar protruding from the sea, rears up from the seaside resort of Calpe (Valencian: Calp).

Two large bays sprawl either side of the Peñon: Playa Arenal on the southern side is backed by the old town, while Playa Levante (La Fossa), to the north, is pretty much wall-to-wall supersized tourist developments with little to offer independent travellers (except the beach, which is glorious).

From the Peñon's Aula de Naturaleza (Nature Centre), a fairly strenuous walking trail – allow 2½ hours for the round trip – heads through a tunnel and then climbs towards the 332m-high summit, offering great seascapes from its end point. In July and August walkers depart every 15 minutes in batches of 20, so you may have a short wait.

🛏 Sleeping & Eating

There are plenty of restaurants and bars around Plaza de la Constitución and along main Avenida de Gabriel Miró, plus a cluster of good fish places down by the port as well as numerous mediocre tourist restaurants.

BENIDORM

Brash Benidorm is an infamous focus for mass tourism along its two wide sandy beaches and the high-rise development that backs them. Bingo, karaoke, fish 'n' chips, all-day fry-ups: it's here, and the profusion of expat bars where not a word of Spanish is spoken give it an atmosphere of its own.

Benidorm's nice side is the old town, set on a hill between the two beaches. From the platform where once a castle stood, the evening light and sunsets can be incredible.

Benidorm is also popular with families for its excellent theme parks: **Terra Mítica** (www.terramiticapark.com; adult/child €37/28, 2nd day free; ⊙10.30am-8pm or midnight Easter & mid-May–mid-Sep, Sat & Sun Oct) and the enormous water park **Aqualandia** (www.aqualandia.net; adult/child €34/26; ⊙10am-dusk mid-May–mid-Oct) among several others. A family could spend a week exploring them all. Various combined passes are available online.

With some 40,000 beds, you won't be short of a place to stay. Perched over the water in the old town, **Villa Venecia** (☑965 85 54 66; www.hotelvillavenecia.com; Plaza San Jaime 1; s €150-220, d €250-380; ㏘꘍@ꚛꚙ) makes a memorable boutique option, while **Hostal Irati** (☑966 81 31 20; www.hostalirati.com; Calle Condestable Zaragoza 5; r €65; ꘍ꚙ) offers top value for its comfy rooms and cute bathrooms. Also in the old town, **La Cava Aragonesa** (☑966 80 12 06; www.lacavaaragonesa.es; Plaza de la Constitución; set menus €10-13, mains €10-18; ⊙1-4pm & 7.30pm-12.30am Sep-May, 1pm-12.30am Jun-Aug) is a legend in its own tapas-time, while, all over town, hundreds of bars and *discotecas* keep things moving nightly.

There are various tourist offices, including one in the **old town** (☑965 86 35 56; www.benidorm.org; Plaza de Canalejos; ⊙9am-9pm Mon-Fri, 10am-5pm Sat, 10am-2pm Sun).

Benidorm is easily accessed by light rail from Alicante or by bus from Valencia.

Hostal Terra de Mar　　　BOUTIQUE HOTEL €€
(☑629 665124; www.hostalterrademar.com; Calle Justicia 31; s/d €97/119; ꘍ꚙ) At this highly original, and artistic, hotel you're greeted by a giant mural of bangled hands, from which rose petals flutter. Each floor has its own style (climb the stairs to travel from Japan to Morocco to Africa and Paris). Some rooms have mini-balconies looking over the old-town street. The low-season tariff is an excellent deal – high-season prices less so. It's very popular so book ahead.

Los Zapatos　　　MODERN EUROPEAN €€
(☑96 583 15 07; www.restaurantseloszapatos.com; Calle Santa María 7; mains €15-23; ⊙12.30-3pm & 7-11pm Thu-Mon) Highly recommended, this German-run restaurant has a short, specialised à la carte menu and a carefully selected wine list of mainly Spanish vintages. In season it does a tempting *menú caza y pescado* (hunting and fish menu) with wild boar and fish of the day.

Shopping

Librería Europa　　　BOOKSHOP
(www.libreria-europa-calpe.com; Calle Oscar Esplá 2; ⊙10am-2pm & 5-8pm or 9pm Mon-Fri, 10am-noon Sat) Good multilingual bookshop with new and secondhand titles, as well as lots of travel guides.

ⓘ Information

Main Tourist Office (☑96 583 85 32; www.calpe.es; Plaza del Mosquit; ⊙9am-5pm or 6pm Mon-Fri, 9am-2pm Sat) In the old town. There's another branch in the beach zone.

ⓘ Getting There & Away

Buses connect Calpe with both Alicante (€7.15, 1½ hours, six to 10 daily) and Valencia (€13.35, 2¾ to 3¾ hours, six or seven daily). The **bus station** (Avenida de la Generalitat Valenciana) is just off the ring road.

Trams travel daily northwards to Denia (€2.50, 40 minutes) and south to Benidorm (€2.50, 30 minutes), connecting with trams for Alicante.

Altea

POP 24,330

Altea, separated from Benidorm only by the thick wedge of the Sierra Helada, is altogether quieter, with beaches mostly of pebbles. The modern part is a bog-standard coastal resort. By contrast, the whitewashed old town, perched on a hilltop overlooking the sea, is a delightfully pretty *pueblo*.

Off Plaza de la Iglesia in Altea's old town, and especially down Calle Major, there's a profusion of cute little restaurants, many open for dinner only, except in high summer.

Altea has tourist offices on the beach and in the old town.

Alicante

POP 335,050

Of all Spain's mainland provincial capitals, Alicante is the most influenced by tourism, thanks to the nearby airport and resorts. Nevertheless this is a dynamic, attractive Spanish city with a castle, old quarter and long waterfront. The eating scene is exciting and the nightlife is absolutely legendary, whether you're chugging pints with the stag parties at 7pm or twirling on the dance floor with the locals seven hours later. On a weekend night, it's impossibly busy and buzzy year-round.

◉ Sights & Activities

Castillo de Santa Bárbara CASTLE
(adult/child €3/1.50; ⊙10am-10pm Apr-Sep, to 8pm Oct-Mar) There are sweeping views over the city from this large 16th-century castle, which houses a **museum** recounting the history of the city. It's a sweaty walk up the hill to the castle, but there's a **lift** (return €2.50; ⊙10am-8pm, last lift up 7.20pm) that rises through the bowels of the mountain to the summit. To return, it's a pleasant stroll down through **Parque de la Ereta** via Calle San Rafael to Plaza del Carmen.

★Museo de Arte Contemporáneo de Alicante GALLERY
(MACA; www.maca-alicante.es; Plaza Santa María 3; ⊙10am-8pm Tue-Sat, to 2pm Sun) This splendid museum, inside the 17th-century Casa de la Asegurada, has an excellent collection of 20th-century Spanish art, including works by Dalí, Miró, Chillida, Sempere, Tàpies and Picasso.

Museo Arqueológico Provincial MUSEUM
(MARQ; www.marqalicante.com; Plaza Dr Gómez Ulla; adult/child €3/free; ⊙11am-2pm & 6pm-midnight Tue-Sat, 11am-2pm Sun Jul-Aug, 10am-7pm Tue-Fri, 10am-8.30pm Sat, 10am-2pm Sun Sep-Jun) This has a strong collection of ceramics and Iberian art. Exhibits are displayed to give the visitor a very visual, high-tech experience. The only drawback is the lack of information in English.

Museu de Fogueres MUSEUM
(Museo de las Hogueras; Rambla de Méndez Núñez 29; ⊙10am-2pm & 5-8pm or 6-9pm Tue-Sat) FREE In addition to a wealth of photographs, costumes and *ninots* (small effigies saved from the flames), this museum has a great audiovisual presentation of what the Fiesta de Sant Joan, all fire and partying, means to *alicantinos*.

Beaches BEACH
Immediately north of the port is the attractively coloured sandy beach of **Playa del Postiguet**. **Playa de San Juan**, easily reached by the tram, is larger and usually less crowded.

Kon Tiki BOAT TRIP
(☑686 994538; www.cruceroskontiki.com; ⊙Mar-Dec) Makes the 45-minute boat trip (from €18 depending on type of trip) to the popular island of Tabarca.

★☆ Festivals & Events

Fiesta de Sant Joan TOWN FIESTA
Alicante's major festival is spread either side of 24 June, when the city stages its own version of Las Fallas (p745), with fireworks and satirical effigies going up in smoke all over town.

⌂ Sleeping

Guest House HOSTAL €
(☑650 718353; www.guesthousealicante.com; Calle Segura 20; s/d/apt €40/50/90; ⊞❋☎) Here's a magnificent budget choice. Each of the eight large, tastefully decorated rooms differs: some have exposed stone walls and others are painted in pale green, daffodil yellow or deep-sea blue. All come with a safe, full-sized fridge and free beverage-making facilities. There are also a couple of well-equipped apartments.

Pensión San Nicolás PENSIÓN €
(☑965 21 70 39; www.alicantesanicolas.com; Calle San Nicolás 14; s/d €25/40, with bathroom €30/45; ❋☎) This small, well-located, family-run guesthouse is beautifully kept, with spotless rooms decorated cheerfully with bright colours and wall-mounted photos. All rooms come with tea- and coffee-making facilities; one room has its own kitchen. It's on one of the quieter central streets.

Hostal Les Monges Palace HOSTAL €€
(☑965 21 50 46; www.lesmonges.es; Calle San Agustín 4; s €37-45, d €53-60; ⊞❋@☎) This agreeably quirky place in the nightlife zone

Alicante

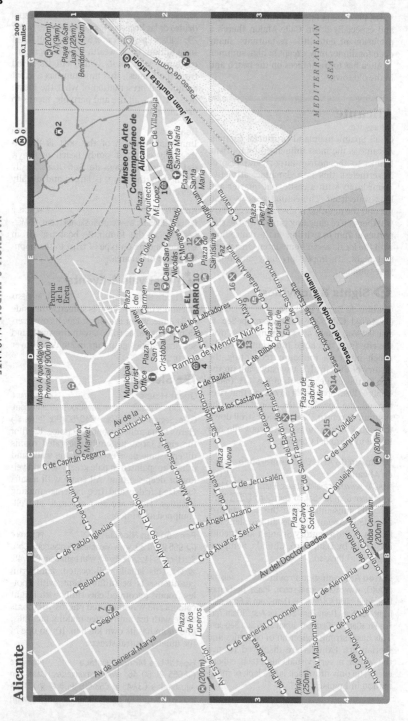

200 m
0.1 miles

Alicante (map labels)

- (200m); A7 (9km); Playa de San Juan (22km); Benidorm (45km)
- Museo Arte Contemporáneo de Alicante
- Basílica de Santa María
- Plaza Santa María
- C de Villavieja
- Av Juan Bautista Lafora
- paseo de Gómiz
- MEDITERRANEAN SEA
- Plaza Arquitecto M Lopez
- C de Toledo
- Calle San C Maldonado Nicolas
- C Monges
- Plaza de Santísima Faz
- C de Rafael Altamira
- C-G
- Plaza Puerta del Mar
- EL BARRIO
- Plaza del Carmen
- Parque de La Ereta
- Museo Arqueológico Provincial (900m)
- C de los Labradores
- C Mayor
- Plaza San Rafael San Cristóbal
- C S Isidro
- Rambla de Méndez Núñez
- Plaza del Portal de Elche
- Plaza de España
- C de Fernando
- Paseo del Conde Vallellano
- Municipal Tourist Office
- Av de la Constitución
- Covered Market
- C de Capitán Segarra
- C de Pablo Iglesias
- C de Poeta Quintana
- C Belando
- Av Alfonso X El Sabio
- C de Médico Pascual Pérez
- Plaza del Teatro
- C San Ildefonso
- C de Bailén
- C de los Castaños
- C de Gerona
- C del Barón de Finestrat
- Plaza de Gabriel Miró
- C Valdés
- C de Lanuza
- (800m)
- C de Bilbao
- Plaza Nueva
- C de Jerusalén
- C de Ángel Lozano
- C de Álvarez Sereix
- C del San Francisco
- C de Canalejas
- Plaza de Calvo Sotelo
- Av del Doctor Gadea
- C de Alemania
- C de Portugal
- C Segura
- Plaza de los Luceros
- Av de General Marva
- Av Estación
- Av de General O'Donnell
- Av Maisonnave
- C del Pintor Cabrera
- C del Pintor Lorenzo Casanova
- Abba Centrum (200m)
- Piripi (250m)
- (200m)
- C del Morell
- Arquitecto

Alicante

is a treasure with its winding corridors, tiles, mosaics and antique furniture. Each room is individually decorated – some are considerably more spacious than others – with somewhat saggy mattresses and plenty of character. The rooftop terrace bar is great and reception couldn't be more welcoming. To really pamper yourself, choose one of the two rooms with sauna and Jacuzzi (€100). Look out for the small Dalí original beside the reception desk.

Abba Centrum   HOTEL €€
(☑965 13 04 40; www.abbahoteles.com; Calle del Pintor Lorenzo Casanova 31; r €62; P❋@☎) Though we don't think they named the chain after the band, there's a certain Scandinavian blond-wood elegance about this business hotel a short walk away from both bus and train stations. Rooms are spacious and comfortable; facilities are excellent and include free gym, sauna and hammam. Online rates are very good.

Hotel Amérigo   HOTEL €€€
(☑965 14 65 70; www.hospes.es; Calle de Rafael Altamira 7; r €160-240; P❋@☎▨) Within an old Dominican convent, this overpriced but commodious five-star choice harmoniously blends the traditional and ultramodern. Enjoy the views from the small rooftop pool, or build up a sweat in the fitness area – if you can tear yourself away from the comfort of your smartly designed room.

🍴 **Eating**

Where's the tapas zone? Virtually the whole centre: wherever it seems that all the action is, you can be sure that there's even more go-

ing on in another node a couple of streets further on. Great scenes.

A number of gourmet ice-cream parlours cool down the centre.

★**Cervecería Sento**   TAPAS €
(Calle Teniente Coronel Chápuli 1; tapas €2-8; ⊙10am-5pm & 8pm-midnight Mon-Sat) Superb, quality *montaditos* (little rolls) and grilled things are the reason to squeeze into this brilliant little bar. Watching the nonstop staff in action is quite an experience too. There's a bigger branch nearby, but this has the atmosphere.

¡**Chico Calla!**   TAPAS €
(Calle de San Francisco 20; tapas €3-11; ⊙8pm-midnight Thu, 1pm-midnight Fri & Sat, 1-5pm Sun; ☎) A short but delicious selection of *montaditos* and other tasty tapas, supplemented by fresh seafood specials, is the stock-in-trade of this handsomely lit bar. Service couldn't be friendlier.

OneOne   BISTRO €€
(☑965 20 63 99; www.restauranteoneone.com; Calle Valdés 9; mains €11-18; ⊙1-4pm & 9pm-midnight Tue-Sat, closed mid-Aug–mid-Sep) It's easier if you speak a little Spanish at this wonderfully eccentric place with its faithful following of regulars but a touch of bravado will get you by (just ask your ebullient host about his travels to Peru). It's a true bistro, the walls scarcely visible for photos and posters, and there's no menu. Just listen carefully as Bartolomé intones...

CésarAnca   MODERN SPANISH €€
(☑965 20 15 80; www.restaurantecesaranca. com; Calle Ojeda 1; dishes €3-20; ⊙1.30-4.30pm & 9-11.30pm Tue-Sat, 1.30-4.30pm Sun & Mon)

Upmarket and buzzy, this is a fun place to sit at the bar and try some high-class gastro creations with the odd touch of molecular wizardry. There's a restaurant too, with the same menu.

Piripi
VALENCIAN €€

(📞 965 22 79 40; www.noumanolin.com; Avenida Oscar Esplá 30; mains €12-26; ⏱1-4.30pm & 8-11.30pm) This highly regarded restaurant is strong on rice, seafood and fish, which arrives fresh and daily from the wholesale markets of Denia and Santa Pola. There's a huge variety of tapas and a *valenciano* speciality that changes daily. It's a short walk west of the centre.

Cantina Villahelmy
VALENCIAN €€

(📞 965 21 25 29; Calle Mayor 37; mains €6-16; ⏱12.30-4pm & 8pm-midnight Tue-Sat, 12.30-4pm Sun, closed Tue & Wed nights winter) One wall's rough stone, another bright orange and blood red, and it's luridly painted with skeletons, creepy-crawlies and a frieze of classical figures. Intimate, funky and popular, this atmospheric cellar-like space has lots of snacks, excellent salads and a menu that features dishes from couscous to octopus as well as a fair helping of rice-based dishes.

Pesca al Peso
SEAFOOD €€

(📞 965 98 13 72; www.pescaalpeso.es; Calle Mayor 22; 2-person set menu €26-35; ⏱noon-5pm & 7pm-1am; 🕤) When people hand out restaurant flyers on the street, it's normally run-a-mile time, but this is an exception. It's simply decorated and simple to understand: choose your seafood by weight from the counter, or go for one of the decent-value set menus for two. It also does rices and has some outdoor tables.

🍷 Drinking & Nightlife

Wet your night-time whistle in the wall-to-wall bars of the Barrio, or historic quarter, around Catedral de San Nicolás. Alternatively, head for the sea. Paseo del Puerto, tranquil by day, is a double-decker line of casino, restaurants, bars and nightclubs.

Desdén
BAR

(Calle de los Labradores 22; ⏱11am-3am) This early opener is a friendly place to kick off the evening that gets loud and packed later.

Desafinado
CLUB

(www.facebook.com/desafinadoalicante; Calle Santo Tomás 6; ⏱11pm-3.30am Thu-Fri, 7pm-3.30am Sat) In the heart of the nightlife zone is this heaving dance bar in an old stone building, but with modern beats.

MareaRock
BAR

(www.marearockbar.com; Calle Virgen de Belén 21; ⏱11pm-4am Thu-Sat) A friendly, bohemian atmosphere and good rock and metal sounds.

ℹ Information

Municipal Tourist Office (📞 965 20 00 00; www.alicanteturismo.com; Rambla Méndez Núñez 41; ⏱10am-6pm Mon-Fri, to 2pm Sat) Extended hours in summer. There are also branches at the train station and airport.

ℹ Getting There & Away

AIR

Alicante's El Altet airport, gateway to the Costa Blanca, is around 12km southwest of the city centre. It's served by budget airlines, charters and scheduled flights from all over Europe.

BUS

From the new bus station destinations include:

TO	PRICE (€)	DURATION (HR)	FREQUENCY (PER DAY)
Barcelona	47	7-9	8
Madrid	31	5	7
Murcia	6.11	1	11-17
Valencia	21	2½	18-21

TRAM & TRAIN

The coastal tram service is a handy option: see the TRAM (www.fgvalicante.com) website. Scenic line 1 heads to Benidorm and on to Denia. Catch it from beside the covered market.

Mainline destinations from the principal train station include the following. For Murcia, there are also very regular *cercanía* trains (€5.70, 1¼ hours) via Elche and Orihuela.

TO	PRICE (€)	DURATION (HR)	FREQUENCY (PER DAY)
Barcelona	58	5	8
Madrid	65	2½	9
Murcia	9.35-18	1	5
Valencia	20-30	1½-2	11

ℹ Getting Around

Bus C-6 (€2.90, 30 minutes, every 20 minutes) runs between Plaza Puerta del Mar and the airport, passing by the north side of the bus station. Special 'resort buses' also run direct from the airport to resort towns up and down the coast. There are numerous car-rental offices at the airport.

Isla de Tabarca

A trip to Tabarca, around 20km south of Alicante as the seagull flies, makes for a pleasant day trip – as much for the boat ride itself as for the island, which heaves with tourists in summer. Pack your towel, mask and snorkel: you'll enjoy some great underwater viewing in permitted areas. There are a few lodging options and campsites on the island if you want to stay.

In summer, daily boats visit the island from Alicante, Benidorm and Torrevieja, and there are less-regular sailings year-round.

Torrevieja

POP 105,210

Torrevieja, set on a wide coastal plain between two lagoons, one pink, one emerald, is a through-and-through resort town with a large, mainly British and Russian, expat population. The beaches are good and in summer the nightlife fairly busy, but the town itself lacks a little soul. Salt production remains an important element of its economy.

◉ Sights & Activities

Museo del Mar y de la Sal MUSEUM
(Calle Patricio Pérez 10; ⊘10am-2pm & 5-9pm Wed-Sat, 10am-2pm Sun-Tue) FREE An appealing clutter of mementoes and bric-a-brac, this museum helps you appreciate why salt still means so much to *torreviejenses*.

Museos Flotantes BOATS
(admission €2; ⊘10am-2pm Wed-Sun) Anchored at the dock are a submarine and an old customs boat, both of which you can clamber aboard to explore. Onshore alongside are various other vessels, and an array of nautical and naval museum pieces. Closed if raining.

Marítimas Torrevieja BOAT TRIP
(www.maritimastorrevieja.com; adult/child 5-10 yr €22/10; ⊘Tue-Thu & Sat) Offers day trips to Isla de Tabarca leaving from near the tourist office.

⌂ Sleeping

Considering how touristy Torrevieja is there's surprisingly little in the way of hotel-style accommodation. Most people are here on a package with prebooked self-catering rooms in apartment blocks.

Hotel Cano HOTEL €
(☑966 70 09 58; www.hotelcano.com; Calle Zoa 53; s/d €40/60; P❄️🛜) Offering great value for its simple, pleasant rooms, this makes a top, central, budget base. In summer the price drops to €45 for a double if you stay more than one night. A selection of rooms have balconies, and wi-fi works better in some than others, so specify when booking.

Fontana Plaza HOTEL €€
(☑966 92 89 25; www.hotelfontanaplaza.com; Calle Rambla Juan Mateo 19; s/d €75/85; P❄️@🛜🏊) This is a classic white minimalist-style, business-class hotel with king-sized doubles and balconies. Some rooms interconnect for families. A few 'economy' rooms have smaller beds and no balcony. There are a few issues like noise between rooms but rates are surprisingly low, and it has a great location in the town centre and just back from the beach. Skip breakfast and find a brew elsewhere.

✗ Eating

Plenty of restaurants around the waterfront offer cheap meals and international menus, though the quality is generally low.

Bahía SPANISH €€
(☑965 71 39 94; www.bahiarestaurante.es; Avenida de la Libertad 3; mains €12-22; ⊘1-4pm & 9pm-midnight) Offering an ample range of fresh seafood, and well-prepared meat dishes with sweet sauces, this traditionally run, but modern-styled place channels sweet-and-savoury traditions from past Mediterranean civilisations. The comfy filing-cabinet chairs, the thoughtful extras like a complimentary vermouth to get you started, and the helpful service make this an oasis among the kebab/fried-fish desert.

Barlovento SEAFOOD €€
(☑966 92 11 82; www.restaurantebarlovento.com; Calle del Cabo 8; mains €12-22; ⊘1.30-4pm & 8pm-midnight) Decked out like the stateroom of a baroque galleon, and with an outdoor terrace overlooking the water, this place, 3km east of the centre, is one of Torrevieja's best-positioned restaurants. Seafood is the way to go here; it's also a nice spot to drop by for a wine and tapa at the bar during a coastal walk.

ℹ Information

Tourist Office (☑ 96 570 34 33; www.turismo-detorrevieja.com; Plaza de Capdepont; ⊙9am-7pm or 8pm Mon-Fri, 10am-2pm Sat) By the marina in the centre of town.

ℹ Getting There & Away

From the **bus station** (Calle Antonio Machado), **Costa Azul** (www.costazul.net) runs seven to 13 buses daily to Alicante (€4.45, one hour), six daily to Cartagena (€4.50, 1½ hours), and two to five to Murcia, with increased services in summer.

INLAND FROM THE COSTA BLANCA

The borderline between the holiday *costa* and the interior is, perhaps appropriately, a motorway. Venture away from the Med, west of the AP7, to find yourself in a different, truly Spanish world. By far the easiest way to explore this hinterland is with your own transport.

Xàtiva

POP 29,400

Xàtiva (Spanish: Játiva) makes an easy and rewarding 50km day trip from Valencia or a stop on the way north or south. It has a small historic quarter and a mighty castle strung along the crest of the Serra Vernissa, at whose base the town snuggles.

The Muslims established Europe's first paper manufacturing plant in Xàtiva, which is also famous as the birthplace of the Borgia Popes Calixtus III and Alexander VI. The town's glory days ended in 1707 when Felipe V's troops torched most of the town.

◉ Sights

★**Castillo**   CASTLE
(adult/child €2.40/1.20; ⊙10am-6pm or 7pm Tue-Sun) Xàtiva's castle, which clasps to the summit of a double-peaked hill overlooking the old town, is arguably the most evocative and interesting in all the Valencia region. Today, behind its crumbling battlements you'll find a mixture of flower gardens (bring a picnic), tumbledown turrets, towers and other buildings, and an excellent museum on medieval life. The walk up to the castle is a long one, but the views are sensational.

If you think it's big today, imagine what it must have looked like 300 years ago at full size. Sadly, an earthquake in 1748 badly damaged it and it never really recovered.

On the way up, on your left is the 18th-century **Ermita de San José** and to the right, the lovely Romanesque **Iglesia de Sant Feliu** (1269), Xàtiva's oldest church. You'll also pass by the very battered remains of part of the old **Muslim town**. A **tourist train** zips up the hill a couple of times a day from the tourist office.

🛏 Sleeping & Eating

★**Mont Sant**   HOTEL €€
(☑962 27 50 81; www.mont-sant.com; Subida al Castillo; r €104-114; ⊙Feb-Dec; P❀🐾🛜🛖) Enthusiastic management make for a wonderful stay at this enchanting place, set amid city walls, the ruins of a convent and palm and citrus gardens between the old town and the castle. It feels as if it's way out in the countryside rather than just a few min-

---

MOROS Y CRISTIANOS

More than 80 towns and villages in the south of Valencia hold their own **Fiesta de Moros y Cristianos** (Moors and Christians Festival) to celebrate the Reconquista, the region's liberation from Muslim rule.

Biggest and best known is in the town of Alcoy (22 to 24 April), when hundreds of locals dress up in elaborate traditional costumes representing different 'factions' – Muslim and Christian soldiers, slaves, guild groups, town criers, heralds, bands – and march through the streets in colourful processions with mock battles.

Processions converge upon Alcoy's main square and its huge, temporary wooden fortress. It's an exhilarating spectacle of sights and sounds.

Each town has its own variation on the format, steeped in traditions that allude to the events of the Reconquista. So, for example, Villena's festival (5 to 9 September) features midnight parades, while La Vila Joiosa (24 to 31 July), near Benidorm, re-enacts the landing of Muslim ships on the beaches. Some are as early as February, so you've a good chance of coinciding with one whenever you visit the region.

utes' walk from town. Stay in the beautifully adapted main building or in one of the spacious modern wood-faced cabins.

All have balcony/terrace spaces and there's a good restaurant. Make sure they show you the amazing medieval cistern.

Casa la Abuela VALENCIAN **€€** (☑ 962 28 10 85; www.casalaabuela.es; Calle de la Reina 17; mains €12-20; ☉ 1.30-4pm & 8.30-11pm Mon-Sat, 1.30-4pm Sun) Renowned for its rice dishes, 'Grandmother's House' is equally strong on meat options. It's more formal than you might imagine granny's place to be.

❶ Information

Tourist Office (☑ 96 227 33 46; www.xativa-turismo.com; Alameda Jaime I 50; ☉ 10am-2pm Tue-Fri, 10.15am-1.30pm Sat & Sun) On the Alameda, Xàtiva's shady main avenue. Hours extend in summer.

❶ Getting There & Away

Frequent *cercanía* trains on line C2 connect Xàtiva with Valencia (€4.30, 40 minutes, half-hourly) and most Valencia–Madrid trains stop here too; though these are more expensive. You can also reach Alicante (€12.20 to €22.30, 1¼ hours, seven daily) from here.

Villena

POP 34,830

Villena, between Alicante and Albacete, is the most attractive of the towns along the corridor of the Val de Vinalopó.

Plaza de Santiago is at the heart of its old quarter. Within the imposing 16th-century town hall is Villena's **Museo Arqueológico** (www.museovillena.com; Plaza de Santiago 1; adult/child €2/1; ☉ 10am-2pm Tue-Fri, 11am-2pm Sat & Sun). There are some magnificent pieces in the normal collection, even before you get to the stunning late Bronze Age treasure hoards, with a series of bowls, bracelets and brooches made from solid gold.

Perched high above the town, the 12th-century **Castillo de Atalaya** (adult/child €3/1.50; ☉ guided tours 10am-noon, 3.30pm-4.30pm Tue-Fri, 11am-1pm, 3.30-4.30pm Sat, 11am-1pm Sun) is splendidly lit at night. Entrance is by guided visit, in Spanish with English summary.

Hotel Restaurante Salvadora (☑ 965 80 09 50; www.hotelsalvadora.com; Av de la Constitución 102; s/d/tw €43/60/66; [P][※][☎]) is the town's sole hotel, featuring simple, clean, well-priced rooms; a popular bar with a great range of tapas; and a **restaurant** (menus €11-19; ☉ 6am-1am) that does a mean *triguico picao*, the local speciality – a stew of wheat, beans, pork and turnip. It's on the main road through town.

The **tourist office** (☑ 966 150 236; www.turismovillena.com; Plaza de Santiago 5; ☉ 9am-2pm Mon-Fri, 11am-2pm Sat & Sun) sells tickets for the town's attractions as does the interpretation centre near the castle.

Nine trains run daily between Alicante and Villena (€6 to €12, 40 minutes); there are also Valencia services. Buses serve both these cities too.

Guadalest

POP 240

You'll be far from the first to discover the village of Guadalest; coaches, heading up from the Costa Blanca resorts, disgorge millions of visitors yearly. But get there early, or stay around after the last bus has pulled out, and the place will be almost your own.

Crowds come because Guadalest, reached by a natural tunnel and overlooked by the **Castillo de San José** (adult/child €3/1.50; ☉ 10.15am-6pm), is indeed very pretty, with stunning views down the valley to the sea, and over a turquoise reservoir below. The ruined castle, perched on a rock, offers the best vistas. To reach it you pass through **Casa Orduña**, a beautiful village house with its original 18th-century furnishings. Entrance is included.

There are half a dozen or so other novelty museums, including the completely bonkers **Museo de Saleros y Pimenteros** (www.museodesalerosypimenteros.es; adult/child €3/1; ☉ 11am-6pm or later), which is a museum of salt and pepper pots: over 20,000 of them.

If you want to stay the night, there is one option that is worth travelling a very long way for. **Cases Noves** (☑ 965 88 53 09; www.casesnoves.es; s/d/superior incl breakfast €85/95/122; [※][@][☎]) is a *casa rural* (village or farmstead accommodation) run by local lass Sofia and her husband, Toni, but put simply they've taken the B&B thing to a whole new level and made a place to stay and eat that is close to perfect. The thoughtfully designed bedrooms come with fresh flowers; you can also relax in the reading room, the film room or the adjacent music room. In winter, toast your toes by the open fireplace; in summer, savour the gorgeous terrace with its views of the distant sea and

EXPLORE THE VALLEYS

Lovely though Guadalest is, it's very touristy. But the parallel valleys to the north of here are much less visited. Head on past Guadalest and follow your nose into the Vall del Pop or the Vall de Ebo. There's some wild country, picturesque villages, and solid game-based mountain food to be had.

the village illuminated at night. The owners give advice on local sights and the splendid opportunities for hill walking and cycling (they'll rent you a bike, too). But the real clincher for this place is the food. The three-course evening meals (€22) are fantastic, but if you can, time your arrival to coincide with the 10-course Saturday-evening affair (€28) – absolutely fabulous!

Buses run from Benidorm to Guadalest. If you drive, you'll be charged €2 to park.

Elche

POP 230,220

Precisely 23km southwest of Alicante, Elche (Valenciano: Elx) is, thanks to Moorish irrigation, an important fruit producer and also a Unesco World Heritage site twice over: for the *Misteri d'Elx,* its annual mystery play, and for its marvellous, extensive palm groves, Europe's largest, originally planted by the Phoenicians. The palms, the mosque-like churches, and the historic buildings in desert-coloured stone give it a North African feel.

◉ Sights

Around 200,000 palm trees, each with a lifespan of some 250 years, make the heart of this busy industrial town a veritable oasis. A signed 2.5km walking trail (ask at the tourist office for the leaflet) leads from the Museu del Palmerar through those palm groves.

★ Huerto del Cura   GARDENS
(www.huertodelcura.com; Calle Porta de la Morera 49; adult/child €5/2.50, audioguide €2; ◎10am-sunset) In the Islamic world, a garden is considered a form of Paradise. Elche's past and culture couldn't therefore be any more obvious than in these privately owned gardens where humanity and nature have joined forces to produce something that truly ap-

proaches that ideal. The highlights are the water features and the cactus gardens. It closes at 3pm Sunday in winter.

Museo Arqueológico y de
Historia de Elche   MUSEUM
(MAHE; Calle Diagonal del Palau 7; adult/child €3/free, Sun free; ◎10am-6pm Mon-Sat, to 3pm Sun) This museum is a superb introduction to the town's long and eventful history. Everything is particularly well displayed and labelled, and it occupies both a purpose-built building and the town's castle.

Museu del Palmerar   MUSEUM
(Porta de la Morera 12; adult/child €1/free; ◎10am-2pm & 3-6pm Tue-Sat, 10am-2pm Sun) In a former farmhouse, this museum is all about the date palm and the intricate blanched, woven fronds used throughout Spain in Palm Sunday rites. Wander through the delightful adjacent palm grove and orchard with its gurgling irrigation channels and typical fruit trees of the *huerta* (area of market gardens).

Basílica de Santa María   CHURCH
(◎7am-1pm & 5.30-9pm) **FREE** This vast baroque church is used for performances of the *Misteri d'Elx*. Climb up its tower (adult/child €2/1, 11am-7pm Jun-Sep, 11am-2pm & 3.30-5pm Oct-May) for a sweeping, pigeon's-eye view over the palms.

L'Alcúdia   RUINS, MUSEUM
(www.lalcudia.ua.es; Ctra de Dolors, Km 1.7; adult/child €5/2; ◎10am-8pm Tue-Sat, to 5pm Sat Oct-Mar) This well-documented site is 3.5km south of the town centre. The *Dama de Elche* was unearthed here, a masterpiece of Iberian art that's now in Madrid. Entry includes the excellent archaeological museum, displaying rich findings from a settlement occupied continuously from Neolithic to late-Visigoth times.

⭤ Sleeping

Hotel Huerto del Cura   BOUTIQUE HOTEL €€
(✆966 61 00 11; www.hotelhuertodelcura.com; Porta de la Morera 14; r €90-113; [P][✳][@][✆][✉][♣]) This is a sublime hotel, with stylish white rooms and antique wooden furnishings. The accommodation is in trim bungalows within lush, palm-shaded gardens. It's a family-friendly place with a playground, large pool and babysitting service. Complete the cosseting at Elche's longest-standing luxury hotel by dining in Els Capellans, its renowned restaurant. It has another, slightly

MISTERI D'ELX

The *Misteri d'Elx*, a two-act lyric drama dating from the Middle Ages, is performed annually in Elche's Basílica de Santa María.

One distant day, according to legend, a casket was washed up on Elche's Mediterranean shore. Inside was a statue of the Virgin and the *Consueta*, the music and libretto of a mystery play describing Our Lady's death, assumption into heaven and coronation.

The story tells how the Virgin, realising that death is near, asks God to allow her to see the Apostles one last time. They arrive one by one from distant lands and, in their company, she dies at peace. Once received into paradise, she is crowned Queen of Heaven and Earth to swelling music, the ringing of bells, cheers all round and spectacular fireworks.

The mystery's two acts, *La Vespra* (the eve of her death) and *La Festa* (the celebration of her assumption and coronation), are performed in Valenciano by the people of Elche on 14 and 15 August respectively (with public rehearsals on the three previous days).

You can see a multimedia presentation – complete with virtual Apostle – in the **Museu de la Festa** (Carrer Major de la Vila 25; adult/child €3/1.50; ⊘10am-2pm & 3-6pm Tue-Sat, 10am-2pm Sun), about a block west of the basilica. The show lasts 35 minutes and is repeated several times daily, with optional English commentary.

less stately, but also palm-surrounded, property nearby, **Hotel Milenio** (☑966 61 20 33; www.hotelmilenio.com; Calle Curtidores; r €78; P✳@🛜🏊).

✖ Eating

Carrer Mare de Déu del Carmé has a cluster of cheap and cheerful eateries. On summer evenings almost the whole length of this short street is set with tables.

★ El Granaino SPANISH €€
(☑966 66 40 80; www.mesongranaino.com; Carrer Josep María Buck 40; mains €14-22; ⊘9.30am-4pm & 8pm-midnight Mon-Sat; 🛜) Across the river from the centre, it's worth the 10-minute walk to get to this place, where the bar is lined with people scarfing down a quick, quality lunch. Top seafood, delicious stews and a fine range of tapas showcase a classic, quintessentially Spanish cuisine. Fuller meals can be enjoyed outside or in the adjacent dining room. Excellent service and quality.

Dátil de Oro VALENCIAN €€
(☑966 45 34 15; www.datildeoro.com; set menus €15-31; ⊘9am-11pm; 🛜) Within the municipal park, the Golden Date is a vast emporium to eating that can accommodate almost 800 diners. Even so, the cuisine is far from institutional and it's one of the best places in town to sample local dishes, such as *arroz con costra* (rice with a crusty egg topping); also date flan and even date ice cream.

ℹ Information

Tourist Office (☑966 65 81 96; www.visitelche.com; Plaza Parque 3; ⊘9am-6pm Mon-Fri, 10am-6pm Sat, 10am-2pm Sun) At the southeast corner of Parque Municipal (Town Park).

ℹ Getting There & Around

Elche is on the Alicante–Murcia *cercanía* train line. About 20 trains daily rattle through, bound for Alicante (€2.65) or Murcia (€3.65) via Orihuela (€2.65). The train and bus stations are beside each other on Avenida de la Libertad (Avenida del Ferrocarril).

From the bus station, destinations include the following:

TO	PRICE (€)	DURATION	FREQUENCY
Alicante	2.20	35min	every ½ hr
Murcia	4.49	45min-2hr	12-13 daily
Valencia	13	2½-4hr	9-10 daily

MURCIA

POP 438,250

Officially twinned with Miami, Murcia is the antithesis of the city of vice; it's a laid-back provincial capital that comes alive during the weekend *paseo* (stroll). Bypassed by most tourists and treated as a country cousin by many Spaniards, the city nevertheless more than merits a visit.

In AD 825 Muslims moved into the former Roman colony and renamed it Mursiya. The town was reconquered in 1243 by Alfonso X

Murcia City

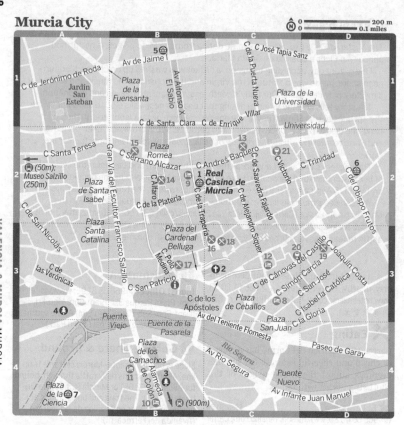

Murcia City

◎ Top Sights

◎ Sights

⬤ Sleeping

⊗ Eating

◎ Drinking & Nightlife

and it's said his shrivelled heart is preserved within the cathedral's altar. Enriched by silk and agriculture, the city was at its grandest in the 18th century, from when the cathedral's magnificent baroque facade dates.

Looted by Napoleonic troops in 1810, and then overcome by plague and cholera, the city fell into decline. A century later, Murcia was the scene of bitter civil-war fighting and many churches were destroyed.

⊙ Sights

Catedral de Santa María CATHEDRAL

(Plaza del Cardenal Belluga; ⊙7am-1pm & 6-8pm daily, to 9pm Sat & Sun Jul-Aug, 7am-1pm & 5-8pm Tue-Sat, 10am-1pm Sun Sep-Jun) FREE Murcia's cathedral was built in 1394 on the site of a mosque. The initial Gothic architecture was given a playful baroque facelift in 1748, with a stunning facade facing on to Plaza Belluga. The 15th-century Capilla de los Vélez is a highlight; the chapel's flutes and curls resemble icing. The Museo de la Catedral (adult/child €3/2; ⊙9am-3pm Tue-Sat, 10am-1pm Sun Jul–mid-Sep, 10am-1pm & 4-7pm Tue-Sat, 10am-1pm Sun mid-Sep–Jun) displays religious artefacts, but is most striking for the excavations on display: the remains of an 11th-century Moorish dwelling and of a small *mezquita* (mosque), visible below a glass walkway.

★Real Casino de Murcia HISTORIC BUILDING

(www.casinodemurcia.com; Calle de la Trapería 18; adult/child €5/3; ⊙10.30am-7pm) Murcia's resplendent casino first opened as a gentlemen's club in 1847. Painstakingly restored to its original glory, the building is a fabulous combination of historical design and opulence, providing an evocative glimpse of bygone aristocratic grandeur. Beyond the decorative facade are a dazzling Moorish-style patio; a classic English-style library with 20,000 books, some dating from the 17th century; a magnificent ballroom with glittering chandeliers; and a compelling *tocador* (ladies powder room) with a ceiling fresco of cherubs, angels and an alarming winged woman in flames. There is also the neoclassical *patio pompeyano* (Pompeiian courtyard) and the classic wood-panelled *sala de billar* (billiards room).

Museo Arqueológico MUSEUM

(www.museoarqueologicomurcia.com; Avenida Alfonso X El Sabio 7; ⊙10am-2pm Tue-Fri, 11am-2pm Sat & Sun Jul-Aug, 10am-2pm & 5-8pm Tue-Fri, 11am-2pm & 5-8pm Sat, 11am-2pm Sun Sep-Jun) FREE Murcia's archaeological museum has exceptionally well laid-out and documented exhibits, spread over two floors, that start with Palaeolithic times and include audio-visual displays.

CITY PARKS

If you are visiting during midsummer, escape the blazing heat by visiting one of Murcia's lovely parks. The classic, small but beautiful **Jardín Floridablanca** has several magnificent banyan trees distinctive for their massive spread of thick woody roots, as well as jacarandas, Cyprus trees, palms, rose bushes and shady benches, plenty of them, for contemplating the view. A larger park and botanical garden, **Murcia Parque** (Jardín Botánico) lies just west of the Puente del Malecón footbridge and is similarly replete with leafy splendour.

Museo de Bellas Artes GALLERY

(Calle del Obispo Frutos 12; ⊙11am-2pm Tue-Sun Jul-Aug, 10am-2pm & 5-8pm Tue-Fri, 11am-2pm & 5-8pm Sat, 11am-2pm Sun Sep-Jun) FREE An inviting, light gallery devoted to Spanish artists. Much is mediocre, but the 2nd-floor Siglo de Oro gallery has two fabulous Murillos – a Crucifixion and an Ecce Homo – and a powerful chiaroscuro San Jerónimo by Ribera. Look out for the faintest shadow of his tame lion. The 3rd floor holds temporary exhibitions.

Museo de la Ciencia y del Agua MUSEUM

(Plaza de la Ciencia 1; adult/child €1.50/1; ⊙10am-2pm & 5-8pm Mon-Fri mid-Jun–Aug, 10am-2pm & 4.30-7pm Tue-Sat, 11am-2pm Sun Sep–mid-Jun; 🖝) Beside the river and one for the children. Although everything's in Spanish, this small hands-on science museum has plenty of buttons to press and knobs to twirl, plus fish tanks and a small planetarium.

Museo Salzillo MUSEUM

(www.museosalzillo.es; Plaza de San Agustín 1-3; admission €3; ⊙10am-2pm Mon-Fri mid-Jun–mid-Sep, 10am-8pm Mon-Sat, 11am-2pm Sun mid-Sep–mid-Jun) Located in the baroque chapel of Ermita de Jesús and devoted to Murcian sculptor Francisco Salzillo (1707–83). Highlights are his exquisite *pasos* (figures carried in Semana Santa processions) and nativity figurines. To get here head west from Gran Vía del Escultor Francsico Salzillo along Calle Santa Teresa.

✲ Festivals & Events

Semana Santa   HOLY WEEK

The city's Easter processions rival Lorca's in their fervour.

Bando de la Huerta   SPRING FESTIVAL

Two days after Easter Sunday, the mood changes as the city celebrates this annual spring festival with parades, food stalls, folklore and carafe-fulls of fiesta spirit.

🛏 Sleeping

The range of accommodation in Murcia is fairly limited – most hotels are chain affairs – but prices are very low.

Cathedral Hostel   HOSTEL €

(☑ 968 93 00 07; www.thecathedralhostel.com; Calle de la Trapería 19; incl breakfast dm €15-20, tw €29; @🛜) This perfectly located hostel has bright comfortable rooms and nice tilework on the walls and floors. Dorms have from four to 10 berths, so it's worth a little upgrade for less crowding. Private rooms are a great deal. There's a communal kitchen and common bathrooms.

Pensión Segura   HOSTAL €

(☑ 968 21 12 81; www.pensionsegura.es; Plaza de Camachos 14; r €35; ✳🛜) Just across a bridge from the heart of town, this makes for a fine budget base. Staff go the extra mile to make you feel welcome, and the rooms are decent and clean, though bathrooms are tiny.

Hotel Casa Emilio   HOTEL €

(☑ 988 22 06 31; www.hotelcasaemilio.com; Alameda de Colón 9; s/d €33/40; ✳🛜) Across from Jardín Floridablanca, near the river, this well-maintained hotel is run by helpful people and has spacious, brightly lit rooms and good firm mattresses. There's a small charge for wi-fi.

Arco de San Juan   HOTEL €€

(☑ 968 21 04 55; www.arcosanjuan.com; Plaza de Ceballos 10; d €55-75; P✳🛜) In a former 18th-century palace this hotel hints at its past with a massive 5m-high original door and some hefty repro columns. The rooms are classic and comfortable, with hardwood details and classy fabrics, and the low prices and top location are a big plus.

Tryp Rincón de Pepe   HOTEL €€

(☑ 968 21 22 39; www.tryphotels.com; Calle de los Apóstoles 34; r €60-100; P✳@🛜) Acres of marble lobby greet guests at this corporate-style hotel. Rooms are spacious with large

TAPAS IN MURCIA

Murcia is excellent for tapas, with plenty of variety, generous portions and a considerable vegetarian choice for non-carnivorous folk. Most of the restaurants listed in this chapter are fronted by tapas bars or serve *raciones* (large/full-plate-size tapas servings; literally 'rations'), which are great for sharing. Overall, Murciano tapas are more inventive than the norm and reflect the province's comprehensive agriculture with their use of fresh seasonal ingredients.

luxurious bathrooms and should have been spruced up by the time you read this. The facilities and location are both pleasing; there's a small casino here as well.

🍴 Eating

Murcia has some excellent eating, with a vibrant old-town tapas scene.

Los Zagales   SPANISH €

(www.barloszagalesmurcia.com; Calle Polo Medina 4; dishes €3-12; ⏱9.30am-4pm & 7pm-midnight) Lying within confessional distance of the cathedral, Los Zagales dishes up superb, inexpensive tapas, *raciones, platos combinados* (mixed platters) and homemade chips and desserts. It's locally popular so you may have to wait for a table. It's worth it.

Salmentum   DELI €

(Plaza de la Cruz; tapas €2-5; ⏱10am-9pm Mon-Sat, 11am-3pm Sun) By the cathedral, this has a great selection of salted-fish products. Sit down and try the delicious *mojama* (dried tuna) with a glass of wine.

Alborada   MODERN SPANISH €€

(☑ 968 23 23 23; www.alboradarestaurante.com; Calle Andrés Baquero 15; mains €15-22; ⏱1-4.30pm & 8.30-11.30pm Mon-Sat, 1-4.30pm Sun) This is a very discreet restaurant that you could easily pass by thinking it was merely another so-so place to eat, but in fact, this is one of the most talked-about restaurants in town. And with good reason! Its dishes are gourmet variations on traditional specialities and it also has a small but impressive tapas list.

El Jardín de Oli   SPANISH €€

(☑ 968 24 22 00; www.facebook.com/eljardindeoli; Calle Alfaro 12; mains €10-18; ⏱9.45am-4pm Mon-

ORIHUELA

Beside the Río Segura and flush with the base of a barren mountain of rock, the historical heart of Orihuela, with superb Gothic, Renaissance and, especially, baroque buildings, well merits a detour. The old town is strung out between the river and a mountain topped by a ruined castle. The main sights are dotted along it, more or less in a line.

A few of the buildings are particularly worth looking out for. The **Convento de Santo Domingo** (Calle Adolfo Claravana; admission €2; ⊙9.30am-1.30pm & 4-7pm or 5-8pm Tue-Sat, 10am-2pm Sun) is a 16th-century convent with two fine Renaissance cloisters and a refectory clad in 18th-century tilework. One of the town's splendid ecclesiastical buildings is the 14th-century Catalan Gothic **Catedral de San Salvador** (Calle Doctor Sarget; ⊙10.30am-2pm & 4-6.30pm Tue-Fri, 10.30am-2pm Sat) FREE, with its three finely carved portals and a lovely little cloister. The Renaissance facade of **Iglesia de las Santas Justa y Rufina** (Plaza Salesas 1; ⊙10am-1pm & 4-6pm Mon-Fri) FREE is worth admiring, its Gothic tower graced with gargoyles.

Also noteworthy are the mainly 14th-century **Iglesia de Santiago Apóstol** (Plaza de Santiago 2; ⊙10am-1pm & 4-6pm Mon-Fri, 10am-1pm Sat), with an impressive Gothic facade and a more extrovert baroque portal alongside, and the **Murales San Isidro**, a *barrio* (district) decorated with dozens of murals by well-known artists. Ask for the leaflet from the helpful **tourist office** (☑965 30 46 45; www.orihuelaturistica.es; Plaza de la Soledad; ⊙8am-2pm or 3pm Mon, 10am-2pm or 3pm and 4-7pm or 5-8pm Tue-Sat, 10am-2pm or 3pm Sun).

Orihuela has a vibrant **Moros y Cristianos festival** in mid-July, and reprises the atmosphere with an enormous medieval market at the end of January.

Fri, plus 8.30-11.30pm Thu & Fri, 1.30-4.30pm & 8.30-11.30pm Sat; 🐾) Cheerful, colourful and family-run, this place is immediately likeable and doesn't disappoint on the food front either. Tasty salads, quality meat and whatever's fresh from the market that day make it a winner. On weekdays a €10 lunch is available: a bargain.

La Tienda de Susano　TAPAS €€
(www.facebook.com/latiendadesusano; Calle de la Trapería 2; tapas €1.50-5; ⊙10am-midnight Mon-Thu, 10.30am-midnight Fri-Sun; 🐾) It's always tough to find elbow room at the bar at this deservedly popular place, so try for an outdoor table on the cathedral square. It specialises in seafoody tapas – delicious anchovies are a given, as are *ortiguillas* (sea anemones): tastier than you'd think.

La Lechera de Burdeos　DELI €€
(www.lalecheradeburdeos.com; Plaza Julián Romea 6; plates €5-15; ⊙10.30am-2.30pm & 5.30-9pm Mon-Thu, to 10pm Fri & Sat) This sweet little place is a shop selling delicious cheeses. In most civilised fashion, you can also sample them in-store, with a glass of wine.

Salzillo　SPANISH €€€
(☑968 22 01 94; www.restaurantesalzillo.com; Calle de Cánovas del Castillo 28; mains €18-24; ⊙1-6pm & 8pm-midnight Mon-Sat, 1-6pm Sun) Favoured by well-heeled conservative Murcians, this elegant but comfortable spot has a lively bar and truly excellent eating in its split-level restaurant area. Starters run to elaborate creations with local artichokes, and the quality of the meaty mains is sky-high: order *a la brasa* for the barbecue flavours.

🍷 Drinking & Nightlife

Most through-the-night life buzzes around the university.

Sala Revolver　CLUB
(www.facebook.com/salarevolver.murcia; Calle Victorio 36; ⊙10pm-late Wed-Sat) There are some vibrant bars and clubs around the university, including this one with its emphasis on Latin and Spanish rock.

★ **La Ronería y La Gintonería**　BAR
(www.la-roneria-y-la-gintoneria.com; Calle de Cánovas del Castillo 17; ⊙3pm-3am) A quite incredible selection of rum greets you on entering this excellent bar. There are some 700 available, with Caribbean travel videos playing to get you in the mood. Once you've tried them all, stagger up the stairs and start on the G&Ts. Hundreds of gins, dozens of tonics. And you.

ℹ️ Information

Tourist Office (📞968 358 749; www.murcia-turistica.es; Plaza del Cardenal Belluga; ⏰10am-7pm Mon-Sat, to 2pm Sun; @ 📶)

ℹ️ Getting There & Away

Murcia's San Javier airport is situated beside the Mar Menor, closer to Cartagena than Murcia. There are budget connections to the UK and other European nations.

At least 10 buses run daily to both Cartagena (€4.10, one hour) and Lorca (€5.70, 1½ hours).

Up to six trains travel daily to/from Madrid (€47, 4¼ hours). *Cercanía* trains run regularly to Alicante (€5.70, 1¼ hours) and Lorca (€5.70, 50 minutes).

ℹ️ Getting Around

From the bus station, take bus 3 into town; from the train station, hop aboard bus 9 or 39. A taxi between the airport and Murcia costs about €55.

MURCIA PROVINCE

The Murcia region offers a tantalising choice of landscapes and sights, ranging from the chill-out beaches of the Costa Cálida to the medieval magic of its towns and a wealth of reminders of the Roman empire. To appreciate fully the unspoiled hinterland, you will need your own wheels.

Cartagena

POP 217,640

Cartagena's fabulous natural harbour has been used for thousands of years. Stand on the battlements of the castle that overlooks this city and you can literally see layer upon layer of history spread below you. There is the wharf where Phoenician traders docked their ships; there is the street where Roman legionaries marched; there is the plaza that once housed a mosque where Islamic Spain prayed to Allah; there are the hills over which came the armies of the Christian Reconquista; and there are the factories of the industrial age, the Modernista buildings and the contemporary warships of what is still an important naval base. As archaeologists continue to reveal a long-buried – and fascinating – Roman and Carthaginian heritage, the city is finally starting to get the recognition it deserves as one of Spain's most historically fascinating places.

History

In 223 BC Hasdrubal marched his invading army into what had been the Iberian settlement of Mastia, refounding it as Qart Hadasht. The town prospered as Carthago Nova during Roman occupation and, under Muslim rule, became the independent emirate of Cartajana, finally reconquered by the Christians in 1242. Though badly bombed in the civil war, industry and the population flourished during the 1950s and '60s.

👁️ Sights

⭐ **Museo del Teatro Romano** MUSEUM, RUINS (www.teatroromanocartagena.org; Plaza del Ayuntamiento 9; adult/child €6/5; ⏰10am-6pm or 8pm Tue-Sat, to 2pm Sun) This super museum was designed by top Spanish architect Rafael Moneo. The tour transports visitors from the initial museum on Plaza del Ayuntamiento, via escalators and an underground passage beneath the ruined cathedral, to the magnificent, recently restored Roman theatre dating from the 1st century BC. The tour and layout of the museum are designed to reflect Cartagena's fascinating layers of urban history and include Roman statues and artefacts as well as the cathedral's crypt and remains of an original Moorish dwelling.

Roman Cartagena RUINS (www.cartagenapuertodeculturas.com) Other Roman sites can be visited around Murcia:

➡ **Barrio del Foro Romano**

(Calle Honda; adult/child €5/4; ⏰10am-5.30pm or 7pm Tue-Sun) This has evocative remains of a whole town block and street linking the port with the forum, and including an arcade and thermal baths. A recently excavated house preserves a courtyard and important fragments of wall paintings.

➡ **Casa de la Fortuna**

(Plaza Risueño; adult/child €2.50/2; ⏰10am-2.30pm or 3pm Tue-Sun mid-Mar–mid-Dec, Sat & Sun mid-Dec–mid-Mar) The Casa de la Fortuna consists of fascinating remains of an aristocratic Roman villa dating back to the 2nd and 3rd centuries, complete with murals and mosaics, and part of an excavated road.

➡ **Muralla Púnica**

(Calle de San Diego; adult/child €3.50/2.50; ⏰10am-5.30pm or 7pm Tue-Sun, plus Mon Jul–mid-Sep) The Muralla Púnica, built around a section of the old Punic wall, concentrates on the town's Carthaginian and Roman legacy. It also contains the tumbledown walls

ℹ MUSEUM PASS

Visiting all the different archaeological sites and museums – and there are a couple more we've not got space to include – in Cartagena can work out quite expensive. Fortunately help is at hand in the form of a variety of passes (admission to four/five/six museums adult €12/15/18, child €9/11.25/13.50) that provide cheaper admission. Passes are available from the tourist office or the sites themselves. The Museo del Teatro Romano counts as two museum entries.

of a 16th-century hermitage complete with tombs filled with human bones.

★ Museo Nacional de Arqueología Subacuática   MUSEUM
(ARQUA; http://museoarqua.mcu.es; Paseo del Muelle Alfonso XII 22; adult/child €3/free; ⊙10am-8pm or 9pm Tue-Sat, to 3pm Sun) This excellent, attractive space delves into the depths of the fascinating world of underwater archaeology. It starts off by explaining the work of underwater archaeologists and then sails on into the maritime history and culture of the Mediterranean. There's lots of old pots, flashy lights, buttons to press, films to watch and a replica Phoenician trading ship to marvel over. Free entry on Saturday afternoon and all day Sunday.

Modernista Cartagena   ARCHITECTURE
Cartagena is rich in Modernista buildings. Particularly magnificent are Casa Cervantes (Calle Mayor 11); Casa Llagostera (Calle Mayor 25); the zinc-domed Gran Hotel (Calle del Aire); the strawberries-and-cream confection of Casa Clares (Calle del Aire 4); and the splendid Palacio Aguirre (Plaza de la Merced), now an exhibition space for modern art (known as Muram).

Castillo de la Concepción   CASTLE
(adult/child €3.75/2.75; ⊙10am-5.30pm or 7pm Tue-Sun, plus Mon Jul–mid-Sep) For a sweeping panoramic view, stride up to Castillo de la Concepción, or hop on the lift (adult/child €2/1). Within the castle's gardens, decorated by strutting peacocks, the Centro de Interpretación de la Historia de Cartagena offers a mid-tech potted history of Cartagena through the centuries via audio screens and a 10-minute film (in English and Spanish).

Museo Arqueológico Municipal   MUSEUM
(Calle Ramón y Cajal 45; ⊙10am-2pm & 5-8pm Tue-Fri, 11am-2pm Sat & Sun) FREE Built above a late-Roman cemetery with a rich display of Carthaginian, Roman, Visigoth and Islamic artefacts. To get here, head northwest of the city centre, via Calle La Palma.

⚜ Festivals & Events

Semana Santa   HOLY WEEK
(www.semanasanta.cartagena.es) During Easter week Cartagena's haunting processions are as elaborate as anything Andalucía can offer.

La Mar de Músicas   WORLD MUSIC
(www.lamardemusicas.com) Bringing the best of world music to Cartagena, this annual festival is held in the castle's auditorium throughout July.

Carthagineses y Romanos   HISTORICAL
(www.cartaginesesyromanos.es) For 10 days during the second half of September, locals play war games in a colourful fiesta that re-enacts the battles between rival Carthaginian and Roman occupiers during the second Punic War.

🛌 Sleeping

Cartagena has few central hotels, and even fewer with any character.

Carlos III   HOTEL €
(📋968 52 00 32; www.carlosiiihotel.com; Calle Carlos III 49; s/d €50/55; 🅿 ✳ 🐾 @ 🤶) Modernisation has been undertaken by a fan of bright colours here, with subtlety gone out the window in a shower of reds, blues, greens and blacks. The beds could be comfier, but it's a good deal in a reasonably central location, and the rooms have plenty of space and reliable wi-fi. The sister hotel behind, Alfonso XIII, will be another good option after its scheduled refit.

Pensión Oriente   PENSIÓN €
(📋968 50 24 69; Calle Jara 27; s/d with shared bathroom €25/35; 🤶) Behind a Modernista facade in a central street, this offers simple, comfortable rooms in a noble building that preserves original features like colourful floor tiles and ceiling mouldings. It's by far Cartagena's most characterful option; helpful management make it a solid all-round choice. All but the spacious room with private bathroom (€40) have well-modernised shared bathrooms. Don't confuse it with a nearby bar, also numbered 27.

VALENCIA & MURCIA CARTAGENA

Hotel Los Habaneros HOTEL €

(968 50 52 50; www.hotelhabaneros.com; Calle de San Diego 60; s/d €50/55; P❄@🛜) Located across from the Muralla Púnica and near the bus station, this hotel is something of a bargain, with good-sized rooms decorated in cream and burgundy and good facilities if a slightly downbeat atmosphere. The better rooms are more modern, with balconies (€75).

✖ Eating

La Fuente TAPAS €

(www.facebook.com/bodegalafuente; Calle Jara 17; drink & tapa €1.80; ⏱9am-4pm & 7pm-midnight Mon-Sat, 11am-4pm Sun) Bright and busy, this place, which lives up to its name by indeed featuring a fountain, makes a top stop for a quick drink and a tapa. The speciality is anchovies, long and tasty, from the Bay of Biscay. Its sister bar opposite offers a similarly cheap drink-and-snack deal.

Techos Bajos SEAFOOD €€

(www.techosbajos.com; Calle Joaquín Madrid; dishes €7-16; ⏱9.30am-4pm Tue-Sun, plus 7pm-midnight Fri & Sat) Locals absolutely flood this large, no-frills kind of place at lunchtime for its well-priced portions of fresh fish and seafood. You'll find it down the hill from the bus station, right opposite the fishing port.

A La Brasa GRILL €€

(www.grupocasatomas.es; Plaza Juan XXIII; mains €11-25; ⏱10.30am-midnight; 🛜) One of a few places run by the same people in this picturesque small park, once the artillery HQ. It features an open kitchen and tables overlooking a small pond. Service is slow but willing, and it's good on the simple stuff – big steaks with a real grill flavour, good-value tapas portions, and tasty burgers.

❶ Information

Ayuntamiento Tourist Office (968 12 89 55; www.cartagenaturismo.es; Plaza del Ayuntamiento 1; ⏱10am-2pm & 4-6pm or 5-7pm Mon-Fri, 10am-1.30pm & 4-6pm or 5-7pm Sat, 10.30am-1.30pm Sun) Near the waterfront in the heart of town.

Muralla Tourist Office (968 50 64 83; www.cartagenaturismo.es; Calle San Diego 25; ⏱10am-5.30pm or 7pm Tue-Sun, plus Mon Jul–mid-Sep) Plenty of excellent information. In the Muralla Púnica complex.

❶ Getting There & Around

Buses run eight times daily to Alicante (€8.88, three hours), and roughly hourly to Murcia (€4.10, 45 minutes to 1¼ hours).

For Renfe train destinations, change in Murcia (€5.35, 50 minutes, four to seven daily). Beware: take the local train, as the Talgo express alternative costs a hefty €17.

A taxi to or from San Javier airport costs approximately €40.

Costa Cálida

With more than 300 days of annual sunshine and an average temperature of 18°C, the Costa Cálida (Hot Coast) is aptly named.

Mar Menor

The Mar Menor is a 170-sq-km saltwater lagoon. Its waters are a good 5°C warmer than the open sea and excellent for water sports, including jet-skiing, kitesurfing, kayaking and waterskiing. From the southern side juts La Manga (the Sleeve), a narrow 22km peninsula of land jutting out between lagoon and sea, overdeveloped with close-packed high-rise accommodation; the world would lose little if it one day cut loose and drifted away.

Cabo de Palos, at the peninsula's southern limit, is much nicer, with a picturesque small harbour filled with pleasure boats and surrounded by low-rise restaurants and holiday apartments. The waters around the tiny offshore (and protected) Islas Hormigas (Ant Islands) are great for scuba diving and the harbour is lined with dive shops.

At the northern end of the lagoon, Lo Pagán is a mellow, low-rise resort with great water views, a long promenade, a pleasant beach, and plenty of bars and restaurants. Get locals to show you where to walk out on jetties for natural mud treatments.

Just east of Lo Pagán lie the Salinas de San Pedro (salt pans), where you can follow

---

CUT-PRICE CAVIAR

A locally produced variant of caviar (huevas de mújol) is produced on the Mar Menor. It's available in jars in most local supermarkets at a very reasonable price compared to the real thing, but tastes very good. There's also a toothsome dried form.

a well-signposted *senda verde* (footpath). This relatively easy walk of just over 4km passes by several lagoons favoured by flocks of pink flamingos trawling for small fry.

Mazarrón

The rugged coast west of Cartagena is fretted with small coves and unspoilt beaches, best reached by car. Inland, where agricultural business prevails, the shimmering silver lakes turn out to be entire valleys sheathed in plastic where vegetables are force-grown in greenhouses for local and export markets.

If speed matters, take the AP7 toll motorway. Otherwise, opt for the more picturesque N332, which swoops and snakes through the coastal mountains. Both bring you to Mazarrón, a bustling, likeable resort with a port section and an inland centre. Head west of the centre for the best beaches, with diving, nudism and seafood on offer.

Águilas

Continuing on another 30km you come to low-key Águilas, with a slowish vibe and an older expat population. The waterfront in town is beautiful, and still shelters a small fishing fleet. Town beaches are divided from each other by a low headland topped by an 18th-century **fortress**. The real interest, though, are the **Cuatro Calas** a few kilometres south of town. These four coves are largely unmolested by tourist development (though they get very busy in summer) and have shimmering waters which merge into desert rock: about as perfect as you'll find on the Spanish Med coast.

🛌 Sleeping & Eating

The central options are disappointing, but if you've got wheels there are some top spots nearby. There's plenty of camping and an official hostel near the Cuatro Calas too. Eating options are strung out along the waterfront and mostly mediocre.

Hotel Mayari   HOTEL €€
(📞964 41 97 48; www.hotel-mayari.com; Calle Río de Janeiro 14, Calabardina; s/d incl breakfast €65/98; 🅿✳🛜) In the seaside settlement of Calabardina, 7km from Águilas, this villa offers exceptional hospitality among dry hillscapes. Rooms are all themed differently, with cool, fresh decor. Some have sea views, and there are brilliant home-cooked dinners available, as well as helpful hillwalking advice.

El Tiburón   SEAFOOD €€
(www.restaurantetiburon.es; Calle Iberia 8; mains €7-15; ⊙12.30-4pm & 7-11pm Tue-Sat, 1-4pm Sun) A cheerful bar-restaurant with more of a local feel than most, this is in the southwestern part of the centre, across a bridge on the main road through town. It does tasty fish tapas, good rices, and has an excellent-value €15 night-time set menu.

ℹ Information

Tourist Office (📞968 493 285; www.aguilas. es; Plaza Antonio Cortijos; ⊙9am-2pm & 5-7pm Mon-Fri, 10am-2pm & 5-7pm Sat, 10am-2pm Sun).

ℹ Getting There & Around

Lycar (www.lycar.es) buses go to Lorca (€3.40, one hour, three to 10 daily) and Murcia (€10, two hours, three to seven daily) as well as Almería. *Cercanía* trains on the C2 line run from Murcia (€7.85, 1¾ hours) via Lorca thrice daily.

Lorca

POP 92,720

The market town of Lorca has long been known for its pretty old town crowned by a 13th-century castle and for hosting one of Spain's most flamboyant Semana Santa (Holy Week) celebrations. In 2011 an earthquake struck here, leaving nine people dead, many injured and homeless, and causing significant damage to the town; the old town was particularly affected. Though some buildings are still closed, it's well worth visiting.

⊙ Sights

⭐**La Fortaleza del Sol**   CASTLE
(www.lorcatallerdeltiempo.com; adult/child €5/4; ⊙10.30am-dusk; 👶) The castle, high over the town, offers dioramas, actors in costume and various gadgetry. It's an impressive place. Two of the castle towers were damaged in the earthquake: you can see the scars on one and the other is yet to be restructured. Entry includes an audioguide; there are also various guided visits available within, including to a synagogue, and some specifically aimed at kids. A €10 entrance includes three guided trips.

★ **Plaza de España** NOTABLE BUILDINGS

The highlight of the old town is a group of baroque buildings around Plaza de España, including the **Pósito**, a 16th-century former granary; the 18th-century **Casa del Corregidor**; and the **town hall**. Lording over the square is the golden limestone **Colegiata de San Patricio**, a church with a handsome baroque facade and predominantly Renaissance interior. Although it looks good from the outside, it did suffer earthquake damage and is currently closed to the public.

Semana Santa Museums MUSEUMS

Peculiar to Lorca are various small museums exhibiting the magnificent Semana Santa costumes. Some cloaks are up to 5m in length and all are elaborately hand-embroidered in silk, depicting colourful religious and historical scenes. The **Museo de Bordados del Paso Azul** (www.pasoazul.com; Calle Nogalte 7; adult/child €2.50/2; ⊙10am-1.30pm & 5-7.30pm Mon-Fri, 10am-1.30pm Sat), competes in splendour with the **Museo de Bordados del Paso Blanco** (MUBBLA; www.mubbla.org; Calle Santo Domingo 8; adult/child €2.50/2; ⊙10.30am-2pm & 5-7.30pm Tue-Sat, 10.30am-2pm Sun), annexed to the church of Santo Domingo.

Casa de Guevara PALACE

(Calle Lope Gisbert 21; ⊙10am-2pm & 4-7pm or 5-7.30pm Tue-Sat, 10am-2pm Sun) The wonderful baroque facade of the 17th-century Casa de Guevara suffered serious earthquake damage but is now looking spruce again. The interior, with elegant patio and halls, is used for temporary exhibitions.

🛏 Sleeping & Eating

Jardines de Lorca HOTEL €

(☑968 47 05 99; www.hotelesdemurcia.com; Alameda de Rafael Méndez; r/superior €54/80;

P ✳ @ 🛜 ⊠) If you're normally travelling on a budget, Lorca is the sort of place where it's worth shelling out a little bit more and getting a whole lot more, and this large complex with a resort feel is exactly what you should be aiming for. It has slick, corporate-style rooms with excellent facilities, including a spa. The price is great. Parking included.

Pensión del Carmen PENSION €

(☑968 46 64 59; Rincón de los Valientes 3; s/d €25/50; ✳🛜) A sound budget choice. Cheerful and family-run, Carmen has seven doubles and seven singles, all spotless. You'll find it in a cul-de-sac just off Calle Nogalte.

Parador de Lorca PARADOR €€

(☑968 40 60 47; www.parador.es; Castillo de Lorca; s/d €70/85; P ✳ @ 🛜 ⊠) Memorably situated in the castle complex way above town, this modern *parador* still smells new. Rooms are tip-top, there's an indoor pool and spa and the views are just stunning. Various archaeological fragments are integrated into the hotel, including the ruins of a synagogue accessed via the car park. Expect prices to rise once it's been open a while.

Mesón la Bodeguica SPANISH €€

(☑649 908993; Calle Montero 4; mains €11-18; ⊙1-4pm & 8.30-11pm Mon-Sat, 1-4pm Sun) Tucked away on a small street in the pedestrian zone, this is a handy find in a town that is no gastro capital. Tasty tapas, creative salads, and toothsome *raciones* make it a good all-rounder.

ℹ Information

Centro de Visitantes (☑968 47 74 37; www.lorcatallerdeltiempo.com; Puerto de San Ginés; ⊙10am-2pm & 5.30-7.30pm Tue-Fri, 10am-2pm & 4.30-6.30pm Sat, 10am-2pm Sun) Located in a former convent with a multimedia

---

ADDING COLOUR TO SEMANA SANTA

In Lorca you'll find issues are clearly blue and white – the colours of the two major brotherhoods that have competed every year since 1855 to see who can stage the most lavish Semana Santa display.

Lorca's Easter parades move to a different rhythm, distinct from the slow, sombre processions elsewhere in Murcia. While still deeply reverential, they're full of colour and vitality, mixing Old Testament tales with the Passion story.

If you hail from Lorca, you're passionately Blanco (White) or Azul (Blue). Each brotherhood has a statue of the Virgin (one draped in a blue mantle, the other in white, naturally), a banner and a spectacular museum. The result of this intense and mostly genial year-round rivalry is just about the most dramatic Semana Santa you'll see anywhere in Spain.

exhibition (adult/child €1/free) illustrating Lorca's long history.

Tourist Office (☑ 968 44 19 14; www.lorca-turismo.es; Puerto de San Ginés; ☉ 9.30am-8.30pm Mon-Fri, 10am-3pm & 5.30-8.30pm Sat, 10am-3pm Sun) Currently housed in the Centro de Visitantes after its old-town offices were destroyed in the earthquake. It may change location in the next few years.

❶ Getting There & Around

Hourly buses (€5.70, 1½ hours) and C2 line *cercanía* trains (€5.70, 50 minutes) run between Lorca and Murcia. Various bus services run into Almería province and beyond.

Parque Natural de Sierra Espuña

The Sierra Espuña, a 40-minute drive southwest of Murcia towards Lorca, is an island of pine forest rising high into the sky above an ocean of heat and dust down below. Sitting just north of the N340, the natural park that protects this fragile and beautiful environment has more than 250 sq km of unspoilt highlands covered with trails and popular with walkers and climbers.

Limestone formations tower above the sprawling forests. In the northwest of the park are many *pozos de la nieve* (ice houses) where, until the arrival of industrial refrigeration, snow was compressed into ice, then taken to nearby towns in summer.

Access to the park is best via **Alhama de Murcia**. The informative **Ricardo Codorniu Visitors Centre** (☑ 968 43 14 30; www.sierraespuna.com; ☉ 10am-2pm & 3-6pm Tue-Sun Sep-Jun, 8.30am-3.30pm Jul & Aug) is located in the heart of the park. A few walking trails leave from here, and they can provide good maps for these and several other picturesque hikes.

The village of **El Berro** makes for a great base for the sierra. It has a couple of restaurants and the friendly **Camping Sierra Espuña** (☑ 968 66 80 38; www.campingsierraespuna.com; sites per person/tent/car €5/5/5, 2-/6-person bungalows €55/106; P 🛜 ☎), with superb facilities, including barbecue pits, swimming pool, minigolf and a cafeteria. For something altogether more luxurious you can't beat the **Bajo el Cejo** (☑ 968 66 80 32; www.bajoelcejo.com; s/d €80/90; P ✳ 🛜 ☎). This delicious countryside hideaway is located inside a converted watermill and is absolutely dripping in style and glamour. The 13 rooms are superb but it's the swimming pool and the setting, overlooking the lemon groves and a deep valley, that are the real stars of the show. There's an excellent in-house restaurant.

Another base for the sierra, and for northern Murcia in general, is the town of **Mula**. The town is a web of old streets squashed up against a pinnacle of dry rock topped by the very battered remnants of a **castle**. From a distance the town actually looks like it's dropped straight out of a Middle Eastern fairy tale. Excellent accommodation is available at **El Molino de Felipe** (☑ 968 66 20 13; www.hospederiaruralmolinodefelipe.es; Carretera Ribera de los Molinos 321; d €60, apt €70-130; P ✳ 🛜 ☎). This is another peaceful rural retreat set among citrus and olive groves in a still-working mill. It has beautifully equipped and spacious duplex apartments and a couple of stylish rooms. It's a bargain. Follow the road signs to the castle until you see it signposted; it's about 4km from town.

Mallorca, Menorca & Ibiza

Best Places to Eat

➡ Simply Fosh (p784)
➡ Comidas Bar San Juan (p811)
➡ Es Racó d'es Teix (p788)
➡ S'Espigó (p800)
➡ S'Eufabi (p824)

Best Places to Stay

➡ Casa Alberti (p799)
➡ Can Cera (p783)
➡ Urban Spaces (p811)
➡ Es Marès (p820)
➡ Ca N'Aí (p789)

Why Go?

The Spain of a million wish-you-were-here postcards, the Balearic Islands have all the sun and sea attributes to write home about. But there is much more to these four sisters than often meets the media eye. Beyond the 'Brits abroad' madness in Mallorca's southwest lies an astonishingly beautiful island, where gold-stone hill towns peek out from above olive groves, cliffs loom above secluded coves and the wild limestone peaks of the Serra de Tramuntana make for spectacular hikes, bike rides and hair-raising drives.

A breezy ferry hop away, low-key Menorca entices with prehistoric sites, delectable beaches and the forts her conquerors built and left behind. Unless she's still sleeping off her latest excess, Ibiza will wax lyrical about her megaclubs, boutiques and boho-cool vibes. Tiny Formentera, for her part, will pipe up to remind you of her sugar-white sands and sapphire seas – one of Europe's few true island escapes, but please whisper it quietly.

When to Go
Palma de Mallorca

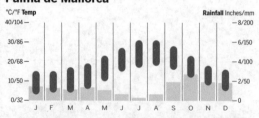

| **Mar & Apr** Spring flowers brush your boots as you walk Mallorca's rugged Serra de Tramuntana. | **Jun–Sep** Beach by day, club by night, raving round the Ibiza clock. | **Jul & Aug** Torchlit re-enactments at Maó's Castell San Felipe on Menorca. |

Walk on the Wild Side

Strike out on foot to see a wilder side to the Balearics. On Mallorca, trails weave through the limestone heights and olive groves of the **Serra de Tramuntana** (p786) – the GR221 Ruta de Pedra en Sec is an epic week-long hike. **Camí de Cavalls** (p805) loops around Menorca, taking in striking coastlines, forts and watchtowers. Ibiza and Formentera share the marshes, cliffs and salt lagoons of the Unesco-listed **Parque Natural de ses Salines** (p823), where birds like Audouin's gulls, Balearic shearwaters and migrating flamingos are often spotted.

TOP FIVE FOOD EXPERIENCES

➡ Dig into Mallorcan meat dishes, such as *lechona asada* (roast suckling pig), *frit mallorquí* (a hearty lamb offal and vegetable fry-up), *llom amb col* (pork wrapped in cabbage with pine nuts and raisins) and *arròs brut* (literally 'dirty rice', soupy rice with pork, rabbit and vegetables).

➡ Bite into *ensaïmades* (sweet pastry spirals dusted with icing sugar) at Ca'n Joan de S'Aigo (p783) in Palma, an antique-filled milk bar dating from 1700.

➡ Sit on a sea-facing terrace in Fornells, Menorca, while enjoying *caldereta de llagosta* (lobster stew).

➡ Go traditional in Ibiza with hearty stews such as *frito de pulpo* (baked octopus, potatoes, paprika and herbs) and *bullit de peix* (fish and potato stew).

➡ Taste the tangy cheese, mayonnaise *(salsa mahonesa)* and gin, made in Maó, Menorca's laid-back seafront capital.

Top Five Beaches

➡ **Cala Saona** (p821) A dreamy arc of frost-white sand and azure water.

➡ **Cala Sant Vicenç** (p794) Jewel-like coves and pristine sea.

➡ **Cala Mitjana** (p799) Pine-stippled cliffs wrap around this soft-sand cove with crystal-clear water for snorkelling.

➡ **Cala Llenya & Cala Mastella** (p815) A twinset of secluded, soft-sand bays massaged by the turquoise Med.

➡ **Cala d'Algaiarens** (p799) Gorgeous tucked-away bay on Menorca's north coast.

MENORCAN GIN

Drink it the usual way, long with tonic. Or do as the Menorcans do and ask for a *gin con limonada* (called locally a *pomada*), a shot of gin in a small glass, topped up with real lemonade. If you like your drink strong, order a *saliveta* for a shot of neat gin, graced with a green olive.

Drive Time

Buckle up for a helter-skelter drive to Sa Calobra (p790) and cliff-hugging stunner Cap de Formentor (p794) on Mallorca. Give the crowds the slip en route to Formentera's lighthouse-tipped Far de sa Mola (p824) and the rocky cape of Cap de Favàritx (p804) on Menorca.

Resources

➡ Illes Balears (www.illesbalears.es) Official tourism website for all the islands.

➡ Platges de Balears (www.platgesdebalears.com) The low-down on every beach.

➡ Balears Cultural Tour (http://balearsculturaltour.net) Walking trails, cultural events, gastronomy and more.

Ibizan Megaclubs

➡ Space (p812)

➡ Pacha (p812)

➡ Amnesia (p812)

ℹ️ Getting There & Around

AIR

In summer, masses of charter and regular flights converge on Palma de Mallorca and Ibiza from all over Europe. All of the islands (bar Formentera) are serviced by low-cost airlines like **EasyJet** (www.easyjet.com), **Ryanair** (www.ryanair.com) and **Jet2** (www.jet2.com).

Major operators from the Spanish mainland include **Iberia** (www.iberia.es), **Air Europa** (www.aireuropa.com), **Air Berlin** (www.airberlin.com) and **Vueling** (www.vueling.com).

BOAT

Compare prices and look for deals at **Direct Ferries** (www.directferries.com). Here are the main operators:

Acciona Trasmediterránea (☎ 902 454645; www.trasmediterranea.es)

Baleària (☎ 902 160180; www.balearia.com)

Iscomar (☎ 902 119128; www.iscomar.com)

MALLORCA

Ever since the first charter flight touched down on a small airstrip in 1950, Mallorca has been the little miss popular of the Med. And the love affair continues. Every year some 10 million visitors flock to the largest Balearic island. But while some sunseekers are here on fly-and-flop packages, many travellers are now discovering Mallorca's alter ego.

Beyond the Brits abroad and nefarious nightlife clichés lies one beautiful island. In the east are ravishing white-sand coves only reachable by boat or on foot, in the north gold-stone hill towns peek enticingly above olive groves, citrus orchards and pine forest, while heading west brings you to the rugged limestone heights of the Tramuntana, which fall abruptly to a sea of bluest blue. The soulful capital, Palma, adds a drop of culture into the mix, with its colossal Gothic

MALLORCA, MENORCA & IBIZA MALLORCA

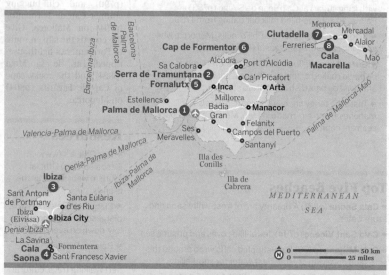

Mallorca, Menorca & Ibiza Highlights

❶ Admire the Gothic splendour of the cathedral in **Palma de Mallorca** (p780).

❷ Hit the trail in Mallorca's spectacularly rugged **Serra de Tramuntana** (p786).

❸ Get your all-night groove on in the megaclubs of **Ibiza** (p807).

❹ Chill out on one of Formentera's breathtaking beaches such as **Cala Saona** (p821).

❺ Enjoy scented strolls in villages like **Fornalutx** (p790) in Mallorca's northwest.

❻ Gasp at the turquoise hues of the sea around

the promontory of **Cap de Formentor** (p794).

❼ Peer into prehistory at Naveta des Tudons and the other ancient monuments around **Ciutadella** (p801).

❽ Slip into Menorca's limpid waters at **Cala Macarella** (p799).

Mallorca

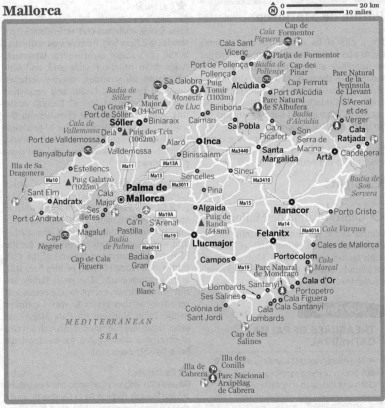

cathedral, town palaces and galleries showing Picasso and Miró. The secret of Mallorca's true staying power today? Well, it's more than sunburn and sangria, that's for sure.

ℹ Getting Around

BOAT
Palma and the major resorts and beaches around the island are connected by boat tours and water-taxi services. Most feature in the tourist-office brochure, *Excursions En Barca*, available in English.

BUS
Most of the island is accessible by bus or train from Palma. All services depart from or near Estació Intermodal de Palma (p785).

CAR & MOTORCYCLE
You can rent cars and bikes, and often scooters too, in even the smallest resort. Palma alone has over 30 agencies. The big league has representatives at the airport and along Passeig Marítim, along with several cheaper companies.

TRAIN
Two train lines run from Plaça d'Espanya in Palma de Mallorca. The popular, old train runs to Sóller and is a pretty ride. A standard train line runs inland to Inca where the line splits with a branch to Sa Pobla and another to Manacor. **Transport de lesIlles Balears** (TIB; ☑ 971 17 77 77; www.tib.org) has details.

ℹ MALLORCA WEBSITES

www.infomallorca.net Official Mallorca tourism website.

www.mallorcahotelguide.com Website of the Mallorca hoteliers' association.

www.tib.org Information on Mallorca's public transport.

Palma de Mallorca

POP 398,162

For a city of its diminutive size, Palma's sights play in the premier league with major metropolises: an immense Gothic cathedral, moored like the prow of a great ship on the Mediterranean's edge, baroque palaces, a pristine old quarter and galleries showcasing Mirós, Picassos and Barcelós are just the tip of the cultural iceberg.

An exciting food scene, happening nightlife and great beaches on the doorstep are other major drawcards.

◉ Sights

◉ Central Palma de Mallorca

Central Palma is known especially for the elegant courtyards, called *patis*, of its many noble houses and mansions. Most are in private hands, but you can often peek through wrought-iron grilles.

> **DON'T MISS**
>
> ### TREASURES OF PALMA CATHEDRAL
>
> ➜ The monumental **facade** is a pot-pourri of Renaissance and neo-Gothic styles, with its interlaced flying buttresses and soaring pinnacles.
>
> ➜ Modernist master Antoni Gaudí carried out renovations from 1904 to 1914. Topped by a fanciful sculpture of Christ crucified, his strange **baldachin** hovers over the main altar.
>
> ➜ Shimmering ruby, gold and sapphire, the **oculus maior** or 'great eye' is the world's largest Gothic rose window. Visit in the morning to see the stunning effect of its light and shapes reflected on the west wall.
>
> ➜ Mallorquin artist Miquel Barceló's **Capella del Santíssim i Sant Pere** in the right apse is a dreamscape representing the miracle of the loaves and fishes done in 15 tonnes of ceramics.
>
> ➜ The **baroque chapter house** is exquisite, with its delicately carved stonework and 16th-century *relicario de la vera cruz* (reliquary of the true cross).

★ Catedral
CATHEDRAL

(La Seu; www.catedraldemallorca.org; Carrer del Palau Reial 9; adult/child €6/free; ⏰ 10am-6.15pm Mon-Fri, to 2.15pm Sat) Palma's vast cathedral is the city's major architectural landmark. Aside from its sheer scale and undoubted beauty, its stunning interior features, designed by Antoni Gaudí and renowned contemporary artist Miquel Barceló, make this unlike any cathedral elsewhere in the world. The awesome structure is predominantly Gothic, apart from the main facade, which is startling, quite beautiful and completely mongrel.

★ Palau de l'Almudaina
PALACE

(Carrer del Palau Reial; adult/child €9/4, audioguide €4, guided tour €6; ⏰ 10am-8pm Apr-Sep, to 6pm Oct-Mar) Originally an Islamic fort, this mighty construction opposite the cathedral was converted into a residence for the Mallorcan monarchs at the end of the 13th century. The King of Spain resides here still, at least symbolically. The royal family are rarely in residence, except for the occasional ceremony, as they prefer to spend summer in the Palau Marivent (in Cala Major). At other times you can wander through a series of cavernous stone-walled rooms that have been lavishly decorated.

★ Es Baluard
GALLERY

(Museu d'Art Modern i Contemporani; www.esbaluard.org; Plaça de Porta de Santa Catalina 10; adult/child €6/free, temporary exhibitions €4; ⏰ 10am-8pm Tue-Sat, to 3pm Sun) Built with flair and innovation into the shell of the Renaissance-era seaward walls, this contemporary art gallery is one of the finest on the island. Its temporary exhibitions are worth viewing, but the permanent collection – works by Miró, Barceló and Picasso – give the gallery its cachet.

The 21st-century concrete complex is cleverly built among the fortifications, which include the partly restored remains of an 11th-century Muslim-era tower (on the right as you arrive from Carrer de Sant Pere).

★ Palau March
MUSEUM

(Carrer de Palau Reial 18; adult/child €4.50/free; ⏰ 10am-6.30pm Mon-Fri, to 2pm Sat) This house, palatial by any definition, was one of several residences of the phenomenally wealthy March family. Sculptures by 20th-century greats, such as Henry Moore, Auguste Rodin, Barbara Hepworth and Eduardo Chillida, grace the outdoor terrace. Within lie many

Palma de Mallorca

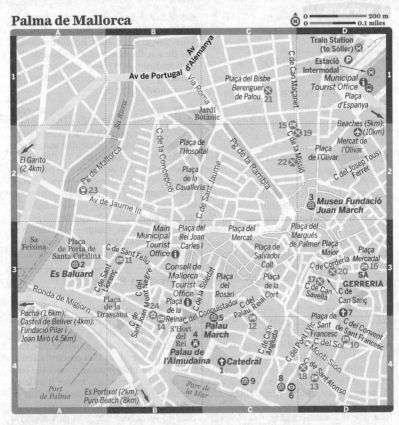

Palma de Mallorca

more artistic treasures from some of Spain's big names in art, such as Salvador Dalí, and Barcelona's Josep Maria Sert and Xavier Corberó, as well as an extraordinary 18th-century Neapolitan baroque *belén* (nativity scene).

DON'T MISS

MALLORCA'S TOP FIVE BEACHES

➡ Platja de Formentor (p794)

➡ Cala Llombards (p796)

➡ Cala Sant Vicenç (p794)

➡ Cala de Deià (p788)

➡ Sa Calobra (p790)

★ **Museu Fundació Juan March**   GALLERY
(www.march.es/arte/palma; Carrer de Sant Miquel 11; ⊙10am-6.30pm Mon-Fri, 10.30am-2pm Sat) FREE This 17th-century mansion gives an insightful overview of Spanish contemporary art. On permanent display are some 70 pieces held by the Fundación Juan March. Together they constitute a veritable who's who of mostly 20th-century artists, including Miró, Juan Gris (of cubism fame), Dalí and the sculptors Eduardo Chillida and Julio González.

Museu Diocesà   MUSEUM
(Carrer del Mirador 5; adult/child €3/free; ⊙10am-2pm Mon-Sat) Opened in 2007 in its magnificent new home of the Palau Episcopal (bishop's residence), the Museu Diocesà, behind the cathedral to the east, is a fascinating excursion for those interested in Mallorca's Christian artistic history. It contains works by Antoni Gaudí, Francesc Comes and Pere Niçard, and a mind-boggling *retaule* (*retablo* in Spanish; an altarpiece) depicting the Passion of Christ (c 1290–1305) and taken from the Convent de Santa Clara.

Museo Can Morey de Santmartí   GALLERY
(www.museo-santmarti.es; Carrer de la Portella 9; adult/child €9/5; ⊙9.30am-8.30pm Apr-Oct, shorter hours rest of year) A grand town mansion set around an inner courtyard was revamped and reopened as this museum in 2012. A dream come true for German art dealer Wolfgang Hörnke, the museum is an ode to the wonderfully weird world of Catalan surrealist artist Salvador Dalí (1904–89). Some 226 original works from the 1930s to the 1970s are displayed on three levels.

Basílica de Sant Francesc   CHURCH
(Plaça de Sant Francesc 7; admission €1.50; ⊙9.30am-12.30pm Mon-Sun, 3.30-6pm Mon-Sat) One of Palma's oldest churches, the Franciscan Basílica de Sant Francesc was begun in 1281 in Gothic style and its baroque facade was completed in 1700. In the splendid Gothic cloister – a two-tiered, trapezoid affair – the elegant columns indicate it was some time in the making. Inside the lugubrious church, the fusion of styles is clear. The high vaulted roof is classic Gothic, while the glittering high altar is a baroque lollipop, albeit in need of a polish.

Banys Àrabs   BATHHOUSE
(Carrer de Serra 7; adult/child €2/free; ⊙9am-7.30pm) These modest Arab baths are the single most important remaining monument to the Muslim domination of the island, although all that survives are two small underground chambers, one with a domed ceiling supported by a dozen columns, some of whose capitals were recycled from demolished Roman buildings. The site may be small, but the two rooms – the caldarium (hot bath) and the tepidarium (warm bath) – evoke a poignant sense of abandonment.

◉ Western Palma

Castell de Bellver   CASTLE
(Bellver Castle; www.cultura.palma.es; Carrer de Camilo José Cela 17; adult/child €4/2, Sun free; ⊙8.30am-1pm Mon, to 8pm Tue-Sat, 10am-6pm Sun) Straddling a wooded hillside, the Castell de Bellver is a 14th-century circular castle (with a unique round tower), the only one of its kind in Spain. Jaume II ordered the castle built atop a hill known as Puig de Sa Mesquida in 1300 and it was largely complete 10 years later. The best part of a visit is to mosey around the castle and enjoy the spectacular views over the woods to Palma, the Badia de Palma and out to sea.

Fundació Pilar i Joan Miró   GALLERY
(http://miro.palma.cat; Carrer de Saridakis 29; adult/child €6/free; ⊙10am-7pm Tue-Sat, to 3pm Sun) Inland from the waterfront is a major art stop, the Fundació Pilar i Joan Miró. Top Spanish architect Rafael Moneo designed the main building in 1992, next to the studio in which Miró had thrived for decades. With more than 2500 works by the artist (including 118 paintings), along with memorabilia, it's a major collection.

🛏 Sleeping

Hostal Pons   HOSTAL €
(📞971 72 26 58; www.hostalpons.com; Carrer del Vi 8; s €30, d €60-70, tr €85; 🛜🎛) Bang in the heart of old Palma, this is a sweet, simple family-run guesthouse. Downstairs a cat slumbers in a plant-filled patio, upstairs

you'll find a book-lined lounge and rooms with rickety bedsteads and tiled floors. Cheaper rooms share communal bathrooms. The roof terrace offers peaceful respite.

Hotel Santa Clara
BOUTIQUE HOTEL **€€**

(☏971 72 92 31; www.santaclarahotel.es; Carrer de Sant Alonso 16; d €104-225, ste €168-360; ❄@🛜) Boutique meets antique in this historic mansion, converted with respect, where subdued greys, steely silvers and cream blend harmoniously with the warm stone walls, ample spaces and high ceilings of the original structure. There's an intimate spa in which to unwind. Palma is reduced to postcard format from the decked roof terrace, ideal for a sunbathe or a sundowner.

Palma Suites
APARTMENT **€€**

(☏971 72 79 00; www.palma-suites.com; Plaça Mercadal 8; ste €137-250; ❄🛜🏊🚶) This stylish newcomer twins hotel luxury with home-style independence. Playful artworks and splashes of bold colour lend character to sizeable, slickly designed apartments, with smart TVs and well-equipped kitchens with Nespresso machines. The triplex suites have bags of room for families. For surround views of Palma's skyline, step up to the roof terrace. There's a minimum three-night stay.

Hotel Dalt Murada
HISTORIC HOTEL **€€**

(☏971 42 53 00; www.daltmurada.com; Carrer de l'Almudaina 6A; s €105, d €99-170, ste €199; ❄🛜) Gathered around a medieval courtyard, this carefully restored old town house, dating from 1500, has 14 rooms with antique furnishings (including chandeliers and canopied beds) and art belonging to the family who run the place. That said, mattresses are too springy for some tastes and street-facing rooms can be noisy. The 21st-century penthouse suite has incomparable cathedral views. Breakfast costs €7.50.

Misión de San Miguel
BOUTIQUE HOTEL **€€**

(☏971 21 48 48; www.urhotels.com; Carrer de Can Maçanet 1; r €75-163, ste €115-203; P❄@🛜) This 32-room boutique hotel is an astounding deal with stylish designer rooms; it does the little things well with firm mattresses and rain showers, although some rooms open onto public areas and can be a tad noisy. Its restaurant, Misa Braseria, is part of the Fosh group. Service is friendly and professional.

★Can Cera
BOUTIQUE HOTEL **€€€**

(☏971 71 50 12; www.cancerahotel.com; Carrer del Convent de Sant Francesc 8; r €165-495; ❄🛜🚶) Welcome to one of Palma's most romantic boutique bolt-holes, entered via an inner courtyard, where cobbles have been worn smooth over 700 years and a wrought-iron staircase sweeps up to guest rooms that manage the delicate act of combining history with modern design flourishes. The decor is stylish but never overblown, with high ceilings, period furnishings and richly detailed throws.

★Hotel Tres
BOUTIQUE HOTEL **€€€**

(☏971 71 73 33; www.hoteltres.com; Carrer dels Apuntadors 3; s €160-280, d €170-290, ste €313-544; ❄@🛜🚶) Hotel Tres swings joyously between 16th-century town palace and fresh-faced Scandinavian design. Centred on a courtyard with a single palm, the rooms are cool and minimalist, with cowhide benches, anatomy-inspired prints and nice details like rollaway desks and Durance aromatherapy cosmetics. Head up to the roof terrace at sunset for a steam and swim as the cathedral begins to twinkle.

🍴 Eating

Plenty of eateries and bars huddle in the maze of streets between Plaça de la Reina and the port. The seaside Es Molinar area around Es Portixol has cheerful seafood eateries and laid-back bars.

Ca'n Joan de S'Aigo
PASTELERÍA, CAFE **€**

(Carrer de Can Sanç 10; pastries €1.30-3; ⏱8am-9pm) Tempting with its sweet creations since 1700, this is *the* place for thick hot chocolate (€2) and pastries in what can only be described as an antique-filled milk bar. The house speciality is *quart,* a feather-soft sponge cake that children love, with almond-flavoured ice cream.

ℹ️ FINDING A BED

The Balearics in high summer (late June to mid-September) can be incredibly busy. Palma alone turns around some 40 inbound and outbound flights a day. Most of the millions of visitors have pre-booked package accommodation. Independent travellers should book at least the first couple of nights around this time. In July and August hotel prices peak. In most places you can expect to pay considerably less in quieter times. Check hotel websites for special offers and promotions.

Restaurant Celler Sa Premsa   SPANISH €

(☑971 72 35 29; www.cellersapremsa.com; Plaça del Bisbe Berenguer de Palou 8; mains €9-14; ⊙12.30-4pm & 7.30-11.30pm Mon-Sat) A visit to this local institution is almost obligatory. It's a cavernous tavern filled with huge old wine barrels and has walls plastered with faded bullfighting posters – you find plenty such places in the Mallorcan interior but they're a dying breed here in Palma. Mallorcan specialities dominate the menu.

Can Cera Gastro Bar   MEDITERRANEAN €€

(☑971 71 50 12; www.cancerahotel.com; Carrer del Convent de Sant Francesc 8; mains €14-22, menus €18-31; ⊙1-3.30pm & 7.30-10.30pm) How enchanting: this restaurant spills out into one of Palma's loveliest inner patios at the hotel of the same name, housed in a 13th-century *palacio*. Dine by lantern light on tapas or season-focused dishes such as watermelon and tomato gazpacho and creamy rice with aioli, saffron and calamari. Note the vertical garden that attracts plenty of attention from passers-by.

Quina Creu   TAPAS €€

(☑971 71 17 72; www.quinacreu.com; Carrer de Cordería 24; mains €9-35, lunch menu €9.90; ⊙noon-1am Mon-Sat) With its mishmash of vintage furniture, flickering haunted-house chandeliers and poster-plastered walls, Quina Creu works the shabby-chic look. The bar has a designer feel, as do the tapas lined up along the bar and chalked on the blackboard. Each is a mini taste sensation, from *sobrassada* (paprika-flavoured cured pork sausage) with quail egg to cod with *gambas* (prawns) and salsa verde.

Misa Braseria   MEDITERRANEAN €€

(☑971 59 53 01; www.misabraseria.com; Carrer de Can Maçanet 1; mains €17-23; ⊙1-3.30pm & 7.30-10.30pm Mon-Sat) Marc Fosh's second baby is this nouveau-rustic brasserie, which combines a basement restaurant with an attractive upstairs patio. The food is slickly presented and tastes are typically fresh. Dishes that change with the seasons star alongside classics such as butter-soft roast chicken and grilled beef with truffle-potato purée. The three-course day menu (€15.50) is outstanding value.

La Taberna del Caracol   SPANISH €€

(☑971 71 49 08; www.tabernacaracol.com; Carrer de Sant Alonso 2; tapas €1.50-17, tapas tasting plate €14; ⊙7.30-11pm Mon, noon-3pm & 7.30-11pm Tue-Sat) Descend three steps into this high-ceilinged Gothic basement. Through a broad vault at the back you can see what's cooking – tasty tapas that include grilled artichokes, snails and a host of other Spanish delicacies. Amid soothing background music, a broad assortment of tapas (four choices for €14, minimum of two people) is a meal in itself.

★ Simply Fosh   MODERN EUROPEAN €€€

(☑971 72 01 14; www.simplyfosh.com; Carrer de la Missió 7A; mains €23-29, menus €21.50-76; ⊙1-3.30pm & 7-10.30pm Mon-Sat) Lovingly prepared Mediterranean cooking with a novel flourish is the order of the day at this 17th-century convent refectory, one of the home kitchens of chef Marc Fosh, whose CV twinkles with Michelin stars. A slick, monochrome interior and courtyard provide the backdrop for high-quality, reasonably priced menus. The three-course lunch menu for €21.50 is a terrific deal.

🍷 Drinking & Entertainment

Nightlife revolves mostly around the city's old quarter, particularly in the narrow streets between Plaça de la Reina and Plaça de la Drassana, which are jammed with bars, pubs and bodegas. Check out the Santa Catalina and Es Molinar districts too. About 2km west of the centre, along and behind Passeig Marítim, is a concentration of taverns, girlie bars and clubs.

S'Arenal and Magaluf, the seaside resorts east and west of Palma respectively, throb with bars and discos. Magaluf (nicknamed 'Shagaluf') gets lairy with Brits behaving badly abroad.

Ginbo   BAR

(Passeig de Mallorca 14; ⊙9.30pm-3am Mon-Sat, 6pm-3am Sun) Ginbo does the best G&T in Palma for our money. Besides around 100 different kinds of gin, the bartenders mix some superb cocktails, including the Porn Star Martini (the mind boggles), which you can sip in the buzzy, stylishly urban, backlit bar or on the terrace.

Puro Beach   LOUNGE, BAR

(www.purobeach.com; ⊙11am-1am May-Sep, to 7pm Apr & Oct; 🛜) This laid-back lounge carries more than a hint of Ibiza with a tapering outdoor promontory over the water and an all-white bar that's perfect for sunset cocktails, DJ sessions and open-air spa treatments. Most of the toned, bronzed bods here wear white to blend in with the slinky decor.

It is a two-minute walk east of Cala Estancia (itself just east of Ca'n Pastilla).

Pacha CLUB
(www.pachamallorca.es; Passeig Marítim 42; ⏱11.30pm-6am daily Jul-Aug, Thu-Sat rest of year) This new glamour puss of a club brings a splash of Ibiza to the dance floor. Opened in 2013, it's a three-floor temple to hedonism, with regular fiestas, DJs pumping out house and chill-out terraces. Entry costs about €15.

El Garito LIVE MUSIC
(www.garitocafe.com; Dàrsena de Can Barberà; ⏱8pm-4.30am) DJs and live performers, doing anything from nu jazz to disco classics and electro beats, heat up the scene from around 10pm. Admission is generally free, but you're expected to buy a drink.

Jazz Voyeur Club LIVE MUSIC
(☎971 90 52 92; www.jazzvoyeurfestival.com; Carrer dels Apuntadors 5; admission free–€25; ⏱8.30pm-1am Mon-Thu & Sun, to 3am Fri & Sat) A tiny club no bigger than most people's living rooms, Voyeur hosts live bands nightly for much of the year – jazz is the focus, but you'll also hear flamenco, blues, funk and the occasional jam session. Red candles burn on the tables and a few plush chairs are scattered about – get here early if you want to grab one. In autumn it hosts a fine jazz festival.

ℹ Information

Airport Tourist Office (☎971 78 95 56; Aeroport de Palma; ⏱8am-8pm Mon-Sat, to 4pm Sun) Tourist information.

Consell de Mallorca Tourist Office (☎971 17 39 90; www.infomallorca.net; Plaça de la Reina 2; ⏱8am-6pm Mon-Fri, 8.30am-3pm Sat; 🐾) Covers the whole island.

Main Municipal Tourist Office (☎971 72 96 34; www.imtur.es; Casal Solleric, Passeig d'es Born 27; ⏱9am-8pm)

Municipal Tourist Office (☎902 102365; ⏱9am-8pm Mon-Sat) In one of the railway buildings off Plaça d'Espanya.

Visit Palma (www.visit-palma.com) Palma's hotel association's website.

ℹ Getting Around

A number of airlines service Mallorca. All buses to other destinations on Mallorca depart from (or near) the **Estació Intermodal de Palma** (☎971 17 77 77; www.tib.org; Plaça d'Espanya). Two train lines run from Plaça d'Espanya; one to Sóller, the other to Inca.

FANCY FOOTWORK

Mallorca is better known for its shoe-making tradition (especially with the international success of the Camper company), but Menorca, too, has long had its share of cobblers. The best-loved local product is the *avarca* (*abarca* in Spanish), a loose, comfortable slip-on sandal that straps around the heel. Sometimes with soles fashioned from recycled car tyres, they make great summer shoes. Shops sell them all over the Balearics.

TO/FROM THE AIRPORT

Palma de Mallorca Airport (PMI) lies 8km east of the city. Bus 1 runs every 15 minutes from the airport to Plaça d'Espanya in central Palma (€3, 15 minutes) and on to the entrance of the ferry terminal. A taxi costs €18 to €22.

BUS

There are extensive local bus services around Palma and its bay suburbs with **EMT** (☎971 21 44 44; www.emtpalma.es). Single-trip tickets cost €1.50, or you can buy a 10-trip card for €10. For the beaches en route to S'Arenal, take bus 15 from Plaça d'Espanya.

TAXI

For a taxi, call ☎971 75 54 40.

Southwest Coast

A freeway skirts around the Badia de Palma towards Mallorca's southwest coast. Along the way you'll pass the resorts of Cala Major, Ses Illetes (lovely little beaches), Palma Nova and Magaluf (nice long beaches and mass British tourism), all basically a continuation of Palma's urban sprawl. From Andratx (worth a stop for a taste of an inland Mallorca town), two turn-offs lead down to the coast: one goes to Port d'Andratx, and the other to the seaside hamlet of Sant Elm, which is surrounded by leafy hills, has a pretty (but busy) sandy beach and the possibility of boat tours to the nearby, uninhabited, Illa de Sa Dragonera and its good walking trails.

Port d'Andratx

Port d'Andratx spreads around low hills surrounding a narrow bay, where yachties hang out. A couple of dive schools are based here, including Diving Dragonera (☑ 971 67 43 76; www.aqua-mallorca-diving.com; Avinguda de l'Amirante Riera Alemany 23; 6-/10-dive package €204/320, 2hr snorkel adult/child €19.50/15; ⊘ 8am-7pm mid-Mar–Oct).

Family-run Hostal-Residencia Catalina Vera (☑ 971 67 19 18; www.hostalcatalinavera.es; Carrer Isaac Peral 63; s €60-65, d €65-85; P ❒) sits a block back from the water in a garden filled with cacti and jasmine. The rooms are simple but immaculate, with occasional antique furnishings and balconies or terraces – some with sea views.

Chef Domenico Curcio has made Trespaís (☑ 971 67 28 14; www.trespais-mallorca.com; Carrer Antonio Callafat 24; mains €10-30, 3-course menu €29.90; ⊘ 6pm-midnight Tue-Sun) the top table in town, with memorable dishes that play up integral flavours, such as John Dory with artichoke mash and pancetta potatoes.

Northwest Coast & Serra de Tramuntana

Dominated by the rugged limestone Serra de Tramuntana range, Mallorca's northwest coast is the Mediterranean before mass tourism. Here steep, forest-shrouded cliffs and mountain slopes tumble down towards a handful of idyllic coves with luminous blue waters. The few towns and villages are built largely of local stone and blend harmoniously into Mother Nature's dreamy canvas. The mountainous interior is much loved by walkers for its stirring landscapes of pine forests, olive groves and springtime eruption of wildflowers like yellow wattles and blood-red poppies. It's a peaceful, virtually year-round destination for walkers and cyclists.

The main road through the mountains (the Ma10) runs roughly parallel to the coast between Andratx and Pollença. It's a stunning, scenic drive, with plenty of *miradors* (viewpoints) to punctuate your trip.

Estellencs
POP 369

Estellencs is a coquettish village of stone buildings scattered around rolling hills below the Puig Galatzó (1025m) peak. A rugged walk of about 1.5km leads down a terraced hillside of orchards and olives to a cove with crystal-clear water and a cute little boat ramp.

The higgledy-piggledy, stone Petit Hotel Sa Plana (☑ 971 61 86 66; www.saplana.com; Carrer de Eusebi Pascual; d incl breakfast €95-125; ⊘ mid-Jan–Nov; ❄ ❒ ❒), with its tousled garden and six rustic farmhouse rooms, is as gorgeous as the village it sits in. It's family owned and particularly welcoming.

Banyalbufar
POP POP 517

Surrounded by steep, stone-walled farming terraces carved into the hillside, delightful Banyalbufar melds into the mountain slopes high above the coast.

One kilometre out of town on the road to Estellencs, the Torre des Verger (Torre de Ses Animes; Carretera de Banyalbufar-Andratx) FREE is a 1579 *talayot* (watchtower), an image you'll see on postcards all over the island. It's one of the most crazily sited structures – one step further and it would plunge into the Mediterranean far below.

Squirreled away at the top end of the village is a quaint 15th-century townhouse, Son Borguny (☑ 971 14 87 06; www.sonborguny.com; Carrer de Borguny 1; s/d €75/95, ste €100-130; ❒). Its attractive rooms feature occasional stone walls and wooden beams, and some have partial sea views. A generous breakfast will fire you up for a day's hiking.

The Palma–Estellencs bus passes through Banyalbufar four to eight times daily.

OFF THE BEATEN TRACK

RUTA DE PEDRA EN SEC

A week's walk would see you traverse the Serra de Tramuntana from Port d'Andratx to Pollença, mostly following old cobbled mule trails. You'd be following the GR221 long-distance trail Ruta de Pedra en Sec (Dry Stone Route). Currently some 167km of the route is completed and open. The 'dry stone' refers to an age-old island building method. In the mountains farming terraces, houses, walls and more are built of stone without mortar. Eventually the signed trail will have eight stages, with a *refugi* (mountain hostel) waiting for you at the end of each day. For a detailed guide to the route so far, pick up *GR221: Mallorca's Dry Stone Way* by Charles Davis. Also check out www.conselldemallorca.net/mediambient/pedra.

Valldemossa

POP 2042

Valldemossa is an attractive blend of tree-lined streets, old stone houses and impressive new villas. The ailing composer Frédéric Chopin and his lover, writer George Sand, spent their 'winter of discontent' here in 1838–39.

◉ Sights & Activities

★Real Cartuja de Valldemossa MONASTERY
(www.cartujadevalldemossa.com; Plaça Cartoixa; adult/child €8.50/4; ⊙9.30am-6.30pm Mon-Sat, 10am-1.30pm Sun) This grand old monastery and former royal residence has a chequered history and was once home to kings, monks and a pair of 19th-century celebrities: composer Frédéric Chopin and George Sand. A series of cells now shows how the monks lived, bound by an oath of silence they could only break for half an hour per week in the library. Various items related to Sand's and Chopin's time here, including Chopin's pianos, are also displayed.

The building's origins date back to 1310 when Jaume II built a palace on the site. After it was abandoned, the Carthusian order took over and converted it into a monastery, which, in 1388, was greatly expanded. The monastery was turned into rental accommodation (mostly to holiday-makers from Palma) after its monks were expelled in 1835. Following the rules of the order, just 13 monks lived in this cavernous space. Entry includes piano recitals (eight times daily in summer) and Jaume II's 14th-century Palau de Rei Sanxo, a muddle of medieval rooms jammed with furniture and hundreds of years of mementos, gathered around a modest cloister.

Miranda des Lledoners VIEWPOINT
For an exquisite view taking in the terraces, orchards, gardens, cypresses, palms, the occasional ochre house through the mountains and the distant plains leading to Palma, walk down Carrer de Jovellanos to Miranda des Lledoners.

Costa Nord CULTURAL CENTRE
(☑971 61 24 25; www.costanord.es; Avinguda de Palma 6; adult/child €6/free; ⊙9am-5pm) The brainchild of part-time Valldemossa resident and Hollywood actor Michael Douglas, Costa Nord describes itself as a 'cultural centre' and begins well with a 15-minute portrayal of the history of Valldemossa, narrated by Douglas himself. The subsequent virtual trip aboard *Nixe*, the 19th-century yacht of Austrian archduke Luis Salvador, who owned much of western Mallorca, will be of less interest to most.

Camino del Archiduque WALKING
More actively, stretch those legs by walking this 3½-hour circular route from Valldemossa that offers dizzyingly spectacular coastal views and seascapes.

Port de Valldemossa WALKING/DRIVING
From Valldemossa, a torturous 7km road leads down to this rocky cove with a dozen or so buildings.

🛏 Sleeping & Eating

★Es Petit Hotel de
Valldemossa BOUTIQUE HOTEL €€
(☑971 61 24 79; www.espetithotel-valldemossa.com; Carrer d'Uetam 1; s €117-158, d €130-175; ❄@🐾) What better way to admire Valldemossa than from the rocking chair on your verandah at this family home turned boutique hotel? Five of its eight sunny, high-ceilinged rooms have gorgeous valley views. In the shady garden you could be an island away from the flow of Cartuja visitors outside. Fresh-baked cakes and pastries make breakfast a sweet treat.

★QuitaPenas TAPAS €
(☑675 993082; www.quitapenasvalldemossa.com; Carreró de la Amargura 1; tapas €3-15; ⊙noon-4pm & 6-8pm) Descend cobbled steps to this sweet deli for tapas prepared with care and first-class seasonal ingredients. Grab one of the half-dozen spots outside for interesting takes on *pa amb oli* (bread with olive oil and vine-ripened tomatoes) or tangy *sobrassada* (cured pork sausage flavoured with paprika and spices) with caramelised fig. Couple with chilled Mallorcan wine and magical mountain views and this is a little slice of heaven.

ℹ Getting There & Away

Bus 210 from Palma to Valldemossa runs five to 12 times daily.

Deià

POP 747

Deià is as pretty as a picture, with its cobbled lanes curling up past honey-stone houses that cower beneath steep hillsides terraced with vegetable gardens, vineyards and fruit orchards.

Such beauty has always been a drawcard and Deià was once second home to an international colony of writers, actors and musicians. The most famous member was the English writer Robert Graves, who died here in 1985 and is buried in the town's hillside cemetery.

Sights & Activities

★ Casa Robert Graves   HISTORIC BUILDING

(Ca N'Alluny; www.lacasaderobertgraves.com; Carretera Deià-Sóller; adult/child €7/3.50; ☺10am-5pm Mon-Fri, 10am-3pm Sat) Casa Robert Graves is a fascinating tribute to the writer who moved to Deià in 1929 and had his house built here three years later. It's a well-presented insight into his life; on show you'll find period furnishings, audiovisual displays and various items and books that belonged to Graves himself.

Cala de Deià   BEACH

A 3km drive from Deià (take the road towards Sóller), or a slightly shorter walk, is Cala de Deià, one of the most bewitching of the Serra de Tramuntana's coastal inlets. Accessible only on foot, the enclosed arc of the bay is backed by a handful of houses and the small shingle beach gives onto crystal-clear water. Competition for a parking spot a few hundred metres back up the road can be intense; get here early.

ⓘ BUSING AROUND THE NORTHWEST

Between May and October, buses trundle frequently along the northwest coast; the services are particularly popular with walkers. The following list shows the duration of the bus trip between each stop:

Port de Sóller–Sóller five minutes

Sóller–Monestir de Lluc one hour

Monestir de Lluc–Cala Sant Vicenç 30 minutes

Cala Sant Vicenç–Port de Pollença 15 minutes

Port de Pollença–Alcúdia 15 minutes

Alcúdia–Port d'Alcúdia 10 minutes

Port d'Alcúdia–Ca'n Picafort 25 minutes

Deià Coastal Path   WALKING

Some fine walks criss-cross the area, such as this gentle path to the pleasant hamlet of Lluc Alcari (three hours return). Another nearby option is the old mule trail between Deià and Sóller (two hours each way).

🛏 Sleeping & Eating

★ Hostal Miramar   HOTEL €€

(☎971 63 90 84; www.pensionmiramar.com; Carrer de Ca'n Oliver; r incl breakfast €75-120; ☺Mar–mid-Nov; ℗) Hidden within lush vegetation and with views across to Deià's hillside church and the sea beyond, this 19th-century stone house with gardens is a shady retreat with nine rooms. Various artists (you can scarcely see the breakfast room walls for canvases) have stayed here over the years. The rooms are petite, antique-furnished and as clean as new pins.

Sa Pedrissa   HISTORIC HOTEL €€€

(☎971 63 91 11; www.sapedrissa.com; Carretera de Valldemossa-Deià; s €180-350, d €210-350, ste €350-490; ℗🌐@🛜🏊) Sublime. From a high rocky bluff looking down along the coast and inland to Deià, this stunning mansion (which once lorded it over an olive farm and may date back to the 17th century) is a luxurious choice. The service is faultless, the views from the pool terrace and many rooms are glorious, and the rooms are unpretentiously classy.

The Village Cafe   INTERNATIONAL €

(☎971 63 91 99; www.villagecafedeia.com; Carrer Felipe Bauzà 1; mains €9-15; ☺noon-11pm Wed-Mon Mar-Oct; 🍴) Swathed in flowers and vines, the terrace at this stone-walled cafe has broad views of the Tramuntana. The gourmet burgers are a fine pick, as are the salads and *bocadillos* (filled rolls). As the ceramic lanterns flick on and the cicadas chirp at dusk, it's a highly atmospheric spot for a G&T and tapas.

★ Es Racó d'es Teix   FUSION €€€

(☎971 63 95 01; www.esracodesteix.es; Carrer de San Vinya Vella 6; mains €36-38, 3-course lunch menu €35, 4-/6-course tasting menu €72/98; ☺1-3pm & 7-10pm Feb-Oct) An island legend, Josef Sauerschell has one Michelin star and it is well deserved. He tends to concentrate on elaborate but hearty meat dishes – anything from braised veal shoulder in sherry-vinegar sauce with marrow to Mallorcan suckling pig and trotters with foie gras.

A SLOW CHUG NORTH TO SÓLLER

Journey into the past heading north from Palma to Sóller. Since 1912, a narrow-gauge train with timber-panelled carriages has trundled along this winding 27km route from Plaça de l'Estació (one way/return €13/20, 1¼ hours, up to seven times daily). You pass through ever-changing countryside that becomes dramatic in the north as it crosses the Serra de Alfàbia, offering fabulous views over Sóller and the sea on the final descent into town.

ℹ️ Information

Deià Mallorca (www.deia.info) Check out this website for information about the town.

Sóller

POP 14,229

As though cupped in celestial hands, the ochre town of Sóller lies in a valley surrounded by the grey-green hills of the Serra de Tramuntana and orange and lemon groves.

Worth exploring in its own right, with its vintage train and tram rides, graceful Modernist architecture and galleries showcasing Picasso and Miró, Sóller is a wonderful base for exploring the west coast and the Tramuntana. It is also the trailhead for some stirring mountain hikes.

👁️ Sights & Activities

Sóller's heart and soul is Plaça de la Constitució, which hums with street life from cafes, bars, kids playing and, on Saturdays, a market.

⭐ Ca'n Prunera –
Museu Modernista   GALLERY, HISTORIC BUILDING
(www.canprunera.com; Carrer de Sa Lluna 86-90; adult/child €5/free; ⏰10.30am-6.30pm Mar-Oct, closed Mon Nov-Feb) One of Mallorca's stand-out galleries, Ca'n Prunera occupies a landmark Modernista mansion. The list of luminaries here is astonishing – works by Joan Miró, along with single drawings by Toulouse-Lautrec, Picasso, Gauguin, Klimt, Kandinsky, Klee, Man Ray and Cezanne. Also part of the permanent collection is a gallery devoted to Juli Ramis (1909–90), a Sóller native and world-renowned painter who had his studio in the neighbouring village of Biniaraix, plus works by Miquel Barceló, Antoni Tapiès and Eduardo Chillida.

⭐ Sala Picasso & Sala Miró   GALLERY
(Plaça d'Espanya 6, Estación de Tren; ⏰10am-6.30pm) FREE Few train stations have such a rich artistic legacy. In two rooms at street level in Sóller's station, there are two intriguing art exhibitions: the Sala Picasso and Sala Miró. The former has more than 50 ceramics by Picasso from 1948 to 1971, many bearing the artist's trademark subjects: dancers, women, bullfighting. The latter is home to a series of playful, colour-charged prints by the Catalan master; Miró's maternal grandfather was from Sóller.

Església de Sant Bartomeu   CHURCH
(Plaça de la Constitució; ⏰11am-1.15pm & 3-5.15pm Mon-Thu, 11am-1.15pm Fri & Sat, noon-1pm Sun) FREE A disciple of architect Antoni Gaudí, Joan Rubió got some big commissions in Sóller. The town didn't want to miss the wave of modernity and so Rubió set to work in 1904 on the renovation of the 16th-century Església de Sant Bartomeu. The largely baroque church (built 1688–1723) preserved elements of its earlier Gothic interior, but Rubió gave it a beautiful if unusual Modernista facade.

Trams   VINTAGE TRAM
(Tranvías; one way €5; 7am-11.30pm; 🚊) A real blast from the past, Sóller's old-world, open-sided trams trundle 2km down to Port de Sóller on the coast. They depart from outside the train station every half-hour or hour; pick up a timetable from the tourist office.

🛏️ Sleeping & Eating

Hostal Nadal   HOSTAL €
(📞971 63 11 80; Carrer de Romaguera 20; s/d/tr €24/37/48, without bathroom €20/29/39; 📶) It may be simple but it's home, and about as cheap as it gets on the island. Rooms are no-frills basic but spotless, and there's a courtyard out the back to flop in after a day's hiking.

⭐ Ca N'Aí   RURAL HOTEL €€€
(📞971 63 24 94; www.canai.com; Camí de Son Sales 50; ste €150-310; 🅿🌀@🛜♿🐾) Nestling among orange groves, family-run Ca N'Aí is a blissful escape, with its serene pools, garden hammocks and turtle-filled ponds. The

MOORS & CHRISTIANS IN IMMORTAL COMBAT

Every second weekend in May, Sóller is invaded by a motley crew of Muslim pirates. **Es Firó**, involving over 1000 townsfolk, is a good-natured mock battle between *pagesos* (locals) and *moros* (Moors). Sóller's take on **Moros i Cristians** (Moors and Christians) celebrates the repelling of a Moorish raiding party on 11 May 1561. Locals dress up and black up as scimitar-waving Moorish pirates, pitched against pole-toting defenders in a series of mock engagements, to the thunder of drums and blunderbusses.

nine spacious suites play up rural luxury, with high ceilings, Moorish-inspired tiles, antique furnishings and private terraces. The restaurant's candlelit patio is an incredibly romantic setting for a meal that puts a refined twist on *finca* (farm) produce.

It's around 2km northwest of the town centre.

Ca'l Bisbe
MALLORCAN €€

(✆ 971 63 12 28; www.hotelcalbisbe.com; Carrer del Bisbe Nadal 10; menus €29.50-38.50; ⊙8-10.30pm Mar-Oct) An old olive mill has been reincarnated into this restaurant, where you eat below heavy wood beams in the lantern-lit dining room or on the poolside terrace. The menu transcends the norm with refined dishes like slow-cooked cod with calamari noodles and black-olive crusted lamb with basil risotto, all expertly matched with local wines.

ⓘ Information

Tourist Office (✆ 971 63 80 08; www.visit-soller.com; Plaça d'Espanya 15; ⊙9.45am-4.15pm Mon-Fri, 9am-1pm Sat) Sóller's tourist office is in an old train carriage beside the station.

Biniaraix & Fornalutx

From Sóller it's a pleasant 2km drive, pedal or stroll through narrow laneways up to the hamlet of Biniaraix. From there, a classic walk ascends the Barranc de Biniaraix, following part of the old pilgrim route from Sóller to the Monestir de Lluc.

Climbing northwards, the narrow, twisting scenic road climbs to Fornalutx, through terraced citrus groves.

Fornalutx is a pretty village of distinctive stone houses with green shutters, colourful flower boxes and well-kept gardens, many now owned by expats.

Fornalutx Petit Hotel (✆ 971 63 19 97; www.fornalutxpetithotel.com; Carrer de l'Alba 22, Fornalutx; s €92.50-128, d €168-195; ⊙mid-Feb–mid-Nov; ❀◉❅❄), a tastefully converted former convent just below the main square, is as much art gallery as boutique hotel. Each of the eight rooms is named after a contemporary Mallorcan painter and displays the painter's canvases. It has a sauna and a hot tub and a wonderful terrace with views over the fertile valley.

Ca'n Reus (✆ 971 63 11 74; www.canreushotel.com; Carrer de l'Alba 26, Fornalutx; d €130-160, ste €170; ᴾ❀◉❅❄) is a tempting romantic escape. The British-owned country mansion was built by a Mr Reus, who got rich on the orange trade with France. The eight rooms are all quite different and all have views; each is stunning and has restrained antique furnishings and exposed stonework, with plenty of light throughout. Children under five are not welcome.

Sa Calobra

The road between the Ma10 and Sa Calobra is a 12km helter-skelter of a drive. Carved through weird mountainous rock formations, it skirts narrow ridges and twists down to the coast in an endless series of hairpin bends. If you think driving is tough, spare a thought for the cyclists slogging it uphill. You won't be alone in Sa Calobra. Armies of buses and fleets of pleasure boats disgorge battalion after battalion of visitors. A short trail through a rock tunnel leads around the coast to a rocky river gorge, the **Torrent de Pareis**, and a small white-pebble cove with fabulous (but usually crowded) swimming spots.

Boats make spectacular excursions beneath the cliffs from Port de Sóller to Sa Calobra, some calling by Cala Tuent.

Monestir de Lluc

Legend has it that, sometime in the 13th century, a shepherd boy and a monk stumbled across a small statue of the Virgin Mary beside a stream and took it to the parish church. The next day, it had vanished and reappeared on the stream bank. After this happened twice more, the villagers got the message and built a chapel to shelter the sacred statue where it was originally found.

A monastery, **Monestir de Lluc** (www. lluc.net; Plaça dels Peregrins; monastery & gardens free, museum adult/child €2/free, Lluc ticket €3; ◎10am-5pm), was established shortly thereafter. Since then thousands of pilgrims come every year to pay homage to the statue of the Virgin of Lluc, known as La Moreneta (the Little Dark One). If you're lucky you might hear Els Blauets, the famed boys' choir, singing. Founded nearly 500 years ago, they're called The Blues after the colour of their cassocks.

The present monastery is a huge, austere complex, dating from the 18th century. Off the central courtyard is the entrance to the **Basílica de la Mare de Déu**; the statue of the Virgin is in the ambulatory behind its main altar. There's also a **museum** of local archaeological finds and a modest art collection.

Pollença

POP 16,200

On a summer evening, when its ochre-hued houses glow in the fading light, cicadas strike up their tentative drone and the burble of chatter floats from cafe terraces below the Gothic church on Plaça Major, Pollença is like the Mallorca you always hoped you would discover.

If you're around on 2 August and notice a bunch of wild buccaneers disembarking, don't worry. It's just Pollença enjoying its **Festes de la Patrona**, celebrating the whupping of Muslim invaders back in 1550.

◎ Sights & Activities

★**Calvari**　　　　　　PILGRIMAGE SITE
(Carrer del Calvari) They don't call it Calvari (Calvary) for nothing. Some pilgrims do it on their knees, but plain walking up the 365 cypress-lined steps from the town centre to the 18th-century hilltop chapel, the **Oratori del Calvari**, is penance enough. This may not be a stairway to heaven, but there are soul-stirring views to savour back over the town's mosaic of terracotta rooftops and church spires to the Tramuntana beyond.

Món d'Aventura　　　　ADVENTURE SPORTS
(☑971 53 52 48; www.mondaventura.com; Plaça Vella 8; canyoning €40-50; ◎10am-2pm & 5-9pm Mon-Fri, 10am-2pm Sat & Sun) Canyoning, cav-

ing, kayaking, climbing, coasteering, hiking – you name the pulse-racing sport, Món d'Aventura has it covered. This is one of the most reputable adventure-sports operators on the north coast.

🛏 Sleeping & Eating

Hotel Desbrull　　　　　BOUTIQUE HOTEL €
(☑971 53 50 55; www.desbrull.com; Carrer del Marqués Desbrull 7; incl breakfast s €71-88, d €77-99; ❄🔌) The best deal in town, with six pleasantly fresh if coquettishly small doubles in a modernised stone house. White dominates the decor in rooms and bathrooms, offset with splashes of colour, and if you like the contemporary art on the walls, you can buy it. It's run by a friendly brother-sister combination.

★**Manzanas y Peras**　　　　TAPAS €
(☑971 53 22 92; www.manzanasyperas.es; Carrer del Martell 6; tapas tasting menu €25; ◎10am-4pm & 7-11pm Mon-Sat, 10am-4pm Sun; 🔌🍴) Tiny but brilliant, Manzanas y Peras (apples and pears) is a friendly oasis next to the Calvari steps, with tables set under trees lit by fairy lights. The tapas menu is a real feast, with taste sensations like crostini topped with melted goats cheese, blueberry jelly and walnuts, and chicken cooked in Moroccan spices with dates. Kids have their own dedicated menu (€11).

OFF THE BEATEN TRACK

CELESTIAL VIEWS

South of Pollença, one of Mallorca's most torturous roads bucks and weaves up 1.5km of hairpin bends to the14th-century **Santuari de la Mare de Déu des Puig** (◎9am-6pm Oct-Mar, 8.30am-8.30pm Apr-Sep) **FREE**, which sits atop 333m Puig de Maria. If you come pilgrim style, the stiff hike through holm oak, pine and olive woods takes around an hour. Explore the Gothic chapel, refectory and heirloom-filled corridors at the top – that's if you can tear yourself away from the spirit-lifting views of the north coast.

Stay the night at this former **nunnery** (☑971 18 41 32; s €10-14, d €17-22; 🔌🍴) and you'll have goat bells as your wake-up call. Rooms are basic, but hey, what do you expect?

SCOTT R BARBOUR / GETTY IMAGES ©

MICHELE FALZONE / GETTY IMAGES ©

1. Catedral (p780), Palma de Mallorca
Palma's cathedral has features designed by Antoni Gaudí and contemporary artist Miquel Barceló.

2. Dalt Vila (p808), Ibiza City
Ibiza City's whitewashed old quarter is home to some of the island's best cafes, clubs and bars.

3. Cala Macarella (p806), Menorca
One of the unspoilt beaches between Son Xoriguer and Cala Galdana.

4. Fornalutx (p790), Mallorca
Stroll along narrow alleys past the stone houses and gardens of this pretty village in the island's north west.

KONRAD WOTHE / GETTY IMAGES ©

WORTH A TRIP

CAP DE FORMENTOR

A splendid drive leads from Port de Pollença out high along this rocky promontory. Stop at the **Mirador de Sa Creueta** (232m), 3km out of Port de Pollença, for a dramatic view. Midway along the promontory is the plush **Hotel Formentor**, a 1920s jewel, which overlooks the pine-shaded strand of **Platja de Formentor** (Platja del Pi). Another spectacular 11km brings you to the lighthouse on the cape that marks Mallorca's northernmost tip. A few kilometres short of the lighthouse two trails lead from a dirt car park down to the splendid beaches of the wild cove of **Cala Figuera** on the northern flank and delightfully secluded **Cala Murta** on the southern side. Both have mesmerising blue waters.

❶ Information

Tourist Office (☑971 53 50 77; www.pollensa.com; Carrer de Guillem Cifre de Colonya; ☺8.30am-1.30pm & 2-4pm Mon-Fri, 10am-1pm Sun May-Oct, shorter hours rest of year) A mine of information on Pollença and its surrounds.

Cala Sant Vicenç

This is a tranquil resort in a magnificent setting: a series of four jewel-like coves with water so limpid you feel you could see to the centre of the world. It's very low-key indeed, and outside the main holiday season you'll pretty much have the place to yourself.

Set between Cala Molins and Cala Carbo, **Hostal los Pinos** (☑971 53 12 10; www.hostal-lospinos.com; Urbanització Can Botana, Cala Sant Vicenç; s €33-46, d €66-88, f €98-114; ☺May–mid-Oct; P❋☀☂) has two gleaming white villas sitting on a leafy hillside. Superior doubles have partial sea views and are wonderfully large with separate lounge areas and balconies.

For the freshest catch of the day, you can't beat beachside fisherman's shack **Cal Patró** (☑971 53 38 99; Cala Barques; mains €14-22; ☺12.30-3.30pm & 7.30-10.30pm Jul & Aug, shorter hours rest of year).

Badia d'Alcúdia

The long beaches of this bay fringe Mallorca's northeast coast, its broad sweeps of sand stretching from Port d'Alcúdia to Ca'n Picafort.

Alcúdia

POP 20,163

Wedged between the Badia de Pollença and Badia d'Alcúdia, Alcúdia was once a Roman settlement. The pretty old town is still partly protected by largely rebuilt **medieval walls** (parts of which you can stroll along). The highlight of the faded Roman ruins of **Pollentia** (www.pollentia.net; Avinguda dels Prínceps d'Espanya; adult/child incl Museu Monogràfic €3/2; ☺9.30am-8.30pm Tue-Sat, 10am-2pm Sun May-Sep, shorter hours rest of year), just outside the ramparts, is the small theatre. Alcúdia makes a great base for this corner of the island.

🛏 Sleeping & Eating

★**Can Tem** BOUTIQUE HOTEL €€
(☑971 54 82 73; www.hotelcantem.com; Carrer de l'Església 14; s €75-80, d €90-125; ❋☀☂) Set in a 17th-century town house, Can Tem is a boutique delight. Designed with flair, its light-flooded, white-walled rooms manage the delicate act of combining original features like beams and wood-carved bedsteads with contemporary artworks and slick bathrooms. Fresh pastries and homemade cake bring a sweet touch to breakfast, served in a pretty cobbled courtyard.

S'Arc INTERNATIONAL €€
(☑971 53 91 78; www.restaurantsarc.com; Carrer d'en Serra 22; mains €18-24; ☺noon-3.30pm & 6.30-11.30pm; ☂) Part of the Petit Hotel Ca'n Simó, this old-town charmer with a pretty inner courtyard and exposed stone walls offers Mediterranean cuisine with some inventive twists, such as Iberian pork with lemon couscous. World flavours also shine here, from Peruvian ceviche to Thai red curry.

❶ Getting There & Away

Bus 351 from Palma (€5.30, one hour) calls at Alcúdia hourly.

Port d'Alcúdia & Around

A lovely stretch of sand arcs southwards from the large harbour, from where boat trips leave daily to destinations such as Platja de Formentor. Nearby **Cap des Pi-**

nar is a craggy, pine-draped peninsula that lends itself to cycling, hiking and wild-goat spotting.

Parc Natural de S'Albufera (☑971 892 250; www.mallorcaweb.net/salbufera; ☺ visitor centre 9am-6pm Apr-Sep, 9am-5pm Oct-Mar) FREE, west of the Ma12 between Port d'Alcúdia and Ca'n Picafort, is prime birdwatching territory, with 303 recorded species (more than 80% of recorded Balearic species), 64 of which breed within the park's boundaries; more than 10,000 birds overwinter here, among them both residents and migrants. Entrance to the park is free, but permits must be obtained from the visitor centre, which is the trailhead for several walks through these protected wetlands.

East Coast

Many of the fine beaches along Mallorca's east coast have succumbed to the ravages of mass tourism. But further south the coastline is corrugated with caves, coves and inlets, some of which are accessible only on foot – among these are Mallorca's most beautiful, with turquoise waters and nary a hotel in sight.

Artà

POP 7415

Rising high and mighty above the graceful inland town of Artà is 14th-century **Santuari de Sant Salvador** (Via Crucis; ☺ 8am-8pm Apr-Oct, shorter hours rest of year) FREE, built atop an earlier Moorish enclave. A much-restored 4000-sq-metre complex, it reveals all the hallmarks of a medieval fortress, down to the stone turrets ringing the top and the metre-thick walls. The views from here sweep over the rooftops of medina-like old town and beyond to the bald, bumpy peaks of the Serra de Llevant.

On the coast, 11km southeast of Artà at the limit of the Ma4042, the **Coves d'Artà** (www.cuevasdearta.com; Carrer Coves de s'Ermita; adult/child 7-12yr/child under 7yr €13/7/free; ☺ 10am-6pm Apr-Oct, to 7pm Jun-Sep, 10am-5pm Nov-Mar), sunken into the cliffs, are a less-visited rival to Porto Cristo's Coves del Drac. Tours of the caves leave every 30 minutes.

🛏 Sleeping & Eating

Hotel Casal d'Artà   HOTEL €
(☑971 82 91 63; www.casaldarta.de; Carrer de Rafael Blanes 19; incl breakfast s €57-75, d incl breakfast €88-96; ✿ 🛜) Hotel Casal d'Artà is a wonderful old mansion in the heart of town. The decor may be old-fashioned, but a sense of light and space pervades this place. Rooms are full of individual charm; some have four-poster beds, while others feature sunken bathtubs. There's a flower-filled roof terrace, with a bubbling fountain and incomparable views over the village.

⭐ **Forn Nou**   MEDITERRANEAN €€
(☑971 82 92 46; www.fornnou-arta.com; Carrer del Centre 7; lunch menu €12, dinner menus €28-38; ☺ noon-4pm & 7pm-midnight Thu-Tue) Forn Nou's bird's nest of a terrace perches high above Artà's medieval maze and peers across the rooftops to the church and fortress. The season-driven menu changes twice monthly, but you can expect clean, bright Mediterranean flavours, along the lines of prawn-filled avocado with truffle mayonnaise and hake with garlic and crispy beetroot.

ℹ Information

Tourist Office (☑971 82 97 78; Carrer de l'Estel 4; ☺ 10am-5pm Tue-Fri, 10am-2pm Sat & Sun) A helpful tourist office with plenty of info and maps of the area. Sells the Artà Card.

ℹ Getting There & Away

Bus 411 to Palma (€9.50, 80 minutes, two to five daily).

ℹ RENTING A FARMHOUSE IN PARADISE

Renting apartments, studios, bungalows and villas is popular on the islands. Rural accommodation, often in stylishly transformed and tranquil country retreats (almost always with a pool), has become especially popular. Mallorca leads the way with some truly beautiful, bucolic options. A great deal more can be found in Lonely Planet's *Mallorca* guidebook. Otherwise, these websites will get you started:

➜ www.fincas4you.com

➜ www.agroturismo-mallorca.com

➜ www.rusticbooking.com

➜ www.mallorca.co.uk

➜ www.rusticrent.com

Portocolom

A tranquil village set on a generous harbour, Portocolom has managed to resist the tourist onslaught with dignity. It cradles a natural harbour, and within a couple of kilometres are fine beaches, such as the immaculate cove of Cala Marçal.

Right on the waterfront, Hostal Porto Colom (☑971 82 53 23; www.hostalportocolom. com; Carrer d'en Cristòfol Colom 5; s €43-65, d €60-112; ❋ 🛜) has breezy rooms with big beds and colourful, sunny decor. Downstairs it has a cool restaurant and lounge bar.

Up to seven buses link with Palma (€6.90, 1½ hours).

Cala d'Or to Cala Mondragó

Once a quaint fishing village, Cala d'Or is now an overblown big-dollar resort. Its sleek marina is lined with glistening megayachts and blindingly whitewashed villas crowd the surrounding hills.

Immediately south of Cala d'Or (and virtually joined to it by urban sprawl) is the smaller and more tranquil Portopetro. Centred on a boat-lined inlet and surrounded by residential estates, it has a cluster of harbourside bars and restaurants, and a couple of small beaches nearby.

Two kilometres south of Portopetro are the three cove beaches of Cala Mondragó, sheltered by large rocky outcrops, fringed by pine trees and connected by footpaths. These coves are among the loveliest on the east coast and form part of the Parc Natural de Mondragó, a natural park encompassing beaches, dunes, wetlands and coastal cliffs. Trails give birdwatchers plenty of opportunities to spot falcons, turtledoves, peregrines and Audouin's gulls. The whole area is protected, so park up above the beaches and walk from there.

Cala Figuera

The fisherfolk here really still fish, threading their way down the winding inlet before dawn. What has probably kept the place in one piece is the fact that the nearest beach, pretty Cala Santanyí, is a few kilometres drive southwest.

Nicer still is Cala Llombards, a petite cove with dazzling turquoise water, which you can walk to (scaling endless stairs) in about 30 minutes from Cala Santanyí or drive to via Santanyí (follow signs to Llombards, then Cala Llombards).

Perched on a bluff at the edge of the resort, the pleasant two-star Hotel Villa Sirena (☑971 64 53 03; www.hotelvillasirena.com; Carrer de la Verge del Carme 37, Cala Figuera; s/d €63/83, 2-/4-person apt €86/135; ⊙ hotel Apr-Oct, apt year-round; ❋ ❋) has enviable views of the sea. Rooms aren't fancy, but extras like a breezy seaside terrace make this a great choice. The well-priced apartments across the road are ideal if you're here for a longer stay.

Bus 502 makes the trip from Palma (€7, 1½ hours) via Colònia de Sant Jordi up to three times a day.

MENORCA

Arrive on the sun-bleached shores of Menorca after a spell on Mallorca or Ibiza and notice the drop in volume – here it's more birdsong than Pete Tong. The easternmost Balearic island moves to its own mellow beat. Its twinset of sea-splashed cities, Anglo-Spanish Maó and medina-like Ciutadella, are delightfully low-key, and the white-sand bays that stud its 216km coastline are among the loveliest in the Med. Inland, criss-crossing its fields and rolling hills are an estimated 70,000km of dry-stone walls.

In 1993 Unesco declared Menorca a Biosphere Reserve, aiming to preserve environmental areas, such as the Parc Natural S'Albufera d'es Grau wetlands, and its liberal sprinkling of mysterious Bronze Age sites.

ⓘ Getting Around

TO/FROM THE AIRPORT

Bus 10 (€2.60) runs between Menorca's airport, 7km southwest of Maó, and the city's bus station every half-hour. A taxi costs around €15.

BUS

You can get to most destinations from Maó with TMSA (www.tmsa.es) or Autos Fornells (www. autosfornells.com), but services elsewhere on the island are patchy at best.

CAR & MOTORCYLCE

Daily hire costs €35 to €45 for a modest sedan. All of the big operators have representatives at the airport. Most also have rental options in Ciutadella. In Maó, try the following:

Autos Mahon Rent (☑971 36 56 66; www. autosmahonrent.com; Moll de Llevant 35-36) Rents out bikes (€15 per day), scooters and cars.

Autos Valls (☑971 57 37 40; www.autosvalls. com; Plaça d'Espanya 13)

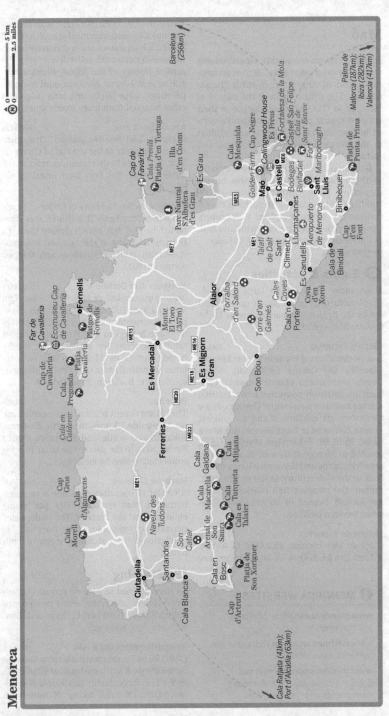

Menorca

5 km
2.5 miles

Barcelona
(256km)

Palma de
Mallorca (187km);
Ibiza (282km);
Valencia (417km)

Far de
Cavalleria

Ecomuseu Cap
de Cavalleria

Fornells

Platges de
Fornells

Cap de
Cavalleria

Cala
Pregonda

Platja
Cavalleria

Cala en
Culderer

Cap de
Favàritx

Cala Presili
Platja d'en Tortuga

Illa
d'en Colom

Es Grau

Cala
Mesquida

Pare Natural
S'Albufera
d'es Grau

Golden Farm Cap Negre

Fortalesa de la Mola
Es Freus

Maó Collingwood House

Es Castell Castell San Felipe
Bodegas Cala de
Binifadet Fort Sant Esteve

Sant Marlborough
Lluís

Binibèquer

Cap
d'en
Font

Cala de
Binidalí

Talatí
de Dalt

Sant
Climent

Aeropuerto
de Menorca

Es Canutells

Cova
d'en
Xoroi

Platja de
Punta Prima

ME7

Monte
El Toro
(357m)

Es Mercadal

ME15

Alaior

Torralba
d'en Salord

Torre d'en
Galmés

Cala n'en
Porter

Cales
Coves

Llucmaçanes

**Es Migjorn
Gran**

ME16

ME18

ME20

Ferreries

ME22

Cala
Galdana

Cala
Macarella

Cala
Mitjana

Cala
Turqueta

Son Bou

ME1

Cap
Gros

Cala
Morell

Cala
d'Algaiarens

Naveta des
Tudons

Son
Catlar

Arenal de
Son
Saura

Cala es
Talaier

Santandria

Ciutadella

Cala Blanca

Cala en
Bosc

Platja de
Son Xoriguer

Cap
d'Artrutx

Cala Ratjada (41km);
Port d'Alcúdia (63km)

Maó

POP 28,972

Sitting pretty on the world's second-largest natural harbour (5km long), Maó is an unusual blend of Anglo and Spanish characteristics. The British made it the capital of Menorca in 1713, and the influence of their almost-100-year presence (the island reverted to Spanish rule in 1802) is still evident in the town's architecture, traditions and culture.

Built atop the cliffs that line the harbour's southern shore, the town is a bright, breezy, easy-going place. Although some older buildings still remain, the majority of the architecture is in the restrained 18th-century Georgian style (note the sash windows and, as the Menorcans say to this day, *boínders* – bow windows).

Sights & Activities

Maó's main plaza is the large Plaça de s'Esplanada, originally a parade ground, laid out by the British. The narrow streets to the east are Maó's oldest.

Plaça d'Espanya   SQUARE

Just above Plaça d'Espanya is the Mercat Claustre del Carme (⊘Mon-Sat), where former neoclassical church cloisters have been imaginatively converted into a buzzing market and shopping centre. Upstairs, enjoy temporary art exhibitions and the modest Museu Hernández Sanz Hernández Mora (⊉971 35 05 97; ⊘10am-1pm Mon-Sat) FREE, devoted to Menorcan themes, illustrated by artworks, maps and decorative items dating back to the 18th century. In the square itself, explore the pungent fish market (⊘8am-1pm Tue-Sat), housed in an attractive olive-green wooden building.

Museu de Menorca   MUSEUM

(Plaça de Sant Francesc; adult/child €2.40/free; ⊘10am-2pm & 6-8.30pm Tue-Sat, 10am-2pm Sun)

This 15th-century former Franciscan monastery has also been a nautical school, a public library, a high school and a children's home. Its well-documented collection covers the earliest history of the island, Roman, Byzantine and Islamic Menorca, and includes paintings, some fascinating early maps and other material from more recent times, too.

Arc de Sant Roc   FORTRESS

(Carrer de Sant Roc, Old Quarter) This 16th-century archway at the top end of Carrer de Sant Roc is the only remaining relic of the medieval walls that once surrounded the old city.

Església de Santa Maria la Major   CHURCH

(Plaça de la Constitució) This church was completed in 1287 but rebuilt during the 18th century. Looming at the east end is a massive organ, built in Barcelona and shipped across in 1810.

Xoriguer Gin Distillery   DISTILLERY

(www.xoriguer.es; Moll de Ponent 93; ⊘8am-7pm Mon-Fri, 9.30am-1.30pm Sat) FREE At this showroom, you can taste and buy the distinctively aromatic Menorcan gin. From the range of sample liqueurs, try a shot of camomile-based Hierbas de Menorca, Palo with its bitter gentian flavour or Calent, cinnamon-scented and traditionally served hot.

Beaches   BEACH

The closest decent beaches to the capital are Sa Mesquida, 7km to the north, Es Grau, 10km to the north, and Platja de Punta Prima, 8km to the south. The latter two are connected to Maó by local bus.

Harbour Cruises   BOAT TOUR

A cluster of operators does one-hour glass-bottomed boat cruises (€11/5 per adult/child) around the harbour. The underwater perspective, enjoyable for its own sake, is outclassed by the stunning views of both banks.

Sleeping

To sleep steeped in history, stay at Collingwood House (p800), the former residence of British admiral Cuthbert Collingwood, Lord Nelson's right-hand man.

Hostal-Residencia La Isla   HOSTAL €

(⊉971 36 64 92; www.hostal-laisla.com; Carrer de Santa Caterina 4; s/d/tr incl breakfast €35/60/80; ❄⊜) This large, family-run *hostal* is excellent value. Its small rooms all come with

---

ℹ MENORCA WEBSITES

www.menorca.es Official Menorca tourism website.

www.visitmenorca.com Website of the hoteliers' association.

www.menorcamonumental.net Excellent presentation of Menorca's monuments and historical sites.

MENORCA'S TOP FIVE BEACHES

Menorca is blessed with some of the most gorgeous beaches in the Med. Tiptoe far from the sunbathing crowd to find your own secluded slice of heaven on the island's 216km coastline. Here's our top five:

Cala Mesquida A narrow country lane leads 7km north of Maó to this sweep of pale and translucent sea. It's a favourite among locals at weekends, fairly quiet otherwise. One end is given over to nudists.

Cala Mitjana Ah, bliss! Pine-brushed cliffs enshroud this white-sand cove on the southwest coast. Take the track that veers off the road between Ferreries and Cala Galdana, then walk for around 20 minutes to reach it.

Cala d'Algaiarens Tucked between Cala Morell and Cala en Carbó on the island's northwest coast, this stunning crescent of powder-soft sand with azure water is fringed by dunes and pines. Take the road to Cala Morell, following signs east to Algaiarens.

Cala Pregonda Swing around the headland of Far de Cavalleria from Fornells to reach this curvy golden beauty, which is backed by dunes and part of a marine reserve. It's a 20- to 30-minute walk from Binimel-la beach, where you can park. Bring a snorkel – the water is crystal clear.

Cala Macarella An exquisite horseshoe bay on the southwest coast, with white sand, unbelievably turquoise water and cliffs cloaked in pines and holm oaks. It can be popular so visit early, late or in low season. Neighbouring Cala Turqueta is lovely, too. There's a free car park 15 minutes' walk away.

their own bathroom and all have air-con. The decor is uninspiring, but the folks are friendly and run a bustling workers' bar-restaurant downstairs.

★ **Casa Alberti** HISTORIC HOTEL €€€
(☑ 686 393569; www.casalberti.com; Carrer d'Isabel II 9; incl breakfast s €70-130, d €90-190, q €140-235; ☑ May-Sep; ⊕) Climb the marble staircase with wrought-iron banisters to your high-ceilinged, white-walled room. Each of the six bedrooms within this 18th-century mansion is traditionally furnished, and you can relax in the grand chandelier-lit salon or on the roof terrace. Breakfast emphasises local organic produce, with squeeze-your-own juice, freshly baked bread and pastries and Menorcan cheese. Rates drop substantially outside of high season.

Hotel Port Mahón HOTEL €€€
(☑ 971 36 26 00; www.sethotels.com; Avinguda del Port de Maó; d €135-200; ☀ ☎ ☎ ⊕) This fine four-star hotel, built in traditional colonial style, has 73 nicely turned-out rooms, a pool and a pleasant garden with plenty of green. Rooms with balcony offer a grand view over the harbour. Decor varies from room to room and rates vary enormously from season to season.

✗ Eating

The harbourside is stacked with fish restaurants. Also worth investigating are many waterfront eateries in Cales Fonts, just 3km away in Es Castell.

La Mejor PASTELERÍA €
(Plaça Carme 6; snacks €1-5; ☑ 7am-11pm, shorter hours Oct-May) This wonderful old-school *pastelería* stocks all kinds of homemade sweet and savoury goodies. Feather-light *ensaïmades* (pastry spirals) filled with *cabell d'àngel* (pumpkin jam) and dusted with icing sugar are the house speciality.

Ses Forquilles SPANISH €€
(☑ 971 35 27 11; www.sesforquilles.com; Carrer de Sa Rovellada de Dalt 20; tapas €2.50-7.50, mains €12-22; ☑ 1-3.30pm & 8.30-11.30pm Mon-Sat) 'The Forks' is run by a friendly young team. This scarlet-walled, art-slung bistro does a roaring trade in fish and meat mains, *montaditos* (mini open sandwiches) and creative tapas – from rabbit spare ribs with aioli to a *sobrassada* (tangy cured sausage) and honey 'lollipop'.

Santa Rita TAPAS €€
(☑ 971 35 22 97; Plaça Bastió 14; tapas €4-9; ☑ 1-3.30pm & 7pm-midnight Mon-Sat) Spilling out onto Plaça Bastió, petite Santa Rita puts its own innovative spin on tapas. There's a

FORTS & MANSIONS

Great Britain occupied Menorca principally to gain possession of Maó's deep natural harbour, captured by the Royal Navy in 1708. It built **Fort Marlborough** (adult/child €3/1.80; ☉10am-1pm & 5-8pm Tue-Sat, 10am-1pm Sun) to defend the sound. A short video sets the historical background to a walk through the tunnels, enlivened by figurines, explosions and commentary. From the central hillock there's a fine view of the emerald-green inlet, Cala de Sant Esteve, the scant remains of Castell San Felipe and, to the south, the circular Torre d'en Penjat.

Across the Cala de Sant Esteve, **Castell San Felipe** (www.museomilitarmenorca.com; adult/child €5/2.50; ☉guided tours 10am Sat Oct-Nov & Mar-May, 10am Thu & Sun Jun-Sep), originally constructed in the 16th century, became, under British control, one of Europe's largest fortresses. When Spain recovered the island, King Carlos III had the fort largely destroyed. However, its labyrinth of underground tunnels has remained more or less intact.

To immerse yourself fully in the area's British colonial past, stop at **Collingwood House** (📋971 36 27 00; www.hoteldelalmirante.com; Hotel del Almirante; s/d incl breakfast €85/112; 🅿🛜🐾), once the residence of Admiral Cuthbert Collingwood, Nelson's fellow commander-at-sea. It's now a charming hotel halfway between Maó and Es Castell, replete with maritime reminiscences, pool, terrace, bar and wonderful views over the harbour.

In the 19th century Queen Isabel II ordered the construction of the extensive **Fortalesa de la Mola** (www.fortalesalamola.com; adult/child €8/5.50, audioguide €3; ☉10am-8pm Jun-Sep, shorter hours rest of yr), built between 1848 and 1875, which sprawls over the promontory of the same name on the northern shore of the bay. It's about a 12km drive from Maó. Ramble through galleries, gun emplacements and barracks.

On the way back towards Maó, you'll notice a rose-coloured stately home. At **Golden Farm** (Granja Dorada), they say, Nelson and his lover Lady Hamilton enjoyed a tryst in 1799. It's closed to the public.

distinctly global feel in dishes along the lines of tuna carpaccio with ponzu sauce, slow-cooked pork cheeks and marinated sardines with aubergines and curry sauce – all presented with flair and a smile.

S'Espigó
SEAFOOD €€€
(📋971 36 99 09; www.sespigo.com; Moll de Llevant 267; mains €21-28; ☉1-3.30pm & 8-11.30pm Tue-Sat, 8-11.30pm Sun-Mon) Among the long line of restaurants that offer delicacies pulled from the seas that surround Menorca, S'Espigó stands out. A brisk walk along the quayside will work up an appetite for dishes that are based upon what's hauled from the Mediterranean the previous day.

Jàgaro
SEAFOOD €€€
(📋971 36 23 90; www.jagaromenorca.com; Moll de Llevant 334; mains €15-38; ☉1-4pm & 8-11pm) Harbourside Jàgaro is good enough for royalty (see the photos of the Crown Prince and Princess at the entrance). Hauled from the restaurant's own boat, the fish couldn't be fresher, and the *caldereta de llagosta* (lobster stew) is superb. The more adventurous can begin with *ortiga de mar* (sea anemone).

🍷 Drinking & Entertainment

Nightlife in Maó is low-key compared with Mallorca or Ibiza. Most of the action is on the waterfront.

Mirador Café
BAR
(Plaça d'Espanya 2; ☉noon-12.30am Mon-Sat) Take a ringside seat outside for port views with your tapas and beer or glass of wine. The Mirador is a perennial favourite thanks to its cracking views, reasonable prices and occasional live music, including gigs at 9pm on Saturdays. Find it beside a short cul-de-sac at the top of Costa de ses Voltes.

Ars Café
CAFE, RESTAURANT
(www.arscafe.info; Plaça del Príncep 12; ☉11am-11pm Mon-Sat) Arty and boho at the edges, this is a warm, relaxing place to drink or eat. For maximum atmosphere, choose the front, main bar – except after midnight on Friday and Saturday, when you need to head down to the cellar bar, with its DJ and live music.

ℹ Information

Opening hours from November to April are much reduced.

Airport Tourist Office (☎971 15 71 15; ☺8am-8.30pm Wed-Mon, 8am-3pm Tue)

Main Tourist Office (☎971 36 37 90; Plaça de Sa Constitució 22; ☺10am-6.45pm Mon-Fri, 10.30am-1.30pm & 6-8pm Sat) Pick up maps and info here.

Port Tourist Office (☎971 35 59 52; Moll de Llevant 2; ☺8am-8.30pm Fri-Tue, 8am-2.30pm Wed & Thu)

ℹ Getting There & Around

Acciona Trasmediterránea (p778) and Baleària (p778) run ferries to Palma de Mallorca (around €31, six hours) several times a week.

TMSA (www.tmsa.es) operates a roughly hourly bus service to Alaior (€1.55, 10 minutes), Es Mercadal (€2.55, 25 minutes), Ferreries (€3.35, 35 minutes), Ciutadella (€5, one hour) and Sant Lluís (€1.60, 15 minutes), as well as to Cala'n Porter (€1.65, 30 minutes, three daily) and Es Migjorn Gran (€2.80, 25 minutes, four daily).

Autos Fornells (www.autosfornells.com) has daily services linking Maó to north-coast destinations including Es Grau (€1.65, 15 minutes) and Fornells (€3.25, 50 minutes).

The Interior – Maó to Ciutadella

The Me1, Menorca's main road connecting Maó and Ciutadella, runs east–west through undulating farmland, passing by the sun-bleached villages of Alaior, Es Mercadal and Ferreries. Along the way smaller roads branch off towards the beaches and resorts of the north and south coasts.

Many of Menorca's most significant archaeological sites are signposted off the main road.

Es Mercadal

Es Mercadal, one of the oldest villages on the island (a market has been held here since at least 1300), is at the turn-off north for Fornells.

Good old-fashioned home cooking and a familiar atmosphere is what you'll find at Ca N'Aguedet (☎971 37 53 91; Carrer de Lepanto 30; mains €11-26; ☺1-4pm & 8-11.30pm), which prides itself on dishes such as the melt-in-your-mouth *lechón* (suckling pig) or *conejo con cebolla y alcaparras* (rabbit with onion and capers).

Ferreries

Ferreries is renowned for its cheese, shoes and leather goods. At its market (Plaça Espanya; ☺9am-1pm Sat), stallholders sell fresh produce, along with traditional Menorcan crafts, and there's folk dancing in high season. The turn-off to the resort of Cala Galdana is just west of town.

The beautiful, 200-year-old rambling whitewashed house and pretty garden at Mesón El Gallo (☎971 37 30 39; www.mesonelgallo.com; mains €9-21; ☺1.30-3pm & 7.30-11pm Tue-Sun Feb-Nov) merit a visit for their own sake. Enjoy meat dishes, grilled just as you wish them, on the vine-clad terrace or in the rustic interior with its beams and terracotta floor. From Ferreries, head down the Cala Galdana turn-off for 1.5km.

Ciutadella

POP 29,580

Known as Vella i Bella ('Old and Beautiful'), Ciutadella is an attractive, distinctly Spanish city with a picturesque port and an engaging old quarter. Its character is quite distinct from that of Maó, and its historic centre is far more appealing.

Founded by Carthaginians and known to the Muslims as Medina Minurqa, Ciutadella was almost destroyed following the 1558 Turkish invasion and much of the city was subsequently rebuilt in the 17th century. It was Menorca's capital until the British arrived in the early 18th century.

⊙ Sights

The glory of central Ciutadella is that it's almost entirely traffic free.

Plaça d'es Born   SQUARE
Ciutadella's main square is a gracious affair, with 19th-century buildings such as the fortress-like ajuntament (town hall) and Palau Torresaura. The obelisk at the centre was raised to commemorate those townsfolk who died trying to ward off the Turks on 9 July 1558. For the finest view of the port and the town's remaining bastions and bulwarks, sneak behind the town hall and up to the 14th-century Bastió d'Es Governador (☺9am-7pm Tue-Sun).

Old Ciutadella   HISTORIC NEIGHBOURHOOD
The narrow cobbled lanes between Plaça d'es Born and Plaça de ses Palmeres hold plenty of interest, with whitewashed buildings

WORTH A TRIP

MENORCA'S PREHISTORIC ROCK STARS

Get a handle on Menorca's history by visiting its liberally scattered archaeological sites (in winter, these are unattended and can be visited freely). The monuments span three main periods: the Pre-Talayotic (or cave era) from 2000 BC to 1300 BC; the Talayotic (Bronze Age) from 1300 BC to 800 BC; and the Post-Talayotic (Iron Age) from 800 BC to around 100 BC. Similarly, there are three general types of structures: *navetas*, thought to be tombs or meeting places; *talayots*, large stone mounds used as watchtowers; and *taulas*, horseshoe-shaped sanctuaries with tall T-shaped pillars at their heart, which could have been used as sacrificial altars.

Torre d'en Galmés (adult/child €3/1.80; ⊙9.15am-8.45pm Tue-Sat, 9.15am-3pm Sun & Mon) If you only visit one Talayotic site, let it be this. Stop by the small information centre for a 10-minute video presentation, then wander at will over the site with its three hilltop *talayots*, rambling circular dwellings, deep underground storage chambers and sophisticated water-collection system. It's signposted on the road between Alaior and Son Bou.

Son Catlar (admission free; ⊙10am-sunset) This is the largest Talayotic settlement in the Balearic Islands, with five *talayots* and ruined dwellings covering around 6 hectares. Find it south of Ciutadella (from the *ronda* ring road follow the road for Cala Macarella and after 2.8km veer right).

Naveta des Tudons (adult/child €2/1.20; ⊙9.15am-8.30pm Tue-Sat, 9.30am-3pm Sun & Mon) East of Ciutadella (near the Km 40 road marker), the Naveta des Tudons is a stone burial chamber constructed around 1000 BC.

Talatí de Dalt (adult/child €4/3; ⊙10am-sunset) At this Talayotic settlement, 3km west of Maó, the roots of wild olive trees force apart the weathered stones of the large central *talayot*. There's also a particularly well-preserved *taula*.

Torralba d'en Salord (adult/child €3.50/free; ⊙10am-8pm Mon-Sat) Torralba d'en Salord is located 15km from Maó. Follow the signposts and take a left turn off the Me1 to reach this Talayotic settlement, whose outstanding feature is an impressive *taula*.

Cales Coves Further south on the coast at Cales Coves, some 90 caves dug into the coastal cliffs were apparently used for ritual burials.

abutting elegant noble palaces and ornate churches like baroque 17th-century **Església del Roser** (Carrer del Roser; ⊙11am-1.30pm & 6-9.30pm Mon-Sat). **Església dels Socors** (Carrer del Seminari 9) is home to the **Museu Diocesà** (adult/child €3/free; ⊙10.30am-1.30pm Tue-Sat May-Oct), a fine little museum, secular as much as religious. Attractively arcaded **Carrer ses Voltes** is lined with smart shops, restaurants and bars. The town's **fish market** (Plaça de la Llibertat; ⊙7am-1pm Tue-Sat) is in a pleasing 1895 Modernista building.

Catedral　　　　　　　　　　CATHEDRAL
(Plaça de la Catedral; ⊙10am-4pm Mon-Sat) The 14th-century cathedral was built in Catalan Gothic style (but with a baroque facade) on the site of Medina Minurqa's central mosque.

Museu Municipal　　　　　　　MUSEUM
(Bastió de sa Font; adult/child €2.50/free; ⊙10am-2.30pm & 6-9pm Tue-Sat May-Sep, morning only Oct-Apr) The single, vaulted gallery of the town museum has a small display of Talayo-

tic, Roman and Islamic finds from the area. Ask to borrow its comprehensive documentation in English.

Castell de Sant Nicolau　　　　TOWER
(Plaça del Almirante Ferragut; ⊙11am-1pm & 6-8pm Tue-Sat) **FREE** West of the town centre, this stout little 17th-century watchtower stands guard at the southern head of the port entrance. Views over the waters to Mallorca and southwards along the coast are stunning.

🏃 Activities

Menorca Blava　　　　　　　　BOAT TOUR
(www.menorcablava.com; adult/child €44/22; ⊙9.30am-1.30pm & 5-8.30pm) Runs boat trips to the beaches of the southern coast, departing at 10am, returning at 5pm and including a paella lunch.

Diving Centre Ciutadella　　　　DIVING
(☑971 38 60 30; Plaça de Sant Joan 10; per dive €48; ⊙May-Oct) One of three dive centres in and around Ciutadella. It's located in the port.

🛏 Sleeping

Hostal-Residencia Oasis
HOSTAL €

(☑ 630 018008; www.hostaloasismenorca.es; Carrer de Sant Isidre 33; d €40-66, tr €56-87, q €82-103; 🐾) Run by delightful friendly owners, this quiet place is close to the heart of the old quarter. Rooms, mostly with bathroom, are set beside a spacious garden courtyard. Their furnishings, though still trim, are from deep into the last century.

⭐ Tres Sants
BOUTIQUE HOTEL €€€

(☑ 971 48 22 08; www.grupelcarme.com; Carrer Sant Cristòfol 2; s €140-175, d €180-210; ❄ 🐾 🏊) Buried deep in Ciutadella's medina-like heart, Tres Sants is a slice of breezy, boho cool. The owners' attentive eye for detail shines in this beautifully converted 18th-century manor house, with frescoed walls, candlelit passageways and whitewashed rooms with nice touches like four-poster beds, sunken bathtubs and iPod docks. The subterranean pool and steam bath evokes the hotel's Roman origins.

Hotel Sant Ignasi
RURAL HOTEL €€€

(☑ 971 38 55 75; www.santignasi.com; Carretera de Cala Morell; incl breakfast s €130-166, d €191-265, ste €235-380; ❄ 🐾 🏊) This venerable 18th-century mansion, planted solidly in grounds shaded by mature wild olive trees, is in open country, a mere 3km outside Ciutadella. Each of the 20 serene rooms has its own individual style and there's a first-class restaurant. Prices more than halve over winter months. From the Cala Morell road, take a narrow lane signed 'Hotel Rural' for 1.6km.

🍴 Eating

Ciutadella's small port teems with restaurants and cafes, many of which are set in the old city walls or carved out of the cliffs that line the waterfront.

Smoix
INTERNATIONAL €€

(☑ 971 48 05 16; www.smoix.com; Carrer de Sant Isidre 33; mains €12-22, 3-course lunch €17; ◔ 1-3.30pm & 8-11.30pm Tue-Sat, 1-3.30pm Mon) A pinch of creativity spices up dishes at this pretty courtyard restaurant. You might begin with, say, endive, salmon, rocket and seaweed salad, followed by cod with aubergine, tomatoes and gorgonzola. The food is fresh and local, the ambience low-key and romantic.

Cas Ferrer de sa Font
MENORCAN €€

(☑ 971 48 07 84; www.casferrer.com; Carrer del Portal de sa Font 16; mains €15-20; ◔ 1-3.30pm & 8-11pm Tue-Sat, 8-11pm Sun & Mon) Nowhere on the island will you find more authentic Menorcan cuisine – the menu is based upon meats and vegetables from the owner's organic farm. Dine on the delightful interior patio of this charming 18th-century building or inside, below beams and soft curves, in what was once a blacksmith's forge.

Cas Cònsol
TAPAS, MEDITERRANEAN €€

(☑ 971 48 46 54; www.casconsol.com; Plaça des Born 17; menú del día €14, mains €13-18; ◔ 12.30-3.30pm & 8-11.30pm Mon-Sat) Occupying the former French consulate, Cas Cònsol harmoniously blends the modern and minimalist within a historic setting. It serves tapas and creative mains such as quail with apple sauce and raisins. From the small wedge of terrace, there are great views of the harbour.

⭐ C'an Bep
SPANISH €€€

(☑ 971 48 78 15; www.canbep.com; Passeig Sant Nicolau 4; mains €14-25; ◔ 1-4pm & 8pm-midnight Mon-Sat) Dine at the marble-topped bar, where locals congregate to chat, or in the smart rear restaurant. Like the port-side restaurants below it, C'an Bep offers plenty of fresh fish dishes, including *cap roig*, a delicious Balearic speciality that off-puttingly translates as 'sea scorpion'.

Café Balear
SEAFOOD €€€

(☑ 971 38 00 05; www.cafe-balear.com; Plaça de Sant Joan 15; mains €15-45, 3-course menu €19; ◔ 1-4pm & 7.30pm-midnight Mon-Sat) Sometimes the old-timers are the best. Set apart from the town's more frenetic restaurant activity, this remains one of Ciutadella's classic seafood stops. You can eat outside on the quayside while tucking into local prawns, *navajas* (razor shells) or fresh fish, caught from Café Balear's own boat.

MAYONNAISE

Menorcans claim to have given the world the name 'mayonnaise', arguing that the term is derived from *salsa mahonesa*, meaning 'sauce of Mahón (Maó)'. The French, too, claim it as their own, but the islanders argue that it was originally brought to the mainland by the troops of the Duc de Richelieu after they defeated the British in 1756. A plausible story (in fact, it's widely used all around the northern Mediterranean), but perhaps best taken with a pinch of salt – like the best mayonnaise.

MALLORCA, MENORCA & IBIZA CIUTADELLA

♟ Drinking & Entertainment

The bulk of the town's nightlife is concentrated along the waterfront, in particular around both sides of Plaça de Sant Joan.

La Margarete BAR
(Carrer de Sant Joan Baptista 6; ⊙10am-3.30am) Tucked away down a side street, this is a stylish option. The interior is slick with modern, arty decor. On warmer nights, enjoy its pleasant cropped lawn.

Space CLUB
(www.spacemenorca.com; Plaça de St Juan 15; ⊙midnight-6am) Opened in 2012, this little sibling of the Ibiza megaclub has given Ciutadella's nightlife a jump-start. Top DJs spin everything from house to disco, and there's a glam roof terrace overlooking the city for chilling.

Jazzbah LIVE MUSIC
(Plaça de San Joan 3; ⊙10pm-5.30am) This venue, dug deep into the cliff face, is worth watching for its live concerts, happening house nights and chill-out sessions.

🛍 Shopping

Ciutadella has two magnificent and long-established delicatessens.

El Paladar FOOD
(www.elpaladar.es; Camì de Maó 10; ⊙9am-1pm & 5-8.30pm Mon-Sat) Penetrate deep into this boutique for wines, pickles, pâtés, ripe local cheeses and plenty of pig products.

Ca Na Fayas FOOD
(www.canafayas.es; Carrer Murada d'Artrutx 32 & Avinguda de Jaume I El Conqueridor 47; ⊙8am-2pm & 5-9pm Mon-Sat) This richly scented

---

OFF THE BEATEN TRACK

CAP DE FAVÁRITX

The drive up to this narrow rocky cape at the northern extremity of the Parc Natural S'Albufera d'es Grauis is a treat. The last leg is across a lunar landscape of black slate. At the end of the road (on the way, ignore the *propiedad privada* – private property – sign; it's public access), a lighthouse stands watch. South of the cape stretch some fine remote sandy bays and beaches, including Cala Presili and Platja d'en Tortuga, both accessible only on foot.

---

gourmet emporium has entrances on two streets. Whole cheeses, shelf upon shelf of them, fill the shop window.

ℹ Information

Tourist Office (☑971 38 26 93; Plaça de la Catedral 5; ⊙9.30am-3pm Mon, 9am-8.30pm Tue-Sun Jun-Sep, shorter hours Oct-May)

ℹ Getting There & Away

Twice-daily ferries for Port d'Alcúdia in Mallorca (€35 to €38, two hours) leave with Baleària (p778) and Iscomar (p778) from Son Oleo, just south of town.

Torres (www.bus.e-torres.net) buses serve the coast south of Ciutadella as far as Son Xoriguer, departing from Plaça dels Pins. The hourly **TMSA** (www.tmsa.es) service to Maó (€5, one hour) stops en route in Ferreries (€2, 15 minutes) and Es Mercadal (€2.85, 25 minutes).

ℹ Getting Around

Autos Ciutadella (☑971 48 00 24; www.autosciutadella.com; Avinguda del Capità Negrete 49bis) Local car-rental agency offering competitive prices.

Velos Joan (☑971 38 15 76; www.velosjoan.com; Carrer de Sant Isidre 30; ⊙8.30am-1.30pm & 4-8.30pm Mon-Fri, 10am-1pm & 7-8.30pm Sat, 10.30am-noon Sun) Bike rental here costs between €12 and €25 per day.

North Coast

Menorca's north coast is rugged and rocky, punctured by small, scenic coves. It's less developed than the south, and with your own transport and a bit of footwork, you'll discover some of the Balearics' best off-the-beaten-track beaches.

Es Grau & Around

This spruce, whitewashed hamlet sits beside a pretty arc of a bay. The beach's shallow waters are ideal for young families. Inland from Es Grau and separated from the coast by a barrier of high sand dunes is S'Albufera, the largest freshwater lagoon in the Balearics.

◉ Sights & Activities

★ **Parc Natural S'Albufera d'es Grau** NATURE PARK
(☑971 35 63 03; ⊙park 9am-7pm Tue-Thu, 9am-3pm Fri-Mon, information office 9am-3pm Mon-Fri) Home to many species of wetland birds, this lagoon and its shores form the 'nucleus zone'

of Menorca's Unesco Biosphere Reserve, a natural park protected from development. It's a safe haven for birdlife (kites and fish eagles for instance) and species like Lilford's wall lizards and Hermann's tortoises. The park's information office is 1km off the Me5/Es Grau road. From here you can follow two easy, signed trails (a third leads from Es Grau), each lasting under an hour.

Menorca en Kayak   KAYAKING
(☑ 669 097977; www.menorcaenkayak.com; Carrer S'Arribada 8, Es Grau; ☺ Easter-Oct) Rent a kayak or bike here to explore the nature park from the sea or land.

Fornells
POP 950

This whitewashed fishing village sits on a long slim bay, with sheltered, unruffled waters ideal for novice windsurfers. Fornells is renowned for its waterfront seafood restaurants, most of which serve up the local, decidedly pricey speciality, *caldereta de llagosta* (lobster stew). Swinging 4km west around the coast brings you to the resort of Platges de Fornells and its fine sandy beach.

◉ Sights & Activities

Castell Sant Antoni   FORTRESS
FREE 'Castle' is a grand word for this insensitively 'restored' fort with its excess of crude concrete. All the same, it's worth a brief visit. You can browse around at will and learn about the history of Fornells from the well-documented informative panels.

Dia Complert   ADVENTURE SPORTS
(☑ 609 670996; www.diacomplert.com; Passeig Marítim 41; ☺ Apr-Oct) This is your one-stop shop in Fornells for action on water and land – from diving, jet-skiing and guided kayak outings to mountain-bike sorties and half-day hikes along the coast. It also rents out bikes and kayaks.

Kayatak   WATER SPORTS
(☑ 626 486426; www.katayak.net; Passeig Marítim 69; ☺ Apr-Oct) This outfit runs four-hour catamaran (adult/child €65/35) and kayaking (adult/child €40/25) excursions. It also rents bicycles, stand-up paddleboards and kayaks for €15/15/30 per day respectively.

Wind Fornells   WATER SPORTS
(☑ 664 335801; www.windfornells.com; ☺ May–mid-Oct) Ramon and co at Wind Fornells offer windsurfing and dinghy sailing courses

WORTH A TRIP

CAMÍ DE CAVALLS
This signed walking trail, the GR223, revives an 18th-century defensive route that linked coastal watchtowers, fortresses and artillery batteries. Well signed (look for the horseshoe symbol), it snakes around the coastline for 184km, with occasional forays inland, and can be walked in easy sections. Most stretches are attackable by mountain bike, too. Ask for details at tourist offices or buy *Camí de Cavalls Guidebook: 20 Routes to Discover Menorca* (€22). The Camí de Cavalls is mostly flat along Menorca's southern shores and makes for splendid, undemanding walking.

(two-hour sessions €47). They also rent out stand-up paddleboards (two hours €25).

🍽 Sleeping & Eating

Hostal La Palma   HOSTAL €€
(☑ 971 37 66 34; www.hostallapalma.com; Plaça s'Algaret 3; s €50, d €66-115; ☺ Easter-Oct; ❊ 🛜 🛜) Behind this busy bar-restaurant are cheerful rooms with balconies and views of the surrounding countryside. Singles aren't available in August. Rates inlcude breakfast and halve in the low season.

Hostal S'Algaret   HOSTAL €€
(☑ 971 37 65 52; www.hostal-salgaret.com; Plaça s'Algaret 7; s/d/tr €50/90/110; ☺ May-Sep; ❊ 🛜 🛜 🛜) In business since the 1950s, this pleasant, simple *hostal* offers crisp, clean rooms with balconies and a warm welcome.

Es Port   SEAFOOD €€
(☑ 971 37 64 03; Passeig Marítim 5; mains €12-65; ☺ 1-4pm & 8-11pm Tue-Sun May-Oct) The fish and other seafood are the freshest here – unsurprisingly since Es Port has its own boat and lobster pots. Like most of its neighbours, it does *caldereta de llagosta*, but less financial outlay goes into a sizzling *paella de llomanto* (lobster paella).

Café del Nord   SPANISH €€
(☑ 971 37 66 97; www.cafedelnord.com; Local 5, Platja de Fornells; mains €11-65, 3-course menu €15; ☺ 1-3.30pm & 7-11pm; 🛜) In a cracking spot above the bay, Café del Nord offers tantalising sea views and rustles up great seafood and rice dishes. The shellfish and

CAVE CLUBBING

For a night on the rocks, head to Cova d'en Xoroi (www.covadenxoroi.com; Cala'n Porter; entry incl drink adult/child day €7.50/4, night €10-20; ⊙ noon-6am May-Sep), perched like an eyrie in the cliffs above Cala'n Porter. Go by day for glittering sea views or at sunset for chill-out beats and cocktails. DJs hit the decks as the night wears on, pumping out everything from house to hippie grooves. With its troglodyte nooks and crannies, this is one the most atmospheric clubs in the Balearics.

anglerfish *caldereta* will set you back a reasonable €20.

Cap de Cavalleria & Around

At a roundabout 3km south of Fornells, follow signs for Far de Cavalleria, to reach a parking area after 7km. From here a walk of less than 10 minutes brings you to the stunning double-crescent, golden beach of Platja Cavalleria.

A further spectacular 2km drive north brings you to the tip of Cap de Cavalleria, abrupt cliffs, Far de Cavalleria (Spain's oldest lighthouse) and a series of crumbling civil-war Republican gun emplacements.

Ecomuseu Cap de Cavalleria (www. ecomuseudecavalleria.com; Predi de Santa Teresa; adult/child €3/free; ⊙ 10am-7.30pm Apr-Oct) is a small, private museum 1km north of Platja Cavalleria's car park. Panels and videos illustrate the north coast, its fauna, the lighthouse, ancient inhabitants and Roman occupation. Borrow the booklet with full English translations of the captions. The museum's *Les 7 Rutes* is a detailed multilingual map showing every feature of the peninsula.

South Coast

Menorca's southern flank tends to have the better beaches – and thus the greater concentration of development. The jagged coastline is occasionally interrupted by a small inlet with a sandy beach, backed by a cluster of gleaming-white villas, largely small-scale and in Moorish-Mediterranean style.

Ciutadella to Son Bou

The rugged coastline south of Ciutadella gives way to a couple of smallish beaches at the resorts of Santandria and Cala Blanca. On the island's southwest corner looms the large resort of Cala en Bosc, a busy boating and diving centre. Not far east are the popular beaches of Platja de Son Xoriguer, connected to Ciutadella by frequent buses.

Between Son Xoriguer and Cala Galdana lie some of the island's least-accessible coves. A narrow country road leads south of Ciutadella (follow the 'Platjes' sign from the *ronda* – ring road) and then forks twice to (almost) reach the unspoiled beaches (from west to east) of Arenal de Son Saura, Cala es Talaier, the especially lovely little Cala en Turqueta and Cala Macarella.

Southwest of Ferreries is Cala Galdana, settled snugly around its lovely horseshoe-shaped bay, marred by three monster hotels. The Camí de Cavalls (p805) leads west through pine trees to Cala Macarella (30 minutes) and eastwards to Cala Mitjana (20 to 30 minutes), another enticing strand that's also accessible by road.

The resort of Son Bou, southwest of Alaior, boasts the island's longest beach and most depressing development. Just beyond the beach's eastern limit are the remains of a 5th-century Christian basilica.

South of Maó

The coast south of Maó is more intensively developed (well, by Menorcan standards), but it has a sprinkling of pretty coves, the island's top winery and mysterious archaeological sites that delight anyone with an interest in prehistory.

◉ Sights & Activities

Binibèquer   VILLAGE
Binibèquer looks like a charming fishing village; in fact, it was modelled on one in the early 1970s. Gleaming white and something of a tourist beehive, its sugar-cube houses and tight alleys are appealing, whatever their genesis. A 15-minute walk east of the village centre brings you to a sandy cove with clear water. Buses from Maó stop here.

Platja de Punta Prima   BEACH
Platja de Punta Prima is a small holiday resort with a pleasant 200m-long beach. Although it's protected by the low expanse of offshore Illa de l'Aire, distinguished by the

thin pencil of its lighthouse, the waves still roll in gently and enticingly. Regular buses run here from Maó.

Molí de Dalt
WINDMILL

(☎971 15 10 84; adult/child €1.20/0.60; ⏱10am-2pm Mon-Sat) Sant Lluís, a bright, white, grid-pattern inland town, was built by the French during their brief occupation of the island between 1756 and 1763. Stop to visit the Molí de Dalt, the town's last surviving working windmill, constructed during the French era. Within it, there's a small museum of rural implements and tools.

★ Bodegas Binifadet
WINERY TOURS

(☎971 15 07 15; www.binifadet.com; Carretera Sant Lluís-Es Castell Km 1; ⏱10am-8pm, to 10pm Jul & Aug) At Menorca's largest winery, you can amble around the vineyards at your own pace. Or join a free 30-minute guided tour that concludes with a tasting of its wines, grape jelly and tangy Menorcan goat cheese. It's just outside San Lluís, on the road to Es Castell.

🛏 Sleeping & Eating

★ Hotel Biniarroca
HOTEL €€€

(☎971 15 00 59; www.biniarroca.com; Camí Vell 57, Sant Lluís; incl breakfast s €125-150, d €150-300, ste €320-385; ⏱May-Oct; @🛜🛎) Crank up the romance at this rambling rural retreat. It's Irun with panache by a pair of British lady artists and designers. Ducks peck and sheep graze just beyond the fence of their lovely garden, planted with flowers, tamarisk and almond trees. Their gourmet restaurant is open to all-comers. Rates are much lower outside high summer.

Pan y Vino
MEDITERRANEAN, FRENCH €€

(☎971 15 02 01; www.panyvinomenorca.com; Camí de la Coixa 3, Torret, Sant Lluís; 4- to 9-course menus €37-50; ⏱7.15-11pm Wed-Mon) Patrick and Noelia are your hosts at this Menorcan country-house restaurant, where Med-meets-French cuisine is prepared with finesse. Sit on the terrace for the seasonal tasting menu, which might include dishes like wild mushroom risotto with truffle oil and Mahon cheese. There's a well-edited wine list.

IBIZA

The all-night raver, the boho-cool hippie chick, the sexiest babe on the beach – Ibiza is all this and more to those who have a soft spot for the party-loving sister of the Balearics. The cream of Europe's DJs (David Guetta, Luciano, Sven Väth et al) makes the island holy ground for clubbers. And no-where does sunset chilling like Sant Antoni de Portmany's strip of mellow cafes.

Ibiza

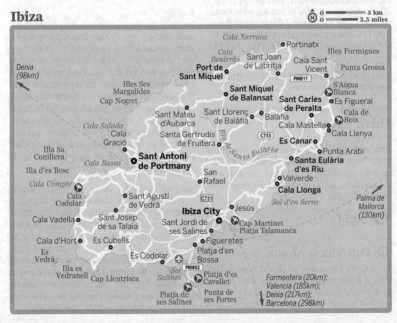

MALLORCA, MENORCA & IBIZA IBIZA

❶ IBIZA WEBSITES

www.ibiza.travel Official Ibiza tourism website.

www.ibiza-spotlight.com Up-to-date website with clubbing, hotel and activity reviews.

www.essentialibiza.com Beaches, activities, clubs and more.

www.ibizahotelsguide.com Official website of Ibiza's hoteliers' association.

www.ibizaruralvillas.com For rural villas and houses.

Ibiza's modest population of 132,637 is swallowed whole by the six-million-odd tourists that descend on it each year. But there's more to this pine-clad, sun-kissed, beach-bejewelled island than meets the bleary eye. Step off the beaten track for a spell in a rural hotel, a hilltop hamlet or on a secluded north-coast cove to discover Ibiza's surprisingly peaceful side. Or roam the ramparts of Ibiza City's Unesco-listed Dalt Vila to immerse yourself in the island's rich heritage.

❶ Getting Around

TO/FROM THE AIRPORT

Bus 10 from Ibiza City runs to the airport every 20 minutes; during summer bus 9 goes to the airport from Sant Antoni every 1½ hours and bus 24 from Es Canar via Santa Eulària every two hours. Out of season you'll have to go to Ibiza City first.

BUS

Fares don't exceed €4.30 for the longest journey. Online, check out www.ibizabus.com.

Ibiza City

POP 49,390

Ibiza's capital is a vivacious, enchanting town with a captivating whitewashed old quarter topped by a cathedral. It's also a focal point for some of the island's best cafes, bars and clubs.

◉ Sights

◉ Dalt Vila & Around

Ibiza City's bird's nest of an old town is Dalt Vila, a Unesco World Heritage site. It rises in a helter-skelter of cobbled lanes, white-washed houses and lookouts, crowned by a cathedral and embraced by massive Renaissance ramparts. The Romans were the first to fortify this hilltop. The existing walls were raised by Felipe II in the 16th century to protect against invasion by French and Turkish forces. It's a joy to wander around (comfy shoes essential).

Ramparts   HISTORIC SITE

A ramp leads from Plaça de Sa Font in Sa Penya up to the Portal de ses Taules, the main entrance. Above it hangs a commemorative plaque bearing Felipe II's coat of arms and an inscription recording the 1585 completion date of the fortification – seven artillery bastions joined by thick protective walls up to 22m in height.

You can walk the entire perimeter of these impressive Renaissance-era walls, designed to withstand heavy artillery, and enjoy great views along the way.

Catedral   CATHEDRAL

(Plaça de la Catedral; ⊙9.30am-1.30pm & 3-8pm) Ibiza's cathedral elegantly combines several styles: the original 14th-century structure is Catalan Gothic, but the sacristy was added in 1592 and a major baroque renovation took place in the 18th century. Inside, the **Museu Diocesà** (admission €1.50; ⊙9.30am-1.30pm Tue-Sun, closed Dec-Feb) contains centuries of religious art.

Bastions   TOWERS

In the **Baluard de Sant Jaume** (Ronda Calvi; adult/child €2/free; ⊙10am-2pm & 5-8pm Tue-Fri, 10am-2pm Sat & Sun), an exhibition of military paraphernalia includes soldiers' cuirasses that you can try for size (and weight!) and cannonballs to heave. An exhibition within the **Baluard de Sant Pere** (Portal Nou; adult/child €2/free; ⊙10am-2pm & 5-8pm Tue-Fri, 10am-2pm Sat & Sun), the next bastion northwards, demonstrates the tricks of artillery warfare and how to mount a cannon and has an audiovisual illustration of how the city walls were constructed.

Madina Yasiba La Cúria   MUSEUM

(Carrer Major 2; adult/child €2/free; ⊙10am-2pm & 6-9pm Tue-Fri, 10am-2pm Sat & Sun) This small display replicates the medieval Muslim city of Madina Yabisa (Ibiza City) prior to the island's fall to Christian forces in 1235. Artefacts, audiovisuals and maps transport visitors back in time. The centre is housed in what was, from the 15th century, the Casa de la Cúria (law courts). Parts of its walls were the original Islamic-era defensive walls.

Ibiza City

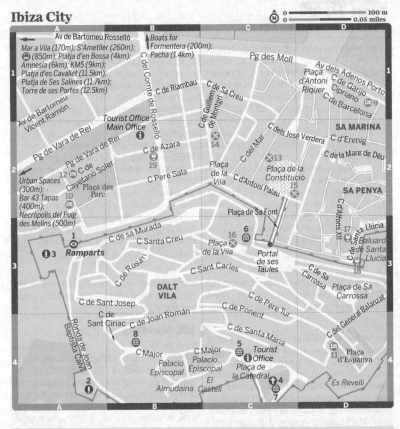

N 0 ____ 100 m
0 ____ 0.05 miles

Ibiza City

◎ Top Sights
1 Ramparts	A3

◎ Sights
2 Baluard de Sant Jaume	A4
3 Baluard de Sant Pere	A3
4 Catedral	C4
5 Madina Yasiba La Cúria	C4
6 Museu d'Art Contemporani (MACE)	C3
7 Museu Diocesà	C4
8 Museu Puget	B4

⊜ Sleeping
9 Hostal La Marina	D1

10 Hostal Parque	A2
11 Hotel Mirador de Dalt Vila	D4
12 Vara de Rey	A2

◉ Eating
13 Bistrot El Jardin	C2
14 Comidas Bar San Juan	C2
15 Croissant Show	C2
16 El Olivo	C3

⊜ Drinking & Nightlife
17 Angelo	D3
18 Soap	D3
19 Teatro Pereira	B2

MALLORCA, MENORCA & IBIZA IBIZA CITY

Necròpolis del Puig des Molins

HISTORIC SITE

(Carrer de la Via Romana 31; adult/child €2.40/free; ☺10am-2pm & 6.30-9pm Tue-Sat, 10am-2pm Sun) The earliest tombs within this ancient burial ground date from the 7th century BC and

Phoenician times. Follow the path around and peer into the *hypogea* (burial caverns), cut deep into the hill. You can descend into one interlocking series of these. The site museum displays finds such as amulets and terracotta figurines discovered within the

WORTH A TRIP

A TALE OF TWO BEACHES

Ibiza City is a short hop from some first-class beaches. The party set hangs out at Platja d'en Bossa, the island's longest beach, for daytime clubbing at Ushuaïa (p812) and DJs pumping chill-out beats at lounges like Bora Bora Beach Club (p813) and Nassau Beach. Here you can work on or off a hangover, or try your hand at water sports like jet-skiing, kitesurfing, stand-up paddleboarding and windsurfing.

Edging south, dune-backed Platja d'es Cavallet is queen of the gay and nudist scene. Nearby is Platja de ses Salines, a fine strip of pale sand with glass-clear sea. Here celebs, beach babes, party posers and all-comers work the bronzed, blissed-out look. Shuffle away from them and you are in the tranquil heart of the Unesco-listed Parque Natural de ses Salines ([☎] 971 30 14 60; www.balearsnatura.com), a nature reserve of marshes, salt pans and pine-cloaked coastal cliffs that southern Ibiza shares with Formentera. It's a safe haven for birdlife such as the Audouin's gull, the Balearic shearwater and migrating flamingos (August to October).

From the 16th-century defence tower Torre de ses Portes at Ibiza's southernmost tip, you can glimpse the islands that speckle the Es Freus strait separating Ibiza and Formentera. Among them are Illa des Penjats (Hangman's Island), where captured pirates were once sent to the gallows, and Illa des Porcs (Pig Island), where plump pigs smuggled over from Formentera were once kept.

more than 3000 tombs that honeycomb the hillside. Both museum and site were closed for restoration works at the time of writing.

Museu d'Art
Contemporani (MACE) MUSEUM
(www.mace.eivissa.es; Ronda de Narcís Puget; ⊙10am-2pm & 5-8pm Tue-Fri, 10am-2pm Sat & Sun) FREE Housed within an 18th-century powder store and armoury, this museum is a showcase for contemporary art. The permanent collection contains drawings by Ibizan artist Marí Ribas Portmany, Japanese prints and photographic works. Descend to the archaeological site to map out Ibiza's history through the ages – from the Phoenicians to the Islamic period.

Museu Puget MUSEUM
(Carrer Major 18; ⊙10am-2pm & 5-8pm Tue-Fri, 10am-2pm Sat & Sun May-Jul) FREE A historic mansion with typical late-Gothic courtyard and stairs to the upper floor houses 130 paintings by Ibizan artist Narcís Puget Viñas (1874–1960) and his son, Narcís Puget Riquer (1916–83).

◉ Sa Penya

There's always something going on portside – people-watchers will be right at home. Sa Penya bursts with funky and trashy clothing boutiques. The so-called hippie markets, street stalls along Carrer d'Enmig and the adjoining streets, sell everything under the sun. But don't let the

word 'hippie' make you think you're getting a bargain. Quite the opposite – prices are sky high!

🛏 Sleeping

Vara de Rey GUESTHOUSE €€
([☎] 971 30 13 76; www.hibiza.com; Passeig de Vara de Rey 7; s €50-65, d €65-115, ste €115-170; [❉]) Housed in a restored town mansion, this boho-flavoured guesthouse sits on the tree-lined Passeig Vara de Rey boulevard. The look is shabby-chic in rooms with touches like chandeliers, wrought-iron bedsteads and diffused light. Suites notch up the romance with four-poster beds and Dalt Vila views.

Hostal La Marina HOSTAL €€
([☎] 971 31 01 72; www.hostal-lamarina.com; Carrer de Barcelona 7; s €75-80, d €95-130, ste €150-190; [❉]) Looking onto both the waterfront and bar-lined Carrer de Barcelona, this mid-19th-century building has rooms done out in breezy blues and whites. A handful of (predictably noisier) rooms face the street, but you can opt for pricier doubles and attics with terraces and panoramic port and/ or town views. The same people run other lodgings along the street.

Hostal Parque HOSTAL €€
([☎] 971 30 13 58; www.hostalparque.com; Plaça des Parc 4; s €60-90, d €110-190, tr €150-190, q €180-240; [❉][☎]) Overlooking palm-dotted Plaça des Parc, this *hostal's* rooms have recently

been spruced up with boutique touches like wood floors, contemporary art and ultra-modern bathrooms. There's a price hike for Ático (penthouse) rooms, but their roof terraces with Dalt Vila views are something else. Street-facing rooms might be a tad noisy for light sleepers.

★**Urban Spaces** DESIGN HOTEL €€€
(☎871 51 71 74; www.urbanspacesibiza.com; Carrer de la Via Púnica 32; ste €200-270; ❄📶) Ira Francis-Smith is the brains behind this design newcomer with an alternative edge. Some of the world's most prolific street artists (N4T4, INKIE, JEROM, et al) have pooled their creativity in the roomy, mural-splashed suites, with clever backlighting, proper workstations and balconies with terrific views. Extras like yoga on the roof terrace and clubber-friendly breakfasts until 1pm are sure-fire people-pleasers.

Hotel Mirador de Dalt Vila BOUTIQUE HOTEL €€€
(☎971 30 30 45; www.hotelmiradoribiza.com; Plaça d'Espanya 4; s €310, d from €480 Aug, s €250, d from €390 Jul & Sep; ⊙Easter-Dec; ❄@📶🏊) This rose-hued mansion is the Fajarnés family home, with 13 stunningly renovated rooms. Public areas display paintings and exquisite objets d'art, all from the family's private collection. The spa-pool has a counter-current swim jet for the active and the restaurant is a gourmet's delight.

Eating

Bistrot El Jardin CAFE €
(Plaça de la Constitució 11; light meals €6-12; ⊙9.30am-2am, closed Sun in winter) Pot plants and herbs fill the terrace of this cafe on the market square. It's a laid-back spot for fresh-pressed juices and smoothies, and we love the creative take on salads – from goat cheese with pears, nuts and honey to artichoke hearts with endives and gorgonzola, which are attractively presented on slate.

Mar a Vila TAPAS €
(Avinguda d'Ignasi Wallis 16; mains €8.50-14; ⊙10am-midnight Mon-Sat) This sweet tapas place brings a dash of the sea to the city centre and conceals a pretty inner courtyard. The tapas and *pintxos* (Basque tapas) are bang on the money, as are satisfying mains like sticky pork cheeks with carrot-potato cream and macadamia nuts.

Croissant Show CAFE €
(☎971 31 76 65; Plaça de la Constitució; snacks & light mains €2-17; ⊙6am-11pm) Opposite the food market, this is where *everyone* goes for an impressive range of pastries, gourmet salads and post-partying breakfast goodies. It is quite a scene all on its own. Grab a table on the people-watching terrace.

★**Comidas Bar San Juan** MEDITERRANEAN €
(Carrer de Guillem de Montgrí 8; mains €4-12; ⊙1-3.30pm & 8.30-11pm Mon-Sat) More traditional than trendy, this family-run operation, with two small dining rooms, harks back to the days before Ibiza became a byword for glam. It offers outstanding value, with fish dishes and steaks for around €10. It doesn't take reservations, so arrive early and expect to have other people at the same table as you.

El Olivo MEDITERRANEAN €€
(☎971 30 06 80; www.elolivoibiza.org; Plaça de Vila 7; mains €19-24, tapas menu €28; ⊙7pm-1am Tue-Sun) Standing head and shoulders above most places in the Dalt Vila, this slick little bistro has plenty of pavement seating. The menu goes with the seasons in clean, bright flavours as simple as rack of lamb in a fennel-mustard crust and octopus carpaccio drizzled in Ibizan olive oil – all delivered with finesse.

S'Ametller IBIZAN €€
(☎971 31 17 80; www.restaurantsametller.com; Carrer de Pere Francès 12; menus €22-35; ⊙1-4pm & 8-1am Mon-Sat, 8pm-1am Sun) The 'Almond Tree' specialises in local, market-fresh cooking. The daily menu (for dessert, choose the house *flaó,* a mint-flavoured variant on cheesecake and a Balearic Islands speciality) is inventive and superb value. S'Ametller also offers cookery courses – including one that imparts the secrets of that *flaó.*

Bar 43 Tapas TAPAS €€
(☎971 30 09 92; www.ibiza-43.com; Avinguda d'Espanya 43; ⊙8.30pm-2am Tue-Sat; 📶) This cosy, unfussy bar distinguishes itself with its warm welcome and generously portioned tapas – *gambas al ajillo* (prawns sautéed in garlic), *boquerones* (marinated anchovies) and the like. Go for the good buzz and reasonable prices.

Drinking & Entertainment

Sa Penya is the nightlife centre. Dozens of bars keep the port area jumping from sunset until the early hours. Alternatively, various bars at Platja d'en Bossa combine sounds, sand and sea with sangria and other tipples. After they wind down, you can continue at one of the island's world-famous nightclubs.

CLUBBING ON IBIZA

Ibiza's clubs are the stuff of legend – huge, throbbing temples to which thousands of disciples flock to pay homage to the gods of hedonism. From late May to the end of September, the west of the island is one big, non-stop dance party from sunset to sunrise and back again. Space, Pacha and Amnesia were all in *DJ Mag*'s top 10 in 2013.

The major clubs operate nightly from around midnight to 6am from mid-May or June to early October. Theme nights, fancy-dress parties and foam parties are regular features. Some places go a step or two further, with go-go girls (and boys), striptease acts and even live sex as the (ahem) climax.

Entertainment Ibiza-style doesn't come cheaply. Admission can cost anything from €20 to €65 (mixed drinks and cocktails then go for around €10 to €15).

If you hang out around Sa Penya, you might score a discount flyer if they think you've got the look. Buying club tickets online (for instance at www.ibiza-spotlight.com) is €5 to €15 cheaper and less hassle than buying them at the door. You can cancel for a full refund up to 24 hours ahead.

Amnesia (www.amnesia.es; Carretera Ibiza a San Antonio Km 5, San Rafael; admission €35-75; ⊙ midnight-6am) Amnesia's sound system gives your body a massage. Beats skip from techno to trance, while the decks welcome DJ royalty like Paul Van Dyk and Sven Väth. A huge glasshouse-like terrace surrounds the central dance area. Big nights include Cocoon (Mondays), Cream (Thursdays) and foam-filled Espuma (Wednesdays and Sundays).

Space (www.space-ibiza.es; Platja d'en Bossa; admission €20-75; ⊙ 11pm-6am) The aptly named Space can pack in as many as 40 DJs and up to 8000 clubbers and is considered one of the world's best clubs. Come for the terrace, electro and parties like We Love (Sundays) and Carl Cox (Tuesdays).

Pacha (www.pacha.com; Avinguda 8 d'Agost, Ibiza City; admission €20-70; ⊙ 11pm-6am) Going strong since 1973, Pacha is Ibiza's original glamourpuss – a cavernous club that can hold 3000 people. The main dance floor, a sea of mirror balls, heaves to deep techno. On the terrace, tunes are more relaxing. Cherry-pick your night: David Guetta works the decks at Thursday's F*** Me I'm Famous, while hippies groove at Tuesday's Flower Power.

Ushuaïa (www.ushuaiabeachhotel.com; Platja d'en Bossa 10; admission €25-70; ⊙ 3pm or 5pm-midnight) Queen of daytime clubbing is ice-cool Ushuaïa on Platja d'en Bossa. The open-air megaclub gets the party started early with superstar DJs like David Guetta, Luciano and Sven Väth, and poolside lounging by a lagoon with Bali beds. Check out the Sky Lounge for sparkling sea views or stay the night in the minimalist-cool hotel (there are even swim-up rooms!).

Es Paradis (www.esparadis.com; Carrer de Salvador Espriu 2, Sant Antoni de Portmany; admission €15-50; ⊙ 11pm-6am) Go for the amazing sound system, fountains and outdoor feel (there's no roof, but who needs one in summer?). It's one of the prettiest of the macro-clubs, with loads of marble, greenery and a glass pyramid. Queues can be enormous, so get there early. Es Paradis is known for its water parties (Tuesdays and Fridays). Prepare to get soaked!

Privilege (www.privilegeibiza.com; San Rafael; admission €20-50; ⊙ 11pm-6am) Welcome to the world's biggest club. Five kilometres along the road to San Rafael, Privilege is a mind-blowing space with 20 bars, an interior pool and capacity for 10,000 clubbers. The main domed dance temple is an enormous, pulsating area, where the DJ's cabin is suspended above the pool.

KM5 BAR
(www.km5-lounge.com; Carretera de Sant Josep, Km 5.6; ⊙ 8pm-4am May-Sep) This bar, named after its highway location, is where you go to glam it up. Head out of town towards Sant Josep and dance in the gardens as you gear up for the clubs. Lounging is the second major activity – there are plenty of pillows strewn about the Bedouin-style tents.

IBIZA CLUBS IN THE SPOTLIGHT

Michael (Stivi) Stivanello is the clubbing expert at Ibiza Spotlight and a massive electronic music fan. He filled us in on his clubbing tips.

Ticket Tips Buy them online in advance. It's less hassle as you can just rock up and budget costs better, too.

Favourite Clubs Space for its crystal-clear sound system, Amnesia for its terrace and big-name DJs, Privilege for the sheer size of it, Pacha because it's Pacha! Try to find all the hidden rooms.

Best Nights Two of the best are Cream at Amnesia (house, electro and top DJs) and Flower Power at Pacha, where you can dress up, trawl the hippie market and dance to the Beatles.

First Timers Check out 'Ibiza Virgins' on www.ibiza-spotlight.com for need-to-know info like drink prices, dress codes and tickets.

After Parties Clubbing doesn't stop when the clubs close. Keep an ear to the ground for after parties like the one at Sal Rossa in Platja d'en Bossa. Check social media or ask PRs and workers to find out what's happening.

Teatro Pereira   MUSIC BAR
(www.teatropereyra.com; Carrer del Comte de Rosselló 3; ⊙ 8am-4am) Away from the waterfront hubbub, this time warp is all stained wood and iron girders. It was once the foyer of the long-abandoned 1893 theatre at its rear. It's often packed and offers nightly live music.

Bora Bora Beach Club   BAR
(www.boraboraibiza.net; ⊙ noon-6am May-Sep) At Platja d'en Bossa, 4km from the old town, this is *the* place to be– a long beachside bar where sun and fun worshippers work off hangovers and prepare new ones. Entry's free and the ambience is chilled, with low-key club sounds wafting over the sand.

Angelo   GAY
(www.angeloibiza.com; Carrer d'Alfons XII 11; ⊙ 10pm-4am) In the shadow of the old city walls, Angelo is a busy gay bar with several levels. The atmosphere is relaxed and heteros wind up here too. Nearby are a handful of other gay-leaning bars, such as the slicker Soap (Carrer de Santa Llúcia 21; ⊙ 10pm-4am).

❶ Information

The **tourist office** (☑ 971 39 92 32; www.eivissa.es; Plaça de la Catedral; ⊙ 10am-2pm & 6-9pm Mon-Sat, 10am-2pm Sun) in the old town loans free audioguides to the city; bring your passport or identity document. There is also an **island-wide office** (☑ 971 30 19 00; www.ibiza.travel; Passeig de Vara de Rei 1; ⊙ 9am-8.30pm Mon-Sat, to 2pm Sun, shorter hours in winter).

❶ Getting There & Away

AIR

Ibiza's airport (Aeroport d'Eivissa), just 7km southwest of Ibiza City, receives direct flights from mainland Spanish cities and a host of UK and other European centres.

BOAT

All ferries leave from the port 300m north of the centre, but the Formentera ferries have their own terminal.

Aquabus (www.aquabusferryboats.com; 1-way/return €3.50/6) Hourly ferries to/from Playa d'en Bossa and Figueretes, May to October.

Baleària (☑ 902 16 01 80; www.balearia.com) Regular crossings to Formentera (€17 to €22, one hour) and Palma de Mallorca (€35 to €60, 4½ hours).

Cruceros Santa Eulària (www.ferrysantaeulalia.com) Boats to Cala Llonga (adult/child return €12/6), Santa Eulària d'es Riu (adult/child return €18/10) and Formentera (adult/child return €32/17), May to October.

❶ Getting Around

Bus 10 (€3.35, every 20 minutes) runs from the airport to the central port area via Platja d'en Bossa.

Buses to other parts of the island depart from the bus station on Avenida de la Pau, northwest of the town centre.

Bus 14 (€2.35) runs every 20 minutes to Platja d'en Bossa.

ℹ ALL ABOARD THE DISCOBUS

Much cheaper than a taxi, the Discobus (www.discobus.es; per person €3; ⊙ midnight-6am Jun-Sep) does an all-night whirl of the major clubs, bars and hotels in Ibiza City, Platja d'en Bossa, San Rafael, Es Canar, Santa Eulària and Sant Antoni.

East Coast

A busy highway (C733) speeds you north out of Ibiza City towards Santa Eulària d'es Riu on the east coast. More scenic is the slower coastal road via Cala Llonga, which winds through low hills and olive groves, with detours along the way to several beaches. To follow it, take the turn-off to Jesús a couple of kilometres northwest of Ibiza City.

Cala Llonga is set on an attractive bay with high rocky cliffs sheltering a lovely sandy beach, but the town itself is blighted by high-rise hotels.

Santa Eulària d'es Riu

POP 13,737

Ibiza's third-largest town is a bustling place, with a couple of child-friendly, gently sloping beaches, a large harbour and plenty of 20th-century tourist-resort architecture.

◉ Sights

The hillock of Puig de Missa, a world away from the beaches, is the core of the original town, where you'll find the pleasant 16th-century church, the Església de Santa Eulària.

Museu Barrau   MUSEUM
(Calle Puig de Missa 33; ⊙ 10am-2pm Tue-Sat) A white house with blue shutters dedicated to local artist Laureà Barrau.

Museu Etnogràfic   MUSEUM
(☑ 971 33 28 45; Can Ros, Puig de Missa; adult/child €3/free; ⊙ 10am-2pm Mon-Sat, 11am-1.30pm Sun) Displays farming and household implements.

🛏 Sleeping & Eating

Hostal-Residencia Sa Rota   HOSTAL €
(☑ 971 33 00 22; www.hostalsarota.com; Carrer de San Vicente 59; s €35-45, d €50-74; 🕾) Open year-round, this bargain *hostal* features bright, generous rooms (the doubles in par-

ticular), with modern bath or shower. The downstairs cafe has a relaxing outdoor extension with an ivy-shaded pergola.

Ca's Català   HOTEL €€
(☑ 971 33 86 49; www.cascatala.com; Carrer del Sol; s €55, d €80-118; 🕾 ✷ 🐾) Kerstin is your kindly host at this cheerful option, which has the feel of a private villa. Most of its 12 large rooms overlook a tranquil garden courtyard and pool with bar. Most bedrooms have ceiling fans and a few come with aircon. Doubles, all with four-poster bed, are in attractive, gleaming white. It's very close to the bus station.

El Naranjo   SEAFOOD €€
(☑ 971 33 03 24; Carrer de Sant Josep 31; mains €9-17; ⊙ 1-4pm & 7pm-midnight Tue-Sun; 🐾) Hidden away from the bustle, 'The Orange Tree' has a pretty courtyard draped in bougainvillea and twinkling with fairy-lights. The fish (for instance sea bass in a salt crust) is always fresh and cooked to retain its juices. Carnivore options include suckling pig with apple sauce.

Ses Savines   INTERNATIONAL €€
(☑ 971 33 18 24; Cala ses Estaques; snacks €5-10, mains €12-34; ⊙ noon-midnight late Apr-Oct) This slick, seafront lounge-restaurant has sofas and loungers for drinking in the stunning views. Go for drinks, snacks (goat cheese salad, baguettes and the like) or Med-meets-Asia mains like cod loin in a soy reduction with tempura vegetables. Service can be lethargic, so bring time.

🍷 Drinking & Entertainment

Guarana   CLUB
(www.guaranaibiza.com; Passeig Marítim; ⊙ 8pm-6am May-Oct) By the marina, this is a cool club away from the Ibiza–San Rafael–Sant Antoni circuit. There's live music on Sunday evenings.

ℹ Information

Tourist Office (☑ 971 33 07 28; www.santa eulariadesriu.com; Carrer Marià Riquer Wallis 4; ⊙ 9.30am-1.30pm & 5-7.30pm Mon-Fri, 10am-1pm Sat) Just off the main street. There are also a couple of summer-only information booths.

ℹ Getting There & Away

BUS

Regular buses connect Santa Eulària with Ibiza City, Sant Antoni and the northern beaches.

FERRY

In summer, Cruceros Santa Eulària (p813) runs boats to several destinations, including the following:

DESTINATION	BOATS PER DAY	ADULT/CHILD (€)
Cala Llonga	8	12/6
Ibiza	6	18/10
Formentera	2	32/17

Santa Eulària d'es Riu to S'Aigua Blanca

◉ Sights & Activities

Sant Carles de Peralta   VILLAGE

This sleepy village sits on the main road north of Santa Eulària. Just outside the village, at Km 12, is Las Dalias market.

Cala Llenya & Cala Mastella   BEACH

Situated 9km northeast of Santa Eulària, Cala Llenya is a serene pine-fringed sandy bay (easterly breezes mean the water can get wavy). Its sister is the even tinier, just as pretty, Cala Mastella, which outside high season you could have totally to yourself. At the latter, scramble around the rocks at the eastern end to reach Es Bigotes restuarant.

Cala de Boix, Es Figueral & S'Aigua Blanca   BEACH

Curving Cala de Boix is massaged by tempting waters. Back on the main road, the next turn-off leads to the low-key resort Es Figueral, with a golden-sand beach and turquoise water. A little further on, a turn-off takes you to the still-lovelier beaches of S'Aigua Blanca (clothing optional). All these beaches can be very, very busy in high season.

🛏 Sleeping & Eating

Hostal Restaurante Es Alocs   HOSTAL €

(📞971 33 50 79; www.hostalalocs.com; Platja Es Figueral; s €35-40, d €55-65; ☻May-Oct; ❋🛜) This very friendly choice sits right on the beach at Es Figueral. Rooms occupy two floors and most have a small fridge and balcony. The bar-restaurant has a wonderful terrace, deeply shaded with tangled juniper and chaste trees.

Hostal Cala Boix   HOSTAL €

(📞618 813019; www.hostalcalaboix.com; Cala de Boix; s/d €53/86; ☻May-Oct; 🅿❋@🛜) Set uphill and back from Cala de Boix, this op-

tion couldn't be further from the Ibiza madness. Spruced up in 2013, its bright, colour-splashed rooms have balconies and many have sea views. Pines afford shade around the lovely pool area overlooking the bay. Its restaurant, S'Arribada, specialises in fish and paellas.

Es Bigotes   SEAFOOD €€

(Cala Mastella; meals €25-35; ☻noon-3pm Easter-Oct) Offering whatever fish was caught that morning simmered with herbs, mixed vegetables and potatoes in a huge vat, this simple shack is known far and wide. In July and August, turn up in person at least the day before to book a spot. To arrive by car, take the last turning left before Cala Mastella.

Bar Anita   SPANISH €

(Sant Carles de Peralta; mains €8-16; ☻7.30am-2am) A timeless tavern opposite the village church of Sant Carles de Peralta, Bar Anita has been attracting all sorts since the hippies rocked up here in the 1960s. The kitchen churns out great tapas, pizza and mains like roast pork and chicken – or simply drink and chat.

Cala Sant Vicent

The package-tour resort of Cala Sant Vicent extends around the shores of a protected bay on the northeast coast. Its long stretch of sandy beach is backed by a string of modern midrise hotels. A 2.5km drive northwards winds through a leafy residential area high up to Punta Grossa, with spectacular views over the coast and east out to sea.

MALLORCA, MENORCA & IBIZA EAST COAST

WORTH A TRIP

HIPPIE CHICK

The little village of Sant Carles de Peralta springs to life for Las Dalias (www.lasdalias.es; ☻10am-8pm Sat year-round, plus 7pm-1am Mon Jun-Sep) hippie market. Rainbow throws, Indian beads, feathered bikinis, books, ethnic CDs, bongo drums, paintings, incense, hats and hand-embroidered bags are all for sale here. It's just as much about the show as the shopping, with juice bars, massages, fortune-telling, live music and more.

North Coast & Interior

The north of Ibiza has some of the island's most attractive landscapes. Its winding back roads, coastal hills and inland mountains are popular with both walkers and cyclists.

Portinatx

Portinatx is the north coast's major tourist resort. Busy, yes, but a good spot for families and positively underpopulated when set against the megaresorts around Ibiza town. Its three adjoining beaches – S'Arenal Petit, S'Arenal Gran and Platja Es Port – are each beautiful but often crowded.

Cala Xarraca, west of Portinatx, is a picturesque, partly protected bay with a rocky shoreline and dark-sand beach. Development is limited to a solitary bar-restaurant and a couple of private houses.

🛏 Sleeping

★ Ca Sa Vilda Marge   RURAL HOTEL €€€
(☑971 33 32 34; www.casavildamarge.com; Carretera de Portinatx; incl breakfast s €98-139, d €149-169, f €259; P❋🕸🐕🛏) This petite rural guesthouse is a little slice of heaven, with owners who bend over backwards to please. The quiet rooms are done out in natural hues, floaty drapes, beams and exposed stone. Crash on a poolside cabana bed or hire a bicycle to pedal through the countryside. It's located 2km off the main C733 towards Portinatx.

Sant Miquel de Balansat & Around

One of the largest inland villages, Sant Miquel offers a slice of low-key Ibizan life. Swing 4km north and you'll reach its former fishing village, Port de Sant Miquel, which is now a busy resort, with fine beaches dominated by the huge concrete honeycomb of Hotel Club San Miguel.

◉ Sights

Iglesia Sant Miquel   CHURCH
(⊙9.30am-1.30pm & 4.30-7.30pm Tue-Fri, 9.30am-12.30pm Sat) Sant Miquel de Balansat is overlooked by its shimmering white 14th-century fortress church. The restored early 17th-century frescoes in the Capella de Benirràs are a swirl of flowers and twisting

---

DON'T MISS

ACTIVE IBIZA

Not all the action in Ibiza revolves around the club dance floors. Go beyond the beats and the sun lounger to discover a more active side to the island. Here's our pick:

Walking Ibiza (☑608 692901; www.walkingibiza.com) Hit the trails of Ibiza's coast and interior with pro guide Toby. His guided walks cover everything from community hikes every Friday (suggested donation €10) to three-day treks (€350) and two-week around-the-island treks (€1200); the latter include food and accommodation.

Ibiza Mundo Activo (☑676 075704; www.ibizamundoactivo.blogspot.co.uk) This one-stop adventure-sports shop takes you hiking, biking, caving, climbing and kayaking across the island. Find times and prices online.

Scuba Ibiza Diving (www.scubaibiza.com) Based at Marina Botafoch in Ibiza City, this PADI Five Star dive centre runs the full shebang of courses, from three-hour intro sessions to the four-day Open Water Diver (€399). It also offers speciality courses such as wreck diving and underwater photography. Equipment rental for qualified divers costs €12 per dive. Dive sites include the pristine Freus Marine Reserve.

Ibiza Horse Valley (☑680 624911; www.ibizahorsevalley.com; Sant Joan de Labritja) Nestled in a lush valley, this sanctuary and riding centre for mistreated horses offers everything from half-day treks into the hills to camping with horses and beach hacks. Full details are on the website.

Ibiza MTB (☑616 129929; www.ibizamtb.com) Ibiza has some fantastic mountain-bike terrain. Ibiza MTB offers bike rental (€15 to €50), with free delivery and pick-up in the Santa Eulària area. Or slip into the saddle for three-hour guided mountain-bike tours, which reach from the west coast to forest singletracks, sunset rides and excursions to Parque Natural Ses Salines.

SANTA GERTRUDIS DE FRUITERA

Blink and you might miss tiny Santa Gertrudis, south of Sant Miquel – and what a shame that would be! This once sleepy, whitewashed village at the island's heart is a gem. You'll find art-and-craft galleries, antique and bric-a-brac shops and several good cafes and bars around the central, pedestrianised Plaça de l'Església. At Bar Costa (Plaça de l'Església 11; ⊙8am-2am Wed-Mon Apr-Mar), some of the original paintings lining the walls were contributed by penniless artists who couldn't pay their tab. Sit on the terrace for drinks and *bocadillos* (filled rolls).

For such a pipsqueak of a village, Santa Gertrudis has some terrific restaurants. Among the best is DiMi's (☑971 19 73 87; Carrer Venda des Poble; tapas €3.90-15, mains €12-25; ⊙7pm-midnight May-Oct, 1-11pm Nov-Apr). Belgium meets Ibiza at this convivial bistro, with a pretty garden terrace. The menu globetrots, skipping from tapas (baby squid, Iberian hams and the like) to nicely spiced wok curries and Belgian classics like *moules-frites* (mussels with fries) cooked to a T.

vines. Each Thursday from June to September, there's traditional island dancing on the pretty patio at 6.15pm.

Port de Sant Miquel
BEACH
In this attractive, deep-sunk bay, you can waterski, canoe and hire snorkelling gear to explore the rocky shoreline.

Cova de Can Marçà
CAVE
(www.covadecanmarsa.com; adult/child €10/6; ⊙10.30am-1.30pm & 2.30-8pm May-Oct, shorter hours Nov-Apr) A turn-off to the right just before Port de Sant Miquel takes you around a headland to this underground caverns spectacularly lit by coloured lights. Tours in various languages take around 30 minutes. After resurfacing, pause for a drink on its terrace and savour the panorama of sheer cliffs and deep blue water.

Cala Benirràs
BEACH
From Port de Sant Miquel, an unsealed road continues 4km around the coast to the unspoiled bay of Cala Benirràs, with high, forested cliffs and a couple of bar-restaurants that back onto the beach. At dusk you may well encounter hippies with bongos banging out a greeting to the sunset, something they have been doing for decades.

🛏 Sleeping

Can Planells
RURAL HOTEL €€€
(☑971 33 49 24; www.canplanells.com; Carrer de Venda Rubió 2; incl breakfast d €175-220, ste €220-300; ❄🏊🛜🐕) This country mansion, just 1.5km outside Sant Miquel on the road to Sant Mateu d'Aubarca, exudes relaxed rural luxury in its handful of tastefully arranged doubles and suites (the best have private terraces). Mellow out by the pool or with strolls

through the gardens and fruit-tree groves. Farm-fresh produce makes breakfast that bit special.

Sant Llorenç de Balàfia & Around

Overlooking the quiet hamlet of Sant Llorenç is a brilliant-white 18th-century fortress-church, built at a time when attacks by Moorish pirates were the scourge of the island. From Sant Llorenç head 500m east to the C733 road and turn north. Take a lane off the C733 beside the restaurant Balàfia to reach the minuscule, once-fortified hamlet of Balàfia, with two towers, flowers and lots of *privado* signs around its half-dozen houses – but don't let these deter you from exploring its couple of lanes.

🛏 Sleeping & Eating

Can Gall
RURAL HOTEL €€€
(☑971 33 70 31; www.agrocangall.com; incl breakfast d €242-297, f €451; ⊙closed Dec; ❄🏊🛜🚗🐕) A few kilometres north from Sant Llorenç de Balàfia along the C733, a signed turn-off just after Km 17 leads to this 200-year-old *finca* (country estate) turned tranquil hideaway set amid citrus and olive groves. The rooms play up rural luxury, with wooden ceilings and exposed stone. Tear yourself away to wallow in the infinity pool or savour the breeze from its chill-out terrace.

Agroturismo Atzaró
RURAL HOTEL €€€
(☑971 33 88 38; www.atzaro.com; Carretera Sant Joan Km 15; d €390-440, ste €510-810; 🅿❄🛜🏊) Combining Japanese zen with tribal Africa and farmhouse Ibiza, Atzaró is the ultimate in rural luxury. Its stunning rooms feature new-wave design flourishes and comforts like iPod docks, robes and DVD players that

justify the price tag; some rooms have private terraces, fireplaces and four-posters. Besides a well-regarded restaurant, there is an astoundingly lovely spa set in fragrant Mediterranean gardens.

★ **La Paloma** ITALIAN €€
(☑971 32 55 43; Sant Llorenç; mains €16-26; ☺cafe 10.30am-4.30pm, restaurant 7.30-11.30pm Mar-Oct; 🖶) 🖉 There's a mellow vibe at this boho-cool restaurant set in lush gardens, 100m downhill from the church. The food is Italian with a creative slant – herby salads with garden veg, homemade focaccia, Tuscan antipasti and a terrific *solomillo* (entrecôte steak) with balsamic and thyme. The cafe serves great quiches, carrot cake and organic smoothies on its shady, overgrown terrace.

West Coast

Sant Antoni de Portmany
POP 23,314
Sant Antoni, widely known as 'San An', is about as Spanish as bangers and mash. While its still known for its booze-ups, brawls and lairy Brits-abroad reputation, it does have a more mellow side, particularly along the cafe-lined sunset strip, home of the legendary Café del Mar.

◉ Sights

Not far north of Sant Antoni are several undeveloped beaches, such as Cala Salada, a wide bay with sandy shores backed by pine forest. Closer to Sant Antoni are the pretty inlet beaches of Cala Gració and Cala Gracioneta, separated by a small rocky promontory.

🛏 Sleeping & Eating

Hostal la Torre HOTEL €€
(☑971 34 22 71; www.hostallatorre.com; incl breakfast s €75, d €100-130; ☺Easter-Oct; 🕸🛜) Though barely 2km north of Sant Antoni on the headland of Cap Negret, it's a world away from the town's bustle. Sea views from the bar-restaurant terrace are magnificent – even more so from the upper area, exclusive to guests. The 18 rooms are plain, but it all adds up to a relatively peaceful stay in San Antoni.

★ **Can Pujolet** RURAL HOTEL €€€
(☑971 80 51 70; www.canpujolet.com; Santa Inés; s €119-140, d €170-260, apt €400-460; 🕸🛜🖳🖶) Swap partying for pin-drop peace at dreamy Can Pujolet, 10km north of Sant Antoni. Rooms play up simple luxury, with tiled floors, exposed stone and terraces rising from the olive groves. Lounge by the pool and Jacuzzi, or wander through pine forest to cliffs with sea views. The *finca's* organic

---

DON'T MISS

SUNSET STRIP

Nowhere is the sun plopping into the Med more of an event than Sant Antoni. From the port, head for the small rock-and-sand strip on the north shore to join hundreds of others for drinks at a string of lounge bars. All serve food too. Between mid-May and September, once the sun goes down, all turn up the rhythmic heat and pound on until late. Our top five:

Café del Mar (www.cafedelmarmusic.com; ☺4pm-1am) An Ibiza institution that's been serving up the same mix of ambient tunes, pricey drinks and staggering sunsets for over 30 years. Every year it brings out a CD of the summer's best chill-out tracks.

Café Mambo (www.cafemamboibiza.com; ☺1pm-2am) The cool kid of the moment, Mambo is a pre-party hot-spot and welcomes the crème of Ibiza's DJs to the decks.

Mint (www.mintloungeibiza.com; ☺5pm-2am mid-May–Sep, 11am-11pm rest of year) Sidling up to Mambo, this fresh-faced lounge is a super-relaxed spot for drinking in the sunset over a cocktail.

Savannah (www.savannahibiza.com; ☺11am-3am) With its amazing views, glam decor and sunset terrace, Savannah is a fine pick for a strawberry daiquiri, dinner or pre-club partying.

Kama Sushi (☑971 59 67 67; ☺6pm-1am) A slinky lounge for winningly fresh sushi, zingy lychee mojitos and sunset DJ beats.

fruit and veg end up on the lunch and dinner table.

Es Rebost
SPANISH €€

(☑971 34 62 52; www.esrebostdecanprats.com; Carrer Cervantes 4; mains €15-24; ⊙1-4pm & 8pm-midnight Wed-Mon) Authentic, family-run Ibizan restaurants are a rare breed in Sant Antoni – all the more reason to visit Es Rebost. Go for spot-on mains like *arroz meloso* (creamy seafood rice), fish and steaks. The three-course day menu is a bargain at €13.50.

Villa Mercedes
FUSION €€

(☑971 34 85 43; www.villamercedesibiza.com; Molls dels Pescadors; mains €14-23; ⊙1pm-2am; ☑) Set in gorgeous gardens, this boho-chic Ibizan mansion overlooks the marina and offers eclectic cooking, from wok-fried vegetables through rice and noodle dishes to the local catch of the day, as well as cocktails and live music almost every day.

Drinking & Entertainment

Sunset strip bars face stiff competition from stylish lounge bars about 300m further north along the pedestrian walkway.

Golden Buddha
LOUNGE

(⊙10am-3.30pm) Named after its namesake golden buddha, this seafront lounge at Caló des Moro has fair prices, comfy sofa beds, chilled music and a tapas menu.

Sun Sea Bar
LOUNGE

(Carrer Cervantes 50B; ⊙10am-2am) Waterfront choice at Caló des Moro, with a pool, Med-style food and tapas, all-day DJs and a sunset terrace

Ibiza Rocks
LIVE MUSIC

(www.ibizarocks.com; Carrer Cervantes 27) Ibiza does indeed rock at this hotel, with the best gigs on the island (Dizzee Rascal, the Prodigy and Arctic Monkeys have all starred in recent years). The full line-up is posted on the website.

❶ Information

Tourist Office (☑971 34 33 63; Passeig de ses Fonts; ⊙9.30am-8.30pm Mon-Fri, 9.30am-1pm Sat & Sun) Beside the harbour.

❶ Getting There & Away

Cruceros Portmany (www.crucerosportmany.com; adult/child €9/4.50) boats depart around every half-hour to Cala Bassa (20 minutes) and

IBIZA'S TOP FIVE BEACHES
➡ Cala Mastella (p815)
➡ Cala de Boix (p815)
➡ Cala Benirràs (p817)
➡ Cala Xarraca (p816)
➡ Cala Codolar (p819)

Cala Compte (30 minutes). To Ibiza City (40 minutes), bus 3 runs every 15 to 30 minutes. Bus 7 (eight daily June to October) serves Cala Bassa.

Cala Bassa to Cala d'Hort

Heading west and south from Sant Antoni, you'll come to the bay of Cala Bassa, a pretty swoop of sand backed by junipers, pines and tamarind trees. It's popular for its turquoise water and blissed-out beach club. Walk in beyond the rocks to this lovely, sandy horseshoe bay. The next few coves around the coast hide some extremely pretty beaches including Cala Compte, with crystal-clear water, and tiny, cliff-flanked Cala Codolar. All are accessible by local bus and/or boat from Sant Antoni. Further south, Cala Vadella is a modest resort, with a fine crescent-shaped beach in the centre of town.

A gorgeous drive through scented pine trees brings you to bijou Cala d'Hort, overlooked by Es Vedrà, a craggy limestone islet that rears 380m up from the sea like the epic ruins of some fantasy fortress. It's steeped in local legend – sea nymphs, Atlantis, you name it. The water here is an inviting shade of blue and the beach is a long arc of sand sprinkled with pebbles and rocks.

🛏 Sleeping & Eating

Hotel Calador
HOTEL €€

(☑971 80 84 24; www.calador-ibiza.com; Cala Carbo; d €80-110, apt €140-260; 🅿❄🛜🐾🐕) Wow, what a view of Es Vedrà! You'll be captivated by the vista from this charming pick between Cala Vadella and Cala d'Hort. It's a restful base, with sunny rooms and apartments (most with sea-facing terraces), palm-fringed gardens, a pool, tennis courts and kids' splash pool. Breakfast costs an extra €11. Rates nosedive in the low season.

El Carmen
SEAFOOD

(☑971 18 74 49; Cala d'Hort; paella per person from €21, min 2 people; ⊙noon-midnight; 🐕) Sunset is primetime viewing of Es Vedrà from the terrace of this friendly bar-restaurant, from where you tumble onto the beach. Locals and visitors flock here for the seafood, in particular the paellas.

FORMENTERA

If Ibiza is the party queen, her little sister, Formentera (population 10,757), is the shy, natural beauty, who prefers barefoot beach strolls by starlight to all-night raving in superclubs. Dangling off the south coast of Ibiza, a mere half an hour away by fast ferry, this 20km-long island is a place of lazy days spent lounging on some of Europe's (dare we say the world's?) most ravishing beaches.

Nowhere is the lure of the sea more powerful in the Balearics than here, where enticing, frost-white slithers of sand are smoothed by water in unbelievable shades of azure, turquoise and lapis lazuli that will have you itching to leap in the moment you step off the boat. Ask people what they've done for the week here and watch them shrug their shoulders, shake the last sand out of their shoes, grin and reply: 'Nothing, it was awesome.'

❶ Information

Tourist Office (☑971 32 20 57; www.formentera.es; Carrer de Calpe; ⊙10am-2pm & 5-7pm Mon-Fri, 10am-2pm Sat) Formentera's main tourist office is beside the ferry landing point in La Savina. There are smaller branches in Es Pujols and Sant Francesc Xavier.

---

❶ STAYING IN FORMENTERA

Formentera looks like a beautiful spot to pitch a tent. Alas, camping is prohibited to preserve the island's fragile coastline. With just over 50 *hostales* (budget hotels) and hotels, beds are like gold dust in midsummer and are often booked in a flash.

Rental apartments are a better deal for stays of a week or more. Check out www.formenterahotelsguide.com and www.guiaformentera.com, www.homelidays.co.uk and www.homeaway.co.uk. Astbury Formentera (www.formentera.co.uk) is a UK-based specialist in house and apartment rentals in Formentera.

---

❶ Getting There & Around

BOAT

Regular passenger ferries run between Ibiza City and La Savina. Return fares are a little under double that of a one-way fare. There are substantial discounts for children.

Baleària-Trasmapi (www.balearia.com) Four to 10 daily. Foot passengers pay around €18 one way. A small car (with passenger) costs €93 one way; motorcycle, €33; bicycle, free.

Mediterranea-Pitiusa (www.medpitiusa.net) Passengers only; two to eight fast ferries daily. One-way tickets cost between €24 and €27.

BUS

Autocares Paya (☑971 32 31 81; www.autocarespaya.com) Runs a regular bus service connecting the main villages, but hiring a scooter or bicycle is more flexible.

CAR & BICYCLE

Kiosk after kiosk offering car, scooter and bicycle hire greet you on arrival at La Savina's harbour. Daily rates start at around €8 for a bike, €29 for a motor scooter. A car is superfluous on this tiny island, but rental starts at around €35 per day.

TAXI

Call ☑971 32 23 42.

Sant Francesc Xavier & La Savina

Formentera's languorous capital, Sant Francesc Xavier is an attractive whitewashed village, with cafes overlooking small, sunny plazas. The town's older buildings include a 14th-century chapel and an 18th-century fortress church.

It's worth staying the night simply for Es Marès (☑971 32 32 16; www.hotelesmares.com; Carrer Santa María 15; incl breakfast d €330-420, ste €540-590; ▣❋❂❊❀), a slinky boutique hotel. Flooded with natural light, its all-white rooms are dressed with funky driftwood, blonde wood furnishings and locally quarried sandstone. Unwind on the pool deck or in the beautifully tiled spa, with hydro-massage jets and treatments from oxygen facials to lomi massages. Balearic food with a modern, seasonal twist stars on the restaurant menu.

Just 3km to the north is the lakeside port village of La Savina, where ferries from Ibiza dock and yachts tinkle in the harbour. The village is a low-key base for exploring the gorgeous beaches immedi-

Formentera

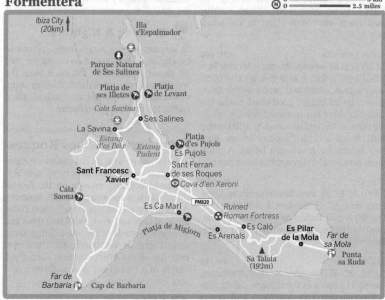

ately north. Or go below Formentera's dazzlingly clear water with **Blue Adventure** (☑636 817419, 971 32 11 68; www.blue-adventure. com; Calle Almadrava 67-71, La Savina; dives with/ without equipment €50/36). The centre offers a full array of PADI-accredited diving courses.

Cala Saona

Delectable Cala Saona is on the road south of Sant Francesc Xavier, a third of the way to Cap de Barbaria. The water is a startling shade of luminous blue and the sand salt white. In our opinion this is one of, if not *the*, best beach on the Spanish Med. Fortunately there's not a lot of development here, bar a couple of laid-back beach shacks serving fried fish and good vibes in the summer.

A white behemoth of a building, **Hotel Cala Saona** (☑971 32 20 30; www.hotelcala-saona.com; d €198-270, ste €297-607 ; Ⓟ❄@ 🛜🏊♿) offers a pool, an ultramodern spa, tennis courts and a restaurant. The rooms are minimalist chic, with white walls, nature-inspired art and streamlined bathrooms; the best overlook the beach and out to sea. Its bar-restaurant is perfect for a sundowner. Prices halve in low season.

Es Pujols

Once a sleepy fishing village, Es Pujols is now the closest Formentera comes to a proper beach resort, but in comparison to those in neighbouring Ibiza that's not very close at all! Rows of sun-bleached timber boat shelters still line the beachfront. If the beaches are too crowded for your liking, more-secluded options lie within easy striking distance (keep walking northwest towards Platja de Llevant).

⊙ Sights & Activities

Wet4Fun   WATER SPORTS
(☑971 32 18 09; www.wet4fun.com; Carrer Roca Plana 51; ⊙10am-6pm Mon-Sat, 2-6pm Sun May-Oct) Wet4Fun offers the chance to learn windsurfing, paddle-surfing, catamaran sailing, canoeing and kayaking. You can also rent out canoes (€10 per hour) and bicycles (€25 for four days) here.

🛏 Sleeping & Eating

Hostal Voramar   HOSTAL €€
(☑971 32 81 19; www.hostalvoramar.com; Av Miramar 25-33; s/d incl breakfast €127/167; ⊙May-Oct; ❄@🛜🏊) Ochre fronted and about 100m inland from the beach, Hostal Voramar has

comfortable rooms, most with balcony. For night owls, breakfast is served from 8.30am until noon. Have a workout in the small gym.

Hotel Sa Volta
HOTEL €€€

(☑ 971 32 81 25; www.savolta.com; Av Miramar 94; s €88-120, d €150-210; P ❄ @ 🛜 ☀ 🚲) This bijou hotel stands white and proud in the town centre. Its 22 bright, good-sized rooms are tastefully done out in muted colours, while the three suites up the romance with canopy beds. It has a chilled rooftop lounge, pool and Jacuzzi for post-beach lazing. A minimum seven-night stay applies in summer.

Claro
SNACKS €

(☑ 971 32 83 25; www.claroformentera.es; Carrer Espalmador 97; ☺9am-4pm & 6.30-10pm Jun-Sep; 🛜) A cool Italian pit stop for breakfast, *piadini* (flatbread sandwiches) and coffee. Free wi-fi.

El Caminito
GRILL €€

(☑ 971 32 81 06; www.caminitoformentera.es; Carretera La Savina-Es Pujols; mains €18-48; ☺8-11.30pm Apr-Oct) This Argentine grill brings a touch of the Pampas to the Med, serving juicy steaks. It's 1km outside Es Pujols on the road to La Savina.

Bocasalina
MEDITERRANEAN €€

(☑ 971 32 91 13; Passeig Marítim; mains €20-42; ☺9am-1.30am mid-Apr–Sep) This glass-fronted waterfront restaurant rustles up homemade pasta, spot-on seafood and steaks. Snag a

---

OFF THE BEATEN TRACK

CAP DE BARBARIA

A narrow sealed road heads south of Sant Francesc Xavier through stone-walled farmlands to Cap de Barbaria, the island's southernmost point. It's a pleasant ride to the lonely white lighthouse at the road's end. Gazing out to sea and watching the waves crash against the cliffs below is captivating, especially at sunset. From the *far* (lighthouse) a 10-minute walk eastwards leads to the Torre d'es Cap de Barbaria, an 18th-century watchtower.

On the road to the lighthouse is Cap de Barbaria (www.capdebarbaria. com; Carretera de Cap de Barbaria Km 5.8) winery, which produces some fine reds from the merlot, cabernet sauvignon and monastrell grape varieties.

---

candlelit table on the terrace overlooking the sea.

Drinking & Nightlife

In summer Es Pujols gets lively. Its intense tangle of intertwined bars along or just off Carrer d'Espardell (just back from the waterfront) stay open until 3am or 4am. Customers are 90% Italian – indeed, you'd hardly know you were in Spain!

Sant Ferran de ses Roques

A dinky village with an old sandstone chapel, a plaza and a handful of cafes, Sant Ferran looks ordinary enough on the face of things. Back in the swingin' 1960s, however, it was a stop on the hippie trail – Bob Dylan jammed here and Pink Floyd had their guitars custom-made at the still-existing workshop (Carrer de Sant Jaume 17). The purple haze has all but lifted, but Sant Ferran still moves to a chilled-out beat and you might spot the odd bongo.

Sights

Cova d'en Xeroni
CAVE

(☑ 971 32 82 14; adult/child €4/2.50; ☺10am-1.30pm & 5-8pm Mon-Sat May-Oct) On the main road east of Sant Ferran just beyond Km 6, turn right for the Cova d'en Xeroni. This underground cavern rich in stalactites and stalagmites was revealed in 1975 when the landowner was digging a well. It's a one-man band, so treat opening times with a grain of salt (the most likely times are 1pm and 6pm).

Sleeping

Hostal Illes Pitiüses
HOSTAL €€

(☑ 971 32 81 89; www.illespitiuses.com; Avinguda Juan Castelló Guasch 48; incl breakfast s €82-119, d €93-135, tr €128-184; ❄ 🛜 🚲) It's nothing fancy, but this simple, central *hostal* is a tidy base for soaking up laid-back Sant Ferran life and the welcome is friendly. There's free wi-fi but it is slooow. Prices almost halve in the low season.

Eating & Drinking

Pedestrianised Carrer Major has a string of summer eateries.

Can Forn
SEAFOOD €€

(☑ 971 32 81 55; Carrer Major 39; mains €10-15; ☺noon-2.30pm & 7-11pm Mon-Sat) Family-run Can Forn rustles up authentic island cuisine

PARQUE NATURAL DE SES SALINES

The Ses Salines nature park, a protected area and a Unesco World Heritage site, begins just north of Estany Pudent (the aptly named 'Smelly Lake'). It extends along the slim finger of land that pokes northwards towards Ibiza and across the narrow intervening strait to also embrace Ses Salines, the salt pans of Ibiza's southern tip. Platja de Llevant and Platja de ses Illetes, a pair of ravishingly beautiful, dune-flanked strips of white sand, line the promontory. A 3km partly dirt road heads north from the La Savina–Es Pujols road.

A 4km walking trail leads from the La Savina–Es Pujols road to the far end of the promontory, from where you can glimpse Illa s'Espalmador across the narrow strait. The tiny uninhabited islet has beautiful, quiet beaches (especially S'Alga, on the southeast side) and mud baths. Wading across isn't recommended because of strong currents and incoming tides. The Barca Bahia boat runs up to three times daily from La Savina ferry port to the island via Platja de ses Illetes.

and has a cosy, old-school vibe. Go for dishes such as *calamar a la bruta* ('dirty calamari', with potato, Mallorcan sausage and squid ink), local lamb chops and *habas* (broad beans) fried up with onions and garlic.

Fonda Pepe BAR
(Carrer Major 55; ☺8-11.30pm) An island classic and former Dylan hang-out, Fonda Pepe is a knockabout bar that attracts a lively crowd of locals and travellers. It does great *pomadas* (shots of gin and lemon) and decent tapas, but service was a bit gruff during our last visit.

Platja de Migjorn

The island's southern arc is necklaced with rugged, sandy bays lapped by placid waters, known collectively as Platja de Migjorn. Development (and clothes) are kept to a bare minimum on this swath of coast, beloved of naturists and escapists. The best beaches are at the eastern end around Es Arenals.

Reached by a series of bumpy tracks, most of these beach settlements are no more than a handful of houses, a couple of bar-restaurants and the odd *hostal*.

🛏 Sleeping & Eating

Hostal Ca Marí HOSTAL €€
(☑971 32 81 80; www.hotelcamari.com; Es Ca Marí; r €107-145, apt €109-165; ☺May-Oct; P🅿@ 🛜🚼🅿) At Hostal Ca Marí, rooms and apartments all share gardens, a central bar, a restaurant, a pool and a grocery shop. The beach, where the *hostal* has its own bar-restaurant, is barely 100m away.

Gecko Beach Club BOUTIQUE HOTEL €€€
(☑971 32 80 24; www.geckobeachclub.com; Es Ca Marí; r incl breakfast €270-325; P🅿🛜🚼🅿) Formentera slips into the glam shoes of its sister Ibiza at this gorgeous boutique hotel. Right on the beach, it pairs minimalist rooms with a chilled vibe and A-list credentials – think yoga by the poolside, cabana beds, cocktails and hammocks strung between the palms.

Sa Platgeta SEAFOOD €€
(☑971 18 76 14; Es Ca Marí; mains €15, meals €35; ☺1pm-midnight May-Sep) Planted amid pines just back from a narrow, rock-studded beach, this simple bar-restaurant is one of the best spots on the island for fresh fish. It's 500m west of Es Ca Marí (follow the signs through the backstreets or take the waterfront boardwalk).

Vogamari SPANISH €€
(☑971 32 90 53; www.vogamari.es; mains €15-30; ☺1-4.30pm & 7.30-11pm May-Oct) Set amid a greenery-filled dune, Vogamari is a simple island restaurant with a broad verandah. It's great for fresh fish, paella or solid meat dishes. Turn off the PM820 at Km 9.5.

FORMENTERA'S TOP BEACHES

➡ Platja de Migjorn (p823)

➡ Cala Saona (p821)

➡ Platja de ses Illetes (p823)

➡ Platja de Llevant (p823)

MALLORCA, MENORCA & IBIZA PLATJA DE MIGJORN

TO THE LIGHTHOUSE

From Es Caló, the road twists precipitously up through pine woods to the island's highest point. Close to the top, beside Restaurante El Mirador, there are spectacular views along this slip of an island, whose eastern extremity is elevated on a limestone plateau. Most of the coastline is only accessible by boat. A road runs arrow-straight to the island's eastern tip, passing through Es Pilar de la Mola, which comes alive for hippie markets, held from 4pm to 9pm each Wednesday and Sunday. The road continues, bringing you to Far de sa Mola lighthouse, a monument to Jules Verne (who used the end-of-the-world setting in one of his novels), a bar and a sublime seascape.

Es Cupiná   SEAFOOD €€

(☑ 971 32 72 21; meals around €35) At the eastern extremity of the beach and in business for nearly 40 years, this breezy restaurant is noted for its freshly cooked fish of the day.

Drinking & Nightlife

Above the long strand, the scattering of bars range from sophisticated (often Italian-run) chill-out cocktail scenes to more rough-and-ready affairs.

Blue Bar   BAR

(☑ 666758190;   www.bluebarformentera.com; ⊗ noon-4am Apr-Oct) This funky, sea-splashed shack is prime sunset cocktail material. Back in the '60s, legend says it even played host to hippies par exellence Bob Marley and Jimi Hendrix. Everything is blue – seats, sunshades, tables, loos and walls. Why, they even mix a blue Curacao-based cocktail!

Take the sandy track at Km 7.9 of the Carretera San Ferran-La Mola, off the PM820.

10.7   BAR

(☑ 660 985248; www.10punto7.com; ⊗ 11am-1am late May-Sep) Milan meets the sea at this super-stylish Italian number, with a menu of sushi and international wines. The rolling waves below, black-and-white decor and good vibes are perfect for lingering. Take the dirt track at Km 10.7 of the Carretera San Ferran-La Mola, off the PM820.

Es Caló

The tiny fishing hamlet of Es Caló is on a rocky cove ringed by faded timber boat shelters. The coastline is jagged, but immediately west you'll find stretches of blisteringly white sand massaged by what will probably turn out to be the most translucent water you will ever gleefully dive into.

Sleeping & Eating

Hostal Rafalet   HOSTAL €

(☑ 971 32 70 16; www.hostal-rafalet.com; s/d €80/110; ❀❀) Overlooking a small rocky harbour, Hostal Rafalet is a welcoming *hostal*, where many of the whistle-clean rooms have sea views. Did we say 'sea views'? Sorry, we meant it's so close to the sea that fish might try to cuddle up next to you in bed at night. Downstairs, there's a popular bar and fish restaurant with a portside terrace.

S'Eufabi   SPANISH €€

(☑ 971 32 70 56; www.seufabi.com; Carretera La Mola, Km 12.5; mains €10-18; ⊗ noon-3.30pm & 8-11pm) S'Eufabi dishes up some of the best paella and *fideuá* (a fine noodle variant) on Formentera at a reasonable price. This shady eatery is about 1km east of Es Caló, on the left as you begin the gentle ascent towards Es Pilar de la Mola.

Understand Spain

Spain Today

Although you may not notice it as a visitor – this is *Spain*, after all, and its streets and bars are as full as ever – Spain is experiencing a time of profound economic crisis. As if that weren't enough, Catalonia wants to secede. Amid all the gloom, however, Spaniards cling to the hope that the country may have hit rock bottom and is once again on the rise.

Best on Film

Jamón, jamón (1992) Dark comedy that brought Penélope Cruz and Javier Bardem to prominence.

Todo sobre mi madre (1999) Classic Pedro Almodóvar romp through sex and death.

Mar adentro (2004) Alejandro Amenábar's study of a Galician quadriplegic.

Volver (2006) Almódovar's lush and offbeat portrait of a Spanish family in crisis.

Alatriste (2006) War and betrayal pursue a Spanish musketeer in this 17th-century epic.

Best in Print

A Late Dinner: Discovering the Food of Spain (Paul Richardson) Erudite journey through Spain's fascinating culinary culture.

A Handbook for Travellers (Richard Ford) This 1845 classic is witty, informative and downright rude.

The Train in Spain (Christopher Howse) Amusing yet insightful reflections from a veteran Spain-watcher.

The New Spaniards (John Hooper) A journey through three decades (until 2006) of democratic Spain.

Don Quixote (Miguel de Cervantes) Spain's best-known novel remains a classic journey through inland Spain.

Economic Crisis

Six years after Spain's economic crisis took hold in late 2008, the country is still reeling. Unemployment, which had dropped as low as 6% as Spain enjoyed 16 consecutive years of growth, now sits stubbornly above 26%, which equates to six million people. The International Monetary Fund (IMF) says that it could be a further five years before that figure falls below 25%. Suicide rates are on the rise, Spain's young professionals are fleeing the country in unprecedented numbers and Oxfam recently predicted that a staggering 18 million Spaniards – 40% of the population – are at risk of social marginalisation within the next decade.

And if all of this sounds bad, it's nothing compared to the catastrophic youth unemployment rates which recently topped 57.7%. Old-timers you speak to can't remember a time this bad, with businesses closing their doors forever, including many that weathered civil war and dictatorship down through the decades. And the government's punishing austerity drive is hardly improving the mood of Spaniards.

Signs of Hope?

These things are always easier to quantify in hindsight than they are at the time, but there are small signs that Spain's economy is recovering, albeit *very* slowly. After five years of contracting, the economy has begun to grow – yes, it may be at a snail's pace, and yes, it may take another decade to return to the growth rates of the pre-crisis boom years. But economists at Spain's largest banks have predicted that the economy may grow by almost 1% in 2014.

Talk to business owners and many will tell you that an imperceptible shift occurred late in 2013. As one restaurant owner told us, 'people started going out to eat again. Maybe everyone just reached a point where they just threw up their hands and said, enough! Whatever the reason, there has been a change, even if it is a small one.' At the very least, the worst seems to have passed. Long may it continue.

A New Politics

One of the most visible responses of Spaniards to the crisis has been to get organised. On 15 May 2011, the *indignados* (those who are indignant) took over the iconic Plaza de la Puerta del Sol in the centre of Madrid in a peaceful sit-in protest. Their popularity maintained by social-media networks, they stayed for months, the forerunner to numerous such movements around the world, including Occupy Wall Street and its offshoots.

Driven by dissatisfaction with Spain's major political parties – the Popular Party government is already on the nose due to a major corruption scandal, while the still-disgraced Socialists appear unelectable in the short term having presided over the onset of Spain's catastrophic economic collapse – the 15-M movement (as they are known) has set up social and political grassroots networks across the country. These community-based networks provide social welfare, prevent the evictions of those unable to pay their mortgages, and agitate for reforms to laws that require defaulting mortgage holders to hand over their homes *and* continue paying off their mortgage.

No-one quite knows where it will all lead, but many Spaniards are hopeful of what may lie ahead.

Catalan Independence?

More than any other country in continental Europe, Spain often seems at risk of falling apart. For almost four decades, the Basque terrorist group ETA waged a low-level but violent struggle for independence. ETA is now a spent force, but now, it seems, Catalonia wants to leave the Spanish fold.

Angered by what it considers to be its unfair shouldering of the economic burden during Spain's economic crisis, Catalonia announced that a referendum on independence would take place on 9 November 2014. Unlike in the UK where Scotland is being allowed to decide its own future, Spain's national government has denounced the plan as illegal and has vowed not to let the referendum go ahead. The only certain outcome for now appears to be an increasingly strident war of words between the national government and the restive region.

POPULATION: **46.61 MILLION**

AREA: **505,370 SQ KM**

GDP PER CAPITA: **US$30,100**

ANNUAL INFLATION: **1.8%**

UNEMPLOYMENT: **26.3%**

POPULATION BELOW POVERTY LINE: **21.1%**

if Spain were 100 people

74 would speak Castilian Spanish
17 would speak Catalan
7 would speak Galician
2 would speak Basque

belief systems
(% of population)

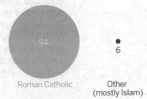

94 — Roman Catholic
6 — Other (mostly Islam)

population per sq km

SPAIN USA ENGLAND

👤 ≈ 30 people

History

Spain's story is one of Europe's grand epics. It is a story shaped by ancient and not-so-ancient civilisations sweeping down through the Iberian Peninsula, and by the great ideological battles between Muslims and Christians of the Middle Ages. Later it became the tale of an empire upon which the sun never set and of near endemic conflict over the spoils. And the 20th century was a match for anything that went before with Civil War, dictatorship and a stunning return to democracy.

Top Roman Remains

Mérida

Segovia

Itálica

Tarragona

Baelo Claudia, Bolonia

Lugo

Villa Romana La Olmeda

Spain & the Ancient Civilisations

Spain can make a convincing claim to be the cradle of European humanity – in 2007, Europe's oldest human remains (a mere 1.2 million years old) were discovered at Atapuerca, near the northern city of Burgos. But it was not until around 3000 years ago that Spain finally entered history's mainstream.

Phoenicians & Greeks

The Phoenician Empire (1500–300 BC) was the first of the grand civilisations of the Ancient World to set their sights on Spain. From their base along what is now the southern Lebanese coast, the Phoenicians may have been the world's first rulers of the sea. They were essentially traders rather than conquerors, and it was indeed commerce that first brought them to Spain around 1000 BC. They arrived on Spanish shores bearing perfumes, ivory, jewellery, oil, wine and textiles, which they exchanged for Spanish silver and bronze.

Conquest may not have been the Phoenicians' aim, but as their reach expanded, so too did their need for safe ports around the Mediterranean rim. One of these was Carthage in modern-day Tunisia, founded in 814 BC, and in Iberia they established coastal trading colonies at Almuñécar (which they called Ex or Sex), Huelva (Onuba) and Cádiz (Gadir). Cádiz, that breezy and thoroughly Andalucian city in Spain's deep south, can as a result make a pretty strong claim to be the oldest continuously inhabited settlement in Europe.

TIMELINE	c 1.2 million BC	c 22,000 BC	c 15,000– 10,000 BC
	Europe's earliest-known humans leave their fossilised remains in the Sima del Elefante at Atapuerca, near the northern city of Burgos.	Neanderthal humans die out on the Iberian Peninsula – possibly due to climatic changes during the last Ice Age, or possibly because they were displaced by Homo sapiens arriving from Africa.	Palaeolithic (Old Stone Age) hunters of the Magdalenian culture paint beautiful, sophisticated animal images in caves at Altamira and other sites along Spain's northern coastal strip.

While the Phoenicians were setting up shop around Spain's southern coastline, Ancient Greek traders were arriving further north. In the 7th century BC the Greeks began to establish trading settlements mainly along the Mediterranean coast – the biggest was Emporion (Empúries) at L'Escala in Catalonia.

The most important gifts of the Phoenicians and Greeks to Spain were not cities, only fragments of which remain today, but rather the things they brought with them, such as iron and several things now considered quintessentially Spanish – the olive tree, the grapevine and the donkey – along with other useful skills and items such as writing, coins, the potter's wheel and poultry.

The Romans

They might have been here first, but the hold of the Phoenicians and Greeks over their Spanish 'territories' was always rather tenuous and never destined to last.

From about the 6th century BC the Phoenicians and Greeks were pushed out of the western Mediterranean by newly independent Carthage, a former Phoenician colony that established a flourishing settlement on Ibiza. For a brief period during the third century BC, during the so-called Punic Wars in which Rome and Carthage battled for control over the Mediterranean, Carthage conquered southern Spain. The Second Punic War (218–201 BC) saw Carthaginian general Hannibal march his elephants on from here and over the Alps to threaten Rome, but Rome's victory at Ilipa, near Seville, in 206 BC, ultimately gave it control over the Iberian Peninsula. The first Roman town in Spain, Itálica (p598), was founded near the battlefield soon afterwards.

The Romans held sway on the Iberian Peninsula for 600 years. It took them 200 years to subdue the fiercest of local tribes, but by AD 50 most of Hispania (as the Romans called the peninsula) had adopted the Roman way of life.

Rome's legacy to Spain was huge, giving Hispania a road system, aqueducts, temples, theatres, amphitheatres and bathhouses, along with the religion that still predominates today – Christianity – and a Jewish population who were to play a big part in Spanish life for over 1000 years. The main languages still spoken on the Iberian Peninsula – Castilian Spanish, Catalan, Galician and Portuguese – are all versions of the colloquial Latin spoken by Roman legionaries and colonists, filtered through 2000 years of linguistic mutation; the Basques, though defeated, were never Romanised like the rest and hence their language never came within the Latin orbit.

It was also the Romans who first began to cut (for timber, fuel and weapons) the extensive forests that in their time covered half the *meseta*. In return, Hispania gave Rome gold, silver, grain, wine, fish, soldiers,

AL-ANDALUS

HISTORY SPAIN & THE ANCIENT CIVILISATIONS

Richard Fletcher's *Moorish Spain* is an excellent short history of Al-Andalus (the Muslim-ruled areas of the peninsula) and assumes little or no prior knowledge of the subject. For a modern take on Spain's Moorish history, track down Jason Webster's *Andalus: Unlocking the Secrets of Moorish Spain*.

6th century BC	218 BC	1st to 3rd centuries AD	AD 53
Carthage, a former Phoenician colony in North Africa, supplants the Phoenicians and Greeks as the major trading power in the western Mediterranean.	Roman legions arrive in Spain during the Second Punic War against Carthage, initiating the 600-year Roman occupation of the Iberian Peninsula; it takes two centuries to subdue all local resistance.	Pax Romana (Roman Peace), a period of stability and prosperity. The Iberian Peninsula is divided into three provinces: Baetica (capital: Córdoba); Lusitania (Mérida) and Tarraconensis (Tarragona).	Future Roman Emperor Trajan is born in Itálica to a wealthy senator. His imperial rule will begin in 98 and see the Roman Empire reach its greatest extent.

Almohad rule saw a cultural revival in Seville, and the great Cordoban philosopher Averroës (1126–98) exerted a major influence on medieval Christian thought with his commentaries on Aristotle, trying to reconcile science with religion.

emperors (Trajan, Hadrian, Theodosius) and the literature of Seneca, Martial, Quintilian and Lucan.

The Roman centuries were something of a golden age for Spain, but the Pax Romana (Roman Peace; the long, prosperous period of stability under the Romans) in Spain began to crumble in the 3rd and 4th centuries AD when Germanic tribes began to sweep down across the Pyrenees. The Visigoths, another Germanic people, sacked Rome itself in 410, but later became Roman allies. When the Germanic Franks pushed the Visigoths out of Gaul in the 6th century, they settled in the Iberian Peninsula, making Toledo their capital.

The roughly 200,000 Visigoths maintained a precarious hold over the millions of more-sophisticated Hispano-Romans, and culturally, the Visigoths tended to ape Roman ways. Nonetheless, the Roman era had come to an end.

Moorish Spain & La Reconquista

A recurring theme in early Spanish history is Spain's susceptibility to foreign invasion, to empires that rose and fell on Spanish soil but which invariably came from elsewhere. And so it would prove again, although that would slowly change over the next eight centuries, during an epic struggle for the soul of Spain.

The Moorish Arrival

The death of the Prophet Mohammed in far-off Arabia in 632 would send shockwaves across the known world. Under Mohammed's successors, known as caliphs (from the Arabic word for 'follower'), the new religion spread with extraordinary speed. Much of the Middle East was theirs by 656 and by 682 Islam had reached the shores of the Atlantic in Morocco. Spain, and with it Europe, now lay within sight and within reach.

They had chosen a good moment to arrive: with the disintegration of the Visigothic kingdom through famine, disease and strife among the aristocracy, the Iberian Peninsula was in disarray and ripe for invasion.

For all its significance, there is an element of farce to what happened next. If you believe the myth, the Muslims were ushered into Spain by the sexual misadventures of the last Visigoth king, Roderic, who reputedly seduced Florinda, the daughter of the governor of Ceuta on the Moroccan coast. The governor, Julian, sought revenge by approaching the Muslims with a plan to invade Spain, and in 711 Tariq ibn Ziyad, the Muslim governor of Tangier, landed at Gibraltar with around 10,000 men, mostly Berbers (indigenous North Africans).

Roderic's army was decimated, probably near Río Guadalete or Río Barbate in western Andalucía, and he is thought to have drowned while fleeing the scene. Visigothic survivors fled north and within a few years

Top Prehistoric Sites

Cueva de Altamira, near Santillana del Mar

Atapuerca, near Burgos

Cueva de Tito Bustillo, Ribadesella

Dolmens, Antequera

Cueva de la Pileta, near Ronda

Siega Verde, near Ciudad Rodrigo

4th to 7th centuries AD	711	718	756
Germanic tribes enter the Iberian Peninsula, ending the Pax Romana. The Visigoths establish control and bring 200 years of relative stability in which Hispano-Roman culture survives.	Muslims invade Iberia from North Africa, overrunning it within a few years, becoming the dominant force on the peninsula for nearly four centuries, and then a potent one for four centuries more.	Christian nobleman Pelayo establishes the Kingdom of Asturias in northern Spain. With his victory over a Muslim force at the Battle of Covadonga around 722, the Reconquista begins.	Abd ar-Rahman I establishes himself in Córdoba as the emir of Al-Andalus (the Islamic areas of the peninsula) and launches nearly three centuries of Cordoban supremacy.

THE VISIGOTH LEGACY

The Visigoths left little mark on the Spanish landscape – they were better conquerors than they were builders of monuments meant to last. Of what remains, the most noteworthy structure is the modest Visigothic church (p175) at Baños de Cerrato, near Palencia, which dates from 661, and is reckoned to be Spain's oldest surviving church. Otherwise, archaeological fragments are all that remain in archaeological museums around the country, and in Mérida's Museo de Arte Visigodo (p564).

Aside from their meagre contribution to Spanish architecture, the Visigoths' principal lasting impact on Spanish history lies in the fact that Visigothic nobility headed the small Christian kingdoms that survived the Muslim conquest of 711 and began the eight-century Reconquista, which eventually reasserted Christianity in the Iberian Peninsula. Common names of Visigothic origin, such as Fernando, Rodrigo, Fernández and Rodríguez, are still reminders of the Visigoths' role in the Spanish story.

the Muslims had conquered the whole Iberian Peninsula, except for small areas behind the mountains of the Cordillera Cantábrica in the north. Their advance into Europe was only checked by the Franks at the Battle of Poitiers in 732.

Al-Andalus: The Early Years

The enlightened Islamic civilisation that would rule much of the Iberian Peninsula for centuries would be called Al-Andalus.

Initially Al-Andalus was part of the Caliphate of Damascus, which ruled the Islamic world. Once again, Spain was a distant outpost of someone else's empire. In 750, however, the Umayyads were overthrown in Damascus by a rival clan, the Abbasids, who shifted the caliphate to Baghdad. One aristocratic Umayyad survivor made his way to Spain and established himself in Córdoba in 756 as the independent emir of Al-Andalus, Abd ar-Rahman I. It was he who began construction of Córdoba's Mezquita (p641), one of the world's greatest Islamic buildings. Just as importantly, Córdoba was the capital of an empire that relied on no foreign powers. For almost the first time in Spanish history, Spain (in this case, Al-Andalus) was both powerful and answerable only to itself.

Córdoba's Golden Age

From the middle of the eighth century to the mid-11th century, the frontier between Muslim and Christian territory lay across the north of the peninsula, roughly from southern Catalonia to northern Portugal, with a protrusion up to the central Pyrenees. South of this line, Islamic cities such as Córdoba, Seville and Granada boasted beautiful palaces, mosques and gardens, universities, public baths and bustling *zocos* (markets).

Best Moorish Monuments

Alhambra, Granada

Mezquita, Córdoba

Albayzín, Granada

Alcázar, Seville

Giralda, Seville

Aljafería, Zaragoza

Alcazaba, Málaga

929	1031	1035	1085
Abd ar-Rahman III inaugurates the Córdoba Caliphate, under which Al-Andalus reaches its zenith and Córdoba, with up to half a million people, becomes Europe's biggest and most cultured city.	The Córdoba Caliphate disintegrates into dozens of *taifas* (small kingdoms) after a devastating civil war. The most powerful *taifas* include Seville, Granada, Toledo and Zaragoza.	Castilla, a county of the northern Christian kingdom of León (successor to the kingdom of Asturias), becomes an independent kingdom and goes on to become the leading force of the Reconquista.	Castilla captures the major Muslim city of Toledo in central Spain after infighting among the *taifas* leaves them vulnerable to attack.

Reconquista
Castles on
the Web
....
www.castillosnet.
org
....
www.castlesof
spain.co.uk

Al-Andalus' rulers allowed freedom of worship to Jews and Christians (known as Mozárabes and Mozarabs respectively). Jews mostly flourished, but Christians had to pay a special tax, so most either converted to Islam (to be known as *muladíes* or *muwallad*) or left for the Christian north.

In 929 the ruler Abd ar-Rahman III gave himself the title caliph, launching the Caliphate of Córdoba (929–1031), during which Al-Andalus reached its peak of power and lustre. Córdoba in this period was the biggest and most dazzling city in Western Europe. Astronomy, medicine, mathematics and botany flourished and one of the great Muslim libraries was established in the city.

Later in the 10th century the fearsome Cordoban general Al-Mansour (or Almanzor) terrorised the Christian north with 50-odd forays in 20 years. He destroyed the cathedral at Santiago de Compostela in northwestern Spain in 997 and forced Christian slaves to carry its doors and bells to Córdoba, where they were incorporated into the great mosque. There was, it seemed, no limit to Córdoba's powers.

Al-Andalus: The Later Years

Just when it seemed that Córdoba's golden age would last forever, Al-Andalus turned the corner into a long, slow decline.

After Al-Mansour's death the caliphate collapsed in a devastating civil war, ending Umayyad rule. Córdoba remained powerful but in 1031, the emirate finally broke up into dozens of *taifas* (small kingdoms).

Gile Tremlett's
*Catherine of
Aragón: The
Spanish Queen
of Henry VIII*
brings to life all
the scheming
and intrigue of
royal Europe in
the 16th century
through the
story of Isabel
and Fernando's
daughter.

Political unity was restored to Al-Andalus by the invasion of a strict Muslim sect of Saharan or Berber nomads, the Almoravids, in 1091. The Almoravids had conquered North Africa and were initially invited to the Iberian Peninsula to support Seville, one of the strongest *taifas*, against the growing Christian threat from the north. Sixty years later a second Berber sect, the Almohads, invaded the peninsula after overthrowing the Almoravids in Morocco. Both sects roundly defeated the Christian armies they encountered in Spain, and maintained the Muslim stranglehold over the southern half of the peninsula.

The near-constant infighting of Muslim versus Muslim was, however, starting to take its toll. While the Almohad's successors, the Nasrids, retreated to Granada and contributed to the splendours of the Alhambra (p655), the Christian armies of the Reconquista were closing in.

The Reconquista

The Christian Reconquest of the Iberian Peninsula began in about 722 at Covadonga, Asturias, and ended with the fall of Granada in 1492. In between these two dates lay almost eight centuries of misadventures, stirring victories and missed opportunities.

1091	1160–73	1195	1218
North African Muslim Almoravids invade the peninsula, unifying Al-Andalus, ruling it from Marrakesh and halting Christian expansion. Almoravid rule crumbles in the 1140s; Al-Andalus splits into *taifas*.	The Almohads, another strict Muslim sect from North Africa, conquer Al-Andalus. They make Seville their capital and revive arts and learning.	The Almohads inflict a devastating defeat on Alfonso VIII of Castilla at the Battle of Alarcos, near Ciudad Real – the last major Christian reverse of the Reconquista.	The University of Salamanca is founded by Alfonso IX, King of León, making it the oldest – and still the most prestigious – university in the country.

THE MOORISH LEGACY

Muslim rule left an indelible imprint upon the country. Great architectural monuments such as the Alhambra in Granada and the Mezquita in Córdoba are the stars of the Moorish legacy, but thousands of other buildings large and small are Moorish in origin (including the many churches that began life as mosques). The tangled, narrow street plans of many a Spanish town and village, especially in the south, date back to Moorish times, and the Muslims also developed the Hispano-Roman agricultural base by improving irrigation and introducing new fruits and crops, many of which are still widely grown today. The Spanish language contains many common words of Arabic origin, including the names of some of those new crops – *naranja* (orange), *azúcar* (sugar) and *arroz* (rice). Flamenco, though brought to its modern form by Roma people in post-Moorish times, has clear Moorish roots. It was also through Al-Andalus that much of the learning of ancient Greece and Rome – picked up by the Arabs in the eastern Mediterranean – was transmitted to Christian Europe, where it would exert a profound influence on the Renaissance.

An essential ingredient in the Reconquista was the cult of Santiago (St James), one of the 12 apostles. In 813 the saint's supposed tomb was discovered in Galicia. The city of Santiago de Compostela grew around the site, to become the third-most-popular medieval Christian pilgrimage goal after Rome and Jerusalem. Christian generals experienced visions of Santiago before forays against the Muslims, and Santiago became the inspiration and special protector of soldiers in the Reconquista, earning the sobriquet Matamoros (Moor-slayer). Today he is the patron saint of Spain.

Castilla Rises

Covadonga lies in the Picos de Europa mountains, where some Visigothic nobles took refuge after the Muslim conquest. Christian versions of the 722 battle there tell of a small band of fighters under their leader, Pelayo, defeating an enormous force of Muslims; Muslim accounts make it a rather less important skirmish. Whatever the facts of Covadonga, by 757 Christians had clawed back nearly a quarter of the Iberian Peninsula.

The Asturian kingdom eventually moved its capital south to León and became the Kingdom of León, which spearheaded the Reconquista until the Christians were set on the defensive by Al-Mansour in the 10th century. Castilla, initially a small principality within León, developed into the dominant Reconquista force as hardy adventurers set up towns in the no-man's-land of the Duero basin. The capture of Toledo in 1085, by Alfonso VI of Castilla, led the Seville Muslims to call in the Almoravids from North Africa.

Aragón was one of the most powerful kingdoms in medieval Spain, a crown created in 1137 when Ramón Berenguer IV of Catalonia married Petronilla, heiress of Aragón, to create a formidable new Christian power block in the northeast, with Barcelona as its power centre.

1229–38	1248	1469	1478
Catalonia enjoys its golden age under King Jaume I of Aragón, who takes the Balearic Islands and Valencia from the Muslims and makes Catalonia the major power in the western Mediterranean.	Having captured Córdoba 12 years earlier, Castilla's Fernando III takes Seville after a two-year siege, making the Nasrid Emirate of Granada the last surviving Muslim state on the peninsula.	Isabel, the 18-year-old heir to Castilla, marries Fernando, heir to Aragón and one year her junior, uniting Spain's two most powerful Christian states.	Isabel and Fernando, the Reyes Católicos (Catholic Monarchs), stir up religious bigotry and establish the Spanish Inquisition that will see thousands killed between now and its abolition in 1834.

In 1212 the combined armies of the Christian kingdoms routed a large Almohad force at Las Navas de Tolosa in Andalucía. This was the beginning of the end for Al-Andalus: León took key towns in Extremadura in 1229 and 1230; Aragón took Valencia in the 1230s; Castilla's Fernando III El Santo (Ferdinand the Saint) took Córdoba in 1236 and Seville in 1248; and Portugal expelled the Muslims in 1249. The sole surviving Muslim state on the peninsula was now the Emirate of Granada.

Echoes of the Middle Ages

....
Sos del Rey Católico, Aragón
....
Albarracín, Aragón
....
Santiago de Compostela
....
Morella, Valencia
....
La Taha, Las Alpujarras
....
Santo Domingo de la Calzada, La Rioja
....
Ávila
....
Albayzín, Granada

Granada Falls

In 1476 Emir Abu al-Hasan of Granada refused to pay any more tribute to Castilla, spurring Isabel (queen of Castilla) and Fernando (king of Aragón) to launch the Reconquista's final crusade against Granada, with an army largely funded by Jewish loans and the Catholic Church. The Christians took full advantage of a civil war within the Granada emirate, and on 2 January 1492 Isabel and Fernando entered the city of Granada at the beginning of what turned out to be the most momentous year in Spanish history.

The surrender terms were fairly generous to Boabdil, the last emir, who got the Alpujarras valleys south of Granada and 30,000 gold coins. History has been less kind. Whether true or not, it is often recounted how Boabdil turned for one last tearful look at his beloved Granada as he headed into exile, whereupon his mother scolded him by saying: 'Do not weep like a woman for that which you were unable to defend like a man!' The remaining Muslims were promised respect for their religion, culture and property, but this didn't last long.

Eight centuries after it began, Al-Andalus was no more.

The Spanish Inquisition

Spain's new Catholic rulers made it clear from the beginning that Islam's enlightened policies of religious coexistence were a thing of the past.

Not content with territorial conquest, the Catholic Monarchs' Christian zeal led to the founding of the Spanish Inquisition to root out those believed to be threatening the Catholic Church. The Inquisition's leading figure was Grand Inquisitor Tomás de Torquemada, who was appointed Queen Isabel's personal confessor in 1479. He was, centuries later, immortalised by Dostoevsky as the articulate Grand Inquisitor who puts Jesus himself on trial in *The Brothers Karamazov,* and satirised by Monty Python in the *Flying Circus*.

The Inquisition focused first on *conversos* (Jews converted to Christianity), accusing many of continuing to practise Judaism in secret; in an interesting footnote to history, Torquemada was himself born to *converso* parents.

January 1492	April 1492	October 1492	1494
Isabel and Fernando capture Granada, completing the Reconquista. Boabdil, the last Muslim ruler, is scorned by his mother for weeping 'like a woman for what you could not defend like a man'.	Isabel and Fernando expel Jews who refuse Christian baptism. Some 200,000 leave, establishing Jewish communities around the Mediterranean; Spain's economy suffers from the loss of their knowledge.	Christopher Columbus, funded by Isabel and Fernando, lands in the Bahamas, opening up the Americas to Spanish colonisation. The bulk of Spanish maritime trade shifts from Mediterranean to Atlantic ports.	The Treaty of Tordesillas (near Valladolid) divides recently discovered lands west of Europe between Spain and Portugal, giving the Spanish the right to claim vast territories in the Americas.

During the Inquisition, the 'lucky' sinners had their property confiscated, which had, prior to the fall of Granada, served as a convenient fund-raiser for the war of Reconquista against the Muslims. The condemned were then paraded through towns wearing the *sambenito,* a yellow shirt emblazoned with crosses that was short enough to expose their genitals, then marched to the doors of the local church and flogged.

If you were unlucky, you underwent unimaginable tortures before going through an *auto-da-fé,* a public burning at the stake. Those that recanted and kissed the cross were garrotted before the fire was set, while those that recanted only were burnt quickly with dry wood. If you stayed firm and didn't recant, the wood used for the fire was green and slow-burning.

In the 15 years Torquemada was Inquisitor General of the Castilian Inquisition, he ran some 100,000 trials and sent about 2000 people to burn at the stake. On 31 March 1492, Fernando and Isabel, on Torquemada's insistence, issued their Edict of Expulsion, as a result of which all Jews who refused Christian baptism were forced to leave Spain within two months on pain of death. Up to 100,000 converted, but some 200,000 – the first Sephardic Jews – left Spain for other Mediterranean destinations. The bankrupt monarchy seized all unsold Jewish property. A talented middle class was gone.

Cardinal Cisneros, Torquemada's successor as overseer of the Inquisition, tried to eradicate Muslim culture too. In the former Granada emirate he carried out forced mass baptisms, burnt Islamic books and banned the Arabic language. After a revolt in Andalucía in 1500, Muslims were ordered to convert to Christianity or leave. Most (around 300,000) underwent baptism and stayed, becoming known as *moriscos* (converted Muslims), but their conversion was barely skin deep and they never assimilated. The *moriscos* were finally expelled between 1609 and 1614.

Spain's Empires

Having secured the Iberian Peninsula as their own, the Catholic monarchs turned their attention elsewhere. The conquest of Granada coincided neatly with the opening up of a whole new world of opportunity for a confident Christian Spain. Columbus' voyage to the Americas, in the very same year as Granada fell, presented an entire new continent in which the militaristic and crusading elements of Spanish society could continue their efforts.

Conquering a New World

In April 1492 the Catholic Monarchs granted the Genoese sailor Christopher Columbus (Cristobel Colón in Spanish) funds for his long-desired voyage across the Atlantic in search of a new trade route to the Orient.

> **Medieval Jewish Sites**
> ....
> *Judería (Jewish quarter), Toledo*
> ....
> *The Call, Girona*
> ....
> *Ribadavia, Galicia*
> ....
> *Judería, Córdoba*
> ....
> *Hervás, Extremadura*

1512	1517–56	1521	1533
Fernando, ruling as regent after Isabel's death in 1504, annexes Navarra, bringing all of Spain under one rule for the first time since Roman days.	Reign of Carlos I, Spain's first Habsburg monarch, who comes to rule more of Europe than anyone since the 9th century, plus rapidly expanding areas of South and Central America.	Hernán Cortés, from Medellín, Extremadura, conquers the Aztec empire in present-day Mexico and Guatemala in the name of the Spanish crown.	Francisco Pizarro, from Trujillo, Extremadura, conquers the Inca empire in South America with a small band of conquistadors.

Echoes of Spain's American Colonies

Trujillo, Extremadura

Lugares Colombinos, near Huelva

Casa-Museo de Colón, Valladolid

Columbus' Tomb, Seville Cathedral

Tordesillas, near Valladolid

Palacio de Sobrellano, Comillas

Museo de América, Madrid

Columbus sailed from the Andalucian port of Palos de la Frontera on 3 August 1492, with three small ships and 120 men. After a near mutiny as the crew despaired of sighting land, they finally arrived on the island of Guanahaní, in the Bahamas, and went on to find Cuba and Hispaniola. Columbus returned to a hero's reception from the Catholic Monarchs in Barcelona, eight months after his departure. Columbus made three more voyages, founding the city of Santo Domingo on Hispaniola, finding Jamaica, Trinidad and other Caribbean islands, and reaching the mouth of the Orinoco and the coast of Central America. But he died impoverished in Valladolid in 1506, still believing he had reached Asia.

Brilliant but ruthless conquistadors such as Hernán Cortés and Francisco Pizarro followed Columbus' trail, seizing vast tracts of the American mainland for Spain. By 1600 Spain controlled Florida, all the biggest Caribbean islands, nearly all of present-day Mexico and Central America, and a large strip of South America. The new colonies sent huge cargoes of silver, gold and other riches back to Spain, where the crown was entitled to one-fifth of the bullion (the *quintoreal,* or royal fifth). Seville enjoyed a monopoly on this trade and grew into one of Europe's richest cities.

Entangled in the Old World

It wasn't just the Americas that the monarchs thought should be theirs. Ever scheming, Isabel and Fernando embroiled Spain in European affairs by marrying their five children into the royal families of Portugal, the Holy Roman Empire and England. After Isabel's death in 1504 and Fernando's in 1516, their thrones passed to their grandson Carlos I (Charles I), who arrived in Spain from Flanders in 1517, aged 17. In 1519 Carlos also succeeded to the Habsburg lands in Austria and was elected Holy Roman Emperor (as Charles V) – meaning he now ruled all of Spain, the Low Countries, Austria, several Italian states, parts of France and Germany, and the expanding Spanish colonies in the Americas.

For all Spain's apparent power, European conflicts soaked up the bulk of the monarchy's new American wealth, and a war-weary Carlos abdicated shortly before his death in 1556, retiring to the Monasterio de Yuste (p557) in Extremadura and dividing his many territories between his son Felipe II (Philip II; r 1556–98) and his brother Fernando.

Felipe got the lion's share, including Spain, the Low Countries and the American possessions, and presided over the zenith of Spanish power, though his reign is a study in contradictions. He enlarged the American empire and claimed Portugal on its king's death in 1580, but lost Holland after a long drawn-out rebellion. His navy defeated the Ottoman Turks at Lepanto in 1571, but the Spanish Armada of 1588 was routed by England. He was a fanatical Catholic, who spurred the Inquisition to new persecu-

1556–98	1561	1571	c 1600–1660
Reign of Felipe II, the zenith of Spanish power. The American territories expand into the modern United States and enormous wealth arriving from the colonies is used for grandiose architectural projects.	The king makes the minor country town of Madrid capital of his empire. Despite many new noble residences, the overwhelming impression of the new capital is one of squalor.	The Holy League fleet, led by Spain and Venice and commanded by Felipe II's half-brother Don Juan de Austria, defeats the Ottoman fleet at Lepanto, ending Ottoman expansion into Europe.	Spain enjoys a cultural golden age with the literature of Cervantes and the paintings of Velázquez, Zurbarán and El Greco scaling new heights of artistic excellence as the empire declines.

THE CATHOLIC MONARCHS

Few individuals in any time or place have had such an impact on their country's history as Spain's Reyes Católicos, Isabel of Castilla and Fernando of Aragón. Indeed, Spain owes its very existence to their marriage in 1469 (which effectively united the Iberian Peninsula's two biggest Christian kingdoms) and to their conquest of Granada (1492) and annexation of Navarra (1512).

Isabel, by all accounts, was pious, honest, virtuous and very determined, while Fernando was an astute political operator – a formidable team. Isabel resisted her family's efforts to marry her off to half a dozen other European royals before her semi-clandestine wedding to Fernando at Valladolid – the first time the pair had set eyes on each other. They were second cousins; she was 18 and he 17. Isabel succeeded to the Castilian throne in 1474, and Fernando to Aragón's in 1479. By the time Isabel died in 1504, the pair had achieved the following:

➡ set up the Spanish Inquisition (1478)

➡ completed the Reconquista by conquering Granada (1492)

➡ expelled all Jews (1492) and Muslims (1500) who refused to convert to Christianity

➡ helped to fund Columbus' voyage to the Americas (1492), opening the door to a vast overseas empire for Spain

➡ crushed the power of Castilla's rebellious nobility

Today Isabel and Fernando lie side by side in the beautiful Gothic church they commissioned as their own mausoleum, Granada's Capilla Real (p664).

tions, yet readily allied Spain with Protestant England against Catholic France. He received greater flows of silver than ever from the Americas, but went bankrupt.

Felipe too died in a monastery – the immense one at San Lorenzo de El Escorial (p134), which he himself had commissioned, and which stands as a sombre monument to his reign and to the follies of Spain's colonial era.

A Country Divided

In the moment of Spain's finest hour, at a time when it ruled large swaths of the known world, the country's rulers sowed the seeds for the country's disintegration. So much of the fabulous wealth that accrued from Spain's American and other colonies was squandered on lavish royal lifestyles and on indulgences that did little to better the lives of ordinary Spaniards. The result was a deeply divided country that would for centuries face almost constant battles of royal succession and its fair share of external wars.

Echoes of the Napoleonic Wars

Cabo de Trafalgar, Los Caños de Meca

Trafalgar Cemetery, Gibraltar

Museo de las Cortes de Cádiz, Cádiz

Xardín de San Carlos, A Coruña

1609–14	1676	1701	1702–13
The *moriscos* (converted Muslims) are expelled from Spain in a final purge of non-Christians that undermines an already faltering economy.	The devastation caused by the third great plague to hit Spain in a century is compounded by poor harvests. In all, more than 1.25 million Spaniards die through plague and starvation during the 17th century.	Felipe V, first of the Bourbon dynasty, takes the throne after the Habsburg line dies out with Carlos II. Felipe being second in line to the French throne causes concern across Europe.	Rival European powers support Charles of Austria against Felipe V in the War of the Spanish Succession: Felipe survives as king but Spain loses Gibraltar and the Low Countries.

Out of Step with Europe

Bourbon Baubles

....

Palacio Real, Madrid

....

Palacio Real, Aranjuez

....

La Granja de San Ildefonso, near Segovia

At one level, a flourishing arts scene in 17th-century Spain created the illusion of a modern European nation. It was at this time that Spain was immortalised on canvas by great artists such as Velázquez, El Greco, Zurbarán and Murillo, and in print by the likes of Miguel de Cervantes (author of *Don Quixote*) and the prolific playwright Lope de Vega.

And yet weak, backward-looking monarchs, a highly conservative Church and an idle nobility allowed the economy to stagnate, leading to food shortages in a country where there were gross inequalities between the haves and the have-nots. Spain lost Portugal and faced revolts in Catalonia, Sicily and Naples. Silver shipments from the Americas shrank disastrously. And the sickly Carlos II (Charles II; r 1665–1700), known as El Hechizado (the Bewitched), failed to produce children, a situation that led to the War of the Spanish Succession (1702–13).

During the war, things got even worse – Spain lost its last possessions in the Low Countries to Austria, and Gibraltar and Menorca to Britain. Felipe V (Philip V; r 1700–46), to whom Carlos II had bequeathed the Spanish throne, renounced his right to the French throne but held on to Spain. He was the first of the Bourbon dynasty, still in place today.

This was Europe's Age of Enlightenment, but Spain's powerful Church and Inquisition were at odds with the rationalism that trickled in from France. Two-thirds of the land was in the hands of the nobility and Church, and inequality and unrest were rife.

France Invades

During the First Republic some Spanish cities declared themselves independent states, and some, such as Seville and nearby Utrera, even declared war on each other.

When France's Louis XVI, cousin to Spain's Carlos IV (Charles IV; r 1788–1808), was guillotined in 1793 in the aftermath of the French Revolution of 1789, Spain declared war on France, only for Spain to make peace with the French Republic two years later. In 1805 a combined Spanish–French navy was beaten by the British fleet, under Admiral Nelson, off the Cabo de Trafalgar, putting an end to Spanish sea power.

In 1807, French forces poured into Spain, supposedly on the way to Portugal, but by 1808 this had become a French occupation of Spain, and Carlos IV was forced to abdicate in favour of Napoleon's brother Joseph Bonaparte (José I).

In Madrid crowds revolted, as immortalised by Goya in his paintings *El dos de mayo* and *el tres de mayo,* which now hang in Madrid's Museo del Prado (p83). Across the country Spaniards took up arms guerrilla-style, reinforced by British and Portuguese forces led by the Duke of Wellington. A national Cortes (Parliament) meeting at Cádiz in 1812 drew up a new liberal constitution, incorporating many of the principles of the American and French prototypes. The French were finally driven out after their defeat at Vitoria in 1813.

1793	1805	1808–13	1809–24
Spain declares war on France after Louis XVI is beheaded, but within a couple of years the country is supporting the French in their struggles against the British.	A combined Spanish–French fleet is defeated by British ships under Nelson at the Battle of Trafalgar. Spanish sea power is effectively destroyed, and discontent against the king's pro-French policies grows.	French forces occupy Spain; Carlos IV abdicates in favour of Napoleon's brother, José I. The ensuing Peninsular War sees British forces helping the Spanish defeat the French.	Most of Spain's American colonies win independence as Spain is beset by problems at home. By 1824 only Cuba, Puerto Rico, Guam and the Philippines are under Spanish rule.

Spain's Decline

Although momentarily united to see off the French, Spain was deeply divided, not to mention increasingly backward and insular. For much of the 19th century, internal conflicts raged between liberals (who wanted vaguely democratic reforms) and conservatives (the Church, the nobility and others who preferred the earlier status quo).

Uncertainties over royal succession resulted in the First Carlist War (1833–39). During the war, violent anticlericalism emerged, religious orders were closed and, in the Disentailment of 1836, church property and lands were seized and auctioned off by the government. It was the army alone that emerged victorious from the fighting. Another Carlist War (1872–76) followed, again between different claimants to the throne.

In 1873 the liberal-dominated Cortes proclaimed the country a federal republic. But this First Republic had lost control of the regions and the army put Isabel II's son Alfonso on the throne as Alfonso XII (r 1874–85), in a coalition with the Church and landowners.

Barely able to hold itself together, Spain had little chance of maintaining its few remaining colonies. In 1898, Spain lost Cuba, the Philippines, Guam and Puerto Rico.

For a country that had ruled one of the greatest empires of the age, this sealed an ignominious fall from grace.

The Spanish Civil War

Spain's Civil War (1936–39) was a long time coming. In many ways, the seeds of division were sown centuries before in the profound inequalities that flowed from Spain's colonial riches, and in the equally profound divisions that began to surface in the 19th century.

The Road to War

Spain was by the early years of the 20th century locked in an unending power struggle between liberal and conservative forces, with neither able to maintain the upper hand for long.

For a time, the left seemed ascendant. In the 1890s and the 1900s anarchists bombed Barcelona's Liceu opera house, assassinated two prime ministers and killed 24 people with a bomb at King Alfonso XIII's wedding to Victoria Eugenie of Battenberg in May 1906. Along with the rise of the left came the growth of Basque and Catalan separatism. In the Basque country, nationalism emerged in the 1890s in response to a flood of Castilian workers into Basque industries: some Basques considered these migrants a threat to their identity. In 1909 a contingent of Spanish troops was wiped out by Berbers in Spanish Morocco. The government's decision to call up Catalan reservists sparked the so-called

Pre–Civil War Books

As I Walked Out One Midsummer Morning – Laurie Lee

··

South from Granada – Gerald Brenan

··

The Spanish Labyrinth – Gerald Brenan

··

Modern Spain, 1875–1980 – Raymond Carr

1814	1833–39	1872–76	1898
Fernando VII becomes king and revokes the 1812 Cádiz Constitution (an attempt by Spanish liberals to introduce constitutional reforms) just weeks after agreeing to uphold its principles.	The First Carlist War, triggered by disputes over the succession between backers of Fernando VII's infant daughter, Isabel, and his brother, Carlos. Isabel will eventually become queen.	The Second Carlist War, between three different monarchist factions, brings Isabel II's son, Alfonso XII, to the throne after the brief, chaotic First Republic of 1873.	Spain loses Cuba, Puerto Rico, Guam and the Philippines, its last remaining colonies, after being defeated in the Spanish–American War by the US, which declared war in support of Cuban independence.

Semana Trágica (Tragic Week) in Barcelona, which began with a general strike and turned into a frenzy of violence. The government responded by executing many workers.

Spain stayed neutral during WWI, but it remained a deeply troubled nation. In 1921, 10,000 Spanish soldiers were killed by Berbers at Anual in Morocco, and two years later General Miguel Primo de Rivera, an eccentric Andalucian aristocrat established his own mild dictatorship.

National elections in 1931 brought in a government composed of socialists, republicans and centrists. A new constitution gave women the vote, granted autonomy-minded Catalonia its own parliament, legalised divorce, stripped Catholicism of its status as official religion, and banned priests from teaching. But Spain lurched back to the right in the 1933 elections. One new force on the right was the fascist Falange, led by José Antonio Primo de Rivera, son of the 1920s dictator.

By 1934 violence was spiralling out of control. Catalonia declared itself independent (within a putative federal Spanish republic), and workers' committees took over the northern mining region of Asturias. A violent campaign against the Asturian workers by the Spanish Legion (set up to fight Moroccan tribes in the 1920s), led by generals Francisco Franco and José Millán Astray, split the country firmly into left and right.

In the February 1936 elections the right-wing National Front was narrowly defeated by the left-wing Popular Front, with communists at the fore.

Something had to give.

Civil War Reads

For Whom the Bell Tolls – Ernest Hemingway

Homage to Catalonia – George Orwell

Blood of Spain – Ronald Fraser

The Spanish Civil War – Hugh Thomas

The Battle for Spain – Antony Beevor

The Civil War Begins

On 17 July 1936 the Spanish army garrison in Melilla, North Africa, rose up against the Popular Front government, followed the next day by garrisons on the mainland. The leaders of the plot were five generals, among them Francisco Franco. The civil war had begun.

The civil war split communities, families and friends, killed an estimated 350,000 Spaniards (some writers say 500,000), and caused untold damage and misery. Both sides committed atrocious massacres and reprisals. The rebels, who called themselves Nationalists because they believed they were fighting for Spain, shot or hanged tens of thousands of supporters of the republic. Republicans did likewise to Nationalist sympathisers, including some 7000 priests, monks and nuns.

At the start of the war many of the military and the Guardia Civil police force went over to the Nationalists, whose campaign quickly took on overtones of a crusade against the enemies of God. In Republican areas, anarchists, communists or socialists ended up running many towns and cities, and social revolution followed.

1909	1923–30	1931	1933–35
The Semana Trágica (Tragic Week) in Barcelona begins after Catalan reservists are called up to fight in Morocco; a general strike becomes a violent riot and dozens of civilians are killed.	General Miguel Primo de Rivera launches an army rising in support of King Alfonso XIII and then establishes himself as dictator. He retires and dies in 1930.	Alfonso XIII goes into exile after Republicans score sweeping gains in local elections. Spain's Second Republic is launched, left-wing parties win a national election, and a new constitution enfranchises women.	Right-wing parties win a new election; political violence spirals and a ruthless army operation against workers in Asturias irrevocably polarises Spain into left- and right-wing camps.

Nationalist Advance

Most cities with military garrisons fell immediately into Nationalist hands – this meant almost everywhere north of Madrid except Catalonia and the north coast, as well as parts of Andalucía. Franco's force of legionnaires and Moroccan mercenaries was airlifted to Seville by German warplanes in August. Essential to the success of the revolt, they moved northward through Extremadura towards Madrid, wiping out fierce resistance in some cities. At Salamanca in October, Franco pulled all the Nationalists into line behind him.

Madrid, reinforced by the first battalions of the International Brigades (armed foreign idealists and adventurers organised by the communists), repulsed Franco's first assault in November and then endured, under communist inspiration, over two years' siege. But the International Brigades never numbered more than 20,000 and couldn't turn the tide against the better armed and organised Nationalist forces.

Nazi Germany and Fascist Italy supported the Nationalists with planes, weapons and men (75,000 from Italy, 17,000 from Germany), turning the war into a testing ground for what was to come during WWII. The Republicans had some Soviet planes, tanks, artillery and advisers, but other countries refused to become involved (although some 25,000 French fought on the Republican side).

Republican Quarrels

With Madrid besieged, the Republican government moved to Valencia in late 1936 to continue trying to preside over the quarrelsome factions on its side, which encompassed anarchists, communists, moderate democrats and regional separatists.

In April 1937 German planes bombed the Basque town of Guernica (Gernika), causing terrible casualties; this became the subject of Picasso's famous pacifist painting, which now hangs in Madrid's Centro de Arte Reina Sofía (p89). All the north coast fell to the Nationalists that year, while Republican counter-attacks near Madrid and in Aragón failed. Meanwhile divisions among the Republicans erupted into fierce street fighting in Barcelona, with the Soviet-influenced communists completely crushing the anarchists and Trotskyites who had run the city for almost a year. The Republican government moved to Barcelona in autumn 1937.

Nationalist Victory

In early 1938 Franco repulsed a Republican offensive at Teruel in Aragón, then swept eastward with 100,000 troops, 1000 planes and 150 tanks, isolating Barcelona from Valencia. In July the Republicans launched a last offensive in the Ebro Valley. This bloody encounter, won by the Nationalists,

Paul Preston's searing *The Spanish Holocaust: Inquisition and Extermination in Twentieth-Century Spain* lays bare the brutality of Spain's civil war (neither side comes out well) and the oppression by victorious Franco forces after the war.

1936	1936–39	1938	1939
The left-wing National Front wins a national election. Right-wing 'Nationalist' rebels led by General Francisco Franco rise up against it, starting the Spanish Civil War.	The Spanish Civil War: the Nationalist rebels, under Franco, supported by Nazi Germany and Fascist Italy, defeat the USSR-supported Republicans. About 350,000 people die in fighting and atrocities.	The Nationalists defeat the Republicans' last major offensive, in the Ebro Valley, with 20,000 killed. The Soviet Union ends its support for the Republican side.	The Nationalists take Barcelona in January. The Republican government flees to France, Republican forces evaporate and the Nationalists enter Madrid on 28 March. Franco declares the war over on 1 April.

cost 20,000 lives. The USSR withdrew from the war in September 1938, and in January 1939 the Nationalists took Barcelona unopposed. The Republican government and hundreds of thousands of supporters fled to France. The Republicans still held Valencia and Madrid, and had 500,000 people under arms, but in the end their army simply evaporated. The Nationalists entered Madrid on 28 March 1939 and Franco declared the war over on 1 April.

Franco's Dictatorship

Bloodied and battered Spain may have been, but there was no peace dividend: Spain's new ruler, General Francisco Franco, began as he meant to continue.

The Early Franco Years

An estimated 100,000 people were killed or died in prison in the years immediately following the war. The hundreds of thousands imprisoned included many intellectuals and teachers; others fled abroad, depriving Spain of a generation of scientists, artists, writers, educators and more.

Despite Franco's overtures to Hitler, Spain remained on the sidelines of WWII. In 1944 Spanish leftists launched a failed attack on Franco's Spain from France; small leftist guerrilla units continued a hopeless struggle in parts of the north, Extremadura and Andalucía until the 1950s.

After WWII Franco's Spain was excluded from the UN and NATO, and suffered a UN-sponsored trade boycott that helped turn the late 1940s into Spain's *años de hambre* (years of hunger). But the onset of the Cold War saved Franco: the US wanted bases in Spain, and Franco agreed to the establishment of four, in return for large sums of aid. In 1955 Spain was admitted to the UN.

Franco's Spain

By the late 1950s, the essential elements of Franco's rule were in place. Regional autonomy aspirations were simply not tolerated. The army provided many government ministers and enjoyed a most generous budget. And Catholic supremacy was fully restored.

In 1959 a new breed of technocrats in government, linked to the Catholic group Opus Dei, engineered a Stabilisation Plan, which brought an economic upswing. Spanish industry boomed, modern machinery, technology and marketing were introduced, transport was modernised and new dams provided irrigation and hydropower.

The recovery was funded in part by US aid, and remittances from more than a million Spaniards who had gone to work abroad, but above all by tourism, which was developed initially along Andalucía's Costa del Sol and Catalonia's Costa Brava. By 1965 the number of tourists arriving

Films Set in Franco's Spain

....
Pan's Labyrinth (2006)
....
The Spirit of the Beehive (1973)
....
¡Bienvenido, Mr Marshall! (Welcome, Mr Marshall!; 1952)
....
Las 13 rosas (The 13 Roses; 2007)

1939–50	1955–65	1959	1975
Franco establishes a right-wing dictatorship, imprisoning hundreds of thousands. Spain stays out of WWII but is later excluded from NATO and the UN and suffers a damaging international trade boycott.	Spain is admitted to the UN after agreeing to host US bases. The economy is boosted by US aid and mass tourism on the Costa Brava and Costa del Sol.	Euskadi Ta Askatasuna (ETA) is founded with the aim of gaining Basque independence. The terrorist group will go on to murder more than 800 people, including Franco's prime minister in 1973.	Franco dies and is succeeded by King Juan Carlos I. The monarch had been schooled by Franco to continue his policies but soon demonstrates his desire for change.

in Spain was 14 million a year. These were the so-called *años de desarollo* (years of development). Industry took off, foreign investment poured in and the services and banking sector blossomed. In 1960 fewer than 70,000 cars were on the road in Madrid. Ten years later more than half a million clogged the capital's streets.

Spaniards' standard of living was improving, but the jails were full of political prisoners and large garrisons were still maintained outside every major city. From 1965 opposition to Franco's regime became steadily more vocal. The universities were repeatedly the scene of confrontation and clandestine trade unions also began to make themselves heard again. The waves of protest were not restricted to Madrid. In the Basque Country the terrorist group Euskadi Ta Askatasuna (ETA; Basque Homeland and Freedom) began to fight for Basque independence. Their first important action outside the Basque Country was the assassination in Madrid in 1973 of Admiral Carrero Blanco, Franco's prime minister and designated successor.

In what seemed like a safe bet, Franco chose as his successor Prince Juan Carlos, the Spanish-educated grandson of Alfonso XIII. In 1969 Juan Carlos swore loyalty to Franco and the Movimiento Nacional. Cautious reforms by Franco's last prime minister, Carlos Arias Navarro, provoked violent opposition from right-wing extremists.

Franco finally died on 20 November 1975.

Democratic Spain

Spain appeared destined to sink into chaos without Franco: the country remained as divided as ever and at its helm was an as-yet-untested Franco protégé. But not for the first time in Spanish history, not all was as it seemed.

The Transition

Juan Carlos I, aged 37, took the throne two days after Franco died. The new king's links with the dictator inspired little confidence in a Spain now clamouring for democracy, but Juan Carlos had kept his cards close to his chest. In July 1976 he appointed Adolfo Suárez, a 43-year-old former Franco apparatchik with film-star looks, as prime minister. To general surprise, Suárez got the Cortes to approve a new, two-chamber parliamentary system, and in 1977 political parties, trade unions and strikes were all legalised. Franco's Movimiento Nacional was abolished.

Suárez's centrist party, the Unión de Centro Democrático (UCD; Central Democratic Union), won nearly half the seats in the new Cortes in 1977. A new constitution in 1978 made Spain a parliamentary monarchy with no official religion. In response to the fever for local autonomy, by 1983 the country was divided into 17 'autonomous communities' with

HISTORY DEMOCRATIC SPAIN

FRANCO

Paul Preston's *Franco* is the big biography of one of history's little dictators – and it has very little to say in the man's favour. Conspiracy theorists will love Peter Day's *Franco's Friends: How British Intelligence Helped Bring Franco to Power in Spain.*

1976	1978	1981	1982–96
The king appoints Adolfo Suárez as prime minister. Suárez engineers a return to democracy. Left-wing parties are legalised, despite military opposition, and the country holds free elections in 1977.	A new constitution, overwhelmingly approved by referendum, establishes Spain as a parliamentary democracy with no official religion and the monarch as official head of state.	On 23 February a group of armed Guardia Civil led by Antonio Tejero attempt a coup by occupying the parliament building. The king denounces them on national TV; the coup collapses.	Spain is governed by the centre-left Partido Socialista Obrero Español, led by Felipe González. The country has an economic boom but the government becomes increasingly associated with scandals and corruption.

their own regional governments controlling a range of policy areas. Personal and social life enjoyed a rapid liberation after Franco. Contraceptives, homosexuality and divorce were legalised, and the Madrid party and arts scene known as *la movida madrileña* formed the epicentre of a newly unleashed hedonism that still reverberates through Spanish life.

The Suárez government granted a general amnesty for deeds committed in the civil war and under the Franco dictatorship. There were no truth commissions or trials for the perpetrators of atrocities. For the next three decades Spain cast barely a backward glance.

A Maturing Democracy

The main left-of-centre party, the Partido Socialista Obrero Español (PSOE; Spanish Socialist Workers' Party), led by a charismatic young lawyer from Seville, Felipe González, came second in the 1977 election and then won power with a big majority in 1982. González was to be prime minister for 14 years. The PSOE's young and educated leadership came from the generation that had opened the cracks in the Franco regime in the late 1960s and early 1970s. Unemployment rose from 16% to 22% by 1986. But that same year Spain joined the European Community (now the EU), bringing on a five-year economic boom. The middle class grew ever bigger, the PSOE established a national health system and improved public education, and Spain's women streamed into higher education and jobs.

Spaniards got the fright of their lives in February 1981 when a pistol-brandishing, low-ranking Guardia Civil (Civil Guard) officer, Antonio Tejero Molina, marched into the Cortes in Madrid with an armed detachment and held parliament captive for 24 hours. Throughout a day of high drama the country held its breath. With the nation glued to their TV sets, King Juan Carlos I made a live broadcast denouncing Tejero and calling on the soldiers to return to their barracks. The coup fizzled out.

In 1992 – the 500th anniversary of the fall of Granada and Columbus' first voyage to the Americas – Spain celebrated its arrival in the modern world by staging the Barcelona Olympics and the Expo 92 world fair in Seville. But the economy was in a slump and the PSOE was mired in scandals. It came as no surprise when the PSOE lost the 1996 general election.

The party that won the 1996 election was the centre-right Partido Popular (PP; People's Party), led by José María Aznar, a former tax inspector from Castilla y León. Aznar promised to make politics dull, and he did, but he presided over eight years of solid economic progress, winning the 2000 election as well. The PP cut public investment, sold off state enterprises and liberalised sectors such as telecommunications, and during

---

Spanish History Index (vlib.iue.it/hist-spain) provides countless internet leads for those who want to dig deeper, with everything from geographical studies to society, culture and politics.

Spain History Books

The Story of Spain – Mark Williams

Spain: A History – Raymond Carr

A History of Spain – Simon Barton

A Concise History of Spain – WD & CR Phillips

1986	1992	1996	11 March 2004
Spain joins the European Community (now the EU). Along with its membership of NATO since 1982, this is a turning point in the country's post-Franco international reacceptance.	Barcelona holds the Olympic Games, putting Spain in the international spotlight and highlighting the country's progress since 1975. Madrid is European Capital of Culture and Seville hosts a world expo.	Disaffection with PSOE sleaze gives the centre-right Partido Popular (PP), led by José María Aznar, a general election victory at the start of a decade of sustained economic growth.	A terrorist bombing kills 191 people on 10 Madrid commuter trains. The following day, an estimated 11 million people take to the streets across Spain.

the Aznar years Spain's economy grew a lot faster than the EU average, while unemployment fell dramatically.

Perhaps just as importantly, Spain's changes of government were orderly, electoral affairs, the economic graphs moved in a general upward direction and the improvement in ordinary people's lives was steady.

Troubled Times

On 11 March 2004, just three days before the national elections, Madrid was rocked by 10 bombs on four rush-hour commuter trains heading into the capital's Atocha station. When the dust cleared, 191 people had died and 1755 were wounded, many of them seriously. It was the biggest such terror attack in the nation's history.

In a stunning reversal of pre-poll predictions, the PP, who insisted that ETA was responsible despite overwhelming evidence to the contrary, was defeated by the PSOE in elections three days after the attack.

The new Socialist government of José Luis Rodríguez Zapatero gave Spain a makeover by introducing a raft of liberalising social reforms. Gay marriage was legalised, Spain's arcane divorce laws were overhauled, almost a million illegal immigrants were granted residence, and a law seeking to apportion blame for the crimes of the Civil War and Franco dictatorship entered the statute books. Although Spain's powerful Catholic Church cried foul over many of the reforms, the changes played well with most Spaniards. Spain's economy was booming, the envy of Europe.

And then it all fell apart.

Spain's economy went into freefall in late 2008 and remains in desperate straits. Zapatero's government waited painfully long to recognise that a crisis was looming and was replaced, in November 2011, with a right-of-centre one promoting a deep austerity drive that threatens the generous welfare state on which Spaniards have come to depend. The conservative government also turned back the liberalising reforms of the Socialists, introducing some of Europe's strictest anti-abortion laws and restoring the role of the Catholic Church in education.

That the country remains firmly democratic, however, suggests that modern Spaniards have, for the first time in Spain's tumultuous history, found means other than war for resolving the many differences that divide them. And perhaps that is the strongest sign of just how far Spain has come.

Modern Spain Reading

Ghosts of Spain – Giles Tremlett

The New Spaniards – John Hooper

Juan Carlos: Steering Spain from Dictatorship to Democracy – Paul Preston

Roads to Santiago: Detours & Riddles in the Land and History of Spain – Cees Nooteboom

---

14 March 2004	October 2008	July 2010	November 2011
The PSOE led by José Luis Rodríguez Zapatero sweeps to power and ushers in eight years of Socialist rule, characterised by sweeping changes to social legislation.	Spain's unemployment rate soars from less than 6% to 12.3% in a single month. Spain's finance minister admits that Spain has entered 'its deepest recession in half a century'.	After years of under-achievement, Spain's national football team wins the World Cup for the first time, two years after its maiden European Championship trophy.	The conservative Popular Party, led by Mariano Rajoy (who had been defeated in 2004 and 2008), sweeps to power in national elections, ending eight years of Socialist Party rule.

Architecture

You can almost see centurions marching beneath the great Roman aqueduct in Segovia, while the Alhambra similarly conjures up Spain's Islamic era. Elsewhere, the Middle Ages comes alive amid the Monasterio de Santo Domingo de Silos' Romanesque cloisters, castles dot the countryside from Catalonia to Castilla, and great Gothic cathedrals adorn Burgos, Palma de Mallorca and Toledo. And who in Barcelona isn't carried away by Gaudí's Modernista fantasies? Welcome to Spain, one of Europe's most intriguing architectural stories.

The Introduction of Islam

In 784, with Córdoba well established as the new capital of the western end of the Umayyad Empire, Syrian architects set to work on the grand Mezquita (p641), conjuring up their homeland with details that echo the Umayyad Mosque in Damascus, such as delicate horseshoe arches and exquisite decorative tiles with floral motifs. But the building's most distinctive feature – more than 500 columns that crowd the interior of the mosque – was repurposed from Roman and Visigothic ruins.

In the centuries that followed, Moorish architecture incorporated trends from all over the Islamic empire. The technique of intricately carved stucco detailing was developed in 9th-century Iraq, while *muqarnas* (honeycomb) vaulting arrived via Egypt in the 10th century. Square minarets, such as the Giralda (p575) in Seville (now a church tower), came with the Almohad invasion from Morocco in the 12th century.

The finest remnants of the Islamic era are in Andalucía, although the Aljafería (p365) in Zaragoza is a beautiful exception. Perhaps the most magnificent creation is the core of Granada's Alhambra (p655), the Palacios Nazaríes (Nasrid Palaces). From the 13th to the 15th century, architects reached new heights of elegance, creating a study in balance between inside and outside, light and shade, spareness and intricate decoration. Eschewing innovation, the Alhambra refined well-tried forms, as if in an attempt to freeze time and halt the collapse of Moorish power, which, at the time, was steadily eroding across the peninsula.

Hybrid Styles: Mozarabic & Mudéjar

By the 10th century, Moorish rule had produced a class of people called Mozarabs – practising Christians who lived in Islamic territory and spoke Arabic. When Mozarab artisans moved or travelled north into Christian Spain, they took elements of classic Islamic construction with them.

For example, the Monasterio de San Miguel de Escalada (p183), east of León, imitates the Mezquita, with horseshoe arches atop leafy Corinthian capitals reused from Roman buildings. Many arches are boxed in by an *alfiz* (rectangular decorative frame typically filled with geometric or abstract vegetal decoration) around the upper portion of the arch. This became a signature detail in Mozarabic architecture. The 11th-century Ermita de San Baudelio (p196), beyond Berlanga de Duero in Soria province, is another example. Because these Mozarabic buildings crossed religious boundaries, they could be called the first truly Spanish architectural style to emerge after the rise of Islam.

Later, as the Reconquista started to gain ground, another border-crossing class emerged: Mudéjars (the Muslims who stayed on in

Only one unruly part of northern Spain, in what is now Asturias, was never conquered by the Muslims. During the 9th century a unique building style emerged there, exaggerating Visigothic styles. Oviedo's Palacio de Santa María del Naranco, for instance, has dramatically elongated proportions, delicate relief carvings and tall, thin arches.

SPANISH ARCHITECTURE: THE BASICS

Roman (210 BC–AD 409) Bridges, waterworks, walls, whole cities that inspired later traditions.

Visigothic (409–711) Sturdy stone churches with simple decoration and horseshoe arches.

Moorish (711–1492) Horseshoe arches, square minarets, intricate geometric design.

Mudéjar (1100–1700) Post-Reconquista work by Muslims adapting the Moorish tradition of decoration to more common materials.

Romanesque (1100–1300) Spare decoration and proportions based on Byzantine churches.

Gothic (1200–1600) Flying buttresses enable ceilings to soar, and arches become pointy to match.

Plateresque (1400–1600) A dazzling ornate style of relief carving on facades.

Churrigueresque (1650–1750) Spain's special twist on baroque with spiral columns and gold-leaf everything.

Modernisme (1888–1911) The Spanish version of art nouveau took a brilliant turn in Barcelona.

Contemporary Architecture (1975–present) Previously unimaginable directions since the death of Franco.

Casa Batlló (p253), Barcelona

now-Catholic Spain). Mudéjar artisans, largely disenfranchised, offered cheap labour and great talent. The Mudéjar style, in evidence from the 12th century on, is notable first for the use of relatively inexpensive materials – gone were the days of lavish government commissions, and the Roman stones had all been used up. Instead, brick, tile and plaster were worked with incredible skill to conjure opulence. Teruel (p390) in particular is dotted with intricate brick towers, trimmed in glazed tiles.

Another tell-tale Mudéjar feature is extravagantly decorated timber ceilings done in a style called *artesonado*. They can be barrel vaults, but the most typical style is a flat wood ceiling made of interlocking beams that are inset with multicoloured wood panels in geometric patterns.

Roman Relics & a Visigoth Church

Aqueduct, Segovia

Teatro Romano, Mérida

City walls, Lugo, Galicia

Museu d'História de Tarragona, Catalonia

Itálica, Seville

Baelo Claudia, Andalucía

Villa Romana La Olmeda, Castilla y León

Basílica de San Juan, Castilla y León

From Romanesque to Gothic

While the tide was turning against the Muslims, the Romanesque style was sweeping medieval Europe, taking root in Spain in part because it was the aesthetic opposite of Islamic fashions – architect and art historian Josep Puig i Cadafalch posited that each Romanesque detail was a systematic riposte to an Islamic one. These buildings were spare, angular and heavy, inspired by the proportions of classical structures. Many of these structures were not-so-subtle statements about the success of the Reconquista.

Romanesque structures had perfectly semicircular arches – none of the stylised horseshoe look that had come before. In churches, this was expressed in a semicylindrical apse (or, in many cases, triple apse), a shape previously found in Byzantine churches. The round arch also graced doorways, windows, cloisters and naves. Entrances supported stacks of concentric arches – all the more eye-catching because they were often the only really decorative detail. Some great, lesser-known examples include the Iglesia de San Martín (p175) in Frómista, and Sant Climent de Taüll (p336), one of many fine examples in the Catalan Pyrenees. Later, during

Albarracín (p393)

the 12th century, the Spanish began to modify these semicircles, edging towards the Gothic style, as they added pointed arches and ribbed vaults. The Monasterio de la Oliva (p443) in Navarra was among the first to show such features, and cathedrals in Ávila (p142), Sigüenza (p227), Tarragona (p354) and Tudela all display at least some transitional elements.

The trend elsewhere in Europe towards towering cathedrals made possible by the newfangled flying buttresses caught on in Spain by the 13th century, when the cathedrals at Burgos (p185), León (p177) and Toledo (p204) were built. Some changes were subtle, such as placing choir stalls in the centre of the nave, but one was unmissable: the towering, decorative *retablo* (altarpiece) that graced the new churches. Spanish Gothic architects also devised the star vault, a method of distributing weight with ribbed vaults projecting out from a central point.

Many great buildings were begun at the height of Romanesque fashion but not completed until long after the Gothic style had gained the upper hand. The cathedral in Burgos, for instance, was begun in 1221 as a relatively sober construction, but its 15th-century spires are a product of German-inspired late-Gothic imagination. Mudéjar influences also still made themselves felt. Toledo boasts many gloriously original buildings with a Gothic-Mudéjar flair, as does part of Aragón, where the fanciful brick structures have been declared a Unesco World Heritage site.

The Catalan approach to the Gothic was more sober, bereft of pinnacles. Architects developed incredibly broad, unsupported vaults without the use of flying buttresses. In contrast, the Isabelline Gothic look, inspired by the Catholic queen, reflects her fondness of Islamic exotica and heraldic imagery. It's on display in Toledo's San Juan de los Reyes (p206) and the Capilla Real (p664) in Granada, where she and Fernando are buried.

Most of the innumerable castles scattered across the country also went up in Gothic times – an extraordinary example is the sumptuous castle

The Camino de Santiago is also an architecture pilgrimage route, for such Romanesque beauties as the Monasterio de Santo Domingo de Silos, the smaller cloister in the Monasterio de las Huelgas in Burgos, the restored Iglesia de San Martín in Frómista and the cathedral itself in Santiago de Compostela.

at Coca (p171), in Segovia. In Barcelona, some marvellous civil Gothic architecture can be admired, including the once-mighty shipyards now home to the Museu Marítim (p244).

The Gothic fascination lasted into the 16th century, when there was a revival of pure Gothic, perhaps best exemplified in the new cathedral (p149) in Salamanca, although the Segovia cathedral (p160) was about the last, and possibly most pure, Gothic structure raised in Spain.

Renaissance & Plateresque

Arising from the pan-European Renaissance, the uniquely Spanish vision of plateresque drew partly on Italian styles and was also an outgrowth of the Isabelline Gothic look. It is so named because facade decoration was so ornate that it looked as though it had been wrought by *plateros* (silversmiths). To visit Salamanca, where the Spanish Renaissance first took root, is to receive a concentrated dose of the most splendid work in the genre.

A more purist Renaissance style, reflecting classical proportions and styles already established in Italy and France, prevailed in Andalucía, such as in the Palacio de Carlos V in Granada's Alhambra.

The Renaissance wild card was Juan de Herrera, whose work bears almost no resemblance to anything else of the period because it is so austere. His masterpiece is the palace-monastery complex of San Lorenzo de El Escorial (p134), in which he discarded typical classical decorative orders, leaving vast granite surfaces bare. The look was imitated in numerous monasteries for more than a century.

Baroque & Churrigueresque

Aside from the late-18th-century Cádiz cathedral (p607), there are very few from-scratch baroque buildings in Spain. But the exuberant decoration is so eye-catching that it easily overtakes the more sober earlier buildings to which it's attached. The leading exponents of this often overblown style were the Churriguera brothers, three sons of a respected sculptor who specialised in *retablos*, the enormous carved-wood altar backdrops. One of the sons, José Benito, was court architect for Carlos II from 1690 to 1702; in his obituary he was dubbed 'the Michelangelo of Spain'.

The hallmark of Churrigueresque is the so-called Solomonic column, a delightful twisting pillar that, especially when covered in gold leaf or vines, seems to wiggle its way to the heavens. Later practitioners took the Churrigueras' innovations and ran with them.

Modernisme & Art Deco

At the end of the 19th century, Barcelona's prosperity unleashed one of the most imaginative periods in Spanish architecture. The architects at work here, who drew on prevailing art nouveau trends as well as earlier Spanish styles, came to be called the Modernistas. Chief among them, Antoni Gaudí sprinkled Barcelona with jewels of his singular imagination. They range from his immense, unfinished Sagrada Família (p249) to the simply weird Casa Batlló (p253) and the only slightly more sober La Pedrera (p257). Gaudí's structural approach owed much to the austere era of Catalan Gothic, which inspired his own inventive work with parabolic arches. The works of two other Catalan architects, Lluís Domènech i Montaner and Josep Puig i Cadafalch, are also Barcelona landmarks.

While Barcelona went all wavy, Madrid embraced the rigid glamour of art deco. This global style arrived in Spain just as Madrid's Gran Vía (p79) was laid out in the 1920s. One of the more overwhelming caprices from that era is the Palacio de Comunicaciones on Plaza de la Cibeles (p91).

The 1936–39 Civil War and more than three decades of dictatorship brought such frivolities to an abrupt end.

Ildefonso Falcones' best-selling historical novel *La catedral del mar* (The Cathedral of the Sea) tells the juicy tale of the construction of the Santa María del Mar cathedral in Barcelona in the 13th century.

Best Baroque

....

Monasterio de Nuestra Señora de la Asunción, Granada

....

Plaza Mayor, Salamanca

....

Cathedral facade, Santiago de Compostela

....

Catedral de Santa María, Murcia

....

Real Academia de Bellas Artes de San Fernando, Madrid

....

Altarpiece, Catedral de Toledo

Top Puente Romano
(p644) and Mezquita
(p641), Córdoba

Bottom Catedral (p204),
Toledo

Ciudad de las Artes y las Ciencias (p729), architect Santiago Calatrava

Contemporary Innovation

Post-Franco, Spain has made up for lost time and, particularly since the 1990s, the unifying theme appears to be that anything goes.

Local heroes include Santiago Calatrava, who built his reputation with swooping, bone-white bridges. In 1996 he designed the futuristic Ciudad de las Artes y las Ciencias (p729) complex in Valencia. In 2000 he also built the Sondika Airport, in Bilbao, which has been nicknamed La Paloma (the Dove), for the winglike arc of its aluminium skin.

Catalan Enric Miralles had a short career, dying of a brain tumour in 2000 at the age of 45, but his Mercat de Santa Caterina (p245) in Barcelona shows brilliant colour and inventive use of arches. His **Gas Natural building** (Map p248; Passeig de Salvat Papasseit; M Barceloneta), also in Barcelona, is a poetic skyscraper that juts both vertically and horizontally.

In 1996 Rafael Moneo won the Pritzker Prize, the greatest international honour for living architects, largely for his long-term contributions to Madrid's cityscape, such as the revamping of the Atocha railway station (p90). His **Kursaal Palace** (Map p418) in San Sebastían is eye-catching – still staunchly functional, but shining, like two giant stones swept up from the sea.

In the years since, Spain has become something of a Pritzker playground. It's perhaps this openness – even hunger – for outside creativity that marks the country's built environment today. Norman Foster designed the metro system in Bilbao, completed in 1995; the transparent, wormlike staircase shelters have come to be called *fosteritos*. But it was Frank Gehry's 1998 Museo Guggenheim (p399) in the same city that really sparked the quirky-building fever. Now the list of contemporary landmarks includes Jean Nouvel's spangly, gherkin-shaped Torre Agbar (p257), in Barcelona; Richard Rogers' dreamy, wavy Terminal 4 at Madrid's Barajas airport; Oscar Niemeyer's flying-saucerish Centro Cultural Internacional Avilés (p484) in Asturias; and Zaha Hadid's whalelike bridge-cum-pavilion for the Zaragoza Expo.

Outside Spain, Rafael Moneo is best known for the 2002 Cathedral of Our Lady of Angels, in downtown Los Angeles, California.

Robert Hughes' *Barcelona* is a thorough, erudite history of the city, with an emphasis on architecture. The Gaudí chapters provide special insight into the designer's surprisingly conservative outlook.

Spain's Master Painters

Spain has an artistic legacy that rivals anything found elsewhere in Europe. In centuries past, this impressive portfolio (dominated by Goya and Velázquez in particular) owed much to the patronage of Spanish kings who lavished money upon the great painters of the day. In the 20th century, however, it was the relentless creativity of artists such as Pablo Picasso, Salvador Dalí and Joan Miró, all of whom thumbed their noses at artistic convention, who became the true masters.

The Golden Century – Velázquez & Friends

The star of the 17th-century art scene, which became known as Spain's artistic Golden Age, was the genius court painter, Diego Rodríguez de Silva Velázquez (1599–1660). Born in Seville, Velázquez later moved to Madrid as court painter and composed scenes (landscapes, royal portraits, religious subjects, snapshots of everyday life) that owe their vitality not only to his photographic eye for light, contrast and the details of royal finery, but also to a compulsive interest in the humanity of his subjects so that they seem to breathe on the canvas. With Velázquez, any trace of the idealised stiffness that characterised the previous century's spiritless mannerism fell by the wayside. His masterpieces include *Las meninas* (Maids of Honour) and *La rendición de Breda* (Surrender of Breda), both in the Museo del Prado (p83).

Another shining light of the period was Francisco de Zurbarán (1598–1664), who is best remembered for the startling clarity and light in his portraits of monks.

> Velázquez so much wanted to be made a Knight of Santiago that in *Las meninas* he cheekily portrayed himself with the cross of Santiago on his vest, long before his wish was finally fulfilled.

Goya & the 19th Century

There was nothing in the provincial upbringing of Francisco José de Goya y Lucientes (1746–1828), who was born in a tiny village in Aragón, to suggest that he would become one of the towering figures of European art. Goya began his career as a cartoonist in the Real Fábrica de Tapices (Royal Tapestry Workshop) in Madrid. Illness in 1792 left him deaf; many critics speculate that his condition was largely responsible for his wild, often merciless style that would become increasingly unshackled from convention. By 1799 Goya was appointed Carlos IV's court painter.

Several distinct series and individual paintings mark his progress. In the last years of the 18th century he painted enigmatic masterpieces, such as *La maja vestida* (The Young Lady Dressed) and *La maja desnuda* (The Young Lady Undressed), identical portraits but for the lack of clothes in the latter. The Inquisition was not amused by the artworks, which it covered up. Nowadays all is bared in Madrid's Museo del Prado.

The arrival of the French and the war in 1808 had a profound impact on Goya. Unforgiving portrayals of the brutality of war are *El dos de mayo* (The Second of May) and, more dramatically, *El tres de mayo*

(The Third of May). The latter depicts the execution of Madrid rebels by French troops.

Goya spent the last years of his life in voluntary exile in France, where he continued to paint until his death.

Goya saved his most confronting paintings for the end. After he retired to the Quinta del Sordo (Deaf Man's House) in Madrid, he created his nightmarish Pinturas negras (Black Paintings), which now hang in the Madrid's Museo del Prado (p83). The *Saturno devorando a su hijo* (Saturn Devouring His Son) captures the essence of Goya's genius, and *La romería de San Isidro* (The Pilgrimage to San Isidro) and *El akelarre* (aka *El gran cabrón*; The Great He-Goat) are profoundly unsettling. The former evokes a writhing mass of tortured humanity, while the latter two are dominated by the compelling individual faces of the condemned souls of Goya's creation.

> Check out www. arteespana.com, an interesting website that covers broad swaths of Spanish art history, and where you can buy art books or even models of monuments.

Picasso, Dalí & the Others – the Shock of the New

In the early years of the 20th century, the genius of the mischievous *malagueño* (Málaga native) Pablo Ruiz Picasso (1881–1973) came like a thunderclap. A child when he moved with his family to Barcelona, Picasso was formed in an atmosphere laden with the avant-garde freedom of Modernisme.

Picasso must have been one of the most restless artists of all time. His work underwent repeated revolutions as he passed from one creative phase to another. From his gloomy Blue Period, through the brighter Pink Period and on to cubism – in which he was accompanied by Madrid's Juan Gris (1887–1927) – Picasso was nothing if not surprising. Picasso consistently cranked out paintings, sculptures, ceramics and etchings until the day he died. A good selection of his early work can be viewed in Barcelona's Museu Picasso (p246), while the Museo Picasso Málaga (p683) has more than 200 Picasso works. The remaining works are scattered around different galleries, notably Madrid's Centro de Arte Reina Sofía (p89).

Separated from Picasso by barely a generation, two other artists reinforced the Catalan contingent in the vanguard of 20th-century art: Dalí and Miró. Although he started off dabbling in cubism, Salvador Dalí (1904–89) became more readily identified with the surrealists. This complex character's 'hand-painted dream photographs', as he called them, are virtuoso executions brimming with fine detail and nightmare images dragged up from a feverish and Freud-fed imagination. Preoccupied with Picasso's fame, Dalí built himself a reputation as an outrageous showman and shameless self-promoter. The single best display of his work can be seen at the Teatre-Museu Dalí (p322) in Figueres, but you'll also find important works in the Museu de Cadaqués (p320) in Cadaqués, the

---

WHERE TO SEE GOYA

Reach into the tortured mind of one of Spain's greatest artists with the help of Robert Hughes' riveting work *Goya*. And to see what all of the fuss is about, Madrid's Museo del Prado (p83) has the richest collection of Goyas, but the city's Real Academia de Bellas Artes de San Fernando (p79) is also good, while the Ermita de San Antonio de la Florida (p95) has fabulous ceiling frescoes painted by Goya. Beyond Madrid, Zaragoza's Museo Ibercaja Camón Aznar (p364) has an outstanding collection of Goya etchings, while Fuendetodos, the Aragonese village south of Zaragoza where Goya was born, has the Casa Natal de Goya (p369) and the Museo del Grabado de Goya (p369).

PICASSO'S GUERNICA

It was market day in the small Basque town of Guernica on the morning of 26 April 1937. At the same time that market-goers poured into the town from outlying villages, a squadron of aeroplanes was making its way to Guernica. Over the next few hours Hitler's Condor Legion, in agreement with Franco, dropped hundreds of bombs on the town and killed between a couple of hundred to well over a 1000 civilians.

Shortly afterwards, Picasso, who was based in Paris at the time, was commissioned by the Republican government of Madrid to produce paintings for the Spanish contribution to the Paris Exposition Universelle. As news of the bombings filtered out of Spain, Picasso committed his anger to canvas: it was a poignant memorial to the first use of airborne military hardware to devastating effect. You can see the *Guernica* in Madrid's Centro de Arte Reina Sofía (p89).

Casa Museu Dalí (p320) in Portlligat and Madrid's Centro de Arte Reina Sofía (p89).

Slower to find his feet, Barcelona-born Joan Miró (1893–1983) developed a joyous and almost childlike style that earned him the epithet 'the most surrealist of us all' from the French writer André Breton. His later period is his best known, characterised by the simple use of bright colours and forms in combinations of symbols that represented women, birds (the link between earth and the heavens) and stars (the unattainable heavenly world, source of imagination). The Fundació Joan Miró (p264) in Barcelona and the Fundació Pilar i Joan Miró (p782) in Palma de Mallorca are the pick of the places to see his work, with some further examples in Madrid's Centro de Arte Reina Sofía (p89).

Spain's Best Contemporary Artists

The death of Franco acted as a catalyst for the Spanish art movement. New talent sprang up, and galleries enthusiastically took on anything revolutionary, contrary or cheeky. The 1970s and 1980s were a time of almost childish self-indulgence. Things have since calmed down but there's still much activity.

Basques Eduardo Chillida (1924–2002) and Jorge Oteiza (1908–2003) were two of Spain's leading modern sculptors. During the same period, Seville's Luis Gordillo (b 1934) started his artistic career with surrealism, from where he branched out into pop art and photography. His later work in particular features the serialisation of different versions of the same image.

Antonio López (b 1936) is considered the father of the so-called Madrid hyperrealism. One of his grandest works is the incredibly detailed *Madrid desde Torres Blancas* (Madrid from Torres Blancas).

Mallorcan Miquel Barceló (b 1957) is one of the country's big success stories. His work is heavily expressionist, although it touches on classic themes, from self-portraiture to architectural images.

Barcelona's Susana Solano (b 1946) is a painter and, above all, sculptor, considered to be one of the most important at work in Spain today.

Jaume Plensa (b 1955) is possibly Spain's best contemporary sculptor and has displayed his work around the world.

Flamenco

Flamenco's passion is clear to anyone who has heard its melancholic strains in the background of a crowded Spanish bar or during an uplifting live performance. And yet, flamenco can at times seem like an impenetrable world. If you're lucky, you'll experience that single uplifting moment when flamenco's raw passion suddenly transports you to another place (known as *duende*), where joy and sorrow threaten to overwhelm you. If you do, you'll quickly become one of flamenco's lifelong devotees.

The Birth of Flamenco

Flamenco's origins have been lost to time. Some have suggested that it derives from Byzantine chants used in Visigothic churches. But most musical historians agree that it probably dates back to a fusion of songs brought to Spain by the Roma people, with music and verses from North Africa crossing into medieval Muslim Andalucía.

Flamenco as we now know it first took recognisable form in the 18th and early 19th centuries among Roma people in the lower Guadalquivir valley in western Andalucía. The Seville, Jerez de la Frontera and Cádiz axis is still considered flamenco's heartland and it's here, purists believe, that you'll encounter the most authentic flamenco experience.

Flamenco – the Essential Elements

A flamenco singer is known as a *cantaor* (male) or *cantaora* (female); a dancer is a *bailaor* or *bailaora*. Most of the songs and dances are performed to a blood-rush of guitar from the *tocaor* or *tocaora* (male or female flamenco guitarist). Percussion is provided by tapping feet, clapping hands, and sometimes castanets.

Flamenco *coplas* (songs) come in many different types, from the anguished *soleá* or the intensely despairing *siguiriya* to the livelier *alegría* or the upbeat *bulería*. The first flamenco was *cante jondo* (deep song), an anguished instrument of expression for a group on the margins of society. *Jondura* (depth) is still the essence of pure flamenco.

The traditional flamenco costume – shawl, fan and long, frilly *bata de cola* (tail gown) for women, and flat Cordoban hats and tight black trousers for men – dates from Andalucian fashions in the late 19th century.

Flamenco Legends

Seville's Museo del Baile Flamenco trawls through flamenco's past and present and, with its frequent flamenco classes, gives you the chance to perfect your *sevillana*.

The great singers of the 19th and early 20th centuries were Silverio Franconetti and La Niña de los Peines, from Seville, and Antonio Chacón and Manuel Torre, from Jerez de la Frontera. Torre's singing, legend has it, could drive people to rip their shirts open and upturn tables. The dynamic dancing and wild lifestyle of Carmen Amaya (1913–63), from Barcelona, made her the Roma dance legend of all time. Her long-time partner Sabicas was the father of the modern solo flamenco guitar, inventing a host of now-indispensable techniques.

After a trough in the mid-20th century, when it seemed that the *tablaos* (touristy flamenco shows emphasising the sexy and the jolly) were in danger of taking over, *flamenco puro* got a new lease of life in the

1970s through singers such as Terremoto, La Paquera, Enrique Morente, Chano Lobato and, above all, El Camarón de la Isla (whose real name was José Monge Cruz) from San Fernando near Cádiz.

Some say that Madrid-born Diego El Cigala (b 1968) is El Camarón's successor. This powerful singer's biggest-hitting albums are *Lágrimas negras* (Black Tears; 2003) and *Dos lágrimas* (Two Tears; 2008), which mix flamenco with Cuban influences.

Paco de Lucía, born in Algeciras in 1947, is the doyen of flamenco guitarists. So gifted is he that by the time he was 14 his teachers admitted that they had nothing left to teach him. De Lucía has transformed the flamenco guitar into an instrument of solo expression with new techniques, scales, melodies and harmonies that have gone far beyond traditional limits.

> Many of the most talented flamenco stars have spent time in prison, and each year Spain's penitentiary system holds *El Concurso de Cante Flamenco del Sistema Penitenciario* (The Prison Flamenco Competition).

Flamenco Today

Rarely can flamenco have been as popular as it is today, and never so innovative.

Universally acclaimed is José Mercé, from Jerez. Estrella Morente from Granada (Enrique's daughter and internationally best known for being the 'voice' behind the 2006 film *Volver),* Miguel Poveda (from Barcelona) and La Tana from Seville are young singers steadily carving out niches in the first rank of performers.

Dance, always the readiest of flamenco arts to cross boundaries, has reached its most adventurous horizons in the person of Joaquin Cortés, born in Córdoba in 1969. Cortés fuses flamenco with contemporary dance, ballet and jazz in spectacular shows with music at rock-concert amplification.

Among guitarists, listen out for Manolo Sanlúcar from Cádiz; Tomatito from Almería; and Vicente Amigo from Córdoba and Moraíto Chico from Jerez, who both accompany today's top singers.

Flamenco Fusion

What started with the experimentation of Paco de Lucía has seen musicians mixing flamenco with jazz, rock, blues, rap and other genres.

The seminal recording was a 1977 flamenco-folk-rock album *Veneno* (Poison) by the group of the same name, centred on Kiko Veneno and Raimundo Amador, both from Seville. Kiko remains an icon of flamenco fusion, mixing rock, blues, African and flamenco rhythms with witty lyrics focusing on snatches of everyday life. Amador later formed the

THE SHRIMP OF THE ISLAND

Possibly the most important flamenco singer of all time, José Monge Cruz (aka Camarón de la Isla; Shrimp of the Island) did more to popularise flamenco over the last 30 years than anyone else. Born to Roma parents, Camarón started his career at a young age by singing in local bars. Eventually he met that other great of flamenco, guitarist Paco de Lucía, with whom he recorded nine much-praised albums between 1969 and 1977. Later in his career Camarón worked with one of Paco's students, Tomatito.

Camarón was an intense introvert and hated publicity, but so extraordinary was his talent that publicity was to hound him everywhere he went and, so many say, it was eventually to lead him to an early grave in the best live-fast, die-young rock-star fashion. He was idolised for his voice by flamenco fans across the world, and it was his fellow Roma who really elevated him almost to the status of a god.

He died of lung cancer in 1992 at the age of just 42. It's estimated that more than 100,000 people attended his funeral. The Shrimp's best recordings include *La leyenda del tiempo, Soy gitano* and *Una leyenda flamenca*.

group Pata Negra, and produced four fine flamenco-jazz-blues albums before going solo.

The group Ketama, originally from Granada, has successfully mixed flamenco with African, Cuban, Brazilian and other rhythms for two decades. Cádiz' Niña Pastori arrived in the late 1990s with an edgy, urgent voice singing jazz- and Latin-influenced flamenco.

Eleven-strong Barcelona-based band Ojos de Brujo mixes flamenco with reggae, Asian and even club dance rhythms, while Málaga's Chambao successfully combines flamenco with electronic beats on its albums such as *Flamenco Chill* (2002) and *Pokito a poko* (Little by Little; 2005) and *En el fin del mundo* (At the End of the Earth; 2009).

Concha Buika, a Mallorcan of Equatorial Guinean origin, possesses a beautiful, sensual voice. Her albums *Buika* (2005) and *Mi niña Lola* (2006) are a captivating melange of African rhythms, soul, jazz, hip hop, flamenco and more.

Probably nobody upsets the purists quite as much as Mala Rodríguez does with her socially aware combination of flamenco and rap. *Malamarismo* (2007) is a classic of her unique genre; she's since released *Dirty Bailarina* (2010) and *Bruja* (2103).

> Flamenco World (www.flamenco-world.com) is an online shop that stocks absolutely everything and anything flamenco-based. Its website also contains numerous interviews and news features.

Seeing Flamenco

Flamenco is easiest to catch in Seville, Jerez de la Frontera, Granada and Madrid. The best places for live performances are *peñas (*clubs where flamenco fans band together). The atmosphere in such places is authentic and at times very intimate, proof that flamenco feeds off an audience that knows its flamenco. Most Andalucian towns have dozens of *peñas,* and most tourist offices have lists of those that are open to visitors. The other, easier, option is to attend a performance at a *tablao,* which hosts regular shows put on for largely undiscriminating tourist audiences – the quality can be top-notch, even if the gritty atmosphere of the *peñas* is lacking.

Festivals also attract the best artists. The following are some of the best flamenco festivals:

➡ Festival de Jerez (p622), Jerez de la Frontera

➡ Suma Flamenca (p101), Madrid

➡ Festival Internacional de la Guitarra (p645), Córdoba

➡ Festival Internacional del Cante de las Minas, La Unión, Murcia, in August

➡ Bienal de Flamenco (p589), Seville

Bullfighting

An epic drama of blood and sand or a cruel blood 'sport' that has no place in modern Spain? This most enduring and controversial of Spanish traditions is all this and more, at once compelling theatre and an ancient ritual that sees 40,000 bulls killed in around 17,000 fights every year in Spain. Perhaps it was best summed up by Ernest Hemingway – a bullfighting aficionado – who described it as a 'wonderful nightmare'.

The Basics

The matador (more often called the *torero* in Spanish) is the star of the team. Adorned in his glittering *traje de luces* (suit of lights), it is his fancy footwork, skill and bravery before the bull that has the crowd in raptures or in rage, depending on his (or very occasionally her) performance. A complex series of events takes place in each clash, which can last from about 20 to 30 minutes (there are usually six fights in a program). *Peones* (the matador's 'footmen', whose job it is to test the strength of the bull) dart about with grand capes in front of the bull; *picadores* (horsemen) drive lances into the bull's withers; and *banderilleros* (flagmen) charge headlong at the bull in an attempt to stab its neck. Finally, the matador kills the bull, unless the bull has managed to put him out of action, as sometimes happens.

If you do plan to attend a bullfight, it's important to understand what you're about to experience. The bull's back and neck are repeatedly pierced by the lances, resulting in quite a lot of blood. The bull gradually becomes weakened through blood loss before the *torero* delivers the final sword thrust. If done properly, the bull dies instantly from this final thrust, albeit after bleeding for some time from its other wounds. If the coup de grace is not delivered well, the animal dies a slow death. When this happens, the scene can be extremely disturbing.

When & Where

The bullfighting season begins in the first week of February with the fiestas of Valdemorillo and Ajalvir, near Madrid, to mark the feast day of San Blas. Madrid's season, the most prestigious in Spain, begins during the Fiestas de San Isidro in mid-May. Elsewhere – especially in the two Castillas and Andalucía – *corridas* (bullfights) and *encierros* (running of the bulls through town), as in Pamplona, are part of town festivals. By October, you'd be hard-pressed to find a *corrida* anywhere in the country.

Bullfighting Legends

The most extraordinary matador of the moment is Madrid's José Tomás. After a stellar career, he suddenly retired in 2002, only to make a spectacular return a few years later. At the fiestas of San Isidro in Madrid on 5 June 2008, he cut four bulls' ears (the cutting off of an ear, or in rare cases both ears, of the dead bull is a mark of admiration) – something that hadn't been seen for decades. Says the austere Tomás: 'Living without bullfighting isn't living.' Two weeks later, in another epic afternoon, bulls gored him severely in the thighs three times. After recovering from

Whether or not you watch a bullfight is a personal decision. The spectacle is about many things – death, bravery, performance. No doubt the fight is bloody and cruel, but aficionados say the bull is better off dying at the hands of a matador than in the *matadero* (abattoir). To witness it is not necessarily to approve of it, but doing so might give an insight into the tradition and thinking behind it all.

GREAT ANGLO-AMERICAN BULLFIGHTERS

Ernest Hemingway loved watching the bullfight, but some of his countrymen preferred action to observation. Sidney Franklin was the first English-speaking *torero* (bullfighter) to do so, in 1945 in Madrid's Las Ventas, one of the largest rings in the bullfighting world. He was followed by Californian John Fulton (a painter and poet) in 1967. Best of all was Arizona-born Robert Ryan. Now retired, he is a man of many facets – writer, poet, painter, sculptor and photographer. Englishman Henry Higgins, known in Spain as Enrique Cañadas, something of an adventurer and pilot, was also keen to take to the ring, while his countryman, Mancunian Frank Evans (known as 'El Inglés'), only retired in 2005.

his injuries, he once again returned to the ring and continued to dazzle audiences, but in April 2010, during a fight in Mexico, he was severely injured after being gored in the groin. At the time of writing, his career hangs in the balance.

Other great fighters include El Cordobés, El Juli, Manuel Jesú (El Cid) and Miguel Ángel Perera.

The Bullfighting Debate

The popular image of Spain would have us all believe that every Spaniard is a die-hard bullfighting fan, but this couldn't be further from the truth. While bullfighting remains strong in some parts of the country, notably Andalucía, in other areas such as Galicia, Cantabria and other northern regions it's never really been a part of local culture. A recent poll found that just 17% of Spaniards under 25 had any interest in bullfighting, compared with 41% of those aged over 64. Similar polls suggest that 75% of Spaniards have no interest in the sport.

Today there's a growing anti-bullfighting movement in Spain. The Socialist government banned children under 14 from attending bullfights in 2006 and forbade state-run TV from broadcasting live coverage of bullfights (some private broadcasters continued to televise). This latter decision was later overturned by the newly elected Popular Party government, and live broadcasts of bullfighting (at 6pm) resumed on the state-run channel. The bullfighting world was given a further blow when the Catalan government's ban on bullfighting officially became law on 1 January 2012. On the flip side, though, bullfighting does still have some fans in high places. King Juan Carlos is on record as saying: 'The day the EU bans bullfighting is the day Spain leaves the EU'.

That this is a debate at all in Spain owes a little to bullfighting's waning popularity and arguably more to the country's growing integration with the rest of Europe since Spain's return of democracy in the late 1970s. The fall in bullfighting's popularity has fostered some anti-bullfighting organisations, but the greatest impetus still comes from groups beyond Spanish shores.

The ADDA (www.addaong.org) is a Spanish animal-rights and anti-bullfighting organisation. Other anti-bullfighting organisations are the WSPA (www.wspa.org.uk), PETA (www.peta.org) and the League Against Cruel Sports (www.leagueagainstcruelsports.org). For info on creative protests against bullfighting, see www.runningofthenudes.com.

Survival Guide

Directory A–Z

Accommodation

Spain's accommodation is generally of a high standard, from small, family-run *hostales* (budget hotels) to the old-world opulence of *paradores* (state-owned hotels).

Officially, places to stay are classified into *hoteles* (hotels; one to five stars), *hostales* (one to three stars) and *pensiones* (basically small private *hostales*, often family businesses in rambling apartments; one or two stars). These are the categories used by the annual *Guía Oficial de Hoteles*, sold in bookshops, which lists almost every such establishment in Spain (except for one-star *pensiones*), with approximate prices. Tourist offices and their websites also have lists of local accommodation options.

Checkout time in most establishments is noon.

Reservations

Although there's usually no need to book ahead for a room in the low or shoulder seasons, booking ahead is a good idea, if for no other reason than to avoid a weary search for a room. Most places will ask for a credit-card number or will hold the room for you until 6pm unless you let them know that you'll be arriving later.

Seasons

Prices throughout this guidebook are generally high-season maximums. You may be pleasantly surprised if you travel at other times. What constitutes low or high season depends on where you are and when. Most of the year is high season in Barcelona or Madrid, especially during trade fairs that you're unlikely to know about. August can be dead in the cities, but high season along the coast. Winter is high season in the ski resorts of the Pyrenees and low season in the Balearic Islands (indeed, the islands seem to shut down between November and Easter).

Finding a place to stay without booking ahead in July and August in the Balearics and elsewhere along the Mediterranean Coast can be difficult and many places require a minimum stay of at least two nights during high season. Weekends are high season for boutique hotels and *casas rurales* (rural homes), but low season for business hotels (which often offer generous specials) in Madrid and Barcelona. Always check out hotel websites for discounts.

Prices

At the lower end of the budget category there are dorm beds (from €17 per person) in youth hostels or private rooms with shared bathrooms in the corridor. If you're willing to pay a few euros more, there are many budget places, usually *hostales*, with good, comfortable rooms and private bathrooms. In relatively untouristed or rural areas, the prices of some boutique or other hotels can sometimes drop into the budget category, especially during low season.

Spain's midrange hotels are generally excellent; you should always have your own private bathroom, and breakfast is sometimes included in the room price. Boutique hotels, including many that occupy artistically converted historical buildings, largely fall into this category and are almost always excellent choices.

And a final word about terminology. A *habitación doble* (double room) is frequently just that: a room that has two beds (which you can often shove together to make a double bed). If you want to be sure that you get a double bed, ask for a *cama matrimonial*.

Accommodation Types

Airbnb (www.airbnb.com) is a popular online booking service that covers a range of accommodation types, from apartments and houses to private rooms in somebody's house.

APARTMENTS, VILLAS & CASAS RURALES

Throughout Spain you can rent self-catering apartments and houses from one night upwards. Villas and houses are widely available on the main holiday coasts and in popular country areas.

A simple one-bedroom apartment in a coastal resort for two or three people might cost as little as €40 per night, although more often you'll be looking at nearly twice that much, and prices jump even further in high season. More luxurious options with a swimming pool might come in at anything between €200 and €400 for four people.

Rural tourism has become immensely popular, with accommodation available in many new and often charming *casas rurales*. These are usually comfortably renovated village houses or farmhouses with a handful of rooms. They often go by other names, such as *cases de pagès* in Catalonia, *casas de aldea* in Asturias, *posadas* and *casonas* in Cantabria and so on. Some just provide rooms, while others offer meals or self-catering accommodation. Lower-end prices typically hover around €30/50 for a single/double per night, but classy boutique establishments can easily charge €100 or more for a double. Many are rented out by the week.

Agencies include the following:

Apartments-Spain (www.apartments-spain.com)

Associació Agroturisme Balear (www.rusticbooking.com)

Atlas Rural (www.atlasrural.com)

Casas Cantabricas (www.casas.co.uk)

Cases Rurals de Catalunya (www.casesrurals.com)

Escapada Rural (www.escapadarural.com)

Fincas 4 You (www.fincas4you.com)

Guías Casas Rurales (www.guiascasasrurales.com)

Holiday Serviced Apartments (www.holidayapartments.co.uk)

Owners Direct (www.ownersdirect.co.uk)

Ruralka (www.ruralka.com)

Rustic Rent (www.rusticrent.com)

Rusticae (www.rusticae.es)

Secret Destinations (www.secretdestinations.com)

Secret Places (www.secretplaces.com)

Top Rural (www.toprural.com)

Traum Ferienwohnungen (www.traum-ferienwohnungen.de)

Villas 4 You (www.villas4you.co.uk)

Vintage (www.vintagetravel.co.uk)

CAMPING & CARAVAN PARKS

Spain has around 1000 officially graded *campings* (camping grounds). Some of these are well located in woodland or near beaches or rivers, but others are on the outskirts of towns or along highways. Few of them are near city centres, and camping isn't particularly convenient if you're relying on public transport. Tourist offices can always direct you to the nearest camping ground.

Camping grounds are officially rated as 1st class (1ªC), 2nd class (2ªC) or 3rd class (3ªC). There are also some that are not officially graded, usually equivalent to 3rd class. Facilities generally range from reasonable to very good, although any camping ground can be crowded and noisy at busy times (especially July and August). Even a 3rd-class camping ground is likely to have hot showers, electrical hook-ups and a cafe. The

SLEEPING PRICE RANGES

Throughout this guidebook, accommodation listings are grouped according to price bracket. Establishments within each bracket are then listed in order of author preference. Each place to stay is accompanied by one of the following symbols (the price refers to a double room with private bathroom):

€ less than €65

€€ from €65 to €140

€€€ more than €140

The price ranges for Madrid and Barcelona are inevitably higher:

€ less than €75

€€ from €75 to €200

€€€ more than €200

best ones have heated swimming pools, supermarkets, restaurants, laundry service, children's playgrounds and tennis courts.

Camping grounds usually charge per person, per tent and per vehicle – typically €4.50 to €9 for each. Children usually pay a bit less than adults. Many camping grounds close from around October to Easter. You occasionally come across a *zona de acampada* or *área de acampada*, a country camping ground with minimal facilities (maybe just tap water or a couple of barbecues), little or no supervision and little or no charge. If it's in an environmentally protected area, you may need to obtain permission from the local environmental authority to camp there.

With certain exceptions – such as many beaches and environmentally protected areas and a few municipalities that ban it – it is legal to camp outside camping grounds (but not within 1km of official ones!). Signs usually indicate where wild camping is not allowed. If in doubt, you can always check with tourist offices. You'll need permission to camp on private land.

Useful websites:

Guía Camping (www.guiacampingfecc.com) Online version of the annual *Guía Camping* (€13.60), which is available in bookshops around the country.

Campinguía (www.campinguia.com) Comments (mostly in Spanish) and links.

Campings Online (www.campingsonline.com/espana) Booking service.

CAMAS, FONDAS & HOSPEDAJES

At the budget end of the market, places listing accommodation use all sorts of overlapping names to describe themselves. In broad terms, the cheapest are usually places just advertising *camas* (beds), *fondas* (traditionally a basic eatery and inn combined, though one of these functions is now often missing) and *casas de huéspedes* or *hospedajes* (guesthouses). Most such places will be bare and basic. Bathrooms are likely to be shared, although if you're lucky you may get an in-room *lavabo* (washbasin). In winter you may need to ask for extra blankets.

PENSIONES

A *pensión* is usually a small step up from the *camas*, *fondas* and *hospedajes* in

standard and price. Some cheap establishments forget to provide soap, toilet paper or towels. Don't hesitate to ask for these necessities.

HOSTALES

Hostales are a small step up from *pensiones*. The better ones can be bright and spotless, with rooms boasting full en-suite bathroom – *baño privado*, most often with a *ducha* (shower) rather than bathtub – and usually a TV, air-conditioning and/or heating.

HOTELS

The remainder of establishments call themselves *hoteles* and run the gamut of quality, from straightforward roadside places, bland but clean, through to charming boutique gems and on to superluxurious hotels. Even in the cheapest hotels, rooms are likely to have an attached bathroom and there will probably be a restaurant.

Among the more tempting hotels for those with a little fiscal room to manoeuvre are the 90 or so **paradores** (✆in Spain 902 54 79 79; www.parador.es), a state-funded chain of hotels in often stunning locations, among them towering castles and former medieval convents. Similarly, you can find beautiful hotels in restored country homes and old city mansions, and these are not always particularly expensive.

A raft of cutting-edge, hip design hotels with cool staff and a New York feel can be found in the big cities and major resort areas. At the top end you may pay more for a room with a view – especially sea views or with a *balcón* (balcony) – and will often have the option of a suite.

Many places have rooms for three, four or more people where the per-person cost is lower than in a single or double, which is good for families.

Many of the agencies listed under Apartments, Villas & Casas Rurales also have a full portfolio of hotels.

MONASTERIES

An offbeat possibility is staying in a monastery. In spite of the expropriations of the 19th century and a sometimes rough run in the 20th, numerous monastic orders have survived across the country. Some offer rooms to outsiders – often fairly austere monks' or nuns' cells.

Monastery accommodation is generally a single-sex arrangement, and the idea in quite a few is to seek refuge from the outside world and indulge in quiet contemplation and meditation. On occasion, where the religious order continues ancient tradition by working on farmland, orchards and/or vineyards, you may have the opportunity to work too.

Useful resources include the following:

Guía de Monasterios (www.guiasmonasterios.com)

Alojamientos Monásticos de España A guidebook to Spain's monasteries by Javier de Sagastizabal and José Antonio Egaña, although it needs an update (the latest edition dates to 2003).

REFUGIOS

Refugios (hostels) for walkers and climbers are liberally scattered around most of the popular mountain areas (especially the Pyrenees), except in Andalucía, which has only a handful. They're mostly run by mountaineering and walking organisations.

Accommodation, usually bunks squeezed into a dorm, is often on a first-come, first-served basis, although for some *refugios* you can book ahead. In busy seasons (July and August in most areas) they can fill up quickly, and you should try to book in advance or arrive by mid-afternoon to be sure of a place. Prices per person range from nothing to €15 or more a night. Many *refugios* have a bar and offer meals (dinner typically costs €8 to €12), as well as a cooking area (but no cooking equipment). Blankets

are usually provided, but you'll have to bring any other bedding yourself (or rent it at the *refugio*). Bring a torch too.

The Aragonese Pyrenees are particularly well served with *refugios;* check out the following:

Albergues & Refugios de Aragón (www.alberguesyrefugiosdearagon.com) To make reservations in *refugios* and *albergues*.

Federación Aragonesa de Montañismo (FAM; ☑976 22 79 71; www.fam.es; 4th fl, Calle Albareda 7) The FAM in Zaragoza can provide information, and a card will get you substantial discounts on *refugio* stays.

HOSTELS

Spain has 250 or so youth hostels – *albergues juveniles*, not to be confused with *hostales* (budget hotels) – as well as hundreds of backpackers' hostels dotted around the country. These are often the cheapest places for lone travellers, but two people can usually get a better double room elsewhere for a similar price.

The hostel experience in Spain varies widely. Some hostels are only moderate value, lacking in privacy, often heavily booked by school groups, and with night-time curfews and no cooking facilities (although if there's nowhere to cook there's usually a cafeteria). Others, however, are conveniently located, open 24 hours and composed mainly of small dorms, often with a private bathroom. An increasing number have rooms adapted for people with disabilities. Some even occupy fine historic buildings.

Most Spanish youth hostels are members of the **Red**

Española de Albergues Juveniles (REAJ, Spanish Youth Hostel Network; www.reaj.com), the Spanish representative of Hostelling International.

Most of the REAJ member hostels are also members of the youth hostel association of their region (Andalucía, Catalonia, Valencia etc). Each region usually sets its own price structure and has a central booking service where you can make reservations for most of its hostels. You can also book directly with hostels themselves. Central booking services include the following:

Andalucía (☑902 51 00 00; www.inturjoven.com)

Catalonia (☑93 483 83 41; www.xanascat.cat)

Valencia (☑902 22 55 52; www.gvajove.es)

Prices at youth hostels often depend on the season, and vary from about €15 to €21 for those under 26 (the lower rate is usually applied to people with ISIC cards too) and between €18 and €28 for those 26 and over. In some hostels the price includes breakfast. A few hostels require you to rent sheets (around €2 to €5 for your stay) if you don't have your own or a sleeping bag.

For youth hostels, most require you to have an HI card or a membership card from your home country's youth hostel association. You can obtain an HI card in Spain at most hostels.

A growing number of hostel-style places not connected with HI or REAJ often have individual rooms as well as the more typical dormitory options. Prices can vary

BOOK YOUR STAY ONLINE

For more accommodation reviews by Lonely Planet authors, check out http://lonelyplanet.com/hotels/. You'll find independent reviews, as well as recommendations on the best places to stay. Best of all, you can book online.

greatly as, not being affiliated to any organisation, they are not subject to any pricing system. A good resource for seeking out hostels, affiliated or otherwise, is **Hostel World** (www.hostelworld.com).

Finally, you will sometimes find independent *albergues* offering basic dormitory accommodation for around €10 to €18, usually in villages in areas that attract plenty of Spanish walkers and climbers. These are not specifically youth hostels – although the clientele tends to be under 35. They're a kind of halfway house between a youth hostel and a *refugio*. Some will rent you sheets for a couple of euros, if you need them.

Customs Regulations

Duty-free allowances for travellers entering Spain from outside the EU include 2L of wine (or 1L of wine and 1L of spirits), and 200 cigarettes or 50 cigars or 250g of tobacco.

There are no restrictions on the import of duty-paid items into Spain from other EU countries for personal use. You *can* buy VAT-free articles at airport shops when travelling between EU countries.

Discount Cards

At museums, never hesitate to ask if there are discounts for students, young people, children, families or seniors.

Senior Cards Reduced prices for people over 60, 63 or 65 (depending on the place) at some museums and attractions (sometimes restricted to EU citizens only) and occasionally on transport.

Student Cards Discounts (usually half the normal fee) for students. You will need some kind of identification (eg an International Student Identity Card; www.isic.org) to prove student status. Not accepted everywhere.

Youth Card Travel, sights and youth hostel discounts with the European Youth Card (www.euro26.org), known as Carnet Joven in Spain. The International Youth Travel Card (IYTC; www.istc.org) offers similar benefits.

Electricity

Electrical plugs in Spain can also be round, but will always have two round pins. The second image is for Gibraltar.

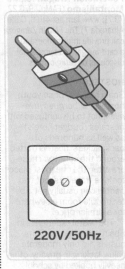

220V/50Hz

240V/50HZ

Embassies & Consulates

The embassies are in Madrid. Some countries also maintain consulates in major cities, particularly in Barcelona.

Australian Embassy Madrid (☑91 353 66 00; www.spain.embassy.gov.au; 24th fl, Paseo de la Castellana 259D)

Canadian Embassy Madrid (☑91 382 84 00; www.canadainternational.gc.ca/spain-espagne/; Torre Espacio, Paseo de la Castellana 259D; underground rail Velázquez); Barcelona (☑932 70 36 14; Carrer d'Elisenda de Pinós 10); Málaga (☑95 222 33 46; Plaza de la Malagueta 2)

French Embassy Madrid (☑91 423 89 00; www.ambafrance-es.org; Calle de Salustiano Olózaga 9); Barcelona (☑93 270 30 00; www.consulfrance-barcelone.org; Ronda de la Universitat 22B) Further consulates in Bilbao and Seville.

German Embassy Madrid (☑91 557 90 00; www.spanien.diplo.de; Calle de Fortuny 8); Barcelona (☑93 292 10 00; www.barcelona.diplo.de; Passeig de Gràcia 111)

Irish Embassy Madrid (☑91 436 40 93; www.embassyofireland.es; Paseo de la Castellana 46); Barcelona (☑93 491 50 21; Gran Via de Carles III 94)

Japanese Embassy Madrid (☑91 590 76 00; www.es.emb-japan.go.jp; Calle de Serrano 109; MGregorio Marañon)

Moroccan Embassy Madrid (☑91 563 10 90; www.embajada-marruecos.es; Calle de Serrano 179; MSanto Domingo); Barcelona (☑932 89 25 30; Calle Béjar 91) Further consulates-general in Algeciras, Almería, Bilbao, Seville, Tarragona and Valencia.

Netherlands Embassy Madrid (☑91 353 75 00; www.espana.nlembajada.org; Torre Espacio, Paseo de la Castellana 259D); Barcelona (☑934 19

95 80; Avinguda Diagonal 611) Further consulates in Palma de Mallorca, Seville and Torremolinos.

New Zealand Embassy Madrid (☑91 523 02 26; www.nzembassy.com/spain; 3rd fl, Calle de Pinar 7, Madrid)

UK Embassy Madrid (☑91 714 62 00; www.gov.uk/government/world/spain; Paseo de la Castellana 259D, Torre Espacio, Madrid); Barcelona (☑93 366 62 00; Avinguda Diagonal 477; underground rail Hospital Clinic); Palma de Mallorca (☑902 109356; Edifici B, Carrer del Convent dels Caputxins 4) Further consulates in Alicante, Bilbao, Ibiza and Málaga.

US Embassy Madrid (☑91 587 22 00; www.spanish.madrid.usembassy.gov; Calle de Serrano 75); Barcelona (☑93 280 22 27; www.barcelona.usconsulate.gov; Passeig de la Reina Elisenda de Montcada 23-25; ☑FGC Reina Elisenda) Consular agencies in A Coruña, Fuengirola, Palma de Mallorca, Seville and Valencia.

Gay & Lesbian Travellers

Homosexuality is legal in Spain and the age of consent is 13, as it is for heterosexuals. In 2005 the Socialist president, José Luis Rodríguez Zapatero, gave the country's conservative Catholic foundations a shake with the legalisation of same-sex marriages in Spain.

Lesbians and gay men generally keep a fairly low profile, but are quite open in the cities. Madrid, Barcelona, Sitges, Torremolinos and Ibiza have particularly lively scenes. Sitges is a major destination on the international gay party circuit; gays take a leading role in the wild **Carnaval** (www.sitges.com/carnaval) there in February/March. As well, there are gay parades, marches and events in several cities on and around the last Saturday in June, when Madrid's **gay and lesbian pride march** (www.orgullogay.org) takes place.

Useful Resources

In addition to the following resources, Barcelona's tourist board publishes *Barcelona – The Official Gay and Lesbian Tourist Guide* biannually, while Madrid's tourist office has a useful 'Gay & Lesbian Madrid' section on the front page of its website (www.esmadrid.com).

Chueca (www.chueca.com) Forums, news and reviews.

GayBarcelona (www.gaybarcelona.com) News and views and an extensive listings section covering bars, saunas, shops and more in Barcelona and Sitges.

Gay Iberia (Guía Gay de España; www.gayiberia.com) Gay guides to Barcelona, Madrid, Sitges and 26 other Spanish cities.

Gay Madrid 4 U (www.gaymadrid4u.com) A good overview of Madrid's gay bars and nightclubs.

Guía Gay de España (www.guia.universogay.com) A little bit of everything.

LesboNet (www.lesbonet.org) Lesbian forums, chat and news.

Night Tours.com (www.nighttours.com) A reasonably good guide to gay nightlife and other attractions in Madrid, Barcelona and seven other Spanish locations.

Orgullo Gay (www.orgullogay.org) Website for Madrid's gay and lesbian pride march and links to gay organisations across the country.

Shangay (www.shangay.com) For news, upcoming events, reviews and contacts. It also publishes *Shanguide*, a Madrid-centric biweekly magazine jammed with listings (including saunas and hard-core clubs) and contact ads. Its companion publication *Shangay Express* is better for articles with a handful of listings and ads. They're available in gay bookshops and gay and gay-friendly bars.

Organisations

Casal Lambda (☑93 319 55 50; www.lambda.cat; Carrer de Verdaguer i Callís 10; ☑5-9pm Mon-Sat; ☑Uquinaona) A gay and lesbian social, cultural and information centre in Barcelona's La Ribera.

Colectivo de Gais y Lesbianas de Madrid (Cogam; ☑91 522 45 17; www.cogam.es; Calle de la Puebla 9; ☑10am-2pm & 5-9pm Mon-Fri; ☑Callao or Gran Vía) Offers activities, has an information office and social centre, and runs an information line (☑91 523 00 70; ☑10am-2pm Mon-Fri).

Coordinadora Gai-Lesbiana Barcelona (☑93 298 00 29; www.cogailes.org; Carrer de Violant d'Hongria 156; ☑Plaça del Centre) Barcelona's main coordinating body for gay and lesbian groups. It also runs an information line, the Línia Rosa (☑900 601601).

Federación Estatal de Lesbianas, Gays, Transexuales & Bisexuales (Map p96; ☑91 360 46 05; www.felgtb.org; 4th fl, Calle de las Infantas 40; ☑8am-8pm Mon-Thu, 8am-3.30pm Fri) A national advocacy group, based in Madrid, that played a leading role in lobbying for the legalisation of gay marriages.

Fundación Triángulo (☑91 593 05 40; www.fundaciontriangulo.org; 1st fl, Calle de Melendez Valdés 52; ☑10am-2pm & 5-8pm Mon-Fri; ☑Iglesia) One of several sources of information on gay issues in Madrid; it has a separate information line, Información LesGai (☑91 446 63 94).

Health

Spain has an excellent health-care system.

Availability & Cost of Health Care

If you need an ambulance, call ☑061. For emergency treatment, go straight to the *urgencias* (casualty) section of the nearest hospital.

Farmacias offer valuable advice and sell over-the-counter medication. In Spain, a system of farmacias de guardia (duty pharmacies) operates so that each district has one open all the time. When a pharmacy is closed, it posts the name of the nearest open one on the door.

Medical costs are lower in Spain than many other European countries, but can still mount quickly if you are uninsured. Costs if you attend casualty range from nothing (in some regions) to around €80.

Altitude Sickness

If you're hiking at altitude, altitude sickness may be a risk. Lack of oxygen at high altitudes (over 2500m) affects most people to some extent. Symptoms of Acute Mountain Sickness (AMS) usually develop during the first 24 hours at altitude but may be delayed by up to three weeks. Mild symptoms include headache, lethargy, dizziness, difficulty sleeping and loss of appetite. AMS may become more severe without warning and can be fatal. Severe symptoms include breathlessness, a dry, irritative cough (which may progress to the production of pink, frothy sputum), severe headache, lack of coordination and balance, confusion, irrational behaviour, vomiting, drowsiness and unconsciousness.

Treat mild symptoms by resting at the same altitude until recovery, usually for a day or two. Paracetamol or aspirin can be taken for headaches. If symptoms persist or become worse, immediate descent is necessary; even 500m can help. Drug treatments should never be used to avoid descent or to enable further ascent.

Hypothermia

The weather in Spain's mountains can be extremely changeable at any time of year. Proper preparation will reduce the risks of getting hypothermia: always carry waterproof garments and warm layers, and inform others of your route.

Hypothermia starts with shivering, loss of judgment and clumsiness. Unless rewarming occurs, the sufferer deteriorates into apathy, confusion and coma. Prevent further heat loss by seeking shelter, wearing warm dry clothing, drinking hot sweet drinks and sharing body warmth.

Bites & Stings

Nasty insects to be wary of are the hairy reddish-brown caterpillars of the pine processionary moth (touching the caterpillars' hairs sets off a severely irritating allergic skin reaction), and some Spanish centipedes have a very nasty but nonfatal sting.

Jellyfish, which have stinging tentacles, are an increasing problem at beaches along the Mediterranean coastline.

The only venomous snake that is even relatively common in Spain is Lataste's viper. It has a triangular-shaped head, grows up to 75cm long, and is grey with a zigzag pattern. It lives in dry, rocky areas, away from humans. Its bite can be fatal and needs to be treated with a serum, which state clinics in major towns keep in stock.

Water

Tap water is generally safe to drink in Spain. If you are in any doubt, ask ¿Es potable el agua (de grifo)? (Is the (tap) water drinkable?). Do not drink water from rivers or lakes as it may contain bacteria or viruses that can cause diarrhoea or vomiting.

Insurance

A travel-insurance policy to cover theft, loss, medical problems and cancellation or delays to your travel arrangements is a good idea. Paying for your ticket with a credit card can often provide limited travel-accident insurance and you may be able to reclaim the payment if the operator doesn't deliver. Worldwide travel insurance is available at lonelyplanet. com/travel_services. You can buy, extend and claim online anytime – even if you're on the road.

Internet Access

Wi-fi is almost universally available at most hotels, as well as in some cafes, restaurants and airports; generally (but not always) it's free. Connection speed often varies from room to room in hotels (and coverage sometimes is restricted to the hotel lobby), so always ask when you check in or make your reservation. Some tourist offices may have a list of wi-fi hot spots in their area.

Good internet cafes are increasingly hard to find; ask at the local tourist office. Prices per hour range from €1.50 to €3.

Language Courses

Among the more popular places to learn Spanish are Barcelona, Granada, Madrid, Salamanca and Seville. In these places and elsewhere, Spanish universities offer good-value language courses.

The **Escuela Oficial de Idiomas** (EOI; www.eeooiinet. com) is a nationwide language institution where you can learn Spanish and other local languages. Classes can be large and busy but are generally fairly cheap. There are branches in any major cities. On the website's opening page, hit 'Centros' under 'Comunidad' and then 'Centros en la Red' to get to a list of schools.

Private language schools as well as universities cater for a wide range of levels, course lengths, times of year, intensity and special requirements. Many courses have a cultural component as well as language. University courses often last a semester, although some are as short as two weeks or as long as a year. Private colleges can be more flexible. One with a good reputation is **Don Quijote** (www.donquijote.com), with branches in Barcelona, Granada, Madrid, Salamanca and Valencia.

It's also worth finding out whether your course will lead to any formal certificate of competence. The Diploma de Español como Lengua Extranjera (DELE) is recognised by Spain's Ministry of Education and Science.

Legal Matters

If you're arrested, you will be allotted the free services of an *abogado de oficio* (duty solicitor), who may speak only Spanish. You're also entitled to make a phone call. If you use this to contact your embassy or consulate, the staff will probably be able to do no more than refer you to a lawyer who speaks your language. If you end up in court, the authorities are obliged to provide a translator.

In theory, you are supposed to have your national ID card or passport with you at all times. If asked for it by the police, you are supposed to be able to produce it on the spot. In practice it is rarely an issue and many people choose to leave passports in hotel safes.

The Policía Local or Policía Municipal operates at a local level and deals with such issues as traffic infringements and minor crime. The Policía Nacional (☑091) is the state police force, dealing with major crime and operating primarily in the cities. The military-linked Guardia Civil (created in the 19th century to deal with banditry) is largely responsible for highway patrols, borders, security, major crime and terrorism. Several regions have their own police forces, such as the Mossos d'Esquadra in Catalonia and the Ertaintxa in the Basque Country.

Cannabis is legal but only for personal use and in very small quantities. Public consumption of any illicit drug is illegal. Travellers entering Spain from Morocco should be prepared for drug searches, especially if you have a vehicle.

Maps
Small-Scale Maps
Some of the best maps for travellers are by Michelin, which produces the 1:1,000,000 *Spain Portugal* map and six 1:400,000 regional maps covering the whole country. These are all pretty accurate and are updated regularly, even down to the state of minor country roads. Also good are the GeoCenter maps published by Germany's RV Verlag.

Probably the best physical map of Spain is *Península Ibérica, Baleares y Canarias* published by the **Centro Nacional de Información Geográfica** (☑955 56 93 20; www.cnig.es; edificio Sevilla 2, 8th fl, módulo 7, Avenida San Francisco Javier 9, Madrid), the publishing arm of the **Instituto Geográfico Nacional** (IGN; www.ign.es; Calle General de Ibáñez de Ibero 3, Madrid). Ask for it in good bookshops.

Walking Maps
Useful for hiking and exploring some areas (particularly in the Pyrenees) are Editorial Alpina's *Guía Cartográfica* and *Guía Excursionista y Turística* series. The series combines information booklets in Spanish (and sometimes Catalan) with detailed maps at scales ranging from 1:25,000 to 1:50,000. They are an indispensable hikers' tool (and some come in English and German), but they have their inaccuracies. The Institut Cartogràfic de Catalunya puts out some decent maps for hiking in the Catalan Pyrenees that are often better than their Editorial Alpina counter-

parts. Remember that for hiking only, maps scaled at 1:25,000 are seriously useful. The CNIG also covers most of the country in 1:25,000 sheets.

You can often pick up Editorial Alpina publications and CNIG maps at bookshops near trekking areas, and at specialist bookshops such as these:

Altaïr (Map p250; ☑93 342 71 71; www.altair.es; Gran Via de les Corts Catalanes 616) In Barcelona.

Altaïr (☑91 543 53 00; www.altair.es; Calle de Gaztambide 31; ⊙10am-2pm & 4.30-8.30pm Mon-Fri, 10.30am-2.30pm Sat; Ⓜ Argüelles) In Madrid.

De Viaje (Map p94; ☑91 577 98 99; www.deviaje.com; Calle de Serrano 41; ⊙10am-8.30pm Mon-Fri, 10.30am-2.30pm & 5-8pm Sat; Ⓜ Serrano) In Madrid.

La Tienda Verde (☑91 535 38 10; www.tiendaverde.es; Calle de Maudes 23) In Madrid.

Librería Desnivel (Map p80; ☑90 224 88 48; www.libreriadesnivel.com; Plaza de Matute 6) In Madrid.

Quera (Map p236; ☑93 318 07 43; www.llibreriaquera.com; Carrer de Petritxol 2) In Barcelona.

Money
The most convenient way to bring your money is in the form of a debit or credit card, with some extra cash for use in case of an emergency.

ATMs
Many credit and debit cards can be used for withdrawing money from *cajeros automáticos* (automatic teller machines) that display the relevant symbols such as Visa, MasterCard, Cirrus etc. Remember that there is usually a charge (around 1.5% to 2%) on ATM cash withdrawals abroad.

Cash

Most banks and building societies will exchange major foreign currencies and offer the best rates. Ask about commissions and take your passport.

Credit & Debit Cards

These can be used to pay for most purchases. You'll often be asked to show your passport or some other form of identification. Among the most widely accepted are Visa, MasterCard, American Express (Amex), Cirrus, Maestro, Plus and JCB. Diners Club is less widely accepted. If your card is lost, stolen or swallowed by an ATM, you can call the following telephone numbers toll free to have an immediate stop put on its use:

Amex (☑900 994426)

Diners Club (☑902 401112)

MasterCard (☑900 971231)

Visa (☑900 991124, 900 991216)

Moneychangers

You can exchange both cash and travellers cheques at exchange offices – which are usually indicated by the word *cambio* (exchange). Generally they offer longer opening hours and quicker service than banks, but worse exchange rates and higher commissions.

Taxes & Refunds

In Spain, value-added tax (VAT) is known as IVA (ee-ba; *impuesto sobre el valor añadido*). Visitors are entitled to a refund of the 21% IVA on purchases costing more than €90.16 from any shop, if they are taking them out of the EU within three months. Ask the shop for a cash back (or similar) refund form showing the price and IVA paid for each item, and identifying the vendor and purchaser. Then present the refund form to the customs booth for IVA refunds at the airport, port or border from which you leave the EU.

Tipping

Menu prices include a service charge. Most people leave some small change if they're satisfied: 5% is normally fine and 10% extremely generous. Porters will generally be happy with €1. Taxi drivers don't have to be tipped but a little rounding up won't go amiss.

Travellers Cheques

Can be changed (you'll often be charged a commission) at most banks and building societies. Visa, Amex and Travelex are widely accepted brands with (usually) efficient replacement policies. Get most of your cheques in fairly large denominations (the equivalent of €100 or more) to save on any per-cheque commission charges. It's vital to keep your initial receipt, and a record of your cheque numbers and the ones you have used separate from the cheques themselves.

Opening Hours

Standard opening hours are for high season only and tend to shorten outside that time.

Banks 8.30am to 2pm Monday to Friday; some also open 4pm to 7pm Thursday and 9am to 1pm Saturday

Central post offices 8.30am to 9.30pm Monday to Friday, 8.30am to 2pm Saturday; most other branches 8.30am to 8.30pm Monday to Friday and 9.30am to 1pm Saturday

Nightclubs midnight or 1am to 5am or 6am

Restaurants lunch 1pm to 4pm, dinner 8.30pm to 11pm or midnight

Shops 10am to 2pm and 4.30pm to 7.30pm or 5pm to 8pm; big supermarkets and department stores generally open 10am to 10pm Monday to Saturday

Post

The Spanish postal system, **Correos** (☑902 197197; www. correos.es), is generally reliable, if a little slow at times.

Postal Rates & Services

Sellos (stamps) are sold at most *estancos* (tobacconists' shops with 'Tabacos' in yellow letters on a maroon background), as well as at post offices.

A postcard or letter weighing up to 20g costs €0.75 from Spain to other European countries, and €0.90 to the rest of the world. For a full list of prices for *certificado* (certified) and *urgente* (express post), go to www.correos.es (in Spanish) and click on 'Calculador de Tarifas'.

Sending Mail

Delivery times are erratic but ordinary mail to other Western European countries can take up to a week (although often as little as three days); to North America up to 10 days; and to Australia or New Zealand (NZ) between 10 days and three weeks.

Public Holidays

The two main periods when Spaniards go on holiday are Semana Santa (the week leading up to Easter Sunday) and July and/or August. At these times accommodation in resorts can be scarce and transport heavily booked, but other places are often half-empty.

There are at least 14 official holidays a year – some observed nationwide, some locally. When a holiday falls close to a weekend, Spaniards like to make a *puente* (bridge), meaning they take the intervening day off too. Occasionally when some holidays fall close, they make an *acueducto* (aqueduct)! Here are the national holidays:

Año Nuevo (New Year's Day) 1 January

Viernes Santo (Good Friday) March/April

Fiesta del Trabajo (Labour Day) 1 May

La Asunción (Feast of the Assumption) 15 August

Fiesta Nacional de España (National Day) 12 October

La Inmaculada Concepción (Feast of the Immaculate Conception) 8 December

Navidad (Christmas) 25 December

Regional governments set five holidays and local councils two more. Common dates:

Epifanía (Epiphany) or **Día de los Reyes Magos** (Three Kings' Day) 6 January

Jueves Santo (Good Thursday) March/April. Not observed in Catalonia and Valencia.

Corpus Christi June. This is the Thursday after the eighth Sunday after Easter Sunday.

Día de Santiago Apóstol (Feast of St James the Apostle) 25 July

Día de Todos los Santos (All Saints Day) 1 November

Día de la Constitución (Constitution Day) 6 December

Safe Travel

Most visitors to Spain never feel remotely threatened, but a sufficient number have unpleasant experiences to warrant an alert. The main thing to be wary of is petty theft (which may of course not seem so petty if your passport, cash, travellers cheques, credit card and camera go missing). What follows is intended as a strong warning rather than alarmism. In other words, be careful but don't be paranoid.

Scams

There must be 50 ways to lose your wallet. As a rule, talented petty thieves work in groups and capitalise on distraction. Tricks usually involve a team of two or more (sometimes one of them an attractive woman to distract male victims). While one attracts your attention, the other empties your pockets. More imaginative strikes include someone dropping a milk mixture on to the victim from a balcony. Immediately a concerned citizen comes up to help you brush off what you assume to be pigeon poo, and thus suitably occupied you don't notice the contents of your pockets slipping away.

Beware: not all thieves look like thieves. Watch out for an old classic: the ladies offering flowers for good luck. We don't know how they do it, but if you get too involved in a friendly chat with these people, your pockets almost always wind up empty.

On some highways, especially the AP7 from the French border to Barcelona, bands of thieves occasionally operate. Beware of men trying to distract you in rest areas, and don't stop along the highway if people driving alongside indicate you have a problem with the car. While one inspects the rear of the car with you, his pals will empty your vehicle. Another gag has them puncturing tyres of cars stopped in rest areas, then following and 'helping' the victim when they stop to change the wheel. Hire cars and those with foreign plates are especially targeted. When you do call in at highway rest stops, try to park close to the buildings and leave nothing of value in view. If you do stop to change a tyre and find yourself getting unsolicited aid, make sure doors are all locked and don't allow yourself to be distracted.

Even parking your car can be fraught. In some towns fairly dodgy self-appointed parking attendants operate in central areas where you may want to park. They will direct you frantically to a spot. If possible, ignore them and find your own. If unavoidable, you may well want to pay them some token amount not to scratch or otherwise damage your vehicle after you've walked away. You definitely don't want to leave anything visible in the car (or open the boot – trunk – if you intend to leave luggage or anything else in it) under these circumstances.

Theft

Theft is mostly a risk in tourist resorts, big cities and when you first arrive in a new city and may be off your guard. You are at your most vulnerable when dragging around luggage to or from your hotel. Barcelona, Madrid and Seville have the worst reputations for theft and, on very rare occasions, muggings.

Anything that you leave lying on the beach can disappear in a flash when your back is turned. At night avoid dingy, empty city alleys and backstreets, or anywhere that just doesn't feel 100% safe.

Report thefts to the national police. You are unlikely to recover your goods but you need to make this formal *denuncia* for insurance purposes. To avoid endless queues at the *comisaría* (police station), you can make the report by phone (☑902 102112) in various languages or on the web at www.policia. es (click on Denuncias). The following day you go to the station of your choice to pick up and sign the report, without queuing.

Telephone

The reasonably widespread blue payphones are easy to use for international and domestic calls. They accept coins, *tarjetas telefónicas* (phonecards) issued by the national phone company Telefónica and, in some cases, various credit cards. Calling from your computer using an internet-based service such as Skype is generally the cheapest option.

Collect Calls

Placing *una llamada a cobro revertido* (an international collect call) is simple. Dial ☑99 00 followed by the code for the country you're calling (numbers starting with 900 are national toll-free numbers):

Australia ☑900 990061

Canada ☑900 990015

France ☑900 990033

Germany ☑900 990049

Ireland ☑900 990353

Israel ☑900 990972

New Zealand ☑900 990064

UK for BT ☑900 990044

USA for AT&T ☑900 990011, for Sprint and various others ☑900 990013

Mobile Phones

Spain uses GSM 900/1800, which is compatible with the rest of Europe and Australia but not with the North American system unless you have a GSM/GPRS-compatible phone (some AT&T and T-Mobile cell phones may work), or the system used in Japan. From those countries, you will need to travel with a tri-band or quadric-band phone.

You can buy SIM cards and prepaid time in Spain for your mobile (cell) phone, provided you own a GSM, dual- or tri-band cellular phone. This only works if your national phone hasn't been code-blocked; check before leaving home. Only consider a full contract if you plan to live in Spain for a while.

All the Spanish mobile-phone companies (Telefónica's MoviStar, Orange and Vodafone) offer *prepagado* (prepaid) accounts for mobiles. The SIM card costs from €10, to which you add some prepaid phone time. Phone outlets are scattered across the country. You can then top up in their shops or by buying cards in outlets, such as *estancos* (tobacconists) and newsstands. Pepephone (www. pepephone.com) is another option.

If you plan on using your own phone while in Spain, check with your mobile provider for information on roaming charges, especially if you're using a phone from outside the EU.

Phone Codes

Mobile (cell) phone numbers start with 6. Numbers starting with 900 are national toll-free numbers, while those starting 901 to 905 come with varying costs. A common one is 902, which is a national standard rate number, but which can only be dialled from within Spain. In a similar category are numbers starting with 800, 803, 806 and 807.

International access code ☑00

Spain country code ☑34

Local area codes None (these are incorporated into listed numbers)

Phonecards

Cut-rate prepaid phonecards can be good value for international calls. They can be bought from *estancos* (tobacconists), small grocery stores, *locutorios* (private call centres) and newsstands in the main cities and tourist resorts. If possible, try to compare rates. Many of the private operators offer better deals than those offered by Telefónica. *Locutorios* that specialise in cut-rate overseas calls have popped up all over the place in bigger cities.

Useful Phone Numbers

Emergencies ☑112

English-speaking Spanish international operator ☑1008 (for calls within Europe) or ☑1005 (rest of the world)

International directory enquiries ☑11825 (calls to this number cost €2)

National directory enquiries ☑11818

Operator for calls within Spain ☑1009 (including for domestic reverse-charge – collect – calls)

Time

Time zone Same as most of Western Europe (GMT/UTC plus one hour during winter and

GMT/UTC plus two hours during the daylight-saving period).

Daylight saving From the last Sunday in March to the last Sunday in October.

UK, Ireland, Portugal & Canary Islands One hour behind mainland Spain.

Morocco Morocco is on GMT/UTC year-round. From the last Sunday in March to the last Sunday in October, subtract two hours from Spanish time to get Moroccan time; the rest of the year, subtract one hour.

USA Spanish time is USA Eastern Time plus six hours and USA Pacific Time plus nine hours.

Australia During the Australian winter (Spanish summer), subtract eight hours from Australian Eastern Standard Time to get Spanish time; during the Australian summer, subtract 10 hours.

12- and 24-hour clock Although the 24-hour clock is used in most official situations, you'll find people generally use the 12-hour clock in everyday conversation.

Tourist Information

All cities and many smaller towns have an *oficina de turismo* or *oficina de información turística*. In the country's provincial capitals you will sometimes find more than one tourist office – one specialising in information on the city alone, the other carrying mostly provincial or regional information. National and natural parks also often have their own visitor centres offering useful information.

Turespaña (www.spain. info) is the country's national tourism body, and it operates branches around the world. Check the website for office locations.

Travellers with Disabilities

Spain is not overly accommodating for travellers with disabilities but some things

are slowly changing. For example, disabled access to some museums, official buildings and hotels represents a change in local thinking. In major cities more is slowly being done to facilitate disabled access to public transport and taxis; in some cities, wheelchair-adapted taxis are called 'Eurotaxis'. Newly constructed hotels in most areas of Spain are required to have wheelchair-adapted rooms. With older places, you need to be a little wary of hotels who advertise themselves as being disabled-friendly, as this can mean as little as wide doors to rooms and bathrooms, or other token efforts.

Worthy of a special mention is Barcelona's **Inout Hostel** (☏93 280 09 85; www.inouthostel.com; Major del Rectoret 2; dm €18; ✳@ 🛜🚭♿; ☖FGC Baixador de Vallvidrera) ♿, which is completely accessible for those with disabilities, and nearly all the staff that work there have disabilities of one kind or another. The facilities and service is first-class.

Organisations

Accessible Travel & Leisure (☏01452-729739; www.accessibletravel.co.uk) Claims to be the biggest UK travel agent dealing with travel for people with a disability, and encourages independent travel.

Barcelona Turisme (☏932 85 38 34; www.barcelona-access.com) Website devoted to making Barcelona accessible for visitors with a disability.

Accessible Madrid (www.esmadrid.com) Madrid's tourist-office website has some useful information (type 'Accessible' into the search box). You can download the free, generally outstanding 152-page *Madrid Accessible Tourism Guide;* it covers everything from sights, restaurants and transport to itineraries through the city. The site also allows you to download a list of wheelchair-accessible hotels, and a PDF called 'Madrid Accessible Tourism Guide', a list

of wheelchair-friendly restaurants, shopping centres and museums.

ONCE (Organización Nacional de Ciegos Españoles; Map p96;☏91 577 37 56, 91 532 50 00; www.once.es; Calle de Prim 3, Madrid; ⓂChueca or Colón) The Spanish association for the blind. You may be able to get hold of guides in Braille to a handful of cities, including Madrid and Barcelona, although they're not published every year.

Society for Accessible Travel & Hospitality (SATH; ☏212-447-7284; www.sath.org; 347 Fifth Ave at 34th St, New York, USA, Suite 605; ◷9am–5pm; 🚇M34 to 5th Ave, M1 to 34th St, Ⓢ6 to 33rd St) A good resource, that gives advice on how to travel with a wheelchair, kidney disease, sight impairment or deafness.

Visas

Spain is one of 26 member countries of the Schengen Convention, under which 22 EU countries (all but Bulgaria, Cyprus, Ireland, Romania and the UK) plus Iceland, Norway, Liechtenstein and Switzerland have abolished checks at common borders. Bulgaria and Romania were due to become a part of the Schengen Area in January 2014, but their accession was postponed after disagreement among EU-member countries.

The visa situation for entering Spain is as follows:

Citizens or residents of EU & Schengen countries No visa required.

Citizens or residents of Australia, Canada, Israel, Japan, New Zealand and the USA No visa required for tourist visits of up to 90 days.

Other countries Check with a Spanish embassy or consulate.

To work or study in Spain A special visa may be required – contact a Spanish embassy or consulate before travel.

Extensions & Residence

Schengen visas cannot be extended. You can apply for no more than two visas in any 12-month period and they are not renewable once in Spain. Nationals of EU countries, Iceland, Norway, Liechtenstein and Switzerland can enter and leave Spain at will and don't need to apply for a *tarjeta de residencia* (residence card), although they are supposed to apply for residence papers.

People of other nationalities who want to stay in Spain longer than 90 days have to get a residence card, and for them it can be a drawn-out process, starting with an appropriate visa issued by a Spanish consulate in their country of residence. Start the process well in advance.

Volunteering

Volunteering possibilities in Spain:

Earthwatch Institute (www.earthwatch.org) Occasionally Spanish conservation projects appear on its program.

Go Abroad (www.goabroad.com) At last count it had links to 54 different volunteering opportunities in Spain.

Sunseed Desert Technology (📞950 52 57 70; www.sunseed.org.uk) This UK-run project, developing sustainable ways to live in semi-arid environments, is based in the hamlet of Los Molinos del Río Agua in Almería.

Transitions Abroad (www.transitionsabroad.com) A good website to start your research.

Women Travellers

Travelling in Spain as a woman is as easy as travelling anywhere in the Western world. That said, you should be choosy about your ac-

commodation. Bottom-end fleapits with all-male staff can be insalubrious locations to bed down for the night. Lone women should also take care in city streets at night – stick with the crowds. Hitching for solo women travellers, while feasible, is risky.

Spanish men under about 40, who've grown up in the liberated post-Franco era, conform far less to old-fashioned sexual stereotypes, although you might notice that sexual stereotyping becomes a little more pronounced as you move from north to south in Spain, and from city to country.

Work

Nationals of EU countries, Switzerland, Liechtenstein, Norway and Iceland may freely work in Spain. If you are offered a contract, your employer will normally steer you through any bureaucracy.

Virtually everyone else is supposed to obtain a work permit from a Spanish consulate in their country of residence and, if they plan to stay more than 90 days, a residence visa. These procedures are almost impossible unless you have a job contract lined up before you begin them.

You could look for casual work in fruit picking, harvesting or construction, but this is generally done with imported labour from Morocco and Eastern Europe, with pay and conditions that can often best be described as dire.

Translating and interpreting could be an option if you are fluent in Spanish and have a language in demand.

Language Teaching

This type of work is an obvious option for which language-teaching qualifications are a big help. Language schools abound and are listed under 'Academias de Idiomas' in the *Yellow

Pages*. Getting a job is harder if you're not an EU citizen, and the more reputable places will require prospective teachers to have TEFL qualifications. Giving private lessons is another avenue, but is unlikely to bring you a living wage straight away.

Sources of information on possible teaching work – in a school or as a private tutor – include foreign cultural centres such as the British Council and Alliance Française, foreign-language bookshops, universities and language schools. Many have noticeboards where you may find work opportunities or can advertise your own services.

At **Pueblo Inglés** (www.puebloingles.com), native English-speakers (not necessarily qualified teachers) can get work conversing with Spaniards in English at summer camps and other locations.

Tourist Resorts

Summer work on the Mediterranean coasts is a possibility, especially if you arrive early in the season and are prepared to stay a while. Check any local press in foreign languages, such as the Costa del Sol's *Sur in English* (www.surinenglish.com), which lists ads for waiters, nannies, chefs, babysitters, cleaners and the like.

Yacht Crewing

It is possible to find work as crew on yachts and cruisers. The best ports at which to look include (in descending order) Palma de Mallorca, Gibraltar and Puerto Banús.

In summer the voyages tend to be restricted to the Mediterranean, but from about November to January, many boats head for the Caribbean. Such work is usually unpaid and about the only way to find it is to ask around on the docks.

Transport

GETTING THERE & AWAY

Spain is one of Europe's top holiday destinations and is well linked to other European countries by air, rail and road. Regular car ferries and hydrofoils run to and from Morocco, and there are ferry links to the UK, Italy, the Canary Islands and Algeria.

Flights, tours and rail tickets can be booked online at lonelyplanet.com/bookings.

Entering Spain

Immigration and customs checks (which usually only take place if you're arriving from outside the EU) normally involve a minimum of fuss, although there are exceptions.

Your vehicle could be searched on arrival from Andorra. Spanish customs look out for contraband duty-free products destined for illegal resale in Spain. The same may apply to travellers arriving from Morocco or the Spanish North African enclaves of Ceuta and Melilla. In this case the search is for controlled substances. Expect long delays at these borders, especially in summer.

The tiny principality of Andorra is not in the EU, so border controls remain in place.

Passport

Citizens of the 27 other EU member states and Switzerland can travel to Spain with their national identity card alone. If such countries do not issue ID cards – as in the UK – travellers must carry a valid passport. All other nationalities must have a valid passport.

By law you are supposed to carry your passport or ID card with you in Spain at all times.

Air

There are direct flights to Spain from most European countries, as well as North America, South America, Africa, the Middle East and Asia. Those coming from Australasia will usually have to make at least one change of flight.

High season in Spain generally means Christmas, New Year, Easter and roughly June to September. It can be worth playing around with dates close to these times – we found, for example, a massive difference on prices for some Spain-bound intercontinental flights on 12 January (peak season) when compared to a few days later. The applicability of seasonal fares varies, of course, depending on the specific destination. You may find reasonably priced flights to Madrid from elsewhere in Europe in August, for example, because it is stinking hot

CLIMATE CHANGE & TRAVEL

Every form of transport that relies on carbon-based fuel generates CO_2, the main cause of human-induced climate change. Modern travel is dependent on aeroplanes, which might use less fuel per kilometre per person than most cars but travel much greater distances. The altitude at which aircraft emit gases (including CO_2) and particles also contributes to their climate change impact. Many websites offer 'carbon calculators' that allow people to estimate the carbon emissions generated by their journey and, for those who wish to do so, to offset the impact of the greenhouse gases emitted with contributions to portfolios of climate-friendly initiatives throughout the world. Lonely Planet offsets the carbon footprint of all staff and author travel.

and everyone else has fled to the mountains or the sea. As a general rule, November to March is when airfares to Spain are likely to be at their lowest, and the intervening months can be considered shoulder periods.

Airports & Airlines

All of Spain's airports share the user-friendly website and flight information telephone number of **Aena** (www.aena.es; ☎902 404704), the national airports authority. To find more information on each airport, choose 'English' and click on the drop-down menu of airports. Each airport's page has details on practical information (including parking and public transport) and a full list of (and links to) airlines using that airport. It also has current flight information.

Madrid's Aeropuerto de Barajas is Spain's busiest (and Europe's fourth- or fifth-busiest) airport. Other major airports include Barcelona's Aeroport del Prat and the airports of Palma de Mallorca, Málaga, Alicante, Girona, Valencia, Ibiza, Seville and Bilbao. There are also airports at Almería, Asturias, Jerez de la Frontera, Murcia, Reus, Santander, Santiago de Compostela and Seville.

Land

Spain shares land borders with France, Portugal and Andorra.

Apart from shorter cross-border services, **Eurolines** (www.eurolines.com) are the main operators of international bus services to Spain from most of Western Europe and Morocco.

In addition to the rail services connecting Spain with France and Portugal, there are direct trains between Zurich and Barcelona (via Bern, Geneva, Perpignan and Girona), and between Milan and Barcelona (via Turin, Perpignan and Girona). For these and other services, visit the 'Internacional' section of the website for **Renfe** (www.renfe.com), the Spanish national railway company.

Andorra

Regular buses connect Andorra with Barcelona (including winter ski buses and direct services to the airport) and other destinations in Spain (including Madrid) and France. Regular buses run between Andorra and Barcelona's Estació d'Autobusos de Sants (€33.50, three hours).

France

BUS

Eurolines (www.eurolines.fr) heads to Spain from Paris and more than 20 other French cities and towns. It connects with Madrid (17¾ hours), Barcelona (14¾ hours) and many other destinations. There is at least one departure per day for main destinations.

CAR & MOTORCYCLE

The main road crossing into Spain from France is the highway that links up with Spain's AP7 tollway, which runs down to Barcelona and follows the Spanish coast south (with a branch, the AP2, going to Madrid via Zaragoza). A series of links cuts across the Pyrenees from France and Andorra into Spain, as does a coastal route that runs from Biarritz in France into the Spanish Basque Country.

TRAIN

The principal rail crossings into Spain pierce the Franco-Spanish frontier along the Mediterranean coast and via the Basque Country. Another minor rail route runs inland across the Pyrenees from Latour-de-Carol to Barcelona.

In addition to the options listed below, two or three TGV (high-speed) trains leave from Paris-Montparnasse for Irún, where you change to a normal train for the Basque Country and on towards Madrid. Up to three TGVs also put you on track to Barcelona (leaving from Paris Gare de Lyon), with a change of train at Montpellier or Narbonne. For more information on French rail services, check out the **SNCF** (www.voyages-sncf.com) website.

There are plans for a high-speed rail link between Madrid and Paris. In the meantime, high-speed services travel via Barcelona. These are the major cross-border services:

➡ **Paris to Madrid** (€198 to €228, 9¾ to 17½ hours, five daily) The slow route runs via Les Aubrais, Blois, Poitiers, Irun, Vitoria, Burgos and Valladolid. It may be quicker

---

BUS PASSES

Travellers planning broader European tours that include Spain could find one of the following passes useful:

Busabout (☎in the UK 084 5026 7514; www.busabout.com; 7-11 Bressenden Pl, London) UK-based hop-on/hop-off bus service aimed at younger travellers. Its network includes more than 30 cities in nine countries, and the main passes are of interest only to those travelling a lot beyond Spain (where there are five stops).

Eurolines (www.eurolines.com) Offers a high-season pass valid for 15 days (adult/under 26 years €355/300) or 30 days (€465/385). This pass allows unlimited travel between 51 European cities, but the only Spanish cities included are Barcelona, Madrid and Alicante.

RAIL PASSES

InterRail Passes

InterRail (www.interrailnet.eu) passes are available to people who have lived in Europe for six months or more. They can be bought at most major stations and student travel outlets, as well as online.

Children's InterRail passes (half the cost of the adult fare) are for children aged four to 11; youth passes for people aged 12 to 25; and adult passes for those 26 and over. Children aged three and under travel for free.

InterRail has a **Global Pass** encompassing 30 countries that comes in four versions, ranging from five days' travel in 10 days to a full month's travel. Check out the website for a full list of prices.

The InterRail **one-country pass** for Spain can be used for three, four, six or eight days in one month. For the eight-day pass you pay €512/326/216 for adult 1st class/ adult 2nd class/youth 2nd class.

Eurail Passes

Eurail (www.eurail.com) passes are for those who've lived in Europe for less than six months and are supposed to be bought outside Europe. They're available from leading travel agencies and online.

For most of the following passes, children aged between four and 11 pay half-price for the 1st-class passes, while those aged under 26 can get a cheaper 2nd-class pass. The website has a full list of prices, including special family rates and other discounts.

Eurail Global Passes are good for travel in 23 European countries; forget it if you intend to travel mainly in Spain. Passes are valid for 15 or 21 consecutive days, or for 10 or 15 days within one month. There are also one-, two- or three-month passes.

The **Eurail Select Pass** provides between five and 15 days of unlimited travel within a two-month period in three to five bordering countries.

Eurail also offers a one-country **Spain Pass** and several **two-country regional passes** (Spain-France, Spain-Italy and Spain-Portugal). You can choose from three to 10 days' train travel in a two-month period for any of these passes. The 10-day Spain Pass costs €455/365 for 1st/2nd class.

As with all Eurail passes, be sure you will be covering a lot of ground to make these worthwhile. To be sure, check the **Renfe** (www.renfe.com) website for sample prices in euros for the places in which you intend to travel.

---

to take the high-speed AVE train to Barcelona and change from there.

➡ **Paris to Barcelona** (from €59, 6½ hours, two daily) A recently inaugurated high-speed service runs via Valence, Nimes, Montpellier, Beziers, Narbonne, Perpignan, Figueres and Girona. Also high-speed services run from Lyon (from €49, five hours) and Toulouse (from €39, three hours).

➡ **Montpellier to Lorca** (€79.55, 12 to 13 hours, daily) Talgo service along the Mediterranean coast via Girona, Barcelona, Tarragona and Valencia.

Portugal

BUS

Avanza (☎902 020999; www. avanzabus.com) runs three daily buses between Lisbon and Madrid (€42.10, 7½ hours, two daily).

Other bus services run north via Porto to Tui, Santiago de Compostela and A Coruña in Galicia, while local buses cross the border from towns such as Huelva in Andalucía, Badajoz in Extremadura and Ourense in Galicia.

CAR & MOTORCYCLE

The A5 freeway linking Madrid with Badajoz crosses the Portuguese frontier and continues on to Lisbon, and there are many other road connections up and down the length of the Spain–Portugal border.

TRAIN

From Portugal, the main line runs from Lisbon across Extremadura to Madrid.

➡ **Lisbon to Madrid** (chair/ sleeper class from €36/50, nine to 10¾ hours, one daily)

➡ **Lisbon to Irún** (chair/ sleeper class €41/56, 14 hours, one daily)

➡ **Oporto to Vigo** (from €14.75, 2¼ hours, two daily)

Sea

Ferries run to Morocco from mainland Spain. Most services are run by the Spanish national ferry company, **Acciona Trasmediterránea** (☏902 454645; www.trasmediterranea.es). You can take vehicles on most routes.

A useful website for comparing routes and finding links to the relevant ferry companies is www.ferrylines.com.

Algeria

Acciona Trasmediterránea operates year-round ferries between Almería and Ghazaouet.

France

A new service operated by **LD Lines** (www.ldlines.co.uk) now sails between Gijón and Saint-Nazaire (15 to 16 hours, three times weekly) for passengers travelling with a car. It continues on to Rosslare in Ireland, stopping for 10 hours in Saint-Nazaire on the way north, and three hours heading south.

Italy

Most Italian routes are operated by **Grimaldi Lines** (www.grimaldi-lines.com) or **Grand Navi Veloci** (www.gnv.it).

➡ **Genoa to Barcelona** (19 hours, once or twice weekly)

➡ **Civitavecchia (near Rome) to Barcelona** (20 hours, six weekly)

➡ **Livorno (Tuscany) to Barcelona** (20½ hours, weekly)

➡ **Porto Torres (Sardinia) to Barcelona** (12 hours, five to seven times weekly)

Morocco

➡ **Tangier to Algeciras** (1½ hours, up to eight daily) Buses from several Moroccan cities converge on Tangier to make the ferry crossing to Algeciras, then fan out to the main Spanish centres.

➡ **Tangier to Barcelona** (24 to 35 hours, weekly)

➡ **Tangier to Tarifa** (35 minutes, up to eight daily)

➡ **Nador to Almería** (six hours, up to three daily)

UK

In 2014 **LD Lines** (www.ldlines.co.uk) inaugurated a new year-round route between Gijón and Poole (25 hours, weekly).

Brittany Ferries (☏0871 244 0744; www.brittany-ferries.co.uk) runs the following services:

➡ **Plymouth to Santander** (20 hours, weekly, mid-March to October only)

➡ **Portsmouth to Santander** (24 hours, twice weekly)

➡ **Portsmouth to Bilbao** (24 hours, twice weekly)

GETTING AROUND

Spain's network of train and bus services is one of the best in Europe and there aren't many places that can't be reached using one or the other. The tentacles of Spain's high-speed train network are expanding rapidly, while domestic air services are plentiful over longer distances and on routes that are more complicated by land.

Air

Spain has an extensive network of internal flights. These are operated by both Spanish airlines and a handful of low-cost international airlines, which include the following:

Air Europa (www.aireuropa.com) Madrid to Ibiza, Palma de Mallorca, Vigo, Bilbao and Barcelona as well as other routes between Spanish cities.

Iberia (www.iberia.com) Spain's national airline and its subsidiary, Iberia Regional-Air Nostrum, have an extensive domestic network.

Ryanair (www.ryanair.com) Some domestic Spanish routes include Madrid to Palma de Mallorca.

Volotea (www.volotea.com) Budget airline; flies domestically and internationally. Domestic routes take in Ibiza, Palma de Mallorca, Malaga, Valencia, Vigo, Bilbao, Zaragoza and Oviedo (but not Madrid or Barcelona).

Vueling (www.vueling.com) Spanish low-cost company with loads of domestic flights within Spain, especially from Barcelona.

Bicycle

Years of highway improvement programs across the country have made cycling a much easier prospect than it once was, although there are few designated bike lanes. Cycling on *autopistas* (tollways) is forbidden. Driver attitudes are not always that enlightened, so beware, and cycling in most major cities is not for the faint-hearted.

If you get tired of pedalling, it is often possible to take your bike on the train. All regional trains have space for bikes (usually marked by a bicycle logo on the carriage), where you can simply load the bike. Bikes are also permitted on most *cercanías* (local-area trains around big cities such as Madrid and Barcelona). On long-distance trains there are more restrictions. As a rule, you have to be travelling overnight in a sleeper or couchette to have the (dismantled) bike accepted as normal luggage. Otherwise, it can only be sent separately as a parcel. It's often possible to take your bike on a bus – usually you'll just be asked to remove the front wheel.

Hire

Bicycle rental is not as widespread as in some European countries, although it's becoming more so, especially in the case of *bici todo terreno* (mountain bikes), and in Andalucía, Barcelona and popular coastal towns. Costs vary considerably, but expect to pay around €8 to €10 per hour, €15 to €20 per day, or €50 to €60 per week.

Zaragoza, Córdoba, Málaga and Seville are among those cities to have introduced public bicycle systems with dozens of automated pick-up/drop-off points around the city. These schemes involve paying a small subscription fee, which then allows you to pick up a bicycle at one location and drop it off at another.

Boat

Ferries and hydrofoils link the mainland (La Península) with the Balearic Islands and Spain's North African enclaves of Ceuta and Melilla.

The main national ferry company is **Acciona Trasmediterránea** (☎902 454645; www.trasmediterranea.es). It runs a combination of slower car ferries and mod-ern, high-speed, passenger-only fast ferries and hydrofoils. On overnight services between the mainland and the Balearic Islands you can opt for seating or sleeping accommodation in a cabin.

Bus

There are few places in Spain where buses don't go. Numerous companies provide bus links, from local routes between villages to fast intercity connections. It is often cheaper to travel by bus than by train, particularly on long-haul runs, but also less comfortable.

Local services can get you just about anywhere, but most buses connecting villages and provincial towns are not geared to tourist needs. Frequent weekday services drop off to a trickle, if they operate at all, on Saturday and Sunday. Often just one bus runs daily between smaller places during the week, and none operate on Sundays. It's usually unnecessary to make reservations; just arrive early enough to get a seat.

On many regular runs (say, from Madrid to Toledo) the ticket you buy is for the next bus due to leave and *cannot* be used on a later bus. Advance purchase in such cases is generally not possible. For longer trips (such as Madrid to Seville or to the coast), and certainly in peak holiday season, you can (and should) buy your ticket in advance. On some routes you have the choice between express and stopping-all-stations services.

In most larger towns and cities, buses leave from a single *estación de autobuses* (bus station). In smaller places, buses tend to operate from a set street or plaza, often unmarked. Locals will know where to go and where to buy tickets.

ROAD DISTANCES (KM)

	Alicante	Badajoz	Barcelona	Bilbao	Córdoba	Granada	A Coruña	León	Madrid	Málaga	Oviedo	Pamplona	San Sebastián	Seville	Toledo	Valencia	Valladolid
Badajoz	696																
Barcelona	515	1022															
Bilbao	817	649	620														
Córdoba	525	272	908	795													
Granada	353	438	868	829	166												
A Coruña	1031	772	1118	644	995	1043											
León	755	496	784	359	733	761	334										
Madrid	422	401	621	395	400	434	609	333									
Málaga	482	436	997	939	187	129	1153	877	544								
Oviedo	873	614	902	304	851	885	340	118	451	995							
Pamplona	673	755	437	159	807	841	738	404	407	951	463						
San Sebastián	766	768	529	119	869	903	763	433	469	13	423	92					
Seville	609	217	1046	933	138	256	947	671	538	219	789	945	1007				
Toledo	411	368	692	466	320	397	675	392	71	507	510	478	540	458			
Valencia	166	716	349	633	545	519	961	685	352	648	803	501	594	697	372		
Valladolid	615	414	663	280	578	627	455	134	193	737	252	325	354	589	258	545	
Zaragoza	498	726	296	324	725	759	833	488	325	869	604	175	268	863	396	326	367

BEATING PARKING FINES

If you've parked in a street parking spot and return to find that a parking inspector has left you a parking ticket, don't despair. If you arrive back within a reasonable time after the ticket was issued (what constitutes a reasonable time varies from place to place, but it is rarely more than a couple of hours), don't go looking for the inspector, but instead head for the nearest parking machine. Most machines in most cities allow you to pay a small penalty (usually around €5) to cancel the fine (keep both pieces of paper just in case). If you're unable to work out what to do, ask a local for help.

Bus travel within Spain is not overly costly. The trip from Madrid to Barcelona starts from around €32 one way. From Barcelona to Seville, which is one of the longest trips (15 to 16 hours), you pay up to €102 one way.

People under 26 should enquire about discounts on long-distance trips.

Among the hundreds of bus companies operating in Spain, the following have the largest range of services:

ALSA (902 422242; www.alsa.es) The biggest player, this company has routes all over the country in association with various other companies.

Avanza (902 020999; www.avanzabus.com) Operates buses from Madrid to Extremadura, western Castilla y León and Valencia via eastern Castilla-La Mancha (eg Cuenca), often in association with other companies.

Socibus & Secorbus (902 229292; www.socibus.es) These two companies jointly operate services between Madrid and western Andalucía, including Cádiz, Córdoba, Huelva and Seville.

Car & Motorcycle

Every vehicle should display a nationality plate of its country of registration and you must always carry proof of ownership of a private vehicle. Third-party motor insurance is required throughout Europe. A warning triangle and a reflective jacket (to be used in case of breakdown) are compulsory.

Automobile Associations

The **Real Automóvil Club de España** (RACE; 900 100992; www.race.es; Calle de Eloy Gonzalo 32, Madrid) is the national automobile club. They may well come to assist you in case of breakdown, but in any event you should obtain an emergency telephone number for Spain from your own insurer or car-rental company.

Driving Licence

All EU member states' driving licences are fully recognised throughout Europe. Those with a non-EU licence are supposed to obtain a 12-month International Driving Permit (IDP) to accompany their national licence, which your national automobile association can issue, although in practice car-rental companies and police rarely ask for one. People who have held residency in Spain for one year or more should apply for a Spanish driving licence.

Fuel & Spare Parts

Gasolina (petrol) in Spain is pricey, but generally slightly cheaper than in its major EU neighbours (including France, Germany, Italy and the UK). Petrol is about 10% cheaper in Gibraltar than in Spain and 15% cheaper in Andorra.

You can pay with major credit cards at most service stations.

Hire

To rent a car in Spain you have to have a licence, be aged 21 or over and, for the major companies at least, have a credit or debit card. Smaller firms in areas where car hire is particularly common (such as the Balearic Islands) can sometimes live without this last requirement. Although those with a non-EU licence should also have an IDP, you will find that national licences from countries such as Australia, Canada, New Zealand and the USA are usually accepted without question.

Atesa (902 100101; www.atesa.es)

Auto Europe (www.autoeurope.com) US-based clearing house for deals with major car-rental agencies.

Autos Abroad (www.autosabroad.com) UK-based company offering deals from major car-rental agencies.

Avis (902 180854; www.avis.es)

Europcar (902 105030; www.europcar.es)

Hertz (91 749 77 78; www.hertz.es)

Holiday Autos (900 838014; www.holidayautos.es) A clearing house for major international companies.

Ideamerge (www.ideamerge.com) Renault's car-leasing plan, motor-home rental and more.

Pepecar (807 414243; www.pepecar.com) Local low-cost company, but beware of 'extras' that aren't quoted in initial prices.

SixT (902 491616; www.sixt.es)

Insurance

Third-party motor insurance is a minimum requirement in Spain and throughout Europe. Ask your insurer for a European Accident Statement form, which can simplify matters in the event of an accident. A European breakdown-assistance policy such as the AA Five Star Service or RAC Eurocover Motoring Assistance is a good investment.

Car-hire companies also provide this minimum insurance, but be careful to understand what your liabilities and excess are, and what waivers you are entitled to in case of accident or damage to the hire vehicle.

Road Rules

➡ **Blood-alcohol limit:** 0.05%. Breath tests are common, and if found to be over the limit, you can be judged, condemned, fined and deprived of your licence within 24 hours. Fines range up to around €600 for serious offences. Nonresident foreigners may be required to pay up on the spot (at 30% off the full fine). Pleading linguistic ignorance will not help – the police officer will produce a list of infringements and fines in as many languages as you like. If you don't pay, or don't have a Spanish resident to act as guarantor for you, your vehicle could be impounded, although this is rare.

➡ **Legal driving age for cars:** 18 years.

➡ **Legal driving age for motorcycles & scooters:** 16 (80cc and over) or 14 (50cc and under) years. A licence is required.

➡ **Motorcyclists:** Must use headlights at all times and wear a helmet if riding a bike of 125cc or more.

➡ **Overtaking:** Spanish truck drivers often have the courtesy to turn on their right indicator to show that the way ahead of them is clear for overtaking (and the left one if it is not and you are attempting this manoeuvre).

➡ **Roundabouts (traffic circles):** Vehicles already in the circle have the right of way.

➡ **Side of the road:** Drive on the right.

➡ **Speed limits:** In built-up areas, 50km/h (and in some cases, such as inner-city Barcelona, 30km/h), which increases to 100km/h on major roads and up to 120km/h on *autovías* and *autopistas* (toll-free and tolled dual-lane highways, respectively). Cars towing caravans are restricted to a maximum speed of 80km/h.

Hitching

Hitching is never entirely safe in any country in the world, and we don't recommend it. Travellers who decide to hitch should understand that they are taking a small but potentially dangerous risk. People who do choose to hitch will be safer if they travel in pairs and let someone know where they are planning to go.

Hitching is illegal on *autopistas* and *autovías*, and difficult on other major highways. Choose a spot where cars can safely stop before highway slipways, or use minor roads. The going can be slow on the latter, as the traffic is often light.

Local Transport

Most of the major cities have excellent local transport. Madrid and Barcelona have extensive bus and metro systems, and other major cities also benefit from generally efficient public transport. By European standards, prices are relatively cheap.

MEMORABLE TRAIN JOURNEYS

The romantically inclined could opt for an opulent and slow-moving, old-time rail adventure with numerous options across the peninsula.

Catch the **Transcantábrico** (☏902 555902; www.renfe.com/trenesturisticos) for a journey on a picturesque narrow-gauge rail route, from Santiago de Compostela (by bus as far as O Ferrol) via Oviedo, Santander and Bilbao along the coast, and then a long inland stretch to finish in León. The eight-day trip costs from €2950 per person in high season. The trip can also be done in reverse or in smaller chunks. There are 13 departures from April to October. Check if your package includes various visits along the way, including the Museo Guggenheim in Bilbao, the Museo de Altamira, Santillana del Mar, and the Covadonga lakes in the Picos de Europa. The food is exceptional, with some meals being eaten on board but most in various locations.

The other option is **Al-Andalus** (www.renfe.com/trenesturisticos), which, despite the name, covers a significant proportion of the peninsula, from loops through Andalucía to roots that take the slow route between Madrid and Seville, Madrid and Zaragoza, Zaragoza to León, and León to Santiago de Compostela. Options vary from three to five nights. Prices for the six-day/five-night itineraries start at €3125 per person in high season.

The trains don't travel at night, making sleeping aboard easy and providing the opportunity to stay out at night.

A much shorter but still enchanting train ride is the narrow-gauge train from Palma de Mallorca to Sóller.

Bus

Cities and provincial capitals all have reasonable bus networks. You can buy single tickets (usually between €1 and €2) on the buses or at tobacconists, but in cities such as Madrid and Barcelona you are better off buying combined 10-trip tickets that allow the use of a combination of bus and metro, and which work out cheaper per ride. These can be purchased in any metro station and from some tobacconists and newspaper kiosks.

Regular buses run from about 6am to shortly before midnight and even as late as 2am. In the big cities a night bus service generally kicks in on a limited number of lines in the wee hours. In Madrid they are known as búhos (owls) and in Barcelona more prosaically as nitbusos (night buses).

Metro

Madrid has the country's most extensive metro network. Barcelona has a reasonable system. Valencia, Zaragoza, Bilbao and Seville also have limited but useful metro systems. Tickets must be bought in metro stations (from counters or vending machines), or sometimes from estancos (tobacconists) or newspaper kiosks. Single tickets cost the same as for buses (around €1.50). The best value for visitors wanting to move around the major cities over a few days are the 10-trip tickets, known in Madrid as Metrobús (€12.20) and in Barcelona as T-10 (€10.30). Monthly and seasonal passes are also available.

Taxi

You can find taxi ranks at train and bus stations, or you can telephone for radio taxis. In larger cities taxi ranks are also scattered about the centre, and taxis will stop if you hail them in the street – look for the green light and/or the libre sign on the passenger side of the windscreen. The bigger cities are well populated with taxis, although you might have to wait a bit longer on a Friday or Saturday night. No more than four people are allowed in a taxi.

Daytime flagfall (generally to 10pm) is, for example, €2.40 in Madrid, and up to €2.90 after 10pm and on weekends and holidays. You then pay €1 to €1.25 per kilometre depending on the time of day. There are airport and

Train Routes

luggage surcharges. A cross-town ride in a major city will cost about €10 – absurdly cheap by European standards – while a taxi between the city centre and airport in either Madrid or Barcelona will cost €30 with luggage.

Tram

Trams were stripped out of Spanish cities decades ago, but they're making a timid comeback in some. Barcelona has a couple of new suburban tram services in addition to its tourist Tramvia Blau run to Tibidabo. Valencia has some useful trams to the beach, while various limited lines also run in Seville, Bilbao, Murcia and, most recently, Zaragoza.

Train

Renfe (☎902 243402; www. renfe.com) is the excellent national train system that runs most of the services in Spain. A handful of small private railway lines also operate.

You'll find *consignas* (left-luggage facilities) at all main train stations. They are usually open from about 6am to midnight and charge from €4 to €6 per day per piece of luggage.

Spain has several types of trains, and *largo recorrido* or *grandes líneas* (long-distance trains) in particular have a variety of names.

➡ **Alaris, Altaria, Alvia, Arco and Avant** Long-distance intermediate-speed services.

➡ **Cercanías** For short hops and services to outlying suburbs and satellite towns in Madrid, Barcelona and 11 other cities. Called *rodalies* in Catalonia.

➡ **Euromed** Similar to the Tren de Alta Velocidad Española (AVE) trains, they connect Barcelona with Valencia and Alicante.

➡ **FEVE (Ferrocarriles de Vía Estrecha)** Narrow-gauge network along Spain's north coast between Bilbao and

> ### CHEAPER TRAIN TICKETS
>
> Train travel can be expensive in Spain but there is one trick worth knowing. Return tickets cost considerably less than two one-way tickets. If you're certain that you'll be returning on the same route sometime over the coming months (usually three months is the limit), buy a return ticket and you can later change the return date, which works out a lot cheaper than buying two one-way tickets.

Ferrol (Galicia), with a branch down to León.

➡ **Regionales** Trains operating within one region, usually stopping all stations.

➡ **Talgo and Intercity** Slower long-distance trains.

➡ **Tren de Alta Velocidad Española (AVE)** High-speed trains that link Madrid with Albacete, Barcelona, Burgos, Córdoba, Cuenca, Huesca, Lerida, Málaga, Seville, Valencia, Valladolid and Zaragoza. There are also Barcelona–Seville and Barcelona–Málaga services. In coming years Madrid–Cádiz and Madrid–Bilbao should also come on line.

➡ **Trenhotel** Overnight trains with sleeper berths.

Classes & Costs

All long-distance trains have 2nd and 1st classes, known as *turista* and *preferente*, respectively. The latter is 20% to 40% more expensive.

Fares vary enormously depending on the service (faster trains cost considerably more) and, in the case of some high-speed services such as the AVE, on the time and day of travel. Tickets for AVE trains are by far the most expensive. A one-way trip in 2nd class from Madrid to Barcelona (on which route only AVE trains run) could cost as much as €139 (it could work out significantly cheaper if you book well in advance).

Children aged between four and 12 years are entitled to a 40% discount; those aged under four travel for

free (except on high-speed trains, for which they pay the same as those aged four to 12). Buying a return ticket often gives you a 10% to 20% discount on the return trip. Students and people up to 25 years of age with a Euro<26 Card (Carnet Joven in Spain) are entitled to 20% to 25% off most ticket prices.

If you're travelling as a family, ask for one of a group of four seats with a table when making your reservation.

On overnight trips within Spain on *trenhoteles* it's worth paying extra for a *litera* (couchette; a sleeping berth in a six- or four-bed compartment) or, if available, single or double cabins in *preferente* or *gran clase* class. The cost depends on the class of accommodation, type of train and length of journey. The lines covered are Madrid–A Coruña, Barcelona–Córdoba–Seville, Barcelona–Madrid (and on to Lisbon) and Barcelona–Málaga, as well as international services to France.

Reservations

Reservations are recommended for long-distance trips, and you can make them in train stations, **Renfe** (☎902 243402; www.renfe. com) offices and travel agencies, as well as online. In a growing number of stations you can pick up prebooked tickets from machines scattered about the station concourse.

Language

Spanish (*español*) – or Castilian (*castellano*), as it is also called – is spoken throughout Spain, but there are also three co-official, regional languages: Catalan (*català*), spoken in Catalonia, the Balearic Islands and Valencia; Galician (*galego*), spoken in Galicia; and Basque (*euskara*), which is spoken in the Basque Country and Navarra.

The pronunciation of most Spanish sounds is very similar to that of their English counterparts. If you read our coloured pronunciation guides as if they were English, you'll be understood. Note that kh is a throaty sound (like the 'ch' in the Scottish *loch*), r is strongly rolled, ly is pronounced as the 'lli' in 'million' and ny as the 'ni' in 'onion'. You may also notice that the 'lisped' th sound is pronounced as s in Andalucia. In our pronunciation guides, the stressed syllables are in italics.

Where necessary in this chapter, masculine and feminine forms are marked with 'm/f', while polite and informal options are indicated by the abbreviations 'pol' and 'inf'.

BASICS

Hello.	Hola.	o·la
Goodbye.	Adiós.	a·dyos
Yes./No.	Sí./No.	see/no
Excuse me.	Perdón.	per·don
Sorry.	Lo siento.	lo syen·to
Please.	Por favor.	por fa·vor

WANT MORE?

For in-depth language information and handy phrases, check out Lonely Planet's *Spanish Phrasebook*. You'll find it at **shop.lonelyplanet.com**, or you can buy Lonely Planet's iPhone phrasebooks at the Apple App Store.

Thank you.	Gracias.	gra·thyas
You're welcome.	De nada.	de na·da
How are you?	¿Qué tal?	ke tal
Fine, thanks.	Bien, gracias.	byen gra·thyas

What's your name?

¿Cómo se llama Usted?	ko·mo se lya·ma oo·ste (pol)
¿Cómo te llamas?	ko·mo te lya·mas (inf)

My name is ...

Me llamo ...	me lya·mo ...

Do you speak English?

¿Habla inglés?	a·bla een·gles (pol)
¿Hablas inglés?	a·blas een·gles (inf)

I don't understand.

No entiendo.	no en·tyen·do

ACCOMMODATION

hotel	hotel	o·tel
guesthouse	pensión	pen·syon
youth hostel	albergue juvenil	al·ber·ge khoo·ve·neel
I'd like a ... room.	Quisiera una habitación ...	kee·sye·ra oo·na a·bee·ta·thyon ...
single	individual	een·dee·vee·dwal
double	doble	do·ble
air-con	aire acondicionado	ai·re a·kon·dee·thyo·na·do
bathroom	baño	ba·nyo
window	ventana	ven·ta·na

How much is it per night/person?

¿Cuánto cuesta por noche/persona?	kwan·to kwes·ta por no·che/per·so·na

Does it include breakfast?

¿Incluye el desayuno?	een·kloo·ye el de·sa·yoo·no

NUMBERS

1	uno	oo·no
2	dos	dos
3	tres	tres
4	cuatro	kwa·tro
5	cinco	theen·ko
6	seis	seys
7	siete	sye·te
8	ocho	o·cho
9	nueve	nwe·ve
10	diez	dyeth
20	veinte	veyn·te
30	treinta	treyn·ta
40	cuarenta	kwa·ren·ta
50	cincuenta	theen·kwen·ta
60	sesenta	se·sen·ta
70	setenta	se·ten·ta
80	ochenta	o·chen·ta
90	noventa	no·ven·ta
100	cien	thyen
1000	mil	meel

DIRECTIONS

Where's ...?
¿Dónde está ...? don·de es·ta ...

What's the address?
¿Cuál es la dirección? kwal es la dee·rek·thyon

Can you please write it down?
¿Puede escribirlo, pwe·de es·kree·beer·lo
por favor? por fa·vor

Can you show me (on the map)?
¿Me lo puede indicar me lo pwe·de een·dee·kar
(en el mapa)? (en el ma·pa)

at the corner	en la esquina	en la es·kee·na
at the traffic lights	en el semáforo	en el se·ma·fo·ro
behind ...	detrás de ...	de·tras de ...
in front of ...	enfrente de ...	en·fren·te de ...
left	izquierda	eeth·kyer·da
next to ...	al lado de ...	al la·do de ...
opposite ...	frente a ...	fren·te a ...
right	derecha	de·re·cha
straight ahead	todo recto	to·do rek·to

EATING & DRINKING

What would you recommend?
¿Qué recomienda? ke re·ko·myen·da

What's in that dish?
¿Que lleva ese plato? ke lye·va e·se pla·to

I don't eat ...
No como ... no ko·mo ...

Cheers!
¡Salud! sa·loo

That was delicious!
¡Estaba buenísimo! es·ta·ba bwe·nee·see·mo

Please bring us the bill.
Por favor, nos trae por fa·vor nos tra·e
la cuenta. la kwen·ta

I'd like to book a table for ...	Quisiera reservar una mesa para ...	kee·sye·ra re·ser·var oo·na me·sa pa·ra ...
(eight) o'clock	las (ocho)	las (o·cho)
(two) people	(dos) personas	(dos) per·so·nas

Key Words

bottle	botella	bo·te·lya
breakfast	desayuno	de·sa·yoo·no
(too) cold	(muy) frío	(mooy) free·o
dinner	cena	the·na
food	comida	ko·mee·da
fork	tenedor	te·ne·dor
glass	vaso	va·so
highchair	trona	tro·na
hot (warm)	caliente	ka·lyen·te
knife	cuchillo	koo·chee·lyo
lunch	comida	ko·mee·da
market	mercado	mer·ka·do
(children's) menu	menú (infantil)	me·noo (een·fan·teel)
plate	plato	pla·to
restaurant	restaurante	res·tow·ran·te
spoon	cuchara	koo·cha·ra
vegetarian food	comida vegetariana	ko·mee·da ve·khe·ta·rya·na

SIGNS

Abierto	Open
Cerrado	Closed
Entrada	Entrance
Hombres	Men
Mujeres	Women
Prohibido	Prohibited
Salida	Exit
Servicios/Aseos	Toilets

BASQUE

Basque is spoken at the western end of the Pyrenees and along the Bay of Biscay – from Bayonne in France to Bilbao in Spain, and inland, almost to Pamplona. No one quite knows its origin, but the most likely theory is that Basque is the lone survivor of a language family that once extended across Europe, and was wiped out by the languages of the Celts, Germanic tribes and Romans.

Hello.	Kaixo.
Goodbye.	Agur.
How are you?	Zer moduz?
Fine, thank you.	Ongi, eskerrik asko.
Excuse me.	Barkatu.
Please.	Mesedez.
Thank you.	Eskerrik asko.
You're welcome.	Ez horregatik.
Do you speak English?	Ingelesez ba al dakizu?
I don't understand.	Ez dut ulertzen.

Meat & Fish

beef	carne de vaca	kar·ne de va·ka
chicken	pollo	po·lyo
duck	pato	pa·to
lamb	cordero	kor·de·ro
lobster	langosta	lan·gos·ta
pork	cerdo	ther·do
prawns	camarones	ka·ma·ro·nes
tuna	atún	a·toon
turkey	pavo	pa·vo
veal	ternera	ter·ne·ra

Fruit & Vegetables

apple	manzana	man·tha·na
apricot	albaricoque	al·ba·ree·ko·ke
banana	plátano	pla·ta·no
beans	judías	khoo·dee·as
cabbage	col	kol
capsicum	pimiento	pee·myen·to
carrot	zanahoria	tha·na·o·rya
cherry	cereza	the·re·tha
corn	maíz	ma·eeth
cucumber	pepino	pe·pee·no
fruit	fruta	froo·ta
grape	uvas	oo·vas
lemon	limón	lee·mon
lettuce	lechuga	le·choo·ga
mushroom	champiñón	cham·pee·nyon
nuts	nueces	nwe·thes
onion	cebolla	the·bo·lya
orange	naranja	na·ran·kha
peach	melocotón	me·lo·ko·ton
peas	guisantes	gee·san·tes
pineapple	piña	pee·nya
plum	ciruela	theer·we·la
potato	patata	pa·ta·ta
spinach	espinacas	es·pee·na·kas
strawberry	fresa	fre·sa
tomato	tomate	to·ma·te
vegetable	verdura	ver·doo·ra
watermelon	sandía	san·dee·a

Other

bread	pan	pan
cheese	queso	ke·so
egg	huevo	we·vo
honey	miel	myel
jam	mermelada	mer·me·la·da
rice	arroz	a·roth
salt	sal	sal
sugar	azúcar	a·thoo·kar

Drinks

beer	cerveza	ther·ve·tha
coffee	café	ka·fe
(orange) juice	zumo (de naranja)	thoo·mo (de na·ran·kha)
milk	leche	le·che
red wine	vino tinto	vee·no teen·to
tea	té	te
(mineral) water	agua (mineral)	a·gwa (mee·ne·ral)
white wine	vino blanco	vee·no blan·ko

EMERGENCIES

Help!	¡Socorro!	so·ko·ro
Go away!	¡Vete!	ve·te
Call ...!	¡Llame a ...!	lya·me a ...
a doctor	un médico	oon me·dee·ko

QUESTION WORDS

How?	¿Cómo?	ko·mo
What?	¿Qué?	ke
When?	¿Cuándo?	kwan·do
Where?	¿Dónde?	don·de
Who?	¿Quién?	kyen
Why?	¿Por qué?	por ke

the police	la policía	la po·lee·thee·a

I'm lost.
Estoy perdido/a. es·toy per·dee·do/a (m/f)

I'm ill.
Estoy enfermo/a. es·toy en·fer·mo/a (m/f)

It hurts here.
Me duele aquí. me dwe·le a·kee

I'm allergic to (antibiotics).
Soy alérgico/a a soy a·ler·khee·ko/a a
(los antibióticos). (los an·tee·byo·tee·kos) (m/f)

Where are the toilets?
¿Dónde están los don·de es·tan los
servicios? ser·vee·thyos

SHOPPING & SERVICES

I'd like to buy ...
Quisiera comprar ... kee·sye·ra kom·prar ...

I'm just looking.
Sólo estoy mirando. so·lo es·toy mee·ran·do

Can I look at it?
¿Puedo verlo? pwe·do ver·lo

I don't like it.
No me gusta. no me goos·ta

How much is it?
¿Cuánto cuesta? kwan·to kwes·ta

That's too expensive.
Es muy caro. es mooy ka·ro

Can you lower the price?
¿Podría bajar un po·dree·a ba·khar oon
poco el precio? po·ko el pre·thyo

There's a mistake in the bill.
Hay un error en ai oon e·ror en
la cuenta. la kwen·ta

ATM	cajero	ka·khe·ro
	automático	ow·to·ma·tee·ko
internet cafe	cibercafé	thee·ber·ka·fe
post office	correos	ko·re·os
tourist office	oficina	o·fee·thee·na
	de turismo	de too·rees·mo

TIME & DATES

What time is it?	¿Qué hora es?	ke o·ra es
It's (10) o'clock.	Son (las diez).	son (las dyeth)
Half past (one).	Es (la una)	es (la oo·na)
	y media.	ee me·dya
At what time?	¿A qué hora?	a ke o·ra
At ...	A la(s) ...	a la(s) ...

morning	mañana	ma·nya·na
afternoon	tarde	tar·de
evening	noche	no·che

yesterday	ayer	a·yer
today	hoy	oy
tomorrow	mañana	ma·nya·na
Monday	lunes	loo·nes
Tuesday	martes	mar·tes
Wednesday	miércoles	myer·ko·les
Thursday	jueves	khwe·bes
Friday	viernes	vyer·nes
Saturday	sábado	sa·ba·do
Sunday	domingo	do·meen·go

BASQUE SIGNS

In many towns in the Basque region street names and signs are changing from Spanish to Basque. Not everyone uses these new names though, and many maps remain in Spanish, which can make navigating a little tricky for travellers. In this book we've provided the most commonly used version or have included both Spanish and Basque. Here are some Basque words commonly used in signs, followed by their Spanish counterpart and English translation:

aireportua	aeropuerto (airport)
erdialdea	centro (city centre)
jatetxea	restaurante (restaurant)
kalea	calle (street)
kale nagusia	calle mayor (main street)
komunak	servicios (toilets)
kontuz	atención (caution/beware)
nekazal turismoak	casas rurales (village/ farmstead accommodation)
ongi etorri	bienvenido (welcome)
turismo bulegoa	oficina de turismo (tourist office)

GALICIAN

Galician is the official language of the Autonomous Community of Galicia and is also widely understood in the neighbouring regions of Asturias and Castilla y Léon. It's very similar to Portuguese. Galicians are likely to revert to Spanish when addressing a stranger, especially a foreigner, but making a small effort to communicate in Galician will always be welcomed.

Hello.	*Ola.*
Good day.	*Bon dia.*
Goodbye.	*Adeus./Até logo.*
Many thanks.	*Moitas grácias.*
Do you speak English?	*Fala inglés?*
I don't understand.	*Non entendo.*
Could you speak in Castilian, please?	*Pode falar en español, por favor?*
What's this called in Galician?	*Como se chama iso en galego?*

TRANSPORT

Public Transport

boat	*barco*	bar·ko
bus	*autobús*	ow·to·boos
plane	*avión*	a·vyon
train	*tren*	tren
first	*primer*	pree·mer
last	*último*	ool·tee·mo
next	*próximo*	prok·see·mo
a ... ticket	*un billete de ...*	oon bee·lye·te de ...
1st-class	*primera clase*	pree·me·ra kla·se
2nd-class	*segunda clase*	se·goon·da kla·se
one-way	*ida*	ee·da
return	*ida y vuelta*	ee·da ee vwel·ta
aisle seat	*asiento de pasillo*	a·syen·to de pa·see·lyo
station	*estación*	es·ta·thyon
ticket office	*taquilla*	ta·kee·lya
timetable	*horario*	o·ra·ryo

window seat	*asiento junto a la ventana*	a·syen·to khoon·to a la ven·ta·na

I want to go to ...
Quisiera ir a ... kee·sye·ra eer a ...

At what time does it arrive/leave?
¿A qué hora llega/sale? a ke o·ra lye·ga/sa·le

Does it stop at (Madrid)?
¿Para en (Madrid)? pa·ra en (ma·dree)

Which stop is this?
¿Cuál es esta parada? kwal es es·ta pa·ra·da

Please tell me when we get to (Seville).
¿Puede avisarme cuando lleguemos a (Sevilla)? pwe·de a·vee·sar·me kwan·do lye·ge·mos a (se·vee·lya)

I want to get off here.
Quiero bajarme aquí. kye·ro ba·khar·me a·kee

Driving and Cycling

I'd like to hire a ...	*Quisiera alquilar ...*	kee·sye·ra al·kee·lar ...
4WD	*un todo-terreno*	oon to·do-te·re·no
bicycle	*una bicicleta*	oo·na bee·thee·kle·ta
car	*un coche*	oon ko·che
motorcycle	*una moto*	oo·na mo·to
child seat	*asiento de seguridad para niños*	a·syen·to de se·goo·ree·da pa·ra nee·nyos
helmet	*casco*	kas·ko
mechanic	*mecánico*	me·ka·nee·ko
petrol	*gasolina*	ga·so·lee·na
service station	*gasolinera*	ga·so·lee·ne·ra

How much is it per day/hour?
¿Cuánto cuesta por día/hora? kwan·to kwes·ta por dee·a/o·ra

Is this the road to (Barcelona)?
¿Se va a (Barcelona) por esta carretera? se va a (bar·the·lo·na) por es·ta ka·re·te·ra

(How long) Can I park here?
¿(Por cuánto tiempo) Puedo aparcar aquí? (por kwan·to tyem·po) pwe·do a·par·kar a·kee

The car has broken down (at Valencia).
El coche se ha averiado (en Valencia). el ko·che se a a·ve·rya·do (en va·len·thya)

I have a flat tyre.
Tengo un pinchazo. ten·go oon peen·cha·tho

I've run out of petrol.
Me he quedado sin gasolina. me e ke·da·do seen ga·so·lee·na

CATALAN

The recognition of Catalan as an official language in Spain is the end result of a regional government campaign that began when the province gained autonomy at the end of the 1970s. Until the Battle of Muret in 1213, Catalan territory extended across southern France, taking in Roussillon and reaching into the Provence. Catalan was spoken, or at least understood, throughout these territories and in what is now Catalonia and Andorra. In the couple of hundred years that followed, the Catalans spread their language south into Valencia, west into Aragón and east to the Balearic Islands. It also reached Sicily and Naples, and the Sardinian town of Alghero is still a partly Catalan-speaking outpost today. Catalan is spoken by up to 10 million people in Spain.

In Barcelona you'll hear as much Spanish as Catalan. Your chances of coming across English speakers are also good. Elsewhere in the province, don't be surprised if you get replies in Catalan to your questions in Spanish. However, you'll find that most Catalans will happily speak to you in Spanish, especially once they realise you're a foreigner. This said, the following Catalan phrases might win you a few smiles and perhaps help you make some new friends.

Hello.	*Hola.*	**Monday**	*dilluns*
Goodbye.	*Adéu.*	**Tuesday**	*dimarts*
Yes.	*Sí.*	**Wednesday**	*dimecres*
No.	*No.*	**Thursday**	*dijous*
Please.	*Sisplau./Si us plau.*	**Friday**	*divendres*
Thank you (very much).	*(Moltes) gràcies.*	**Saturday**	*dissabte*
You're welcome.	*De res.*	**Sunday**	*diumenge*
Excuse me.	*Perdoni.*		
May I?/Do you mind?	*Puc?/Em permet?*	**1**	*un/una* (m/f)
I'm sorry.	*Ho sento./Perdoni.*	**2**	*dos/dues* (m/f)
		3	*tres*
What's your name?	*Com et dius?* (inf)	**4**	*quatre*
	Com es diu? (pol)	**5**	*cinc*
My name is ...	*Em dic ...*	**6**	*sis*
Where are you from?	*D'on ets?*	**7**	*set*
Do you speak English?	*Parla anglès?*	**8**	*vuit*
I understand.	*Ho entenc.*	**9**	*nou*
I don't understand.	*No ho entenc.*	**10**	*deu*
Could you speak in	*Pot parlar castellà*	**11**	*onze*
Castilian, please?	*sisplau?*	**12**	*dotze*
How do you say ... in	*Com es diu ... en*	**13**	*tretze*
Catalan?	*català?*	**14**	*catorze*
		15	*quinze*
I'm looking for ...	*Estic buscant ...*	**16**	*setze*
How do I get to ...?	*Com puc arribar a ...?*	**17**	*disset*
Turn left.	*Giri a mà esquerra.*	**18**	*divuit*
Turn right.	*Giri a mà dreta.*	**19**	*dinou*
near	*a prop de*	**20**	*vint*
far	*a lluny de*	**100**	*cent*

GLOSSARY

Unless otherwise indicated, the following terms are from Castilian Spanish. The masculine and feminine forms are indicated with the abbreviations 'm/f'.

ajuntament – Catalan for *ayuntamiento*
alameda – tree-lined avenue
albergue – refuge
albergue juvenil – youth hostel
alcázar – Muslim-era fortress
aljibe – cistern
artesonado – wooden Mudéjar ceiling with interlaced beams leaving a pattern of spaces for decoration
autopista – tollway
autovía – toll-free highway
AVE – Tren de Alta Velocidad Española; high-speed train
ayuntamiento – city or town hall

bailaor/bailaora – m/f flamenco dancer
baile – dance in a flamenco context
balneario – spa
barrio – district/quarter (of a town or city)
biblioteca – library
bici todo terreno (BTT) – mountain bike
bodega – cellar (especially wine cellar); also a winery or a traditional wine bar likely to serve wine from the barrel
búhos – night-bus routes

cabrito – kid
cala – cove
calle – street
callejón – lane
cama – bed
cambio – change; also currency exchange
caña – small glass of beer
cantaor/cantaora – m/f flamenco singer
capilla – chapel
capilla mayor – chapel containing the high altar of a church
carmen – walled villa with gardens, in Granada

Carnaval – traditional festive period that precedes the start of Lent; carnival
carretera – highway
carta – menu
casa de huéspedes – guesthouse; see also *hospedaje*
casa de pagès – *casa rural* in Catalonia
casa rural – village, country house or farmstead with rooms to let
casco – literally 'helmet'; often used to refer to the old part of a city; more correctly, *casco antiguo/histórico/viejo*
castellano/a (m/f) – Castilian; used in preference to *español* to describe the national language
castellers – Catalan human-castle builders
castillo – castle
castro – Celtic fortified village
català – Catalan language; a native of Catalonia
catedral – cathedral
cercanías – local train network
cervecería – beer bar
churrigueresco – ornate style of baroque architecture named after the brothers Alberto and José Churriguera
ciudad – city
claustro – cloister
CNIG – Centro Nacional de Información Geográfica; producers of good-quality maps
cofradía – see *hermandad*
colegiata – collegiate church
coll – Catalan for *collado*
collado – mountain pass
comarca – district; grouping of *municipios*
comedor – dining room
comunidad – fixed charge for maintenance of rental accommodation (sometimes included in rent); community
conquistador – conqueror
copa – drink; literally 'glass'
cordillera – mountain range
coro – choir: part of a church, usually the middle
correos – post office
Cortes – national parliament

costa – coast
cruceiro – standing crucifix found at many crossroads in Galicia
cuesta – lane, usually on a hill
custodia – monstrance

dolmen – prehistoric megalithic tomb

embalse – reservoir
encierro – running of the bulls Pamplona-style; also happens in many other places around Spain
entrada – entrance
ermita – hermitage or chapel
església – Catalan for *iglesia*
estació – Catalan for *estación*
estación – station
estación de autobuses – bus station
estación de esquí – ski station or resort
estación marítima – ferry terminal
estany – Catalan for *lago*
Euskadi Ta Askatasuna (ETA) – the name stands for Basque Homeland & Freedom
extremeño/a (m/f) – Extremaduran; a native of Extremadura

fallas – huge sculptures of papier mâché (or nowadays more often polystyrene) on wood used in Las Fallas festival of Valencia
farmacia – pharmacy
faro – lighthouse
feria – fair; can refer to trade fairs as well as to city, town or village fairs that are basically several days of merrymaking; can also mean a bullfight or festival stretching over days or weeks
ferrocarril – railway
festa – Catalan for *fiesta*
FEVE – Ferrocarriles de Vía Estrecha; a private train company in northern Spain
fiesta – festival, public holiday or party
fútbol – football (soccer)

gaditano/a (m/f) – person from Cádiz

gaita – Galician version of the bagpipes

gallego/a (m/f) – Galician; a native of Galicia

gitanos – Roma people

glorieta – big roundabout (traffic circle)

Gran Vía – main thoroughfare

GRs – *(senderos de) Gran Recorrido;* long-distance hiking paths

guardia civil – military police

hermandad – brotherhood (including men and women), in particular one that takes part in religious processions

hórreo – Galician or Asturian grain store

hospedaje – guesthouse

hostal – cheap hotel

huerta – market garden; orchard

iglesia – church

infanta/infante – princess/prince

IVA – *impuesto sobre el valor añadido,* or value-added tax

jamón – cured ham

jardín – garden

judería – Jewish *barrio* in medieval Spain

lago – lake

librería – bookshop

lidia – the art of bullfighting

locutorio – private telephone centre

madrileño/a (m/f) – person from Madrid

malagueño/a (m/f) – person from Málaga

manchego/a (m/f) – La Manchan; a person from La Mancha

marcha – action, life, 'the scene'

marismas – wetlands

marisquería – seafood eatery

medina – narrow, maze-like old section of an Arab or North African town

mercado – market

mercat – Catalan for *mercado*

meseta – plateau; the high tableland of central Spain

mihrab – prayer niche in a mosque indicating the direction of Mecca

mirador – lookout point

Modernista – an exponent of Modernisme, the architectural and artistic style influenced by art nouveau and sometimes known as Catalan Modernism, whose leading practitioner was Antoni Gaudí

monasterio – monastery

morería – former Islamic quarter in a town

movida – similar to *marcha*; a *zona de movida* is an area of a town where lively bars and discos are clustered

mozárabe – Mozarab (Christian living under Muslim rule in early medieval Spain)

Mozarabic – style of architecture developed by Mozarabs, adopting elements of classic Islamic construction to Christian architecture

Mudéjar – Muslims who remained behind in territory reconquered by Christians; also refers to a decorative style of architecture using elements of Islamic building style applied to buildings constructed in Christian Spain

muelle – wharf or pier

municipio – municipality, Spain's basic local administrative unit

muralla – city wall

murgas – costumed groups

museo – museum

museu – Catalan for *museo*

nitbus – Catalan for 'night bus'

oficina de turismo – tourist office; also *oficina de información turística*

parador – luxurious state-owned hotels, many of them in historic buildings

parque nacional – national park; strictly controlled protected area

parque natural – natural park; protected environmental area

paseo – promenade or boulevard; to stroll

paso – mountain pass

pasos – figures carried in *Semana Santa* parades

pelota vasca – Basque form of handball, also known simply as *pelota*, or *jai-alai* in Basque

peña – a club, usually of flamenco aficionados or Real Madrid or Barcelona football fans; sometimes a dining club

pensión – small private hotel

pinchos – tapas

pintxos – Basque tapas

piscina – swimming pool

plaça – Catalan for *plaza*

plateresque – early phase of Renaissance architecture noted for its intricately decorated facades

platja – Catalan for *playa*

playa – beach

plaza – square

plaza de toros – bullring

port – Catalan for *puerto*

PP – Partido Popular (People's Party)

PRs – *(senderos de) Pequeño Recorrido;* short-distance hiking paths

PSOE – Partido Socialista Obrero Español (Spanish Socialist Workers Party)

pueblo – village

puente – bridge; also means the extra day or two off that many people take when a holiday falls close to a weekend

puerta – gate or door

puerto – port or mountain pass

punta – point or promontory

ración/raciones – large/full-plate-size tapas serving; literally 'rations'

rambla – avenue or riverbed

rastro – flea market; car-boot sale

REAJ – Red Española de Albergues Juveniles; the Spanish HI youth hostel network

real – royal

Reconquista – Christian reconquest of the Iberian Peninsula from the Muslims (8th to 15th centuries)

refugi – Catalan for *refugio*

refugio – mountain shelter, hut or refuge

Renfe – Red Nacional de los Ferrocarriles Españoles; the national rail network

retablo – altarpiece

Reyes Católicos – Catholic monarchs; Isabel and Fernando

ría – estuary

río – river

riu – Catalan for *río*

rodalies – Catalan for *cercanías*

romería – festive pilgrimage or procession

ronda – ring road

sacristía – sacristy; the part of a church in which vestments, sacred objects and other valuables are kept

sagrario – sanctuary

sala capitular – chapter house

salinas – salt-extraction lagoons

santuario – shrine or sanctuary

Semana Santa – Holy Week; the week leading up to Easter Sunday

Sephardic Jews – Jews of Spanish origin

seu – cathedral (Catalan)

sidra – cider

sidrería – cider bar

sierra – mountain range

tablao – tourist-oriented flamenco performances

taifa – small Muslim kingdom in medieval Spain

tasca – tapas bar

techumbre – roof

teleférico – cable car; also called *funicular aéreo*

terraza – terrace; pavement cafe

terrazas de verano – open-air late-night bars

tetería – teahouse, usually in Middle Eastern style, with low seats around low tables

torero – bullfighter

torre – tower

trascoro – screen behind the *coro*

turismo – means both tourism and saloon car; *el turismo* can also mean 'tourist office'

urgencia – emergency

vall – Catalan for *valle*

valle – valley

villa – small town

VO – abbreviation of *versión original;* a foreign-language film subtitled in Spanish

zarzuela – Spanish mix of theatre, music and dance

Behind the Scenes

SEND US YOUR FEEDBACK

We love to hear from travellers – your comments keep us on our toes and help make our books better. Our well-travelled team reads every word on what you loved or loathed about this book. Although we cannot reply individually to your submissions, we always guarantee that your feedback goes straight to the appropriate authors, in time for the next edition. Each person who sends us information is thanked in the next edition – the most useful submissions are rewarded with a selection of digital PDF chapters.

Visit **lonelyplanet.com/contact** to submit your updates and suggestions or to ask for help. Our award-winning website also features inspirational travel stories, news and discussions.

Note: We may edit, reproduce and incorporate your comments in Lonely Planet products such as guidebooks, websites and digital products, so let us know if you don't want your comments reproduced or your name acknowledged. For a copy of our privacy policy visit lonelyplanet.com/privacy.

OUR READERS

Many thanks to the travellers who used the last edition and wrote to us with helpful hints, useful advice and interesting anecdotes:

Crawford Daly, Tone Earwaker, Luisella Furlan, Marlon Goos, Lisa Greenquist, Anne Hodges, Greg Kroll, Michael Marquardt, Lisa Maslove, Amanda McGough, Katia Moretti, Charles Mullins, James Nickel, Sally Norris, Sue O'Brien, Stefano Patara, Isidro J. Piñeiro, Suzanne Poncha, Nathalie Potvin, Nick de Ruiter, Ken Westmoreland

AUTHOR THANKS

Anthony Ham

Special thanks above all to Itziar Herrán, who brought both wisdom and an eye for detail to her many contributions in the Madrid chapter. Thanks also to Francisco Palomares, Miguel Ángel Simón, Astrid Vargas and Andy Tucker; to Marina and Alberto for their unwavering hospitality; to Sandra, Javi, Alex, Dulce and Dolores, among many other friends in Spain; to Dora Whitaker, Jo Cooke and my exceptional team of coauthors. And to Marina, Carlota and Valentina – you are everything that is good about this wonderful country.

Stuart Butler

First and foremost I must, once again, thank my wife, Heather and children Jake and Grace for their patience with this project and for being good travel companions (and don't worry Jake the dinosaurs in Enciso won't really eat you). I'd also like to thank Oihana Lazpita, Itziar Herrán, Leire Rodríguez Aramendía, Pilar Martínez de Olcoz, Clara Navas, Amaya Urberuaga and everyone else who has helped me out on this and other Basque-based projects.

Kerry Christiani

A heartfelt *gràcies* to all the locals and tourism pros I met on the road. Special thanks go to Antonia for the apartment in Pollença, Carmen Vila Altimir for tips and good times and clubbing pro Michael 'Stivi' Stivanello at Ibiza Spotlight. Last but never least, a big thank you to my husband, Andy, for being a great travel companion, a savvy map-reader and skilful mountain driver.

Isabella Noble

Thanks to everyone who helped out along the way, on the road and at home, especially tourism staff for dealing with my endless stream of strange questions and to Carlos for the life advice. *Muchísimas gracias* to John Noble for the endless words of wisdom and to Jacky for support. Finally to Mum, Susan Forsyth, for the inspiration.

John Noble

Special thanks to the Casa das Crechas crew for a great night of music and to Izzy for companionship and assistance on the road and at the desk.

Josephine Quintero

I would like to thank coordinating author Anthony Ham for his suggestions and support. *Gracias* also to Robin Chapman for his good humour, great map-reading skills and adventurous spirit on the road. I would also like to thank all the helpful folk at tourist information offices and tour companies, as well as my daughter Isabel Quintero and her partner, Luis Barrio Ruíz for their insight into Segovia and thereabouts, and use of the spare rooms.

Brendan Sainsbury

Thanks to all the untold bus drivers, chefs, hotel receptionists, tour guides, and flamenco singers who helped me in this research. Special thanks to José in Córdoba and Dario in Seville for their tips and insights. Kudos, as ever, to my wife Liz and eight-year-old son Kieran for their company on the road.

Regis St Louis

I'm grateful to the many friends and acquaintances who provided guidance and tips along the way. Biggest thanks go to coauthor Sal Davies for her hard work, Manel Casanovas for gourmet insight at Barcelona Turisme, Sol Polo and friends, Margherita Bergamo, Carine Ferry, Gonzalo Salaya, Anna Aurich, Núria Rocamora, Manel Baena, Malén Gual and Bernardo Laniado-Romero. Thanks also to Alan Waterman for making the trip down from London. Finally big hugs to my family for all their support.

Andy Symington

I owe gratitude to many people in tourist offices, on streets and in cabs. Particular thanks to Joan Francesc Peris García, to the LP team, Anthony Ham, my co-authors and to my family for their constant support. I am deeply in debt to many people from Valencia for splendid hospitality and help. Rosa Martínez Sala, Delfina Soria Bonet, Dolors Roca Ferrerfabrega, Enrique Lapuente Ojeda and Laura Martínez Rudilla went out of their way to provide information and show me new places. Elsewhere, I am indebted to Nieves Pérez Álvarez, Mar Pérez Álvarez, Francisco Javier Fernández Álvarez, Violeta Álvarez Braga & Rebeca Fernández Álvarez. I also owe thanks for various favours to José Eliseo Vázquez González, Javier De Celis Sánchez, Alberto Sánchez Fernández, Richard Prowse and Mike Burren.

ACKNOWLEDGMENTS

Climate map data adapted from Peel MC, Finlayson BL & McMahon TA (2007) 'Updated World Map of the Köppen-Geiger Climate Classification', Hydrology and Earth System Sciences, 11, 1633¬44.

Barcelona metro map © Ferrocarril Metropolità de Barcelona, SA 2011

Madrid Metro Map © Metro de Madrid

Illustrations p86-7, 254-5, 268-9, 580-81, 642-3, 660-61 by Javier Zarracina

Cover photograph: Alhambra, Granada, Alan Copson/Corbis.

THIS BOOK

This 10th edition of Lonely Planet's *Spain* guidebook was researched and written by Anthony Ham, Stuart Butler Kerry Christiani, Isabella Noble, John Noble, Josephine Quintero, Brendan Sainsbury, Regis St Louis and Andy Symington. This guidebook was commissioned in Lonely Planet's London office, and produced by the following:

Destination Editors Jo Cooke, Dora Whitaker

Coordinating Editor Simon Williamson
Product Editor Luna Soo
Senior Cartographers David Kemp, Valentina Kremenchutskaya
Book Designer Jessica Rose
Assisting Editors Michelle Bennett, Elin Berglund, Penny Cordner, Melanie Dankel, Carly Hall, Kristin Odijk, Monique Perrin, Martine Power, Alison Ridgway, Gabrielle Stefanos, Tracy Whitmey

Assisting Cartographers Corey Hutchison, James Leversha, Gabriel Lindquist, Alison Lyall, Anthony Phelan
Cover Researcher Naomi Parker
Thanks to Anita Banh, Sasha Baskett, Carolyn Boicos, Kate Chapman, Ryan Evans, Larissa Frost, Jouve India, Briohny Hooper, Wayne Murphy, Katherine Marsh, Claire Naylor, Karyn Noble, Katie O'Connell, Trent Paton, Eleanor Simpson, Lyahna Spencer

Index

Map Pages **000**
Photo Pages **000**

Map Legend

Sights
- Beach
- Bird Sanctuary
- Buddhist
- Castle/Palace
- Christian
- Confucian
- Hindu
- Islamic
- Jain
- Jewish
- Monument
- Museum/Gallery/Historic Building
- Ruin
- Sento Hot Baths/Onsen
- Shinto
- Sikh
- Taoist
- Winery/Vineyard
- Zoo/Wildlife Sanctuary
- Other Sight

Activities, Courses & Tours
- Bodysurfing
- Diving
- Canoeing/Kayaking
- Course/Tour
- Skiing
- Snorkelling
- Surfing
- Swimming/Pool
- Walking
- Windsurfing
- Other Activity

Sleeping
- Sleeping
- Camping

Eating
- Eating

Drinking & Nightlife
- Drinking & Nightlife
- Cafe

Entertainment
- Entertainment

Shopping
- Shopping

Information
- Bank
- Embassy/Consulate
- Hospital/Medical
- Internet
- Police
- Post Office
- Telephone
- Toilet
- Tourist Information
- Other Information

Geographic
- Beach
- Hut/Shelter
- Lighthouse
- Lookout
- Mountain/Volcano
- Oasis
- Park
- Pass
- Picnic Area
- Waterfall

Population
- Capital (National)
- Capital (State/Province)
- City/Large Town
- Town/Village

Transport
- Airport
- Border crossing
- Bus
- Cable car/Funicular
- Cycling
- Ferry
- Metro station
- Monorail
- Parking
- Petrol station
- S-Bahn/Subway station
- Taxi
- T-bane/Tunnelbana station
- Train station/Railway
- Tram
- Tube station
- U-Bahn/Underground station
- Other Transport

Note: Not all symbols displayed above appear on the maps in this book

Routes
- Tollway
- Freeway
- Primary
- Secondary
- Tertiary
- Lane
- Unsealed road
- Road under construction
- Plaza/Mall
- Steps
- Tunnel
- Pedestrian overpass
- Walking Tour
- Walking Tour detour
- Path/Walking Trail

Boundaries
- International
- State/Province
- Disputed
- Regional/Suburb
- Marine Park
- Cliff
- Wall

Hydrography
- River, Creek
- Intermittent River
- Canal
- Water
- Dry/Salt/Intermittent Lake
- Reef

Areas
- Airport/Runway
- Beach/Desert
- Cemetery (Christian)
- Cemetery (Other)
- Glacier
- Mudflat
- Park/Forest
- Sight (Building)
- Sportsground
- Swamp/Mangrove

John Noble

Santiago de Compostela & Galicia John, originally from England's Ribble Valley, has lived in an Andalucian mountain village since 1995. He has travelled lengthily all over Spain and helped write every edition of Lonely Planet's Spain and Andalucía guides. He loves returning to Galicia's green countryside, stone architecture, magnificent coastline and wonderful music, food and wine. The novelty of his latest trip was experiencing Galicia in its winter clothes, disappearing in the fog at Cabo Fisterra and getting stuck in the snow at O Cebreiro.

Josephine Quintero

Castilla y León, Aragón Josephine moved to Spain some 25 years ago, fleeing from the invasion of Kuwait (but that's another story). She still revels in the relaxed way of life in Andalucía and loves to explore the rest of the country, seeking out hidden corners, appreciating the unsung glories and meeting some extraordinary people along the way. During research for this title, one of the highlights was visiting Zaragoza's fascinating origami museum, another was finally appreciating the appeal of birdwatching, particularly in the magnificent Aragón Pyrenees.

Read more about Josephine at:
lonelyplanet.com/members/Josephine.Quintero

Brendan Sainsbury

Seville & Andalucía's Hill Towns, Granada & South Coast Andalucía Originally from Hampshire, England, Brendan first went to Spain on an Interrail ticket in the 1980s. He went back as a travel guide several years later and met his wife-to-be in a small village in rural Andalucía in 2003. He has been writing books for Lonely Planet for a decade, including two previous editions of the *Spain* guide. Brendan loves Granada, the writing of Federico Lorca, cycling along via verdes, and attending as many flamenco shows as his research allows.

Regis St Louis

Barcelona Regis first fell in love with Barcelona on a grand journey across Iberia in the late 1990s. Since then he has returned frequently to explore this endlessly fascinating city. Favourite memories from his most recent trip include earning a few scars at a *correfoc* in Gràcia and watching fearless *castellers* build human towers at the Santa Eulàlia festival. Regis is also the author of *Barcelona*, and he has contributed to dozens of other Lonely Planet titles. He lives in Brooklyn, New York.

Andy Symington

Catalonia, Valencia & Murcia Andy hails from Australia but has been living in Spain for over a decade, where, to shatter a couple of stereotypes of the country, he can frequently be found huddled in subzero temperatures watching the tragically poor local football team. He has authored and coauthored many LP guidebooks and other publications on Spain and elsewhere; in his spare time he walks in the mountains, embarks on epic tapas trails, and co-bosses a rock bar.

OUR STORY

A beat-up old car, a few dollars in the pocket and a sense of adventure. In 1972 that's all Tony and Maureen Wheeler needed for the trip of a lifetime – across Europe and Asia overland to Australia. It took several months, and at the end – broke but inspired – they sat at their kitchen table writing and stapling together their first travel guide, *Across Asia on the Cheap*. Within a week they'd sold 1500 copies. Lonely Planet was born.

Today, Lonely Planet has offices in Franklin, London, Melbourne, Oakland, Beijing and Delhi, with more than 600 staff and writers. We share Tony's belief that 'a great guidebook should do three things: inform, educate and amuse'.

OUR WRITERS

Anthony Ham
Coordinating Author, Madrid, Toledo & Castilla-La Mancha, Extremadura
In 2001, Anthony fell in love with Madrid on his first visit to the city. Less than a year later, he arrived on a one-way ticket, without knowing a word of Spanish or a single person. After 10 years of living in the city, he recently returned to Australia with his Spanish-born family, but he still adores his adopted country as much as the first day he arrived. His most recent Spanish passions, among many, are trying to track down the critically endangered Iberian lynx and sharing stories of Spain's wild places. When he's not writing for Lonely Planet, Anthony writes about and photographs Spain, Scandinavia, Australia and Africa for newspapers and magazines around the world. Read more about Anthony at www.anthonyham.com

Stuart Butler
Bilbao, the Basque Country & La Rioja Stuart's first childhood encounters, in Parque Nacional de Doñana and on family holidays along the north coast, left lasting impressions. When he was older he spent every summer on the Basque beaches, until one day he found himself unable to tear himself away – he has been there ever since. His travels for Lonely Planet, and a wide variety of magazines, have taken him beyond Spain to the shores of the Arctic, the deserts of Asia and the forests of Africa. His website is www.stuartbutlerjournalist.com

Read more about Stuart at:
lonelyplanet.com/members/stuartbutler

Kerry Christiani
Mallorca, Menorca & Ibiza Kerry met her now husband in Mallorca in 1999 and has jumped at every chance to return to the Balearics since. Memorable moments for this edition include waking up to a goat bells at a monastery near Pollença, watching fiery sunsets at Ibiza's beach cafes and walking barefoot on Formentera's sugar-white beaches. Kerry studied Spanish to MA level and has authored some 20 guidebooks. She contributes frequently to magazines and websites and tweets about her adventures @kerrychristiani.

Read more about Kerry at:
lonelyplanet.com/members/kerrychristiani

Isabella Noble
Cantabria & Asturias Isabella's in-depth investigation of distant northern regions far from her Andalucian home began at the age of 12, and she was thrilled to discover that the two bears of the Senda del Oso are still there a decade later. English/Australian on paper but Spanish at heart, she has lived and travelled in Spain since 1994. Adventures this trip include exploring after-dark Gijón, tackling snowy mountain passes, and falling in love with Oviedo. For now, she lives between Andalucía and London.

Read more about Isabella at:
lonelyplanet.com/members/isabellanoble

OVER PAGE | MORE WRITERS

Published by Lonely Planet Publications Pty Ltd
ABN 36 005 607 983
10th edition – Nov 2014
ISBN 978 1 74321 575 3
© Lonely Planet 2014   Photographs © as indicated 2014
10 9 8 7 6 5 4 3 2 1
Printed in China

Although the authors and Lonely Planet have taken all reasonable care in preparing this book, we make no warranty about the accuracy or completeness of its content and, to the maximum extent permitted, disclaim all liability arising from its use.